6/08

BIOGRAPHICAL ENCYCLOPEDIA
OF THE SUPREME COURT

THE LIVES AND LEGAL PHILOSOPHIES
OF THE JUSTICES

Edited by Melvin I. Urofsky

Virginia Commonwealth University

CQ PRESS

A Division of Congressional Quarterly Inc.
Washington, D.C.

CQ Press
1255 22nd Street, NW, Suite 400
Washington, DC 20037

Phone: 202-729-1900; toll-free, 1-866-427-7737 (1-866-4CQ-PRESS)

Web: www.cqpress.com

Cover design: Tony Olivis, of Studio 2

Cover photos: *(Top row, from left)* Stephen Gerald Breyer, Clarence Thomas, Ruth Bader Ginsburg, Samuel Anthony Alito Jr. *(Second row)* Anthony McLeod Kennedy, John Paul Stevens, John Glover Roberts Jr., Antonin Scalia, David Hackett Souter *(Third row)* William Orville Douglas, John Marshall, William Howard Taft *(Bottom row)* Earl Warren, Thurgood Marshall, Louis Dembitz Brandeis, Roger Brooke Taney, Oliver Wendell Holmes Jr. *From the Collection of the Supreme Court of the United States*

Interior photo credits are located on page 665.

∞ The paper used in this publication exceeds the requirements of the American National Standard for Information Sciences—Permanence of Paper for Printed Library Materials, ANSI Z39.48-1992.

Printed and bound in the United States of America

10   09   08   07   06   1   2   3   4   5

Library of Congress Cataloging-in-Publication Data

Biographical encyclopedia of the Supreme Court : the lives and legal philosophies of the justices / edited by Melvin I. Urofsky.
    p. cm.
 Includes bibliographical references and index.
 ISBN 1-933116-48-X (alk. paper)
 1. United States. Supreme Court—Officials and employees—Biography—Encyclopedias.
 2. Judges—United States—Biography—Encyclopedias. I. Urofsky, Melvin I. II. Title.

 KF8744.B56 2006
 347.73'2634--dc22
 [B]
               2006011563

For David W. Levy

Scholar, colleague, and friend
on the occasion of his retirement

CONTENTS

CONTENTS

CHRONOLOGICAL LISTING OF THE SUPREME COURT JUSTICES

In this listing, the year in which a justice took the judicial oath is used as the starting date of service on the Court. Similar chronological listings using appointment or confirmation dates will result in a different order for the justices, particularly for the earliest members of the Court.

Two sets of year ranges appear after the names of chief justices who served previously as associate justices.

James Wilson (1789–1798)	612	James Moore Wayne (1835-1867)	592
John Jay (1789–1795)	294	Roger Brooke Taney (1836–1864)	532
John Blair Jr. (1790–1796)	34	Philip Pendleton Barbour (1836–1841)	10
William Cushing (1790–1810)	151	John Catron (1837–1865)	119
John Rutledge (1790–1791, 1795)	440	John McKinley (1838–1852)	346
James Iredell (1790–1799)	280	Peter Vivian Daniel (1841–1860)	155
Thomas Johnson (1792–1793)	301	Samuel Nelson (1845–1872)	378
William Paterson (1793–1806)	390	Levi Woodbury (1845–1851)	615
Samuel Chase (1796–1811)	132	Robert Cooper Grier (1846–1870)	233
Oliver Ellsworth (1796–1800)	180	Benjamin Robbins Curtis (1851–1857)	148
Bushrod Washington (1799–1829)	588	John Archibald Campbell (1853–1861)	112
Alfred Moore (1800–1804)	369	Nathan Clifford (1858–1881)	145
John Marshall (1801–1835)	326	Noah Haynes Swayne (1862–1881)	522
William Johnson (1804–1834)	303	Samuel Freeman Miller (1862–1890)	357
Henry Brockholst Livingston (1807–1823)	320	David Davis (1862–1877)	160
Thomas Todd (1807–1826)	556	Stephen Johnson Field (1863–1897)	183
Gabriel Duvall (1811–1835)	178	Salmon Portland Chase (1864–1873)	125
Joseph Story (1812–1845)	503	William Strong (1870–1880)	513
Smith Thompson (1823–1843)	554	Joseph P. Bradley (1870–1892)	41
Robert Trimble (1826–1828)	560	Ward Hunt (1873–1882)	277
John McLean (1830–1861)	349	Morrison Remick Waite (1874–1888)	571
Henry Baldwin (1830–1844)	7	John Marshall Harlan (1877–1911)	236

CONTRIBUTORS

About the Editor

Melvin I. Urofsky is professor of public policy and law at the L. Douglas Wilder School of Government and Public Affairs at Virginia Commonwealth University. He is the author or editor of more than two dozen books on constitutional law, Supreme Court history, and religious freedom. His other publications with CQ Press include *The Public Debate over Controversial Supreme Court Decisions* (2006); *100 Americans Making Constitutional History* (2004); and *Landmark Decisions of the United States Supreme Court*, with Paul Finkelman (2003).

About the Contributors

Henry J. Abraham is the James Hart Professor of Politics Emeritus at the University of Virginia. His numerous books include *Freedom and the Court: Civil Rights and Liberties in the United States*, 8th ed. with Barbara A. Perry (2003); *Justices, Presidents, and Senators: A History of the U.S. Supreme Court Appointments from Washington to Clinton*, new and revised ed. (1999); *The Judicial Process: An Introductory Analysis of the Courts of the United States, England, and France*, 7th ed. (1998); and *The Judiciary: The Supreme Court in the Governmental Process*, 10th ed. (1996).

Richard M. Abrams is professor emeritus of history and former associate dean of international and area studies at the University of California, Berkeley. He is the author of *America Transformed: Sixty Years of Revolutionary Change, 1941–2001* (2006), in which the Supreme Court figures prominently. His research interests include political, business, and industrial history.

Judith A. Baer is professor of political science at Texas A&M University. She is the coauthor of *The Constitutional and Legal Rights of Women: Cases in Law and Social Change* (2006). Professor Baer is a former fellow at the Woodrow

Wilson International Center for Scholars and Fulbright Senior Lecturer.

Michal R. Belknap is professor of law at California Western Law School and adjunct professor of American history at the University of California, San Diego. He is the author of several books, including *The Supreme Court under Earl Warren* (2005); *The Vietnam War on Trial: The My Lai Massacre and the Court Martial of Lieutenant Calley* (2002); and *Federal Law and Southern Order: Racial Violence and Constitutional Conflict in the Post-Brown South* (1987). He is also the editor of *American Political Trials*, rev. ed. (1993).

Gayle Binion is professor of political science and former chair of the Law and Society Program at the University of California, Santa Barbara. Her law review articles include "Feminist Jurisprudence and the First Amendment: Hearing Another Voice" (1998) and "On Politics, Constitutional Interpretation and Abortion Rights' Jurisprudence" (1997). Her research focuses on the areas of civil rights and civil liberties within the U.S. constitutional structure, with special emphasis on the status of women, ethnic minorities, and the poor. She is particularly interested in understanding the role of the judiciary in defining and protecting constitutional rights.

David J. Bodenhamer is professor of history and executive director of the Polis Center at Indiana University/Purdue University, Indianapolis. He is the author of *Our Rights* (forthcoming) and *Fair Trial: Rights of the Accused in American History* (1993). He also is editor of *The Bill of Rights in Modern America*, with James W. Ely Jr. (forthcoming) and *The History of Indiana Law*, with Randall T. Shepard (2006). His research interests include the history of individual rights and rights of the accused.

William Bosch, S.J., is professor emeritus and college archivist at Le Moyne College in Syracuse, New York. He is the author of *Judgment on Nuremberg: American Attitudes toward the Major German War-Crime Trials* (1970).

Craig M. Bradley is the James Louis Calamaras Professor of Law at Indiana University School of Law–Bloomington. He is the editor and coauthor of *Criminal Procedure: A Worldwide Study*, 2d ed. (forthcoming) and *The Rehnquist Legacy* (2006). He is a former Fulbright fellow and law clerk to Justice William H. Rehnquist. His teaching and research covers such areas as criminal procedure, comparative criminal procedure, and federal criminal law.

Daniel L. Breen is professor of history at Newbury College. In addition, he teaches legal studies and philosophy at Brandeis University. He is currently working on an article on the influence of Judge Henry J. Friendly upon the contemporary jurisprudence of the Supreme Court.

William R. Casto is the Allison Professor of Law at Texas Tech University. He is the author of *Foreign Affairs and the Constitution in the Age of Fighting Sail* (2006) and *The Supreme Court in the Early Republic* (1995). His research interests include the law, foreign affairs, and Calvinism in the early republic.

Stephen Cresswell is professor of history at West Virginia Wesleyan College. He is the author of *Rednecks, Redeemers and Race* (2006); *Multiparty Politics in Mississippi* (1995); and *Mormons and Cowboys, Moonshiners and Klansmen: Federal Law Enforcement in the South and West* (1991).

Barry Cushman is the Percy Brown Jr. Professor of Law and History at the University of Virginia. He is the author of many articles on constitutional development in the late nineteenth and early twentieth centuries. His book, *Rethinking the New Deal Court: The Structure of a Constitutional Revolution* (1998), was awarded the American Historical Association's Littleton-Griswold Prize.

David J. Danelski is the Boone Centennial Professor Emeritus at Stanford University. Among his publications are *The Autobiographical Notes of Charles Evans Hughes*, with Joseph Tucchin (1973) and *A Supreme Court Justice Is Appointed* (1964). He received the Hughes-Gossett Award for Historical Excellence from the Supreme Court Historical Society in 1997. His research focuses chiefly on judicial decision making and biography.

Donald O. Dewey is professor emeritus of history at California State University, Los Angeles, where he was also dean of natural and social sciences from 1970 to 1996. Previously, he served as associate editor of *The Papers of James Madison,* an ongoing publication. He is the author of *Lessons on the Bill of Rights and Limited Government,* with Kenneth A. Wagner and John T. Hyland (1995) and *Marshall versus Jefferson: The Political Background of* Marbury v. Madison (1970).

Norman Dorsen is the Stokes Professor of Law and counselor to the president at New York University. He has written extensively on constitutional law and on Supreme Court justices, and he has participated in many leading cases in the U.S. Supreme Court. He served as law clerk to Justice John Marshall Harlan II from 1957 to 1958, and as president of the ACLU from 1976 to 1991. He has received many awards, including honorary degrees and the Eleanor Roosevelt Medal for Human Rights from President Clinton in 2000.

James W. Ely Jr. is the Milton R. Underwood Professor of Law and professor of history at Vanderbilt University. He is the author of numerous articles and books on U.S. legal and constitutional history, including *The Fuller Court: Justices, Rulings, and Legacy* (2003); *Railroads and American Law* (2001); *The Guardian of Every Other Right: A Constitutional History of Property Rights,* 2nd ed. (1998); and *The Chief Justiceship of Melville W. Fuller, 1888–1910* (1995). His research interests include the history and evolution of property rights and the jurisprudence of the Gilded Age.

Daniel A. Farber is the Sho Sato Professor of Law at the University of California, Berkeley. He is the author of *Lincoln's Constitution* (2003); *The First Amendment,* 2d ed. (2003); and *Eco-Pragmatism* (1999). His research concentrates on constitutional law and history, jurisprudence, and environmental law. Professor Farber is a member of the American Academy of Arts and Sciences.

Ward Farnsworth is professor of law and Nancy Barton Scholar at Boston University Law School. He is the author, most recently, of the law review article "Signatures of Ideology: The Case of the Supreme Court's Criminal Docket" (2005). He served as law clerk to Justice Anthony M. Kennedy during the October 1996 term.

John M. Ferren is a senior judge on the District of Columbia Court of Appeals. He is the author of *Salt of the Earth, Conscience of the Court: The Story of Justice Wiley Rutledge* (2004), which won the 2004 Langum Prize for Legal History and shared the 2005 George Pendleton Prize from the Society for History in the Federal Government.

Paul Finkelman is the President William B. McKinley Professor of Law and Public Policy and senior fellow in the Government Law Center at Albany Law School. He is the author or editor of more than twenty books. He is the author of *Landmark Decisions of the Supreme Court*, with Melvin Urofsky (2003), and *A March of Liberty: A Constitutional History of the United States* (2001).

Michael J. Gerhardt is the Samuel Ashe Distinguished Professor of Constitutional Law and director of the Center on Law and Government at the University of North Carolina at Chapel Hill Law School. He is the author of *The Federal Appointments Process*, rev. ed. (2003) and *The Federal Impeachment Process: A Constitutional and Historical Analysis*, 2d ed. (2000).

Dorothy J. Glancy is professor of law at Santa Clara University School of Law. Her writings cover a wide range of topics, including Justice William O. Douglas, historical aspects of the right to privacy, historic preservation, and intellectual property. An expert regarding privacy and intelligent transportation systems (ITS), she is also a research fellow of the Gruter Institute for Law and Behavioral Research and a member of the State of California Court Technology Advisory Committee.

Robert M. Goldman is professor of history at Virginia Union University. He is the author of *Reconstruction and Black Suffrage* (2001) and other works on U.S. constitutional history.

Mark A. Graber is professor of government at the University of Maryland, College Park, and professor of law at the University of Maryland School of Law. He is the author of *Dred Scott and the Problem of Constitutional Evil* (2006); *Rethinking Abortion* (1996); and *Transforming Free Speech* (1991), as well as essays on constitutional politics, law, history, and development.

Michael Grossberg is the Sally M. Reahard Professor of History and a professor of law at Indiana University. He is the coeditor of the forthcoming three-volume *Cambridge History of Law in the United States*. His research focuses on the legal history of American family law and social relations.

Kermit L. Hall is professor of history and president of the University at Albany. He is the author of *The Magic Mirror: Law in American History* (1989), editor in chief of *The Oxford Companion to the Supreme Court*, 2d ed. (2005), and editor of *Institutions of Democracy: The Judicial Branch*, with Kevin McGuire (2005). His research interests include the Supreme Court, judicial selection, and American legal and constitutional history.

Marci A. Hamilton is the Paul R. Verkuil Chair in Public Law at the Benjamin N. Cardozo School of Law at Yeshiva University. She is a former law clerk to Justice Sandra Day O'Connor (1989) and the author of *The Religious Origins of Disestablishment Principles*, with Rachel Steamer (2006) and *God vs. the Gavel: Religion and the Rule of Law* (2005).

Richard F. Hamm is professor of history and public policy at the University at Albany. He is the author of *Murder, Honor, and Law* (2003) and *Shaping the Eighteenth Amendment* (1995). His research interests focus on history of crime, social movements and the law, and legal biography. He is the recipient of the 1996 Henry Adams Award for History in the Federal Government.

Susan N. Herman is the Centennial Professor of Law at Brooklyn Law School. Her recent publications include *The Sixth Amendment Right to a Speedy and Public Trial* (forthcoming) and "The USA Patriot Act and the Submajoritarian Fourth Amendment" (2006). Her research covers the Supreme Court and a range of constitutional and criminal procedure issues. She serves as a member of the Board of Directors and as general counsel to the American Civil Liberties Union.

Scott Horton is a partner with Patterson, Belknap, Webb & Tyler in New York. In his spare time, he writes about nineteenth-century legal history.

Timothy S. Huebner is associate professor of history and director of the Rhodes Institute for Regional Studies at Rhodes College. He is the author of *The Taney Court: Justices, Rulings, Legacy* (2003) and *The Southern Judicial Tradition: State Judges and Sectional Distinctiveness, 1790–1890* (1999). In 2004 the Carnegie Foundation for the Advancement of Teaching and the Council for the Advancement and Support of Education named him Tennessee Professor of the Year.

Joseph Gordon Hylton is professor of law at Marquette University, where he teaches American constitutional history and comparative constitutional law. He is the author of *Property Law and the Public Interest*, 3d ed. (forthcoming); *Sports Law and Regulation* (1998); and *Professional Values and Individual Autonomy: The United States Supreme Court and Lawyer Advertising* (1998). Professor Hylton is currently at work on a biography of Supreme Court Justice David Josiah Brewer. He is a former Fulbright Scholar to Ukraine.

Peter Irons is professor emeritus of political science at the University of California, San Diego. His books include *God on Trial* (forthcoming); *A People's History of the Supreme*

Court, rev. ed. (2006); *War Powers* (2005); and *Jim Crow's Children* (2003). His research and writing focus on the Supreme Court and constitutional litigation.

Herbert A. Johnson is distinguished professor of law emeritus at the University of South Carolina. He is the author of *The Chief Justiceship of John Marshall, 1801–1835* (1997) and coauthor of the *Oliver Wendell Holmes Devise History of the Supreme Court* volume entitled *Foundations of Power, John Marshall, 1801–1815*, with George L. Haskins (1981). His current research involves the relationship between seventeenth-century English constitutional development and the rise of American constitutionalism.

John W. Johnson is professor of history at the University of Northern Iowa. Among his books are Griswold v. Connecticut: *Birth Control and the Constitutional Right of Privacy* (2005); *The Struggle for Student Rights:* Tinker v. Des Moines *and the 1960s* (1997); *Insuring Against Disaster: The Nuclear Industry on Trial* (1986); and *American Legal Culture, 1908–1940* (1981). He received Thomas Jefferson awards from the Society for History in the Federal Government for both editions of his edited work *Historic U.S. Court Cases: An Encyclopedia* (2001 and 1992). He also received the Distinguished Scholar Award (2006) and the Donald N. McKay Faculty Research Award (2001) from the University of Northern Iowa. He is currently working on a book on the history of affirmative action in the United States.

John Paul Jones is professor of law at the University of Richmond, where he teaches administrative law, constitutional law, and the law of admiralty. He served as a judicial clerk for the Honorable David Schwartz of the United States Court of Claims and has been a visiting scholar at the Central Intelligence Agency. Professor Jones writes and lectures about comparative constitutional law, judicial administration, and maritime law.

Kenneth Jost is Supreme Court editor for CQ Press and associate editor of the *CQ Researcher*. He teaches media law as an adjunct professor at Georgetown University Law Center. Jost has covered legal affairs as a reporter, editor, or columnist since 1970 and has contributed to a variety of legal publications. He is the editor of *The Supreme Court A to Z*, 4th ed. (forthcoming), and a frequent commentator about the Court on television and radio programs. He was a member of the *Researcher* team that won the American Bar Association's Silver Gavel Award in 2002 for magazine coverage of law and justice issues.

Jonathan Kahn is assistant professor of law at Hamline University School of Law. He is the author of *How A Drug Becomes 'Ethnic': Law, Commerce, and the Production of Racial Categories in Medicine* (2004); *Privacy as a Legal Principle of Identity Maintenance* (2003); and *Budgeting Democracy* (1997). His research encompasses law and biotechnology, critical legal theory, and social studies of science.

Paul Kens is professor of political science and history at Texas State University–San Marcos. He is the author of Lochner v. New York: *Economic Regulation on Trial* (1998) and *Justice Stephen Field: Shaping Liberty from the Gold Rush to the Gilded Age* (1997). He was awarded National Endowment for the Humanities fellowships in 1993–1994 and 2005–2006. He has also received awards for articles on constitutional history and Western history.

Ken I. Kersch is assistant professor of politics at Princeton University. He is the author of *The Supreme Court and American Political Development*, with Ronald Kahn (2006); *Constructing Civil Liberties: Discontinuities in the Development of American Constitutional Law* (2004); and *Freedom of Speech: Rights and Liberties under the Law* (2003), as well as numerous articles, book chapters, and reviews. His interests lie in American constitutional and political development and American political thought.

Jonathan Lurie is professor of history and adjunct professor of law at Rutgers University. He is the author of *The Slaughterhouse Cases: Regulation, Reconstruction and the Fourteenth Amendment*, with Ronald M. Labbe (2003), which received the Scribes Award in 2004 from the American Society of Writers on Legal Subjects. He is also the author of *Military Justice in America* (2001); *Pursuing Military Justice* (1998); and *Arming Military Justice* (1992). In 2005 he was a Fulbright Lecturer at Uppsala University School of Law.

Thomas C. Mackey is professor of history at the University of Louisville and adjunct professor of law at the Louis D. Brandeis School of Law, University of Louisville. A specialist in U.S. legal and constitutional history, he is the author of *Pursuing Johns: Criminal Law Reform, Defending Character, and New York City's Committee of Fourteen, 1920–1930* (2005). His research interests include law and society issues and criminal law history.

Maeva Marcus is research professor of law at the George Washington University Law School. She is editor of *The Documentary History of the Supreme Court of the United States, 1789–1800* (eighth and final volume, forthcoming) and director of the Institute for Constitutional Studies at the George Washington University. She is a member of the Permanent Committee for the Oliver Wendell Holmes Devise (2001–2009) and president-elect of the American

Society for Legal History. Her publications include *Truman and the Steel Seizure Case* (1994) and *Origins of the Federal Judiciary: Essays on the Judiciary Act of 1789* (editor and contributor, 1992), as well as many articles and essays in books and law reviews.

Tony Mauro is Supreme Court correspondent for *Legal Times* and American Lawyer Media. He is the author of *Illustrated Great Decisions of the Supreme Court*, 2d ed. (CQ Press, 2006). Mauro has covered the Supreme Court since 1980.

Elizabeth Brand Monroe is associate professor of history at Indiana University–Purdue University Indianapolis. She is the author of multiple entries to encyclopedias and companions on legal and constitutional topics and *The Wheeling Bridge Case: Its Significance in American Law and Technology* (1992). She is currently working on a biography of William Wirt, the famous constitutional lawyer and U.S. attorney general from 1817 to 1829.

A. E. Keir Nash is professor emeritus at the University of California, Santa Barbara. He is the author of numerous articles on environmental law and policy and nineteenth-century American legal history, especially the legal history of slavery.

Jenni Parrish is director of the law library and professor of law at the University of California Hastings College of the Law. She is the author of the article "Litigating Time in America at the Turn of the Twentieth Century" (2002). She teaches immigration legal history and is involved in the complete renovation and seismic retrofit of her law library. Her research currently focuses on the legal history of daylight savings time in the United States.

Michael E. Parrish is professor of history at the University of California, San Diego. He is the author of *The Hughes Court: Justices, Rulings and Legacy* (2002); *Anxious Decades: America in Prosperity and Depression, 1921–1941* (1992); and *Felix Frankfurter and His Times: The Reform Years* (1982).

Richard Polenberg is the Goldwin Smith Professor of American History and Stephen H. Weiss Presidential Fellow at Cornell University. He is the author of *The World of Benjamin Cardozo: Personal Values and the Judicial Process* (1997) and *Fighting Faiths: The Abrams Case, The Supreme Court, and Free Speech* (1987), which received the American Bar Association's Silver Gavel Award.

Robert C. Post is the David Boies Professor of Law at Yale Law School. He is an expert in constitutional law and the editor of *Civil Society and Government*, with Nancy Rosenblum (2002) and author of *Constitutional Domains: Democracy, Community, Management* (1995), among other books. He is currently writing the tenth volume of the *Oliver Wendell Holmes Devise History of the Supreme Court*, which will cover the period from 1921 to 1930, when William Howard Taft was chief justice. Professor Post served as law clerk to Justice William J. Brennan Jr. from 1978 to 1979.

H. Jefferson Powell teaches at the Duke University School of Law and holds a joint appointment at the Divinity School. He has served as principal deputy solicitor general in the U.S. Department of Justice and as special counsel to the attorney general of North Carolina, and he has briefed and argued cases before the Supreme Court. He is the author of "That Heaven of Which We Have Heard," in *Places of God: Theological Conversations with Wendell Berry* (forthcoming), and *A Community Built on Words* (2005). Professor Powell received the Duke Bar Association's Excellence in Small Section Teaching Award and was University Scholar/Teacher of the Year 2001–2002.

Linda Przybyszewski is associate professor of history at the University of Notre Dame. She is the editor of *Some Memories of a Long Life, 1854–1911*, by Malvina Shanklin Harlan (2002) and the author of *The Republic According to John Marshall Harlan* (1999). Her research covers the subjects of constitutional law and church-state issues.

Eric W. Rise is associate professor of sociology and criminal justice at the University of Delaware. He is the author of *The Supreme Court of Florida and Its Predecessor Courts, 1821–1917*, with Walter W. Manley and E. Canter Brown (1997); *The Martinsville Seven: Race, Rape, and Capital Punishment* (1995); and *From Local Courts to National Tribunals: The Federal District Courts of Florida, 1821–1991* (1991). His research interests include the history of civil rights litigation, freedom of speech, and federal and state judiciaries.

Daniel B. Rodriguez is the Warren Distinguished Professor of Law at the University of San Diego School of Law. He is the author of numerous articles and book chapters on state and federal constitutional law. His scholarship on the history and theory of American federalism has been published in various venues, including the *University of Pennsylvania Law Review* (2003); the *Encyclopedia of the American Constitution* (2000); the *Yale Journal on Regulation* (1996); and the *Duke Law Journal* (1995). He is the author of a forthcoming monograph on constitutional police power and is the coauthor of a forthcoming book on statutory interpretation.

Ralph A. Rossum is director of the Rose Institute of State and Local Government and the Henry Salvatori Professor of American Constitutionalism at Claremont McKenna College. He is the author of eight books, including *Antonin Scalia's Jurisprudence: Text and Tradition* (2006); *Federalism, the Supreme Court, and the Seventeenth Amendment: The Irony of Constitutional Democracy* (2001); and *American Constitutional Law*, with G. Alan Tarr (1986), as well as numerous articles in law reviews and professional journals. He has written extensively on the American founding, federalism, and modes of constitutional interpretation.

Margaret M. Russell is professor of law at the Santa Clara University School of Law. She is chair of the board of directors of the American Civil Liberties Union of Northern California and a vice president of the national American Civil Liberties Union. Among her recent publications are "Civil Liberties in the U.S.: Why They Matter in a Post 9/11 World" (2003) and "Cleansing Moments and Retrospective Justice" (2003). Her areas of specialization include civil procedure, constitutional law, and contemporary legal theory.

Herman Schwartz is professor of law at American University Washington College of Law. He is the author of *Right Wing Justice* (2004) and *The Struggle for Constitutional Justice in Post-Communist Europe* (2000). He is also the editor of *The Rehnquist Court* (2002) and *The Burger Years* (1987). His research interests are religion in America, judicial selection, and comparative constitutional law.

Philip J. Schwarz is professor emeritus of history at Virginia Commonwealth University. He is the author of *Gabriel's Rebellion: A Documentary History*, with Douglas R. Egerton (forthcoming); *Migrants Against Slavery: Virginians and the Nation* (2001); *Slave Laws in Virginia* (1996); and *Twice Condemned: Slaves and the Criminal Laws of Virginia* (1988).

Rebecca Shepherd Shoemaker is professor of history at Indiana State University in Terre Haute, where she teaches constitutional history. She is the author of *The White Court: Justices, Rulings, Legacy* (2004). Her areas of interest include civil liberties history. She is currently completing a book-length history of the Indiana Civil Liberties Union.

Robert Stanley is professor of political science at California State University, Chico. He is the author of "The Income Tax Cases," in Melvin I. Urofsky, ed., *The Public Debate over Controversial Supreme Court Decisions* (CQ Press, 2006); "When Monopoly Mattered," in *Historic U.S. Court Cases: An Encyclopedia* (2001); and *Dimensions of Law in the Service of Order: Origins of the Federal Income Tax, 1861–1913* (1993).

Philippa Strum is director of the United States Studies division at the Woodrow Wilson International Center for Scholars and Breuklundian Professor Emerita at CUNY. Her books include *Women in the Barracks: The VMI Case and Women's Rights* (2002); *When the Nazis Came to Skokie* (1999); *Privacy: The Debate in the United States since 1945* (1998); and *Louis D. Brandeis: Justice for the People* (1984).

Thad W. Tate is the Forrest G. Murden Professor of Humanities Emeritus at the College of William and Mary and emeritus director of the Institute of Early American History and Culture. He is the author of *Colonial Virginia: A History*, with Warren Billings and John Selby (1986) and *The Negro in Eighteenth-Century Williamsburg* (1972).

James A. Thomson has studied and practiced law in the United States and Australia, where he is currently a barrister of the supreme courts of Western Australia and Victoria as well as the High Court of Australia. He teaches law part-time at the Western Australia and Murdoch University Law School and is the author of articles on federal and constitutional law that have appeared in the United States and Australia. He has been admitted to the New York Supreme Court bar.

Mark V. Tushnet is professor of law at Harvard Law School. He is the coauthor of four casebooks, including the most widely used casebook on constitutional law, the author of fourteen other books, including a two-volume work on the life of Justice Thurgood Marshall, and the editor of eight others. He served as president of the Association of American Law Schools in 2003 and was elected a fellow of the American Academy of Arts and Sciences in 2002.

Sandra F. VanBurkleo is associate professor of history and adjunct professor of law at Wayne State University. She is lead editor of *Constitutionalism and American Culture: Writing the New Constitutional History* (2002) and author of *Belonging to the World: Women's Rights and American Constitutional Culture* (2001). She is completing a study of the development of modern citizenship in the Pacific Northwest and soon will begin a detailed account of Americans' experiences related to liberty of speech, press, and assembly from colonial times to the present.

Stephen J. Wermiel is the associate director of the Marshall-Brennan Constitutional Literacy Project at American University Washington College of Law. The project enlists and prepares law students to teach a course in constitutional law in Washington, D.C., public high schools. He was a Supreme Court reporter for the *Wall Street Journal* from

1979 to 1991. Wermiel also teaches constitutional law and a seminar on the Supreme Court.

Natalie Wexler is a lawyer and historian. She is currently an associate editor of the ongoing multivolume series *The Documentary History of the Supreme Court of the United States, 1789–1800* (7 volumes, 1985–).

G. Edward White is University Professor and David and Mary Harrison Distinguished Professor of Law at the University of Virginia. He is the author of thirteen books, including *Alger Hiss's Looking-Glass Wars: The Covert Life of a Soviet Spy* (2004); *The Constitution and the New Deal* (2000); *Justice Oliver Wendell Holmes: Law and the Inner Self* (1993); *The Marshall Court and Cultural Change, 1815–1835* (1991); *Earl Warren: A Public Life* (1982); and *The American Judicial Tradition: The Profiles of Leading American Judges* (1976). His books have received the Silver Gavel Award from the American Bar Association, the Littleton-Griswold Prize from the American Historical Association, the James Willard Hurst Prize from the Law and Society Association, and the Triennial Coif Award from the Association of American Law Schools. His research encompasses American legal and constitutional history and American intellectual history.

Lou Falkner Williams is associate professor of history at Kansas State University. She is the author of *The Ellenton Riot Cases and Federal Enforcement of Black Rights in Post-Redemption South Carolina* (2000) and *The Great South Carolina Ku Klux Klan Trials* (1996). Her research focuses primarily on Reconstruction Era civil rights issues.

Victoria Saker Woeste is senior research fellow at the American Bar Foundation in Chicago. She has published *The Farmer's Benevolent Trust: Law and Agricultural Cooperation in Industrial America, 1856–1945* (1998), which won the 2000 J. Willard Hurst Prize of the Law and Society Association. Her research interests range from agricultural and business history to anti-Semitism, group libel, and the meaning of civic equality in the twentieth-century United States.

Michael Allan Wolf is the Richard E. Nelson Chair in Local Government Law at the University of Florida Levin College of Law. His teaching and scholarly interests center on land-use planning, property, and environmental law as well as constitutional history and economic development. His publications include *Strategies for Environmental Success in an Uncertain Judicial Climate* (2005) and *Land-Use Planning*, with C. M. Haar (1989). He is also the general editor of the multivolume *Powell on Real Property* (2000–).

PREFACE

The Supreme Court of the United States is the oldest and most powerful constitutional court in the world. As provided for in Article III of the Constitution, the First Congress established a supreme court as well as lower federal courts in the Judiciary Act of 1789. Initially, the Supreme Court appeared to be the weakest of the three branches of government. In *The Federalist* Alexander Hamilton predicted that it would be "the least dangerous branch" because it lacked the power of the purse and the sword, the chief tools of the legislature and executive, respectively. The first chief justice, John Jay, resigned, believing that the Court would never play an important role in government affairs.

Hamilton's and Jay's views of the Court have not been borne out by history, however. Under the leadership of John Marshall, the "great Chief Justice," the Court demonstrated that it has significant powers, primarily in its role as the ultimate arbiter of what the Constitution means. Congress may enact laws, and presidents may promulgate policies, but at times states, institutions, and individuals raise challenges to these laws and policies, and some of these challenges end up as appeals to the Supreme Court. Then, when the Court speaks, it speaks with the power Marshall envisioned for it nearly two centuries ago—to say what the Constitution means and whether the laws and policies under review are constitutional.

The Court's role as ultimate arbiter is not always wisely exercised, however. Occasionally, the Court misjudges the popular mood or the determination of Congress and the executive branch to have their way. Few would argue about its worst miscalculation: the decision in *Dred Scott v. Sandford* (1857), in which the Court, led by Chief Justice Roger B. Taney, tried to impose a judicial solution to the most vexing social, political, and economic problem of the time—slavery. In the words of Charles Evans Hughes in 1927, the decision was a "self-inflicted wound," and one that took the Court a generation to overcome. In *Plessy v. Ferguson* (1896), the Court, passing judgment on a segregation case from Louisiana, again missed an opportunity to make the citizens of the United States equal under the law. Justice John Marshall Harlan's dissent contained this prophecy: "In my opinion, the judgment this day rendered will, in time, prove to be quite as pernicious as the decision made by this tribunal in the *Dred Scott* case." In the 1930s, when the nation was in the grip of the worst depression in its history, the Court came very near to inflicting another wound on itself by declaring one popular law of the New Deal after another unconstitutional. That it survived the constitutional crisis is due in no small measure to the adroit political skills of Chief Justice Hughes.

If the Court has rendered decisions that changed the course of American history for the worse, it also has prescribed remedies to change it in positive ways. Under the leadership of Chief Justice Earl Warren in the 1950s, the Court effectively gutted *Plessy* in *Brown v. Board of Education* (1954), which said, among other things, that separate schools could never be equal. This decision was one of many that attempted to reverse the policies of Jim Crow governments, and not only in the South. Cases involving equal rights for African Americans were soon followed by appeals on gender discrimination. Today, no one would tell a woman that she cannot practice law because of her gender, but that is exactly what the Court told the well-qualified Myra Bradwell in the 1873 decision *Bradwell v. Illinois.*

But what is it that causes the Court to change its collective mind over the years? After all, today's justices are bound by the Constitution and the laws passed under it, just as their predecessors were. Moreover, as an institution the Court is a continuum, and when the justices refer to earlier decisions, they speak of them as opinions of "this tribunal," as if every justice who ever served was responsible for everything the Court has said. Even though society's issues, ideals, and goals change over time, the justices are mindful of those who came before them, no matter how different their backgrounds, education, and politics. I hope that you can begin to find the answer to that question in the essays in this book.

The development of the Court, its powers, and its jurisprudential policies are the work—a mixture of individual brilliance and persuasiveness and of collaboration—of the 108 men and 2 women who have sat on its bench since 1789. These essays illustrate the abilities of those who have made a decisive impact on American constitutional development as well as note whose tenure on the Court left little or no trace.

The contributors to *Biographical Encyclopedia of the Supreme Court: The Lives and Legal Philosophies of the Justices* were asked to concentrate primarily on the Supreme Court careers of their subjects. What they did before joining the Court is covered only briefly, but serves to place them in historical context. Perhaps the information on the justices' Court careers will arouse readers' curiosity about their lives. To help satisfy that curiosity, each essay includes an annotated bibliography, which lists biographies of the justice as well as materials on decisions and judicial philosophy. But the primary intention of these essays is to present the issues that confronted the justices during their tenure, interpret and evaluate their work, and assess their importance in our constitutional doctrine and their lasting influence on future Court decisions.

In reading these essays and trying to assess the importance of individual justices, one should keep several factors in mind. First, we need to treat chief justices on a different scale than the associate justices, whether they were brilliant, mediocre, or weak. Although John Marshall, Charles Evans Hughes, and Earl Warren all made significant doctrinal contributions, their real impact is found in how they led the Court. Officially, the chief justice is no more than "first among equals," and all members of the Court cast only one vote apiece. But the chief justice is the political head of the Court and in modern times, with the development of an extensive judicial system of district and circuit courts, presides over the entire judicial system in the constitutional role as "chief justice of the United States." The chief justice is the liaison between the courts and the other branches of government. The chief justice presides over the Court and is responsible for assigning opinions. The person in this position is also the one who, if capable, can lead the Court through times of crisis. We remember Marshall not only for his magisterial opinions but also because during his thirty-five year tenure he helped make a weak tribunal into an equal part of government and led the Court in assuming its powers as the ultimate interpreter of the Constitution.

William Howard Taft, a former president, used his considerable political skills far more effectively as chief justice than he had ever done in the White House, securing for the Court not only a home of its own, but more important, control over its docket. Hughes headed the Court during the constitutional crisis of the 1930s, and his great political skills, not his written opinions, helped bring the judiciary through that crisis unscathed, with its authority and powers intact. Warren wrote eloquent opinions striking down racial segregation and legislative malapportionment, but he is remembered primarily for his ability to move the Court to expand the meaning of constitutionally protected rights.

Other chiefs have fared poorly among historians. Taney, despite a long tenure in which he actually expanded the authority of the Court, is remembered today as the architect of the disastrous *Dred Scott* decision and as the man who tried to undermine Abraham Lincoln's authority to save the Union. Harlan Fiske Stone and Frederick Vinson are portrayed in recent works as ill-suited to the job, unable to keep order in conferences or lead the Court. The evaluation of Warren Burger is that he was neither an effective chief nor a very bright judge. And only constitutional historians even remember the names of other chief justices such as Morrison Waite or Salmon Chase.

The second point to keep in mind is that our assessment of the associate justices tends to focus on their jurisprudential contributions. Chief Justice Marshall could concentrate on the political implications of decisions because Joseph Story worked out the legal issues. Similarly, Chief Justice Warren relied heavily on William Brennan to make sure that his efforts to expand rights were not only just, but based on the Constitution. Intellectually, Story and Brennan dominated the Courts on which they sat.

Because issues change over time, justices who had a major impact in one era may be all but forgotten in another. Few of Story's opinions are cited by current courts, because the issues he considered are no longer relevant in the twenty-first century. If there was a giant on the Court in the late nineteenth century, it was surely Stephen Field, who laid the basis for protection of property rights through the Fourteenth Amendment's due process clause. But Field's ideas have little impact today because the failure of what historian William Wiecek has called "classical legal thought" during the Depression of the 1930s led the Court to abandon substantive due process.

Scholars who try to assess what makes a justice "great" have proposed a number of criteria. One would seem self-evident: is the person learned in the law? One might expect that all of the people nominated to the nation's highest court would have this quality, but that is not, in fact, the case. The true legal scholars on the bench (Story, Oliver Wendell Holmes Jr., Benjamin Cardozo, and Felix Frankfurter come to mind) were few in number, and through much of the Court's history, political connection, not learning, was the decisive factor in appointment. As these essays show, once on the Court, many of these people, especially in the nineteenth century, proved to be little

more than ciphers, leaving no jurisprudential legacy at all. At the same time, some justices whom few expected to leave an impact, such as Louis Brandeis, Hugo Black, and John Marshall Harlan II, turned out to be highly influential.

Another criterion for greatness is the understanding a justice demonstrated of the relationship of law to the aims, values, and needs of society. The truly great justices could mold their opinions—whether decisions for the Court or dissents—in a way that spoke to the American people. Despite his limited individual contributions to legal doctrine, Earl Warren always understood that the law his Court expounded, be it to end racial segregation in schools, reapportion legislative districts, or ensure the rights of persons accused of crimes, would reach millions of people and affect their lives. Justice Brandeis patiently explained in his dissents why the country should cherish and protect free speech and the right to privacy, and how changes in the economy and the society had to be reflected in the law. More recently, Sandra Day O'Connor tried to establish criteria in the jurisprudence of both abortion and church-state relations that reflected the society she saw around her and did not merely parrot ideological fulminations.

A great justice must be able to communicate. The meaning of his or her words cannot be buried in a law review article masquerading as a judicial opinion, understood by only a few law professors. It is important that those teaching the law understand what the Court says, but it is even more important that the people do. When Justice Holmes denounced warrantless wire-tapping, he did so in a way that immediately caught popular attention. Instead of talking in abstract legal principles, he condemned it as "a dirty business," a phrase that nonlawyers could clearly understand. Chief Justice Warren fashioned his opinion in *Brown v. Board of Education* so that it would be short, could fit on one page of a newspaper, and be in language that everyone could understand. Some critics claimed that Warren's opinion was a little short in constitutional analysis, but he understood that in the end it was the people who had to understand the meaning of equal protection.

There are other criteria as well, such as whether the justice could operate effectively within the institutional structure of the Court. Some, such as Black and Brennan, often acted like politicians in developing a majority to support their positions. William O. Douglas, on the other hand, had no use for such persuasion. "The only soul I have to save is my own," he said, a position that Antonin Scalia also seems to have adopted.

The analysis can and does go on, and different scholars apply their own standards. For liberals, the question may be how well a justice can adapt constitutional standards to fit the needs of a modern society, and conservatives may take just the opposite tack and admire a justice who hews closely to what they see as the original intent of the Framers. Nearly every scholar prizes integrity, and, unlike the executive or legislative branches, the judiciary has been remarkably free of scandal. Only one justice has been impeached: Samuel Chase became the target of the Jeffersonians' political war on the judiciary, but in the end the Senate refused to convict. Abe Fortas resigned because of an alleged conflict of interest and his acceptance of large speaking fees after he joined the Court, but his real crime seems to have been his continuing friendship with President Lyndon Johnson and his lack of sensitivity to the separation of powers.

Finally, I would suggest that a truly great justice must be an educator, a justice whose opinions are constructed and written to teach constitutional lessons. It is said of Brandeis that in crafting his dissents, he would say to his clerks, "The opinion is now convincing, but how can we make it more instructive?" The opinions of the great chief justice John Marshall, although addressed to matters that no longer concern us directly, such as chartering banks, nevertheless remain important because they explicated the constitutional authority of a national government so that it may govern effectively. Brandeis, in turn, laid out the bases for understanding our rights and for tying issues such as free speech and privacy to the needs of a democratic society.

Had this book been written fifty years ago, the criteria used by the contributors to assess the justices' careers on the Court might have been different. Prior to the Warren era, the Court's docket had many important cases, but the great expansion of rights was yet to come. Should another editor undertake such a collection fifty years from now, I have no doubt that although some constitutional questions will remain the same, the contributors will have additional criteria and will be judging the men and women of the Supreme Court against a different social, economic, and political background.

This volume is an updated edition of *The Supreme Court Justices: A Biographical Dictionary* (1994). Among its features are new entries for Chief Justice John Roberts and Justice Samuel Alito, updated profiles on all members of the Roberts Court, and revised essays on selected former justices.

The 110 essays in this volume open with the justices' biographical data—birth and death dates, education, official positions, and Supreme Court service. For the date of a justice's appointment, the editors settled on the day the Senate received the nomination as the official date, and that information is courtesy of a report from the Congressional Research Service. The entries close with concise bibliographic essays that point readers to the justices' personal and professional papers, the most notable biographies, and journal articles on topics related to their careers. Last is a list of each justice's noteworthy opinions. Each biography includes a photograph or other illustration of the justice profiled. The book concludes with useful reference items that include a selected bibliography, a succession chart of Supreme Court seats, and a description of the Court's supporting personnel.

Acknowledgments

Unlike a monograph, for which one author does all of the research and writing, a book like this one happens only because a lot of talented people have a serious flaw—they have not learned to say "no" to editors like me who cajole them, often more than once, into contributing to such collections. There is an important dividend, however, in having a book like this written by multiple hands. We not only get the expertise of scholars who have written extensively about their subject, but we also get multiple viewpoints. The men and women who have contributed to this book are law professors, historians, political scientists, documentary editors, newspaper reporters, and freelance writers. They have brought to the project not only knowledge about their subject but also their ability to make substantive judgments about the justice's work and legacy. For their willingness to work with me, I am very grateful.

Their work, however, would not be in your hands without the skill and dedication of the staff at CQ Press. This is the fourth book I have done with CQ Press, and I am fortunate to have established good working relations with an editorial crew that is, in my mind, among the best in the business.

Acquisitions editor Doug Goldenberg-Hart enthusiastically believed that there should be an updated and revised version of the original edition, and he smoothed the way to making it happen. January Layman-Wood, the development editor, took on the often tedious but absolutely necessary task of making sure that all of the details fell into place, work in which she was helped by production editor Joan Gossett and editorial assistant Timothy Arnquist. My sometimes testy relationship with Carolyn Goldinger, in which I rail at the questions she raises, is more than tempered by the realization that she is one of the best copy editors in the business and that far more often than not her questions are right on target. Inge Lockwood did the proofreading, Indexing Partners LLC compiled the index, and intern Josh Stager pulled together the material for the selected bibliography. To all of them a sincere thank you for a job—once again—well done.

This edition is dedicated to my friend and colleague David W. Levy, who is retiring from academe but not from scholarship.

—*Melvin I. Urofsky*
Virginia Commonwealth University

SAMUEL ANTHONY ALITO JR.

Birth: April 1, 1950, Trenton, New Jersey.

Education: Princeton University, A.B., 1972; Yale Law School, J.D., 1975.

Official Positions: Law clerk to Judge Leonard I. Garth, U.S. Court of Appeals for the Third Circuit, 1976 1977; assistant U.S. attorney, District of New Jersey, 1977–1981; assistant to the solicitor general, U.S. Department of Justice, 1981–1985; deputy assistant attorney general, Office of Legal Counsel, U.S. Department of Justice, 1985–1987; U.S. attorney for the District of New Jersey, 1987–1990; judge, U.S. Court of Appeals for the Third Circuit, 1990–2006.

Supreme Court Service: Nominated associate justice by President George W. Bush, November 10, 2005, to replace Sandra Day O'Connor, who had retired; confirmed by the Senate, January 31, 2006, by a 58–42 vote; took judicial oath January 31, 2006.

In the 1972 Princeton University yearbook, the entry for Samuel A. Alito Jr. includes this whimsical sentence: "Sam intends to go to law school and eventually to warm a seat on the Supreme Court." Thirty-four years later, that prediction came true when Alito was sworn in to replace Justice Sandra Day O'Connor, the first female member of the Supreme Court.

Just months earlier, few commentators would have guessed that Alito was destined for the Supreme Court. President George W. Bush had already made two nominations to replace O'Connor, who on July 1, 2005, had announced her intention to retire as soon as her successor was confirmed. The first nominee was John Roberts Jr., whose name was withdrawn after the death of Chief Justice William Rehnquist and resubmitted to the Senate as nominee for chief justice. Bush then nominated his White House counsel, Harriet Miers, who withdrew from consideration after questions were raised about her suitability for the job

and her participation in controversial Bush administration decisions.

At this point, President Bush was under pressure to come back quickly with another female or minority nominee as a replacement for O'Connor. Instead, he reached into the ranks of federal appeals court judges to select Alito, a white male who had quietly served on the U.S. Court of Appeals for the Third Circuit for fifteen years. The president was quick to point out that Alito had "more prior judicial experience than any Supreme Court nominee in more than seventy years."

Because Alito was replacing O'Connor, a swing vote on a range of issues, his experience and reputation were not enough to fend off intense scrutiny and criticism from Senate Democrats and liberal groups. His nomination received more negative Senate votes than any justice since Clarence Thomas, who was confirmed by a 52–48 vote in 1991.

Alito was born in Trenton, New Jersey, in 1950. His father, an Italian immigrant, had grown up in poverty but was able to obtain a college education and become a teacher, as did Sam's mother. The elder Alito eventually obtained a position as a senior civil servant in a nonpartisan research position for the New Jersey legislature. His son Sam also had scholarly inclinations and was a star debater in high school. According to family members, the young Alito never was part of the rebellious antiestablishment climate of the times, preferring instead a sense of order and tradition.

Princeton University was a short distance from where Alito grew up, but when he began his college years there, it was as if he had entered "another world," as he told the Senate in his opening testimony, January 9, 2006. Alito was a rare conservative at a campus where students rallied against the Vietnam War and questioned authority on many fronts. In his senior year, the *Washington Post* reported, while Washington, D.C., was filled with antiwar protesters, Alito and several other Princeton students visited the chambers of Justice John Marshall Harlan, a conservative member of the Supreme Court. Alito's interest in the law was evident in the topic he picked for his thesis: the history of Italy's constitutional court. He graduated Phi Beta Kappa and was a selected scholar of the Woodrow Wilson School of Public and International Affairs.

Samuel Anthony Alito Jr.

Alito went on to Yale Law School, where he also excelled, winning awards for his moot court arguments and his contribution to the *Yale Law Journal*. Alito applied for a Supreme Court clerkship but wound up instead clerking for Leonard Garth, a conservative Third Circuit judge with whom he would later serve.

Alito enjoyed the intellectual world of appellate courts and in 1977 became an assistant U.S. attorney in New Jersey, in its appellate division. There, he met Martha-Ann Bomgardner, an office librarian who later became his wife.

With the election of Ronald Reagan as president in 1980, a brilliant appellate lawyer like Alito became a prized commodity in a Justice Department intent on changing the direction of the courts and the law. Attorney General Edwin Meese III and other top lawyers in the administration wanted to move away from what they saw as the "judicial activism" of the 1960s and 1970s toward a more modest role for judges limited to interpreting the words of statutes and the Constitution rather than imposing their own social policy preferences.

In 1981 Alito accepted an offer to serve as an assistant to the solicitor general, where he took on some of the conservative causes—including ending affirmative action—that some career lawyers were reluctant to pursue. Drawing on his lifelong love for baseball, Alito coined a phrase that resonated well with administration opponents of affirmative action. Alito wrote in a brief that homerun champion Hank Aaron, an African American, would not be regarded as highly "if the fences had been moved in whenever he came to the plate." On abortion, he advised that a frontal assault on the 1973 decision in *Roe v. Wade* would be unproductive, favoring instead a more incremental approach with a goal of "mitigating its effects." Alito also argued a dozen cases before the Supreme Court.

In 1985 Alito applied for a promotion to the position of deputy assistant attorney general in the Office of Legal Counsel, headed by Charles Cooper. His application letter, which would later trigger much of the concern about his nomination among liberals, declared, "I am and always have been a conservative." He went on to disparage liberal Warren Court precedents and to say he was "particularly proud" that he has been able to work toward convincing the Supreme Court that "the Constitution does not protect a right to abortion." Alito got the job and soon was helping devise legal strategy in a number of politically tinged issues, including the Iran-contra scandal. But Alito continued to be viewed as a fair-minded lawyer who stayed above the political fray.

He did not stay in the Office of Legal Counsel for long. In late 1986 he sought appointment as the U.S. attorney in New Jersey, a high profile prosecutorial position. He was motivated in part by the desire to return to New Jersey, where he hoped to raise his family near his parents and in-laws. But friends say Alito had already decided he wanted to become a federal judge, and serving as a U.S. attorney is usually a good stepping-stone toward achieving that goal.

For their part, Alito's superiors also wanted conservative lawyers such as Alito and Roberts, who also had served in the Reagan Justice Department, to position themselves for eventual judgeships and thereby have a long-lasting impact on the law. Cooper, who helped Alito at several stages during his Reagan years, said, "Nobody sat down and said back then that we are going to choreograph the rise of John Roberts and Sam Alito to become members of the Supreme Court." But the fact that both Alito and Roberts eventually became appeals court and then Supreme Court justices is a tribute to the deep impact the Reagan years had on the judiciary.

Alito served as U.S. attorney based in Newark from 1987 to 1990, prosecuting a range of organized crime, corruption, and even terrorism defendants. Again, he had a reputation for nonpartisanship. When a Third Circuit appeals judge retired in 1990, Alito set his sights on the next step in his career and was soon confirmed to fill that seat. The Third Circuit sits in Philadelphia, but Alito's chambers were in Newark, in his native New Jersey.

On the Third Circuit, Alito became known as one of its most conservative members, if not the most conservative. A study by University of Chicago Law School professor Cass Sunstein found that when Alito dissented, his position was almost always to the right of the judges in the majority, even judges appointed by Republican presidents. Alito became known by the nickname "Scalito," in part because he, like Justice Antonin Scalia, was a conservative Italian American jurist from Trenton, New Jersey.

In one dissent that received attention after he was nominated to the Supreme Court, Alito argued that Congress had acted outside its authority under the commerce clause when it outlawed possession of machine guns. In *United States v. Rybar* (1996), Alito said he was applying the 1995 Supreme Court precedent in *United States v. Lopez,* which used the same rationale to strike down a law banning possession of firearms near schools. But the majority on Alito's court distinguished between *Lopez* and *Rybar,* ruling that Congress could have reasonably found a connection between machine gun possession and interstate commerce, whereas the link between commerce and having guns near schools was more attenuated.

Another Alito dissent highlighted the contrast between Alito and O'Connor, the justice he was appointed to replace. In 1992, when the Supreme Court upheld the right to abortion in *Planned Parenthood v. Casey,* it was ruling on a 1991 case from Alito's Third Circuit. Alito had written a partial concurrence and partial dissent in the case that interpreted and applied O'Connor's prior abortion rulings to uphold a Pennsylvania law requiring women to notify their husbands of their plan to have an abortion. Alito reasoned that under O'Connor's test, the law did not severely burden enough women to be unconstitutional. When the case got to the Supreme Court, the joint opinion written by Justices David Souter, Anthony Kennedy, and O'Connor specifically rejected that argument, finding that the spousal notice provision did in fact impose an undue burden on women.

These rulings and others in the area of Fourth Amendment search and seizure and civil rights formed the basis for the strong belief among liberals that once Alito was nominated to the Supreme Court he would be a significantly more reliable conservative than O'Connor and should be opposed.

By the same token, conservatives were heartened that their long campaign to steer the Supreme Court to the right was bearing fruit. In particular, a series of establishment clause rulings by Alito gave the Christian Right confidence that he would be more accommodating than O'Connor was toward religious expression in the public square. One 1999 ruling, *American Civil Liberties Union of New Jersey v. Schundler,* upheld a holiday display on public property in Jersey City that included a crèche and a menorah as well as plastic figures of Santa Claus and Frosty the Snowman.

This background made the quiet judge from Newark an attractive candidate when the Miers nomination crumbled. "He has a deep understanding of the proper role of judges in our society," Bush said on October 31, 2005, announcing his intention to nominate Alito. "He understands that judges are to interpret the laws, not to impose their preferences or priorities on the people."

Liberal groups lined up to state their concerns, in hopes of mobilizing widespread opposition to Alito. Unlike other recent nominees whose views on many issues were unknown, Alito had more than 300 opinions and dissents, as well as other writings, to scrutinize and attack. "While his words are carefully chosen and his demeanor is measured, Judge Alito's ultraconservative judicial philosophy is nothing short of radical," said the liberal group People for the American Way. But conservative groups were quick to answer every charge and praise Alito's qualifications. "The portrait that is drawn of him by those who know him and know his writings is of a man of great intelligence, integrity, fairness, humility and justice," said Wendy Wright of the conservative Concerned Women for America.

As the date of Alito's hearing approached, he became unwittingly enmeshed in a seemingly unrelated Washington controversy. Revelations in the press about a secret domestic surveillance program approved by President Bush in the aftermath of the terrorist attacks of September 11, 2001, raised widespread concern about the extent of executive power, especially in wartime. In a 2000 speech before the Federalist Society, Alito made it clear that he was a proponent of the "unitary executive" theory, which seemed to fit into Bush's muscular view of presidential power. Under this theory, Alito argued that the framers of the Constitution vested all executive power in the president, and that the growth of independent agencies detracted from the effectiveness and accountability of the "vigorous executive" that the framers had in mind.

With the controversial Bush program in mind, Democrats tried repeatedly to determine if, because he espoused this theory, Alito would be too deferential to executive power and less respectful of legislative power. Alito said his views had been misunderstood and did not represent an endorsement of broad presidential power beyond the powers enumerated in the Constitution. But Democrats were not satisfied. "We cannot count on Judge Alito to blow the whistle when the president is out of bounds," said Sen. Edward Kennedy, D-Mass., a member of the Judiciary Committee, when he announced his opposition to Alito. When the nomination reached the Senate floor, he and John Kerry, D-Mass., mounted an unsuccessful filibuster against Alito.

The grilling of Alito on questions about executive power almost overshadowed Democrats' earlier concerns about his views on abortion. In light of his statements about *Roe v. Wade* as a Reagan administration attorney, Democrats persisted in asking him how much weight he would give *Roe* as a precedent in deciding future abortion cases. Alito was noncommittal in response. He said, "When a precedent is reaffirmed, each time it's reaffirmed that is a factor that should be taken into account in making the judgment about *stare decisis.*" But he also said the doctrine of *stare decisis*—respect for precedent—was "not an inexorable command." Because he was willing to describe other precedents as settled doctrine that were unlikely to be disturbed, Alito's reluctance to say the same thing about *Roe* only increased concern among liberals that he was open to the idea of reversing *Roe*.

Two other issues provoked concern about the Alito nomination. Alito held mutual fund investments in the Vanguard Group, and when he was confirmed for his appeals court seat, he pledged not to vote in cases in which Vanguard was a party. Yet in 2002 he did vote in just such a case: a widow sued Vanguard to obtain her late husband's investments that Vanguard had frozen because of a business dispute. When the litigant learned of Alito's investments, she complained, prompting Alito to recuse himself after the fact and ask that the case be decided by a new panel of judges. The American Bar Association, in giving Alito its highest "well qualified" rating, said his failure to recuse himself was an oversight, but several Democrats remained upset.

Alito also came under attack for his membership in Concerned Alumni of Princeton, a group that was unhappy with the admission of women and allegedly unqualified minorities to the elite institution. Alito cited his membership in his infamous 1985 job application, but at his confirmation hearings said he could not recall having any connection to the organization. He speculated that he might have joined because he supported the return of ROTC to Princeton, but he found the organization's other tenets "repugnant." Democratic senators criticized Alito for joining the group in the first place.

One of the more unusual features of Alito's confirmation hearing was the testimony of seven of his Third Circuit colleagues, both current and retired. It is rare, although not unprecedented, for fellow judges to act as character witnesses for nominees. These judges, appointed by both Republicans and Democrats, sang Alito's praises as a careful, fair-minded, and modest judge. Several made comments aimed at rebutting concerns that Alito might be an agenda-driven jurist.

Judge Garth, who had hired Alito as a law clerk and then served with him on the bench, offered these comments: "Make no mistake, he is no revolutionary. He is a sound jurist, always respectful of the institutions and the precepts that led to the decisions in the cases under review." Garth added, "His fairness, his judicial demeanor and actions, and his commitment to the law—all of those qualities which my colleagues and I agree he has—do not permit him to be influenced by individual preferences or any personal predilection."

Witnesses like Garth helped Alito defuse the criticisms leveled by Democrats. In contrast to Robert Bork in 1987, Alito's demeanor was modest and unflappable; he displayed no sharp edges, arrogance, or combativeness. He took the criticism in stride, although it took a toll on his wife seated behind him. One of the enduring televised images from the hearing was of Alito's wife in tears near the end of a long day of contentious questioning. She left the room while her husband, unaware of her distress, continued to testify until a recess was called.

In the end, Alito's hearing seemed to produce widespread dissatisfaction with the process. Adhering to a practice among recent nominees, Alito declined to state his personal views on a range of issues so as not to prejudge future cases. Democrats were frustrated at their inability to extract substantive answers from Alito, and Republicans attacked Democrats for shrill and unsubstantiated attacks on the nominee. After it was all over, Sen. Joseph Biden, D-Del., who had been criticized for long-winded statements that left little time for questioning Alito, suggested that the hearings were a waste of time and that nominees' qualifications should be debated on the floor of the Senate without testimony from the nominees themselves.

—*Tony Mauro*

BIBLIOGRAPHY

There is no biography of Alito, but these articles by Alito illuminate his views on legal issues: "Presidential Oversight and the Administrative State," *Engage* 2 (2001): 11; "The Role of the Lawyer in the Criminal Justice System," *Federalist Society Criminal Law News* 2 (1998): 3; *Change in Continuity at the Office of Legal Counsel, Cardozo Law Review* 15

(1993): 507; "The First Amendment: Information, Publication and the Media," *Seton Hall Constitutional Law Journal* (1991): 327; "The Next Page in Federal Sentencing," *Legal Times,* August 28/September 4, 1989, 19; "Introduction to After the Independent Counsel Decision: Is Separation of Powers Dead?" *American Criminal Law Review* 26 (1989): 1667; "The Year Wasn't So Bad," *National Law Journal,* September 26, 1998, 12; "Documents and the Privilege Against Self-Incrimination," *University of Pittsburgh Law Review* 48 (1986): 27; "The 'Released Time' Cases Revisited: A Study of

Group Decisionmaking by the Supreme Court," *Yale Law Journal* (1974): 1202.

NOTEWORTHY OPINIONS

United States v. Rybar, 103 F.3d 273 (3d Cir. 1996)

Planned Parenthood v. Casey, 947 F.2d 683 (3d Cir. 1991); 505 U.S. 833.

American Civil Liberties Union of New Jersey v. Schundler, 168 F.3d 92 (3d Cir. 1999)

HENRY BALDWIN

Birth: January 14, 1780, New Haven, Connecticut.

Education: Hopkins Grammar School, 1793; Yale College, 1797, LL.D., 1830; attended the law lectures of Judge Tapping Reeve; clerked for Alexander James Dallas.

Official Positions: U.S. representative; chairman, Committee on Domestic Manufactures.

Supreme Court Service: Nominated associate justice by President Andrew Jackson, January 5, 1830, to replace Bushrod Washington, who had died, confirmed by the Senate, January 6, 1830, by a 41–2 vote; took judicial oath January 18, 1830; served until April 21, 1844; replaced by Robert C. Grier, nominated by President James K. Polk.

Death: April 21, 1844, Philadelphia, Pennsylvania.

Henry Baldwin was raised in rural Connecticut but returned to New Haven to attend Yale College, from which he graduated in 1797. He moved to Philadelphia to study law in the office of Alexander J. Dallas, a prominent lawyer, and was admitted to the Philadelphia bar. In 1799 he headed west and settled in the bustling town of Pittsburgh. He joined the local bar in 1801 and started a firm with two other young, ambitious lawyers. Baldwin and his partners soon held prominent places in western Pennsylvania legal and political circles, for a time owning a Republican newspaper, *The Tree of Liberty*.

In 1816 Baldwin won a seat in the U.S. House of Representatives and was reelected twice. Representing the manufacturing interests of Pittsburgh, and himself an iron and textile manufacturer, Baldwin favored a protective tariff and courted southern support by opposing conditional admission of Missouri to statehood. He also staunchly defended Gen. Andrew Jackson's prosecution of the war against the Florida Seminoles.

Baldwin resigned from the House in 1822 due to illness, but he maintained his support of Jackson and corresponded with Jackson adherents about the general's political chances in Pennsylvania. In the 1828 presidential election, Baldwin ardently campaigned for "Old Hickory." The Jackson victory did not bring an immediate reward to Baldwin, whose candidacy for various federal appointments was opposed by Vice President John C. Calhoun. But in late 1829, when Justice Bushrod Washington died, Jackson named Baldwin to the Supreme Court.

In his early years, Baldwin was noted as an amiable, pleasant, and moderate man; Justice Joseph Story initially found the appointment of this Democrat "quite satisfactory." But Baldwin became more contentious with the years, apparently suffering a breakdown in 1832, which prevented his attendance at the 1833 term of the Court. This absence relieved his brethren of what had become an unpredictable, argumentative presence. By 1833 Story was complaining to a federal district judge that Baldwin's "distaste for the Supreme Court and especially for [Chief Justice Marshall] is so familiarly known to us that it excites no surprise."

By the mid-1830s, however, Baldwin had mellowed to the extent that his work on the Third Circuit had produced a volume of well-respected decisions and had raised the prestige of that circuit. He also managed to mend his relationship with the chief justice and was a frequent visitor during Marshall's last illness. According to Story, Baldwin held no one in higher "reverence or respect."

Although Baldwin's initial dissatisfaction with service on the Court might be attributed to its Federalist flavor, Democratic appointments of the 1830s should have assuaged his sense of political isolation. But Baldwin's relationship with the new justices was far from harmonious. In addition, he provoked constant arguments with Court reporter Richard Peters over the presentation of his numerous dissents. In an age when consensus (or at least the appearance of it) was the hallmark of Supreme Court decisions, Baldwin was a misfit.

Henry Baldwin

Baldwin's activity on the bench falls into two major periods: a series of dissents and concurrences in 1831–1832 and a second series of concurrences in 1837. In the 1831 term, the new justice dissented seven times—probably a record for a junior justice. In *Ex parte Crane* (1831), Baldwin criticized the majority decision to issue a writ of *mandamus* as an unwarranted and dangerous extension of federal jurisdiction. His intemperate language no doubt antagonized

Marshall, who had written the opinion, as well as other members of the majority.

In *United States v. Arredondo* (1832), Baldwin's majority opinion placed the burden of proof in public land claims on the government and annoyed President Jackson in the process. The Arredondo claim dated to a vague Spanish land grant in Florida. According to Baldwin, courts must protect even ill-defined land titles predating American possession to ensure security of landownership. The Jackson administration had vigorously opposed the Arredondo claim and now found its recent appointee to the bench issuing a stern lecture on the duties of the government.

In *Cherokee Nation v. Georgia* (1831) and *Worcester v. Georgia* (1832), Baldwin's usual unpredictable thinking appeared more consistent than the majority's. In the first case, Marshall's decision held that the Cherokee had no standing to bring suit under the Court's original jurisdiction because the Cherokee were a "domestic, dependent nation." Although Baldwin did not reiterate Marshall's expression of sympathy for the plight of the Cherokee, his concurrence with the chief justice's opinion appeared to place him squarely in the Marshall camp. In the subsequent case, Baldwin dissented from the majority view (again written by Marshall) that the Cherokee were a special foreign nation and the Georgia act that violated this status was unconstitutional. According to Baldwin, the Cherokee were not a "nation" and "treaties" with them were merely agreements. Over the course of the two cases, Baldwin's consistency of outlook in the face of the majority's apparent reversal managed to irritate the other members of the Court.

The most remarkable product of Baldwin's tenure was *A General View of the Origin and Nature of the Constitution . . . Together with Opinions in the Cases decided at January Term, 1837,* which he wrote and published in pamphlet form. Baldwin had concurred with the majority in these cases of the 1837 judicial "revolution," particularly *Charles River Bridge v. Warren Bridge, New York v. Miln,* and *Briscoe v. Bank of Kentucky,* but had subsequently decided that the Court had not paid sufficient attention to constitutional precepts. To Baldwin, liberal and narrow interpreters of the Constitution continued to err in their judgments, and the 1837 cases were proof of his contention. Correct interpretation, according to Baldwin, lay somewhere between these extremes and had been most consistently delivered by "the late venerated Chief Justice" and Baldwin himself. As Marshall could no longer speak for himself, Baldwin proceeded to explain the "few and simple" principles that would provide "an easy solution" to all questions regarding the Constitution. In the process, he again disrupted the appearance of a harmonious and dignified Court. The last seven years of his tenure witnessed recurrent mental instability and very little productive activity.

—*Elizabeth Brand Monroe*

BIBLIOGRAPHY

Baldwin's judicial career has excited little research. The most extensive treatment is Frank Otto Gatell's essay in Leon Friedman and Fred L. Israel (eds.) *The Justices of the United States Supreme Court, 1789–1969,* vol. 1, 571 (1969) (hereafter cited as Friedman and Israel, *Justices*). G. Edward White addresses Baldwin's early judicial career in *The Marshall Court and Cultural Change, 1815–1835,* volume 3 of the *Holmes Devise History of the Supreme Court* (1988); and Carl Swisher discusses Baldwin's later career in *The Taney Period, 1836–1864* (1974), volume 5 of the series.

NOTEWORTHY OPINIONS

Ex parte Crane, 30 U.S. 190 (1831) (Dissent)

United States v. Arredondo, 31 U.S. 691 (1832)

PHILIP PENDLETON BARBOUR

Birth: May 25, 1783, Orange County, Virginia.

Education: Read law on his own; attended one session at College of William and Mary, 1801.

Official Positions: Member, Virginia House of Delegates from Orange County, 1812–1814; U.S. representative, 1814–1825, 1827–1830; Speaker of the House, 1821–1823; state judge, General Court for the Eastern District of Virginia, 1825–1827; president, Virginia Constitutional Convention, 1829–1830; U.S. district judge, Court of Eastern Virginia, 1830–1836.

Supreme Court Service: Nominated associate justice by President Andrew Jackson, February 28, 1835, to replace Gabriel Duvall, who had resigned; confirmed by the Senate, March 15, 1836, by a 30–11 vote; took judicial oath May 12, 1836; served until February 25, 1841; replaced by Peter V. Daniel, nominated by President Martin Van Buren.

Death: February 25, 1841, Washington, D.C.

Although he served less than five years on the Supreme Court, Philip Pendleton Barbour played a more important role in American constitutional history than is generally acknowledged. Prior to his appointment to the Court, Barbour had contributed significantly to the development of a reinvigorated states' rights interpretation of the Constitution that would increase in importance between the time of his death in 1841 and the outbreak of the Civil War two decades later.

The son of Thomas Barbour, a neighbor and an early political sponsor of James Madison who broke with Madison over the issue of Virginia's ratification of the Constitution, Barbour was educated at a local school. After attempting to practice law in Kentucky, he returned to Virginia and studied law for one term under St. George Tucker at the College of William and Mary.

Barbour was elected to the Virginia House of Delegates in 1812, and then to the U.S. House of Representatives in 1814. During his tenure in Congress, Barbour was a leader of the conservative faction of the Republican Party. Between 1821 and 1823 he served as Speaker of the House. In 1825 he declined an invitation to join the University of Virginia faculty as its first professor of law but stepped down from Congress to accept a position on the Virginia General Court.

In 1827 he returned to Congress where he remained until 1830 when President Andrew Jackson appointed him U.S. district judge for the Eastern District of Virginia. In this capacity he also served as a member of the Fifth Circuit Court of the United States with his longtime political opponent, Chief Justice John Marshall. In addition, Barbour served as president of both the Virginia Constitutional Convention of 1829–1830 and the 1831 Philadelphia Free Trade Convention.

In Congress, Barbour opposed the Bonus Bill of 1817, federally funded internal improvements, restrictions on the ability of Missouri to enter the Union as a slave state, the Second Bank of the United States, and the protective tariff. He opposed the efforts of the South Carolina nullifiers but accepted the premise that a state had the right to withdraw from the Union as a last resort.

In addition to being a principal exponent for the states' rights cause, he was also instrumental in developing its central constitutional arguments. For example, he was the first major political figure to argue that the protective tariff was not only unfair, but also unconstitutional. In this capacity, he helped define the basic tenets of states' rights constitutionalism that would later be endorsed by Supreme Court justices John Catron, Peter Daniel, John Campbell, and, to a limited extent, by Chief Justice Roger Taney. Barbour had been critical of the Marshall Court in the late 1810s, and, in his capacity as counsel for the state of Virginia, he argued unsuccessfully that the Court lacked jurisdiction in the landmark case, *Cohens v. Virginia* (1821). As a member of Congress, he had also sought (unsuccessfully) to require the concurrence of five of the seven justices of the Court in any case involving a constitutional question.

The possibility of Barbour's appointment to the Supreme Court had been rumored since his appoint-

Philip Pendleton Barbour

ment to the lower federal bench in 1830. In February 1831, former president John Quincy Adams predicted that if John Marshall were to retire "some shallow-pated wild-cat like Philip P. Barbour fit for nothing but to tear the Union to rags and tatters, would be appointed in his place." Barbour's chances for appointment improved considerably in 1832 when he withdrew his support for a movement on the part of disgruntled southerners to place his name on the Democratic ticket as the vice presidential candidate in place of Jackson's own choice, Martin Van Buren. By withdrawing when he did, he earned Jackson's gratitude, and his gesture allowed the president to offer Barbour's appointment as a concession to his southern critics.

The resignation of Gabriel Duvall of Maryland in 1835 and the death of John Marshall later that year created two openings on the Court. Although he had been initially rebuffed in his effort to replace Duvall with Roger Taney, Jackson ultimately submitted the names of Taney and Barbour to the Senate. After much controversy, both were approved on March 15, 1836. Two efforts to delay the vote on Barbour's nomination failed by votes of 25 to 20 and 26 to 16, and he was subsequently confirmed, 30–11.

During his first term on the Court, he was part of the majority in a trio of 1837 cases—*Briscoe v. Bank of Kentucky, Charles River Bridge v. Warren Bridge,* and *New York v. Miln*—that repudiated the nationalistic jurisprudence that had been associated with the Marshall Court. Barbour wrote the majority opinion in

Miln, using it as an opportunity to argue for a narrow definition of the federal commerce power and an expansive definition for the state police power, which he characterized as "unqualified and exclusive."

Otherwise, Barbour's four years on the Supreme Court were characterized by a near unanimity of opinion. During his tenure, the Court heard 155 cases, all but 30 of which were decided without a dissenting vote. Barbour sided most frequently with his fellow southerners Catron (97.8 percent of the time) and Taney (97.4 percent) and least frequently with Justices Henry Baldwin (89.6 percent) and Joseph Story (94.1 percent).

Barbour dissented only on two occasions, but evidence suggests that had he lived, his states' rights principles would have eventually put him at odds with his more nationalistic colleagues. Although only Story dissented from Barbour's opinion in *Miln,* Smith Thompson and Baldwin refused to endorse its particulars at the time, and subsequent evidence showed that neither John McLean nor James Wayne accepted his comments on the limits of the federal commerce power. Furthermore, in cases in which the Court was called on to interpret the scope of federal authority, Barbour consistently advocated a narrow construction of all delegations of authority to the national government. This view was apparent in his dissents in *Kendall v. United States ex rel Stokes* (1838)

and *Lessee of Pollard's Heirs v. Kibbe* (1840). In cases such as *Holmes v. Jennison* (1840), which involved questions of implied restrictions upon state sovereignty, Barbour opposed such limitations. Given more time on the bench, Barbour almost surely would have been as strident a defender of the states' rights position as his successor and fellow Virginian, Peter Daniel.

Barbour was apparently well respected by his colleagues, including Justice Story, who eulogized him as "a very conscientious, upright, and laborious judge, whom we all respected for his talents and virtues, and his high sense of duty."

—*Joseph Gordon Hylton*

BIBLIOGRAPHY

There is unfortunately no biography of Barbour. The best sources for information concerning his career are Charles D. Lowery's biography of his brother, *James Barbour: A Jeffersonian Republican* (1984); and Carl B. Swisher's *The Taney Period, 1836–64,* volume 5 of the *Holmes Devise History* (1974).

NOTEWORTHY OPINIONS

New York v. Miln, 36 U.S. 102 (1837)

Kendall v. United States, 37 U.S. 524 (1838) (Dissent)

Holmes v. Jennison, 39 U.S. 540 (1840) (Dissent)

HUGO LAFAYETTE BLACK

Birth: February 27, 1886, Harlan, Alabama.

Education: Birmingham Medical School, 1903–1904; University of Alabama Law School, LL.B., 1906.

Official Positions: Police court judge, Birmingham, 1910–1911; county solicitor, Jefferson County, Alabama, 1914–1917; U.S. senator, 1927–1937.

Supreme Court Service: Nominated associate justice by President Franklin D. Roosevelt, August 12, 1937, to replace Willis Van Devanter, who had retired; confirmed by the Senate, August 17, 1937, by a 63–16 vote; took judicial oath August 19, 1937; retired September 17, 1971; replaced by Lewis F. Powell Jr., nominated by President Richard Nixon.

Death: September 25, 1971, Bethesda, Maryland.

Few Supreme Court justices have achieved the exalted status of Hugo Black, who is widely viewed as one of the Court's most influential justices and perhaps its most committed textualist. Yet much of what the public knows about Justice Black consists of the more colorful aspects of his character and judicial performance.

For example, his contemporaries believed that President Franklin Roosevelt selected Black as his first Supreme Court appointment in 1937 because of the nominee's ardent support in the Senate for the New Deal and the president's Court-packing plan. Black's reputation for trying to read the Constitution as literally as possible is memorialized through his practice of carrying a copy of the document in his pocket for ready reference and his persistently unique reading of the First Amendment as absolutely prohibiting any government interference with the freedom of speech and press. He is also widely remembered for his capacity for hard work, as reflected in his lifelong habits of reading extensively on his own and researching thoroughly any subject of personal or professional interest to him. Moreover, conservatives and liberals alike have admired Black: conservatives commend his steadfast commitment to judicial restraint and opposition to substantive due process, and liberals praise his efforts to secure the constitutional foundations of the New Deal and the incorporation of most of the Bill of Rights. Yet, many people still speculate about whether Black should even have been confirmed in light of his membership, while a young lawyer, in the Ku Klux Klan.

These glimpses into Hugo Black's life and judicial career do not fully reflect the skills he brought to the Court, his judicial philosophy, or his influence on the development of American constitutional law. Black was a seminal figure in constitutional history, but for more complex reasons than his popular image suggests.

Black came to the Court far better prepared and with more settled views on constitutional interpretation than is commonly thought. He graduated at the top of his University of Alabama Law School class, in spite of concurrently taking a full liberal arts curriculum, and began practice in Ashland. In 1907 he moved his practice to Birmingham. Within his first five years in Birmingham, he served for a year and a half as a part-time municipal court judge and for three years as the Jefferson County prosecuting attorney. These positions taught him about police misconduct and the need for efficient but equal justice. In perhaps his most famous case as a prosecutor, he investigated and prosecuted several area police officers for abusing and forcing confessions from black defendants. These personal experiences helped to guide him later as a senator to declare that he would not vote to confirm a former prosecutor as a federal judge if he felt that the latter had abused fair criminal procedures, and as a Supreme Court justice to recognize criminal defendants' constitutional rights.

Hugo Lafayette Black

His private practice included a substantial number of personal injury cases. This work enabled him to sharpen his talents as an eloquent, passionate advocate in countless jury trials and in more than 100 cases in the Alabama appellate courts. His oratorical skills helped him to get elected in 1927 to the U.S. Senate, where he developed an understanding of the relationship between the federal political process and the Supreme Court. On the floor of the Senate and in committees, he often passionately and eloquently defended New Deal legislation and criticized the activist conservative Court. His skills as an orator were also evident in his first public act as an associate justice, when, immediately after his confirmation, he gave a brief but dramatic radio address to verify newspaper reports that he was once a member of the Klan, but to add that he had resigned many years before and would comment no further.

Significantly, Black's second term as a senator coincided with Roosevelt's 1932 election victory. Black quickly caught the president's attention as a committed New Deal liberal who had sponsored a statute that later became the Fair Labor Standards Act of 1938, supported antitrust and other commercial or economic regulations, and oversaw Senate investigations that exposed the abuses of private shipping operators, major commercial airlines, and large utility holding companies. In numerous committee hearings and floor debates, Black espoused the beliefs that Congress had the authority under the commerce clause to pass appropriate legislation to deal with any problem that directly or indirectly affected the national economy and that the federal courts lacked any constitutional authority to interfere with such enactments.

In his unequivocal support for the president's Court-packing plan, he confirmed the power of Congress to change the number of members of the Supreme Court, and he declared that "neither the people who wrote nor the people who approved the Constitution ever contemplated that the Supreme

Court should become all powerful." Foreshadowing the philosophy he would later espouse on the Court, Black suggested that the five conservative justices who dominated the Court made it necessary for the president to take extreme action:

> The time has arrived when those who favor fitting laws to modern needs in order to correct and cure social and industrial injustice must face their problems squarely and fairly. Everybody knows that Supreme Court decisions by a bare majority have for years been thrown as impassable barriers in the way of the solemn and well-matured legislative plans supported by the people.

Once on the Court, Black quickly synthesized his views on constitutional interpretation into a coherent judicial philosophy. He declared a jurisprudence of certainty, with clear, precise standards that would limit judicial discretion, protect individual rights, and give government room to address a significant range of social problems. He saw the Constitution as a set of commands designed to prevent the recurrence of certain historic evils. Once he had determined the scope of a constitutional mandate through its literal language or its framers' intent when its text was unclear, he rigorously applied it, regardless of the consequences or conflicting precedent.

Black gave one of the fullest expressions of his approach to judicial decision making in the inaugural James Madison lecture at New York University Law School in 1960. He denounced the practice of other justices, such as Felix Frankfurter and John Marshall Harlan, to engage in judicial balancing, which "regard[ed] the prohibitions of the Constitution, even its most unequivocal commands, as mere admonitions which Congress need not always observe." Rather, Black recognized that "the whole history and background of our Constitution and Bill of Rights [belie] the assumption or conclusion that our ultimate constitutional freedoms are no more than our English ancestors had when they came to this new land to get new freedoms." He believed that the framers had resolved all of the necessary balancing of

constitutional liberties in 1791: "Where conflicting values exist in the field of individual liberties protected by the Constitution, that document settles the conflict."

Despite its clarity, Black's methodology, as well as many of the results it produced, rarely commanded a majority of the Court. For example, he repeatedly argued that the Constitution meant exactly what it said in the First Amendment's command that government could never abridge freedom of speech and press. In his Madison lecture, he explained:

> The phrase "Congress shall make no law" is composed of plain words, easily understood. . . . The Framers knew this. The language used by Madison in his proposal was different, but no less emphatic and unequivocal.
>
> Of course, the decision to provide a constitutional safeguard for a particular right, such as the right of free speech . . . involves a balancing of conflicting interests. I believe, however, that the Framers themselves did this balancing when they wrote the Constitution and the Bill of Rights. . . . Courts have neither the right nor the power to . . . make a different evaluation of the importance of the rights granted in the Constitution.

Nevertheless, a majority of the Court consistently favored a balancing approach over Black's absolutist reading of the First Amendment. Even in the last opinion he ever wrote, in the Pentagon Papers case, *New York Times v. United States* (1971), only William O. Douglas joined Black's reiteration of his view that even when national security might be at stake, "the history and language of the First Amendment support the view that the press must be left to publish news, whatever the source, without censorship, injunctions, or prior restraints."

Ironically, Black's unique methodology led him to consistently take a far more hospitable stance toward the government in Fourth Amendment cases. He almost always gave the government wide latitude in determining the "reasonableness" of its searches, even those without a warrant. For example, in a heated dissent in *Berger v. New York* (1967), he rejected the majority's invalidation of a conviction based on electronic eavesdropping. Seemingly oblivious to the dangers of wiretapping, he argued that there was nothing in the Fourth Amendment's history to suggest that its framers intended to prohibit governments from using technological innovations to investigate crimes and enforce the law.

In spite of the rarity with which a majority of the Court fully endorsed his methodology—but partly as a consequence of his strong reasoning and persistent advocacy during his long tenure on the Court—Black left his mark on constitutional law in two significant ways. First, he wrote a number of influential opinions that helped to keep critical debates open long enough to allow other justices to change their thinking or to take a position similar to his own but for different reasons. Second, he cast a number of critical votes that helped to shape several areas of constitutional law.

Through his opinions, Black exerted influence in diverse fields such as freedom of speech, incorporation, criminal procedure, and reapportionment. For example, his constant assertion that the First Amendment did not permit the government to regulate obscenity eventually led the Warren Court to define obscenity in a way that made its regulation more difficult. Similarly, his persistent criticism of the government's investigations of and prosecutions for so-called anti-American activities in the 1950s ultimately helped to guide the Warren Court to overturn a number of convictions in the McCarthy era based on "subversive activities."

Black also exerted considerable influence in keeping the debate on incorporation open and facilitating the Court's movement to make most of the Bill of Rights applicable to the states. He sought to reconcile the history and language of the Fourteenth Amendment with the basic need for judicial restraint in the American constitutional scheme. His solution was to propose total incorporation—in other words, to define the term *liberty* in the Fourteenth Amendment's due process clause as including no more or less than the guarantees specified in the first eight amendments.

He first expressed his views on total incorporation in his dissent in *Adamson v. California* (1947). Joined by Douglas, he laid down the formulation that guided him for the rest of his judicial career:

> My study of the historical events that culminated in the Fourteenth Amendment . . . persuades me that one of the chief objects that the provisions of the Amendment's first section, separately, and as a whole, were intended to accomplish was to make the Bill of Rights applicable to the states. . . .
>
> . . . I fear to see the consequences of the Court's practices of substituting its own conceptions of decency and fundamental justice for the language of the Bill of Rights as its point of departure in interpreting and enforcing that Bill of Rights. . . . To hold that this Court can determine what, if any, provisions of the Bill of Rights will be enforced, and if so to what degree, is to frustrate the great design of a written Constitution.

Black sought to restrict judicial discretion by urging the Court to define liberty in terms of another part of the constitutional text in which the original framers had explicitly defined the basic components of liberty as consisting of the specific guarantees set forth in the first eight amendments.

For the next twenty years and in numerous cases, Black continued to call on his fellow justices to apply the first eight amendments to the states. During that period, he often came into conflict with Justice Frankfurter, who rejected total incorporation and argued vigorously instead that the Fourteenth Amendment applied certain guarantees to the states as a matter of fundamental fairness. Although the Court never endorsed total incorporation, it inexorably moved away from the Frankfurter position it had initially adopted in *Wolf v. Colorado* (1949) in the direction of incorporating most of the Bill of Rights. For example, in *Mapp v. Ohio* (1961), Black concurred with the majority's declaration that the states must uphold the guarantees of the Fourth Amendment as incorporated through the Fourteenth Amendment. With this announcement, the Court overruled *Wolf,* which had applied the established constitutional theory that the Fourteenth Amendment's due process clause contained all the authority necessary to strike down state conduct that was fundamentally unfair.

By the time Black retired from the Court in 1971, the incorporation debate had ended. His persistent advocacy had facilitated the Court's move to incorporate all of the Bill of Rights, with the exceptions of the Second and Third Amendments, the Fifth Amendment's requirement of grand jury indictment, and the Seventh Amendment.

His success in the incorporation debate helped to set the stage for the nationalization and reformation of state criminal procedures. In contrast to his narrow reading of the Fourth Amendment, he read the Fifth and Sixth Amendments expansively. Drawing on his experiences as a police court judge and county prosecutor, he constantly tried to lead the Court to strictly enforce the Constitution's provisions defining the conditions of trial by jury and availability of counsel and prohibiting coerced confessions, compulsory self-incrimination, and double jeopardy. Indeed, one of the first Court opinions he wrote, *Johnson v. Zerbst* (1938), held that in a federal prosecution counsel must be appointed to represent a defendant who cannot afford to hire an attorney. He also wrote the Court's unanimous opinion in *Chambers v. Florida* (1940), which held that the confessions obtained by Florida authorities to condemn four black defendants to death were clearly coerced and, therefore, a violation of the Fourteenth Amendment's due process clause. In language to which he and other justices often turned in subsequent criminal procedure cases, he wrote:

Under our constitutional system, courts stand against any winds that blow as havens of refuge for those who might otherwise suffer because they are helpless, weak, outnumbered, or because they are non-conforming victims of prejudice and public excitement. Due process of law, preserved for all by our Constitution, commands that no such practice as that disclosed

[in this case] shall send any accused to his death. No higher duty, no more solemn responsibility, rests upon this Court, than that of translating into living law and maintaining this constitutional shield deliberately planned and inscribed for the benefit of every human being to our Constitution—of whatever race, creed, or persuasion.

When the Court refused to make assistance of counsel mandatory in state felony trials in *Betts v. Brady* (1942), he vigorously dissented. Even though he had not yet fully developed his incorporation theory, and the Court had not yet agreed to apply the Sixth Amendment to the states, Black argued in *Betts* that a state's failure to provide counsel for defendants in state felony trials clearly violated the majority's own "[standard] that due process of law is denied if a trial is conducted in such a manner that it is 'shocking to the universal sense of justice' or 'offensive to the common and fundamental ideas of fairness and right.' " Eventually, Black's persistence paid off. In his opinion for a unanimous Court in *Gideon v. Wainwright* (1963), which overruled *Betts,* he declared:

The right of one charged with crime to counsel may not be deemed fundamental and essential to fair trials in some countries, but it is in ours. From the very beginning, our state and national constitutions and laws have laid great emphasis on procedural and substantive safeguards designed to assure fair trials before impartial tribunals in which every defendant stands equal before the law. This noble ideal cannot be realized if the poor man charged with a crime has to face his accusers without a lawyer to assist him.

Black also helped to shape the Court's establishment clause doctrine. He wrote the Court's opinion in *Everson v. Board of Education of Ewing Township* (1947), which was the first case to declare that the clause applied to the states. Although the *Everson* Court ultimately concluded that the state's payment of the bus fares of all pupils, including those in parochial schools, served a secular purpose and therefore did not violate the establishment clause, Black expressly agreed with Thomas Jefferson that the clause was intended to erect "a wall of separation between Church and State" and noted that government cannot "contribute tax-raised funds to the support of an institution which teaches the tenets and faith of any church." In *Illinois ex rel. McCollum v. Board of Education* (1948), the Court, in yet another Black opinion, held unconstitutional a released time program in which religious instruction took place in public school. Fourteen years later, Justice Black wrote perhaps his most controversial opinion on the separation of church and state in *Engel v. Vitale* (1962), which held that a state-sponsored "non-denominational prayer" was "wholly inconsistent" with the establishment clause. In his view, that clause prohibited any laws that "establish an official religion whether [they] operate directly to coerce non-observing individuals or not." He wrote, "Religion is too personal, too sacred, too holy, to permit its 'unhallowed perversion' by a civil magistrate."

In addition, Black helped to lead the Warren Court to strike down enactments permitting disproportionate legislative representation at the state and federal levels. Indeed, he supported the equal protection claim in every reapportionment case that came before the Court during his tenure. He argued that Article I conferred on qualified voters the rights to vote and to have their votes counted on an equal basis in congressional elections. Yet, over his dissent, the Court declared in *Colegrove v. Green* (1946) that such matters were "political questions" whose merits the Court could not reach. Justice Frankfurter explained that the reapportionment was business for politicians to handle. By entering the "political thicket," Frankfurter warned, the Court risked political reprisals that could ultimately undercut its institutional authority. Black's dissent denounced the Court's preoccupation with political considerations rather than its paramount responsibility of determining whether legislative malapportionment violated the Constitution. He explained that both Article I and the equal protection clause required that congressional district lines be

drawn "to give approximately equal weight to each vote cast." Eventually, four other justices adopted Black's views on the justiciability of apportionment in *Baker v. Carr* (1962). Just two years later, Black delivered the Court's opinion in *Wesberry v. Sanders* (1964), which formally overturned *Colegrove*. As he explained, "The right to vote is too important in our free society to be stripped of judicial protection by such an interpretation."

Black made a second significant impact on constitutional law, not through his opinions, but through his votes in a number of pivotal cases. In this way, he influenced the Court's approaches to the commerce power, criminal procedure, school desegregation, reapportionment, and freedom of religion.

For example, Black consistently supported the Court's abandonment of its substantive due process review of economic regulations and the rise of a more deferential judicial reading of the commerce clause. Within his first five years on the Court, he joined unanimous decisions rejecting a substantive due process challenge to the provisions of the Fair Labor Standards Act in *United States v. Darby Lumber Co.* (1941) and sustaining, in *Olsen v. Nebraska* (1941), a state statute fixing the maximum fee that an employment agency could collect from employees. In explaining the Court's unanimous decision upholding a state right-to-work law that prohibited closed shops in *Lincoln Federal Union v. Northwestern Iron & Metal Co.* (1949), Black declared that the Court had abandoned substantive due process in economic cases and returned "to the earlier constitutional principle that states have power to legislate against what are found to be injurious practices in their internal commercial and business affairs, so long as their laws do not run afoul of some specific federal constitutional prohibition." In fact, during Black's thirty-four-year tenure, the Court never struck down a federal law for violating the commerce clause. For his part, Black consistently voted in the 1960s to uphold the constitutionality of congressional enactments premised on the commerce clause and Section 5 of the Fourteenth Amendment for the purpose of remedying racial discrimination in private accommodations and voting practices.

In addition, Black consistently joined the Court's opinions aimed at ending segregation in the United States. For example, when *Brown v. Board of Education* (1954) was first argued, and the Court under Chief Justice Fred Vinson was first considering whether to overrule *Plessy v. Ferguson* (1896), Black was one of only four justices who voted to overturn *Plessy* and to order the end of segregation in public schools. When *Brown* was reargued after Vinson's death and the appointment of Earl Warren, Black was one of the first to join the new chief justice's subsequently unanimous opinion in *Brown*.

In *Griffin v. County School Board* (1964), Black strengthened *Brown* by writing the Court's opinion holding illegal the action of a county school board that had closed its public schools to avoid integration and thereby contributed to the support of private segregated schools. He wrote, "The time for mere 'deliberate speed' has run out, and that phrase can no longer justify denying these Prince Edward County school children their constitutional rights to an education equal to that afforded by the public schools in the other parts of Virginia." He explained that the trial court could, if necessary, close all the schools in Virginia if the public schools were not reopened in the affected county. Black also joined another important, unanimous school desegregation decision in *Green v. County School Board* (1968), which struck down a "freedom of choice" plan that failed to satisfy a district's obligation to develop a scheme to end its segregated school system immediately.

In the criminal procedure area, Black not only delivered some important opinions, but he also cast critical votes in several others. He was one of the five justices who formed the slim majorities in two seminal criminal procedure cases. The first was *Escobedo v. Illinois* (1964), which invalidated a conviction based on statements obtained from a criminal defendant who had been interrogated by the police, but not granted any of his requests to consult his counsel or to have his counsel present. The second case was *Miranda v. Arizona* (1966), which established one of the Warren Court's most lasting but controversial principles—that a criminal defendant's Fifth Amendment right against self-incrimination and Sixth Amendment right to assistance of counsel require the police to observe or comply with certain procedural safeguards for any individual who has been "taken into custody or otherwise deprived of his freedom by the authorities in any significant way and is subjected to questioning."

Ironically, for all of the influence Hugo Black wielded, his failures often proved as notable as his successes on the Court. For example, he opposed but failed to prevent the Court's recognizing a constitutionally protected right of privacy. In his dissent in *Griswold v. Connecticut* (1965), he harshly criticized the majority's striking down a Connecticut law prohibiting the sale of contraceptives to married couples on the basis of a right of privacy implicitly protected by the "penumbras" of the Bill of Rights, the liberty component of the Fourteenth Amendment due process clause, or the Ninth Amendment. He argued that the original framers had already made a decision in the Bill of Rights as to which aspects of a person's privacy to give constitutional protection and which aspects to leave to the majoritarian process for protection or regulation. He viewed the Court's recognition of any implied fundamental right (such as a general marital right of privacy), other than those applied to the states by virtue of total incorporation, as the revival of substantive due process. As he argued, "Use of any such broad, unbounded judicial authority would make of this Court's members a day-to-day constitutional convention." Two years later, in his dissent in *Berger v. New York* (1967), he similarly lamented that a right of privacy was nothing more than a "vague judge-made goal" and "like a chameleon, has a different color for every turning."

A second notable failure occurred in cases involving equal protection/fundamental rights, which were interests found by the Warren Court to be of such importance that distinctions made on the basis of their exercise required compelling justifications. Black maintained that the Fourteenth Amendment equal protection clause had been designed primarily to end racial discrimination, and he insisted that the Court should apply no more than a rational basis test to review any equal protection claim other than those involving racial discrimination. He therefore dissented when the Court used strict scrutiny under the equal protection clause to strike down laws that made it more difficult for people to exercise their right to travel in *Shapiro v. Thompson* (1969) and their right to vote in *Harper v. Virginia State Board of Elections* (1966) and *Kramer v. Union Free School District No. 15* (1969).

Yet Black also failed to oppose uniformly the Warren Court's equal protection/fundamental rights decisions. Despite his qualms about expanding the equal protection clause to strike laws down on the basis of something other than racial discrimination, his recognition of the needs for equal justice and fair criminal procedures led him to write the plurality opinion in *Griffin v. Illinois* (1956), in which the Court held that a state must furnish an indigent criminal defendant with a free trial transcript if such a transcript is necessary "for adequate and effective appellate review" of his conviction. Black wrote:

[O]ur own constitutional guaranties of due process and equal protection both call for procedures in criminal trials which allow no invidious discriminations between persons and different groups of persons. . . .

In criminal trials a State can no more discriminate on account of poverty than on account of religion, race, or color. Plainly the ability to pay costs in advance bears no rational relationship to a defendant's guilt or innocence and could not be used as an excuse to deprive a defendant of a fair trial. . . .

It is true that a State is not required by the Federal Constitution to provide appellate courts or a right to appellate review at all. But that is not to say that a State that does grant appellate review can do so in a way that discriminates against some convicted defendants on account of their poverty.

Similarly, he joined *Douglas v. California* (1963), in which the Court struck down a state law requiring state appellate courts, on the request of an indigent criminal defendant for counsel on appeal, to make "an independent investigation of the record" and "to appoint counsel [only] if in their opinion it would be helpful to the defendant or the court." Nevertheless, when the Burger Court in *Boddie v. Connecticut* (1971) struck down a state law that required individuals to pay court fees and costs of about sixty dollars in order to sue for divorce, Justice Black dissented on the grounds that neither the due process nor the equal protection clause permitted "judges [to] hold laws constitutional or not on the basis of a judge's sense of fairness."

Another failure involved Black's misapplication of an equal protection standard he initially had helped to define. In his controversial majority opinion in *Korematsu v. United States* (1944), he made the first reference in the Court's history to race as a suspect classification, which, he explained, must be subjected to the "most rigid scrutiny." Under this standard, he then upheld, over the heated dissents of Frank Murphy, Robert Jackson, Owen Roberts, and Wiley Rutledge, the constitutionality of the internment of Japanese Americans during World War II. Even though historians have subsequently established that the military in fact had no reliable evidence to substantiate its claims that Japanese Americans on the West Coast posed a threat to the national security of the United States, Black never expressed any regret over the *Korematsu* decision. Rather, as criticism of *Korematsu* mounted in subsequent years, he boldly defended it: "There's a difference between peace and war. You can't fight a war with the courts in control." He even added that all people of Japanese ancestry "look alike to a person not a Jap. [Had] they attacked our shores you'd have a large number fighting with the Japanese troops. And a lot of innocent Japanese Americans would have been shot in the panic. Under these circumstances I saw nothing wrong in moving them away from the danger area."

A fifth, and particularly significant, failure involved Black's inability during his last decade or so on the Court to build coalitions, maintain consistency in his votes and opinions, and exhibit the tolerance he had demonstrated in the previous twenty-five years. It is difficult to determine whether these changes in the style and substance of his constitutional decision making were attributable to his failing health, a changing world, or some combination of the two. In the 1960s, while new issues confronted the Court, Black fought the problems of old age, particularly cataracts, which interfered with his practice of researching his opinions thoroughly. During this period, his opinions grew shorter and often contained an unprecedented note of anger and exasperation. He also became more curt with his colleagues and his law clerks.

For example, despite his support for *Brown* and opposition to racial discrimination and the abridgement of freedom of speech, Black resisted extending the Constitution's protection to civil rights protesters' demonstrations on private property. Even though he had earlier written the majority opinion in *Marsh v. Alabama* (1946), in which the Court applied the First Amendment to a privately owned company town, Black later dissented in another case on the ground that the trespass convictions of civil rights demonstrators attempting to coerce a private restaurant to serve them should have been sustained. He contended that "none of our prior cases has held that a person's right to freedom of expression carries with it a right to force a private property owner to furnish his property as a platform to criticize the property owner's use of that property." He argued that a property owner, whether governmental or private, was under no obligation to provide a forum for speech; if owners could not control their property, Black feared, the result would be mob violence. In his view, the rule of law should take precedence over encouraging public discourse and protest. Focusing on maintaining "tranquility and order" in cases such as *Gregory v. Chicago* (1969), Black criticized protestors who "think they have been mistreated or [have] actually been mistreated," and their supporters who "do no service [to] their cause, or their country." These statements contrast sharply with his prior respect for dissenters, toleration of the unorthodox, and receptivity to new ideas.

During his last decade on the Court, Black also failed to persuade a majority of justices to accept fully his distinction between freedom of speech and expressive conduct. He argued that the First Amendment's guarantee of freedom of speech did not include expressive conduct. Yet, he was unable to persuade the Court to agree that activities such as flag burning or wearing a jacket with a profane epithet about the draft were not insulated by the First Amendment from criminal sanction. Indeed, he joined Justice Blackmun's dissent in *Cohen v. California* (1971), characterizing the jacket-wearing as conduct and not speech, while in the same year reiterating his commitment to protecting freedom of the press in the Pentagon Papers case. Black defended his stance in *Cohen* as necessary line-drawing, but it does not comfortably coexist with his position in other cases to grant First Amendment protection to some expressive conduct, such as movies.

Black also assumed an ambivalent posture with respect to First Amendment protection for picketing. In *Giboney v. Empire Storage and Ice Co.* (1949), he wrote that legislatures could regulate picketing, but in *Barenblatt v. United States* (1959), he noted that they could not abridge "views peacefully expressed in a place where the speaker had a right to be." In *Cox v. Louisiana* (1965), however, he said, "Picketing, though it may be utilized to communicate ideas, is not speech, and therefore is not of itself protected by the First Amendment." This position contrasts with his statement in *Feiner v. New York* (1951), in which he had labeled the Court's decision sanctioning police action to silence a speaker as "a long step toward totalitarian authority."

Finally, Black never succeeded in persuading any other justices to join his views on *stare decisis*. He often argued that any erroneously reasoned precedent should be overruled, but throughout his tenure his colleagues refused to endorse his standard, which they believed would have introduced greater instability into constitutional adjudication.

By the time Hugo Black left the Court in 1971, more had changed than just his health, tone, and substantive views on many constitutional issues. He had succeeded in moving from being perceived at the time of his appointment as a Roosevelt loyalist to being regarded as a fiercely independent justice. Part of the explanation for this change in perception may be that many of the issues presented to the Court during his tenure were unforeseen at the time of his appointment.

Indeed, social and political conditions have changed to such an extent that today the justice who comes closest to carrying on the legacy of Hugo Black, a New Deal liberal, is Antonin Scalia, an ardent conservative. Justice Scalia seems to share Black's deference to majoritarian decisions (particularly on noneconomic matters), strict adherence to the literal or plain reading of the Constitution, and preferences to overrule wrongly decided cases and to adopt bright-line tests. Scalia has gone even further than Black as a textualist to include expressive conduct within the ambit of First Amendment protection and to argue that the Sixth Amendment confrontation clause must be read literally to mean that every criminal defendant has a right to confront his or her accusers face-to-face in the courtroom.

But Black's legacy goes further than the areas in which he and Scalia might have concurred. Besides helping to secure the incorporation of most of the Bill of Rights and the foundations of the New Deal, to enliven legal and judicial debates over substantive due process and equal protection fundamental rights, and to shape First Amendment and criminal procedure principles that persist, Hugo Black exhibited an independence, integrity, and consistency against which all subsequent justices have measured themselves. Ironically, no one would have been more disappointed than Black himself that even he could not always meet his own high standards.

—*Michael J. Gerhardt*

BIBLIOGRAPHY

A small body of Hugo Black papers is housed in the Library of Congress. Black expressed his own constitutional views not only in his opinions but also in *A Constitutional Faith* (1968), and in the famous Madison lecture, "The Bill of Rights," *New York University Law Review* 35 (1960). Both personal and professional insights can be found in Hugo L. Black Jr., *My Father: A Remembrance* (1975).

There is a great deal of secondary literature on Black the man and the justice. One study that traces his thought to his roots and early career in Alabama is Steve Suitts, *Hugo Black of Alabama* (2005). See especially William Leuchtenburg, "A Klansman Joins the Court: The Appointment of Hugo Lafayette Black," *University of Chicago Law Review* 41 (1973): 1; Charles Reich, "Mr. Justice Black and the Living Constitution," *Harvard Law Review* 76 (1963): 673; and the profiles by John P. Frank in Friedman and Israel, *Justices* vol. 3, 2321; and by G. Edward White in chapter 14 of his *The American Judicial Tradition: Profiles of Leading American Judges,* exp. ed. (1988).

For fuller biographies, see Roger K. Newman, *Hugo Black: A Biography* (1994); Gerald T. Dunne, *Hugo Black and the Judicial Revolution* (1977); James J. Magee, *Mr. Justice Black: Absolutist on the Court* (1980); and Tinsley E. Yarbrough, *Mr. Justice Black and His Critics* (1988). A unique dual biography is James F. Simon, *The Antagonists: Hugo Black, Felix Frankfurter, and Civil Liberties in Modern America* (1989).

NOTEWORTHY OPINIONS

Johnson v. Zerbst, 304 U.S. 458 (1938)

Chambers v. Florida, 309 U.S. 227 (1940)

Betts v. Brady, 316 U.S. 455 (1942) (Dissent)

Korematsu v. United States, 323 U.S. 214 (1944)

Marsh v. Alabama, 326 U.S. 501 (1946)

Colegrove v. Green, 328 U.S. 549 (1946) (Dissent)

Everson v. Board of Education of Ewing Township, 330 U.S. 1 (1947)

Adamson v. California, 332 U.S. 46 (1947) (Dissent)

Illinois ex rel. McCollum v. Board of Education, 333 U.S. 203 (1948)

Griffin v. Illinois, 351 U.S. 12 (1956)

Engel v. Vitale, 370 U.S. 421 (1962)

Gideon v. Wainwright, 372 U.S. 335 (1963)

Wesberry v. Sanders, 376 U.S. 1 (1964)

Griffin v. County School Board , 377 U.S. 218 (1964)

Griswold v. Connecticut, 381 U.S. 479 (1965) (Dissent)

HARRY ANDREW BLACKMUN

Birth: November 12, 1908, Nashville, Illinois.

Education: Harvard College, B.A., summa cum laude, 1929; Harvard Law School, LL.B., 1932.

Official Positions: Clerk, U.S. Court of Appeals for the Eighth Circuit, 1932–1933; judge, U.S. Court of Appeals for the Eighth Circuit, 1959–1970.

Supreme Court Service: Nominated associate justice by President Richard Nixon, April 15, 1970, to replace Abe Fortas, who had resigned; confirmed by the Senate, May 12, 1970, by a 94–0 vote; took judicial oath June 9, 1970, retired August 3, 1994; replaced by Stephen G. Breyer, nominated by President Bill Clinton.

Death: March 4, 1999, Arlington, Virginia.

"I suppose I'll carry Roe to my grave," Blackmun told a reporter, referring to *Roe v. Wade* (1973), the famous case in which he enunciated the constitutional right to abortion. He received thousands of letters following the decision: "Think of any name; I've been called it in these letters." Conversely, he was lauded by women's groups as a hero. It was an odd position for someone who, when nominated for the Court, was called a "strict constructionist" by conservative senator Strom Thurmond, R-S.C., and who had said, "I'd like to regard myself as being a member of the center of the Court." But *Roe* signaled a major change of emphasis in Blackmun's opinions, from a deference to government institutions to what one of his clerks called an "openness to knowledge beyond the lawbooks" and a marked empathy for those disadvantaged by society.

Blackmun was nominated by President Nixon after the Senate rejected two other nominees whom Nixon had counted on to be "tough on criminals" and supportive of government policies. Blackmun's decisions for the Eighth Circuit Court of Appeals fit that description. Nevertheless, his modesty, innate decency, and intelligence impressed dubious senators, and he was confirmed unanimously within a month. Both the modesty and a wry self-deprecating sense of humor were apparent in his labeling himself thereafter as "Old Number Three."

Born in Illinois, Blackmun grew up in St. Paul, Minnesota, where his father opened a grocery and hardware store. Blackmun went to Harvard on a scholarship presented by the Harvard Club of Minnesota. He supplemented it by working as a janitor, milkman, paper grader, and handball court painter. He would take his memories of poverty to the Court with him, telling an interviewer: "Maybe I'm oversensitive, but these are very personal cases. We're dealing with people—the life, liberty and property of people. And because I grew up in poor surroundings, I know there's another world out there that we sometimes forget." He majored in mathematics, graduated summa cum laude (1929) and Phi Beta Kappa, and went on to receive his law degree at Harvard (1932). His impressive record earned him a clerkship with the U.S. Court of Appeals for the Eighth Circuit (1932–1933).

A year later, Blackmun joined a Minneapolis firm and by 1949 had risen from associate to junior partner and then general partner, specializing in estates, taxation, and general civil litigation. He also taught an occasional course at the St. Paul College of Law and the University of Minnesota Law School.

Blackmun had wavered between medicine and law after graduating from college. Delighted at the opportunity "to have a foot in both camps," in 1950 he became resident counsel for the Mayo Clinic in Rochester, Minnesota. The job ended in 1959, when President Dwight Eisenhower appointed him to the appeals court for which he had clerked.

Blackmun wrote more than 200 signed opinions while on the Eighth Circuit court. He tended to defer to the federal and state legislatures and to the Supreme Court and to decide disputes between the government and individuals in favor of the government, particularly in criminal justice cases, but to speak out strongly in support of civil rights. He personally opposed capital punishment, for example, but ruled on the basis of what he considered a state's right to impose it in *Maxwell v. Bishop* (1968). Believing that prior Supreme Court decisions gave a white homeowner the right to refuse to sell to a black would-be purchaser, he suggested that the Court alter its doctrine—which it subsequently did in *Jones v. Alfred H.*

Harry Andrew Blackmun

Mayer Co. (1967, 1968). At the same time, he wrote opinions forbidding the perpetuation of *de facto* segregated schools (*Kemp v. Beasley,* 1970), ordering the rehiring of black faculty members after an all-black school was closed pursuant to a desegregation order (*Smith v. Board of Education,* 1966), and striking down racial discrimination on juries (*Bailey v. Henslee,* 1961). Demonstrating a somewhat cavalier attitude toward free speech, he upheld the convictions of religious protesters against the Vietnam War who demonstrated on a military reservation (*Holdrige v. United States,* 1960). He then upheld the suspension of college students also protesting the war (*Esteban v. Central Missouri State,* 1965), chiding them for not acting more maturely. He saw no violation of double jeopardy when a person was subjected to two successive trials for the robbery of two victims playing in one card game (*Ashe v. Swenson,* 1968), which the Supreme Court reversed two years later. He almost invariably turned down appeals based on Fourth or Fifth Amendment grounds, for example *Cox v. United States* (1967) and *Jarrett v. United States* (1970). His fellow judges remembered him as "the most studious member of the court," and "deliberate, courageous and moderate."

Blackmun continued to defer to government and precedent in his early years on the Supreme Court. In his first opinion, a dissent from a *per curiam* decision overturning a Minnesota obscenity conviction (*Hoyt v. Minnesota,* 1970), he protested against treating state courts as "so obviously misguided" that they could be summarily reversed. His first opinion for the Court, *Wyman v. James* (1971), also upheld state action. Accepting New York's argument that home visits by caseworkers did not abridge a welfare recipient's protection against unreasonable searches, he noted that seventeen additional states believed that the visits were "rehabilitative" and in the best interests of the child. Agreeing in *Furman v. Georgia* (1972) that the death penalty was constitutional, he declared, "I yield to no one in the depth of my distaste, antipathy, and, indeed, abhorrence, for the death penalty." But he added, "We should not allow our personal preferences as to the wisdom of legislative and congressional action, or our distaste for such action, to guide our judicial decisions such as these."

Gradually, he adjusted to the wide-ranging implications of many of the cases handled by the Supreme Court and the exciting and sobering realization that each case affected not merely one plaintiff or defendant but the entire country. He suggested in interviews that he was also affected by the change of justices and the Court's concomitant shift to the right, viewing his obligation as maintaining the Court's center. Whatever the explanation, his opinions became more reflective of his views and more empathetic to individuals. He had no less respect for institutions but insisted that they be held accountable, particularly by the Court. He began using the phrases "real life" and "real world," resembling an equity judge in his reliance upon balancing tests to decide most cases, trying to ascertain where fairness and justice lay.

His sense of the "real world" was apparent in *Roe*, which, with its companion case *Doe v. Bolton*, struck down a Texas abortion law that permitted abortion only to save the life of the mother and a Georgia statute requiring that a doctor's decision to perform an abortion be approved by two additional physicians and a hospital committee. Drawing upon the right of privacy implied by the Fourteenth Amendment and the Court's decisions in *Griswold v. Connecticut* (1965) and *Eisenstadt v. Baird* (1972), Blackmun suggested a legal rule based on the medically recognized stages of pregnancy: no state health interest and therefore no permissible interference by the state during the first trimester, during which medicine had made abortions at least as safe as childbirth and any decision about abortion was to be made by the woman and her physician; a state interest in protecting the woman's health during the second trimester, when regulations concerning the qualifications of persons performing abortions and the facilities in which abortions were performed were legitimate; state power to prohibit abortions during the third trimester (except those necessary for the woman's life or health), when the fetus had reached "viability" and could live outside the womb. Blackmun read the constitutional reference to "person" as applying postnatally and declined to be drawn into a theological argument about whether personhood began before birth.

Justices Byron White and William Rehnquist, dissenting, questioned the Court's favoring "the convenience of the pregnant mother" over the fetus. In fact, the person Blackmun focused on was the physician, not the pregnant woman. In *United States v. Vuitch* (1971), involving a statute prohibiting physicians from performing any abortion not necessary to save the woman's life, the Court had found no constitutional right to abortion. Justice William O. Douglas criticized the relevant statute as overly vague, giving neither the physician nor a possible jury guidelines for deciding whether an abortion was necessary. During oral argument in *Roe*, Blackmun followed Douglas's *Vuitch* approach and emphasized the physician's rights. The justices' conference reportedly centered on that issue, and Blackmun, after two weeks' intensive research in the Mayo Clinic library, wrote a decision that, while it ensured women's access to abortion, was couched largely in language protective of the physician's right to exercise professional judgment. In subsequent cases, however, Blackmun's opinions centered on a woman's right to reproductive privacy rather than physicians' professionalism.

In the years following *Roe*, Blackmun wrote the opinion of the Court or concurred whenever the Court extended the right to abortion by striking down, for example, spousal or parental consent requirements and waiting periods; he dissented from decisions limiting the right (*Planned Parenthood v.*

Danforth, 1976; *Bellotti v. Baird*, 1979; *H. L. v. Metheson*, 1981; *Akron v. Akron Center for Reproductive Health*, 1983; and *Planned Parenthood v. Ashcroft*, 1983). When the Court legitimized bans on government funding of abortions in *Beal v. Doe* (1977); *Maher v. Roe* (1977); and *Harris v. McRae* (1980), Blackmun dissented, going beyond his earlier medical concerns to condemn the hardships wrought on indigent women thereby deprived of their rights. In *Rust v. Sullivan* (1991), a First Amendment case with major implications for abortion rights, he dissented from the Court's finding of no constitutional violation in the federal government's making health care facilities' receipt of federal funds for family planning contingent on their avoiding any mention of abortion.

In *Webster v. Reproductive Health Services* (1989), the Court upheld Missouri's prohibition on the performance of abortions by public employees or in public facilities unless the procedures were to save the life of the woman. The Court also legitimated its requirement that women seeking an abortion be counseled about alternatives, declaring that "the rigid *Roe* framework is hardly consistent with the notion of a Constitution cast in general terms." Blackmun accused the majority of "turn[ing] a stone face" to the right of reproductive freedom. "I fear for the future," he lamented. "I fear for the liberty and equality of . . . millions of women." The majority had not overturned *Roe*, but "the signs are evident and very ominous, and a chill wind blows." It blew even colder in *Planned Parenthood v. Casey* (1992). There, although a three-justice plurality reiterated the right enunciated in *Roe*, it also permitted limitations such as consent and "information" requirements to be imposed on that right. In place of the *Roe* trimester formula, the *Casey* Court created a state power to regulate abortions at any stage of pregnancy, as long as the regulations did not place an "undue burden" upon the right. A separate four-justice bloc would have overturned *Roe*. That left only the plurality and two others justices, including Blackmun, adhering to the shreds of *Roe*. "The distance is but a single vote," Blackmun warned in dissent. "I am 83 years old. I cannot remain on this Court forever."

After *Roe*, Blackmun evinced increasing concern both for "the right to be let alone" and women's rights. As the right to bodily privacy began to influence lower court decisions in, for example, *In re Quinlan* (1976) and *Superintendent of Belchertown State School v. Saikewicz* (1977), Blackmun attempted to extend it. Dissenting from the Court's endorsement of a Georgia sodomy statute and its implicit condemnation of homosexuality, Blackmun argued, "In a Nation as diverse as ours . . . there may be many 'right' ways of conducting . . . relationships" (*Bowers v. Hardwick*, 1986). He came to view *Roe* as a women's rights case, telling a colloquium that he believed the abortion decisions "broke some of the statutorily imposed fetters on women's freedom traceable in our country to Victorian times." He wrote decisions striking down a state law ending parental obligation for support payments sooner for female than for male children (*Stanton v. Stanton*, 1975) and a federal statute providing Aid to Families with Dependent Children only when the mother rather than the father was unemployed (*Califano v. Westcott*, 1979). Each justice is allotted four clerks per year, and it was telling that in 1985 Blackmun became the first justice ever to hire three women clerks. By the time he retired, he had hired more female clerks than any other justice in the history of the Court.

His dissent in *Ford Motor Co. v. Equal Employment Opportunity Commission* (1982) reflected his disquiet at society's treatment of women, particularly poor women. The EEOC had sued Ford under Title VII of the 1964 Civil Rights Act for refusing to hire specific women at one of its warehouses that had never employed any woman, and the trial court had awarded the women back pay. Justice Sandra Day O'Connor wrote for the Court, however, that because Ford had offered to hire the women when the suit was filed and they had turned down the jobs, Ford's back pay liability had halted. Blackmun, dissenting, drew from the "real-life concerns of the parties." Rejected by Ford, the women had gone to work for General Motors and had accumulated seniority by the time Ford offered them jobs without it. Had they moved to Ford, Blackmun noted, they would have received fewer benefits: "lower wages, less eligibility for promotion and transfer, and greater vulnerability to layoffs than persons hired after they were unlawfully refused employment." He quoted from one employee's trial testimony: "I was just wanting that job so bad because you can't, a woman, when you've got three children, I needed the money, and I was wanting the job so bad. I worked so hard. . . . It broke my heart because I knew I had worked so hard." That, said Blackmun, showed how much job security meant and how irrationally the Court had decided.

Blackmun gradually emerged as protective of the rights of those he considered disadvantaged, not only women, but racial minorities, consumers, aliens, and the elderly. He described the Court as "the resort of . . . 'discrete and insular minorit[ies]' " and argued that justice required viewing the world from the perspectives of different people. Recognizing both the country's race problem and the potential role of law in alleviating it, his concurrence in *Regents of the University of California v. Bakke* (1978) argued that affirmative action programs were necessary: "In order to get beyond racism, we must first take account of race." He wrote for the Court in cases validating school desegregation efforts (*Columbus v. Penick*, 1979; *Dayton v. Brinkman*, 1979; and *Washington v. Seattle School Dist. No. 1*, 1982). As the Court chipped away at affirmative action in the late 1980s, he accused it of "regressing" (*City of Richmond v. J. A. Croson*, 1989) and wondered "whether the majority still believes that discrimination . . . is a problem in our society, or even remembers that it ever was" (*Ward's Cove v. Atonio*, 1989). Bringing his training as a mathematician to the issue of race, he appended a footnote to *Castaneda v. Partida* (1977) that established the now-accepted statistical method for proving race discrimination. He wrote an opinion validating statutory employment preferences for Native Americans in the Bureau of Indian Affairs (*Morton v. Mancari*, 1974), and, when he dissented from the Court's decision in an Indian land claims case, he spoke of Native Americans as "a people whom our Nation long ago reduced to a state of dependency" (*South Carolina v. Catawba Indian Tribe*, 1980). Dissenting again when the Court held that

Native Americans could be prosecuted for using peyote in religious ceremonies, he lamented the country's "unfulfilled and hollow promise" of religious liberty for Native Americans (*Employment Division, Department of Human Resources of Oregon v. Smith*, 1990).

Blackmun played a central role in bringing aliens under the protection of the Fourteenth Amendment. Writing for the Court that states could not condition welfare payments to aliens on a durational residency requirement, he declared that classifications based on alienage are suspect and subject to strict scrutiny (*Graham v. Richardson*, 1971). Aliens needed the protection accorded to a "discrete and insular minority" because communities could exclude them from the political process. States therefore could not prohibit aliens from employment in the civil service (*Sugarman v. Dougall*, 1973) or the public schools (*Ambach v. Norwick*, 1979), although they could be barred from the state police (*Foley v. Connelie*, 1978). Although he agreed with the Court in *San Antonio Independent School District v. Rodriguez* (1973) that there was no federal constitutional right to education, Blackmun argued ten years later that it was such a basic right that a state could not exclude the children of illegal aliens from public schools (*Plyler v. Doe*, 1982). He dissented when the Court upheld an Immigration and Naturalization Service decision denying asylum to a Guatemalan whom a guerrilla organization had attempted to coerce into joining its army (*INS v. Elias-Zacarias*, 1992); when it decided that the government could kidnap a Mexican citizen and bring him to the United States for trial (*United States v. Alvarez-Machain*, 1992); and when it decreed that the INS could detain children, pending deportation proceedings, even when an unrelated adult was willing to house them (*Reno v. Flores*, 1993). Eight justices held in 1993 that in spite of both international and domestic law, the United States could intercept Haitian refugees at sea and return them to Haiti (*Sale v. Haitian Centers Council*). In an impassioned dissent, Blackmun lambasted the "land of refugees and guardian of freedom" for "forcibly driving" the refugees "back to detention, abuse and death" and castigated the Court for "strain[ing] to sanction that conduct."

He remained deferential to criminal justice officials, voting to limit the "judicially created exclusionary rule," as he put it in *United States v. Janis* (1976). In 1971 he dissented in *Bivens v. Six Unknown Fed. Narcotics Agents*, seeing no cause of action for a plaintiff whose home had been entered illegally by federal agents and who had been subjected to unreasonable force and a strip search, and he found no due process requirement of juries in juvenile delinquency proceedings (*McKeiver v. Pennsylvania*). He dissented when the Court upheld use of evidence gathered by a warrantless overflight of a suspect's home by a police helicopter, but did so on the limited ground that the frequency of police overflights for nonsearch purposes and therefore the extent to which a reasonable expectation of privacy against such flights existed had not been established (*Florida v. Riley*, 1989).

His pragmatic, case-by-case approach emphasized facts and led to his relatively rare disagreements with criminal justice verdicts. Dissenting from the punishing of an escaped prisoner who presented evidence of continued brutality by guards, Blackmun declared that the prisoner had fled to "extricate" himself from "hell" and emphasized the "beatings, fires, lack of essential medical care, and sexual attacks" suffered by prisoners (*United States v. Bailey*, 1980). He was unenthusiastic about overturning convictions on procedural grounds, urging instead that greater use be made of Section 1983 of Title 42 of the United States Code, which criminalizes deprivation of civil rights. Disagreeing with the decision in *Rizzo v. Goode* (1976), that denied injunctive relief for Philadelphia citizens alleging police brutality, for example, Blackmun argued that the police behavior constituted a pervasive pattern of such deprivation under Section 1983. He also advocated use of Section 1983 to challenge illegal searches (*Allen v. McCurry*, 1980), to act against ineffective public defenders (*Polk v. Dodson*, 1981), and to punish police officers who committed perjury (*Briscoe v. LaHue*, 1983).

His factual approach resulted in the gradual alteration of his view of the death penalty's constitutionality. Statistical evidence persuaded him to vote against Georgia's capital sentencing process as racially

discriminatory (*McCleskey v. Kemp*, 1987). Although he agreed that a mentally retarded person found competent to stand trial could be executed (*Penry v. Lynaugh*, 1989), he dissented from the Court's holding that subjecting minors to execution did not constitute cruel and unusual punishment (*Stanford v. Kentucky*, 1989). (In *Roper v. Simmons*, decided in 2005, ten years after Blackmun left the bench, the Court in effect announced that he had been correct.) Eventually, he concluded that the death penalty as applied on the basis of *Furman v. Georgia* (1972) violated the Eighth Amendment, because twenty years' experience had demonstrated that attempts made after *Furman* to satisfy the "constitutional goal of eliminating arbitrariness and discrimination" in sentencing a convicted criminal to death "can never be achieved without compromising an equally essential component of fundamental fairness—individualized sentencing" (*Callins v. Collins*, 1994). In a lone and emotional dissent from a denial of certiorari in *Callins*, sought by a defendant sentenced to death, Blackmun added that capital punishment was used disproportionately in cases involving members of racial minorities, thereby violating the equal protection clause as well, and he declared, "From this day forward, I no longer shall tinker with the machinery of death." Blackmun kept that promise. He drafted a phrase, "Adhering to my view that the death penalty cannot be imposed fairly within the constraints of the Constitution," and directed the clerk of the Court to attach it as his dissent to every subsequent death penalty decision.

In 1987 the American Society of Law, Medicine, and Ethics gave Blackmun its first Presidents' Award for Outstanding Contributions to Law and Medicine, mentioning, among other cases, *Barefoot v. Estelle* (1983). There, explaining that the American Psychiatric Association had declared that subsequent dangerousness was not predictable, he voted against the imposition of capital punishment on the basis of a prediction of future dangerousness by psychiatrists who had not even examined the defendant. With Blackmun goading it, the Court eventually began to overturn the careless use of psychiatry in capital trials

(*Ake v. Oklahoma,* 1985; *Ford v. Wainwright,* 1986). Blackmun also argued unsuccessfully that the equal protection clause mandated heightened scrutiny in examining state action that discriminated against the mentally retarded (*Cleburne v. Cleburne,* 1985). He held that someone declared incompetent to stand trial could be placed only in a facility that offered appropriate treatment or training (*Jackson v. Indiana,* 1972). He dissented when the Court later backed away from this standard; see, for example, *Jones v. United States* (1983).

Although he placed a high value on speech, Blackmun considered it as subject to a balancing test as any other part of the Constitution. He dissented in *New York Times Co. v. United States* (1971) because the right of the press had not been weighed against possible national security interests. He voted against giving First Amendment protection both to what he labeled the "absurd and immature antic" of a young protester who walked into a courtroom wearing a jacket sporting the words "Fuck the Draft" (*Cohen v. California,* 1971) and to another young man who "harm[ed] the physical integrity of the flag by wearing it affixed to the seat of his pants" (*Smith v. Goguen,* 1974). Although he concurred with the Court in remanding for trial the allegations of students that a school board's decision to remove from their libraries books it labeled "anti-American, anti-Christian, anti-Semitic, and just plain filthy" violated their First Amendment rights, Blackmun emphasized that the case involved "two competing principles of constitutional stature," one being speech and the other, the "properly inculcative purpose" of public education to "'promote civic virtues'" (*Island Trees v. Pico,* 1982). Students had no absolute right to receive ideas, but "certain forms of state discrimination between ideas are improper," and state discrimination against ideas because of their political content was particularly impermissible. For that reason, he joined the Court in striking down a flag desecration statute in *Texas v. Johnson* (1989). He dissented on First Amendment grounds when the Court said a public indecency statute could be applied to nude dancing in a commercial establishment, because the state had not

proved a sufficient interest to balance the right of expression (*Barnes v. Glen Theatre,* 1991). He disagreed with the Court's approach in the "hate speech" case of *R. A. V. v. St. Paul* (1992) but concurred in overturning the statute as overly broad.

Blackmun made a major contribution to the law of commercial speech by treating it as subject to the same balancing test. His first commercial speech opinion for the Court involved abortions, overturning the convictions of a Virginia newspaper's director and managing editor, who published a New York City organization's advertisements for low-cost abortions in accredited facilities (*Bigelow v. Virginia,* 1975). The Court had held in *Valentine v. Chrestensen* (1942) that the First Amendment did not apply to commercial speech. In the incremental manner most likely to secure agreement among the justices, Blackmun narrowed the holding in *Chrestensen* instead of overruling it, saying that the state limitations on the distribution of handbills at issue in *Chrestensen* were a "reasonable regulation." But the reasonableness of regulation of commercial speech depended upon the nature of the speech involved, Blackmun continued, suggesting that the Court adopt a test balancing the right of the speaker against that of the state. As there was nothing fraudulent about the speech in *Bigelow,* it was unreasonable for the state to punish it.

The following year, in *Virginia State Bd. of Pharmacy v. Virginia Citizens Consumer Council* (1976), Blackmun wrote for the Court when it overturned a statute prohibiting pharmacists from advertising the prices of prescription drugs. In finding for the consumers who had brought the case, the district court had adopted Blackmun's suggested balancing test and declared that the First Amendment interest in free flow of price information outweighed any asserted state interest in maintaining pharmacists' professionalism by banning advertisements. Blackmun's opinion in *Virginia State Bd. of Pharmacy* illuminated both his evolving attitude toward the role of speech in a democratic society and his awareness of those less favored by it. Calling advertising the "dissemination of information," he asserted that such information was necessary to enlightened public decision making. The area of democratic decision making was up to the individual: "the particular consumer's interest in the free flow of commercial information . . . may be as keen, if not keener by far, than his interest in the day's most urgent political debate." Financial decisions also might be linked to political choices: "the free flow of commercial information is indispensable . . . to the proper allocation of resources in a free enterprise system . . . [and] to the formation of intelligent opinions as to how that system ought to be regulated or altered." The only interest of the state was the limited one of maintaining professionalism; anything else was "highly paternalistic." Blackmun, unlike the state, assumed "that this information is not in itself harmful, that people will perceive their own best interests only if they are well enough informed, and that the best means to that end is to open the channels of communication rather than to close them." Describing the elderly as the group least physically fit to comparison shop and equally likely to have "diminished resources," Blackmun added: "Those whom the suppression of prescription drug price information hits the hardest are the poor, the sick, and particularly the aged. . . . [T]hey are the least able to learn . . . where their scarce dollars are best spent. . . . [I]nformation as to who is charging what . . . could mean the alleviation of physical pain or the enjoyment of basic necessities."

Striking down a ban on advertising by lawyers in *Bates v. State Bar of Arizona* (1977), Blackmun again questioned the state's view of the public as "not sophisticated enough to realize the limitations of advertising." "We view as dubious any justification that is based on the benefits of public ignorance," he wrote, adding that the ban "likely has served to burden access to legal services, particularly for the not-quite-poor and the unknowledgeable." There was, however, a difference between commercial and noncommercial speech. Blackmun recognized the validity of state regulation aimed at speech that did not "serv[e] individual and societal interests in assuring informed and reliable decision making." Specifically, this meant the state could ban commercial speech that was basically false, deceptive, or misleading; pro-

posed illegal activities; established time, place, and manner limitations; or depended upon coercive in-person solicitation.

Three years later, in *Central Hudson v. Public Service Commission* (1980), the Court edged away from its protection of commercial speech by holding that it was entitled to no more than an intermediate level of constitutional protection and developing a four-part test by which to judge the legitimacy of government regulation. Blackmun concurred only because the Court overturned the restriction on the speech at issue. He applauded when the Court refused to allow Cincinnati to ban freestanding news racks that held "commercial handbills" while permitting such news racks for newspapers (*City of Cincinnati v. Discovery Network,* 1993). The Court held that the differentiation between newspapers and commercial speech was neither neutral nor a reasonable way to reach Cincinnati's stated goals of reducing litter and street obstructions and that it "seriously underestimate[d] the value of commercial speech," suggesting that Cincinnati had misread earlier Court decisions. Blackmun, concerned about the listener rather than the speaker, added that the commercial speech here was listings of homes for sale and of adult education courses, which was information of major value to individuals.

In another First Amendment area, Blackmun's position on church and state reflected an adherence to "Madison's view that both religion and government function best if each remains independent." School districts should not lend instructional materials and equipment to private schools because of the difficulty of distinguishing the sectarian and secular functions (*Wolman v. Walter,* 1977). He dissented in *Committee for Public Education v. Regan* (1980), saying that parochial schools should not be reimbursed for state-mandated testing and reporting services that are "an essential part of the sectarian schools' activities." In a somewhat confusing sequence of cases, he criticized the Court's decision to treat Christmas symbols as neutral holiday decorations as a denial of the symbols' religious meaning (*Lynch v. Donnelly,* 1984) but argued that although a crèche on public property was unconstitutional a menorah combined with a Christmas tree and a sign saluting liberty was not (*Allegheny County v. ACLU*, 1989). He considered the Court wrong to endorse the Air Force's refusal to allow an Orthodox Jew to wear a yarmulke on duty (*Goldman v. Weinberger*, 1986). In 1987 he expressed concern that the wall between church and state "has been crumbling a little of late ... particularly at the Supreme Court level." He repeated his concern when the Court validated a state's hiring a translator for a deaf student in a parochial school, both because the Court could have decided the case on statutory rather than constitutional grounds and because the translator was propagating religious doctrine (*Zobrest v. Catalina Foothills School District*, 1993).

Blackmun described his approach to judging when he told a law school audience in 1988, "The Court moves first in one direction and then it shifts to another as it probes new facts, new legislation, and new theories and the issues that emerge from them." His own change of position enabled the Court to shift precisely in that manner in cases concerning federalism.

In 1968, before Blackmun joined the Court, the justices handed down a decision consistent with the post-1936 practice of upholding federal regulatory statutes based on congressional power over interstate commerce (*Maryland v. Wirtz*). It permitted the federal government to extend the Fair Labor Standards Act (FLSA) to public hospitals, nursing homes, and educational institutions and, by doing so, to impose federal maximum hour and overtime pay standards on those institutions. In 1976, however, with Blackmun in the majority, a 5–4 Court reversed *Wirtz* in *National League of Cities v. Usery*.

Amendments to the FLSA had extended federal wage and hour regulations to almost all employees of state and local governments. In striking them down, Justice Rehnquist said that Congress could not tell the states how to make "essential decisions" about "integral governmental functions." "Integral" was not defined but was described as including functions "essential to [the] separate and independent existence of the states" and "within the area of traditional oper-

ations of state and local governments." Blackmun's unhappy concurrence reflected his fear that the decision might have a negative impact on environmental protection, traditionally within the less-than-zealous jurisdiction of the states. Focusing on "balancing," however, he concluded that the *Usery* doctrine struck the appropriate balance between federal regulatory power and state autonomy.

In 1982 Blackmun joined and wrote for the four *Usery* dissenters in upholding a part of President Jimmy Carter's energy program that limited the autonomy of state utility regulatory commissions. In *Federal Energy Regulatory Commission v. Mississippi*, Blackmun asserted that the federal government was merely utilizing its commerce clause power to preempt conflicting state regulations when in fact it could have preempted the entire field of energy policy. Justice O'Connor, in a dissent Blackmun called "rather loud," attacked the result as inconsistent with *Usery*, "antithetical to the values of federalism, and inconsistent with our constitutional history." Blackmun, unmoved, voted again with the *Usery* dissenters in a case extending the congressional commerce power to regulation of the mandatory retirement ages of state employees, a step designed to avoid discrimination against the elderly (*Equal Employment Opportunity Commission v. Wyoming*, 1983). Finally, in *Garcia v. San Antonio Transit Authority* (1985), the Court effectively overruled *Usery*, with Blackmun writing for the five-justice majority.

Garcia involved federal power to set guidelines under the FLSA for overtime wages paid by a metropolitan transit authority. Explaining his vote, Blackmun said, "In the years that intervened between the two cases . . . I had become convinced that the 'traditional governmental function' test was unworkable. A little reflection demonstrated that mass transportation was not such a function. Indeed, nearly all transportation systems originally were privately owned." "We find it difficult, if not impossible," he wrote in *Garcia*, "to identify an organizing principle that places each of the cases in the first group on one side of a line and each of the cases in the second group on the other side." Lower courts attempting "to draw guidance

from this model [*Usery*] have proved it both impracticable and doctrinally barren," issuing contradictory
holdings. What was shown by *Usery* and *Garcia*,
Blackmun later commented, was "how the Court
veers from one side to the other or, if one will, takes
two steps ahead and one back or one step ahead and
two back, depending on the point of view. If the issues
were to arise again today, even with facts identical to
those of *Garcia*, would the result be the same with the
Court as presently constituted?" In other words, the
Constitution was not a static entity, the justices were
fallible people limited by their own viewpoints but
trying to learn from experience and societal needs,
and the Court's doctrines inevitably would change
again. He announced himself "mildly surprised," and
presumably pleased, when *Garcia* was explicitly reaffirmed in *South Carolina v. Baker* (1988).

Blackmun commented on the "constant development of the concepts of Justice" and the continual
learning process undergone by the justices. And he
said:

> The Court is a very special place from which to
> observe, for one has a view there of what is hap-
> pening in the courtrooms of America. One sees
> what people are litigating about. . . . One gets a
> sense of their desires and of their frustrations,
> of their hopes and of their great disappoint-
> ments, of their profound personal concerns,
> and of what they regard as important and as
> crucial.

This view of the "real world" affected Blackmun's
evolution as a justice. He told interviewers that his
ideas did not change after he became a justice, but if
his fervor for individual rights as against government
institutions was as great when he joined the Court as
in later years, that was not apparent either in the way
he voted or in his language. In *United States v. Kras*
(1973), upholding the constitutionality of bankruptcy
filing fees for indigents, he commented that the filing
fee—for someone without resources—was "less than
the price of a movie and little more than the cost of a
pack or two of cigarettes." It is difficult not to see the
difference between that language and the empathy he

displayed in *Ford v. EEOC* or *Webster* as reflecting the
view from the Court's special window on society. His
own description of the alteration of his thinking
between *Usery* and *Garcia* suggests the openness to
the "real world"—whether of social realities or the
gradually unfolding impact of Supreme Court doctrine on lower court decisions—that he urged upon
his colleagues and that logically would result in
growth and change in any justice's ideas, because the
real world is not static.

A justice who is doctrinaire is unlikely to find
cases difficult to resolve. Blackmun, however, did. "I
probably agonize over cases more than I should," he
reflected during his last year on the Court. He also
referred to the justices as being "locked in combat"
over the outcome of cases, "struggling for the fifth
vote." Whether it was the need to secure a majority
that was responsible for the difference between *Roe*,
with its emphasis on physicians' rights, and *Webster*,
with its understanding of the difficult decisions faced
by an unhappily pregnant woman, is unclear. The
decisive factor could as easily have been the concern
that Blackmun later articulated about maintaining a
strong center as the Court's membership changed, or
what he referred to as the "educational process" that
takes place on the Court. Whatever the reason, the
difference expressed in his opinions during his first
years on the Court and in those that followed was
notable.

Blackmun arrived at the Court as a man with
great faith in institutions and a tendency to defer to
them. His years on the nation's highest bench, and the
annual seminars he ran at the Aspen Institute in Colorado during the Court's summer breaks, exposed
him to people, problems, and ways of thinking that
were far removed from those he had encountered earlier in life. He read every piece of mail the public sent
to his desk, whether laudatory or abusive, and became
less isolated from the pulse of the country than he had
been in his pre-Court years. Sometimes, he realized,
the government did its job of protecting individuals.
When it did not, however, when the individuals
involved were outsiders with very little power, then it
was the function of the Court to step in.

The one thing that did not change during Blackmun's Court years was the need to maintain integrity. "I hope you will always be yourself," he told the Mayo Medical School's 1980 graduating class, defining "yourself" as "human, a little sentimental, possessed of a sense of humor and a sense of humility, not possessed of a pride of authorship or accomplishment." The lack of pride was important. Blackmun may have been thinking of *Roe* when he added, "The Bench . . . is no place to grow rich, and it certainly is no place to become popular."

—*Philippa Strum*

BIBLIOGRAPHY

Blackmun's voluminous papers, housed in the Library of Congress, were opened to researchers in March 2004. Linda Greenhouse's *Becoming Justice Blackmun: Harry Blackmun's Supreme Court Journey* (2005) is based on the papers and focuses primarily on his relationship with Chief Justice Warren Burger and his opinions in the areas of privacy, federalism, the death penalty, and speech. A comprehensive examination of Blackmun's approach to judging and areas of the law such as capital punishment, speech, taxation, federalism, personal autonomy, and race can be found in the articles that constitute *Hastings Constitutional Law Quarterly* 26 (1998). A number of his former clerks have analyzed his jurisprudence, both in the Hastings compilation and in Pamela S. Karlan, "Jurisprudence: Bringing Compassion into the Province of Judging," *North Dakota Law Review* 71 (1995): 173; Harold H. Koh, "Rebalancing the Medical Triad: Justice Blackmun's Contributions to Law and Medicine," *American Journal of Law & Medicine* 13 (1987): 315; and "Justice Blackmun and the 'World Out There,'" *Yale Law Journal* 104 (1994): 12; Karen N. Moore, "Justice Blackmun's Contributions on the Court: The Commercial Speech and State Taxation Examples," *Hamline Law Review* 8 (1985): 29; and Diane P. Wood, "Justice Blackmun and Individual Rights," *Dickinson Law Review* 97 (1993): 421. Stephen L. Wasby, "Justice Blackmun and Criminal Justice: A Modest Overview," *Akron Law Review* 28 (1995): 125, is a good summary of Blackmun's opinions in that field. Philippa Strum, "Change and Continuity on the Supreme Court: Conversations with Justice Harry A. Blackmun," *University of Richmond Law Review* 34 (2000): 285, draws on interviews with the justice during his last year on the Court.

Blackmun's own words about the Court, the problems facing society, and specific areas of the law appear in a number of law review articles. The most significant of them is "Section 1983 and Federal Protection of Individual Rights—Will the Statute Remain Alive or Fade Away?" *New York University Law Review* 60 (1985): 1. Among the others are "The First Amendment and Its Religion Clauses," *Nova Law Review* 14 (1989): 29; "Thoughts About Ethics," *Emory Law Journal* 24 (1974): 3; "Some Goals for Legal Education," *Ohio Northern Law Review* 1 (1974): 403; "Movement and Countermovement," *Drake Law Review* 38 (1989): 747; "The Supreme Court and the Law of Nations," *Yale Law Journal* 104 (1994): 39; and "Reflections of Justice Blackmun," *Bench & Bar of Minnesota* 58 (2001): 34.

NOTEWORTHY OPINIONS

Graham v. Richardson, 403 U.S. 365 (1971)

New York Times Co. v. United States, 403 U.S. 713 (1971) (Dissent)

Bigelow v. Virginia, 421 U.S. 809 (1975)

Virginia State Bd. of Pharmacy v. Virginia Citizens Consumer Council, 425 U.S. 748 (1976)

Califano v. Westcott, 443 U.S. 76 (1979)

Ford Motor Co. v. Equal Employment Opportunity Commission, 458 U.S. 219 (1982) (Dissent)

Garcia v. San Antonio Metropolitan Transit Authority, 469 U.S. 528 (1985)

Bowers v. Hardwick, 478 U.S. 186 (1986) (Dissent)

Stanford v. Kentucky, 492 U.S. 361 (1989) (Dissent)

Webster v. Reproductive Health Services, 492 U.S. 490 (1989) (Dissent)

Employment Division, Department of Human Resources of Oregon v. Smith, 494 U.S. 872 (1990) (Dissent)

Planned Parenthood of Southeastern Pennsylvania v. Casey, 505 U.S. 833 (1992) (Dissent)

Sale v. Haitian Centers Council, 509 U.S. 155 (1993) (Dissent)

Callins v. Collins, 510 U.S. 1141 (1994) (Dissent)

JOHN BLAIR JR.

Birth: 1732, Williamsburg, Virginia.

Education: Graduated with honors from College of William and Mary, 1754; studied law at Middle Temple, London, 1755–1756.

Official Positions: Member, Virginia House of Burgesses, 1766–1770; clerk, Virginia Governor's Council, 1770–1775; delegate, Virginia Constitutional Convention, 1776; member, Virginia Governor's Council, 1776; judge, Virginia General Court, 1777–1778; chief justice, 1779; judge, first Virginia Court of Appeals, 1780–1789; delegate, U.S. Constitutional Convention, 1787; judge, Virginia Supreme Court of Appeals, 1789.

Supreme Court Service: Nominated associate justice by President George Washington, September 24, 1789; confirmed by the Senate, September 26, 1789, by a voice vote; took judicial oath February 2, 1790; resigned January 27, 1796; replaced by Samuel Chase, nominated by President Washington.

Death: August 31, 1800, Williamsburg, Virginia.

When John Blair Jr. joined the Supreme Court at the time of its creation by the Judiciary Act of 1789, he brought with him extensive experience on the courts of his native state. Blair, who had studied at the Middle Temple in the mid-1750s, entered practice before the general court of the colony of Virginia and also became a legislator. Active in the Revolutionary movement, he was a member of the Virginia convention of May 1776, serving on the committee that framed a new state constitution and declaration of rights. With the establishment of a system of state courts, between 1777 and 1789 he sat at one time or another on the general court, the high court of chancery, and the supreme court of appeals. He also became a Virginia delegate to the federal Constitutional Convention of 1787— one of three, including George Washington and James

Madison, who approved the final document—and a Federalist delegate to the Virginia ratifying convention of 1788.

Blair's Virginia experience had already associated him with an early precedent for judicial review. In *Commonwealth v. Caton* (1782), the Virginia Court of Appeals claimed the right to declare an act of the legislature void if it contradicted the state constitution. The case concerned the legality of a pardon granted by the lower house of the legislature to convicted Loyalists in alleged violation of the Virginia Treason Act of 1776. The Supreme Court concluded, however, that the law was valid and had been violated by the legislators themselves. Blair's opinion avoided a forceful affirmation of the Court's right to decide constitutionality that other justices advanced, but he did not explicitly deny it. Rather, in upholding the legality of the statute, he waived the question of constitutionality. He was also a signer of a "Remonstrance" by the judges of the court of appeals in 1788 protesting new legislation that added significantly to their duties, including riding circuit. The judges called the law a violation of the independence of the judiciary guaranteed by the state constitution. That experience must have influenced him, as he joined his fellow Supreme Court justices in attempting to alleviate the heavy burden of their service on the federal circuit courts.

Blair was not among the more outspoken justices of the Court, being more likely to base his opinions on a close reading of the laws or the Constitution than on sweeping principle. Yet he seems generally to have sided with the early efforts of the Court to establish its independence and the right of judicial review. On April 10, 1792, while sitting on the circuit for the Philadelphia district, he joined in a letter to President Washington protesting the terms of the Pension Act of 1792 that required circuit judges to certify veterans' pension claims to the secretary of war, who could in turn

John Blair Jr.

overrule them. The justices objected not only to the nonjudicial character of the duty but also to the power of an officer of the executive branch to override a judge. Some circuit judges agreed to review the claims as commissioners rather than judges, but Blair and his colleagues refused to consider the claim of William Hayburn, who thereupon appealed to Congress. In *Hayburn's Case* (1792), Attorney General Edmund Randolph then sought from the Supreme

Court a writ of *mandamus* commanding the circuit court to proceed on Hayburn's petition.

The Supreme Court divided 3–3 on the motion, with Blair voting in support of Randolph. Although a subsequent revision of the Pension Act ended the necessity of deciding the case, the justices here gave an early demonstration of their refusal to enforce legislation they regarded as unconstitutional.

The most significant case to come before the Court during Blair's tenure was unquestionably *Chisholm v. Georgia* (1793), in which the justices ruled, 4–1, on a debt claim by the executors of an estate of a citizen of South Carolina against the state of Georgia that a state could be sued in the federal courts by a citizen of another state. The core issue was whether the Constitution extended federal judicial power to suits in all cases, or only if the state was the plaintiff, but, ultimately, the issue was state sovereignty. The justices wrote their opinions *seriatim*, and although Blair voted with the majority he avoided the broad claims to the force of popular sovereignty advanced by two of his colleagues and rested his decision on a close reading of the language in Article III, Section 2, of the Constitution. The bold decision stirred strong political opposition and was overturned by the adoption of the Eleventh Amendment, the first instance of such a reversal.

Near the end of his service on the Court, Blair also heard *Penhallow v. Doane's Administrators* (1795). This case involved a suit for damages that tested the right of the federal courts to assume jurisdiction over the objection of the state of New Hampshire in a case that had originally been decided in the defunct court of appeals under the Articles of Confederation. In ruling against New Hampshire, the Court again advanced its strongly nationalist views, and Blair again agreed, while remaining far less explicit than his colleague William Patterson.

Blair's health was by now declining—he had complained on one occasion of "a rattling distracting noise in my head"—and he soon retired to his home in Williamsburg, where he lived until his death.

—*Thad W. Tate*

BIBLIOGRAPHY

For Blair's Court decisions, see Julius Goebel Jr., *History of the Supreme Court of the United States, Antecedents and Beginnings to 1801* (1971); and Wythe Holt, "John Blair: 'A Safe and Conscientious Judge,'" in Scott Douglas Gerber, *Seriatim: The Supreme Court Before John Marshall* (1998).

NOTEWORTHY OPINIONS

Chisholm v. Georgia, 2 U.S. 419 (1793)

SAMUEL M. BLATCHFORD

Birth: March 9, 1820, New York City.

Education: Columbia College, A.B., 1837.

Official Positions: Judge, Southern District of New York, 1867–1872; judge, U.S. Court of Appeals for the Second Circuit, 1872–1882.

Supreme Court Service: Nominated associate justice by President Chester A. Arthur, March 13, 1882, to replace Ward Hunt, who had retired; confirmed by the Senate, March 27, 1882, by a voice vote; took judicial oath April 3, 1882; served until July 7, 1893; replaced by Edward D. White, nominated by President Grover Cleveland.

Death: July 7, 1893, Newport, Rhode Island.

Born into a wealthy New York family with strong connections to the state's financial community, Samuel Blatchford entered Columbia College at age thirteen, graduated in 1837, and gained admission to the bar in 1842. As a lawyer, Blatchford achieved a reputation as a specialist in admiralty law and, after 1852, as a reporter of federal court decisions. His tireless efforts in compiling federal case law, combined with his loyalty to the Republican Party, earned Blatchford a place on the federal bench after the Civil War. He served first as a judge of the Southern District of New York and later as a judge on the Court of Appeals for the Second Circuit. With fifteen years of federal judicial experience, the moderate and noncontroversial Blatchford was a logical choice for the Supreme Court vacancy created by the resignation of Ward Hunt. The Senate approved his nomination on a voice vote.

Although he wrote more than his share of opinions, Blatchford received little attention for most of his work on the Court. In the early part of his tenure, many of his decisions involved admiralty, patents, bankruptcy, and copyrights—not the stuff of landmark cases. Nevertheless, his achievements were notable, particularly in admiralty and patent law. In *Ex parte Boyer* (1884), for example, Blatchford extended the admiralty jurisdiction to canals. His decisions in *Dobson v. Hartford Carpet Co.* (1885) and *Dobson v. Dornan* (1886), both of which involved patents for carpet design granted to Dobson, established rules for the infringement of design. After the second *Dobson* case, Congress passed legislation in this area, adopting many of the principles Blatchford laid down.

As a member of the Court during the 1880s, Blatchford also took part in a number of cases involving the civil rights of African Americans and Chinese immigrants. Both groups were the subject of important federal legislation during the late nineteenth century, and Blatchford's record on such matters—like that of the Court's—was a mixed one. On the one hand, in the *Civil Rights Cases* (1883),

Blatchford voted with the eight-person majority to strike down the Civil Rights Act of 1875 as an unconstitutional attempt to outlaw discrimination in privately owned public accommodations. And, in a case involving a group of Chinese aliens, *Baldwin v. Franks* (1887), Blatchford was part of a seven-justice majority that refused to interpret a treaty between the United States and China so as to protect foreign nationals from violence.

On the other hand, Blatchford supported black voting rights. He was part of a unanimous Court in *Ex parte Yarbrough* (1884) that voted to uphold congressional measures penalizing those who conspired to prevent African Americans from exercising the franchise. Blatchford similarly stood for the protection of civil rights in *Yick Wo v. Hopkins* (1886), in which he joined the rest of the justices in applying the Fourteenth Amendment's equal protection clause to a group of Chinese laundry owners, and in *United States v. Jung Ah Lung* (1888), for which he wrote the majority opinion granting the release of an illegally detained Chinese immigrant.

Samuel M. Blatchford

Like his stands on civil rights issues, Blatchford's opinions in cases involving the Bill of Rights also were uneven. In *Auffmordt v. Hedden* (1890), he refused to extend the Seventh Amendment's guarantee of trial by jury to decisions of customs appraisers regarding the value of imports, and in *O'Neil v. Vermont* (1892), he held that the Eighth Amendment's ban on cruel and unusual punishment did not apply to the states.

Nevertheless, his most notable opinion regarding the Bill of Rights, *Counselman v. Hitchcock* (1892), granted extensive protection to individuals under the Fifth Amendment's self-incrimination provision. Charles Counselman, a grain commission dealer, was called to testify concerning violations of the Interstate Commerce Act, and he had refused to answer questions involving illegal rates he may have received for grain shipments. Although an act of Congress provided that no testimony by an individual could be used against that person in such a proceeding, Counselman thought the statute an insufficient protection against self-incrimination and refused to testify. Lower federal courts held him in contempt, and Counselman appealed to the Supreme Court. In his opinion for the Court, Blatchford accepted Counselman's claim and broadly construed the self-incrimination clause. Rejecting the opposition's argument that the Fifth Amendment applied only to cases in which the witness himself was on trial—and, therefore, not to Counselman's case—Blatchford held that the amendment extended to all criminal proceedings. Moreover, he also believed that the congressional self-incrimination statute offered inadequate protection of Counselman's rights. "It is quite clear that legislation cannot abridge a constitutional privilege," Blatchford wrote, "and that it cannot replace or supply one, at least unless it is so broad as to have the same extent in scope and effect." In *Counselman,* Blatchford stood for an expansive interpretation of individual rights under the Fifth Amendment.

More significant than Blatchford's interpretation of the Bill of Rights, however, was his view of economic liberty. After the Reconstruction period, state and federal courts throughout the nation gradually began to interpret the due process clause of the Fourteenth Amendment as a guarantee of certain fundamental rights, often associated with an individual's pursuit and use of property. "Substantive due process," as it came to be called, became the means by which courts struck down regulatory measures designed to adjust the operation of the marketplace in the public interest. Blatchford's opinion in *Chicago, Milwaukee & St. Paul Railway Co. v. Minnesota* (1890) was the first instance in which the Supreme Court used the due process clause to invalidate a state railroad regulation.

The case involved the Minnesota legislature's establishment of a commission charged with setting equal and reasonable rates for railroad transportation within the state. Under the law, rates established by the commission were "final and conclusive," and not subject to judicial inquiry. The railroad company's refusal to comply with the commission's rates launched a dispute over the Minnesota law's constitutionality that ended up in the Supreme Court. Attorneys for the railway contended that the regulation of rates violated fundamental rights, including the right to obtain the benefits from the use of one's property. Counsel for Minnesota, on the other hand, emphasized a line of precedents, including the Supreme Court's decision in *Munn v. Illinois* (1877), that sustained state legislatures' power to establish reasonable rates for transportation.

Writing for a 6–3 majority, Blatchford concluded that because it offered no check on the commission's rate-setting authority, the Minnesota statute conflicted with the Constitution. "Although the railroad company is forbidden to establish rates that are not equal and reasonable," he wrote, "there is no power in the courts to stay the hands of the commission, if it chooses to establish rates that are unequal and unreasonable." Lacking provisions for judicial investigation into the reasonableness of rates, the statute creating the commission stripped railway companies of their property without due process of law. "[The law] deprives the company of its right to a judicial investigation, by due process of law . . . ," Blatchford wrote, "and substitutes . . . the action of a railroad commission which, in view of the powers conceded to it by the state court, cannot be regarded as clothed with judicial functions." The question of reasonableness, Blatchford believed, was a judicial one, and, by granting the authority to establish rates to a commission without judicial investigation, the Minnesota statute failed to pass constitutional muster.

To contemporary observers, Blatchford's opinion in *Chicago, Milwaukee & St. Paul* seemed to overrule *Munn v. Illinois*, in which the Court had upheld an Illinois law regulating rates for grain elevators, and appeared to signal the Court's willingness to protect property from interference by state legislatures. Just two years after he held that the due process clause could be used against state regulation, however, the enigmatic Blatchford, in *Budd v. New York* (1892), steered the Court back toward an acceptance of regulatory measures. The New York statute at issue in *Budd*, like the law in *Munn*, provided for maximum rates for grain elevators. Although counsel urged that the New York legislature's establishment of reasonable rates violated the principles enunciated in *Chicago, Milwaukee & St. Paul*, Blatchford held otherwise. Following the *Munn* precedent, he concluded that the New York law did not constitute a violation of due process. He explained the apparent contradiction between his opinions in *Chicago, Milwaukee & St. Paul* and *Budd* by making a factual distinction between the two cases: in *Budd* the legislature itself determined reasonable rates, whereas in *Chicago, Milwaukee & St. Paul* a legislatively created commission had done so. "What was said in the opinion in [*Chicago, Milwaukee & St. Paul*] as to the question of the reasonableness of the rate of charge being one for judicial investigation," he concluded, "had no reference to a case where the rates are prescribed directly by the legislature."

Blatchford's murky explanation of his behavior in *Budd* and his generally incongruous record should not detract from the contributions he made as a member of the Court. Among the most steady and dependable of justices, Blatchford wrote 430 majority opinions in a mere eleven years on the Court. He wrote only two dissents, a fact that earned him a reputation as a consensus-builder. Overall, Blatchford served admirably in a particularly crucial period of the Court's history, when the justices were only beginning to come to grips with the massive social changes wrought by the nation's transition to industrial capitalism. Blatchford did not live long enough to witness the Court's continuing struggle to adapt the Constitution to modern American society.

—*Timothy S. Huebner*

BIBLIOGRAPHY

There is no biography of Blatchford, only brief sketches of his life in scattered reference volumes. The best such sketch is by Arnold Paul in Friedman and Israel, *Justices,* vol. 2, 1401. The most useful discussion of Blatchford's best-known opinion is James W. Ely Jr., "The Railroad Question Revisited: *Chicago, Milwaukee & St. Paul Railway v. Minnesota* and Constitutional Limits on State Regulations," *Great Plains Quarterly* 12 (1992): 121.

NOTEWORTHY OPINIONS

Dobson v. Dornan, 118 U.S. 10 (1886)

United States v. Jung Ah Lung, 124 U.S. 621 (1888)

Chicago, Milwaukee & St. Paul Railway Company v. Minnesota, 134 U.S. 418 (1890)

Counselman v. Hitchcock, 142 U.S. 547 (1892)

Budd v. New York, 143 U.S. 517 (1892)

JOSEPH P. BRADLEY

Birth: March 14, 1813, Berne, New York.

Education: Rutgers University, graduated 1836.

Official Positions: None.

Supreme Court Service: Nominated associate justice by President Ulysses S. Grant, February 8, 1870, succeeding James Wayne, who died in 1867 and whose seat remained vacant by act of Congress until 1870; confirmed by the Senate, March 21, 1870, by a 46–9 vote; took judicial oath March 23, 1870; served until January 22, 1892; replaced by George Shiras Jr., nominated by President Benjamin Harrison.

Death: January 22, 1892, Washington, D.C.

The oldest of twelve children, Joseph Bradley was enrolled at Rutgers College in 1833 through the intervention of a former teacher. He graduated in three years and was later described by one scholar as "a desperately serious young man." Shortly after graduation, he undertook to study law—largely with himself as the instructor. Bradley appears to have been rigorous in his preparation. One entry in his notes cites five different sources: one in Latin, two in French, and two in English. Admitted to the New Jersey bar in 1839, for the next thirty years Bradley centered his life and legal career around Newark. By the Civil War era, he had become a prominent attorney, well known among the leaders of Newark's business and legal community.

In 1862 Bradley agreed to run for Congress as a conservative Republican. He lost, but given some of his later opinions as a Supreme Court justice, his position on racial integration as a candidate is of interest. Like many Republicans, including Abraham Lincoln, Bradley had no difficulty supporting the end of slavery but at the same time foreseeing little change in racial attitudes toward blacks. It was perfectly consistent to be pro-Union, antislavery, and antiblack—all at the same time. Candidate Bradley's views would be echoed by Justice Bradley's decision in the *Civil Rights Cases* in 1883. A strong supporter of Ulysses Grant in the 1868 presidential election—indeed, he was a presidential elector pledged to Grant—Bradley was nominated to the Supreme Court in 1870 and served on that bench for almost twenty-two years.

He had been on the Court for six years when he was asked to perform a nonjudicial duty—to serve as a member of the electoral commission in the disputed 1876 presidential election. With Congress deadlocked over the counting of the electoral votes, the solution appeared to be a fifteen-member commission to consist of five members apiece from the House, the Senate, and the Supreme Court. With fourteen commissioners divided equally between the two parties, it was widely assumed that Bradley would cast the deciding vote, and indeed he did. Bradley voted with his fellow Republicans on every question before them, giving Rutherford Hayes sufficient votes to become president.

Possibly because Bradley's views on racial relations were virtually identical with those of the southern Democrats (all the Democratic senators who voted on his confirmation had supported him), these party members may have assumed that he would vote with them. Instead, he did what every other member of the commission did: voted for the candidate of his party. In so doing, however, he may have switched his vote, it is alleged, after two old friends, both Republicans and strong supporters of his judicial selection, visited him the evening before the vote was to be taken. What actually happened will probably never be known, but in the face of Democratic denunciation, Bradley maintained a blend of olympian aloofness, self-righteousness, and self-pity: his dignity, if not his integrity, remained substantially intact.

Bradley's generation fought the Civil War; his party framed the Fourteenth Amendment; and his Court formulated the new enactment's first judicial interpretation. It took the form of a major decision handed down in 1873. The *Slaughterhouse Cases* involved a group of New Orleans butchers challenging a state statute that confined all New Orleans butchering to a specific area and mandated further that it be done on the premises of a particular meat-packing corporation. Disgruntled if not destitute, the butchers invoked the Fourteenth Amendment, claiming that the statute denied them their right to pursue a lawful calling and therefore deprived them of their liberty and property in contravention of the new provision. Speaking for the majority in the 5–4 decision, Justice Samuel Miller rejected this contention, insisting that the butchers had to seek relief from either the state court or state legislature; the Fourteenth Amendment had been intended to deal with the ex-slaves, not the general population. It did not, in other words, apply to their case.

Bradley strongly disagreed. The statute restricting butchering to the premises of a favored company was "onerous, unreasonable, arbitrary, and unjust." The butchers were indeed deprived of their liberty as well as property, without due process of law. "Their right of choice is a portion of their liberty; their occupation is their property." Moreover, although ex-slaves may have been the primary cause of the Amendment, "its language [was] general, embracing all citizens, and . . . was purposely so expressed." Bradley reiterated these views in two later decisions, *Bartermeyer v. Iowa* (1874) and *Butchers' Union Slaughter-House et al. v. Crescent City Live-Stock Landing and Slaughter-House Co.* (1884). In spite of his repeated emphasis on the Fourteenth Amendment's scope, however, he seems to have been somewhat selective in the callings to which he attached the amendment's protection.

In *Bradwell v. Illinois* (1873), Bradley's Court considered the efforts of a woman to gain admittance to the Illinois bar so that she could practice law. Myra Bradwell argued, not unreasonably, that the Four-

Joseph P. Bradley

teenth Amendment prevented Illinois from abridging her "privileges and immunities," one of which was surely her right to practice her chosen calling. The Court, Bradley included, disagreed. Because Bradley had vigorously emphasized the contrary in the *Slaughterhouse Cases,* the question of his inconsistency arises. If a group of butchers had a constitutionally protected right to practice their profession, why did not a woman qualified to practice law have a similar privilege?

In a concurring opinion, Bradley conceded no inconsistency whatsoever. Law had to reflect nature, and in the "nature of things it is not every citizen of every age, sex, and condition that is qualified for every calling and position." One needed to consider "the peculiar characteristics, destiny, and mission of woman." After all, he intoned, the chief purpose of woman was "to fulfill the noble and benign offices of wife and mother. This is the law of the creator, and the rules of civil society must be adapted to the general constitution of things, and cannot be based upon exceptional cases." Perhaps the best assessment of Bradley's concurrence in *Bradwell* came from a writer in the Boston *Daily Advertiser,* who observed, "Judge Bradley's opinion seemed to cause no little amusement upon the bench and on the Bar."

In terms of civil rights, Bradley appears to have placed certain categories of rights higher than others. Indeed, perhaps he can be accused of suffering from a hardening of the categories. In 1872 he dissented from the decision in *Blyew v. United States,* a case involving a brutal murder of an elderly, blind black woman whose death had been witnessed by several of her relatives. Kentucky law, however, forbade a black person to testify at the trial of a white defendant. Federal authorities sought, therefore, to move the case into federal court. In an opinion that seems less than persuasive, Justice William Strong blocked the transfer, arguing that the federal law applied only to persons "affected by the cause," and this limitation did not include witnesses. In his dissent, Bradley denounced Strong's reasoning with forceful language. The result of the decision for potential witnesses "is to brand them with a badge of slavery . . . to expose

them to wanton insults and fiendish assaults . . . to leave their lives, their families, and their property unprotected by law," he wrote.

Passage of the 1875 Civil Rights Act only three years later inspired a nuanced response from Bradley. The new statute mandated integration in certain public establishments such as restaurants and theaters. The right to expect the law to protect one's ability to testify as a witness was very different and far more important, according to Bradley, than a desire on the part of blacks to sit next to whites while dining or at a theater. The former was a vital component of one's privileges as a citizen, and the latter merely a matter of social preference. In his copybook, Bradley wrote of the new law that "surely Congress cannot guarantee to the colored people admission to every place of gathering and amusement. To deprive white people of the right of choosing their own company would be to introduce another kind of slavery." Blacks were entitled to "freedom and all legal and essential privileges, [but] the antipathy of race cannot be crushed and annihilated by legal enactment."

Given these views, one should not be surprised to read Bradley's opinion for the Court in the *Civil Rights Cases* (1883), in which he merely reiterated sentiments he had long held. The Fourteenth Amendment, he insisted, applied only to state action; private discrimination seemed perfectly appropriate to him. Here, Justice Bradley echoed in 1883 what congressional candidate Bradley had asserted in 1862. Moreover, every member of the Court who had participated in the *Slaughterhouse Cases* ten years before agreed with him.

Bradwell and the *Civil Rights Cases* are certainly no tribute to Bradley as a civil libertarian, but one of his later decisions is of great positive significance. In the landmark case of *Boyd v. United States* (1886), Bradley explored the scope of the Fourth Amendment and its relationship to self-incrimination. He rejected the argument "that the seizure of a man's private books and papers to be used in evidence against him is substantially different from compelling him to be a witness against himself." Anticipating later constitutional doctrine, he claimed that "a compulsory production of the private books and papers of the owner compel[s] him to be a witness against himself, within the meaning of the Fifth Amendment and is the equivalent of a search and seizure—within the meaning of the Fourth Amendment." Moreover, the scope and motive for the search were irrelevant.

If Bradley seemed bound to his times in matters of race and gender, he demonstrated flexibility and creativity in the areas of railroad regulation and interpretation of the commerce clause. He had been a very successful railroad lawyer, representing the Camden and Amboy Railroad, which was widely regarded as one of the most notorious contributors to "political pressure and bribery." As a judge, however, his independent attitude toward these common carriers was noteworthy. Bradley strongly supported the Court's refusal to use the Fourteenth Amendment to block state regulation of private corporations—such as railroads or grain elevators—in the public interest. The economic clout of railroad corporations, he insisted, should not permit them to "abdicate their essential duties."

Writing a private note to Chief Justice Morrison Waite concerning the forthcoming decision in *Munn v. Illinois* (1876), one that went against the proprietor of a grain elevator objecting to state regulation, Bradley denounced the railroads in language that seems unusually harsh. Perhaps he had in mind his long experience as director and counsel for the Camden and Amboy. Bradley persuaded the chief justice to hold that when such a corporation "becomes a matter of public consequence so as to affect the whole public and to become a common charge, it is subject to legislative regulation and control." He insisted that there are "in this country no more absolute monopolies of public service than [the railroads] are. The public stands on no equality with them. . . . They have every thing in their own hands. . . . They impose a common charge of greater value to themselves and burden to the public than any other which exists in the present age."

When interpreting the scope of the commerce clause, Bradley demonstrated impressive sensitivity toward the need of an effective federalism. He explored with skill and insight the controversial boundaries between federal regulation of interstate commerce and the state taxing power, frequently upholding regulation at the expense of taxing power. In *Robbins v. Shelby County Taxing District* (1887), for example, he stated for the Court that:

> the United States are but one country, and are and must be subject to one system of regulations, and not to a multitude of systems. . . . It seems to be forgotten that the people of this country are citizens of the United States, as well as of the individual states, and that they have some rights under the Constitution and laws of the former independent of the latter, and free from any interference or restraint from them.

Of Grant's four appointments to the Court, Bradley was undoubtedly the strongest in intellect and learning. Familiar with the American, English, and Continental legal systems, he brought added insights to his decisions through practical experience in the business world, as well as a familiarity with other fields, including mathematics, philosophy, and natural sciences. He was equally at home when expounding on the appropriate, if not invariably complex, methods for calculating the earnings of a railroad, or discussing the intricacies of patent litigation. He reveled in tracking legal doctrines back through a variety of sources, and sometimes his decisions became vehicles for extended research. In an 1890 opinion, for example, Bradley traced an obscure legal doctrine back to the Pandects of Justinian and cited Latin, French, and Spanish sources, including a footnote in French.

In company with other tough-minded and able judges, such as Samuel Miller or Stephen Field, Bradley more than held his own. Miller recalled of Bradley that "if there is a principle on which a case can be decided that no one else has thought of, it has for that reason a charm for him." Nevertheless, Miller believed that given "some allowance for eccentricity, he is a useful and valuable man on the bench." A Rutgers classmate noted that, as with "most men who resemble him in the possession of logical power and habit, he had little or no deference for the mere opinion of others." Bradley, he added, had a compulsion "not only to be, but to know."

Bradley, wrote another contemporary, "was amusingly petulant—naturally eccentric; and he had stimulated eccentricity by its indulgence throughout his life." In 1890 an observer described Bradley as

> a little dried-up anatomy of a man. . . . His skin hangs in wrinkles and all of his fat has long since gone to figures and judicial decisions. He is seventy-seven years old, but there is a fair chance for his lasting at least twenty-three years longer. There is not much of him to die, and when his soul is disembodied it will not be much freer than it is now.

How can one assess Bradley's twenty-two years as a Supreme Court justice? Each generation determines for itself judicial greatness, but there is no doubt that Bradley had superb legal qualifications and was an outstanding technician of the law. Self-taught, he brought to his decisions a seasoned practicality in business affairs. Indeed, his greatest opinions in terms of influence appear to have been in the field of commercial regulation. Further, his writings indicate that Bradley passionately believed both in progress and the perfectibility of man.

Yet Bradley could not translate his broad faith in this perfectibility of man into sound judicial doctrine that went beyond gender and race. In fields of the law that later generations have considered more important than interstate commerce, he seems to have been unable to transcend the limits of his own time. The truly great judge is somehow able to do that, by "nudging" the future rule of law into some sort of shape that goes beyond the current role of law— through decisions that have retained validity, vitality, and significance for our own time, holdings that continue to influence American constitutionalism.

Bradley, according to constitutional law professor Leon Friedman, "had little of the skepticism and tol-

erance of a Holmes, and came to a conclusion about a law or legal rule because it was the *right* law or rule under the circumstances, and not because imperfect men should be allowed to bungle their way freely within broad limits of government." The assessment of Bradley's life and career offered by the *Washington Post* upon his death in 1892 remains valid and accurate. He was "a man of profound and varied learning, legal acumen, and moral rectitude." Beyond this, deponent sayeth not.

—Jonathan Lurie

BIBLIOGRAPHY

Bradley's papers are housed in the New Jersey Historical Society. Some Court-related materials are among them, but the entire collection appears to have been "edited" by his son before donation to the society. There is no extant scholarly biographical study of Bradley, but Charles Fairman contributed three articles, which, when taken together, may make such a biography unnecessary. See "Mr. Justice Bradley's Appointment to the Supreme Court and the Legal Tender Cases," parts 1 and 2, *Harvard Law Review* 54 (1941): 977, 1128; "The Education of a Justice: Justice Bradley and Some of His Colleagues," *Stanford Law Review* 1 (1949): 217; and "What Makes a Great Justice? Mr. Justice Bradley and the Supreme Court, 1870–1892," *Boston University Law Review* 30 (1950): 46. An attempt to integrate much of the existing scholarship on Bradley may be seen in Jonathan Lurie, "Mr. Justice Bradley: A Reassessment," *Seton Hall Law Review* 16 (1986): 343. See also M. G. Collins, "Justice Bradley's Civil Rights Odyssey Revisited," *Tulane Law Review* 70 (1996); and K. D. Whitten, "The Fourteenth Amendment: Justice Bradley's Twentieth Century Legacy," *Cumberland Law Review* 29 (1998/1999): 143.

NOTEWORTHY OPINIONS

Slaughterhouse Cases, 83 U.S. 36 (1873) (Dissent)

Bradwell v. Illinois, 83 U.S. 130 (1873) (Concurrence)

Civil Rights Cases, 109 U.S. 3 (1883)

Boyd v. United States, 116 U.S. 616 (1886)

LOUIS DEMBITZ BRANDEIS

Birth: November 13, 1856, Louisville, Kentucky.

Education: Harvard Law School, LL.B., 1877.

Official Positions: Attorney, Public Franchise League and Massachusetts State Board of Trade, 1897–1911; counsel, New England Policyholders' Protective Committee, 1905; special counsel, wage and hour cases in California, Illinois, Ohio, and Oregon, 1907–1914; counsel, Ballinger-Pinchot investigation, 1910; chairman, arbitration board, New York garment workers' labor disputes, 1910–1916.

Supreme Court Service: Nominated associate justice by President Woodrow Wilson, January 28, 1916, to replace Joseph R. Lamar, who had died; confirmed by the Senate, June 1, 1916, by a 47–22 vote; took judicial oath June 5, 1916; retired February 13, 1939; replaced by William O. Douglas, nominated by President Franklin D. Roosevelt.

Death: October 5, 1941, Washington, D.C.

When Louis Brandeis was nominated to the Supreme Court in 1916, his wife wrote to his brother, "I tell Louis, if he is going to retire, he is certainly doing it with a burst of fireworks." Although Brandeis would become the first Jew to sit on the Court, the fireworks resulted less from his religion than from the political philosophy and the approach to law for which he had already become famous. Both the philosophy and the approach were considered unacceptably radical by influential elements of the business and legal communities. From their point of view, Brandeis's opponents were correct: when Brandeis took his seat on the Court after a fierce and bitter confirmation process, he quickly demonstrated that his ideology and jurisprudence would illuminate his decisions as a justice. In doing so, they also permanently altered American constitutional jurisprudence.

Brandeis graduated at the top of his class (1877) at Harvard Law School, where Christopher Columbus Langdell had introduced the case method and taught that law was a dynamic entity based on social realities. When Brandeis went on to practice law in Boston, he insisted on understanding not only his clients' immediate problems but also the economic and, occasionally, the political context in which they arose. He did so, he told a young associate, because "knowledge of the decided cases and of the rules of logic cannot alone make a great lawyer. . . . The controlling force is the deep knowledge of human necessities. . . . The duty of a lawyer today is not that of a solver of legal conundrums: he is indeed a counsellor at law." He noted in a memorandum on "The Practice of the Law" that a lawyer was "far more likely to impress clients by knowledge of facts than by knowledge of law."

By 1916 Brandeis had impressed enough clients to support a highly lucrative law firm. He had also made an impact on a variety of leaders in public life and on the public itself. The media referred to him as the "people's attorney" because of his involvement in movements for social justice: legalization of unions, women's suffrage, maximum hours and minimum wage legislation, and the use of natural resources for the public rather than the private good. He had fought with some success against the trusts that controlled much of the U.S. economy. His investigation of the insurance industry resulted in his invention of savings bank life insurance. He earned a reputation for integrity by engaging in most of his battles without pay and through his continual criticism of government and corporate corruption. He campaigned vigorously for Woodrow Wilson in the 1912 presidential election; in fact, Arthur Link, Wilson's chief biographer, has attributed Wilson's New Freedom platform to Brandeis's economic thought. Such pre-Court battles both reflected and shaped Brandeis's political ideas, which in turn underlay his judicial opinions. As Paul Freund, one of his law clerks, commented, "It is hardly likely that anyone came to the Supreme Court with a more closely articulated set of convictions than those which Brandeis held."

The opinions Brandeis wrote as a justice were logical extensions of his ideas about the nature of the democratic state and the role of the individual within it. In the ideal society, government enabled individuals to reach their full potential as self-fulfilled members of a just community, and individuals willingly assumed their civic responsibilities. Development of human potential required that each individual have access to ideas, a concept given concrete form in the legal doctrine of freedom of speech and press. Human development also depended on the leisure to learn about potential public policies and associate with others for discussion of public matters, and in the opportunity to participate in the processes through which the policies were determined. A democratic state responsive to the electorate was one in which neither economic nor political institutions were large enough to make individual beliefs irrelevant or to stultify experimentation. To Brandeis, federalism was not just a historically useful system that had enabled thirteen colonies to unite as a nation; rather, it was a productive mechanism for experimentation with new government policies. He insisted on each citizen's civic responsibility and was adamant about education, which continued in one way or another throughout life, as a precondition for a democratic electorate.

Louis Dembitz Brandeis

Brandeis's sociological jurisprudence followed logically from his democratic philosophy. Law represented the will of the people, which in turn reflected their perception of society's needs. As the needs changed, so should the laws, including the Constitution, which judges had an obligation to read according to current societal necessities. Society's needs could be ascertained only by examining facts, either in legislative hearings or by evaluating data accumulated during societal experimentation. He scorned the late nineteenth- and early twentieth-century attorneys who made themselves servants of corporations, telling the Harvard Ethical Society in 1905 that his vision of the ideal lawyer was drawn from the early United States, when "nearly every great lawyer was . . . a statesman: and nearly every statesman, great or small, was a lawyer," holding "a position of independence, between the wealthy and the people, prepared to curb the excesses of either." The role of lawyers in a democratic polity was to defend legislative social experiments by providing judges with sufficient factual material for a determination that the experiments constituted reasonable responses to problems.

Brandeis had done precisely that in the innovative and almost immediately famous "Brandeis brief" that he and his sister-in-law, Josephine Goldmark, prepared for *Muller v. Oregon* (1908). Faced with a challenge to an Oregon statute limiting the maximum number of hours women could work for pay, Brandeis and Goldmark presented the Supreme Court with two pages of traditional legal argument and more than 100 pages of factual data demonstrating the deleterious effect of overly long hours on women's health and the well-being of their families. After winning the case, Brandeis and Goldmark went on to use similar and equally successful arguments to defend other statutes establishing maximum hours and minimum wages for women. Brandeis realized that although it would negate his gender-based argument in *Muller,* the same approach should be taken toward hours and wage legislation for men, and he therefore helped secure publication of Goldmark's careful collections of data supporting that argument. In 1916 they labored for six months on a brief defending an Oregon law setting maximum hours for men. The case, *Bunting v. Oregon* (1917), was turned over to Felix Frankfurter when Brandeis was appointed to the Supreme Court.

Brandeis is perhaps best known for his judicial opinions in the areas of social experimentation, the size of economic and political institutions, and civil liberties, but his reputation also lies in part on his advocacy of limited judicial intervention in policy

making. He did not ignore the judicial properties in pursuit of his goals for the country. Judicial restraint was central to his sociological jurisprudence. It was as undemocratic and unwise for judges to make social policy as it was for them to jump into cases when matters were not ripe for decision. When Arizona sued to prevent the construction of Boulder Dam and the possible diversion of water to California, for example, Brandeis pointed out that construction of the dam had not yet begun and so there was no need for the Court to decide whether waters that might never be taken from Arizona could legitimately be diverted (*Arizona v. California,* 1931). If a party based its case on a right new to American law, as happened when the Associated Press claimed that it had a property right in its dispatches, Brandeis, in dissent, objected to the Court's usurpation of the legislative function by creating and legitimizing a largely undefined right (*International News Service v. Associated Press,* 1918). Similarly, he dissented from the Court's declaration in *Eisner v. Macomber* (1920) that stock dividends were a category of untaxable property, saying that it was up to a legislature to decide.

His most explicit statement about the limits of judicial review came in *Ashwander v. Tennessee Valley Authority* (1936), in which the power of the Tennessee Valley Authority to construct the Wheeler Dam was challenged by a stockholders' suit. Although Brandeis concurred in the Court's holding that the project was constitutionally valid, he stated that he would not have reached the constitutional issue because the plaintiffs had no real standing to sue. He drew on earlier Court decisions to list the restrictive guidelines he believed the Court ought to follow in dealing with constitutional questions: declining to hear "a friendly, non-adversary, proceeding," a case where the complainant has suffered no real injury, or one in which a complainant challenged a statute from which he had benefited; making no decision on constitutional grounds if others were available; and issuing rules of constitutional law that were as narrow as possible.

As a lawyer, he had fulminated against the Court's interpretation of the Fourteenth Amendment's due process clause to promulgate what he considered judge-made doctrines such as liberty of contract in order to strike down social policy enacted by state legislatures. As a judge, he maintained his insistence on judicial restraint, even when he disagreed with the legislative experiment at issue. In 1932 the Court struck down an Oklahoma law forbidding any new ice company to open without first acquiring a certificate of public convenience and necessity from the state (*New State Ice Co. v. Liebmann*). The rationale was that licensing would minimize the higher consumer costs caused by wasteful duplication of plants and delivery service. Justice Sutherland, however, speaking for the Court, said that the ice business was not "affected with a public interest" and that all the Oklahoma statute did was create the possibility of monopoly.

Brandeis had fought against monopoly and the suppression of competition as a lawyer. He nevertheless dissented from the Court's decision in the Oklahoma case and wrote fourteen heavily footnoted pages to show that social conditions in Oklahoma might well have led the legislature to believe that excessive competition had added to the impact of the Depression on unemployment and low prices. He indicated that he disliked the law, asserting that most people "realize that failure to distribute widely the profits of industry has been a prime cause of our present plight." But his own view, or that of "most" people, was irrelevant to him as a justice: Oklahoma's experiment was rational, and the Court ought to permit it to continue.

Frankfurter commented that Brandeis believed that the Constitution "provided for the future partly by not forecasting it and partly by the generality of its language." The Constitution, according to Brandeis, was designed to be flexible. It was as amenable to legislative experimentation as to judicial imagination, and he frequently reminded his colleagues of John Marshall's statement in *McCulloch v. Maryland* (1819): "We must never forget that it is a constitution we are expounding." Brandeis wrote in *New State Ice*:

> There must be power in the States and the Nation to remould, through experimentation, our economic practices and institutions to meet

changing social and economic needs. To stay experimentation in things social and economic is a grave responsibility which might be fraught with serious consequences to the nation.

He noted his belief that federalism enabled states to serve as laboratories for social change and urged the Court not to hinder federalism by "erect[ing] our prejudices into legal principles." "If we would guide by the light of reason," he declared, "we must let our minds be bold."

One of Brandeis's *bêtes noires* was the Court's 1842 decision in *Swift v. Tyson* that federal courts were not bound by state common law, but could follow their own doctrines. Brandeis had joined fellow justice Oliver Wendell Holmes's campaign to overrule the decision, which enabled businesses to circumvent local law by litigating in federal rather than state courts. *Swift* violated Brandeis's belief in federalism, accountability of economic power, and state experimentation with controlling economic institutions. At the successful conclusion of a lengthy campaign, Brandeis was able to write the Court's opinion in *Erie Railroad Co. v. Tompkins* (1938), negating *Swift* by declaring that whenever a state's laws were at issue, federal courts hearing cases in the state would be bound by the decisional rules of the state's highest court. On the same day, he wrote for the Court in *Hinderlider v. La Plata River & Cherry Creek Ditch Co.* (1938), a case concerning an interstate compact, that when cases involved only federal issues and state decisional rules would be inappropriate, decisions were to be made under federal common law. He thereby protected federal supremacy while retaining an emphasis on federalism and state power for experimentation.

These themes, linked closely to his distaste for bigness, ran through many of his opinions. His first dissent, in *New York Central Railroad v. Winfield* (1917), rejected the Court's declaration that the Federal Employers Liability Act filled the field of compensation for injuries to interstate railroad employees. Brandeis refused to read the act as reflecting congressional intent to preclude state protection for workers, because:

it is the state which is both primarily and ultimately concerned with the care of the injured. . . . Upon the state falls the financial burden of dependency, if provision be not otherwise made. . . . Upon the state also rests, under our dual system of government, the duty owed to the individual, to avert misery and promote happiness so far as possible.

Clearly, he perceived the state as a positive institution that could increase individual happiness by alleviating economic injustices.

In *Winfield,* he signaled the way he would approach cases, discussing "world experience in dealing with industrial accidents" and relying on facts to bolster his argument that it was reasonable to believe that further compensation was necessary. When the Court overturned a state statute prohibiting employment agencies from charging workers for whom they found jobs, Brandeis dissented again, writing at length in *Adams v. Tanner* (1917) about the abusive practices of employment agencies that were the target of the legislation and reiterating his contention that courts lacked authority to strike down social legislation unless examination of the facts demonstrated that it was unreasonable.

Brandeis quickly realized that many attorneys appearing before the Court failed to prepare the kind of fact-laden argument he had used in *Muller.* Undaunted, he decided that if attorneys did not perform that function, the justices would have to do it for themselves. In *Jay Burns Baking Co. v. Bryan* (1924), which examined the constitutionality of a Nebraska consumer protection law that set weight standards, including maximum weight limits, for commercially sold loaves of bread, the Court's majority held that the law took bakers' and dealers' property without due process of law. Brandeis disagreed and chastised his brethren for not examining the relevant facts. We justices, he said somewhat disingenuously, had

merely to acquaint ourselves with the art of breadmaking and the usages of the trade; with the devices by which buyers of bread are imposed upon and honest bakers or dealers are

subjected by their dishonest fellows to unfair competition; with the problems which have confronted public officials charged with the enforcement of the laws prohibiting short weights, and with their experience in administering those laws.

Brandeis fulfilled this "mere" task by presenting the Court with fifteen pages of information about the baking industry, most of it in lengthy and forbidding footnotes.

Brandeis's penchant for upholding state experimentation continued throughout his years on the Court. In 1933 the Court overturned a Florida law that, seeking to discourage chain stores, imposed heavier license fees on stores that were part of multicounty chains than on independent shops. The Court declared that Florida's classification of stores lacked a rational basis (*Liggett v. Lee*). Brandeis disagreed and wrote a long essay on the evils of economic bigness, and particularly of the corporations he believed had grown so large that they were a menace to American democracy. They were able to dominate states and citizens, he warned the Court, saying, "The lives of tens or hundreds of thousands of employees and the property of tens or hundreds of thousands of investors are subjected, through the corporate mechanism, to the control of a few men." The United States was in the grip of "the rule of a plutocracy." Five of the twelve plaintiff corporations in the case had assets of more than $90 million each; among them, they controlled more than 19,718 stores throughout the country. Florida might well have believed that this "concentration of wealth and of power and . . . absentee ownership" was "thwarting American ideals," making equality of opportunity impossible, "converting independent tradesmen into clerks; and that it is sapping the resources, the vigor and the hope of the smaller cities and towns."

Brandeis had declared war on concentrated power, warning that unbridled bigness ultimately would prove a false panacea for the country's economic ills. This theme resounded throughout many of his 528 judicial opinions. He was equally certain that concentrated government power was undemocratic, however worthy particular government policies might be. He saw federalism as similar to separation of powers: both arrangements were aspects of the Constitution's solution to the problem of government size. Just as jurisdictional rules helped keep the Court within the boundaries prescribed by the Constitution and prevented it from intervening in problems that were too complicated or remote for any nine justices to solve, so part of the Court's function was to maintain the margins of separation between the federal executive and Congress, and between the federal government and the states.

He therefore dissented when the Court held that a president could fire a civil servant unilaterally in spite of a statute requiring Senate advice and consent before such a removal. Answering the argument that it was more efficient for the chief executive to act unilaterally against civil servants he found unacceptable, Brandeis declared that "the doctrine of the separation of powers was adopted by the Convention of 1787 not to promote efficiency but to preclude the exercise of arbitrary power" (*Myers v. United States*, 1926). "The purpose," he continued, "was not to avoid friction, but, by means of the inevitable friction incident to the distribution of the governmental powers among three departments, to save the people from autocracy."

He held to this principle even when it meant infuriating President Franklin Roosevelt, most of whose New Deal programs Brandeis endorsed. Brandeis was not willing to permit the emergency of the Depression to be used as an excuse for concentration of power within the executive branch. His reluctance became clear when the Court pondered the constitutionality of the National Industrial Recovery Act of 1933 (NIRA), which Roosevelt considered a cornerstone of his recovery plan for the country. The legislation created the National Recovery Administration (NRA) to carry out the law, which exempted industries from antitrust laws if they adopted codes providing for specific wages, hours, conditions of employment, and prices. The act provided no guidelines for the codes, however, giving the president total power to approve or disapprove them.

During oral argument in two 1935 cases resulting from the prosecution of oil company officials for ignoring the code Roosevelt had promulgated (*Panama Refining Co. v. Ryan* and *Amazon Petroleum Corporation v. Ryan*), one company's attorney asserted that his client had not known the law existed and that the only copy he knew of was in the "hip pocket of a government agent sent down to Texas from Washington." Brandeis turned to the government's lawyer and demanded, "Who promulgates these orders and codes that have the force of law?" The lawyer replied that, as they were promulgated by the president, "I assume they are on record at the State Department." This reply was insufficient, and Brandeis pressed further: "Is there any official or general publication of these executive orders?" "Not that I know of," came the answer, with the lawyer finally admitting lamely, "I think it would be difficult, but it is possible to get certified copies of the executive orders and codes from the NRA." Brandeis joined seven of his colleagues in striking down this portion of NIRA as an improper delegation of congressional powers to the executive.

He went further a few months later and voted to nullify the entire act, agreeing with Chief Justice Charles Evans Hughes's opinion for the Court that the massive delegation of power to the president was unconstitutional in all situations (*Schechter Poultry Corp. v. United States*, 1935). Among the other decisions handed down the same day was *Humphrey's Executor v. United States*, in which the Court effectively and unanimously overturned its ruling in *Myers*, vindicating Brandeis by holding that the president could not remove members of independent regulatory commissions. Brandeis announced a third opinion, again for a unanimous Court, holding unconstitutional the Frazier-Lemke Act of 1933, which had permitted farmers to defer mortgage payments. Brandeis and the Court declared that the statute, which authorized bankruptcy courts to take title to the property from the banks that held the mortgages, violated the Fifth Amendment's property clause (*Louisville Joint Stock Land Bank v. Radford*, 1935). The reason for Brandeis's distaste for a law that seemed on its face to protect farmers became apparent when he noted that, under the act, the definition of farmer included "persons who are merely capitalist absentees." "Capitalist absentees" was Brandeis's language for owners of land or stock whose concentrations of money gave them excessive power, and here they were being protected by the federal government.

"This is the end of this business of centralization," Brandeis told Roosevelt adviser Thomas G. Corcoran. "I want you to go back and tell the President that we're not going to let this government centralize everything." Brandeis approved of Roosevelt and used occasions such as his well-known weekly teas to tell New Dealers of his enthusiasm for the economic policies he hoped Roosevelt would propose, many of which the president in fact adopted. But bigness in government could be every bit as oppressive as bigness in business, and Brandeis would have no part of it.

Brandeis's opinions differed from those of his colleagues because he included in them the social realities leading to the legislation that came before the Court. This point of view reflected both his belief that factual information had to underlie all constitutional adjudication and his desire to use judicial opinions as educational devices. It was as important for citizens to understand the reasons behind the law as it for was for them to know what the law was. His clerks were expected to help him make his opinions not only "persuasive" but "instructive." They were sent regularly to find additional relevant statistics in the Library of Congress, even after an opinion had been written, and they frequently discovered that in his endless rewriting Brandeis had made as many as sixty changes in a draft of ten pages and had revised an opinion for the twentieth or thirtieth time. He tried to make clear not only who was suing whom, but why.

The decisions written by his colleagues, such as Mahlon Pitney, William Howard Taft, or George Sutherland, hold little information about the nature of the struggle between labor and management, for example, but Brandeis's opinions reflect and explain the struggle. When the workers at Duplex, a manufacturer of newspaper printing presses, were enjoined from striking or calling on workers in similar plants to refuse to work on Duplex machines, he made sure that anyone reading the resultant case knew that there were only four such companies in the United States, and that the other three were unionized and had instituted minimum wages and maximum hours. Duplex had refused to recognize the union, which led two of the other manufacturers to threaten to break their agreements with the union, jeopardizing its existence. Dissenting in *Duplex Printing Press Co. v. Deering* (1921), Brandeis told his readers that the laborers were neither irrational nor greedy: "May not all with a common interest join in refusing to expend their labor upon articles whose very production constitutes an attack upon their standard of living and the institution which they are convinced supports it?"

Similarly, Brandeis explained at length why he dissented when the Court overturned an Arizona law forbidding its courts to issue injunctions against strikes and picketing (*Truax v. Corrigan*, 1921). Chief Justice Taft wrote about the equal protection and due process clauses of the Fourteenth Amendment; Brandeis, although touching on the relevant constitutional provisions, described the factual situation. Cooks and waiters at the English Kitchen on Main Street in Bisbee, Arizona, struck and encouraged a boycott of the restaurant by picketing and distributing leaflets. Brandeis could find nothing irrational in a state's decision to permit disgruntled workers to tell their story to the public and to refuse courts the power to stop them from doing so. The law admittedly was a societal experiment, he declared, and wrote fourteen pages showing that England, the British dominions, the federal government, and other states had similar experiments: that was sufficient to demonstrate that the statute could not be brushed aside as either arbitrary or unreasonable.

Brandeis was as impassioned and influential in the area of civil liberties as he was in the economic sphere. His seminal contribution to the development of free speech jurisprudence has sometimes been underrated by scholars who have given Justice Holmes credit for the "clear and present danger" doctrine. Although Holmes first formulated the doctrine, writing in *Schenck v. United States* (1919) that the federal government could punish only speech that presented a clear and present danger, he did not define the terms *clear, present,* or *danger;* he suggested no criteria for doing so; and he stated that the doctrine was similar in peacetime and wartime. Brandeis subsequently elaborated on the doctrine, altering it substantially.

Brandeis considered free speech crucial to individual development and a necessity for the educated citizens that a democratic state demands. Speech, privacy, education, and democracy all were elements of the ideal political system. Democracy meant majority rule with full protection for the rights of individuals. Sociological jurisprudence, which in other spheres mandated judicial deference to the will of the majority, required that the judiciary play a central role in preventing government from interfering with individual rights. An educated electorate had to be able to engage in free and open discussion if law was to reflect felt necessities, experimentation was to occur, and socially responsive policies were to be developed.

Although Brandeis silently concurred in Holmes's opinion in *Schenck,* his rethinking became apparent in three dissents he wrote the following year. The first came in *Schaefer v. United States* (1920), an appeal from a conviction under the 1917 Espionage Act for printing misleading articles about the American war effort. Brandeis declared that the constitutional right of free speech was the same in wartime as it was during peace. In fact, he continued, it was precisely in time of war that free speech was most necessary, for it was then that "an intolerant majority" was most likely to be "swayed by passion or by fear."

The second was *Pierce v. United States* (1920), in which the Court upheld a second Espionage Act conviction, this one for distribution of Socialist leaflets that allegedly had interfered with the operation of the war effort and had caused insubordination. Brandeis's dissent reiterated his belief that the speech doctrine was identical in war and peace and that "the fundamental right of free men to strive for better conditions through new legislation and new institutions will not be preserved, if efforts to secure it by argument to fellow citizens may be construed as criminal incitement to disobey the existing law." His third dis-

sent came in *Gilbert v. Minnesota* (1920), a case challenging Minnesota's statute prohibiting any interference with the military enlistment effort, as applied to a speaker who had criticized the war and the draft during a public meeting. Describing the law as one that criminalized the teaching of pacifism, Brandeis condemned it for violating the rights of speech, privacy, and religion. In addition, he argued strenuously that if the Court used the Fourteenth Amendment's due process clause to strike down states' economic legislation, as it regularly did, surely the Court should apply the clause to state legislation that limited something as important as speech.

The *Gilbert* dissent laid the foundation for a major alteration of American law and for a reassessment of political values. In 1925, adopting Brandeis's argument, the Court declared that freedom of speech and press were "among the fundamental rights and 'liberties' " protected by the due process clause (*Gitlow v. New York*). This case and subsequent cases in which the Court held one or another of the Bill of Rights' liberties to be "incorporated" into the due process clause are responsible for the assumption, now part of American law and polity, that the Bill of Rights is a barrier to state, as well as federal, violation of individual liberties.

Brandeis's most eloquent contribution to free speech jurisprudence came in *Whitney v. California* (1927). Attacking a California statute outlawing political parties that advocated the use of illegal force, Brandeis aligned himself with the Founding Fathers, who, he asserted, "believed that the final end of the State was to make men free to develop their faculties." This goal could be accomplished only if "deliberate forces" prevailed over those that were "arbitrary"; if citizens were not only free to speak their thoughts, but encouraged to exercise their responsibility to do so; and if the nation understood "that the fitting remedy for evil counsels is good ones." Recognizing that by the time he wrote, the American government had become more active than it had been during its early years and that citizens now had reason to be concerned about how to keep the government within acceptable boundaries, he argued that "fear of serious injury" was insufficient justification for punishing speech, and he suggested a different standard:

> There must be reasonable ground to believe that the danger apprehended is imminent. There must be reasonable ground to believe that the evil to be prevented is a serious one . . . even advocacy of violence, however reprehensible morally, is not a justification for denying free speech where the advocacy falls short of incitement and there is nothing to indicate that the advocacy would be immediately acted on. . . . In order to support a finding of clear and present danger it must be shown either that immediate serious violence was to be expected or was advocated, or that the past conduct furnished reason to believe that such advocacy was then contemplated.

Brandeis transformed Holmes's "clear and present danger" by defining *present* to mean that "the incidence of the evil apprehended is so imminent that it may befall before there is opportunity for full discussion. If there be time to expose through discussion the falsehood and fallacies, to avert the evil by the processes of education, the remedy to be applied is more speech, not enforced silence." Brandeis also rejected Holmes's assumption that the government could act against speech presenting a danger of any evil the government had the right to prevent. The evil of "some violence or . . . destruction of property" was not enough; the evil had to be "the probability of serious injury to the State." If, as Brandeis suggested, it was unconstitutional to prevent or punish speech unless all reasonable people would agree that it represented a serious and imminent danger of probable injury to the state itself, the government's power to interfere with speech was minimal.

Although it came in equal measure from his pre-Court career and the eventual influence of his dissents from the bench, Brandeis had as great an impact on privacy jurisprudence as he had on free speech jurisprudence. In 1890 the *Harvard Law Review* had published "The Right to Privacy" by Brandeis and his law partner, Samuel D. Warren Jr. When Brandeis was

nominated to the Court, Dean Roscoe Pound of Harvard Law School told the Senate that the article had added a chapter to American law. Combining a formulation of law as a changing entity with the concept of privacy, the article argued that new inventions with the potential for violations of privacy had to be brought under law in the name of protecting the individual's "right to be let alone."

Brandeis and Warren were reacting to invasions of privacy by the press. By the time Brandeis joined the Court, government had access to the kind of technology that the article had warned about and had become big enough to represent a serious privacy threat. Brandeis now became concerned not only about the enhanced possibilities of government intrusion and their impact on the right of privacy, so central to the individual's development, but about the nature of a government that might resort to invasions of privacy. He therefore dissented when the Court upheld a conviction, under the Harrison Anti-Narcotic Act, obtained after the government induced two state prisoners to offer an attorney money for drugs and record their conversations with him.

As Holmes wrote for the Court in sustaining the conviction in *Casey v. United States* (1928), there was no doubt that the law had been broken. Brandeis agreed but declared that the conviction should be overturned because the government had instigated the crime and, absent government action, there would have been no evidence for the government to record. "The government . . . may not provoke or create a crime and then punish the criminal, its creature," he argued. He explained that he was less concerned about Casey than about the government, and voted as he did "not because some right of Casey's has been denied, but in order to protect the Government. To protect it from illegal conduct of its officers. To protect the purity of its courts."

Similarly, Brandeis objected to a conviction under the National Prohibition Act, obtained as a result of evidence gathered during five months of government wiretapping. The Court held in *Olmstead v. United States* (1928) that wiretapping did not constitute the kind of physical trespass or seizure prohibited by the Fourth Amendment's search and seizure clause. Incredulous, Brandeis asked, "Can it be that the Constitution affords no protection against such invasions of individual security?" and answered his question by recalling the Founding Fathers' concern about writs of assistance and general warrants. Wiretapping was even more insidious than those devices because it was more intrusive. Brandeis urged the Court to adopt a socially responsive interpretation of the Constitution, including the search and seizure clause. "Rights of . . . the liberty of the individual must be remolded from time to time," he had written in *Truax,* "to meet the changing needs of society." He was referring to the specific manifestations of the rights, not the rights themselves, which were unchanging, and which Brandeis found at the core of the Constitution. In *Olmstead,* he wrote:

> The makers of our Constitution undertook . . . to protect Americans in their beliefs, their thoughts, their emotions, and their sensations. They conferred, as against the Government, the right to be let alone—the most comprehensive of rights and the right most valued by civilized men.

Privacy and speech were connected in their centrality to the free flow of ideas and to individual growth. It was insufficient to claim, as the Court did, that the government had violated an individual right in the name of the greater good, because the greater good actually was being hurt by a well-intentioned but misguided government: "Experience should teach us to be most on our guard to protect liberty when the Government's purposes are beneficent. . . . The greatest dangers to liberty lurk in insidious encroachment by men of zeal, well-meaning but without understanding." The government, by acting illegally, was encouraging disdain for law. Brandeis had warned in his dissent in *Burdeau v. McDowell* (1921): "At the foundation of our civil liberty lies the principle which denies to government officials an exceptional position before the law and which subjects them to the same rules of conduct that are commands to the citizen. . . . Respect for law will not be advanced

by resort, in its enforcement, to means which shock the common man's sense of decency and fair play." He added in *Olmstead,* "Our Government is the potent, the omnipresent teacher. For good or for ill, it teaches the whole people by its example. Crime is contagious. If the Government becomes a lawbreaker, it breeds contempt for law: it invites every man to become a law unto himself; it invites anarchy." And he warned: "To declare that in the administration of the criminal law the end justifies the means—to declare that the Government may commit crimes in order to secure the conviction of a private criminal—would bring terrible retribution. Against that pernicious doctrine this Court should resolutely set its face."

American constitutional law today is fact-oriented largely because of the Brandeis brief and the fact-based sociological jurisprudence embodied in almost all of Brandeis's judicial opinions. Joining a Court whose members were born in the nineteenth century, he helped wrench its collective face toward the twentieth century, constantly reminding the justices and the larger legal and political communities of changing societal realities. His fervent sense of democracy and the need of the political system for free, involved, and fulfilled citizens resounds through the words he wrote while on the bench. His conception of judicial opinions as lessons has been adopted, possibly to occasional excess, by subsequent justices. His innovative reaching out to the academic branch of the legal profession through citation of law review articles has now become routine in Court opinions. His insistence that both economic and political institutions had to be accountable to the people was adopted in part by the New Deal and later administrations. His perception of the law as a dynamic, changing entity and his delineation of the right of privacy have become embedded in American jurisprudence. Federal and state court decisions are replete with references to his opinions, particularly in the fields of speech and privacy. Dean Acheson, another of Brandeis's former clerks, told the mourners at the justice's funeral that "his faith in the human mind and in the will and capacity of people to understand and grasp the truth never wavered or tired."

Such was his legacy to the Supreme Court and to the American people.

—Philippa Strum

BIBLIOGRAPHY

The largest collections of Brandeis's Court papers, including the Brandeis papers and the Frankfurter papers, are in the Harvard Law School Library. Court-related items can be found in the Frankfurter papers at the Library of Congress and in the major Brandeis archives at the University of Louisville. Brandeis's letters, including many from the Court years, are in the well-annotated *Letters of Louis D. Brandeis,* eds. Melvin I. Urofsky and David W. Levy (5 volumes, 1971–1978); and *"Half Brother, Half Son": The Letters of Louis D. Brandeis to Felix Frankfurter* (1991). Two useful compilations of his Court drafts are Alexander M. Bickel, ed., *The Unpublished Opinions of Mr. Justice Brandeis* (1957); and Philippa Strum, ed., *Brandeis on Democracy* (1995), which has material on the Court as well as documents from other aspects of his career.

Among the major biographies of Brandeis are Alpheus Thomas Mason, *Brandeis: A Free Man's Life* (1946); and Philippa Strum, *Louis D. Brandeis: Justice for the People* (1984). Alden Todd, *Justice on Trial* (1964), is a thorough account of the fight over the Brandeis nomination. Other volumes containing information about the Court years are Alpheus Thomas Mason, *Brandeis: Lawyer and Judge in the Modern State* (1933); Felix Frankfurter, ed., *Mr. Justice Brandeis* (1932); Samuel J. Konefsky, *The Legacy of Holmes and Brandeis* (1956); and Philippa Strum, *Brandeis: Beyond Progressivism* (1993). A major and extremely insightful article on Brandeis's First Amendment jurisprudence is Vincent Blasi, "The First Amendment and the Ideal of Civil Courage: The Brandeis Opinion in Whitney v. California," *William and Mary Law Review* 29 (Summer 1988); see also Pnina Lahav, "Holmes and Brandeis: Libertarian and Republican Justifications for Free Speech," *Journal of Law and Politics* 4 (1988). An excellent account of Brandeis's views on federal jurisdiction and the *Erie Railroad* case is Edward A. Purcell Jr., *Brandeis and the Progressive Constitution* (2000). For changing historical views on Brandeis's and Holmes's reputations, see the Symposium on "The Canonization of Holmes and Brandeis," *New York University Law Review* 70 (1995).

NOTEWORTHY OPINIONS

Schaefer v. United States, 251 U.S. 466 (1920) (Dissent)

Gilbert v. Minnesota, 254 U.S. 325 (1920) (Dissent)

Truax v. Corrigan, 257 U.S. 312 (1921) (Dissent)

Myers v. United States, 272 U.S. 52 (1926) (Dissent)

Whitney v. California, 272 U.S. 357 (1927) (Concurrence)

Olmstead v. United States, 277 U.S. 438 (1928) (Dissent)

New State Ice Co. v. Liebmann, 285 U.S. 262 (1932) (Dissent)

Liggett v. Lee, 288 U.S. 517 (1933) (Dissent)

Louisville Joint Stock Land Bank v. Radford, 295 U.S. 555 (1935)

Ashwander v. Tennessee Valley Authority, 297 U.S. 288 (1936) (Concurrence)

Erie Railroad Co. v. Tompkins, 304 U.S. 64 (1938)

WILLIAM JOSEPH BRENNAN JR.

Birth: April 25, 1906, Newark, New Jersey.

Education: University of Pennsylvania, B.S., 1928; Harvard Law School, LL.B., 1931.

Official Positions: Judge, New Jersey Superior Court, 1949–1950; judge, appellate division, New Jersey Superior Court, 1950–1952; associate judge, New Jersey Supreme Court, 1952–1956.

Supreme Court Service: Recess appointment as associate justice by President Dwight D. Eisenhower, October 15, 1956, to replace Sherman Minton, who had resigned; nominated as associate justice by President Eisenhower January 14, 1957; confirmed by the Senate March 19, 1957, by a voice vote; took judicial oath October 16, 1956; retired July 20, 1990; replaced by David H. Souter, nominated by President George H. W. Bush.

Death: July 24, 1997, Arlington, Virginia.

Few justices in history played as great a leadership role in shaping the direction of the Court than Justice William J. Brennan Jr. Yet for much of his thirty-four-year tenure, his part was largely unknown to the public, as Brennan labored in the shadows of Chief Justice Earl Warren and Justices Hugo L. Black, William O. Douglas, Felix Frankfurter, and John M. Harlan. Only in the final decade of his service did the public come to recognize Brennan as the architect of much of the revolution in constitutional law that took place in the 1960s and 1970s. Although his influence on the Court was complex and varied, Brennan's message was relatively simple and unwavering: the role of law in society, and of judges in giving meaning to that role, is to protect the essential human dignity of every individual. The Constitution must be interpreted toward that end, he believed, and governments must be held accountable if they fail to act accordingly. Court procedures and rules must also be drawn to further that goal.

The constitutional landmarks to this philosophy span three decades, but the erection of new monuments grew sparse in the late 1970s and 1980s, replaced by frequent dissenting opinions. Still, only a few of the monuments were toppled as the changing membership of the Court caused the pendulum to swing in the direction of a more restrained view of the Constitution and a narrower approach to the role of judges.

When he arrived at the Supreme Court, Justice Brennan was virtually unknown outside of New Jersey, even though he had achieved prominence in the legal community in his home state. A 1931 graduate of Harvard Law School, he joined one of New Jersey's leading law firms and soon became a specialist on the side of management in the fledgling field of labor law. His credibility was based, at least in part, on the memory of his late father's popularity as a union leader whose reputation helped him to win election as Newark's commissioner of public safety.

In fifteen years of private practice before and after World War II, Brennan demonstrated his considerable skills as an advocate and trial lawyer, as a legal tactician and draftsman, and as a conciliator who could get along with all parties in a dispute. These qualities would prove invaluable during his Supreme Court tenure.

After the war Brennan joined with a group of young lawyers who were urging reform of the state judicial system. In 1947 New Jersey adopted a new constitution, including restructured courts, and Brennan could not resist the temptation to help put the new plan into effect. He was appointed to the new superior court bench in 1949 by a Republican governor, even though Brennan was a Democrat. The young reformer's mentor was New Jersey's chief justice, Arthur Vanderbilt. Brennan quickly became Vanderbilt's trusted lieutenant, leading his efforts to eliminate congestion and long delays in the state's courts.

This interest in court reform was not simply a matter of efficiency for Brennan; it was directly connected to his view of the need for fairness and compassion in the law. Efficient court procedures, he observed in 1956, lead to "attainment of the ideal of dispositions according to right and justice."

Brennan was quickly promoted to the superior court's appellate division, and in 1952 to the New Jersey Supreme Court. Brennan cemented his relationship as Vanderbilt's right-hand man, no small achievement because Brennan frustrated Vanderbilt

William Joseph Brennan Jr.

by disagreeing with him on a number of important court decisions. When Brennan was appointed to the U.S. Supreme Court in 1956, Vanderbilt let it be known that he had planned to recommend Brennan as his successor as New Jersey's chief justice.

Brennan's record on the New Jersey Supreme Court has long been the subject of debate. The popular view is that he was a moderate who turned liberal once on the federal bench, much to the surprise and disappointment of President Dwight Eisenhower. (Eisenhower expressed his disagreement with Brennan in a number of conversations with friends and acquaintances, but there is no evidence that he ever said the words often attributed to him with reference to Brennan and Warren: "My two worst mistakes are both sitting on the Supreme Court.") But Brennan's friends in New Jersey and other local legal observers knew that he was unmistakably liberal, and his record of decisions affirms that view.

Although the state court had little occasion to deal with federal constitutional questions, Brennan touched on a number of issues that later became hallmarks of his decisions on the U.S. Supreme Court. He took a broad view of the privilege against self-incrimination in *In re Pillo* (1952), finding the privilege in New Jersey to be based on common law tradition, rather than the Fifth Amendment. He took a strong position against prior restraint of free expression in *Adams Theatre Co. v. Keenan* (1953). In his most famous state court dissent, in *State v. Tune* (1953), he excoriated the majority for refusing to allow an accused murderer to inspect his own confession. He expressed strong support for the guarantee against double jeopardy in *State v. Midgeley* (1954).

In May 1956 Brennan addressed a Justice Department conference on court delays and came to the attention of U.S. Attorney General Herbert Brownell. When Justice Sherman Minton announced plans to retire a few months later, President Eisenhower said he wanted to look for a Democrat, to appear more bipartisan for the impending presidential election, and a Catholic, as the Court had not had a Catholic member for some time. Brennan fit the bill: he was supported by Vanderbilt and by Brownell's conclusion, after reading all of his New Jersey opinions, that Brennan was a moderate. Justice Brennan took his seat on October 16, 1956, one week into the Court term, as a recess appointment chosen while the Senate was not in session.

The Senate confirmed his appointment five months later, on March 19, 1957. Sen. Joseph McCarthy, R-Wis., cast the only negative vote. McCarthy opposed Brennan because of two speeches Brennan gave in 1954 criticizing congressional investigations that threaten the rights of individuals. These remarks are among the earliest records of Brennan's concern with law and human dignity. "We cannot and must not doubt our strength to conserve, without the sacrifice of any, all of the guarantees of justice and fair play and simple human dignity which have made our land what it is," Brennan said in an address to the Irish Charitable Society in Boston. Ours, he said, is "a system of government based upon the dignity and inviolability of the individual soul."

Although Brennan did not come to the Supreme Court with a fully developed constitutional philosophy, it did not take him long to arrive at the view that the Constitution must be interpreted for the time, not based on some fixed, permanent original understanding of its authors. "What due process under the 14th Amendment meant to the wisdom of other days cannot be its measure to the vision of our time," he said in the 1961 James Madison lecture at New York University Law School.

In the twilight of his tenure, Brennan became closely identified with this approach in a national debate over constitutional interpretation, spawned in part by the bicentennial of the Constitution, in part by the failed Supreme Court nomination of conservative judge Robert H. Bork, and in part by the vigorous attack of aides to President Ronald Reagan. Brennan's most sweeping discussion of constitutional interpretation came in a 1986 speech at Georgetown University Law School in which he boldly criticized those who advocate that determining the "original intent" of the framers is the only proper way to read the Constitution:

> In its most doctrinaire incarnation, this view demands that Justices discern exactly what the Framers thought about the question under consideration and simply follow that intention in resolving the case before them. It is a view that feigns self-effacing deference to the specific judgments of those who forged our original social compact. But in truth it is little more than arrogance cloaked as humility. It is arrogant to pretend that from our vantage we can gauge accurately the intent of the Framers on application of principle to specific, contemporary questions. . . .
>
> We current Justices read the Constitution in the only way that we can: as Twentieth Century Americans. We look to the history of the time of framing and to the intervening history of interpretation. But the ultimate question must be, what do the words of the text mean in our time. For the genius of the Constitution rests not in any static meaning it might have had in a world that is dead and gone, but in the adaptability of its great principles to cope with current problems and current needs.

This focus on adapting the Constitution to the needs of the day was only one facet of Brennan's judicial philosophy. Another principal tenet of his jurisprudence was that the law must be compassionate, preserving the essential dignity of individuals. "Law is again coming alive as a living process responsive to changing human needs," he said in a 1964 speech. "The shift is to justice and away from fine-spun technicalities and abstract rules." This approach was apparent in a multitude of Brennan decisions, cutting across different areas of the law, from the rights of the accused to government treatment of welfare recipients and illegal alien children.

One example of this approach in criminal cases provided continuity between Brennan's New Jersey tenure and his service on the U.S. Supreme Court. Building on the theme of his dissent in *State v. Tune*, Brennan, in his first term in Washington, wrote the Court's opinion in *Jencks v. United States* (1957), establishing the right of defendants in federal criminal prosecutions to inspect documents upon which the government is relying rather than leaving it to the trial judge to decide which documents are relevant for the defense.

No one better captured this aspect of Brennan's philosophy than Chief Justice Warren in a 1966 *Harvard Law Review* tribute:

> He administers the Constitution as a sacred trust, and interprets the Bill of Rights as the heart and life blood of that great charter of freedom. His belief in the dignity of human beings—all human beings—is unbounded. He also believes that without such dignity men cannot be free. These beliefs are apparent in the warp and woof of all his opinions.

Perhaps no case better illustrates these facets of Brennan's constitutional view than *Goldberg v. Kelly* (1970), in which he wrote for the majority that the Fourteenth Amendment guarantee of due process applies to the termination of welfare benefits and requires notice and a hearing before benefits are discontinued. "Termination of aid pending resolution of a controversy over eligibility may deprive an eligible recipient of the very means by which to live while he waits," he wrote.

This view was always subject to the criticism, as expressed by Justice Black's dissent in *Goldberg*, that the Court was making political judgments, acting like a legislature rather than a group of judges. Such criti-

cism rarely fazed Brennan, who believed unfailingly in the need for the judiciary to be the final arbiter of what is constitutionally fair and necessary.

Yet another feature of Brennan's approach was a belief that it was not simply the substance of rights that had to be protected; rather, he maintained, the procedures that governments use to regulate modern society must be fair and must not unduly interfere with the exercise of individual rights. This focus on the unfairness of procedures—burden of proof, vagueness of laws, statutes that were too broad—was a new concept in constitutional law, particularly in the realm of First Amendment protection for freedom of speech and freedom of religious beliefs.

One example of this approach was the majority opinion in *Speiser v. Randall* (1958), striking down a California law that denied a tax exemption to individuals who refused to swear an oath that they did not advocate overthrow of the United States. The law was unconstitutional, Brennan wrote, not based on whether California could require such an oath to qualify for a tax break, but because California in effect required taxpayers to show that they had not engaged in prohibited speech. This procedure, although arguably within California's authority, posed too great a danger of self-censorship by individuals who wanted to avoid difficulty in demonstrating their eligibility for the tax break. Therefore, it was the process that was deficient, not the substantive right itself. This willingness to examine the practical effects of otherwise legitimate exercises of government power also set Brennan apart.

No discussion of William Brennan is complete without an examination of the way he approached the job, not so much the constitutional philosophy, but his outlook on day-to-day details. No doubt each justice aspires to influence his colleagues and to alter the course of constitutional law, but none has had a more single-minded focus than Brennan on the importance of seeking a majority. It has become almost a cliché, but the story is nevertheless true that Brennan would ask his new law clerks to identify the most important principle of constitutional law and then, holding up the five fingers of one hand, exclaim with glee, "You can't do anything around here without five votes." His success was aided by an almost encyclopedic memory of the Court's work during his tenure. Another often-cited story is of how, in the middle of discussing a case, Brennan would say that he had written on the particular subject in the past. He would swivel to the bookcase of *U.S. Reports* behind his desk, pluck the correct volume from the shelves, and open it to the proper page.

From his earliest days on the bench, Brennan displayed an extraordinary ability to take a position and then work with his colleagues to shape and modify it until a majority was secured. He was never too set in his views to consider a colleague's request for adjustments, especially when the suggestion came from a justice who represented the potential fifth vote.

The means to this end were numerous. Sometimes he would gain support through his characterization of the issue. In *Goldberg v. Kelly,* he described the issue for decision as a "narrow one," although that was hardly the case. At other times, he would dispatch his law clerks to find out from their counterparts what other justices were thinking or what it would take to secure their votes. Once so engaged, there was no greater conciliator in the annals of the Court. His effervescent personality and unfailing warmth became a legend among Court employees, particularly among his colleagues.

This approach to the job fit nicely with his approach to constitutional solutions. Brennan rejected the rigid absolutes of Black and Douglas, who believed that the First Amendment prohibited any regulation of free speech. Brennan preferred a jurisprudence of balancing and tests that evolved into a vast body of practical constitutional doctrine, but a body to which adjustments and variations were easily made to accommodate changed situations and to which new tests could be added to accommodate the views of other justices.

In *Plyler v. Doe* (1982), Brennan wrote for the Court that under the Fourteenth Amendment guarantee of equal protection of the laws, the state of Texas could not single out the children of illegal aliens for denial of free public education. Brennan spent months negotiating with Justice Lewis Powell, who was concerned about the children but wanted to avoid a sweeping constitutional pronouncement about education or the status of illegal aliens. In the end, Brennan was forced to lower the level of constitutional scrutiny to which the Texas law was subjected, so that an "important" government objective would suffice to justify the law, instead of the more rigorous "compelling" interest. This compromise meant that illegal aliens and their children would not receive the same high degree of protection from discrimination that applies to racial minorities or to legal aliens. Even with this change, however, the Texas law was still invalid, with Powell's crucial fifth vote providing the majority, and Brennan's opinion made it difficult for governments to discriminate against illegal aliens.

The recognition that he was a talented lawyer and craftsman was part of the basis for the extraordinary bond of trust that developed quickly between Brennan and Chief Justice Warren. It is no coincidence that Warren turned to Brennan, his colleague for only two years at the time, to draft the Court's opinion, signed by all nine justices, in *Cooper v. Aaron* (1958), the Little Rock, Arkansas, school desegregation case that affirmed the obligation of state officials to heed the dictates of the Supreme Court. Brennan quickly demonstrated an ability to write a narrow, unflamboyant, workmanlike opinion.

Indeed, Brennan's demonstrated legal craftsmanship, his ability to anticipate the other justices, and his personal warmth and charm made him a valuable ally of Warren throughout the chief justice's tenure, and the two men met regularly to discuss cases and map strategy. A few commentators have even suggested that the period ought to be described as the "Brennan Court," instead of the Warren Court, because the strategies and constitutional doctrines were his more than the chief justice's. Brennan, however, scoffed at such suggestions, always revering the name and memory of Earl Warren and coining the term "superchief" to refer to him.

The aspects of American constitutional law in which Justice Brennan effected change are far too numerous to cover in a brief essay, but a handful stand out on the legal landscape. There are also a few places in which his legacy has been diluted or even erased by subsequent actions of the Supreme Court.

When Brennan arrived at the Court in 1956, the Bill of Rights was still largely a shield against abuse of individual liberties by the federal government. A debate had raged for nearly a decade between Black and Frankfurter over whether the adoption of the Fourteenth Amendment in 1868, with its guarantee of "liberty" protected by "due process," meant that the Bill of Rights was also intended to curb the authority of the states. Black argued for wholesale application of the entire Bill of Rights, and Frankfurter argued that the Fourteenth Amendment had brought about no such result. By 1956 the First Amendment guarantees of freedom of speech and religion were the principal rights that had been incorporated into the Fourteenth Amendment, and they were still not vigorously enforced. Although Black's advocacy created the climate for incorporation, it was Brennan, in consultation with Warren, who set about the practical task of selecting those amendments that should logically apply to the states because they were among the "principles of a free government," and of choosing cases in which to achieve that goal. Brennan outlined his motivation in the 1961 Madison lecture:

> The need for vigilance to prevent government from whittling away the rights of the individual was never greater. . . .
>
> Far too many cases come from the states to the Supreme Court presenting dismal pictures of official lawlessness. . . . Judicial self-restraint which defers too much to the sovereign powers of the states and reserves judicial intervention for only the most revolting cases will not serve to enhance Madison's priceless gift of "the great rights of mankind secured under this Constitution."

Although he rejected Black's advocacy of wholesale incorporation of all of the first eight amendments, Brennan helped guide the application of most provisions of the Bill of Rights to limit state authority.

Only the Second and Third Amendments, the Fifth Amendment grand jury provision, and the Seventh Amendment remain unincorporated. For Brennan's part, he directly contributed *Malloy v. Hogan* (1964), which held that the Fifth Amendment privilege against self-incrimination applied in state criminal courts, not just federal. It is not surprising that this piece of incorporation is included among Brennan's works, as he had expressed strong views about the privilege against self-incrimination on the New Jersey Supreme Court in *In re Pillo*.

Among his most visible and lasting achievements are those in the field of the First Amendment, where the law's broad tolerance for controversial and offensive speech is due in some significant degree to his opinions. Consistent with his criticism of prior restraint in New Jersey in *Adams Theatre Co. v. Keenan,* he took a strong stand against prior restraint on speech or publication in *New York Times Co. v. United States* (1971), which thwarted the government's efforts to halt publication of the Pentagon Papers.

In *New York Times Co. v. Sullivan* (1964), Brennan's opinion gave new protection to freedom of expression, ruling that the First Amendment limits the authority of states to punish libelous speech about the conduct of public officials. A public official may recover only when a defamatory statement has been made with "actual malice—that is, with knowledge that it was false or reckless disregard of whether it was false or not." His position was later expanded to cover speech about public figures as well.

The decision revolutionized the field of libel law, but it also included one of the strongest statements of purpose for the First Amendment, memorializing "a profound national commitment to the principle that debate on public issues should be uninhibited, robust, and wide-open, and that it may well include vehement, caustic, and sometimes unpleasantly sharp attacks on government and public officials." His commitment to this view never wavered, and he extended in *Texas v. Johnson* (1989) and *United States v. Eichman* (1990), which struck down state and federal laws, respectively, prohibiting burning of the American flag as a protest. "If there is a bedrock principle underlying the First Amendment," he wrote in the Texas case, "it is that the government may not prohibit the expression of an idea simply because society finds the idea itself offensive or disagreeable."

Brennan's vision of free expression took the Court to places that had not previously been thought to involve the First Amendment. In a number of these opinions, his emphasis on the practical effect of government actions, as in the *Speiser* case, was most pronounced. In *NAACP v. Button* (1963), he invalidated a Virginia law and those of a number of other states that prohibited organizations such as the National Association for the Advancement of Colored People from becoming involved in cases in which they had no direct interest. The effect of these laws was to thwart the NAACP's litigation strategy, which relied heavily on reaching out to the community to find and assist clients in school desegregation cases and other racial bias disputes. Brennan rejected the defense that such laws were a valid regulation of solicitation and held that, regardless of the label attached by the state, the laws violated the freedoms of expression and association.

In two other cases, *Elrod v. Burns* (1976) and *Rutan v. Republican Party of Illinois* (1990), Brennan established that the First Amendment protects nonpolitical public employees from patronage practices—being fired or transferred (as well as hired or promoted) on the basis of their loyalty to a political party.

The religion clauses represent another First Amendment sphere on which Brennan left his mark, functioning as one of the Court's most zealous advocates of strict separation between church and state. His position in these cases is ironic because, during his confirmation hearings in 1957, some people raised concern about whether, as a Catholic, he could repress his allegiance to the pope in the interests of fealty to the Constitution. Justice Brennan left no doubt as to his answer in a long concurring opinion outlining his own strong belief in separation in *Abington School District v. Schempp* (1963), in which the Court struck down as a violation of the establishment clause a state

law that required Bible reading in public school classrooms. He continued to be effective in cases invalidating government aid to religious schools in the 1970s, but his adherence to strict separation pushed him into the dissenter's camp in the 1980s, as the Court opened windows in the wall of separation.

In the other religion clause, guaranteeing the free exercise of religion, Brennan's pathbreaking decision in *Sherbert v. Verner* (1963) is now in eclipse. Brennan held that South Carolina's denial of unemployment benefits to a worker who was fired for refusing to work on Saturday, her Sabbath, violated her freedom of religious worship. His decision required states and employers to take reasonable steps to accommodate workers' free exercise rights. That principle was largely undisputed until the decision in *Employment Division v. Smith* (1990), in which Justice Antonin Scalia ruled in the case of prohibited religious use of peyote in Oregon that the First Amendment does not require states to make exceptions to generally applicable laws simply to accommodate religious freedom.

Equality and the elimination of societal discrimination are also fields on which Justice Brennan left an indelible mark. *Cooper v. Aaron* was only his first encounter with the school desegregation issue. In *Green v. New Kent County School Board* (1968), he spoke for the Court, expressing frustration with the slow pace of school desegregation and insisting that recalcitrant school officials find a solution that "promises realistically to work now." A few years later, in *Keyes v. Denver School District No. 1* (1973), the first desegregation case outside of the South, Brennan held that once a violation is shown in one part of a system, the school board bears the burden of showing that the rest of the system is not unconstitutionally segregated as well.

Brennan also led the Court in a number of major decisions—controversial and widely criticized by conservatives—upholding the constitutionality or statutory validity of affirmative action plans in the face of challenges that such programs discriminate against those who are not advantaged by them. Among these were: *United Steelworkers of America v. Weber* (1979), upholding private employers' voluntary affirmative action under Title VII of the 1964 Civil Rights Act, which prohibits employment discrimination; *Johnson v. Transportation Agency* (1987), upholding a public employer's voluntary affirmative action plan for women under Title VII; *United States v. Paradise* (1987), upholding a promotion preference for black state troopers in Alabama, under the equal protection clause of the Fourteenth Amendment and finding that the plan was justified to correct past discrimination; and *Metro Broadcasting v. Federal Communications Commission* (1990), upholding, under the Fifth Amendment's equal protection component, a broadcast licensing preference for minority-owned businesses to promote diversity in programming.

Until Brennan tackled the issue in the early 1970s, gender discrimination was largely unrecognized as a violation of the equal protection clause. But in a line of cases beginning with *Frontiero v. Richardson* (1973) and leading up to *Craig v. Boren* (1976), he succeeded in elevating constitutional recognition of sex discrimination, although not to as high a plane as he had hoped. In *Frontiero,* the Court struck down a federal law that made it easier for spouses of male military personnel than for spouses of female service personnel to receive increased benefits. Brennan argued that such gender-based discrimination should be viewed as every bit as "suspect" as racial bias and should be subjected to the equal protection clause's most rigorous scrutiny. He fell one vote short of a majority for this approach, however, and gender discrimination has never again been subjected to the highest levels of constitutional inquiry. Nevertheless, in *Craig* he successfully proffered a new intermediate level of scrutiny for sex discrimination, requiring government to have an important, although not a compelling, justification for discriminatory conduct. In this case, the Court invalidated an Oklahoma law that allowed women to buy 3.2 percent beer at age eighteen, but men not until age twenty-one, finding that the law discriminated against males between ages eighteen and twenty-one.

Justice Brennan's views reflected those of the 1960s civil rights era that access to the federal courts to protect individual rights was essential, and that

state courts could not always be trusted to have the necessary sensitivity to do the job. The successes he had in this realm during the Warren Court were undercut or even overruled during the tenures of Chief Justices Warren E. Burger and William H. Rehnquist. Yet Brennan continued to frame the debate, even after these setbacks.

No opinion by Justice Brennan has received more widespread recognition, nor had more practical effect, than *Baker v. Carr* (1962), which declared for the first time that challenges to the fairness of state legislative apportionments presented legitimate issues under the equal protection clause that could properly be decided in federal courts. Although a classic example of a narrow and carefully crafted opinion, the ruling forced legislatures throughout the country to face the redrawing of fairer district lines and led directly to the subsequent principle of one person, one vote. Although the degree of precision required in line-drawing has varied in later decisions, the battles have been fought largely in federal court. Chief Justice Warren remarked later that the ruling was the "most important" of his tenure.

Other efforts by Brennan to expand access to federal courts met with varying degrees of temporary success. His major civil rights decision giving federal courts broad power to issue injunctions to prevent state court interference with First Amendment rights, *Dombrowski v. Pfister* (1965), was substantially undercut in the name of federalism by *Younger v. Harris* (1971), raising the threshold of injury necessary to justify federal court intervention in pending state court proceedings.

The availability of *habeas corpus* for state prisoners in federal court was another roller coaster doctrine for Brennan. *Habeas corpus* is a civil proceeding generally providing postconviction review of the rights of criminal defendants, and traditionally such review was conducted in the state courts. In *Fay v. Noia* (1963), Brennan significantly expanded the availability of federal court review of the fairness of state criminal convictions, allowing federal *habeas* petitions for claims such as unconstitutional confessions or improper searches and seizures. This step gave state prisoners, especially those on death row, a chance to be heard for many years. By the late 1970s, however, the Court was cutting back sharply on this Brennan doctrine, and in *Coleman v. Thompson* (1991), it was expressly overruled not even a year after Brennan had left the Court.

Despite significant setbacks to his aspirations for access to the federal courts, Brennan was not one to give up. In a seminal article in the *Harvard Law Review* in 1977, and again in his second James Madison lecture in 1986, he urged civil rights lawyers to look to the state courts and state constitutions to protect individual liberties on a broader scale than the U.S. Supreme Court was willing to do. These urgings helped to spawn an entire constitutional movement toward rediscovery of the guarantees of state constitutions.

Brennan's legacy in the field of equality was not his only contribution to our understanding of the Fourteenth Amendment. He is also directly responsible for the contemporary view that there are "fundamental" rights that are not expressly named in the Bill of Rights, but that are entitled to the highest levels of protection under the equal protection or due process clause. This concept has become integral to the body of constitutional law. It was also an important vehicle for expression of the themes of his jurisprudence—reading the Constitution as a twentieth-century document, one that was intended to promote and protect the virtues of human dignity and fairness.

In *Shapiro v. Thompson* (1969), one of the last Warren Court decisions, Brennan wrote for the majority that a one-year residency requirement to qualify for local welfare benefits violated the Constitution's right to travel. The decision declared this a fundamental right entitled to the strictest Fourteenth Amendment scrutiny because it directly affected the means of subsistence—"food, shelter and other necessities of life."

The decision by Brennan one year later in *Goldberg v. Kelly*, finding that welfare benefits were protected by the due process clause, was another significant step in this conception of fundamental rights. The decision squarely rejected the long-developing constitutional distinction between rights and privileges, finding that fundamental fairness was required regardless of the label placed on the program. The Court has since curtailed the rigor of the due process required under such circumstances, but the basic principle remains intact for government benefits, public employment, and other activities.

No fundamental right has been more controversial than the right to privacy and the related right of women to choose abortion. Here, too, Brennan's influence is significant, although not always in ways that are readily apparent. In *Griswold v. Connecticut* (1965), an opinion by Justice Douglas recognizing a right to marital privacy that protected the use of contraceptives, Brennan worked behind the scenes to provide the rationale for finding privacy implicit in numerous portions of the Bill of Rights. It was Brennan who led the Court to the next step in *Eisenstadt v. Baird* (1972), holding that the equal protection clause prevented treating single women differently from married women for contraceptives.

When the privacy fight moved to yet another field the following year, Brennan once again exerted his influence. The opinion upholding a right to abortion in *Roe v. Wade* (1973) was written by Justice Harry A. Blackmun, but Brennan was a moving force in internal Court deliberations to find the strongest possible rationale for the newly declared fundamental right. He remained a staunch defender of *Roe*, which was under fire throughout his tenure, but his support was largely internal, and he never wrote an opinion about the substantive right to abortion.

A final facet of Justice Brennan's jurisprudence is the seemingly simple but important idea that government must be accountable to the people in court. Prior to the ruling in *Monell v. Dept. of Social Services* (1978), city and county governments were largely immune from lawsuits for damages under the Reconstruction-era federal civil rights law, commonly known as Section 1983. But in *Monell*, Brennan held that local governments may be sued for damages under Section 1983, which provides liability for any deprivation of rights by persons acting "under color of" state law. The decision and others that followed it prompted a virtual revolution in civil rights litigation.

Similar accountability may apply to federal officials, not under Section 1983, because federal officials never act under color of state law, but directly under provisions of the Bill of Rights. This doctrine, also part of the revolution in accountability, was established by Brennan in *Bivens v. Six Unknown Fed. Narcotics Agents* (1971), in which a lawsuit for damages was allowed directly under the Fourth Amendment against federal narcotics agents for an egregious warrantless arrest and search. In *Davis v. Passman* (1979), a similar damages action was allowed against a member of Congress directly under the Fifth Amendment for sex discrimination in employment.

In a few areas Brennan's efforts might be classified as failures, although these judgments are subjective and can be seen from different points of view. For example, some critics would consider Brennan's efforts in the gender discrimination arena less than successful because gender bias never achieved equal status with race discrimination. Others argue, however, that the middle level of scrutiny applied to gender bias cases is a significant step forward and not a failure. Two subjects on which Brennan clearly made fewer inroads than he would have liked are the constitutional status of obscenity and the death penalty.

In Brennan's first term, Warren turned to him for a solution to the legal problem of obscenity. The result was the decision in *Roth v. United States* (1957), holding that obscene materials were not protected by the First Amendment and offering the first of a number of definitions of obscenity produced over the next decade. This and other attempts to define obscenity in some practical way so that courts could enforce the law proved unworkable, but Brennan led the Court throughout the 1960s in trying to find a solution. He repeatedly rejected the absolutism of Black and Douglas, who believed that the Court should not be in the business of picking and choosing protected speech.

Finally, however, Brennan also came to believe that no definition of obscenity could be developed that would allow individuals to conform their conduct to the law with some degree of certainty. He abandoned the definitional effort in a dissenting

opinion in *Paris Adult Theatre I v. Slaton* (1973), arguing that obscene materials should be covered within the broad sweep of the First Amendment as long as there is no suggestion of exploiting or selling to minors. This recognition came too late, however, because by then the First Amendment constituency on the Court had dissipated, and, on the same day, the majority ruled in *Miller v. California* (1973) that the definition of obscenity and judgments about its prosecution should be left to local community standards. Thereafter, Brennan dissented from virtually every obscenity decision, including the denial of review by the Supreme Court. Although his dissents forced the Court to confront his position in each instance, they had little substantive impact on the majority.

Brennan's first visible concern with the death penalty came in a dissenting opinion in *McGautha v. California* (1971), in which he expressed strong concerns about the need for fairness in the procedures allowing juries to impose a death sentence. Within a year, however, Brennan had concluded that the death penalty posed not simply due process problems, but was itself inherently a form of cruel and unusual punishment in violation of the Eighth Amendment. This view, expressed in *Furman v. Georgia* (1972), was shared entirely only by Justice Thurgood Marshall. Other justices joined in *Furman* to find the death penalty unconstitutional as then applied in most states, but that coalition was short-lived, and a procedurally acceptable death penalty was reinstated in *Gregg v. Georgia* (1976).

Ironically, the decision in *Gregg* reflected some of the concerns Brennan had expressed in *McGautha*, but by that time he had moved on to the view that the death penalty in any form violated the Eighth Amendment. Thereafter, as in the obscenity cases, Brennan dissented in every death penalty case that came before the Court. His standard "cruel and unusual punishment" dissent had little impact on other justices, but on rare occasions he was able to persuade a majority in a lengthier memorandum of the unfairness of the procedures in a particular case.

Still, Brennan felt as passionately about the death penalty at the end of his service on the Court as he had almost two decades earlier when he first raised the cruel and unusual punishment argument. As he explained in the Oliver Wendell Holmes lecture at Harvard Law School in 1986:

> As I read them, the Bill of Rights generally and the Eighth Amendment specifically insist that the state treat its members with respect for their intrinsic worth as human beings, and this is true even as the state punishes the commission of the most brutal crimes. . . .
>
> A punishment is "cruel and unusual" if it does not comport with human dignity. The calculated killing of a human being by the state involves, by its very nature, an absolute denial of the executed person's humanity, and thus violates the command of the Eighth Amendment.

Throughout his tenure, Justice William Brennan was a constant target of critics who rejected his approach to the Constitution and to the proper role of the courts. These ranged from colleagues on the bench—Frankfurter, Harlan, Black, and Scalia—to luminaries in the academy. For example, Raoul Berger, the retired Harvard Law School scholar, argued in a 1988 article that Justice Brennan "brings his own agenda to the Constitution and is committed to a course that cannot be reconciled with the Constitution or with long established methods of construction." The level of criticism escalated in the 1980s, when the young conservatives who populated the Reagan administration Justice Department treated Brennan as if he were the cause of the deficit, the cold war, and the rest of the world's ills. Yet Brennan was never fazed by this barrage and stood by his approach proudly until his last moment on the bench.

Many colleagues and leaders of the profession have paid tribute to his career, but two such commentaries spanning a decade sum up his legacy particularly well. Dedicating its annual survey of American law to Brennan in 1981, New York University Law School wrote: "By his strong advocacy of the Bill of Rights, he has changed the very way in which we look at the role of government and government's relation to the individual. Those searching for compassion and humanity in the law need only read the opinions of Justice Brennan."

A decade later in the *Harvard Civil Rights-Civil Liberties Review* of 1991, Justice Blackmun wrote, "By any measure, Justice Brennan must be regarded as one of the great names among those who have served on the Supreme Court of the United States. Whether one makes that evaluation by length of service, influential leadership, or number of significant opinions, the result is the same. Reflection upon Justice Brennan's accomplishments in all three areas makes it inevitable."

—Stephen J. Wermiel

BIBLIOGRAPHY

Justice Brennan's collection of personal Court files is housed at the Library of Congress in Washington, D.C. Access to some portions of the collection is open to researchers, but other portions require the permission of the trustees, administered through the Manuscript Library's Division. The collection includes files on thousands of cases, complete with exchanges, memoranda, and draft opinions. His most recent files, for the Rehnquist Court, beginning in 1986, remain closed.

Other general sources include Stephen J. Friedman, "William J. Brennan," in Friedman and Israel, *Justices*, vol. 4, 2849; and Nathan Lewin, "William J. Brennan," in the supplemental volume to that series, page 239. Other useful essays are collected in "The Jurisprudence of Justice William J. Brennan, Jr.," *University of Pennsylvania Law Review* 139 (1991): 1317; and "A Tribute to Justice William J. Brennan, Jr.," *Harvard Law Review* 104 (1990): 1.

More recent scholarship includes E. Joshua Rosenkranz and Bernard Schwartz, eds., *Reason & Passion: Justice Brennan's Enduring Influence* (1997); Stephen L. Sepinuck and Mary Pat Treuthart, eds., *The Conscience of the Court: Selected Opinions of Justice William J. Brennan Jr. on Freedom and Equality* (1999); and Roger Goldman with David Gallen, eds., *Justice William J. Brennan, Jr.: Freedom First* (1994).

Some of Justice Brennan's major off-the-bench writings are: "Constitutional Adjudication and the Death Penalty: A View from the Court," *Harvard Law Review* 100 (1986): 313; "The Constitution of the United States: Contemporary Ratification," *South Texas Law Review* 27 (1986):

433; "State Constitutions and the Protection of Individual Rights," *Harvard Law Review* 90 (1977): 489; and "The Bill of Rights and the States," *New York University Law Review* 36 (1961): 761.

NOTEWORTHY OPINIONS

Roth v. United States, 354 U.S. 476 (1957)

Speiser v. Randall, 357 U.S. 513 (1958)

Baker v. Carr, 369 U.S. 186 (1962)

Sherbert v. Verner, 371 U.S. 398 (1963)

NAACP v. Button, 371 U.S. 415 (1963)

Fay v. Noia, 372 U.S. 391 (1963)

Abington School District v. Schempp, 374 U.S. 203 (1963)

New York Times Co. v. Sullivan, 376 U.S. 254 (1964)

Malloy v. Hogan, 378 U.S. 1 (1964)

Green v. New Kent County School Board, 391 U.S. 430 (1968)

Shapiro v. Thompson, 394 U.S. 618 (1969)

Goldberg v. Kelly, 397 U.S. 254 (1970)

McGautha v. California, 402 U.S. 183 (1971) (Dissent)

Eisenstadt v. Baird, 405 U.S. 438 (1972)

Frontiero v. Richardson, 411 U.S. 677 (1973)

Monell v. Dept. of Social Services, 436 U.S. 658 (1978)

United Steelworkers of America v. Weber, 443 U.S. 193 (1979)

Plyler v. Doe, 457 U.S. 202 (1982)

Johnson v. Transportation Agency, 480 U.S. 616 (1987)

DAVID JOSIAH BREWER

Birth: June 20, 1837, Smyrna, Asia Minor.

Education: Wesleyan University, 1852–1853; Yale University, A.B., 1856; Albany Law School, LL.B., 1858.

Official Positions: Commissioner, U.S. Circuit Court, Leavenworth, Kansas, 1861–1862; judge of probate and criminal courts, Leavenworth County, 1863–1864; judge, First District of Kansas, 1865–1869; Leavenworth city attorney, 1869–1870; justice, Kansas Supreme Court, 1870–1884; judge, U.S. Court of Appeals for the Eighth Circuit, 1884–1889; president, Venezuela-British Guiana Border Commission, 1895.

Supreme Court Service: Nominated associate justice by President Benjamin Harrison, December 4, 1889, to replace Stanley Matthews, who had died; confirmed by the Senate, December 18, 1889, by a 53–11 vote; took judicial oath January 6, 1890; served until March 28, 1910; replaced by Charles Evans Hughes, nominated by President William Howard Taft.

Death: March 28, 1910, Washington, D.C.

David J. Brewer was born to the Reverend Josiah Brewer, a New England Congregational clergyman and missionary noted for his opposition to slavery and war, and Emilia Field, the sister of Supreme Court justice Stephen J. Field and prominent law reformer David Dudley Field. Brewer was raised in privilege in Wethersfield, Connecticut, and at age fifteen entered Wesleyan College. He subsequently graduated from Yale University, studied briefly with his uncle, David Field, and then attended Albany Law School.

Adventurous in spirit and eager to free himself of the overpowering reputation of his uncle, Brewer decided in the late 1850s to launch his professional career in the rough-and-tumble environment of Kansas Territory. He quickly earned a reputation for his skill in representing railroad and business inter-

ests. A Republican, he filled several lower political and legal offices in the state before serving on the Kansas Supreme Court of and the Eighth Circuit federal court. In 1890 President Benjamin Harrison elevated Brewer to the Supreme Court, in part because the well-qualified Kansas judge was a reluctant aspirant, a quality that Harrison admired.

A justice of considerable intelligence and energy, Brewer was fated to serve on a court that at various periods of his tenure included Stephen Field, John Marshall Harlan, and Oliver Wendell Holmes Jr., justices genuinely brilliant and even more energetic than he. Brewer nevertheless played a critical role in the history of the Court at the turn of the century. He joined with Justice Rufus W. Peckham to become the intellectual leaders of the conservative bloc. Brewer believed strongly that the Court should limit government interference in the economy and permit the marketplace to distribute the inevitable rewards produced by capitalism. Brewer also had an almost unyielding adherence to the idea that the states should be free, under the Tenth Amendment, from federal interference. His orthodox conservatism resulted in more than 200 dissents during his years on the Court. Yet Brewer's views were not altogether predictable. His Congregational, missionary, and anti-slavery roots meant that he had a sympathetic ear for the disadvantaged.

Brewer's first important majority opinion came in *Reagan v. Farmers' Loan & Trust Co.* (1894), a case that showed clearly that although he might believe in the idea of states' rights, Brewer was wary of giving the states too much authority to interfere in the marketplace. *Reagan* stemmed from a decision by the Texas Railroad Commission to regulate railroad rates on commerce within the state. Brewer spoke for the Court in finding the regulation violated the rights of investors in the railroad because they were not receiving any return on their invested capital.

David Josiah Brewer

Brewer's opinion limited the impact of *Munn v. Illinois* (1877), which had provided an opening wedge to state regulatory efforts, and in that respect exposed a philosophical link between Brewer and Field, who had originally dissented in *Munn* on the grounds that protection of property rights was the highest goal of the Constitution.

Brewer's conservative sympathies appeared most dramatically a year later in *In re Debs* (1895), in which he wrote a unanimous opinion for the Court upholding an injunction against striking workers at the Pullman Palace Sleeping Car Company. Eugene Debs was the president of the American Railroad Union whose members protested an abrupt reduction in pay by the Pullman Company. The strike spread to other unions, and a call went out for a general boycott of all Pullman rail cars, an action that disrupted interstate rail transportation and the movement of the mails.

Conservatives denounced the Pullman strike as a harbinger of an even more fearsome general working-class uprising. When the railroad owners refused to drop Pullman cars from service, violence ensued. U.S. Attorney General Richard Olney won an order from the federal district court in Chicago enjoining the strikers from interrupting the flow of the mails. When Debs ignored the injunction, he was found guilty of contempt of court. President Grover Cleveland subsequently broke the strike by dispatching federal troops to restore order and safe passage of the mails. Debs appealed his contempt conviction to the Supreme Court.

Brewer's unanimous opinion affirmed the injunctions and contempt citations against labor leaders accused of conspiring to block interstate commerce. Brewer held that the federal courts had broad powers to issue such injunctions in order to keep interstate commerce moving. He also concluded that the federal government had a duty to protect the general welfare, the execution of which depended on a complementary power to apply to its own courts for assistance. Brewer realized that the best way to dilute the threat of labor unions was to severely restrict the strike as a tool by which to wring concessions from management.

Brewer championed conservative property interests in other cases. He took part in the majority opinion in *Pollock v. Farmers' Loan and Trust Co.* (1895), which declared the federal income tax unconstitutional. His agreement with the majority, over the sharp dissents of four other justices, thwarted the federal government's attempt to impose a tax on income until the adoption of the Sixteenth Amendment in 1913.

He objected on constitutional and philosophical grounds to most other efforts that interfered with economic activity. He was, for example, a silent dissenter in *Holden v. Hardy* (1898), in which the majority upheld the constitutionality of a Utah law that restricted miners and other workers employed in smelters to an eight-hour day except in case of emergency. The majority sustained the statute based on the scope of the police power of the states to provide for the health, safety, morals, and welfare of their citizenry. In this instance, the Court found the regulations particularly appropriate because they dealt with hazardous occupations. Brewer's disagreement with the decision no doubt stemmed from a dilemma in his own thinking. He favored the rights of states to manage their internal affairs and at the same time opposed state actions that would strengthen labor unions and weaken employers. When forced to choose between these competing principles, Brewer usually sided with employers.

Much the same situation confronted him in the landmark case of *Lochner v. New York* (1905), where he silently joined the majority. The state of New York had fined Joseph Lochner for violating a labor law prohibiting employment in bakeries for more than sixty hours a week or more than ten hours a day. Lochner appealed his conviction to the Supreme Court on the grounds that he should be free to contract for wages and working conditions.

Justice Peckham's majority opinion held that the New York law did indeed interfere with Lochner's freedom to contract. While recognizing that the state had lawful police powers, Peckham emphasized that the legislation based on those powers had to be reasonably related to the ends asserted by the state. A majority of the Court held that New York State had failed to show that the hours worked by bakers in excess of the statute endangered either them or the public. The Court concluded that the due process guarantee of liberty under the Fourteenth Amendment outweighed the state's competing interest in protecting an individual from excessive toil. Brewer joined with the majority because he feared that statutes such as the New York bake shop law undermined traditional capitalistic notions, such as the freedom to contract.

Brewer was not altogether blinded by his devotion to capitalism, however. He was persuaded on occasion, for example, that the power of business could be properly restrained by government when it posed a threat to the market. He provided the decisive vote in *Northern Securities Co. v. United States* (1904), in which the justices sustained President Theodore Roosevelt's effort to set aside a merger between two corporate barons of the day, James Hill and J. P. Morgan.

Moreover, Brewer's Congregational background and the missionary experiences of his parents disposed him to a patronizing view of the disadvantaged. For example, his opinion for the Court in *Muller v. Oregon* (1908) seems on first impression to be at odds with his positions in *Lochner* and *Holden*. In *Muller*, Brewer sustained the constitutionality of an Oregon statute that limited the workday for women to ten hours, distinguishing this case from *Holden* and *Lochner* on the grounds that these cases involved male workers. Brewer explained that women required special protection by the state and, arguably, less in the way of protection for their right to contract out their labor. Brewer explained that the ten-hour restriction was altogether appropriate, because "women's physical structure and the performance of maternal functions place her at a disadvantage in the struggle for subsistence." Such paternalistic assumptions about women were the rule, not the exception, during his time. Brewer's opinion, for example, reached its conclusion by drawing on much of the argument made in support of it by Louis D. Brandeis, a social and legal reformer otherwise hostile to most of the justice's beliefs.

Brewer also regularly protested the treatment accorded the Chinese. Once again, his behavior on the Court reflected something of his childhood. Just as his father had opposed slavery, Brewer balked at the discriminatory treatment accorded the Chinese under the Chinese Exclusion Acts of 1882 and 1892. These measures imposed strict bureaucratic burdens on Chinese aliens living in the United States and on those seeking resident status. In *United States v. Sing Tuck* (1904), for example, a Chinese alien sued the federal government on the grounds that he had been denied due process in gaining prompt access to the courts. Brewer's powerful dissent in favor of the defendant asked rhetorically: "Why should anyone who claims the right of citizenship be denied prompt access to the courts?" He insisted that a denial of due process had occurred because Chinese immigrants had failed to receive adequate administrative procedure to gain resident status. Brewer concluded by admonishing the majority that its position undermined American foreign relations with the most populous nation on earth and demeaned the Chinese people without cause.

Brewer built an impressive record in support of Chinese immigrants, although he usually did so in the minority. For example, he dissented not only from the Court's opinion in *Sing Tuck,* but also in *United States v. Ju Toy* (1905), which denied resident Chinese access to the federal courts to try their claims of citizenship. He disagreed with Justice Harlan's majority opinion in *Kaoru Yamataya v. Fisher* (1903), also known as the *Japanese Immigrant Case,* which struck down a Japanese alien's claim for due process in deportation proceedings. And he dissented from the majority in *Fong Yue Ting v. United States* (1893), which involved the use of a pass system for resident Chinese. Brewer strongly believed that Chinese who had been converted to Christianity should be given better protection under the federal Constitution.

His record concerning the rights of African Americans was mixed. He shared many of the racist sentiments of his day, affirming that a strong antislavery background did not immediately translate into support for government action designed to promote equality for blacks. In *Berea College v. Kentucky* (1908), for example, Brewer wrote for the Court in upholding a state statute prohibiting private schools and colleges from providing instruction on an integrated basis. He held in *Hodges v. United States* (1906) that the federal government did not have power to prosecute a gang of whites who had forced blacks to leave their jobs in Arkansas.

Both of these decisions show his strong states' rights beliefs. In *Berea,* he concluded that the state had total power over the corporations and other entities that it created by law, and in *Hodges,* he affirmed that the police power equipped the states to deal exclusively with criminal acts carried out by whites against blacks. The only significant exception to this approach was his dissent in *Giles v. Harris* (1903), in which he joined Harlan against an opinion by Holmes that sustained the massive disfranchisement of African Americans in the South.

Brewer's states' rights views informed other parts of his jurisprudence. For example, he delivered the opinion of the Court in *Kansas v. Colorado* (1907), a case raising the question of whether, under the Tenth Amendment, the federal government was a government of delegated powers and, if so, whether those powers not specifically delegated were reserved to the states. In this instance, Kansas had sought to enjoin Colorado from diverting waters of the Arkansas River to the detriment of Kansas. The United States had joined the suit, claiming that it had the right under the commerce power to control the waters.

Brewer dismissed the position of the federal government on the grounds that the Constitution did not expressly grant to Washington the right to control the waters. Such a right was, according to Brewer, clearly reserved to the states. "The proposition that there are legislative powers," he wrote, "not expressed in the grant of powers, is in direct conflict with the doctrine that this is a government of enumerated powers." Brewer concluded that under the enumerated powers doctrine, the federal government had no constitutional prerogative to control water simply because of its interstate nature.

Brewer was adamant in his belief that the states controlled the bulk of power in the federal system. In *Leisy v. Hardin* (1890), for example, he dissented when the majority held that the interstate nature of liquor shipped into a state prevented that state from regulating it. The police powers were reserved exclusively to the states, Brewer insisted in a dissent joined by Justices Harlan and Horace Gray. If a state did not wish to have liquor brought across its borders, then the federal government could not make it do so. Brewer made a similar point in *Champion v. Ames* (1903), when he argued in dissent against the constitutionality of a federal law that tried to regulate the sale of lottery tickets across state lines. He explained that to "hold that Congress has general police power would be to hold that it may accomplish objects not entrusted to the general government, and to defeat the operation of the Tenth Amendment."

His commitment to states' rights even extended to preventing the federal government from outlawing the keeping of an alien woman for the purposes of prostitution. In *Keller v. United States* (1909), Brewer held that the regulation of prostitution was clearly a matter for the states, one that fell within their exclusive police powers. Even though the Constitution gave Congress broad powers over aliens, that authority did not extend to the punishment of crimes. The reasoning here was particularly disingenuous in light of his ruling in *Muller* because the alien woman in question was not charged with a crime; rather, those forcing her into prostitution were criminally liable. Brewer's quest to curb federal power, therefore, yielded somewhat strained results.

David Brewer was a conservative judge with an activist vision of the judge's role. He distrusted most of the popular movements of his day, especially the rise of organized labor, which he viewed as an agent of anarchism and a threat to civilization. In this regard, he was much like Holmes. Yet unlike Holmes, Brewer was eager to join the fray and refused to defer to the legislative branch. He believed that he and his judicial contemporaries should lead, not follow, in attempting to ensure a free market for capitalism, some appropriate procedural protection for the disadvantaged, and

in releasing the states to realize fully their police powers.

Brewer's views seem antique today. His substantive conservatism on issues of federalism and economic reform disturbs modern-day liberals, while his expansive notion of the power of the judiciary flies in the face of conservatives who believe that judges should defer to the legislative branch. Brewer was an idealist for his conservative times, one sufficiently committed to his beliefs that he thought judicial power an appropriate means of securing them.

—*Kermit L. Hall*

BIBLIOGRAPHY

Michael J. Broadhead, *David J. Brewer: The Life of a Supreme Court Justice* (1994), provides a thorough analysis of Brewer's life and times with a sound discussion of his major opinions. Shorter sketches include Owen M. Fiss in Kermit L. Hall, ed. *The Oxford Companion to the Supreme Court of the United States* (1992), 89–91; and Arnold M. Paul in Friedman and Israel, *Justices*, vol. 2, 1515. Henry J. Abraham, *Justices and Presidents: A Political History of Appointments to the Supreme Court*, 2d. ed. (1985), provides a thoughtful analysis of Brewer's appointment to the Court and the political impact of his jurisprudence. See also Joseph Gordon Hylton, "David Josiah Brewer: A Conservative Justice Reconsidered," *Journal of Supreme Court History* (1994), 45–64; and S. K. Green, "Justice David Josiah Brewer and the 'Christian Nation' Maxim," *Albany Law Review* 63 (1999): 427.

NOTEWORTHY OPINIONS

Leisy v. Hardin, 135 U.S. 100 (1890) (Dissent)
Reagan v. Farmers' Loan & Trust Co., 154 U.S. 362 (1894)
In re Debs, 158 U.S. 564 (1895)
Champion v. Ames, 188 U.S. 321 (1903) (Dissent)
Giles v. Harris, 189 U.S. 475 (1903) (Dissent)
United States v. Sing Tuck, 194 U.S. 161 (1904) (Dissent)
Kansas v. Colorado, 206 U.S. 46 (1907)
Muller v. Oregon, 208 U.S. 412 (1908)
Berea College v. Kentucky, 211 U.S. 45 (1908)
Keller v. United States, 213 U.S. 138 (1909)

STEPHEN GERALD BREYER

Birth: August 15, 1938, San Francisco, California.

Education: Stanford University, A.B., 1959; Oxford University, B.A., 1961; Harvard Law School, LL.B., 1964.

Official Positions: Law clerk to Justice Arthur J. Goldberg, 1964–1965; assistant to assistant attorney general, Antitrust Division, U.S. Justice Department, 1965–1967; assistant to the special prosecutor, Watergate Special Prosecution Force, 1973; special counsel, Senate Judiciary Committee, 1974–1975; chief counsel, Senate Judiciary Committee, 1979–1980; judge, U.S. Court of Appeals for the First Circuit, 1980–1994.

Supreme Court Service: Nominated associate justice by President Bill Clinton, May 17, 1994, to replace Harry A. Blackmun, who had retired; confirmed by the Senate, July 29, 1994, by an 87–9 vote; took judicial oath August 3, 1994.

When President Bill Clinton appointed Stephen G. Breyer to the U.S. Supreme Court, many observers initially viewed the nominee as a talented but bland technocrat. Justice Breyer has, however, emerged over the course of more than a decade of service as one of the Court's most brilliant and jurisprudentially ambitious justices. Breyer arrived at the Court with a broad background in academia, government service, and the federal judiciary, and with sophisticated, well-developed views on law, economics, and regulatory policy. In subsequent years, he has refined those views in light of his experiences on the Court and worked self-consciously toward developing a systematic theory of judging. Along the way, Breyer has earned a place as a worthy liberal intellectual counterpart—and sparring partner—to conservative justice Antonin Scalia.

Stephen Breyer was born into a middle-class Jewish family in San Francisco, California, where his father was a lawyer for the San Francisco Board of Education and his mother a politically and civically active homemaker. Breyer majored in philosophy at Stanford, where he evinced a nascent interest in philosophical pragmatism. He pursued advanced studies in philosophy, politics, and economics as a Marshall scholar at Magdalen College, Oxford, and then went on to the Harvard Law School, where he was an editor of the *Harvard Law Review.* Breyer subsequently clerked for Justice Arthur Goldberg at the height of the Warren Court's rights revolution (1964–1965) and wrote the first draft of Goldberg's famous concurrence in the landmark right to privacy decision of *Griswold v. Connecticut* (1965). Breyer next worked for the Antitrust Division of the Justice Department (1965–1967), where he met his wife, Joanna Hare, the Oxford-educated daughter of an English aristocrat and Tory MP.

Breyer then returned to Harvard Law School and to the Kennedy School of Government to teach antitrust, administrative law, and regulation. In the ensuing years, he moved back and forth between Cambridge and Washington, serving briefly as an assistant to the Watergate special prosecutor (1973) and, at the invitation of Sen. Edward Kennedy, D-Mass., as special counsel to the Senate Judiciary Committee (1975), where he rose to become the chief counsel (1979–1980). There, Breyer worked with one of his intellectual heroes, Cornell economist Alfred Kahn, and made his mark as one of the architects of the deregulation of the airline industry. With broad bipartisan support, President Jimmy Carter appointed Breyer to the U.S. Court of Appeals for the First Circuit in 1980, and he became chief judge in 1990. While serving on the federal bench, Breyer was an influential member of the commission that developed the federal sentencing guidelines (1985–1989). In academia, Breyer earned a reputation as one of the nation's leading scholars of risk and the design of rational and efficient regulatory systems. In government, he won plaudits for his ability to work effectively with politicians of both parties and for his mastery of the intricacies of the legislative and administrative process. And on the bench, he earned a reputation as a talented pragmatist and consensus builder.

Stephen Gerald Breyer

Breyer was President Clinton's second appointment to the Court. A Democrat presiding in an era of growing Republican dominance, Clinton was known for his strategy of "triangulation," by which he tried to lead by finding a pragmatic middle ground between old-style liberalism and ascendant conservative trends. As a leader who placed a high value on the art of finding workable solutions through compromise, Clinton had initially expressed an interest in appointing a politician to the Court, on the model of liberal judicial icons Earl Warren or Hugo Black. When these efforts fell through, Clinton set his sights on experienced, moderate, and pragmatic judges who might win consensus political support. Breyer fit the bill—he had been high on the list of many in Washington for Clinton's first Supreme Court appointment. Many Republicans not only liked Breyer personally but also valued his sophisticated understanding of the problems and processes of business and economics. But, in an interview with Clinton, Breyer reportedly came across as too cold and technocratic for the president's taste, and the nod went to Ruth Bader Ginsburg instead. When Justice Harry Blackmun retired the following year, however, Breyer's friends in Washington convinced the president that he had misjudged him, and Clinton named him as his second and final Court pick. Most of the limited opposition to Breyer's appointment came not from Republicans, but from the left wing of the Democratic Party, which saw him as too cozy with business interests and insufficiently committed to civil rights and civil liberties. He was nevertheless confirmed overwhelmingly by a vote of 87–9.

Most accounts of Justice Breyer's jurisprudence begin and end by characterizing him as a "common sense" moderate and judicial "pragmatist," with a predisposition for looking beyond the application of formal, *a priori* principles in favor of the attainment of concrete, real-world objectives. The often casual way the term *pragmatism* is used in ordinary political parlance—for example, as applied to politicians perpetually open to compromise, such as Bill Clinton—however, can obscure the well thought-out and systematic nature of Breyer's pragmatism, which is rooted in his academic study of philosophy and of the design of effective and efficient regulatory systems. Prior to his appointment to the bench, Breyer's chief scholarly and intellectual interests were in the relatively arcane areas of administrative and regulatory law. As a Supreme Court justice, however, he has been called upon to extend the compass of his thought over a much broader range of questions, many of which, such as civil rights, civil liberties, and federalism, are, for many Americans, more familiar territory. The key to understanding how Breyer approaches questions in these areas is to see his points of entry as extensions of an outlook forged initially with regulatory systems in mind. That outlook is characterized by an animating concern with the identification and achievement of government objectives, an attentiveness to the complexities and uniqueness of distinct regulatory contexts, and a focus on questions of institutional design and incentive structures.

As an academic, Breyer approached regulatory questions from a "law and economics" perspective, which emphasizes the role of law in achieving collective social goals. The liberal Harvard wing of the law and economics movement, with which Breyer was associated, shared with the movement's conservative (or free-market) University of Chicago wing a focus on the web of law as a system of functional regulatory incentives. The Harvard wing departed from the Chicago school, however, in the relative confidence it placed in the competence of government experts to design systematically rational and efficient regulatory regimes at the national level. In so doing, it evinced an affinity for European technocracy of the sort visible today in Breyer's thought and jurisprudence. Indeed, Breyer's much-discussed leadership in promoting recent conversations amongst judges across national borders (and, most prominently,

with European judges) is an outgrowth of these affinities.

Breyer's pragmatism is best understood in this context. In his view, law is purposive: it is designed with a particular objective in mind. And that objective typically involves an effort to solve a concrete problem (or set of problems). For this reason, legal analysis must be undertaken in light of the law's overarching policy objectives. Reflecting his training at the Harvard Law School in the "legal process" approach to law pioneered by his teachers, New Deal veterans Henry Hart and Albert Sacks, he understands that judges are only one part of a broader national-level regulatory apparatus. The role of the judge is to be mindful of the system as a whole's collective purpose (and the limited institutional capacities of judges) and to work as part of a broader team of institutions focused on achieving statutory and constitutional objectives.

In approaching a policy problem or a case, Breyer is mindful that an appropriate judgment about whether either a set of institutional arrangements or the incentive structures set by certain legal rules (or judicial interpretations of them) advances or thwarts the achievement of discernable policy objectives is possible only when a wealth of empirical data is close at hand. For this reason, Breyer is a committed empiricist. Because legislators and expert administrators routinely have a wealth of empirical information at their command that judges do not, Breyer often reminds us they are typically better situated than judges to make these assessments. For this reason, he counts himself as an apostle of judicial restraint. He also defends his transnationalism primarily in terms of his empiricism. In a dissent to *Printz v. United States* (1997), he argues that the best reason for American judges to take note of how their counterparts in other countries have decided cases is that, in looking around the world, they will find a wealth of information that will "cast an empirical light" on many of the same purposive policy questions that commonly come before American courts.

Justice Breyer has recently capped his jurisprudential vision with a foray into democratic theory.

Formerly, he was content to take up a succession of relatively narrow questions that involved discerning the purpose of particular statutes and constitutional provisions and principles, each viewed more or less in isolation from the other. In his book *Active Liberty: Interpreting Our Democratic Constitution* (2005), however, he has taken to arguing that that Constitution as a whole has a central purpose—the promotion of "active liberty" or "democracy." Although the Constitution's "democratic objective" in many cases counsels judicial restraint, Breyer insists that it also should serve as a "source of judicial power and an interpretive aid to making protection of [individual liberty] more effective." He contends that is important for a judge to see his interpretive task as involving "a quest for . . . workable democratic government protective of individual (negative) liberty." As his use of the word *quest* suggests, this process is perpetual and provisional, always open to appropriate experimentation and the consideration of new empirical evidence. To the judge befalls the especially important task of keeping the conduits of evidence open, and the lines of discussion free.

Breyer's rulings on the relationship between the national government and the states is part and parcel of this overarching jurisprudential vision. Constitutional federalism, for Breyer, is not first and foremost about the original constitutional bargain, the locus of sovereignty, or the foundational principles of American government. It is, rather, a tool, a handy component part of broader regulatory system designed to serve broader national governing purposes. Breyer has argued that what many take to be American federalism's foundational questions—those involving the allocation of basic authority and of state autonomy—are "no longer of practical importance," having been settled in the 1930s at the time of New Deal, when "a changing world . . . demanded the [new] kind of federalism that ultimately emerged." Today, the Court's most important federalism cases call for fact-based, technical calibrations to the governing order most appropriate to achieving a concrete objective in an altering technological and regulatory context. "American federalism," he has written, "is metamorphic, con-

tinuously re-inventing itself, radically adopting to changing circumstances over time." The important questions are "what level of government is best suited to the making of which decisions" under these circumstances, and how to preserve the democratic objectives of federalism in a context characterized by increasing technological complexity. The role of the Supreme Court in federalism cases is to "help the three branches of government together arrive at better answers."

Breyer classifies this outlook as evincing a commitment to "cooperative federalism," a touchstone of twentieth-century constitutional liberalism. Cooperative federalists understand the federal system, not as an arena defined by legally stipulated and formally separate spheres of authority, but as a problem-solving endeavor in which the various governments—local, state, and federal—work together as partners to solve common problems. Under such a system, Breyer has written, "within broad limits, political, not legal, considerations determine which entity, state or federal, will enact which law." Cooperative federalists believe that the interests of the states are represented and protected by their representatives in Congress, and, therefore, the judiciary plays only a small part in limiting national power over them. Effective governance is, and must be, the touchstone, as Justice Blackmun, writing for the Court, explained in *Garcia v. San Antonio Transit Authority* (1985).

Justice Breyer's understanding of American federalism has led him to adopt a broad—indeed, sweeping—reading of the national government's enumerated power under the commerce clause, which gives Congress the power to "regulate commerce . . . among the several states." He dissented vigorously, for example, from the Rehnquist Court's decision in *United States v. Lopez* (1995), in which, for the first time since before the New Deal constitutional revolution of 1937, the Court voided an attempt by Congress to regulate activity pursuant to its commerce powers on the grounds that the activity—the possession of a gun in a school zone—did not involve commerce. Following precedent set in the 1930s, Breyer argued that the relevant test was whether the activity in question had a "significant effect" on interstate commerce. This determination, he wrote, "requires an empirical judgment of a kind that a legislature is more likely than a court to make with accuracy." Breyer then went on to list many of the ways in which, after a broad consideration of the question, Congress found that guns near schools significantly affected commerce. Congress found, for example, that by creating a climate of fear in which teachers have difficulty teaching and students have difficulty learning, guns in school zones depressed educational achievement. This, in turn, affected domestic productivity. This, in turn, affected the prospect of U.S. success in international economic markets. It was therefore reasonable for Congress to conclude that the activity had a "substantial effect" on interstate commerce. When the Court voided the federal Violence Against Women Act of 1994 in *United States v. Morrison* (2000) on similar grounds, Breyer was once again in dissent.

Justice Breyer's decisions in the Court's Eleventh Amendment/state sovereign immunity cases reflect the same commitment to an expansive understanding of national power that was evident in his commerce clause rulings. In a run of those cases, the Rehnquist Court held that Congress has only limited authority (typically grounded in Section 5 of the Fourteenth Amendment) to authorize private lawsuits in federal courts against the states without their consent. These cases were: *Seminole Tribe of Florida v. Florida* (1996); *Alden v. Maine* (1999); *Board of Trustees of the University of Alabama v. Garrett* (2001), in which Breyer wrote a dissent; and *Tennessee v. Lane* (2004). Like the Court's other liberals, Breyer resisted these rulings. Given his reading of the constitutional relationship between the states and the federal government as essentially instrumental—and, therefore, mutable, in light of changing national policy goals and altering judgments made at the national level about the best means of achieving them—appeals to a state's sovereign immunity in such contexts ring hollow to him. It is not helpful, in his view, to treat state sovereign immunity as an abstract formal principle, which the founders enshrined in dividing sovereignty into distinctively separate spheres. The appropriate question

is whether the principle serves or frustrates the relevant regulatory purpose, in light of broader considerations of democratic self-government. In his *Garrett* dissent, Breyer alluded to the extensive evidentiary record that Congress had compiled concerning discrimination against people with disabilities in his argument that it was constitutionally appropriate for Congress, pursuant to its powers under the Fourteenth Amendment, to authorize suits against the states in the Americans with Disabilities Act. In *Federal Maritime Commission v. South Carolina Ports Authority* (2002), the Court held that claims of state sovereign immunity of the sort validated by the Rehnquist Court in its earlier decisions were equally applicable when the federal government subjected the states to adjudicatory proceedings before federal administrative agencies. Breyer argued, however, that "however much they might resemble the activities of legislature or a court," the activities of these agencies are properly classified as executive, not judicial. These arrangements involve "the exercise of political responsibility" by executive branch agents enforcing official national policy against the states, which, as a practical matter, bring no more pressure to bear against a state than an array of efforts by private citizens to complain to the federal government about state conduct. As such, they are simply an alternative means the executive branch uses to achieve a constitutionally permissible end. They do not subject the states to "the judicial power of the United States" under the Constitution's Article III, and therefore do not impinge on state sovereign immunity.

Justice Breyer's dissent from the Court's decision striking down a federal law ordering state officials to conduct criminal background checks on gun buyers as an affront to fundamental principles of federalism is written from a similar perspective. In *Printz v. United States* (1997), Breyer looked to what he saw as constitutional federalism's broader objectives, which involve both the achievement of national objectives in the interest of democratic self-government and the preservation of local authority and control. He reasoned that, as a practical matter, Congress's decision to avail itself of local sheriffs to conduct background checks substituted for the creation of a national bureaucracy to perform the same function. He arrived at this conclusion in part by analyzing the way that similar regulatory dynamics worked in European federal systems. For this reason, in a contemporary context, Congress's decision to commandeer local officials in effect actually minimized federal bureaucratic intrusions and advanced rather than contravened the purposes of American federalism.

Justice Breyer approaches questions of government powers, including separation of powers, in a similar spirit. Structural questions arising under the Constitution (unlike civil liberties questions, he hastens to add) must be analyzed in light of the Constitution's "structural aim," which is "the creation of a representative form of government capable of translating the people's will into effective public action." The Constitution's separation of powers provisions, like its other structural provisions, "must be read with the structural flexibility sufficient to adapt substantive laws and institutions to rapidly changing social, economic, and technological conditions." This approach may often involve the creation of "new administrative forms." To read these constitutional provisions this way, he explained in dissent in *Federal Maritime Commission,* is not to depart from the founders' wishes, but to vindicate "the Framers' own aspiration to write a document that would 'constitute' a democratic, liberty-protecting form of government that would endure through centuries of change."

Breyer's attentiveness to altered institutional contexts and consequences in separation of powers cases motivated his concurrence in *Clinton v. Jones* (1997), in which the Court spurned separation of powers and executive privilege objections to allow a sexual harassment lawsuit against President Clinton to go forward while he was in office. There, Breyer, noting a contemporary context characterized by growing litigiousness and an increasingly intrusive discovery process, placed little stock in Justice John Paul Stevens's point that, in the past, civil suits against sitting presidents were extremely rare and therefore unlikely to prove disruptive. Breyer suggested that the Court consider formulating "a constitutionally based requirement

that district courts schedule proceedings so as to avoid significant interference with the President's ongoing discharge of his official responsibilities."

Citing "the genius of the Framers' pragmatic vision," and proclaiming it the duty of the Court "to interpret nonliteral separation of powers principles in light of the need for 'workable government,' " Breyer joined Justice Scalia and Justice Sandra Day O'Connor in dissenting from the Court's decision in *Clinton v. City of New York* (1998), which invalidated the line-item veto on separation of powers grounds. In an era characterized by the problem of omnibus bills loaded up with thousands of unrelated "pork barrel" provisions, and by runaway budget deficits, modern presidents typically face the stark choice of vetoing these bills in their entirety or swallowing them whole. Breyer noted that it was a practical impossibility for Congress to "divide such a bill into thousands or tens of thousands of separate appropriations bills." The line-item veto legislation, he noted, "represent[s] an experiment that may, or may not, help representative government work better."

Although a professed partisan of judicial restraint, Breyer defended the distinctive prerogatives of judicial power in *Plaut v. Spendthrift Farms* (1995), in which he concurred in the Court's decision holding it a separation of powers violation for Congress to reopen and revise final court judgments entered into prior to the legislation's enactment. In *Hamdi v. Rumsfeld* (2004) and *Rumsfeld v. Padilla* (2004), two cases involving broad claims of authority by the president to detain U.S. citizens deemed "enemy combatants" as part of the "war on terror," Breyer voted in favor of the position that some degree of judicial oversight of the detentions is constitutionally required. He expressed similar concerns in his opinion for a closely divided Court holding that an alien ordered to be deported based on his criminal record could not be held indefinitely, but only for a period of time that was "reasonable," and subject to federal court review (*Zadvydas v. Davis,* 2001).

Breyer had spent little time reflecting on civil liberties (or civil rights) before coming to the Court. In systematizing his jurisprudence in recent years, however, he has worked to integrate civil liberties into his broader vision. Sometimes he does so by interpreting provisions of the Bill of Rights, such as the First Amendment's free speech and establishment clauses, with pragmatic, consequentialist, and purposive considerations in mind, defending them as derivatives of his commitment to "active liberty" and "participatory" democracy. At other times, however, he does so by reading the various provisions of the Bill of Rights as "negative liberty" exceptions to a more general "active liberty" approach.

In the end, Breyer's approach to rights and liberties absorbs the substantive commitments of the Warren-era rights revolution but defends those commitments in institutional and process-oriented terms—as opposed to deriving them from foundational moral principles. In this regard, in a recent colloquy with legal philosopher Ronald Dworkin, the leading proponent of the latter approach, Breyer argued that it was more appropriate to ask whether a reading of one of the Constitution's rights provisions was "sound," rather than whether it was "principled." That said, the process-oriented Breyer and the foundationalist Dworkin are basically on the same page as far as civil liberties are concerned. Most of the time, their disagreement is less over the result than the appropriate legal justification. Breyer is able to uphold the rights revolution legacy of the Warren Court without the need to defend it as a matter of substance, because, situated as he is in time, he inherited that substance as a matter of precedent. His position in legal time also allows him to avail himself of earlier waves of activist judging while positioning himself as a practitioner of judicial restraint.

Breyer is, in most respects, a liberal when it comes to the freedom of speech. Like many liberals, he encourages some forms of expression in some contexts, often on negative liberty grounds, but in others supports limits on speech on active liberty grounds when they are aimed at achieving substantive liberal objectives. In defending the constitutionality of limits on campaign contributions, for example, Breyer emphasized the democracy-promoting aspects of the speech restrictions. "To understand the First Amendment as . . . protect[ing] active liberty," he wrote in *Active Liberty*, "is to understand it as . . . seeking to facilitate a conversation among ordinary citizens that will encourage their informed participation in the electoral process." Government efforts to "democratize the influence that money can bring to bear upon the electoral process" and to "maintain the integrity of the political process," when they "strike a reasonable balance between electoral speech-restricting and speech-enhancing consequences"—that is, when they are considered in light of a "proportionality" test—are constitutionally acceptable. In these efforts, he has added, government must be given "the leeway to make regulatory mistakes." He voted with the Court's majority, for example, to hold that a prohibition on the distribution of anonymous campaign literature was a free speech violation (*McIntyre v. Ohio Elections Commission*, 1995). In a series of complex campaign finance decisions, Breyer wrote for a plurality of the Court's centrist justices to hold that a federal law restricting political party expenditures that were not coordinated with a candidate's campaign was unconstitutional (*Colorado Republican Federal Campaign Committee v. Federal Elections Commission* (1996); agreed with a 6–3 majority that the Court's landmark campaign finance decision in *Buckley v. Valeo* (1976) set the constitutional standards applicable to state elections, and validated state-level rules limiting campaign contributions aimed at avoiding corruption or the appearance of corruption (*Nixon v. Shrink Missouri Government PAC*, 2000); and voted to uphold, against a free speech challenge, the Bipartisan Campaign Finance Reform Act of 2002 (often called McCain-Feingold, after its sponsors), which, among other things, restricted "soft money" contributions, in pursuit of the same anticorruption objectives (*McConnell v. Federal Election Commission*, 2003).

Breyer's "democratic" vision purports to place an especially high value on protecting political speech, despite his views on the constitutionality of campaign finance regulations. This leaves significant room, in Breyer's view, for the regulation of commercial speech, particularly when such regulations are aimed at the achievement of federal regulatory objectives. In

United States v. United Foods (2001), for example, he dissented from a decision of the Court to strike down a federal statute forcing handlers of fresh mushrooms to contribute to a fund for the promotion of mushroom sales. In an echo of his dissent in the firearms background check case, Breyer noted that "compared with traditional 'command and control' price or output regulation, this kind of regulation . . . is more consistent, not less, with producer choice." The Court in this case, he warned, "introduce[es] into First Amendment law an unreasoned legal principle that may well pose an obstacle to the development of beneficial economic regulation." He expressed similar concerns in his dissent from the Court's holding that federal restrictions on the solicitation for, and advertising of, compound drugs amounted to an unconstitutional restriction on commercial speech (*Thompson v. Western States Medical Center,* 2002). Nevertheless, he agrees with the Court's other members that commercial speech is constitutionally protected. In *Rubin v. Coors Brewing* (1995), for example, Breyer joined a unanimous Court in holding that a federal ban on beer labels that disclosed the drink's alcohol content contravened the First Amendment.

Breyer approaches free speech questions through a characteristically empirical and pragmatic prism. His free speech opinions are narrowly drawn and anticategorical, and they parse facts and forms of speech closely. They pay close attention to the relationship between altering and distinctive contexts and efforts to engineer the achievement of legitimate government purposes, as they are supported by relevant empirical evidence. To date, his most extensive and elaborately crafted free speech opinions have been in cases involving regulatory regimes, such as the legal regulation of elections and of broadcast and cable technologies. In *Denver Area Educational Telecommunications Consortium v. FCC* (1995), for example, he wrote for the Court invalidating federal regulations requiring cable television companies to segregate and block "patently offensive" sexual programming. In doing so, he rejected the categorical and concept-focused analogical approach to the question adopted by many of the Court's other justices. Breyer argued

that less-restrictive means were available for accomplishing the same (legitimate) end. He added, moreover, that a fact-based consideration of the question was especially appealing when the case involved a regulatory arena characterized by ongoing technological change. A few years later, he concurred in the Court's decision to uphold against a free speech challenge the FCC's regulations obligating cable television companies to carry certain stations with the aim of providing a diversity of views. After noting that the free speech costs were undeniable, Breyer went on to argue in *Turner Broadcasting System v. FCC* (1997) that, in the current technological context, the public purposes sought by the agency were important and outweighed the attendant costs. Similar considerations suffuse Breyer's decisions in federal campaign finance cases, such as *McConnell.*

Breyer can also be fairly deferential to the government in free speech cases in areas where many liberals would not be. He frequently sides with the Court's conservatives in First Amendment cases involving sex, public decency, and drug use. In *Ashcroft v. American Civil Liberties Union* (2004), for example, he dissented (along with Scalia, Rehnquist, and O'Connor) from the Court's decision to void a federal requirement aimed at shielding children from obscenity on the Internet by requiring commercial pornographers to impose effective age-verification screens on their Web sites. Breyer argued that although the legislation at issue was properly subjected to the most exacting First Amendment scrutiny, the law, on the facts of the case, was the least restrictive means available to advance a compelling government interest. Breyer joined the same conservative justices in dissenting from the Court's decision in *United States v. Playboy Entertainment Group* (2000) to strike down a law requiring cable television channels providing primarily sexually oriented material to either block or scramble their signal or limit their programming to hours deemed less accessible to children. Justice Breyer voted with the Court's majority in *Erie v. Pap's A. M.* (2000) to hold that a city's public indecency ordinance banning nude dancing did not contravene the First Amendment. In a case in which the Court's three most liberal justices dissented, he wrote a concurrence to the majority opinion agreeing that the federal government could insist, as a condition of federal funding, that public libraries install Internet filtering software on their computers (*United States v. American Library Association,* 2003). These tendencies are far from absolute, however. Breyer voted with the Court's majority in *Ashcroft v. Free Speech Coalition* (2002) to strike down a federal law banning "simulated" child pornography that either used an individual who "appear[ed] to be a minor" or advertised in a way that "convey[ed] the impression" that a minor was appearing in the pictures—even if no actual minor was involved. He also voted with the majority in *Reno v. American Civil Liberties Union* (1997), which invalidated an earlier attempt by Congress to regulate obscenity on the Internet. In these cases, Breyer shied away from applying general rules in favor of a close scrutiny of the facts, a balancing of related interests, and (often) a detailed and technologically savvy assessment of whether, in that particular case, the government had availed itself of the least restrictive means to achieve its objective.

Breyer's opinions on the freedom of association are similarly variable. When antidiscrimination laws are involved, Breyer frequently spurns free association claims. For example, he voted, in dissent, in *Boy Scouts of America v. Dale* (2000) for a narrow understanding of free association and expression rights in a case involving the Scouts' dismissal of a gay scoutmaster. In *Hurley v. Irish-American Gay Group of Boston* (1995), however, he voted with a unanimous Court to allow the group organizing a parade to exclude an organization that represents gays, lesbians, and bisexuals. Citing free association claims, in *California Democratic Primary v. Jones* (2000), Breyer teamed up with the Court's conservatives to strike down California's open primary law, which forbade the state's political parties from limiting the votes in party primaries to party members.

Breyer typically votes with the Court's liberals in establishment clause cases. But, perhaps out of an awareness that other advanced western democratic countries have managed fairly well with less rigid

church-state boundaries, Breyer, to date, has been less dogmatic and alarmist in approaching constitutional questions concerning religion than many contemporary liberals. From time to time—although not consistently—he sides with the Court's conservatives in these cases. For example, he wrote a concurrence holding that a public school's decision to bar a student Christian group from holding after-school meetings on school grounds was an unconstitutional imposition on the freedom of speech (*Good News Club v. Milford,* 2001), and he concurred with the Court's holdings that financial grants-in-aid to parochial schools for secular purposes did not violate the establishment clause (*Mitchell v. Helms,* 2000), and that the erection of a Ku Klux Klan cross in a public square at Christmastime was constitutionally protected religious speech (*Capitol Square v. Pinette,* 1995). Although he is willing to apply the major Court-devised tests in this area, such as the *Lemon* test (derived from *Lemon v. Kurtzman,* 1971) and the endorsement test, when he finds them helpful, Breyer insists that what is ultimately determinative is not whether the action being assessed meets the terms of any doctrinal test, but whether it is consistent with the underlying purpose of the establishment clause.

That said, Breyer is by no means an accommodationist on church-state questions. He joined the Court's strict separationists in an array of important establishment clause decisions, for example, in *Rosenberger v. University of Virginia* (1995), in which he dissented from the Court's holding that a state university's ban on funding to a student religious publication amounted to a free speech violation; *Agostini v. Felton* (1997), in which he dissented from the Court's opinion that found no establishment clause violation when public school teachers were assigned to provide instruction in parochial schools; and *Santa Fe Independent School District v. Doe* (2000), in which he voted with the Court's liberal majority to find that student-initiated, student-led payers at a public school's varsity home football games amounted to a violation of the establishment clause. He dissented in *Zelman v. Simmons-Harris* (2003), in which the Court upheld the constitutionality of a public school voucher scheme that provided tuition money to parents for use at private secular and religious schools alike. In this case, Breyer read the establishment clause consequentially, arguing that it is aimed, in significant part, at quelling "religiously based social conflict" and that the voucher scheme at issue would exacerbate that conflict.

Breyer acknowledged that for much of American history looser constitutional standards of church-state separation were followed and may have been well-suited to their context. "Under . . . modern day circumstances" of increased religious diversity, however, the consistent goal of preventing religious strife was best advanced as a practical matter through more exacting standards of church-state separation. Reaffirming a crucial prong of the *Lemon* test, Breyer voted with the Court's majority in *McCreary County v. American Civil Liberties Union* (2005) to hold that a Kentucky county's decision to display the Ten Commandments was unconstitutional because it was motivated by the intent to advance religion. In the companion case of *Van Orden v. Perry* (2005), where the facts were slightly different, however, he parted company with the Court's strict separationists. In *McCreary*, the commandments had been placed on public property only recently and at the behest of a set of readily identifiable religious groups. In *Van Orden*, by contrast, the commandments had been placed on the Texas State Capitol grounds forty years earlier at the behest of a largely secular civil group, with the aim of conveying both a religious and a secular moral message. Moreover, in *Van Orden*, but not in *McCreary*, the commandments were situated alongside a large number of other nonreligious monuments and historical markers. Breyer explained that a fact-specific determination of how the text of the commandments was actually used determined his votes. (It is worth noting that Breyer also moved in two separate directions when faced with slight factual variations in the 2003 University of Michigan affirmative action decisions *Gratz v. Bollinger* and *Grutter v. Bollinger*. In those he voted to strike down the undergraduate affirmative action plan but uphold the law school's plan.)

When it comes to economic rights, Breyer tends to vote with the Court's liberals in defense of government power. He sided with the majority in the controversial *Kelo v. City of New London* (2005) case, in which the Court upheld a municipality's right to appropriate private property and turn it over to private developers, when the appropriation was aimed at the economic revitalization of a decaying downtown business district. He has supported against takings clause challenges a state requirement that accrued interest on deposits of client funds in lawyers' trust accounts be used to pay for legal service for the poor (*Brown v. Legal Foundation of Washington*, 2003), and a moratorium on new construction imposed during the development of a comprehensive regional land use plan (*Tahoe-Sierra Preservation Council v. Tahoe Regional Planning Agency*, 2002). Breyer wrote a concurring opinion in *BMW v. Gore* (1996), in which, for the first time since the New Deal, the Court applied the doctrine of fundamental economic rights under the Constitution's due process clause. But his position in this case appeared to stem as much from his concern with the rationality of a regulatory system than with economic rights, per se. In this case, Breyer voted to invalidate an Alabama state court's $2 million punitive damages award to a man who was sold a $40,000 new car that, unbeknownst to him, had sustained $600 worth of damages. Crucial for Breyer was the award's arbitrariness. Due process, he insisted, "require[s] the application of law, rather than a system of caprice." It is worth noting that these were the same sensibilities that had motivated his work on the commission that wrote the federal sentencing guidelines. He later confronted the question of the constitutionality of those guidelines as a Supreme Court justice. He dissented when the Court invalidated the sentencing guideline scheme set by the state of Washington in *Blakely v. Washington* (2004). In *United States v. Booker* (2005), he partly concurred and partly dissented from the Court's decision to invalidate the federal guidelines on Sixth Amendment right to jury trial grounds, a decision that let the guidelines stand in an advisory capacity. In his *Booker* opinion, in an echo of the concerns he expressed in *BMW v.*

Gore, Breyer voted to allow appeals courts to void sentences as "unreasonable."

Breyer's views on criminal process matters vary significantly, depending on the area in question. He has sided reliably with the Court's liberals in capital punishment (and *habeas corpus*) cases. For example, he voted with the majority in *Atkins v. Virginia* (2002), which held that the execution of the mentally retarded violated the Eight Amendment's prohibition on cruel and unusual punishment, and in *Roper v. Simmons* (2005), which held that the execution of an individual who was under age eighteen at the time he committed capital murder was a violation of the Eighth Amendment. In both of these opinions, the Court made reference to international standards and the jurisprudence of other countries, an approach Breyer has encouraged in many areas of the law.

It is not uncommon, however, for Breyer to side with the Court's conservatives in Fourth Amendment search and seizure cases. In *Minnesota v. Carter* (1998), for example, Breyer joined the Court's conservatives to hold that a guest visiting an apartment did not have a legitimate expectation of privacy when a policeman, who had been tipped off by a neighbor, saw him engaged in illegal activities while peering from outside the apartment through imperfectly closed blinds. He has voted to uphold random drug testing for high school athletes and, subsequently, for all students wishing to participate in extracurricular activities in *Vernonia School District 47J v. Acton* (1995) and *Board of Education v. Earls* (2002), respectively. In his concurrence in *Earls,* Breyer justified his decision, in part, by alluding to a raft of social scientific evidence concerning the seriousness of the drug problem among American youth and the failure of supply-side interdiction efforts to effectively address the problem. Joined only by Scalia, Breyer dissented in *Bond v. United States* (2000) and asserted that passengers have no legitimate expectation of privacy in the soft luggage they store in a bus's overhead storage bins. In *Illinois v. Cabalas* (2005), Breyer voted with the Court's conservatives (and Justice Stevens) that there was no Fourth Amendment violation when police ran a drug-sniffing dog around a car during an

ordinary traffic stop and used the dog's barking as probable cause for searching the trunk (where they found marijuana). This is not to say that he is always to be found with the conservatives in these cases. In *Groh v. Ramirez* (2004), he joined a 5–4 opinion by Stevens that a suspect's Fourth Amendment rights were violated because of a faulty warrant. Moreover, even when he is with the Court's conservatives, the opinions are not easily categorizable as "conservative." For example, he joined Scalia's opinion in *Kyllo v. United States* (2001) to hold that police could not use thermal imaging to detect the lights needed to grow marijuana. Breyer is not a predictably liberal vote in all Fourth Amendment contexts.

As a "minimalist" justice committed to anticategorical, narrow rulings that closely parse the case facts, Breyer is not inclined to the sorts of bold excursions that identify new unenumerated rights, such as the right to privacy. His caution in this regard is evident, for example, in his discussion of the issue of constitutional privacy in *Active Liberty,* in which Breyer chooses to approach the topic of privacy rights through the prism of considerations of technological change, rather than through more expansive philosophical theories. Arriving at the Court in the aftermath of its decision in *Planned Parenthood of Southeastern Pennsylvania v. Casey* (1992), however, Breyer has voted consistently to uphold constitutional privacy rights in abortion and gay rights cases. He wrote the Court's opinion in *Stenberg v. Carhart* (2000), a case voiding a Nebraska law prohibiting a particular late-term abortion procedure under all circumstances, with no exception for either the life or the health of the mother. In doing so, he reaffirmed his (and the Court's) commitment to abortion rights under the "undue burden" standard set out in *Casey.* Breyer has defended his decision in abortion rights cases as involving the "straightforward application" of the relevant precedent established "over the course of a generation." Precedent notwithstanding, however, Breyer voted with the Court's majority, but did not write separately, in *Lawrence v. Texas* (2003) to overrule *Bowers v. Hardwick* (1986), in the process striking down the state of Texas's prohibition on same-sex sodomy. Breyer also voted in *Saenz v. Roe* (1999) to uphold an earlier identified "right to travel" under the Fourteenth Amendment's privileges and immunities clause.

As a thinker with a special interest in the challenges posed by technological change, Breyer seems particularly intrigued by the Court's "right to die" cases that are typically argued before the Court under substantive due process, privacy rights grounds. Breyer concurred in the Court's unanimous opinion in *Washington v. Glucksberg* (1997), which upheld the constitutionality of a state statute criminalizing assisted suicide for terminally ill patients in the face of a Fourteenth Amendment "liberty" challenge. This is an area of the law that Breyer understands to be very much in flux. In his *Glucksberg* opinion, Breyer rejected the majority's characterization of the right at issue as "the right to commit suicide with another's assistance," preferring instead the speculative "the right to die with dignity." He, in turn, interpreted this right as an individual's liberty not to be forced to endure severe pain, should he choose not to do so, during the dying process. Because evidence indicated that palliative care was available, Breyer read the Washington law as not impinging on this right. In *Gonzales v. Oregon* (2006), however, Breyer voted with the majority to uphold a state law permitting a physician to prescribe a lethal dose of drugs to a terminally ill patient.

Breyer's views on civil rights evince the mix of substantive empiricism, stereotypes, and prejudices that characterize the constitutional liberalism of the second half of the twentieth century. Despite his ostensibly sweeping commitment to ruling on the data, he chooses, in many civil rights cases, to dismiss empirically observable differences between groups as "stereotypes" rather than social or biological facts. In *Miller v. Albright* (1998), for example, Breyer dissented from the Court's decision to uphold a statutory provision granting automatic citizenship at birth to an out-of-wedlock, foreign-born child of an alien father and an American mother, but required a similar child of an alien mother and an American father to provide proof of identity and relationship, writing that the statute's distinctions "depend for their validity upon the generalization that mothers are significantly more likely than fathers to care for their children or to develop caring relationships with their children." In doing so, Breyer relied in part on the Court's precedent in *United States v. Virginia* (1996), in which he had joined Ginsburg's opinion holding that the Virginia Military Institute's all-male admissions policy relied on impermissible generalizations about the respective natures of the sexes in violation of the Fourteenth Amendment's equal protection clause.

Despite his ostensible skepticism about judicial power, Breyer has voted to allow increasing judicial involvement in a broad array of discrimination contexts. In a series of statutory sexual harassment cases brought under Title VII of the Civil Rights Act of 1964, he has warned employers to chill sex-related speech in the workplace and encouraged plaintiffs to file lawsuits to force these restrictions (*Burlington Industries v. Ellerth*, 1998, and *Faragher v. Boca Raton*, 1998). In *Alexander v. Sandoval* (2001), he joined Stevens's dissent, which argued that Title VI of the Civil Rights Act of 1964 provided a private right of action to individual plaintiffs alleging that the activities by federally funded or assisted institutions had a "disparate impact" on the basis of race, color, or national origin. He extended his commitment to broadening private rights of action through the expansive construction of federal statutes in *Jackson v. Birmingham Board of Education* (2005), a Title IX case, in which he voted with the Court's liberals (and O'Connor) to hold that the statute implicitly created an individual right to sue when a school district employer allegedly retaliated against an employee for complaining about sex discrimination affecting the school's women's sports program. Breyer also voted to read Title IX broadly in *Davis v. Monroe County* (1999) and in his dissent in *Gebser v. Lago Vista* (1998). This general inclination to open up the courts to litigation in discrimination cases is further evidenced by Breyer's jurisprudence in the Court's Eleventh Amendment/sovereign immunity cases.

Breyer's relatively favorable disposition toward the goals-focused judicial policing of the workplace is also evident in his broad interpretations of the Americans with Disabilities Act (ADA). For example, he joined Stevens in dissent from the Court's decision in *Sutton v. United Airlines* (1999), which held that an airline did not violate the ADA by requiring its pilots to have perfect, uncorrected vision. In *Murphy v. United Parcel Service* (1999), Breyer again joined Stevens in dissent when the Court ruled that a package delivery company did not violate the ADA when it refused to give a job requiring strenuous manual labor to an employee with chronically high blood pressure. In *PGA Tour v. Martin* (2001), Breyer voted with the Court's majority in holding that the PGA golf tour's failure to grant a player with a circulatory disorder a waiver of a tournament regulation forbidding the use of golf carts amounted to an ADA violation. These opinions were similarly buttressed by his votes in sovereign immunities cases arising out of the ADA, for example, *Garrett* and *Tennessee v. Lane* (2004), in which Breyer concurred in the Court's holding that the Eleventh Amendment does not prevent Congress, pursuant to its Fourteenth Amendment enforcement powers, from authorizing suits against the states, when those suits were aimed at vindicating the fundamental due process rights of the disabled, such as access to a state's courtrooms.

This is not to say that Breyer rejects empirical evidence or stereotypes in all civil rights contexts. He shares the inclination of contemporary liberals to treat people in jurisprudential contexts as part of racial groups rather than as individuals. He gives considerable weight in voting rights cases to the empirical observation that black Americans tend to vote for black candidates, and he has worked to place the authority of the state behind reinforcing these tendencies. In his dissenting opinion in the Voting Rights Act case of *Abrams v. Johnson* (1997), for example, Breyer cited extensive evidence of racial polarization in voting in support of the proposition that drawing legislative districts with race in mind was a form of "benign" rather than "invidious" discrimination. Like many contemporary liberals, Breyer holds that benign racial discrimination in university admissions is justifiable in service of a compelling state interest, in part

because of the distinctively black point of view such students bring to the educational process. In the University of Michigan affirmative action cases, Breyer joined O'Connor in disapproving of the awarding of explicit numerical points to applicants who were members of racial minority groups. In effect, he encouraged schools to instead adopt a more obfuscatory approach by using race as a "plus factor" in their admissions process, as the University of Michigan Law School did. Breyer did not mention, however, that, as a practical matter, there was no significant difference between these two approaches.

Breyer's disposition towards judicial power is derivative of his liberalism. In many respects, both rhetorical and real, he is a partisan of judicial restraint. As a devotee of the "legal process" school, Breyer has long been mindful that the Court is only one of government's many institutions, and that the claims it can make to the expertise necessary to make appropriate policy judgments may be quite limited. As a pragmatist, his opinions evince an awareness that the Court's judgments are often made in distinctive and changing contexts. In such contexts, he believes broad rulings and bold pronouncements of the sort commonly associated with the liberal judicial activism of an earlier era are ill-advised. Breyer is deferential to the powers of Congress in many contexts, and, statistically speaking, is among the justices least likely to void a federal statute on constitutional grounds. That said, Breyer's substantive interpretations of the Constitution diverge significantly from their original meaning and are typically made in a forward-looking, policy-oriented spirit. Moreover, in the absence of explicit congressional authorization, Breyer commonly interprets federal statutes and constitutional language in ways that expand the scope of federal judicial involvement in a broad array of policy areas.

Breyer's thought and jurisprudence embody many of the tensions that have long been inherent in progressive political philosophy. He has written of his enthusiasm for "participatory self-government" or even "participatory democracy," where "changes . . . bubble up from below." At the same time, however, he also has described democracy as "a national conversation involving, amongst others, scientists, engineers, businessmen and women, the media, along with legislators, judges, and many ordinary citizens"—a rather academic and elitist formulation that is a far cry from the democracy expounded by earlier Democrats such as Thomas Jefferson, Andrew Jackson, or William Jennings Bryan. Breyer's democracy—like that of his earlier twentieth-century liberal progenitors, such as Woodrow Wilson, Louis Brandeis, and political thinker and editor Herbert Croly—is poised on the fault line between popular self-rule and rule by a national technocratic elite.

This fault line runs in many ways through his work. Substance aside, Breyer is democratic in the way he writes opinions and approaches his job. He is deliberate about drafting his opinions in accessible language, to invite engagement from actors outside the Court into what he regards as an ongoing dialogue about only provisionally resolved issues. He is, moreover, a regular on the lecture circuit and regards it as part of his job to explain the Court to the public, both at home and abroad, and to invite the public into a continuing conversation about its performance and its position within America's broader political system.

Breyer's commitment to transparency, however, can be offset when he imputes purposes to either statutes or constitutional provisions that many would argue differ from the actual purpose of those who wrote them. His enthusiasm for both cooperative federalism and for transnational judicial consultation also offset his commitment to transparency by blurring the formal lines of government authority and therefore of constitutional accountability. Like the European model with which it shares so many affinities, Breyer's thought raises questions about whether it too suffers from a "democratic deficit" and whether, as such, it is genuinely faithful to the "purposes" and "objectives" of America's constitutional founders.

It is often said of Breyer that his opinions are simply focused on facts and consequences, and are admirably free of ideology. But this is not accurate. Breyer works pragmatically and close to the ground within the confines of the ideologies of twentieth-century political liberalism. His approach to inter-

preting statutes and the U.S. Constitution is marked by a set of distinctive touchstones. His outlook is, in style, spirit, and substance, regulatory, economistic, scientistic, empirical, consequentialist, comparativist, and systematic. He has now begun to argue that it is also fundamentally democratic. Justice Breyer has assumed the status of one of liberalism's leading juridical voices in an increasingly conservative age. Whether, in their core commitments or in their most original innovations, the method and substance of his jurisprudence represent the dying gasp of the past or a roadmap for America's constitutional future—or both—remains to be seen.

—*Ken I. Kersch*

BIBLIOGRAPHY

The only comprehensive scholarly overview of Justice Breyer's jurisprudence and thought to date is Ken I. Kersch's "The Synthetic Progressivism of Stephen G. Breyer," in *Rehnquist Justice: Understanding the Court Dynamic*, ed. Earl M. Maltz (2003). See also Ken I. Kersch, "Justice Breyer's Mandarin Liberty," *University of Chicago Law Review* 73 (2006): 759–822. Justice Breyer himself, however, has written and spoken widely over the years, and his own extrajudicial writings provide a relatively clear portrait of his understandings and approach to law. He is the author of several books. The most accessible are *Breaking the Vicious Circle: Toward Effective Risk Regulation* (1993); *Active Liberty: Interpreting Our Democratic Constitution* (2005); and *Judges in Contemporary Democracy: An International Conversation* (2004) (with Robert Badinter).

Justice Breyer has also written numerous articles that provide a window on important aspects of his jurisprudence. Among these are "Does Federalism Make a Difference?" *Public Law* (Winter 1999): 651–662; "Judicial Review: A Practicing Judge's Perspective," *Texas Law Review* 78 (2000): 761–775; "On the Uses of Legislative History in Interpreting Statutes," *Southern California Law Review* 65 (1991): 846–874; "Our Democratic Constitution," *New York University Law Review* 77 (2002): 245–272; "Changing Relationships Among European Constitutional Courts," *Cardozo Law Review* 21 (1999-2000): 1045–1061; "The Interdependence of Science and Law," *Judicature* 82 (July/August 1998): 24–27; "Antitrust, Deregulation, and the Newly Liberated Marketplace," *California Law Review*

75 (May 1987): 1005–1047; and "Economics for Lawyers and Judges," *Journal of Legal Education* 33 (1983): 294–305. Among his speeches (some published, and others available on the U.S. Supreme Court's Web site at www.supremecourtus.gov) are "The Supreme Court and the New International Law," Keynote Address, *American Society of International Law Proceedings* 97 (2003): 265–268; and "The Constitutional Relevance of Foreign Court Decisions," Discussion with Justice Antonin Scalia, Moderated by Norman Dorsen, American University, Washington College of Law, Washington, D.C., January 13, 2005.

NOTEWORTHY OPINIONS

United States v. Lopez, 514 U.S. 549 (1995) (Dissent)

Denver Area Educational Telecommunications Consortium v. FCC, 518 U.S. 717 (1995)

BMW v. Gore, 517 U.S. 559 (1996) (Concurrence)

Colorado Republican Federal Campaign Committee v. Federal Elections Commission, 518 U.S. 604 (1996)

Clinton v. Jones, 520 U.S. 681 (1997) (Concurrence)

Abrams v. Johnson, 521 U.S. 74 (1997) (Dissent)

Washington v. Glucksberg, 521 U.S. 702 (1997) (Concurrence)

Printz v. United States, 521 U.S. 898 (1997) (Dissent)

Stenberg v. Carhart, 530 U.S. 914 (2000)

Board of Trustees of the University of Alabama v. Garrett, 531 U.S. 356 (2001) (Dissent)

Zadvydas v. Davis, 533 U.S. 678 (2001)

Federal Maritime Commission v. South Carolina Ports Authority, 535 U.S. 743 (2002) (Dissent)

Zelman v. Simmons-Harris, 536 US 639 (2003) (Dissent)

Ashcroft v. American Civil Liberties Union, 536 US 639 (2004) (Dissent)

Van Orden v. Perry, 545 U.S. __ (2005) (Concurrence)

HENRY BILLINGS BROWN

Birth: March 2, 1836, South Lee, Massachusetts.

Education: Yale University, A.B., 1856; studied briefly at Yale Law School and Harvard Law School.

Official Positions: U.S. deputy marshal for Detroit, 1861; assistant U.S. attorney, 1863–1868; circuit judge, Wayne County, Michigan, 1868; federal judge, Eastern District of Michigan, 1875–1890.

Supreme Court Service: Nominated associate justice by President Benjamin Harrison, December 23, 1890, to replace Samuel Miller, who had died; confirmed by the Senate, December 29, 1890, by a voice vote; took judicial oath January 5, 1891; retired May 28, 1906; replaced by William H. Moody, nominated by President Theodore Roosevelt.

Death: September 4, 1913, Bronxville, New York.

W e consider the underlying fallacy of the plaintiff's argument," wrote Justice Henry Billings Brown for the majority in *Plessy v. Ferguson* (1896), to consist in the assumption "that the enforced separation of the two races stamps the colored race with a badge of inferiority. If this be so, it is not by reason of anything found in the act, but solely because the colored race chooses to put that construction upon it." In this opinion, Brown's most famous and infamous, can be detected the intellectual and social assumptions of the late nineteenth century.

Born into an upper-middle-class family in South Lee, Massachusetts, educated at prep schools and Yale College, and trained in law through apprenticeship and study at the Yale and Harvard law schools, Brown personified the dominant class of his time. As a man of ability, a lawyer of talent, and a judge for his era, Brown was a justice who could forthrightly say that

separation did not imply the inferiority of blacks. He also, however, demonstrated flexibility in his judicial thought, as he did in cases such as *Pollock v. Farmers' Loan & Trust Co.* (1895) and *Holden v. Hardy* (1898).

Before joining the Court, Brown lived and worked in Detroit, Michigan. In 1860 he became a deputy U.S. marshal and soon became acquainted with the work of the federal district court in Detroit. Because of the court's location on Lake Erie, he became knowledgeable in admiralty issues. In 1863 President Abraham Lincoln appointed Brown an assistant U.S. attorney, a position he held until 1868 when he received appointment to the Wayne County circuit court. He lost his bid to be elected to that court and entered private practice. In 1875 President Ulysses S. Grant appointed Brown to the U.S. District Court for the Eastern District of Michigan, his bench for the next fourteen years.

As a federal district judge, Brown became noted for his grasp of technical issues and admiralty law.

One historian has argued that Brown was "a lawyer's judge," that he disciplined himself to "carefully analyze complex factual situations." This quality of Brown's jurisprudence meant that although he could master the issues and rules in dispute, he was not intellectually disposed to establish new directions for judicial and public policy, as can be seen in *Plessy*, in which Brown validated existing discrimination. Using careful planning and politicking, Brown sought a Supreme Court position, and in December 1890, on the death of Justice Samuel Miller, President Benjamin Harrison appointed him to the Court.

Brown disposed of his share of the routine business of the Court. Because of his knowledge of the lower federal courts, he often decided cases involving the calculation of fees for lower federal officials and the payment of federal fines, as in, for example, *Massachusetts Benefit Association v. Miles* (1891) and *United States v. Kingsley* (1891). He also wrote the usual spectrum of minor cases, such as *Cope v. Cope* (1891), resolving a conflict of laws question, and *Barbed Wire Patent* (1892), resolving the tangled barbed wire controversy on behalf of Joseph Glidden. In addition, because of his admiralty knowledge, Brown often wrote the decisions regarding shipping, such as *The Oregon* (1895).

Although Brown brought important skills to the Supreme Court, what most informed his approach to judging was his background and the dominant intellectual assumptions of his era. Brown viewed the world from a white, male, upper-middle-class per-

Henry Billings Brown

spective that embraced social Darwinism. This view of society held that certain groups had achieved social and economic prominence because, through "natural selection," they had proven to be the most "fit." In the late nineteenth century America's dominant groups eagerly adopted this ideology, first, because it justified their control of society, and second, because the theory made it appear as though their dominance was "natural"; therefore, any attempt to ameliorate the social or economic conditions of "lesser" peoples or races was not only wrong-headed and unscientific, but unnatural.

Although Brown shared these ideas and assumptions, he was not always prepared to press the law into those intellectual channels. For example, when the Court invalidated the income tax in *Pollock*, Brown dissented. He might have been expected to decide that the tax was a taking from the worthy and a redistribution to the unworthy (as the majority did), but Brown disagreed. Instead, he argued that the income tax was a common instrument used throughout the world as a basis for supporting governments, and by striking down the proposed income tax the Court had surrendered to the fears of the "moneyed class." Brown would have upheld the tax as an appropriate government policy.

In *Holden v. Hardy*, which involved Utah's regulation to protect men in the dangerous occupation of hard-rock mining, Brown upheld the power of the states to use their police power to protect workers' health and safety. Although the Supreme Court had already built the judicial doctrine of substantive due process as a device to overturn state legislation that interfered with private property rights, in *Holden,* Brown carved out a protected class of persons the states could legitimately legislate for—male miners. In cases such as *Holden,* Brown emphasized that the judicial test of a state's statute was whether it was "an exercise of reasonable discretion, or whether its action be a mere excuse for an unjust discrimination, or the oppression, or spoliation of a particular class."

In *Plessy,* Brown relied on the reasonableness of the equal but separate doctrine in ruling in favor of Jim Crow railroad cars. In fact, the decision in the case so mirrored the spirit of its times that its announcement failed to generate any controversy. As historian Charles A. Lofgren, the most careful student of this case, has demonstrated, Brown's decision in *Plessy,* although poorly crafted, reflected the era's racial, social, and legal assumptions. Most whites believed that blacks were an inferior race, and, therefore, even if the Thirteenth and Fourteenth Amendments may have established a rough legal equality between the races, those amendments certainly did not establish social equality. So, if the state of Louisiana separated the races on railroad cars, not only was it free to do so without violating any black rights, but such a policy was also a "reasonable regulation" and a valid use of the state's power. If blacks took offense at the separation, in Brown's thinking, it was because blacks were inferior; they failed to understand the true purpose (and benefit for both races) of separation. "If one race be inferior to the other socially," he explained, "the

Constitution of the United States cannot put them on the same plane."

Justice John Marshall Harlan disagreed with Brown's opinion, writing a dissent that remarkably foreshadowed the Supreme Court's reversal of *Plessy* nearly a half-century later in *Brown v. Board of Education* (1954). Harlan's was practically the only voice in the country—and the only judicial voice—opposing racial segregation. *Plessy* may offend the sensibilities of modern readers, but it is a testament to the changing values of the country and an example of how American law conveys those values into public policy. Although Brown is often censured for his opinion in *Plessy,* perhaps he was guilty only of being a "reasonable" American in the Gilded Age.

—*Thomas C. Mackey*

BIBLIOGRAPHY

On Brown and especially the *Plessy* case, see Charles A. Lofgren, *The Plessy Case: A Legal-Historical Interpretation* (1987). Also see Joel Goldfarb, "Henry Billings Brown," in Friedman and Israel, *Justices,* vol. 2, 1553; and Robert J. Glennon Jr., "Justice Henry Billings Brown: Values in Tension," *University of Colorado Law Review* 44 (1973): 553.

NOTEWORTHY OPINIONS

Pollock v. Farmers' Loan & Trust Co. II, 158 U.S. 601 (1895) (Dissent)

Plessy v. Ferguson, 163 U.S. 537 (1896)

Holden v. Hardy, 169 U.S. 366 (1898)

WARREN EARL BURGER

Birth: September 17, 1907, St. Paul, Minnesota.

Education: Attended the University of Minnesota, 1925–1927; St. Paul College of Law (now William Mitchell College of Law), LL.B., magna cum laude, 1931.

Official Positions: Assistant U.S. attorney general, Civil Division, Justice Department, 1953–1956; judge, U.S. Court of Appeals for the District of Columbia Circuit, 1956–1969.

Supreme Court Service: Nominated chief justice by President Richard Nixon, May 23, 1969, to replace Chief Justice Earl Warren, who had retired; confirmed by the Senate, June 9, 1969, by a 74–3 vote; took judicial oath June 23, 1969; retired September 26, 1986; replaced as chief justice by William H. Rehnquist, nominated by President Ronald Reagan.

Death: June 25, 1995, Alexandria, Virginia.

The influence of a chief justice is difficult to evaluate. Although nominally the leader of the Court, except for administrative matters, he has almost no formal power over the Court's decision making. He does decide who writes the Court's opinion, and he can always take the important decisions for himself. Even then, however, he must be among the majority, or he loses the opinion-assignment power to the senior justice on the other side.

The chief's ability to use the exalted status of "Chief Justice of the United States" to exercise leadership on the Court therefore depends on intangible qualities of character, intellect, persuasiveness, and respect. Whichever of these it was that Warren Burger lacked, he will not be remembered as one of the Court's great leaders. Earl Warren would have been a difficult act to follow under any circumstances, especially by someone chosen to undo much of Warren's legacy while some of the strong figures who were Warren's allies—William J. Brennan, Thurgood Mar-

shall, and William O. Douglas—still sat on the Court. Warren Burger, however, did not even come close.

Nevertheless, Chief Justice Burger had a great impact on American life, if only by exercising the one-ninth of the Court's enormous power that every justice has. That power was especially important during Burger's tenure, because, although it is not generally realized, during his term of service the Court dealt with some of the most controversial aspects of American life. Much that the previous Court did is no longer contested. *Miranda v. Arizona* (1966), *Mapp v. Ohio* (1961), *Brown v. Board of Education* (1954), and the apportionment cases—these highlights of the Warren Court are now accepted parts of American life and law, despite continued periodic mutterings about *Miranda* and *Mapp*. But the abortion decision, the affirmative action cases, the church-state decisions, issues of presidential power, and of access to the courts—the subjects of the great cases of the Burger era—are still surrounded by heated controversy.

Warren Earl Burger is one of America's great personal success stories. Born into a working-class family in Minnesota, he attended night school at the St. Paul College of Law. He then practiced law in Minnesota for more than twenty years and worked with Harold Stassen in Minnesota politics from the 1930s until the 1950s, managing Stassen's unsuccessful presidential campaigns in 1944 and 1948. In 1952 he backed Gen. Dwight D. Eisenhower for the Republican nomination for the presidency and was rewarded by being made assistant attorney general in charge of the Civil Division of the Department of Justice. There he attained some notoriety by arguing a Supreme Court case, *Peters v. Hobby* (1955), defending the use of faceless accusers when the solicitor general, Simon Sobeloff, refused to do so. In 1955 President Eisenhower nominated him to the U.S. Court of Appeals for the District of Columbia Circuit, where he began a bitter lifelong feud with Judge David Bazelon, then chief judge of the court and one of its leading liberals.

After *Miranda v. Arizona* was decided, Burger became a persistent critic of the decision. Law and order was a major issue in the 1968 election, and Burger's articles and views came to Richard Nixon's attention. Conservative, but not known as an extremist, and very strong on law and order, Burger seemed the ideal person for Nixon to appoint as Earl Warren's successor.

Shortly after becoming chief justice, Burger made it clear that, in addition to reducing protection for the rights of the criminally accused, he had at least one

Warren Earl Burger

other item on his agenda: discouraging the efforts of public interest lawyers and others to go to the federal courts for some kind of redress for social injustice. Encouraged by the *Brown* case, lawyers for women, prisoners, the handicapped, and other disadvantaged groups had turned to the federal courts to obtain the justice they could not get elsewhere. In 1971 Burger told *New York Times* correspondent Fred Graham that young lawyers should not look to the courts for social change and promised them "some disappointments" if they did.

As it happened, however, the first controversial cases to face Burger involved school desegregation. Part of Nixon's southern strategy was to allow southern school boards to continue to resist or evade desegregation. They had managed to do that quite successfully since 1955, but in 1968 the Supreme Court finally ordered that desegregation be achieved "NOW." The federal courts of appeals promptly began to issue orders requiring school boards to comply with plans drawn up by officials of the Department of Health, Education, and Welfare (HEW) under its guidelines.

Some six months after Nixon became president, however, HEW withdrew its guidelines. Southern trial judges, many of whom had always been hostile to the *Brown* ruling, immediately ordered delays in implementing desegregation plans. Within a few months, one of these cases, *Alexander v. Holmes County Board of Education* (1969), was on the Court's calendar as the very first case facing the new chief justice.

The drama of the situation was obvious. For the first time since *Brown*, the Justice Department was supporting a school board against black litigants, and the entire southern school desegregation effort was at stake. The time usually given for oral argument in the Court was doubled. According to Bob Woodward and Scott Armstrong in *The Brethren*, the case produced a great deal of dispute within the Court, with Burger initially inclined to support the delay. When the Court unanimously ordered immediate desegregation, it was clear that Burger had changed his position.

Thereafter, Burger generally supported efforts at school desegregation. During the term after the *Alexander* case, Burger wrote a major decision for a unanimous Court authorizing federal courts to use busing and other remedies to achieve desegregation (*Swann v. Charlotte-Mecklenburg Board of Education*, 1971). Two years later, in 1973, he joined Justice Brennan's opinion for the Court in *Keyes v. School District No. 1, Denver, Colorado* (1973), setting down certain rules that made it possible to desegregate northern and western schools, where, unlike in the South, segregation was not mandated by a state statute, but was a result of state or local school board actions. And six years later, in 1979, in the last of the Court's major school desegregation cases during Burger's tenure, he split his vote in two cases from Ohio, *Dayton Board of Education v. Brinkman* and *Columbus Board of Education v. Penick*.

All in all, Burger's record in school desegregation showed a cautious sympathy, but that sympathy was undercut by his joining a 5–4 decision in 1974 in which he chose to write the Court's opinion. In *Milliken v. Bradley*, a case involving Detroit and its suburbs, the Court blocked efforts to bring suburbs into the desegregation process, except in rare circumstances. The effect on school desegregation efforts verged on the catastrophic. The United States was fast becoming a nation of black central cities and white suburbs, and the ruling made it virtually impossible to prevent the proliferation of impoverished black center-city school districts surrounded by a ring of affluent white districts. The Court's 5–4 decision the previous year in a Texas case refusing to require

equalization of state financing, which Burger also joined, only made things worse (*San Antonio Independent School District v. Rodriguez*, 1973).

Oscillation characterized other aspects of Burger's civil rights record. He was the author of *Griggs v. Duke Power Co.* (1971), which may still be the most important civil rights decision since *Brown*. Title VII of the Civil Rights Act of 1964 banned discrimination in employment. In *Griggs*, the Court unanimously interpreted Title VII to prohibit employers from using a hiring method that produced a work force that did not reflect the relevant labor pool unless the employer can show a business necessity for using that method. Whether the employer intends to discriminate is irrelevant, Burger wrote.

> The Act proscribes not only overt discrimination but also practices that are fair in form but discriminatory in operation . . . that operate as "built-in headwinds" for minority groups and are unrelated to job performance.

This recognition that the problems facing minorities in America are attributable to institutionalized racism and prejudice, as much as to overt intentional discrimination, has been rare in Supreme Court jurisprudence.

The chief justice was also supportive of efforts to cope with discrimination against minorities in a decision upholding the authority of the federal government to set aside a certain portion of federal contracts for minority businesses (*Fullilove v. Klutznick*, 1980). On the other hand, except for *Fullilove*, Burger consistently voted against affirmative action efforts in education and employment, whether in dissent or in the majority. Also, apart from *Griggs*, he usually voted for a narrow interpretation of Title VII's ban on discrimination in employment. And although he wrote the first major decision striking down discrimination against women (*Reed v. Reed*, 1971), he usually voted against efforts to eliminate sex discrimination.

As the years went on, Chief Justice Burger's conservatism grew stronger. This rightward tilt was not restricted to civil rights. In his last five years on the Court, his most frequent ally was the Court's most extreme conservative, William H. Rehnquist; the two voted together at least 80 percent of the time. By the time Burger retired, he had become one of the most conservative members of his Court.

Although Burger's record on civil rights was mixed, it was anything but that where access to the courts to redress official injury was concerned. During his seventeen-year tenure, he consistently wrote or joined decisions denying litigants such access, stating that the plaintiffs either did not have enough of an interest to prosecute the action or that in some other way they had not sufficiently demonstrated the existence of the "case or controversy" that a federal court was constitutionally allowed to adjudicate. In many of these decisions, the vote was 5–4, so that Burger's vote was crucial, and he often chose to write the opinions himself. In 1972, for example, he wrote for a 5–4 majority in *Laird v. Tatum,* in which the Court refused to allow a challenge to the Army's systematic surveillance of antiwar demonstrations. Two years later, 5–4 and 6–3 decisions, both written by Burger, denied citizens the right to assert a constitutional right to see the CIA budget (*United States v. Richardson,* 1974) and to block Sen. Barry Goldwater, R-Ariz., and other members of Congress from violating a constitutional ban on serving in both Congress and the military (*Schlesinger v. Reservists Committee to Stop the War,* 1974). During the next two years, two other close decisions denied poor blacks and others the right to challenge a housing ordinance that effectively kept them out of a Rochester, New York, suburb (*Warth v. Seldin,* 1975) and an Internal Revenue Service regulation that lifted hospitals' incentive to serve poor people (*Simon v. Eastern Kentucky Welfare Rights Organization,* 1976). And ten years later, he joined a 5–3 decision that denied parents of black children the right to challenge the IRS's failure to deny tax exemptions to racially discriminatory private schools (*Allen v. Wright,* 1984). But when the Court wanted to uphold a law encouraging nuclear power, the chief justice had no trouble affirming the federal judiciary's authority to hear the case, even though the standing issue—the right to bring the suit—seemed quite similar to cases where that authority had been denied (*Duke Power Co. v. Carolina Environmental Study Group, Inc.,* 1978).

Despite this virtually unbroken line of hostile decisions, the efforts to deny litigants the opportunity to have a federal court hear their claims appear to have failed. The 1970s saw a burst of consumer, environmental, civil rights, and other social legislation, and, in most of these, Congress included a right to go to federal court to enforce the rights created by the legislation. Burger and his allies could do little about that.

Chief Justice Burger's efforts to undo the Warren Court's legacy in enhancing the rights of the accused were far more successful, although not quite in the way it was originally expected. The three peaks of the Warren Court's jurisprudence in criminal justice were *Mapp,* which required state courts to exclude unconstitutionally obtained evidence from state criminal trials; *Gideon v. Wainwright* (1963), which unanimously ruled that criminal defendants were entitled to a court-appointed lawyer if they could not afford one; and *Miranda,* which required police to warn suspects in custody of their right not to be compelled to incriminate themselves. *Gideon* has been relatively noncontroversial, but *Mapp* and *Miranda* each produced hostile reactions from police prosecutors and their political allies.

Many, therefore, assumed that when Harry Blackmun joined the Court a few months after Burger, and the law-and-order conservatives had gained a majority on the Court, they would immediately overturn *Mapp* and *Miranda.* The Court did not, and the decisions are still good law and likely to remain so.

One reason is simply that the decisions have not proven to be much of a hindrance to effective law enforcement. If anything, *Mapp* has probably improved police efficiency. A more significant reason was stated by Burger in one of his earliest efforts to reverse the Court's direction. The case was *Bivens v. Six Unknown Fed. Narcotics Agents* (1971), which dealt with the right to sue federal officers for a constitutional violation, such as entering someone's house without a warrant. There is no statute that provides compensation in such a case, but in *Bivens* the Court decided that the Constitution itself authorized a remedy. Burger protested. In his dissent, he went beyond the issues in the case to attack the rule excluding unconstitutionally obtained evidence from criminal trials. He tempered his assault, however, with this obviously regretful qualification:

I do not propose . . . that we abandon the suppression doctrine until some meaningful alternative can be developed. . . . Obviously the public interest would be poorly served if law enforcement officials were suddenly to gain the impression, however erroneous, that all constitutional restraints had been removed.

These two considerations—the lack of an effective alternative and the possibility of encouraging police misconduct by giving the wrong impression—have probably been the main reasons that a fiercely prosecution-oriented Court refrained from overturning *Mapp*.

Instead, the Court continually chipped away and undermined it so that few restraints on police searches and seizures remained. The standard for when the police may search a person or place or arrest someone was diluted and diminished; many exceptions to the exclusionary rule were created or expanded; and privacy interests given constitutional protection were reduced.

As chief justice, Burger participated in all of these developments, and in the few cases where the Court did protect the privacy rights of an accused, he usually dissented. Despite the reasons for his appointment, however, he chose to write infrequently, assigning the opinions in this field to others and contenting himself with simply voting.

The *Miranda* interrogation ruling received the same treatment as *Mapp*—it remained on the books, but much diminished. Creating exceptions, loosening its requirements, and denying it constitutional status drained the decision of much of its significance. Here, too, Burger wrote little but simply voted consistently for upholding police action. In one interrogation case involving not *Miranda* but a related doctrine, he did refuse to allow a government informer to circumvent an indicted prisoner's right to counsel and wrote for the Court in *United States v. Henry* (1980); a few years later, however, he joined a majority that backed off that ruling in *Kuhlmann v. Wilson* (1986).

Without doubt, the most controversial decision during Burger's tenure was *Roe v. Wade* (1973), which legalized abortion nationwide. Seven members of the Court supported Justice Blackmun's opinion, including Burger, who silently went along. Although the ruling came under fire almost immediately from self-styled right-to-life groups, the decision itself held firm throughout Burger's years on the Court. The attacks came largely in the form of restrictions and obstacles that some states and localities tried to erect in order to prevent women from exercising the right to choose.

The first major challenge came in a 1983 case from Ohio, and here the chief justice joined a majority striking down restrictions such as a requirement that first trimester abortions be performed in a hospital (*City of Akron v. Akron Center for Reproductive Health, Inc.,* 1983). This case was, however, practically the only time that Burger voted against restrictions. He joined narrow majorities upholding the right of the federal government and state governments to refuse to fund abortions for poor women, and almost all the Rehnquist, Byron White, and Sandra Day O'Connor dissents from decisions striking down restrictions, including the ruling that husbands may not veto abortions. By the time he retired, Burger was considered an automatic vote for virtually any plausible restriction. Indeed, in his last year on the Court he suggested that given the Court's rulings striking down state and locally imposed regulations, "we should reexamine *Roe*" (*Thornburgh v. American College of Obstetricians and Gynecologists,* 1986). What kind of "reexamination" he had in mind is not known because he retired that year, but in view of his consistent support for almost any restriction, it is fairly certain that he would at least have joined the Rehnquist opinions in *Webster v. Reproductive Health Services* (1989) and in *Planned Parenthood v. Casey* (1992) significantly diluting *Roe,* although perhaps not Justice Antonin Scalia's opinions calling for its overruling.

In light of Burger's post-*Roe* record, it comes as no surprise that in other matters affecting privacy and the family, Burger consistently voted to uphold restrictions or regulation. With a particularly harsh concurring opinion, he joined the Court's 5–4 opinion allowing states to criminalize homosexual behavior; he voted to uphold state restrictions on the distribution of contraceptives, even to adults; and he consistently voted to deny free speech and other rights to children.

Burger's occasionally peculiar mix of positions is apparent in his church-state decisions. During the 1970s a fundamental reconstruction of the law regulating relations between religion and the state took place, and Burger usually wrote on this topic, often the majority opinion, but also many concurrences and dissents.

The Court had first grappled with church-state relationships in *Everson v. Board of Education* (1947). With its Janus-faced combination of doctrine and outcome, this decision proved a forerunner of things to come. The opinion by Justice Hugo Black still ranks as one of the strongest statements ever made for a virtually complete separation of religion and the state. Nevertheless, Black and a 5–4 majority of the Court *allowed* substantial assistance to religious schools. In dissent, Justice Robert Jackson wrote:

> The undertones of the opinion, advocating complete and uncompromising separation of Church from State, seem utterly discordant with its conclusion yielding support to their commingling in educational matters.

Then, in the 1960s, the Court issued two decisions banning officially mandated school prayers, *Engel v. Vitale* (1962), and Bible readings, *Abington School District v. Schempp* (1963), which are still among the Court's most controversial and least accepted rulings in some parts of the country and by some groups.

Despite the great significance and impact of these cases, relatively few church-state cases came to the Court during the Warren years. The Court's primary concerns were elsewhere—race, criminal justice, and apportionment. Since 1970, however, hardly a year has passed without at least one or two important church-state separation cases. Burger's influence can be seen

in the fact that almost all of these decisions invoke one or the other of his two earliest church-state opinions in decisions that face in very different directions.

In the 1962 school prayer case, the Court stated that to survive a challenge under the First Amendment's establishment clause, official action must have "a secular legislative purpose and a primary effect that neither advances nor inhibits religion." Then in 1970, Burger's first year on the Court, he was forced to deal with one of the most delicate issues the Court would encounter in its entire church-state jurisprudence: tax exemptions for property used for religious purposes. The Court responded with surprising concord. In an opinion Burger wrote for eight members of the Court—only Justice Douglas dissented—he permitted the exemption. "[An] unbroken practice of according the exemption to the Churches . . . is not something to be lightly cast aside," he wrote in *Walz v. Tax Commission* (1970). In prior cases, history had been used to justify separation of church and state. Now it was being used by the Court to allow state involvement, a tactic that opponents of separation would resort to more often in later cases.

The following year, the chief justice wrote *Lemon v. Kurtzman* (1971), the first of many Burger Court cases involving state grants of money or services to religious schools and the source of what became the controversial *Lemon* test. Pennsylvania and Rhode Island had provided supplemental salary payments to teachers of secular subjects in private schools, most of them religious. In finding these payments inconsistent with the establishment clause, Burger drew on the prior decisions to put together a three-part test that became the standard for state legislation involving religious entities: (1) the statute must have a *secular purpose* (although there may also be a religious purpose); (2) the *primary effect* of the statute must not be either the advancement or the inhibition of religion; and (3), quoting *Walz*, "the statute must not foster an excessive government entanglement with religion."

The *Lemon* test provided the dominant criteria. Although continually under fire both by members of the Court and scholars as vague, unhelpful, and confusing, it has lasted since 1971, and in 1992 the Court declined an invitation to abandon it. The best indication of how little guidance it provided is its author's own record. Although the Court has purported to apply the *Lemon* test in nearly all of its establishment clause decisions (with a few notable exceptions), Burger dissented from almost all those that found the state involvement unconstitutional and voted with the majority in all those that upheld the state action. Whether the issue was free services or other aid to parochial schools, a moment of silence for prayer, religious symbols on public property, or tax deductions or credits, Burger almost always read his three-part test to uphold the state involvement. Most of the time he, White, and Rehnquist dissented, because during this period the Court, often by the narrowest of majorities, voted to erect a substantial barrier of separation between church and state.

In justifying his effort to uphold the state action aiding or otherwise involving government in religion, Burger said that he was relying "more on experience and history than on logic," as he did in his ruling on the property tax case. "Experience and history" were the criteria for his opinion for the Court in the legislative chaplain case, *Marsh v. Chambers* (1983). Burger wrote for a 6–3 majority to uphold Nebraska's employment of a Presbyterian chaplain because legislative chaplains had existed "from colonial times through the founding of the Republic and ever since."

Burger's two-part legacy to the church-state issue—the *Lemon* test and the reliance on historical practice—is not likely to last. Those who seek more leeway for state involvement and support for religion hope to undo the *Lemon* test. On the other hand, they are not likely to support a substantial reliance on history, for they recognize that doing so would allow practices that are inappropriate for the present, regardless of how well established they were 200 years ago. What Burger did accomplish with the *Lemon* test, probably unintentionally, was to provide a simple-sounding formula synthesizing preexisting tendencies, which was used by the dominant majority of the 1970s and 1980s to strengthen the wall of separation.

Burger was especially interested in executive power. In retrospect, it is likely that the most momentous decision of his years on the Court was *United States v. Nixon* (1974), which forced the president to surrender his Watergate tapes. By providing the smoking gun that proved Nixon's complicity in the Watergate cover-up, the decision led to Nixon's resignation from office. With Nixon's compliance with the Court's order to release his tapes—which was hardly a foregone conclusion when the suit began—the case established the primacy of the rule of law. And, by exploring the nature of executive privilege in the context of both criminal and impeachment proceedings, it was a major statement on the American system of separation of powers.

As related by Woodward and Armstrong in an account that has not been challenged, it was not one of the chief justice's finest hours. Although the opinion in the case appeared under his name, his original draft was rejected by the other justices, and the final product was a patched-up compromise to which he contributed relatively little. Compromise over controversial issues is quite normal, but it is clear that Burger showed little leadership here. The compromise itself, as set forth in the Court's opinion, seems sound: the president has a constitutionally based executive privilege, but absent sensitive national security, military, or diplomatic considerations, evidence essential to the fair administration of criminal justice must be turned over to a grand jury; and a general claim of executive privilege will not suffice to prevent this. Perhaps most important, the president must submit to the courts for an adjudication of the matter. The president is not above the law.

That Warren Burger was not a great leader of the Court seems generally acknowledged. He is not considered to have run the Court efficiently, and he certainly did not minimize conflict. Few justices apparently respected either his intellect or his character. Some felt that he played fast and loose with Court rules to manipulate the outcome or the assignment of opinions—it is believed that he sometimes shifted his position from the minority to the majority to take advantage of the chief justice's authority to assign the opinion-writing when in the majority. And there have been repeated charges that he breached the Court's confidentiality by discussing pending cases with President Nixon.

History is more likely to rate Burger as a competent and cautious conservative, who, despite his conservative instincts and calls for judicial restraint, presided over one of the most activist periods in the Court's history, when it produced results that were anything but conservative. For a man who came to the Court committed to reducing its role in the quest for social justice, the great irony is that during his tenure the Court greatly enhanced the rights of women, minorities, prisoners, and other disadvantaged groups; erected a relatively high wall of separation of church and state; did not significantly reduce the amount of litigation seeking social change; and wound up drawing the ire of right-wing conservatives at least as much, if not more, than its predecessor. It also contributed to the downfall of the president who had appointed almost half of its membership. Neither expected *that* when Richard Nixon made Warren Earl Burger chief justice of the United States.

—*Herman Schwartz*

BIBLIOGRAPHY

There is no biography of Burger, and his professional and personal papers housed at the College of William and Mary will be closed to researchers until 2026. Good overviews of the Court during the Burger years are Vincent Blasi, ed. *The Burger Court: The Counter-Revolution That Wasn't* (1986); Arthur L. Galub, *The Burger Court: 1968–1984* (1986); Charles M. Lamb and Stephen C. Halpern, eds., *The Burger Court: Political and Judicial Profiles* (1991); Herman Schwartz, ed. *The Burger Years: Rights and Wrongs in the Supreme Court 1969–1986* (1987); and Bernard Schwartz, *The Burger Court: Counter-Revolution or Confirmation* (1998). Bob Woodward and Scott Armstrong, *The Brethren* (1979) is an "inside" view of the Court during Burger's early tenure.

A good overview of his judicial philosophy is Philip Craig Zane, "An Interpretation of the Jurisprudence of Chief Justice Warren Burger," *Utah Law Review* (1995): 975; and the symposium on his jurisprudence in *Oklahoma Law Review* 45 (1992): 1. On criminal law, see Jerold H. Israel, "Criminal Procedure, the Burger Court, and the Legacy of the Warren Court," *Michigan Law Review* 75 (1977): 1320; Wayne R. La Fave and Jerold Israel, *Criminal Procedure* (1984). For religion cases, see Norman Redlich, "Separation of Church and State: The Burger Court's Tortuous Journey," *Notre Dame Law Review* 60 (1985): 1094. The Nixon case is discussed in the symposium "United States v. Nixon," *UCLA Law Review* 22 (1974): 4; and on abortion, see Sarah Weddington, *A Question of Choice* (1992).

Burger's views on a number of topics are covered in "Symposium: The Jurisprudence of Chief Justice Warren E. Burger," *Oklahoma Law Review* 45 (1992): 1; and in Warren E. Burger, *It Is So Ordered: A Constitution Unfolds* (1995).

NOTEWORTHY OPINIONS

Griggs v. Duke Power Co., 401 U.S. 424 (1971)

Swann v. Charlotte-Mecklenburg Board of Education, 402 U.S. 1 (1971)

Bivens v. Six Unknown Fed. Narcotics Agents, 403 U.S. 388 (1971) (Dissent)

Lemon v. Kurtzman, 403 U.S. 602 (1971)

Reed v. Reed, 404 U.S. 71 (1971)

United States v. Nixon, 418 U.S. 683 (1974)

Milliken v. Bradley, 418 U.S. 717 (1974)

Marsh v. Chambers, 463 U.S. 783 (1983)

HAROLD HITZ BURTON

Birth: June 22, 1888, Jamaica Plain, Massachusetts.

Education: Bowdoin College, A.B., 1909; Harvard University, LL.B., 1912.

Official Positions: Member, Ohio House of Representatives, 1929; director of law, Cleveland, 1929–1932; acting mayor of Cleveland, November 9, 1931–February 20, 1932; mayor of Cleveland, 1935–1940; U.S. senator, 1941–1945.

Supreme Court Service: Nominated associate justice by President Harry S. Truman, September 18, 1945, to replace Owen J. Roberts, who had resigned; confirmed by the Senate, September 19, 1945, by a voice vote; took judicial oath October 1, 1945; retired October 13, 1958; replaced by Potter Stewart, appointed by President Dwight D. Eisenhower.

Death: October 28, 1964, Washington, D.C.

Harold Burton was the first of President Harry Truman's four appointments to the Supreme Court. A career politician with no prior judicial experience, Burton brought a pragmatic style of decision making to a Court characterized by ideological conflict. Burton never earned great distinction, but his moderating influence helped to ease the Court through one of its more divisive periods.

Born in a suburb of Boston and educated in eastern schools, Burton decided after graduating from Harvard Law School in 1912 that leaving the East would bring him greater opportunities for a satisfying legal career. He ultimately settled in Cleveland, where he established a successful law practice, taught corporate law at Western Reserve University, and served for four years as the city's law director.

Burton's first love was politics, however, and he wasted no time cultivating his ties to the local Republican Party organization. From 1935 to 1940 he served as Cleveland's mayor, during which time he lowered

the city's crime rate, reduced its deficit, and broke the patronage network. In 1940 Ohio voters easily elected the popular mayor to the U.S. Senate, where he assumed a moderate stance on domestic issues and vigorously supported President Franklin Roosevelt's interventionist foreign policy.

On September 18, 1945, President Truman nominated Burton to replace Justice Owen Roberts, who had resigned at the end of the 1944 term. Burton and Truman had worked closely together in the Senate, and many observers attributed Burton's appointment to the cronyism that characterized Truman's administration, especially as Burton had no prior judicial experience. In fact, Burton's nomination satisfied several mandates. The retirement of Roberts left Chief Justice Harlan Fiske Stone as the Court's only Republican member. Burton's appointment met the demands of Republican leaders in Congress that Truman restore some political balance to the Court. At the same time, Burton's moderate and pragmatic politics convinced Truman that his nominee would be neither intensely partisan nor fiercely ideological on the Court. Finally, Burton's status as a sitting member of the Senate promised easy confirmation. Truman's calculations proved accurate, for the Senate approved Burton unanimously the day after he was nominated.

Burton's tenure at the Supreme Court was characterized by heated disagreements between judicial activists, who favored expansive powers of judicial review, and advocates of judicial restraint, who encouraged deference to legislative judgments. Burton gravitated toward restraint, writing opinions that generally upheld legislative enactments and decided cases on narrow procedural grounds.

His restraint was more a product of his political beliefs than a commitment to judicial ideology, however. For example, he supported national security measures because he subscribed to cold war politics; he favored desegregation because he found racial discrimination personally abhorrent; and he urged restrictions on the right to picket because he feared the effect of organized labor on corporate power. In short, he deferred to legislative judgments because he agreed with them, not necessarily because he believed the political branches had the exclusive power to formulate public policy.

Burton's political beliefs closely resembled Truman's, and the president was rarely disappointed with his selection. In several cases, Burton supported the Justice Department's efforts to regulate business through the antitrust statutes. In *Lichter v. United States* (1948), he upheld the government's power to renegotiate wartime contracts to curb fraud and profiteering, a subject that Burton and Truman had investigated when they served in the Senate. In fact, Burton's only significant disagreement with Truman's executive policies occurred in *Youngstown Sheet & Tube Co. v. Sawyer* (1952), which rejected Truman's authority to seize the nation's steel mills and avert a strike during the Korean War. Burton's concurring opinion rested on the grounds that the Taft-Hartley Act of 1947 prescribed other methods for resolving labor disputes and specifically reserved to Congress the power to authorize seizure. Although he was generally sympathetic to the exercise of executive power, Burton's congressional experience had instilled in him a respect for the separation of powers, leading him to limit the president's authority when Congress had specifically prohibited certain actions.

Burton's pragmatic approach to adjudication appeared in his decisions regarding national security during the cold war. He usually upheld government regulations against espionage and subversion over claims that they violated First Amendment freedoms. By closely construing the facts of a case to limit the effects of his rulings, however, he occasionally convinced more libertarian justices to join his opinions. For example, in *Beilan v. Board of Education* (1958), Burton upheld the dismissal of a Philadelphia teacher who refused to tell school officials whether he was a member of a communist organization. Two years earlier, in *Slochower v. Board*

Harold Hitz Burton

of Higher Education of New York City (1956), Burton had dissented from a ruling that public employers could not fire workers for refusing to discuss Communist Party membership. In *Beilan,* however, Burton convinced two justices from the *Slochower* majority to modify their views. Although school boards could not legally infer disloyalty from a teacher's silence, Burton reasoned, they could use the teacher's lack of candor as evidence of professional incompetence.

Burton sometimes joined his more libertarian colleagues, but he curbed their activism by focusing on procedural rather than constitutional remedies. In *Joint Anti-Fascist Refugee Committee v. McGrath* (1951), Burton ordered the U.S. attorney general to remove the names of three allegedly communist organizations from a list of subversive groups. Unlike the other four members of the majority, however, who considered the very practice of listing suspected organizations unconstitutional, Burton held only that the attorney general must first offer proof of subversion in a court of law.

Burton's circumspection also dictated his concurrence in *Jencks v. United States* (1957), which involved a perjury conviction of a man who falsely swore that he was not a Communist. Five justices held that a defendant was entitled to examine evidence against him contained in FBI reports, but Burton preferred that the trial judge first screen the files so that information affecting national security could be withheld. Later that year, Congress enacted a statute that regulated the use of FBI records in criminal trials in a manner similar to that recommended by Burton.

Burton's eclectic jurisprudence was not limited to the national security arena. In establishment clause cases, for example, he favored a fairly strict separation of church and state, while permitting some government support of religion. He dissented from Justice Hugo Black's opinion in *Everson v. Board of Education of Ewing Township* (1947) because he not only agreed with Black that the First Amendment erected a wall of separation between church and state, but, unlike Black, he also believed that a New Jersey statute that authorized school boards to reimburse parents for transportation to parochial school breached that wall.

He then joined Black's opinion in *Illinois ex rel. McCollum v. Board of Education* (1948), which struck down a program that permitted clergymen to provide weekly religious instruction in public school classrooms, but only after Black agreed not to extend his ruling to similar programs that granted students released time to receive off-campus religious training.

In cases involving criminal procedure, Burton generally granted states broad powers to maintain law and order. This pattern was consistent with the political views he had held as mayor of Cleveland, where he had been elected on a platform that promised to rid the city of organized crime. In cases alleging coerced confessions, he rarely presumed police misconduct, giving local judges and juries responsibility for determining the reliability of confessions. He also left decisions regarding the appointment of defense counsel in the hands of local jurisdictions.

Despite his support for law enforcement, some of Burton's most libertarian opinions involved criminal cases. Although he usually granted the police broad discretion to obtain evidence, he condemned the use of secret radio transmitters on private property to eavesdrop on a suspect's conversations. His dissent in *Louisiana ex rel. Francis v. Resweber* (1947) forcefully argued that to execute a prisoner after two earlier attempts had failed violated the double jeopardy and cruel and unusual punishment provisions of the Bill of Rights. Burton criticized only the botched attempt at electrocution; he did not challenge the authority of a state to carry out a death sentence. He also limited his dissent to the actions taken by prison officials; if state law had permitted repeated attempts, he would not have objected.

Burton's civil rights decisions aptly revealed the congruence between his jurisprudential and political beliefs. A member of the Cleveland NAACP, Burton had adopted a moderately progressive stance on race relations, supporting the abolition of poll taxes and the establishment of a fair employment practices commission. Many observers were therefore surprised when, during his first term, Burton refused to join the otherwise unanimous opinion in *Morgan v. Virginia* (1946), which invalidated a Virginia statute that required segregation on public transportation. Burton pointed out that ten other states had a law similar to Virginia's, and he asked, if, as the Court said, interstate passengers should be treated equally, why had Congress neglected to pass such a law. In subsequent cases involving the desegregation of graduate and professional schools, however, Burton urged the wholesale reversal of the "separate but equal doctrine," and he heartily supported Chief Justice Earl Warren's efforts to craft a unanimous opinion in *Brown v. Board of Education* (1954). Still, Burton hesitated to invoke constitutional guarantees of equality if narrower remedies were available. His opinion for a unanimous Court in *Henderson v. United States* (1950), for example, relied on the Interstate Commerce Act, rather than the equal protection clause of the Fourteenth Amendment, to void the practice of partitioning railroad dining cars to separate black and white passengers.

By the time Parkinson's disease forced Burton to retire, he had garnered a reputation as a mediocre jurist, generally conservative but never doctrinaire, who made no significant jurisprudential contributions to the Court. Scholars of the Court have concurred in that judgment, but the appraisal is somewhat unfair. Several of his opinions interpreting federal statutes such as the Fair Labor Standards Act and the Taft-Hartley Act remain valid law. His opinion in *American Tobacco Co. v. United States* (1946) greatly expanded the government's power under the Sherman Antitrust Act. At the same time, Chief Justice Fred Vinson routinely assigned opinions to wavering justices in order to maintain his slim coalition. This practice gave Burton, a faithful member of the Truman bloc, few opportunities to write important constitutional opinions.

Nevertheless, Burton's style of judging constrained his ability to influence his colleagues. During oral arguments he rarely asked questions. He found preparing opinions extremely difficult, yet he insisted on researching precedent exhaustively and writing his own draft opinions, thereby limiting his judicial output. His lack of a guiding jurisprudential philosophy and his tendency to decide cases on narrow grounds

also hindered his ability to formulate significant constitutional doctrine.

Burton's main contribution to the Supreme Court was to bring a sense of stability to a tribunal that was undergoing a significant transformation. During his tenure, five new associate justices came to the Court, and he served under three chief justices, two of whom, Vinson and Warren, symbolized the extremes of judicial restraint and activism. His affable personality brought together colleagues who sometimes regarded one another with acrimony. His attention to the technical details of a case often provided solutions when other justices disagreed on the merits. During a period when most members of the Court wanted to avoid political controversy, Burton proved a reliable ally.

—Eric W. Rise

BIBLIOGRAPHY

The standard biography of Harold Burton is Mary Frances Berry, *Stability, Security, and Continuity: Mr. Justice Burton and Decision-Making in the Supreme Court, 1945–1958* (1978), which is useful primarily for its examination of the internal politics of the Court during Burton's tenure. For substantive analysis of the cases that Burton decided, see Ronald Marquardt, "The Judicial Justice: Mr. Justice Burton and the Supreme Court" (Ph.D. diss., University of Missouri, 1973). David N. Atkinson provides an intriguing discussion of Burton's work habits, based on interviews with his former law clerks, in "Justice Harold H. Burton and the Work of the Supreme Court," *Cleveland State Law Review* 69 (1978): 69. In "American Constitutionalism Under Stress: Mr. Justice Burton's Response to National Security Issues," *Houston Law Review* 9 (1971): 271, Atkinson assesses the impact of cold war politics on Burton's jurisprudence. Arthur S. Miller, *Death by Installments: The Ordeal of Willie Francis* (1988), examines the circumstances surrounding one of Burton's most notable dissents.

Justice Burton's papers, including his personal diary and extensive correspondence files, are located in the Library of Congress. This unusually rich collection documents his terms as mayor of Cleveland and U.S. senator, as well as his judicial career. *The Occasional Papers of Mr. Justice Burton*, edited by Edward C. Hudon (1969), is a compilation of Burton's extrajudicial writings, mostly on the history of the Supreme Court.

NOTEWORTHY OPINIONS

American Tobacco Co. v. United States, 328 U.S. 781 (1946)

Louisiana ex rel. Francis v. Resweber, 329 U.S. 459 (1947) (Dissent)

Everson v. Board of Education of Ewing Township, 330 U.S. 1 (1947) (Dissent)

Lichter v. United States, 334 U.S. 742 (1948)

Henderson v. United States, 339 U.S. 816 (1950)

Joint Anti-Fascist Refugee Committee v. McGrath, 341 U.S. 123 (1951)

Youngstown Sheet & Tube Co. v. Sawyer, 343 U.S. 579 (1952) (Concurrence)

Slochower v. Board of Higher Education of New York City, 350 U.S. 551 (1956) (Dissent)

Beilan v. Board of Education, 357 U.S. 399 (1958)

PIERCE BUTLER

Birth: March 17, 1866, Pine Bend, Minnesota.

Education: Carleton College, A.B., B.S., 1887.

Official Positions: Assistant county attorney, Ramsey County, Minnesota, 1891–1893; county attorney, 1893–1897.

Supreme Court Service: Nominated associate justice by President Warren G. Harding, November 23, 1922, to replace William R. Day, who had retired; renominated December 5, 1922; confirmed by the Senate, December 21, 1922, by a 61 8 vote; took judicial oath January 2, 1923; served until November 16, 1939; replaced by Frank Murphy, nominated by President Franklin D. Roosevelt.

Death: November 16, 1939, Washington, D.C.

Pierce Butler was born in a log cabin on a Minnesota farm on St. Patrick's Day, 1866, to Irish Catholic immigrants who had left Ireland after the 1848 famine. Graduating from Carleton College in 1887, Butler read law and was admitted to the bar in 1888. That year he cast his first vote for Grover Cleveland, and he remained a Democrat for the rest of his life. After serving as assistant county attorney for two years, he was elected county attorney of Ramsey County, Minnesota, in 1893. Reelected two years later, he declined to seek a third term and entered private practice. A railroad lawyer and an expert in rate and valuation cases, Butler represented several railroads before the Supreme Court in the *Minnesota Rate Cases* (1913). Thereafter, he represented the Canadian government in the Grand Trunk arbitration, in which William Howard Taft was an arbitrator. The two Americans became friends, and when President Warren G. Harding nominated Taft chief justice in 1921, Taft and Butler celebrated the event together.

In 1922, anticipating Justice William R. Day's retirement, Taft surveyed candidates to recommend to President Harding. Taft's first choice was John W. Davis, but Davis gave no clear sign of interest, so Taft considered other possible candidates. Meanwhile, Martin T. Manton, a judge on the U.S. Court of Appeals for the Second Circuit, emerged independently as a leading candidate from New York. Taft thought that Manton's appointment to the Court would be a "disaster." In Taft's eyes, Manton was "utterly unfit" for the Court. From what Taft had heard, Manton had been a shady lawyer, an ambulance chaser who had risen to the bench entirely through political connections. When Justice Willis Van Devanter suggested Pierce Butler, who was also a Catholic and a Democrat, as a alternate candidate, Taft pursued the idea vigorously by first persuading Butler to become a candidate. Next, he advised him to seek the support of the midwestern and western Catholic hierarchy, as well as Democrats, the bench, the bar, and the business community. Finally, Taft personally urged the president to nominate Butler.

Senate progressives opposed Butler's confirmation, principally because of his conservative economic views. They also maintained that he lacked a judicial temperament because, as a regent at the University of Minnesota during World War I, he had taken the lead in dismissing professors for their "unpatriotic" views. After examining the evidence against Butler, a subcommittee of the Senate Judiciary Committee recommended unanimously that his nomination be confirmed. The subcommittee specifically concluded that Butler's economic views did not disqualify him for the Court. The vote on Butler's confirmation was 61–8, with 27 abstentions.

Taft was greatly pleased by Butler's confirmation. It meant that the chief justice would have a strong, able, and hardworking colleague who would be a team player. Butler wrote 323 majority opinions in his seventeen years on the Court, averaging nineteen opinions a term, but only a few of those opinions are of historic significance. During his early years as a justice, he seldom dissented. He explained his views on dissent on the back of one of Justice Harlan Stone's slip opinions as follows: "I voted to reverse. While this sustains your conclusions to affirm, I still think reversal would be better. But I shall in silence acquiesce. Dissents seldom aid in the right development of the law. They often do harm. For myself I say: 'Lead us not into temptation.' " Butler's opinions contain few statements as quotable as the one above, and

Pierce Butler

that was no accident. One of his sons said that Butler carefully went over each of his opinions with a blue pencil and deleted any statement he thought might he quotable.

Justice Oliver Wendell Holmes described Butler in a single word—"monolith," adding, "there are no seams the frost can get through." Once, after persuading Holmes to acquiesce in a case being discussed in conference, Butler said, "I am glad we have finally arrived at a just decision," and Holmes replied, "Hell is paved with *just* decisions." To Butler, principle was everything and could never be sacrificed to expediency. Butler had a system of values that oriented his life and his decisions, and he had articulated those values long before he came to the Court. As one would expect of a lawyer, he prized law, order, tradition, and freedom, but an analysis of his pre-Court public addresses shows that he also highly valued laissez-faire, patriotism, and morality.

Laissez-faire was especially important to Butler. "Contemporaneously with the ever increasing activities of government," he said in 1916, "there is a school of thought leading toward a kind of state socialism. Too much paternalism, too much wet-nursing by the state, is destructive of individual initiative and development. An athlete should not be fed on predigested food, nor should the citizens of tomorrow be so trained that they will expect sustenance from the public 'pap.' " It was Butler's view that the state may not transgress "its true function" and become a vast charitable machine, furnishing employment, doling out aid, and meeting the needs of the people. Such a program would ruin the nation, "weaken character and leave the individual man and woman without the motive or hope or inspiration necessary to freedom and morality."

Butler's commitment to patriotism was as strong as his commitment to laissez-faire. In 1915 he said that the strength of the state was limitless when erected by "loving patriotism." Patriotism to Butler was not simply flag-waving; he acknowledged that such activity was easy and often pleasant, but "real patriotism" required the bearing of the burdens of taxation gladly as well as discharging the other duties of citizenship. The primary duty of citizenship, he said, was undivided allegiance to the nation. "Allegiance to government and protection by it are reciprocal obligations, and, stripped of all sentiment, the one is the consideration for the other; that is, allegiance for protection and protection for allegiance. Because the citizen is entitled to its protection, he owes allegiance in full measure to his country." This idea, he thought, was implicit in the oaths taken by public officials and aliens, and although most native citizens took no oaths, they owed the same loyalty. "Thus," he concluded, "it is that all, from the highest to the lowliest of our naturalized citizens, are, by legal obligation strong and binding, held to full and faithful loyalty."

Patriotism and laissez-faire were intimately connected with Butler's central value: morality. "The educated man," he told a Catholic audience in 1915, "whose character is not sound, whose conscience is not well-instructed and whose conduct is not guided by religion or morality, is a danger to the State and his fellowmen." One of his favorite quotations was from Archbishop John L. Spalding: "The end of all worthy struggles is to establish morality as the basis of individual and national life."

If these three tenets informed Butler's decisions on the Court, so too did tradition, which to him meant a strong commitment to precedent. Few justices in the history of the Court have shown stronger resistance to overruling precedents. "Our decisions ought to be sufficiently definite and permanent," he wrote in *Railroad Commission v. Pacific Gas & Electric Co.* (1938), "to enable counsel usefully to advise clients. Generally speaking, at least, our decision of yesterday ought to be the law of today."

No justice in the twentieth century voted more consistently for laissez-faire than Butler. Believing that contracts freely and fairly entered into were "sacred," he never voted against the assertion of a contract right when the Court divided on the issue. Also believing that the government had no right to regulate the hours or wages of workers, he voted accordingly every time the issue arose during his tenure, and he was on the winning side in every such decision until 1937. In *Morehead v. New York ex rel. Tipaldo* (1936), which invalidated New York's law regulating wages for women, Butler wrote the majority opinion, one of his most important.

Although Butler valued individual freedom, patriotism almost always prevailed when the two values were in conflict, as in *United States v. Schwimmer* (1929), in which the Court held that a forty-nine-year-old woman was not entitled to become a citizen of the United States because she could not in good conscience swear to bear arms in defense of the nation. Writing for the majority, Butler identified Rosika Schwimmer with pacifists and conscientious objectors who, during World War I, not only refused to bear arms, but who also refused to obey the laws and encouraged disobedience in others. Pacifists, he wrote, lack a "sense of nationalism"; they do not have the "ties of affection" to the government of the United States that are requisite for aliens seeking naturalization. Butler had expressed similar ideas in public addresses in 1915 and 1916. In every divided decision involving Communists, International Workers of the World, or aliens who refused to swear unqualified allegiance, Butler voted against the individual.

A possible illustration of morality as the basis of Butler's decisions is *Buck v. Bell* (1927), in which the Court upheld the constitutionality of compulsory sterilization of the feeble-minded in Virginia. Holmes, who wrote the Court's opinion, quickly won the approval of all his colleagues, except Butler. "I bet you Butler is struggling with his conscience as a lawyer on this decision," Holmes was quoted as saying to a fellow justice. "He knows the law is the way I have written it. But he is afraid of the Church. I'll lay you a bet that the Church beats the law." Butler dissented without opinion. One might conclude that because Butler was a Catholic, he believed that compulsory sterilization was immoral and for that reason dissented. One might also conclude that he thought that the Virginia sterilization statute was unconstitutional because it deprived persons of liberty in violation of due process of law. So the basis of his dissent is unclear. But there is no doubt that Butler strongly disagreed with Holmes, who wrote for the Court: "It is better for all the world, if instead of waiting to execute degenerate offspring for crime, or to let them starve for their imbecility, society can prevent those who are manifestly unfit from continuing their kind. The principle that sustains compulsory vaccination is broad enough to cover cutting the Fallopian tubes."

Butler was also the lone dissent in *Hansen v. Haff* (1934). Hansen, an unmarried alien woman, had left the United States in the company of a married man with whom she had been having sexual relations for some years. The intimate relationship continued abroad, and Hansen intended it to continue on her return to the United States until she reached the city of her residence, where she was employed as a domestic. Based on these facts, the immigration authorities refused to readmit her into the country because a federal statute excluded aliens who came to the United States "for the purpose of prostitution or for any other immoral purpose." The Court held that the woman was entitled to readmission because her extramarital relations fell short of concubinage, and, at any rate, she was not reentering the country for the purpose of having such relations. Butler countered, citing Webster's definition, that the woman was indeed a concubine. Further, he said, she entered the country for an immoral purpose, and it made no difference whether that purpose was dominant or subordinate.

Although Butler seldom articulated the value of due process in his public addresses prior to his appointment to the Supreme Court, he had a strong commitment to the principle. During his tenure on

the Court, no justice—not even Louis Brandeis—supported due process claims more than Butler. The fact that he often dissented in favor of due process claims is a measure of the intensity of his commitment. At times, however, because of value conflicts, loyalty to the opinion of the Court, or respect for those with whom he differed, Butler found it difficult to express his dissenting views, even in defense of due process.

Olmstead v. United States (1928), which upheld the constitutionality of wiretapping, was just such a case. Chief Justice Taft, who wrote the Court's opinion for a majority of five, saw the problem primarily in terms of his values of law and order. So did Butler, but his early experience at the criminal bar had taught him about unfair police practices, the zeal of prosecutors to convict, and the great advantage the state has over the individual in criminal prosecutions. He disliked crime as much as Taft did, but, as he put it in one of his opinions as circuit justice, "Abhorrence, however great, of persistent and menacing crime will not excuse transgression in the courts of the legal rights of the worst offenders." And Butler believed it did not excuse the use of evidence obtained by wiretapping. He decided to write a dissenting opinion in *Olmstead,* but apparently not without some inner struggle, for he began the opinion by saying he "sincerely regret[ted]" that he was unable to agree with Taft and the majority and concluded with the statement: "With great deference, I think [the defendants] should be given a new trial."

One of Butler's most important due process dissents was in *Palko v. Connecticut* (1937), in which the majority included the liberal justices Brandeis, Stone, Charles Evans Hughes, Nathan Cardozo, and Hugo Black. The majority held that a state could try a defendant more than once for the same offense without violating due process of law. Frank Palka (the Court records misspelled his name) had been tried for murder and given a life sentence. Dissatisfied with the sentence, the Connecticut prosecutor tried him again, which state law permitted, and this time Palka received the death penalty. Butler was the only dissenter, and, as in *Buck v. Bell,* he dissented without opinion, but he expressed his attitude. During the oral argument, he was "very tough" on counsel and shouted at the state's attorney: "What do you want? Blood?"

Supreme Court scholars have questioned Butler's ability. Fred Rodel considered Butler the "least intellectually gifted of the Nine Old Men, a second-rate successor, of sorts, to far abler Justice [Edward] White." William F. Swindler wrote that Butler had "manifest intellectual limitations." There is some evidence that Butler's critics underestimated his ability. Robert H. Jackson recalled Butler as "a man of great ability and devotion to the job as he saw it." The day Butler died, a lawyer remarked that Jackson must be glad not to have Butler on the bench vigorously questioning him when he argued for the government as solicitor general. Jackson replied, "I'm sorry that he is not, for nothing kept our office on its toes as the certainty that our arguments would have to face the scrutiny of Justice Butler." William O. Douglas, who had been Butler's colleague, said in an unpublished interview in 1961 that Butler was a "very friendly, likeable man. When you crossed swords with Butler you knew you were crossing swords with an expert. He had a very extraordinary mind and great powers of argumentation. He was a great adversary. . . . He has been greatly . . . misunderstood." In his memoirs, Douglas confirmed this assessment of Butler. "While he was extremely conservative," Douglas wrote, "I had great admiration for his intellect. . . . Butler was able—very able."

Douglas's statements suggest why Butler was able to keep intact the Court's conservative bloc—the "Four Horsemen"—in the 1930s. As Chief Justice Hughes pointed out, Butler automatically had the vote of the arch-conservative James McReynolds, and he had "a strong influence on Justices Van Devanter and [George] Sutherland." Until 1937 Butler was frequently able to attract Owen Roberts's vote in economic cases and forge the majorities that invalidated many New Deal laws. These decisions in turn led to a confrontation between Franklin Roosevelt and the Court. Justice Butler's success in forging conservative majorities in the 1930s was historically more important than his judicial opinions.

Butler's death in 1939 marked the end of an era in the Court's history. He was one of the last justices appointed to the Court who had not attended law school. He was also one of the last great champions of substantive due process as a means of protecting property rights, a constitutional doctrine that no longer commanded a majority during his final three years of service. It is therefore not surprising that he recorded more dissents in that period than he did in his previous fourteen years on the Court. Finally, Butler's death gave President Roosevelt his fifth Supreme Court appointment, which brought into being a new era of constitutional interpretation.

—*David J. Danelski*

BIBLIOGRAPHY

There are no Butler Court papers, but material on his earlier years constitute a small collection at the Minnesota Historical Society in St. Paul. Papers relating to his confirmation are in the University of Washington Library in Seattle. Material on Butler can also be found in the Robert Jackson, Harlan Fiske Stone, and William Howard Taft collections in the Library of Congress.

David J. Danelski, *A Supreme Court Justice Is Appointed* (1964), provides a detailed description and analysis of Butler's appointment. Francis Joseph Brown, *The Social and Economic Philosophy of Pierce Butler* (1945), remains useful for its comprehensive coverage of Butler's judicial opinions. See also Phillip Thompson, "Silent Protest: A Catholic Justice Dissents in *Buck v. Bell*," *Catholic Lawyer* 43 (2004): 125; and Barry Cushman, "The Secret Lives of the Four Horsemen," *Virginia Law Review* 83 (1997): 559–645.

NOTEWORTHY OPINIONS

Olmstead v. United States, 277 U.S. 438 (1928) (Dissent)

United States v. Schwimmer, 279 U.S. 644 (1929)

Hansen v. Haff, 291 U.S. 559 (1934) (Dissent)

Morehead v. New York ex rel. Tipaldo, 298 U.S. 587 (1936)

Palko v. Connecticut, 302 U.S. 319 (1937) (Dissent)

JAMES FRANCIS BYRNES

Birth: May 2, 1879, Charleston, South Carolina.

Education: St. Patrick's Parochial School (never graduated); studied law privately; admitted to the bar in 1903.

Official Positions: Court reporter, second judicial circuit of South Carolina, 1900–1908; solicitor, second judicial circuit of South Carolina, 1908–1910; U.S. representative, 1911–1925; U.S. senator, 1931–1941; director, Office of Economic Stabilization, 1942–1943; director, Office of War Mobilization, 1943–1945; secretary of state, 1945–1947; governor of South Carolina, 1951–1955.

Supreme Court Service: Nominated associate justice by President Franklin D. Roosevelt, June 12, 1941, to replace James McReynolds, who had retired; confirmed by the Senate, June 12, 1941, by a voice vote; took judicial oath July 8, 1941; resigned October 3, 1942; replaced by Wiley B. Rutledge, appointed by President Roosevelt.

Death: April 9, 1972, Columbia, South Carolina.

Justice Byrnes's memoirs devote but eleven pages to his experience on the Supreme Court, and with good reason: he served only one term. His tenure on the Court was sandwiched between service as a senator from South Carolina and a post bearing the unofficial title of "assistant president," in which he assisted his close friend Franklin D. Roosevelt with domestic and foreign policy during World War II. Byrnes contributed to the Court mainly by enlivening its social life; he regularly gathered the justices for dinner at his home and led them in postprandial songs. Byrnes's short service on the Court and impressive political career combined to truncate his judicial legacy. He was impatient with the Court's slow pace while the world was at war: "I don't think I can stand the abstractions of jurisprudence at a time like this."

By today's standards, his legal training, like his formal education, was incomplete. His father died before his birth, and to help his mother support the family, Byrnes quit school at the age of fourteen and began working as a clerk for Charleston lawyers. In a sense, he was a throwback to the early nineteenth century; he read law as an apprentice in the office of a local judge, who eventually sponsored his admission to the bar. His political ambitions surfaced early, and his career in public service began with his election to Congress in 1910.

His most memorable Supreme Court opinion came in *Edwards v. California* (1942). The case involved a California statute that penalized any resident who brought into the state a person known to be indigent—a law obviously aimed at reducing the number of "Okies" emigrating to California during the Great Depression. Byrnes, influenced by Felix Frankfurter, struck down the law on the grounds that the commerce clause protected the right of citizens to interstate travel. Employing an unfortunate analogy, Byrnes concluded that people, like healthy cattle, ought to be free to cross state lines. His reasoning infuriated the civil libertarians on the Court, particularly William O. Douglas, who believed the statute violated the privileges and immunities clause of the Fourteenth Amendment.

In other decisions, Byrnes exhibited an unremarkable disposition to construe strictly the intent of Congress in interpreting federal statutes. In general, he was a judicial conservative who disdained legislating from the bench. In view of his active participation in the New Deal, however, one suspects that a case involving the powers of the executive would have put Byrnes's convictions to the test. He maintained an ideological distance from the more nationalistic New Dealers Roosevelt appointed to the Court and cleaved instead to centrists such as Frankfurter and Chief Justice Harlan F. Stone. In all, he wrote sixteen majority opinions for the Court, but no concurrences or dissents, a record that leaves his jurisprudence essentially uncharted.

Byrnes eventually revealed his true colors on the major social issue of his day: civil rights. From 1951 to 1955 he served as governor of South Carolina, which furnished one of the cases collectively decided as *Brown v. Board of Education* (1954). As governor, he urged the Eisenhower administration to uphold segregation on the grounds that education was a matter for local authorities to handle and that forced integration would lead to race riots.

—*Victoria Saker Woeste*

James Francis Byrnes

BIBLIOGRAPHY

The only biographical sketch that deals primarily with his Court career is in Friedman and Israel, *Justices,* vol. 4, 2517. His memoirs, *All in One Lifetime* (1958), do not shed much light on the Court. There are several biographies of Byrnes, but understandably none give much emphasis to his judicial career or his legal philosophy.

NOTEWORTHY OPINIONS

Edwards v. California, 314 U.S. 160 (1942)

JOHN ARCHIBALD CAMPBELL

Birth: June 24, 1811, Washington, Georgia.

Education: Franklin College (now the University of Georgia), graduated with first honors, 1825; attended U.S. Military Academy at West Point, 1825–1828.

Official Positions: Alabama state representative, sessions of 1837 and 1843; assistant secretary of war, Confederate States of America, 1862–1865.

Supreme Court Service: Nominated associate justice by President Franklin Pierce, March 21, 1853, to replace Justice John McKinley, who had died; confirmed by the Senate, March 22, 1853, by a voice vote; took judicial oath April 11, 1853; resigned April 30, 1861; replaced by David Davis, nominated by President Abraham Lincoln.

Death: March 12, 1889, Baltimore, Maryland.

John Campbell was a product of the plantation South, and his record on the U.S. Supreme Court reflected his region's identification with a states' rights/strict constructionist interpretation of the Constitution. The son of a Georgia lawyer-planter, Campbell attended Franklin College (now the University of Georgia) and West Point before beginning a legal career at the precocious age of eighteen. He relocated to Alabama in 1830 and established himself as a leader of the legal and mercantile community in Mobile.

Although he was twice elected to the Alabama legislature and twice declined appointment to the state supreme court, Campbell's reputation was built primarily on his record as an effective advocate and his thorough knowledge of the law. His personal law library was reputed to be the most extensive in the United States, and his familiarity with the literature of the Anglo-American and continental legal traditions was said to rival that of Joseph Story. Within Alabama politics, Campbell was identified as a Democrat, but as a member of a faction that favored both a strong southern rights position and the commercial development of the state. This group was loosely identified with South Carolina's John C. Calhoun and the cause of southern nationalism. Campbell freed his slaves on his appointment to the Supreme Court and occasionally speculated on the ultimate demise of the "peculiar institution," but his orientation was generally proslavery.

Campbell was appointed to the Court to replace his fellow Alabaman, John McKinley, who had died in July 1852. The sitting members of the Court urged the newly inaugurated Franklin Pierce to nominate Campbell after observing him argue six separate cases before them during the December 1851 term. On the eve of his confirmation, a correspondent to the *New York Tribune* wrote of Campbell that he was "a gentleman of shining and profound talents, vast legal attainments and withal is irreproachable in character;

but he is a fire-eater [a southern nationalist] of the blazing school."

During his eight years as an associate justice, Campbell wrote 116 opinions, which included 92 majority opinions, 18 dissents, 5 concurrences, and 1 statement. He also dissented eleven additional times without opinion. This pattern reflected the generally high degree of agreement on the Taney Court in the 1850s, which is not surprising, given that nine of the ten judges that served on the Court during Campbell's tenure were identified as Jacksonian Democrats at the time of their appointment.

Campbell concurred with the proslavery majority in *Dred Scott v. Sandford* (1857), the best known of the cases in which he participated. He was also thought to be Chief Justice Roger Taney's choice as his successor, but Campbell's constitutional views differed from those of Taney in important respects. In a number of cases involving the expansion of federal jurisdiction, limitations of state sovereignty, and the rights of corporations, Campbell combined with Justices Peter Daniel and John Catron to form a solid states' rights bloc on the Court in contrast to the moderate nationalism that most of their colleagues embraced. As such, they constituted the first discrete, multimember faction in the Court's history.

During his first term on the Court, Campbell issued powerful dissents rejecting arguments that a corporation could be treated as a citizen for purposes of federal jurisdiction (*Marshall v. Baltimore & Ohio Railroad*, 1853), and that the contracts clause of the Constitution prohibited a state from repealing a previously granted tax exemption (*Piqua v. Knoop*, 1854). He reiterated these views in his dissent in *Dodge v. Woolsey* (1856). In each case, he was joined in dissent by Daniel and Catron. By one count, the Taney Court decided twenty-one constitutional cases between the time of Campbell's appointment in 1853 and the end of the 1858 term. Campbell and Daniel each dissented in six of these cases, doing so jointly on five occasions and being joined by Catron in four.

A unionist in 1861, Campbell did not resign from the Court immediately upon Alabama's January secession; instead, he worked for a peaceable resolution of the sectional crisis. On April 26, however, less than two weeks after President Lincoln's declaration that an "insurrection" existed, Campbell left the Court. During the Civil War, he served as the Confederate assistant secretary of war.

At the end of the conflict, Campbell reestablished himself as one of the South's outstanding lawyers and one of the leading members of the bar of the Supreme Court. He argued at least forty-three cases before his former tribunal, beginning in February 1873 with his representation of the disadvantaged butchers in the *Slaughterhouse Cases* (1873) and concluding with his argument in *Robinson v. Fair* on October 22, 1888. Had he stayed on the Court during the Civil War, as did his fellow southerners Catron and James Wayne, and remained on the bench until his death, he would have served longer

John Archibald Campbell

than any justice in the Court's history except William O. Douglas.

—*Joseph Gordon Hylton*

BIBLIOGRAPHY

The only recent full-length biography of Campbell is R. J. Saunders, *John Archibald Campbell: Southern Moderate, 1811–1899* (1997). His role in Alabama politics, which has often been misunderstood, is explored in J. Mills Thornton III, *Politics and Power in a Slave Society: Alabama, 1800–1860* (1978). For his career after his resignation, see Jonathan Lurie, "Ex-Justice Campbell: The Case of the Creative Advocate," *Journal of Supreme Court History* 30 (2005): 17.

NOTEWORTHY OPINIONS

Marshall v. Baltimore & Ohio Railroad, 57 U.S. 314 (1853) (Dissent)

Piqua v. Knoop, 57 U.S. 369 (1854) (Dissent)

Dodge v. Woolsey, 59 U.S. 331 (1856) (Dissent)

BENJAMIN NATHAN CARDOZO

Birth: May 24, 1870, New York City.

Education: Columbia University, A.B., 1889; A.M., 1891; Columbia Law School, 1891, no degree.

Official Positions: Justice, New York Supreme Court, 1913; judge, New York State Court of Appeals, 1913–1932; chief judge, 1926–1932.

Supreme Court Service: Nominated associate justice by President Herbert Hoover, February 15, 1932, to replace Oliver Wendell Holmes Jr., who had retired; confirmed by the Senate, February 24, 1932, by a voice vote; took judicial oath March 14, 1932; served until July 9, 1938; replaced by Felix Frankfurter, nominated by President Franklin D. Roosevelt.

Death: July 9, 1938, Port Chester, New York.

Benjamin N. Cardozo is generally regarded as being among the most liberal of Supreme Court justices, and that is one of the great ironies of American legal history. A liberal he surely was during his tenure on the Court, but only because his belief in judicial restraint predisposed him to accept congressional statutes regulating the economy. Along with Louis D. Brandeis and Harlan Fiske Stone, Cardozo was one of the three justices most likely to uphold New Deal legislation. But Cardozo's philosophical position was best summed up in the phrase "ordered liberty," which he made famous in *Palko v. Connecticut* (1937). Herbert Hoover had used the same words in his unsuccessful 1932 campaign for reelection, and, in important respects, Cardozo's cautious, middle-of-the-road stance, in which order was as important as liberty, was similar to that of the president who appointed him.

Hoover's nomination of Cardozo to replace Oliver Wendell Holmes Jr. may have been the most popular act of a president whose reputation was otherwise shattered by his inability to solve the problems of the Great Depression. Cardozo, nominally a Democrat, had enjoyed the confidence of all political factions throughout his career as a lawyer, judge, and chief judge. He had written several highly regarded books, the most influential of which was *The Nature of the Judicial Process* (1921). He had received honorary degrees from many universities, including Yale, Harvard, and his alma mater, Columbia. Many of his decisions in areas such as torts, contracts, and liability had influenced judges and courts throughout the United States. Hailed as "a profound scholar, a lucid and courageous thinker and a saintly character," Cardozo was widely regarded as the most suitable successor to the venerable Holmes. As one observer said at the time, "Cardozo is a judge in the fundamental sense of holding the balance even between violently contending shades of thought."

The attempt to hold that balance in the face of the contention surrounding the New Deal would tax even Cardozo's considerable ability. Greatly prizing collegiality and good manners, Cardozo was troubled by the rancor that marked the justices' deliberations and surfaced in their opinions. Personal considerations also made his years on the Supreme Court the unhappiest of Cardozo's professional career. A bachelor, Cardozo had lived for most of his life with his older sister, Ellen, who needed constant medical attention. She had died in 1929, leaving him a lonely man. In Albany, he had resided at the same hotel as the other members of the court of appeals, had enjoyed close personal relations with them, and had found it easy to commute to his home in New York City. In Washington, by contrast, he lived and worked by himself and felt, he often said, as if he were a "homesick exile." Most of the justices did the actual drafting of decisions at their homes, meeting at the Court only to hear arguments, hold weekly conferences, and deliver their opinions. Cardozo was friendly with Justice Stone and, to a lesser extent, with Owen Roberts. Yet he was dismayed by the icy disdain shown to him, as a Jew, by James C. McReynolds, a notorious anti-Semite.

In 1935 and 1936, when the Supreme Court's conservative majority did most of its damage to the New Deal, Cardozo generally sided with the Roosevelt administration. True, in May 1935 he concurred when the Court unanimously struck down the National Industrial Recovery Act (NIRA) on the dual grounds that it represented an overly broad delegation of legislative authority and violated the commerce clause. But Cardozo had earlier been the only justice who had been willing to sustain the NIRA's efforts to raise oil prices by permitting the president to prohibit the interstate shipment of petroleum—so-called "hot oil"—produced in excess of an amount prescribed by state authority in *Panama Refining Co. v. Ryan* (1935). The following year, Cardozo wrote dissenting opinions for the liberal minority in three crucial cases: *Carter v. Carter Coal Co.*, which struck down an act establishing minimum wages and maximum hours in the bituminous coal industry; *Jones v. Securities and Exchange Commission*, which restricted the agency's investigative authority; and *Ashton v. Cameron County Water Improvement Dist. No. One*, which nullified a statute designed to provide bankruptcy relief to state and local governments.

Cardozo was prepared to accept the expansion of federal power under the commerce clause largely because, on his theory of judicial review, the Supreme Court should overturn statutes only when they were clearly arbitrary or oppressive. Nothing revealed his fundamentally cautious view better than another dissenting opinion, also written in 1935, involving a state's right to impose a tax based on a business's gross sales rather than its profits (*Stewart Dry Goods Co. v. Lewis*). In enacting the levy,

Benjamin Nathan Cardozo

Cardozo asserted, the legislature had not acted arbitrarily. It had engaged in

> no act of sheer oppression, no abandonment of reason, no exercise of the general will in a perverse or vengeful spirit. Far from being these or any of them, it is a pursuit of legitimate ends by methods honestly conceived and rationally chosen. More will not be asked by those who have learned from experience and history that government is at best a makeshift, that the attainment of one good may involve the sacrifice of others, and that compromise will be inevitable until the coming of Utopia.

In 1937, when the Court did an about-face and accepted pivotal New Deal measures, Cardozo's commitment to judicial restraint continued to shape his decisions, which were now written for the majority. In *Helvering v. Davis,* the justices upheld the government's authority to impose taxes on employees and employers to fund old-age pensions under the Social Security Act. How, Cardozo asked, was one to decide when Congress was using the spending power in aid of the "general welfare," as Article I, Section 8, of the Constitution required?

> The line must still be drawn between one welfare and another, between particular and general. Where this shall be placed cannot be known through a formula in advance of the event. There is a middle ground or certainly a penumbra in which discretion is at large. The discretion, however, is not confided to the courts. The discretion belongs to Congress, unless the choice is clearly wrong, a display of arbitrary power, and not an exercise of judgment.

Cardozo added that the concept of the general welfare necessarily changed over time: "The hope behind this statute is to save men and women from the rigors of the poor house as well as from the haunting fear that such a lot awaits them when journey's end is near."

Cardozo's approach produced a different outcome when the issue before the Court was not economic regulation but individual rights. One such case involved the University of California's requirement that all able-bodied male undergraduates take four semesters of military science. Two students, both devout members of the Methodist Episcopal Church and conscientious objectors to war, petitioned for an exemption on the grounds that training for war was immoral and contrary to their Christian faith. They were suspended, lost an appeal in the California Supreme Court, and took their case to the U.S. Supreme Court. In *Hamilton v. Regents of the University of California* (1934), the justices unanimously rejected their claim and upheld the requirement. Justice Pierce Butler delivered the majority opinion, but Cardozo wrote a separate concurrence. Conceding that the California regents' requirement "may be condemned by some as unwise or illiberal or unfair when there is violence to conscientious scruples, either religious or merely ethical," Cardozo nevertheless concluded that "more must be shown to set the ordinance at naught. In controversies of this order courts do not concern themselves with matters of legislative policy, unrelated to privileges or liberties secured by the organic law." To grant the exemption, in effect, would be to exalt the right of private judgment "above the powers and the compulsion of the agencies of government."

In cases involving the criminal law, Cardozo's deference to legislative initiative had similar consequences. An early example was *Snyder v. Commonwealth of Massachusetts* (1934). Herman Snyder had been convicted of murdering a gas station attendant during a holdup. During the trial, the judge had taken the jury, the district attorney, and the defense attorney to "view" the scene of the crime but had refused to allow Snyder to be present. The question, then, was whether the judge's decision had deprived the defendant of due process of law under the Fourteenth Amendment. Writing for a narrow five-member majority, Cardozo held that the risk of injustice to the defendant was, at most, a "shadowy" one. Massachusetts, he continued, "is free to regulate the procedure of its courts in accordance with its own conception of policy and fairness, unless in so doing it offends some principle of justice so rooted in the traditions and conscience of our people as to be ranked as fundamental."

The same viewpoint shaped Cardozo's most famous and influential Supreme Court opinion, *Palko v. Connecticut* (1937). Frank Palka (his name was misspelled in the briefs) had been accused of murdering a policeman after burglarizing a store in Bridgeport. Connecticut asked for a first-degree murder conviction, but the jury returned a verdict of second-degree murder after the judge had ruled that a confession was inadmissible. Asserting that the judge had erred, the state won a new trial, at which the confession was admitted and Palka was sentenced to death. The questions before the Supreme Court were whether this constituted double jeopardy and, if so, whether it was forbidden by the Fifth Amendment. Writing for the Court in December 1937, Cardozo decided that there was no double jeopardy, but in any event, the federal prohibition did not apply to the states, by reason of the Fourteenth Amendment's due process clause, because protection against double jeopardy was not "of the very essence of a scheme of ordered liberty."

To substantiate his argument, Cardozo had to explain why some provisions of the Bill of Rights were more fundamental than others and consequently were binding on the states. The due process clause, he reasoned, would indeed prohibit a state from abridging freedom of speech, freedom of the press, the free exercise of religion, the right of peaceable assembly, and the right to benefit of counsel, all of which are "implicit in the concept of ordered liberty." But other rights—such as trial by jury, protection against compulsory self-incrimination, guarantees against double jeopardy—were less deserving of protection. To Cardozo, there was a bright and shining line between the two kinds of rights. With the line clearly drawn, he reasoned, the Court and the people could rest assured that "The edifice of justice stands, its symmetry, to many, greater than before."

Palko was Cardozo's last Supreme Court decision. Shortly after delivering it, he suffered a heart attack, which was followed by a stroke in January 1938. In the six months left to him, he was never able to resume his duties. So he did not live to see how the doctrine of judicial restraint, which in the 1930s had served to legitimize New Deal measures, would later become a chief weapon in the arsenal of conservative critics of the Warren Court's activism. Nor could Cardozo have foreseen that the Warren Court would eventually erase the line he had attempted to draw between rights that were fundamental and those that were not and would declare that the rights he had considered peripheral were, in fact, essential to American liberty.

—*Richard Polenberg*

BIBLIOGRAPHY

Most of Benjamin Cardozo's personal papers were destroyed after his death, but some letters may be found in collections at Columbia University and the American Jewish Archives. For Cardozo's extrajudicial writings and essays, see Margaret Hall, ed., *Selected Writings of Benjamin Nathan Cardozo* (1947). The only full-scale biography is Andrew L. Kaufman, *Cardozo* (1998). His jurisprudence is examined in Richard Polenberg, *The World of Benjamin Cardozo: Personal Values and the Judicial Process* (1997); and Stanley Charles Brubaker's unpublished doctoral dissertation, "Benjamin Nathan Cardozo: An Intellectual Biography" (University of Virginia, 1979). For an early assessment, see Beryl Harold Levy, *Cardozo and Frontiers of Legal Thinking, with Selected Opinions* (1938). For a modern view, see Richard A. Posner, *Cardozo: A Study in Reputation* (1990).

NOTEWORTHY OPINIONS

Snyder v. Massachusetts, 291 U.S. 97 (1934)

Hamilton v. Regents of the University of California, 293 U.S. 245 (1934) (Concurrence)

Jones v. Securities and Exchange Commission, 298 U.S. 1 (1936) (Dissent)

Carter v. Carter Coal Co., 298 U.S. 238 (1936) (Dissent)

Ashton v. Cameron County Water Improvement Dist. No. One, 298 U.S. 513 (1936) (Dissent)

Helvering v. Davis, 301 U.S. 619 (1937)

Palko v. Connecticut, 302 U.S. 319 (1937)

JOHN CATRON

Birth: Circa 1786, Pennsylvania or Virginia.

Education: Self-educated.

Official Positions: Judge, Tennessee Supreme Court of Errors and Appeals, 1824–1831; first chief justice of Tennessee, 1831–1834.

Supreme Court Service: Nominated associate justice by President Andrew Jackson, March 3, 1837, to fill a newly created seat; confirmed by the Senate March 8, 1837, by a 28–15 vote, took judicial oath May 1, 1837; served until May 30, 1865; seat abolished by Congress.

Death: May 30, 1865, Nashville, Tennessee.

Little is certain of John Catron's earliest years, not even the state or year of his birth. He grew up poor in Virginia, then Kentucky, moved to Tennessee's Cumberland Mountains, and served under Andrew Jackson in the War of 1812. Largely self-educated, he gained admission to the Tennessee bar in 1815 and thereafter began a rapid ascent.

Relocating to the state capital, Nashville, in 1818, Catron successfully invested in the early Tennessee iron industry while building a profitable practice centered on land title litigation, then a massive Tennessee problem. His 1824 appointment to the Tennessee Supreme Court had its source in legislators' knowledge that he favored confirmation of de facto landholders despite title defects. In 1829 he fortified his Jacksonian political credentials statewide by publishing articles that anticipated Jackson's first presidential message to Congress attacking the Bank of the United States. Catron was named Tennessee's chief justice in 1831, and during the nullification crisis he was instrumental in causing Tennessee to fall in behind Jackson. An 1834 reorganization of the state judiciary elimi-

nated the chief justiceship, and, briefly back in private practice, Catron managed the 1836 Tennessee campaign for Jackson's designated successor, Martin Van Buren. On his last day as president, Jackson nominated Catron to the U.S. Supreme Court.

Catron's twenty-eight-year term of Supreme Court service has been exceeded by only 13 of the 110 justices appointed since 1789. During Catron's second year on the Court, Chief Justice Roger Taney wrote to Jackson: "I have been impressed with . . . his judgment, legal knowledge, and high integrity . . . a most valuable acquisition to the . . . Supreme Court." Late nineteenth-century justices still cited Catron's opinions as did, for example, Stephen Field in *Bowman v. Chicago and North Western Railway* (1888): Referring to Catron as "the learned justice," Field wrote, "The language of Mr. Justice Catron on this subject . . . is instructive. . . ."

Scholars have been widely divided over Catron's jurisprudence. Writing in 1898, Joshua Caldwell placed Catron in the Taney Court's doctrinal middle, between "high-toned Federalists" James Wayne, John

McLean, and Benjamin Curtis and an anti-Federalist bloc of Taney, Levi Woodbury, Peter Daniel, and Samuel Nelson. Caldwell found in Catron's opinions a "leaning toward Federalist principles . . . rather surprising . . . as he had been a lifelong friend of Andrew Jackson." Contrariwise, John Schmidhauser in 1961 placed Taney at the Court's center and Catron among the pro-southern "extreme justices." More recently, Frank Otto Gatell described Catron as following "a reasonable line between . . . federal and state power, with a preferential bias . . . [for] the latter," whereas John Scheb concluded that throughout his tenure "Catron was a stalwart defender of states' rights and of . . . slavery."

Not all of these scholars can be on target, and Caldwell and Gatell come closer than Scheb and Schmidhauser. The interpretive difficulties stem less from Catron's politically complex jurisprudence than from missing its underlying ordering of values. By focusing too heavily on best-remembered constitutional decisions, scholars have neglected other significant "telltale texts," especially Catron's state opinions concerning slaves and his federal opinions in other areas prominent on the nineteenth century's public agenda. An additional confusion may be in assuming that a justice politically active in off-duty hours, which Catron certainly was, would be a jurisprudential activist, which Catron frequently was not.

First, Catron's support of slavery fell short of "fire-eating" status. Unlike some southern justices who found threats to slavery lurking under many a federalism or economic issue, Catron often seemed chiefly driven by other considerations. Respecting federal powers, these considerations included sustaining a Jacksonian model of a fairly powerful presidency and preventing states from impinging unduly on the commerce powers of Congress.

Catron's states' rights jurisprudence poses a complex puzzle. The clue is that he did not entirely share the common states' rights view that less federal power was almost always desirable. His regional reflexes were both new western (when the West meant "trans-Appalachian") and old southern. The West wanted geographic expan-sion and economic modernization and, on issues such as federal admiralty jurisdiction and the disposition of public lands, unlike the old South, sometimes saw federal power as beneficial. But on one major issue, the contract clause's limitations on state legislatures modifying contracts, the two regions eyed the same enemy—entrenched, northeastern capital—and wanted a weak clause. In contract clause cases, Catron's decision making closely resembled that of his two strongly sectional southern colleagues, Alabama's John Campbell and Virginia's Peter Daniel.

Before considering how Catron's western orientation played out in other areas, it is helpful to examine several slavery cases from Catron's Tennessee court years and his related, unique pattern in federal slavery cases. *Bob v. State* (1830) found Catron dis-

John Catron

playing "text-bound" judicial passivism in dissenting from overriding a state circuit judge's refusal to grant a slave's appeal of a death sentence. Catron considered the lower court trials unfair. "I have never known any person convicted ... upon evidence so slight," he declared, but thought an 1811 statute vested absolute discretion to grant or refuse an appeal in the circuit judge. Catron's colleagues, John Haywood and Jacob Peck, asserting "color, rank, or station can make no difference," decided the circuit judge's discretion was not arbitrary "to do as he pleases, but to discover ... what is right, ... otherwise his unrighteous discretion shall be purified."

When not constrained by statute, Catron joined decisions that put the Tennessee court to the left of other southern courts. For example, a white murderer of a slave was held subject to common law conviction after acquittal of the statutory crime in *Fields v. State* (1829), a case later scorned by the Georgia court as the "wholly untenable" consequence of "fervid zeal in behalf of humanity to the slave" (*Neal v. Farmer*, 1851). A slave, winning freedom in one suit, was permitted to bring another suit seeking monetary damages in *Matilda v. Crenshaw* (1833).

Telling was Catron's rejection of other slave states' resolutions of a thorny issue: did the unmentioned children of a slave mother with a bequest of future freedom eventually go free also or were they doomed to lifelong slavery? The Kentucky and Virginia courts had already decided on slavery, but in *Harris v. Clarissa* (1834), Catron stated that "we are not satisfied" with the Kentucky court's reasoning and that the Virginia decision was "a most strict construction, not to say a strained one, in prejudice of human liberty."

Catron's unique approach developed from the first two major Supreme Court slavery cases. He was the only southern justice to find unnecessary a qualifying concurrence with, or a dissent from, northerner Joseph Story's Court opinions in the *Amistad* case (1841), which awarded freedom to black mutineers on a ship engaged in illegal slave trading, and in *Prigg v. Pennsylvania* (1842), which held void state laws that conflicted with exclusive federal power under the fugitive slave clause.

Catron eschewed the southern proclivity for bringing slavery issues into nonslavery cases. In fact, in *Strader v. Graham* (1850) and *Dred Scott v. Sandford* (1857), when slaves unsuccessfully argued that northern sojourns gave them freedom, Catron brought nonslavery issues into slavery cases. Catron's *Dred Scott* concurrence that the 1820 Missouri Compromise was unconstitutional limited its passivist differences with Taney's sweeping opinion to opposing as unnecessary Taney's ruling that blacks could not bring suit in federal court. He also made a plaintive reference to a nonslavery implication of Taney's pruning of congressional power over territories:

It is due to myself to say that it is asking much of a judge who has for nearly twenty years been exercising jurisdiction from the western Missouri line to the Rocky Mountains and, on this understanding of the Constitution, inflicting the extreme penalty of death for crimes committed where the direct legislation of Congress was the only rule, to agree that he had been all the while acting in mistake, and as an usurper.

The better example is *Strader*. It had reached the Court seven years earlier, almost contemporaneously with Catron's taking positions incompatible with southern extremism: favoring Oregon's admission as a free state, thundering in his Nashville courtroom against southern expansionists bent on invading and extending slavery to Cuba, and holding that the 1850 Fugitive Slave Act, repealing its 1793 predecessor, aborted the pending suit of a slave owner to recover $500 from one who had aided his slave's escape. Taney's *Strader* opinion cited, somewhat misleadingly, one precedent that Catron had written, *Permoli v. First Municipality of New Orleans* (1845), and another from which Catron had dissented, *Pollard v. Hagan* (1845), and tossed out the entire 1787 Northwest Ordinance as superseded by the Constitution's 1789 ratification. As its third article had prohibited slavery northwest of the Ohio, the ordinance was anathema to ardent slavery supporters who saw the best course as holding precisely what Taney did.

Catron, together with the Court's fiercest opponent of slavery, John McLean, objected that jettisoning the ordinance's other five articles was *"obiter dictum uncalled for."* Catron particularly objected to voiding the fourth article's provision of perpetual rights to free, untaxed navigation of the Mississippi and St. Lawrence River systems. He saw in this provision—and liked—the potential for an *intrastate* federal power over navigation, a federal power additional to congressional powers over *interstate* commerce and to the federal judiciary's admiralty powers. Taney, on the other hand, saw the potential for limiting state power—and did not like it.

That not deciding more than necessary was an independent value for Catron is suggested by its appearance in issues other than slavery. *McCracken v. Hayward* (1844) provides an illustration. Catron refused to join in holding, contrary to the contract clause, an Illinois stay law barring the sale of debtor's property at less than two-thirds of real worth. He preferred the narrower course of voiding a circuit court rule that had made the Illinois statute enforceable. Similarly indicative were his criticisms of opinions by Taney and Story, the Court's chief rivals during Catron's first decade. Although he concurred in *Swift v. Tyson* (1842), Catron criticized Story's opinion for deciding an unnecessary additional issue rather than waiting "until it fairly arose," and he correctly predicted some state courts would not follow Story's dictum. When Taney, in *Cutler v. Rae* (1849), rushed to decide an admiralty jurisdiction issue without prior written or oral argument, and unionist justice James Wayne, a Georgian, called that a regrettable "first" in the Court's history, Catron completely refused to participate in deciding the case.

Catron's capacity for a lonely, nationalist path was well displayed in *Pollard v. Hagan* (1845), a case that he "deemed the most important controversy ever brought before this court, either as . . . respects the amount of property involved, or the principles." Evaluations of importance change, but modern legal

scholars appear to have overlooked that the majority's ruling contradicts the received wisdom that between *Marbury v. Madison* in 1803 and the Civil War, the Court only once, in *Dred Scott*, ruled a congressional enactment void. At stake was title to Mobile, Alabama, properties created by filling in tidelands, chiefly by the labors of small landowners. Eight justices held that the "equal footing doctrine" (under which new states were admitted on terms no less favorable than the original thirteen) coupled with an earlier case awarding title to certain oyster beds to New Jersey, as sovereign heir to rights of the British Crown, required upholding the Alabama Supreme Court's award of title to Alabama, and in turn to claimants other than the fillers-in of the tidal lands.

Catron, objecting that at stake in *Pollard* was U.S. sovereignty, took a nationalist position similar to the New Deal Court's in the tidal oil lands controversy of the 1940s and 1950s (*United States v. California,* 1947). Catron argued that provisions for federal ownership of these lands written into the 1819 congressional act admitting Alabama to the Union, as well as 1824 and 1836 congressional acts confirming claims deriving from federal title, should be controlling.

Pulsing beneath Catron's *Pollard* opinion was another Jacksonian motivation—preference for the small entrepreneur and diligent settler. It was the same new West disposition to settle title doubts in favor of pioneers that had led to his state court appointment. It burst through the surface of his writing in California controversies pitting eastern corporations' claims under often fraudulent pre-1848 Mexican "floating grants" ("floating" because the boundaries were ill-defined) versus farmer-settlers' claims under federal preemption laws. There was no doubt where Catron's populist heart lay, as can also be seen in his dissent in *Fremont v. United States* (1854):

> Cultivators of the soil should . . . [be] safe from the ruin that lurks in a floating claim, familiar to western ploughmen, many of whom remember exhausting litigation in their own families for the paternal hearth, and who relied on the

firm and consistent decisions of this court to protect their new homes on the Pacific.

Western and southern interests dovetailed in corporation cases, and Catron often backed his southern colleagues' desire to minimize protective federal jurisdiction extending "person-like" or "citizen-like" status to corporations, as when he dissented with Daniel and Campbell in *Marshall v. Baltimore & Ohio Railroad* (1854). Catron also shared these colleagues' hostility to allowing broad coverage to wealthy or corporate patent holders. Certainly, class-consciousness is apparent in his objection to the 5–4 ruling in *Hogg v. Emerson* (1850) that allowed the holder of letters-patent on one steam engine improvement to add later, via a patent schedule, what Catron saw as two separate inventions, and then sue for an infringement of the latter. Catron argued that treating the three as a unity undercut the salutary limiting of patents to single inventions. If three could be run together, any number may be. What would result? And "although the claim may be fictitious, still this does not protect the public from harassment, as usually men using cheap implements cannot afford to litigate in the United States Courts."

When new western aims (that would be enhanced by greater national power) and old southern aims (that would be hindered) diverged, Catron's decision making sometimes stammered—as in federal admiralty jurisdiction, which Hamiltonian proponents of rapid industrialization wanted to expand against the wishes of Jeffersonian agrarians. English law had limited admiralty jurisdiction to tide-affected waters. An inadvertently well-named 1825 decision, *The Thomas Jefferson,* had retained English limits.

The Taney Court majority first ventured in a new direction by accepting evidence of what Justice Robert Grier, an expansionist, sarcastically dubbed "occult tides" invisibly present at inland locations and extending federal jurisdiction to places such as, in *Waring v. Clarke* (1847), a Mississippi River collision scene almost 100 miles north of New Orleans. In *Propeller Genesee Chief v. Fitzhugh* (1852), the majority upheld an 1845 act extending federal jurisdiction to

the Great Lakes. Where Daniel dissented consistently, Catron either wrote cautious concurrences (as in *Waring*) or voted with the majority (as in *Genesee Chief*). As the Civil War approached, he zigzagged, siding with southerners on some issues and with northern expansionists on others.

Once armed conflict began, Catron's order of values became swiftly clear: Union, national government, West—all first; secession, South, last; and the future of slavery, a dependent variable, on the back burner. Catron's wartime actions were hard-line Unionist. When Campbell resigned his seat and joined the Confederacy, Catron hastened to hold circuit court in Kentucky, then on secession's brink. When Taney, back in Baltimore, issued *habeas corpus* for a suspected traitor held in military custody and chastised Lincoln verbally, Catron, holding court in Missouri, refused *habeas corpus* and blistered secessionists in his comments. Catron paid for his stance. Returning to his Nashville home in the wake of Tennessee newspaper reports of his Missouri comments, he was threatened by Confederate vigilantes who gave him twenty-four hours to resign his Supreme Court seat or get out of town. He chose to leave Nashville, even though the consequence was confiscation by the rebel government of $90,000 of his property. He declined to uphold the presidential embargo in the *Prize Cases* (1863), but he was not afraid to issue a writ for arrest of the Kentucky governor and to uphold the confiscation of a pro-Confederacy newspaper in *United States v. Republican Banner Officers,* an 1863 circuit holding. Catron lived just long enough to see the final surrender of the Confederacy; the Court's most ardent Jacksonian died May 30, 1865.

—*A. E. Keir Nash*

BIBLIOGRAPHY

The scarcity of, and conflict among, secondary sources about even elementary facts of Catron's life is astonishing, requiring unusual reliance on deduction from the cases and on the Catron papers in the Tennessee State Archives in Nashville. A fair amount of relevant data and sensible interpretation are scattered through Carl B. Swisher, *The Taney Period, 1836–1864* (1974), volume 5, in the *Oliver Wendell Holmes Devise History.*

See also Joshua Caldwell, *Sketches of the Bench and Bar of Tennessee* (1898); Frank Otto Gatell, "John Catron," in Friedman and Israel, *Justices,* vol. 1, 737; John Schmidhauser, "Judicial Behavior and the Sectional Crisis of 1837–1860," *Journal of Politics* (1961); and John M. Scheb II, "John Catron," in Kermit L. Hall, ed., *The Oxford Companion to the Supreme Court of the United States* (1992).

NOTEWORTHY OPINIONS

Pollard v. Hagan, 44 U.S. 212 (1845) (Dissent)

License Cases, 46 U.S. 504 (1847) (Dissent)

Piqua Branch of State Bank of Ohio v. Knoop, 57 U.S. 369 (1854) (Dissent)

Dred Scott v. Sandford, 60 U.S. 393 (1857) (Concurrence)

SALMON PORTLAND CHASE

Birth: January 13, 1808, Cornish, New Hampshire.

Education: Dartmouth College, 1826.

Official Positions: U.S. senator, 1849–1855, 1861; governor of Ohio, 1856–1860; secretary of the Treasury, 1861–1864.

Supreme Court Service: Nominated chief justice by President Abraham Lincoln, December 6, 1864, to replace Chief Justice Roger B. Taney, who had died; confirmed by the Senate, December 6, 1864, by a voice vote; took judicial oath December 15, 1864; served until May 7, 1873; replaced by Morrison R. Waite, appointed by President Ulysses S. Grant.

Death: May 7, 1873, New York City.

One of ten children born to a New Hampshire farmer-legislator, Chase moved to Ohio in 1820 with his uncle, an Episcopal bishop, three years after his father's death left the family impoverished. He graduated Phi Beta Kappa from Dartmouth College in 1826, briefly considered a career in the ministry, but instead studied law—and politics—in Washington, D.C., as an apprentice to Attorney General William Wirt. Admitted to the bar in Cincinnati, he established a successful practice and then involved himself in various reform causes, especially temperance and antislavery. By the 1840s Chase's earnest but radical views on slavery and his legal efforts on behalf of runaways earned him the label "Attorney General for the Runaway Negroes."

Although active in Whig and then Liberty Party politics from the 1830s, Chase did not hold public office until 1849. The compromise choice of the state legislature for U.S. senator from Ohio, once in Washington Chase opposed the Kansas-Nebraska Act and participated in the anti-Nebraska movements that led to formation of the Republican Party. Chase returned to Ohio in 1855 and won two terms as governor before gaining election again to the Senate, this time as a Republican. An unsuccessful candidate for the Republican presidential nomination in 1860, he joined the Lincoln administration as secretary of the Treasury and skillfully managed wartime finances. He resigned abruptly from the cabinet in 1864 and considered running against the president, but eventually declined to do so. After the election, Lincoln fulfilled earlier promises to Radical Republicans by nominating Chase to succeed Roger B. Taney, who had died two months before, as chief justice.

Chase's staunch opposition to slavery and his alliance with congressional radicals caused concern among political conservatives, but the new chief justice steered a moderate course. He was, in truth, a one-issue radical. He emphasized the national character of freedom and insisted on equality before the law for all citizens: the Declaration of Independence, the Constitution's general welfare provision, and the Bill of Rights contained individual rights that the nation should protect in the states. On other issues, especially fiscal and monetary matters, Chase held conservative views. A states' rights nationalist, he believed the federal government, although supreme, had no permanent role in state affairs so long as states treated equally all residents engaged in lawful pursuits. Above all, Chase was pragmatic: law, like politics, required compromise. His pragmatism served him well on the Court.

Few men have become chief justice with a more thorough grounding in the art of governing, and Chase needed these political skills because he assumed leadership of a weakened Court struggling to regain its stature as an equal branch of government. The self-inflicted wound of *Dred Scott v. Sandford* (1857) had damaged the Court's reputation, and the emergencies of war had shifted power decisively to the president and Congress. At first, the opportunities to restore the balance appeared meager. Trivial issues crowded the docket, much to the dismay of the activist Chase. Missing were the momentous race-centered concerns that occupied the attention of Congress and the president. Also absent were important issues about the nature of a reconstructed Union and its impact on prewar understandings of federal-state power.

This state of affairs changed quickly beginning in 1865. Although few decisions during Chase's tenure addressed matters of race, questions about Recon-

Salmon Portland Chase

struction loomed large on the Court's agenda. Also important were economic and social issues given impetus by the Civil War, issues that reflected the nation's nascent transformation from an agrarian to an industrial power. Led by Chase, the justices took advantage of the cases before them. By 1867 the Court had seized a far greater share of federal power than had seemed possible a scant three years earlier. By the time of Chase's death in 1873, the Court had regained near equality with the legislative and executive branches, at times aggressively extending its authority to review state and national actions. Symbolic of this renewed authority was the Court's invalidation of congressional statutes. Before 1865 only two acts of Congress had ever been declared unconstitutional; by 1873 the total was twelve, seven of them since 1869.

Yet for all its assertiveness, a cautious moderation was the dominant tone on the Chase Court. The justices reflected the uncertainties and divisions of the Reconstruction era, when Congress and president vied for the power to set conditions for the rebellious states' reentry into the Union. They also sat during a gradual shift from an instrumentalist to a formalist conception of law. Antebellum jurists and commentators had accepted the state legislatures' right to use law as an instrument of social and economic policy, even if it meant abandoning precedent or modifying rights, especially property rights. Although permissive instrumentalism was still the norm in 1865, Civil War experiences tempered its thrust. Not only did war aims emphasize individual and minority rights, but the conflict also spurred the creation of a national market and raised constitutional questions about the role of state legislatures in the regulation of business and interstate commerce. Legal theorists increasingly promoted formalism, or an emphasis on formal legal procedures and judicial review, as a means of protecting many kinds of individual rights from legislative interference, including property rights of the corporation, recognized in law as an artificial person. Taken as a whole, the Chase Court's decisions reflected these various conflicts, serving as a bridge between two political and constitutional eras.

Before the Chase Court, no group of justices had ever been as politically oriented as this one. Each justice maintained close political connections outside the Court. More important, the associate justices generally held conceptions of national power different from the Republican Congress, which took an expansive view of its constitutional authority. Three justices—Robert C. Grier, Nathan Clifford, and Samuel Nelson—were holdover appointees of prosouthern Democratic presidents before the war, and these justices clung to a narrow view of federal constitutional power. Two others—John Catron, who died in 1865, and James Wayne—had been appointed by Andrew Jackson and shared his states' rights nationalism. Even most of the justices appointed by Lincoln held more conservative views than Congress, especially its radical Republican bloc. The headstrong Stephen J. Field was a "War Democrat" who supported the Union but held an antimajoritarian, laissez-faire conception of federal power in peacetime. Lincoln's friend and political ally, David Davis, was a moderate Republican who ultimately left the party over the impeachment of Andrew Johnson. Only Noah Swayne and Samuel Miller, together with Chase, were initially sympathetic to the arguments of congressional radicals that the federal government could override state power to achieve Reconstruction policies or that Congress's authority in these matters was greater than the president's.

As chief justice, Chase faced several challenges: managing the Court's affairs so as not to create factions among his colleagues; claiming an independent role for the Court in the struggle between Congress and president over Reconstruction; addressing the changed nature of federal-state relations that resulted from the Civil War; securing the rights of all citizens as promised by the Union victory; and helping the Court to reconcile the constitutional problems posed by the new industrial economy and the shift in law from instrumentalism toward formalism. In all five areas, his political skills proved useful.

Chase was foremost a politician, even while serving as the nation's highest judicial officer. He neither hid his interest in politics nor severed his political connections. So strong was his attachment that, in 1868, he actively considered another bid for the Republican presidential nomination. His political experience and connections were not unmixed blessings, however, because his deeply felt commitment to equal rights for black Americans was often at odds with majority public sentiment. Also, at times an aloof and formal personal manner blunted his effectiveness as a conciliator. Still, it is questionable whether a less-experienced chief justice could have maneuvered the Court successfully through the politically charged postwar climate.

The dominant issues before the Court during Chase's tenure concerned the scope of national power. Many of the cases, though not all, addressed the constitutionality of wartime and Reconstruction measures. At first—and on an issue that arose from prewar actions—the Court proceeded quietly, extending legal doctrines from the Taney era that upheld national power, while in the process creating doctrines that increased options for the justices. The pivotal case involved bond litigation from Iowa. In *Gelpcke v. Dubuque* (1863), the Court greatly expanded its review power over state court judgments by requiring Iowa to honor municipal bonds that the Iowa Supreme Court had held to be invalid. The decision was popular with creditors. When combined with the Taney Court's ruling in *Swift v. Tyson* (1842), it allowed federal courts through the 1930s to oversee municipal debts, contracts, and tort liability, among other matters. For Chase, the case sustained the nation's authority in terms reminiscent of his predecessor's views, especially later when the chief justice joined the majority in upholding Taney's innovative use of the Court's *mandamus* power to compel Iowa's compliance with its decision. It also justified federal judicial restraints on state excesses, an issue that arose often during Reconstruction.

Other actions from 1864 and 1865 reveal the chief justice and his colleagues working in less-visible ways to restore the Court's credibility and to reassert its independence. One of Chase's first acts as chief was to admit a black attorney, John S. Rock of Massachusetts, into practice, the first so honored. Although not predictive of the Court's halting decisions on civil rights, the symbolism of an African American at work where the *Dred Scott* decision had been issued less than a decade earlier was a powerful restorative of public confidence. In another gesture, Chase ordered the clerk to list West Virginia as a state on the Court's docket, thereby confirming Lincoln's recognition of its wartime separation from Confederate Virginia. A more substantive action was Chase's brief opinion denying Supreme Court jurisdiction of appeals assigned to it by an 1855 statute establishing a federal court of appeals. The decision was only the fourth time that the Court had invalidated a federal law or a portion of it, and it foreshadowed the Court's later vigorous use of judicial review, yet avoided a confrontation with either Congress or the president.

The Court in 1866 and 1867 decided against congressional and state laws in three cases that directly involved Reconstruction, but not always with the full support of its chief. The first such case was *Ex parte Milligan* (1866), testing the constitutionality of an 1864 military trial and death sentence for an Indiana man convicted of disloyal activities in a state where civilian courts remained open. The justices held unanimously that the military had not followed the requirements of the 1863 Habeas Corpus Act requiring it to report civilian prisoners to the local federal district court. But Chase and three justices differed from the majority on the basic point of whether the judiciary could decide when a crisis justified the use of military courts. To the chief justice, this issue, like Reconstruction policy generally, was political, not

legal; it was for Congress and the president to decide, not the courts.

The adverse implications of this decision for Reconstruction became clear a few months later in early 1867 with the *Test Oath Cases (Ex parte Garland; Cummings v. Missouri)*. The justices concluded, 5–4, that the congressional and state loyalty oaths required of southern activists and sympathizers violated the Constitution's ban on *ex post facto* laws and bills of attainder. Chase joined in Miller's dissent. Although later calling the state oath "detestable," Chase explained in an 1870 letter that he believed it safer not to interfere with a state's right to regulate its internal concerns. The chief justice was able to reconcile his support of radical Reconstruction with his advocacy of "freedom national," the belief that the Constitution protected liberty for all citizens against state restraints. In this instance, the state had withheld the privileges of full civil participation from individuals who acted willfully against its interests. Chase was also concerned that the *Test Oath Cases,* when combined with *Milligan,* sharply diminished the ability of federal and state governments to prevent former rebels from controlling the governments of the reconstructed states.

Chase's support of congressional policies on Reconstruction stemmed from his belief, shared by the Radical Republicans, that the war had changed the American constitutional system. Nowhere was this change more evident than in the 1865 adoption of the Thirteenth Amendment. Although subsequent interpretations restricted its meaning to the elimination of slavery, Chase took a much broader interpretation in the circuit court case *In re Turner* (1867), when he upheld the Civil Rights Act of 1866 under the Thirteenth Amendment in the course of striking down an apprenticeship law for blacks. He clearly viewed the amendment as the triumph of the abolitionists' broader goal to nationalize the right to freedom. And the amendment also required Congress to enforce this open-ended right, which Chase defined in terms of the Declaration of Independence and Bill of Rights, a definition that suggested the equality of all citizens. Finally, it kept open, perhaps required, the possibility of black suffrage. The vote, Chase believed, gave all men, black and white, the ability to protect their and their neighbors' welfare.

In the *Milligan* and *Test Oath Cases,* the chief justice had balanced his support of congressional reconstruction with his desire to maintain the Court's independence as a coequal branch of government. Rather than challenge Congress, as a majority of his colleagues appeared ready to do—a challenge the Court was sure to lose—Chase argued that reconstructing the Union was a political rather than a judicial process. This pragmatic stance allowed the Court to avoid confrontation while preserving its authority to address future Reconstruction legislation.

Chase's success in winning support for this position can be seen in subsequent Reconstruction cases. In two 1867 decisions, *Mississippi v. Johnson* and *Georgia v. Stanton,* the chief justice led a unanimous Court in refusing to accept jurisdiction or rule on the constitutionality of the Reconstruction Acts of March 1867 establishing military governments in the former Confederate states. Chase, invoking the separation of powers principle in his opinion, recognized the impracticality of issuing an injunction against the president. More important, he wisely kept the Court from using a dubious opportunity to declare the Reconstruction Acts unconstitutional, which isolated it from the brewing conflict between the president and Congress over who would set the terms of Reconstruction.

The same pragmatic assessment of political realities governed the Court's action in subsequent Reconstruction cases during Chase's tenure. In *Ex parte McCardle* (1868), which occurred during and shortly after the impeachment of President Andrew Johnson, a Mississippi editor convicted of writing incendiary articles about Reconstruction questioned the authority of the Congress to establish military tribunals to try civilians. When Chase, speaking for the Court, concluded that it could hear McCardle's *habeas corpus* petition under an 1867 statute, Congress changed the law to prevent the justices from considering this challenge to its authority. A year later the justices unanimously dismissed McCardle's suit, although Chase's opinion emphasized the Court's general power of review.

As the Court considered these cases, Chase faced a different challenge, one that ultimately separated him from many of his former abolitionist colleagues. The House of Representatives impeached President Johnson for violating the Tenure of Office Act, a measure requiring the Senate to approve dismissals of any executive appointee it had confirmed. Chase, as chief justice, was the presiding officer at the trial in the Senate. For some time, Chase had been moving away from positions held by congressional radicals who wanted to use military government to ensure the proper reconstruction of southern states. Early in 1867 he questioned the legitimacy of continued military rule and refused to sit with the circuit court wherever military rule existed. By the summer of that year he openly advocated a less harsh policy toward the South. Although the Court under his leadership had avoided a direct confrontation with Congress, the *McCardle* case suggested that differences could not be submerged indefinitely.

Chase prepared diligently for his role as presiding judge, carefully studying the history and law of impeachment. He insisted that the Senate follow court rules and clashed frequently with a prosecution that often proceeded on political grounds. Twice overruled on important evidentiary matters, Chase nevertheless won much sympathy and support for his efforts to require the Senate to conduct itself as a judicial rather than a legislative body. The trial had another effect on the chief justice: it led to his decision to break with his fellow Republicans. After 1868, when he unsuccessfully pursued the Democratic presidential nomination, Chase was much less involved in partisan matters, even though his political interests and ambitions did not wane.

After *McCardle,* the *Test Oath Cases,* and the impeachment trial, Reconstruction issues faded from the Court's docket, at least for the remainder of Chase's tenure. A major exception was *Texas v. White* (1869), in which the reconstructed state government tried to recover bonds sold by the Confederate government to pay for the war effort. For the majority, Chase endorsed the theory of congressional reconstruction as expressed in the Reconstruction Acts of

1867, that the Constitution had created a nation, even as it had invested certain powers in the states: "The Constitution, in all its provisions," he wrote, "looks to an indestructible Union, composed of indestructible states." The rebellious states had forfeited their rights. Congress, under its constitutional power to guarantee republican governments, had the power to set the terms for their reentry to the Union. Significantly, Chase pointedly avoided ruling on the constitutionality of the Military Reconstruction Acts, following the Court's previous stance that reconstruction was a political question, not a judicial one.

Late in 1869 the Supreme Court faced another wartime issue, the constitutionality of the Legal Tender Act of 1862, in *Hepburn v. Griswold,* decided in February 1870. The act, which Chase had supported as a necessary expedient during his days at Treasury, had created a government-issued paper currency, "greenbacks," to finance the war effort. This inflationary currency also could be used to retire debts incurred before 1862, even if the original contract called for repayment in specie, or gold and silver. The justices divided sharply over the case, with Chase leading a 5–4 majority in declaring the act unconstitutional as it applied to contracts made before the measure became law. The decision was highly controversial. Republicans bitterly condemned Chase for reversing his earlier position, and Democrats generally applauded. Critics especially feared that the Court would extend its ruling to contracts made subsequent to the 1862 law, thus disrupting financial markets.

The controversy heightened when President Ulysses S. Grant appointed two new justices, William Strong and Joseph P. Bradley, both assumed to oppose the *Hepburn* decision, and the attorney general moved for a reconsideration of the case. The motion created a bitter dispute among the justices, with Chase pitted against Miller, the leader of the minority in the earlier case. Chase made every effort to keep the case from being reopened, but lost. A new 5–4 majority in the *Legal Tender Cases* (1871) held that the notes were valid for repayment of both prior and subsequent debts.

Chase's failing health—he suffered a series of strokes in 1870—limited his activities on the bench for the remainder of his term. Although his condition improved during 1872, he was never able to write effectively, his speech remained partially slurred, and his ability to lead the Court waned markedly. He closed his career by joining the dissent in the *Slaughterhouse Cases* (1873), announced three weeks before his death. His role was minor; he offered no separate opinion. But the case, which limited the scope of the Fourteenth Amendment and restricted the ability of the federal government to protect citizens against the states, offered the chief justice one last chance to reaffirm his belief in equal rights for blacks, a principle that he had promoted throughout his public life.

Chase was a worthy heir to the legacy of his predecessors, Marshall and Taney. The Court under his leadership substantially increased its jurisdiction, influence, and reputation. Chase helped the Court invigorate and extend judicial review, even though at times the justices appeared to differ with Congress over policy, not constitutionality, a result that foreshadowed the actions of subsequent Courts. Under Chase, the Court's Reconstruction decisions—or, more often, its nondecisions—placed the justices squarely in the middle of national politics. But the chief justice led his colleagues to exercise their newfound authority with discretion and always with a pragmatic and essentially conservative view to what was possible. This, indeed, was his greatest achievement and his greatest legacy as a jurist: he skillfully guided the Supreme Court through the trying years of Reconstruction to reclaim its place as a coequal branch of the federal government.

—*David J. Bodenhamer*

BIBLIOGRAPHY

Important manuscript collections for Salmon Chase can be found at the Library of Congress and the Historical Society of Pennsylvania. Edward G. Bourne et al., eds., "Diary and Correspondence of Salmon P. Chase," *Annual Report of the American Historical Association,* vol. 2 (1902), offers a valuable collection of several hundred Chase letters over his entire career. The best recent study is John Niven, *Salmon P. Chase: A Biography* (1995).

Charles Fairman, *History of the Supreme Court of the United States,* vol. 6, *Reconstruction and Reunion, 1864–1888,* part 1 (1971), provides an exhaustive but balanced treatment of the Supreme Court during Chase's tenure as chief justice. Harold M. Hyman and William M. Wiecek, *Equal Justice Under Law, Constitutional Development, 1835–1875* (1982), constitutes a critical yet sympathetic analysis of Chase's role in Reconstruction issues, tying the Chase Court to the Taney Court, which preceded it, and the Waite Court, which followed. See also the various articles in the "Symposium on Salmon P. Chase and the Chase Court," *Northern Kentucky Law Review* 21 (Fall 1993).

In regard to postwar issues, see also David F. Hughes, "Salmon P. Chase: Chief Justice," *Vanderbilt Law Review* 18 (1965): 569, a careful portrait of Chase's leadership of the Court on the most important Reconstruction questions. Stanley I. Kutler, in *Judicial Power and Reconstruction Politics* (1968), convincingly argues that the Chase Court reasserted judicial independence during Reconstruction.

NOTEWORTHY OPINIONS

Ex parte Milligan, 71 U.S. 2 (1866) (Concurrence)

Cummings v. Missouri, 71 U.S. 277 (1867)

Ex parte Garland, 71 U.S. 333 (1867)

Mississippi v. Johnson, 71 U.S. 475 (1867)

Ex parte McCardle, 73 U.S. 318 (1868); 74 U.S. 506 (1869)

Texas v. White, 74 U.S. 700 (1869)

Hepburn v. Griswold, 75 U.S. 603 (1870)

SAMUEL CHASE

Birth: April 17, 1741, Somerset County, Maryland.

Education: Tutored by father; studied law in Annapolis law office; admitted to bar in 1761.

Official Positions: Member, Maryland General Assembly, 1764–1784; delegate, Continental Congress, 1774–1778, 1784–1785; member, Maryland Committee of Correspondence, 1774; member, Maryland Convention and Council of Safety, 1775; judge, Baltimore Criminal Court, 1788–1796; chief judge, General Court of Maryland, 1791–1796.

Supreme Court Service: Nominated associate justice by President George Washington, January 26, 1796, to replace John Blair, who had resigned; confirmed by the Senate, January 27, 1796, by a voice vote; took judicial oath February 4, 1796; served until June 19, 1811; replaced by Gabriel Duvall, nominated by President James Madison.

Death: June 19, 1811, Baltimore, Maryland.

Samuel Chase served on the Supreme Court for only fourteen years and missed all or much of some of those years because of frequent illness. Yet in that time he compiled a lifetime of controversy. He fulfilled the destiny that he had foretold as a riotous leader of the Sons of Liberty in the 1770s. Chase's opposition to the royal governor of Maryland was so extreme that the mayor and aldermen of Annapolis branded him a "busy, restless incendiary, a ringleader of mobs, a foul-mouthed and inflaming son of discord."

Chase supported Gen. George Washington in the Continental Congress from 1775 to 1778, amassing credits on which he would collect in 1796. But in the meantime, his efforts to corner the market on flour forced him to leave Congress in disgrace. He was severely attacked in a pamphlet by Alexander Hamilton, writing as "Publius." In 1778 Chase survived an attempt to remove him from his position as chief judge of the Baltimore Criminal Court. A majority of the Maryland Assembly supported his removal, but not the required two-thirds. Political observers probably were not surprised when Chase became the first, and only, member of the U.S. Supreme Court to be impeached.

Chase implored President Washington to grant him a federal office because of financial need. Washington considered him for attorney general before appointing him to the Supreme Court. He had, in fact, been a leader of the Maryland opposition to the Constitution and, as recently as 1793, had been violently and publicly anti-British. Yet by the time of his advancement to the Court he had become equally pro-Federalist and anti-Jeffersonian in his language. Although he was unanimously approved by the Federalist-dominated Senate, he was not welcomed with open arms. Treasury Secretary Oliver Wolcott had "but an unworthy opinion" of Chase. Justice James

Iredell's comment provided an accurate, though unintended, forecast of Chase's judicial career: "I have no personal acquaintance with Mr. Chase, but am not impressed with a very favorable opinion of his moral character, whatever his professional abilities may be."

Chase's judicial abilities would earn him praise at the same time his injudicious temperament brought him condemnation. Joseph Story, who followed Chase on the bench, presented a different picture. He called Chase a "rough, but very sensible man . . . bold, impetuous." When Story compared Chase to Dr. Samuel Johnson, he had Chase's size, appearance, and manner in mind, but Story added that the resemblance was "above all" because of Chase's intellect. No less an authority than Edward S. Corwin described Chase as the most notable of any of Chief Justice John Marshall's predecessors.

Despite all of Chase's excess baggage and the turmoil that was yet to come, few appearances on the Supreme Court have been so auspicious. The constitutionality of state legislation sequestering debts owed by Virginia citizens to British creditors was challenged in *Ware v. Hylton* (1796). Virginia's counsel, led by the young John Marshall, argued that the legislation was unaffected by the protection of British creditors negotiated in the treaty of 1783, because the legislation preceded the treaty by several years. As the junior member, Chase spoke first. His thorough analysis of the case left little for justices William Paterson, James Wilson, and William Cushing to add. Chase's first opinion has been described as the most brilliant

Samuel Chase

Supreme Court opinion prior to *Marbury v. Madison* (1803). Chase laid out every conceivable justification for the Virginia legislation and then demolished them one by one. Most important, "A treaty cannot be the supreme law," as the Constitution promises, "if any act of a state legislature can stand in its way." *Ware v. Hylton* remains the basic text for future discussions of the supremacy of national treaties over legislation.

The next day, Chase interpreted the direct tax clause of the Constitution in *Hylton v. United States.* His performance here did not compare with *Ware,* and it appears he had focused his best efforts on the treaty case. Chase did, however, offer an *obiter dictum* that was accepted until 1895, when Chief Justice Melville Fuller corrected "a century of error" while ruling a federal income tax unconstitutional. "I am inclined to think," Chase remarked, "but of this I do not give judicial opinion, that the direct taxes contemplated by the constitution, are only two, to wit, a capitation or poll tax simply without regard to property, profession or any other circumstances; and a tax on land." Paterson made the same ruling, with much less hedging, but Chase said it first.

Chase asserted judicial supremacy in interpreting the Constitution on a number of occasions. In *Calder v. Bull* (1798), he declared, "An act of the legislature (for I cannot call it a law), contrary to the great first principles of the social compact, cannot be considered a rightful exercise of legislative authority." He was confident that "certain vital principles in our free republican governments . . . will determine and overrule an apparent and flagrant abuse of legislative power." He assigned full responsibility for interpreting state constitutions to the state judiciaries, which the Supreme Court confirmed in *Cooper v. Telfair* (1800).

His notebook of "Instructions to Grand Jury" contains this powerful charge, probably written in 1799:

> If the *Federal* Legislature should, at any time, pass a Law *contrary to the Constitution of the United States, such law* would be *void*; because the Constitution is *the fundamental Law* of the United States, and *paramount* to any Act of the Federal Legislature, whose authority is derived from, and delegated by that Constitution; and which imposes *certain restrictions* on the Legislative Authority that can only be preserved through the . . . Courts of Justice. The *Judicial* power of the United States is *coexistent, co-extensive*, and *coordinated* with, and altogether independent of the *Legislature* & the *Executive*; and the Judges of the Supreme and District Courts are bound by the oath of office to regulate their decisions *agreeably to the Constitution*. The Judicial powers, therefore, are the only proper and competent authority to decide whether any Law made by Congress, or any of the State Legislatures is contrary to or in violation of the *federal* Constitution.

John Marshall was an interested observer in 1800, when Chase refused to allow James T. Callender's counsel to argue that the Sedition Act was unconstitutional: "The judicial power of the United States is the only proper and competent authority to decide whether any statute made by Congress (or any of the State Legislatures) is contrary to, or in violation of, the Federal Constitution." This authority is "expressly granted to the judicial power of the United States and is recognized by Congress by a perpetual statute," meaning the Judiciary Act of 1789. He proposed to go a dangerous step further when he was the only member who argued that Supreme Court justices should rule the Circuit Court Act of 1802 unconstitutional and refuse to return to circuit duty. "The distinction

of taking the *Office* from the *Judge*, and not the *Judge* from the *Office*" he considered to be "puerile and nonsensical." Fortunately, calmer heads prevailed in Paterson's opinion in *Stuart v. Laird* (1803).

Chase's longest decision, *Calder v. Bull* (1798), is famous for the ruling that the *ex post facto* clause of the Constitution is applicable only to criminal proceedings, which deprived the clause of potential significance as a protection of property against state legislation. This ruling still stands. Chase was most un-Hamiltonian in *Calder,* when he ruled that "all the powers delegated by the people of the United States to the federal government are defined, and no *constructive* power can be exercised by it." The states, in contrast, possessed all authorities allowed by the state constitutions, so long as they were "not expressly taken away by the constitution of the United States." This statement is reminiscent of his remark in *Ware v. Hylton* that the people grant to state governments "the supreme and sovereign power of the state" to pass legislation, so long as it does not conflict with the federal Constitution. Chase seemed on the verge of discussing the police power doctrine, which would receive so much attention in the Taney Court.

Ironically, Chase's most memorable circuit decision was quite Jeffersonian in its insistence that there is no federal common law in criminal cases. He ruled in *United States v. Worrall* (1798) in the Pennsylvania circuit court that neither the Constitution nor an act of Congress had conferred common law jurisdiction on the federal courts. Therefore, it would be "improper to exercise a jurisdiction to make bribery punishable by resort to common law precedent." His precedent was not at the time followed in other circuit courts, but it was upheld by the Supreme Court in *United States v. Hudson and Goodwin* (1812). Where common law could be used, Chase was more consistent than his brethren in following standardized principles of construction and procedure.

Unfortunately, Chase squandered much of the favorable notice gained from these decisions when he became a Federalist "hanging judge" in the sedition and treason trials of 1799–1800. He had openly advocated adoption of the Alien and Sedition Acts, and he intended to see them used to fullest effect. Chase sentenced David Brown to a year and a half in jail, the harshest of any sedition sentence. His forceful rulings in the sedition trial of Callender and the treason trial of John Fries, both in 1800, provided the basis of his impeachment in 1804. Counsel for both defendants were so offended by his rulings that they withdrew from the cases. Chase shocked Fries's counsel by showing them his opinion *before* the trial in order to expedite proceedings. He was surprised when they expressed disgust and withdrew. He condemned Fries to death despite his lack of counsel; fortunately, President John Adams pardoned Fries. Most Philadelphia counsel refused to practice before Chase. District court judge Richard Peters, a Federalist, complained, "I never sat with him without pain, as he was forever getting into some intemperate and unnecessary squabbles." Even at his worst moments, however, Chase demonstrated judicial skill. In *United States v. Callender* (1800), he demonstrated more knowledge of libel and slander law and of recent British precedents than his colleagues.

Chase might have avoided impeachment if he had not bitterly attacked Congress's repeal of the Judiciary Act of 1801 in an intemperate jury charge in Maryland on May 2, 1803. He declared that "Mobocracy" threatened to destroy "peace & order, freedom and property." A Maryland legislator demanded that the next Congress "wipe off this defilement from our courts by removing from the bench the obnoxious rubbish which has occasioned it." President Thomas Jefferson relayed the charge to his lieutenant in the House, suggesting impeachment of this "insolent and overbearing man"; having interfered, Jefferson cautioned that "it is better that I should not interfere." Jefferson could not have forgotten that Chase had missed the entire August 1800 term because he was in Maryland campaigning for the reelection of President Adams.

After months of delay, the House of Representatives approved eight charges of impeachment, six of them based on the Callender and Fries trials, by a 73–32 vote. Chase went to trial in the Senate on January 3, 1805, where he anticipated defeat and removal. But he had assembled a brilliant team of Federalist attorneys, and they simply overwhelmed John Randolph, the erratic and sometimes spectacularly foolish House manager. Five of the eight charges did not even receive a majority, and one received no votes, even though twenty-five of the thirty-four senators were Jeffersonian Republicans. Six Republicans voted not guilty on all eight charges. The charge based on Chase's conduct in 1803 fared best, with nineteen voting for conviction.

Chase was a changed man during his last six years on the Court, partly because of the chastening experience of impeachment, but more likely because of persistent illness. He was always in need of money, frequently borrowing, and he clung to the bench for his salary despite attacks of gout which left him in misery for his remaining days. He was seldom on duty in 1804 and 1805; he missed the entire sessions of 1806 and 1810; and there was no 1811 term. Under Marshall, Chase wrote only one opinion of the Court (because Marshall had ruled on circuit), a brief concurring opinion, and a dissent against Justice William Johnson's opinion in *Croudson v. Leonard* (1808). Johnson's vindictive assessment in 1822 that "Chase could not be got to think or write" was characteristically unfair, but it was not as far afield as some of his other partisan assessments of Chase's Federalist colleagues, so long as it is limited to his waning years.

—*Donald O. Dewey*

BIBLIOGRAPHY

The only full biography, James Haw, Francis F. Beirne, Rosamond R. Beirne, and R. Samuel Jett, *Stormy Patriot, The Life of Samuel Chase* (1980), is thorough and useful, although it bears some of the weight of its many authors and many years in preparation. Irving Dilliard's essay in Friedman and Israel, *Justices*, vol. 1, 185, is entertaining and informative. The best account of the impeachment is Jane Elsmere's unpublished doctoral dissertation, "The Impeachment Trial of Justice Samuel Chase" (Indiana University, 1962).

NOTEWORTHY CASES

Ware v. Hylton, 3 U.S. 199 (1796)

Calder v. Bull, 3 U.S. 386 (1798)

TOM CAMPBELL CLARK

Birth: September 23, 1899, Dallas, Texas.

Education: Virginia Military Institute, 1917–1918; University of Texas, A.B., 1921; LL.B., 1922.

Official Positions: Assistant district attorney, Dallas County, 1927–1932; special assistant, Justice Department, 1937–1943; assistant U.S. attorney general, 1943–1945; U.S. attorney general, 1945–1949; director, Federal Judicial Center, 1968–1970; judge, U.S. Court of Appeals, various circuits, by special arrangement, 1967–1977.

Supreme Court Service: Nominated associate justice by President Harry S. Truman, August 2, 1949, to replace Frank Murphy, who had died; confirmed by the Senate, August 18, 1949, by a 73–8 vote; took judicial oath August 24, 1949; retired June 12, 1967; replaced by Thurgood Marshall, nominated by President Lyndon B. Johnson.

Death: June 13, 1977, New York City.

During his eighteen years on the Supreme Court, Tom C. Clark was not an intellectual leader. He wrote only a handful of memorable opinions and articulated no coherent judicial philosophy. Yet when he retired in June 1967, Clark was one of the Court's most widely known and influential members. The reason was his off-the-bench campaign to reform judicial administration. A hobby that became a consuming passion, that crusade even affected his decision making. In adjudicating cases, Clark adhered to a few simple principles that he believed would promote effective judicial management.

That he should have viewed judging with an administrator's eye is understandable, for Clark came to the Court after more than a decade of service in a variety of executive positions within the U.S. Department of Justice. Born into a family of Texas lawyers, he had attended public schools in Dallas, then enrolled at the Virginia Military Institute, only to

drop out after one year to enlist in the army. Following service in an infantry division during World War I, Clark returned home to train for the family vocation at the University of Texas, receiving his law degree in 1922. He then joined his father's Dallas law firm. In 1927 Clark was appointed assistant district attorney of Dallas County. He returned to private practice in 1933 but, although successful, abandoned it again for public service in 1937 when Sen. Tom Connally, D-Texas, secured him a position with the Justice Department.

Starting there as special assistant in the War Risk Insurance Section, Clark faced some 3,000 claims by injured servicemen. A year later he moved to the Antitrust Division, heading up its wage and hour unit and later its New Orleans field office and West Coast region. Following the attack on Pearl Harbor, President Franklin D. Roosevelt appointed Clark civilian coordinator of the Western Defense Command, in which capacity he handled legal aspects of the relocation and internment of Japanese Americans. Clark then took over the war frauds unit of the Antitrust Division. He worked closely with Sen. Harry Truman, D-Mo., who chaired a committee investigating waste and corruption in defense industries. In 1944 Clark moved up to head the Antitrust Division, and the following year, when many of its functions were transferred to the Criminal Division, Attorney General Francis Biddle placed him in charge of that function.

Clark kept in touch with Truman, however, and at the 1944 Democratic National Convention helped him to obtain the vice presidential nomination. After Roosevelt's death made Truman president in 1945, he selected Clark to replace Biddle.

As attorney general, Clark retained his interest in antitrust, initiating 160 new enforcement actions and personally arguing a major case before the Supreme Court. He also took an interest in civil rights. Clark pressured the FBI to investigate lynchings and called for the enforcement of federal legislation that penalized lynchers. In addition, he had his department

Tom Campbell Clark

file an *amicus curiae* brief with the Supreme Court that helped persuade it to declare judicial enforcement of racially restrictive housing covenants unconstitutional (*Shelley v. Kraemer,* 1948). Exhibiting an interest in fair and orderly administration, Clark used his position to promote adoption of the Administrative Procedures Act of 1946. He also played a large role in the development of the Truman administration's internal security policies. He advocated a loyalty program for federal employees, and under him, the Justice Department drafted the first attorney general's list of allegedly subversive organizations. He secured an expansion of his department's investigative authority that included authorization for the FBI to make greater use of wiretaps. In 1948, despite a dearth of evidence against the accused, Clark personally authorized prosecution of the top leaders of the American Communist Party under the Smith Act.

When Truman nominated him to the Supreme Court in 1949 to succeed liberal justice Frank Murphy, liberals and radicals protested the choice; they considered Clark a Red-baiting extremist. Some opponents alleged that he was indifferent to the rights of persons accused of crime. With vastly less justification, critics accused him of being antilabor and antiblack. Nevertheless, the Senate confirmed Clark, 73–8.

He soon demonstrated that concerns about his commitment to individual rights were well founded. Clark became an ally of the conservative chief justice, Fred Vinson. During the four years they served together, Clark rejected the libertarian claims in civil liberties cases 76 percent of the time, only slightly below Vinson's 86 percent. Clark generally supported anti-Communist loyalty-security programs. In *Garner v. Board of Public Works* (1951), for example, he spoke for a 5–4 majority that upheld a Los Angeles ordinance under which city employees had to file affidavits affirming that they were not then, and never had been, members of the Communist Party, and to execute loyalty oaths that involved swearing they had not taught or advocated the overthrow of the government.

As law professor John P. Frank correctly observes, however, Clark was not an arrant Red-baiter. When, in *Wieman v. Updegraff* (1952), the Court unanimously struck down an Oklahoma law requiring government employees to swear they had not been members of any organization on the attorney general's list during the past five years, Clark wrote the opinion condemning this statute for penalizing even persons who had joined such groups without being aware of their character.

Wieman presented a brief shift to a more libertarian position that followed Vinson's death and the appointment of Earl Warren as chief justice in 1953. Warren launched a successful drive to increase the number of cases the Court was deciding, an effort in which the administratively minded Clark cooperated gladly. As the Warren Court began to move in a libertarian direction in civil liberties cases, Clark went along. He supported a 1956 ruling that the existence of the Smith Act precluded states from punishing sedition against the United States, and in *Slochower v. Board of Higher Education* (1956), he wrote a majority opinion holding that the dismissal of a Brooklyn College professor under a provision of the New York City charter violated the Fifth Amendment. The charter required summary discharge of any employee who invoked the privilege of self-incrimination during an investigation of his official conduct.

In 1957, however, Clark became a vigorous dissenter in civil liberties cases. Warren had been drifting closer to the Court's liberal stalwarts, Hugo Black and William O. Douglas, and the 1956 appointment of William Brennan completed the formation of a four-man liberal bloc that Clark perceived as a threat to internal security programs he considered essential. He spoke out first in an intemperate dissent from the Court's May 1957 ruling in *Jencks v. United States,* which held that the government must permit defense attorneys to see written statements furnished to the FBI by prosecution witnesses. The result of this decision, Clark lamented, would be a "Roman holiday for

rummaging through confidential information as well as vital national secrets."

On "Red Monday," June 17, 1957, he dissented three more times. In *Yates v. United States,* Clark protested when the majority overturned the convictions of California Communist Party leaders under the Smith Act and rendered a central provision of that law virtually unusable against the party. He also denounced the Court's rulings in *Watkins v. United States* and *Sweezy v. New Hampshire,* overturning contempt sentences imposed on individuals who had refused to cooperate with federal and state legislative investigations of subversive activities.

Clark continued to dissent the following year, but in cases upholding the dismissals of a teacher and a subway conductor who had refused to answer questions about their involvement in Communist activities, he found himself on the winning side. Responding to congressional outrage against the Court's latest internal security decisions, Justices Felix Frankfurter and John Marshall Harlan ceased cooperating with the liberal bloc, and by 1959 Clark was frequently in the majority. In a decision seemingly inconsistent with *Sweezy,* he spoke for the Court in *Uphaus v. Wyman* (1959), which rejected a First Amendment attack on a one-man legislative investigation by the attorney general of New Hampshire, declaring that the state's need to unearth subversive activities outweighed any invasion of privacy it might involve. The following year Clark wrote a majority opinion holding that Los Angeles County had not denied a temporary employee due process when it fired him for invoking the Fifth Amendment before a congressional committee.

After Frankfurter retired in 1962, the liberal bloc regained control, and Clark again found himself dissenting in internal security cases. As popular concern about communism abated and the Court devoted more of its attention to other issues, however, Clark appeared to be more content as a member of the Warren Court. He concurred in its pathbreaking ruling in *Baker v. Carr* (1962), subjecting the apportionment of state legislatures to control by the federal judiciary, and he consistently supported its efforts to enhance the rights of African Americans. In *Burton v. Wilmington Parking Authority* (1961), he wrote an innovative opinion holding that a private restaurant must comply with the equal protection clause of the Fourteenth Amendment because it rented space from a government agency. Clark also spoke for the Court in *Heart of Atlanta Motel v. United States* (1964), which affirmed the constitutionality of the public accommodations provisions of the Civil Rights Act of 1964, and in *Katzenbach v. McClung* (1964), which held that, although based on the commerce clause, these provisions could be enforced against a local business having only limited contact with interstate commerce. Other Clark opinions overturned criminal trespass convictions against sit-in demonstrators and invalidated transfer policies designed to forestall school integration in Knoxville, Tennessee.

Although he made significant contributions to the work of the Warren Court in civil rights, Clark was even more productive in other areas. Predictably, the former head of the Antitrust Division became the Court's antitrust specialist. He also produced numerous important opinions on state taxation of interstate business and frequently spoke for the Court in cases involving other tax issues, interstate commerce, and labor law. He wrote often in immigration cases as well. But his real specialty was criminal procedure. Of the 341 opinions that he wrote during his eighteen years on the bench, more than 26 percent dealt with some aspect of that subject. Nearly 20 percent of his majority opinions involved criminal procedure.

Among them was *Mapp v. Ohio* (1961), which required state courts to join the federal judiciary in excluding evidence that was the product of unreasonable searches or seizures. *Mapp* initiated a constitutional revolution in which the Warren Court made almost all of the criminal procedure provisions of the Bill of Rights fully applicable to the states and dramatically increased the protection they afforded to defendants.

Clark appeared somewhat out of character as the Court's spokesman in *Mapp,* because he usually voted against persons convicted of crimes. He was firmly committed to the maintenance of law and order and

believed that government could retain the respect of its citizens only if it punished the guilty. As a former prosecutor, Clark identified with those responsible for law enforcement and sympathized with their concerns. He dissented from the Court's landmark ruling in *Miranda v. Arizona* (1966), requiring police to inform suspects of their rights before attempting to interrogate them. Clark would not vote to reverse a conviction, even when it was clear that law enforcement personnel had violated the rights of the accused, unless the defendant could prove the violation had contributed to the guilty verdict.

Despite his conditional approach to lapses in pretrial criminal procedure, Clark became an absolutist concerning violations of the right to a fair trial. When first confronted with the problem of prejudicial publicity in criminal cases, he balanced the Sixth Amendment rights of the accused against First Amendment rights of freedom of expression, announcing in a majority opinion in *Irvin v. Dowd* (1961), and a dissent in *Rideau v. Louisiana* (1963), that a defendant was entitled to have a conviction reversed only if he could prove that press coverage had actually biased the jury. While wrestling in *Estes v. Texas* (1965) with the question of whether live television coverage violated the right to a fair trial, however, Clark changed his mind. Ignoring the First Amendment, he adopted an unconditional approach to Sixth Amendment violations that did not require proof of harm. He then followed *Estes* with an opinion in a notorious pretrial publicity case, *Sheppard v. Maxwell* (1966), presuming harm from the infringement of the defendant's constitutional right to a fair trial. Clark changed his position because he concluded that as violations of that right (unlike the improper eliciting of confessions) occurred in the courtroom, judges (who, he believed, should meet higher standards than police officers) could and should prevent them. If jurists appeared to condone violations of the Constitution, public confidence in the judiciary and the fair administration of justice would be undermined. Similar reasoning led Clark to favor requiring state courts to comply with the exclusionary rule; he considered this necessary to ensure the "judicial integrity so necessary to the true administration of justice."

The administration of justice, not the plight of criminal defendants, was his overriding concern. Indeed, this interest was the adhesive that bound the disparate elements of Clark's jurisprudence together. He had no real judicial philosophy. Clark considered flexibility the attribute most essential to success on the Supreme Court, and his opinions reflected common sense rather than commitment to activism, self-restraint, or any other jurisprudential strategy.

Law school dean Thomas Mengler aptly characterizes the opinion Clark wrote in *Abington School District v. Schempp* (1963), holding that Bible reading in the public schools violated the First Amendment's establishment of religion clause, as designed "for the readership of *Time,* rather than the *Harvard Law Review.*" A year earlier the Court had excited a popular outcry by holding unconstitutional the New York regents' prayer to be recited in that state's schools. Disturbed by the reaction to *Engel v. Vitale* (1962), Clark, a practicing Presbyterian, determined to reassure the public that the Court was not undermining religion. In *Schempp,* he wrote a short opinion that eschewed sophisticated legal analysis and addressed the concerns of the average citizen. It was, in short, an exercise in public relations.

That is not to say that Clark's decision making was unprincipled. His public relations effort was designed to persuade Americans to accept an exclusion of religious exercises from public schools, which he regarded as constitutionally required. Although he was devoted to President Truman, Clark concurred when the Court ruled in *Youngstown Sheet & Tube Co. v. Sawyer* (1952) that Truman had acted unconstitutionally in seizing the nation's steel mills during the Korean War. He believed the seizure was illegal and that duty required him to say so.

Clark was a principled man, but pragmatic in his approach to opinion writing. A skillful negotiator, he was always willing to accommodate another justice to achieve a majority or unanimity, even if doing so required conceding a disputed point. Clark did have convictions to which he adhered firmly, but the principles he implemented most consistently were tenets of judicial administration rather than constitutional law.

These precepts were three in number. The first—based on a belief that once courts had determined a legal issue, even those conscientiously opposed to the result were bound by it—was that he would dissent from a precedent with which he disagreed only in the term in which it was established. The second was that doctrines that embodied bad public policy should be overruled whenever he could persuade four other justices to join him in doing so. Third, if the Court concluded that a precedent was no longer to be followed, Clark believed it should say so explicitly.

His handling of search and seizure cases illustrates these principles at work. Shortly before his appointment, the Court held in *Wolf v. Colorado* (1949) that the exclusionary rule did not apply to the states. Clark, who had been outraged years earlier when he was unable to prevent the use against one of his first clients of evidence obtained during a particularly heinous search by police in Dallas, disagreed with its position. Yet when the Court reaffirmed it in *Irvine v. California* (1954), he reluctantly concurred, rather than dissent. Although writing then that *Wolf* remained "the law, and as such . . . entitled to the respect of the Court's membership," he subsequently lobbied his colleagues to persuade them to use *Mapp* to overrule the 1949 decision, even though the defendant's attorneys had based their appeal on issues other than whether the exclusionary rule applied to the states.

Clark followed the course he did in these search and seizure cases because he was convinced this was the best way to promote the effective administration of justice. In his opinion, the Court's job was to establish rules for a vast array of social institutions. To avoid confusion at lower levels in the justice system, it had an obligation to make as clear as possible precisely what those rules were. Adherence to his three principles was the best way to achieve that objective, Clark believed.

Achieving clarity was necessary to maximize efficiency, and an efficiently run legal system would provide a higher level of justice. Clark was convinced that the growth of popular discontent with the courts during the 1960s was due largely to a "breakdown of judicial procedures," and that the way to halt this collapse was to enhance efficiency. Despite his law and order mentality, he became a supporter of decriminalizing victimless crimes because cases of this type clogged the courts, impairing their capacity to administer justice promptly.

Ensuring that justice was administered promptly, efficiently, and effectively became Tom Clark's passion during the last two decades of his life. In 1957 he assumed the chairmanship of the American Bar Association's moribund section of judicial administration. For someone who was also a sitting Supreme Court justice, Clark devoted an incredible amount of time to that job. By the end of his term he had revitalized the section, and, according to John Frank, "the foundation was laid for the American Bar's modern activities to improve the administration of justice." Clark subsequently played a leading role in the establishment of the Joint Committee for the Effective Administration of Justice, a body that between 1961 and 1964 worked to coordinate the efforts of the ABA section and a number of other organizations active in this field. In addition to serving as chair of the joint committee and participating in many of its citizens conferences on court modernization and seminars for judges, Clark was also instrumental in obtaining a grant from the Kellogg Foundation to fund its operations. Later, he won financial backing from Kellogg for the National College of State Trial Judges, an outgrowth of the joint committee that Clark helped to found and whose board of directors he chaired.

Constantly flying around the country giving speeches and chairing meetings, Clark became in Frank's words "the traveling salesman of justice." For a decade he carried on this sales campaign while also performing his duties on the Court. Clark always gave priority to his Court responsibilities, but meeting them while crusading across the country for the reform of the administration of justice required a travel schedule that would have worn out most men.

Clark retired from the Supreme Court in 1967 so that his son, Ramsey Clark, could become attorney general. President Lyndon Johnson wanted to name the younger Clark to head the Justice Department, but because Justice Clark would have to recuse himself from all of the department's many cases before the Court, he hesitated to do so. Clark solved this problem by stepping down.

Although he was willing to leave the Court to advance his son's career, at sixty-seven and in good health Tom Clark was not ready for complete retirement. He traveled around the country, serving as a trial judge and becoming the first jurist ever to sit on all of the U.S. circuit courts of appeal. He also continued his campaign to improve the administration of justice. After Earl Warren persuaded Congress to establish the Federal Judicial Center, Clark became its first director in March 1968. He chaired the ABA's special committee on the evaluation of disciplinary enforcement and continued to participate in seminars and give speeches. In addition, Clark wrote on his favorite subject; 95 percent of the articles he published during the latter part of his life addressed problems of court management. "I can categorically state, without fear of legitimate contradiction," his former clerk, Larry Temple, wrote after Clark died in 1977, "that Tom Clark made a greater favorable impact on the administration of justice than any individual in our legal history."

Clark's influence on that field was far more important than his impact on constitutional law. During his eighteen years on the Supreme Court, he wrote a comparatively small number of really important opinions. *Mapp* was by far the most significant, but his *Schempp* opinion, which began the creation of a test the Court would use for two decades to assess alleged violations of the establishment clause, is also notable. *Burton* was an innovative attack on the hoary principle that only government can violate the Constitution, and it might have led to this doctrine being severely circumscribed had congressional enactment of civil rights legislation forbidding many private businesses to discriminate not soon rendered such revolutionary judicial action unnecessary. *Heart of Atlanta* and *McClung* were important because they upheld a landmark law, but doctrinally they did little more than underscore what the Justice Department lawyers who drafted the Civil Rights Act of 1964 already knew: Congress can use its power to regulate interstate commerce to do anything it wants, a doctrine the Court began to dismantle in the 1990s. Clark made major contributions to the development of the law governing prejudicial pretrial publicity, and he also produced a significant opinion holding that motion pictures are protected by the First Amendment.

Nothing he did on the bench, however, matched the importance of his work to improve the administration of justice. It was this and not his contributions to constitutional law that won him acclaim from the bar and the public. His efforts on behalf of judicial reform earned him a reputation that redounded to the benefit of the institution he served. When the Warren Court was under attack for its controversial rulings on race relations, criminal procedure, legislative redistricting, and separation of church and state, Clark was often able to mollify those it had angered.

He was by most standards not a great justice. His memorable opinions were few in number, and he made no significant contribution to the fierce jurisprudential debates that raged within the Supreme Court during the years that he served on it. But, as Temple notes, "When the chronicles of the development and betterment of the administration of justice in this country are recorded, the name of Tom C. Clark will be paramount."

—*Michal R. Belknap*

BIBLIOGRAPHY

Justice Clark's papers are divided between the Harry S. Truman Presidential Library in Independence, Missouri, and the Tarlton Law Library of the University of Texas School of Law in Austin, Texas. The material housed in the Truman Library relates to his pre-Court career, and the Texas collection includes Clark's Supreme Court case files and correspondence and other items reflecting his involvement in efforts to improve judicial administration. There is no biography of Tom Clark. Chapter 5 of John P. Frank, *The Warren Court* (1964); and Richard Kirkendall, "Tom C. Clark," in Friedman and Israel, *Justices*, vol. 4, 2665, provide good overviews of his career, but unfortunately the first of these

pieces was written while Clark was still on the Court, and the second nearly a decade before his death.

Reflecting the intensity of Clark's interest in judicial administration and the importance of his efforts to reform it, more articles can be found on this subject than on any aspect of his work on the bench. The most important are John P. Frank, "Justice Tom Clark and Judicial Administration," *Texas Law Review* 46 (1967): 5; James A. Gazell, "Justice Tom C. Clark as Judicial Reformer," *Houston Law Review* 15 (1978): 307; and Dennis D. Dorin, "Tom C. Clark: The Justice as Administrator," *Judicature* 61 (December-January 1978): 271. Marc Srere, "Note: Justice Tom C. Clark's Unconditional Approach to Individual Rights in the Courtroom," *Texas Law Review* 54 (1985): 421; Thomas M. Mengler, "Public Relations in the Supreme Court: Justice Tom Clark's Opinion in the School Prayer Case," *Constitutional Commentary* 6 (1989): 331; Paul R. Baier, "Justice Clark, the Voice of the Past, and the Exclusionary Rule," *Texas Law Review* 64 (1985): 415; and Dennis D. Dorin, "Marshalling Mapp: Justice Tom Clark's Role in *Mapp v. Ohio*," *Case Western Reserve Law Review* 52 (2001): 401, all provide useful insights into aspects of Clark's jurisprudence. A good overview of the cases involving national security is Arthur Sabin, *In Calmer Times: The Supreme Court and Red Monday* (1999).

NOTEWORTHY OPINIONS

Wieman v. Updegraff, 344 U.S. 183 (1952)

Slochower v. Board of Higher Education, 350 U.S. 551 (1956)

Jencks v. United States, 352 U.S. 657 (1957) (Dissent)

Watkins v. United States, 354 U.S. 178 (1957) (Dissent)

Sweezy v. New Hampshire, 354 U.S. 234 (1957) (Dissent)

Yates v. United States, 354 U.S. 298 (1957) (Dissent)

Uphaus v. Wyman, 360 U.S. 72 (1959)

Burton v. Wilmington Parking Authority, 365 U.S. 715 (1961)

Irvin v. Dowd, 366 U.S. 717 (1961)

Mapp v. Ohio, 367 U.S. 643 (1961)

Abington School District v. Schempp, 374 U.S. 203 (1963)

Reynolds v. Sims, 377 U.S. 533 (1964) (Concurrence)

Heart of Atlanta Motel v. United States, 379 U.S. 241 (1964)

Katzenbach v. McClung, 379 U.S. 294 (1964)

Estes v. Texas, 381 U.S. 532 (1965)

Sheppard v. Maxwell, 384 U.S. 333 (1966)

JOHN HESSIN CLARKE

Birth: September 18, 1857, Lisbon, Ohio.

Education: Western Reserve University, A.B., 1877, A.M., 1880.

Official Positions: Federal judge, U.S. District Court for Northern District of Ohio, 1914–1916.

Supreme Court Service: Nominated associate justice by President Woodrow Wilson, July 14, 1916, to replace Charles Evans Hughes, who had resigned; confirmed by the Senate, July 24, 1916, by a voice vote; took judicial oath October 9, 1916; resigned September 18, 1922; replaced by George Sutherland, nominated by President Warren G. Harding.

Death: March 22, 1945, San Diego, California.

John Hessin Clarke had been a prominent railroad and corporate attorney, a newspaper publisher, an activist in Ohio's Democratic reform politics, and an unsuccessful candidate for the U.S. Senate when President Woodrow Wilson appointed him to serve as a federal district court judge in 1914. Two years later Wilson elevated Clarke to the Supreme Court.

As Wilson had hoped, Clarke displayed on the Court the progressive politics that had characterized his pre-judicial career. Indeed, Chief Justice William Howard Taft complained that Clarke acted "as if each case was something to vote on as he would vote on it in the Senate or the House, rather than to decide as a judge." Clarke's confidence in the ability of government to solve social problems was manifest in his voting record in cases involving exercises of federal and state regulatory power. He dissented in two cases striking down federal laws regulating the use of child labor, *Hammer v. Dagenhart* (1918) and *Bailey v. Drexel Furniture* (1922). He voted to uphold the federal Adamson Act's eight-hour day for railway workers in *Wilson v. New* (1917) and joined the Court's

opinion upholding a federal statute regulating meat-packers and stockyards in *Stafford v. Wallace* (1922). Rejecting the doctrines of substantive due process, which he denounced as "Fourteenth Amendment nonsense," Clarke voted to uphold Oregon's minimum wage and maximum hour laws in *Stettler v. O'Hara* (1917) and *Bunting v. Oregon* (1917). He endorsed the Court's opinion sustaining New York's workmen's compensation statute in *New York Central Railroad Co. v. White* (1917) and joined Justice Louis Brandeis's landmark fact-intensive dissent from a decision striking down a Washington statute regulating the fees charged by employment agencies in *Adams v. Tanner* (1917).

Clarke's sympathy for working people also led him to resist the use of injunctions to enforce anti-union contracts in *Hitchman Coal & Coke Co. v. Mitchell* (1917) to support the right of employees to picket their employer in *Truax v. Corrigan* (1921) and *American Steel Foundries v. Tri-City Central Trades Council* (1921), and to oppose the use of the antitrust laws against labor unions in *United Mine*

Workers v. Coronado Coal Co. (1922) and *Duplex Printing Press Co. v. Deering* (1921). Clarke consistently maintained a stern trustbusting position in the leading business antitrust cases of the period: *United States v. U.S. Steel Corp.* (1920), *United States v. United Shoe Machinery Co.* (1918), *United States v. Reading Railroad Co.* (1920), *United States v. Lehigh Valley Railroad* (1920), and *American Column and Lumber Co. v. United States* (1921).

In Clarke's legal progressivism, however, diminished solicitude for economic liberty was not accompanied by an incipient concern for modern civil liberties. He joined Justice Oliver Wendell Holmes's landmark 1919 opinions upholding federal prosecutions under the Espionage Act during World War I in *Schenck v. United States, Frohwerk v. United States,* and *Debs v. United States,* and he wrote the majority opinion in *Abrams v. United States* (1919), which extended the power of Congress to punish antigovernment speech even beyond what Holmes was willing to countenance.

Finding himself dissatisfied with the life of a justice, Clarke disappointed many liberals by resigning unexpectedly from the Court in September 1922. Thereafter, he spent much of his time promoting the cause of American participation in the World Court and the League of Nations. In the 1930s Clarke joined other legal progressives in believing that many of the decisions of the Court declaring New Deal initiatives unconstitutional were unsound. He supported the "Court-packing" plan and delivered a national radio address defending its constitutionality. Clarke resisted offers to write his biography, insisting that his life had not been "sufficiently unusual or important."

—*Barry Cushman*

John Hessin Clarke

BIBLIOGRAPHY

The definitive biography of Clarke is Hoyt Landon Warner, *The Life of Mr. Justice Clarke: A Testament to the Power of Liberal Dissent in America* (1959). Also useful are David M. Levitan, "The Jurisprudence of Mr. Justice Clarke," *Miami Law Quarterly* 7 (1952): 44; and Carl Wittke, "Mr. Justice Clarke in Retirement," *Western Reserve Law Review* 1 (1949): 28. A small collection of correspondence in the Clarke papers may be found at the Case Western Reserve University Library in Cleveland.

NOTEWORTHY OPINIONS

Abrams v. United States, 250 U.S. 616 (1919)

Schaefer v. United States, 251 U.S. 466 (1920) (Dissent)

NATHAN CLIFFORD

Birth: August 18, 1803, Rumney, New Hampshire.

Education: Haverhill Academy; studied law in office of Josiah Quincy in Rumney; admitted to New Hampshire bar, 1827.

Official Positions: Maine state representative, 1830–1834; attorney general of Maine, 1834–1838; U.S. representative, 1839–1843; U.S. attorney general, 1846–1848; minister to Mexico, 1848–1849.

Supreme Court Service: Nominated associate justice by President James Buchanan, December 9, 1857, to replace Benjamin R. Curtis, who had resigned; confirmed by the Senate, January 12, 1858, by a 26–23 vote; took judicial oath January 21, 1858; served until July 25, 1881; replaced by Horace Gray, nominated by President Chester A. Arthur.

Death: July 25, 1881, Cornish, Maine.

Soon after starting his legal career in 1827, Nathan Clifford became active in Maine's Democratic politics, serving in the state legislature and as attorney general. In 1839 he entered the House of Representatives, and three years later President James K. Polk appointed him attorney general. In 1857, when James Buchanan chose him for the Supreme Court's "New England seat," the nomination raised considerable criticism. Some northern senators objected to him as a "doughface" because of his close links with southern Democrats, his friendship with Chief Justice Roger B. Taney, and his attacks on the abolitionists; other senators considered him merely a party hack. He was confirmed nevertheless and served as an associate justice for twenty-three years, from 1858 to 1881.

Although Clifford wrote no famous opinions, he did have an impact on the Court because he consistently voted according to a strict conservative philosophy, which defended states' rights against federal intervention. In the Civil War cases, his political ideology conflicted with the rising policies of nationalism and expansion of federal power and led to numerous dissents. In the *Prize Cases* (1863), he concurred in Justice Samuel Nelson's dissent, which affirmed that the federal government's seizing of neutral shipping was unconstitutional because the conflict was President Abraham Lincoln's "personal war" until Congress officially declared hostilities. He was with the majority in limiting federal activity in *Ex parte Milligan* (1866), which declared unconstitutional the military commission's trial of civilians outside of the war zone. In *Hepburn v. Griswold* (1870), he voted with the majority against the federal government's power to issue paper money as legal tender even in a time of emergency. When the Court reversed itself in *Knox v. Lee* (1871), Clifford wrote a strong dissent of nearly 18,000 words arguing that legal tender must be exclusively gold and silver.

In two Reconstruction cases, Clifford's opinions were unfortunately the voice of the future. *Williams v. Mississippi* (1898), which held that blacks could be excluded from jury rolls because they were not registered voters, was foreshadowed in his dissent in *United States v. Reese* (1876). Here, Clifford argued that although the Fifteenth Amendment strictly limited racial discrimination in voting, other qualifications by cities or states that restricted the franchise were legitimate, and, therefore, Lexington's poll tax, used to disenfranchise African Americans, was constitutional. In *Hall v. DeCuir* (1878), a case concerning segregated accommodations on a Mississippi River passenger ship, Clifford coined the phrase "equality is not identity," which was later translated by *Plessy v. Ferguson* (1896) into "separate but equal." He followed this conservative philosophy on racial matters in cases such as *Strauder v. West Virginia* (1880) and *Ex parte Virginia* (1880), in which he joined in the dissent against the Court's invalidating statutes that excluded blacks from jury service. Jury selection, the dissent contended, was a state prerogative, and the majority's declarations were attempts to destroy true dual federalism.

The best-known cases of this period concern the Civil War and Reconstruction, but most of Clifford's nearly 400 opinions dealt with maritime and commercial law. He became the Court's expert on the assigning of fault and accountability in ship collisions, which were a relatively common occurrence in a commercially expanding nation. Given his being

Nathan Clifford

labeled a "doughface," it might seem ironic that he wrote most of the Court's decisions upholding the forfeiture of slave ships. His affirmation of the government's seizures had none of the moral indignation of Chief Justice Salmon P. Chase's opinions in regard to slavers, but Clifford strictly applied the laws banning slave importation.

Because he had been sent as a special commissioner to arrange the treaty of Guadalupe Hidalgo, which ended the U.S.-Mexican war, Clifford also specialized in southwestern land disputes. His decisions often favored the appeals of new American claimants rather than those holding the original Spanish land grants.

Although Clifford was a conservative Jeffersonian Democrat, his opinions on economic matters strongly supported business expansion. He held firmly for limited liability, "inevitable accident" in maritime cases, a strict interpretation for written contracts, protection for the innocent third party, and an acceptance of the *caveat emptor* principle. He also maintained that "patents for inventions are not to be treated as mere monopolies and, therefore, odious in the eyes of the law; but they are to receive a liberal construction ... to be so interpreted as to uphold and not to destroy the right of the inventor" (*Turrill v. Railroad Company*, 1863). He demanded real novelty for a patent, however, and affirmed that once a patented item was sold, the inventor had no claim whatsoever.

Clifford presided over the commission that determined the 1876 disputed presidential election and, as a staunch Democrat, voted for Samuel J. Tilden. In 1880 he suffered a stroke that ended his active participation in the Court's decisions. Critics suggested that this was no great legal loss because they believed that he had become senile some time before. Even in failing health, Clifford, ever the party stalwart, clung to his position in the hope that a future Democratic president might name his successor. He refused to resign to the bitter end, which came with his death in July 1881.

—*William Bosch*

BIBLIOGRAPHY

The papers of Nathan Clifford are in the Maine Historical Society. There is no modern biography, but David M. Silver's *Lincoln's Supreme Court* (1956) is a richly researched mother lode from which other authors have mined much on Clifford's character and wartime activities. His later career is considered in Robert Fridlington, *The Reconstruction Court, 1864–1888* (1987).

NOTEWORTHY OPINIONS

Turrill v. Railroad Company, 68 U.S. 491 (1863)

Knox v. Lee, 79 U.S. 457 (1871) (Dissent)

United States v. Reese, 92 U.S. 214 (1876) (Dissent)

Hall v. DeCuir, 95 U.S. 485 (1878) (Concurrence)

BENJAMIN ROBBINS CURTIS

Birth: November 4, 1809, Watertown, Massachusetts.

Education: Harvard College, graduated 1829 with highest honors; Harvard Law School, graduated 1832.

Official Positions: Massachusetts state representative, 1849–1851.

Supreme Court Service: Recess appointment as associate justice by President Millard Fillmore, September 22, 1851, to replace Justice Levi Woodbury, who had died; nominated December 12, 1851, confirmed by the Senate, December 23, 1851, by a voice vote; took judicial oath October 10, 1851; resigned September 30, 1857; replaced by Nathan Clifford, nominated by President James Buchanan.

Death: September 15, 1874, Newport, Rhode Island.

After receiving degrees from Harvard College in 1829 and Harvard Law School in 1832, Benjamin R. Curtis spent the next seventeen years in law practice in Massachusetts. In 1849 he was elected to the Massachusetts House of Representatives and served for two years. President Millard Fillmore, following the advice of his secretary of state, Daniel Webster, then chose Curtis to fill the "New England" seat on the U.S. Supreme Court vacated by the death of Levi Woodbury.

Justice Curtis's six-year tenure was marked by enormous transition in the Court's jurisprudence, particularly with regard to the commerce clause and the Fifth Amendment's guarantee of due process. In his first term, the junior justice forged a valuable consensus in *Cooley v. Board of Wardens of the Port of Philadelphia* (1851), a challenge to a Pennsylvania law that required all vessels using the port of Philadelphia to employ local pilots or pay a substantial fine. Shipmaster Cooley contended on appeal that the statute violated the federal government's "exclusive" commerce clause power to regulate pilotage. Curtis, in a majority opinion noted for its balanced approach to the thorny conflict of national and state concerns, rejected Cooley's argument and upheld the law:

> Either absolutely to affirm, or deny that the nature of this power requires exclusive legislation by Congress, is to lose sight of the nature of the subjects of this power, and to assert concerning all of them, what is really applicable but to a part. Whatever subjects of this power are in their nature national, or admit only of one uniform system or plan of regulation, may justly be said to be of such a nature as to require exclusive legislation by Congress. That this cannot be affirmed of laws for the regulation of pilots and pilotage is plain.

In fact, he continued, Congress had expressly stated in the Judiciary Act of 1789 that such matters should be governed by existing state laws until further congressional enactment.

In crafting the "selective exclusiveness" standard later known as the *Cooley* doctrine, Curtis set forth a pragmatic method for distinguishing subjects of exclusive federal control from those that might be governed locally or concurrently between the federal government and the states. Although ultimately supplanted by a more flexible balancing approach to delineating the boundaries of the commerce power, the *Cooley* doctrine nevertheless provided a useful analytical transition from the rigidity of earlier commerce clause decisions.

Curtis also influenced the Court's nascent due process jurisprudence. In *Murray's Lessee v. Hoboken Land & improvement Co.* (1856), he wrote on behalf of a unanimous Court that the Fifth Amendment guarantee of due process applied to the actions of Congress as well as to those of the executive and judicial branches. In so doing, Curtis proffered an instrumental definition of due process as procedures that did not conflict with specific written constitutional provisions or with the "settled modes and usages" of English and early American practice. Curtis's other noteworthy opinions include: *Steamboat New World v. King* (1854), in which the Court broadened the scope of federal admiralty jurisdiction to include inland rivers on the basis of their navigability rather than the ebb and flow of the ocean tides, and *Lafayette Insurance Company v. French* (1856), in which the Court clarified the jurisdictional

Benjamin Robbins Curtis

status of corporations as "citizens" of their state of incorporation.

Aside from *Cooley,* however, Curtis's most memorable opinion is his forceful dissent in *Dred Scott v. Sandford* (1857). In response to the majority's denial of Scott's appeal on the grounds that Congress was powerless to prohibit slavery and that blacks were not entitled to the privileges and immunities of national citizenship, Curtis methodically, thoroughly, and devastatingly dissected the flaws of the majority's reasoning. In the mistaken belief that the majority decision had already been filed, Curtis prematurely released a copy of his dissent to a Boston reporter. The story exacerbated the already tense atmosphere of disagreement over the decision. Shortly thereafter, Curtis resigned from the Court, citing the inadequate salary—he had a large family to support—and conflicting "private duties" as his motivations. It is quite likely that his loss of confidence in the Court following the *Dred Scott* decision was a significant contributing factor.

While on the Court, Curtis edited two significant reference works, *Reports of Cases in the Circuit Courts of the United States* (2 vols., 1854), and *Decisions of the Supreme Court of the United States* (22 vols., 1856). The latter accomplishment was one of the earliest compilations of condensed decisions in the history of the Court.

After leaving the bench, Curtis devoted the rest of his life to private law practice and argued fifty-four cases before the Court. In 1868 he successfully defended President Andrew Johnson in his Senate impeachment trial. After several years of poor health, he died on September 15, 1874, in Newport, Rhode Island.

—*Margaret M. Russell*

BIBLIOGRAPHY

Curtis's papers are available at both the Library of Congress and the American Antiquarian Society in Boston. *The Life and Writings of Benjamin Robbins Curtis* and *A Memoir of Benjamin Robbins Curtis, LL.D., with Some of His Professional and Miscellaneous Writings*, both edited by the justice's son, Benjamin R. Curtis, in 1879, are wide-ranging collections of Curtis's correspondence, speeches, judicial opinions, and other writings. The most complete study of Justice Curtis to date is an unpublished doctoral dissertation by Richard H. Leach, "Benjamin R. Curtis: Case Study of a Supreme Court Justice" (Princeton, 1951). Portions of this project have been published in three articles: "Benjamin Robbins Curtis: Judicial Misfit," *New England Quarterly* 25 (1952): 507; "Benjamin Robbins Curtis: A Model for a Successful Legal Career," *American Bar Association Journal* 41 (1955): 225; and "Justice Curtis and the *Dred Scott* Case," *Essex Institute Historical Collection* 94 (1958): 37. Recent scholarship tends to focus on his *Dred Scott* opinion; see Sanford Levinson, "Abraham Lincoln, Benjamin Curtis, and the Importance of Constitutional Fidelity," *Green Bag* 4 (n.s. 2001): 419; and Earl Maltz, "The Unlikely Hero of Dred Scott: Benjamin Robbins Curtis and the Constitutional Law of Slavery," *Cardozo Law Review* 17 (1996): 1995.

NOTEWORTHY OPINIONS

Cooley v. Board of Wardens of the Port of Philadelphia, 53 U.S. 299 (1851)

Murray's Lessee v. Hoboken Land & Improvement Co., 59 U.S. 272 (1856)

Dred Scott v. Sandford, 60 U.S. 393 (1857) (Dissent)

WILLIAM CUSHING

Birth: March 1, 1732, Scituate, Massachusetts.

Education: Graduated Harvard, 1751, honorary LL.D., 1785; Yale, honorary A.M., 1753; studied law under Jeremiah Gridley; admitted to the bar in 1755.

Official Positions: Judge, probate court for Lincoln County, Massachusetts (now Maine), 1760–1761; judge, Superior Court of Massachusetts Bay province, 1772–1777; chief justice, Superior Court of the Commonwealth of Massachusetts, 1777–1780, Supreme Judicial Court, 1780–1789; member, Massachusetts Constitutional Convention, 1779; vice president, Massachusetts Convention, which ratified U.S. Constitution, 1788; delegate to Electoral College, 1788.

Supreme Court Service: Nominated associate justice by President George Washington, September 24, 1789; confirmed by the Senate, September 26, 1789, by a voice vote; took judicial oath February 2, 1790; served until September 13, 1810; replaced by Joseph Story, nominated by President James Madison.

Death: September 13, 1810, Scituate, Massachusetts.

William Cushing served longer with minimal effect than any of the fourteen Supreme Court justices whose terms overlapped his. His lengthy judicial career in Massachusetts made him an obvious, almost automatic, choice by President George Washington. Indeed, on paper, he was the most highly qualified of any of his brethren. It was only after his twenty-one uneventful years on the Court that historians looked back and discovered that there was not a great deal to show for his twenty-nine years on the state bench either—with one possible exception. Legend holds that Cushing proclaimed an end to slavery in Massachusetts in 1783 because it was a violation of the new state constitution. The evidence to support such a claim, however, is scanty and unconvincing.

Cushing seemed to have been born for political influence in Massachusetts. On his mother's side, he descended from the patriarch John Cotton, and his father and grandfather were both judges of the Massachusetts Superior Court. When John Cushing retired after twenty-three years, he was succeeded by William, who had for the past twelve years been register of deeds and judge of probate for a county in the Maine district, as well as that county's only attorney. Cushing was the only judge who was retained when the new state supreme court was formed in 1775. He had endeared himself to the radicals by refusing his salary from the Crown in 1774, yet also managed to remain on friendly terms with loyalists. He was justly described by contemporaries as "remarkable for the secrecy of his opinions." He was state chief justice from 1777 until his appointment to the U.S. Supreme Court. Cushing seems to have contributed little enlightenment as a member of the convention that wrote the Massachusetts Constitution of 1780, or as vice president of the state convention that ratified the federal Constitution.

Cushing was officially the senior associate justice on the Supreme Court, as well as the oldest of Washington's appointees. John Rutledge was appointed first after Chief Justice John Jay, but he never occupied the second seat. Seniority did not make Cushing more voluble. It may even have had the opposite effect. The justices spoke in reverse seniority, so Cushing preceded only the chief justice. Younger and more creative thinkers would already have expounded on the issues prior to Cushing, so he was often in a position of simply concurring with them. Even before Chief Justice John Marshall persuaded his colleagues to abandon *seriatim* decisions, Cushing could rationalize his relative silence. President Thomas Jefferson had Cushing primarily in mind when he proposed that the Court be required to return to *seriatim* decisions, in hopes that it would highlight the weaknesses of the silent majority.

William Cushing

Cushing delivered only nineteen brief opinions during his twenty-one years on the bench, and his decisions were direct, noncomplex, or as some have said, "simple." If succinctness is a blessing, then Cushing was a saint. He wrote just two sentences in *Calder v. Bull* (1798), a case which he considered "clear of all difficulty." He did not even refer to the *ex post facto* clause. This opinion is an extraordinary example, but even his longer opinions generally deal with a single point. In *Ware v. Hylton* (1796), a case involving prewar debts owed to British merchants, he focused entirely on the language of the Treaty of 1783, avoiding the discussions of federal relationships, which characterized Justice Samuel Chase's lead opinion. Cushing's first sentence gives an accurate picture of the opinion: "My statement of this case will, agreeable to my view of it, be short." *Chisholm v. Georgia* (1793), which upheld the right of a citizen to sue a state in federal court, is regarded as Cushing's best opinion, but it adds nothing significant to the opinions that had preceded it. He declared that the rights of individuals are "as dear and precious as those of states." He challenged the states that "if the constitution is found inconvenient . . . , it is well that a regular mode is pointed out for amendment." Congress and the states quickly initiated that process, which led to the Eleventh Amendment.

Under Marshall, Cushing was called on most often to deal with cases turning on procedural technicalities—frequently issues involving loyalist or British property claims. Sadly, his most impressive later opinion, *McIlvaine v. Coxe's Lessee* (1808), which established guidelines for naturalization policy, was described by a major historian of the Marshall Court as "well beyond his capacities at that time, and perhaps beyond his professional ability even at a younger age." Law professor Herbert A. Johnson has speculated that the quality of this opinion, with Cushing's name attached, brings into question "the commonly accepted assumption that *delivery* of a majority opinion implied *authorship* of the opinion."

On circuit in Connecticut, Cushing and John Jay were the first federal judges to invalidate a state law for violation of the Treaty of 1783. On the Supreme Court, he took a unique position on the judicial review of state constitutions. He was the only justice who thought the Supreme Court could void an act in violation of the Georgia constitution (*Cooper v. Telfair,* 1800). He added, however, that the case did not warrant judicial review because the authority to banish citizens and to confiscate property was inherent in every government and was a matter for legislative, rather than judicial, determination.

President Washington was obviously not disappointed in his senior associate justice. He appointed Cushing chief justice on January 26, 1796, and the Senate, after rejecting John Rutledge, confirmed him the next day. He kept the commission for a week before declining because of age and ill health. Alexander Hamilton and Patrick Henry had also declined before the Cushing appointment, so he was in good company. Sen. William Plumer, F-N.H., was distressed by Cushing's nomination to head the Court.

He is a man I love and esteem. He once possessed firmness and other qualities for that office, but Time, the enemy of man, has much impaired his mental faculties. When Jay resigned, Cushing was the eldest Justice, and I fear that the promotion will form a precedent for making Chief Justice from the eldest Judge though the other candidates may be much better qualified.

Washington next considered Justices William Paterson and James Iredell before looking outside the Court to Oliver Ellsworth. An associate justice would not be advanced to the center chair until 1910, when Edward D. White became chief justice. President John Adams cited the possible offense to Cushing as a reason not to advance Paterson to chief justice in 1801, but that was intended to justify not appointing Paterson rather than to imply serious consideration of Cushing.

Cushing was always dignified, even in his declining years. He was probably the last American judge to wear the full English wig, ceasing only when he realized that this formidable headgear was the reason that scores of New York City boys followed him in the streets. He was well read, both in legal and general literature. His earlier travels to the state courts in a horse-drawn wagon that contained many of the comforts of home, including a library, provisions, and his wife, who read to him as they proceeded, surely contributed to his knowledge. Distances and roads were such for a Supreme Court justice that he had to travel them by horseback, despite his age, to ride his circuit.

Cushing was also remarkably dedicated and conscientious, except when his health impeded him. He set a record for responsibility that can never be matched. He was the one justice who was present on the first day that the Court sat in each of the three capitals of the United States. He was in New York with John Jay and James Wilson when the Court first convened on February 1, 1790; he was in Philadelphia with three others when they first met there one year later; and he was the only one who reported for duty in Washington, D.C., at the beginning of the February 1801 term.

When Justice Iredell complained about the unfairness of being confined to the distant southern circuit, Cushing characteristically replied that he would do his share, whatever the rotation. He was too optimistic when he consoled Iredell that "the System may ere long meet with a legislative remedy." Indeed, the chief justice had asked him to negotiate with Congress to lessen the burden of circuit riding. He suggested that cases should be heard at the capital, rather than at the periphery, which would have improved the lives of six Supreme Court justices, while placing a severe burden on many litigants and their counsel. It is indicative of Cushing's sense of duty that in 1790 he delayed the acceptance of his appointment to the Supreme Court so that he could make one last circuit in the state courts to ensure that they met.

Generally good spirited both on and off the bench, Cushing was never as partisan as most of his colleagues. His peak of extremism came in 1798, when he warned the grand jury in Virginia about a French "plot against the rights of Nations and of mankind and against all religion and virtue, order and decency."

Sadly, Cushing had no private fortune and was forced to remain too long on the Court in order to keep his salary. He had never been notably successful as an attorney, so he had no legal practice to rely on for survival. Not an outstanding judge either, Cushing remained long enough to justify Justice William Johnson's characterization of him twelve years after his death as "incompetent." Perhaps the best assessment of the senior associate justice was expressed fourteen years before he died, by Senator Plumer, who considered Cushing a friend. Plumer described the retiring John Blair, who had certainly been no star on the Supreme Court, as "a man of good abilities, not indeed a Jay, but far superior to Cushing."

—*Donald O. Dewey*

BIBLIOGRAPHY

The best published review of Cushing's career is Herbert A. Johnson's essay in Friedman and Israel, *Justices* vol. 1, 57. John Cushing's unpublished doctoral dissertation, "A Revolutionary Conservative: The Public Life of William Cushing, 1732–1810" (Clark University, 1960), is thorough, critical, and valuable. His article "The Cushing Court and the Abolition of Slavery in Massachusetts," *American Journal of Legal History* 5 (1961): 118, takes a dim view of Cushing's leadership on this issue. Dated, but still useful, is Arthur P. Rugg, "William Cushing," *Yale Law Journal* 30 (1920): 120.

NOTEWORTHY OPINIONS

Chisholm v. Georgia, 2 U.S. 419 (1793)

Ware v. Hylton, 3 U.S. 199 (1796)

McIlvaine v. Coxe's Lessee, 6 U.S. 280 (1808)

PETER VIVIAN DANIEL

Birth: April 24, 1784, Stafford County, Virginia.

Education: Privately tutored; attended Princeton University, 1802–1803.

Official Positions: Member, Virginia House of Delegates, 1809–1812; Virginia Privy Council, 1812–1835; lieutenant governor of Virginia, 1818–1835; U.S. district judge, Eastern District of Virginia, 1836–1841.

Supreme Court Service: Nominated associate justice by President Martin Van Buren, February 27, 1841, to replace Justice Philip Barbour, who had died; confirmed by the Senate, March 2, 1841, by a 22–5 vote; took judicial oath January 10, 1842; served until May 31, 1860; replaced by Samuel F. Miller, nominated by President Abraham Lincoln.

Death: May 31, 1860, Richmond, Virginia.

Born in Stafford County, Virginia, nearly midway between Washington and Richmond, Peter V. Daniel was educated by private tutors and attended the College of New Jersey (later Princeton) for a few months. He moved to Richmond in 1805 to study law with Edmund Randolph, was admitted to the bar in 1808, and elected to the Virginia legislature the next year. He soon rose to membership in the Virginia Privy Council and became lieutenant governor in 1818. Daniel was active in leadership of the Old Dominion Democratic-Republicans, later the Jacksonian Democrats. He owned slaves, but was never a planter. Within the strictures of Virginia's slave system, he gave careful attention to details of fact and to opportunities for mercy in the Virginia Privy Council's review of trials of slaves for rape and of allegations that a slave suspect had been tortured.

Supporting William H. Crawford in 1824 and Andrew Jackson in 1828, Daniel became Jackson's, and later Martin Van Buren's, main supporter in Virginia. His own political career was only moderately successful. When he ran for governor in 1830, he lost to John Floyd. By February 1835 he was off the council, having been defeated for reelection under the new state constitution. Jackson finally found a way to reward Daniel; in March 1836 the president appointed Daniel federal district judge for the Eastern District of Virginia. The day Justice Philip Barbour (a Virginian) died in 1841, President Van Buren, with just nine more days in office, decided to appoint Daniel to the Supreme Court. Whigs mounted a fruitless effort to obstruct the appointment, but the Senate confirmed him, and Daniel served from January 1842 until his death in May 1860. He wrote seventy-four majority opinions, filed fifty dissents, and wrote a number of concurring opinions.

As a justice, Daniel had little lasting influence on the Supreme Court. He wrote more than twice as many lone dissenting opinions as did any other justice on the Taney Court. He had to, if he were to live up to Van Buren's description of him as "a Democrat *ab ovo*" who was "not in so much danger of falling off in the true spirit." States' rights was his unbending position; hostility to banks and corporations and opposition to internal improvements were his tenets until his death. The reason that Justice Daniel frequently was in the minority on the Court—often a minority of one—was his extreme devotion to antifederalism and agrarianism. There are some clues concerning his zealous attachment to states' rights and lingering antifederalism. Daniel's first wife was the daughter of Edmund Randolph, who had displayed ambivalence about the Constitution of 1787. In addition, Daniel came of age and joined the Old Dominion government when fellow Virginian John Taylor of Caroline was publishing his passionate arguments against mercantile oppression of agriculture through control of federal power, and when Spencer Roane and other Virginians challenged the Marshall Court's decisions concerning federal judicial supremacy.

His background, however, does not fully explain Daniel's perseveration in the face of inevitable change. Randolph, Roane, and Taylor could exert no immediate influence on Justice Daniel: all were eulogized well before Daniel joined the Court. While justices such as Roger Brooke Taney led the Court in reinterpretation of the Constitution to remove obstacles to early corporate growth, other members of the bench and bar were expanding the coverage of federal admiralty jurisdiction, as steamboats changed the nature of waterborne commerce, corporations and banks asserted their legal rights in case after federal case, and a minority of northern jurists looked

Peter Vivian Daniel

for ways to use the power of the federal government against slavery. Daniel fought a rearguard action against corporations and banks, attempted to limit federal admiralty jurisdiction to the traditional tidewater, strenuously opposed internal improvements, and vigorously championed state and federal protection of the "peculiar institution," slavery. Only in the last two battles did he have a significant number of allies. Had Daniel lived beyond 1860, he would doubtlessly have joined another group—Confederate sympathizers or Confederates—whose cause was lost.

Daniel faced the special uphill battle of anyone who wishes to limit the federal government's power. Where an omission from the Constitution is not obvious and there is no express denial of a power to the federal government, the necessary and proper clause can be cited to claim a federal power. So it was with internal improvements such as roads and canals. When the national government offered none of these improvements or services, nor was expressly required to, it was certainly a matter of argument as to whether the Constitution allowed it to. That Daniel held one of the more extreme positions about internal improvement—that it was never allowed—did not place him on the untenable side of the argument. He stood with millions of other Americans. Unelected, Daniel had no constituency, but his point of view did.

Daniel argued in *Searight v. Stokes* (1845), therefore, that the Constitution granted no power to the central government to create roads or any other internal improvement within the states. He chose a poor way to emphasize his point. The Constitution did, he admitted, confer on the government the power to establish post roads; but, in a tour de force of denial, he insisted that power did not extend beyond designating routes. Here was a perfect opportunity for someone to respond that the necessary and proper clause gave full power to the central government to build, own, and maintain post roads where there were none, or where existing roads frustrated the delivery of the U.S. mail. By Daniel's implication, however, the sovereign federal government was dependent on state or local governments or on private enterprise to provide the roads by which the mail was to be delivered.

Daniel carried his restrictive interpretation of the limits of federal power into his opinions in three of the most important regulatory cases that came before the Taney Court. In the *License Cases* (1847), he concurred with the majority that states could regulate the importation of liquor, but, true to form, he did so on the basis of his particularly intense states' right philosophy. He would not be open to later shifts in the Court's position concerning exclusivity of the federal commerce power. He dissented from the majority decision in the *Passenger Cases* (1849) that states could not tax immigrants to finance a hospital for ship passengers. That decision, he declared, was guilty of "trampling down ... some of the strongest defenses of the safety and independence of the States of this confederacy." Daniel split the difference in his separate opinion in *Cooley v. Board of Wardens* (1851), concurring with the decision but dissenting from the majority's arguments. The issue was whether pilotage in harbors was within the federal power to regulate commerce. It was not, said five justices, because pilotage was of local rather than national importance. It was not, said Daniel, because the power to regulate pilotage always had been a state power and admitted neither federal interference nor even tolerance.

Unlike some of his contemporaries, Daniel never explicitly pointed out the connection between the federal regulatory cases and the troublesome question of federal jurisdiction over slavery. But his opinion in

Prigg v. Pennsylvania (1842), a major fugitive slave case, shows that his attitude toward federal power over commerce was in uneasy harmony with his opinions concerning the domestic institution. He firmly believed that the states had the duty to carry out, by legislation if necessary, the legitimate powers of the central government. In *Prigg,* the Court majority appeared to hold any state legislation concerning fugitive slaves to be in conflict with the exclusive power of the federal government to aid owners in the return of their human property. But Daniel believed that state action to aid the capture and return of fugitive slaves upheld—indeed, must uphold—federal power to protect the property rights of owners. He never explicitly acknowledged the extent to which such state aid to the functioning of the federal government would increase the federal government's power. It increased that power over slavery, but Daniel understood the practical problem that motivated slavery supporters to campaign for adequate assistance from the central government to recapture runaway slaves until the Fugitive Slave Act of 1850 was passed—and after even it proved to be inadequate. There were not enough federal officials in the states to enforce the Fugitive Slave Law of 1793, so state government help was essential to make the fugitive slave provision of the Constitution effective. And Daniel was hardly alone in this dissent from part of Justice Joseph Story's opinion for the Court: Chief Justice Taney stood firmly with him.

Daniel's *Dred Scott v. Sandford* (1857) opinion showed his most consistent thinking: he was both proslavery and opposed to the exercise of one kind of federal power, that of Congress over slavery in the territories. (Still, he recognized no right of a state to create a citizen of the national government.) Daniel emphasized the role of Congress as "agent or trustee" of the United States and the people thereof and concluded that Congress could not thereby take upon itself the power to confer on one group of citizens a privilege that it denied to another group. In other words, Daniel argued that Congress had no right to prohibit slave owners from bringing their human property into the area designated by the Missouri

Compromise as free when Congress allowed non-slaveholders to bring in other kinds of property. To do so was discrimination against slaveholders and southerners and therefore went beyond the constitutional authority of any branch of the federal government. Daniel maintained another kind of consistency. If Congress had no power to legislate concerning slavery in the territories, then how could the Northwest Ordinance's prohibition of slavery be valid? Daniel was the only justice to say it was not—in fact, it was "*ab initio* void." Daniel left nothing to chance in this concurring opinion. He found every way possible to deny federal power over slavery in the territories.

It was in admiralty cases that Daniel became most anachronistic and eccentric. The framers of the Judiciary Act of 1789 took the admiralty clause of the Constitution to mean that the federal courts must have exclusive jurisdiction over admiralty cases. This interpretation left common law cases concerning inland water transportation to state and local courts but shifted control of admiralty cases away from the states to the new federal government. The older that government became and the more miles of river and lake that could be covered by migrating people and faster boats, the more many people argued for the extension of admiralty jurisdiction beyond the tidewater to inland waterways, especially those connected with tidewater areas. Daniel had to uphold admiralty jurisdiction over the tidewater, but the moment anyone sought to move beyond that traditional realm, Daniel blocked the way as best he could. As inland, interstate, waterborne commerce grew in complexity, however, problems of jurisdiction began to affect commerce adversely. One commentator stated that purportedly corrective legislation of 1845 granted nothing more than "quasi admiralty jurisdiction" to federal courts because it applied only to lakes and their connecting rivers and relied for its legitimacy on the federal commerce power rather than on admiralty jurisdiction. When the denial of admiralty jurisdiction in *The Thomas Jefferson* (1825) was finally overturned by a nearly unanimous Taney Court in *Propeller Genesee Chief v. Fitzhugh* (1852), Daniel predictably filed the sole dissent, even though the Court

countenanced jurisdiction only over interstate waterborne commerce. (It may be pointed out that waterborne commerce in other regions of the United States outweighed such commerce in Daniel's native South by four to one.)

It would be a mistake to dismiss Daniel completely because he chose to fight a losing battle and exhibited a prickly stubbornness and partisanship seldom seen among the very best jurists. His brothers on the bench took him very seriously because he labored with care over all decisions, expending great time and industry in his research for them and exhibiting great learning in them. His opinion in the *Passenger Cases* is one of his most interesting because his position was almost as credible as those of the rest of the divided Court. When he was assigned to write an opinion for the Court, he obviously was in harmony with the majority on the issue at hand. His opinion for the Court in *West River Bridge Co. v. Dix* (1848), which upheld an eminent domain action, stands out for its clarity and forcefulness. Even on the point of prickly stubbornness, one can find something to praise. He was nothing if not independent of the pressure of general opinion, an achievement to be admired in principle in a member of the highest judiciary. That his intellectual independence often pitted him against inevitable change is the tragedy of his career. His stiff backbone attracted little love from friends, but being lovable has never been a requirement for appointment to the supreme tribunal.

—*Philip J. Schwarz*

BIBLIOGRAPHY

The most comprehensive judicial biography is John P. Frank, *Justice Daniel Dissenting: A Biography of Peter V. Daniel, 1784–1860* (1964). A succinct account of Daniel's agrarian philosophy is Lawrence Burnette Jr., "Peter V. Daniel: Agrarian Justice," *Virginia Magazine of History and Biography* 60 (1954): 289. Carl Swisher effectively assesses Daniel's role in the major decisions of the Taney Court in *The Taney Period, 1836–64* (1974), volume 5 of the *Holmes Devise History*. The best assessment of Daniel's *Dred Scott* opinion is in Don E. Fehrenbacher, *The Dred Scott Case: Its*

Significance in American Law and Politics (1978). There is no major collection of Daniel papers, but important letters are in the Martin Van Buren papers, Library of Congress, and in scattered other collections.

NOTEWORTHY OPINIONS

Prigg v. Pennsylvania, 41 U.S. 539 (1842) (Concurrence)

Searight v. Stokes, 44 U.S. 151 (1845)

License Cases (*Thurlow v. Massachusetts*) 46 U.S. 504 (1847) (Concurrence)

West River Bridge Co. v. Dix, 47 U.S. 507 (1848)

Passenger Cases (*Smith v. Turner* and *Norris v. City of Boston*), 48 U.S. 283 (1849) (Dissent)

Cooley v. Board of Wardens of the Port of Philadelphia, 53 U.S. 299 (1851) (Concurrence)

Propeller Genesee Chief v. Fitzhugh, 53 U.S. 443 (1852) (Dissent)

Dred Scott v. Sandford, 60 U.S. 393 (1857) (Concurrence)

DAVID DAVIS

Birth: March 9, 1815, Cecil County, Maryland.

Education: Graduated Kenyon College, 1832; Yale Law School, 1835.

Official Positions: Illinois state representative, 1845–1847; member, Illinois Constitutional Convention, 1847; Illinois state circuit judge, 1848–1862; U.S. senator, 1877–1883.

Supreme Court Service: Recess appointment as associate justice by President Abraham Lincoln, October 17, 1862, to replace John A. Campbell, who had resigned; nominated December 3, 1862, confirmed by the Senate, December 8, 1862, by a voice vote; took judicial oath December 10, 1862; resigned March 4, 1877; replaced by John Marshall Harlan, nominated by President Rutherford B. Hayes.

Death: June 26, 1886, Bloomington, Illinois.

The Supreme Court career of David Davis, Abraham Lincoln's friend, campaign manager, and appointee, is most closely identified with one case—*Ex parte Milligan* (1866)—in which the Court challenged the trial of civilians by military tribunals during the Civil War. Davis's fifteen-year career on the Court was, otherwise, relatively undistinguished. Indeed, not only did Davis seek the Liberal-Republican nomination for president while sitting on the Court, but also, when the Illinois legislature elected him to the U.S. Senate, Davis chose to take the Senate oath. Moreover, Davis's decision to leave the bench disturbed the delicate political balance envisioned for the commission created to resolve the dispute over the presidential election of 1876.

David Davis was born on his maternal grandfather's plantation on Maryland's eastern shore March 9, 1815, eight months after his father, a young physician, died. He began studies at Kenyon College at age thirteen and, after graduation, moved to Lenox, Mass-

achusetts, to study law with attorney Henry W. Bishop. He attended the New Haven Law School for less than a year and returned to Lenox. At the age of twenty, Davis headed west to Illinois, ultimately settling in Bloomington. A successful law practice and an active political life, including service in the state legislature in the mid-1840s, led to his election in 1848 as a state judge in the Eighth Circuit. He held that position until his elevation to the Supreme Court in 1862, two years after orchestrating Lincoln's nomination as the Republican presidential candidate in 1860.

One would have to go beyond the opinions Justice Davis wrote during his first three years on the Supreme Court to realize that the Union was engulfed in a life-or-death struggle. Of the thirteen decisions he wrote during the December 1863 and December 1864 terms (Davis was confined to bed by illness the following term), nine concerned property disputes. But Davis's presence on the Court was significant because he voted with the slender five-member majority in the *Prize Cases* of 1863, upholding the Lincoln administration's blockade of southern ports, even absent a formal declaration of war.

While fulfilling his circuit court duties, Davis was closer to the exigencies of war. His biographer includes the following excerpt from Davis's charge to a grand jury sitting at the circuit court in Indianapolis:

> It is charged that there are secret organizations . . . with 'grips, signs and passwords' having for their objects—resistance to Law, and the overthrow of the Government. . . . If anywhere in this State bad men have combined together for such wicked purposes, I pray you, bring them to light and let them receive the punishment due to their crime.

In *Ex parte Milligan,* a case that first came before Davis when he was sitting on the circuit court for the district of Indiana, the issue concerned where such disloyal citizens would stand trial to "receive the[ir] punishment."

In May 1865 Davis, along with district judge David McDonald, heard the petition of Lambdin P. Milligan, a Peace Democrat, to be "discharged from an allegedly unlawful imprisonment." Milligan argued there and, after Davis and McDonald could not agree, before the Supreme Court that because he was a civilian, the military commission that tried, convicted, and sentenced him to death by hanging for disloyal activities had no jurisdiction. On December 17, 1866, nine months after extensive oral argument by a group of

advocates that included Maj. Gen. Benjamin Butler for the government and David Dudley Field for the defense, Davis announced a ruling in Milligan's favor.

Davis, who to that point had been circumspect and conservative in his rhetoric as a justice, dramatically noted that the issue posed by Milligan's challenge "involves the very framework of the government and the fundamental principles of American liberty"; indeed, "no graver question was ever considered by this court, nor one which more nearly concerns the rights of the whole people." Now that the "late wicked Rebellion" was over, constitutional questions regarding the conduct of the Civil War could "be discussed and decided without passion or the admixture of any element not required to form a legal judgment." Davis's opinion in *Milligan* signaled the Court's reassertion of its antebellum role as ultimate arbiter and defender of the Constitution.

David Davis

Davis concluded that the military commission had no jurisdiction to try or sentence Milligan. The dire conditions of war could not excuse the violation of essential constitutional rights. In the most memorable passage from his entire Supreme Court opus, Davis proclaimed:

> The Constitution of the United States is a law for rulers and people, equally in war and in peace, and under all circumstances. No doctrine, involving more pernicious consequences, was ever invented by the wit of man than that any of its provisions can be suspended during any of the great exigencies of government.

The price for uttering these noble phrases was, according to Supreme Court historian Charles Warren, "a storm of invective and opprobrium" from Radical Republican quarters. Stung by this reaction, Davis wrote, in private correspondence: "The people can change their Constitution, but until it is done all attempts to evade it, override it, or disregard it, end either in anarchy or despotism." This principle would resurface in Supreme Court history not only in cases specifically concerning military trial of civilians in subsequent wars, but also in the opinions of the Court's conservatives who later struggled against the wave of liberal legislation designed to deliver the nation from the depths of the Great Depression.

Davis's remaining years on the Court would prove to be neither as stormy nor as stimulating, particularly for someone as politically active and interested as he. Much of the Court's work was taken up with problems posed by the outcome and conduct of the Civil War, the relationship between the states and the newly ascendant federal government, and the nation's increasingly complex industrial economy.

One puzzle Davis and his fellow justices faced was the question of when the Civil War had, in fact, ended. In *Burke v. Miltenberger* (1874), for example, the Supreme Court had to decide, in a real property dispute, whether the Provisional Court of Louisiana, established by President Lincoln during the war, maintained its authority as late as June 1865. Davis noted that no single event, such as the surrender of Confederate general Kirby Smith on May 26, 1865, marked the cessation of the war; rather, "the war did not begin or close at the same time in all the States, that its commencement and termination in any State is to be determined by some public act of the political departments of the government."

In *United States v. Anderson* (1870), the dispute concerned the effect of a two-year statute of limitations on a claim brought by a loyal citizen in June 1868 under the Abandoned or Captured Property Act. As in *Burke,* Davis refused to identify one universal date for the end of the war. In the absence of clear guidance from Congress, Davis opted for a relatively late date, August 20, 1866, in the process making clear

his pro-Union bias: "It is clear the point of time should be construed most favorably to the person who adhered to the National Union, and who has proved the government took his property."

Although slavery was abolished by the Thirteenth Amendment, the Supreme Court still had to contend with the legacy of the "peculiar institution." In *Boyce v. Tabb* (1873), the Court affirmed a federal circuit court holding that a creditor could enforce a promissory note given by a debtor for slaves purchased in 1861. Despite the fact that the Louisiana Supreme Court had declared such contracts void, Davis, citing the principles of *Swift v. Tyson* (1842), did not feel bound to follow the state's lead, noting that state court decisions "are not conclusive authority, although they are entitled to, and will receive from us, attention and respect."

In an earlier case, *Payne v. Hook* (1869), Davis had also championed federal law, notwithstanding contrary state rulings. In a probate matter brought by a Virginian against a Missouri official, Davis concluded that the equity jurisdiction of federal courts "is subject to neither limitation or restraint by State legislation, and is uniform throughout the different States of the Union."

He did, however, recognize a limit to judicial power, even of the federal courts. For example, in *Wilmington and Raleigh Railroad Co. v. Reid* (1871), the Supreme Court, in an opinion by Davis, thwarted North Carolina's attempt to tax railroad property, despite a provision in the railroad's charter exempting the company "from any public charge or tax whatsoever." The tax exemption provision was deemed "plain and unambiguous"; despite his sympathy for the state's plight, especially since "the necessities of government cannot always be foreseen," Davis concluded that the courts of the country "are not the proper tribunals to apply the corrective to improvident legislation of this character." In this regard, see also *Washington University v. Rouse* (1869), a Davis opinion protecting the school's tax-exempt status.

Another railroad benefited from Davis's jurisprudence in *Union Pacific Railroad Company v. Hall* (1875). This time it was the federal government that was seeking payment from the carrier, but the Supreme Court refused to hold Union Pacific liable for interest on federal bonds before the maturity of the principal. Davis adhered closely to the terms of the 1862 act of Congress authorizing and financing railroad construction and to the realities then prevailing: "Vast as was the work, limited as were the private resources to build it, the growing wants as well as the existing and future military necessities of the country demanded that it be completed." The Court's role was not to "sit in judgment upon [the statute's] wisdom or policy," but to "interpret its provisions." Although Davis privately expressed concern about "railroad mania" in Illinois localities anxious to lend support through bond issues, in the *Union Pacific* case he did not allow his personal bias to interfere with his judicial obligations.

Davis's years on the Supreme Court were frustrating, exacting, and ultimately unsatisfying. He enjoyed circuit court duties but confessed privately that he found appellate work "too much like hard labor." In February 1872 Davis received the presidential nomination at the Labor Reform (or National Labor Union) convention in Columbus. His dreams of the White House evaporated two months later when, despite some active campaigning on his behalf, he lost the Liberal Republican nomination to Horace Greeley.

Davis had a chance to play a more prominent role in the next presidential election, as it was generally expected that, unaligned as he was with the leaders of either party, he would be named to the electoral commission charged with deciding the winner in the Hayes-Tilden contest. Instead, Davis accepted his election to the U.S. Senate from Illinois and resigned his seat on the Court. He served six years as a senator and, as an independent leader of that body, was named president pro tem in 1881. As the first in the line of succession following the death of President James A. Garfield and the accession of Chester A. Arthur, Davis had finally realized his national political aspirations.

—*Michael Allan Wolf*

BIBLIOGRAPHY

The standard biographical treatment, Willard King, *Lincoln's Manager: David Davis* (1960), is especially strong on Davis's political life. The Davis family papers can be found at the Illinois State Historical Society in Springfield. In addition, an impressive collection of Davis papers and other materials was placed by King into the collection of the Chicago Historical Society. Davis's Court career is skillfully woven into Charles Fairman's broader account in *Reconstruction and Reunion: 1864–88, Part One* (1971), volume 6 of the *Holmes Devise History*. Stanley Kutler's *Judicial Power and Reconstruction Politics* (1968) contains quite a provocative account of the Milligan affair.

NOTEWORTHY OPINIONS

Ex parte Milligan, 71 U.S. 2 (1866)

Wilmington and Raleigh Railroad Co. v. Reid, 80 U.S. 264 (1871)

Boyce v. Tabb, 85 U.S. 546 (1873)

Burke v. Miltenberger, 86 U.S. 519 (1874)

Union Pacific Railroad Co. v. Hall, 91 U.S. 343 (1875)

WILLIAM RUFUS DAY

Birth: April 17, 1849, Ravenna, Ohio.

Education: University of Michigan, A.B., 1870; University of Michigan Law School, 1871–1872.

Official Positions: Judge, Court of Common Pleas, Canton, Ohio, 1886; first assistant U.S. secretary of state, 1897–1898; U.S. secretary of state, 1898; member, U.S. delegation, Paris Peace Conference, 1898–1899; judge, U.S. Court of Appeals for the Sixth Circuit, 1899–1903; umpire, Mixed Claims Commission, 1922–1923.

Supreme Court Service: Nominated associate justice by President Theodore Roosevelt, February 19, 1903, to replace George Shiras Jr., who had resigned; confirmed by the Senate, February 23, 1903, by a voice vote; took judicial oath March 2, 1903; resigned November 13, 1922; replaced by Pierce Butler, nominated by President Warren G. Harding.

Death: July 9, 1923, Mackinac Island, Michigan.

Until late in the fourth decade of his life, save for the few years he spent at the University of Michigan, most of William Day's life was centered in Ohio. In 1872 he formed a partnership with a locally established lawyer, William S. Lynch, in Canton. While Lynch built the firm's corporate client base, Day earned a reputation as a litigator. Lynch introduced Day to the woman who became his wife and to William McKinley. Day and McKinley became close friends and remained so until McKinley's death. In 1897 President McKinley brought Day to Washington, and, as first assistant secretary of state, secretary of state, and peace commissioner, Day was a major participant in the Spanish-American War. In 1899 McKinley returned Day to Cincinnati, Ohio, as a judge of the Sixth Circuit, where he sat with two other future members of the Supreme Court, Horace Lurton and William Howard Taft. President Theodore Roosevelt, perhaps to secure the support of the

McKinley wing of the party, named Day to the Supreme Court in 1903.

Day served for nineteen years on the Court and made a record as a liberal formalist. In an era dominated by government reaction to economic change and judicial scrutiny of such action, Day generally favored government action. The centerpiece of his constitutional faith was the concept of dual sovereignty, especially as expressed in the Tenth Amendment; within limits, he sanctioned government regulation of economic and social activity. Day believed that the federal and state governments could extensively regulate the economy, but they could do so only within their proscribed spheres. Day therefore voted to sustain state use of police powers, but he also favored exercise of limited federal powers.

The states were central to Day's jurisprudence of government action. Under the Tenth Amendment, which reserved to the states the powers not delegated to the federal government, Day believed that the states possessed broad police powers. He therefore dissented in two notable cases in which the Court struck down state regulation: *Lochner v. New York* (1905) and *Coppage v. Kansas* (1915). He refused to join the majority in *Lochner* when it struck down a New York health regulation that limited the working hours of bakers. He wrote a strong dissent in *Coppage*. Day defended the state police power when the Court struck down, as an infringement of the liberty to contract, a state ban on yellow dog contracts, which made it a condition of employment that the worker not belong to or join any union.

Day was not just a dissenter. In *McLean v. Arkansas* (1909), he wrote the opinion for the Court upholding mining safety regulations; likewise, in *Minnesota ex rel. Whipple v. Martinson* (1921), he wrote the Court's opinion sustaining the states' power to regulate drug use. In Day's jurisprudence, states could legislate to protect public health, safety, and morals; but he did not believe that the federal government had a similar power.

William Rufus Day

Although the Constitution gives Congress no general power to legislate in the interest of health and public welfare, many progressives sought such legislation. Reformers hung their proposals on certain constitutional hooks based on the delegated powers. The most important of these was the commerce power, and, from the late nineteenth century to the New Deal, its use grew dramatically. Day never countenanced the unlimited growth of the commerce power, and he was unwilling to expand it beyond its late nineteenth-century bounds. His limitations of the commerce power derived from Chief Justice Melville Fuller's opinion in *United States v. E. C. Knight Company* (1895). In his opinion, Fuller separated manufacturing and commerce, saying Congress could regulate interstate commerce, but it could not regulate manufacturing, which remained a matter for state control.

Day's reading of the commerce clause did not mean that Congress was powerless, but only limited. He supported federal legislation that regulated those engaged in interstate trade. He believed the Interstate Commerce Act, the Sherman Antitrust Act, and the Clayton Antitrust Act were all legitimate. He refused to go along, most notably in his dissent in *United States v. United States Steel Corp.* (1920), with his brethren who limited these laws. He also allowed the federal government to use its commerce power to ban from transportation impure and harmful products. In *Hoke v. United States* (1913), he even permitted the commerce power—through the Mann Act—to be used to ban the transportation of women across state lines for immoral purposes. But this was as far as Day would go. The limits he placed on federal action through the commerce power were clearly seen in his opinion for the Court in *Hammer v. Dagenhart* (1918). In a 5–4 decision, the Court struck down a federal ban from interstate commerce of goods made with child labor. To Day, the law was regulation of manufacturing—a subject reserved to the states—and not a legitimate use of the commerce power. The law, Day thought, threatened to eliminate local powers and threatened the federal nature of the nation. William Day represented a liberal strain of the formalist judicial tradition of the nineteenth century and early twentieth century: he was willing to use government power, but only within the known rules.

—*Richard F. Hamm*

BIBLIOGRAPHY

A good study of Day's judicial career is Joseph E. McLean, *William Rufus Day: Supreme Court Justice from Ohio* (1946). Stephen B. Wood, *Constitutional Politics in the Progressive Era: Child Labor and the Law* (1968), is the best treatment of the circumstances surrounding his most famous opinion.

NOTEWORTHY OPINIONS

McLean v. Arkansas, 211 U.S. 539 (1909)

Coppage v. Kansas, 236 U.S. 1 (1915) (Dissent)

Hammer v. Dagenhart, 247 U.S. 251 (1918)

United States v. United States Steel Corp., 251 U.S. 417 (1920) (Dissent)

WILLIAM ORVILLE DOUGLAS

Birth: October 16, 1898, Maine, Minnesota.

Education: Whitman College, B.A., 1920; Columbia Law School, LL.B., 1925.

Official Positions: Member, Securities and Exchange Commission, 1936–1939; chairman, 1937–1939.

Supreme Court Service: Nominated associate justice by President Franklin D. Roosevelt, March 20, 1939, to replace Louis D. Brandeis, who had retired; confirmed by the Senate, April 4, 1939, by a 62–4 vote; took judicial oath April 17, 1939; retired November 12, 1975; replaced by John Paul Stevens, nominated by President Gerald R. Ford.

Death: January 19, 1980, Washington D.C.

Justice William O. Douglas served longer on the U.S. Supreme Court than any other justice. Irony, variety, and nonconformity were the characteristics of the restless intelligence of this independent-minded man, whose thirty-six-year tenure on the Court spanned major transformations in mid–twentieth-century American society. Justice Douglas was very much a creature of his times. From the New Deal and World War II at the beginning of his judicial career, through the cold war, the civil rights and environmental movements, to the withdrawal from Vietnam as he retired from the Court, Douglas responded to the challenges of his era.

Douglas's judicial opinions do not fit within any particular school of legal doctrine, although he is associated with the legal realists and considered both an activist and a liberal jurist. In fact, Douglas resisted the very concept of legal doctrine and rejected any foreordained set of propositions from which resolutions of legal controversies could be deduced. Instead, he believed that his job as a justice was to make decisions about particular sets of facts in their particular

social, economic, and political contexts. As the situations changed, his decisions changed.

Although he resisted doctrine, Douglas believed passionately in the power of ideas. His judicial opinions sometimes have an oracular style, articulating a wide variety of values and ideals such as democracy, equality, free enterprise, privacy, diversity, and conservation. Many of the opinions of his late judicial career sound like manifestos. Both on and off the Court, Douglas tirelessly advocated progressive views and liberal democratic values. Most of all, he believed that individuals should think for themselves. Douglas genuinely despised conformity and fought against the regimentation of individuals by big business or big government.

During his long tenure on the bench, Douglas wrote more than 1,200 judicial opinions, countless articles and speeches, and thirty-one books, including a two-volume autobiography. After World War II, during Court recesses, Douglas traveled to Russia, China, Burma, India, and other remote parts of the world and wrote about them in popular books and articles. He said that these explorations of diverse societies gave him a fresh perspective on the issues that came before the Supreme Court. For Douglas, theory and life always went together.

In 1939 President Franklin D. Roosevelt nominated Douglas to replace Justice Louis D. Brandeis, who knew Douglas and was reportedly pleased by his successor. Roosevelt no doubt considered Douglas, then the young, vigorous, iconoclastic, and obviously bright chairman of the Securities and Exchange Commission, as insurance against a recurrence of Supreme Court obstruction of New Deal regulatory programs. Forty years old when he was appointed, Douglas was the second-youngest justice to join the Court, after Joseph Story. Moreover, Douglas was from the West, which was demanding representation on the Court. Hailing from a poor family in Yakima, Washington, Douglas seemed to be the quintessential westerner and a self-made "common man" to boot. But Douglas came to the Court equipped with more than his often-ridiculed five-gallon western hat. Under that hat was a keen mind sharpened by an eastern legal education at Columbia Law School and service on the law faculties of Columbia and Yale.

In addition to being a New Deal loyalist, Douglas was also one of Roosevelt's personal friends. In fact, Douglas was one of the president's "poker buddies," a group that included Washington power brokers such as Interior Secretary Harold Ickes and Treasury Secretary Henry Morgenthau. Surprisingly, in light of later

William Orville Douglas

attempts to impeach Douglas, his confirmation was noncontroversial. No witnesses spoke for or against Douglas's confirmation at the Senate Judiciary Committee hearing. In the Senate, the vote was 62–4, with thirty senators not voting.

During his first decade or so on the Court, Douglas kept at least one eye on politics. He was considered a possible candidate for the Democratic ticket in 1940. In late 1941 Roosevelt suggested that Douglas resign from the Court and take charge of what became the War Production Board, but Douglas remained on the Court. There are conflicting accounts of how and why Douglas was considered but not chosen to run as vice president with Roosevelt in 1944. Although Roosevelt liked Douglas, he left the vice presidential decision up to the Democratic convention, which chose Harry Truman, who became president when Roosevelt died in 1945. Douglas apparently always felt bitter about not being president of the United States. Although he had turned away from electoral ambition by the 1950s, politics continued to intrude on his judicial life in the form of several politically motivated but unsuccessful efforts to impeach him.

Douglas brought to the Court a distinctive approach to law and judging. For him, law was a practical process that operated in a particular political, social, and economic context to serve societal goals. Judging was, in part, applied psychology. As a student and faculty member at Columbia Law School, he adopted what was then called a functional, as opposed to theoretical, view of law. As a member of the Yale Law School faculty from 1928 to 1934, Douglas worked with legal realists who took a dynamic, pragmatic view of law and insisted on an empirical approach to legal problems in the light of actual social, political, economic, and psychological realities. For realists, concentration on doctrine and precedents perniciously masked the vital actuality of present circumstances. Although Justice Douglas sometimes referred approvingly to "sociological jurisprudence," he avoided describing himself as a legal realist or as a functionalist. He was far too independent-minded to associate himself with anything that sounded like orthodoxy.

Having rejected legal doctrine as a basis for judicial decision making, Douglas gradually developed a distinctive judicial style. In simplest terms, he thought his job was to decide cases. Douglas believed he was responsible for making his own decision in each case that came before the Court, and he said he agreed with Thomas Jefferson that each judge should give his individual opinion in every case. That belief may account for Douglas's numerous dissenting and concurring opinions, including his notorious dissents without opinion in tax cases, in which he almost invariably voted for the taxpayer because he distrusted big government. During some periods, he filed a separate opinion in every case decided by the Court. Douglas became adept at deciding cases rapidly. Noted for his restlessness on the bench, he often grew impatient during oral arguments and would write letters or engage in other tasks. He hated to waste time. In his later years on the Court, he complained that accomplishing Court work, deciding cases, and ruling on petitions and stays required only working four days a week.

Explaining decisions was of secondary importance to deciding cases. Douglas generally avoided established legal doctrine. He said he was opposed to *stare decisis,* the judicial practice of deciding cases based on precedent, because present controversies should be decided on their own terms, rather than by applying past cases. Particularly in constitutional cases, Douglas thought *stare decisis* was an excuse for not making hard choices about how to apply constitutional values to new circumstances. He often said that he would rather create a precedent than find one.

The Douglas approach to judicial decision making has often been criticized as results-oriented: first deciding the result he wanted to reach and then building an argument for the correctness of that outcome. Critics also have disparaged some of his judicial opinions as careless, slapdash polemics. But Douglas was generally unperturbed by complaints that he was results-oriented or intellectually untidy. For him, life, including law, was just like that. Spinning webs of legal doctrine in order to entrap future decisions in foreordained conclusions was not the role Douglas thought the Constitution assigned to Supreme Court justices. For him, judicial opinions should provide solutions to real-life problems, not academic dissertations about legal doctrine. Sometimes he gave no reasons at all. Because deciding the case was the point of judging, and supporting reasons were far less important, it is not surprising that he often did not invest much time developing the latter. Prof. Vern Countryman, who was Douglas's law clerk and later his literary executor, reports Douglas as saying, "For those who liked the result, it was scholarship."

Douglas had an uncanny ability both to understand what was at issue in complicated cases and to envision new ways of looking at them. A typical Douglas opinion is filled with facts and may even have an appendix or two to provide even more background for his view of the case. He would first focus on the facts at issue and then find a pivotal issue at the heart of the legal controversy. In the latter part of his judicial career, he grasped cases especially quickly because he believed that legal controversies, like much of human behavior, fall into cyclical patterns, recurring every decade or so.

Douglas's opinion for the Court in *Griswold v. Connecticut* (1965), which recognized a penumbral right of privacy in the Constitution, provides a typical as well as famous example of Douglas's characteristic approach to judicial decision making. In *Griswold,* the Court held unconstitutional a Connecticut criminal statute prohibiting the use and distribution of contraceptives. Douglas saw marital privacy as the heart of the case: "Would we allow the police to search the sacred precincts of marital bedrooms for telltale signs of the use of contraceptives?" Douglas asked. Then he answered: "The very idea is repulsive to the notions of privacy surrounding the marriage relationship." Douglas's opinion found that the penumbras of various constitutional guarantees establish a "right of privacy older than the Bill of Rights," which protects marriage as "a coming together for better or for worse, hopefully enduring, and intimate to the degree of being sacred." His insight into what was really at stake in *Griswold* retains remarkable vitality.

Douglas took seriously the political status of the Supreme Court, which the Constitution places at the head of the judicial branch of government. Just as the executive or the legislative branches do, the Supreme Court exercises political power. He felt that, as a justice, he had a political role in deciding cases based on his own understanding of constitutional values. More than once, Douglas described the Court as "the keeper of the conscience. And the conscience is the Constitution." He felt that it was "very important to have a keeper of the conscience, an independent group, above the storm." Part of the Court's political role under the Constitution was independently to apply constitutional values to keep the other branches in check.

Douglas's distrust of the executive grew stronger, particularly after Roosevelt's death. For example, in *Youngstown Sheet & Tube Co. v. Sawyer* (1952), the Court held unconstitutional President Truman's seizure of the steel mills to prevent a lockout in connection with a labor dispute. Douglas concurred in the decision, but he had his own grounds for holding Truman's action unlawful. Seizure of the steel mills was expropriation of private property, which under the Constitution could be accomplished only by legislative action. Douglas warned: "All executive power—from the reign of ancient kings to the rule of modern dictators—has the outward appearance of efficiency." He repudiated the idea that the Constitution gave "the President not only the power to execute the laws but to make some."

His views regarding the political responsibilities of the judiciary led Douglas to dissent in numerous cases in which the Court dismissed constitutional challenges because those bringing the challenges were found to lack standing to sue. A good example is *Laird v. Tatum* (1972), in which the Court held that individuals and groups that had been under army surveillance because of antiwar activities lacked standing to complain about it in court. Douglas's dissenting opinion asserted that the case involved "a cancer in our body politic" in the form of a dangerously unlawful exercise of executive power that would remain unchecked if the Court did not allow these individuals and groups to bring their case to court. Douglas explained in his autobiography that his "view always has been that anyone whose life, liberty or property was threatened or impaired by any branch of government . . . had a justiciable controversy and could properly repair to a judicial tribunal for vindication of his rights."

According to Douglas, the Constitution not only established the Supreme Court's political role, but also provided a set of general principles that the Court was to apply. These constitutional principles provided a philosophy that judges must interpret and apply in light of their own lives and experiences. For Douglas, such a dynamic approach to constitutional interpretation was not at all incompatible with strict construction. He considered himself a strict constructionist, like Hugo Black, because he believed strict construction meant not subtracting from or making exceptions to constitutional freedoms. Douglas also considered himself a strict incorporationist, because he believed that all of the rights contained in the Bill of Rights were incorporated into the Fourteenth Amendment's due process guarantee against state and local action that deprives individuals of liberty.

Among the more interesting examples of Douglas's adjustment of constitutional guarantees to contemporary circumstances was his 1946 opinion in *United States v. Causby*. The case was brought by a North Carolina chicken farmer whose property served as a glide path for military aircraft using an adjacent airport during World War II. The farmer sought compensation under the just compensation clause of the Fifth Amendment because the overflights made his property less valuable. Justice Douglas's opinion recognized two important realities. First, modern air transport requires use of the air space above private property as part of the public domain, where airplanes can fly without restriction by those who own the land below. Second, the farmer's particular circumstances involved frequent low-level takeoffs and landings. That pattern of overflights, so low that they frightened the farmer's chickens literally to death, was a government use of the farmer's land. Because the government's use made the farmer's land less valuable, the farmer was entitled to recover just compensation for his loss. For Douglas, applying constitutional guarantees that the government will not take property without paying just compensation required focusing on what was really at stake: the devaluation of the chicken farmer's land by the government's overflights. In a sense, the decision is results-oriented: big government should bear the financial loss rather than the small farmer. But the opinion's apt focus on the particular circumstances of the case also exemplifies Douglas's characteristic ability to apply the Constitution to new circumstances and technologies.

Psychological aspects of the work of the Supreme Court were also important to Douglas, who believed with the realists that each individual justice brings a unique life experience to bear on making each decision. Douglas's interest in psychology was personal as well as theoretical. He noted in his autobiography that he undertook psychoanalysis with Dr. George Draper in New York to overcome his migraine headaches and his fear of water and lightning. Douglas believed that an active life outside the Court was essential to keep a justice in touch with the realities of the society in which he lived and to maintain a psychological balance. He often warned that judges who insulate themselves from life tend to become dried-up husks of human beings, incapable of growth and change.

Change was at once inevitable and beneficial in his view. Unconstrained by commitment to doctrinal consistency, Douglas was notably uninhibited about changing his mind, simply admitting that an earlier decision or view was wrong. In the 1940s the Court decided two well-known cases that involved the constitutionality of compelling school children to salute the American flag. In *Minersville School District v. Gobitis* (1940), Douglas first voted with the majority of the Court that Jehovah's Witnesses children could be compelled to salute the flag, even though doing so violated their religious beliefs. Three years later, in *Board of Education v. Barnette* (1943), he changed his mind and joined Justice Black in a concurring opinion that argued that forced expression contrary to an individual's religious principles violates the First Amendment.

In 1952 Justice Douglas forthrightly declared that he had changed his views with regard to the constitutionality of electronic surveillance. Dissenting in *On Lee v. United States*, a case involving a narcotics agent carrying a hidden microphone, Douglas stated that his earlier tolerance of electronic surveillance in *Goldman v. United States* (1942) had been mistaken. "I now more fully appreciate the vice of the practices spawned by ... *Goldman*. Reflection on them has brought new insight to me. I now feel that I was wrong in the *Goldman* case," in not voting to overrule *Olmstead v. United States* (1928), which had found wiretapping to be constitutional, over a stirring dissent from Justice Brandeis.

In addition to cases in which Justice Douglas changed his mind and said so, his flexible approach in deciding particular cases greatly annoyed some of his judicial colleagues, especially Felix Frankfurter. The Japanese exclusion cases and the Rosenberg espionage case are two prominent examples. In these cases, which involved highly charged political controversies, Douglas did not see himself or his decisions as inconsistent. In his view, he simply responded to the particular circumstances of various aspects of the cases, to help resolve difficult tensions among strongly held values and interests.

The three Japanese exclusion cases, *Hirabayashi v. United States* (1943), *Korematsu v. United States* (1944), and *Ex parte Endo* (1944), contested the legality of military orders that imposed curfews, relocation, and detention of Japanese on the West Coast after the attack on Pearl Harbor. Douglas filed a concurring opinion in *Hirabayashi*, upholding the legality of a curfew order against persons of Japanese ancestry. He voted with the majority in *Korematsu*, in which the Court upheld an order excluding persons of Japanese ancestry from military areas of the West Coast and providing for their relocation and detention. Although Douglas opposed racial and ethnic discrimination and said so repeatedly in his opinions, he thought that the wartime circumstances presented by *Korematsu* and *Hirabayashi* involved a genuine national emergency sufficiently grave to warrant interference with individual civil rights. Douglas's sense that the nation was in imminent danger was probably particularly acute because during this time he was a frequent visitor at the White House, where the fear of a Japanese invasion of the West Coast must have been palpable. Douglas's opinion for the Court in *Ex parte Endo*, however, focused on the conceded fact that Mitsuye Endo was a loyal American citizen who posed no danger to the war effort or national security. Douglas's context-bound realist view saw that the government's exclusion of Ms. Endo was unjustified and, therefore, unconstitutional.

In the Rosenberg espionage case, Douglas's shifting votes apparently outraged Frankfurter and Robert H. Jackson, who saw them as irresponsible political grandstanding for his civil libertarian constituencies. Julius and Ethel Rosenberg had been convicted of conspiracy and violations of the Espionage Act for giving atomic and military secrets to the Soviet Union, and the judge in the case sentenced both of them to death. In reacting to numerous petitions brought to the Supreme Court on behalf of the Rosenbergs, Douglas seems to have thought that he was just considering each petition, as he considered any other petition, on its own merits. First, he voted to deny a hearing before the Supreme Court, then dissented from such denial, and eventually granted a last-minute stay of execution after the Court had adjourned. That final extraordinary stay was immediately overturned by the full Court meeting in special session in *Rosenberg v. United States* (1953). Douglas was undoubtedly ambivalent about the situation. A

militant anti-Communist, he was also concerned about individual rights and procedural fairness. Although not a consistent opponent of the death penalty, Douglas strongly believed in strict enforcement of constitutional protection of the rights of people accused of crimes.

As he considered the various Rosenberg petitions, he apparently began to sense that the sensationalized prosecution of the Rosenbergs had deprived them of a fair trial. In granting the emergency stay of execution, Douglas did not feel constrained to be consistent with earlier decisions on different petitions, even though they involved the same case. In deciding this particular petition, Douglas became convinced that, under provisions of the Atomic Energy Act, the Rosenbergs could not legally be executed without a jury recommendation of the death penalty. Whether he was subconsciously swayed by the public controversy on all sides of the Rosenberg case is difficult to determine. In later speeches and articles, Douglas insisted that the Supreme Court was and should be above the storm of public pressures. He always maintained that he had been unaffected by the public outcry and protest marches for and against the Rosenbergs and merely decided the legal issues in the petitions presented to him.

Douglas's many decisions in cases involving the economy reflected his roots in legal realism. His views about economics generally favored free enterprise, although early opinions often favored the regulatory power of government. A bankruptcy expert and corporate regulator before he came to the Court, Douglas insisted that corporate directors, officers, and controlling shareholders have fiduciary duties of care and fairness with regard to their investors and creditors.

Although over time Douglas came to fear too much power on the part of regulatory agencies, many of his decisions favored economic regulation. Among the best known is his opinion for the Court in *Federal Power Commission v. Hope Natural Gas Co.* (1944). This decision greatly enhanced the discretion of regulatory agencies to set the rates utility companies charge their customers. Douglas held that "fixing of 'just and reasonable' rates involves a balancing of the investor and the consumer interests," by the regulatory agency, with very little role for the courts in reviewing the reasonableness of the rates.

Like Brandeis before him, Douglas was wary of big business and believed in vigorous enforcement of the antitrust laws. Echoing the populism of his times, Douglas was skeptical about the power of large business and financial interests over the economy and especially over small businesses and small investors. For example, he dissented in *United States v. Columbia Steel Co.* (1948), in which the majority found no violation of the Sherman Antitrust Act when the nation's largest unfinished steel producer acquired the largest independent steel fabricator on the West Coast. "We have here the problem of bigness," Douglas insisted. "Industrial power should be decentralized. It should be scattered into many hands so that the fortunes of the people will not be dependent on the whim or caprice, the political prejudices, the emotional stability of a few self-appointed men."

From his childhood, when he overcame the debilitation of polio by hiking in the Cascade Mountains, Douglas loved the natural world. The outdoors provided a source of personal strength and comfort for the restless justice, even though a riding accident nearly cost him his life in 1949. An avid naturalist, conservationist, hiker, and rider, Douglas actively promoted environmental causes, such as the preservation of the C & O Canal in and near Washington, D.C., which in 1977 became a national historic park named for him. Some of his most impassioned nonjudicial writing, such as *A Wilderness Bill of Rights* (1965), concerned the environment. It is therefore somewhat surprising that he did not write a great many judicial opinions on this subject. The last opinion Douglas filed as a Supreme Court justice was, however, a concurring opinion in *Northern Indiana Public Service v. Walton* (1975), in which, in addition to voicing concern about unconstrained discretion on the part of an administrative agency, Douglas expressed his apprehension about the environmental hazards of nuclear power.

Douglas's well-known dissenting opinion in *Sierra Club v. Morton* (1972) suggested a whole new strategy for bringing environmental problems before the courts. The majority held that the Sierra Club lacked standing to object to government approval of a recreational resort in the Mineral King Valley in the Sierra mountains of California. Douglas filled his dissenting opinion, its footnotes, and its appendix with examples of threatened environmental destruction. He argued that natural features and creatures, from trees and rivers to mountains and woodpeckers, should be allowed to bring their own legal actions, through guardians, to prevent destruction of their ecological systems.

Douglas also wrote important opinions supporting land-use regulation. His opinion in *Berman v. Parker* (1954) upheld the urban renewal powers of government to condemn whole neighborhoods, including blighted and not-so-blighted properties, to make way for rebuilding a more attractive and healthy community. He also wrote the majority opinion in *Village of Belle Terre v. Boraas* (1974), in which the Court approved a zoning regulation that restricted occupancy of single family residences by groups other than traditional families. Justice Thurgood Marshall dissented, saying that the restriction violated rights of association, but Douglas did not think that freedom of association was involved in the case at all. He was concerned about "The regimes of boarding houses, fraternity houses, and the like [that] present urban problems. More people occupy a given space; more cars rather continuously pass by; more cars are parked; noise travels with crowds." In Douglas's view, "A quiet place where yards are wide, people few, and motor vehicles restricted are legitimate guidelines in a land-use project addressed to family needs." The power to regulate land use "is not confined to elimination of filth, stench, and unhealthy places. It is ample to lay out zones where family values, youth values, and the blessings of quiet seclusion and clean air make the area a sanctuary for people." He knew from personal experience that a healthy environment is essential for the development of strong, independent individuals.

Much of Douglas's judicial philosophy focused on the importance of individual freedom and equality. Even his economic and environmental interests were frequently based on his overriding belief in the independent, self-reliant individual. In his 1958 book, *Right of the People,* he declared, "Our Society is built upon the premise that it exists only to aid the fullest individual achievement of which each of its members is capable. Our starting point has always been the individual, not the state."

Early in his judicial career, however, he was sometimes willing to subordinate individual rights to broader government interests, as in the Japanese internment cases. But in the early 1950s, he became concerned about the dangers posed by government regimentation of individual freedom. He came to believe that one of the most important purposes of the Constitution was to restrain government. Dissenting in *Laird v. Tatum,* Douglas declared, "The Constitution was designed to keep government off the backs of the people. The Bill of Rights was added to keep the precincts of belief and expression, of the press, of political and social activities free from surveillance." In Douglas's view, "The aim [of the Bill of Rights] was to allow men to be free and independent and to assert their rights against government."

Douglas provided the most comprehensive discussion of his views regarding individual freedoms guaranteed by the Constitution in connection with the 1973 abortion cases, *Roe v. Wade* and *Doe v. Bolton,* in which the Supreme Court invalidated Texas and Georgia abortion statutes on privacy grounds. In his concurring opinion in *Bolton,* Douglas described what he called "a reasoning" about individual rights that are guaranteed by the Bill of Rights and are included within the right to liberty protected against state government interference under the Fourteenth Amendment.

Douglas suggested three concentric circles of individual rights: "First is the autonomous control over the development and expression of one's intellect, interests, tastes, and personality." He saw these rights, including freedom of conscience and free exercise of religion, as aspects of freedom of thought and conscience that were absolutely protected under the First Amendment without any exceptions or qualifications. In this absolutely protected area, Douglas also placed the Fifth Amendment's right to remain silent.

"Second is freedom of choice in the basic decisions of one's life respecting marriage, divorce, procreation, contraception, and the education and upbringing of children." These fundamental rights, including the right of privacy involved in *Griswold* and the abortion cases, were outside the absolute protection of the First Amendment and were therefore subject to some reasonable control by the regulatory power of government. But any regulation had to be narrowly drawn and supported by a compelling state interest.

"Third is the freedom to care for one's health and person, freedom from bodily restraint or compulsion, freedom to walk, stroll, or loaf." These rights protected individuals as they interacted with others out in the world where the individual, although not exactly immune from government regulation, nevertheless retained certain rights to be let alone by the government, even in relatively public circumstances.

The particular individual freedom with which Douglas is most closely associated is the right of privacy. Douglas derived many of his views about protecting individual privacy against government interference from Brandeis, his predecessor on the Court. But Douglas nearly always referred to a right *of* privacy, rather than Brandeis's right *to* privacy. Moreover, Douglas's right of privacy was solely focused on government threats to privacy. He rejected imposing damage liability for invasions of privacy by the news media, which Brandeis had suggested many years earlier. For example, dissenting in *Public Utilities Commission v. Pollak* (1952), Douglas argued that when the government forced a "captive audience" of riders on the publicly licensed street cars in the District of Columbia to listen to radio broadcasts, such action infringed the privacy rights of individuals to be let alone by the government. After repeatedly calling for recognition of a constitutional right of privacy in a series of dissenting opinions, Douglas eventually persuaded a majority of the Court to adopt his views about privacy in *Griswold.* In that case, Douglas characterized the right of privacy as based on "several fundamental constitutional guarantees," of individual freedom, including the First Amendment right of association, the Third Amendment's prohibition of quartering soldiers, the Fourth Amendment's prohibition of unreasonable searches and seizures, and the Fifth Amendment's prohibition of compelled self-incrimination. Douglas's opinion for the Court found the right of privacy in the penumbras of these constitutional guarantees. In Douglas's view, "specific guarantees of the Bill of Rights have penumbras, formed by emanations from those guarantees that help give them life and substance. Various guarantees create zones of privacy."

For Douglas, the right of privacy was part of the meaning of the Constitution, even though the word "privacy" does not appear in the text. One had but to open one's eyes and one's mind to see it. Douglas believed that the right of privacy is consistent with strict construction of the Constitution, because it is part of what the Bill of Rights means. Because he also believed that all of the guarantees of individual freedom in the Bill of Rights are included as aspects of the liberty protected against state action under the due process clause of the Fourteenth Amendment, states such as Connecticut were constrained to respect the right of privacy along with the rest of the Bill of Rights. Douglas did not believe that the right of privacy was the same thing as substantive due process, which he rejected as simply fastening extraconstitutional personal views and economic preferences of particular justices on the Constitution. The right of privacy was, for Douglas, part and parcel of the Constitution itself.

Douglas came to agree with Black that First Amendment guarantees of freedom of expression and religion permit no government regulation of any kind with regard to speech, press, religion, conscience, or association. In the appeal of the conviction of the Communist Party leaders, *Dennis v. United States* (1951), Douglas entered a short but extremely effective dissent that tore apart the weak reasoning of Chief Justice Fred Vinson's majority opinion upholding the convictions. He searched the record to find evidence—any evidence—that the defendants had done anything other than talk, and he could find no proof that they had committed a single act of any sort, even conspiracy to act. Although vilified at the time for his defense of free speech even for Communists, Douglas's dissent has become one of the great markers in free speech jurisprudence. Law Professor Thomas Emerson noted an essential ingredient in Douglas's thought, a "remarkable ability to grasp the realities of the system of free expression." For Douglas, free speech could be understood only in the larger context of facts. The power of his dissent lies in his reliance on the facts of the case.

Douglas dissented in obscenity cases such as *Roth v. United States* (1957), in which he stated: "The First Amendment, its prohibition in terms absolute, was designed to preclude courts as well as legislatures from weighing the values of speech against silence. The First Amendment puts free speech in the preferred position." Even though Douglas was a victim of obnoxious press accounts about his personal life, he believed that awarding damages for defamation or invasion of privacy was unconstitutional because it involved penalizing the media for disseminating information. For example, he concurred in rejecting the invasion of privacy action in *Time v. Hill* (1957), which involved a sensationalized magazine account of a family's experience as hostages of escaped criminals. He was concerned that the possibility of having to pay damages might discourage publication.

Because he believed in the intrinsic worth of each individual, Douglas consistently favored equality of opportunity. A case involving a special admissions program for minority applicants to the University of Washington Law School, *DeFunis v. Odegaard* (1974), presented a particularly difficult equal protection question. The majority found the case moot because the nonminority plaintiff was in his last semester of law school and would graduate no matter what the Court decided. Douglas thought the Court should decide the case. Repeatedly insisting on racial neutrality and decrying racial, religious, and ethnic quotas, he took a hard look at law school admissions practices. After carefully considering the circumstances, Douglas concluded that the law school's special admissions process was constitutional because, in his view, it was designed to individualize and to equalize the treatment of applicants from minority backgrounds. "I think a separate classification of these applicants is warranted, lest race be a subtle force in eliminating minority members because of cultural differences," Douglas wrote. At the same time, he also insisted, "There is no constitutional right for any race to be preferred." For Douglas, equal protection, like many constitutional values, involved a complex balancing of the realities of the situation. Individualized treatment in this instance satisfied Douglas's understanding of the spirit of equal protection.

Douglas's concerns about individual equality are also reflected in his application of equal protection guarantees to strictly scrutinize legislative classifications that affect fundamental rights. Among the most interesting examples of this approach to equal protection guarantees was Douglas's inventive opinion for the Court in *Skinner v. Oklahoma* (1942). His opinion describes the law at issue in the case, Oklahoma's Habitual Criminal Sterilization Act, as "legislation which involves one of the basic civil rights of man. Marriage and procreation are fundamental to the very existence and survival of the race. There is no redemption for the individual whom the law touches. . . . He is forever deprived of a basic liberty." Therefore, the opinion concludes, the Court should apply "strict scrutiny of the classification" that differentiated between those convicted of grand larceny and others convicted of similar property crimes such as embezzlement. Careful scrutiny was required "lest unwittingly, or otherwise, invidious discriminations are made against groups or types of individuals in violation of the constitutional guaranty of just and equal laws." Because Oklahoma provided no reasons why it needed to sterilize people who had been convicted of grand larceny three times, but not people who had been convicted of embezzlement three times, the statute was unconstitutional. "The equal protection clause would indeed be a formula of empty words if such conspicuously artificial lines could be drawn," when fundamental individual rights were at stake. Douglas later applied this strict scrutiny approach in invalidating Virginia's $1.50 annual poll tax as a condition for voting in state elections in *Harper v. Virginia State Board of Elections* (1966). His idea that legislative classifications that affect fundamental individual rights must be strictly scrutinized by the courts has proved to be both powerful and enduring.

A self-conscious nonconformist, Douglas saw himself as an individual who, through native ability, self-reliance, and hard work, had overcome adversity and challenge, to make his way in the world. In 1970, when Rep. Gerald Ford, R-Mich., sought to impeach Justice Douglas, the effort was based in part on Douglas's unconventional lifestyle, as well as his alleged financial misdealings. Douglas had been divorced three times while sitting as a justice and was, at the age of sixty-seven, happily married to a twenty-three-year-old fourth wife. His off-the-bench activities included leading environmental protest marches and traveling to strange and faraway places. At times he seemed to have his own foreign policy, including opposition to the Vietnam War. As long as he did his Court work, he reasoned, he could live as he liked.

Much of Douglas's sense of his individuality was founded on his relationship with the natural world. He thrived in the outdoors and relished strenuous hikes, particularly in remote places of wild beauty, such as his vacation home at Goose Prairie, Washington. He valued the natural world as a source of personal challenge, which brought him satisfaction as well as growth. For Douglas, wilderness was an essential environment where, by literally getting lost in nature, he could find himself. He counted his life span in terms of the destruction of the American wilderness.

William O. Douglas's judicial work was as eclectic as it was prolific. People tend either to strongly agree or disagree with his independent-minded judicial philosophy, much as they intensely liked or disliked the blunt-spoken and impatient man. Some of his judicial opinions have a remarkable resonance and eloquence. Some are political tracts. Still others appear to have been carelessly thrown together. Through it all, Douglas had an insight into the American spirit, an ability to articulate constitutional values, and a power to provoke thought and argument that few Supreme Court justices have equaled.

—*Dorothy J. Glancy*

BIBLIOGRAPHY

Extensive Douglas papers are in the Library of Congress. Melvin I. Urofsky, ed. *The Douglas Letters* (1987), contains an intriguing selection of those private papers, such as letters, memoranda, and personal files. William O. Douglas, *Go East, Young Man: The Early Years* (1974), and *The Court Years: The Autobiography of William O. Douglas* (1980), make up Douglas's autobiography. Douglas also wrote twenty-nine additional books on subjects varying from the environment to international travel to political freedom.

James Simon, *Independent Journey* (1980), provides a readable and thought-provoking account of the essential qualities of Douglas's character as they developed over the course of his long life. Bruce Allen Murphy, *Wild Bill: The Legend and Life of William O. Douglas* (2003), focuses on Douglas's private life and scandals and, unfortunately, is weak on his jurisprudential ideas and legacy.

A number of writers have analyzed Douglas's judicial career, and these works include Howard Ball and Philip J. Cooper, *Of Power and Right: Hugo Black, William O. Douglas and America's Constitutional Revolution* (1992); Bernard Wolfman, Jonathan L. F. Silver, and Marjorie A. Silver, *Dissent Without Opinion: The Behavior of Justice William O. Douglas in Federal Tax Cases* (1975); and Stephen L. Wasby, ed., *"He Shall Not Pass This Way Again": The Legacy of Justice William O. Douglas* (1990), which contains a useful collection of essays and commentary about Douglas from nearly thirty legal scholars and historians.

Vern Countryman, Douglas's former law clerk and the literary executor of his estate, wrote a number of books about him. One of the more interesting is *The Judicial Record of Justice William O. Douglas* (1974), which was written in reaction to the last impeachment effort brought against him. Professor Countryman also published selections of Douglas opinions, including *Douglas of the Supreme Court* (1959), and *The Douglas Opinions* (1977). Two interesting appraisals of his Court work are L. K. Ray, "Autobiography and Opinion: The Romantic Jurisprudence of Justice William O. Douglas," *University of Pennsylvania Law Review* 60 (1999): 707; and P. Manus, "Wild Bill Douglas's Last Stand: A Retrospective on the First Supreme Court Environmentalist," *Temple Law Review* 72 (1999): 111. Douglas's views on speech are analyzed in Thomas Emerson, "Mr. Justice Douglas' Contribution to the Law: The First Amendment," *Columbia Law Review* 74 (1974): 354. See also Michal R. Belknap, *Cold War Political Justice: The Smith Act, the Communist Party, and American Civil Liberties* (1977).

G. Edward White's *The American Judicial Tradition* (1988) contains a provocative chapter on Douglas entitled "The Anti-Judge: William O. Douglas and the Ambiguities of Individuality." For a contrary view, see Melvin I. Urofsky, "William O. Douglas as a Common Law Judge," *Duke Law Journal* 41 (1991): 133.

At least two plays have been written about Justice Douglas's colorful life. Douglas Scott's *Mountain* (1990) enjoyed success off-Broadway in New York. A biographical monodrama, *Douglas,* by Robert Litz, was presented in Seattle, Washington, in September 1992.

NOTEWORTHY OPINIONS

Skinner v. Oklahoma, 316 U.S. 535 (1942)

Hirabayashi v. United States, 320 U.S. 81 (1943) (Concurrence)

Federal Power Commission v. Hope Natural Gas Co., 320 U.S. 591 (1944)

Ex parte Endo, 323 U.S. 283 (1944)

United States v. Causby, 328 U.S. 256 (1946)

Dennis v. United States, 341 U.S. 494 (1951) (Dissent)

Youngstown Sheet & Tube Co. v. Sawyer, 343 U.S. 579 (1952) (Concurrence)

On Lee v. United States, 343 U.S. 747 (1952) (Dissent)

Rosenberg v. United States, 346 U.S. 273 (1953) (Dissent)

Berman v. Parker, 348 U.S. 26 (1954)

Roth v. United States, 354 U.S. 476 (1957) (Dissent)

Griswold v. Connecticut, 381 U.S. 479 (1965)

Harper v. Virginia State Board of Elections, 383 U.S. 663 (1966)

Sierra Club v. Morton, 405 U.S. 727 (1972) (Dissent)

Laird v. Tatum, 408 U.S. 1 (1972) (Dissent)

Roe v. Wade, 410 U.S. 113 (1973) (Concurrence)

Village of Belle Terre v. Boraas, 416 U.S. 1 (1974)

DeFunis v. Odegaard, 416 U.S. 312 (1974) (Dissent)

GABRIEL DUVALL

Birth: December 6, 1752, Prince George's County, Maryland.

Education: Classical preparatory schooling; studied law.

Official Positions: Clerk, Maryland Convention, 1775–1777; clerk, Maryland House of Delegates, 1777–1787, 1787–1794; member, Maryland State Council, 1782–1785; U.S. representative, 1794–1796; chief justice, General Court of Maryland, 1796–1802; presidential elector, 1796, 1800; first comptroller of the Treasury, 1802–1811.

Supreme Court Service: Nominated associate justice by President James Madison, November 15, 1811, to replace Samuel Chase, who had died; confirmed by the Senate, November 18, 1811, by a voice vote; took judicial oath November 23, 1811; resigned January 14, 1835; replaced by Philip Barbour, nominated by President Andrew Jackson.

Death: March 6, 1844, Prince George's County, Maryland.

Gabriel Duvall was nominated to the Supreme Court to fill the vacancy created by the death of Samuel Chase of Maryland. On the same day, Joseph Story was named to the seat left vacant by the death of William Cushing. Both were confirmed only three days later. The striking contrast between the two nominees suggests a presidential stratagem by which Duvall's confirmation could be cast as balancing Story's. Although both men had served in their state legislatures and in the House of Representatives, at the time of their nominations, Story had just turned thirty-two, and Duvall was nearly fifty-nine. Story had no judicial experience, but Duvall had served for six years as chief judge of the Maryland General Court and recorder of the mayor's court. Certainly, their ages and backgrounds gave no hint either to the length of their tenures or to the extent of their jurisprudential legacies.

Notwithstanding his prior experience as a judge, Duvall sat quietly in the Supreme Court; in twenty-three years, he wrote opinions in only seventeen cases. All were nicely crafted examples of the judicial art, but none were of much significance other than to the parties involved. As he had been the first comptroller of the Treasury, Duvall wrote most often for the Court in disputes arising from audits of public accounts.

Duvall's most frequently cited opinion appears in *Walton v. United States* (1824), in which the Court held that a bill of exceptions (the formal list of objections made at trial) properly prepared at, or immediately following, trial was the jurisdictional *sine qua non* of appeal. In another frequently cited case, *Boyd's Lessee v. Graves* (1819), he adopted for the Court the rule that a boundary line marked out and honored by the parties over many years prevails over the terms of a land patent with which it varies.

In *Prince v. Bartlett* (1814), a federal marshal, in pursuit of goods against which to levy a federal judgment, burgled the storehouse in which they had been placed by a county sheriff after execution of a state writ of attachment. Notwithstanding the provocative facts of the case, the Court eschewed a ruling on federalism and found lacking the statutory conditions for affording priority to the federal claim. Subsequently, courts have relied on *Prince v. Bartlett* for the distinction drawn by Duvall in that case between bankruptcy and mere insolvency.

In *United States v. January* (1813), Duvall fashioned the federal rule that the ordinary practice permitting first the debtor and alternatively the creditor to designate to which among competing obligations a payment should be applied did not pertain when different sureties, under distinct obligations, were interested.

During Duvall's entire tenure on the bench, John Marshall headed the Supreme Court. In only two cases did Duvall offer for the record a dissent from the position taken by the great chief justice. In the famous case of *Trustees of Dartmouth College v. Woodward* (1819), Duvall dissented without offering a full opinion, entering in the record only a brief note calling attention to the apparent consensus of French lawyers in 1786 that had a royal charter been properly issued to the French East India Company, it would have been irrevocable.

Duvall's most moving opinion came in *Mima Queen and Child v. Hepburn* (1813), when he alone disagreed with Marshall's opinion refusing admission in the courts of the District of Columbia of hearsay evidence to prove a person was not a slave. Marshall wrote for the Court with great sympathy for the plight of petitioners and others in their condition but failed to see any distinction between freedom cases like this and others "in which a right to property may be asserted." Duvall rested his dissent on the practice of admitting hearsay in such cases by the courts of Maryland, the laws of which were supposed by act of Congress to be adopted in the courts for that part of the District formerly part of Maryland. He also based his dissent on the more serious consequences for "persons of color" of excluding hearsay in freedom cases than in other boundary, pedigree, custom, and prescription disputes in which hearsay exceptions were already widely recognized.

—*John Paul Jones*

Gabriel Duvall

BIBLIOGRAPHY

Very little has been written on Duvall. But see Irving Dillard, "Gabriel Duvall" in Friedman and Israel, *Justices*, vol. 1, 419; and G. Edward White, *The Marshall Court and Cultural Change, 1815–35* (1988), 321–327.

NOTEWORTHY OPINIONS

Mima Queen and Child v. Hepburn, 11 U.S. 290 (1813) (Dissent)

Prince v. Bartlett, 12 U.S. 431 (1814)

Boyd's Lessee v. Graves, 17 U.S. 513 (1819)

Walton v. United States, 22 U.S. 651 (1824)

OLIVER ELLSWORTH

Birth: April 29, 1745, Windsor, Connecticut.

Education: Princeton, A.B., 1766; honorary LL.D., Yale (1790), Princeton (1790), Dartmouth (1797).

Official Positions: Member, Connecticut General Assembly, 1773–1776; state's attorney, Hartford County, 1777–1785; delegate to Continental Congress, 1777–1784; member, Connecticut Council of Safety, 1779; member, Governor's Council, 1780–1785, 1801–1807; judge, Connecticut Superior Court, 1785–1789; delegate, Constitutional Convention, 1787; U.S. senator, 1789–1796; commissioner to France, 1799–1800.

Supreme Court Service: Nominated chief justice by President George Washington, March 3, 1796, to replace John Jay, who had resigned; confirmed by the Senate, March 4, 1796, by a 21–1 vote; took judicial oath March 8, 1796; resigned December 15, 1800; replaced by John Marshall, nominated by President John Adams.

Death: November 26, 1807, Windsor, Connecticut.

Oliver Ellsworth was a thoroughgoing Calvinist who experienced his election by God for salvation. He was born into a prosperous (though not wealthy) Connecticut farming family. His parents intended him for the ministry, and he was educated by famous new divinity ministers before and after he graduated from the College of New Jersey (now Princeton) in 1766. But Ellsworth found his calling in law and politics. He became—in the Calvinist parlance of his times—a "Righteous Ruler."

After marrying the daughter of a prominent Connecticut family, Ellsworth developed a lucrative law practice and entered politics. From 1773 to 1789 he was a state legislator and then a judge. He also was an active and influential delegate, first to the Continental Congress and later to the Constitutional Convention, after which he became Connecticut's most

effective advocate for ratification. Ellsworth then represented Connecticut in the Senate and was the Federalist senators' de facto floor leader until he became chief justice of the United States in 1796.

None of his contemporaries—except for John Marshall—had a more profound and long-lasting influence on the federal judicial system. At Philadelphia he was a member of the Committee of Detail that wrote the Constitution's judicial article. More significant, in the First Congress, he personally drafted and was widely recognized as the "leading projector" of the Judiciary Act of 1789, which established and prescribed the federal courts' judicial powers. Finally, he concluded his national public service as chief justice of the court he had helped to create.

Ellsworth was a gifted politician and known to be self-disciplined. William Vans Murray, who served with Ellsworth on a diplomatic mission to France in 1800, wrote that Ellsworth "has a head of iron—just iron—that works with the precision of a mill, without its quickness and giddy manner. I profoundly admire the neatness and accuracy of his mind." Ellsworth also understood the art and utility of political compromise. He believed human events to be absolutely predestined by God according to a perfect plan that was beyond human comprehension. His educators had taught him that evil was also part of God's plan and served a divine purpose. Because he had experienced his personal salvation, he knew that his own conduct was righteous. At the same time, he could accept political compromises as part of God's unknowable plan. These psychological dynamics added up to an immensely confident man who acted from principle, but who nevertheless could enthusiastically embrace compromise as a desirable component of political life.

Ellsworth's ability to craft workable compromises played a major role in the drafting and enactment of the Judiciary Act. He was adamant on the need for vesting the federal courts with plenary power over a comparatively narrow range of litigation, including revenue collection cases, criminal prosecutions, and prize cases. He warned that "there will be Attacks on the General Government that will go to the Very Vitals of it [and state] Judges may Swerve." Without adequate revenues and effective criminal laws, the government could not defend itself. To obtain these absolutely essential powers, Ellsworth agreed to exclude the federal courts from trying many other suits that implicated important but lesser national interests.

As chief justice, Ellsworth revisited the major themes of the Judiciary Act. In *Wiscart v. Dauchy* (1796) and *Turner v. Bank of North America* (1799), he reaffirmed Congress's extensive powers to limit the federal courts' jurisdiction. In *United States v. La Vengeance* (1796), he significantly expanded the federal admiralty judges' authority to enforce federal revenue laws without the intercession of juries.

Oliver Ellsworth

Ellsworth also took an active role in the vigorous enforcement of criminal law. He believed that God had predestined human history to bring order out of chaos and that the federal government was obviously part of God's plan. He instructed grand juries that "national laws . . . are the means by which it pleases heaven to make of weak and discordant parts, one great people; and to bestow upon them unexampled prosperity." But he also believed in original sin and had a pessimistic view of human nature. "Numerous are the vices," he warned, "and as obstinate the prejudices, and as daring as restless is the ambition, which perpetually hazard the national peace." He therefore urged "constant vigilance" in the enforcement of federal criminal law. "No transgression is too small, nor any transgressor too great, for animadversion."

Given this concern for the enforcement of criminal law, it comes as no surprise that in 1799, his last year of service on the Court, Ellsworth delivered a grand jury charge providing the most comprehensive explanation and justification of the federal courts' controversial enforcement of federal common law crimes. That same year, while riding circuit, Ellsworth wrote a controversial opinion in the common law prosecution of Isaac Williams. In *United States v. Williams* (1799), he insisted that the federal common law of crimes extended even to conduct outside the United States by an individual who had renounced his American citizenship and became the naturalized citizen of a foreign country.

In addition to his contributions to federal criminal law, Ellsworth was an effective administrator who convinced his fellow justices to accept a significant change in the structure of the Court's public opinions. Before his time, the Court followed the English practice in which each justice would deliver his own opinion *seriatim*. Under Ellsworth, however, the Court began to follow the Connecticut practice of pronouncing a single opinion presenting the majority's view together with dissenting opinions, if any. During his tenure, *seriatim* opinions were delivered in only one case in which he participated in the Court's decision. Ellsworth's practice of delivering a single majority opinion continues to the present and has enormous implications for the Court's role as the ultimate expositor of constitutional law. Instead of multifarious pronouncements from the individual justices, the single majority opinion permits the Court to speak with one voice.

Like Chief Justice John Jay before him, Ellsworth spent the last months of his judicial tenure as a diplomat. In 1799 he sailed to Europe to negotiate a conclusion to the undeclared naval war between the United States and France. Following the conclusion of successful negotiations, he resigned his office on the grounds of ill health. Ellsworth spent the rest of his life in Connecticut where he was an active participant in state politics.

—*William R. Casto*

BIBLIOGRAPHY

William Garrott Brown, *The Life of Oliver Ellsworth* (1905), is the best biography of Ellsworth, but is quite out of date in terms of the author's style and access to primary sources. "Biographical Sketch of Chief Justice Ellsworth," *Analectic Magazine* 3 (1814): 382, is an insightful and reasonably frank sketch by Gulian Verplanck, who knew Ellsworth. The various volumes of *The Documentary History of the Supreme Court of the United States, 1789–1800* (1985 et seq.) provide the best tools for tracing Ellsworth's drafting of the Judiciary Act and his subsequent service as chief justice. See also William Casto, "Two Advisory Opinions by Chief Justice Oliver Ellsworth," *Green Bag* 6 (n.s. 2003): 413; and Casto, "Oliver Ellsworth," *Journal of Supreme Court History* 20 (1966).

NOTEWORTHY OPINIONS

United States v. La Vengeance, 3 U.S. 297 (1796)

Wiscart v. Dauchy, 3 U.S. 321 (1796)

Turner v. Bank of North America, 4 U.S. 8 (1799)

United States v. Williams, 29 F. Cases 1330 (C.C.D. Conn. 1799)

STEPHEN JOHNSON FIELD

Birth: November 4, 1816, Haddam, Connecticut.

Education: Graduated Williams College, 1837; studied law in private firms; admitted to the New York bar in 1841.

Official Positions: Alcalde of Marysville, 1850; California state representative, 1850–1851; justice, California Supreme Court, 1857–1863.

Supreme Court Service: Nominated associate justice by President Abraham Lincoln, March 7, 1863, for a newly created seat; confirmed by the Senate, March 10, 1863, by a voice vote; took judicial oath May 20, 1863; retired December 1, 1897; replaced by Joseph McKenna, nominated by President William McKinley.

Death: April 9, 1899, in Washington, D.C.

Stephen J. Field, the justice with the second-longest tenure in Supreme Court history, spent his early youth in Connecticut and Massachusetts. He then lived in Europe for several years with a sister and brother-in-law before returning to Massachusetts to attend Williams College in the early 1830s.

Field was part of a large and accomplished family, which most likely helped to stoke his ambitious and independent spirit. After college graduation, he read law in the office of his eldest brother, David Dudley Field Jr., a noted New York attorney who would later gain prominence for the Field Code, an effort to provide a streamlined codification of New York law. Stephen Field's bar preparation was interrupted briefly by a disabling accident, after which he resumed studies in the Albany office of John Van Buren, the attorney general of New York. Field was admitted to practice in New York in 1841 and for the next six years practiced law with David Field, ending the partnership to return to Europe in 1848. Intrigued

by tales of fame and fortune from the burgeoning gold-rush territory, Field decided in 1849 to move to California, where he was to spend the remainder of his prominent pre-Court career.

He sailed to San Francisco and quickly became active in political and business affairs. Within three weeks of his arrival in California, he helped to found the town of Marysville at the junction of the Yuba and Feather Rivers, purchased a significant amount of property, and was elected the town's alcalde, a quasi-political, quasijudicial office that entailed service as both mayor and chief civil magistrate. By Field's own account, he used this position to establish Marysville as a "model town" through a combination of bold leadership and legal acumen. When the office of alcalde was abolished by the adoption of the 1850 California Constitution, Field then established a successful law practice in Marysville. He also won election to a Democratic seat in the California legislature, where he assumed a critical role in drafting the new state's civil and criminal codes. He left the legislature to run for the state senate in 1851, but did not win. He returned to law practice for six years before winning election to the California Supreme Court in 1857 and was elevated to the position of chief justice in 1861.

In his turbulent half-decade on the California Supreme Court, Field honed a reputation for personal brashness, frontier spirit, and stubborn independence that later characterized his lengthy tenure on the U.S. Supreme Court. Self-confident and outspoken, Field developed during this period well-publicized friendships with Leland Stanford and other famous tycoons of industry. These conspicuous connections to California business catalyzed his professional success, but they also fueled public criticism of him as arrogant and corrupt. Ultimately, however, the more positive aspects of Field's reputation prevailed: in 1863, when Congress added a tenth seat to the Supreme Court to ensure a majority of pro-Union votes and to avail itself of a westerner's likely expertise in land and mining cases, Field handily won unanimous acclamation from Stanford and the California congressional delegation as the best jurist to represent the new Pacific Coast circuit.

Stephen Johnson Field

From his earliest years on the Court, Field's opinions displayed tenacity, clarity, and boldness of vision; he was an ardent critic of government—especially federal—interference in private business and never hesitated to be the lone dissenter when his tireless powers of persuasion failed to win over his colleagues. Field's

admonition shortly before his death that judges must speak out with "absolute fearlessness" was evidently embraced throughout his judicial career. From a prolific lifetime oeuvre of 640 opinions on the Court, he wrote dissenting opinions in 86 cases and dissented a total of 220 times, 64 times alone. As he proclaimed in departing from the Court's judgment in the *Second Legal Tender Cases* (1871): "The only loyalty which I can admit consists in obedience to the Constitution and the laws made in pursuance of it." Such avowed singularity of vision, however, can also foster intellectual myopia, and Field's jurisprudence may be characterized by his adherence at least as often to his own peculiar brand of judicial dogmatism as to the Constitution itself.

Field's first ten years on the Court involved significant challenges, not only to the exercise of federal executive and legislative authority following the Civil War, but also to the nature and scope of postbellum judicial review. Certainly, the Court's tragic decision in *Dred Scott v. Sandford* (1857) was a "self-inflicted wound" to its own legitimacy during this period, and, as Edward S. Corwin noted:

During neither the Civil War nor the period of Reconstruction did the Supreme Court play anything like its role of supervision, with the result that during the one period the military powers of the President underwent undue expansion, and during the other, the legislative powers of Congress. The Court itself was conscious of its weakness. . . . [A]t no time since Jefferson's first administration has its independence been in greater jeopardy than between 1860 and 1870.

Into this arena of ambivalence entered Field, who sought to puncture any assumptions regarding the politically precarious circumstances of his own wartime appointment as the "tenth justice" by resolutely determining "to apply the Constitution as strictly as though no war had ever existed." (In fact, Field was the tenth justice for only two years: John Catron's death in 1865, James M. Wayne's death in 1867, and Robert C. Grier's resignation in 1870 gradually reduced the Court's membership to seven, and it was not restored to the newly fixed full membership of nine until 1870.) In *Ex parte Milligan* (1866), Field joined a unanimous Court in holding that President Abraham Lincoln had acted unconstitutionally by permitting military commission trials for civilians in nonwar areas in which civil courts had continued to function, and joined a 5–4 majority in holding that even Congress and the president acting together during wartime lacked the constitutional power to authorize such tribunals. Such clear-cut Court repudiations of presidential and congressional authority were not well received, and Field soon became the target of venomous public criticism for his views.

Consternation over the *Milligan* opinions was further heightened by the controversial *Test Oath Cases* (*Cummings v. Missouri* and *Ex parte Garland*, 1867), in which Field wrote for each 5–4 majority in striking down laws requiring retrospective Union loyalty oaths as conditions of employment. In *Cummings,* the Court invalidated a Missouri regulation requiring persons in the professions to swear past and present loyalty to the Union; in *Garland,* the Court struck down a federal statute imposing a similar oath on attorneys seeking to practice law in the federal courts. In declaring both test oath laws invalid under the bill of attainder and *ex post facto* provisions of the Constitution, Field demonstrated a willingness to exercise fully and seriously the Court's power of review, even in the face of vociferous objections from

Congress and the public. In an intriguing harbinger of future jurisprudential concerns, Field's majority opinions also focused particularly on the importance of preserving the individual's inalienable right to pursue a lawful occupation free from government restraint—a central tenet that Field would invoke frequently in the decades to come. In the meantime, congressional and public reaction to the decisions in *Milligan* and the *Test Oath Cases* ranged from legislative proposals for impeachment of the majority justices to press condemnation of the decisions as "Dred Scott Number Two" and "Dred Scott Number Three."

Despite—or perhaps because of—such trenchant criticism so early in his Court career, Field began to carve a niche for himself on the Court and in the national spotlight. Nominated for the presidency by the California delegation at the Democratic National Convention of 1868, he was hailed as "a wall of fire against the encroachments of Radical domination" and "the guardian of the Constitution of his country against all the power of the Radical party." Field's paltry showing in convention ballots quashed any hope of election, but his willingness to be considered for the presidency so early in his Court career may be an indication not only of his lingering political ambitions, but also of the power and influence he hoped to wield in shaping the direction of the Court.

Field's first decade on the Court drew to a close with a series of cases concerning Reconstruction-era legislation, and they illustrate both the tenuous nature of the postbellum Court and the ready iconoclasm with which Field criticized the views of his brethren. In *Ex parte McCardle* (1869), the Court considered a southern editor's *habeas corpus* petition for release from military imprisonment for obstructing Reconstruction efforts. The Court first heard the case in its 1868 term. Shortly after oral argument, Congress—fearing that William McCardle's appeal would afford the Court the opportunity to declare the Reconstruction Acts unconstitutional—began to consider legislation to revoke the Court's jurisdiction over *habeas corpus* appeals, including McCardle's. When a majority of the Court agreed to postpone the case until Congress had voted on the jurisdiction-stripping bill, Field joined Justice Grier's acerbic dissent from what they termed the Court's "shameful" abdication of judicial responsibility. Nevertheless, Field's dismay did not affect his ultimate position regarding the proper procedural disposition of the case. When Congress eventually voted to pass the bill, Field and Grier, without comment, joined the rest of the Court in dismissing the appeal.

Another example of Field's outspokenness during this era was his unswerving criticism of the Legal Tender Acts, wartime statutes authorizing the substitution of paper money—"greenbacks"—for gold and silver in the payment of debts. In two decisions in the 1870 and 1871 terms concerning the constitutionality of these acts, Field displayed a characteristically staunch determination to hold fast to his position, even as changes in the Court's composition transformed his view from the majority to the minority. The Court had heard oral arguments in both the 1867 and 1868 terms in the first of these challenges, *Hepburn v. Griswold*. Because of strong pressures, both internal and external, the Court was unable to reach a decision until late 1869; even then, its tentative preliminary vote of 5–3 to strike down the acts quickly unraveled when an ailing and confused Grier absentmindedly voted in conference first to uphold the acts and then to strike them down. Field persuaded Grier to resign because of his failing health, and Grier left the bench on February 1, 1870.

A week later the Court issued a decision in *Hepburn,* voting 4–3 to invalidate the Legal Tender Acts as an abrogation of congressional powers and an impairment of freedom of contract as applied to debts incurred before their passage. That same day, President Ulysses S. Grant nominated William Strong, a Pennsylvania state judge, and Joseph P. Bradley, a New Jersey attorney, to fill the vacancies created by Wayne's death and Grier's retirement. Strong and Bradley were confirmed and seated on the Court in March. Within weeks of their arrival, the Court agreed to reconsider the constitutionality of the Legal Tender Acts. This second challenge, *Knox v. Lee* and *Parker v. Davis* (known as the *Second Legal Tender Cases*), was argued in the 1870 term and concerned

the same central issue—the power of Congress to pass the acts and apply them to preexisting debts.

This time the Court voted 5–4 to overrule the *Hepburn* decision of fifteen months before. Field issued a lengthy and vehement dissent, arguing that the acts authorized the repudiation of debts, a "dishonor" and "public crime" unwarranted by the Constitution. Invoking natural law principles in support of his method of constitutional interpretation, Field contended, "It is only by obedience [to the Constitution and its dictates] that affection and reverence can be shown to a superior having a right to command. So thought our Master when he said to his disciples: 'If ye love me, keep my commandments.'"

Field's other significant opinions in his first decade on the Court include *Low v. Austin* (1872), in which a unanimous Court held that the constitutional ban on state taxes on imports or exports prohibits state taxes on goods brought in from foreign countries only if those goods retain their character as "imports"; and *Bradley v. Fisher* (1872), in which the Court recognized the doctrine of judicial immunity, ruling that judges may not be sued in their official capacities, regardless of the error of their actions.

Although Field was quick to establish a bold judicial style on the Court, he did not fully develop his nascent judicial philosophies until his second decade of service, when many of his inchoate leanings coalesced into a distinctive jurisprudence. The period from 1873 to 1888 was by far the most prolific and influential phase of his Supreme Court career. Critical to the development of his jurisprudence were the Civil War amendments: the Thirteenth Amendment, ratified in 1865, which officially abolished slavery; the Fourteenth Amendment, ratified in 1868, which prohibited the exercise of state action to deny persons the equal protection and due process of the law and the privileges or immunities of national citizenship; and the Fifteenth Amendment, ratified in 1870, which forbade states to deny anyone the right to vote on the basis of race, color, or previous condition of servitude. Understood in the context of the Civil War/Reconstruction era in which they were promulgated, these amendments were clearly intended to limit state encroachment on individual liberties in order to undo the evils of slavery and to effect far-reaching goals of racial equality. In their first several decades of implementation, however, the Court construed the Civil War amendments in such a narrow and crabbed fashion that they were virtually unrecognizable as constitutional guarantees.

Field's unique contribution to this interpretive debate lay not in his refusal to view the Civil War amendments as guarantors of personal liberty, but rather in his consistently broad application of the amendments to protect economic and property interests as core human rights, while at the same time endorsing a constricted interpretation of the applicability of the amendments to the eradication of racial discrimination—the amendments' original purpose. These constitutional perspectives, forcefully advanced in majority opinions and in dissents, provided the Court with interpretive tools that would continue to affect its jurisprudence concerning the Civil War amendments throughout the next half-century.

The Court's first definitive statement on the meaning and scope of the Fourteenth Amendment came in the *Slaughterhouse Cases* (1873), cases that had nothing to do with the vestiges of slavery or with the civil rights of blacks. Instead, these cases concerned a challenge by a group of New Orleans butchers against the state of Louisiana's decision to grant a monopoly on the city's slaughterhouse business to one company. This arrangement, the butchers contended, interfered with their right to do business and violated guarantees under the Thirteenth Amendment and the Fourteenth Amendment's privileges or immunities, equal protection, and due process clauses. By a vote of 5–4, the Court rejected the butchers' argument, holding that their "right to do business" was neither a "privilege or immunity" of U.S. citizenship nor a "property" interest protected by the due process clause. Defending a narrow interpretation of the privileges or immunities clause as protecting only those limited preexisting rights that had previously been recognized as concomitants of federal rather than state citizenship, Justice Samuel Miller wrote on behalf of the majority that any broader

interpretation would allow the Court to be "a perpetual censor upon all legislation of the States on the civil rights of their own citizens."

Field's dissent in the *Slaughterhouse Cases* is an intriguing exemplar of his concern with the subject of economic liberty and his use of natural law principles in defense of his constitutional reasoning. He said that the privileges or immunities clause of the Fourteenth Amendment should be interpreted to protect the right of man "to pursue his happiness by following any of the known established trades and occupations ... subject only to such restraints as equally affected all others." Moreover, he asserted, the Fourteenth Amendment should be read broadly to protect such "inalienable rights, rights which are the gift of the Creator, which the law does not confer, but only recognizes." Despite the implications of such hortatory language concerning "inalienable rights," however, Field's forthcoming decisions in interpreting the Civil War amendments would reveal an overarching concern not with the recognition of individual civil—that is, social and political—rights, but with the protection of individual and corporate property rights, economic freedoms, and other forms of private enterprise.

Field's sharply circumscribed definition of "inalienable rights" in social and political terms may be seen in a series of cases throughout the 1870s and early 1880s. In *Bradwell v. Illinois* (1873), a ruling announced the day after the release of the *Slaughterhouse* opinions, Field joined with the 8–1 majority to reject Myra Bradwell's privileges or immunities clause challenge to the state of Illinois's refusal, on the grounds of gender, to grant her a license to practice law in its courts. In the context of a female's "right to do business," Field agreed with the Court's holding that the right to practice law was not a privilege or immunity of American citizenship. A few years later, in *Minor v. Happersett* (1875), Field joined a unanimous Court in holding that the privileges or immunities clause of the Fourteenth Amendment does not guarantee women the right to vote. "The Constitution of the United States does not confer the right of suffrage on anyone," the Court said.

Even for challenges concerning congressional authority to protect blacks' suffrage rights—a constitutional mandate directly traceable to the history and language of the Fifteenth Amendment—Field shared the rest of the Court's refusal to recognize an expansive definition of federally protected individual civil rights under the Civil War amendments. In *United States v. Reese* (1876), Field agreed with the Court's 8–1 majority in holding that Congress had exceeded its power to enforce the Fifteenth Amendment in enacting a statute that penalized state officials who denied or otherwise obstructed the right of blacks to vote. The Court held that the Fifteenth Amendment did not guarantee the right to vote, but only the right to be free from racial discrimination in the exercise of the state-created right to vote.

In the companion case of *United States v. Cruikshank* (1876), the Court unanimously dismissed federal indictments brought against Louisiana citizens charged with using fraud and violence to prevent blacks from exercising their right to vote. Here, the Court held that because the indictments at issue had not explicitly averred the existence of racial animus on the part of the defendants, they were therefore not truly federal offenses under the Fifteenth Amendment.

In *Ex parte Siebold* (1880), Field dissented from the Court's decision upholding the convictions of two state election officers under federal laws for interfering with federal elections, arguing for a narrower construction of congressional power. Although Field occasionally acceded to a broader interpretation of congressional authority under the Fifteenth Amendment's enabling clause—for example, in *Ex parte Yarbrough* (1884)—his overarching philosophy endorsed severe limitations on the use of the Fifteenth Amendment to protect blacks in the exercise of the franchise.

Field's position with respect to constitutional protections of the civil rights of blacks in other areas was similarly stinting. In the companion cases of *Strauder v. West Virginia* and *Ex parte Virginia and J. D. Coles* (1880), Field dissented from two of the few decisions of the era in which the rights of blacks were upheld in challenges under the Civil War amend-

ments. In *Strauder*, the Court reversed the conviction of a black defendant who had unsuccessfully petitioned during his state court trial for removal to federal court on the grounds that West Virginia's statute excluding blacks from juries deprived him of equal protection of the laws. The majority in *Strauder* noted that not only was the impartial selection of a jury a "legal right" protected by the Fourteenth Amendment, but also that congressionally authorized removal from state to federal court under circumstances of invidious discrimination was "an ordinary mode of protecting rights and immunities conferred by the Federal Constitution and Laws." In *Ex parte Virginia*, the Court upheld a provision of the Civil Rights Act of 1875 that prohibited racial discrimination in jury selection, affirming that the purpose of the Fourteenth Amendment was indeed to eliminate state bias on the grounds of race and color. Field's dissent asserted that "the equality of protection assured by the Fourteenth Amendment to all persons . . . does not imply that they shall be allowed to participate in the administration of its laws . . . or to discharge any duties of public trust."

Finally, in a devastating blow to congressional attempts under the Civil War amendments to reach and prohibit private racial discrimination, Field joined the 8–1 majority in the *Civil Rights Cases* (1883), holding that neither the Thirteenth nor the Fourteenth Amendment authorized Congress to ban discrimination against blacks in privately owned public accommodations. In so doing, Field agreed with the Court's conclusions that private racial bias did not constitute a badge of slavery or involuntary servitude impermissible under the Thirteenth Amendment, and that private racially discriminatory acts were unreachable under the Fourteenth Amendment absent state action.

In salient contrast to his narrow construction of the Civil War amendments with regard to individual civil rights in areas such as the franchise and jury selection, Field vigorously advanced a broadly expansive interpretation of the amendments with respect to the protection of economic liberties and private enterprise concerns. Indeed, Field's jurisprudence of "property rights" as developed in the 1870s and 1880s has led many historians to label him the most prominent and successful proponent of laissez-faire economics in Court history. Certainly, Field forged a clear-cut impression of probusiness, antistatist predilections that make the laissez-faire label apt and accurate today.

Field's dissent in the *Slaughterhouse Cases* provided an early indication of the importance with which he regarded economic freedom as a core right enshrined with constitutional protections. Field further developed this concept in *Bartemeyer v. Iowa* (1874), in which he asserted that the due process and privileges or immunities clauses of the Fourteenth Amendment should be interpreted to protect an individual's right to use, enjoy, sell, and dispose of property free from government interference. He dissented in *Munn v. Illinois* (1876) and in the other "Granger Cases," which concerned the constitutionality of state legislation regulating the rates to be set by grain elevator owners. The majority held that such laws were permissible exercises of state police power so long as the use of the grain elevators was "affected with a public interest." In dissent, Field wrote, "I deny the power of any Legislature under our government to fix the price which one shall receive for his property of any kind."

In the *Sinking Fund Cases* (1879), two appeals involving the validity of a 1878 federal law that had required two Pacific railroads (one incorporated by Congress, the other by the state of California) to set aside portions of their earnings in a "sinking fund" to ensure the payment of their debts, Field issued a particularly vehement and detailed dissent. Claiming that the majority endorsed an impairment of contract and a violation of the due process clause, he warned:

> The decision will, in my opinion, tend to create insecurity in the title to corporate property in the country. . . . Where contracts are impaired, or when operating against the government are sought to be evaded and avoided by legislation, a blow is given to the security of all property. If the government will not keep its faith, little better can be expected from the citizen. If contracts are not observed, no property will in the end be respected; and all history shows that rights of persons are unsafe where property is insecure. Protection to one goes with protection to the other; and there can be neither prosperity nor progress where this foundation of all just government is unsettled. "The moment," said the elder Adams, "the idea is admitted into society that property is not as sacred as the laws of God, and that there is not a force of law and public justice to protect it, anarchy and tyranny commence."

Through a combination of forceful rhetoric and unrelenting adherence to his views, Field effectively used his dissents to promulgate notions of "substantive due process" in the realm of economic rights—notions that would gradually gain credence among his brethren and be recognized decades later by a majority of the Court. Therefore, in assessing Field's influence on the Court's jurisprudence during this period, it is instructive to note not only his majority opinions and concurrences, but also the opinions and dissents he issued while riding circuit in his role as designated justice for the Ninth Circuit Court of Appeals.

A classic example is his statement in the Ninth Circuit case of *San Mateo v. Southern Pacific R.R. Co.* (1882), in which the court ruled unconstitutional under the equal protection and due process clauses a tax the state of California imposed on its railroads. Despite the lack of clear Supreme Court precedent supporting such a result, Field held that the Fourteenth Amendment's protection of "persons" should be interpreted to include the protection of corporations and corporate property. He observed, "It would be a most singular result if a constitutional provision intended for the protection of every person should cease to exert such protection the moment the person becomes a member of a corporation." Field's contributions to "Ninth Circuit law" concerning the Fourteenth Amendment apparently found a sympathetic ear with his colleagues; by the time a similar challenge reached the U.S. Supreme Court a few years later, in

Santa Clara County v. Southern Pacific Railroad Co. (1886), the Court summarily noted in dictum that the Fourteenth Amendment's protection of "persons" applied to corporations as well as individuals.

Field's other notable opinions during this period were *Pennoyer v. Neff* (1878), in which he spoke for an 8–1 majority in a landmark decision delineating the constitutional and procedural bases under the Fourteenth Amendment for a state's exercise of personal jurisdiction over a noncitizen, nonresident defendant who is not physically present in the state at the time of service; and *Mugler v. Kansas* (1887), in which he dissented from the majority decision upholding a Kansas law that forbade the manufacture and sale of intoxicating liquor in the state as a valid exercise of state police power to protect public health and morals.

Finally, full consideration of Field's evolving judicial philosophy during this era needs some mention of his ongoing political interests, activities, relationships, and even possible aspirations to elective office. He counted among his prestigious friends well-known figures such as Leland Stanford and Collis P. Huntington, and rumors about Field's prospects as a presidential candidate continued to percolate throughout the 1870s and much of the 1880s. When a special commission was appointed in 1877 to resolve a bitter dispute over electoral votes in the presidential election of 1876, Field was one of five members of the Court chosen to serve. After heated partisan deliberations, the commission ruled that Republican Rutherford B. Hayes had won the electoral count by one vote. Field showed his indignation at the result and his support for the Democratic cause by absenting himself from Hayes's inauguration ceremonies. Still, at the Democratic Convention of 1880, Field received a mere sixty-five votes on the first ballot. Four years later, at the 1884 Democratic state convention in California, Field's adopted home state overwhelmingly refused to support his candidacy, and his name was not proposed at all at that year's national convention. By the late 1880s, as Field reached his early seventies, he abandoned all serious presidential aspirations and turned instead to the further solidification of his influence on the Court and to his hopes of someday becoming chief justice.

Field's last ten years on the Court were marked by high drama, great disappointment with respect to personal ambitions, but ultimately the tremendous satisfaction of seeing many of his maverick conservative judicial views gain ascendancy. In 1888 Field's longtime hope of becoming chief justice was dashed when President Grover Cleveland instead chose Melville W. Fuller to fill the vacancy created by the death of Morrison R. Waite. Field apparently regarded Cleveland's rejection of him as a great personal insult and never forgave him for the slight.

That same year, while serving as Ninth Circuit judge in California, Field became embroiled in a bizarre personal feud with litigants in his courtroom that nearly cost him his life. The complicated imbroglio began when David S. Terry, former chief justice of the California Supreme Court and an old enemy of Field's, appeared in Field's court with his wife, Sarah Hill, in a dispute concerning an alleged secret marriage contract between Hill and the late William Sharon. In response to several comments made in open court by Field about Hill's character, Terry and Hill noisily objected, and Field promptly held them in contempt and sentenced them to jail. As a result, Terry waged a bitter vendetta against Field, and Field was advised not to resume his circuit court duties in California.

In 1889 Field did return to California, accompanied by a bodyguard, Deputy Marshal David Neagle. By chance, Field and Neagle encountered Terry and Hill in a railway station restaurant. When Terry lunged at Field, Neagle drew a gun in his defense and shot Terry to death. In the ensuing state criminal proceedings against Neagle, the federal circuit court issued a writ of *habeas corpus,* which was in turn challenged before the U.S. Supreme Court. The Court (sitting without Field) upheld the writ as a proper exercise of federal power in *In re Neagle* (1890), on the grounds that the attorney general's order to Neagle to protect Field was "a law of the United States." Ironically, despite its odd and idiosyncratic factual underpinnings, the case remains a leading precedent concerning the scope of federal executive and judicial powers.

In his waning years on the Fuller Court, Field began to see that his decades-old defenses of private property rights and other conservative ideologies were, with increasing frequency, no longer minority viewpoints. Field's nephew, Justice David J. Brewer, appointed in 1890 by President Benjamin Harrison, shared many of Field's beliefs with respect to economic concerns and appeared ready to carry those beliefs into the next century's jurisprudence. In Field's view, much remained to be accomplished; in one of his final opinions, a concurrence in the Court's decision to strike down the federal income tax in *Pollock v. Farmers' Loan & Trust Co.* (1895), Field warned:

> If the provisions of the Constitution can be set aside by an act of Congress, where is the course of usurpation to end? The present assault on capital is but the beginning. It will be but the stepping-stone to others, larger and more sweeping, till our political contests will become a war of the poor against the rich—a war constantly growing in intensity and bitterness.

By 1896 Field's health was frail, and his inability to fulfill his judicial duties was becoming apparent to his colleagues. According to Charles Evans Hughes, various justices thought that Field would surely be encouraged to retire if he were reminded of his own role in persuading the aging Justice Grier to retire some twenty-six years earlier:

> Justice Harlan was deputed to make the suggestion. He went over to Justice Field, who was sitting alone on a settee in the robing room apparently oblivious of his surroundings, and after arousing him gradually approached the question, asking if he did not recall how anxious the Court had become with respect to Justice Grier's condition and the feeling of the other Justices that in his own interest and in that of the Court he should give up his work. Justice Harlan asked if Justice Field did not remember what had been said to Justice Grier on that occasion. The old man listened, gradually became alert and finally, with his eyes blaz-

ing with the old fire of youth, he burst out: "Yes! And a dirtier's day work I never did in my life!" That was the end of that effort of the brethren of the Court to induce Justice Field's retirement; he did resign not long after.

In fact, Field's lingering last months on the Court were undoubtedly prolonged by his determination to break the record of thirty-four-plus years of service set by Chief Justice John Marshall in 1835. By early 1897 it was clear that he would, so Field announced that his resignation would take effect on December 1. On that date, Field retired after a total of thirty-four years, eight months, and twenty days—a record that has since been surpassed only by Justice William O. Douglas.

Field died on April 9, 1899, in Washington, D.C. Perhaps the most fitting epitaph for his irascible spirit, fervently held convictions, and lifetime of public service can be found in his own words, written in his last year on the Court:

> Timidity, hesitation and cowardice in any public officer excite and deserve only contempt, but infinitely more in a judge than in any other, because he is appointed to discharge a public trust of the most sacred character. To decide against his conviction of the law or judgment as to the evidence, whether moved by prejudice, or passion, or the clamor of the crowd, is to assent to a robbery as infamous in morals and as deserving of punishment as that of the highwayman or the burglar; and to hesitate or refuse to act when duty calls is hardly less the subject of just reproach.

—*Margaret M. Russell*

BIBLIOGRAPHY

The writings of Justice Stephen Field include the following: *Personal Reminiscences of Early Days in California with Other Sketches* (1893); two retrospectives on the work of the Court, "The Supreme Court of the United States, Centennial Celebration of the Organization of the Federal Judiciary," 134 U.S. 729 (1890); and "The Centenary of the

Supreme Court of the United States," *American Law Review* 24 (1890): 351; and "The Late Chief Justice Chase," *Overland Monthly* 11 (October 1873): 305. By far the most informative of the four works is the first, Field's relatively informal recollections of his early life and work; the others are more carefully tailored and staid presentations of his opinions and judicial perspectives.

Carl Brent Swisher, *Stephen J. Field: Craftsman of the Law* (1930), was for many years considered to be the definitive study of Field's life; it should now be supplemented by Paul Kens, *Justice Stephen Field: Shaping Liberty from the Gold Rush to the Gilded Age* (1997).

Field's judicial philosophy, particularly as a proponent of laissez-faire and other conservative economic ideologies, is discussed at great length in the following works: Robert Goedecke, "Justice Field and Inherent Rights," *Review of Politics* 27 (1965): 198; Howard J. Graham, "Justice Field and the Fourteenth Amendment," *Yale Law Journal* 52 (1943): 851; William C. Jones, "Justice Field's Opinions on Constitutional Law," *California Law Review* 5 (1917): 108; Robert G. McCloskey, *American Conservatism in the Age of Enterprise* (1951); Charles W. McCurdy, "Justice Field and the Jurisprudence of Government-Business Relations; Some Parameters of Laissez-Faire Constitutionalism, 1863–1897," *Journal of American History* 61 (1975): 970; and Wallace Mendelson, "Mr. Justice Field and Laissez-Faire," *Virginia Law Review* 36 (1950): 45.

NOTEWORTHY OPINIONS

Cummings v. Missouri, 71 U.S. 277 (1867) (Test Oath Cases)

Ex parte Garland, 71 U.S. 333 (1867) (Test Oath Cases)

Second Legal Tender Cases (*Knox v. Lee* and *Parker v. Davis*), 79 U.S. 457 (1871) (Dissent)

Low v. Austin, 80 U.S. 29 (1872)

Bradley v. Fisher, 80 U.S. 335 (1872)

Slaughterhouse Cases, 83 U.S. 36 (1873) (Dissent)

Bartemeyer v. Iowa, 85 U.S. 129 (1874)

Munn v. Illinois, 94 U.S. 113 (1876) (Dissent)

Pennoyer v. Neff, 95 U.S. 714 (1878)

Sinking Fund Cases, 99 U.S. 700 (1879) (Dissent)

Strauder v. West Virginia, 100 U.S. 303 (1880) (Dissent)

Ex parte Virginia, 100 U.S. 339 (1880) (Dissent)

Ex parte Siebold, 100 U.S. 371 (1880) (Dissent)

Mugler v. Kansas, 123 U.S. 623 (1887) (Dissent)

Pollock v. Farmers' Loan & Trust Co., 158 U.S. 601 (1895)

ABE FORTAS

Birth: June 19, 1910, Memphis, Tennessee.

Education: Southwestern College, A.B., 1930; Yale Law School, LL.B., 1933.

Official Positions: Assistant director, corporate reorganization study, Securities and Exchange Commission, 1934–1937; assistant director, Public Utilities Division, Securities and Exchange Commission, 1938–1939; general counsel, Public Works Administration, 1939–1940, and counsel to the Bituminous Coal Division, 1939–1941; director, Division of Power, Department of the Interior, 1941–1942; undersecretary, Department of the Interior, 1942–1946.

Supreme Court Service: Nominated associate justice by President Lyndon B. Johnson, July 28, 1965, to replace Arthur J. Goldberg, who had resigned; confirmed by the Senate, August 11, 1965, by a voice vote; took judicial oath October 4, 1965; nominated chief justice June 26, 1968; nomination withdrawn October 4, 1968; resigned May 14, 1969; replaced by Harry A. Blackmun, nominated by President Richard Nixon.

Death: April 5, 1982, Washington, D.C.

Abe Fortas is remembered more for the circumstances surrounding his abortive nomination as chief justice and his subsequent resignation than for his judicial opinions. This is unfortunate. Trained as a Washington lawyer during the 1930s, and later trusted as a close adviser to President Lyndon Johnson, Fortas, perhaps more than any other justice, provided a link between Franklin Roosevelt's New Deal and Johnson's Great Society. Although his tenure was brief and controversial, Fortas played a significant role in shaping some of the most important cases handed down by the Warren Court.

Fortas was born into a modest, working-class family steeped more in the cultural than the religious traditions of Judaism. From his father, an amateur musician, Fortas inherited a deep and abiding love of

music and became an avid violinist, who later counted Pablo Casals and Isaac Stern among his friends and clients.

An outstanding student, Fortas won scholarships to Southwestern College in Memphis and to Yale Law School. At Yale, he served as editor in chief of the *Yale Law Journal* and came under the influence of two powerful exponents of legal realism: Thurman Arnold and William O. Douglas. After graduating in 1933, Fortas joined Yale's faculty while also accepting a position with Jerome Frank in the New Deal's Agricultural Adjustment Administration. In 1937, while serving at the Interior Department, Fortas befriended a young member of Congress from Texas named Lyndon Johnson.

In the 1940s Fortas left government service but remained in Washington to found a law firm with

Thurman Arnold and Paul Porter. Fortas came to exemplify the Washington lawyer of the postwar era. An able and aggressive advocate, trained in government by the New Deal, he effectively navigated clients through the intricacies of federal policies and programs. Always drawn to men of power and influence, Fortas maintained his friendship with Lyndon Johnson during the 1950s, serving as his lawyer and close adviser until Johnson, as president, nominated his friend to the Court in 1965.

On the Court, Fortas developed a reputation as a liberal in civil rights and a conservative in areas involving government regulation of business. His opinions demonstrate an instrumental approach to the law but reveal no coherent legal philosophy. This is not to say Fortas was unprincipled—although some accused him of this—but that, true to his education in legal realism, he saw the law as a tool to achieve specific results.

Fortas's experience as a corporate lawyer led him to take a dim view of judicial interference in business matters. For example, in *Baltimore & Ohio Railroad Co. v. United States* (1967), Fortas in dissent argued that the Court had no business questioning the informed decision of the Interstate Commerce Commission to allow a merger of two railroads.

His greatest concern, however, was protecting the rights of minorities, the disenfranchised, and the powerless. He fiercely championed the rights of criminal defendants, especially their Fifth Amendment right against self-incrimination. In *In re Gault* (1967),

Fortas wrote a strong opinion that effectively created a "Bill of Rights" for juvenile criminal offenders by extending certain basic Fourteenth Amendment due process rights into juvenile courts. Writing in a realist vein, Fortas relied more on historical, sociological, and psychological studies of the juvenile justice system than on legal precedent to support his holding.

Free speech was an area of special concern for Fortas, especially in the era of civil rights and anti–Vietnam War demonstrations. He was not, however, a First Amendment absolutist. To the contrary, he could not abide disruptive civil disobedience or symbolic speech that violated valid laws merely to dramatize dissent. The musician in him cherished harmony and decorum. He allowed for tension and conflict but insisted it be contained or structured. Therefore, in *Brown v. Louisiana* (1966), Fortas found a Louisiana breach of the peace statute unconstitutional as applied to several blacks who conducted a peaceful sit-in of a segregated public library. But in *Street v. New York* (1969), Fortas, in a stinging dissent, drew the line at flag burning, declaring that "protest does not exonerate lawlessness." In his landmark opinion in *Tinker v. Des Moines School District* (1969), Fortas held unconstitutional a school's prohibition on black armbands worn by students to protest the Vietnam War. Echoing his support for juvenile rights enunciated in *Gault*, Fortas declared that students did not surrender their First Amendment rights upon entering a school. Wearing the armbands, he asserted,

Abe Fortas

was akin to "pure speech" that did not involve "aggressive, disruptive actions" and did not interfere with the school's work.

Fortas also had a strong commitment to privacy as a constitutional right. Indeed, he saw the right to privacy as a significant limitation on freedom of the press. Consistent with his free speech cases (and with his deep personal antipathy toward the press), Fortas refused to extend First Amendment protections to press activities he considered to be intrusive or disruptive. His dissent in *Time Inc. v. Hill* (1967), which dealt with an alleged defamation by the press, is an example.

In 1968 President Johnson nominated Fortas to replace the retiring Earl Warren as chief justice. It was an honor from which he never recovered. The confirmation hearings took place after Johnson had decided not to seek reelection and had become a lame duck. Fortas soon became the target of a conservative backlash against the activism of the Warren Court and Johnson's Great Society programs. Revelations of his ongoing business connections with millionaire businessman Louis Wolfson added to the drama. Johnson was forced to withdraw Fortas's name. One year later, amid further allegations of improper business dealings, Fortas resigned from the Court, although he maintained his innocence. Back in the private sector, he was rebuffed by his old law firm, but continued to practice law until his death in 1982.

—*Jonathan Kahn*

BIBLIOGRAPHY

Fortas's own views can be found in his *Concerning Dissent and Civil Disobedience* (1968), a fascinating look into his ideas on the nature and limits of free expression in a civil society, made even more interesting by the fact that he wrote it while sitting on the Supreme Court.

There are two major biographies: Laura Kalman, *Abe Fortas: A Biography* (1990); and Bruce Allen Murphy, *Fortas: The Rise and Fall of a Supreme Court Justice* (1988). Murphy's book concentrates on Fortas's life as a Washington insider and is primarily a political biography. Kalman's is a solid study of Fortas's life and the first to be based on complete access to Fortas's private papers. Her work is therefore more complete than Murphy's and provides a good review of the development of Fortas's legal ideas. See also Kalman, "Does Character Affect Judicial Performance?" *University of Colorado Law Review* 71 (2000): 1385. John W. Johnson explores Fortas's most important opinion decision in *The Struggle for Student Rights: Tinker v. des Moines and the 1960s* (1997).

NOTEWORTHY OPINIONS

Brown v. Louisiana, 383 U.S. 131 (1966)

Baltimore & Ohio Railroad Co. v. United States, 385 U.S. 3 (1967) (Dissent)

Time, Inc. v. Hill, 385 U.S. 374 (1967) (Dissent)

In re Gault, 387 U.S. 1 (1967)

Tinker v. Des Moines School District, 393 U.S. 503 (1969)

Street v. New York, 394 U.S. 576 (1969) (Dissent)

FELIX FRANKFURTER

Birth: November 15, 1882, Vienna, Austria.

Education: College of the City of New York, A.B., 1902; Harvard Law School, LL.B., 1906.

Official Positions: Assistant U.S. attorney, Southern District of New York, 1906–1909; law officer, Bureau of Insular Affairs, War Department, 1910–1914; assistant to the secretary of war, 1917; secretary and counsel, President's Mediation Commission, 1917; assistant to the secretary of labor, 1917–1918; chairman, War Labor Policies Board, 1918.

Supreme Court Service: Nominated associate justice by President Franklin D. Roosevelt, January 5, 1939, to replace Benjamin Cardozo, who had died; confirmed by the Senate, January 17, 1939, by a voice vote; took judicial oath January 30, 1939; retired August 28, 1962; replaced by Arthur Goldberg, nominated by President John F. Kennedy.

Death: February 22, 1965, Washington, D.C.

Closely identified with the social and economic reforms of President Franklin D. Roosevelt's New Deal, and long associated with liberal causes and organizations ranging from the American Civil Liberties Union to the *New Republic* magazine, Felix Frankfurter generated fear and paranoia among conservatives when the Senate considered his nomination in 1939. Elizabeth Dilling, author of *The Red Network,* a volume published at her own expense and highly recommended by the American Legion, warned members of the Senate Judiciary Committee that the nominee had "long been one of the principal aids of the 'red' revolutionary movement in the United States."

A spokesman for the American Federation Against Communism, while denying any anti-Semitic intentions, cautioned "in America, an anti-Jewish sentiment is growing by leaps and bounds. . . . To place, at this time, upon the highest court another one of that race is not only a political mistake but a social one." The national director of the Constitutional Crusaders wondered why the president had not chosen "an American from Revolutionary times instead of a Jew from Austria just naturalized," to which Sen. George Norris, R-Neb., a Frankfurter ally, responded, "an American from Revolution times would be too old."

New Dealers and liberals, on the other hand, greeted Frankfurter's nomination and confirmation with euphoria. Secretary of the Interior Harold Ickes pronounced it "the most significant and worth-while thing the President has done." The *Nation* magazine believed "no other appointee in our history has gone to the Court so fully prepared for its great tasks. There will be no *Dred Scott* decisions from a Supreme Court on which he sits." *Newsweek* predicted the newest justice would be "a magnificent champion of the underdog."

Supreme Court justices have a habit of disappointing, amazing, and confounding the presidents who selected them, as well as the groups and individuals who supported and opposed their appointment. There are few clearer examples of this axiom than Felix Frankfurter, the vibrant Harvard Law School professor, who arrived at the Court with a resumé attesting to three decades of participation in some of the most controversial social, legal, and political battles of his generation. As a teacher, author, public servant, litigator, and adviser to presidents, he had usually thrown his considerable energy and intellect into the fray on the side of what contemporaries called the progressive direction of affairs.

Joining the Harvard faculty shortly before World War I, Frankfurter pioneered the development of courses in administrative law and federal jurisdiction and fired the imagination of three generations of students to serve the public interest rather than private gain. As one of the federal government's chief labor administrators during the Great War, he sought protection for union members and pushed for improved working conditions, including an eight-hour day in the steel industry. He severely criticized California's prosecution of Tom Mooney, a militant labor organizer sent to prison on dubious evidence, and later leveled similar charges against Massachusetts authorities in the Sacco-Vanzetti case.

Frankfurter condemned Attorney General A. Mitchell Palmer and the post–World War I Red Scare, opposed American military intervention against the Bolsheviks in Russia, represented alien Communists threatened with deportation, and argued for the constitutionality of a federal minimum wage law in the famous case of *Adkins v. Children's Hospital* (1923). In the pages of the *New Republic*, he regularly criticized the judicial vetoes of the Supreme Court under Chief Justices William Howard Taft and Charles Evans Hughes. His fingerprints were all over landmark pieces of legislation in the 1930s, including the Norris-LaGuardia anti-injunction law, the Securities Act of 1933, and the Public Utility Holding Company Act of 1935. By the time of his appointment, Frankfurter's former students, often labeled "Felix's hot dogs," were occupying positions in many New Deal departments and agencies.

Frankfurter's intimate association with Oliver Wendell Holmes, Louis Brandeis, and Benjamin Cardozo, members of the Court who had displayed the greatest judicial toleration for social reform, as well as concern for safeguarding civil liberties, also encouraged his supporters to predict that he would follow much the same path. Archibald MacLeish, a former Frankfurter student, noted that the late 1930s marked a major watershed in the nation's constitutional history as the Court approved New Deal reforms, permitted more latitude to the political branches on economic measures, and became more assertive with regard to issues that touched civil liberties and civil rights. MacLeish predicted Frankfurter would do likewise, a point of view shared by Yale law professor Walton Hamilton: "Frankfurter defends

Felix Frankfurter

Holmes and Cardozo alike when they elevate the authority of the legislature above freedom of contract, yet make it yield before freedom of speech."

MacLeish, Hamilton, and other observers made the faulty assumption that Holmes and Brandeis shared a common vision about civil liberties and that Frankfurter stood shoulder to shoulder with them. In fact, Brandeis displayed far more regard for individual rights in the First Amendment area and elsewhere than Holmes, who treasured civil liberties far less than legislative discretion to regulate a splintered, fractious society. And, before joining the Court, Frankfurter usually sided with Holmes. He backed the latter's dissent in *Meyer v. Nebraska* (1923), when the majority, including Brandeis, struck down a law that prohibited public school instruction in the German language. Holmes's position, he noted to Judge Learned Hand, might encourage legislative attacks against "despised minorities," but "we are back at the old issue of the denial of power because of the potentiality of its abuse."

Two years later, he again sided with Holmes when the other justices invalidated an Oregon statute intended to ban education in private, church-run schools. Writing in the *New Republic* under the heading, "Can the Supreme Court Guarantee Toleration?" Frankfurter concluded it could not. "We expect our Courts to do it all," he lamented. Had Frankfurter's supporters paid closer attention to his pre-Court views about judicial power and civil liberties, they would not have been so shocked later by his stand in similar cases. He remained throughout his life a quintessential Bull Moose progressive, who believed in strong, energetic government to promote the general welfare. He read from the book of Rousseau, not Locke, a classical republican who placed the interests of the commonwealth above private rights, economic or otherwise.

As a young lawyer fresh from Harvard Law School in 1906, Felix Frankfurter joined the Wall Street firm of Hornblower, Miller & Potter. Soon after his arrival, a senior partner suggested that he might rise faster there if he anglicized his name. Recalling his mother's admonition to "always hold yourself dear," he politely but firmly refused. Later in life, as a justice

of the U.S. Supreme Court, he expressed anger when told that one of his former Jewish students, faced with the same decision, had chosen to do otherwise. Although a descendant of several generations of Central European rabbis, he seldom set foot in a synagogue or temple after adolescence and usually described himself as a "reverent agnostic."

Much to his mother's chagrin, he married a Congregational minister's daughter. He followed Brandeis into the Zionist crusade more out of fealty to Brandeis than out of deep devotion to the cause. He insisted that his funeral be conducted without a rabbi, but wanted the Kaddish, the ritual prayer for the dead, read by a former law clerk, a practicing, orthodox Jew. "I came into this world a Jew and although I did not live my life entirely as a Jew," he told playwright Garson Kanin, "I think it is fitting that I should leave as a Jew."

Of all the justices who ever served on the Supreme Court, Frankfurter, it can be argued, was both the least and the most influenced by his ethnocultural heritage. Among the most secular of our jurists, he displayed a faith in the powers of reason on a par with figures from the Enlightenment. But he was also, in the shrewd assessment of one scholar, "first and foremost a teacher in the rabbinic style," who relished "complexities, balanced truths, entertained questions, and understood puzzles." Instead of the Torah, however, he quoted copiously and endlessly from the opinions of Holmes and Brandeis, much to the annoyance of his brethren on the bench. "We would have been inclined to agree with Felix more often in conference," Justice William Brennan once remarked, "if he quoted Holmes less frequently to us."

A Jew, an immigrant, and a naturalized citizen, Frankfurter never attempted to conceal these attributes, but his journey from New York's Lower East Side to the Supreme Court shaped his almost mystical faith in assimilation, in the transforming powers of American culture, especially public education, to forge what St. Jean de Crevecoeur had called in 1782 "the American . . . a new man . . . who, leaving behind him all his ancient prejudices and manners, receives new ones from the new mode of life he has embraced, the new government he obeys, and the new rank he holds. . . . Here individuals of all races are melted down into a new race of men, whose labors and posterity will one day cause great changes in the world."

Frankfurter's robust belief in cultural assimilation, in the melting pot, in the ideal of a meritocratic social order where talent, brains, and energy counted for more than race, religion, or class led him to hire the Court's first black law clerk in 1948, William Coleman Jr. And it inspired perhaps his greatest contribution to American law: helping Chief Justice Earl Warren forge a unanimous Court to strike down segregated public schools in *Brown v. Board of Education* in 1954.

In addition to Coleman, he actively promoted the careers of other black lawyers, notably Charles H. Houston, the chief legal strategist of the NAACP, and William Hastie, the first black named to the federal bench by Roosevelt and later dean of the Howard University Law School. But Frankfurter also wrote the Court's 1950 opinion in *Hughes v. Superior Court of California*, which upheld an injunction prohibiting blacks from picketing at supermarkets to persuade the owners to fill a certain percentage of jobs with African Americans. California had no law against racial hiring quotas, but the local court and Frankfurter found the goals of the picketing to be inimical to the state's policy of nondiscrimination.

A longtime supporter of the NAACP's original program of nondiscrimination and the ideal of "a color-blind" legal order, Frankfurter did not move beyond that position during his lifetime. A decade after the *Hughes* case, as the civil rights struggle escalated in the South, Frankfurter expressed grave doubts about the militant tactics of young black college students and the Court's response to the first sit-in demonstrations. In Louisiana and elsewhere, black protesters in department stores, theaters, amusement parks, and restaurants had been jailed for trespass on private property. Following a heated conference about one of these cases, he told Hugo Black, another skeptic: "It will not advance the cause of constitutional equality for Negroes for the court to be taking short cuts to discriminate as partisans in favor of Negroes or even to appear to do so."

Although felled by illness before the final decision in *NAACP v. Button* (1963), Frankfurter was prepared to sustain a Virginia law that forbade solicitation of clients by an agent of an organization that litigates cases in which it is not a party and has no pecuniary interest. The NAACP argued that the Virginia legislature had aimed the statute explicitly at their organization and other civil rights groups that advised persons about their legal rights and remedies. Frankfurter, however, argued "there's no evidence . . . this statute is aimed at Negroes as such," and he concluded, "I can't imagine a worse disservice than to continue being the guardians of Negroes." Aside from *Hughes,* he never faced the dilemma of affirmative action programs, but it does seem likely that his views would have been closer to those of Antonin Scalia than to Thurgood Marshall's.

The same commitment to assimilation, derived from his own successful experience as a Jew, an immigrant, and a naturalized citizen, had other less happy consequences. Who can doubt that they profoundly shaped his views in *Meyer v. Nebraska* (1923) and *Pierce v. Society of Sisters* (1925) before he joined the Court, or in *Minersville School District v. Gobitis* (1940) at the start of his judicial career, and *Braunfeld v. Brown* (1961) near its end?

In *Gobitis,* the first flag salute case, he affirmed the power of school officials to compel children to salute the flag against the claims of a religious minority that such coerced participation violated the free exercise of their faith. In *Braunfeld,* he concurred in rejecting claims that Sunday closing laws were both a forbidden establishment of religion and an interference with religious liberty. In Felix Frankfurter's universe, secular public policies and rituals, when backed by a strong popular consensus, always trumped narrow sectarian religious beliefs, however passionately held. Neither Jehovah's Witnesses nor Orthodox Jews, he believed, could escape the common burdens and shared responsibilities of American citizenship.

Like most mortals, Frankfurter was a person of paradox and contradiction, someone who frequently acted and thought in ways that were not always consistent. Warm, charming, and supportive with his law clerks, he could be rude, abrasive, and petty with his brethren on the Court. Because of his intimate relationship with Justice Brandeis, probably no person came to the Court with greater inside information about how that institution functioned and about the importance of collegial relations among its members. Yet he failed to put what he knew into practice. Always critical of those who, like Justice Black, read constitutional provisions in absolute terms, he could be a strict constructionist when it came to issues of church and state or the Fourth Amendment. No one denounced with more fervor the extrajudicial activities of his colleagues, while himself engaging furiously in off-the-bench politics and policy making.

Frankfurter's extrajudicial political activities, especially during World War II, require some discussion, because they raise troubling questions about his fidelity to the important principle of the separation of powers. He was not the first sitting justice to dabble behind the scenes in politics. The examples are numerous. John Jay advised President George Washington on his State of the Union address and served as a commissioner of the mint. Under various pseudonyms, the great John Marshall pilloried his Jeffersonian critics in the press. Joseph Story drafted federal bankruptcy legislation and encouraged friends in Congress to sponsor it. Roger Taney helped write Andrew Jackson's message vetoing the recharter of the Second Bank of the United States.

But even in light of these historical precedents, Frankfurter's extrajudicial efforts were unusual in scope and volume. They have no parallel until the Abe Fortas–Lyndon Johnson relationship during the 1960s. Frankfurter assisted White House lawyers with the drafting of the executive agreement that transferred American destroyers to England in exchange for leases on British naval bases. He wrote sections of the Lend-Lease Act and suggested to congressional allies that it bear the title of H.R. 1776. Fortunately for Frankfurter, legal issues touching on these matters never came before the justices. The same cannot be said of his role in the famous case of the Nazi saboteurs.

In the summer of 1942 the German government landed eight saboteurs at locations on Long Island and Florida with the assignment of blowing up bridges, factories, and other military installations. The scheme failed miserably. The saboteurs and their few American confederates were quickly apprehended by local police, the FBI, and military intelligence. President Roosevelt ordered them tried by a special military tribunal. He also issued a proclamation closing the federal courts to any enemy alien then in custody on charges of sabotage. Seeking advice on how to constitute the military tribunal, Secretary of War Henry L. Stimson consulted his old protégé, Frankfurter, who recommended that it be composed solely of regular officers and exclude any civilian leaders from the department. Frankfurter also took Stimson's side when the secretary became embroiled in an argument with Attorney General Francis Biddle over permitting press coverage of the trial. Frankfurter opted for secrecy.

Stimson's diary entries probably reveal only a fraction of Frankfurter's conversations with him about the saboteurs' case. It seems likely that Frankfurter also discussed the issues regularly with John McCloy, his newest confidant in the War Department, who lived near Frankfurter in Georgetown and walked with him regularly in the evening. Having helped the government structure its proceedings against the German spies, Frankfurter then became the most vigorous defender of the administration's position when the accused sought judicial relief in the federal courts. Frankfurter was influential in shaping Chief Justice Harlan F. Stone's opinion that rejected their *habeas corpus* plea and sealed their fate in *Ex parte Quirin* (1942).

Frankfurter's extrajudicial activities ended abruptly with Roosevelt's death in 1945 and the conclusion of the war, when he lost access to the White House and executive branch agencies. They resumed briefly but significantly during the long struggle over school desegregation in the Eisenhower years. Frankfurter regularly advised his former clerk, Philip Elman, then in the office of the solicitor general, about the administration's strategy in *Brown v. Board of Education* I and II.

Were Frankfurter present today to defend his actions during the war and the desegregation cases, he would no doubt claim that he only stepped over the bounds of judicial neutrality on behalf of two noble causes: defeating Nazi Germany and ensuring an effective strategy for ending racial segregation in the public schools. His critics might respond that Mr. Justice Frankfurter, normally uncompromising when it came to questions of process, seldom argued that the ends justified the means. Or, at the very least, they would wish he had displayed more charity toward those of his judicial colleagues who dabbled, often less effectively than he, in affairs beyond the Court.

His law clerks affectionately called him "the Little Judge." Most of them recalled Frankfurter bouncing (he apparently never walked) down the corridors of the Supreme Court building while he whistled (usually off key) "Stars and Stripes Forever," the sextet from *Lucia di Lammermoor,* or the adagio from Mozart's great clarinet quintet. Bursting into their office after a long conference with the other justices, he regaled them with amusing stories about the behavior of his brethren: when Justice Stanley F. Reed, nicknamed "Dopey," said something especially absurd; when Justice Charles E. Whittaker, unable to make up his mind, switched his vote for the third time; or how Chief Justice Warren, grappling with the issue of the foreseeability of lightning in a torts case, finally threw up his hands in despair and said: "Oh, hell, how can I know if it's foreseeable? I don't know that much about lightning. We don't have much lightning in California!"

Dean Acheson, who often walked to work with Justice Frankfurter in the early 1950s, spoke of "the general noisiness of the man," an opinion shared by Court staff and clerks who often heard his voice piercing above others from the justices' private conference room. Just being Felix Frankfurter, wrote one journalist, "is in itself a violent form of exercise." He often tested his clerks' intellectual mettle by goading them into long arguments over legal history, current events, constitutional doctrine, and music: name ten milestones in Anglo-American law and defend your choices. Who was home secretary in the Atlee government? Who was the greater composer, Bartok or Bruch? To win these debates, he did not hesitate to

intimidate his younger opponents by invoking his seniority or his intimate knowledge of the persons and events under discussion. Sometimes sensing defeat, he would bolt from the office in disgust, leaving a shaken clerk behind. But next morning, within earshot of the same clerk, he would say to his secretary: "Wasn't that a terrific argument last night? Wasn't Al just great. Did you hear what he said to me?"

With less affection, attorneys who appeared before the Supreme Court from the late 1930s until the early 1960s recalled how Frankfurter peppered them with vexing questions. Perched forward on his high-backed chair, looking at times like a brittle, bespectacled, irritated sparrow, he turned the proceedings into a law school seminar. He could be especially brutal in his interrogation of former students and clerks, who often became targets for their mentor's display of judicial impartiality. "How," he asked one lawyer about a jurisdictional issue, "did you get to our Court?" "I came in on the Baltimore & Ohio, Mr. Justice," was the befuddled reply.

For twenty-three years on the bench, in chambers, and in conference, Frankfurter's judicial colleagues suffered his wit, learning, vanity, and fury. "If you had gone to the Harvard Law School," he once quipped to the brilliant Robert Jackson, "there would have been no stopping you." Chief Justice Fred Vinson, he noted, had made only two contributions to the rhetoric of jurisprudence: the expressions "for my money" and "in my book." During one heated exchange with Earl Warren, he shouted: "Be a judge, God damn it, be a judge."

After another tense conference battle, Justice Black told his son: "I thought Felix was going to hit me today, he got so mad." No doubt speaking for others, Warren told a friend, wearily: "All Frankfurter does is talk, talk, talk. He drives you crazy." "When I came into this conference," Justice William O. Douglas said on one occasion, "I agreed in the conclusion that Felix has just announced, but he's talked me out of it."

His first law clerk and longtime friend, Joseph L. Rauh Jr., once observed that Frankfurter's historical reputation would have been more secure had he never served on the Supreme Court. It is difficult to imagine that statement being made about many of the other individuals nominated and confirmed for the nation's highest judicial tribunal since 1789. For virtually all of them, service on the Supreme Court was the capstone of a career and the arena of public life that most clearly defined their place in American history. But for service on the Court, John Marshall would be remembered as simply another diplomat and secretary of state; Roger Taney as a partisan politician and Treasury secretary; Hugo Black as a loyal New Deal senator from Alabama; Earl Warren as a moderately progressive three-term governor and vice presidential candidate; and William Brennan as an able appellate jurist from New Jersey.

History, often unsympathetic to those on the losing side, has not been kind to Mr. Justice Frankfurter. The publication of his Court diaries and letters in the 1970s revealed a man of enormous insecurities, one frequently consumed and crippled by anger, vanity, and self-pity. Apart from Justice James McReynolds, it is difficult to name a member of the Court who had worse personal relations with his colleagues. Moreover, the almost universal scholarly consensus is that, as a justice, Frankfurter was a failure, a jurist who, in Joseph Lash's memorable phrase, became "uncoupled from the locomotive of history" sometime during World War II and left little in the way of an enduring doctrinal legacy. He would have made a superb contribution to the Court in an earlier era when its rampant activism often thwarted the creation of the modern welfare state, but his brand of judicial restraint became an anachronism when the nation's agenda shifted to the expansion of civil rights and civil liberties. Like the judicial conservatives of the New Deal years, Frankfurter saw many of his cherished constitutional structures demolished during his own lifetime—notably in the case of the exclusionary rule and legislative reapportionment. And unlike the two jurists he admired most—Holmes and Brandeis—his dissents assumed less significance over time.

Frankfurter's appointment in 1939 simply confirmed the triumph of New Deal jurisprudence, especially its deference to social and economic legislation.

His retirement in 1962, however, fundamentally altered the course of constitutional development. When Arthur Goldberg took Frankfurter's seat, he gave Chief Justice Warren a dependable fifth vote and opened the most expansive era in the Court's history in its defense of civil rights and civil liberties. In pending cases that challenged portions of the Immigration and Nationality Act in *Rusk v. Cort* (1962) and *Kennedy v. Mendoza-Martinez* (1963), the contempt powers of the House Un-American Activities Committee in *Russell v. United States* (1962), and the authority of Florida to compel certain disclosures by the NAACP in *Gibson v. Florida Legislative Investigation Committee* (1963), Frankfurter had been prepared to sustain the government in each instance. Goldberg tipped the balance in the other direction.

In the following decade, a majority of the justices spurned virtually all of Frankfurter's views on justiciability, political questions, due process, incorporation, and the speech clause of the First Amendment. Many of the neoconservatives who resisted the new judicial activism in the 1970s and 1980s attempted simultaneously to claim him as their own, but had great difficulty doing so in view of Frankfurter's defense of government economic regulation, his frequent stance against capital punishment, and his near-absolute position on both the Fourth Amendment and the establishment clause. He became a jurist almost without jurisprudential progeny.

Scholars trying to reconstruct Frankfurter's judicial world have employed a range of intellectual tools. Conventional legal analysis stresses his links to a tradition of judicial restraint from nineteenth-century legal scholar James Bradley Thayer to Justices Holmes and Brandeis. Those who use social-psychological or social-cultural explanations emphasize his immigrant background, unresolved identity crisis, and desire for acceptance by a Protestant establishment symbolized by Harvard, Henry Stimson, Holmes, and Franklin Roosevelt. Robert Burt offers the most severe indictment. In his view, Frankfurter was the Jewish insider, the parvenu who "struggled against acknowledging his outcast status . . . and always remained homeless in spite of himself." By failing to accept his own marginal status, Burt concludes, "Frankfurter lost all sympathy for outsiders anywhere."

That judgment is probably unduly harsh and reductionist. It fails to take into account numerous instances in Frankfurter's judicial career when, despite having reached the pinnacle of "insider" status, he manifested deep sympathy for outsiders and outcasts—most notably in his sustained opposition to capital punishment from the case of *Chambers v. Florida* (1940) to *Culombe v. Connecticut* (1961). Arthur Culombe, a thirty-three year-old illiterate with a mental age of nine, who had been in trouble with the law since adolescence, was convicted of murder and sentenced to death on the basis of a confession secured after five days of continuous and isolated interrogation by the police. No one can read Frankfurter's concurring opinion reversing this conviction without sensing both his outrage at the police tactics and his sympathy for the defendant.

Even more revealing is Frankfurter's dissenting opinion in a little-noted capital murder case from the District of Columbia in 1947, *Fisher v. United States*. The defendant, a black janitor, was convicted and sentenced to death for killing his white employer during an argument and brawl. Led by Justice Reed, the Court majority affirmed this conviction, despite powerful evidence that Fisher had been provoked, fought in self-defense, and that the trial judge had failed to properly instruct the jury on the issue of premeditation. Frankfurter's scathing dissent noted the judge's incompetence, highlighted the long history of conflict between Fisher and his boss, and stressed that the fight had started when the employer called Fisher "a black nigger." This section of the opinion outraged the other justices, who urged Frankfurter to delete the racial slur from his opinion. He refused. President Truman also refused to commute Fisher's death sentence, despite Frankfurter's personal appeal. Time and again over the course of his judicial career, Frankfurter spoke out in capital cases in which outsiders faced execution under circumstances that suggested to him their accusers had played fast and loose with the basic rules of criminal justice—notably in the cases of Julius and Ethel Rosenberg, convicted atomic spies, and Caryl Chessman, California's alleged "red light" bandit.

Finally, in cases during the Warren years in which resident aliens, accused of subversive activities, were facing deportation by the government, one might have expected the insider, parvenu justice to don his patriotic attire and sanction the government's conduct. But in *Carlson v. Landon* (1952), Frankfurter dissented against the proposition that Congress could deny bail to five alien Communists pending a final decision. And in *Rowoldt v. Perfetto* (1957), he provided the fifth and decisive vote to reverse the deportation of an elderly Jewish alien who had briefly joined the Communist Party in the 1930s. Earl Warren, ironically, always pointed to *Rowoldt* as an example of Frankfurter's failure to practice judicial restraint when his personal sympathies got the better of him. "I think Frankfurter is capable of a human instinct now and then," Warren told one of his clerks. "Frankfurter really obviously just felt sorry for this poor old immigrant. . . . I think Frankfurter may well have thought that there but for the grace of God go I."

Although virtually all of his important constitutional decisions failed to survive the judicial revolution of the 1960s and 1970s, Frankfurter left behind a number of critical legacies that merit emphasis today—the importance of judicial restraint in a democratic society, the value of federalism, the necessity for the Court to articulate an evolving concept of due process, and a passionate belief in the role of the courts and in the rule of law. Courts, he told us, are not the only or the primary institutions of government in this society. They could not, he often repeated, guarantee toleration where that spirit had withered among the people at large.

If his greatest failing on the Court was an all-too-eager deference to majorities, it sprang from a unique historical context where the judiciary had for decades thwarted the popular will and from a passionate belief in the virtues of self-education through the trial-and-error of messy democratic politics. The pre–New Deal judiciary often confused disputes over policy with debates over constitutional fundamentals. Reacting to those judicial excesses, Frankfurter sometimes forgot that the Constitution does articulate basic values and that it is the duty of the Court to give preference to them over the competing policy choices of transitory majorities.

As one of Roosevelt's closest advisers, he eagerly embraced the social and economic reforms of the New Deal. But among post–New Deal justices, he became something of a rarity in resisting the spirit of economic nationalism that would have swept away state regulatory power under the broad banner of the commerce clause. He did not believe, for example, that Congress intended to oust the states from their primary role in policing the insurance industry or managing the underwater resources of the outer continental shelf. His judicial brethren scorned these views, but Congress confirmed them in later legislation. He rejected the notion that the marketing of milk required a single, uniform national rule. He sought to preserve the fiscal integrity of the states by demolishing the vast array of tax immunities erected by judicial decisions.

Frankfurter's robust state-centered federalism was vividly demonstrated in cases touching the interpretation of state laws and state constitutions by local courts. "The state courts belong to the States," he wrote in *Flournoy v. Wiener* (1944). "Not only do we not review a case from a state court that can rest on a purely state ground, but we do not even review state questions in a case that is properly here from a state court on a federal ground." Such deference to federalism can perpetuate injustice, but civil libertarians and environmentalists who look to state courts and state constitutional provisions to defend individual rights and save local resources by invoking "independent state grounds" owe a debt to Felix Frankfurter.

Long identified with the ideal of judicial restraint, Frankfurter was, in fact, an activist when it came to the due process clause, where he believed the Court had a special constitutional obligation to articulate the community's evolving moral consensus toward more civilized standards of conduct and human relations. As he wrote in *Wolf v. Colorado* (1949):

Due process of law conveys neither formal nor fixed nor narrow requirements. It is the compendious expression for all those rights which the courts must enforce because they are basic to our free society. But basic rights do not become petrified as of any one time, even though, as a matter of human experience, some may not too rhetorically be called eternal verities. It is of the very nature of a free society to advance in its standards of what is deemed reasonable and right. Representing as it does a living principle, due process is not confined within a permanent catalogue of what may at a given time be deemed the limits or the essentials of fundamental rights.

His great constitutional adversary, Justice Black, who wished to cabin due process within the specific boundaries of the Bill of Rights, denounced Frankfurter's approach as dangerously subjective: "this stretching-contracting meaning of due process" or "the accordion-like meaning of due process." Black feared it would produce a judicial despotism reminiscent of the pre–New Deal Court. But Frankfurter's more open-ended, evolutionary approach to due process allowed him to strike down racial segregation in the District of Columbia, even without an equal protection clause in the Fifth Amendment, and it did not run aground when the Court was called upon to vindicate rights not explicitly catalogued in the Bill of Rights. Here, Frankfurter's approach to due process, carried on by Justice John Harlan and reaffirmed in a 1992 abortion decision, has helped to advance the revolution in human rights. The writers of *Planned Parenthood of Southeastern Pennsylvania v. Casey* quoted Frankfurter's opinion for the Court in *Rochin v. California* (1952): "To believe that this judicial exercise of judgment could be avoided by freezing 'due process of law' at some fixed stage of time or thought is to suggest that the most important aspect of constitutional adjudication is a function for inanimate machines, and not for judges."

Frankfurter, the apostle of judicial restraint, nevertheless claimed for the judiciary an activist role with respect to due process. And here one perceives another major contradiction in his conception of the institutional function of courts in American society. He preached ad nauseam the virtues of judicial restraint and judicial humility with respect to legislative policy choices and ultimate constitutional questions. At the same time, he possessed one of the most exalted conceptions of the judiciary's competence and importance of any jurist in the modern era.

He seldom voted to invalidate a legislative choice. But he also rarely reversed a judicial contempt order. That power, he wrote in *Offutt v. United States* (1954), "is a mode of vindicating the majesty of law." In conflicts between the press and the courts, disputes that usually pitted the First Amendment against the Fifth or Sixth Amendments, he normally sided with the judges. And he reserved his greatest scorn for judges—Webster Thayer in the Sacco-Vanzetti case, Harold Medina in the Smith Act prosecutions, Irving Kaufman in the Rosenberg trial—who dropped the veil of judicial impartiality to engage in blatant political partisanship. They destroyed confidence in "the majesty of the law" as surely as reckless newspapers during a murder trial, defiant miners who ignored judicial decrees, or blacks engaged in massive civil disobedience.

Shortly before his last illness in 1962, Frankfurter attended a performance of Robert Bolt's play about Thomas More, *A Man for All Seasons*. He sat with Garson Kanin, Ruth Gordon, and Howard Beale, the Australian ambassador to the United States. At a crucial moment in the drama, More warns his future son-in-law, William Roper, not "to cut a great road through the law to get after the Devil." When Roper insists that the ends may sometimes justify the means, More snaps back: "Oh? And when the last law was down, and the Devil turned round on you—where would you hide, Roper, the laws being flat? Yes, I'd give the Devil benefit of law, for my own safety's sake."

According to Beale, Frankfurter was enthralled by the speech and kept jabbing him in the ribs. "That's the point!" he said. "That's it, that's it!" Indeed, that was the final point for Justice Frankfurter, a true romantic, who could speak without irony about "the majesty of the law." He never accepted the proposition

of legal realists that law was simply a manifestation of arbitrary human desires, perhaps the residue of what a particular judge had for breakfast or lunch. And he surely scorned the fascist or communist notion that law came from the barrel of a gun.

Sometimes, in pursuit of this ideal—the rule of law—Felix Frankfurter defied the better angels of his own nature. The results could be disastrous, as they were in the flag salute cases, or his concurrence in *Dennis v. United States* (1951), affirming the conviction of American Communists under the Smith Act. Sometimes, off the bench, temporarily shedding his judicial robes, he did not always practice what he preached. He aspired to be Thomas More, but he sometimes acted like William Roper, ready "to cut a great road through the law to get after the Devil," especially when the Devil happened to be the Nazi regime or racial segregation. But the alternative to that ideal—no rule of law and a judiciary swept away by a blind faith in its own rectitude—could be equally fatal to the health of a democratic society. That, too, Felix Frankfurter knew.

— *Michael E. Parrish*

BIBLIOGRAPHY

Felix Frankfurter's pre-Court papers are housed at the Library of Congress, and his judicial papers are available at the Harvard Law Library. Several volumes of Frankfurter's essays have been edited: see Archibald MacLeish and E. F. Pritchard Jr., eds., *Law and Politics: Occasional Papers of Felix Frankfurter, 1913–1939* (1939); Philip H. Kurland, ed., *Felix Frankfurter on the Supreme Court: Extrajudicial Essays on the Court and the Constitution* (1970); and Philip Elman, ed., *Of Law and Men: Papers and Addresses of Felix Frankfurter, 1939–1956* (1956).

Melvin I. Urofsky has written the best short biography, *Felix Frankfurter: Judicial Restraint and Individual Liberties* (1992). On Frankfurter's pre-judicial career, see Michael E. Parrish, *Felix Frankfurter and His Times: The Reform Years* (1982). Two provocative psychological interpretations of Frankfurter are offered by Harry N. Hirsch, *The Enigma of Felix Frankfurter* (1981); and Robert A. Burt, *Two Jewish Justices: Outcasts in the Promised Land* (1988). Frankfurter offered an interpretation of his own life in an oral memoir published as *Felix Frankfurter Reminisces* (1960), ed., Harlan Philips. His diaries, focusing on the Court years, have been edited with an insightful introduction by Joseph P. Lash, ed., *From the Diaries of Felix Frankfurter* (1975).

For sympathetic accounts of Frankfurter's jurisprudence, see Sanford W. Levinson, "The Democratic Faith of Felix Frankfurter," *Stanford Law Review* 25 (1973): 430; and Mark Silverstein, *Constitutional Faiths: Felix Frankfurter, Hugo Black, and the Process of Judicial Decision-Making* (1984). J. D. Fassett looks at Frankfurter and one of his colleagues in "The Buddha and the Bumblebee: The Saga of Stanley Reed and Felix Frankfurter," *Journal of Supreme Court History* 28 (2003): 165. Frankfurter's complex relationship with Hugo Black is well explored in James F. Simon, *The Antagonists: Hugo Black, Felix Frankfurter and Civil Liberties in Modern America* (1989).

A jurisprudential analysis of Frankfurter and his colleagues is offered in J. D. Hockett, *New Deal Justice: The Constitutional Jurisprudence of Hugo L. Black, Felix Frankfurter, and Robert H. Jackson* (1996). For his views on the federal system, see M. B. McManamon, "Felix Frankfurter: The Architect of 'Our Federalism,' " *Georgia Law Review* 27 (1993): 697.

NOTEWORTHY OPINIONS

Minersville School District v. Gobitis, 310 U.S. 586 (1940)

Flournoy v. Wiener, 321 U.S. 253 (1944)

Fisher v. United States, 328 U.S. 463 (1947) (Dissent)

Wolf v. Colorado, 338 U.S. 25 (1949)

Hughes v. Superior Court of California, 339 U.S. 460 (1950)

Dennis v. United States, 341 U.S. 394 (1951) (Concurrence)

Rochin v. California, 342 U.S. 165 (1952)

Carlson v. Landon, 342 U.S. 524 (1952) (Dissent)

Braunfeld v. Brown, 366 U.S. 599 (1961) (Concurrence)

Culombe v. Connecticut, 367 U.S. 568 (1961) (Concurrence)

MELVILLE WESTON FULLER

Birth: February 11, 1833, Augusta, Maine.

Education: Bowdoin College, A.B., 1853; studied at Harvard Law School and read law, 1853–1855.

Official Positions: Member, Illinois House of Representatives, 1863–1864; member, Venezuela-British Guiana Border Commission, 1899; member, Permanent Court of Arbitration at The Hague, 1900–1910.

Supreme Court Service: Nominated chief justice by President Grover Cleveland, May 2, 1888, to replace Morrison R. Waite, who had died; confirmed by the Senate, July 20, 1888, by a 41–20 vote; took judicial oath October 8, 1888; served until July 4, 1910; replaced as chief justice by Edward D. White, nominated by President William Howard Taft.

Death: July 4, 1910, Sorrento, Maine.

Melville Fuller spent his childhood in Augusta, Maine, and entered Bowdoin College in September 1849 at age sixteen. He was active in a debating society and pursued his strong interest in literature. Graduating in 1853, Fuller promptly began his legal studies. As was then common practice, he received most of his legal training by apprenticeship. In 1854 Fuller entered Harvard Law School, where he attended lectures for six months. Admitted to the Maine bar the next year, Fuller moved back to Augusta and began to practice law with an uncle. Leaving behind his advantageous family contacts in Augusta, Fuller abruptly decided to move to Chicago in 1856. Like many New Englanders of his generation, Fuller felt that Chicago, which was emerging as the commercial center of the Midwest, offered attractive business and professional opportunities.

In Chicago, Fuller formed a series of short-lived partnerships with other attorneys. Although he appeared regularly in court and earned recognition as a skillful appellate advocate, he found it difficult to establish a financially successful law practice. He became active in Democratic Party politics and was a supporter of Stephen A. Douglas, which put him in an awkward political position when the Civil War began. Fuller was loyal to the Union and favored military action to crush secession. At the same time, he opposed abolitionism and was unhappy about the Lincoln administration's conduct of war. Fuller did not serve in the military. Instead, he was elected to the Illinois Constitutional Convention of 1862 and served in the Illinois House of Representatives during the 1863 legislative session. He supported a proposed state constitutional amendment to deny blacks the right to vote, denounced the Emancipation Proclamation, and assailed Lincoln's suspension of *habeas corpus*. Despite this controversial political record, Fuller excelled in establishing harmonious personal relations with persons of diverse legal and political views. He had a genial nature, with an urbane sense of humor and unfailing courtesy.

Fuller's professional status was substantially enhanced by each of his two marriages. He inherited land in Chicago from his first wife, Calista Reynolds, who died after six years of marriage. In May 1866 Fuller married Mary Ellen Coolbaugh. Her father was a wealthy banker and president of the Union National Bank, the largest financial institution in Chicago. Aided by his father-in-law's contacts, Fuller developed a large and successful practice focused on real estate and corporate law. He began to represent the Union National Bank and frequently appeared on behalf of other Illinois banks. In addition, Fuller defended railroad companies in personal injury litigation arising out of railroad accidents. But, in addition to appearing in behalf of Chicago's business elite, he also served as counsel for municipal bodies such as the South Park commissioners. Similarly, he handled various legal matters for the city of Chicago, including the famous case involving ownership of lakefront land along Lake Michigan, *State of Illinois v. Illinois Central Railroad Co.* (1888).

Melville Weston Fuller

In time, Fuller became one of the busiest attorneys in Chicago, trying approximately 2,500 cases during his career. He was also a skillful appellate advocate; in 1872 he argued his first of many cases before the U.S. Supreme Court. Before his appointment to the bench, Fuller had a wide experience with many diverse fields of law. He secured professional recognition as well as financial success and was elected president of the Illinois State Bar Association in 1886.

The death of Chief Justice Morrison R. Waite in March 1888 opened the door for Fuller's surprise appointment to the nation's top judicial post. After considering other individuals, President Grover Cleveland, the first Democrat in that office since the Civil War, selected Fuller. The nominee had been an enthusiastic backer of the Cleveland administration, and the president had consulted him concerning the distribution of political patronage in Illinois. Indeed, Cleveland had earlier asked Fuller to accept the post of solicitor general, which he declined. With his strong ties to Chicago, Fuller was reluctant to accept the nomination to the Court, but he acquiesced to the president's wishes. The Republican-controlled Judiciary Committee delayed action on Fuller's nomination for months hoping to prevent a confirmation vote until after the upcoming presidential election. In July 1888, however, after a brief debate that centered on Fuller's conduct during the Civil War, the Senate confirmed the appointment, 41–20.

By any standard, Fuller was eminently successful as a judicial administrator. His initial task was to exert leadership over his colleagues. A likable man, Fuller soon succeeded in establishing warm personal relations and proved a masterful social leader of the Court. Despite sharp divisions in some important cases and inevitable personality conflicts, Fuller's skills as a mediator prevented destructive personal feuds. As part of his effort to foster harmonious working relations,

Fuller introduced the practice of requiring each justice to shake hands with the other justices before hearing arguments or meeting in conference. He hoped that this custom, which has endured to the present, would minimize personal rifts among the justices.

Fuller also skillfully managed the Supreme Court's business. He expedited the handling of cases and presided with dignity over public sessions and oral arguments. Fuller's easy manners and genial temperament served him well in managing judicial conferences. He softened differences among the justices and used humor to dispel tension.

As chief justice, Fuller was responsible for assigning the preparation of opinions when he was in the majority. Early in his tenure Fuller kept some of the major opinions, such as *Pollock v. Farmers' Loan & Trust Co.* (1895), for himself. Thereafter, he generally assigned significant cases to others, a policy that reflected Fuller's self-effacing nature and his desire to promote judicial harmony. There is no evidence that Fuller used assignments to reward or punish colleagues for their views. An indefatigable worker, Fuller shouldered far more than his share of opinions for the Court, choosing the unglamorous opinions dealing with jurisdictional and procedural matters or commercial transactions. Like many of his colleagues, Fuller's prose style was verbose and diffuse. He wrote only a handful of dissenting opinions, usually in cases where Fuller sought to protect state autonomy from federal encroachment.

When Fuller became chief, the Court was laboring under an antiquated federal court structure and a staggering workload. Fuller helped to secure passage of the 1891 Evarts Act, which established the modern circuit courts of appeals system. In so doing, he demonstrated effective political skills and became the first chief justice to lobby Congress for legislation to reform the federal judicial system. Fuller also ably discharged a variety of extrajudicial duties and twice served as a member of arbitration panels dealing with international disputes.

Fuller led the Supreme Court during an era of sweeping social and economic transformation. The growth of large-scale corporate enterprise, rapid urbanization, and the emergence of a national market gave rise to vexing questions for the Court. If Fuller did not have a systematic judicial philosophy when he became chief, he was markedly influenced by the Jacksonian political legacy with its insistence on limited government, preservation of states' rights, and opposition to paternalism. Fuller's success in the practice of law reinforced his acceptance of such principles. The key to understanding Fuller's judicial outlook is his persistent attachment to Jacksonian principles. He exemplifies the link between Jacksonian democracy and the emergence of laissez-faire constitutionalism in the late nineteenth century.

Faith in state autonomy, dedication to the rights of property owners, and attachment to free trade among the states formed the cornerstone of Fuller's constitutional thought. He was, therefore, prepared to read national power broadly to protect economic rights under the due process clause of the Fourteenth Amendment and the dormant commerce power. Still, Fuller was willing to allow the states wide latitude in shaping social policy with respect to race relations, criminal justice, and public morals.

His reverence for private property was a crucial ingredient of his jurisprudence. Like many nineteenth-century Americans, Fuller regarded the right to acquire, possess, use, and transfer property as among the most important individual liberties. Freedom was defined largely in economic terms. He was convinced that the Constitution and Bill of Rights erected barriers against majoritarian rule to protect economic liberty. Moreover, he believed that private property and other types of individual liberty were inseparable. Respect for property rights, therefore, safeguarded individuals by limiting the reach of legitimate government authority. Under his leadership, the Court sought to protect private property as a personal right. Anchoring this commitment to property ownership was Fuller's awareness of the vital role of investment capital in the economic transformation of the United States. He was eager to safeguard capital formation and to facilitate the development of a national market.

The chief issues before the Court during Fuller's tenure concerned the rights of property owners and the extent to which Congress or the states could control economic activity. Throughout the nineteenth century the justices had defended property and contractual rights from legislative infringement. But Fuller's appointment as chief justice marked a dramatic shift in the formulation of constitutional doctrine. The Fuller Court took an activist role in protecting the rights of property owners, striking down federal and state economic legislation. In so doing, Fuller had no trouble supporting a host of bold constitutional innovations. For example, the Court adopted a substantive interpretation of the due process clause in *Chicago, Milwaukee & St. Paul Railway Co. v. Minnesota* (1890), fashioned the novel liberty of contract doctrine in *Allgeyer v. Louisiana* (1897), and placed constitutional limits on rate regulation in *Smyth v. Ames* (1898). Fuller provided the fifth vote in *Lochner v. New York* (1905), in which the Court struck down as an interference with the liberty of contract a state law regulating the hours of labor in bakeries. The rationale of *Lochner* made the Court the overseer of state regulatory laws.

Likewise, Fuller favored an expansive use of injunctions by federal courts to secure effectively property rights. He joined his associates in upholding a groundbreaking injunction against interference by strikers with interstate commerce in *In re Debs* (1895) and in affirming the issuance of injunctions to prevent state officials from enforcing unconstitutional laws in *Ex parte Young* (1908). In another important step, in *Chicago, Burlington & Quincy Railroad Company v. Chicago* (1897), the Court held that the just compensation requirement of the Fifth Amendment was an essential element of due process as guaranteed by the Fourteenth Amendment. Just compensation became, in effect, the first provision of the Bill of Rights to be applied to the states. This decision set the stage for the gradual extension of other provisions of the Bill of Rights in the twentieth century. In short, a profound commitment to property and private economic ordering gave a distinct cast to the jurisprudence of the Fuller years.

Yet Fuller was no doctrinaire adherent to laissez-faire philosophy. He frequently invoked the state police power and sustained legislation that he perceived as protecting the health, safety, and morals of the public. For example, Fuller supported decisions that sustained state laws limiting the hours of employment in mines, mandating payment of wages in cash, and imposing licensure requirements on certain businesses. In *Muller v. Oregon* (1908), Fuller agreed that a state could restrict the working hours for women in factories and laundries. Despite its reputation as a conservative economic bastion, the Court under Fuller validated more regulatory legislation than it overturned. In practice, the liberty of contract doctrine was employed sparingly.

Fuller was well aware of the political dimension to constitutional adjudication. In sensitive areas such as race relations and public morals, Fuller and his associates were disinclined to challenge popular attitudes. Even in the sharply contested economic terrain, where Populists and Progressives assailed some of his rulings, Fuller was usually in harmony with the dominant currents of political thought. Indeed, there was a forward-looking dimension to Fuller's handling of economic issues. He identified with burgeoning industrial capitalism, and under his direction the Court was more receptive to the new realities of American economic life than many other sectors of the polity.

Overshadowed by highly visible justices such as Stephen J. Field and Oliver Wendell Holmes, Fuller never gained intellectual ascendancy over his colleagues. Yet he was adept at massing the Court behind zealous defense of the rights of property owners. He exercised considerable leadership through informal consensus building.

Fuller wrote relatively few of the leading constitutional decisions handed down during his tenure. Perhaps his most famous opinions were written in connection with *Pollock*, in which Fuller, speaking for a majority of five, invalidated the 1894 income tax legislation. Distinguishing earlier authority that upheld the Civil War income tax, he ruled that an income levy was a direct tax, which, under the Constitution, had to be apportioned among the states according to population. Fuller was motivated in part to protect accumulated capital and to preserve the existing balance in state-federal relations. He instinctively realized that an income tax would expand federal revenue and power as well as portend further moves to reallocate wealth. Although Populists fiercely denounced the *Pollock* decision, evidence shows that the outcome was in line with public sentiment. Nor it is convincing to portray Fuller as a champion of the wealthy. He voted to sustain both state and federal inheritance taxes.

Fuller's handling of the commerce power reflected unresolved tensions between the needs of a national industrial market and the persistence of localism and states' rights sentiments. He consistently championed free trade among the states and joined numerous decisions holding that state regulations unreasonably burdened interstate commerce. At the same time, he was reluctant to recognize broad congressional authority to regulate commerce.

In *United States v. E. C. Knight Co.* (1895), the first case under the Sherman Antitrust Act to reach the Supreme Court, the justices accepted the constitutionality of the measure but restricted congressional power to prevent manufacturing monopolies. Speaking for a majority of eight justices, Fuller followed the established view that manufacturing was local in nature and subject to state control. He drew a sharp line between manufacturing and the sale of goods in interstate markets. The *E. C. Knight* decision narrowed the reach of the Sherman Act and hampered antitrust enforcement. Modern eyes can clearly see the economic unreality of Fuller's opinion. His distinction between manufacturing and commerce ignores the basic interdependence of economic activity.

But to Fuller, the issues transcended the threat of business consolidation and went to the very foundation of the constitutional scheme. Consistent with his dedication to a limited federal government, Fuller insisted that large areas of economic life remained outside the authority of Congress. He did not read the commerce clause as a comprehensive grant of power because such a step would upset the federal system and leave the states with little economic activity to control. If Fuller took a narrow view of congressional power, he nevertheless voted to apply the Sherman

Act in several cases. Moreover, in *Swift & Company v. United States* (1905), Fuller supported the stream of commerce doctrine that extended the federal commerce power to local enterprises that were an integral part of interstate transactions. Despite this development, the line Fuller drew between manufacturing and commerce in *E. C. Knight* endured until the New Deal and the constitutional revolution of 1937.

Fuller could not consistently marshal a majority behind the principle of limited government. For example, in *Champion v. Ames* (1903), the justices, 5–4, construed congressional commerce authority broadly to uphold legislation suppressing the interstate transportation of lottery tickets. In perhaps his best-known dissenting opinion, Fuller pointed out that Congress was, in effect, seeking to exercise a police power to regulate public morals. He argued that this goal was inconsistent with the intent of the framers and threatened to upset the constitutional balance between the national and state governments.

One of Fuller's most far-reaching opinions came in *Loewe v. Lawlor* (1908). At issue was a private damage suit under the Sherman Act against union officials for instituting a secondary boycott against the plaintiff employer. Speaking for a unanimous court, Fuller maintained that the Sherman Act prohibited any combination that obstructed the free flow of commerce. Accordingly, the law applied to union activities. Although controversial with labor unions, which feared large damage suits, Fuller followed the prevailing view that the Sherman Act reached all combinations that restrained trade.

Despite his preoccupation with economic issues, Fuller also made contributions in other areas of law. He wrote several opinions that helped to define the Supreme Court's original jurisdiction. In *Virginia v. West Virginia* (1907), Fuller concluded that the Court had jurisdiction over an original action by Virginia seeking to allocate part of its pre–Civil War debt to West Virginia. He occasionally demonstrated concern over civil liberties. He filed an eloquent dissent in *Fong Yue Ting v. United States* (1893), arguing that the Constitution protected resident Chinese aliens against summary deportation. Again in dissent, Fuller contended in the *Insular Cases* that the Bill of Rights extended to overseas territories on their acquisition by the United States. He joined the opinion in *Twining v. New Jersey* (1908), which intimated that some of the personal guarantees in the Bill of Rights might be effective against the states. This opinion paved the way for eventual nationalization of procedural rights for criminal defendants. In addition, Fuller demonstrated sympathy for the plight of injured workers. He regularly voted to restrict application of the so-called fellow servant rule, which protected employers from liability for injury to their workers. In *Johnson v. Southern Pacific Co.* (1904), Fuller insisted that the Safety Appliance Act should be liberally construed to secure the safety of railroad employees. In *United States v. Shipp* (1909), he vigorously used the contempt power to punish law officers who connived in the lynching of a black prisoner despite the issuance of a stay pending appeal. This case was the first instance of the Court's instituting a contempt proceeding, and Fuller's ringing condemnation of this incident served to focus national attention on lynching.

Over time, many of Fuller's achievements have been eclipsed. The nation no longer adheres to a constitutional order based on the principles of limited government, states' rights, and respect for private property. Fuller's attempts to cabin congressional tax and regulatory authority ultimately proved futile. Indeed, after a lacerating struggle over the New Deal program, the Supreme Court largely abandoned its long-standing concern with economic rights in 1937. Because much of Fuller's handiwork seems to belong to another era, few scholars would place Fuller among the great justices.

Yet Fuller left his mark on American jurisprudence and has perhaps received inadequate attention. He saw the federal judiciary as an active participant in governance and greatly strengthened its role in American life. Many of the doctrinal innovations associated with his name have continuing vitality. Contrary to popular belief, the Supreme Court has never really abandoned a substantive interpretation of the due process clause; rather, it uses the doctrine as a safeguard for noneconomic rights instead of property interests. Expansive use of federal equity power in the

late twentieth century built on precedent from the Fuller era. Indeed, many of the issues that predominated during his tenure—the reach of regulatory authority, the rights of property owners—reappeared during the Rehnquist Court. Renewed scholarly and judicial interest in economic rights suggests enduring recognition that property ownership and individual liberty are linked, and Chief Justice Fuller was a major contributor to the ongoing debate over the place of property in American constitutional law.

—*James W. Ely Jr.*

BIBLIOGRAPHY

The Fuller papers are divided between the Library of Congress and the Chicago Historical Society. The standard, although somewhat outdated, biography is Willard L. King, *Melville Weston Fuller: Chief Justice of the United States, 1888–1910* (1950). Fuller's leadership is also explored in Robert J. Steamer, *Chief Justice: Leadership and the Supreme Court* (1986).

Studies of the Court and its doctrine during the Fuller years include: James W. Ely Jr., *The Chief Justiceship of Melville W. Fuller* (1995); Loren P. Beth, *The Development of the American Constitution, 1877–1917* (1971); David P. Currie, *The Constitution in the Supreme Court: The Second Century, 1888–1986* (1990); Arnold Paul, *Conservative Crisis and the Rule of Law: Attitudes of Bar and Bench, 1887–1895* (1960); and John F. Semonche, *Charting the Future: The Supreme Court Responds to a Changing Society, 1890–1920* (1978).

For studies focusing more on doctrinal issues, see James W. Ely Jr., *The Guardian of Every Other Right: A Constitutional History of Property Rights* (1992); Herbert Hovenkamp, *Enterprise and American Law, 1836–1937* (1991); and Paul Kens, *Judicial Power and Reform Politics: The Anatomy of Lochner v. New York* (1990).

NOTEWORTHY OPINIONS

Fong Yue Ting v. United States, 149 U.S. 698 (1893) (Dissent)

United States v. E. C. Knight Co., 156 U.S. 1 (1895)

Pollock v. Farmers' Loan & Trust Co., 157 U.S. 429 (1895)

Champion v. Ames, 188 U.S. 321 (1903) (Dissent)

Johnson v. Southern Pacific Co., 196 U.S. 1 (1904)

Virginia v. West Virginia, 206 U.S. 290 (1907)

Loewe v. Lawlor, 208 U.S. 204 (1908)

United States v. Shipp, 214 U.S. 386 (1909)

RUTH BADER GINSBURG

Birth: March 15, 1933, Brooklyn, New York.

Education: Cornell University, B.A., 1954; attended Harvard University Law School, 1956–1958; graduated Columbia Law School, J.D., 1959.

Official Positions: Judge, U.S. Court of Appeals for the District of Columbia Circuit, 1980–1993.

Supreme Court Service: Nominated associate justice by President Bill Clinton, June 22, 1993, to replace Byron R. White, who had retired; confirmed by the Senate, August 3, 1993, by a 96–3 vote; took judicial oath August 10, 1993.

Ruth Bader Ginsburg reached the Supreme Court after directing the litigation strategy in the 1970s that established the first constitutional rules against sex discrimination. Her experience in combating the institutionalized prejudice against women that initially slowed her own advancement in the legal profession played a major part in President Bill Clinton's decision to appoint her to the Court in 1993 to succeed Justice Byron R. White.

On the Court, Ginsburg became a strong voice and consistent vote in support of efforts to combat discrimination against women, minorities, and gays. Although she resisted ideological labels in her Senate confirmation hearings, she aligned herself generally with the Court's liberal justices in most other areas as well, including criminal law, federalism, and church-state relations.

Ruth Joan Bader was born in Brooklyn's Flatbush section to Jewish parents of modest means. Her father, Nathan Bader, worked as a furrier and later as a haberdasher; her mother, Celia Amster Bader, worked in New York's garment district. Celia Bader installed in her daughter from an early age a love of learning and a spirit of independence. She was stricken with

cancer while Ruth was in high school and died on the eve of her daughter's high school graduation in 1950.

More than forty years later, Ginsburg paid tribute to her mother when she spoke about women's equality in a moving conclusion to her remarks after Clinton announced her selection for the Court. "I pray that I may be all that she would have been," Ginsburg said, "had she lived in an age when women could aspire and achieve and daughters are cherished as much as sons." Clinton reportedly teared up as Ginsburg finished.

Financing her education from scholarships and her mother's savings, Ruth Bader excelled at Cornell University, where she graduated first among the women in her class in 1954. She also met her future husband, Martin Ginsburg, who became a tax lawyer and later—after she was appointed to the federal appeals court in Washington—a professor at Georgetown University Law Center. Along with Martin, Ruth enrolled in Harvard Law School, where she made law review, cared for their infant daughter, and then helped him finish his studies after he was diagnosed with cancer. He recovered, graduated, and took a job in New York. She transferred to Columbia for her final year of law school.

Although tied for first place in her graduating class in 1959, Ginsburg could not get a job with a top New York law firm or a Supreme Court clerkship. One of her professors recommended her to Justice Felix Frankfurter, but he replied that he was not ready to hire a woman as a clerk. Instead, Ginsburg got a two-year clerkship with a federal district court judge. She then studied civil procedure in Sweden as part of a comparative law project at Columbia. She also began to take an interest in feminist thought.

After her return from Sweden, Ginsburg became the second woman to join the law faculty of Rutgers University in New Jersey, where she taught from 1963 to 1972. She also helped the New Jersey chapter of the American Civil Liberties Union (ACLU) litigate sex discrimination cases, including suits on behalf of teachers who had to give up their jobs after becoming pregnant. Ginsburg herself had obscured her second pregnancy while at Rutgers for fear of losing her then-untenured position.

Ginsburg left Rutgers in 1972 for Columbia Law School, where she became the school's

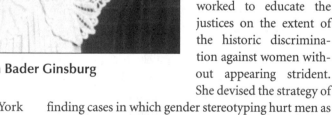

Ruth Bader Ginsburg

first tenured woman faculty member. In New York she also became director of the ACLU's Women's Rights Project. In that role, she conceived and directed the legal strategy that moved the Supreme Court in a series of cases to rule that laws treating men and women differently because of sex are subject to heightened constitutional scrutiny. Admirers, likening her work to the NAACP Legal Defense Fund's campaign against school desegregation, com-

monly describe her as "the Thurgood Marshall of gender equality law."

Ginsburg had first worked with the ACLU's national office on a brief challenging an Idaho law that preferred men to women as administrators of decedents' estates. Sally Reed blamed her estranged husband, Cecil, for the suicide of their son, Richard, and wanted to manage Richard's estate, but the Idaho law favored his father. The brief that Ginsburg helped write with the ACLU's chief lawyer argued that gender discrimination should be automatically suspect for constitutional purposes and in any event that the law had no rational basis. The Court in *Reed v. Reed* (1971) struck the law down, 9–0, but on the narrower rational-basis ground.

The success encouraged the ACLU to create the women's rights unit, and Ginsburg negotiated an arrangement with Columbia to direct the project while teaching half time. To continue the campaign, Ginsburg worked to educate the justices on the extent of the historic discrimination against women without appearing strident. She devised the strategy of finding cases in which gender stereotyping hurt men as well as women. As she explained later, she wanted to show "the disadvantage to men of being pigeonholed."

In the first case she argued before the Court, Ginsburg challenged a federal law governing benefits for the dependent spouses of married members of the military. Under the law, wives of men in the military were automatically eligible for the benefits, but the husbands of women in the military had to show that they were dependent on their wives for more than half their income. Sharon Frontiero, a lieutenant in the Air Force, asked lawyers at the Southern Poverty Law Center to help her obtain benefits for her husband after the Air Force said he was ineligible. The center filed a lawsuit challenging the provision and then asked the ACLU Women's Rights Project to assist at the Supreme Court.

In her argument, Ginsburg pointed out that the provision effectively paid men more than women and that it was premised on a gender stereotype of the sort disapproved in *Reed*. The Court in *Frontiero v. Richardson* (1973) agreed by an 8–1 vote, but the victory was muddled. Justice William J. Brennan Jr. concluded in a plurality opinion for four justices that gender discrimination was subject to "strict scrutiny"—the most demanding constitutional standard. But the other four justices simply found the discrimination improper without defining a test for future cases. Justice William H. Rehnquist was the lone dissenter.

Three years later the Court settled on a constitutional standard for sex discrimination in a case challenging an Oklahoma law that allowed young women between the ages of eighteen and twenty-one to buy low-alcohol-content "near beer," but men had to be twenty-one. The state defended the differential treatment by citing the higher incidence of drunken driving among young men than among young women. Ginsburg filed an amicus brief in support of the young man and bar owner challenging the law. The Court's decision in *Craig v. Boren* (1976) established what came to be known as "intermediate scrutiny" for laws discriminating between men and women. Writing for six justices, Brennan said that previous cases had established the rule that "classifications by gender must serve important governmental objectives and must be substantially related to achievement of those objectives." While acknowledging the importance of traffic safety, Brennan concluded that the Oklahoma law was a "tenuous fit" with the state's goal.

In all, Ginsburg argued six cases before the Court while heading the ACLU Women's Rights Project and won five of them. At the same time, she was working to win ratification of the Equal Rights Amendment (ERA) to establish a firm constitutional bar against sex discrimination. By 1978 supporters had fallen short of ratification by three-fourths of the states. Ginsburg helped craft the legal arguments to justify extending the time to ratify the amendment past the original deadline of 1979 and to disregard any efforts by state legislatures to rescind previous votes to ratify. Congress extended the deadline, but even with additional time the ERA failed to win a place in the Constitution.

President Jimmy Carter named Ginsburg to the U.S. Court of Appeals for the District of Columbia Circuit in 1980. Over the next thirteen years, Ginsburg earned a reputation for thorough preparation, prompt opinion-writing, careful reasoning, and cautious decision making. Her views and judicial approach often put her in the middle of a court that had been dominated by liberal, Democratic appointees but came to be ideologically fractious with the appointment of conservative jurists by Presidents Ronald Reagan and George H. W. Bush.

Among the Republican appointees was Antonin Scalia, who served on the D.C. Circuit for four years until his elevation to the Supreme Court in 1986. Despite the ideological differences, Ginsburg and her husband became close friends of Scalia and his wife. Among other things, the two justices shared a common interest in opera. After Ginsburg joined Scalia on the Supreme Court, they both appeared on stage as extras, in full costume, in a 1994 Washington Opera production of *Ariadne auf Naxos*.

Despite her record on women's rights, Ginsburg disquieted abortion rights advocates with a critique of the landmark *Roe v. Wade* (1973) decision in a speech at New York University Law School in March 1993. Invited to deliver the school's James Madison Lecture, Ginsburg contrasted the Supreme Court's step-by-step approach on gender discrimination with the broader sweep of *Roe*, which effectively invalidated all existing state laws on abortion. The Court's decision to "fashion a regime blanketing the subject," Ginsburg said, "invited no dialogue with legislators" and "served to fuel rather than reduce controversy." When Ginsburg was chosen for the Supreme Court, some abortion rights supporters cited the speech as cause for concern, while others called her a reliable supporter of abortion rights.

Justice White's decision to retire from the Court—announced in mid-March 1993, more than three months before the end of the term—gave President Clinton the first opportunity for a Democrat to choose a justice in twenty-six years. Clinton had promised during the campaign to appoint justices who supported abortion rights and took "an expansive view of the Constitution and the Bill of Rights." On the day of White's announcement, Clinton said he would look for a justice with experience, judgment, and "a big heart."

Clinton's search took an unusually long eighty-seven days. Initially, he considered choosing New York's governor Mario Cuomo, but Cuomo surprised the White House by saying he was not interested. Clinton also focused on Interior Secretary Bruce Babbitt, a former Arizona governor; but environmentalists urged Clinton to keep Babbitt in the cabinet instead. As a result, the list of more than forty candidates was dominated by sitting federal judges. At the top of the list was Stephen G. Breyer, a well-regarded judge on the federal appeals court in Boston, who had been a Senate aide and a Harvard Law School professor. But Breyer's interview with Clinton went poorly, and the president asked his aides to give him another candidate even while news reports were describing Breyer as the all-but-certain choice.

Ginsburg had been on the early lists of possible candidates but had dropped out of later speculation. Her judicial reputation was excellent and as a Jewish woman she would be a "two-fer" in terms of diversity. But her age—sixty—counted against her. And Clinton had initially been unimpressed with what he heard and read about her. When aides arranged a Sunday morning interview at the White House, however, Clinton was won over by Ginsburg's life story of combating discrimination against women both in her own life and in the courtroom.

Announcing his decision the next day, Clinton cited Ginsburg's "truly historic record of achievement" on women's rights. In her acceptance remarks, Ginsburg spoke of the advances she had seen for women in the law. She recalled that she had been one of fewer than ten women in a law school class of nearly 500. Now, she said, few law schools had less than 40 percent female enrollment. The number of women on federal courts had increased from only one in 1976 to "close to twenty-five." And for herself, Ginsburg noted that her daughter, Jane, had written in her high school yearbook that her ambition was to "to see her mother appointed to the Supreme Court."

Ginsburg's nomination moved smoothly and quickly through the Senate—in sharp contrast to the confirmations of Justices David H. Souter in 1990 and Clarence Thomas in 1991. In her opening statement Ginsburg depicted herself as an advocate—and a practitioner—of judicial restraint. "My approach is neither liberal or conservative," she said. "Rather, it is rooted in the place of the judiciary in our democratic society." She promised that she would not write her own convictions into the Constitution and described the judicial process as one of gradual change.

In subsequent comments, however, Ginsburg aligned herself with legal views generally described as liberal. She said courts had a role in forcing social changes when groups were "shut out of the political process." She endorsed a constitutional right to privacy and approvingly cited decisions taking expansive views of contemporary standards to evaluate new claims of individual liberties. She supported affirmative action while opposing "rigid quotas" and struck separationist notes on church-state issues.

Ginsburg also reassured women's groups by strongly endorsing abortion rights. "This is something central to a woman's life, to her dignity," Ginsburg said. "And when government controls that decision for her, she's being treated as less than a fully adult human responsible for her choices." For good measure, Ginsburg also explicitly endorsed the dormant Equal Rights Amendment. The Constitution should include "a clarion call that women and men are equal before the law," she said.

In the only major conflict during the hearings, Ginsburg resisted Republicans' attempts to pin her down on capital punishment. While promising to be "scrupulous in applying the law on the basis of legislation and precedent," Ginsburg pointedly declined to say whether she agreed with rulings holding the death penalty constitutional. "If you want me to take a pledge," Ginsburg said, "that is one thing you must not ask a judge to do." With less conflict, she also ducked questions on a range of other issues, including gun control, *habeas corpus,* property rights, racial gerrymandering, and school vouchers. The Judiciary Committee, 18–0, approved Ginsburg's nomination on July 29. The full Senate was nearly unanimous five days later, confirming Ginsburg, 96–3; three conservative Republicans cast the only no votes. In swearing-in ceremonies a week later, Ginsburg again returned to the theme of advancing opportunities for women. "A system of justice will be richer for a diversity of background and experience," she said.

Justice Ginsburg began making her presence felt from her first day on the bench, when she was counted as having asked seventeen questions during one hour-long argument. After receiving some critical comments, she eased up somewhat but remained one of the Court's most active questioners throughout her first term and thereafter. She also made a point of introducing gender-free terminology into arguments and opinions. During one argument, when one of the justices posed a hypothetical involving a "postman," Ginsburg changed the term in a follow-up question to "letter carrier."

More substantively, Ginsburg aligned herself generally with the justices viewed as constituting the Court's liberal wing: John Paul Stevens, David Souter, and Stephen Breyer, whom Clinton appointed in 1994 to succeed Harry A. Blackmun. For the next decade, these four justices comprised a fairly cohesive bloc that—in contrast to the five more conservative justices—took a broader view of civil rights and civil liberties and supported an expansive construction of federal powers vis-à-vis the states. Statistical compilations showed that Ginsburg voted more than 80 percent of the time with each of the three liberal justices; by comparison, she agreed with conservatives Scalia and Thomas in fewer than two-thirds of the cases.

As a junior justice, Ginsburg drew few assignments of special note in her first two years on the bench. But in the 1995–1996 term, she received an assignment that built on and carried forward her life-long work on gender equality. The issue was the constitutionality of an all-male, state-supported military college: Virginia Military Institute. In her opinion in *United States v. Virginia* (1996), Ginsburg forcefully ruled the state's policy unconstitutional and in the process appeared to tighten somewhat the standard for reviewing government actions that treat men and women differently.

The case drew national attention in part because of VMI's stout defense of its all-male enrollment. Founded in 1839, the school had a prominent place in Virginia's political and business circles. VMI graduates comprised an influential network within the state, and they rallied to defend the all-male policy when it came under challenge. For its part, the school said the men-only policy was essential to the rigorous regimen imposed on first-year students as a means of instilling the importance of strictly following rules and closely bonding with their fellow cadets. But the Justice Department, acting on a complaint from a never-identified female high school student, filed suit against the school, claiming that the policy amounted to illegal sex discrimination under the Fourteenth Amendment's equal protection clause.

The case went up and down in lower federal courts. Initially, a federal district court judge upheld the all-male policy, saying that the state's interest in preserving VMI's distinctive educational methods satisfied the test set out in a 1982 decision, *Mississippi University for Women v. Hogan.* In that decision—written by Justice Sandra Day O'Connor—the Court held that sex classifications could be upheld only if they served "important governmental objectives" and were "substantially related to the achievement of those objectives." The U.S. Court of Appeals for the Fourth Circuit disagreed and sent the case back to the district court to craft a remedy. The state then proposed to set up a separate, all-female military program at a different campus. The district court judge and the appeals court upheld the plan, and the Justice Department brought the case to the Supreme Court.

In ruling the all-male policy unconstitutional, Ginsburg neatly turned the state's celebration of VMI's educational methods against the school. "This case concerns an incomparable military college," Ginsburg began. Women sought admission precisely because of its "unique program and unparalleled record." Under the Court's precedents, she continued, defenders of sex-based government actions must demonstrate an "exceedingly persuasive justification" and cannot rely on "overbroad generalizations . . . about the way that most women (or most men) are." As for the new program for women, it was inadequate. "Women seeking and fit for a VMI-quality education cannot be offered anything else," she concluded.

Ginsburg's special concern with gender equality could be seen in other opinions, including separate concurrences or dissents. In her first opinion as a justice, for example, she wrote a concurrence in a sexual harassment case, *Harris v. Forklift Systems, Inc.* (1994), to say that a plaintiff needed to show only that the claimed discriminatory conduct "unreasonably interfered with plaintiff's work performance" and that it was unnecessary to show an actual loss of productivity. In a footnote, she also said that it was "an open question" whether gender-based classifications are inherently suspect for constitutional purposes.

In later years, Ginsburg voted in dissent in *Gebser v. Lago Vista Independent School District* (1998) to allow suits against school districts for teacher-against-student sexual misconduct and with the majority in *Davis v. Monroe County Board of Education* (1999) to permit suits against school districts for severe student-on-student sexual harassment. She also joined a pair of 1999 decisions that allowed sexual harassment suits for workplace conduct even if no tangible adverse consequences resulted. Despite her consistent support for strong enforcement against sexual harassment, Ginsburg also showed an awareness of the practical needs for employers or government defendants. With a dissenting opinion in *Gebser* and with her votes in the two workplace cases, Ginsburg suggested that defendants with effective internal policies against sexual harassment could avoid liability if plaintiffs failed to use those remedies.

Ginsburg had served for nearly seven years before the Court heard its first argument in a law challenging an abortion regulation. The issue was a Nebraska law—one of many similar state statutes—that banned a procedure properly called "dilation and evacuation" but dubbed "partial birth abortion" by antiabortion groups. Ginsburg voted with the 5–4 majority in *Stenberg v. Carhart* (2000) to strike down the law on the grounds that it was too broad and that it failed to include an exception to the ban when necessary to protect the woman's health. Earlier, Ginsburg had voted in dissent in two summary rulings that upheld state abortion regulations challenged by abortion providers.

As with women's rights, Ginsburg proved to be a strong supporter of efforts to eliminate discrimination against racial minorities. In only her second term, she wrote an acerbic dissent to a decision that threw out an ambitious if controversial desegregation plan ordered by a federal judge for Kansas City schools. "Given the deep, inglorious history of segregation in Missouri," Ginsburg wrote in *Missouri v. Jenkins* (1995), "to curtail desegregation at this time and in this manner is an action at once too swift and too soon."

The same year, Ginsburg led the four dissenters in the decision, *Miller v. Johnson* (1995), that made it difficult for state legislatures to deliberately create congressional or legislative districts to help elect minority candidates. The Court's conservative majority had first opened federal courts to racial redistricting suits before Ginsburg joined the Court. In *Shaw v. Reno* (1993), the Court held that white voters in North Carolina could challenge on equal protection grounds a congressional districting plan that created a majority-black district by combining predominantly black neighborhoods in three cities in the center of the state. O'Connor's opinion emphasized the "highly irregular" shape of the resulting district in allowing the suit to challenge what she called a "racial gerrymander." Justice White led the four dissenters in the case in his last opinion before he retired.

The next racial redistricting case to reach the Court involved a challenge to a more conventionally shaped, majority-black congressional district in Georgia. By the same vote as in *Shaw,* however, the Court in *Miller v. Johnson* ruled the redistricting plan unconstitutional, not because it was oddly shaped, but because race had been the "dominant and controlling rationale" in drawing the lines. In dissent, Ginsburg said this new standard would throw redistricting plans into uncertainty and turmoil, invite litigation, and give federal judges an "unwarranted" role in the process. She emphasized the history of excluding racial minorities from political participation as justification for "vigilant judicial inspection to protect minority voters," a consideration not needed for majority white voters. And she pointedly noted that no constitutional objection had previously been raised to drawing other ethnic districts, Irish or Italian, for example.

Eight years later, Ginsburg again cited the history of racial discrimination in the United States in voting to uphold affirmative action plans at the University of Michigan's law school and undergraduate college challenged by unsuccessful white applicants. The Court upheld the law school's plan but ruled the undergraduate system unconstitutional in *Gratz v. Bollinger* (2003) because of its fixed numerical bonus for minority candidates. Applying the "strict scrutiny" standard, Chief Justice Rehnquist said the plan violated equal protection principles because it was not "narrowly tailored" to attain the state's goal in achieving a diverse student body. Dissenting from that decision, Ginsburg observed, "We are not far distant from an overtly discriminatory past, and the effects of centuries of law-sanctioned inequality remain painfully evident in our communities and schools." On that basis, she argued that racial policies aimed at "inclusion" should not be subject to the strict scrutiny standard applied to policies aimed at "exclusion."

During her confirmation hearing, Ginsburg had been asked about a statement she made in 1979, before her appointment to the appeals court, opposing discrimination against homosexuals. She reaffirmed her position, but only in general terms. "I think rank discrimination against anyone is against the tradition of the United States and is to be deplored," she said. True to her word, she joined two landmark gay rights decisions. *Romer v. Evans* (1996) struck down a Colorado initiative barring enactment of state or local laws to prohibit discrimination on the basis of sexual orientation, and *Lawrence v. Texas* (2003) struck down state antisodomy laws. She joined the dissenters in *Boy Scouts of America v. Dale* (2000), which upheld on First Amendment grounds the Boy Scouts' policy excluding gay men as adult leaders.

Ginsburg also demonstrated sensitivity to the needs of persons with disabilities in a several cases. In the most significant, Ginsburg wrote for a narrow majority in holding that the federal Americans with Disabilities Act (ADA) gives mental patients a qualified right to be placed in a community setting instead of in an institution. "Unjustified isolation" of people with mental illnesses "is properly regarded as discrimination based on disability," Ginsburg wrote in *Olmstead v. L. C.* (1999). With customary caution, however, Ginsburg put conditions on patients' rights to choose community placement. The state could require institutionalization, she said, if community placement was not recommended by mental health professionals or could not be "reasonably accommodated, taking into account the resources available . . . and the needs of others with mental disabilities."

Despite the qualifications, admirers described Ginsburg's opinion as the disability rights movement's *Brown v. Board of Education* (1954). They point to a concurring opinion in another case as further evidence of Ginsburg's sensitivity to issues affecting persons with disabilities. In *Bragdon v. Abbott* (1998), Ginsburg joined a decision ruling that a person with HIV had a disability for purposes of the ADA. While the majority emphasized the physical consequences of the plaintiff's condition, Ginsburg stressed in a brief concurrence that the condition satisfied the ADA's definition because society "perceived" it as a disability and that perception affected access to employment, health care, education, and other activities.

In a series of other decisions, however, Ginsburg joined in somewhat narrowing application of the ADA in private employment cases. For example, in *Sutton v. United Air Lines* (1999), she joined in rejecting an ADA suit challenging an airline's refusal to hire two severely myopic women as pilots. With eyeglasses, the women had 20/20 vision or better, but the airline said they did not meet its requirement of 20/100 uncorrected vision. The Court, in an opinion by O'Connor, said the women were not "disabled" under the law because their condition was correctable. Two of Ginsburg's liberal colleagues, Stevens and Breyer, called that interpretation "a crabbed vision" of the law's scope.

In civil cases, Ginsburg has generally supported easier access to courts and broader legal remedies. In the Rehnquist Court's most important decisions in the area, she dissented from rulings to use the due process clause to set federal limits on punitive damages in state cases. In *Honda Motor Co. v. Oberg* (1994), she disagreed with the ruling to invalidate a provision of Oregon's constitution limiting judicial review of damage awards. The state's procedures, she wrote in dissent, allowed sufficient safeguards to satisfy due process. But she also dissented from the ruling in *State Farm Mutual Automobile Insurance Co. v. Campbell* (2003), which suggested punitive damages should typically be no greater than compensatory damages and rarely if ever greater than ten times the compensatory amount. "The numerical controls . . . seem to me boldly out of order," she wrote.

Ginsburg wrote for a majority in a somewhat unexpected ruling to uphold $4 million in damage awards won by six former railway workers in West Virginia for workplace exposure to asbestos. The railroad sought to bar any compensation for the workers' fear of developing cancer, apparently the principal basis for the award. But in *Norfolk & Western Railway Co. v. Ayers* (2003), Ginsburg concluded that, under established liability principles, the workers were entitled to damages for their asbestos-related diseases and for any "mental anguish" resulting from their injuries.

In several other, less noticed cases, Ginsburg has been a strong voice for ensuring access to the courts, especially for indigent litigants. She wrote for a 6–3 majority in *M. L. B. v. S. L. J.* (1996), ruling that states cannot prevent someone from appealing a parental termination order solely because of inability to pay for a transcript. The ruling extended an earlier decision, *Griffin v. Illinois* (1956), which had relied on the due process and equal protection clauses to guarantee

indigent criminal defendants a trial transcript for use in appeals. Quoting that decision, Ginsburg said that the state should also not be allowed to "bolt the door to equal justice" in a parental termination case. Nine years later, Ginsburg again wrote for the Court in another extension of the *Griffin* decision, this time guaranteeing appointed counsel for indigent criminal defendants appealing after a guilty plea (*Halbert v. Michigan,* 2005). In both cases, Ginsburg brushed aside dissenters' concerns that the ruling would unduly burden the courts.

Ginsburg's concern about access to courts is evident in her dissent in *Buckhannon Board & Care Home, Inc. v. West Virginia Department of Health and Human Resources* (2001), which barred attorney fee awards in cases—for example, civil rights or environmental suits—in which a defendant settles the dispute out of court. She said the ruling would "impede access to court for the less well-heeled," and she emphasized her disagreement by reading portions of the opinion from the bench. A year earlier, however, she had given environmental groups a significant victory by upholding the right of citizen groups to sue alleged polluters under the Clean Water Act even if any financial penalties are to be paid to the federal government. Civil penalties "afford redress to citizen plaintiffs," Ginsburg wrote in *Friends of the Earth, Inc. v. Laidlaw Environmental Services (TOC), Inc.* (2000), because they "encourage defendants to discontinue current violations and deter them from committing future ones."

Ginsburg had no experience with criminal law before her appointment to the federal appeals court in 1980, and on the D.C. Circuit she did not handle cases in two of the Supreme Court's most divisive areas: capital punishment and *habeas corpus*. (The District of Columbia did not use the death penalty, and it is not a state for purposes of federal *habeas corpus* law.) But her votes and her opinions on the Court demonstrated themes similar to those in her work on civil cases: an interest in substantive justice and procedural regularity.

Her views could be seen clearly in her frequent support for challenges in death penalty cases. In her first term, for example, Ginsburg led the dissenters in a 5–4 decision that barred a death row inmate's plea for a new sentencing hearing because the jury was told he had been sentenced to death for a previous offense. The evidence created "a grave" risk that the jury could have believed the defendant's fate had already been sealed, she wrote in *Romano v. Oklahoma* (1994). A decade later, Ginsburg wrote a forceful opinion reversing a Texas death row inmate's conviction because prosecutors had withheld damaging information about an important government witness. "A rule ... declaring 'prosecutor may hide, defendant must seek,' is not tenable in a system constitutionally bound to accord defendants due process," she wrote in *Banks v. Dretke* (2004).

Ginsburg also joined the Court's two landmark decisions prohibiting execution of mentally retarded or juvenile offenders—*Atkins v. Virginia* (2002) and *Roper v. Simmons* (2005)—but she did not write separately in either. And in a number of cases, she generally sided with other liberal justices in interpreting the *habeas corpus* provisions of the Antiterrorism and Effective Death Penalty Act (AEDPA) in ways that softened its impact in limiting death penalty challenges, sometimes in the majority, but more often in dissent.

In one significant line of decisions, Ginsburg joined a cross-ideological, five-justice majority that limited the role of judges vis-à-vis juries in criminal sentencing, but then stopped short of extending the doctrine to totally scrap the federal guidelines system. In *Apprendi v. New Jersey* (2000), the Court struck down as an infringement of the right to trial by jury a state "hate crime" law allowing a judge to impose an enhanced sentence after finding the offense motivated by, for example, racial prejudice. Ginsburg wrote for the Court in *Ring v. Arizona* (2002) applying a similar rule to death penalty statutes, and she joined the opinion in *Blakely v. Washington* (2004) in extending the doctrine to invalidate a state sentencing guideline law.

When the Court heard arguments challenging the federal sentencing guidelines scheme, however, Ginsburg helped to partly save the system. In a bifurcated ruling in *United States v. Booker* (2005), Ginsburg followed the earlier rulings in barring mandatory use of the guidelines, but siding with the

Blakely dissenters, she voted to allow federal judges to use the complex calculations as advisory guides for sentences.

In search and seizure law, Ginsburg, like the other liberal justices, reflected the shift toward a more relaxed view of Fourth Amendment restrictions, but she was as likely as any of her colleagues to find challenged law enforcement practices had gone too far. For example, she dissented in the decision in *Illinois v. Caballes* (2005) to allow police to use a drug-sniffing dog without probable cause for a search in an otherwise lawful traffic stop. The ruling, she warned, "clears the way for suspicionless, dog-accompanied drug sweeps on parked cars along sidewalks and in parking lots."

On similar Fourth Amendment grounds, Ginsburg opposed broad, suspicionless drug-testing in several contexts after initially joining an opinion allowing mandatory drug screening for high school athletes. Ginsburg cautioned in her concurring opinion in *Vernonia School District 47J v. Acton* (1995) that allowing random drug tests for high school athletes did not necessarily sanction routine drug testing of all students. She then led four dissenters when the Court extended the ruling in *Board of Education of Independent School District No. 92 of Pottawatomie County v. Earls* (2002) to allow drug testing for any student participating in extracurricular activities. The safety justification for testing athletes did not apply to students participating in such activities as bands or chess clubs, Ginsburg said. And the policy would have a "capricious, even perverse" effect, she said, by discouraging at-risk students from participating in activities that could palliate drug problems. Ginsburg wrote for a nearly unanimous Court in *Chandler v. Miller* (1997), which struck down a Georgia law requiring drug testing of candidates for state office. Four years later, she joined without separate opinion the decision in *Ferguson v. Charleston* (2001), which overturned a public hospital's policy of drug-testing pregnant women and turning positive results over to law enforcement authorities.

In church-state cases, Ginsburg has been a consistent vote for interpreting the establishment clause to limit government-sponsored religious expression.

She also joined with dissenters in opposing Rehnquist's successful efforts to ease rules against use of government funds at religious schools. She voted with the majority in *Santa Fe Independent School District v. Doe* (2000) to prohibit school-sponsored prayers at high school football games and with the dissenters two years later in the ruling, *Zelman v. Simmons-Harris* (2002), that allowed tax-paid vouchers for students attending church-affiliated schools. In 2005 she voted once with the majority and once in dissent to bar officially sponsored displays of the Ten Commandments in or around government buildings.

Among the eight decisions on church-state cases, however, Ginsburg wrote separately only once, and that was on a procedural issue. In *Agostini v. Felton* (1997), Ginsburg objected to the majority's decision to allow New York City to reopen a decade-old case to challenge—and overrule—the Court's 1985 decision in *Aguilar v. Felton,* barring use of federal funds to pay public school teachers to provide remedial services at parochial schools. The city had invoked Rule 60(b) of the Federal Rules of Civil Procedure to reopen the case, but Ginsburg quoted the rule to show that it applied only to federal district courts. Using the rule in effect to ask the Court to reconsider a prior ruling was "unprecedented" and "aberrational," she said.

Ginsburg has also aligned herself with the liberal bloc in opposing another significant Rehnquist legacy—the use of federalism principles to limit Congress's power vis-à-vis the state—but without writing opinions herself. She dissented but did not write separately from the six decisions between 1996 and 2000 that barred private damage suits against state governments for violating federal law. Two of those cases involved major federal civil rights statutes: *Kimel v. Florida Board of Regents* (2000) prohibited actions under the Age Discrimination in Employment Act; and *Board of Trustees of the University of Alabama v. Garrett* (2001) protected states from damage suits under the employment provisions of the ADA.

Ginsburg's concern with disability rights and access to courts did prompt a brief concurring opinion when the Court allowed a suit against the state of Tennessee for violating the ADA's provisions requir-

ing barrier-free access to public buildings, including courthouses. She noted that Congress had considered "a body of evidence" showing that persons with disabilities faced obstacles in using public facilities and services. That evidence, Ginsburg wrote, "sufficed to warrant the barrier-lowering, dignity-respecting national solution the People's representatives in Congress elected to order."

Ginsburg also dissented from a second line of cases limiting Congress's use of the commerce clause to adopt laws touching on areas traditionally left to the states. One of those rulings, *United States v. Morrison* (2000), struck down the Violence Against Women Act, a law strongly backed by women's groups that allowed federal court suits for victims of "gender-motivated" violence. Even though the case involved an area of Ginsburg's special concern, she chose to join Breyer's dissent without writing herself.

In September 1999, three weeks before the beginning of her seventh term, Ginsburg underwent surgery for colon cancer. Ginsburg provided detailed information about her illness and course of treatment and did not miss a single Court session during the term despite receiving "precautionary" chemotherapy from January through June. Some observers thought Ginsburg appeared weak or tired, and her written work for the term was somewhat diminished. Still, one law professor aptly credited her with "a remarkable display of will power." By the start of the 2000 term, Ginsburg appeared completely recovered. And as she reached her tenth year on the Court, the *Columbia Law Review* assembled a symposium to analyze her contributions to the law and pay tribute to her accomplishments.

Among the many who sang Ginsburg's praises, perhaps no one better captured the essence of her judicial philosophy than David Shapiro, a Harvard Law School professor, who noted that he had worked with Ginsburg on several law reform projects related to civil procedure and federal jurisdiction. Ginsburg's work "represents the best qualities a judge can have," Shapiro wrote. He cited first "lawyerly precision" and then her "strong sense of the importance of context and of resolving the controversy at hand without reaching well beyond that controversy to resolve disputes not yet presented." But he closed with the tacit recognition that Ginsburg was no mere legal technocrat by citing as well her "determination to interpret and apply statutes, rules, and the common law with respect for the humane and efficient administration of justice."

—*Kenneth Jost*

BIBLIOGRAPHY

Columbia Law School marked the tenth anniversary of Justice Ginsburg's appointment to the Court with a symposium in her honor on September 12, 2003. The papers prepared for the symposium, published in *Columbia Law Review* 104 (January 2004), include an introductory overview by Prof. Herma Hill Kay of the University of California, Berkeley, School of Law, and five separate essays examining Ginsburg's jurisprudence in civil procedure and federal jurisdiction, opportunity and equality, constitutional interpretation, disability rights, and affirmative action.

Biographical essays in two recent books on members of the Rehnquist Court focus on Ginsburg's work on gender discrimination before and after becoming a justice. See "Ruth Bader Ginsburg's Equal Protection Clause," in Mark Tushnet, *A Court Divided: The Rehnquist Court and the Future of Constitutional Law* (2005); and Judith Baer's essay "Advocate on the Court: Ruth Bader Ginsburg and the Limits of Formal Equality," in Earl Maltz, ed., *Rehnquist Justice: Understanding the Court Dynamic* (2003).

NOTEWORTHY OPINIONS

Harris v. Forklift Systems, Inc., 510 U.S. 17 (1994) (Concurrence)

Romano v. Oklahoma, 512 U.S. 1 (1994) (Dissent)

Honda Motor Co. v. Oberg, 512 U.S. 415 (1994) (Dissent)

Missouri v. Jenkins, 515 U.S. 70 (1995) (Dissent)

Miller v. Johnson, 515 U.S. 900 (1995) (Dissent)

United States v. Virginia, 518 U.S. 515 (1996)

Chandler v. Miller, 520 U.S. 305 (1997)

Agostini v. Felton, 521 U.S. 203 (1997) (Dissent)

Olmstead v. L. C., 527 U.S. 581 (1999)

Ring v. Arizona, 536 U.S. 584 (2002)

Gratz v. Bollinger, 539 U.S. 244 (2003) (Dissent)

Illinois v. Caballes, 543 U.S. 405 (2005) (Dissent)

Halbert v. Michigan, 545 U.S. ____ (2005)

ARTHUR JOSEPH GOLDBERG

Birth: August 8, 1908, Chicago, Illinois.

Education: Northwestern University, B.S.L., 1929; J.D., summa cum laude, 1930.

Official Positions: Secretary of labor, 1961–1962; U.S. ambassador to the United Nations, 1965–1968.

Supreme Court Service: Nominated associate justice by President John F. Kennedy, August 31, 1962, to replace Felix Frankfurter, who had retired; confirmed by the Senate, September 25, 1962, by a voice vote; took judicial oath October 1, 1962; resigned July 25, 1965; replaced by Abe Fortas, nominated by President Lyndon B. Johnson.

Death: January 19, 1990, Washington, D.C.

Nominated by John F. Kennedy to fill the seat of the more conservative Felix Frankfurter, Arthur J. Goldberg became the justice who completed the Warren Court. Serving on the Court for only three years, Goldberg never achieved the reputation for judicial craftsmanship of his predecessor, but he nevertheless made a significant mark on the history of the Court and of the country by joining Earl Warren, Hugo Black, William Douglas, and William Brennan to provide a majority for what became known as the Warren Court agenda: judicial reinforcement of constitutional rights and civil liberties, particularly the equality rights of minorities, the rights of those suspected or accused of crime, and the freedom to differ.

Goldberg's career began early. He galloped though college and law school and was admitted to the bar of Illinois in 1929, at the age of twenty. He practiced law in Chicago for some twenty years, representing a number of labor unions, before becoming general counsel to the Congress of Industrial Organi-

zations (CIO) and then the United Steel Workers. After moving to a Washington law firm in the 1950s, Goldberg helped to effect the merger of the American Federation of Labor (AFL) and CIO and became special counsel to the AFL-CIO Industrial Union Department. It was in this capacity that he met and began to advise John Kennedy during the 1960 presidential campaign. From January 1961 to September 1962 Goldberg served as an outspoken secretary of labor, advocating an enhanced federal role in mediating labor disputes and also on foreign affairs.

After joining the Court in October 1962, Goldberg predictably took an active role in cases involving labor law and antitrust, often writing opinions interpreting federal legislation such as the Sherman Act and Clayton Act to permit an expansive role for the federal government in these areas. Examples are *United States v. Loew's, Inc.* (1962), *Silver v. New York Stock Exchange* (1963), and *United States v. Ward Baking Co.* (1964).

But Goldberg's most significant contribution to the Court was his conviction that individual rights frequently outweigh countervailing government interests and concerns about federalism. Goldberg joined and often created majorities deciding that particular Bill of Rights guarantees should be incorporated and applied in state proceedings. In *Malloy v. Hogan* (1964), he supported the claim that the Fifth Amendment privilege against self-incrimination applies to the states. He concurred in *Pointer v. Texas* (1965), which incorporated the right to confront witnesses, and he was part of the unanimous landmark decision in *Gideon v. Wainwright* (1963), in which the Court ruled that the Sixth Amendment right to counsel, including obligation to provide assigned counsel for indigent defendants, applies to the states. Goldberg also proved willing to expand the scope of particular rights, such as the right to counsel. For example, in *Massiah v. United States* (1964), Goldberg voted with the majority to hold that the Sixth Amendment right to counsel attaches at the beginning of formal judicial proceedings and prohibits the police or prosecutors from "deliberately eliciting" information from a defendant in the absence of counsel.

Arthur Joseph Goldberg

Goldberg's belief in the importance of the right to counsel during the accusatory stage of a criminal proceeding is clear in the opinion he wrote for the 5–4 majority in one of the Warren Court's most controversial opinions—*Escobedo v. Illinois* (1964). Goldberg's opinion, declaring a right to counsel during police interrogation, even before the commencement of formal proceedings, led law enforcement officials to fear that the Court's expanding view of the Sixth Amendment would severely curtail the utility of interrogation as an investigatory technique. Civil libertarians, on the other hand, forecast an end to inherently coercive police tactics. After Goldberg resigned, however, the Court found a compromise in the Fifth Amendment rule of *Miranda v. Arizona* (1966) instead of building on the rationales Goldberg had offered in *Escobedo*.

Goldberg also supported or wrote opinions designed to improve the access of indigent criminal defendants to full and fair appeals. *Douglas v. California* (1963) extended the right to counsel on appeal, and *Lane v. Brown* (1963) provided indigents free transcripts. Joined by Justices Douglas and Brennan, Goldberg expressed some of the Supreme Court's first serious doubts about the constitutionality of a state's use of the death penalty, dissenting from the Court's refusal to hear *Rudolph v. Alabama* (1963). His prescient dissent in *Swain v. Alabama* (1965) argued for a right to be free from racial discrimination in jury selection and anticipated that peremptory challenges would have to be limited in the interest of equal protection, a realization that commanded a majority on the Court only two decades later.

With Goldberg's participation, the Warren Court also sought to promote civil rights by protecting demonstrators trying to secure such rights. *Cox v. Louisiana* (1965) reversed convictions of demonstrators on First Amendment grounds, and *Heart of*

Atlanta Motel v. United States (1964) affirmed the power of Congress to enact powerful civil rights legislation. In one of the landmark cases of the century, the Court equalized voting power through reapportionment in *Reynolds v. Sims* (1964).

Goldberg's commitment to the principle of equality is documented in his book *Equal Justice* (1971), published after he had left the Court. But his opinions show an equally fervent commitment to other constitutional guarantees, especially the First Amendment. In a concurring opinion in *New York Times Co. v. Sullivan* (1964), a case limiting libel actions brought against public figures, Goldberg stated his view that the First Amendment confers "an absolute, unconditional privilege to criticize official conduct despite the harm which may flow from excesses and abuses." His generous interpretation of the First Amendment also led him to argue against restrictions created by obscenity prosecutions or ideological restrictions on the right to travel.

Goldberg's last opinion, a concurrence in *Griswold v. Connecticut* (1965), argued that a constitutional right of privacy, protecting decisions such as the right to use contraceptives, exists in part because of the Ninth Amendment's guarantee that the people retain rights not enumerated in the Constitution. This opinion, like many others Goldberg wrote, reflected his conviction that it is the constitutional role of the courts to vindicate equality or liberty rights of minorities who are unlikely to command the support of legislatures. It also reflected his disagreement with the usual Warren Court dissenters, John Marshall Harlan, Tom Clark, Potter Stewart, and Goldberg's fellow Kennedy appointee, Byron White, who believed that the Supreme Court should play a modest role in deference to Congress and to state legislatures.

In July 1965 President Lyndon Johnson asked Goldberg to leave the Court to replace Adlai Stevenson as ambassador to the United Nations. Anxious to pursue his interest in international relations, Goldberg agreed. Goldberg is quoted as having described the difference between his role on the Court and at the United Nations as captured in four words: "It is so ordered." After serving as ambassador until 1968, Goldberg returned to private practice, teaching, and an unsuccessful campaign to become governor of New York. Before his death on January 9, 1980, Arthur Goldberg was awarded the Presidential Medal of Freedom, capping a legal career that began when Goldberg became interested in the law while watching Clarence Darrow, another champion of equality, justice, and the underdog.

—*Susan N. Herman*

BIBLIOGRAPHY

After leaving the Supreme Court, Arthur Goldberg wrote prolifically on the topics that had been important to him as a justice. He published several books on the constitutional issues that had dominated the Warren Court. See *Equal Justice: The Warren Era of the Supreme Court* (1971); *The Evolving Constitution: Essays on the Bill of Rights* (1989). He wrote dozens of articles in law reviews and other publications about criminal justice, the death penalty, and other constitutional issues, including the First Amendment. He wrote extensively on the Supreme Court and judicial administration, and he was a frequent contributor to symposia evaluating the work of other justices and judges. He also maintained his interest in labor law and international affairs, writing and speaking frequently on these topics. Biographies of Goldberg include Dorothy Goldberg's *A Private View of a Public Life* (1975); and Victor Lasky's *Arthur J. Goldberg: The Old and the New* (1970).

NOTEWORTHY OPINIONS

Rudolph v. Alabama, 375 U.S. 889 (1963) (Dissent)

New York Times Co. v. Sullivan, 376 U.S. 254 (1964) (Concurrence)

Escobedo v. Illinois, 378 U.S. 478 (1964)

Heart of Atlanta Motel v. United States, 379 U.S. 241 (1964) (Concurrence)

Cox v. Louisiana, 379 U.S. 536 (1965)

Griswold v. Connecticut, 381 U.S. 479 (1965) (Concurrence)

HORACE GRAY

Birth: March 24, 1828, Boston, Massachusetts.

Education: Harvard College, A.B., 1845; Harvard Law School, 1849.

Official Positions: Reporter, Massachusetts Supreme Judicial Court, 1854–1864; associate justice, 1864–1873; chief justice, 1873–1881.

Supreme Court Service: Nominated associate justice by President Chester A. Arthur, December 19, 1881, to replace Nathan Clifford, who had died, confirmed by the Senate, December 20, 1881, by a 51–5 vote; took judicial oath January 9, 1882; served until September 15, 1902; replaced by Oliver Wendell Holmes Jr., nominated by President Theodore Roosevelt.

Death: September 15, 1902, Nahant, Massachusetts.

No other Supreme Court justice was quite so "well-born" as Horace Gray. In the early 1800s his grandfather, William Gray, was the richest man in New England. Although he suffered from Thomas Jefferson's 1808 embargo, French and British seizures of his ships, and the War of 1812, William Gray strongly supported the war effort. Becoming a Jeffersonian, he was twice Massachusetts's lieutenant governor. Out of his own pocket, he provided daily relief to the poor and, when the government was nearly broke, paid for refurbishing the U.S.S. *Constitution,* so she could fight. After William died in 1820, his son, Horace Gray, ran the family's businesses well for two decades, but then shifted too much capital from shipping into high-risk iron mill investments that folded during a business slump. His son, Horace—the future Supreme Court justice—graduated at seventeen from Harvard and learned during a European tour soon after that his family's wealth had abruptly disappeared.

Facing these difficulties, young Gray studied law assiduously at Harvard and joined the antislavery Free Soil Party in 1848. Soon after he had a stroke of luck (or rather, of luck and family connections). At twenty-six, while building a profitable legal practice, he was appointed reporter of the Massachusetts Supreme Judicial Court. He continued both activities for nine years, joining the Republican Party and gaining wide attention for an 1857 *Monthly Law Review* article that devastated the historical contentions of Chief Justice Roger Taney's proslavery *Dred Scott* opinion.

In 1864 he was appointed to the Massachusetts high court and in 1873 became its chief justice. In his seventeen years on this court, he wrote 1,367 opinions, only one of which was in dissent. On recommendations from Gray's longtime friend, Sen. George Hoar, R-Mass., and from Justice Samuel Miller, President Chester Arthur nominated Gray to the U.S. Supreme Court. There, while maintaining homes in Washington,

Boston, and on the Massachusetts seashore, he served for twenty-one years and wrote 451 opinions. He wrote only ten dissents—a circumstance that later led to an incorrect assessment of his judicial influence by scholars who overlooked when he did, and when he did not, join in the dissents of others.

At Gray's 1902 funeral, Chief Justice Melville Fuller likened his accomplishments to those of another Massachusetts chief justice, Lemuel Shaw, and two earlier holders of Gray's Supreme Court seat, Joseph Story and Benjamin Curtis: "He will be ranked with them without appreciable interval." In 1909 Harvard law professor Samuel Williston, a former Gray law clerk, repeated the prediction. History has been somewhat less appreciative. In 1961 doctoral candidate Stephen Robert Mitchell put Gray "just below the top rung in the judicial ladder." In 1992 history professor John Semonche seemed more impressed by Gray's formalism in manners and writing style than by his substantive contribution. Gray's constitutional opinions—staples of legal textbooks well into the New Deal era—have almost vanished from recent casebooks, while those of Story and Curtis are still included.

Gray's constitutional opinions had three main themes. The first was support of substantial and effective national government power, but not too much. He endorsed congressional power in both wartime and peacetime to make paper money legal tender in *Julliard v. Greenman* (1884); held that Congress may by statute override an earlier treaty and provide for sum-mary detention and expulsion of aliens in *Fong Yue Ting v. United States* (1893); and ruled that Congress had power, without regard to the Fourteenth Amendment's state action limitation, to provide for punishing persons who deprive citizens in the custody of federal marshals of their civil rights in *Logan v. United States* (1892). But he drew the line when Congress attempted to enact a peacetime income tax (*Pollock v. Farmers' Loan and Trust*, 1895), or tried to exert commerce clause power over manufacturing that only indirectly affected interstate commerce (*United States v. E. C. Knight Co.*, 1895).

The second theme was that states had fairly ample police powers to regulate the economy. In the absence of contrary federal law, a state could require nondiscriminatory railroad rates on journeys beginning within the state even if the destination were out-of-state (concurrence with Joseph Bradley's dissent in *Wabash, St. Louis, and Pacific Railroad Co. v. Illinois*, 1886); prohibit importation and sale of liquor (dissent in *Leisy v. Hardin*, 1890); and could levy a tax based on the railroad's in-state proportion of total track mileage, regardless of how much or little its cars traveled in state (*Pullman's Palace Car Co. v. Pennsylvania*, 1891). But here, also, Gray would not allow states unlimited powers. A state could not, after the railroad built a bypass, require an interstate passenger express to go three miles out of its way on the old track to stop at a county seat (*Illinois Central R. Co. v Illinois*, 1893), nor would a writ of *mandamus* serve to compel a railroad to put a stop where it passed through a

Horace Gray

Washington county seat—Yakima—after the railroad decided it could make more money by platting a new town four miles away on its own land, stopping trains there instead, and depopulating Yakima (*Northern Pacific Ry. v. Washington,* 1892).

The third theme pertained to individual rights. Under the Fourteenth Amendment, persons born in the United States, except Indians living in tribes or separately but not taxed, were citizens regardless of race. Congress could not, pursuing an anti-Chinese immigration policy, deny reentry to the San Francisco-born son of Chinese aliens (*United States v. Wong Kim Ark,* 1898).

Gray also insisted that the government respect Indians' treaty-acquired property interests. In lengthy 1863 negotiations, Chippewa chief Moose Dung expressed a desire for a 640-acre set-aside for him and his heirs: "I have taken the mouth of Thieving River as my inheritance." The federal negotiator, a Minnesota senator, seemingly exasperated, or thinking the United States was "thieving" enough Indian land for the day, directed the interpreter, "Tell him I don't care anything about the mouth of Thieving River. He can have it." Whereupon Moose Dung optimistically said, "I accept . . . because . . . I am going to be raised from want to riches . . . to the level of the white man." Gray held that an 1894 congressional resolution giving the interior secretary power to oversee the rental terms of that land, which was by then urbanized and valuable, collapsed before the vested right of Moose Dung's son (known as Moose Dung the younger) to lease as he pleased (*Jones v. Meehan,* 1899).

Although Gray agreed with *Plessy v. Ferguson* (1896) that state-required racial segregation in intrastate rail transportation was constitutional, a local practice of excluding blacks from state court grand juries, neither prohibited nor prescribed by state law, was unconstitutional (*Carter v. Texas,* 1900). For Gray, due process pertained primarily to criminal procedures, and he initially viewed the doctrine of substantive due process as unsound (*Head v. Amoskeag Manufacturing,* 1885). The Fourteenth Amendment's due process clause did not incorporate the Bill of Rights and make all its provisions applica-

ble to states, which therefore could reduce jury size from twelve to eight. But in federal trials, the Seventh Amendment's guarantee of a trial by jury meant what it historically did in English common law—twelve jurors and a judge (*Capital Traction v. Hof,* 1899). Nor should a judge tamper with historically mixed allocations of powers to decide questions of law and fact by instructing jurors in a way that limited their freedom in deciding whether the circumstances indicated murder or manslaughter (sixty-page dissent in *Sparf v. United States,* 1895).

Many of Gray's positions, particularly regarding government and the economy, were more consistent with New Deal views of good constitutional results than with the strong laissez-faire judicial activism of the *Lochner v. New York* (1905) era. Why then did the apparent slide in Gray's perceived importance occur? One reason is that some decisions thought important at the time were analytical derivations from another judge's earlier "head" opinion, which survives better. For example, *Logan* largely derives from Justice Miller's opinion in *Ex parte Yarbrough* (1884), a "structural" argument that, quite apart from Fourteenth and Fifteenth Amendment demands for fair, nondiscriminatory state behavior in elections, the Constitution's requirement of periodic federal elections entails sufficient federal power to reach individuals' discriminatory behavior hindering other citizens' voting.

A second reason is that it is not Gray's methods and substantive jurisprudence that have changed, but rather succeeding generations' standards of greatness. Standards of late nineteenth-century elite lawyers, trained when Langdellian (Harvard law professor Christopher Columbus Langdell introduced the "case method" to the study of law) legal analysis searched for scientifically objective, formal symmetries thought to underlie the case law, fit well with Gray's preferred decision-making method. His seemingly neutral method soft-pedaled cases' public policy implications. Late twentieth-century standards tend to prize policy explicitness in the constitutional interpretations of activist and passivist judges alike.

A third reason for Gray's decline in reputation pertains to the fields of law thought more and less important to the analysts. For Professor Williston in 1909 race relations and labor rights scarcely rose to the level of consciousness, but international law, the law of charitable trusts, and admiralty law were close to center stage. Much of Gray's contribution lay in the latter fields.

Gray's preferred method and fields of interest were well displayed in what Williston considered two great Gray opinions—*Liverpool and Great Western Steam v. Phenix Insurance* (1889) and *Hilton v. Guyot* (1895). Gray sought out precedents exceedingly far back and then wrote exceedingly long historical essays finding the answers in those precedents. *Liverpool* took sixty-seven pages and citations of more than eighty American, British, Dutch, French, and Italian cases and commentaries to "find" that American law, which held invalid clauses in shipping contracts exempting a common carrier from liability for employee neglgence, prevailed over British law (which held the opposite) where the bill of lading was drawn up in New York by a British ship company's agent for goods bound from New York to Liverpool but lost when the ship sank in a Welsh bay just short of its destination.

Gray's majority opinion in *Guyot* held that because the French judicial system treated other "civilized" countries' court judgments as *prima facie* evidence in—but not conclusive on—related French court proceedings, then American courts could retry on the merits French judgments on American-owned companies with Paris offices. Gray produced a 100-page examination of a 1629 French royal ordinance down through two and a half centuries of the cases and commentaries of twenty-two countries.

Like his predecessor, Morrison Waite—who once wistfully wrote to Gray, "Can't you tell me the secret of your *style*. I wish I had it"—Chief Justice Fuller was frequently persuaded by Gray's meticulous analytic powers. His character, despite its stiffness, attracted several other justices. John Marshall Harlan joked to Waite that Gray's idea of a vacation was searching for precedents in British Columbia. But Waite at age sixty-nine really wanted the company of Gray (a keen hiker) and Gen. William Tecumseh Sherman (good at

expeditions) on an 1883 Montana trip where they "slept . . . on the ground. . . . The thermometer went . . . below freezing . . . had breakfast at five . . . eggs and lambchops . . . superb morning."

Gray in fact had considerable power within the Court. Vacationing in Europe, one of the clearly great justices, Stephen Field, wrote to another, Joseph Bradley, about unwanted Gray impact on their colleagues' thinking. Field urged that Bradley write a very strong dissent in the Pullman-Pennsylvania tax case and pledged "to co-operate with you . . . to defeat the manifest purposes of Gray to overturn our interstate commerce decisions." He also vowed "to purchase a one-horse landau" so that he and Bradley could have strategy chats going to and from Court conferences.

But how much power did Gray have, and to what societal ends did he use it? One scholarly misconception infers from Gray's low number of written dissents relatively low power. A misreading of primary sources led another scholar to state that Gray's "closest friends . . . found attitudes which bordered on prejudice . . . but never so far as can be discovered, committed . . . to writing." The friends, however, probably were not referring in modern fashion to ethnic prejudice (which most of Gray's Brahmin friends shared) but, in nineteenth-century usage, to Gray's being opinionated. In any event, Gray's prejudices or, rather, his Anglo-centered point of view can be found, with a little searching, in his writing, for example, in an unintentionally funny opinion about customs duties on imported tomatoes.

In *Nix v. Hedden* (1893), the importer argued tomatoes were fruits and should enter duty-free. The government insisted they were vegetables and imposed a 10 percent tariff. Gray's favored 100-page historical solution would not work, as only one dubious precedent was available—beans were not seeds in a pod (*Robertson v. Salomon*, 1889). Into Court came dictionaries and experts. Discussion was inconclusive. Then Gray had one of his most original—if Anglo-culture-bound—jurisprudential ideas. Look not to definitions or botany, but to the tomato's societal functions. Said he, tomatoes "are usually served at dinner in, with, or after the soup, fish, or meats which constitute the principal part of the repast, and not, like fruits generally, as dessert." Tomatoes, therefore, are vegetables and taxable.

Gray wrote this cultural-anthropological silliness a few days before his *Fong Yue Ting* majority opinion further displayed his underlying social attitudes (and not just, it appears, his deference to Congress). Fuller, Field, and David Brewer dissented, the latter saying: "In view of this enactment of the . . . foremost Christian nation, may not the thoughtful Chinese disciple of Confucius fairly ask, 'Why do they send missionaries here?' "

By today's standards, these justices were prejudiced, but the question to ask is what else came with, or offset, these upper-class Anglo-Saxon prejudices and also drove their decision making. Comparing Gray on this score with Brewer, generally now remembered only as the Court's staunchest advocate of substantive due process; Henry Billings Brown, author of *Plessy*, who later said he thought Harlan's dissent might have been right; and Bradley, who, dead before *Plessy*, had joined Harlan's dissent in its 1890 precursor, *Louisville, New Orleans, & Texas Railroad Company v. Mississippi*, suggests a final cause of Gray's decline in reputation—his lack of empathy for less-fortunate mortals, his icy, precedent-cloaked judicial passivity.

For example, where Gray let the Northern Pacific Railway devastate Yakima economically, Brewer in dissent objected that the railroad "locates its depot on the site of a 'paper town'; and for private interests, builds up a new place at the expense of the old. . . . A railroad corporation has a public duty to perform as well as a private interest to subserve. . . . I never before believed that the courts would permit it to abandon the one to promote the other."

With respect to First Amendment freedoms, one searches Gray's jurisprudence in vain for anything like Bradley's lone dissent in the Court's earliest free speech case, *Ex parte Curtis* (1882). Objecting to an 1876 statute prohibiting federal employees from soliciting, giving, or receiving money for electoral campaigns, Bradley said bluntly: "The freedom of speech and of the press, and that of assembling together to . . . discuss matters of public interest . . . are expressly secured by the Constitution." That Congress could impose, as a condition of taking employment, entire silence on political subjects struck him as "absurd. Neither men's mouths nor their purses can be constitutionally tied up in this way." Instead, one finds an 1896 obscenity prosecution, *Swearingen v. United States*, in which the Court majority held the publication not obscene, while Gray and three others voted it was, but without explanation.

With respect to treatment of nonwhite ethnic groups, Gray's opinions contain nothing to compare with Brown's condemning the army for firing on unarmed Native Americans in a forced relocation march (*Conners v. United States*, 1901). Moreover, with respect to the rights of working-class whites, despite Gray's historical legal learning, he wrote nothing like Brown's essay in *Holden v. Hardy* (1898) upholding Utah's eight-hour maximum workday for miners, with its sweeping sense of American law's dynamism over the course of the nineteenth century, its realization that changes in industrial techniques required changes in worker-protective legislation, and its realistic analysis of corporation-labor relations.

More typical of Gray's judicial activities as they bore upon less-fortunate groups, and on how the costs and profits of industrialization should be distributed among Americans, was his role concerning expansion or contraction of the "fellow servant rule," then a hotter social justice issue than legislation on working hours. Gray's Massachusetts predecessor, Lemuel Shaw, had held in 1842 that each worker, and not the employer, assumed the risk for the negligence of his coworkers, his "fellow servants"—a convenient rule for the entrepreneurial class, but not for the injured worker whose negligent fellow servant was usually too poor to pay much of a recompense. By the 1870s state legislatures were overturning this judge-made rule. Indeed, Gray, while on the Massachusetts court, originated a rule making the employer liable for unsafe working conditions (*Coombs v. New Bedford Cordage, Massachusetts*, 1869).

Gray's Supreme Court role respecting the fellow servant rule was different. It has, seemingly, been camouflaged by the received scholarly wisdom about dissent on the Court of the Gilded Age that, looking only at written dissents, characterizes Harlan and Field as the "great dissenters." But such a view overlooks not only the tactical value of mutely joining others' dissents but also the difference between the self-expressive value of a solo dissent and the strategic value of appearing to be a consensus-builder, rather than a cantankerous loner, by dissenting only when at least one other justice wants to do so.

Limiting the analysis to cases with two or more dissenters produces a different picture of the Court during Gray's first half-decade. Gray emerges as the leader of the dissenter pack in cases where one justice paired with another in multiple-dissent cases. Gray joined in thirty-seven dissenting pairs, followed by Harlan joining in thirty-four pairs, Bradley in thirty-one, Waite in twenty-nine, and Field—exactly in the Court middle—in twenty-eight. During the first half of the 1890s, however, Gray's frequency of pairing in dissent dropped to the Court middle, while the dissent-pairings of the only two Civil War and Reconstruction-era appointees still alive in 1895 (Field and Harlan) leapt to the top.

What was happening? First, Gray's persuasive impact seemed to be even stronger than when Field expressed his worries to Bradley. Second, a frequent cause of dissent pairings on the later Waite Court had been occasioned by Field's limiting the scope of the fellow servant rule over Bradley's objections (on this they disagreed) joined by Gray and two other 1880s appointees. By the 1890s, as the Civil War–era appointees died, Gray's viewpoint was winning out. By 1897 he was ready to move from debate in chambers and concurring in dissents to writing an expansion of the rule. In *Alaska Treadwell Gold Mine v. Whelan*, Gray ruled that a foreman, even if he had the power of hiring and firing employees under him, was not a company supervisor but a fellow servant of the worker who had been injured by the foreman's negligence. Gray overruled the Alaskan jury and the appeals court, returning to the mining company the award to the injured worker.

Such—a half-century distant from Horace Gray's 1848 days in the Free Soil Party—was his purportedly neutral 1890s jurisprudence. Too much was morally gray in it, and too little in him was William Gray.

—*A. E. Keir Nash*

BIBLIOGRAPHY

Samuel Williston, "Horace Gray," in William Draper Lewis, ed., *Great American Lawyers*, vol. 3 (1907–1909), 189, is the best commentary by Gray's contemporaries. John C. Semonche offers a different view in his brief piece in Kermit Hall, ed., *Oxford Companion to the Supreme Court of the United States* (1992). Stephen Robert Mitchell's unpublished dissertation, "Mr. Justice Horace Gray" (University of Wisconsin, 1961), is the single best secondary source, but is analytically a bit wooden and often has too little distance from the biographical primary sources, including their wording.

NOTEWORTHY OPINIONS

Julliard v. Greenman, 110 U.S. 421 (1884)

Liverpool and Great Western Steam v. Phenix Insurance, 129 U.S. 397 (1889)

Northern Pacific Railway v. Washington, 142 U.S. 492 (1892)

Logan v. United States, 144 U.S. 263 (1892)

Nix v. Hedden, 149 U.S. 304 (1893)

Fong Yue Ting v. United States, 149 U.S. 698 (1893)

Hilton v. Guyot, 159 U.S. 113 (1895)

Alaska Treadwell Gold Mine v. Whelan, 168 U.S. 86 (1897)

United States v. Wong Kim Ark, 169 U.S. 649 (1898)

ROBERT COOPER GRIER

Birth: March 5, 1794, Cumberland County, Pennsylvania.

Education: Dickinson College, graduated 1812.

Official Positions: President judge, District Court of Allegheny County, Pennsylvania, 1833–1846.

Supreme Court Service: Nominated associate justice by President James K. Polk, August 3, 1846, to replace Justice Henry Baldwin, who had died; confirmed by the Senate, August 4, 1846, by a voice vote; took judicial oath August 10, 1846; retired January 31, 1870; replaced by William Strong, nominated by President Ulysses S. Grant

Death: September 25, 1870, Philadelphia, Pennsylvania.

Robert C. Grier entered Dickinson College in 1811 and received his degree a year later. After studying law with a local lawyer and gaining admission to the Pennsylvania bar in 1817, Grier spent the next sixteen years in legal practice. A Jacksonian Democrat, he received a patronage appointment to a state court judgeship in 1833, a position he held for thirteen years. Justice Henry Baldwin's death in 1844 created a vacancy on the U.S. Supreme Court, which took two years to fill. President John Tyler first nominated Edward King and then John M. Read to the seat, but neither gained Senate approval. Tyler's successor, James K. Polk, nominated Grier, and the Senate confirmed him August 4, 1846.

Early in his tenure on the Court, Grier assumed a pivotal and outspoken stance on the complex issue of state infringement on the federal commerce power. In the *License Cases* (1847), Grier concurred separately in the Court's decision to uphold three state laws regulating liquor sales as a valid exercise of state police power. He vigorously defended a state's prerogative to protect its general health and morals by excluding an article of trade such as liquor from its own commerce. Two years later, however, Grier wrote separately in the *Passenger Cases* (1849) to emphasize the limits of state police power. In the *Passenger Cases,* the Court struck down New York and Massachusetts laws that had levied head taxes on each alien passenger brought into their ports. Grier asserted that Massachusetts had exceeded its power by adopting a tax that could directly affect foreign commerce, the regulation of which belonged to Congress alone. In holding that state police power must not interfere with foreign commerce, he struck a careful balance that would continue in his alliance with the majority's reasoning in *Cooley v. Board of Wardens of the Port of Philadelphia* (1851), which declared that unless Congress had said otherwise, some commerce was indeed local.

On other matters pertaining to states' authority, Grier was similarly influential. In *Cook v. Moffat* (1847), he wrote the majority opinion rejecting a Maryland businessman's effort to use his state's insolvency laws to escape debts from another state, reasoning that a state should honor another state's otherwise valid bankruptcy laws only as it chose under comity. In *Peck v. Jenness* (1849), Grier spoke for a unanimous Court in upholding a New Hampshire state court's judgment under an 1841 federal bankruptcy act as the valid decision of a tribunal "equal and independent" to the courts of the United States. In 1851 Grier dissented on behalf of himself and the Court's three most vociferous states' rights advocates—John Catron, Peter Daniel, and Samuel Nelson—in *Woodruff v. Trapnall* (1851). The dissenters decried the majority's denial of the state of Arkansas's right to refuse acceptance of state bank notes proffered by the former state treasurer.

Grier also aggressively defended state autonomy in a number of pre–Civil War cases concerning slavery, for which he was sternly criticized in abolitionist circles. In *Moore v. People of Illinois* (1852), Grier wrote the majority opinion sustaining an Illinois fugitive slave statute over the objection that such laws were exclusively within federal jurisdiction, on the grounds that states entertained the authority to "repel from their soil a population likely to become burdensome and injurious, either as paupers or criminals." In a peculiar turn of events, Grier played a critical—and ethically improper—part in the disposition of the Court's most infamous slavery case, *Dred Scott v. Sandford* (1857). Responding to an inappropriate letter of inquiry from president-elect James Buchanan about the progress of the as-yet-unreleased *Dred Scott* decision, Grier sent Buchanan a detailed account of the pending case and a promise to work closely with other justices in the

Robert Cooper Grier

majority to minimize the breadth of dissent in the final opinions of the Court. In *Dred Scott,* Grier wrote briefly to concur both with Justice Nelson's view that Missouri law should determine Scott's status and with Chief Justice Roger B. Taney's opinion that the Missouri Compromise was unconstitutional.

Despite his earlier affirmations of states' rights against abolitionist challenges, Grier's majority opinion in the *Prize Cases* (1863) expressed a compelling defense of wartime presidential power to quell Confederate resistance. In the *Prize Cases,* the Court was charged with determining the constitutionality of the Union blockade of Confederate ports instituted by President Abraham Lincoln in April 1861, several months before Congress met and approved the action. Grier upheld the president's authority to act immediately to address the Confederate insurrection, reasoning that a formal declaration of war by Congress was unnecessary for a war "which all the world acknowledges to be the greatest civil war known in the history of the human race."

Significant cases in the remaining years of Grier's Court service include *Ex parte Milligan* (1867), in which Grier joined the Court in rejecting the assertion of wartime government power to authorize military tribunals to try civilians in areas with functioning civil courts, and *Texas v. White* (1869), in which Grier joined Justices Noah Swayne and Samuel Miller in dissenting from the majority opinion upholding the status of Texas as a "state," which could not have seceded from an "indissoluble union." Grier also strongly opposed the Court's one-year postponement before passing upon the constitutionality of the Reconstruction Acts in *Ex parte McCardle* (1869). In a statement joined by Justice Stephen J. Field, Grier protested as a dereliction of duty the Court's decision to delay its ruling until Congress had passed a law stripping it of appellate jurisdiction.

After an extended period of declining health in the late 1860s and accompanying widespread criticism of his judicial competence, Grier retired on January 31, 1870, at the urging of his colleagues on the Court. He died on September 25 of that year in Philadelphia.

—*Margaret M. Russell*

BIBLIOGRAPHY

The body of writing on Grier's life and judicial career is relatively small. The most complete sources include: David P. Brown, "Robert Cooper Grier, LL.D," *Forum* 2 (1856): 91; Salmon P. Chase, "Resignation of Mr. Justice Grier," 75 U.S. vii (1870); and Frank Otto Gatell, "Robert C. Grier," in Friedman and Israel, *Justices*, vol. 2, 871.

NOTEWORTHY OPINIONS

Cook v. Moffat, 46 U.S. 295 (1847)

License Cases, 46 U.S. 504 (1847) (Concurrence)

Passenger Cases, 48 U.S. 283 (1849) (Concurrence)

Woodruff v. Trapnall, 51 U.S. 190 (1851) (Dissent)

Prize Cases, 67 U.S. 635 (1863)

JOHN MARSHALL HARLAN

Birth: June 1, 1833, Boyle County, Kentucky.

Education: Centre College, A.B., 1850; studied law at Transylvania University, 1851–1853.

Official Positions: Adjutant general of Kentucky, 1851; judge, Franklin County, 1858; state attorney general, 1863–1867; member, Louisiana Reconstruction Commission, 1877; member, Bering Sea Tribunal of Arbitration, 1893.

Supreme Court Service: Nominated associate justice by President Rutherford B. Hayes, October 17, 1877, to replace David Davis, who had resigned; confirmed by the Senate, November 29, 1877, by a voice vote; took judicial oath December 10, 1877; served until October 14, 1911; replaced by Mahlon Pitney, nominated by President William Howard Taft.

Death: October 14, 1911, Washington, D.C.

When Justice John Marshall Harlan sat down in late 1910 to write down a list of his most important decisions, he chose many that one would expect. For example, his renowned dissents in the *Civil Rights Cases* (1883) and *Plessy v. Ferguson* (1896) are there. But also listed are a great many decisions concerned primarily with economic issues, and some, such as bond repudiation cases, that few would have anticipated. What seems to have bound the various cases together in Harlan's mind was their importance in promoting nationalism. Although Harlan's favorite opinions on civil rights aimed to achieve a nationalized standard of rights, many of his economic cases strove to encourage and protect a national economy, one in which trade flowed freely among the states without regional barriers or discriminations. He believed that the great corporations that arose in the Gilded Age threatened to wipe out the individual entrepreneur trying to do business in that national market. As a result, Harlan backed the federal agencies and legislation that aimed at control-

ling the power of these corporations and so found himself both honored and vilified during the Progressive Era.

In part, Harlan's commitment to nationalism was an inheritance from his father, a Whig politician. But Harlan's Civil War experience as a Union officer in the border state of Kentucky confirmed this tendency and made it into one of the primary concerns of his judicial career. He was born to an elite Kentucky family of lawyering Whigs who owned slaves. He went to Centre College in Danville, Kentucky, and completed his legal studies at Transylvania University at Lexington. He was admitted to the bar in 1853 after working and studying in several law offices, including his father's. Harlan joined the Whig Party and was immediately recognized as a gifted stump speaker. In 1858 he won election as judge of the county court of Franklin County for one year, his only judicial experience before being appointed to the Supreme Court. He ran for a seat in the U.S. House of Representatives in 1859 and lost. From 1863 to 1867 he served as attorney general of Kentucky and made unsuccessful runs for governor in 1871 and 1875 under the Republican banner.

Harlan's shift in political allegiance from the Whig to the Republican Party and his abandonment of the institution of slavery occurred after the Civil War. From the time of secession through the end of the war, Harlan was part of a shifting pro-Union, anti-emancipation coalition that existed under various names in Kentucky. When war broke out, Harlan organized and led a regiment for the Union Army, but he resigned his commission in 1863 when his father's death left the family law office with no competent head. Throughout this time he counseled gradual emancipation and as late as 1865 condemned the Thirteenth Amendment as an unrepublican assault on the property rights of white slaveholders.

The Harlans were never abolitionists; rather, they defined forbearance from the physical abuse of power and goodwill between the races as essential to honorable behavior for white men. The Republican Party rejected the white supremacy that had existed hand in hand with this paternalistic ethos, and Harlan found the GOP's embrace of legal equality far more palatable than the racial terrorism of the Democrats. Still, Harlan would never shake free of paternalism with its assumptions of racial hierarchy and separation.

His journey to the Court began in 1876 when he threw the Kentucky delegation to the Republican presidential convention behind the candidacy of Rutherford B. Hayes. The new president appointed him to the Louisiana commission, which was sent there to decide the disputed state election of 1876. When Hayes nominated Harlan for an associate justiceship in October 1877, some Republicans complained because they still did not trust Harlan to be true to the party's principles.

If they were worried about his devotion to the constitutional amendments the Civil War had produced, they did not know their man. Justice Harlan's record on civil rights, although it betrays the taint of paternalism, was by far the most favorable to blacks and other minorities of any member of the Court during the Gilded Age. Harlan rejected the majority's notion that the Fourteenth and Fifteenth Amendments applied only to the acts of the states or their officials. These jurists did have a point: the Fourteenth Amendment used the words "No State shall" in declaring its prohibitions, and the Fifteenth contained similar language. Yet Congress, made up of many of the same men who had approved of the Civil War amendments, passed laws that punished individuals for their attacks on persons trying to exercise their civil rights, and the Court struck them down. In *Baldwin v. Franks* (1887), Harlan disagreed with a decision involving persecuted Chinese immigrants of the Pacific Coast. He insisted in dissent that "the rights therein granted or guaranteed might be guarded and protected against lawless combinations of individuals, acting without the direct sanction of the states." He also dissented in *James v. Bowman* (1903), in which the Court held that the

John Marshall Harlan

Fifteenth Amendment did not protect blacks from private assaults made upon them for trying to vote.

In applying the Thirteenth Amendment, Harlan was not hampered by the state-action doctrine because the amendment read simply, "Neither slavery nor involuntary servitude, except as punishment for crime . . . shall exist within the United States." The ban on slavery was universal. Harlan invoked this amendment, as well as the Fourteenth, in the two dissents for which he is best remembered—the *Civil Rights Cases* (1883) and *Plessy v. Ferguson* (1896). The first tested the constitutionality of the Civil Rights Act of 1875, a federal statute that decreed "all persons within the jurisdiction of the United States shall be entitled to the full and equal enjoyment of the accommodations" in inns, public transportation, places of amusement, and the like. Harlan had opposed the law as a gubernatorial candidate in 1875, but now, from his protected judicial position, he came out in its defense. In *Plessy,* which was little noticed by the public, the Court reviewed a Louisiana state law that segregated the races on public railroads. The question in both cases was whether the Thirteenth and Fourteenth Amendments to the Constitution prohibited racial segregation.

In both instances, the majority of the Court decided that the Thirteenth Amendment's prohibition on slavery did not extend to racial segregation. Justice Joseph Bradley asked in the *Civil Rights Cases,* "What has [the denial of public accommodation] to do with the question of slavery?" Similarly, Justice Henry Brown wrote in *Plessy,* "A statute which implies merely a legal distinction between the white and colored races—a distinction which is founded in the color of the two races . . . has no tendency to destroy the legal equality of the two races, or reestablish a state of involuntary servitude." Harlan, in contrast, argued in *Plessy* that the Civil War amendments had "removed the race line from our governmental systems." "Our Constitution is color-blind," he declared, warning, "The destinies of the two races, in this country, are indissolubly linked together, and the interest of both require that the common government of all shall not permit the seeds of race hate to be planted under the sanction of law."

Segregation in public accommodation was a badge of slavery, wrote Harlan, that had been used during antebellum times to mark even free blacks out as members of a slave race. Harlan admonished his brethren for failing, as he put it in the *Civil Rights Cases,* "to compel the recognition of the legal right of the black race to take the rank of citizens." He dissented for similar reasons in other cases, including *Louisville, New Orleans, & Texas Railroad Co. v. Mississippi* (1890) and *Chiles v. Chesapeake & Ohio Railway Co.* (1910).

Yet even in his two famous dissents, the limits on the egalitarianism of Harlan's racial thought were apparent. In *Plessy,* for example, he began with a complaint that segregation prevented a white man from having his colored servant with him during a train trip, and in the *Civil Rights Cases,* Harlan did not deny the legitimacy of the dubious notion of social rights but settled for declaring them irrelevant. In other decisions, he failed to follow the color-blind rule, which, one presumes, would have prohibited the mere mention of race in statutes. In *Pace v. Alabama* (1885), the Supreme Court concluded that a state law that punished interracial adultery more harshly than same-race adultery was not a violation of the equal protection of the laws, because both partners of the interracial couple were punished equally. Harlan did not dissent from this legal sophistry. Also, he made a point of not giving an opinion as to the legality of segregation in the public schools when he very well might have in *Cumming v. Richmond County Board* (1899).

His off-the-bench activities as a Presbyterian elder also suggest the ambiguity of his position on race. As a member of the standing committee on freedmen at the Presbyterian General Assembly of 1905, he assented to this statement in their report: "Assimilation is as destructive as it is repugnant." Destructive, possibly, because romantic racialism held at this time that each race possessed a distinct spiritual genius worth preserving; repugnant, undoubtedly, because of racist distaste for interracial sexual relations. In that same year, Harlan fought hard but unsuccessfully against a proposal to allow individual Presbyterian churches to limit themselves to one race exclusively. The front page of the *New York Age* of April 20, 1905, recorded his position "against separate presbyteries for whites and blacks even if the whites and blacks were to agree mutually to have them," which he voiced at a public meeting led by black clergymen.

He asked his fellows to be color-blind and race-blind. In *Berea College v. Kentucky* (1908), Harlan was outraged when the majority of the Court allowed the state to prohibit interracial teaching in a private school. He asked:

> Have we become so inoculated with the prejudice of race that an American government, professedly based on the principles of freedom, and charged with the protection of all citizens alike, can make distinctions between such citizens in the matter of their voluntary meeting for innocent purposes simply because of their respective races?

Perhaps Harlan emphasized the innocence because he was recalling *Pace*. Surely he remembered *Cumming* when he emphasized in *Berea College* that he spoke only of private schools. These actions leave us wondering how he could incorporate his forceful stand against the official imposition of segregation with an acquiescence to some forms of voluntary and involuntary social separation. Perhaps he was trying to create a biracial (not an interracial) society in an egalitarian polity. The habits of thought bred into a slaveholder may have been impossible to shake.

While Harlan worked on a way to integrate free black citizens into the political community, he also fought a rearguard action against the progressive technocrats who wanted to decrease all citizen participation in government. Harlan's concern for popular participation in civic affairs was at the root of his decision to support the idea that the due process clause of the Fourteenth Amendment incorporated all the protections found in the first eight amendments to the Constitution. This idea, called incorporation theory or the nationalization of the Bill of Rights, was first voiced by Harlan in dissent in *Hurtado v. California* (1884).

Joseph Hurtado had been tried and convicted of murder in California, but he had not been indicted by a grand jury; he therefore complained that he had been denied his rights as guaranteed in the Fifth Amendment and applied to state action by the Fourteenth Amendment. The Court majority, although it admitted some exceptions, held that, according to the rules of constitutional draftsmanship, no clause may repeat another; so the term "due process" in the Fifth Amendment could not also signify all the other protections also in the Fifth Amendment, such as a grand jury indictment in felony cases. Therefore, because a given term must mean the exact same thing each time it is used, the due process clause of the Fourteenth Amendment could not encompass all those other protections named in the Fifth Amendment, either. Harlan threw aside the rules of draftsmanship as technicalities that camouflaged the awful fact that the Court was willing to allow the states to abandon elements of criminal procedure that the founders had conceived of as essential to republican government. Many states were experimenting with simplified criminal procedures, and Harlan considered California to be the thin edge of a wedge. By the 1890s legal writers were engaged in a full-scale battle over whether the entire jury system should be discarded because of its inadequacies.

Harlan pursued the doctrinal logic of his *Hurtado* dissent and championed the nationalization of all of the protections found in the first eight amendments of the Bill of Rights. He tried unsuccessfully to have the Court apply to the states the Eighth Amendment's ban on cruel and unusual punishment in *O'Neil v. Vermont* (1892), the Fifth Amendment's traditional grand and petit jury procedures in *Maxwell v. Dow* (1900), the First Amendment's freedom of speech protection in *Patterson v. Colorado* (1907), and the Fifth Amendment's protection against self-incrimination in *Twining v. New Jersey* (1908). His colleagues gave Harlan a small victory in *Chicago, Burlington & Quincy Railroad Company v. Chicago* (1897) by allowing him to deliver an opinion that applied to the states the Fifth Amendment's requirement for fair compensation for property taken for public use. They would not, however, let him use it to bolster his position in any of the other cases, despite his complaint that the brethren seemed to value civil rights only when property was involved.

After the Spanish-American War, Harlan found himself again fighting for the idea that the full protections of the Bill of Rights was applicable to all persons subjected to government authority. Harlan had supported the war as a battle against tyranny and a way to soothe the old wounds of the Civil War by giving the North and South a common enemy. But Congress and the administration did not feel that Filipinos or Puerto Ricans measured up to the responsibilities of citizenship and so made their territories into colonies instead of granting them independence. The question of whether Congress could treat those territories differently from those destined for statehood brought the first of the so-called *Insular Cases* before the Court in 1901. In *De Lima v. Bidwell*, Harlan found himself on the winning side when the Court declared that Puerto Rico was not a foreign country. Unfortunately, on the same day he also had to dissent in *Downes v. Bidwell*, in which the majority declared that Congress could pass special tariff laws applicable only to Puerto Rico, something it might not do to a state.

Intertwined with the tariff question was that of what rights the island inhabitants might claim from the federal government. Many white Americans believed Congress might pick and chose which rights would be granted. Harlan's dissent in *Downes* expressed his fear that the Court would allow Congress to rule the new territories as it pleased without regard to the limits of its constitutionally enumerated powers. "I confess," he wrote in *Downes*, "that I cannot grasp the thought that Congress which lives and moves and has its being in the Constitution and is consequently the mere creature of that instrument" could exclude its creator from the islands.

In his eyes, it was not enough for Americans to congratulate themselves, as Justice Brown did in writing for the majority, that "there are certain principles of natural justice inherent in the Anglo-Saxon character which need no expression in constitution or statutes to give them effect." Harlan pointed out that "the wise men who framed the Constitution, and the patriotic people who adopted it, were unwilling to depend for their safety upon . . . 'certain principles of natural justice inherent in the Anglo-Saxon character.'" "They well remembered," as some of the brethren had apparently forgotten, "that Anglo-Saxons across the ocean had attempted, in defiance of law and justice, to trample upon the rights of Anglo-Saxons on this continent."

Harlan continued his unsuccessful effort in *Hawaii v. Mankichi* (1903), in which he declared that in 1898 "when the flag of Hawaii was taken down . . . and in its place was raised that of the United States," every provision of the Constitution went into force. In 1911 he continued to protest in silent dissents to *Dowdell v. United States* and *Gavieres v. United States* and never reconciled himself to the American empire. When he used the vocabulary of colonialism, he always put the words *dependencies* and *subjects* in quotation marks. He blamed imperialism on the greed of the commercial interests.

Just as Harlan tried to bind the nation together after the Civil War by extracting a national standard of citizenship rights from the Reconstruction amendments, so he attempted to open to all citizens a national marketplace. Interstate economic ties could strengthen national feeling. Harlan wanted goods to travel freely and for a contract between a buyer on one side of the country and a seller on the other side to be enforced in the courts. Like his brethren, Harlan invoked the clause that gave to Congress sole power to "regulate Commerce . . . among the several states," but he surpassed them by spotting unconstitutional burdens on commerce where they did not. In fact, Harlan defended interstate commerce in the broadest practical sense of the term, even when state regulation was not involved.

In municipal and state bond repudiation decisions, Harlan's devotion to commercial nationalism becomes clear. He tended to favor creditors in order to preserve the integrity of the national and international market in local American bonds. In *Antoni v. Greenhow* (1883), Harlan foretold the "disastrous consequences which would result both to the business interest and to the honor of the country" if the state succeeded in defying its creditors. Although some legal scholars believe that judges of the Gilded Age who found repeatedly for property holders were prejudiced by class interest, in Harlan's case, commercial nationalism was responsible.

In the bond case found on his list of favorites, *Presidio County, Texas v. The Noel-Young Bond & Stock Company* (1909), Harlan made it clear that the Court held the county responsible for the promises that its bonds recited on their face because such promises had made sale of those bonds to far-off purchasers possible in the first place. The Court usually followed this logic, but Harlan's concern led him to dissent when they did not. For example, he dissented in *Brenham v. German American Bank* (1892), warning that in light of the "enormous" amounts of similar bonds in circulation, "a declaration by this court that such notes are void . . . will, we fear, produce incalculable mischief." In *Ex parte Young* (1908), however, Harlan swerved from his interpretation that the Eleventh Amendment did not protect the states from being sued on their bonds after railroad attorneys began to put his doctrine to an entirely different, procorporation use. But so long as the issue was localism versus nationalism, his position was clear.

Despite Harlan's devotion to the commerce clause, he also had great respect for the states' police powers, so long as commercial localism was not involved. He spoke for the majority in *Reid v. Colorado* (1902), which allowed Colorado to punish anyone who did not hold out-of-state livestock off the market for ninety days to prevent the spread of Texas fever. Harlan also supported state efforts to protect the people from the immoral effects of liquor in *Mugler v. Kansas* (1887) and dissented when the rest of the Court proved less concerned in cases concerning bootlegging in Iowa: *Bowman v. Chicago & Northwestern Railway Company* (1888), *Rhodes v. Iowa* (1898), and *Adams Express Company v. Iowa* (1905).

He had a similarly clear but only partially successful record on the regulation of lottery tickets. In *Leisy v. Hardin* (1890), he joined Horace Gray's dissent when the Court refused to allow a state to pro-

hibit such tickets, and in *Champion v. Ames* (1903), he managed to deliver a majority opinion that allowed Congress (not the states) to ban lottery tickets from interstate commerce. His record on the regulation of margarine displayed a similar high-minded moralism. In *Powell v. Pennsylvania* (1888) and in *Plumley v. Massachusetts* (1894), Harlan upheld laws prohibiting the sale of oil products treated to pass for dairy products. He met defeat and dissented in *Schollenberger v. Pennsylvania* (1898), when the majority of the Court declared margarine an inherently healthy product that a state might not regulate out of existence.

Harlan's dissent in *Lochner v. New York* (1905), a decision that struck down a labor law for bakers, should be understood in terms of his respect for the police powers of the state where no commercial localism was present. After all, he supported liberty of contract in *Adair v. United States* (1908) when he spoke for the majority in striking down the Erdmann Act, which made it a criminal offense for an interstate railroad to fire a worker because of union membership. Harlan held that such membership had no necessary connection to interstate commerce, while bakers' working conditions had a clear connection to health.

Harlan's respect for state police powers ended at the point where their exercise might amount to a discrimination against out-of-state goods. Speaking for the Court, he condemned the localism displayed in a wharfage fee laid only on ships carrying out-of-state goods in *Guy v. Baltimore* (1879). In his dissent to *Transportation Company v. Parkersburg* (1882), he displayed his dislike of all state-imposed burdens on interstate commerce even when they fell equally on in-state and out-of-state goods. He tried unsuccessfully to have the Court strike down inspection fees for out-of-state fertilizer in *Patapsco Guano Company v. North Carolina Board of Agriculture* (1898). Harlan also dissented in several cases in which the Court allowed states to place embargoes on livestock or people because of the threat of disease, as in *Smith v. St. Louis & Southwestern Railway Company* (1901) and *Compagnie Francaise de Navigation a Vapeur v. Louisiana State Board of Health* (1902). Apparently, Harlan was so suspicious of localism that he wished the Court to make the states allow both cows and people a chance to prove their good health.

Harlan was more successful when states tried to close their borders to out-of-state meat in a heavy-handed manner. In *State of Minnesota v. Barber* (1890), he carried the Court with him in striking down a law that made it practically impossible for anyone to sell out-of-state meat in Minnesota markets. He had similar luck in *Brimmer v. Rebman* (1891), where Virginia placed an inspection fee on all meat slaughtered 100 miles from Norfolk.

Statutory discrimination against out-of-state products was only the tip of the iceberg of localism in Harlan's eyes. He wanted to improve the status of foreign—in other words, out-of-state—corporations. In *Hooper v. California* (1895) and *Nutting v. Massachusetts* (1902), Harlan tried but failed to convince the Court that insurance policies should fall under the constitutional definition of commerce. He always objected to stipulations made by the states that foreign corporations exchange their right to resort to the federal courts for permission to enter; he joined Justice William Day's dissent to that practice in *Blake v. McClung* (1898). The Court's willingness to tolerate the statutory sniping that the states directed at one another's foreign corporations provoked his dissents in *Philadelphia Fire Association v. New York* (1886) and *New York v. Roberts* (1898). Harlan was vindicated late in life by three decisions involving foreign corporations that he delivered in 1910, *Western Union Telegraph Company v. Kansas, Ludwig v. Western Union Telegraph Company,* and *International Textbook Company v. Pigg.* The year 1910 seems to have marked the beginning of the end for unconditional requirements laid upon foreign corporations in exchange for permission to enter a state.

More than his brethren, Harlan feared that state taxation would burden interstate commerce. When he stood before his constitutional law class at the Columbia (now George Washington University) Law School on January 8, 1898, he confided to his students one absolute certainty: "That there is not a state in this union which would not, if it had the power, support its government from top to bottom by levying tribute or

taxes upon the commerce among the states; they have all tried to do it." His accuracy and disapproval were borne out in decisions involving the issue of taxing property used in interstate commerce in which he dissented (sometimes with others) from the Court's less-strict standard of judgment: *Pullman's Palace Car Company v. Pennsylvania* (1891), *Maine v. Grand Trunk Railway Company* (1891), *Horn Silver Mining Company v. New York State* (1892), *Ficklen v. Shelby County Taxing District* (1892), *Adams Express Company v. Ohio State Auditor* (1897), *Pittsburgh, Cincinnati, Chicago and St. Louis Railway Company v. Backus* (1894), and *Kidd v. Alabama* (1903). He had only the occasional victory, such as *Louisville & Jeffersonsville Ferry Company v. Kentucky* (1903), in which Harlan convinced the majority of the Court that the state had tried to tax property that was not actually within its control.

Perhaps this zeal for an unrestricted flow of commerce among the states explains Harlan's support for that most controversial of Gilded Age doctrines—substantive due process. By applying this doctrine to case after case, the Court set itself up as a kind of superagency passing on the reasonableness of railroad and other rates set by state legislatures and state commissions. Harlan explained in his law lecture for April 23, 1898, that:

> since the adoption of the 14th amendment there have been a great many decisions in the country as to what constitutes due process of law, and you will never hear the last of that phrase as long as this is a free country because there are varying circumstances arising and the judges are put at their wits' ends to know whether this, that or the other act transcends the provision of the Constitution.

Harlan's contribution to defining due process were two decisions: *Covington & Lexington Turnpike Road Company v. Sandford* (1896) and, more important, *Smyth v. Ames* (1898), in which he held that the judiciary was best suited to act as an evenhanded dispenser of justice between the corporation's property rights and the public's right to service. He offered a formula for judges to consult in estimating the fair value of the property and therefore the proper rate of carriage. For this, he brought down on his head the opprobrium of a good many constitutional scholars who do not believe the judiciary is constitutionally qualified or institutionally capable of playing such a role. This opinion, however, with its careful balancing of the interests of farmers and merchants on the one hand and of railroads on the other, contains a logic that is often overlooked.

Substantive due process is the doctrine most often cited as proof of the Gilded Age judiciary's favoritism of property holders at the expense of the general population. Although Harlan may have had a hand in creating the legal framework for a marketplace that gave rise to the national corporations that seemed to threaten the country with plutocracy, he was clearly more supportive of federal action to counter such a threat than any of his colleagues. He dissented in *Pollock v. Farmers' Loan & Trust Co.* (1895), in which the Court struck down the income tax on the grounds that as a direct tax it should have been apportioned among the states according to population. "No such apportionment can possibly be made without doing gross injustice to the many for the benefit of the favored few in particular States," he complained, and then urged the populace to amend the Constitution—which it did.

Harlan also supported the Interstate Commerce Commission in a string of cases in which the majority of the Court gutted its powers, including *Texas & Pacific Railway Company v. ICC* (1896), *ICC v. Cincinnati, New Orleans & Texas Pacific Railway* (1897), and *ICC v. Alabama Midland Railway Company* (1897). Harlan complained in this last dissent that "taken in connection with other decisions defining the power of the Interstate Commerce Commission, the present decision, it seems to me, goes far to make that commission a useless body for all practical purposes, and to defeat many of the important objects designed to be accomplished."

He also believed that the Court's interpretation of the Sherman Antitrust Act of 1890 in *United States v. E. C. Knight Co.* (1895) went a long way toward preventing the federal government from controlling monopolies. The Court distinguished between commerce, which Congress might regulate, and manufacturing, which it might not, and held that the sugar monopoly fell into the latter category. Harlan dissented silently from other decisions that limited the scope of the law, such as *Hopkins v. United States* (1898) and *Anderson v. United States* (1898).

Such decisions led to Harlan's being called the Great Dissenter, but he was victorious in *Northern Securities Company v. United States* (1904), in which he held that the Sherman Act authorized the attorney general to stop railroad tycoons J. P. Morgan and James J. Hill from consolidating their roads. The government's effort, he explained, would prevent the public from finding itself "at the absolute mercy of the holding corporation." *Northern Securities* popularized both Harlan and the antitrust effort. He came to public notice again in the 1911 trust cases, *Standard Oil v. United States* and *United States v. American Tobacco.* Harlan supported the Court's finding that the government had a case against both monopolies, but he feared that references to the "rule of reason" were the majority's way of "usurping the constitutional functions of the legislative branch of the Government." He feared that in the future judges might use their discretion to decide that some restraints of trade created by monopolies were not unreasonable, and then disallow efforts to prosecute such corporations. Harlan reminded his fellow justices that when the Sherman Act was passed:

the conviction was universal that the country was in real danger from ... the slavery that would result from aggregations of capital in the hands of a few individuals and corporations controlling, for their own profit and advantage exclusively, the entire business of the country, including the production and sale of the necessaries of life.

That Harlan could use the language of slavery so vividly almost fifty years after the Civil War is one indication of how closely his imagination was bound up with that war's transformative effects. He never completely shook off the habits of his antebellum life, but he came to see nationalism as the central organizing principle of political and constitutional thought when he sat on the bench from 1877 to 1911.

—*Linda C. A. Przybyszewski*

BIBLIOGRAPHY

Two large collections of private papers, one at the Library of Congress and the other at the University of Louisville Law School, contain Court-related materials. The recent interest in Harlan has led to several biographies; see especially Linda C. A. Przybyszewski, *The Republic According to John Marshall Harlan* (1999); and Tinsley E. Yarbrough, *Judicial Enigma: The First Justice Harlan* (1995). Loren Beth, *John Marshall Harlan: The Last Whig Justice* (1992), covers all the important legal issues but is less analytical than one might desire. The best piece on Harlan's pre-Court political career is Louis Hartz's "John Marshall Harlan in Kentucky, 1855–1877," *Filson Club Quarterly* 14 (1950): 17. Before the civil rights movement flourished, several writers attempted to defend Harlan as a man before his time. See, for example, Edward F. Waite, "How 'Eccentric' was Mr. Justice Harlan?" *Minnesota Law Review* 37 (1953): 173; and Richard F. Watt and Richard M. Okiloff, "The Coming Vindication of Mr. Justice Harlan," *Illinois Law Review* 44 (1949): 13.

After *Brown v. Board of Education* (1954), many scholars turned to Harlan's civil rights decisions, and the *Kentucky Law Journal* devoted its Spring 1958 issue to Harlan with articles by Henry J. Abraham, Florian Bartosic, David G. Farrelly, and Alan F. Westin. Probably the best article on civil rights, the seed of a never-finished biography, is Westin's "John Marshall Harlan and the Constitutional Rights of Negroes: The Transformation of a Southerner," *Yale Law Journal* 66 (1957): 637. Monte Canfield Jr. tried to use Harlan's approach to the state-action doctrine in " 'Our Constitution Is Color-Blind': Mr. Justice Harlan and Modern Problems of Civil Rights," *University of Missouri at Kansas City Law Review* 32 (1964): 292. A more recent look at his civil rights legacy is M. T. O'Brien, "Justice John Marshall Harlan as Prophet: The Plessy Dissenter's Color-Blind Constitution," *William & Mary Bill of Rights Journal* 6 (1998): 753, which is possibly an answer to Earl Maltz, "Only Partially Color-Blind: John Marshall Harlan's View of Race and the Constitution," *Georgia State University Law Review* 12 (1996): 973. Perhaps the only piece that looks closely (and caustically) at Harlan's economic decisions is Mary Cornelia Aldis Porter, "John Marshall Harlan the Elder & Federal Common Law: A Lesson from History," *Supreme Court Review* (1972): 1.

Several works that explore important decisions include: David G. Farrelly, "Justice Harlan's Dissent in the Pollock Case," *Southern California Law Review* 24 (1951): 174; J. Morgan Kousser, "Separate but Not Equal: The Supreme Court's First Decision on Racial Discrimination in the Schools," *Journal of Southern History* 46 (1980): 17; and Charles A. Lofgren. *The Plessy Case: A Legal-Historical Perspective* (1987).

NOTEWORTHY OPINIONS

Civil Rights Cases, 109 U.S. 3 (1883) (Dissent)

Hurtado v. California, 110 U.S. 516 (1884) (Dissent)

Baldwin v. Franks, 120 U.S. 678 (1887) (Dissent)

Mugler v. Kansas, 123 U.S. 623 (1887)

State of Minnesota v. Barber, 136 U.S. 313 (1890)

United States v. E. C. Knight Co., 156 U.S. 1 (1895) (Dissent)

Plessy v. Ferguson, 163 U.S. 537 (1896) (Dissent)

Covington & Lexington Turnpike Road Co. v. Sandford, 164 U.S. 578 (1896)

Chicago, Burlington & Quincy Railroad Co. v. Chicago, 166 U.S. 226 (1897)

Smyth v. Ames, 169 U.S. 466 (1898)

Downes v. Bidwell, 182 U.S. 244 (1901) (Dissent)

Champion v. Ames, 188 U.S. 321 (1903)

Northern Securities Company v. United States, 193 U.S. 197 (1904)

Lochner v. New York, 198 U.S. 45 (1905) (Dissent)

Berea College v. Kentucky, 211 U.S. 45 (1908) (Dissent)

Presidio County, Texas v. The Noel-Young Bond & Stock Company, 212 U.S. 58 (1909)

JOHN MARSHALL HARLAN II

Birth: May 20, 1899, Chicago, Illinois.

Education: Princeton University, B.A., 1920; Rhodes scholar, Oxford University, Balliol College, B.A. in jurisprudence, 1923; New York Law School, LL.B., 1924.

Official Positions: Assistant U.S. attorney, Southern District of New York, 1925–1927; special assistant attorney general, New York, 1928–1930; chief counsel, New York State Crime Commission, 1951–1953; judge, U.S. Court of Appeals for the Second Circuit, 1954–1955.

Supreme Court Service: Nominated associate justice by President Dwight D. Eisenhower, November 9, 1954, to replace Robert Jackson, who had died; nomination resubmitted January, 10, 1955; confirmed by the Senate, March 16, 1955, by a 71–11 vote; took judicial oath March 28, 1955; retired September 23, 1971; replaced by William H. Rehnquist, nominated by President Richard Nixon.

Death: December 29, 1971, Washington D.C.

John Marshall Harlan was the son of John Maynard Harlan and Elizabeth Palmer Flagg Harlan. His family was distinguished in the law. His great-grandfather was a lawyer; his grandfather, for whom he was named, was a justice of the U.S. Supreme Court for thirty-four years; his father was a lawyer; and an uncle was a member of the Interstate Commerce Commission.

Harlan studied at Princeton University and was a Rhodes scholar for three years at Balliol College, Oxford, where he began the study of law and formed lifetime attachments. He completed his legal education at New York Law School in 1924 and was admitted to practice in New York in 1925. He began his career with Root, Clark, Buckner & Howland, a large Wall Street firm. When a senior member of the firm, Emory R. Buckner, was appointed U.S. attorney for the Southern District of New York in 1925, Harlan became his assistant. During this period Harlan participated in several notable prosecutions, including that of Harry M. Daugherty, former U.S. attorney general, for official misconduct, and of Thomas W. Miller, former alien property custodian, for fraudulent conspiracy.

Harlan made partner in the Root, Clark firm in 1931 and, after Buckner's death in 1941, became its leading trial lawyer. His practice had unusual range and complexity. For example, he represented the New York City Board of Higher Education in litigation involving the appointment of free-thinking Bertrand Russell to teach at City College; he handled the will of Miss Ella Wendel, involving an extensive fortune and a host of claimants—at least one of whom was subsequently convicted of fraud; and he represented heavyweight champion Gene Tunney in a contract action.

During World War II, Harlan rendered conspicuous service in England as head of the Eighth Air Force's operational analysis section, which was composed of hand-picked civilian experts in mathematics, physics, electronics, architecture, and law, to furnish advice on bombing operations. Harlan was awarded the United States Legion of Merit and the Croix de Guerre of Belgium and France. On his return to private practice in 1945, Harlan was soon recognized as a leader of the New York bar. He argued several appeals before the U.S. Supreme Court, including one case that became a landmark in corporate law and civil procedure.

Although private practice was his professional love, Harlan was again called to public service. From 1951 to 1953 he acted as chief counsel for the New York State Crime Commission, which Republican governor Thomas Dewey had appointed to investigate the relationship between organized crime and state government. Harlan was also active in professional organizations, serving as chairman of the committee on the judiciary and vice president of the Association of the Bar of the City of New York. In January 1954 Harlan was appointed a judge of the U.S. Court of Appeals for the Second Circuit. He served less than a year before President Dwight Eisenhower appointed him to the U.S. Supreme Court.

Throughout most of his years on the Court, Justice Harlan provided a form of resistance to the dominant liberal motifs of the Warren Court. He did this in a way that was intelligent, determined, and, above

John Marshall Harlan II

all, principled. But it would be a mistake to conceive of Harlan solely in this conservative light. To a surprising degree, Harlan concurred in the liberal activism of the Court, picking his spots carefully and remaining true to his core judicial values. In all his work he exhibited outstanding professional competence, leading Judge Henry Friendly to write that "there has never been a Justice of the Supreme Court who has so consistently maintained a high quality of performance or, despite differences in views, has enjoyed such nearly uniform respect from his colleagues, the inferior bench, the bar, and the academy."

Harlan's two principal judicial values were federalism and proceduralism, both directed to keeping the " 'delicate balance of federal-state relations' in good working order." On many occasions, Harlan in dissent criticized the Court's entry into political matters, as in *Reynolds v. Sims* (1964), or into state procedures, as in *Henry v. Mississippi* (1965), as inconsistent with the demands of the federal structure. His view of federalism is perhaps best summarized in a dissenting opinion by Justice Stephen Field in *Baltimore & Ohio Railroad v. Baugh* (1893), which Harlan quoted approvingly:

The Constitution of the United States recognizes and preserves the autonomy and independence of the States. . . . Supervision over either the legislative or the judicial action of the States is in no case permissible except as to matters by the Constitution specifically authorized or delegated to the United States.

Harlan applied federalism principles to restrict the so-called state action doctrine that permits expansion of federal court authority. He thought that such expansion over activities that are properly the responsibility of state government simultaneously impairs "independence in their legislative and independence in their judicial departments." For example, despite his strong commitment to racial equality, Harlan did not believe that land bequeathed in trust to a Georgia city as a "park and pleasure ground" for white people was unconstitutionally administered merely because a state court replaced public trustees with private trustees and the park was municipally maintained (*Evans v. Newton,* 1966). And in a nonracial context, in *Amalgamated Food Employees Union 590 v. Logan Valley Plaza, Inc.* (1968), Harlan dissented from a holding that a privately owned shopping mall was the equivalent of a company town and therefore could not prohibit peaceful picketing of a supermarket in the mall.

It is of special importance that Harlan saw federalism not only as part of the U.S. constitutional design, "born of the necessity of achieving union," but as "a bulwark of freedom as well." In one of his speeches he declared:

We are accustomed to speak of the Bill of Rights and the Fourteenth Amendment as the principal guarantees of personal liberty. Yet it would surely be shallow not to recognize that the structure of our political system accounts no less for the free society we have. Indeed, it was upon the structure of government that the founders primarily focused in writing the Constitution. Out of bitter experience they were suspicious of every form of all-powerful central authority and they sought to assure that such a government would never exist in this country by structuring the federal establishment so as to diffuse power between the executive, legislative, and judicial branches.

Harlan also viewed federalism as essential for preserving pluralism and local experimentation. No other political system "could have afforded so much scope to the varied interests and aspirations of a dynamic people representing such divergencies of ethnic and cultural backgrounds," and still "unify them into a nation." Addressing government power to regulate obscenity, Harlan said, "One of the great strengths of our federal system is that we have, in the forty-eight States, forty-eight experimental social laboratories."

Harlan's dedication to proceduralism was equally firm. The term refers not only to rules that govern trials and appeals, but also to issues that determine when the judicial power will be exercised. In his dissent in *Reynolds v. Sims* from the Court's "one person, one vote" decision, Harlan stated his basic philosophy. He rejected the view:

that every major social ill in this country can find its cure in some constitutional "principle," and that this Court should "take the lead" in promoting reform when other branches of government fail to act. The Constitution is not a panacea for every blot on the public welfare, nor should this Court, ordained as a judicial body, be thought of as a general haven for reform movements.

Harlan urged the Court to steer clear of "political thickets," lest "the vitality of our political system, on which in the last analysis all else depends, is weakened by reliance on the judiciary for political reform; in time a complacent body politic may result."

Harlan embodied his view of the limited role of the courts in a series of doctrines. First, he jealously guarded the Supreme Court's appellate authority, which he believed should be used "for the settlement of [issues] of importance to the public," and "should not be exercised simply 'for the benefit of the particular litigants.' " He repeatedly called on the Court to follow a number of practices designed to avoid unnecessary or premature judicial intervention, such as allowing administrative processes to run their course, not passing on the validity of state statutes that have neither been enforced nor interpreted by state courts, avoiding issues not considered below, and refusing to hear appeals of nonfinal orders.

Second, Harlan urged the Court to show deference to other decision-making authorities. Perhaps from his experience as a trial lawyer, Harlan believed strongly in deference to the fact-finding of trial courts, saying that "appellate courts have no facilities for the examination of witnesses; nor in the nature of things can they have that intimate knowledge of the evidence and 'feel' of the trial scene."

Finally, Harlan was committed to the stable and predictable development of the law. He protested when the Court resolved important issues by way of summary disposition. For example, in the 1971 Pentagon Papers case (*New York Times Co. v. United States*), Harlan in dissent recounted the "frenzied train of events" whereby, within one week from the date of lower court decisions, the Court heard argument and issued a decision. He identified several difficult issues and noted that the "time which has been available to us, to the lower courts, and to the parties has been wholly inadequate for giving these cases the kind of consideration they deserve."

In light of his commitment to federalism and proceduralism, we may now look more closely at Harlan's dissents from the principal civil liberty themes of the Warren Court. Perhaps the most central of these themes is "equality," an idea that, as Archibald Cox put it, "once loosed . . . is not easily cabined." Harlan vigorously opposed egalitarian rulings of many kinds. He was most vehement in condemning the reapportionment decisions, first in *Baker v. Carr* (1962), in which the Court authorized federal jurisdiction to decide the issue whether state legislative districts were malapportioned, and then in *Reynolds v. Sims*, in which the Court established the one person, one vote rule, and in the many sequels to these rulings. Harlan never became reconciled to what he regarded as a wholly unjustified encroachment into the political realm, saying in *Reynolds* that "it is difficult to imagine a more intolerable and inappropriate interference by the judiciary with the independent legislatures of the States."

Closely related to the reapportionment cases are those dealing with the right to vote. Harlan dissented

from the ruling that invalidated Virginia's poll tax, from a decision that opened school board elections to a man who was neither a parent nor a property holder in the district, and from the decision upholding Congress's power to extend the franchise to eighteen-year-olds.

The poll tax case illustrates an aspect of the Court's egalitarianism to which Harlan especially objected: its acceptance of the idea that government has an obligation to eliminate economic inequalities as a way to permit everyone to exercise human rights. The leading case in this regard was *Griffin v. Illinois* (1956), in which a sharply divided bench held that where a stenographic trial transcript is needed for appellate review, a state violates the Fourteenth Amendment by refusing to provide the transcript to an impoverished defendant who alleges reversible errors in his trial. Harlan's dissent maintained that "all that Illinois has done is to fail to alleviate the consequences of differences in economic circumstances that exist wholly apart from any state action." He later dissented in *Douglas v. California* (1963), in which the Court held that a state had to provide counsel to a convicted indigent seeking to appeal. Another example of this genre was Harlan's protests at efforts to transform welfare payments into an entitlement. Harlan maintained in dissent that states could deny such payments to otherwise eligible welfare applicants who had not resided in the state for a year or more (*Shapiro v. Thompson*, 1969).

Harlan also found himself out of step with the prevailing view on criminal procedure in state trials, where the Warren Court rewrote the book, transforming the law relating to confessions and lineups, the privilege against self-incrimination, jury trials, wiretapping and eavesdropping, and the admissibility of illegally obtained evidence. Harlan vigorously dissented from almost all of the major decisions, arguing that the assertion of national judicial power over state criminal justice was inconsistent with a healthy federalism.

Harlan also objected in the interests of federalism to extensions of congressional power. In the two most significant cases, he protested when the Court adopted broad theories in sustaining the authority of Congress to invalidate state English-language literacy tests for voting as applied to individuals who completed the sixth grade in Puerto Rican schools (*Katzenbach v. Morgan,* 1966) and to punish private (as distinguished from state) interference with constitutional rights (*United States v. Guest,* 1966).

At the same time, Harlan, contrary to the majority, deferred to congressional judgments that resulted in an impairment of civil liberties. For example, he conceded broad authority to Congress over citizenship, rejecting any constitutional right to prevent involuntary denationalization in *Afroyim v. Rusk* (1967); protesting a softening of the immigration law that provided for deportation of any alien who had ever been a member of the Communist Party, however nominally, in *Rowoldt v. Perfetto* (1957); and opposing a constitutional right to travel abroad in *Kent v. Dulles* (1958). In these cases he refused to overturn actions of the elected branches of government that resulted in severe and arguably unjustified harm to individuals.

In addition to filing dissents in many of the Warren Court's principal liberal decisions, Harlan was part of a majority that rejected constitutional theories supported by the liberal justices in many other important cases. For example, he wrote the prevailing opinions that rejected First Amendment claims by individuals who were held in contempt by the House Un-American Activities Committee (*Barenblatt v. United States,* 1959); were denied admission to the practice of law for refusing to respond to questions concerning Communist activities (*Konigsberg v. State Bar,* 1961); and sentenced to prison because of membership in the Communist Party (*Scales v. United States,* 1961). He also agreed with rulings that permitted states to question suspects of crime without regard to the privilege against self-incrimination and that denied women the right to serve on juries equally with men.

The Warren Court ended in mid-1969, but Harlan remained for two more terms, a brief period in which he was the leader of the Court. Possessing seniority and an unmatched professional reputation, he took advantage of the replacement of Earl Warren and Abe Fortas by Warren Burger and Harry Blackmun to regain the position of dominance that Felix Frankfurter and he had shared until Frankfurter retired in August 1962. As evidence of his influence, he cast only twenty-four dissenting votes in the 1969 term, and eighteen in the 1970 term. His average for the period between 1963 and 1967 was 62.6 dissenting votes per term. This new situation meant that Harlan could reassert conservative themes in his own opinions or join such expressions in the opinions of others. For example, in *Dandridge v. Williams* (1970), he adhered to his long-standing opposition to expansion of the constitutional right of poor people to public assistance in the leading case rejecting welfare as an entitlement.

Similarly, he prevailed in a series of criminal justice decisions including those that denied a right to jury trial in juvenile delinquency proceedings, and permitted the closing of such hearings to the public (*McKeiver v. Pennsylvania,* 1971) and authorized capital sentencing without guidelines (*McGautha v. California,* 1971). And in *Wyman v. James* (1971), Harlan joined the opinion sustaining the power of caseworkers to make unannounced visits to the homes of welfare recipients to check their eligibility and provide rehabilitative assistance.

In the First Amendment area Harlan also maintained long-standing positions, but here he was more often in dissent than in the majority. The most notable occasion was *New York Times Co. v. United States;* here, Harlan would have permitted the prior restraint of newspaper publication of the Pentagon Papers, an extensive and politically embarrassing history of the Vietnam War. He also dissented in an important libel case, *Rosenbloom v. Metromedia, Inc.* (1971), and in two 1971 decisions restricting the authority of bar examiners to probe into the associations of applicants, *In re Stolar* and *Baird v. State Bar of Arizona.* But he prevailed in another bar admission case the same year, *LSRRC v. Wadmond,* recalling issues from earlier days, that upheld questions about Communist associations. And he was part of the majority that sustained an important obscenity prosecution in *United States v. Reidel* (1971).

But these conservative opinions and votes are far from the whole story. Justice Potter Stewart, one of Harlan's closest colleagues, recognized this when he said at a memorial service for Harlan: "I can assure you that a very interesting law review article could someday be written on 'The Liberal Opinions of Mr. Justice Harlan.'" In virtually every area of the Court's work, there are cases in which Harlan was part of the Warren Court consensus and, indeed, in which he spoke for the Court.

Harlan joined *Brown v. Board of Education II* (1955) and *Cooper v. Aaron* (1958), decisions instrumental in protecting the principle of school desegregation. He also joined every opinion decided while he was on the Court that rejected other sorts of state-enforced segregation.

He concurred in *Gideon v. Wainwright* (1963), the pathbreaking case granting a right to counsel to accused felons, and he wrote the opinion of the Court in *Boddie v. Connecticut* (1971), which held that a state could not deny a divorce to a couple because they lacked the means to pay the judicial filing fee. Although both of these cases were decided under the due process clause, they amounted at bottom to judicially mandated equalization of economic circumstance in situations where Harlan concluded that it would be fundamentally unfair to deny poor people what others could afford.

In the criminal procedure area, Harlan opposed the rule that excluded illegally seized evidence in state prosecutions, but he consistently supported a strong version of the Fourth Amendment protection against unreasonable searches and seizures by federal authorities, as in *Jones v. United States* (1958) and *Giordenello v. United States* (1958), including application of the principle to wiretapping and eavesdropping in *Katz v. United States* (1967). He also supported the ruling that extended criminal due process protections to juveniles accused of delinquency (*In re Gault*, 1967).

One also finds major cases in which Harlan supported the right of free expression. For example, he wrote the opinion in *NAACP v. Alabama ex rel. Patterson* (1958), holding that freedom of association protected the right of individuals to join unpopular civil

rights groups anonymously. He joined *New York Times Co. v. Sullivan* (1964), which first imposed limits on libel judgments against the media, and he joined some (but not all) of the sequels to that case. He joined opinions that barred states from refusing to seat an elected legislator because of his sharply critical views on the Vietnam War (*Bond v. Floyd*, 1966), and from convicting a leader of the Ku Klux Klan for "seditious" speech (*Brandenburg v. Ohio*, 1969). And he wrote for the Court to protect the right of a black man, unnerved by the shooting of a civil rights leader, to burn an American flag in protest (*Street v. New York*, 1969). Harlan also wrote opinions, all curbing variants of McCarthyism, that nominally were decided on nonconstitutional grounds but rested on First Amendment principles (*Cole v. Young*, 1956; *Service v. Dulles*, 1957; *Yates v. United States*, 1957; and *Maisenberg v. United States*, 1958).

Freedom of religion also showed Harlan as frequently, but not invariably, protective of constitutional guarantees. He joined decisions that prohibited organized prayer in the public schools (*Engel v. Vitale*, 1962) and invalidated a requirement that state officials declare a belief in God (*Torcaso v. Watkins*, 1961). And although he approved state loans of textbooks to church schools in *Board of Education v. Allen* (1968), he balked when tax-raised funds were used to reimburse parochial schools for teachers' salaries, textbooks, and instructional materials in *Lemon v. Kurtzman* (1971). He was unwilling to grant constitutional protection to adherents of sabbatarian faiths who objected to Sunday closing laws in *Braunfield v. Brown* (1961) and to unemployment compensation laws that required Saturday work in *Sherbert v. Verner* (1963), but during the Vietnam War he wrote a powerful opinion declaring that a statute limiting conscientious objection to those who believed in a theistic religion offended the establishment clause because it "accords a preference to the 'religious' [and] disadvantages adherents of religions that do not worship a Supreme Being" (*Welsh v. United States*, 1970).

In these cases, Harlan emphasized that "the attitude of government towards religion must . . . be one of neutrality." He was sophisticated enough to appreciate that neutrality is "a coat of many colors." Nevertheless, as Columbia professor Kent Greenawalt, a former Harlan clerk, has observed, "No modern justice has striven harder or more successfully than Justice Harlan to perform his responsibilities in [a neutral] manner."

A final area of civil liberties, sexual privacy, is of particular importance because Harlan produced the most influential opinions on this subject written by anyone during his tenure on the Court. In the first case, *Poe v. Ullman* (1961), a 5–4 majority led by Frankfurter refused to adjudicate, on the ground that there was no threat of prosecution, the merits of a Connecticut law that criminalized the sale of contraceptives to married and unmarried people alike. Harlan's emotional opinion—a rarity for him—not only differed with this conclusion, but extensively defended the proposition that Connecticut's law violated the due process clause of the Fourteenth Amendment, a position that soon prevailed in *Griswold v. Connecticut* (1965), the case that first recognized a right to sexual privacy. It is impossible to know whether Harlan would have extended this reasoning to support the result in *Eisenstadt v. Baird* (1972), which held that a state could not punish the distribution of contraceptives to unmarried persons, or the recognition of abortion as a personal right in *Roe v. Wade* (1973), both decided soon after he retired. But I am confident that, at a minimum, he would have protected the right of a married woman to proceed with an abortion that was dictated by family considerations.

Harlan's participation in the major thrusts of the Warren Court was not confined to civil liberties and civil rights. In economic cases, too, he sometimes went along with the majority's support of government regulation of business, despite the fact that his private practice often involved the defense of antitrust and other actions involving the government.

Harlan fortified his formidable conservative record under Chief Justice Warren Burger after the Warren Court ended. But he nevertheless adhered to a balanced judicial profile by supporting some of the Court's liberal activist rulings. In the equality area, he maintained his support for desegregation, and he

joined the new chief justice's opinion expanding remedies against discriminatory employment tests in *Griggs v. Duke Power Co.* (1971). He continued his deep concern for Fourth Amendment rights in *Coolidge v. New Hampshire* (1971). The opinion in *Boddie* also came during this period. Harlan's reliance on the due process clause to reach this result was criticized, and the doctrine has not survived, but the case stands as a rare example of Harlan's reaching out to right an economic imbalance. In the First Amendment field, he wrote a widely cited opinion that protected the display on a jacket in a state courthouse of a "scurrilous epithet" ("fuck the draft") in protest against conscription (*Cohen v. California,* 1971).

What should one conclude from the many decisions in which Justice Harlan, a conservative, supported constitutional rights, often in highly controversial cases in which the Court was split? That he was in step with the majority of the Warren Court? Plainly not. There are too many instances where he marched separately. That he was essentially a civil libertarian? No again. Not only can one find too many cases to the contrary, but at a basic level, that is not the way Harlan reacted to injustice. This is not to say that he was insensitive to human suffering or unmoved by evidence of arbitrariness. It is rather that something else was at the core.

That something was Harlan's deep, almost visceral, desire to keep things in balance, to resist excess in any direction. Many times during my year as one of his clerks, I heard him say how important it was "to keep things on an even keel." To me, that is the master key to Harlan and his jurisprudence. One recalls Castle, the hero of Graham Greene's novel *The Human Factor,* as he muses on those who are "unable to love success or power or great beauty." Castle concludes that it is not because these people feel unworthy or are "more at home with failure," but that "one wanted the right balance." In reflecting on some of his own perplexing and self-destructive actions, Castle decides that "he was there to right the balance. That was all." Harlan was not a man who avoided success or power or, if one knew Mrs. Harlan, great beauty, but nevertheless, in his own eyes, he was there to right the balance. It is significant that he entitled a major speech at the American Bar Association "Thoughts at a Dedication: Keeping the Judicial Function in Balance."

The evidence of balance is apparent not only in the decisions discussed above, but in his elaborate views on doctrines of justiciability. These views are closely related to his frequent preoccupation with judicial modesty or, put negatively, his opposition to excessive judicial activism, which in turn is linked to the central theme of his judicial universe—federalism. Several years ago, I suggested that "his pervasive concern has been over a judiciary that will arrogate power not rightfully belonging to it and impose its views of government from a remote tower, thereby enervating the initiative and independence at the grass roots that are essential to a thriving democracy."

On the other hand, reflecting his balanced approach, Harlan wrote or joined many opinions that expanded the Court's jurisdiction. One was *Poe v. Ullman,* in which he vigorously dissented from Frankfurter's reasoning in dismissing a challenge to Connecticut's birth control law on the ground that the statute was not being enforced. Again, in *NAACP v. Alabama,* the first case explicitly recognizing a freedom of association, his opinion for the Court overcame difficult procedural obstacles involving the doctrines of standing and independent and adequate state grounds. In the first school prayer case, *Engel v. Vitale,* and again in the ruling that ordered the House of Representatives to seat Adam Clayton Powell, *Powell v. McCormack* (1969), both cases of unusual sensitivity, Harlan joined majority opinions that rejected substantial procedural defenses.

Stare decisis is another area relating to legal process and the judge's role in which Harlan sometimes manifested an activist spirit. He recognized that the doctrine "provides the stability and predictability required for the ordering of human affairs over the course of time and a basis of 'public faith in the judiciary as a source of impersonal and reasoned judgments.'" And although the principle should not be "woodenly applied," and "no precedent is sacrosanct,"

surely if the principle of *stare decisis* means anything in the law, it means that precedent should

not be jettisoned when the rule of yesterday remains viable, creates no injustice, and can reasonably be said to be no less sound than the rule sponsored by those who seek change, let alone incapable of being demonstrated wrong.

And in many cases he vigorously protested the overruling of precedent.

But many contrary instances show Harlan's flexibility. For example, he wrote separately in *Gideon v. Wainwright* (1963) to give *Betts v. Brady* (1942) "a more respectful burial than has been accorded" by the Court. In *Marchetti v. United States* (1968), he spoke for the Court in overruling a decision that denied the privilege against self-incrimination to gamblers prosecuted for failing to register and pay taxes. In *Moragne v. States Marine Line, Inc.* (1970), a celebrated opinion, he overruled a case (*The Harrisburg,* 1886) that "rested on a most dubious foundation when announced, has become an increasingly unjustifiable anomaly as the law over the years has left it behind, and . . . has produced litigation-spawning confusion in an area that should be easily susceptible of more workable solutions."

Finally, one may point to a series of cases in which Harlan exhibited a trait familiar to all of his law clerks—his exceptional open-mindedness and willingness to listen to new arguments. In these cases he dissented from the Court's refusal to hear oral argument on constitutional claims, although in each of them he was not predisposed to endorse the merits of the appeal. He joined Justice William O. Douglas's dissent from the refusal to hear a plea that a group was improperly ordered to register as a Communist-front organization (*Veterans of the Abraham Lincoln Brigade v. Subversive Activities Control Board,* 1965). And in perhaps the most far-reaching action, he would have set down for oral argument a complaint challenging the legality of the Vietnam War, *Massachusetts v. Laird* (1970), although he ordinarily accorded great deference to the elected branches of government on matters of war and peace.

The pattern of decisions provides ample proof that Harlan was not a one-dimensional justice. What is less obvious is the source of his drive to keep things in balance, to eschew an extreme ideology. Two possibilities may be suggested.

The first is the familiar notion that, in any society, patricians such as Harlan are concerned less with results in particular controversies—and certainly less about pressing any group against the wall—than with ensuring the smooth functioning of institutions without the precipitation of volatility or deep-seated enmities. They would hold that dissent should be allowed an outlet, that minorities should be able to hope, that political power should not become centralized and therefore dangerous. This belief explains Harlan's decisions supporting desegregation, a strong federal presence, and law and order. It also explains his fears about court-dominated legislative reapportionment and about the "incorporation" of the Bill of Rights through the Fourteenth Amendment that enhanced judicial authority and represented too dramatic a break with established doctrine. But it also accounts for Harlan's willingness to take reformist steps, to overrule outdated precedent selectively and before a problem worsened, and above all to listen closely to many voices.

These traits are consistent with Harlan's warm embrace of federalism principles. It should be recalled that the idea of federalism itself is a kind of balance—a way of dividing government authority to prevent a too-easy dominance of public life by a single institution or faction. *The Federalist Papers* are explicit in extolling, as a "guard against dangerous encroachments," the division of power "between two distinct governments" so that the "different governments will control each." Years ago I reflected on whether the national government or states and local governments are the more secure bulwark of—or the greater threat to—civil liberty.

Local units are closer to the people but offer more opportunity for undetected discrimination and repression. The national government acts more visibly and with more formal regard for minority interests, but its vast power is a civil liberties time bomb that in this century has brought us the Palmer Raids, McCarthyism, and Watergate.

Whatever the proper resolution of this question, it is clear that Harlan believed, as much as he believed in any principle, that federalism was "a bulwark of freedom."

A second source of Harlan's overall philosophy is legal process theory, which had its heyday during almost exactly the period that he served on the Court. In the early 1950s Henry Hart produced a draft of the work that he and Albert Sacks published at Harvard Law School in a "tentative edition" in 1958 (it was also the final edition). The moderate philosophy embodied in these materials, entitled "The Legal Process: Basic Problems in the Making and Application of Law," was tailor-made to Harlan's personality. It emphasized the central role that procedure plays in ensuring judicial and legislative objectivity and argued that "just" policies will result when each branch of government works within its assigned role. In this way courts through "reasoned elaboration" of decisions, and legislatures through the public-seeking interpretation of statutes, will ensure maximum fulfillment of society's expectations.

Harlan was attracted to this theory, which enabled him to take constitutional steps as long as they were not too long or jarring. At the same time, it offered him ample institutional reasons for resisting excessive judicial authority. This approach was often enlisted in opinions that were inhospitable to civil liberties, but Harlan's reliance on legal process also led him at times to the protection of individual rights and the overruling of outmoded precedent. By 1971, when Harlan left the Supreme Court, legal process theory, buffeted by events in society at large, was beginning to lose its hold, even at Harvard, and the more extreme philosophies of law and economics and critical legal studies soon moved to the forefront. The struggle within the Court became ever more polarized as in succeeding years strong civil libertarians, which Harlan was not, waged battle with doctrinaire conservatives, which he also was not.

It fell to John Marshall Harlan, by nature a patrician traditionalist, to serve on a Supreme Court that, for most of his years, was rapidly revising and liberalizing constitutional law. In these circumstances, it is not surprising that he would protest the direction of the Court and the speed with which it was traveling. He did this in a remarkably forceful and principled manner, thereby providing balance to the institution and the law it generated. Despite this role, Harlan joined civil liberties rulings on the Court during his tenure to the degree that his overall jurisprudence can fairly be characterized as conservative primarily in the sense that it evinced caution, a fear of centralized authority, and a respect for process.

—*Norman Dorsen*

BIBLIOGRAPHY

Justice Harlan's papers are deposited in the Seeley G. Mudd Manuscript Library at Princeton University. Tinsley H. Yarbrough, *John Marshall Harlan: Great Dissenter of the Warren Court* (1992), is the only comprehensive biography, and it provides considerable information on Harlan's life as well as his career on the Supreme Court. David L. Shapiro, ed., *The Evolution of a Judicial Philosophy: Selected Opinions and Papers of Justice John M. Harlan* (1969), is a compilation of opinions, speeches, and tributes through June 1968, carefully selected and edited by a former law clerk. More recent is "John Marshall Harlan II: Remembrances by His Law Clerks," *Journal of Supreme Court History* 27 (2002): 138.

Various articles and symposia worth consulting are: Henry J. Bourguignon, "The Second Mr. Justice Harlan: His Principles of Judicial Decision Making," *Supreme Court Review* (1979): 251; Centennial Conference in Honor of Justice John Marshall Harlan, *New York Law School Law Review* 36 (1991): 1, which includes contributions by judges, former law clerks, and scholars on Harlan as a judicial conservative, Harlan and the Bill of Rights, and Harlan's legal process; "Comment, The Legitimacy of Civil Law Rea-soning in the Common Law: Justice Harlan's Contribution," *Yale Law Journal* 82 (1972): 258; Norman Dorsen, "The Second Mr. Justice Harlan: A Constitutional Conservative," *New York University Law Review* 44 (1969): 249; Daniel A. Farber, "Civilizing Public Discourse: An Essay on Professor Bickel, Justice Harlan, and the Enduring Significance of Cohen v. California," *Duke Law Journal* (1980): 283; and "Mr. Justice Harlan," *Harvard Law Review* 85 (1971): 369, consisting of articles on the occasion of his retirement by Earl Warren, J. Edward Lumbard, John B. F. Wood, Henry J. Friendly, and Charles Nesson.

NOTEWORTHY OPINIONS

Griffin v. Illinois, 351 U.S. 12 (1956) (Dissent)

Kent v. Dulles, 357 U.S. 116 (1958)

NAACP v. Alabama ex rel. Patterson, 357 U.S. 449 (1958)

Barenblatt v. United States, 360 U.S. 109 (1959)

Poe v. Ullman, 367 U.S. 497 (1961) (Dissent)

Baker v. Carr, 369 U.S. 186 (1962) (Dissent)

Gideon v. Wainwright, 372 U.S. 335 (1963) (Concurrence)

Douglas v. California, 372 U.S. 353 (1963) (Dissent)

Reynolds v. Sims, 377 U.S. 533 (1964) (Dissent)

Katzenbach v. Morgan, 383 U.S. 301 (1966) (Dissent)

Afroyim v. Rusk, 387 U.S. 253 (1967)

Marchetti v. United States, 390 U.S. 39 (1968)

Street v. New York, 394 U.S. 576 (1969)

Welsh v. United States, 398 U.S. 333 (1970)

Boddie v. Connecticut, 401 U.S. 371 (1971)

Cohen v. California, 403 U.S. 15 (1971)

New York Times Co. v. United States, 403 U.S. 713 (1971) (Dissent)

OLIVER WENDELL HOLMES JR.

Birth: March 8, 1841, Boston, Massachusetts.

Education: Harvard College, A.B., 1861; LL.B., 1866.

Official Positions: Associate justice, Supreme Judicial Court of Massachusetts, 1882–1899; chief justice, 1899–1902.

Supreme Court Service: Nominated associate justice by President Theodore Roosevelt, December 2, 1902, to replace Horace Gray, who had died; confirmed by the Senate, December 4, 1902, by a voice vote; took judicial oath December 8, 1902; retired January 12, 1932, replaced by Benjamin N. Cardozo, nominated by President Herbert Hoover.

Death: March 6, 1935, Washington, D.C.

Oliver Wendell Holmes Jr. is one of the best-known Supreme Court justices in history, and commentators consistently rank him as one of the "great" justices to sit on the Court. Holmes is also notable in engendering more literature, both scholarly and popular, than any other justice. Today, his life and career continue to be objects of fascination.

Holmes had literary aspirations as an undergraduate at Harvard, but they were postponed in the spring of his senior year, when the Civil War began. Holmes left Harvard, enlisted in the Twentieth Regiment of Massachusetts Volunteers, and in July 1861 secured a commission as a lieutenant.

Holmes's Civil War service was one of the memorable episodes in his life. He served until June 1864 and was wounded three times, in the chest, neck, and heel. The first two wounds were life-threatening, with only the fortunate trajectory of the bullets sparing him. For the remainder of his life, Holmes thought of his experiences in the war as especially vivid and meaningful. He claimed that his generation had been uniquely favored ("touched with fire") in being the first to participate in the "crusade" of the Civil War. He romanticized the experience of participating in war, as opposed to war itself, which he once described as "horrible and dull." In 1895 he wrote an essay, "The Soldier's Faith," in which he characterized the attitude that made a soldier throw his life away for a cause that he could not comprehend as "true and adorable."

After his wartime service, Holmes returned to Boston, attended Harvard Law School, and completed his studies in 1866. The next several years were devoted to practicing law and a variety of related activities. He wrote essays on legal history and jurisprudence for the *American Law Review* and served as its coeditor from 1870 to 1873; he edited a volume of James Kent's *Commentaries on American Law;* wrote an influential book, *The Common Law* (1881); and briefly joined the Harvard law faculty. Holmes was appointed an associate justice of the Supreme Judicial Court of Massachusetts in December 1881. He had always wanted to be a judge, feeling that academic life was "half life" and law practice was insufficiently theoretical. By 1899 he was chief justice of the Massachusetts court.

For all of Holmes's dedication to his work and satisfaction with it, the demands of the Massachusetts court were not sufficient to meet his intellectual energies. During the twenty years he served, he continued to write scholarly articles and to make speeches and addresses, publishing them in a volume, *Speeches,* in 1891. "The Soldier's Faith" was one such address. It came to the attention of Gov. Theodore Roosevelt, R-N.Y., in the late 1890s, who was impressed with its apparently jingoistic sentiment.

On July 9, 1902, Justice Horace Gray, who was gravely ill, sent his resignation to President Roosevelt but said he would remain on the Court until the president named his successor. Roosevelt selected Holmes on August 11, a month before Gray's death on September 15.

Cautious to the end, Holmes did not resign from the Massachusetts court until the Senate received the nomination and formally confirmed him in early December. At age sixty-one Holmes and his wife, Fanny, moved to Washington to start a new life. In the early months of his tenure, Holmes wrote friends of his wonder and delight in the magnitude of the task: the capacities of his fellow judges, the breadth of the legal questions, the energized political atmosphere of Washington. Ten years later, however, Holmes no longer felt that his job was completely absorbing. He had found that he could easily keep up with the work of the Court, being able

Oliver Wendell Holmes Jr.

to dash off his assigned opinions and help recalcitrant justices with their work. In his leisure time he returned to his lifelong hobbies of reading and correspondence, and as his personal contacts narrowed, his correspondence friendships increased. After 1912 the circle of his friends began to change, as his older contemporaries were dying. In their place he sought the company of a younger generation of intellectuals, among them Felix Frankfurter, Harold Laski, Learned Hand, Herbert Croly, Walter Lippmann, and Zechariah Chafee.

In seeking out the company of new friends, Holmes was also seeking recognition. As surprising as it may seem, Holmes in 1912, after ten years on the Court, was still essentially unknown, not only to the lay public, but to all but a handful of lawyers. To the extent he had developed a reputation, it was with a few "progressive" intellectuals who had found in his dissent in *Lochner v. New York* (1905), which tested the constitutionality of a state law fixing minimum hours of work in the baking industry, the outlines of an appropriately deferential judicial attitude toward reformist social legislation. Beyond *Lochner,* which had only begun to be celebrated by 1912, many Court watchers found Holmes enigmatic and his opinions obscure.

A tally sheet of Holmes's major opinions during the first fifteen years of his tenure, 1902–1917, produces a record that seems at variance with subsequent images of Holmes as a judge. Not only was he a largely unrecognized figure during those years, but also the principal attributes of his later images—that he was an enlightened judge in his deference to progressive legislation and that he was a supporter of civil liberties—are hard to square with the thrust of his decisions.

The best evidence of Holmes's attributed enlightenment can be found in a line of decisions, including *Lochner,* in which he made it clear that judges should not supersede the policies of legislatures on questions of economic policy. He had announced this posture in his very first opinion for the Court, *Otis v. Parker* (1903), a case testing the constitutionality of a California statute prohibiting contracts for the sales on margin of corporate capital stock. "It by no means is true," Holmes wrote, "that every law is void which may seem to the judges who pass on it excessive, unsuited to its ostensible end, or based on conceptions of morality with which they disagree." A similar posture marked his dissent in *Lochner* and his dissents in *Adair v. United States* (1907), *Noble State Bank v. Haskell* (1911), and *Coppage v. Kansas* (1914), all of which protested against judicial use of the doctrine of "liberty of contract," ostensibly derived from the Fourteenth Amendment's due process clause, to invalidate social legislation. In all those dissents Holmes deferred judgment on the wisdom of the legislation in question, while reiterating that, as he put it in *Haskell,* "Judges should be slow to read into the [Constitution] a [mandate to void] . . . the legislative power."

Such opinions identified Holmes as having a clear and consistent approach to the scope of constitutional review in cases of social legislation. He was opposed to judicial glosses on the constitutional text, such as "liberty of contract," as a means of substituting the ideology of judges for that of legislators, so long as legislative decisions were rationally based. Judicial intervention, in his view, was reserved for the case of the overwhelming constitutional mandate, such as a statute that offended the exact text of the Constitution. The opinions were not, however, necessarily supportive of any ideological position on the legitimacy of social legislation. Progressives, who supported regulation of the industrial marketplace to foster desirable social ends, endorsed Holmes's results in the cases, but Holmes did not necessarily share that attitude.

Beyond that line of decisions and *Swift & Company v. United States* (1905), in which Holmes found that an agreement among shippers of fresh meat to fix prices came within the reach of the Sherman Antitrust Act of 1887, he wrote few opinions that early twentieth-century progressives would have found congenial. In the most celebrated case of Holmes's early tenure, *Northern Securities Co. v. United States* (1904), he was conspicuously on the "wrong" side. The Roosevelt administration had sought to apply the Sherman Antitrust Act, which outlawed "every contract, combination in the form of trust or otherwise, or conspiracy, in restraint of trade among the several states," against a holding company capitalized from the stock of competitor railroads. The Court ruled, 5–4, that the creation of the holding company violated the act. Holmes dissented, arguing that the meaning of the terms *contract, combination,* and *conspiracy* in the act could only be the technical meaning at common law; otherwise, any two-party agreement between competitors of any size would violate the law. For this arguably commonsensical position, he received the enmity of Roosevelt, who said that Holmes had been "a bitter disappointment . . . on the bench."

Similarly, in *Dr. Miles Medical Company v. John D. Park & Sons Company* (1911), Holmes declined to apply the Sherman act to an agreement between a manufacturer of proprietary medicines and representatives of drugstores in which the prices of patent medicines were fixed. In dissenting from a majority opinion that the price-fixing scheme violated the act, Holmes said that "I think . . . it is safe to say that the most enlightened judicial policy is to let people manage their own business in their own way, unless the ground for interference is very clear." He then went on to say that, in his view, the meaning of the term "fair price" was the "point of most profitable returns." That point "marked the equilibrium of social desires" and determines the fair price. This was an astonishingly unprogressive statement in its espousal of judicial noninterference with the economic marketplace and its assumption that whatever was profitable in that marketplace was fair.

If Holmes's early decisions on social legislation permit him to be labeled a progressive judge only with strain, his early decisions on civil liberties were equally inconsistent with a later stereotype of Holmes as a liberal. Here, context is again important. Early twentieth-century progressives were concerned primarily with redressing economic inequalities and did not address minority rights beyond the sphere of industrial relations. The oft-described tension in American liberal thought between support for government regulation and solicitude for minority rights did not surface until later in the century.

Even so, Holmes's early decisions were notably unsympathetic to minority rights. In the midst of widespread discrimination against blacks in the early decades of the twentieth century, the Court regularly supported the positions of black claimants who sought relief against government-supported racial discrimination. Holmes, however, was not usually part of the Court majorities who upheld minority claims. In *Bailey v. Alabama* (1911), for example, the Court invalidated an Alabama statute that made the breach of a contract *prima facie* evidence of fraud as inconsistent with the Thirteenth Amendment's prohibition of slavery. The Court reasoned that such statutes, invariably applied to contracts between black farm laborers and their employers, effectively prevented laborers from terminating their contracts except in the unlikely event that they were able to repay advanced wages at the time of termination. Holmes, dissenting, argued that given the tendency of black laborers "to remain during a part of the season, receiving advances, and then to depart at the period of need in the hope of greater wages at a neighboring plantation," the statute was a reasonable device to ensure the performance of labor agreements. "The power of the states to make breach of contract a crime," he asserted, "is not done away with by the abolition of slavery."

In *United States v. Reynolds* (1914), however, Holmes joined a decision invalidating a comparable arrangement, the criminal-surety practice. Under that practice, persons convicted of minor offenses and ordered to pay fines could enter into arrangements with other persons to have their fines paid in exchange for labor. Evidence in Alabama and Georgia, which permitted the arrangements, was that they were used overwhelmingly in cases involving black farm laborers and often resulted in laborers being subject to what the Court called "an ever-turning wheel of servitude." A unanimous Court concluded that the practices amounted to peonage and invalidated them.

Holmes wrote a separate concurrence revealing his motivation in supporting the Court's position. After reiterating his view that the Thirteenth Amendment did not prevent states from criminalizing breaches of contract, Holmes indicated that he thought the application of the criminal-surety practice to contracts involving black laborers particularly unfortunate:

> [I]mpulsive people with little intelligence or foresight may be expected to lay hold of anything that affords a relief from present pain, even though it will cause greater trouble by and by. The successive [surety] contracts, each for a longer term than the last, are the inevitable, and must be taken to have been the contemplated, outcome of the Alabama laws.

Holmes's posture in *Reynolds* amounted to a scrutiny of the motives of legislation and a conclusion that those motives were race conscious. This stance was unusual for Holmes, given his deference to legislation and his indifference to claims based on racial discrimination. Yet Holmes's position in *Reynolds* amounted to the exception that proved the rule: his scrutiny was precipitated by his conviction that the system was deliberately designed to take advantage of the "impulsiveness" of black laborers. Ordinarily, Holmes eschewed paternalism in economic relationships, but in *Reynolds* he inclined toward paternalism because he accepted the stereotype of black "impulsiveness." His race consciousness was a consciousness based on white supremacy.

Holmes's general indifference to the claims of minorities surfaced even more starkly in his decisions involving aliens, in which he allowed the federal government and individual states sweeping powers over them. In three cases, *United States v. Sing Tuck* (1904), *United States v. Ju Toy* (1905), and *Patsone v. Pennsylvania* (1914), Holmes wrote majority opinions for the Court denying the constitutional claims of aliens. The first two cases involved efforts on the part of Chinese petitioners to prove that they were U.S. citizens. Holmes upheld as constitutional federal administrative proceedings requiring the testimony of two witnesses that a petitioner had been born in the United States and making the determinations of immigration officials on the question of an applicant's citizenship conclusive without provision for judicial review.

Not only could the federal government summarily exclude aliens from the country, states also had apparent impunity to discriminate against aliens who resided within their borders. That was the message of Holmes's decision in *Patsone*. The Pennsylvania legislature, in the wake of labor unrest, had passed a statute making it unlawful for any unnaturalized foreign-born resident to kill wildlife and thereby prohibited resident aliens from owning or possessing firearms. The statute, enacted a month after an agreement between Pennsylvania coal mine operators and mine workers had expired, was clearly the legislature's attempt to reduce the possibility of violence in the mines. Pennsylvania had made no effort to show that aliens, as a class, were more dangerous to wildlife than citizens. The legislation had nothing to do with the dangers aliens posed to wildlife, but everything to do with the dangers aliens in the labor force purportedly posed to the public at large.

It is easy enough to critique *Patsone,* but seen from the perspective of judicial review, Holmes's opinion is instructive. He may have believed that, given principles of sovereignty, states could exclude aliens entirely from their borders. He may have felt that, given the mandates of sovereignty, legislative pronouncements in an area in which legislative supremacy was unquestioned were in effect unreviewable. That was a consistent and defensible position, but it obliterated the impact of constitutional clauses designed to restrict legislative power. If a state could invoke its sovereignty as a basis for the most arbitrary sort of classification, it was hard to know

the meaning of equal protection of the law as a constitutional principle.

Not much in Holmes's early career on the Court, then, lends support for the characterization of him as a civil libertarian, any more than for the characterization of him as a progressive or liberal judge. The case for Holmes in those capacities has rested largely on two features of his later years on the Court. The first of these was his continued dissenting posture in liberty of contract and other cases in which conservative majorities used doctrinal glosses on constitutional provisions to limit the scope of social legislation. The second was his emergence, after 1919, as a champion of free speech.

One way to resolve the apparent contradiction between Holmes's image and his early decisions is to suggest that his judicial stance changed with time, that he became more liberal as he aged. Perhaps Holmes's new set of friends, the group of younger progressive intellectuals, became his principal intellectual constituency, and through them he became acquainted with the issues that progressives thought important. Strong evidence exists that in the area of free speech Holmes's progressive friends had a direct impact on the way he conceptualized speech issues in the last years of his tenure.

This suggestion, on balance, must be rejected. Holmes's jurisprudence, even taking free speech issues into account, remained largely of a piece during his whole career on the Court. He was only accidentally a progressive, and a liberal only with respect to certain kinds of speech issues. The emergence of his image as a progressive and liberal judge rests largely on the selective publicization of others and on the fortuitous affinity between Holmes's extremely limited theory of judicial review and the social goals of progressives. Even Holmes's allegedly libertarian posture on speech, which emerged very late in his career, arguably rests more on a few memorable sentences in his opinions than on a consistent jurisprudential theory.

Two sets of cases illustrate these conclusions. The first set is Holmes's opinions between 1917 and 1931 on cases testing the constitutionality of social legislation and includes *Hammer v. Dagenhart* (1918), *Truax v. Corrigan* (1921), *Pennsylvania Coal Co. v. Mahon* (1922), *Adkins v. Children's Hospital* (1923), *Tyson & Brother v. Banton* (1927), and *Buck v. Bell* (1927), among others. The second set is Holmes's free speech opinions, ranging from his early decisions in *Patterson v. Colorado* (1907) and *Fox v. Washington* (1915) through his 1919 decisions testing the constitutionality of the Espionage Act of 1917, *Schenck v. United States* and *Abrams v. United States,* to his notable later statements about free speech in *Gitlow v. New York* (1925) and *United States v. Schwimmer* (1929).

The first set of cases does not establish Holmes as an ideological progressive: it merely provides additional evidence of his opposition to substantive judicial readings of open-ended clauses in the Constitution. *Hammer* and *Adkins* were eloquent critiques of the doctrine of liberty of contract, reinforcing the position Holmes had previously advanced in *Lochner, Adair,* and *Coppage.* In all those decisions, Holmes sustained state regulatory power, which he supported because of his positivist inclinations, not because he cared about the evils of child labor (*Hammer*), the level of wages paid hospital workers (*Adkins*), or the regulation of theater ticket prices (*Banton*).

Mahon and *Buck v. Bell* are less easily reconciled with a progressive ideological agenda, although both were arguably consistent with Holmes's ideological instincts as a judge. In *Mahon,* a coal company had sold off its surface land rights for development, retaining its subsurface mineral rights. When Pennsylvania forbade subsurface mining in areas where public buildings, thoroughfares, or private houses were located, the company challenged the statute as a violation of its property and contract rights. In his majority opinion, Holmes maintained that the contract and due process clauses imposed limits on the capacity of legislatures to take property without compensation. He seems to have been motivated by commonsensical propositions. The company had retained subsurface rights, and, given its business, the principal value of the land to it lay in those rights. Those who acquired land from the company could have acquired the subsurface rights as well. Moreover, the contract

and due process clauses were strong textual mandates for constitutional limitations on legislative conduct.

Holmes's progressive friends declined comment on *Mahon.* The opinion, however, has had nothing of the notoriety over the years of Holmes's decision in *Buck v. Bell,* in which he sustained the constitutionality of a Virginia statute providing for compulsory sterilization of certain inmates in state mental institutions. The statute established a procedure by which inmates were labeled "mentally deficient" and sterilized so as to keep them from "perpetuating their kind" and adding to the burden on state facilities. The inmates did not have much opportunity to demonstrate their ineligibility for sterilization, nor did the state advance a convincing justification for why only inmates of state facilities, rather than "mental defectives" in the general population, were singled out for sterilization.

Holmes summarily dismissed both the due process and equal protection arguments. He felt that compulsory sterilization was akin to compulsory vaccination, and that "three generations of imbeciles," a label he mistakenly applied to Carrie Buck and her family, were "enough." He downplayed equal protection as "the usual last resort of constitutional arguments." In contrast to many of his decisions, in *Buck v. Bell,* Holmes did not exhibit indifference toward the social policy embodied in the statute he was sustaining. He was an enthusiast for eugenics, the movement that had precipitated the *Buck* statute. Many progressives embraced eugenics as a worthwhile reform. The movement became somewhat tarnished by its Nazi adherents, but in the 1920s Nazi-style "population control" had not yet been anticipated.

On balance, Holmes's later decisions on social legislation exhibited the same consciousness as his earlier opinions. He began with a presumption that legislatures, being majoritarian and positivist institutions, could do what they wanted: the scope of judge-created constitutional review was narrow. He was at bottom a Darwinist, a Malthusian, and a fatalist, so his enthusiasm for reformist legislation was extremely limited. He believed that the idea that judges were constrained by some disembodied, transcendental entity called "the law" was nonsense. Judges, he concluded, had ample opportunities to be creative law-makers, and consequently should be loath to write their views on public policy into constitutional doctrine. Because a constitution was made "for people of differing views," judges should avoid substituting their doctrinal glosses for the text.

A generation of early twentieth-century intellectuals sought to make Holmes a progressive judge for their own purposes, and the label so attached itself to him that it took forty years, and the more searching scrutiny of a later generation puzzled by Holmes's apparent indifference to civil liberties, to complicate matters and begin a new phase in Holmesian historiography. But one dimension of his jurisprudence has appeared as resolutely progressive or liberal—his apparent sympathy for dissident, "unpopular" speakers, and his apparent championing of what he called "the principle of freedom for the thought we hate."

Here again Holmes has been widely misunderstood, as commentators, seduced by the power of his rhetoric, have ignored the pattern of his decisions. But there are complicating factors. In contrast to his decisions on social legislation, in which Holmes immediately adopted and followed a consistent jurisprudential posture, his opinions on free speech underwent a process of change distinctly in the direction of protecting speech. By the end of his career, Holmes treated freedom of speech issues as raising the most serious constitutional questions, whereas earlier he had apparently assumed that the First and Fourteenth Amendments added little to the doctrinal status of speech at common law.

Up to the end of World War I, Holmes's views on free speech were orthodox and restrictive. In *Patterson v. Colorado* and *Fox v. Washington,* he summarily dismissed free speech claims by newspaper editors who had criticized the motives of Colorado judges and championed the cause of public nudity. In *Patterson,* he stated that First Amendment protection applied only to prior restraints on speech, not speech that had been published. In both cases he indicated that speech could be suppressed if it had a "tendency" to encourage illegal or undesirable conduct, even without evidence that such conduct had occurred. The decisions

treated the First Amendment as adding nothing to the common law, which held objectionable speech as no different from any other socially undesirable act.

In 1919 Holmes confronted the scope of congressional power to suppress speech in four cases testing the constitutionality of the Espionage Act of 1917 and the Sedition Act of 1918, the most sweeping effort on the part of the federal government to restrict "subversive" speech since the Alien and Sedition Acts of 1797. Those statutes criminalized expressions having the effect of causing insubordination in the armed forces or of obstructing the recruitment or enlistment of soldiers, and expressions advocating any "curtailment of production" of the war effort.

Holmes wrote opinions in all the cases. The leading two, doctrinally, were *Schenck* and *Abrams;* the most popularly celebrated was *Debs v. United States,* which involved the incarceration of Eugene Debs, a prominent Socialist politician, for declaring his opposition to the war. (The fourth was *Frohwerk v. United States.*) Holmes laid down an apparently consistent doctrinal position: the constitutional test for whether allegedly subversive speech could be criminally prosecuted was whether it created a "clear and present danger" that the evils described by the statute would occur. In laying down the clear and present danger test, Holmes explicitly abandoned his position in *Patterson* that the First Amendment's protection was confined to prior restraints, and he intimated that the clear and present danger test was intended to supplant the "bad tendency" test he had employed in *Patterson* and *Fox.*

In actuality, the situation was far less clear. After mentioning the clear and present danger test in upholding the legislation in *Schenck,* Holmes did not refer to it again in either *Frohwerk* or *Debs,* even though the facts of those cases suggested that the expressions were too remotely related to interference with the war effort to make out a clear and present danger. Then, in *Abrams,* Holmes, this time in dissent, appeared to deviate from his earlier opinions in his understanding of clear and present danger. The *Abrams* case involved the convictions of Russian-speaking immigrants, sympathetic to the anti-Bolshevik forces in Russia, who distributed leaflets to munitions workers urging them not to manufacture weapons that were going to be used against their Russian comrades. Holmes rephrased the clear and present danger test to read "clear and imminent danger" and argued that the leaflets were too inept in their syntax and content to have any serious effect. He then declared, "We should be eternally vigilant against attempts to check the expression of opinions that we loathe and believe fraught with death, unless they so imminently threaten immediate interference with the lawful and pressing purposes of the law that an immediate check is required to save the country." This statement was a much more speech-protective reading of the "clear and present danger" formula than Holmes had previously made.

From *Abrams* on, one could chart a progression of Holmesian First Amendment decisions in which speech received greater and greater protection, including *Gitlow, Schwimmer,* and *United States ex rel. Milwaukee Social Democratic Publishing Co. v. Burleson* (1921). In *Burleson,* Holmes argued in dissent that the postmaster general could not summarily deny second-class mail privileges on the basis of a publication's content, a marked departure from his opinion in *McAuliffe v. New Bedford* (1892) from his days on the Supreme Judicial Court of Massachusetts. In *McAuliffe,* a policeman had been dismissed for political campaigning, and Holmes had argued that because New Bedford could decline to hire policemen at all, it could establish the terms of their employment. In *Burleson,* he conceded that the United States could terminate its postal service, but that "greater power" did not apparently subsume the "lesser power" to condition access to that service on the content of publications.

Gitlow and *Schwimmer* went even further. In *Gitlow,* the New York legislature had provided criminal penalties for speech advocating the overthrow of the government and had subsequently convicted Benjamin Gitlow for circulating "The Communist Manifesto," a document that called in general terms for "revolutionary mass action" but specifically recommended only "mass political strikes." Even though no

evidence suggested that the publication of the "Manifesto" had "any effect," a majority of the Court held this fact immaterial because the statute proscribed advocacy itself. In such situations the clear and present danger test did not apply because the legislature had predetermined that certain types of advocacy imminently threatened the body politic.

Holmes dissented, and his dissent contained some startling statements. "Every idea is an incitement," he declared, and the "only difference" between the expression of an opinion and "an incitement in the narrower sense" is "the speaker's enthusiasm for the result." "If in the long run the beliefs expressed in proletarian dictatorship are destined to be accepted by the dominant forces of the community," he said, "the only meaning of free speech is that they be given their chance and have their way." These two comments appeared to endorse a view of speech well beyond that embodied in the clear and present danger test. That test had implicitly distinguished between speeches and incitements, with the latter a category of speeches that bore a close enough connection to danger to the state that they could be suppressed. In suggesting that the only difference between a speech and an incitement was the speaker's enthusiasm for the result, Holmes seemed to be suggesting that clear and present danger was a subjective rather than an objective formulation, which robbed it of its utility. One could hardly let a speaker decide whether his or her speech posed a danger to the state if there were to be any restrictions on speech.

Even more puzzling were Holmes's comments about "the only meaning of free speech." They suggested that the test for whether the beliefs of proletarian dictatorship were legitimate was their eventual acceptance or rejection by the dominant forces of the community, not their initially incendiary character. The logic of this statement led to complete protection for all speech, with the market, as signified by the views of dominant forces, being the ultimate determinant of legitimacy. Some speech might not eventually "have [its] way," but all speech needed to be "given [its] chance." The dominant forces, however, could eventually suppress any speech they disapproved of.

As interpreted, the statement seemed inconsistent with all of Holmes's free speech decisions since *Schenck,* in which he had assumed that the First Amendment placed some limits on majoritarian repression of unpopular speech.

If Holmes's dissent in *Gitlow* is read as a libertarian document, his progression from a restrictive to an ultralibertarian conception of free speech was completed in *Schwimmer,* in which he applied the First Amendment in a context where it had never before been applied. That context was the deportation of resident aliens, a class of persons, Holmes had argued in *Sing Tuck* and *Ju Toy,* that were afforded no constitutional protection.

In *Schwimmer,* a forty-nine-year-old citizen of Hungary who had been a resident of the United States for several years filed an application for American citizenship. On her application form she declined to give an affirmative answer to a question as to whether she would take up arms in the defense of the United States, citing her belief in pacifism. The Immigration and Naturalization Service summarily denied her application. When she challenged that denial, a federal appellate court held that the denial was improper because as a forty-nine-year-old woman she would not be asked to take up arms. A majority of the Supreme Court reversed and instituted the original denial of citizenship.

Holmes, in dissent, repeated the argument that Schwimmer's pacifism was irrelevant because she would not be asked to take up arms. He then went on, however, to suggest that *Schwimmer* was a free speech case. He wrote:

> If there is any principle of the Constitution that more imperatively calls for attachment than any other, it is the principle of free thought—not free thought for those who agree with us but freedom for the thought we hate. I think that we should adhere to that principle with regard to admission into, as well as to life within this country.

The oddity of that statement was that Congress had no requirement to adhere to the First Amendment, or any other constitutional provision, in naturalization cases. Congress had the undoubted power to condition American citizenship on the avowal of certain beliefs, just as it had the power to condition citizenship on health requirements. Holmes had made much of that sovereign power in his earlier decisions concerning aliens. Now he was suggesting that the constitutional principle of free speech ought to apply "with regard to admission into, as well as life within this country."

It is hard to imagine that, by the time he wrote *Schwimmer* in 1929, Holmes had reconsidered his position on sovereignty and alien rights and concluded that the Constitution, after all, did apply to aliens. *Schwimmer* was an example of Holmes's tendency, not only in free speech cases but throughout his opinions, to prefer a memorable, sweeping phrase to analytical or doctrinal consistency. *Patterson, Schenck, Abrams, Gitlow,* and *Schwimmer* were doctrinally irreconcilable: Holmes had successively announced a battery of tests and conceptions of the impact of the First Amendment in subversive speech cases, and the tests and conceptions could not be squared with one another. Only in *Schenck* had Holmes explicitly rejected one of his earlier conceptions: in *Schwimmer* he said that the "position and motives" of the petitioner were "wholly different from those of Schenck," as if the two cases should be decided in the same constitutional framework. That suggestion was analytically bizarre.

The *Patterson-Schwimmer* sequence suggests that it is not very fruitful to approach Holmes's free speech opinions seeking doctrinal or even philosophical consistency. Even what might be called a progression in those opinions of greater solicitude for speech requires qualification in light of some other decisions, such as *Gilbert v. Minnesota* (1920) or the companion cases of *Meyer v. Nebraska* and *Bartels v. Iowa* (1923), in which Holmes either permitted state restrictions on speech in circumstances where a clear and present danger did not seem to have been demonstrated, or failed to conceptualize the cases as raising free speech issues at all. In the *Meyer-Bartels* cases, certain states had attempted to prohibit the teaching of foreign languages before the eighth grade, apparently on the grounds of patriotism and anti-German sentiment. Although Holmes conceded that such statutes infringed on the "liberty of teacher and scholar," he thought them constitutional. He either did not see the liberty to receive information about a foreign language or culture as raising First Amendment issues or he thought the states' interest in promoting a common tongue compelling. That position was impossible to square with *Schwimmer*.

On balance, Holmes's free speech opinions were not so much evidence of a progressive or liberal sensibility as they were evidence of the unique complex of values that made up his judicial posture. As a judge, Holmes was deeply interested in exploring the philosophical foundations of legal issues and identifying his philosophical stance toward those issues. He was far less interested in doctrinal or analytical consistency, and his philosophical views, rendered in terms of the political ideologies of his day, did not easily mark him as progressive, liberal, or conservative.

Free speech was the sort of issue that Holmes enjoyed ruminating about. He had first conceived speech as no different from any other social act and therefore entitled to no greater protection than unpopular conduct. As he was forced to think more about speech in the context of the wartime subversive speech cases, he began to recognize a strong social interest in encouraging even unpopular speech as part of the process by which persons exchange ideas in a democratic society. He disengaged speech from an older liberty framework, which had included liberty of contract and of which he was highly skeptical, and began to conceive of it as a philosophical principle of freedom in a democracy—freedom to protest, to express one's individuality, to articulate "fighting faiths." He began to associate this principle with his deterministic views on majoritarian power and historical change, and he concluded that suppressing speech was wrongheaded and ultimately fruitless. In so doing he was not endorsing the substance of unpopular views: he continued to express indifference toward them, as he had toward progressive social legislation. In short, free speech for Holmes was a com-

plicated and important philosophical puzzle. Addressing such puzzles was one of the things he liked best to do as a judge.

Another thing Holmes liked to do as a judge was to write his opinions "with style." Style for Holmes meant an emphasis on the pithy, arresting, often cryptic or ambiguous aphorism. Such Holmesian aphorisms have a capacity to linger in the memories of readers. It is far easier to summon up their language than to explain them. In the area of free speech, Holmes experimented with a number of memorable phrases, and although they vividly encompassed some of the philosophical complexities of free speech issues, they did little to clarify those issues or, for that matter, Holmes's position on them. To affirm the principle of "freedom for the thought we hate" or to suggest that "the only meaning of free speech" is that unpopular doctrines may ultimately "have their way" is to state, in memorable fashion, one of the central philosophical rationales for protection for speech in a society committed to democratic forms of change.

When one asks what follows from the statements for lawyers and judges charged with analyzing and deciding free speech issues, the statements evaporate. Holmes was not particularly interested in that dimension of judicial decision making, nor in the political labels others attached to his work. An irony of Holmes's career is that so few commentators have granted him his preferences. As a judge, he wrote to Canon Patrick Sheehan in 1912, he wanted "to put as many new ideas into the law as I can, to show how particular solutions involve general theory, and to do it with style." He pursued those goals avidly and successfully throughout his judicial career. One may be frustrated by the dimensions of judging that his blueprint leaves out, but one should resist trying to recast his jurisprudential sensibility.

—*G. Edward White*

BIBLIOGRAPHY

The Oliver Wendell Holmes Jr. papers, in the Harvard Law School Library, have been issued in a microfilm edition by University Publications of America (1985). The Holmes papers contain about 29,000 items, the bulk of which is correspondence. Several of Holmes's correspondences, including those with Harold Laski, Frederick Pollock, Lewis Einstein, Clare Castletown, Felix Frankfurter, Morris Cohen, Canon Patrick Sheehan, Franklin Ford, and John C. H. Wu, have been published. The major unpublished correspondence collections in the Holmes papers are those with John Wigmore and John Chipman Gray, and his wife, Nina. Other items in the Holmes papers include travel and Civil War diaries, a list of his yearly readings, engagement calendars, and a sparse collection of judicial papers. Two excellent collections of Holmes's writings are Max Lerner, *The Mind and Faith of Justice Holmes* (2d ed., 1988); and Richard A. Posner, *The Essential Holmes* (1991).

Biographies of Holmes include Liva Baker, *The Justice from Beacon Hill* (1991), a reliable and well-written trade biography that is sparse and derivative in its discussion of Holmes's work as a scholar and judge; Catherine Drinker Bowen, *Yankee from Olympus* (1944), a blend of fact and fiction about Holmes and his family, captivating reading if one is unconcerned with accuracy; Mark DeWolfe Howe, *Justice Oliver Wendell Holmes: The Shaping Years* (1957), and *Justice Oliver Wendell Holmes: The Proving Years* (1963), the authorized biography, and a masterful treatment of Holmes's early life and career through the publication of *The Common Law*, lamentably cut short by Howe's death in 1967; John S. Monagan, *The Grand Panjandrum: The Mellow Years of Justice Holmes* (1988), a delightful account of Holmes's later life, based on interviews with persons who knew him well; Sheldon Novick, *Honorable Justice* (1989), the first nonfiction trade biography covering Holmes's entire life, based on the Holmes papers but erratic in its coverage and insights; and G. Edward White, *Justice Oliver Wendell Holmes: Law and the Inner Self* (1993), an analysis of Holmes's life and work and the relationship between them.

Robert W. Gordon, ed., *The Legacy of Oliver Wendell Holmes, Jr.* (1992), is a collection of essays on Holmes, including some accomplished treatments of various phases of his career. In addition, one should consult Yosal Rogat, "Mr. Justice Holmes: A Dissenting Opinion," *Stanford Law Review* 15 (1963): 254, a major revision of Holmes's image as a civil libertarian, focusing on cases involving aliens and blacks; and Rogat, "The Judge as Spectator," *University of Chicago Law Review* 31 (1964): 213, a brilliant analysis of Holmes as a detached Brahmin figure, comparing him with

his contemporaries, Henry James and Henry Adams. F. R. Kellogg, "Holmes, Common Law Theory, and Judicial Restraint," *John Marshall Law Review* 36 (2003): 457, examines Holmes's views in light of his common law ideas. Albert W. Altschuler, *Law Without Values: The Life, Work, and Legacy of Justice Holmes* (2000), is a stinging attack on Holmes's alleged lack of morals in his jurisprudence.

Edmund Wilson's essay on Holmes in *Patriotic Gore* (1963), Wilson's collection of writings on the Civil War, remains one of the most insightful and best-written analyses of Holmes, demonstrating that one need not have professional legal training to produce lucid evaluations of legal figures.

NOTEWORTHY OPINIONS

Otis v. Parker, 187 U.S. 606 (1903)

Northern Securities Co. v. United States, 193 U.S. 197 (1904) (Dissent)

Swift & Company v. United States, 196 U.S. 375 (1905)

Lochner v. New York, 198 U.S. 45 (1905) (Dissent)

Patterson v. Colorado, 205 U.S. 454 (1907)

Noble State Bank v. Haskell, 219 U.S. 104 (1911) (Dissent)

Bailey v. Alabama, 219 U.S. 219 (1911) (Dissent)

Dr. Miles Medical Company v. John D. Park & Sons Company, 220 U.S. 373 (1911) (Dissent)

United States v. Reynolds, 235 U.S. 133 (1914) (Concurrence)

Coppage v. Kansas, 236 U.S. 1 (1914) (Dissent)

Fox v. Washington, 236 U.S. 273 (1915)

Hammer v. Dagenhart, 247 U.S. 251 (1918) (Dissent)

Schenck v. United States, 249 U.S. 47 (1919)

Frohwerk v. United States, 249 U.S. 204 (1919)

Debs v. United States, 249 U.S. 211 (1919)

Abrams v. United States, 250 U.S. 616 (1919) (Dissent)

Pennsylvania Coal Co. v. Mahon, 260 U.S. 393 (1922)

Adkins v. Children's Hospital, 261 U.S. 525 (1923) (Dissent)

Gitlow v. New York, 268 U.S. 652 (1925) (Dissent)

Buck v. Bell, 274 U.S. 200 (1927)

United States v. Schwimmer, 279 U.S. 644 (1929) (Dissent)

CHARLES EVANS HUGHES

Birth: April 11, 1862, Glens Falls, New York.

Education: Madison College (now Colgate University), 1876–1878; Brown University, A.B., 1881, A.M., 1884; Columbia Law School, LL.B., 1884.

Official Positions: Special counsel, New York State investigating commissions, 1905–1906; governor of New York, 1907–1910; U.S. secretary of state, 1921–1925; U.S. delegate, Washington Armament Conference, 1921; U.S. member, Permanent Court of Arbitration, 1926–1930; judge, Permanent Court of International Justice, 1928–1930.

Supreme Court Service: Nominated associate justice by President William Howard Taft, April 25, 1910, to replace David J. Brewer, who had died; confirmed by the Senate, May 2, 1910, by a voice vote; took judicial oath October 10, 1910; resigned June 10, 1916; replaced by John H. Clarke, nominated by President Woodrow Wilson; nominated chief justice by President Herbert Hoover, February 3, 1930, to replace Chief Justice William Howard Taft, who had retired; confirmed by the Senate, February 13, 1930, by a 52–26 vote; took judicial oath February 24, 1930; retired July 1, 1941; replaced by Harlan F. Stone, nominated by President Franklin D. Roosevelt.

Death: August 27, 1948, Osterville, Massachusetts.

Charles Evans Hughes was born during the Civil War in a small town in upstate New York. He was the only child of a preacher and of a rigidly devout Baptist mother who believed implicitly in the hot fire of Hell and the looming wrath of a just God. Together, they inculcated in their child the stark discipline of hard work, moral diligence, and the paramount importance of order. From such seemingly parochial beginnings would emerge one of the most outstanding, influential, and urbane figures of twentieth-century American law.

A prodigy with a photographic memory and compulsive attention to detail, the young Hughes matured prematurely. At three, he was reading English; at eight, he was reading Greek and German. At age six, and less than a year into first grade, he persuaded his parents to let him leave school by drafting and sending to them a detailed agenda for assiduous study at home. At thirteen, he earned a high school diploma and a year later enrolled in Madison College (now Colgate University), dutifully following his parents' plan for him to prepare for the ministry. But here a spark of rebellion appeared, and the sixteen-year-old Hughes transferred to Brown University in search of broader horizons. His preoccupation with order in an orderly universe remained, but now in a more secular context: he chose law. He graduated from Columbia Law School, immediately began practice with one of the leading law firms in New York City, and became a partner three years later. He was then twenty-five.

Hughes's rejection of his father's calling evoked from his parents desperate anxiety "that," as his father wrote, "you may be turned from the path of rectitude by the influence of your worldly associates." His parents need not have worried. Most of the stern habits that ordered his life during his childhood tutelage endured into his old age. At least twice they would drive him close to physical and mental breakdowns, and they induced a recurrent bleeding ulcer. They would decisively shape the way he approached his duties in his truly remarkable public career. "Whatever I do, wherever I go," Hughes once wrote, "when the question of right or wrong comes up, it is decided by what Pa or Ma will say if I did it."

Never a profound but always a meticulously systematic thinker, Hughes forged for himself one of the most extraordinary careers a man of the law might ever hope for. In a society that formally invested authority in law rather than in persons, his

Charles Evans Hughes

career afforded him high place, public honor, and exceptional opportunity to influence his society's structure of power. During the first half of his life, he earned wealth and widespread respect as a practicing attorney who also willingly gave his time and talents to public service. During the second half he was elected governor of New York; was appointed associate justice of the U.S. Supreme Court; resigned to become the Republican Party's 1916 candidate for

president and very nearly unseated the incumbent, Woodrow Wilson; served as president of the American Bar Association; was appointed secretary of state; served on the Permanent Court of International Justice, or World Court; and was appointed a second time to the Supreme Court—a unique achievement— this time as chief justice. In short, this man, whose intellect was so profoundly shaped by the rigid discipline of early nineteenth-century rural American Protestant fundamentalism, became one of the most influential figures of twentieth-century pluralist, urban America.

During Hughes's lifetime, the United States was dramatically transformed in almost every way. The post–Civil War political settlement provided the framework for a centralized or national constitutional order. Local and regional economies were gradually absorbed into a national matrix by the transportation and industrial revolutions. Small-unit private proprietary business enterprise yielded to large-scale multidivisional, multifunctional public corporations as the dominating force and defining feature of the American business system.

It is not clear that Hughes understood the significance of these changes any better than most other people. As a member of the Court, however, he did understand two things that would help bring American law and constitutional jurisprudence into line with those changes. The first was the paramount need for social and political order. The second was the importance of preserving the integrity of the Court itself as the vital arbiter of conflicting and sometimes mutually exclusive claims on justice that are inevitable in a complex and fast-changing society. "We secure our peace and confidence," he remarked, "by loyal acceptance of the decisions of our umpires."

Consistent with that idea were the immortal words that Hughes, when he was governor of New York, ad-libbed during an address—words that he came to regard as a plague: "The Constitution," he said, "is what the judges say it is." As he explained later, he intended neither denigration of the Constitution nor a complaint about judges. What he meant was that because judges play such a pivotal role in declaring the Constitution's meaning, they should stay out of the business of reviewing the fact-findings of government regulatory agencies. That would, he said, place them too "close to the public impatience." Because the courts are indispensable for protecting "our liberty and . . . our property under the Constitution," and because judges determine what the Constitution says, it is essential that the public continue to regard judges as demigods. Do not weaken them, he pleaded, by exposing them to the public pressures implicit in fact-finding. Keep the judges "for . . . questions of property rights," to sustain the "constitutional right to hold property and not to be deprived of it without due process of law."

Hughes was too sophisticated to believe that judges either did or should disinterestedly apply the principles of law to particular cases of fact without regard to favored social outcomes. He would himself suffer (probably fair) criticism for allegedly tailoring his judicial opinions to outcomes he favored. But in his mind it was the myths of an aloof judiciary and of inalienable property rights that sustained liberty in a democratic polity; those myths represented for him the vital buttresses of the good society. He worked hard throughout his career to protect the strength of those myths, even as his meticulous attention to detail and to facts impelled him to factor the real, everyday consequences of legal decisions into his judicial opinions.

Hughes's concern for order and, perhaps most of all, his remarkably profound, inner-directed sense of right often moved him to digress from legal reasoning

shaped prior to the transportation, industrial, and corporation revolutions. Always acutely conscious of the need to maintain the perception of stability in the law, he strove nevertheless to apply a juridical logic that accommodated to modern times. His efforts resulted in two important long-term outcomes.

The first was to enhance the power of government at both the state and federal levels to regulate American life. In contemplating cases requiring a fine-line interpretation of the commerce or contract clauses of the Constitution, Hughes usually sought outcomes that empowered Americans to use their government to make social and economic policy commensurate with the vast changes they were experiencing. Once on the Court, Hughes almost always favored a strong public direction of economic behavior. As one writer noted, "Hughes's judicial opinions consistently manifested . . . a desire for some central ordering force to supplant the inadequate ordering of markets and contracts."

The second important result of Hughes's work was to give substance to the Constitution's restraints on government when it came to protecting the personal and communicative rights emphasized in the first six amendments. Justice Oliver Wendell Holmes Jr. is usually assigned credit for shaping doctrine that would infuse federal jurisprudence with meaningful limits on the power of government to abridge speech, press, and lawful assembly. His and Justice Louis D. Brandeis's repeated dissents in civil liberties cases during the 1920s surely did build the case for confining such power to circumstances in which the alleged offense presented "a clear and present danger" to public safety or national security. But it was not until the 1930s, with Hughes as chief justice and writing some of the major opinions, that Holmes's principles began to emerge as those of the Court's majority.

Some of Hughes's actions during his first Court tenure (1910–1916) in the era of Taft and Wilson foreshadowed the achievements of the Court over which he would later preside. From the beginning, Hughes showed a tendency to uphold social legislation that, as he put it in a case concerning state regulation of the hours of labor for women (*Miller v. Wilson*, 1915), had a "reasonable relation to a proper purpose." The purpose he usually had in mind concerned civil order, the integrity of government authority, and (although he would have denied it) his own standards of justice. On behalf of federal regulation, he tended to give broad scope to the power granted to Congress in the Constitution to regulate interstate commerce.

When Hughes first came on the Court, as well as during his chief justiceship, that idea was still fiercely in dispute. In *United States v. E. C. Knight Co.* (1895), fifteen years before Hughes began his first tenure, the Court had found that a sugar refining company whose raw sugar came entirely from out of state, and most of whose refined sugar found markets outside the state, nevertheless lay beyond Congress's power to regulate interstate commerce. Notions of state sovereignty dominated constitutional law, except where judges deemed state legislation "confiscatory" or somehow in violation of "due process"—which usually meant in violation of the judges' view of the prerogatives of private property.

As the youngest member of the Court, Hughes moved cautiously, but effectively, toward augmenting government regulatory powers. In the much celebrated *Minnesota Rate Cases* (1913), he asserted the power of the states to control intrastate transportation even when it might seriously affect interstate commerce, as long as Congress had not already acted in the field. But in the same opinion, Hughes insisted that all commerce had become so intricately dependent that Congress might well preempt intrastate rules in order to effectively regulate interstate commerce.

Shortly afterward came the most famous of his early opinions, *Shreveport Rate Cases* (1914):

Congress is empowered to regulate—that is, to provide the law for the government of interstate commerce; . . . "to promote its growth and insure its safety." . . . Its authority . . . necessarily embraces the right to control the operations in all matters having such a close and substantial relation to interstate traffic that the control is essential or appropriate to the security of that traffic, [and] to the efficiency of the interstate service.

In shaping what came to be known as the Shreveport Doctrine, Hughes argued that the states' regulatory power must yield to that of Congress whenever the conduct of even purely intrastate commerce might adversely affect interstate conduct.

Hughes was willing, moreover, to extend this principle to Congress's jurisdiction over businesses when there was "actual movement" of their goods or services across state lines. "In determining whether commerce is interstate or intrastate," he insisted, "regard must be had to its essential character" (*Pennsylvania Railroad Co. v. Clark Bros. Coal Mining Co.,* 1915). These opinions appeared to contrast sharply with the Court's earlier rulings, especially that in the *Knight* case.

Hughes did not remain entirely consistent on such matters. The Court on which he sat did not overturn *Knight*, and, in any case, Hughes himself would later join in supporting comparably narrow decisions. In an opinion he wrote shortly before resigning to run for president, Hughes sustained an injury liability claim against an interstate railroad that was validated by state law, although under federal law, no such claim could stand. In *Chicago, Burlington & Quincy Railroad Co. v. Harrington* (1916), while noting that the injured man had been loading coal brought entirely from outside the state, Hughes could find no "close or direct relation to interstate transportation." In another case that same year, however, Hughes had no difficulty in holding that federal law controlled a railroad's liability if merely the goods involved in the accident had crossed state lines (*Southern Railway v. Prescott,* 1916). Such apparent contradictions led critics to see Hughes's jurisprudence as focusing less on principle than on favored results—albeit results that contrasted with his brethren's more common solicitude for corporate business immunity from government regulation or civil tort actions.

Like Justice Holmes, whom he greatly admired, Hughes refused to accept "liberty of contract" or the sanctity of contract as absolutes. The first, he believed, did not preclude state action to protect certain classes of workers from accepting unduly burdensome contracts. And the second did not preclude the state from modifying or abrogating contracts that it determined obstructed legitimate legislative objectives. In several cases, sometimes in dissent, Hughes argued that a state or city retained the power to revoke a franchise on the grounds that "It is a tacit condition annexed to grants of franchises that they may be lost by misuser or nonuser"; and that the grant of a franchise does not preclude the government from subsequently regulating rates or services (*New York Electric Lines Co. v. Empire City Subway Co.*, 1914).

On the other hand, Hughes would not permit a state to enforce a contract that imposed unconstitutional burdens on an individual. In *Bailey v. Alabama* (1911), Hughes wrote for the Court striking down a statute that compelled an employee to work off his debt to a creditor by stipulating that refusal to do so *ipso facto* constituted a criminal offense as a fraudulent violation of contract. Such a law violated the Constitution's ban on involuntary servitude, Hughes wrote, because it was a crude form of coercion—forcing a person to choose between performing involuntary services or facing criminal charges—an instrument especially effective "against the poor and ignorant, its most likely victims."

Hughes's solicitude for personal rights emerged early in his first Court tenure. He wrote for the Court in overturning an Arizona statute that limited the number of aliens a single employer could hire. Although he usually granted legislatures wide scope in determining means for protecting the public welfare, in this case he saw that the language of the statute showed that "discrimination against aliens [is] . . . an end in itself." That made it an unconstitutional intrusion on "the right to work for a living." Because Congress had full power to invite immigrants to the nation, a state could not effectively nullify that power by forcing an alien into penury (*Truax v. Raich*, 1915).

In *McCabe v. Atchison, Topeka & Santa Fe Railway Co.* (1914), he wrote for the 5–4 majority an opinion that declared unconstitutional a part of an Oklahoma statute permitting railroads to provide luxury cars for whites, but none for nonwhites. Although he accepted the "separate but equal" doctrine laid down in *Plessy v. Ferguson* (1896), Hughes insisted that even if only one nonwhite required a luxury car, the railroad must bear the cost of providing it. "The constitutional right [to such a car does] not depend upon the number of persons who may be discriminated against. . . . The essence of the constitutional right," wrote Hughes, "is that it is a personal one." This decision was probably the first legal victory in the twentieth century for blacks after decades of reverses that effectively nullified the intent of the Fourteenth and Fifteenth Amendments to secure the freedmen's civil rights and guarantee them equal protection of the law. Unfortunately, because Hughes also found that the plaintiffs in the case did not have standing, because they were not the individuals denied access to a luxury car, Hughes's *obiter dictum* about the personal essence of a constitutional right assertion served merely as an invitation for future litigation. And it was not until 1941, Hughes's last year as chief justice, that the Court finally made the principle stick.

Hughes's concern for civil liberties showed up most clearly after he left the Court. Following his defeat for president in 1916, he returned to private practice and, in that capacity, he represented many large corporations, sometimes before his former colleagues on the Court. But his most distinguished service occurred in 1920 when, on his own initiative, he volunteered his services on behalf of five duly elected New York assemblymen who had been peremptorily denied their seats because they belonged to the Socialist Party. In the bigoted American postwar environment following the Bolshevist triumph in Russia, Hughes's efforts proved as futile as comparable good-citizen actions of the McCarthy era of the 1940s and 1950s. But his was a gesture that would eventually help build civil liberties into an important feature of American democracy.

In 1931 Chief Justice Hughes wrote the Court's opinion in *Stromberg v. California*, a decision attorney and educator Harry Kalven Jr. has called "the first case in the history of the Court in which there was an explicit victory for free speech." Even so, Hughes did not move the law very far. He ordered reversal of a conviction on grounds that a part of the California law under which Yetta Stromberg was convicted was unconstitutional because it was too vague, while he explicitly upheld the constitutionality of another part of the law that made it a felony to use provocative flags or symbols that might serve as "an invitation or stimulus to anarchistic action or as an aid to propaganda that is of a seditious character." The Court evidently was not yet prepared to regard "anarchistic action" or "seditious character" as at all vague, to say nothing of what might constitute "an invitation" or "an aid to propaganda."

Hughes and his brethren continued to regard government authority as superior to most private rights, at least when those rights concerned lifestyle or political expression. In *Hamilton v. Regents of the University of California* (1934), a unanimous Court rejected a Methodist's conscientious objection to serving in a university's reserve officer training corps, then required of all able-bodied male students. Even the Court's three most liberal members, Benjamin Cardozo, Harlan Stone, and Brandeis, joined in a concurring opinion that pointedly rejected the claims of private conscience to some measure of immunity from state command. "The right of private judgment," Cardozo wrote, "has never yet been so exalted above the powers and compulsion of the agencies of government."

It would not be until after 1937 that the Court began moving civil liberties into the center of modern liberal law. And that would come primarily after numerous Court vetoes of New Deal economic legislation brought about a major political crisis, and after resignations from the Court permitted President Franklin Roosevelt to appoint new justices. Until that time, Hughes's record was spotty on this issue.

When Hughes was nominated in 1930 to replace William Howard Taft as chief justice, progressives were strongly opposed, regarding Hughes mainly as a Republican lawyer for corporations. The Senate confirmed him by a small majority, with twenty-six opposed and eighteen abstaining. And Hughes did not get off to an auspicious beginning. His first public statement after confirmation, a speech to the American Bar Association, emphasized the importance of preserving states' rights against federal encroachment—at a time when the country was facing a national economic calamity.

Once his term began, Hughes joined again and again with the conservatives—in particular, the four fiercely antireform justices—Willis Van Devanter, George Sutherland, Pierce Butler, and James McReynolds—in overturning state and federal measures designed to alleviate the country's critical conditions. In one case, *Crowell v. Benson* (1932), against even his own declared principles that the courts should refrain from second-guessing the fact-findings of regulatory commissions, he contrived to find that the courts could properly review the facts ascertained by the commission charged with administering a workman's compensation act. In another case, ostensibly out of solicitude for state court jurisdiction, he joined those four again, plus Justice Owen Roberts, in throwing out a case against six top executives of the American Tobacco Company, who had bilked the corporation for millions of dollars in "bonuses" and sold themselves stock for a fifth of its market value. As Justices Stone and Brandeis noted in dissent in *Rogers v. Guaranty Trust Co.* (1933), Hughes revealed (untypically) an almost willful blindness to the obvious interstate character of modern corporate business.

What was going on? A fair guess is that Hughes was troubled by the popular outcry against American business that followed on the stock market crash of 1929 and the devastating Great Depression that followed. His keen concern for order led him to "tilt" against what appeared to be a movement toward radical change that would, among other things, undermine the security of private business property. Like many fundamentally conservative people at the time, Hughes seems to have believed in the nearness of revolution.

His celebrated opinion in *Home Building & Loan Assn. v. Blaisdell* (1934), for a 5–4 majority, revealed this clearly. In upholding a Minnesota law that suspended foreclosures on indebted properties, Hughes acted in line with his earlier opinions on the legitimate power of states to alter or abrogate contracts. But in this case, instead of emphasizing, as Stone, Cardozo, and Brandeis wanted him to, that the states have plenary power to determine the balance between private rights and public welfare (a phrasing Hughes did take from Cardozo to include in his opinion), Hughes preferred to highlight the temporary nature of the act, and to stress how it helped to preserve the public's faith in a just and orderly government amid emergency conditions. Hughes's acknowledgment of the emergence of the state in America as an entity independent of the multiple social forces that made demands on it was an important contribution to modern political thinking. But Cardozo and Stone let it be known at the time that by failing to emphasize the plenary powers of the state to treat the allocation of economic advantages, the Court missed an opportunity to bring constitutional law fully into the twentieth century.

In another 1934 case Hughes joined in sustaining a state's regulatory power. In *Nebbia v. New York*, Justice Roberts wrote for a 5–4 majority to uphold New York's right to counter "destructive competition" by regulating milk prices. With Hughes joining in an expansive assertion of government's power to regulate, Roberts wrote, "There is no closed class or category of businesses affected with a public interest.... The phrase ... can ... mean no more than that an industry, for adequate reason, is subject to control for the public good." But for the next two years, Hughes would be found mostly on the other side, going a long way toward eviscerating the federal government's major programs for coping with the Depression.

On May 27, 1935, a day that came to be called "Black Monday," a unanimous Court overturned the National Industrial Recovery Act (NIRA), the measure that some regarded as the heart of the New Deal, in *Schechter Poultry Corp. v. United States*, as well as the Frazier-Lemke Act, a farm mortgage relief measure, in *Louisville Joint Stock Land Bank v. Radford*. The *Radford* case was not critical because it fell mostly on the act's careless wording. Brandeis, for the Court, stressed that although government may alter contracts for good public purpose, as Hughes had successfully argued during his first Court tenure, the poor wording of the act seemed to give government the right to take property without compensation.

But much more was at stake in the NIRA case, and Hughes again split with his more progressive colleagues, even though his earlier record might have indicated he would do otherwise. The key to the case for Brandeis, Cardozo, and Stone was the virtually unlimited and uninstructed delegation of government power to private trade associations for setting prices, wages, and production levels. The example of fascism, which was then vigorously ascending in Europe and in theory featured a superficially similar form of syndicalism, played a strong role in the justices' view of the NIRA. It was not altogether unreasonable in those years to fear the spread of authoritarian regimes, even in liberal democracies. But Hughes seemed to have a more antiquated concern for states' rights. He threw his support to a distinction between "direct" effects on interstate commerce that Congress could regulate and "indirect" effects that he insisted it could not. That line of reasoning brought the Court back to 1895 and *E. C. Knight* and the sugar trust.

The next year, Brandeis, Cardozo, and Stone found themselves alone again, this time in dissent, when Hughes's Court threw out the New Deal's Agricultural Adjustment Act (AAA) in *United States v. Butler* (1936). Here, Roberts wrote a truly astonishing opinion for the 6–3 majority that Hughes joined. The opinion first asserted that although Congress did have the power to tax and spend for the general welfare, it could not do so for purposes reserved to the states, namely, to regulate agriculture—notwithstanding the plain interstate and international character of modern agriculture. Second, according to Roberts, "A tax ... has never been thought to connote the expropriation of money from one group for the benefit of another"—notwithstanding that nearly all taxation does that. Third, Roberts said that by tying receipt of such benefits to specific regulations, Congress was engaged in "coercion by economic pressure," even though the law required no one to accept the benefits and thereby the regulations, and nearly all government largesse is conditioned by some required behavior. Fourth, he said that if the federal government could purchase compliance by offering grants, one could foresee a condition whereby "the independence of the individual states [will be] obliterated, and the United States converted into a central government exercising uncontrolled police power in every state of the Union, superseding all local control or regulation of the affairs or concerns of the states."

Stone, with Brandeis and Cardozo joining, dispatched such blather with a brief, sharp dissent: "The suggestion that [the government's power of the purse] must now be curtailed by judicial fiat because it may be abused by unwise use hardly rises to the dignity of argument. So may judicial power be abused. . . . Courts are not the only agency of government that must be assumed to have capacity to govern." The Court and the American people, Stone concluded, would benefit most from "the frank recognition that language, even of a constitution, may mean what it says: that the power to tax and spend includes the power to relieve a nationwide economic maladjustment by conditional gifts of money."

But the Court majority remained incorrigible. By a 5–4 margin, with Hughes concurring, it followed the AAA decision by striking down a congressional act that sought to stabilize prices and wages in the troubled bituminous coal industry. In *Carter v. Carter Coal Co.* (1936), Hughes once again seemed to return to the *E. C. Knight* doctrine: "If the people desire to give Congress the power to regulate industries within the state, and the relations of employers and employees in these industries," he pontificated in a concurring opinion, "they are at liberty to declare their will in the appropriate manner, but it is not for the Court to amend the Constitution by judicial decision." As one law school dean complained that year, "What we face now is the question, not how governmental functions shall be shared, but whether in substance we shall govern at all."

By this time, the Hughes Court's collision with Franklin Roosevelt's New Deal program had attracted criticism across the country, and not altogether on partisan political or strictly ideological grounds. A widespread sentiment had formed that the Court, made up mostly of aging men deep into their seventies and eighties, was out of touch with reality and was engaging in blunt political acts aimed at blocking every effort of the Roosevelt administration to deal with the modern corporate economy realistically and to end the crisis of the Depression. Why Hughes was

participating in this obstructive course is still not clear. It is true he was a lifelong Republican who may well have resented his much younger, shallow, patrician-born Democratic neighbor from downstate New York. But then, Harlan Stone was also a New York Republican who distrusted the New Deal experiments and had no personal fondness for Roosevelt. Perhaps the best answer is that Hughes was always profoundly conservative, and his departures from the old came mainly—and usually grudgingly—when he feared that to do otherwise would put order into jeopardy.

Following the *Carter Coal* decision, the Hughes Court in June 1936 took one more dramatic step toward provoking disorder when it overturned a New York minimum wage law. This time Hughes voted with the minority in the 5–4 decision in *Morehead v. New York ex rel. Tipaldo*. But the damage was done. Even conservative students of the law exclaimed their disapproval. Stone, in his dissent, denounced the "economic predilections" of the Court's majority. Calls for revamping the Court grew.

That November, FDR won a landslide reelection victory in which he made "the Republican Supreme Court" a campaign issue. Thinking the time ripe, he asked Congress to pass a reform bill that would have permitted the president to name an additional justice to the Court for every sitting justice over the age of seventy (six of them were). But Roosevelt's plan misfired. Although Congress had changed the number of seats on the Supreme Court several times before, many in the president's own party in Congress opposed him this time. So great had the Supreme Court's authority grown in Americans' sense of nationhood, so important had the myth of its nonpartisanship become, that, even in the face of the manifest partisanship of at least the consistently united four conservatives on the Court, the public recoiled from what the press quickly dubbed "Court-packing." FDR found his plan attacked as if he had challenged the importance of motherhood, religion, and apple pie. To make matters worse, he chose to sidestep the political reasons for the proposal and disingenuously argued the need to relieve the workload of the superannuated justices.

That comment eased the task of his enemies. Although Hughes wished to avoid a direct confrontation with the administration on what he recognized was a proper political issue, FDR's claim that the aging Court members needed help gave him his opening. He responded to FDR's proposal in two ways. The first was to pick apart, in his well-practiced fashion of providing detailed data, the president's contention that the Court's aging members needed relief. Taking cues from Sen. Burton Wheeler, D-Mont., he addressed a letter to the Senate Judiciary Committee as if in answer to a factual inquiry. Hughes easily showed that the Court had had no more trouble handling its full load of cases than had any previous Court. Hughes spoke for himself but claimed that the letter was "in accord with the views of the Justices," although in fact he had consulted only with Van Devanter and Brandeis. Had he consulted all, he would have risked revealing division among the brethren on the issue. And the others, although miffed by their chief's presumption, declined to expose the Court to the embarrassment and controversy that a public challenge would entail. FDR's congressional opponents used Hughes's letter in their successful campaign to sink the plan.

Although he would forever after deny it, Hughes's second response to the Court-packing controversy was essentially to change his judicial posture. The year 1937 marked the beginning of a nearly complete reversal of the Hughes Court's earlier positions on reform legislation, with Hughes and Roberts joining Brandeis, Cardozo, and Stone for a new 5–4 majority in the 1937 term.

By that margin, in March 1937, only months after voiding New York's minimum wage law, the Court upheld Washington State's minimum wage law in *West Coast Hotel Co. v. Parrish* and explicitly reversed the decision in *Morehead* and the main precedent cited in that case, the infamous *Adkins v. Children's Hospital* (1923). In April Hughes gave the New Deal its greatest victory when he and the same four others upheld the 1935 National Labor Relations Act (NLRA) in *National Labor Relations Board v. Jones & Laughlin Steel Corp.* To do so, he almost cavalierly waved aside

his own position in the NIRA, AAA, and coal act cases, as if rediscovering his earlier view that "regard must be had to [the] essential character" of the stream of commerce to determine Congress's jurisdiction. Justice McReynolds had every right to protest in his dissent: "Every consideration brought forward to uphold the [National Labor Relations] Act . . . was applicable to support the Acts held unconstitutional in cases decided within [only the past] two years."

The *Jones & Laughlin* decision represented something new in modern American government. Until 1935 the growth of a government regulatory regime had responded almost entirely to demands made by various elements within the business community. With passage of the NLRA, a major piece of federal regulatory law emanated from concerns of the state itself to establish a controllable order in industrial relations, as well as in response to demands from among nonbusiness interests within the society for the kind of statutory protection from adverse market outcomes that different business groups commonly enjoyed. In upholding the act and in recognizing collective bargaining as a "fundamental right," the Hughes Court dramatically altered the employer-employee relationship, restoring to the state a large part of the mediating role it had had before nineteenth-century changes in law created a free labor market that underwrote industrial capitalism. The restoration of government's active role in regulating industrial relations won firm standing in 1941, the last year of Hughes's stewardship. With the Court largely restructured by six resignations and deaths, Hughes reluctantly joined in a unanimous validation of the Fair Labor Standards Act of 1938, which reversed several precedents that had denied Congress's full power to regulate interstate commerce and the labor and goods that produced that commerce. The case was *United States v. Darby Lumber Co.* (1941).

Before the end of 1938, the Court clearly indicated that it would henceforth presume the legitimacy of legislative efforts to govern the economy. In an obscure case, *United States v. Carolene Products Co.,* Justice Stone, for the Hughes Court, declared: "The existence of facts supporting the legislative judgment [in economic matters] is to be presumed." Then, in what became a famous footnote, Stone added that "legislation which restricts . . . political processes . . . is to be subjected to more exacting judicial scrutiny." Stone included among such restrictions the right to vote, to assemble, to organize politically, and in general, "restraints upon the dissemination of information."

In a vital way, this development marked the maturing of modern liberalism. Traditional liberalism had placed private property at the center of its emphasis on individual liberty, reasoning that from the immunity of property from arbitrary constraint or expropriation all other elements of individual liberty followed. Modern liberalism placed personal freedom—lifestyle, speech, assembly, religious choice—at the center of its concern for individual liberty, recognizing that the industrial and corporation revolutions, by bringing about a concentration of propertied power, had impaired the function of private property to protect individual liberty.

What is often overlooked about the Hughes Court is that it set the first important precedents for developing a civil liberties jurisprudence. In *DeJonge v. Oregon* (1937), in which the Court unanimously overturned the conviction of a man for attending a Communist Party meeting, Hughes declared plainly, "Peaceable assembly for lawful discussion cannot be made a crime." In *Herndon v. Lowry* that same year, for the first time the Court put Justice Holmes's test of "clear and present danger" into a majority opinion that overturned a conviction for illicit speech. In this case, a black organizer for the Communist Party had been convicted for inciting insurrection. Roberts for the Court declared the law under which the state had obtained the conviction "a dragnet which may enmesh anyone who agitates for a change of government" and "an unwarrantable invasion of the right of free speech." In *Hague v. C. I. O.* (1939), the Hughes Court found a municipal ordinance requiring permits for citizens to hold peaceful public meetings to be an unconstitutional burden on free speech and assembly. And in *Thornhill v. Alabama* (1940), the Court held a statute banning peaceful picketing to be "invalid on its face," interfering as it did with the free discussion

"indispensable to the effective and intelligent use of the processes of popular government to shape the destiny of modern industrial society." In all these cases, the Hughes Court set apart certain rights and immunities having to do with the communicative freedoms that no government could abridge without establishing some impelling reason of safety or order. Although a thorough protection for civil liberties still had a long way to go, the Hughes Court prepared a solid base.

Finally, there remains an assessment of the reputation of Charles Evans Hughes as a jurist. Most public accounts of the man's career have treated him with high honor. One scholar called the body of opinions by Hughes to be the most important since those of the great John Marshall. Others also extolled his administrative abilities as chief justice. Some contemporaries even cited his great sense of humor—a quality not obvious from either the character of his writings, including his autobiographical notes, or his public image. The man's very appearance, perhaps most of all his full, well-groomed but imperious beard, suggested a formidable authoritative presence. He appeared the very embodiment of a "great judge." "He radiated authority," which he exerted "by the artistic mastery with which he presided," wrote Justice Felix Frankfurter.

On the other hand, private opinions of Hughes by many of his contemporaries, including some of the same colleagues who publicly extolled him, differ sharply. The papers of Harlan Stone, who succeeded Hughes as chief justice, are full of scorching judgments of both the man's legal opinions and his conduct as chief. "At conference," Stone wrote about one case, "the case was presented by the Chief Justice in his usual fashion of greatly over-elaborating the unimportant details of the case and disposing, by *ipsi dixit*, in a sentence or two, of the vital question." Others found his opinions verbose, often obscuring the critical issues. Some contemporaries jibed that Hughes, who coveted a reputation as a liberal like Holmes and Brandeis, usually chose not to speak for the Court when he joined conservative opinions, but assigned himself the Court's voice when he could agree on a liberal decision. Many stressed his inconsistency, and conservatives especially deplored his results-oriented activism. Archibald Cox of the Harvard Law School gave faint praise in saying that the Hughes Court did "appreciably less violence" than did the Warren Court "to the ideal of a coherent, growing, yet continuing body of law."

Perhaps it may best be said that Charles Evans Hughes presided over the U.S. Supreme Court at a time when great things were happening in constitutional law and that they probably happened as much in spite of Hughes as because of him.

—*Richard M. Abrams*

A revisionist study that argues the Court was not as reactionary as critics or historians have believed is Barry Cushman, *Rethinking the New Deal Court: The Structure of a Constitutional Revolution* (1998). For Hughes's role in the Court fight, see William E. Leuchtenburg, "The Nine Justices Respond to the 1937 Crisis," *Journal of Supreme Court History* (1997): 55; and Leuchtenburg, "Charles Evans Hughes: The Center Holds," *North Carolina Law Review* 83 (2005): 1187. A different view is Richard Friedman, "Chief Justice Hughes's Letter on Court-Packing," *Journal of Supreme Court History* (1997): 76.

One should also consult Alpheus T. Mason, *Harlan Fiske Stone: Pillar of the Law* (1956), which provides an intensive examination of the Hughes period, and a rare less-than-wholly favorable treatment of the chief justice.

BIBLIOGRAPHY

The Hughes papers are in the Library of Congress. The most complete biography remains Merlo J. Pusey, *Charles Evans Hughes*, 2 vols. (1952), which is very much an "official" work. David J. Danelski and Joseph S. Tulchin have edited *The Autobiographical Notes of Charles Evans Hughes* (1973), which provides the most intimate portrait of Hughes we are likely to get.

For various interpretations of the man, see Paul A. Freund, "Charles Evans Hughes as Chief Justice," *Harvard Law Review* 81 (1967): 4; Samuel Hendel, *Charles Evans Hughes and the Supreme Court* (1951), a balanced account that pays more attention than most to Hughes's record on civil liberties; and, in this regard, see Merle William Loper, "The Court of Chief Justice Hughes: Contributions to Civil Liberties," *Wayne Law Review* 12 (1966): 535. The best and most succinct account of Hughes's first tenure on the Court is an anonymous note, "Governor on the Bench: Charles Evans Hughes as Associate Justice," *Harvard Law Review* 89 (1976): 961. Michael F. Parrish provides a critical account of the Hughes Court in "The Great Depression, the New Deal, and the American Legal Order," *Washington Law Review* 59 (1984): 723.

NOTEWORTHY OPINIONS

Minnesota Rate Cases, 230 U.S. 352 (1913)

Shreveport Rate Cases, 234 U.S. 342 (1914)

McCabe v. Atchison, Topeka & Santa Fe Railway Co., 235 U.S. 151 (1914)

Truax v. Raich, 239 U.S. 33 (1915)

Chicago, Burlington & Quincy Railroad Co. v. Harrington, 241 U.S. 177 (1916)

Stromberg v. California, 293 U.S. 359 (1931)

Home Building & Loan Assn. v. Blaisdell, 290 U.S. 398 (1934)

Schechter Poultry Corp. v. United States 295 U.S. 495 (1935)

Carter v. Carter Coal Co., 298 U.S. 238 (1936) (Partial Dissent)

Morehead v. New York ex rel. Tipaldo, 298 U.S. 587 (1936) (Dissent)

DeJonge v. Oregon, 299 U.S. 353 (1937)

West Coast Hotel Co. v. Parrish, 300 U.S. 379 (1937)

National Labor Relations Board v. Jones & Laughlin Steel Corp., 301 U.S. 1 (1937)

WARD HUNT

Birth: June 14, 1810, Utica, New York.

Education: Graduated from Union College, 1828; studied law at the Tapping Reeve School.

Official Positions: Member, New York Assembly, 1839; mayor of Utica, 1844; member, New York Court of Appeals, 1866–1869; New York State commissioner of appeals, 1869–1873.

Supreme Court Service: Nominated associate justice by President Ulysses S. Grant, December 6, 1872, to replace Samuel Nelson, who had retired; confirmed by the Senate, December 11, 1872, by a voice vote; took judicial oath January 9, 1873; retired January 27, 1882; replaced by Samuel Blatchford, nominated by President Chester A. Arthur.

Death: March 24, 1886, Washington, D.C.

Ward Hunt's nine-year term on the Supreme Court was generally undistinguished; he is known in law schools today only because of a vigorous dissent on a still troubling jurisdictional question, and he deserves the limited attention of legal historians because of a brief but eloquent dissent from the Court's abdication of civil rights principles.

Little is known of Hunt's life, although basic data can be gleaned from public records and contemporary newspapers. Born into a comfortable middle-class milieu, Hunt was groomed for a legal career, graduating with honors from Union College and studying law with Judge James Gould at the Tapping Reeve School in Litchfield, Connecticut. He was politically active, aligning himself with Martin Van Buren's Jacksonian branch of the New York Democratic Party. In 1844 he was elected mayor of Utica. Opposition to slavery led him to leave the Democrats, and in 1855–1856 he became a founder of the Republican Party in New York. At the close of the Civil War, he was elected to the New York Court of Appeals,

becoming chief judge in 1868. He was still serving as New York's chief judicial officer when President Ulysses S. Grant named him to the U.S. Supreme Court. The nomination was apparently at the behest of Sen. Roscoe Conkling, R-N.Y., a fellow Utican and longtime friend. His nomination proved uncontroversial, and he was confirmed within a week.

Hunt's jurisprudential production (152 opinions, 7 dissents) may seem scant for a justice who served nearly a decade on the Court. But Hunt suffered a paralytic stroke in 1878, and during the next four and a half years he remained an associate justice but did not participate in any of the Court's proceedings. Hunt lacked an independent income and consented to retire only after Congress enacted a special bill granting him an early pension.

Hunt's most noble contribution came in the form of a dissent to the Court's 1876 decision to gut the Enforcement Act of 1870, which implemented the Fifteenth Amendment's guarantee of the right to vote for black citizens. In extraordinarily twisted and attenuated reasoning, Chief Justice Morrison R. Waite, writing for all but Hunt in *United States v. Reese* (1875), found the congressional act unconstitutional because it was not, in its penalty provisions, limited to denial of the right to vote "on account of race."

In fact, as Hunt correctly demonstrated, the statute did incorporate such a limitation. The Supreme Court's majority was animated, not by fidelity to the laws they were sworn to uphold, but by baser political motives. The Compromise of 1877, marking an end to Reconstruction and the beginning of the Jim Crow era throughout the South, was already in preparation, and the Court's majority was making its contribution to the betrayal of the South's new citizens. Hunt distinguished himself by refusing to participate in this charade.

The balance of Hunt's opinion consisted of a forceful statement of the Radical Republican principles behind the Fifteenth Amendment. Congress had intended to grant the freed slaves the full measure of rights that had been enjoyed by white citizens up to that date. He found that this guarantee plainly extended the right to vote to state elections as well as federal elections and that it had become part of the "republican form of government" that the Union promised the citizens of the states. In the end, Hunt somberly noted, the majority's intent was to render all the Civil War amendments "impotent."

Regrettably, Hunt stood quietly by as Waite's steamroller proceeded to devastate the legal protections granted the freedmen; he seems to have regarded *Reese* as a form of *stare decisis* to which he was bound. In *Cruikshank v. United States* (1876), he went along with a ruling that in effect held that vigilantism and terrorism designed to intimidate freedmen from voting were "rights guaranteed to the people by the Constitution." In *Hall v. DeCuir* (1878), he silently assented to a ruling striking down a Louisiana law guaranteeing former slaves and free blacks access to railroads without discrimination as an "unconstitutional interference with interstate commerce." These opinions collectively may represent the most odious chapter in the history of Supreme Court jurisprudence.

Law students today are most likely to come across Hunt through his dissent to the intriguing case of *Pennoyer v. Neff* (1877). In that case, the Supreme Court invalidated a money judgment rendered against an absentee landowner on the grounds that the state court's exercise of jurisdiction was unconstitutional. The plaintiff had made use of a state statute allowing service by publication if the defendant owned property in the jurisdiction and providing for attachment of the property. Such jurisdiction is called *quasi in rem* today because it rests on the fictional notion that the *res,* in this case the real property, is the subject of the litigation. The Court held that the exercise of jurisdiction was unconstitutional because the property had not been attached first. Hunt found this distinction trifling; more significant, he demonstrated that the Court's opinion rested on mere *obiter dicta* in the cases cited, that is, language that was not necessary

Ward Hunt

to the holding. In opposition, Hunt compiled an impressive assemblage of cases whose holdings squarely contradicted the majority. Although *Pennoyer* is still correct law, Hunt won lasting admiration for his forceful and persuasive argument on a close legal point.

Hunt was more favorably disposed than his immediate successors on the Court toward the exercise of state regulatory authority on economic questions. He joined in *Munn v. Illinois* (1877), authorizing the state to fix a ceiling on storage charges in grain silos; and in the *Slaughterhouse Cases* (1873), he voted to sustain a state-authorized monopoly. In another series of opinions, he regularly supported bondholders who challenged the attempts of government authorities to welsh on their obligations (*Commissioners of Johnson City. v. Thayer*, 1877; *County of Randolph v. Post*, 1877; and *Burlington Township v. Beasley*, 1877). In these and most other opinions, Hunt did not stand out from his colleagues; he seems very much a man of his times, who offers us little that is of more than historical interest.

—*Scott Horton*

BIBLIOGRAPHY

Stanley I. Kutler's "Ward Hunt," in Friedman and Israel, *Justices*, vol. 2, 1221, is the only serious biographical treatment.

NOTEWORTHY OPINIONS

United States v. Reese, 92 U.S. 214 (1875) (Dissent)

Pennoyer v. Neff, 95 U.S. 714 (1877)

JAMES IREDELL

Birth: October 5, 1751, Lewes, England.

Education: Educated in England; read law under Samuel Johnston of North Carolina; licensed to practice, 1770–1771.

Official Positions: Comptroller of customs, Edenton, North Carolina, 1768–1774; collector of customs, Port of North Carolina, 1774–1776; judge, Superior Court of North Carolina, 1778; attorney general, North Carolina, 1779–1781; member, North Carolina Council of State, 1787; delegate, North Carolina convention for ratification of federal Constitution, 1788.

Supreme Court Service: Nominated associate justice by President George Washington, February 9, 1790; confirmed by the Senate, February 10, 1790, by a voice vote; took judicial oath May 12, 1790; served until October 20, 1799; replaced by Alfred Moore, nominated by President John Adams.

Death: October 20, 1799, Edenton, North Carolina.

James Iredell had gained a reputation as a prominent North Carolina Federalist prior to his Supreme Court appointment in 1790. Although he began his career as an official of the colonial government—he served as collector of customs in Edenton and, after studying law, was appointed deputy king's attorney—he wrote several tracts during the 1770s that established him as sympathetic to the Revolutionary cause.

During the Revolutionary War, Iredell served as a member of a committee charged with reviewing state statutes (1776). He also served as a superior court judge and as state attorney general. Returning to private practice, Iredell was able to give vent to his strongly held opinions concerning the fundamental nature of constitutional law and the importance of judicial review. In his *Instructions to Chowan County*

Representatives (1783), he argued that fixed salaries for judges were necessary, for "otherwise they cannot be truly independent, which is a point of the utmost moment in a Republic where the Law is superior to any or all the Individuals, and the Constitution superior even to the Legislature, and of which the Judges are the guardians and protectors." As an attorney in the case of *Bayard v. Singleton* (1787), he successfully argued that a state confiscation act violated the North Carolina Constitution because it denied a jury trial to litigants challenging the confiscation. Iredell's efforts in favor of adoption of the U.S. Constitution during North Carolina's ratifying conventions of 1788 and 1789 brought him to the attention of President George Washington, who named him to the Supreme Court in 1790.

As a justice, Iredell proved himself to be conscientious and careful. His opinions, in which he usually raised and answered the arguments of the parties in methodical fashion, often took a tack independent of his brethren. He was sensitive to the impact that the Court's decisions might have in the larger world, and he frequently expressed his reluctance to decide important or constitutional questions unnecessarily, although he was quite willing to engage in extraneous discussions that would now be termed *dicta*. His primary concerns, as revealed in his opinions, were the principles of separation of powers and judicial review and, perhaps most important, his concern for the interests of the states vis-à-vis the federal government.

Early in his career on the Court, Iredell had the opportunity to act on his beliefs in separation of powers and judicial review of legislation. In 1792 Congress passed the Invalid Pensions Act, assigning to the federal circuit courts the task of determining whether veterans who claimed to have been injured in the Revolutionary War were eligible for pensions. The act made the circuit courts' determinations subject to review by the secretary of war. Shortly after the act's passage, circuit courts around the country, which at that time were composed of one or two Supreme Court justices and the local district judge, confronted the statute, and all found it defective.

Iredell, sitting on the circuit court for the district of North Carolina, and district judge John Sitgreaves sent a letter to President Washington setting out their views on the statute. They had no case before them, so the letter amounted to an advisory opinion. By the terms of the Constitution, they said, each department—legislative, judicial, and executive—must remain separate. Because the act authorized the secretary of war to review a judicial decision, it in effect set up an arm of the executive branch as an appellate court—without investing the secretary of war with life tenure, as required by Article III. The act, therefore, subjected the court's decision to "a mode of revision which we consider to be unwarranted by the Constitution." Essentially, the judges were expressing their conclusion that the act was unconstitutional because it violated the guarantee of separation of powers.

An even clearer statement of Iredell's belief in judicial review of legislation came in *Calder v. Bull* (1798), the first case in which the Supreme Court confronted the meaning of the constitutional prohibition against *ex post facto* laws. Although he agreed with the rest of the justices that the Connecticut law at issue was not an *ex post facto* law because it was civil rather than criminal in nature, Iredell observed that if any federal or state act violated a constitutional provision, it was "unquestionably void"—adding that, "as the authority to declare it void is of a delicate and awful nature, the Court will never resort to that authority, but in a clear and urgent case."

Undoubtedly, Iredell's most famous opinion is his dissent in *Chisholm v. Georgia* (1793)—the case that precipitated the Eleventh Amendment to the Constitution, which bars federal courts from hearing suits brought by individuals against states other than

James Iredell

their own. *Chisholm* was a suit brought by citizens of South Carolina against Georgia for nonpayment of a debt contracted during the Revolution. Georgia, claiming sovereign immunity, refused to enter an appearance, and the plaintiffs moved for a default judgment. In separate opinions issued in February 1793, four of the five justices then on the Court found no constitutional barrier to the suit; on the contrary, they held that suits against states were authorized by Article III, Section 2, which conferred federal jurisdiction over suits "between a state and citizens of another state." Iredell alone dissented.

Having first encountered the case in 1791 while sitting on the circuit court for the district of Georgia— where he dismissed the suit on the ground that the circuit court lacked jurisdiction, but implied that it might be allowable in the Supreme Court—Iredell had had ample time to formulate his views. He presented the question in the narrowest possible terms: would an action of *assumpsit* (an action for damages for the nonperformance of an oral or written contract) lie against a state? Vehemently rejecting the plaintiffs' suggestion that judicial authority could be derived directly from the Constitution, without the benefit of any enabling legislation, Iredell turned to the Judiciary Act of 1789 for clarification. The fourteenth section of that act, he noted, authorized the issuance of all writs *"agreeable to the principles and usages of law."* The "law" referred to, he concluded, could only be "the common law"—that is, the law *"as it existed in England (unaltered by any statute) at the time of the first settlement of the country."* Iredell proceeded to examine the common law of England regarding suits against the Crown, explaining that "every State in the *Union* in every instance where its sovereignty has not been delegated to the *United States,* I consider to be as compleatly sovereign, as the *United States* are in respect to the powers surrendered."

Iredell then embarked on a lengthy disquisition on English case law, which led him to the conclusion that the only method of proceeding against the king in the case of debt was by petition and was dependent on his consent. By analogy, the only remedy against a state in the case of debt was by petition to the legislature. Iredell went on to reject the argument that a state could be analogized to a corporation. As he had done earlier in his opinion when rejecting the idea that judicial power could be derived directly from the Constitution, Iredell set out a sharp division between the spheres of the courts and the legislature: to apply the law of corporations to the very different situation of states would be tantamount to engaging in law-making, "when the *application* of law, not the *making* of it, is the sole province of the Court."

In conclusion, Iredell observed that his decision made it unnecessary for him to consider whether the Constitution itself authorized federal courts to entertain suits against states, noting that "it is of extreme moment that no Judge should rashly commit himself upon important questions, which it is unnecessary for him to decide." He continued, however, that because so much had been said on the subject of the Constitution, "It may not be improper to intimate that my present opinion is strongly against any construction of it, which will admit, under any circumstances a compulsive suit against a State for the recovery of money." His last sentence rang ominously: "I pray to God, that if the Attorney General's doctrine, as to the law, be established by the judgment of this Court, all the good he predicts from it may take place, and none of the evils with which, I have the concern to say, it appears to me to be pregnant."

Iredell's opinion, as it turned out, was more in keeping with the mood of the country than were those of his fellow justices. The day after the opinions came down, a constitutional amendment to overturn the result was introduced in the House of Representatives, and a similar amendment passed both houses of Congress the following year. By 1795 the requisite number of states had ratified the amendment, which, because of bureaucratic errors, was not made official until 1798.

Some commentators, such as Griffith J. McRee— the first editor of Iredell's letters—have seen in Iredell's dissent the germ of what later became known as the doctrine of states' rights. Others, noting Iredell's strong Federalist record and judicial support for unpopular displays of Federalist might such as the

Alien and Sedition Acts, have disputed this view. Jeff B. Fordham has written that what Iredell did "was simply to state a legal opinion instead of writing a political tract." Unwilling to embark on new and uncharted territory when it "was of no great importance to the effectuation of the purposes of the union," Iredell chose the road of caution. Christopher T. Graebe has offered a more instrumentalist analysis of Iredell's dissent, pointing out that a number of its legal arguments do not hold water: "Iredell knew the result that the country needed in light of growing Southern discontent with federal power, and he found the requisite law to achieve his political goal." Certainly, Iredell was influenced by an awareness of the political difficulties inherent in the majority's decision. In a draft of part of the opinion that Iredell ultimately omitted, he considered the impossibility of enforcing a judgment against an unwilling state. Turning on its head the adage that "where there is a right, there is a remedy," Iredell suggested that "where no remedy can be found, there is no right."

Iredell again displayed his concern for state prerogatives in *Ware v. Hylton* (1796), another politically charged case. The suit involved a debt contracted before the Revolution; the debtor was a Virginian, the creditor British. In 1777 Virginia passed a sequestration act, allowing citizens who owed money to British creditors to discharge their debts by paying them to the state. In 1780 the debtor took advantage of this statute to discharge part of the debt, but when peace was negotiated in 1783, the treaty provided that creditors on either side should "meet with no lawful impediment" to the recovery of debts contracted before the Revolution. Relying on the treaty, the British creditor sued the Virginia debtor for recovery of the debt—including that part of the debt that had been paid to the state.

Four justices, in separate opinions, held that the 1783 treaty nullified the Virginia sequestration act. As in *Chisholm*, Iredell was the only one to disagree. Having decided the case in the circuit court, he took no actual part in the decision, but he felt strongly enough about the case that he read his circuit court opinion from the bench. In Iredell's view, the provision of the treaty at issue was executory, requiring legislative action to give it effect. Once the Constitution was ratified, the supremacy clause served to repeal the Virginia sequestration act, but "*everything done under the act while in existence,* so far as private rights at least were concerned," was unaffected by the repeal. The defendant, therefore, was no longer a "debtor" as to that part of the debt paid to the state, and the words of the treaty could not apply. This reasoning ignored the political reality that the treaty was expressly directed at allowing British creditors to surmount legal obstacles such as state sequestration and confiscation acts. But Iredell—who appeared to recognize the shaky legal ground on which his argument rested—chose to defer to another political reality, namely, the hostility of the states to this provision of the treaty.

Although Iredell's reading of the law in these cases was influenced by pragmatism, he was far from unprincipled. If he can be said to have defended states' rights, he did so only when no great harm would result to the interests of the federal government. Indeed, given his generally staunch defense of federal power—most evident in the charges he delivered to grand juries while riding circuit—it is likely that his dissents were motivated by a desire to preserve the Union by mollifying those states, including his own, whose fierce independence threatened to tear it apart.

—*Natalie Wexler*

BIBLIOGRAPHY

W. P. Whichard has written the only modern biography, *Justice James Iredell* (2000). A brief but informative biographical sketch of Iredell is Fred L. Israel, "James Iredell," in Friedman and Israel, *Justices*, vol. 1, 121. Thoughtful analysis of Iredell's opinion in *Chisholm v. Georgia* can be found in Christopher T. Graebe, "The Federalism of James Iredell in Historical Context," *North Carolina Law Review* 69 (1990): 251; and, to a lesser extent, in Jeff B. Fordham, "Iredell's Dissent in Chisholm v. Georgia," *North Carolina Historical Review* 8 (1931): 155. See also William R. Casto, "James Iredell and the American Origins of Judicial Review," *Connecticut Law Review* 27 (1995): 329; and C. F. I.

Hickox et al., "James Iredell and the English Origins of American Judicial Review," *Anglo-American Law Review* 23 (1994): 100.

The bulk of Iredell's papers are in the Charles B. Johnson collection at the North Carolina State Department of Archives and History, and others are deposited at Duke University. Both collections contain some items relating to Iredell's judicial career. Griffith J. McRee, *Life and Correspondence of James Iredell* (1857, 1949), is dated and somewhat unreliable but contains transcripts of a number of letters that have since been lost. Many documents and letters relating to Iredell's tenure on the Supreme Court can be found in the volumes of Maeva Marcus, ed., *The Documentary History of the Supreme Court of the United States, 1789–1800* (1985–). For information on Iredell's early life, see Don Higginbotham, ed., *The Papers of James Iredell* (1976).

NOTEWORTHY OPINIONS

Chisholm v. Georgia, 2 U.S. 419 (1793) (Dissent)

Ware v. Hylton, 3 U.S. 171 (1796) (Dissent)

Calder v. Bull, 3 U.S. 386 (1798)

HOWELL EDMUNDS JACKSON

Birth: April 8, 1832, Paris, Tennessee.

Education: West Tennessee College, A.B., 1850; University of Virginia, 1851–1852; Cumberland University, 1856.

Official Positions: Custodian of sequestered property for Confederate states, 1861–1865; judge, Court of Arbitration for Western Tennessee, 1875–1879; state legislator, 1880; U.S. senator, 1881–1886; judge, Sixth Federal Circuit Court, 1886–1891, U.S. Court of Appeals for the Sixth Circuit, 1891–1893.

Supreme Court Service: Nominated associate justice by President Benjamin Harrison, February 2, 1893, to replace Lucius Q. C. Lamar, who had died; confirmed by the Senate, February 18, 1893, by a voice vote; took judicial oath March 4, 1893; served until August 8, 1895; replaced by Rufus W. Peckham, nominated by President Grover Cleveland.

Death: August 8, 1895, Nashville, Tennessee.

History considers the central event in the public life of Howell Jackson to be the ironic irrelevance of a judicial vote that he had overcome serious illness and great distance to cast. A deeper irony, however, may be that history has misunderstood both iterations of *Pollock v. Farmers' Loan & Trust Co.* (1895) and Jackson's support of the small income tax that was held unconstitutional.

Howell Jackson's legal work as an eminent corporate lawyer and Democrat opposed to state debt repudiation led to his election to the U.S. Senate and important alliances with future presidents Grover Cleveland and Benjamin Harrison. It is a measure of Jackson's political skill that he was appointed to the federal appellate bench by Cleveland and to the Supreme Court by Harrison, during the period of their own presidential rivalry.

Like most of the era's judges, Jackson carved no new directions in either economic or civil rights policies. He voted with the majority in *Fong Yue Ting v. United States* (1893), which denied a resident alien due process protection to challenge his deportation under the Chinese Exclusion Act. In *Brass v. North Dakota* (1894), Jackson concurred in Justice David Brewer's dissent from a ruling upholding the constitutionality of state regulation of grain elevators. In *Mobile & Ohio R.R. v. Tennessee* (1894), Jackson invalidated under the contracts clause a Tennessee effort to repudiate the tax exemption provision in a state-granted charter. In 1894 Jackson contracted tuberculosis, and his illness prevented his participation in the Court's narrow interpretation of the Sherman Antitrust Act in *United States v. E. C. Knight Co.* (1895), and its support of the labor injunction in *In re*

Debs that same year. The evidence, however, suggests that he would have strongly supported both rulings.

But for his role in the income tax cases, therefore, this representative of mainstream legal assumptions would have seemed to progressives a typical member of the rogues' gallery of reactionaries that populated the Court during the Gilded Age. Returning to the capital after the first *Pollock* ruling, which had held the tax unconstitutional as applied to income from land, Jackson appeared to be the swing vote for the tax on the remaining questions that had deadlocked the Court. Yet, after the final hearing, the Court held the entire income tax unconstitutional, with Jackson in vocal dissent, generating the view that a "vacillating jurist" must have switched his vote.

Jackson's *Pollock* opinion is his most celebrated, yet a careful reading integrates it with his centrist premises. His problem with the decision was not that a genuinely redistributive law had been thwarted; rather, he believed that precedent and the traditional "practice of the government" had been abandoned. The decision was less a slap at the poor than "the most disastrous blow ever struck at the constitutional power of Congress."

Howell Edmunds Jackson

Progressives and legal realists who argued for a judicial approach based in social facts and policy results criticized the Court for frustrating a genuinely reformist law. From this point of view, Jackson's vote gave him a "liberal" cachet, despite his lifelong corporate associations. Other scholars have argued that lawmakers across the political spectrum sought to maintain the existing order against economic and political upheaval. This view makes Jackson's career, his brief tenure on the Court, and his most celebrated opinion more easily reconcilable.

—*Robert Stanley*

BIBLIOGRAPHY

The primary biographical source is Irving Schiffman, "Howell E. Jackson," in Friedman and Israel, *Justices,* vol. 2, 1603. For a discussion of progressive interpretive assumptions and recent departures, see Robert Stanley, *Dimensions of Law in the Service of Order: Origins of the Federal Income Tax, 1861–1913* (1993).

NOTEWORTHY OPINIONS

Pollock v. Farmers' Loan & Trust Co. 157 U.S. 429 (1895) (Dissent)

ROBERT HOUGHWOUT JACKSON

Birth: February 13, 1892, Spring Creek, Pennsylvania.

Education: Local schools in Frewsburg, New York; Albany Law School, 1912.

Official Positions: General counsel, Bureau of Internal Revenue, 1934–1936; assistant U.S. attorney general, 1936–1938; U.S. solicitor general, 1938–1939; U.S. attorney general, 1940–1941; chief U.S. prosecutor, Nuremberg war crimes trial, 1945–1946.

Supreme Court Service: Nominated associate justice by President Franklin D. Roosevelt, June 12, 1941, to replace Harlan F. Stone, who was promoted to chief justice; confirmed by the Senate, July 7, 1941, by a voice vote; took judicial oath July 11, 1941; served until October 9, 1954; replaced by John Marshall Harlan, nominated by President Dwight D. Eisenhower.

Death: October 9, 1954, Washington, D.C.

In Feburary 1941 President Franklin Roosevelt elevated Harlan Fiske Stone to the chief justiceship and named Attorney General Robert H. Jackson to replace Stone as associate justice. Jackson had provided Roosevelt with legal advice at several important junctures, including FDR's Court-packing plan and the lend-lease program, which had circumvented a congressional prohibition to provide essential military equipment to Great Britain.

Jackson joined the Court during a transition period. After the so-called "switch in time" in 1937, when Justice Owen Roberts changed his position on some important issues, a new majority of the Court had begun to embrace the modern regulatory state. By the time of Jackson's appointment, all of the justices except Harlan Stone and Roberts were Roosevelt appointees. Although the direction of change was clear, the new doctrines had not yet received their decisive formulations. Having abandoned the effort to protect economic rights from government regulation, the Court was also just beginning to find a new role for itself as a defender of civil liberties. Jackson helped create the modern doctrinal rules governing judicial review of economic regulations. He also participated in the process by which the Court became the guardian of free speech and other individual rights.

Jackson was something of a maverick. He served with Justices Hugo Black and Felix Frankfurter, who created, respectively, the intellectual bases for the Warren Court and for its critics. Unlike those justices, however, Jackson's votes could not be easily predicted on the basis of his general judicial philosophy. His opinions have a far more personal touch than those of most judges of the period or even today. They combine vivid metaphors with a sometimes sardonic humor. Many of his opinions are forgotten now because the evolution of the law took a different path.

But some of them took root and seem as fresh today as when they were written. For example, his opinion in the second flag salute case provided the foundation for the Court's important and controversial flag-burning opinions nearly fifty years later.

Born on a western Pennsylvania farm, Jackson was a fourth-generation Democrat with strong rural roots; his great-grandfather had been a staunch supporter of Andrew Jackson. His father operated a livery stable and country hotel. Although Robert Jackson attended law school for one year, he was self-educated, holding neither an undergraduate nor a law degree. He was the last justice to have qualified as a lawyer by "reading law" rather than through formal legal education. He finished a two-year course in one year at Albany Law School only because he had decided to set up a small practice in Jamestown, New York, and many of the leading lawyers in that town had studied at Albany. Later, his clients included businessmen, labor unions, and farmers. He was active in New York politics and became an adviser to New York's Democratic governor, Franklin Roosevelt. In the 1932 presidential election Jackson campaigned for Roosevelt throughout New York State.

At the age of forty-two, Jackson moved to Washington, D.C., where he worked for the rest of his life as a government lawyer and a judge. As general counsel to the Bureau of Internal Revenue (where he successfully brought tax evasion proceedings against Andrew Mellon, former secretary of the Treasury), then as solicitor general and later attorney general, Jackson was considered a staunchly loyal New Dealer. He would describe the period of his service as solicitor general as the happiest part of his life.

Jackson's horizons were not, however, limited to the law. He was considered a serious possibility for the Democratic Party's presidential nomination in 1940 in the event that Roosevelt decided not to run again. He also received international acclaim for his role as chief prosecutor in the Nuremberg war crimes trial.

Robert Houghwout Jackson

During World War II, Jackson had felt removed from the great events of the period; he remarked that on the Monday after Pearl Harbor, the Court had heard arguments about the taxability of greens fees at country clubs. He welcomed the opportunity to participate in the Nuremberg trials. Although he took the Nuremberg assignment against the advice of Chief Justice Stone, his successful prosecution helped establish important new principles of international law. Indeed, Jackson viewed the Nuremberg prosecution as his most important professional achievement. Unfortunately, at the close of the trials, Jackson learned that for a second time he would be passed over for the position of chief justice. His response was swift and savage. He publicly proclaimed that the Court was split by ideological differences and that his nomination as chief justice had been blocked by the civil libertarian wing of the Court, in particular by Black. The repercussions of this ugly public fight between the justices poisoned Jackson's later years on the Court.

Jackson's most famous opinion is undoubtedly *West Virginia State Board of Education v. Barnette* (1943). In June 1940, before Jackson joined the Court, the justices had decided *Minersville School District v. Gobitis*. In an opinion by Justice Frankfurter, the Court held that a Jehovah's Witness could be expelled from school for refusing to salute the flag for religious reasons. It may be no coincidence that this opinion was announced at a time when the European picture was gloomy indeed. In the same month that *Gobitis* was decided, the British were evacuating Dunkirk, and the Germans were closing in on Paris. Nor, at that time, did the Court have a robust history of defending free speech. It is little wonder, under the circumstances, that Frankfurter wrote for an 8–1 majority in support of national unity. Stone was the only dissenter.

By 1943 it was clear that *Gobitis* had dubious prospects. Justices Black, William O. Douglas, and Frank Murphy took advantage of another case involving the Jehovah's Witnesses to make an extraordinary public announcement that they no longer supported the *Gobitis* ruling. Justice Wiley Rutledge, who was appointed in 1943, was also known to oppose *Gobitis* because of a dissent he had written as a court of appeals judge in another case involving the Witnesses.

Jackson began his opinion overruling *Gobitis* with several pages of factual background. He recounted how, after *Gobitis*, the West Virginia legislature enacted a requirement that all schools present courses on civics. Two years later, the state board of education adopted a resolution ordering all students and teachers to salute the flag, "provided, however, that refusal to salute the flag be regarded as an act of insubordination, and shall be dealt with accordingly." The penalty for this insubordination was expulsion, with the added result that the child was considered a truant, so that he or she could be sent to a reformatory as a delinquent and the parents could be prosecuted criminally.

Jackson began his analysis with the premise that the flag salute, although not verbal, is nevertheless a form of communication. As he said, "Objection to this form of communication when coerced is an old one, well known to the framers of the Bill of Rights."

An accompanying footnote pointed out that William Tell was sentenced to shoot the famous apple off his son's head "for refusal to salute a bailiff's hat." Jackson next observed that censorship of speech, under the Court's precedents, could be allowed only if the speech created a "clear and present danger." "It would seem," he added, "that involuntary affirmation could be commanded only on even more immediate and urgent grounds than silence." But in reality, the state had not even purported to identify a clear and present danger of any kind. Therefore, Jackson said, sustaining the West Virginia rule would imply "that a Bill of Rights which guards the individual's right to speak his own mind, left it open to public authorities to compel him to utter what is not in his mind."

Jackson then turned to the *Gobitis* precedent. He noted that the opinion in that case had focused on the question of religious exemption, assuming that the mandatory flag salute was otherwise constitutional. Notably, Jackson declined to follow *Gobitis* in deferring to state authorities. As to the role of school boards as representatives of the local community, he declared in a frequently quoted passage:

> The very purpose of a Bill of Rights was to withdraw certain subjects from the vicissitudes of political controversy, to place them beyond the reach of majorities and officials and to establish them as legal principles to be applied by the courts. One's right to life, liberty, and property, to free speech, freedom of worship and assembly, and other fundamental rights may not be submitted to vote; they depend on the outcome of no elections.

Nor was Jackson persuaded by the argument that school boards had greater expertise than judges in educational matters, for "we act in these matters not by authority of our competence but by force of our commissions."

This brought Jackson to the heart of the case. In an apparent reference to the Nazis, he said that "those who begin coercive elimination of dissent soon find themselves exterminating dissenters." Compulsory uniformity, in the end, "achieves only the unanimity of the graveyard." He closed the opinion with a passage that has become famous to generations of law students and scholars:

> The case is made difficult not because the principles of its decision are obscure but because the flag involved is our own. . . . But freedom to differ is not limited to things that do not matter much. That would be a mere shadow of freedom. The test of its substance is the right to differ as to things that touch the heart of the existing order.
>
> If there is any fixed star in our constitutional constellation, it is that no official, high or petty, can prescribe what shall be orthodox in politics, nationalism, religion, or other matters of opinion or force citizens to confess by word or act their faith therein.

Barnette historically marked the Court's shift from the protection of economic interests to individual rights. Today, First Amendment doctrine is a complicated skein of rules and standards, and judicial opinions are more likely to discuss the appropriate standard for judicial review than to revisit the basic values underlying the amendment. *Barnette* did not break new ground in the sense of articulating a new test; it essentially retained the existing clear and present danger test. But in a sense, all of the current doctrinal complexities are no more than a series of footnotes to Jackson's resounding affirmation of freedom of thought and speech.

Barnette today overshadows Jackson's other, less powerful First Amendment opinions. For example, in *Terminiello v. Chicago* (1949), the Court reversed the conviction of a vituperatively anti-Semitic, anti-Catholic speaker. The Court held that the jury instructions were fatally flawed because they allowed conviction for speech that "stirs the public to anger, invites dispute, brings about a condition of unrest, or creates a disturbance." Jackson dissented. He saw more at stake than just a street-corner demagogue. Rather, he saw a replay of the street battles of the Weimar Republic, which culminated in Hitler's rise to power. The influence of his Nuremberg experience is evident

here. But *Terminiello* also reflects Jackson's general willingness to distinguish between the suppression of ideas of the kind he rejected in *Barnette* and responses to concrete harms, which he usually found tolerable. For example, in his dissenting opinion in *Douglas v. City of Jeannette* (1943), he was willing to uphold a ban on door-to-door solicitation by Jehovah's Witnesses as a way to protect the privacy of residents.

Apart from *Barnette*, Jackson's most important opinions involved structural constitutional issues—federalism and separation of powers—rather than individual rights. Perhaps because of his extensive experience in government, he was able to make a lasting contribution to the law in these areas.

Jackson wrote a seminal opinion in *Youngstown Sheet & Tube Co. v. Sawyer* (1952), the steel seizure case. Although only a concurring opinion, Jackson's test was later cited more often than Black's majority opinion as the governing test. The case arose during the Korean War. To head off a nationwide strike of steel workers, which was thought to be a threat to the war effort, President Harry S. Truman issued an executive order directing the secretary of commerce to take charge of most of the steel mills. The order was based on "inherent presidential power" rather than on any specific statutory authority. This order presented the Court with difficult and unprecedented questions regarding the scope of presidential power.

For Black, this case was simple. No express constitutional provision gave the president the power to seize the steel mills. Rather than granting the president the authority to formulate public policy, the Constitution gave Congress the lawmaking power. For Black, no more needed to be said.

Although it is officially the "opinion of the Court," Black's majority opinion reflected a frail consensus. Each justice who joined Black's opinion also felt called upon to file a concurring opinion: Justice Tom C. Clark agreed only with the result but not with Black's opinions, and Chief Justice Fred Vinson and Justices Stanley Reed and Sherman Minton dissented. The reason for the dissatisfaction with Black's opinion was probably that although it accurately reflected the constitutional text, it entirely ignored the evolution of the presidency over the course of almost two centuries since the founding.

Jackson began his influential concurrence with a candid disclosure that his experience as a presidential counselor probably had colored his views more than conventional legal sources. In light of that experience, he rejected Black's formalistic approach. For, as Jackson said, the "actual art of governing under our Constitution does not and cannot conform to judicial definitions of the power of any of its branches based on isolated clauses or even single Articles torn from context."

To provide guidance in analyzing the tangled relationships between the branches of government, Jackson offered what he called a "somewhat over-simplified" classification of presidential actions. He distinguished three categories of presidential acts. First, Congress may have authorized the presidential action, either implicitly or explicitly. In this situation, the president's power is at its peak because he acts by virtue of the combined powers of both branches. Second, when Congress has been silent on the subject, the president must rely on the independent constitutional powers of his office, but "there is a zone of twilight" in which those powers overlap with congressional authority. Here, "any actual test of power is likely to depend on the imperatives of events and contemporary imponderables rather than on abstract theories of law." Third, when Congress has forbidden the presidential action, "his power is at its lowest ebb." In this situation of direct conflict between the two branches, the president's claim must be scrutinized with special caution, lest the "equilibrium" of the constitutional system be upset.

Clearly, the steel seizure did not belong to the first category of specifically authorized actions. As to the second category, Jackson could find no basis for a claim of inherent presidential power. He specifically rejected the government's claim that the first clause of Article II, vesting the executive power in the president, was a general grant of all executive powers. Nor was he willing to accept the view that the president had broad inherent powers, beyond those in the constitutional text, to deal with emergencies. After

reviewing recent European history, he concluded that "emergency powers are consistent with free government only when their control is lodged elsewhere than in the Executive."

In closing, Jackson remarked on the evolution of presidential powers:

> The Constitution does not disclose the measure of the actual controls wielded by the modern presidential office. That office must be understood as an Eighteenth-Century sketch of a government hoped for, not as a blueprint of the Government that is. . . . Subtle shifts take place in the centers of real power that do not show on the face of the Constitution.

Given the amount of power that had gravitated to the White House already, Jackson saw no reason for the Court to further aggrandize the presidency.

The consequences of recognizing a broad presidential power to respond to national emergencies were, in Jackson's view, unforeseeable. Acknowledging such a presidential power might erode the very basis of the rule of law, for "with all its defects, delays and inconveniences, men have discovered no technique for long preserving free government except that the Executive be under the law, and that the law be made by parliamentary deliberations." More than twenty-five years later, in *Dames & Moore v. Regan* (1981), a case arising from the Iranian hostage situation, the Court turned to Jackson's concurrence as a guiding framework for analyzing presidential power.

Jackson came to the Court in a period when the relationships between the federal government and the states were in flux. He wrote an opinion that crystallized the new understanding of the scope of federal power. *Wickard v. Filburn* (1942) involved wheat quotas adopted under the Agricultural Adjustment Act. The statute was designed to stabilize wheat production through the use of quotas, which were subject to approval by the farmers themselves in a referendum. Roscoe Filburn owned a dairy and poultry farm in Ohio. He raised a small amount of wheat, sold part, and used the rest for livestock feed, home consumption, and as seed for the following year. The question before the Court was whether, as applied to the wheat Filburn used himself rather than selling, the statute was a valid regulation of interstate commerce.

Jackson's opinion for the Court in *Wickard* is a ringing affirmation of national power. Prior decisions had suggested that Congress could regulate interstate sales and transportation, but not "local" activities such as production or consumption. Jackson rejected the concept that these local activities are beyond the commerce power. By producing wheat for his own use, Filburn was reducing the demand in the interstate market for wheat. Admittedly, the effect of his individual activities was minuscule. But Congress had the power to regulate his activities because "his contribution, taken together with that of many others similarly situated, is far from trivial." This test paved the way for the later adoption of the 1964 Civil Rights Act, which was based on Congress's power to regulate interstate commerce.

The obverse side of congressional power consists of limits on state power. Although the commerce clause on its face is simply a grant of power to Congress, since the early days of the Republic it has also been considered a limitation on the powers of the states. Here again, Jackson took a strong nationalist stand. He believed passionately in the importance of free trade between the states, and he viewed the commerce clause as mandating a national common market. *H. P. Hood & Sons, Inc. v. Du Mond* (1949) is one of his strongest judicial statements of this philosophy. Hood supplied milk to Boston and wanted to make additional purchases in New York State for the Boston market. Under New York law, Hood needed a state license to open an additional facility for receiving milk from farmers. The New York statute required the state agriculture commissioner to determine "that the issuance of the license will not tend to a destructive competition in a market already adequately served." The commissioner denied the license on the grounds that the dairy market was already adequately served and that Hood's purchases would divert milk from local consumption.

As Jackson pointed out, the dairy industry was heavily regulated and had already given rise to several Supreme Court opinions regarding state interference with interstate commerce. In one of those earlier cases, Justice Benjamin Cardozo had remarked that the Constitution was "framed upon the theory that the peoples of the several states must sink or swim together." As Jackson pointed out, one of the primary flaws of the Articles of Confederation had been the existence of trade barriers among the states. The Constitution therefore established the "principle that our economic unit is the Nation."

Jackson's description of the commerce clause culminates in a powerful endorsement of free trade among the states:

> Our system, fostered by the Commerce Clause, is that every farmer and every craftsman shall be encouraged to produce by the certainty that he will have free access to every market in the Nation, that no home embargoes will withhold his export, and no foreign state will by customs duties or regulations exclude them. Likewise, every consumer may look to the free competition from every producing area in the Nation to protect him from exploitation by any. Such was the vision of the Founders, such has been the doctrine of this Court which has given it reality.

He concluded that New York, by attempting to protect local buyers of milk from interstate competition, was directly flouting this basic principle of a national common market.

Jackson remains a somewhat enigmatic figure. Some of his opinions helped lay the foundations for important doctrinal developments. Others seem quaint or even quirky. The latter category is illustrated by his dissent in *Beauharnais v. Illinois* (1952), in which Jackson endorsed the general principle of treating racist speech as "group libel" but argued that the defendant was entitled to a jury trial regarding the truth of his racist credo. Today, this seems a somewhat eccentric position.

Jackson's best opinions, however, are a unique addition to the Court's jurisprudence. Their distinguishing feature is their bold effort to enunciate broad principles. Although Jackson related those principles to the intent of the framers and earlier precedents, he was also candid in admitting that they reflected value judgments based on history and contemporary experience. This technique could misfire when Jackson incorrectly judged the values toward which society was moving. But when it worked—when he called upon values that were to prove basic and enduring—his opinions provided a strong foundation on which other, more legalistic, justices could build.

—*Daniel A. Farber*

BIBLIOGRAPHY

The Jackson papers are in the Library of Congress, and the Columbia University oral history collection holds a large and important memoir. Eugene Gerhart, *America's Advocate: Robert H. Jackson* (1958), is uncritical and relies heavily on a lengthy autobiographical sketch Jackson wrote to defend his point of view in the imbroglio over the chief justiceship.

Jackson's *The Struggle for Judicial Supremacy* (1941) expresses his view of the Court's evolution as an institution, with particular reference to the *Lochner* era and the 1937 "switch-in-time" that upheld the New Deal. His ideas on the Court are well explained in Glendon Schubert, *Dispassionate Justice: A Synthesis of the Judicial Opinions of Robert H. Jackson* (1969). For Jackson's ideas within the context of the Court he served on, see Jeffrey D. Hockett, *New Deal Justice: The Constitutional Jurisprudence of Hugo L. Black, Felix Frankfurter, and Robert H. Jackson* (1996).

For other analyses, see Felix Frankfurter, "Mr. Justice Jackson," *Harvard Law Review* 68 (1955): 938, an appraisal by a judicial ally; the symposium, "Mr. Justice Jackson," in *Stanford Law Review* 8 (1955); Louis Jaffe, "Mr. Justice Jackson," *Harvard Law Review* 68 (1955): 940, a thoughtful overview of Jackson's opinions and legal writings; and G. Edward White, *The American Judicial Tradition: Profiles of Leading American Judges* (1976), which includes a thoughtful essay about Jackson's jurisprudence. Although he did not write separately in the school desegregation cases, Jackson suffered a great deal in coming to terms with the eventual decision; see G. S. Chernak, "The Clash of Two Worlds: Justice Robert H. Jackson, Institutional Pragmatism, and *Brown*," *Temple Law Review* 72 (1999): 51.

NOTEWORTHY OPINIONS

Wickard v. Filburn, 317 U.S. 111 (1942)

West Virginia State Board of Education v. Barnette, 319 U.S. 624 (1943)

H. P. Hood & Sons, Inc. v. Du Mond, 336 U.S. 525 (1949)

Terminiello v. Chicago, 337 U.S. 1 (1949) (Dissent)

Beauharnais v. Illinois, 343 U.S. 250 (1952) (Dissent)

Youngstown Sheet & Tube Co. v. Sawyer, 343 U.S. 579 (1952) (Concurrence)

JOHN JAY

Birth: December 12, 1745, New York City.

Education: Privately tutored; attended boarding school; graduated from King's College (later Columbia University), 1764; clerked in law office of Benjamin Kissam; admitted to the bar in 1768.

Official Positions: Secretary, Royal Boundary Commission, 1773; member, New York Committee of 51, 1774; delegate, Continental Congress, 1774, 1775, 1777, president, 1778–1779; delegate, New York Provincial Congress, 1776–1777; chief justice, New York Superior Court, 1777–1778; minister to Spain, 1779; secretary of foreign affairs, 1784–1789; envoy to Great Britain, 1794–1795; governor, New York, 1795–1801.

Supreme Court Service: Nominated chief justice by President George Washington, September 24, 1789; confirmed by the Senate, September 26, 1789, by a voice vote; took judicial oath October 9, 1789; resigned June 29, 1795; replaced by Oliver Ellsworth, nominated by President Washington.

Death: May 17, 1829, Bedford, New York.

The war for American independence catapulted dozens of young, barely seasoned politicians and lawyers into positions of extraordinary power and influence. Among them was the reserved, eminently capable John Jay of New York—the first chief justice of the United States.

Early experiences powerfully shaped Jay's conception of the "good" political society and the role of judicial statesmen in republics. The eldest son of the wealthy Peter and Mary Van Cortlandt Jay, John followed the path dictated by his parents' social class and connections within the New York mercantile community. He was educated privately until 1760, when he matriculated at King's College (now Columbia University) to deepen his mastery of the classics, natural science, public law, and philosophy (including political economy).

Jay decided to take up the study of law only in his final year at university, partly, as was customary among gentlemen, in preparation for public service. He graduated with honors and began an apprenticeship in the law office of eminent attorney Benjamin Kissam, where, as assistant to the chief clerk, Jay chafed under piles of tedious copy work. When city lawyers struck in 1765 in support of colonial protests of the Stamp Act, Jay happily fled to the family estate in Rye, New York, where he immersed himself in the classics, philosophy, and political theory.

In 1766 Jay returned to Kissam's firm as chief clerk, and two years later gained admission to the New York bar and opened law offices in the city with Robert Livingston Jr., an old schoolmate. There, he threw himself into work, the whirl of high society, debating clubs, and conservative state political groups.

In 1769 Jay accepted his first public office as a commissioner to settle a boundary dispute between New York and New Jersey.

Jay's generation was soon to confront adversity. By 1774 the streets and wharves of American port cities rumbled with rebellious talk about the Intolerable Acts, King George III's abrogation of his coronation oath, and ministerial violations of the ancient English constitution. At first, Jay resisted independence: he helped formulate the conciliatory olive branch petition of 1774 and seriously considered moving to London as an alternative to treason. But by 1775 the transatlantic volley of exchanges about the status of colonies and the merits of continued membership in the British union proved to be powerful attractions to an up-and-coming expert in political economy and foreign affairs. Jay feared, too, that the Crown no longer could protect colonial property and trade—in Jay's view the "great and weighty reasons" underlying genuinely useful alliances and political unions.

Jay therefore remained in New York to serve the cause, both in his home state and in the First and Second Continental Congresses. He sat on state committees of correspondence and safety, synchronizing intercolonial protests and providing a semblance of government as the British magistracy collapsed. Jay helped draft the New York Constitution, and until 1779 he also served (erratically and without distinction) as chief justice of the New York Superior Court.

Independence proved to be a watershed in Jay's career. In the space of a few months, he found himself starring—without much of a script—in the drama of

national establishment. In 1778, while still sitting on the state bench, and only three days after his arrival in Philadelphia as a New York delegate to the general government, Jay was elected president of Congress. A year later he became minister plenipotentiary to Spain, and in 1782 he was one of five commissioners sent to Europe to negotiate what would become the Paris Peace Treaty with Great Britain.

These rapid-fire experiences were formative: Jay quickly came to believe that his original, gloomy assessment of American prospects for success had been appallingly accurate. As a weak quasi-executive in Congress, Jay helplessly watched the confederation collapse. Americans were experiencing growing pains—the invention of modern party politics, for example, and the flexing of capitalist muscle, but Jay saw only degenerate partisan bickering, demagoguery, excessive "leveling," logjams in Congress, a dangerous tendency to fetter diplomats, drifts of worthless paper currency, and interstate competition for trading alliances. In Europe, Jay personally guaranteed repayment of war loans and encouraged entrepreneurs to invest in America; privately, he despaired of Americans' capacity for virtue and Congress's ability to navigate the rapids between independence and nationhood.

When Jay returned to New York in July 1784, he turned down ambassadorships to Britain and France in favor of law practice and state politics. But the respite was brief. Within weeks, Congress drafted Jay to be secretary of foreign affairs, an office he held until 1789. He remained secretary of state ad interim

John Jay

until March 1790, when Thomas Jefferson returned from Europe.

As Jay struggled to prevent disaster in Congress and abroad, his anxieties about the "degraded" condition of New World republicans, and about American prospects for survival in the hurly-burly of international exchange, gave rise to a stringently conservative scheme for unification and stabilization. As early as 1784–1785, he advocated the creation of a coercive, departmentalized federation with enhanced executive prerogative, a Congress capable of ensuring economic growth and the security of property, and a superior federal judiciary possessed of strength sufficient to immobilize self-serving states. On the question of federal power, Jay (with Alexander Hamilton) epitomized high federalism: in 1785 he told John Adams that, in a perfect world, he would have the states "considered . . . in the same light in which counties stand to the States," as mere administrative "districts to facilitate the purposes of domestic order and good government," not as separate seats of sovereignty.

By 1788 observers viewed Jay as a linchpin in the drive to secure ratification of the new federal constitution. Because of illness, he wrote only five articles for *The Federalist Papers* (Nos. 2 through 5 and 64) in areas of his particular expertise—foreign affairs, federal treaty powers, relations between domestic stability and long-term prosperity, and the utility of well-enforced federal laws as Americans struggled to persuade Europeans of republican reliability. Jay fretted about vaguely worded reservations of state power in the federation, and so supported subsequent calls for revisionary constitutional conventions. But, after federation, Jay gladly accepted a commission as the Republic's first chief justice (and, as it turned out, as a judge of the Eastern Circuit established by the First Congress). On February 2, 1790, he called his new Court to order with a quorum of four judges.

Jay's acceptance of the chief justiceship seems odd. Why would a man known widely as an indispensable (if not particularly imaginative) political economist and diplomat, and only secondarily as a lawyer, agree to preside over an untested, controversial tribunal, years before the articulation of the Supreme Court's implied power to review acts of Congress? In the late eighteenth century, legitimacy and prestige attached most completely to firmly established ideas and institutions; the Supreme Court boasted no history, no case law or procedure separate from British law practice, no distinguished bar, no clear role in governance beyond responsibility to decide certain limited categories of legal disputes. Jay himself had exhibited scant interest in his state judgeship or the minutiae of legal research. Why, then, did he leave the political spotlight, abandon a lucrative law practice, and preside over a docketless court in borrowed chambers at the New York City Stock Exchange?

Jay's decision makes sense when viewed in light of his experience and priorities. The years between 1787 and 1803, to borrow historian Bernard Bailyn's phrase, might be termed a "soft ambiguous moment" in the history of the judiciary. No chief justice, then or now, could make of the Court whatever he wished; but within the vague outlines sketched in Philadelphia and in the 1789 Judiciary and Process Acts, the Court—perhaps for the last time in its history—could be pressed into service in decidedly unmodern ways, to reflect the interests and assumptions of the diplomat seated as chief justice. Washington chose a friend he knew to be schooled in the law of nations, economy, and a political philosophy based on the writings of Edmund Burke. Moreover, as the president put it in 1794, Jay had been "personally conversant" with signatories of the 1783 peace treaty, served as foreign affairs secretary, and helped frame republican constitutions, thereby fitting himself for judicial statesmanship at a dangerous moment in American history.

How did John Jay envision the chief justiceship and the Supreme Court's role in government? A staunch Federalist might be expected to hope—and Jay did—that federal courts might be used as a hedge against "Laws dictated by the Spirit of the Times not the Spirit of Justice." But Jay's vision amounted to more than a mindless attempt to impose order. By 1790 Jay believed that the pressing issue of the day was American survival within a skeptical global community; the Republic needed to escape unhealthy economic dependence in relations with Europeans, including a heavy debt load, and move toward healthy, reciprocal trading alliances. Only then, said Jay, could Americans be "honest and grateful to our allies, but . . . think for ourselves." In Jay's judgment, national prosperity—his long-term and most important "object of state"—depended entirely on refurbishing a tarnished reputation and persuading Europeans that Americans would protect property, create stable currencies, and make good on the terms of contracts and treaties.

Jay pinned his hopes for the realization of his "objects" on the federal judiciary and effective deployment of relevant bodies of federal law. By enforcing contracts and treaties, judges could construct images of reliability; they also could force states to accept federal guidelines in the creation of uniform economic legislation. Although Jay did not object to the notion of implied powers of judicial review and indeed encouraged his colleagues to exercise review powers on circuit, he probably did not envision a John Marshall–style Supreme Court aimed primarily at domestic development and consolidation. As more than one scholar has noted, Jay was a cosmopolitan figure, with one eye trained perpetually on Europe, and he hoped to use the Court to ensure domestic stability so that America might experience prosperity as a trading nation.

Federal courts also would expose citizens to the moralizing principles embedded in the bodies of law Jay particularly admired—notably the law of nations, which he took to be a virtual codification of God's will. In this way, imperfect republicans eventually might achieve the perfection that the framers, in a fit of republican zeal, wrongly imputed to the electorate. As Jay explained in 1793, society was not yet "so far improved, and the Science of Government [so perfected] that the whole nation could in the peaceable course of law, be compelled to do justice." Federal courts would educate as well as control the citizenry by means of grand jury charges and the swift execution of well-made laws.

Jay's vision proved chimerical. The associate justices complained incessantly about onerous circuit-riding duties, and their objections eroded morale.

And, although grand jury charges provided a welcome occasion to instruct jurymen and newspaper readers on the fine points of the federal government, Jay had too few occasions to use his new court as an instrument in pursuit of "great objects."

Nevertheless, Jay's contributions probably were more substantial than scholars recognize: the justices laboriously hammered out rules of practice and evidence, established a federal bar, and, by pointedly relying on state practice whenever possible, chipped away at Republican charges of Federalist tyranny. Jay also modestly strengthened the Court's shaky position within the general government. In a 1792 New York circuit court hearing on a writ of *mandamus* in *Hayburn's Case*, he defended the separation of powers by refusing to allow federal courts to pass judgment, as federal statute required, on claims of invalid pensioners. The decision, reinforced in 1794 by suggestive language in *Glass v. Sloop Betsey*, paved the way for later attempts to garner implied review powers.

Finally, Jay was able to wield federal judicial power in defense of the Treaty of Paris and American sovereignty in relations with Europe. His dissent on circuit in *Ware v. Hylton* anticipated the Supreme Court's insistence on adherence to treaty provisions in a 1796 appeal of the same case; and in the *Sloop Betsey* case, Jay ruled against France's use of its American consul as a prize agent, thereby shoring up the precarious U.S. claim of sovereignty.

The Court, however, fell far short of its chief justice's expectations: by 1793 Jay decided to pursue his "objects" through diplomacy and other executive posts. The proximate cause of Jay's dejection was the state of Georgia and, more particularly, its insistence in the 1793 case of *Chisholm v. Georgia* (the first constitutional law case decided by the Supreme Court) on the ongoing utility in republics of the old monarchical doctrine of sovereign immunity.

The case concerned a claim arising from the Revolutionary War. In 1792 Alexander Chisholm, a South Carolinian and the executor of the estate of Robert Farquhar, sought state payment on a war supply contract. He invoked the Court's original diversity jurisdiction in suits between citizens of different states, or between states and noncitizens. The state of Georgia returned the summons, claiming sovereign immunity from federal process. Also in 1792 the Court heard arguments in *Georgia v. Brailsford,* a bill in equity in which Georgia appeared willingly as complainant, hoping to recover the amount of a debt originally owed to South Carolinian Loyalists and a Briton whose property had been either confiscated or sequestered (justices disagreed on the point) during the Revolution.

The amount had become the object of an injunction, and although his colleagues urged otherwise, Jay continued the restraining order (dissolved in 1794, when Georgia brought and lost an action at law), partly so that Jay could exploit Georgia's voluntary appearance in his *Chisholm* opinion. Both disputes generally addressed state obligations to settle Loyalist claims fairly, as the Paris Treaty required. Therefore, they also tested whether federal courts might be useful to Jay in restoring America's reputation in Europe. If "national regularity" depended on "attention and obedience to those rules and principles of conduct which reason indicates and which morality and wisdom prescribe," Jay said, Georgia's recalcitrance threatened not only the Union, but also American prospects on an international stage.

In separate opinions, which was the Court's usual practice before Chief Justice Marshall changed it, Jay and Justice James Wilson contended that the whole people, not the states, had compacted to form a federation and so could hold a state accountable for behavior damaging to the nation. The relevant clause in Article III of the federal Constitution, after all, did not exclude suits by citizens of other states, nor did it require state consent for such suits. By the same logic, the sovereign people surely could summon states. Jay pointed to *Brailsford:* were federal courts mere conveniences, to be heeded only when states benefited from decisions?

The Court's 1793 ruling by default (because Georgia refused to appear) against the state claim of sovereign immunity seemed to render depleted state treasuries vulnerable to the claims of war suppliers and traitors. If the Jay Court had its way, moreover, other states soon would eat humble pie: on February 20, 1793, process had been returned and the state ordered to appear at the next term in *Oswald v. New York.* Simultaneously, the Court awarded a subpoena in *Grayson et al. v. Virginia;* five months later, William Vassal, a Loyalist victim of Massachusetts's confiscation statute, was granted a subpoena, which inspired Gov. John Hancock to deliver a speech warning his countrymen of the perils of runaway judicial federalism.

Because these cases and many others threatened a flood of litigation against states and insupportable pressure on state treasuries, Jay's decisions in the Georgia cases caused widespread alarm. On December 14, 1792, the Georgia Assembly had resolved not to be bound by an unfavorable Court ruling; after *Chisholm,* a Georgia grand jury formally presented a grievance to the governor, Edward Telfair, who in turn urged passage of a statute (enacted two weeks later) affirming state sovereign immunity. On March 18, 1793, Massachusetts legislators in special session spearheaded a movement encouraging Congress to adopt the Eleventh Amendment, which made it impossible for federal officers to summon states as defendants. Virginia officially condemned Jay for attacking the reserved sovereignty of states, and Georgians toyed with hanging federal officers, should they again try to force a state appearance. In 1798, when the amendment took effect, the clerk of the Supreme Court painstakingly entered a list of reversals, including *Chisholm,* in the minute book for "want of jurisdiction."

The comparative ease with which the states humiliated the highest court in the land caused Jay to despair of its potential as an effective agency of government. In 1794, while still serving as chief justice, he sailed to England as envoy extraordinaire to defuse tensions with Britain over unpaid debts, sequestration of Loyalist estates by state governments, and New World trading rights. The Jay Treaty established mixed commissions to resolve economic disputes, granted trade concessions to Britain, and shifted responsibility for payment of defaulted loans to Congress. Despite formidable resistance to the treaty, the Senate ratified it in 1795. Jay was relieved: "Should the treaty prove ... beneficial," he wrote, "justice will *finally* be done. If not, be it so—my mind is at ease." In a revealing letter, Jay told Edmund Randolph that the treaty's debt-related sixth article addressed "that justice and equity which judicial proceedings may, on trial, be found incapable of affording"; commissioners could do "exactly what is right."

In 1795 Jay was elected governor of New York in absentia, and he resigned from the Court. When President John Adams asked him to resume his judicial post in 1800, Jay demurred on the ground that he yearned for retirement and still perceived the Court to be destitute of "energy, weight and dignity." In 1801 he retired to his farm in Westchester County, New York. Jay had no taste for Jeffersonian America; he particularly deplored the public fascination with Jacobinism and weak government. Yet his favored maxim always had been "Fortitude founded on Resignation." Despite poor health, he devoted the rest of his life to the Episcopal Church, an extensive correspondence, and abolitionism.

More completely perhaps than any of his Federalist allies, Jay believed that evil stalked humankind, that order prevailed only within firm legal structures, and that Republicans lacked virtue, wisdom, and discipline. When Alexander Hamilton advocated manipulation of election returns in 1800 to defeat Jefferson, Jay quietly wrote off both Hamilton and federalism: it was better to sacrifice individuals and party than moral principle. Jay probably died without changing his mind about the inadequacy of republicanism. After witnessing the failure of his conception of judicial statesmanship at the hand of licentious states, he simply could not foresee American success. Surely the Republic would succumb to anarchy, he warned in *Chisholm*, if a "pleasure to obey or transgress with impunity should be substituted in the place of a sanction to its laws." Benjamin Kissam's chief clerk, Lindley Murray, said of the young Jay that he had been notable for "strong reasoning powers, comprehensive views, indefatigable application, and uncommon firmness of mind"; in mid-life, these traits crystallized into a sophisticated but rigidly legalistic conservatism. Historian Richard Morris perhaps said it best:

"[Jay's] tireless effort to endow the national government with energy, capacity, and scope ... attests to his vision, courage, and tenacity," he wrote in 1967. "It remained for others to spell out the safeguards for individual liberties and the limitation on national power ... essential to the maintenance of a democratic society."

—*Sandra F. VanBurkleo*

BIBLIOGRAPHY

The Jay papers are in the Columbia University libraries, and various portions are available in a variety of editions. Biographical studies of Jay include Irving Dilliard's sketch in Friedman and Israel, *Justices*, vols. 1, 3, a gracefully written essay, only slightly impatient with the Jay Court's decidedly unmodern appearance and behavior; and Herbert Johnson, *John Jay, 1745–1829* (1970), an older empathetic description of his life, flawed by limited exposure to critical documents and the literature of the Revolution.

The best brief study of Jay's stint on the bench is Richard Morris, *John Jay, the Nation, and the Court* (1967), although it is flawed by its anachronistic determination to rescue Jay by transforming him into a pale imitation of John Marshall. For fuller accounts of the early Court, see Maeva Marcus, ed., *The Documentary History of the Supreme Court of the United States; 1789–1800* (1985–), an invaluable guide to the Supreme Court's business with a sound biographical sketch of Jay; and Julius Goebel, *History of the Supreme Court of the United States: Antecedents and Beginnings to 1801* (1971), the first volume of the *Holmes Devise History*, the most consistently useful compilation of information about the Court's first decade in doctrinal and institutional terms, but staunchly anti-Jay and not particularly sensitive to the context of legal development. More recent studies of the Jay and his Court include Scott Douglas Gerber, *Seriatim: The Supreme Court Before John Marshall* (1998) especially Sandra F. VanBurkleo, " 'Honour, Justice, and Interest': Great Objects of State: John Jay's Republican Politics and Statesmanship on the Federal Bench," a revised and expanded version of her article of the same title in *Journal of the Early Republic* (1984): 239. Both articles are critical of earlier attempts to restore Jay to the judicial pantheon by modernizing him; see also William R. Casto, *The Supreme Court in the Early Republic: The Chief Justiceships of John Jay and Oliver Ellsworth* (1995). Walter Stahr's *John Jay* (2005), a full and generally sensitive biography, devotes only one short chapter to Jay's tenure on the Court.

Specialized studies of particular aspects of Jay's career include: Jerald Combs, *The Jay Treaty* (1970), a balanced account of the negotiation and ratification process; Doyle Mathis, "Chisholm v. Georgia: Background and Settlement," *Journal of American History* 54 (1967): 19, a now-classic corrective to erroneous received wisdom; to be read in conjunction with Clyde Jacobs, *The Eleventh Amendment and Sovereign Immunity* (1972), a detailed study of the early Supreme Court's most humiliating moment.

NOTEWORTHY OPINIONS

Georgia v. Brailsford, 2 U.S. 402 (1792)

Chisholm v. Georgia, 2 U.S. 419 (1793)

Glass v. Sloop Betsey, 3 U.S. 6 (1794)

300

THOMAS JOHNSON

Birth: November 4, 1732, Calvert County, Maryland.

Education: Educated at home; studied law under Stephen Bordley; admitted to the bar, 1760.

Official Positions: Delegate, Maryland Provincial Assembly, 1762; delegate, Committee of Correspondence, 1774; member, Continental Congress, 1774–1777; delegate, first Maryland Constitutional Convention, 1776; first governor of Maryland, 1777–1779; member, Maryland House of Delegates, 1780, 1786, 1787; member, Maryland convention for ratification of the federal Constitution, 1788; chief judge, General Court of Maryland, 1790–1791; member, Board of Commissioners of the Federal City, 1791–1794.

Supreme Court Service: Recess appointment as associate justice by President George Washington, August 5, 1791, to replace John Rutledge, who had resigned; nominated November 1, 1791; confirmed by the Senate, November 7, 1791, by a voice vote; took judicial oath August 6, 1792; resigned January 16, 1793; replaced by William Paterson, nominated by President Washington.

Death: October 26, 1819, Frederick, Maryland.

Thomas Johnson's most significant contributions to the development of the new American nation would not necessarily include his service on the bench of the Supreme Court, although in his very brief tenure he participated in a number of interesting cases. Instead, he may be better known for his part in the success of the American Revolution and in the establishment of the capital of the United States in the District of Columbia. Johnson began to pursue public office soon after his admission to the bar. He served in the lower house of the Maryland Assembly from 1762 to 1773. Because of his ardent support of American rights, Johnson was elected to the Annapolis Committee of Correspondence and to the First and Second Continental Congresses. He returned to Maryland as commander of its militia;

was elected to three one-year terms (1777–1779) as the first governor of the state; became a member of the Maryland House of Delegates (1780, 1786, 1787), as well as of the state's convention to ratify the federal constitution. In 1790 the governor appointed him chief judge of the Maryland General Court. Johnson resigned from this position to become an associate justice of the Supreme Court.

Initially reluctant to serve on the Court because of the duty of riding circuit imposed on the justices by the Judiciary Act of 1789, Johnson overcame his reservations and accepted the temporary commission sent to him by President Washington on August 5, 1791. The Senate, out of session in August, confirmed him on November 7 to a permanent position. Johnson, however, missed the February 1792 term of

Court and did not take his seat on the Supreme Court until August 6, 1792. His entire career on the federal bench consisted of holding a circuit court in Virginia in the fall of 1791, attending the Supreme Court in August 1792, and riding the southern circuit in the fall of 1792. (While holding the court in South Carolina, however, Johnson indicated his belief in judicial review by refusing to allow the court to proceed under the Invalid Pensions Act passed by Congress in 1792.) After that experience, Johnson decided the burdens of circuit riding were too much for him and resigned his position on January 16, 1793. He retired to his estate in Frederick, Maryland.

Despite the brevity of his tenure on the Supreme Court, Johnson had the opportunity to examine two important issues. In *Hayburn's Case* (1792), the Court heard argument as to whether the attorney general had authority ex officio, without the specific permission of the president, to move for a *mandamus* to the U.S. Circuit Court for the District of Pennsylvania requiring it to hear the petition of William Hayburn. The Court divided equally on the

Thomas Johnson

question, so the motion was denied. Johnson joined those members of the Court who thought the attorney general should be permitted to proceed on his own. Had his views prevailed, elements of federal procedure might look very different today.

Johnson also participated in the initial stage of *Georgia v. Brailsford* (1792). The state of Georgia asked the Supreme Court to issue an injunction to prevent Samuel Brailsford, a British subject, from

receiving the money owed him as a result of a judgment in the U.S. Circuit Court for the District of Georgia. Georgia believed the money belonged to it by virtue of a state statute authorizing sequestration of British property during the Revolution. If an injunction were granted, all the parties' interests could be adjudicated in the Supreme Court. The majority voted in favor of issuing the injunction; Johnson, in dissent, stated that Georgia was not entitled to an injunction, because her "right to the debt in question . . . may be enforced at common law." Georgia eventually lost the battle with Brailsford in a jury trial in the Supreme Court (1794), in which the justices unanimously indicated, in a charge to the jury, that they thought that the peace treaty ending the Revolutionary War superseded a state sequestration statute. When this verdict was rendered, Johnson had already left the Court.

—*Maeva Marcus*

BIBLIOGRAPHY

Letters pertaining to Thomas Johnson's Supreme Court service are published in the volumes of Maeva Marcus, ed., *The Documentary History of the Supreme Court of the United States, 1789–1800* (1985–). Edward S. Delaplaine's *The Life of Thomas Johnson* (1927) remains the only full-length biography. A short informative essay about Johnson, written by Herbert Alan Johnson, appears in Friedman and Israel, *Justices*, vol. 1, 149.

NOTEWORTHY OPINIONS

Georgia v. Brailsford, 2 U.S. 402 (1792) (Dissent)

WILLIAM JOHNSON

Birth: December 27, 1771, Charleston, South Carolina.

Education: Graduated Princeton, 1790; studied law under Charles Cotesworth Pinckney; admitted to bar in 1793.

Official Positions: Member, South Carolina House of Representatives, 1794–1798; speaker, 1798; judge, Court of Common Pleas, 1799–1804.

Supreme Court Service: Nominated associate justice by President Thomas Jefferson, March 22, 1804, to replace Alfred Moore, who had resigned; confirmed by the Senate, March 24, 1804, by a voice vote; took judicial oath May 7, 1804; served until August 4, 1834; replaced by James M. Wayne, nominated by President Andrew Jackson.

Death: August 4, 1834, Brooklyn, New York.

William Johnson, the great dissenter of the early Republic, embodied the American dream. Born to blacksmith William Johnson and Sarah Nightingale Johnson, young William went to grammar school in Charleston, completed studies at Princeton University by 1790, read law with South Carolina's renowned lawyer-diplomat Charles Pinckney, and in 1793 gained admission to the Charleston bar. Johnson rose to power with dazzling speed. Once admitted to the bar, he was elected to the South Carolina House of Representatives; by March 1794 he had married and established himself as a society figure, a reliable and colorful Jeffersonian Republican, and a confidant of the master of Monticello. Johnson served as House secretary and speaker and judge of the South Carolina Constitutional Court; at age thirty-two, he accepted Thomas Jefferson's nomination to the U.S. Supreme Court, replacing the ineffectual North Carolinian Alfred Moore.

Chief Justice John Marshall's young associate relished a good scrap, but he also found it necessary to cooperate with his brethren. As he explained in an 1822 letter: "I found that I must either submit to circumstances or become such a cipher . . . as to effect no good at all. I therefore bent to the current." In 1807 Johnson infuriated Jefferson by relying on—and therefore granting credence to—Marshall's ruling in *Marbury v. Madison* (1803) to protest the Court's grant of a writ of *mandamus* in the treason trial of Aaron Burr. A year later on circuit, Johnson—apprehending presidential overreach—refused in *Gilchrist v. Collector of Charleston* (1808) to allow the detention of Gilchrist's vessel, as Republican embargo policies required. Family legend has it that Johnson personally boarded several vessels and issued sailing orders. In his decision of May 28, 1808, he insisted that federal officers never were justified, at the bidding of the executive, to increase "restraints upon commerce"; presidents and collectors were "equally subjected to legal restraint" and so "equally incapable" of "an unsanctioned encroachment upon individual liberty."

Attorney General Caesar Rodney promptly denounced Johnson as a Jeffersonian imposter suffering from "leprosy of the bench," but that judgment was premature. During and after the War of 1812, Johnson came to blows repeatedly with Justice Joseph Story; within a few years, the two men barely spoke. By Story's lights, republicanism required a sturdy, if mutable system of federal law (including an energetic system of admiralty courts and federal criminal jurisdiction) to ensure public morality as capitalists and crooks swarmed over the American continent. Johnson preferred to rely on state courts in criminal cases, and he feared federal tyranny (symbolized for him by the specter of admiralty courts in places like Louisville, Kentucky) more than the moral corruption associated with scrambles for wealth. In *United States v. Hudson* (1812) and *Goodwin* (1812), he refused to grant federal jurisdiction in criminal cases; Story dissented and ignored *Hudson* on circuit. Similarly, in *Ramsey v. Allegre* (1827), Johnson resisted attempts to modify the English "ebb and flow of the tide" doctrine, which limited admiralty jurisdiction to salt water, in order to expand federal authority to inland waterways without the constitutional amendment demanded by critics.

Johnson also perceived tyranny in the attempt by business corporations to persuade judges of their organizational identity with stockholders, whose collective rights and immunities then could be ascribed to a corporate "person." Johnson contended, for example, in his 1808 *Bank of the United States v.*

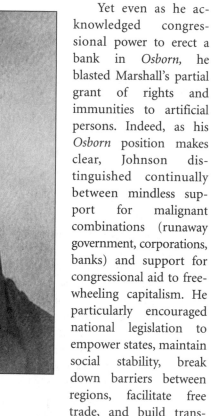

William Johnson

Deveaux circuit court opinion, that banking corporations possessed neither standing nor a right to sue in federal courts. He went along with John Marshall in *McCulloch v. Maryland* (1819); and five years later, in *Osborn v. Bank of the United States* (1824), he supported congressional power under the necessary and proper clause to create a bank, in part because he exalted Congress—described by him in *Anderson v. Dunn* (1821) as a "deliberate assembly, clothed with the majesty of the people."

Yet even as he acknowledged congressional power to erect a bank in *Osborn*, he blasted Marshall's partial grant of rights and immunities to artificial persons. Indeed, as his *Osborn* position makes clear, Johnson distinguished continually between mindless support for malignant combinations (runaway government, corporations, banks) and support for congressional aid to free-wheeling capitalism. He particularly encouraged national legislation to empower states, maintain social stability, break down barriers between regions, facilitate free trade, and build transportation networks—the "arteries" and "veins" of an extensive body politic. He therefore denounced James Monroe's veto of the Cumberland Road Act in 1822 and joined the centrist majority in *Martin v. Hunter's Lessee* (1816), with its ringing affirmation of the Court's authority under Section 25 of the 1789 Judiciary Act to review state court decisions whenever they touched federal statutes or treaties. Johnson also acquiesced in Marshall's anti-Jacksonian *Cherokee*

Nation v. Georgia (1831), which condemned Indian removal policies and state meddling with settled indigenous communities protected by treaty.

Johnson laid out some of the elements of this selectively nationalist philosophy in his concurring opinion in *Gibbons v. Ogden* (1824), the "steamboat case" testing the validity of a New York grant of monopoly to the Fulton-Livingston company to run boats exclusively on the Hudson River. Brushing aside state warnings about the imminent collapse of the Republic, Marshall toyed with but ultimately rejected Daniel Webster's "exclusivity" principle—the idea that Congress, under the commerce clause, might regulate new commercial subjects (such as steamboats) and persons (possibly including fugitive slaves) as well as the interstate exchange of goods. Marshall feared southern resistance to exclusivity and so held, less radically, that steamboat traffic on interstate rivers fell easily within Congress's established power to control navigation.

Johnson felt no such inhibition. Heedless of southern opposition and armed to the teeth with constitutional convention proceedings and the law of nations, he chided Marshall for unwarranted timidity: "The power of a sovereign state over commerce ... must be exclusive," residing in only "one potentate; and hence the grant of this power carries with it the whole subject, leaving nothing for the state to act upon."

As the *Gibbons* opinion suggests, Johnson was ambivalent about complete state control over slavery—perhaps because, as he stated, he opposed absolute state authority over labor and other resources; nor did he worry, with Americans a decade later, that Congress might wield regulatory power to aid fugitive slaves or destroy property rights in persons. He was a slaveholder and opposed abolition, but he also opposed the inhumane treatment of Africans, whether free or bonded. From 1822 to 1824 he tarnished his reputation in South Carolina, first, by sharply criticizing state denial of due process to slave rebel Denmark Vesey; second, by declaring in his 1823 circuit court opinion in *Elkison v. Deliesseline* that South Carolina's Negro Seaman Act, which barred black American sailors from Charleston and other

harbors, was a violation of the civil rights of free blacks seeking trade in the state; and, third, by opposing South Carolina's notorious nullification of the so-called tariff of abominations, again (as he explained in *Osborn*) because he viewed the federal Constitution as an economic document designed to eradicate the Confederation's "Congress of Ambassadors" as well as an unfruitful localism in commerce.

In cases involving the contract clause, Johnson exhibited a markedly thinner skin. Before the Panic of 1819, Marshall had written opinions in contract cases to accommodate dissenting views, and Johnson could therefore join the majority in *Dartmouth College v. Woodward* and *Sturges v. Crowninshield*, both decided in 1819. But as a states' rights rebellion gained force in the West and South, Johnson sounded an alarm. In 1823 he wrote a poignant, politically devastating concurrence in *Green v. Biddle*, in which Story and Bushrod Washington wielded the contract clause against Kentucky's occupying claimant laws to force state compliance with an agreement struck between Kentucky and Virginia in 1792. In *Green*, Johnson distinguished between the law of the case (which, he grudgingly concluded, supported the result) and the decidedly antirepublican tenor of a bench that refused to forge rules appropriate to new, non-English situations. On the one hand, he pointed to provisions of the state constitution outlawing the taking of property without due process or compensation as solid ground for invalidating the occupant laws, and he said the Court was overreaching for no good reason. On the other hand, he condemned his colleagues for destroying the property rights of occupants without jury trial. Ever the champion of free-trading republicanism, Johnson simply could not abide Court support for the antirepublican bankers, speculators, and corporatizers served so well by *Green*; moreover, federal jurisdiction had been expanded at the expense of an assembly rightly concerned about its lack of control over land titling.

In *Green*, Johnson probably reached the end of his unionist tether. While "groping [his] way through the labyrinth" of land and contract law toward his brilliant *Green* opinion, he began to cut himself loose from juridical convention. After 1819 his opinions evince a sea change, away from abstract reasoning rooted in international law, political theory, and natural law and toward a concrete, community-centered jurisprudence capable of reflecting diverse measures of fairness without collapsing into relativism. Johnson, in other words, unwittingly began to pave the way for the economic policies and "dual federalism" of the later Taney Court. Not surprisingly, he often expressed his views in dissent. His apprehensions about judicial support for bankers and other unproductive "nabobs," and his conviction that public morality in economic life depended to a great extent on local control over remedial legislation, underlay his opinion in *Ogden v. Saunders* (1827), in which he supported, to Marshall's horror, a state prohibition of endless claims by creditors against insolvents; characteristically, and in the name of union, he drew the line at New York's discharge of obligations to out-of-state creditors.

The prolific Johnson served almost three decades on the federal bench, and, not counting circuit court rulings, he wrote 112 opinions for majorities, 21 concurring opinions, 34 dissents, and 5 *per curiam* opinions. Only Marshall and Story outdid him. He was castigated regularly—by Federalists for his support of state legislative power and by Jeffersonians for attacks upon executive "tyranny" or radical antiunionism.

Johnson surely could be a loose cannon. As his remarkable *Ogden* and *Green* concurrences make clear, he viewed opinions as occasions for experimentation. He admitted impetuousness and often devoted days or weeks to land speculation or nonjudicial writing, such as a two-volume biography of Nathanael Greene. Yet he was also an engaged and engaging jurist with an uncommon capacity for surprise; only enemies, such as John Quincy Adams, thought of him as "restive, turbulent, hot-headed, [and] flaringly independent."

In the end, it is of small moment that Johnson alienated Court reporters or pigheadedly refused to admit obvious mistakes. Johnson's legacy rests with written evidence of a formidable legal imagination—in opinions, in his richly technical correspondence with Jefferson, and in published replies to critics. Arguably, Johnson established the dissent as a legiti-

mate component of American constitutional discourse. He also articulated a strikingly modern, rights-centered vision of the role of federal courts. When Attorney General Rodney publicly shredded Johnson's *Gilchrist* opinion, the judge took to his pen; no better summary of his philosophy exists than the one written in self-defense. "In a country where laws govern," said Johnson, "courts of justice necessarily are the medium of action and reaction between the government and the governed. The basis of individual security and the bond of union between the ruler and the citizen must ever be found in a judiciary sufficiently independent to disregard the will of power, and sufficiently energetic to secure to the citizen the full enjoyment of his rights."

—*Sandra F. VanBurkleo*

BIBLIOGRAPHY

The standard biography is Donald G. Morgan, *Justice William Johnson: The First Dissenter* (1954); short sketches include Donald G. Morgan, "William Johnson," in Friedman and Israel, *Justices,* vol. 1, 355; and Sandra F. VanBurkleo, "William Johnson," in Kermit Hall, ed., *Oxford Companion to the Supreme Court of the United States* (1992), 449–450. See also Herbert A. Johnson, "The Constitutional Thought of William Johnson," *South Carolina Historical Magazine* 89 (1988): 132; and Timothy Huebner, "Divided Loyalties: Justice William Johnson and the Rise of Disunion in South Carolina, 1822–1834," *Journal of Supreme Court History* (1995): 19.

For Johnson within the context of the Marshall Court and his times, see two volumes of the *Holmes Devise History,* George Haskins and Herbert Johnson, *Foundations of Power: John Marshall, 1801–1815* (1981); and G. Edward White, *The Marshall Court and Cultural Change, 1815–1835* (1991).

NOTEWORTHY OPINIONS

United States v. Hudson, 11 U.S. 32 (1812)

United States v. Goodwin, 11 U.S. 108 (1812)

Green v. Biddle, 21 U.S. 1 (1823) (Concurrence)

Gibbons v. Ogden, 22 U.S. 1 (1824) (Concurrence)

Osborn v. Bank of the United States, 22 U.S. 738 (1824) (Concurrence)

Ogden v. Saunders, 25 U.S. 213 (1827)

ANTHONY McLEOD KENNEDY

Birth: July 23, 1936, Sacramento, California.

Education: Stanford University, A.B., 1958; London School of Economics, 1957–1958; Harvard Law School, J.D., 1961.

Official Positions: Judge, U.S. Court of Appeals for the Ninth Circuit, 1976–1988.

Supreme Court Service: Nominated associate justice by President Ronald Reagan, November 30, 1987, to replace Lewis F. Powell Jr., who had retired; confirmed by the Senate, February 3, 1988, by a 97–0 vote; took judicial oath February 18, 1988.

Growing up in Sacramento, California, Anthony Kennedy knew Earl Warren, that state's wartime Republican governor and afterward the fifteenth chief justice of the United States. As a young lawyer, Kennedy worked for Ronald Reagan, another Republican governor of the state, drafting for him an amendment to the state constitution intended to limit the taxing and spending powers of the legislature. The amendment failed as a ballot initiative, but the governor's grateful patronage led in 1975 to Kennedy's appointment by President Gerald Ford to the U.S. Court of Appeals for the Ninth Circuit and, little more than a decade later, to his appointment by President Reagan to the U.S. Supreme Court.

Kennedy was educated at Stanford University, the London School of Economics, and the Harvard Law School. After law school, he worked briefly for a large law firm in San Francisco and then served a short term of active duty in the National Guard, before succeeding to his father's law practice in Sacramento. He practiced as an attorney and lobbyist for twelve years, meanwhile marrying Mary Davis, another Sacramento native he had known since childhood with whom he has had three children. He also served as a part-time member of the faculty of the McGeorge College of Law at the University of the Pacific, teaching constitutional law classes at night. His course is remembered for its emphasis on the law of the commerce clause.

When Kennedy joined the Ninth Circuit bench, he was just shy of forty—the youngest judge in any of the federal appellate courts and the third youngest ever appointed to a federal appellate court. During his dozen years on the Ninth Circuit, he took part in more than 1,400 decisions and wrote more than 400 opinions. Often in dissent in the circuit regarded as the nation's most liberal, Kennedy nevertheless wrote many influential opinions. His opinion for the court in *American Federation of State, County, and Municipal Employees v. Washington* (1985), holding that federal employment discrimination law did not require the state to base its compensation scheme on a theory of comparable worth, was widely followed in other circuits. In *Pacemaker Diagnostic Clinic of America, Inc. v. Instromedix, Inc.* (1984), he presented a theory for determining the extent of congressional discretion to shift claims from Article III courts to other government tribunals, which the U.S. Supreme Court adopted in 1986, a year before he joined the Court.

His opinion for the Ninth Circuit in *Chadha v. INS* (1980), that a one-house congressional veto for administrative decisions was unconstitutional, was affirmed by the Supreme Court five years later.

When Kennedy left Sacramento for Washington, he carried the reputation of a devoted family man, a devout Roman Catholic, and a loyal Republican. His nomination to the Court followed the Senate's rejection of Judge Robert H. Bork, after a spirited ideological debate, and the withdrawal of Judge Douglas H. Ginsburg, after public exposure of controversial facts about his personal life. That Judge Kennedy would fall third on the short list prepared by Ronald Reagan and Attorney General Edwin Meese might be attributed to White House perception that Bork and Ginsburg were more committed to the president's conservative ideology. That evaluation has proven true. Although Justice Kennedy has taken conservative positions in many important constitu-

Anthony McLeod Kennedy

tional areas and voted more often with Chief Justice William Rehnquist than any other member of the Court, he has in certain high-profile cases exhibited a streak of independence, parting company with those who anchored the Rehnquist Court's right wing, the chief justice and Justices Antonin Scalia and Clarence Thomas.

Among the cases in which Justice Kennedy voted as his sponsors might have expected, none was more climactic than *Bush v. Gore* (2000). Kennedy's was one of five votes that resolved the legal controversy arising from the presidential election of 2000. In *Bush v. Gore*,

he joined in the opinion *per curiam* that the Supreme Court of Florida had violated the equal protection clause of the U.S. Constitution's Fourteenth Amendment by overruling a decision of Florida's secretary of state to refuse recounts not completed by a statutory deadline. According to the majority, the proposed recounts would have been so arbitrary and lacking in standards as to violate the constitutional right of federal voters to equal treatment by state election officials.

Kennedy has been a reliable vote for the Court's reapportioning of American sovereignty that follows from the Court's new interpretation of federalism. He joined in Rehnquist's opinion in *Seminole Indian Tribe of Florida v. Florida* (1996), in which the Court overruled *Pennsylvania v. Union Gas Co.* (1989), and restricted the power of Congress to make states accountable in federal court for violations of rights created by most federal laws, including those protecting the environment or regulating the workplace. Three years later, Kennedy wrote the opinion for the Court in *Alden v. Maine* (1999), holding that Congress could not compel a state to open its courts to cases in which the state is sued by its employees for violation of federal wage laws. Taken together, *Seminole Tribe* and *Alden* left states effectively "above the law" as enacted by Congress, except in cases in which Congress acted pursuant to one of the three Civil War amendments. When, in *Nevada Department of Human Resources v. Hibbs* (2003), the Court, in another Rehnquist opinion, then affirmed the power of Congress to make states accountable for violation of the Family and Medical Leave Act, enacted as an exercise of Fourteenth Amendment power, Kennedy dissented. And he dissented again in *Tennessee v. Lane* (2004), when the Court upheld another act of Congress pursuant to the Fourteenth Amendment that makes states accountable for violation of the Americans with Disabilities Act. As these decisions make clear, Kennedy's commitment to state immunity from suit for violations of federal social welfare laws matches that of Scalia and Thomas.

The Rehnquist Court's new doctrine of federalism not only dictated enhanced state immunity, it also dictated diminished national power. In *United States v. Lopez* (1995), the Court struck down the Gun-Free School Zone Act, which made the possession of a firearm near a school a federal crime. The Court found the law to be unconstitutional on the grounds that Congress had exceeded its authority to regulate interstate commerce, although that law-making authority has long been regarded as sufficient for Congress to regulate local, noncommercial activity that has a substantial impact on interstate commerce. In *Lopez*, the Court refused to accept an unsubstantiated presumption by Congress that guns near schools had an influence on interstate commerce sufficient to warrant national legislation. The impact of *Lopez* on federal regulatory power might have been minimal had it been nothing more than a judicial prompt to Congress to do better homework when legislating in the expectation that courts will later come to the same conclusion about the impact of local activities on a national market. After all, Congress had enacted the Gun-Free School Zone Act on the basis of a virtually blank legislative history, devoid of committee hearings, staff reports, or anything else, apparently, but the intuition of lawmakers that a gun ban was somehow connected with interstate commerce.

That the Rehnquist Court had in mind something more became clear in *United States v. Morrison* (2000), in which a provision of the federal Violence Against Women Act (VAWA) was held unconstitutional. In this instance, the legislation, which created a federal civil remedy for victims of misogynistic violence, had come methodically through the legislative process, and the congressional conclusion that acts of violence against women had costs to the national labor pool was supported by a record consisting of studies and reports that in printed form stacked nine feet high. This case, therefore, was not like *Lopez*, in which it could be said that Congress had jumped to a conclusion about effects on interstate commerce. When the Court in *Morrison* held VAWA's civil remedy provision unconstitutional, it was indisputably the result of a difference in opinion between the branches about what the evidence proved about the consequences for the workplace and marketplace of casualties from such violence. Here, the Court insisted on the substitution of its judgment for that of Congress about what was sufficient impact to cause an effect. Rehnquist wrote for the Court and was joined not only by Kennedy, Scalia, and Thomas but also by Sandra Day O'Connor. The decision in *Morrison*, more than that in *Lopez*, represents a shift in trajectory by the Supreme Court from enabling to limiting national legislation for social welfare, leaving much of that field by default to state lawmakers. It also demonstrates an aggressive assertion by the Court of its own judgment in cases where the branches differ about what Congress is empowered to do. Kennedy has been consistent and forthright in his avowal of this new federalism, notwithstanding its implications for the separation of powers and judicial restraint.

Justice Kennedy is clearly no champion of affirmative action. In *City of Richmond v. J. A. Croson Co.* (1989), he joined the Court in holding unconstitutional the city's program for setting aside a portion of its public contracts for minority businesses. He espoused the view that government programs said to be violations of the equal protection clause because they discriminated against whites ought to be judicially assessed by the same strict standard employed in assessing programs said to discriminate against minorities. He wrote separately to insist that federal programs be treated in the same way as state programs, despite the obvious difference in the relevant texts of the Fifth and Fourteenth Amendments, a position he restated the following year, dissenting in

Metro Broadcasting, Inc. v. Federal Communications Commission (1990).

In its 2002 term, the Supreme Court returned to the constitutionality of affirmative action, taking up two cases in which unsuccessful white applicants relied on the equal protection clause to challenge the way the University of Michigan made admission decisions. In both cases, the university defended its use of affirmative action as compatible with a standard for admission decisions articulated by Justice Lewis Powell in his pivotal concurring opinion in *Regents of the University of California v. Bakke* (1972). According to Powell, a decision-making process in which race defined admission quotas was unconstitutional, but a process in which race was only one factor in the decision on each applicant's case could be constitutional so long as race was not allowed to control the decision. In *Gratz v. Bollinger* (2003), the Court found the process used by the University of Michigan for admission to its undergraduate college unconstitutional because race presumptions effectively displaced individualized decisions. In *Grutter v. Bollinger* (2003), however, the Court found the process used by Michigan's law school sufficiently individualized applicants to satisfy the Constitution, even if race was used as a factor in admission decisions. Kennedy joined the Court in *Gratz* but dissented in *Grutter*. In his view, the decision-making processes in both cases amounted to quota systems, contrary to the standard derived from Powell's *Bakke* opinion.

By means of the writ of *habeas corpus*, the U.S. Constitution affords persons imprisoned after criminal convictions in state courts a right to collateral review of their cases by federal courts. In *Wainwright v. Sykes* (1977), the Supreme Court held that this constitutional right is available only to those who do not abuse the privilege, that is, those who have first fully pursued state procedures for review of their convictions. Where once that restriction applied only to deliberate defaults, it was extended in *Coleman v. Thompson* (1991) to those who unintentionally miss a postconviction opportunity in state court, and in *McCleskey v. Zant* (1991) to prisoners who raise a claim in a subsequent *habeas* petition that might have been made in an earlier petition unsuccessful for

other reasons. Kennedy joined in the opinion of the Court in *Coleman* and wrote the opinion for the Court in *McCleskey*. In short, the restrictions in these cases can make a missed deadline or opportunity fatal for a wrongfully condemned prisoner. Kennedy also supplied the swing vote in *Murray v. Giarratano* (1989), in which the Court, reinterpreting *Ross v. Moffitt* (1974), declined to find in the Constitution any obligation on the part of states to furnish legal counsel for indigent death row prisoners pursuing writs of *habeas corpus* in state courts.

These restrictions on *habeas corpus* imply considerable Supreme Court confidence in state courts and deference to their role in a federal system. Indeed, Kennedy wrote sympathetically for the Court in *McCleskey* about the "injury" to a state from federal second-guessing when the state has not had its own opportunity to review a conviction said to be erroneous. In this regard, his views on *habeas corpus* have since been effectively codified, and indeed extended, by Congress in the Antiterrorism and Effective Death Penalty Act of 1996.

Kennedy's inclination to turn away applicants for federal writs of *habeas corpus* who unintentionally missed a deadline or overlooked an opportunity for postconviction review invites comparison with his sympathy for hapless police. It has long been a part of American law that evidence procured by police acting contrary to the constitutional rights of the accused cannot be admitted as evidence against him. To this exclusionary rule, Kennedy introduced an exception for good-faith mistakes by police in their applications for warrants. While on the Ninth Circuit, he advocated such an exception in his dissent from the decision to refuse a hearing *en banc* in *Harvey v. United States* (1983), and the Supreme Court made it the law of the land a year later in *United States v. Leon* (1984).

Kennedy has played a prominent role in the Court's reconsideration of the law implementing the First Amendment's establishment clause. In *County of Allegheny v. ACLU* (1989), the Court was dealing with the constitutionality of two different holiday displays in two different locations. One display was a crèche on the grand staircase of the county courthouse, and the other was a crèche, along with a Christmas tree, menorah, and various other symbols of the holiday season, in front of the city-county building. The Court said the courthouse display offended the establishment clause, while the outdoor display did not. Kennedy wrote for himself, Rehnquist, Byron White, and Scalia to agree with the Court's ruling on the outdoor display, but to dissent in that he would have found the display inside the courthouse constitutional. According to Kennedy, the establishment clause does not stop government from endorsing religion so long as government does not favor one religion over another and so long as government does not coerce persons into participating. He reiterated this view in *Lee v. Weisman* (1992), in which he wrote for a 5–4 majority that invocations and benedictions delivered during public school graduation exercises were coercive.

In *County of Allegheny*, Kennedy had acquiesced in applying the test for establishment clause constitutionality found in *Lemon v. Kurtzman* (1971). According to that test from the Burger Court era, government action is unconstitutional if its primary purpose is to aid religion, if its primary effect aids religion, or if its consequence is excessive entanglement of the government in religious matters. By 1993, however, Kennedy was willing to join Scalia and Thomas to condemn the *Lemon* test as unworkable in *Lamb's Chapel v. Center Moriches Union Free School District* (1993). In this case, the Court held unconstitutional a school district's policy that discriminated against religious groups applying for use of school facilities after hours. Later in the same term, Kennedy supplied the swing vote in *Zobrest v. Catalina Foothills School District* (1993), in which the Court held that a school district did not violate the establishment clause if it paid for a sign language interpreter to accompany a student to classes at a Roman Catholic high school. Mention of *Lemon v. Kurtzman* was conspicuously absent from the Court's opinion in *Zobrest,* which could reasonably be said to have tacitly overruled it. Having condemned the *Lemon* test as unworkable in 1993, Kennedy nevertheless has since proved willing to pay it lip service when it serves less as a hurdle than as a stepping stone for government aid to religious schools. In *Mitchell v. Helms* (2000),

he voted with the 6–3 majority to uphold a federal statute that authorized expenditures of federal aid for instructional and educational materials used in private schools, most of which are Catholic or otherwise religiously affiliated. Kennedy's view seems to be that the establishment clause should be no barrier to government assistance to schools run by churches, so long as the government is evenhanded in its distribution among faiths. And this view is just one vote away from being the Court's.

If Kennedy has lived up substantially to expectations that he would supply the fifth vote for the right wing of the Rehnquist Court, he has occasionally proven a maverick. He first deviated in *Planned Parenthood of Southeastern Pennsylvania v. Casey* (1992), when he, O'Connor, and Justice David Souter formed a plurality of the not-so-reactionary in refusing to overrule *Roe v. Wade* (1973). The three insisted on continued constitutional recognition for the right to an abortion but called for a relaxed standard in assessing state laws curtailing its exercise. For the rest of the Rehnquist Court era, their position dominated abortion cases. As a consequence, the antiabortion movement was denied a categorical rejection of *Roe v. Wade's* fundamental principle and forced to argue in lower courts the factual circumstances in every challenge to an abortion law.

In *Casey,* Kennedy, O'Connor, and Souter also chose new ground on which to make a stand about exceptions to the rule of *stare decisis,* the unwritten but powerful rule that obliges a court to decide new cases in conformity with its past decisions on the same point of law. All nine of the justices taking part in *Casey* agreed that the Supreme Court could overrule its own precedent when the underlying rule has proven impracticable, anomalous, or out of date. But it was also common ground that *stare decisis* should apply with greater force when reliance on precedent by those subject to the rule would make its repudiation inequitable. To these traditional considerations, the *Casey* plurality proposed adding another: that *stare decisis* should govern more strictly where the precedent in question has been the subject of an intensely divisive controversy. In the view held jointly by Justices Kennedy, O'Connor, and Souter, the

Supreme Court ought to hesitate longer before over-ruling its more controversial precedents because the Court's action would give the appearance of surren-dering to public opinion and thereby subvert the Court's legitimacy.

The joint opinion in *Casey* is less obviously, but just as importantly, about lawmaking by courts as it is about the abortion right. Critics have complained that in *Roe* the Court usurped a legislative role. In *Casey,* Kennedy and his co-authors eschewed an opportunity to make new law in broad terms with a dramatic doctrinal *volte face* (about face). They opted instead to leave the regulation of abortion for consid-eration from time to time, case by case. Their undue burden standard turns out in practice to be less a pre-cept than a differential equation of degree and cir-cumstance, the solution to which has for so long been allotted to judges.

Depending on one's definition of conservatism, it might also be said that Kennedy frustrated ideological expectations in *Texas v. Johnson* (1989), when he sup-plied the swing vote for a decision that a protestor's conviction for burning an American flag during a political demonstration violated constitutionally guaranteed freedom of speech. He joined unre-servedly in Justice William Brennan's opinion for the Court on the merits of the case, but he also wrote sep-arately to describe the position of a jurist duty bound to render a judgment contrary to his personal opin-ion: "The hard fact is that sometimes we must make decisions we do not like. We make them because they are right, right in the sense that the law and the Con-stitution, as we see them, compel the result."

His most notorious detour from the path he was expected to follow came in *Lawrence v. Texas* (2003), in which Kennedy wrote for the 5–4 majority that overruled *Bowers v. Hardwick* (1986) and held uncon-stitutional a Texas law that made homosexual sodomy a crime. Kennedy's opinion for the Court in *Lawrence* begins and ends with a reaffirmation of the contro-versial doctrine of substantive due process, that is, the assumption that the Fifth and Fourteenth Amend-ments implicitly remove certain private acts and per-sonal relationships beyond the reach of majoritarian

regulation. Otherwise, Kennedy found fault with the historical fact-finding in *Bowers* that there was no tra-dition of legal tolerance in America and elsewhere for the private sexual conduct of couples of the same sex, and he rejected the notion that the religious judg-ments of the American majority about the morality of homosexual conduct alone could justify its criminal-ization. None of these ideas sits well with those whom Justice Kennedy's pedigree would suggest he shares a communion of jurisprudence.

As much as Justice Kennedy's approach to the writ of *habeas corpus* might suggest a strict law-and-order jurist, he has disagreed with Rehnquist, Scalia, and Thomas on the continued constitutionality of the death penalty when it has been challenged as cruel and unusual punishment prohibited by the Eighth Amend-ment. All on the Rehnquist Court seemed to agree that the general words "cruel and unusual punishment" should be interpreted in light of evolving social stan-dards as evidenced by changes wrought legislatively since the era of the Constitution's drafting. Where the justices of that Court differed is the point at which a social standard has evolved sufficiently to warrant pro-hibition of practices previously adjudged constitution-ally permissible. In *Penry v. Lynaugh* (1989), for example, Kennedy joined Rehnquist, Scalia, and Thomas in O'Connor's opinion for the Court that held constitutional the death sentence of a man with the mental age of six. The Court found insufficient evi-dence of an emerging national consensus against such executions. But in *Atkins v. Virginia* (2002), Kennedy and O'Connor joined in overruling *Penry* and holding unconstitutional Virginia's capital punishment of mentally retarded criminals. This time, the Court found sufficient evidence of a trend in other states pro-hibiting such executions to conclude that they had become cruel and unusual. Then, in *Roper v. Simmons* (2005), Kennedy, parting company not only with Rehnquist, Scalia, and Thomas, but also with O'Con-nor, wrote the opinion for the Court holding unconsti-tutional the execution of persons who were younger than eighteen when they committed the crime.

The opinions for the Court in *Lawrence* and *Roper* both referred to the laws and practices of other nations, making it clear that they formed at least part of the basis for the Court's conclusion about contemporary social standards and therefore about what the Constitution forbids as contrary to due process or cruel and unusual punishment. This deference to foreign law touched a conservative nerve, and it did not go unnoticed that Kennedy had written these opinions. Dissenting in both cases, Justice Scalia was scathing in his denunciation of resort by the two majorities to what foreign nations think, and even more intemperate criticism followed in a rising storm of indignation. Bills were introduced in Congress prohibiting courts from considering foreign laws, but none has yet passed into law. Public debate continues about the extent to which the American law of human rights should harmonize with that of other nations or the world community.

Supreme Court justices are often invited to voice their opinions from vantage points other than the bench, but when they accept, they almost invariably limit their remarks to the banal. Contrary to this professional protocol, Justice Kennedy in the summer of 2003 publicly criticized the American system of corrections. In a speech at the annual convention of the American Bar Association, he called his audience's attention to the huge number of persons incarcerated in America and the disproportionate presence in that population of African Americans. He expressed reservations about the cost of such a penal system but also called present levels of funding inadequate. He objected to the lengthening of sentences that has resulted from the federal sentencing guidelines and lamented the atrophying of the pardon power. He invited renewed attention to the goal of rehabilitation and then challenged the entire American bar to pursue broad reforms in sentencing and clemency. The ABA took him seriously and formed a commission for the pursuit of these matters. Whether real reform will follow remains to be seen.

In general, Kennedy showed an inclination to vote with the Rehnquist Court's right wing and, in particular, a commitment to the new doctrine of federalism, antipathy for group rights in affirmative action, and sympathy for states called into federal courts to defend criminal convictions against *habeas corpus* attack. Against this backdrop, his positions in *Casey* and *Johnson, Lawrence,* and *Roper* seem evidence of a more individualistic or libertarian form of conservative jurisprudence than those of the Court commonly regarded as further to the right. The civil rights history of the Rehnquist Court is in large measure a product of Kennedy's refusal to make tradition the sole determinant of due process, his embrace of an evolving definition for cruel and unusual punishment, and his insistence that the due process clause is legitimately a source for otherwise unenumerated rights. If this surprises those consulting his pedigree, perhaps they are ignoring his years teaching constitutional law. Lecturing clearly about the meaning of the Constitution can come only from concentrated attention to its contours, and opinions formed in that manner are too well tempered to be pliable.

—*John Paul Jones*

BIBLIOGRAPHY

Good studies of Kennedy and his jurisprudence are in Mark V. Tushnet, *A Court Divided: The Rehnquist Court and the Future of Constitutional Law* (2005); Herman Schwartz, *The Rehnquist Court: Judicial Activism on the Right* (2002); Tinsley E. Yarbrough, *The Rehnquist Court and the Constitution* (2000); and Friedman and Israel, eds., *Justices,* vol. 5 (1997). For analysis of Kennedy's votes, decisions, and role on the Court, see the reviews of the Supreme Court by term, published annually in the *Harvard Law Review*.

NOTEWORTHY OPINIONS

Texas v. Johnson, 491 U.S. 397 (1989) (Concurrence)

County of Allegheny v. American Civil Liberties Union, 492 U.S. 573 (1989)

Metro Broadcasting, Inc. v. Federal Communications Commission, 497 U.S. 547 (1990) (Dissent)

McCleskey v. Zant, 499 U.S. 467 (1991)

Planned Parenthood of Southeastern Pennsylvania v. Casey, 505 U.S. 833 (1992) (Joint Plurality)

Alden v. Maine, 527 U.S. 706 (1999)

Lawrence v. Texas, 539 U.S. 558 (2003)

Tennessee v. Lane, 541 U.S. 509 (2004) (Dissent)

Roper v. Simmons, 543 U.S. 551 (2005)

JOSEPH RUCKER LAMAR

Birth: October 14, 1857, Elbert County, Georgia.

Education: University of Georgia, 1874–1875; Bethany College, A.B., 1877; Washington and Lee University, 1877.

Official Positions: Member, Georgia legislature, 1886–1889; commissioner to codify Georgia laws, 1893; associate justice, Georgia Supreme Court, 1903–1905; member, mediation conference, Niagara Falls, Canada, 1914.

Supreme Court Service: Nominated associate justice by President William Howard Taft, December 12, 1910, to replace William Henry Moody, who had retired; confirmed by the Senate, December 15, 1910, by a voice vote; took judicial oath January 3, 1911; served until January 2, 1916; replaced by Louis D. Brandeis, nominated by President Woodrow Wilson.

Death: January 2, 1916, Washington, D.C.

Descended from two distinguished Georgia families, Joseph Rucker Lamar was a product of the southern establishment. His paternal side in particular had a heritage of public service, with Mirabeau Lamar serving as president of the Republic of Texas and a cousin, Lucius Quintus Cincinnatus Lamar, as associate justice of the U.S. Supreme Court. Joseph Lamar lived up to this heritage. Educated in the South, he attended Richmond Academy, the University of Georgia, Bethany College, and Washington and Lee Law School before studying law in the office of a prominent Georgia attorney. After passing the Georgia bar, Lamar built his reputation as a corporate lawyer. He served in the state legislature from 1886 to 1889 and in 1893 was selected to a commission rewriting the Georgia civil code. While practicing law he also wrote extensively on Georgia legal history. In 1903 Lamar took a seat on the Georgia Supreme

Court but returned to private practice in 1905, which he continued until President William Howard Taft nominated him to the Supreme Court.

Lamar served on the Court just five years, writing only 113 majority opinions. Generally thought of as a conservative on economic matters, his most significant opinion represented a setback for labor unions and civil liberties. Writing in *Gompers v. Bucks Stove & Range* (1911), Lamar ruled that an antitrust order prohibiting the American Federation of Labor from organizing a secondary boycott through the publication of "unfair" and "we don't patronize" lists did not infringe on the First Amendment freedom of expression. Other of Lamar's opinions tended to reinforce this conservative image. Taking a narrow view of the state's regulatory power in *Smith v. Texas* (1914), he ruled that a law requiring that train conductors have previous experience as brakemen violated liberty of contract. In *Kansas City Southern Railway v. Anderson* (1914), he dissented from a decision allowing double damages to be paid to a plaintiff when a railroad refused to pay for livestock killed on its tracks.

Lamar's attachment to laissez-faire economics was even more evident in *German Alliance Insurance Co. v. Lewis* (1914). There, in one of his few dissents, Lamar disagreed with a majority decision upholding state regulation of insurance rates. Insurance, he maintained, was not "a business affected with public interest" and therefore should not be subject to state regulation. Lamar predicted that the expansion of regulation would become all pervading. He warned that citizens would then hold their property and their individual right of contract and of labor under legislative rather than constitutional guarantee.

In contrast to the cases concerning state regulation, Lamar seemed willing to give more latitude to federal agencies than is usually associated with the conservative thinking of his time. In *United States v. Grimaud* (1911), for example, he wrote an opinion expanding Congress's authority to delegate rule-making authority to administrative agencies. He also joined the majority that expanded the Pure Food and Drug Act in *Hipolite Egg Co. v. United States* (1911) and extended the authority of the Interstate Commerce Commission in the *Minnesota Rate Cases* (1913).

In matters of civil rights, Justice Lamar's record was mixed. He concurred in the result of *McCabe v. Atchison, Topeka & Santa Fe Railway Co.* (1914),

Joseph Rucker Lamar

upholding an Oklahoma law that required separate coaches for black passengers. Yet he voted with the majority in invalidating a peonage law in *Bailey v. Alabama* (1911), wrote the opinion invalidating a special tax that discriminated against Chinese laundries in *Quong Wing v. Kirkendall* (1912), and protected the Choctaw and Chickasaw tribes from Oklahoma's attempt to withdraw a tax exemption on their lands in *Choate v. Trapp* (1912).

A forceful dissent in *Diaz v. United States* (1912) hinted that Lamar also had a broader view of criminal justice and civil liberties than might have been expected. There he argued that the constitutional guarantees that an accused has a right to confront witnesses and a right not to be placed in jeopardy twice for the same crime should apply to a case tried in the Philippines. Lamar appeared to have a special disdain for conspiracy laws. In 1912 he joined Justice Oliver Wendell Holmes dissenting in two cases that upheld conspiracy convictions. And in *United States v. Holte* (1915), he dissented from a decision that upheld a woman's conviction for "conspiring to cause her own transportation in interstate commerce for purposes of prostitution." Such a construction of the law would make every victim guilty of conspiracy, he argued. "Even that elastic offense cannot be extended to cover such a case."

When he was being considered for appointment, Joseph Rucker Lamar was described as a man with "no entanglements or extreme tendencies of thought." As moderate as it was conservative, his record as a justice of the Supreme Court appears to bear out that assessment.

—*Paul Kens*

BIBLIOGRAPHY

The best available biography is Leonard Dinnerstein, "Joseph Rucker Lamar," in Friedman and Israel, *Justices,* vol. 3, 978–995 (1973). Clarinda Pendleton Lamar, *The Life of Joseph Rucker Lamar, 1857–1916* (1926), is a biography written by Lamar's wife. A small amount of Lamar correspondence is held by the University of Georgia.

NOTEWORTHY CASES

United States v. Grimaud, 220 U.S. 506 (1911)

Gompers v. Bucks Stove & Range, 221 U.S. 418 (1911)

Diaz v. United States, 223 U.S. 442 (1912) (Dissent)

German Alliance Insurance Co. v. Lewis, 233 U.S. 389 (1914) (Dissent)

Smith v. Texas, 233 U.S. 630 (1914)

United States v. Holte, 236 U.S. 140 (1915) (Dissent)

LUCIUS QUINTUS CINCINNATUS LAMAR

Birth: September 17, 1825, Eatonton, Georgia.

Education: Emory College, A.B., 1845.

Official Positions: Member, Georgia House of Representatives, 1853; U.S. representative, 1857–1860, 1873–1877; U.S. senator, 1877–1885; secretary of the interior, 1885–1888.

Supreme Court Service: Nominated associate justice by President Grover Cleveland, December 12, 1887, to replace William Woods, who had died; confirmed by the Senate, January 16, 1888, by a 32–28 vote; took judicial oath January 18, 1888; served until January 23, 1893; replaced by Howell E. Jackson, nominated by President Benjamin Harrison.

Death: January 23, 1893, Macon, Georgia.

In *Profiles in Courage,* John F. Kennedy analyzed well-known political leaders such as John Quincy Adams and Daniel Webster, but he also looked at Lucius Q. C. Lamar. As a symbol of his age, Lamar served his state, his region, and his country in a long political and legal career culminating with service on the U.S. Supreme Court. Although best known as a politician, Lamar affected the Supreme Court through his devotion to the separation of powers, his interest in interstate commerce, and his suspicion of executive power.

Lamar attended Emory College and apprenticed law in Macon, Georgia. As a young man, he lived in Mississippi and Georgia and dabbled in politics, winning a congressional seat from Mississippi in 1857. In Congress, he worked with the secessionist wing of the Democratic Party, becoming friends with Jefferson Davis. Lamar left Congress upon secession and aided in the establishment of the Confederacy. His support for secession may have influenced his cousin, Justice John A. Campbell, to resign from the Court. Lamar served briefly in the Confederate army before becoming Confederate commissioner to Russia. He traveled as far as London, but never reached Russia. Lamar returned in 1863 and completed the war as a colonel and judge advocate.

After the war, Lamar became a professor of law at the University of Mississippi while pursuing a private practice. Once again elected to Congress in 1872, Lamar became a symbol of those southerners willing to accept the results of the war while opposing Reconstruction. Calling for national reconciliation, Lamar's short but impassioned 1874 eulogy for Sen. Charles Sumner of Massachusetts was "one of the great speeches in the history of the House," and it made him an overnight sensation.

Elected to the Senate in 1876, Lamar participated in the major policy debates regarding the end of Reconstruction and the tariff question. When Democrat Grover Cleveland became president in 1884,

Lamar became interior secretary. With the death of Justice William B. Woods in May 1887, Cleveland nominated Lamar to the Supreme Court.

The nomination was not without controversy. Because Lamar was the first southerner nominated to the Court since the Civil War and because of his age (sixty-two when nominated, the second-oldest appointment made), the Republican-dominated Senate Judiciary Committee reported his nomination to the full Senate with a negative vote. The Senate confirmed Lamar, 32–28, but his nomination emphasized just how sensitive sectional feelings remained in Gilded Age America.

Although he started slowly, Lamar came to be a force on the bench, particularly in 1890 and 1891. He handled routine cases against the federal government for recovery of monies, such as *United States ex rel Redfield v. Windom* (1891), but most of Lamar's decisions dealt with land boundaries, tort issues, and contracts. He wrote for the Court in *Southern Development Corp. v. Silva* (1888), *Hannibal & St. Joseph Railroad Company v. Missouri River Packet Company* (1888), and *Clement v. Packer* (1888), among others.

Lucius Quintus Cincinnatus Lamar

Legal historian Arnold Paul defined Lamar's judicial style as "constitutional formalism." In cases of important public policy, Lamar construed statutes narrowly, and especially so in matters of separation of powers. Lamar believed that the Court should enforce the separation of powers between the branches of the federal government in order to avoid tyranny by any particular branch.

His commitment to the separation of powers can be discerned in his dissent in *In re Neagle* (1890), joined by Chief Justice Melville Fuller. The Court's majority in *Neagle* read executive branch powers broadly. The case arose from a complex situation that resulted in a death in California. The U.S. attorney general's office had appointed a bodyguard to defend Justice Stephen J. Field from personal attack, but Congress had not authorized the bodyguard, David Neagle, who killed Field's attacker. The attorney general's office defended its action as inherent in the president's constitutional duty "to take care that the laws be faithfully executed." Lamar was not convinced. Because Congress had not authorized the appointment of the bodyguard, he argued, the executive department could not read into a constitutional phase executive powers that Congress had not approved. Lamar's dissent demonstrates both his attachment to the separation of powers and his suspicion of executive power.

Lamar also strengthened federal regulation of interstate commerce relative to regulations by the states. In *Chicago, Milwaukee, and St. Paul Railway Co. v. Minnesota* (1890), Justice Samuel Blatchford, for a six-person majority, struck down as unconstitutional the powerful railroad commission of Minnesota on the grounds that the statute did not provide adequate judicial review of the "reasonableness" of the maximum railroad rates set by the commission. Justices Joseph P. Bradley, Horace Gray, and Lamar dissented, arguing that reasonableness was not a judicial issue but a legislative one and therefore the statute should be upheld. Although written by Bradley, the dissent had Lamar's concurrence because of implied judicial restraint—courts ought not interfere with the formation of public policy.

Lamar's position regarding interstate commerce is best seen in *McCall v. California* (1890). Although three justices dissented from Lamar's majority opinion, *McCall* elaborated the rule that a state tax on an agency of an interstate corporation was an unconstitutional burden on interstate commerce. This position parallels his strict separation position because the states and the federal government possess clearly defined powers in the regulation of commerce, and the courts ought to enforce the separation of those powers.

Lamar died while visiting Georgia in the winter of 1893. His life can be read as an accommodation to the changing needs of the South, which he served first, and the nation, which he served well and with honor later.

—*Thomas C. Mackey*

BIBLIOGRAPHY

Lamar's life received full treatment in James B. Murphy, *L. Q. C. Lamar: Pragmatic Patriot* (1973). Also useful are Arnold M. Paul, "Lucius Quintus Cincinnatus Lamar," in Friedman and Israel, *Justices,* vol. 2, 1431; John F. Kennedy, *Profiles in Courage* (1955); and articles to mark the centennial of his death in *Mississippi Law Journal* 63 (1993): 1.

NOTEWORTHY OPINIONS

In re Neagle, 135 U.S. 1(1890) (Dissent)

McCall v. California, 136 U.S. 104 (1890)

HENRY BROCKHOLST LIVINGSTON

Birth: November 25, 1757, New York City.

Education: Graduated from College of New Jersey (Princeton), 1774; studied law under Peter Yates; admitted to bar in 1783.

Official Positions: Member, New York Assembly, 1786, 1800–1802; judge, New York State Supreme Court, 1802–1807.

Supreme Court Service: Recess appointment as associate justice by President Thomas Jefferson, November 10, 1806; nominated December 15, 1806, to replace William Paterson, who had died; confirmed by the Senate, December 17, 1806, by a voice vote; took judicial oath January 20, 1807; served until March 18, 1823; replaced by Smith Thompson, nominated by President James Monroe.

Death: March 18, 1823, Washington, D.C.

Born into one of New York's wealthiest and most powerful eighteenth-century families, Henry Brockholst Livingston received his education at the College of New Jersey (now Princeton) and, after graduating in 1774, joined the Continental Army at the outbreak of the Revolution. After the war, he read law under Albany's Peter Yates, gained admission to the bar in 1783, and soon won a seat in the New York Assembly. Even though he favored the ratification of the nation's new Constitution and developed a professional association with Alexander Hamilton, Livingston became a Jeffersonian during the 1790s. In 1802, after a decade and a half of involvement in state politics, he was appointed to the New York Supreme Court, where he served alongside the venerable chancellor, James Kent. Five years later, on the death of Justice William Patterson of New Jersey, Thomas Jefferson appointed Livingston to the U.S. Supreme Court, primarily because of political and geographical considerations.

Livingston's appointment came at an important time in American constitutional history, as Jefferson was attempting to stifle the power of the Federalist-dominated Supreme Court. Despite an impressive record as a state judge, Livingston offered little resistance to the Court's prevailing course and seemed to fade into obscurity among the likes of John Marshall and Joseph Story. Livingston had been accustomed to writing separate opinions on the New York bench, but he hesitated to challenge John Marshall's policy of having the Court speak in a single voice: moreover, he rarely dissented, even when he privately disagreed with his brethren. For example, after writing a strongly worded circuit opinion in 1817 affirming the constitutionality of state insolvency legislation applied retroactively (*Adams v. Storey*), Livingston kept silent in *Sturges v. Crowninshield* (1819), in which the Court held that similar legislation violated the Constitution's contract clause. And although he expressed some doubts about the Court's decision in

Dartmouth College v. Woodward (1819), the most important contract case decided by the Marshall Court, Livingston voted with the majority on learning that Chancellor Kent favored the Court's position. Livingston's reticence in such instances was characteristic of his Supreme Court career as a whole. As a justice for seventeen years, he wrote only forty-nine opinions, none of which related to the central constitutional questions of the day.

Much of Livingston's work on the Court dealt with commercial issues—the law of promissory notes, bills of exchange, and insurance, for example. In such cases, indicative of his acceptance of the Marshall Court's Federalist position, Livingston tended to take the side of creditors. In *Lenox v. Prout* (1818), he held that in the event of default by the maker of a promissory note, the endorser of that note was not entitled to the protection of a court of equity. Instead, the holder of the unpaid note could bring an action against either the endorser or the maker. Consistent with this line of reasoning, in *Dugan v. United States* (1818), Livingston held that in all cases involving contracts with the United States, the national government has the right to enforce the performance of the contract or to recover damages for its violation. "It would be strange," he reasoned, "to deny to them a right which is secured to every citizen of the United States." Again, in light of his support for retroactive bankruptcy legislation while on circuit, Livingston's strict view of the enforcement

Henry Brockholst Livingston

of contracts in these cases points to the important influence of the Court's Federalist majority on his judicial behavior.

Aside from commercial law, Livingston also made his mark in maritime and prize cases. One of his most notable opinions was *United States v. Smith* (1820), which involved the scope of a congressional piracy statute. In the case, American citizens had been convicted under the law for the capture and robbery of a Spanish ship on the high seas. In dissent, Livingston argued that the act failed to define "piracy" specifically, in accordance with congressional power to do so under the Constitution. Because of the statute's imprecision, he favored the release of the defendants. *Smith* was one of the few cases in which Livingston refused to assent to the majority position.

Despite his scant judicial record, Livingston earned the respect and friendship of his fellow justices, particularly Joseph Story, with whom he carried on a lengthy correspondence. Story described Livingston as "a very able and independent judge," who was "luminous, decisive, earnest, and impressive on the bench." Such comments, coming from a jurist of Story's caliber, speak well for Livingston's abilities. Yet, Livingston's opinions—few in number and terse in style—may have misrepresented his juristic talents and helped make him one of the most obscure justices in Supreme Court history.

—*Timothy S. Huebner*

BIBLIOGRAPHY

There is no major collection of Livingston's papers, although some materials can be found in the large collection of Livingston family papers in the New-York Historical Society. Some of the correspondence between Livingston and Joseph Story has been published. See *Life and Letters of Joseph Story* (1971); and Gerald T. Dunne, "The Story-Livingston Correspondence," *American Journal of Legal His-*

tory 10 (1966): 224. The best overall sketch of Livingston is by Gerald Dunne in Friedman and Israel, *Justices,* vol. 1, 387.

NOTEWORTHY OPINIONS

Dugan v. United States, 16 U.S. 172 (1818)

Lenox v. Prout, 16 U.S. 520 (1818)

United States v. Smith, 18 U.S. 153 (1820) (Dissent)

HORACE HARMON LURTON

Birth: February 26, 1844, Newport, Kentucky.

Education: Douglas University (University of Chicago), 1860; Cumberland Law School, L.B., 1867.

Official Positions: Chancellor in equity, 1875–1878; judge, Tennessee Supreme Court, 1886–1893; judge, U.S. Court of Appeals for the Sixth Circuit, 1893–1909.

Supreme Court Service: Nominated associate justice by President William Howard Taft, December 13, 1909, to replace Rufus W. Peckham, who had died; confirmed by the Senate, December 20, 1909, by a voice vote; took judicial oath January 3, 1910; served until July 12, 1914; replaced by James C. McReynolds, nominated by President Woodrow Wilson.

Death: July 12, 1914, Atlantic City, New Jersey.

Horace Lurton was one of the last men appointed to the Supreme Court to have served in the Civil War. Although only eighteen years of age when the war broke out, he joined the Fifth Tennessee Regular Infantry. Captured in 1862, he escaped from a Union prison and joined the guerrilla forces led by Gen. John Morgan. Morgan's Raiders harassed Union forces and raided supply installations until July 1863, when most of the unit was captured. Once again Lurton found himself a prisoner of war. Suffering from a lung disease, he was released shortly before the war's end.

On his release, Lurton embarked on a career as prudent as his youth had been daring. After completing his education at Cumberland Law School in 1867, he entered a successful practice in Clarksville, Tennessee. He served a stint as a trial judge from 1875 to 1878, returned to private practice, and was then elected to the Tennessee Supreme Court in 1886. He had just become chief justice of that court in 1893

when President Grover Cleveland selected him for the federal court of appeals. Lurton served on the Sixth Circuit with future Supreme Court justice William Day, and future president and chief justice William Howard Taft. It was there that he had his most productive years. Certainly, he was highly regarded. Theodore Roosevelt seriously considered Lurton, a southern Democrat, for the Supreme Court in 1906 but opted instead for a nominee from his own party, William H. Moody. Three years later, however, President Taft made Lurton his first appointment to the Court.

At the time of his appointment, Lurton was sixty-six years old. He served on the Court for only four years, writing just ninety-seven opinions, none of which was a landmark case, and he rarely expressed a written dissent or concurrence. Both on the Sixth Circuit and in the Supreme Court, he was assigned cases that often involved complex questions of financial relations or antitrust. Demonstrating respect for precedent, his opinions tended to trace earlier case law in detail. Professionalism muted expression of a personal philosophy in his writing, which, if anything, reflected a tempered conservatism.

That conservatism was apparent in opinions involving economic regulations. In *Heaton-Peninsular Button-Fastener Co. v. Eureka Specialty Co.* (1896), a Sixth Circuit case, Lurton discounted the argument that certain contracts could be against public policy. "If there is one thing which, more than another, public policy requires," he wrote, "it is that men of full age and competent understanding shall have utmost liberty of contracting." His language left little doubt that Lurton subscribed to liberty of contract, a theory the Court used to oversee state regulations. Yet he was not quick to invalidate state regulations. On the circuit court, for example, he upheld statutory mechanics' and materialmen's lien laws against charges that they violated liberty of contract. On the basis of his voting record, Justice Lurton appeared even more sympathetic to federal economic regulation. He voted with the majority that upheld a federal employer liability insurance statute in the *Second Employer Liability Case* (1912), strengthened the Pure Food and Drug Act in *Hipolite Egg Co. v. United States* (1911), and expanded the power of the Interstate Commerce Commission in the *Minnesota Rate Cases* (1913).

Lurton's most significant opinions dealt with antitrust. *Henry v. A. B. Dick Co.* (1912) involved the sale of patented duplicating machines. As a condition

Horace Harmon Lurton

of sale, the Dick company required purchasers to use only ink and supplies it made. Henry, who sold another company's ink, claimed that this condition amounted to a restraint of trade. Lurton disagreed. The company had a patent on the machine, he reasoned. The very purpose of patent law is monopoly, and the sale of ink is closely enough linked to the patented product to be justified. The decision in *A. B. Dick* restricted the impact of antitrust laws, but some of Lurton's other opinions, such as *Park v. Hartman* (1907) and *United States v. Terminal Railroad Assn.* (1912), demonstrated his willingness to enforce antitrust law in many circumstances.

Although the record is slim, Lurton's conservative inclination was more evident in civil rights matters. *Karem v. United States* (1903), a case decided by the Sixth Circuit, invalidated a federal statute that made it a crime to conspire to keep black citizens from voting. The statute, Lurton reasoned, was inappropriate under the Fifteenth Amendment because it governed acts of individuals rather than those of the state. Later, in *Bailey v. Alabama* (1911), he joined Justice Oliver Wendell Holmes Jr. in dissent when the majority overruled a state peonage law.

What stands out most in Lurton's record, however, is moderation. Not even his most significant opinions broke new legal ground. By the time he applied it in *Karem*, for example, the state action doctrine was well established. Rather than an innovative application of antitrust law, *Henry v. A. B. Dick* reflected a judicious weighing of the purpose of antitrust against the purpose of patent law. By all accounts, Horace Lurton was the consummate professional judge.

—*Paul Kens*

BIBLIOGRAPHY

The best available biography is James F. Watts Jr., "Horace Harmon Lurton," in Friedman and Israel, *Justices,* vol. 3, 1847. A collection of Justice Lurton's correspondence is held by the Library of Congress.

NOTEWORTHY OPINIONS

Karem v. United States, 121 F. 250 (6th Circ. 1903)

Henry v. A. B. Dick Co., 224 U.S. 1 (1912)

United States v. Terminal Railroad Assn., 224 U.S. 383 (1912)

JOHN MARSHALL

Birth: September 24, 1755, Germantown, Virginia.

Education: Tutored at home; self-taught in law; attended one course of law lectures at College of William and Mary, 1780.

Official Positions: Member, Virginia House of Delegates, 1782–1785, 1787–1790, 1795–1796; member, Executive Council of State, 1782–1784; recorder, Richmond City Hustings Court, 1785–1788; delegate, state convention for ratification of federal Constitution, 1788; minister to France, 1797–1798; U.S. representative, 1799–1800; U.S. secretary of state, 1800–1801; member, Virginia Constitutional Convention, 1829.

Supreme Court Service: Nominated chief justice by President John Adams, January 20, 1801, to replace Oliver Ellsworth, who had resigned; confirmed by the Senate, January 27, 1801, by a voice vote; took judicial oath February 4, 1801; served until July 6, 1835; replaced by Roger B. Taney, nominated by President Andrew Jackson.

Death: July 6, 1835, Philadelphia, Pennsylvania.

John Marshall was born on the Virginia colonial frontier to one of the leading families in Fauquier County. His father, Thomas Marshall, a militia officer and surveyor, served as Fauquier's delegate in the House of Burgesses, as a vestryman for Leeds Parish, and as county sheriff. His employment as a surveying assistant to his boyhood friend, George Washington, identified the family with the future president and ultimately involved his son in the purchase of a substantial portion of the Fairfax estate that Washington and Thomas Marshall surveyed. John Marshall's mother, Mary Keith Marshall, was the daughter of a clergyman who had married into the prominent Randolph family. Through her the future chief justice was distantly related to Thomas Jefferson.

Tutored at home by his mother and local clergy, Marshall studied for a time with the Reverend

Archibald Campbell of Westmoreland County. At nineteen, he was appointed lieutenant in the Culpeper Minute Men and saw action at the battle of Great Bridge in southeastern Virginia (December 9, 1775). From August 1776 to the spring of 1780, Marshall served as first lieutenant and captain in the Virginia Continental Line, with additional duties as a judge advocate. He was present during the battles of Brandywine, Germantown, and Stony Point, and he endured the harsh winter encampment at Valley Forge.

After military service, Marshall studied law with George Wythe, the newly appointed professor of law and police at the College of William and Mary, and was admitted to practice law on August 28, 1780. Shortly after his marriage to Mary Willis "Polly" Ambler in January 1783, he shifted the locus of his law practice and political life to Richmond, where, in addition to service in the House of Delegates, he also spent three years as the recorder of the Richmond City Hustings Court, the only judicial position he held before his nomination to the U.S. Supreme Court.

As a delegate to the Virginia convention that ratified the Constitution, Marshall supported ratification and delivered a persuasive speech on the need for a federal judiciary in the proposed government. Once the new government was in operation, he declined several offers of federal office, preferring to remain in private practice. He was particularly prominent in defending Virginia planters against their British creditors, and it was in this context that he argued his only Supreme Court appeal, *Ware v. Hylton* (1796).

Marshall came to national prominence as a result of his membership in a mission to France, 1797–1798, in the course of which he and his colleagues soundly rejected French demands that the United States pay tribute to the French Republic before a treaty of amity could be negotiated. With the publication of their correspondence with the French agents (called Messrs. X, Y, and Z), they became the focal point of partisan debate between the Jeffersonian and Federalist political parties. On Marshall's return from France, and at the urging of former president George Washington, he ran for the Richmond seat in the House of Representatives. Elected as the only Federalist member of Congress from Virginia, he served in the House until his appointment as secretary of state in May 1800. During the last months of the Adams administration, Marshall served concurrently as secretary of state and chief justice of the United States.

The federal judiciary came under heavy attack when the Jeffersonian Republican Party came into power in March 1801. President Jefferson and his supporters in Congress were strongly opposed to the establishment of new federal trial courts. They were even more critical of the composition of the circuit courts, the judges having been selected from among the most loyal members of the Federalist Party. Many federal judges, including some of Marshall's colleagues on the Supreme Court, had been overbearing and unprofessional in their conduct of criminal trials designed to stamp out political opposition. When the Jeffersonian majority in Congress repealed the Judiciary Act of 1801, the Supreme Court justices reluctantly resumed circuit riding to preside over the traditional circuit courts. In *Stuart v. Laird* (1803), the Court upheld the authority of Congress to abolish the circuit courts established under the Judiciary Act.

John Marshall

Against this background, Chief Justice Marshall delivered his famous decision in *Marbury v. Madison* (1803), which held a section of the Judiciary Act of 1789 null and void because it conflicted with provisions of the Constitution. The statute granted the Supreme Court jurisdiction to issue a writ of *mandamus,* which, but for Marshall's invalidation, would have been available to command delivery of William Marbury's commission as a justice of the peace.

Ostensibly, the Court's decision was a formal rejection of jurisdiction, and because it did not require enforcement, it was self-executing. *Marbury*, however, brought earlier American jurisprudence concerning judicial review into the precedents of the Supreme Court, and it therefore represented an important step in establishing the Court as a primary expositor of U.S. constitutional law. *Marbury* also demonstrated the manner in which the Court, through deciding cases concerning its own jurisdiction, could gain institutional power within the federal union. Although judicial nullification of congressional statutes was used sparingly before 1890, courts thereafter would expand the concept of judicial review and assert that the Supreme Court was the sole expounder of constitutional law in the United States, which the justices reiterated in *Cooper v. Aaron* (1958).

Marbury drew on diverse strands of constitutional thought: first, the concept of a written constitution, which implied a sovereign act of the people that was superior to statutes passed by the legislature; second, the implication of the Constitution that federal courts were of limited jurisdiction; third, a corollary on separation of powers doctrine that asserted that judges in administering the law were required by their oath to uphold the Constitution and therefore were independent of both legislative and executive control.

Equally important to the American federal union was the conferral upon the Supreme Court of a limited power to hear appeals from the highest courts of each state in certain federally related cases. In 1816 the Commonwealth of Virginia defied the Court's mandate in a case involving the Fairfax proprietaries. Because Marshall had a personal financial interest in the litigation, he did not participate in the decision, but his close confidante on the bench, Joseph Story, wrote a strong defense in *Martin v. Hunter's Lessee* (1816) of the proposition that for the Union to function, such an appeal was proper and must be binding upon the various states.

Five years later, Marshall decided that matters pending in state courts that were otherwise subject to Supreme Court review might be appealed from the highest state court having jurisdiction over the case.

Cohens v. Virginia (1821) involved a Virginia criminal statute imposing a fine for selling lottery tickets. The Cohen brothers, Philip and Mendes, had sold tickets issued by the District of Columbia lottery managers pursuant to a District statute. They were convicted before the Hustings Court of Norfolk, and under state procedural law there was no right to appeal to Virginia's highest court, the court of appeals. Marshall upheld the validity of the appeal from the Virginia trial court to the Supreme Court, based on the fact that the lottery was authorized by a congressional statute. In 1824, when the case was argued on the merits, however, the Cohens lost because the Court viewed the District statute authorizing the lottery as a mere local regulation, not intended by Congress to be supreme over state law.

Cohens demonstrates Marshall's insistence that the Supreme Court exercise broad authority in reviewing state laws that conflicted with the Constitution or the laws and treaties made pursuant to it. He believed this was essential to the smooth functioning of the constitutional system, a necessary instrument for the implementation of foreign treaties and agreements, and a manifestation of federal supremacy. Consequently, no state should be permitted to so structure its appellate system that federal questions were shielded from appellate review, and the Supreme Court might make its own decisions of fact when its jurisdiction depended upon such a decision.

In *McCulloch v. Maryland* (1819), the chief justice spoke for the Court in explaining the scope of the necessary and proper clause in Article 1, Section 8, of the Constitution. This issue had been debated since the 1792 disagreement between Thomas Jefferson and Alexander Hamilton over the chartering of the Bank of the United States. In *McCulloch*, Marshall essentially adopted Hamilton's position—that the powers of the federal government were delimited by the Constitution, but that under the necessary and proper provision whatever was useful or efficacious in implementing those powers was constitutional. This stance contrasted with Jefferson's view that the clause permitted only those additional powers as were essential to functioning within the enumerated grants of power.

McCulloch is a good example of Marshall's preference for effectiveness in the exercise of government power. He was deeply concerned that political leaders should possess adequate authority to carry out their duties. He drew a distinction between policy decisions, which in his opinion were to be left to the executive and Congress, and matters touching on private individual rights, which courts should protect against overbearing or confiscatory government action. Deference to the political decisions of the president and Congress is implicit in the Marshall Court's acceptance of Jefferson's imposition of the embargo as an instrument of foreign policy. Marshall was quick to intercede, however, when government action threatened the constitutional rights of individuals or groups, as evidenced by his opinions in *Fletcher v. Peck* (1810), *Dartmouth College v. Woodward* (1819), and *Worcester v. Georgia* (1832).

Marshall's opinion in *McCulloch* was based on the supremacy of the federal government within its constitutional sphere. The case involved Maryland's attempt to tax the notes issued by the Bank of the United States branch in Baltimore. The chief justice pointed out that such a tax imposed a burden on a federal activity. Although some equitably imposed taxes might be constitutional, this particular tax operated to place the bank at a competitive disadvantage within Maryland. It was therefore contrary to the Constitution's Article VI, which made the laws of the United States the supreme law of the land and subordinated state statutes and taxes to the provisions of congressional acts. Like many Marshall Court opinions in other fields, *McCulloch* merely initiated the process of defining the tax immunities that existed between the federal government and state governments. Its clear and emphatic assertion of federal supremacy, however, remains Marshall's most enduring contribution to American constitutional law.

Although Marshall has frequently been described as a procapitalist judge, he is best seen as a strong nationalist who sought the prosperity of the United States through economic diversification and legal safeguards for private property. In general, he favored free competition, but he was not unwilling to use government subsidies to encourage new forms of commercial or industrial activity. Commercial activity between the states should not be subjected to artificial mercantilist obstructions, and monopolies were to be regarded with suspicion.

Like many of his contemporaries, Marshall wished to see the United States develop into a free trade area where goods and services might be bought and sold across state boundaries with virtually no restriction. His most famous opinion in this area is *Gibbons v. Ogden* (1824), which involved efforts by New York's state legislature to restrict steamboat navigation in New York harbor and on the Hudson River to vessels operated by the Fulton-Livingston monopoly. Observing that trade among the states included navigation of the waterways, Marshall held that the New York statutes and monopoly violated the Constitution. That document gave Congress the right to regulate commerce among the states, and the state legislation conflicted with that federal constitutional grant. In addition, Congress, in the Federal Coasting Licensing Act of 1793, had already exercised its power to regulate commerce in the waters covered by the New York statutes, preempting the states from making rules for the regulation of commerce. Undoubtedly one of the most encyclopedic of Marshall's opinions, *Gibbons* remains the cornerstone of the federal commerce power to this day. It anticipated future cases that would apply an economic test to determine what was burdensome to the flow of commerce, and it guaranteed that the commerce clause of the Constitution would become one of the focal points of federal power from that point on.

In a nation as undeveloped as the United States was in the first three decades of the nineteenth century, foreign investment was essential to economic prosperity. Investment in turn depended on the legal system's support for the institution of private property. Building on earlier case law that developed legal safeguards for vested property interests, Marshall shaped the contract clause into an additional instrument for controlling state tendencies to trample on private property rights. He accomplished this through a broad, but now antiquated, view of contract. Originally, the Constitution's prohibition against states abridging the obligation of contracts was directed toward seizure of accounts payable in commercial transactions, as had been done in the case of British creditors during the American Revolution, or state laws that favored debtors and impeded creditors from collecting their accounts.

Marshall began his creative work on the contract clause in *Fletcher v. Peck* (1810) by treating a Georgia state land grant as if it were a contract between the grantor state and the grantees, who had bribed the legislature and secured the vast Yazoo land grant that included the rich farmlands of the future states of Alabama and Mississippi. The subsequent reform-minded legislature enacted a statute repealing the land grant, but Marshall held that although a legislature would not normally be bound by the actions of its predecessor, when private rights arose as a consequence of a legislative act, those property interests could not be infringed without violation of the contract clause.

In *Dartmouth College v. Woodward* (1819), Marshall viewed contracts in a more general and equitable context. The pre-Revolutionary charter to Dartmouth College was viewed as the origin of property rights in those who received the charter (that is, the trustees); the Crown, which granted the charter; and those who gave property to the college in reliance upon the charter's terms. Marshall reasoned that these arrangements prevented the state of New Hampshire from seizing the assets and books of the college and making it a state university. As the legal successor to the English Crown, the state was bound by its contractual relation with the trustees and the donors. Although the broad application of the contract clause to business, as well as charitable corporations, was somewhat restricted by the Marshall Court, it was left to the subsequent Court, led by Chief Justice Roger B. Taney, to assert countervailing rights reserved to states when corporate charters were vague.

Marshall's most serious dissent from his colleagues involved the contract clause and its application to state insolvency laws. An economic depression in 1819 caused many mercantile firms to suffer finan-

cial difficulty, and some sought refuge in insolvency, a process whereby creditors agreed not to imprison the debtor provided his or her assets were made available for distribution among them. Although the Constitution authorized Congress to enact a uniform law of bankruptcy, it had not done so, except for a short-lived statute in effect from 1800 to 1803. In *Ogden v. Saunders* (1827), Marshall and his Court had to decide whether the enactment of an insolvency law that discharged a preexisting debt violated the contract clause. A majority of the Court held that state insolvency laws did not abridge the obligations of contract, but simply altered the remedies available to creditors. Marshall dissented, asserting that the parties entered into a contract for payment, and that no state action infringing upon those agreed rights was permissible. By this point in Marshall's career it appears that he viewed contract rights as arising under natural law by virtue of the private agreement of the parties. In opposition, his associates saw contractual rights arising from private agreement, which in turn was subject to the applicable state law. For them, certain contractual rights and obligations might, under some circumstances, be legislatively altered without violating the constitutional mandate.

Marshall's growing acceptance of natural law principles in regard to the contract clause cases began to shape his approach to individual rights in the last decade of his chief justiceship, even though pragmatism and caution limited his resort to abstract principles of natural law. Despite English precedents, including the famous *Somerset's Case* (1772), which held that slavery was contrary to natural law and therefore could exist only by virtue of express municipal law, Marshall preferred a positivist approach. In *The Antelope* (1825), he was asked to rule on the status of Africans captured from a slave trading ship off the American coast. He rejected the invitation to consult the law of nations or some abstract theory of natural justice. Rather, he sought express provisions in the municipal law of the states involved to determine whether the purported slaves were held and transported illegally. Absent proof that the nation of the ship's registry had abolished the slave trade, Marshall felt compelled to surrender both the ship and its human cargo to the owners of the vessel.

In regard to Indian land titles, the chief justice, in *Johnson v. McIntosh* (1823), considered the various tribes to hold a mere possessory interest that did not restrict the right of the Crown, the commonwealth of Virginia, or its grantee, the United States, to confer title to the land. The post-Revolutionary grant of Illinois land therefore extinguished possessory rights held by those claiming under Indian deeds. Subsequently, in *Cherokee Nation v. Georgia* (1831), Marshall asserted that the Cherokee tribe was neither a separate sovereign nation nor a state of the United States, and it lacked standing to obtain an injunction from the Supreme Court against Georgia legislation that undermined the independence of the Cherokee people. Because the Cherokee were living within the limits of the United States, they were subject to state and federal law. They were a dependent domestic nation, and once they surrendered possession of their land, it became available for grant by the states or federal government. Furthermore, Marshall pointed out that the state of Georgia had civil authority over the Cherokee lands, and the Court would exceed its authority by restraining that state's legislature from acting on Indians subject to its jurisdiction.

In deciding *Cherokee Nation*, Marshall indicated that in an appropriate case, such as when Indian rights arose from agreements incorporated in federal treaties, the Supreme Court might intervene to protect these rights. Such a case arose the following year in *Worcester v. Georgia* (1832). Samuel Worcester, a missionary appointed by the American Board of Commissioners for Foreign Missions and approved by the president of the United States as a resident within the Cherokee territory, was convicted under a Georgia criminal law prohibiting residence without a state license. Citing treaties between the tribe and the federal government granting self-government to the tribe, Worcester asserted that he was not subject to Georgia law. Marshall relied on the treaty provisions to declare the Georgia statute null and void and contrary to the authority of Congress to regulate trade with the Indian nations. Because the treaties were in the nature of contracts between the Cherokee and the United States, and because they also involved the supremacy of the United States under the commerce clause, Marshall's firm holding in favor of the Indians was inevitable. Unfortunately, it was to be of no practical value. President Andrew Jackson refused to enforce the decree; the "Trail of Tears," which carried a large portion of the Cherokee to the Oklahoma Territory, continued to operate, and white settlers from Georgia poured into Cherokee lands that contained gold deposits and the rich alluvial soil necessary to grow cotton.

Perhaps more than any other chief justice, Marshall was responsible for altering the way the Supreme Court conducted its business. Within the first years of his tenure he succeeded in convincing the other justices to accept a unitary "opinion of the Court" as the preferred way of announcing decisions. This was not a novel practice; under Marshall's predecessor, Oliver Ellsworth, a number of Supreme Court opinions had been issued *per curiam*. These opinions were on relatively minor points, however, and the practice of *seriatim* opinions persisted for major cases. In the *seriatim* opinion, based on English practice, each judge stated his individual view of the case, and the law of the case had to be extracted from the points on which a majority of the justices seemed to agree.

Agreement on the content of "opinions of the Court" moved the Supreme Court in the direction of unanimity, which was enhanced by Marshall's efforts to have all justices room together in one hotel, where they ate at the same table and discussed the cases pending before them. Although the influx of new associate justices appointed by Thomas Jefferson and Andrew Jackson began to undermine these arrangements, Marshall remained a dominant figure on the Court until about 1825, when his influence began to wane. For almost a quarter of a century, he delivered well over 50 percent of the opinions of the Court, most of them bearing clear marks of his authorship and judicial philosophy.

Marshall's leadership of the Court was marked by political astuteness and exceptional skill in human relations. When the Court was under attack by a hostile president and Congress, he used jurisdictional holdings as a way to defer deciding cases that might prove inflammatory, as in *Marbury v. Madison* and *Cherokee Nation v. Georgia*. After Marshall joined the Court, relatively few original jurisdiction cases involving the states came before the justices, but they heard more cases involving the Court's appellate jurisdiction over state courts construing the Constitution, as well as federal statutes and treaties entered into pursuant to the Constitution. Cases arising in the District of Columbia, where no state interests were involved, made up a substantial portion of the Court's work. The probability of conflict with state authority was limited, and the Court became less controversial in a political sense.

Within the Court, Marshall used his skills at human relations to bring his associates into agreement with his view of the Court as the principal institution for interpretation of the Constitution. He was a robust and outgoing person with a quick sense of humor. In Richmond and in Washington he gained a reputation for modesty in dress and behavior, and his female relatives were frequently appalled at his disregard for the fashionable conventions of the day. From his days as a Continental Line officer he exhibited a rare ability to soothe ruffled feelings and compromise arguments. Generous in his treatment of others, he could count as personal friends virtually all who opposed him politically. The single noteworthy exception to this statement was his kinsman, Thomas Jefferson, who suspected Marshall of a malevolent and calculating disposition toward him and his policies. Marshall was not unaware of these feelings, but still he joined a group of subscribers pledged to raise money for Jefferson's support in the last years of his life.

Marshall's correspondence with Joseph Story and his concern for the health of Justices Bushrod Washington and Gabriel Duvall demonstrate his involvement in the well-being of his colleagues. This extended to Henry Baldwin, a Jacksonian appointee plagued with fits of insanity during his service on the Marshall Court. Both Baldwin and Jefferson's first appointee, the fiery William Johnson, were treated with tolerance and respect. Despite serious health

problems in the last five years of his life, the chief justice continued to carry out his duties, fearing that President Jackson would undo much of his work through the appointment of his successor.

Marshall left to the U.S. Supreme Court a legacy of respect and stature that ensured its continuance as a major institution in American life. His constitutional law articulated clear principles of federal supremacy and laid the legal foundation for economic prosperity and growth in the decades before the Civil War. In thirty-four years on the Supreme Court bench, he succeeded in erecting a structure for constitutional government that would dominate the Court's work until at least the Civil War, and in many cases well beyond.

—*Herbert A. Johnson*

BIBLIOGRAPHY

Marshall's papers are being published in Herbert A. Johnson, Charles T. Cullen, and Charles F. Hobson, eds., *The Papers of John Marshall*, 12 vols. to date (1974–2006).

The most comprehensive biographical study is R. Kent Newmyer, *John Marshall and the Heroic Age of the Supreme Court* (2001). Francis N. Stiles, *John Marshall: Defender of the Constitution* (1981), is a brief and general survey that gives a helpful introduction to Marshall's life and constitutional thought. Marshall's career before he was appointed to the Court has been carefully analyzed and detailed in David Robarge, *A Chief Justice's Progress: John Marshall from Revolutionary Virginia to the Supreme Court* (2000); and his activities as chief justice are analyzed in Herbert A. Johnson, *The Chief Justiceship of John Marshall* (1997).

Robert K. Faulkner's *The Jurisprudence of John Marshall* (1968) is still useful but needs to be read in light of Charles F. Hobson's more exhaustive study, *The Great Chief Justice: John Marshall and the Rule of Law* (1996). Two volumes that cast new light on *Marbury* and provide helpful insights into the significance of Marshall's jurisprudence and decision making are Robert L. Clinton, *Marbury v. Madison and Judicial Review* (1989); and Paul W. Kahn, *The Reign of Law: Marbury v. Madison and the Construction of America* (1997).

The definitive studies of Marshall's work as chief justice are found in the *Holmes Devise History* series: George L.

Haskins and Herbert A. Johnson, *Foundations of Power: John Marshall, 1801–1815* (1981); and G. Edward White, *The Marshall Court and Cultural Change, 1815–1835* (1988).

NOTEWORTHY OPINIONS

Marbury v. Madison, 5 U.S. 137 (1803)

Fletcher v. Peck, 10 U.S. 87 (1810)

McCulloch v. Maryland, 17 U.S. 316 (1819)

Dartmouth College v. Woodward, 17 U.S. 518 (1819)

Cohens v. Virginia, 19 U.S. 264 (1821)

Gibbons v. Ogden, 22 U.S. 1 (1824)

Ogden v. Saunders, 25 U.S. 213 (1827) (Dissent)

Cherokee Nation v. Georgia, 30 U.S. 1 (1831)

Worcester v. Georgia, 31 U.S. 515 (1832)

THURGOOD MARSHALL

Birth: July 2, 1908, Baltimore, Maryland.

Education: Lincoln University, A.B., cum laude, 1930; Howard University Law School, LL.B., 1933.

Official Positions: Judge, U.S. Court of Appeals for the Second Circuit, 1961–1965; U.S. solicitor general, 1965–1967.

Supreme Court Service: Nominated associate justice by President Lyndon B. Johnson, June 13, 1967, to replace Tom C. Clark, who had retired; confirmed by the Senate, August 30, 1967, by a 69–11 vote; took judicial oath October 2, 1967; retired October 1, 1991; replaced by Clarence Thomas, nominated by President George H. W. Bush.

Death: January 24, 1993, Bethesda, Maryland.

President Lyndon Johnson appointed Thurgood Marshall to the Supreme Court because, in Johnson's words, it was "the right thing to do, the right time to do it, the right man and the right place." Marshall was the first African American to sit on the Supreme Court. His nomination came at the right time because by 1967 the Democratic Party's commitment to civil rights required representation of African Americans in high office. Marshall was the right man not only because he had been the strategist of the legal challenge to school segregation that culminated in *Brown v. Board of Education* (1954) and was the nation's most prominent African American lawyer, but also because he was committed to the implementation, through constitutional law, of Johnson's Great Society vision.

When Marshall arrived at the Court, he joined a solid liberal majority that shared that vision. The Court's composition changed rapidly, however, and Marshall spent most of his career on the Court holding up the banner of a vision about which the nation had grown somewhat skeptical.

After graduating from Lincoln University in Pennsylvania, Marshall enrolled in Howard University's law school, from which he graduated first in the class of 1933. Dean Charles Hamilton Houston of Howard took Marshall as a protégé, and Marshall referred throughout his life to the lessons Houston taught him. For Houston, law was a method of social engineering. He urged his students to work through law to improve the legal and social conditions of the African American community.

Marshall became the leader among African American lawyers because he took Houston's message to heart. After a brief attempt to sustain a private practice in Depression-racked Baltimore, Marshall moved to New York in 1936, where he joined Houston on the staff of the National Association for the Advancement of Colored People (NAACP). In 1939, after Houston left New York, Marshall became the

NAACP's chief lawyer, a position he held until 1961. Marshall was one of the NAACP's leading speakers and organizers, but his main contribution came through his work as a lawyer.

The NAACP's legal staff grew from two when Marshall joined it to around a dozen when he left. Marshall's responsibilities as a manager made it difficult for him to sustain his work as a trial lawyer, but his early experience at trials gave him a sense—this infused his work as a judge as well—of how the abstract legal rules appellate judges define actually work in the courtroom. Marshall also was the NAACP's leading appellate advocate. He developed a casual and informal style of argument that worked quite effectively before courts, even the Supreme Court in the late 1940s and 1950s, that were inclined Marshall's way but needed assurance that the course he wanted to pursue was acceptable both legally and morally. When he argued against school segregation in *Brown*, his conversational style contrasted dramatically, and favorably, with the more oratorical style of his great adversary,

Thurgood Marshall

John W. Davis. And even when the Court rejected Marshall's argument for rapid desegregation in its decision on the appropriate remedy in *Brown II* (1955), his insistence that constitutional rights were "present and personal" made the justices appropriately uncomfortable with their own actions.

In 1961 President John F. Kennedy appointed Marshall to the U.S. Court of Appeals for the Second Circuit, where he served four years. In 1965 President Johnson named Marshall solicitor general, intending to elevate him to the Supreme Court when the opportunity arose. Two years later, Johnson created a vacancy on the Court by appointing Ramsey Clark attorney general, which led Justice Tom C. Clark, Ramsey's father, to retire.

Marshall arrived at the Court when it was in the full flush of the Warren Court's liberal activism. Like most new justices, Marshall did not write many significant opinions in his first years of his tenure, and by the time Marshall had enough seniority to do so, the Court's composition had changed. President Richard Nixon's four appointments destroyed the powerful liberal coalition, and although occasionally a majority could be knit together for a liberal result, Marshall's abilities were not those of a coalition builder. His main contributions to constitutional law therefore came in his dissents. The Court's further transformation in the 1980s simply reinforced this situation.

In *Stanley v. Georgia* (1969), for example, Marshall wrote an opinion drawing together free speech and privacy concerns to find it unconstitutional to punish a person for possessing obscene material in his home. In sympathetic hands, Marshall's analysis might have led the Court to ban all regulation of obscene materials, but when the Court confronted the fundamental free speech question in *Miller v. California* (1973), a new conservative majority allowed local communities to apply their own standards to suppress obscenity. Marshall was among the four dissenters.

For most of Marshall's tenure, his colleagues respected him for the role he had played in making constitutional law with the NAACP and for the unique perspective he brought to the Court. Their respect, however, did not translate into making Marshall influential within the institution. His contributions to constitutional law consisted of his work with the NAACP and the public and academic reception of his dissents.

Marshall's jurisprudence embraced Houston's belief that law was a method of social engineering, but without the scientific or systematic overtones that Houston's term conveys. Rather, Marshall approached legal problems with a practical orientation born of his experience as a lawyer. For him, legal issues were practical problems of social organization, and the right legal answers were those that provided the most sensible solutions to the problems. Marshall's experience led him to rely not on expert advice, but on his own judgment to determine what the most sensible solution was. In *Powell v. Texas* (1968), for example, Marshall rejected the position, advanced by most liberals of the time, that alcoholism was a disease that could not be punished through the criminal process. He was skeptical about the claims made by experts based on a rather thin record, but, more important, he emphasized that as society was then organized, no real solution to the problem of public drunkenness seemed available except through the admittedly unattractive use of police to help alcoholics "dry out."

Another early decision, and its ultimate fate, illustrates Marshall's jurisprudence and place on the Court. The NAACP's lawyers had struggled for years to eliminate racial discrimination by private parties such as homeowners and restaurant operators. Their constitutional claims were impeded by the state action doctrine, which required some participation by state officials in enforcing discrimination before the discrimination became unconstitutional. Marshall had argued *Shelley v. Kraemer* (1948), a restrictive covenant case, before the Court, and his argument drew on his insistence that the Constitution had to take social reality into account. As a justice, Marshall found "state action" in the activities of operators of modern shopping malls, which he described as the

modern equivalents of Main Street, in *Amalgamated Food Employees v. Logan Valley Plaza* (1968). The opinion made social reality the basis for what Marshall regarded as sensible constitutional law. Again, however, the Court's new majority first undermined the decision in *Lloyd Corp. v. Tanner* (1972) and then formally overruled it in *Hudgens v. National Labor Relations Board* (1976).

Marshall's pragmatism led him to develop his most enduring contribution to constitutional law, the "sliding scale" approach to equal protection cases. The Court's majority purported to follow a rigid scheme in which the crucial step involved classifying a challenged statute as implicating either a fundamental right or a suspect class; if the statute involved either, it was almost always held unconstitutional. According to Marshall, that approach failed to appreciate the way rights and classifications could interact: the practical and normative impact of a statute that involved a not-quite-suspect class and a not-quite-fundamental right, Marshall argued, could be as problematic as the statutes the Court's majority regularly held unconstitutional. Rather than using a rigid classifying approach to equal protection cases, Marshall said, the Court should balance the severity of the statute's impact on groups and on rights against the goals government was trying to promote. Although the Court purported to reject Marshall's approach, some of its decisions—for example, *City of Cleburne v. Cleburne Living Center* (1985)—are best understood as adopting it. Academic commentators almost uniformly believe that Marshall's approach in *Cleburne* is sounder than the majority's.

Marshall's "sliding scale" or balancing approach allowed him to incorporate his sensitivity to the practical impact of law, particularly its impact on the poor, into constitutional law. When the Court upheld a fifty-dollar filing fee for bankruptcy cases in *United States v. Kras* (1973), Marshall objected to Justice Harry Blackmun's casual suggestion that it would be relatively easy for poor people to raise that sum: "No one who has had close contact with poor people can fail to understand how close to the margin of survival many of them are." Suggesting that the Court would not uphold "compulsory visits to all American homes for the purpose of discovering child abuse," Marshall dissented from the decision in *Wyman v. James* (1971), which allowed social workers to make unannounced searches of welfare recipients' residences. In *Harris v. McRae* (1981), he objected to the Court's use of a "relentlessly formalistic catechism" to uphold Congress's denial of funding for abortions to women receiving Medicaid, noting that the denial had "a devastating impact on the lives and health of poor women."

Most of Marshall's career with the NAACP had been devoted to attempts to persuade the Court that race discrimination pervaded society, but could be eliminated through law. He continued that effort as a justice, even as the Court's conservative majority became skeptical about both parts of the argument. Dissenting from the majority's refusal to find unconstitutional a city's decision to close a street through an exclusively white neighborhood to keep out "undesirable traffic," Marshall applied what he called "a dab of common sense" to explain why the decision was discriminatory in *City of Memphis v. Greene* (1981). His experience as a member of a racial minority allowed him to explain in *Castaneda v. Partida* (1977) why race discrimination could persist even in communities with a majority of racial minorities. "Successful" members of minority groups, he wrote, "frequently respond to discrimination . . . by attempting to disassociate themselves from the group," but the point of the antidiscrimination doctrine was to avoid "broad overgeneralizations concerning minority groups."

Marshall's concern for individual rights might have posed a problem for him in affirmative action cases. Adhering to a Great Society notion of affirmative action, Marshall consistently voted to uphold affirmative action programs. His opinions, however, endorsed affirmative action as a remedy for prior discrimination, not as a means of allocating social benefits to minority groups. He was more willing than the Court's majority to find that past discrimination continued to affect present conditions, but always connected affirmative action to discrimination.

Marshall's affirmative action opinions also contain a second theme. After the Court held segregation

unconstitutional, it gave state governments time to work out programs to eliminate it. The Court, in short, deferred to the judgment of local authorities as they tried to respond to what they, and the Court, understood to be a difficult social problem. Marshall saw affirmative action in much the same way: it too was a difficult social problem, and local authorities should be given substantial leeway in developing their responses. Marshall therefore never suggested that the Constitution required governments to adopt affirmative action programs, but he always voted to uphold the programs they did adopt.

Great Society liberalism generally had a strong nationalizing impulse, and despite Marshall's willingness to defer to legislatures in the affirmative action area, his experience made him skeptical of "states' rights" claims made to insulate local governments from national regulation. He was an active supporter of the Warren Court's innovations in constitutional criminal procedure and wrote one of the Court's important decisions applying Bill of Rights guarantees—protection against double jeopardy—to the states in *Benton v. Maryland* (1969). These decisions imposed national standards of police conduct and overrode claims that states should be free to develop their own approaches to law enforcement. In Marshall's eyes, local police practices were too often directed at racial and economic minorities. Marshall dissented in *Florida v. Bostick* (1991), in which the Court upheld the practice of "working the buses," meaning that police officers board buses and "request" permission to search passengers' belongings. For Marshall, the practice did not give the people who used buses any real choices. Moreover, they tended to be people who could not afford trains or airplanes, and Marshall's opinion suggested that, as in the bankruptcy filing fee case, the majority failed to understand what it was like to be poor. The theme he sounded in criminal procedure cases was the demand for a realistic appreciation of what one observer said Marshall's questions to lawyers asked for—"what really happens between the cops and a criminal suspect in a squad car, or the way social workers really treat welfare clients."

Marshall drew on his life's experience when he became, along with Justice William Brennan, one of two justices who argued that capital punishment violated the Constitution's ban on cruel and unusual punishments. As a practicing lawyer, he had represented defendants executed for capital crimes, and he always believed that, because "death is so lasting," even a small risk of error was intolerable.

His analysis of the constitutional question had two elements. First, as he argued in *Furman v. Georgia* (1972), capital punishment no longer served any acceptable social purpose. Retribution, which he called "vengeance," was simply an appeal to "our baser selves." No convincing case for the death penalty's deterrent effect had been made. And, in an approach that revealed the importance Marshall gave to experience, he argued that the death penalty was "morally unacceptable to the people of the United States," despite widespread legislative approval of capital punishment. The reason for that judgment, Marshall explained, was that "people who were fully informed as to the purposes of the penalty and its liabilities" would find it "shocking, unjust, and unacceptable." An important component of this judgment, to Marshall, was the fact that the death penalty "falls upon the poor, the ignorant, and the underprivileged members of society," who find it difficult to get their voices heard in legislatures. For Marshall, the courts—staffed by people experienced in law, as he was—were the places that such people could get a fair hearing.

The second element in Marshall's approach to the death penalty also relied on his experience, this time as a lawyer who knew how the law was actually administered. After the Court allowed states to reinstitute capital punishment, Marshall's dissents regularly pointed out how unfairness infected capital trials. His most astringent comments were reserved for the competency of counsel. When, in *Strickland v. Washington* (1984), the Court adopted a strict test for determining when counsel's performance was unconstitutionally ineffective, requiring that the lawyer's performance had to be both well below what professional norms required and prejudicial to the defen-

dant, Marshall commented, "How under the sun can a deficient performance not register in the defense?"

Marshall was a Great Society liberal in another way. Although he was not sympathetic to claims by local governments, he did try to insulate some intermediate institutions—those standing between individuals and governments—from government regulation. This idea was a part of the Great Society's institutional settlement in which such intermediate groups, through bargaining in a pluralist political system, could shape public policy and thereby become committed to the existing order.

Labor unions were among the most important of these intermediate institutions, at least in the ideological universe of Great Society liberals. Marshall tended to support the power of centralized labor unions against challenges from individual members. He wrote the Court's opinion in *Emporium Capwell Co. v. Western Addition Community Organization* (1975), finding no violation of federal labor law when an employer fired four African American workers who had created a minority caucus outside their union and tried to bargain with the employer. Marshall's opinion argued that separate bargaining would "divide [workers] along racial or other lines," thereby reducing the bargaining power of all workers.

Marshall's concern for preserving the authority of intermediate groups was also expressed when he became the Court's liberal specialist in Native American law and sought to insulate Native American populations from state regulation. His opinions developed standards for interpreting federal law that, while conceding the power of the national government to do whatever it wanted with respect to those populations, routinely found that Congress had not tried to exercise its power in a way that severely undermined them. Again, a case lying at the intersection of concern for intermediate groups and attention to minority interests shows Marshall's concerns more clearly. *Santa Clara Pueblo v. Martinez* (1978) involved a rule defining membership in the pueblo, which had significant consequences for a person's entitlement to tribal and federal benefits, in a way that discriminated against women. Marshall's opinion for the Court refused to find that Congress, in enacting the 1968 Indian Civil Rights Act, meant to allow lawsuits in federal court to challenge such rules. The challenger's only remedy, Marshall said, was within the Native American system of courts.

That Marshall implemented the liberal vision associated with Johnson's Great Society does not mean, therefore, that he adhered to positions taken by those the media labeled "leading liberals." He supported Johnson in the Vietnam War, for example, and in *Schlesinger v. Holtzman* (1973), he issued an extraordinary order dissolving a stay Justice William O. Douglas had issued against continued bombing of Cambodia. Marshall was also more skeptical than some liberals about some versions of affirmative action as they developed in the 1980s, and he never found black nationalists such as Malcolm X attractive.

Great Society liberalism, however, might be acceptable as a political vision, but not as a constitutional one. The most basic criticism of Marshall's approach to constitutional law emerged in the dialogue between him and the Court's majority over the choice between the majority's rigid approach to equal protection law and Marshall's "sliding scale" approach. Proponents of the majority's approach argued that some rigidity was essential to confine judicial discretion; otherwise, judges who "balanced" competing interests would both duplicate what occurred in the political branches and enact their own policy preferences into constitutional law. Similarly, critics were concerned about Marshall's insistence on a "realistic" appreciation of what happened outside the Court; some degree of abstraction, they argued, was necessary because each judge's assessment of what "really" happened would be shaped by his or her personal perspective, an inadequate basis on which to rest constitutional law.

Precisely because Marshall did not find it important to work out in general terms an overall approach to constitutional law, he never addressed these concerns directly. Indeed, his deep commitment to his realistic and pragmatic approach showed that he rejected these arguments. Here too he relied on his experience. For Marshall, judges whose careers had been confined to the academy or to elite law practice might not truly understand how constitutional law operated in police stations or welfare offices, but Marshall was not this kind of judge. His career had carried him from a struggling private practice, to trial and appellate work in ordinary cases and in celebrated constitutional appeals, to the solicitor general's office where he had an overview of the federal government's litigation, and to the Supreme Court. And unlike any of his colleagues, he had lived the life of an African American in a racially divided society. His range of experience gave him confidence in his assessment of reality. His confidence was bolstered by the trajectory of his career, not just by the range of his experience. As Marshall saw it, he had succeeded as a lawyer and judge because, at each stage in his career, his judgment had been vindicated—for example, when the Supreme Court held segregation unconstitutional and when Johnson selected him to serve on it.

Marshall's approach to constitutional adjudication fit comfortably with his sense of himself and his career. An open and friendly man who found it difficult to have harsh words with or say harsh words about people he worked with, Marshall tried to treat his colleagues on the Court as if they ought to have the same degree of confidence in their ability to exercise sound judgment, to develop sensible solutions to the practical problems that law presented, as he had in his own ability. Within the Court, even those who consistently voted to reject Marshall's positions said that they respected the experience he brought to the conference table. Still, Marshall may not have appreciated that his colleagues, no matter how much they respected him for his achievements, might not be willing to base the edifice of constitutional law solely on the sound good sense of whoever happened to be the justices of the Supreme Court.

For all the misgivings critics might have about directing judges with less experience and generosity of spirit simply to exercise good judgment in making constitutional law, Marshall's career as a practicing lawyer and as a justice does exemplify how far good judgment can take a person.

—*Mark V. Tushnet*

BIBLIOGRAPHY

Thurgood Marshall's papers are in the Library of Congress and were opened shortly after his death. Mark Tushnet, *Making Civil Rights Law: Thurgood Marshall and the Supreme Court, 1936–1961* (1993), deals with Marshall's career with the NAACP; and Tushnet, *Making Constitutional Law: Thurgood Marshall and the Supreme Court, 1961–1991* (1997), deals with his career as a judge and as solicitor general. Tushnet also edited *Thurgood Marshall: His Speeches, Writings, Arguments, Opinions, and Reminiscences* (2001). Juan Williams, *Thurgood Marshall: American Revolutionary* (1998); and Howard Ball, *A Defiant Life* (1999), look at his life as a whole. Roger Goldman with David Gallen, *Thurgood Marshall: Justice for All* (1992), is a compilation of tributes to Marshall, with an essay on and excerpts from his opinions.

For examinations of his opinions on specific subjects, see Victor Kramer, "The Road to City of Berkeley: The Antitrust Positions of Justice Thurgood Marshall," *Antitrust Bulletin* 32 (1987): 335; Mark Tushnet, "Change and Continuity in the Concept of Civil Rights: Thurgood Marshall and Affirmative Action," *Social Philosophy & Policy* 8 (1991): 150; Jonathan Weinberg, "Thurgood Marshall and the Administrative State," *Wayne Law Review* 38 (1991): 115; and Tracey Maclin, "Justice Thurgood Marshall: Taking the Fourth Amendment Seriously," *Cornell Law Review* 77 (1992): 723.

NOTEWORTHY OPINIONS

Amalgamated Food Employees v. Logan Valley Plaza, 391 U.S. 308 (1968)

Stanley v. Georgia, 394 U.S. 557 (1969)

Benton v. Maryland, 395 U.S. 784 (1969)

Wyman v. James, 400 U.S. 309 (1971) (Dissent)

Furman v. Georgia, 408 U.S. 238 (1972)

United States v. Kras, 409 U.S. 434 (1973) (Dissent)

Emporium Capwell Co. v. Western Addition Community Organization, 420 U.S. 50 (1975)

Santa Clara Pueblo v. Martinez, 436 U.S. 49 (1978)

Strickland v. Washington, 466 U.S. 668 (1984) (Dissent)

Florida v. Bostick, 501 U.S. 429 (1991) (Dissent)

STANLEY MATTHEWS

Birth: July 21, 1824, Cincinnati, Ohio.

Education: Kenyon College, graduated with honors in 1840.

Official Positions: Assistant prosecuting attorney, Hamilton County, 1845; clerk, Ohio House of Representatives, 1848–1849; judge, Hamilton County Court of Common Pleas, 1851–1853; member, Ohio Senate, 1855–1858; U.S. attorney for southern Ohio, 1858–1861; judge, Superior Court of Cincinnati, 1863–1865; counsel, Hayes-Tilden electoral commission, 1877, U.S. senator, 1877–1879.

Supreme Court Service: Nominated associate justice by President Rutherford B. Hayes, January 26, 1881, to replace Noah Swayne, who had retired; no action by Senate; nominated by President James A. Garfield, March 18, 1881; confirmed by the Senate, May 12, 1881, by a 24–23 vote; took judicial oath May 17, 1881; served until March 22, 1889; replaced by David J. Brewer, nominated by President Benjamin Harrison.

Death: March 22, 1889, Washington, D.C.

Even the most conventional public figures of the past century occasionally led lives of color and seeming paradox. An antislavery Democrat in Cincinnati in the 1840s, Stanley Matthews was by 1858 a federal district attorney responsible for the prosecution of violators of the Fugitive Slave Act; a Union veteran of the Civil War, he was an author of the Compromise of 1877, which handed the presidency to his friend, Rutherford B. Hayes, in return for the removal of federal troops from the South; a devout Presbyterian, Matthews opposed religious instruction in public schools; an eminent Republican railroad attorney, as a senator from Ohio he favored inflation of the currency and opposed the Chinese Exclusion Act.

It should be no surprise that one biographer found in Matthews "an unusual combination of liberal and conservative premises," yet neither Matthews nor his generally admiring contemporaries found inconsistencies in his views or rulings. Progressive writers have charged Matthews and the other bearded and remote legal figures of the age with manipulating judicial formalism—rigid reliance on precedent and deduction from vague natural law assumptions—in order to prevent reform. Recent scholarship has argued that judges of the era across the political spectrum sought to preserve the existing social order against transformation by the forces of industrialism and political upheaval.

Matthews stands as preeminently a representative of classical legal consciousness, committed to controlling change through the careful definition of spheres of private rights and public powers. He sketched no alternatives to the course of industrial policy or civil rights, voting with the majority to extend Fourteenth Amendment protection to corporations in *Santa*

Clara County v. Southern Pacific Railroad (1886), to expand their protection from state regulation in *Wabash, St. Louis and Pacific Railroad Co. v. Illinois* (1886), and to thwart congressional power to oppose racial discrimination in the *Civil Rights Cases* (1883).

To modern eyes, Matthews's most important opinions were rendered in *Hurtado v. California* (1884), in which he found the grand jury indictment clause of the Fifth Amendment unavailable to defendants in state criminal proceedings, and in *Yick Wo v. Hopkins* (1886), in which he held unconstitutional a San Francisco ordinance requiring permits to operate laundries in wooden buildings, because permits were denied to all Chinese applicants, but not to others. Matthews ruled that a facially neutral law "administered by public authority with an evil eye and an unequal hand" violated equal protection.

It is emblematic of both Matthews's time and his place in it that his most celebrated opinion policed the boundaries of state power and read the common law to defeat the threat of economic turmoil. In *Poindexter v. Greenhow* (1885), Matthews ruled that states lacked authority to repudiate their debts under the contract clause, and that although the Eleventh Amendment protected the states themselves from suits challenging repudiation, state officials could be sued for trying to enforce such illegal acts.

Precisely this kind of legalistic distinction without a "realistic" difference, seemingly designed to protect the wealthy, persuaded progressive writers of Matthews's "conservatism," even while cases such as *Yick Wo* sounded "liberal." On the whole, however, it is Matthews's overall similarity to other and more progressive judges of his era, rather than his particular differences from them, that merits attention.

—*Robert Stanley*

Stanley Matthews

BIBLIOGRAPHY

The primary biographical source is still Louis Filler, "Stanley Matthews," in Friedman and Israel, *Justices,* vol. 2, 1351. The best general introduction to interpretive scholarship is Elizabeth Mensch, "The History of Mainstream Legal Thought," in David Kairys, ed., *The Politics of Law: A Progressive Critique* (2d ed., 1990). The most fully developed interpretive departure is Charles W. McCurdy, "Justice Field and the Jurisprudence of Government-Business Relations: Some Parameters of Laissez-Faire Constitutionalism, 1863–1897," in Lawrence M. Friedman and Harry N. Scheiber, eds., *American Law and the Constitutional Order* (1978).

NOTEWORTHY OPINIONS

Hurtado v. California, 110 U.S. 516 (1884)

Poindexter v. Greenhow, 114 U.S. 270 (1885)

Yick Wo v. Hopkins, 118 U.S. 356 (1886)

JOSEPH McKENNA

Birth: August 10, 1843, Philadelphia, Pennsylvania.

Education: Benicia Collegiate Institute, graduated in 1864; admitted to the bar in 1865.

Official Positions: District attorney, Solano County, California, 1866–1870; member, California Assembly, 1875–1876; U.S. representative, 1885–1892; judge, U.S. Court of Appeals for the Ninth Circuit, 1892–1897; U.S. attorney general, 1897.

Supreme Court Service: Nominated associate justice by President William McKinley, December 16, 1897, to replace Stephen J. Field, who had retired; confirmed by the Senate, January 21, 1898, by a voice vote; took judicial oath January 26, 1898; retired January 5, 1925; replaced by Harlan F. Stone, nominated by President Calvin Coolidge.

Death: November 21, 1926, Washington, D.C.

Joseph McKenna's Irish-Catholic immigrant parents moved their family from Philadelphia to Benicia, California, when he was twelve. Just three years later, his father died, and Joseph became the head of the family. While helping to support his family, McKenna attended parochial schools and, later, Benicia Collegiate Institute where he studied law. He passed the bar in 1865. But law held less of an allure for McKenna than politics, and, except for a brief period, he never practiced as a private lawyer. Instead, he became a staunch Republican politician.

From 1865 on, McKenna was either a candidate or an elected officeholder until he was appointed to the bench. He served in the House of Representatives from 1885 to 1892, where he displayed the knack of gaining the support of powerful figures; Leland Stanford and William McKinley both found him to be a useful ally and played a part in his political rise. Stanford suggested his name to President Benjamin Harrison for a vacancy on the Ninth Circuit Court of

Appeals in 1892. After McKinley became president, he named McKenna his attorney general and then, within the year, nominated him to the Supreme Court to fill the seat of Justice Stephen Field, who had finally been persuaded to retire after thirty-four years on the Court.

McKenna also would serve a long time, and his twenty-six-year tenure broke into three periods: an early period of learning his new role; a middle period when he was an important (although somewhat erratic) member of the Court; and a late period of failing abilities limiting his effectiveness. His career, especially his middle period, essentially showed him as a politician dressed in judicial robes.

At the time of McKenna's appointment, some observers complained that he was unsuited for the Court. The grumbling was politically motivated but contained a germ of truth. Nothing in his background, including his legal positions, prepared him for the Court. He was a poor lawyer and knew it, so he spent some time in the Columbia University law library to ready himself. But the cramming did little good, and a Court librarian later commented that as a new justice, McKenna was overwhelmed by the duties. McKenna's tentativeness as a justice was reflected in his writing: his early opinions—for example, *Magoun v. Illinois Trust and Savings Bank* (1898)—were weighed down with loads of precedent and irrelevant case law. Nor did he have a clear philosophy to guide him, and despite his long tenure, he never developed one.

Throughout his career and across many different issues, McKenna proved inconsistent in his decisions and reasoning. Typical of his lack of consistency were his votes and opinions in cases concerning state and federal regulation of working conditions. He was with the majority in *Lochner v. New York* (1905) when the Court struck down a New York health regulation that limited the working hours of bakers. But in the 1908 case *Muller v. Oregon,* he joined the unanimous majority in upholding the state's hours regulation for women industrial work-

Joseph McKenna

ers. In *Wilson v. New* (1917), McKenna was in the majority upholding the federal Adamson Act, which set an eight-hour day for railroad workers. A belief in dual federalism cannot explain this shift, because in *Bunting v. Oregon* (1917), McKenna's majority opinion sustained a state law mandating a ten-hour day that was in effect a minimum wage law. Then, in *Adkins v. Children's Hospital* (1923), he joined the majority in striking down federal minimum wage leg-

islation for women in the District of Columbia, which brought him back to where he had started in *Lochner.*

Although McKenna never developed a consistent judicial stand, he did adapt his politician's skills to his new role. In the middle of his career, especially in the second decade of the twentieth century, his writing style returned to a more natural form, and he expressed his opinions in strong, clear phrases. His opinion in *United States v. United States Steel Corporation* (1920) is a brief and direct statement of the application of the rule of reason—that not all restraints of trade were unreasonable and therefore illegal—to the Sherman Antitrust Act. Moreover, his sensitive political antenna had earlier picked up the strong support for federal action under the commerce power. His opinions for the Court in *Hipolite Egg Company v. United States* (1911), upholding the constitutionality of the Pure Food and Drug Act, and *Hoke v. United States* (1913), upholding the Mann Act, reflected both his political awareness and maturing judicial powers. These two opinions are lucid and forceful statements of the federal government's power to use the commerce power to promote the general welfare. Moreover, they upheld popular laws passed in the face of supposed national emergencies.

The same pattern emerged in McKenna's votes and opinions in the free speech cases that grew out of the federal and state legislative attempts to limit expression during World War I. In a number of cases, beginning with *Schenck v. United States* (1919) and ending with *Gilbert v. Minnesota* (1920), McKenna joined with the majority in upholding these popular laws. In *Gilbert,* McKenna asserted that although the freedom of speech was inherent, it was not absolute. In a time of emergency, like a war, broad restrictions and limitations could be placed on speech despite the First Amendment.

The wartime speech cases were his swan song. In the 1920s he stayed on the Court even though he no longer had the ability to understand the issues. Chief Justice William Howard Taft, after McKenna's mental decline, dismissed him as a "Cubist" on the bench and several times had to ask McKenna to rework his opinions so they would reflect the accordance of the majority. His colleagues suggested he retire, but he refused. In 1924, as an expedient, the brethren—under the chief justice's direction—agreed not to make any decisions in cases in which his vote would be the deciding one. Whether it was due to the pres-sure of colleagues, his realization of his decline, or his wife's death, McKenna retired in 1925.

—*Richard F. Hamm*

BIBLIOGRAPHY

The standard biography is Matthew McDevitt, *Joseph McKenna: Associate Justice of the United States* (1946), which is sympathetic but honest in its treatment. For McKenna's decline, see Alpheus T. Mason, *William Howard Taft: Chief Justice* (1964).

NOTEWORTHY OPINIONS

Hipolite Egg Company v. United States, 220 U.S. 45 (1911)

Hoke v. United States, 227 U.S. 308 (1913)

Bunting v. Oregon, 243 U.S. 426 (1917)

United States v. United States Steel Corporation, 251 U.S. 417 (1920)

Gilbert v. Minnesota, 254 U.S. 325 (1920)

JOHN McKINLEY

Birth: May 1, 1780, Culpeper County, Virginia.

Education: Read law on his own; admitted to the bar in 1800.

Official Positions: Alabama state representative, sessions of 1820, 1831, and 1836; U.S. senator, 1826–1831 and 1837; U.S. representative, 1833–1835.

Supreme Court Service: Recess appointment as associate justice by President Martin Van Buren, April 22, 1837, for a newly created Supreme Court seat; nominated September 19, 1837; confirmed by the Senate, September 25, 1837, by a voice vote; took judicial oath January 9, 1838; served until July 19, 1852; replaced by John A. Campbell, nominated by President Franklin Pierce.

Death: July 19, 1852, Louisville, Kentucky.

John McKinley migrated with his parents from Virginia to Kentucky, where he spent his boyhood and young adulthood. In 1800 he was admitted to the bar and practiced law in Frankfort and Louisville until 1818, when he moved to Huntsville, Alabama. Soon after Alabama achieved statehood in 1819, McKinley stood for election as one of the state's new circuit judges. Although he was defeated in that election, within a year he was elected a member of the state legislature. In 1822 he was an unsuccessful candidate for the U.S. Senate, but in 1826 he was elected to fill the vacancy in Alabama's other Senate seat caused by the incumbent's death. Failing reelection in 1830, the next year McKinley returned to the state legislature, where his status as a former senator gave him a prominent role. Within a year he was again representing Alabama in Washington, this time as a member of the House of Representatives. At the end of the term, McKinley declined to run again but returned to the Alabama legislature in 1836, and was once again chosen to serve as senator. Before his term began,

however, President Martin Van Buren appointed him to the Supreme Court.

McKinley had begun his fifteen years' service in the state and national legislatures as a supporter of Henry Clay, a former Kentucky acquaintance, but by 1826 acknowledged himself an Andrew Jackson man. In another era or another state, McKinley's conversion might have courted suspicion, but political consistency was not the rule in Alabama politics in the 1820s, and McKinley's attitudes toward public lands, internal improvements, and the Bank of the United States all bore the Democratic stamp.

As a justice, McKinley continued to adhere to Democratic principles, but his difficult circuit duties and poor health caused frequent absences from sessions of the Court. McKinley's circuit was the Ninth, which included parts of Alabama, Mississippi, and Louisiana, and all of Arkansas. For the first years of his service, he had a route of 10,000 miles and a docket of nearly two-thirds of the cases pending in all of the federal circuit courts. His circuit opinions were never published, and his limited attendance in Washington resulted in few Supreme Court opinions—eighteen majority, two concurring, and two dissenting.

McKinley missed the initial cases of the judicial "revolution" of 1837 when the era of the Marshall Court ended and that of Chief Justice Roger B. Taney began. Yet McKinley, as a junior member of the Court, soon informed the more senior members of his Democratic position on states' rights with regard to corporations. On circuit in 1838, he decided *Bank of Augusta v. Earle,* a case involving the right of a bank chartered out-of-state to operate in Alabama. The defendant, refusing to pay a bill of exchange, pointed to the Alabama constitutional provision prohibiting "foreign" banks from doing business in the state. McKinley decided in favor of Earle, citing the state constitution's prohibition and arguing that comity, the respect for the laws of another jurisdiction, did not apply. The bank appealed, and the case was paired with two similar cases.

The Supreme Court heard the cases in January 1839, amid the financial difficulties brought about by the Panic of 1837. The concerns in *Bank of Augusta v. Earle* also resonated with the political issues raised in 1832 over the recharter of the Bank of the United States. McKinley's circuit court opinion had excited commercial and banking interests throughout the country. Joseph Story wrote to Charles Sumner that McKinley's decision had "frightened half the lawyers and all of the corporations of the country out of their proprieties." Arrayed before the justices were the cream of the Supreme Court bar to argue on behalf of the banks. In addition, James Kent, former chancellor of New York and a leading legal commentator, contended in an article in the *Law Reporter* that McKinley's decision had no support in English or international commercial law.

Chief Justice Taney, writing for the majority, reversed McKinley's lower court decision and found for the bank, holding that comity granted "foreign" corporations the right to operate in other states unless specifically forbidden to do so. Because the Alabama constitutional provision had not forbidden out-of-state corporations negotiating bills of exchange, the bank was entitled to collect against Earle. McKinley was the lone dissenter.

Three other cases of the 1840s show McKinley's adherence to state powers. In *Groves v. Slaughter* (1841), McKinley, in a dissenting opinion reminiscent of *Bank of Augusta,* said that the Mississippi constitutional prohibition of slaves from other states was self-executing. The majority, however, found that the provision required specific legislation to be effective.

As a dissenter in *Lane v. Vick* (1845), McKinley found the majority's decision overruling the Mississippi Supreme Court's construction of a will gave too much power to federal courts. According to McKinley, in the absence of a need for national uniformity, state court interpretations should be followed.

In *Pollard v. Hagan* (1845), McKinley expounded for the Court the compact theory and its relationship to the disputed ownership of submerged land. Here,

John McKinley

he found that the national government only held federal lands as the agent of the states and could not exceed its commission as agent. Because territories were to be admitted to the Union on an equal footing with the original states, the national government could not continue to maintain sovereignty over submerged lands.

In the *Passenger Cases* (1849), McKinley surprisingly found that the statutes of New York and Massachusetts regulating the arrival of alien passengers were unconstitutional. Whether his opinion was predicated on the un-Democratic concept that Congress had exclusive power over interstate commerce, or on the belief that the statutes conflicted with existing federal immigration laws, is unclear. Even the justices themselves failed to reach consensus, as eight wrote separate opinions.

With the exception of the *Passenger Cases*, McKinley's opinions during his fourteen years on the Court reflect his political stance before his arrival on the bench. He propounded the typical Democratic attitudes of his region, which for most of his tenure were shared by Jacksonians in the White House and Congress. But McKinley's intermittent attendance in Washington left others to influence contemporary legal attitudes. His death occasioned little notice.

—*Elizabeth Brand Monroe*

BIBLIOGRAPHY

McKinley's judicial career has excited little research. The most extensive treatment is Frank Otto Gatell's essay in Friedman and Israel, *Justices*, vol. 1, 769. Carl Swisher addresses McKinley's limited contributions in the context of the Taney Court in *The Taney Period, 1836–1864*, volume 5 of the *Holmes Devise History of the Supreme Court* (1974).

NOTEWORTHY OPINIONS

Groves v. Slaughter, 40 U.S. 15 (1841)

Lane v. Vick, 44 U.S. 3 (1845)

Pollard v. Hagan, 44 U.S. 212 (1845)

Passenger Cases, 48 U.S. 283 (1849)

JOHN McLEAN

Birth: March 11, 1785, Morris County, New Jersey.

Education: Attended local school; privately tutored; read law with John S. Gano and Arthur St. Clair Jr.

Official Positions: Examiner, U.S. Land Office, 1811–1812; U.S. representative, 1813–1816, chairman, Committee on Accounts; judge, Ohio Supreme Court, 1816–1822; commissioner, General Land Office, 1822–1823; U.S. postmaster general, 1823–1829.

Supreme Court Service: Nominated associate justice by President Andrew Jackson, March 6, 1829, to replace Robert Trimble, who had died; confirmed by the Senate, March 7, 1829, by a voice vote; took judicial oath January 11, 1830; served until April 3, 1861; replaced by Noah H. Swayne, nominated by President Abraham Lincoln.

Death: April 3, 1861, Cincinnati, Ohio.

Despite his long tenure, hard work, and national prominence during his lifetime, John McLean was never an important justice, and his impact on law was minimal. And although he wrote 247 opinions of the Court, McLean was neither a scholar nor a theorist, and, with a few exceptions, his majority opinions are virtually forgotten. Those few that are remembered, such as *Wheaton v. Peters* (1834), *Briscoe v. Bank of Kentucky* (1837), and *Pennsylvania v. Wheeling Bridge Co.* (1852), are recalled more for the parties involved, the high political issue at stake, or the important economic issue in question than for the importance of McLean's opinion. Furthermore, despite his dissent in *Dred Scott v. Sandford* (1857) and fifty-nine other separate opinions, concurrences, and dissents, he did not leave a record of prophetic dissents or concurrences. Few justices have worked so hard, for so long, with such little impact.

McLean was born in New Jersey, the son of Scotch-Irish immigrants, but was raised on the fron-

tier in the Ohio valley. He had little formal education but studied law with Arthur St. Clair, the son of the former governor of the Northwest Territory. McLean began practicing law in Lebanon, Ohio, in 1807. He was a member of Congress from 1813 to 1816 and a vigorous supporter of President James Madison's war policy. McLean then became a judge on the Ohio Supreme Court, serving from 1816 to 1822. While on this court, McLean ruled in *Ohio v. Carneal* (1817) that masters could not employ slaves in Ohio, but that they could probably travel through the state with their slaves. President James Monroe appointed McLean as a commissioner of the General Land Office in 1822 and as postmaster general in 1823. McLean's brilliant administrative skills and adept political maneuvering enabled him to retain his position under President John Quincy Adams. Always politically agile, during the election of 1828, McLean refused to use his office and immense patronage powers to help Adams. Although he had not worked for Andrew Jackson, the president-elect rewarded McLean for his silent "non-partisan" support. Two days after his inauguration, Jackson nominated McLean to the Supreme Court, and one day later the Senate confirmed him.

Although he was Jackson's first Court appointee, McLean was not a true Jacksonian Democrat. He opposed Jackson's wholesale removals of officeholders in order to distribute patronage, and he supported protective tariffs and internal improvements. While on the bench, McLean persistently dabbled in politics, and he seemed available to any party. He was, at various times, discussed as a presidential nominee by the Anti-Masonic Party, Free Soil Democrats, the Whigs, and in 1856 and 1860, the Republicans. McLean never saw any impropriety in continuing to be a politician while on the Court. In this sense he was no different from many others on and off the bench at this time.

Despite his early affiliation with the Democrats, McLean's jurisprudence lay more in the Federalist-nationalist tradition of John Marshall and Joseph Story than the emerging Jacksonian jurisprudence of Chief Justice Roger B. Taney. Three elements characterized that jurisprudence: an inclination to stimulate and allow new economic enterprises through the release of creative energies, a deference to state power and state sovereignty, and strong proslavery tendencies. McLean distanced himself from Taney in the first two of these areas, and whenever possible—within his notion of proper jurisprudence—he opposed slavery.

John McLean

In *Charles River Bridge v. Warren Bridge* (1837), Taney held that the franchise to build a new bridge did not abrogate the rights of the stockholders of the older bridge company. McLean's dissent explicitly rejected older English doctrine that protected virtually all existing enterprises from competition, and to this extent he accepted some of the Jacksonian ideals of enhanced competition. But he was unwilling to apply those ideals to this case. On the substantive issues, McLean agreed with Story's Federalist jurisprudence. The creation of the new Warren Bridge violated the contract clause of the Constitution by abrogating the Charles River Bridge Company's charter, which was clearly a contract between the state and the proprietors.

Unlike everyone else on the Court, however, McLean did not believe the Court had jurisdiction in the case. His view of the jurisdictional issue also reflected some of the Jacksonian deference to the states. McLean did not want the Supreme Court to micromanage the emerging dynamic economy.

Unlike Taney and other Jacksonians, in a number of commercial cases, McLean was ready to intervene in state affairs to strengthen national power. In the *License Cases* (1847), he joined the majority to uphold the challenged regulations of the sale of liquor as legitimately within the scope of a state's police power. But McLean also reaffirmed that in the area of interstate commerce the power of Congress was "supreme."

McLean applied the implications of his *License Case* opinion to the *Passenger Cases* (1849). As the senior judge in the majority, McLean wrote the lead opinion in this case in which every judge wrote something, and the Court split, 5–4. McLean wrote to strike down state laws requiring that ship captains pay a fee for every immigrant they landed. He construed this fee to be a tax and found that any tax on imports, whether "upon tonnage, merchandise, or passengers" was a "regulation of commerce, and cannot be laid by a State, except under the sanction of Congress." Taney, favoring state power over national power, led four hard-core states' rights dissents.

In *Cooley v. Board of Wardens of the Port of Philadelphia* (1851), the Jacksonian majority on the Court upheld Philadelphia's regulation of its port, which included a requirement that most ships hire local pilots. McLean did not dispute the utility of this legislation but believed it violated Congress's power to regulate commerce. He expressed concern that a majority of the Court had now subscribed to the notion that "a State may regulate foreign commerce, or commerce among the States." McLean feared a "race of legislation between Congress and the States" that would produce chaos in interstate and international commerce.

Consistent with his neo-Federalist view of national power, McLean wrote the majority opinion in *Pennsylvania v. Wheeling Bridge Co.* (1852), ordering that the Wheeling Bridge be raised so it would not interfere with commerce on the Ohio River. Here Taney and the extreme states' rights advocate, Peter V. Daniel, dissented.

McLean's jurisprudence on slavery is complex. He was personally and politically opposed to slavery, and the antislavery lawyer and politician Salmon P. Chase, a future chief justice, was a good friend and political ally. In 1848 Chase told Charles Sumner that McLean was "the most reliable man, on the slavery questions, now prominent in either party." As legal scholar Robert M. Cover noted, from a Free Soil perspective, McLean was "sound on slavery, politically and personally, if not judicially."

McLean heard a number of fugitive slave cases in his role as circuit justice, and he also reviewed fugitive slave and other slavery-related cases on the Supreme Court. His early jurisprudence was clearly antislavery. In 1841 he joined Story's opinion ordering the release of the *Amistad* captives. This result was a direct slap at the proslavery policies of Jackson's successor, Martin Van Buren. *Groves v. Slaughter* (1841) pitted McLean's Federalist commercial jurisprudence against his antislavery views. The case turned on a Mississippi constitutional provision that prohibited the importation of slaves. McLean noted that the "necessity of a uniform commercial regulation, more than any other consideration, led to the adoption of the federal Constitution," and he denied that the states had concurrent power to regulate commerce in the absence of congressional legislation. This stance put him squarely in the Federalist-nationalist Whig tradition and clearly in opposition to the Taney-Jacksonian views of commerce and would seem to lead to the conclusion that Mississippi could not prohibit the importation of slaves as articles of commerce. But saying that would have undermined his antislavery views and the laws of most of the North. Instead, in a concurring opinion, McLean declared that slavery was purely a creature of local law, and using his home state as an example, he asserted that although Ohio could not prohibit the importation "of the cotton of the south or the manufactured articles of the north . . . no one doubts its power to prohibit slavery."

Prigg v. Pennsylvania (1842) also forced McLean to choose between a nationalist jurisprudence and an antislavery jurisprudence. Here he broke ranks with both Story and Taney. Story's majority opinion struck down all state personal liberty laws on the grounds that the federal fugitive slave law of 1793 preempted all state regulation of the return of fugitive slaves. The proslavery, states' rights Jacksonians, let by Taney and Daniel, agreed with the result in this case, but they wanted to allow the states to be proactive in aiding the return of fugitive slaves. McLean, on the other hand, abandoned his normal support for a strong national government. In the only dissent in the case, he argued, consistent with his opinion in *Groves,* that slavery was local and therefore the states could constitutionally intervene in the return of fugitive slaves to protect free blacks.

Although he dissented in *Prigg*, McLean accepted the will of the majority of his brethren. In a number of subsequent circuit court cases, he usually (but not always) ruled in favor of masters and against those who wanted to help fugitive slaves. In *Norris v. Newton* (1850), he charged an Indiana jury to find for the slave-holding plaintiff, reminding the jurors that "the law, and not conscience, constitutes the rule of action." McLean's circuit court opinions in *Jones v. Van Zandt* (1843), *Norris,* and *Miller v. McQuerry* (1853) continued to disappoint his friends, as did his failure to dissent from Justice Levi Woodbury's opinion when *Jones v. Van Zandt* reached the Supreme Court in 1847.

McLean was obligated by his notion of *stare decisis* to support fugitive slave renditions, but he remained opposed to slavery. In *Dred Scott v. Sandford* (1857), McLean wrote a thirty-five-page critique of Taney's opinion. As he had throughout his career, McLean argued that slavery was "emphatically a state institution." The only exception to this, he asserted, involved the Constitution's fugitive slave clause. Also consistent with his lifelong views, McLean supported the power of the national government to regulate affairs in the territories. McLean's dissent was admirable but is often forgotten because of Justice Benjamin Curtis's sixty-eight-page attack on Taney's opinion. At the time, however, McLean's dissent led to renewed interest in him as a presidential candidate. In 1860 Thaddeus Stevens, among others, backed him for the presidential nomination, but the presidency was no longer a realistic possibility for the seventy-five-year-old jurist. Moreover, his home state of Ohio backed a more viable candidate, Salmon Chase. McLean remained on the Court during the secession crisis and died a month after Abraham Lincoln's inauguration.

—*Paul Finkelman*

BIBLIOGRAPHY

Francis P. Weisenburger, *The Life of John McLean: A Politician on the United States Supreme Court* (1937), the only scholarly biography of McLean, is dated and overemphasizes his political interests and career. An excellent short summary of McLean's life, followed by some of his opinions, is Frank Otto Gatell, "John McLean," in Friedman and Israel, *Justices,* vol. 1, 535.

Robert M. Cover, *Justice Accused: Antislavery and the Judicial Process* (1975), discusses the dilemmas of judges, such as McLean, who opposed slavery but felt obligated to enforce the constitutional provisions protecting the institution. Paul Finkelman, *An Imperfect Union: Slavery, Federalism, and Comity* (1981), places much of McLean's jurisprudence on slavery in the context of federalism. See also Michael A. Kahn, "The Appointment of John McLean to the Supreme Court: Practical Politics in the Jacksonian Era," *Journal of Supreme Court History* (1993): 59; and Paul Brickner, "The Passenger Cases (1849): Justice John McLean's 'Cherished Policy' as the First of Three Phases of American Immigration Law," *Southwestern Journal of Law and Trade* (2003/2004): 63.

Harold M. Hyman and William M. Wiecek, *Equal Justice Under Law* (1982), is the best book available on the constitutional history of antebellum America. Carl B. Swisher, *The Taney Period, 1836–1864* (1974), volume 5 of the *Holmes Devise History of the Supreme Court,* is a classic history of the Taney Court.

NOTEWORTHY OPINIONS

Charles River Bridge v. Warren Bridge, 36 U.S. 420 (1837) (Dissent)

Groves v. Slaughter, 40 U.S. 449 (1841) (Concurrence)

Prigg v. Pennsylvania, 41 U.S. 539 (1842) (Dissent)

Passenger Cases, 48 U.S. 283 (1849)

Pennsylvania v. Wheeling Bridge Co., 54 U.S. 518 (1852)

Dred Scott v. Sandford, 60 U.S. 393 (1857) (Dissent)

JAMES CLARK McREYNOLDS

Birth: February 3, 1862, Elkton, Kentucky.

Education: Vanderbilt University, B.S., 1882; University of Virginia, LL.B., 1884.

Official Positions: Assistant U.S. attorney, 1903–1907; U.S. attorney general, 1913–1914.

Supreme Court Service: Nominated associate justice by President Woodrow Wilson, August 19, 1914, to replace Horace H. Lurton, who had died; confirmed by the Senate, August 29, 1914, by a 44–6 vote; took judicial oath October 12, 1914; retired January 31, 1941; replaced by James F. Byrnes, nominated by President Franklin D. Roosevelt.

Death: August 24, 1946, in Washington, D.C.

In the annals of U.S. Supreme Court history, James Clark McReynolds is as well known for his disagreeable nature as for his conservative, even reactionary, opposition to the New Deal programs of President Franklin Roosevelt. Like Woodrow Wilson, the president who appointed him, McReynolds was a southerner and a gold Democrat. In fact, both men received their legal training at the University of Virginia in the early 1880s. Unlike Wilson, however, McReynolds took to the law and made it his career, a career that culminated in federal service as attorney general and as an associate justice for twenty-six of the most dynamic years in the history of the nation.

McReynolds, of Scotch-Irish descent, grew up on the family plantation in Elkton, Kentucky, near the Tennessee border; his father had served as a surgeon in the Confederate army. McReynolds excelled at Vanderbilt University, where he was valedictorian, and then studied with the legendary John Minor and others at the University of Virginia. On graduation, McReynolds served briefly as a secretary to Sen. Howell F. Jackson, D-Tenn., then moved on to a successful law practice in Nashville. While there, McReynolds taught commercial law at Vanderbilt's law school, serving with then-circuit court judge Horace Lurton, the man whose seat on the Supreme Court McReynolds would later occupy.

From 1903 to 1907, McReynolds served in Theodore Roosevelt's administration as assistant attorney general, specializing in antitrust law. He divided the next several years between private practice in New York City and service as a special federal prosecutor in the American Tobacco Company antitrust case. In 1913 President Wilson, after vehement opposition arose to his idea of appointing Louis Brandeis as attorney general, named McReynolds. Although McReynolds appears to have filled that job competently, his term was marked by an embarrassing incident concerning the postponement of a Mann Act prosecution of the son of a Democratic politician, and by friction with other members of the administration. When Justice Lurton died in July 1914, Wilson chose McReynolds, another southern Democrat, despite some concern over his irascible temperament.

In the years before the New Deal, McReynolds disagreed with the progressive-leaning majority, siding instead with those who championed private property interests. He dissented in cases such as *Block v. Hirsh* (1921), which supported rent control, and *Village of Euclid v. Ambler Realty Company* (1926), which upheld zoning.

During these pre–New Deal years, McReynolds also revealed, despite his record as a strong trust-buster, an impatience with government regulation of business. For example, in *Federal Trade Commission v. Gratz* (1921), McReynolds spoke for the majority that overturned the FTC's complaint against a cotton bagging manufacturer: "Nothing is alleged which would justify the conclusion that the public suffered injury or that competitors had reasonable ground for complaint. If real competition is to continue, the right of the individual to exercise reasonable discretion in respect of his own business methods must be preserved."

McReynolds's record in the realm of civil liberties is somewhat enigmatic. In *Berger v. United States* (1921) and *Stromberg v. California* (1931), for example, he disagreed with the majority's tolerance. In *Berger,* a case involving the prosecution of German- and Austrian-born Socialist dissenters under the Espionage Act, the Supreme Court was faced with the allegation that Judge Kenesaw Mountain Landis was "prejudiced and biased against [some] defendants because of their nativity." The majority of the Court concluded that Judge Landis had "no lawful right or

James Clark McReynolds

power to preside as judge on the trial of the defendants upon the indictment." In dissent, McReynolds—who throughout his judicial tenure demonstrated his own prejudice against Jews, African Americans, and female professionals—was more understanding of Landis: "Intense dislike of a class does not render the judge incapable of administering complete justice to one of its members. . . . And while 'an overspeaking judge is no well-tuned cymbal,' neither is an amorphous dummy unspotted by human emotions a becoming receptacle for judicial power." These words came from a man who was openly racist and anti-Semitic and who declined to appear at functions attended by Justices Nathan Cardozo and Louis Brandeis.

In *Stromberg,* McReynolds dissented when the majority overturned the conviction of a Communist woman charged with flying a red flag at a summer camp for children. The Court found the state statute under which she was prosecuted to be "repugnant to the guarantee of liberty contained in the Fourteenth Amendment." Yet, only eight years before, McReynolds had articulated an expansive view of the nature of liberty and in the process led the Court as it overturned a state law that forbade teaching foreign languages to children who had not passed the eighth grade. The case was *Meyer v. Nebraska* (1923), and McReynolds's rhetoric is a memorable challenge to the state's police power. McReynolds wrote concerning liberty guaranteed by the Fourteenth Amendment:

Without doubt it denotes not merely freedom from bodily restraint but also the right of the individual to contract, to engage in any of the common occupations of life, to acquire useful knowledge, to marry, establish a home and bring up children, to worship God according to the dictates of his own conscience, and generally to enjoy those privileges long recognized as essential to the orderly pursuit of happiness by free men.

Two years later, in *Pierce v. Society of Sisters* (1925), McReynolds wrote for the Court as it ruled unconstitutional a compulsory public school attendance statute. He cited *Meyer* and concluded that the act "unreasonably interferes with the liberty of parents and guardians to direct the upbringing and education of children under their control." On the foundation of *Meyer* and *Pierce* were cases like *Griswold v. Connecticut* (1965) and *Roe v. Wade* (1973) built by later, more liberal, justices.

It was during Franklin Roosevelt's presidency that McReynolds, aligned with Justices Pierce Butler, Willis Van Devanter, and George Sutherland—they were known as the "Four Horsemen"—earned his reputation as the Supreme Court's most reactionary member. In case after case, McReynolds registered his disagreement as the majority supported radical efforts by state and federal governments to rescue the nation from the Great Depression. One observer of the Court noted that as the liberal justices prevailed, McReynolds replaced Brandeis as the "great dissenter."

In *Home Building & Loan Assn. v. Blaisdell* (1934), he joined Sutherland, who, dissenting from the Court's approval of Minnesota's mortgage moratorium law, warned of "future gradual but ever-advancing encroachments upon the sanctity of private and public contracts." In *Nebbia v. New York* (1934), McReynolds fumed as the majority upheld the state's milk price-control scheme:

If now liberty or property may be struck down because of difficult circumstances, we must expect that hereafter every right must yield to the voice of an impatient majority when stirred by distressful exigency. . . . Certain fundamentals have been set beyond experimentation; the Constitution has released them from control by the state.

He asked skeptically whether "the milk business [is] so affected with a public interest that the Legislature may prescribe prices for sales by stores?" He searched in vain for a "reasonable relation" between means and ends. He ended with the observation that "the highest duty intrusted to the courts" was "zealously to uphold" the "dominance of the Constitution."

In 1935, in a series of decisions known as the *Gold Clause Cases,* McReynolds offered his most memorable dissent, but he did so orally from the bench, not in the pages of the *United States Reports.* In the early days of the New Deal, after the nation left the gold standard and the gold content of the dollar was reduced, Congress, by joint resolution, had canceled the gold clause included in private contracts and government bonds as insurance against inflation. The printed version of McReynolds's objections to the majority's failure to negate this "confiscation of property rights and repudiation of national obligations" can be found following the holding in *Norman v. Baltimore & Ohio Railroad* (1935) and by reference in two subsequent cases. His tone was caustic: "Just men regard repudiation and spoilation of citizens by their sovereign with abhorrence," two policies he regarded as unauthorized for a "federal government . . . of delegated and limited powers," and as contrary to the intent of the framers. His prediction for the future was dire indeed: "Loss of reputation for honorable dealing will bring us unending humiliation; the impending legal and moral chaos is appalling."

The accounts vary concerning what McReynolds said from the bench when he read aloud his dissent. According to one report, he warned that "shame and humiliation are upon us" and "anarchy and despotism are at the door." Others quote the angry justice as declaring, "This is Nero at his worst. The Constitution is gone!" The exact phrases are not as important, however, as the spirit in which they were offered. To the conservative members of the Supreme Court, these were dire times for the constitutional Republic.

As the New Deal progressed, so did McReynolds's pattern of protest at the excesses of government. His was the lone dissenting voice in *Ashwander v. Tennessee Valley Authority* (1936). The majority approved the plan for the sale of surplus power from the Wilson Dam, but McReynolds characterized the TVA's program as disingenuous and illegal:

> If under the thin mask of disposing of property the United States can enter the business of generating, transmitting, and selling power ... with the definite design to accomplish ends wholly beyond the sphere marked out for them by the Constitution, an easy way has been found for breaking down the limitations heretofore supposed to guarantee protection against aggression.

One year later, in *West Coast Hotel Co. v. Parrish* (1937), a case in which the Court upheld a Washington State minimum wage law for women, the victim of the Court's excessive deference, according to McReynolds, was the "liberty of contract" advanced by *Adkins v. Children's Hospital* (1923). In *West Coast Hotel,* McReynolds joined Sutherland, who had written the Court's opinion in *Adkins,* in reiterating the power of the Supreme Court to declare such statutes repugnant to the Constitution. The power base of the Court had shifted to the left, marginalizing McReynolds and the other conservatives as the New Deal built up steam.

McReynolds's dissent in *National Labor Relations Board v. Jones & Laughlin Steel Corporation* (1937) best represents the rapidity of the Court's shift. In an opinion for the Four Horsemen objecting to the sweep of the National Labor Relations Act, McReynolds noted that the majority's holding "departs from well established principles followed in" two cases in which the Court had checked the New Deal program: *Schechter Poultry Corp. v. United States* (1935) and *Carter v. Carter Coal Co.* (1936). As if to add special emphasis to the Court's about-face, McReynolds, in a departure from proper citation form, included the months and

years of those two, now-rejected precedents. McReynolds reacted against a "view of congressional power [that] would extend it into almost every field of human industry." "Any effect on interstate commerce by the discharge of employees shown here would be indirect and remote in the highest degree," wrote McReynolds, rejecting the majority's expansive "stream of commerce" rationale.

McReynolds remained on the Court for another four years and died five years after retiring. During World War II, the cantankerous ex-justice adopted thirty-three British war children, corresponding with them and providing financial support. In his will, the lifelong bachelor left significant bequests to various charities. Even in death, McReynolds remained an enigma.

—Michael Allan Wolf

BIBLIOGRAPHY

The McReynolds papers are collected at the University of Virginia Library in Charlottesville. Justice McReynolds's Supreme Court memorial, 334 U.S. v (1948), contains some helpful details concerning McReynolds's life, but little in the way of criticism or analysis of his judicial philosophy. Alexander Bickel provides some perceptive insights in *The Judiciary and Responsible Government: 1910–1921,* Part One (1984), volume 9 of the *Holmes Devise History.* Bickel relied in part on Barbara Barlin Schimmel's dissertation, "The Judicial Philosophy of Mr. Justice McReynolds" (Yale, 1964). See also two articles by Barry Cushman, "Clerking for Scrooge," *University of Chicago Law Review* 70 (2003): 721; and "The Secret Lives of the Four Horsemen," *Virginia Law Review* 83 (1997): 559.

NOTEWORTHY OPINIONS

Federal Trade Commission v. Gratz, 253 U.S. 421 (1921)

Meyer v. Nebraska, 262 U.S. 390 (1923)

Pierce v. Society of Sisters, 268 U.S. 510 (1925)

Nebbia v. New York, 291 U.S. 502 (1934) (Dissent)

Norman v. Baltimore & Ohio Railroad, 294 U.S. 240 (1935) (Dissent)

Ashwander v. Tennessee Valley Authority, 297 U.S. 288 (1936) (Dissent)

National Labor Relations Board v. Jones & Laughlin Steel Corporation, 301 U.S. 1 (1937) (Dissent)

SAMUEL FREEMAN MILLER

Birth: April 5, 1816, Richmond, Kentucky.

Education: Transylvania University, M.D., 1838; studied law privately; admitted to the bar in 1847.

Official Positions: Justice of the peace and member of the Knox County, Kentucky, court, an administrative body, in the 1840s.

Supreme Court Service: Nominated associate justice by President Abraham Lincoln, July 16, 1862, to replace Justice Peter V. Daniel, who had died; confirmed by the Senate, July 16, 1862, by a voice vote; took judicial oath July 21, 1862; served until October 13, 1890; replaced by Henry B. Brown, nominated by President Benjamin Harrison.

Death: October 13, 1890, Washington, D.C.

Justice Samuel Freeman Miller arrived on the Supreme Court bench in 1862 with the strong endorsement of Republicans from his adopted state of Iowa, but without any formal legal training. Moreover, he had no previous experience in public office higher than justice of the peace and member of the county court in his native Kentucky. Despite this seeming lack of proper credentials, Miller's strength of character, strong pragmatic bent, aggressiveness, analytical ability, and enormous faith in his own intellect proved him worthy of the nation's highest court. Chief Justice Salmon P. Chase labeled this Lincoln appointee the Supreme Court's "dominant personality." During his twenty-eight years of service, Miller wrote 616 opinions, more than any previous Supreme Court justice. He left his mark on American constitutional law, most notably in his construction of the Fourteenth Amendment.

Law was the second career choice for Miller. He attended medical school at Transylvania University at Lexington, graduated in 1838, then served as a country doctor for about ten years. His avid participation in the Barbourville Debating Society convinced him that law and politics suited him better than medicine. Miller read law and passed the bar exam in 1847. Certain that his abolitionist tendencies would be more acceptable elsewhere, he left Kentucky in 1850 and moved his family to Keokuk, Iowa, where he joined a prominent law firm and quickly became one of the area's leading attorneys. A former Whig, Miller joined the Republican Party at its inception and worked hard for its success, although he failed in his bid for state senator in 1856 and was passed over for party nomination for governor in 1861. A strong Lincoln man, Miller was unknown outside Iowa. Reorganization of the federal judicial circuits after the Civil War broke out, however, fostered his chances for appointment to the Supreme Court. Fellow Iowans lobbied intensely for Miller's appointment, and their efforts paid off when Lincoln chose him as the first Supreme Court justice appointed from west of the Mississippi to represent the newly created Ninth Circuit. Lincoln's faith in Miller was rewarded by his vigorous support for the president's war efforts.

Miller's conduct on the bench during the Civil War was strongly nationalistic. For example, he voted with the 5–4 majority in the *Prize Cases* (1863) to uphold the constitutionality of the president's blockade of southern ports. This opinion, perhaps the most significant of the cases approving Lincoln's wartime policies, enabled the government to treat the war as a conventional war for purposes of foreign policy but continue to maintain that it was an insurrection for purposes at home. Miller went along with the Court's refusal to interfere with the wartime suspension of *habeas corpus* and military trials for civilians. When the fighting was over and the danger to the Union was past, however, he joined a belated censure of the wartime military trials in *Ex parte Milligan* (1866). The majority decided that neither the president nor Congress had authority to authorize military trials of civilians when the civilian courts were open; Miller's concurring opinion stated that Congress did possess such power but had not used it.

Miller's early postwar record demonstrated a similar regard for government authority, a view that was often at odds with his judicial brethren. When 5–4 majorities found in *Ex parte Garland* (1867) and *Cummings v. Missouri* (1867) that federal and state required test oaths violated the Constitution as *ex post facto* laws and bills of attainder, Miller dissented. He insisted that the oath was not a punishment but simply another requirement for the privilege of practicing law or serving as a minister. It was absurd to Miller that in one case the Court found the Constitution "to confer no power on Congress to prevent traitors practicing in her courts, while in the other it is held to confer power on this court to nullify a provision of the Constitution of the State of Missouri, relating to a qualification required of ministers of religion." In Miller's estimation, the Court had clearly overstepped the bounds of judicial review.

Miller registered a biting dissent against the majority's tender regard for the property rights of creditors in *Hepburn v. Griswold* (1870), another 5–4 decision. The issue was the constitutionality of paper money or "greenbacks" as legal tender. Invoking the "spirit" of the contract clause, which, in fact, restrains the states rather than the federal government, Chief Justice Chase found greenbacks unconstitutional for repayment of debts contracted prior to the law. The Legal Tender Act also violated the Fifth Amendment, according to Chase, as a deprivation of property without due process of law. Miller, on the other hand, believed that the Constitution granted Congress ample power to define and regulate the money supply. He stressed wartime necessity and opposed "substituting a court of justice for the National Legislature."

Within fifteen months, Miller's dissenting opinion became constitutional law when *Knox v. Lee* (1871) overturned *Hepburn*. President Ulysses S.

Samuel Freeman Miller

Grant appointed William Strong and Joseph Bradley to the Court on the same day that the first legal tender decision was announced. This new majority favorable to administration policy reopened the issue, with Miller, as he put it in a letter to his brother-in-law, serving "as leader in marshalling my forces, and keeping up their courage against a domineering Chief, and a party in court who have been accustomed to carry everything their own way." Miller's aggressiveness and determination paid off in the second legal tender decision written by Strong.

Miller's reaction to congressional Reconstruction policies contrasted sharply to his nationalistic support for the war effort. For its initial interpretation of the rights of citizens under the Fourteenth Amendment, the Supreme Court chose, ironically, a case that involved white butchers rather than former slaves. That the Fourteenth Amendment had made some changes in the rights of citizenship seemed clear, but its precise meaning was surrounded with uncertainty. What changes, if any, had the amendment made in federal-state relationships? What were the privileges and immunities associated with national citizenship? Did the amendment nationalize the Bill of Rights? The backlog of civil rights cases in the South demanded answers to these difficult questions, but the Supreme Court refused to address the issues in Enforcement Act cases and chose the *Slaughterhouse Cases* (1873) instead. Why so strange a choice? The justices obviously recognized that precedent made in these cases would hold enormous implications for the civil and political rights of the freedmen. It seems safe to argue, therefore, that the Court deliberately chose a case that would depoliticize the explosive legal questions involved. The butchers' case enabled the Court to decide some of the controversial issues regarding Reconstruction without seeming to decide them at all. If the *Slaughterhouse Cases* were about white butchers, they nevertheless postponed for a century the establishment of a broad nationalization of rights for black Americans.

The carpetbag government of Louisiana had established a monopoly of butchers in New Orleans. Although the law would ordinarily fall under the police powers of the state, the other butchers sued on the grounds that it violated the Thirteenth and Fourteenth Amendments. John A. Campbell, a former Supreme Court justice, who had resigned to follow his state into the Confederacy, argued that the state monopoly was a form of servitude outlawed by the Thirteenth Amendment. More important, it violated the "privileges and immunities" guaranteed to citizens by the Fourteenth—the right to follow the vocation of one's choice being one of those privileges.

Miller spoke for a closely split majority. Recognizing that "no questions so far reaching and pervading in their consequences . . . have been before this court during the official life of any of its present members," he quickly rejected the Thirteenth Amendment argument and turned to the Fourteenth. Miller seemed genuinely surprised to think that the Reconstruction amendments, written to benefit blacks, could be construed to uphold the rights of white citizens. But Miller's interpretation of national citizenship gave the former slaves little reason to cheer. This previously nationalistic judge rendered an opinion grounded in traditional notions of dual federalism. National citizenship, for Miller, was separate and distinct from state citizenship. The basic rights of citizenship remained where they had always been, under the protection of the states. Miller listed a number of privileges and immunities he considered a part of national citizenship, most of which were of little use to the freed slaves. The United States could protect its citizens on the high seas and in foreign countries, Miller decided, but not in the states where they lived. He emphatically denied that the Fourteenth Amendment was intended "to transfer the security and protection of all the civil rights . . . from the States to the Federal government." It was impossible, he thought, that Congress meant to make such a drastic change in the basic nature of the federal system.

Miller's tortured construction aroused bitter dissent among four of his colleagues. Justice Stephen J. Field maintained, for example, that the fundamental rights of citizenship were no longer dependent on citizenship in a state. If the amendment meant no more than the majority said, it had "most unnecessarily excited Congress and the people on its passage." The dissenting opinions recognized what Miller denied, that rights were no longer to be "separate and exclusive" but "complementary and concentric," allowing the federal government to protect the rights of its citizens when the states failed to do so.

Miller may have been willing to sacrifice the rights of the freedmen, as historian William Gillette has suggested, to preserve the states' right to regulate business and thereby postponing judicial support for big business. Letters to his brother-in-law indicate, however, that Miller was no proponent of equality for blacks. Although he was unwilling to leave the freedmen to the tender mercies of the former Confederates, he feared that Republican Reconstruction policy risked "the eventual destruction of some of the best principles of our existing constitution." Miller's opinion in *Slaughterhouse* went a long way to preserve the "existing constitution." If Miller's opinion put off federal protection for vested property rights, the dissenting opinions of Bradley and Field embraced substantive due process and the laissez-faire principles that pointed the Court's way to the future.

United States v. Cruikshank (1876) reiterated the principles of *Slaughterhouse* in terms of rights for black citizens. Miller voted with the majority in a case involving a massacre of some 100 blacks in Louisiana. Following Miller's logic in *Slaughterhouse,* Chief Justice Morrison R. Waite stated that people must "look to the states" to protect their individual rights. The Fourteenth Amendment had added "nothing to the rights of one citizen as against another." The Supreme Court had allowed the narrow interpretation of national citizenship in *Slaughterhouse* to circumscribe the meaning of the amendment for the people it was intended to endow with all the benefits of citizenship.

In the *Civil Rights Cases* (1883), the Court once again employed a constricted view of the Fourteenth Amendment. At issue was the constitutionality of the Civil Rights Act of 1875, which attempted to secure equality of social rights, including equal access to privately owned public facilities. Because the complaint involved no state action, no discriminatory state law, the national government had no right to intervene.

"Individual invasion of individual rights," Bradley insisted for the majority, "is not the subject of the amendment." The law was clearly unconstitutional, according to this interpretation. Consistent with his interpretation of the Fourteenth Amendment in *Slaughterhouse,* Miller voted with the majority in these cases, as well as in *Cruikshank.*

By today's standards, the conduct of Miller and the Court in the area of civil rights is disappointing. It should be noted, however, that very few Americans were committed to genuine equality for black people during the Reconstruction era. The Republican majority in Congress provided amendments and laws sufficient to establish a broad nationalization of civil and political rights but failed to follow up with the necessary funds to finance the increased caseload in the lower federal courts and the military force necessary to subdue the recalcitrant South. After the election of 1874 returned a Democratic majority to Congress, signaling that the American people had grown weary of the never-ending racial problems in the southern states, federal Reconstruction efforts were in full retreat. Whether the Court began that retreat with the *Slaughterhouse Cases* or merely followed the lead of the legislative branch, it is perhaps too much to expect that the third branch of government with no powers of enforcement could establish the full citizenship of the 4 million freed people.

If Miller's estimation of the Fourteenth Amendment was disappointing, he displayed a stronger regard for the voting rights of blacks. He went along with the Court in *United States v. Reese* (1876), deciding that the Fifteenth Amendment did not grant freedmen the right to vote but rather the right not to be discriminated against in the franchise on the grounds of race. The case struck down two sections of the Enforcement Act of 1870 but nevertheless suggested that the federal government had power to prosecute both state officials and private individuals who interfered with the suffrage on grounds of race.

Ex parte Yarbrough (1884) marked a resounding victory for the voting rights of black Americans. The case involved a conspiracy to deprive a black citizen of the franchise on account of his race. Speaking for the majority, Miller construed the Fifteenth Amendment broadly, and then he went on to hold that neither the case nor the Enforcement Act depended on the Fifteenth Amendment, which forbids only those denials of the franchise that were because of race. Congressional authority to protect voters in national elections derived from Article I. "If this government is anything more than a mere aggregation of delegated agents of other States and governments, each of which is superior to the general government," Miller ruled, "it must have the power to protect the elections on which its existence depends from violence and corruption." Congress had broad powers to protect blacks in federal elections against both private persons and state officials, and because state and local elections were generally held at the same time, the power extended to state elections as well. It was a decision worthy of Miller's Civil War nationalism.

As one of the Republican justices chosen to serve on the electoral commission to settle the disputed presidential election of 1876, Miller had a part in bringing about the official end of Reconstruction. Like all the other participants, he voted his party preference, giving Rutherford B. Hayes a majority of one in the commission and securing the presidency for the Republican Party.

Outside the arena of civil rights, Miller withstood the efforts of big business and his judicial brethren to write laissez-faire economic theory into constitutional law through the Fourteenth Amendment. He had turned a deaf ear to the substantive due process arguments in *Slaughterhouse*, preserving the states' right to regulate. Otherwise, he noted, the Court would become a "perpetual censor" of state legislation. The Supreme Court held firm in the Granger cases. Miller voted with the majority to allow state regulation of railroads and grain elevators, establishing a public interest doctrine in *Munn v. Illinois* (1877). But Chief Justice Waite conceded even in *Munn* that "under some circumstances" a state regulatory statute might be so arbitrary as to be unconstitutional. Such a concession was all that business needed to keep pounding the Court with a substantive reading of the due process clause. Miller complained in *Davidson v. New*

Orleans (1877) that the Court's docket was "crowded with cases in which we are asked to hold that state courts and state legislatures have deprived their own citizens of life, liberty, or property without due process of law." This "strange misconception of the scope of this provision" of the Fourteenth Amendment soon overtook the justices, and Miller fought a losing battle. If his initial construction had postponed the protection of vested interests through the Fourteenth Amendment, the Court had by 1886 made corporations "persons" entitled to equal protection under the amendment intended to protect the citizenship rights of black Americans. And shortly before Miller's death in 1890, the Court expressly adopted substantive due process in *Chicago, Milwaukee & St. Paul Railway Co. v. Minnesota*, with Miller concurring.

Miller made a similar stand against judicial protection of vested interest in a long line of dissenting opinions in state and municipal bond repudiation cases beginning with *Gelpcke v. Dubuque* (1863). However valid the grounds for repudiation seemed to state courts, the nation's highest court generally held that a contract, once made, could not be broken. But Miller was unwilling to make the taxpayers suffer for the wrong judgment of their officials. He thought that state law should be construed by the state courts. It was a "painful matter," Miller complained in a letter to his brother-in-law, that these cases compelled him "to take part in a farce whose result is invariably the same, namely to give more to those who have already, and to take away from those who have little, the little that they have." Miller spoke for the majority for a change when *Loan Association v. Topeka* (1875) invalidated a Kansas law that authorized spending tax money for private purposes.

While the Supreme Court was becoming more deeply entrenched in its determination to protect property rights, the public was becoming aware that regulation of big business, particularly railroads, was necessary at some level of government. Yet the attempts of the various states to regulate intrastate commerce could be seriously detrimental to the smooth flow of interstate commerce. When the constitutionality of an Illinois statute outlawing long haul–short haul rate differentials came before the Court in *Wabash, St Louis, & Pacific Railway v. Illinois* (1886), Miller seized the opportunity to sound a clear call for national regulation. Speaking for the majority in one of his most important decisions, Miller struck down the state law as a violation of the commerce clause. Refusing to speak to the "justice or propriety" of the Illinois regulation, Miller maintained that "regulation can only appropriately exist by general rules and principles, which demand that it should be done by Congress of the United States under the commerce clause." Miller's exhortation led directly to the Interstate Commerce Act of 1887. That neither the Congress nor the Supreme Court was willing to clothe the Interstate Commerce Commission with enough authority to regulate effectively was not the fault of Samuel Miller.

During his twenty-eight years on the Court, Justice Miller stood firm for the right of government to govern. He lacked the fear of government action and the overriding respect for private property that entrenched his colleagues in laissez-faire economic policy. Unfortunately, he stood for the right to regulate at too high a cost to black Americans. Miller was bitterly disappointed when Grant passed him over for the center seat in 1874 but no doubt would have appreciated the *Albany Law Journal's* labeling him in 1890 "the real chief in any court in which he might have sat."

—*Lou Falkner Williams*

BIBLIOGRAPHY

Charles Fairman, *Mr. Justice Miller and the Supreme Court* (1939; reprinted 2002), the standard biography of Miller, is a model of careful scholarship, although Fairman's penchant for getting all his information into print often overrides organization and analysis. Fairman also treats Miller extensively in two articles, "Justice Samuel Miller: A Study of a Judicial Statesman," *Political Science Quarterly* 50 (1935): 15; and "Samuel F. Miller, Justice of the Supreme Court," *Vanderbilt Law Review* 10 (1957): 193; as well as the two volumes he wrote for the *Holmes Devise History, Reconstruction and Reunion,* Parts 1 and 2 (1971, 1987), which is the most exhaustive treatment of the Reconstruction Court. For a short biographical sketch, see William Gillette, "Samuel Miller," in Friedman and Israel, *Justices,* vol. 2, 1011, an excellent, succinct analysis of Miller and his contribution to the law.

For comparative studies, see Paul Albert Weidner' s unpublished dissertation, "Justices Field and Miller: A Comparative Study in Judicial Attitudes and Values" (University of Michigan, 1957); and G. Edward White, "Miller, Bradley, Field, and the Reconstructed Constitution," in *The American Judicial Tradition: Profiles of Leading American Judges* (1988 ed.).

NOTEWORTHY OPINIONS

Gelpcke v. Dubuque, 68 U.S. 175 (1863) (Dissent)

Ex parte Garland, 71 U.S. 333 (1867) (Dissent)

Hepburn v. Griswold, 75 U.S. 603 (1870) (Dissent)

Slaughterhouse Cases, 83 U.S. 36 (1873)

Loan Association v. Topeka, 87 U.S. 655 (1875)

Ex parte Yarbrough, 110 U.S. 651 (1884)

Wabash, St. Louis, & Pacific Railroad Co. v. Illinois, 118 U.S. 557 (1886)

SHERMAN MINTON

Birth: October 20, 1890, Georgetown, Indiana.

Education: Indiana University, LL.B., 1915; Yale University, LL.M., 1917.

Official Positions: Public counselor, Public Service Commission, 1933–1934; U.S. senator, 1935–1941; assistant to president, 1941; judge, U.S. Court of Appeals for the Seventh Circuit, 1941–1949.

Supreme Court Service: Nominated associate justice by President Harry S. Truman, September 15, 1949, to replace Wiley B. Rutledge, who had died; confirmed by the Senate, October 4, 1949, by a 48–16 vote; took judicial oath October 12, 1949; retired October 15, 1956; replaced by William J. Brennan Jr., nominated by President Dwight D. Eisenhower.

Death: April 9, 1965 in New Albany, Indiana.

Sherman Minton, the first Supreme Court justice from Indiana, was President Harry Truman's final appointment to the Court. As a member of the conservative "Truman bloc," led by Chief Justice Fred Vinson, Minton supported the broad exercise of executive and legislative power and approved the restriction of civil liberties in the name of national security. More than any other Truman nominee, however, Minton was ideologically committed to the philosophy of judicial restraint, providing a theoretical grounding for the rulings of his more politically inclined colleagues.

Minton's judicial philosophy grew out of his political experiences during the Great Depression. In 1934 he was elected to the U.S. Senate, where he befriended Truman, another freshman senator. Minton vigorously supported Franklin Roosevelt's economic policies, and when the Supreme Court invalidated New Deal legislation, he harshly attacked the tribunal for substituting its own political judgment for that of Congress. He introduced legislation that would have required the vote of seven justices to declare a federal statute unconstitutional, and he championed Roosevelt's "Court-packing" scheme before a skeptical Senate. In 1940, after Minton lost his bid for reelection, Roosevelt invited his supporter to join the White House staff. Six months later, when a vacancy occurred on the U.S. Court of Appeals for the Seventh Circuit, which included Minton's home state, Roosevelt rewarded him with a judicial appointment.

Following Justice Wiley Rutledge's death in 1949, Truman nominated his old friend to the Supreme Court. The nomination followed Truman's pattern of naming political allies to the bench, although in this case the usual criticism was somewhat muted because Minton had more judicial experience than any of Truman's previous nominees. Perhaps because of a growing concern for judicial professionalism, however, Minton was the last member of Congress to be named to the Court. During the confirmation hearings in the

Senate Judiciary Committee, several Republicans questioned Minton's fierce Democratic loyalties, and other members wondered whether he could fairly serve on a tribunal that he had so recently criticized. The committee reported the nomination favorably, and the Senate confirmed him, 48–16, with most of the opposition coming from Republicans.

Guided by his frustration with the judicial activism of economic conservatives during the Great Depression, Minton adopted a philosophy of judicial restraint. The duty of the Court, he believed, was to determine whether the Constitution granted the political branches the power to enact certain policies, not to judge the wisdom of those policies. He adhered strictly to precedent, interpreted statutes and constitutional provisions narrowly, and deferred to the judgment of the other branches. This practice comported with the views of Truman's other appointees—Harold Burton, Tom C. Clark, and Vinson—and with Stanley Reed, who often joined the Truman bloc. These justices, however, used judicial restraint more as a vehicle for political conservatism than as a coherent philosophy of adjudication. Minton was more faithful to the values of Felix Frankfurter, the Court's leading theorist of judicial restraint, although Frankfurter's concern for the independence of the judiciary and his willingness to look beyond the formalistic application of precedent often led him to disagree with Minton.

In addition to professing judicial restraint, Minton also emphasized to his colleagues the impor-

Sherman Minton

tance of acting as a unified deliberative body. He believed that a judicial opinion should reflect the judgment of the Court, not the personal views of its author, and he willingly altered passages in his opinions if another justice threatened to dissent. He disdained concurring opinions, writing only three in his entire career, because they obscured the singular reasoning of the majority. When writing for the majority, Minton ignored countervailing arguments, so that his opinions resembled the advocacy of an appellate attorney more than the jurisprudential musings of a justice like Frankfurter.

Minton's approach to judging was evident in one of his earliest and most controversial opinions, *United States ex rel. Knauff v. Shaughnessy* (1950). Under the authority of a 1941 statute that allowed the executive branch to exclude aliens who posed a security risk, the attorney general had prohibited Ellen Knauff, the German-born wife of an American soldier, from entering the country. Knauff claimed that she had been denied due process because the government had not conducted a hearing. Minton held that the president's inherent power to conduct foreign affairs included the authority to exclude aliens, placing those decisions outside the scope of judicial review. *Knauff* demonstrated Minton's deference to other branches, particularly when national security issues were involved, but it also revealed his cramped view of statutory interpretation. The War Brides Act of 1945 had relaxed the criteria for admitting the alien spouses of American military personnel, but Minton dismissed its relevance because it had not specifically limited the 1941 statute.

Because of his belief that the political branches of government were best equipped to assess national security interests, Minton also upheld the power of Congress and state legislatures to combat subversion by limiting the freedom of expression and association. In *Adler v. Board of Ed. of the City of New York* (1952), a teacher challenged New York's "Feinberg Law," which allowed school boards to fire teachers for disloyalty if they belonged to certain organizations. Praising the law's goal of shielding children from dangerous ideas, Minton upheld the use of group membership as evidence of disloyalty because "one's reputation [is] determined in part by the company he keeps." He denied that the law infringed on teachers' freedom of association because they were free to choose between public employment or membership in a subversive organization.

Decisions such as *Adler* disappointed civil libertarians, especially because Minton had promised when he joined the Court to "work fiercely for the enforcement of the Bill of Rights." Actually, Minton compiled a libertarian record in free expression cases unrelated to national security issues by supporting the right of speakers to espouse unpopular views without government interference. These opinions were the product not only of a genuine concern for First Amendment freedoms but also of a respect for precedents established in the 1930s and 1940s. In *International Brotherhood of Teamsters v. Hanke* (1950), for example, Minton dissented from Frankfurter's majority opinion, which upheld restrictions on labor picketing, because earlier cases had clearly held that picketing was a form of speech protected by the First Amendment.

In criminal procedure cases, however, he allowed the government wide latitude to control criminal behavior. His most important opinion in this area, *United States v. Rabinowitz* (1950), held that the Fourth Amendment's warrant requirement and its prohibition against unreasonable searches were separate provisions, meaning that searches incident to arrest were to be judged by the reasonableness of the search rather than the reasonableness of obtaining a warrant. This ruling overturned a three-year-old precedent that required police officers to obtain search warrants, when practicable, before searching a suspect. Minton also narrowly interpreted the right to counsel, the privilege against self-incrimination, and the availability of federal *habeas corpus* relief for state prisoners. He was especially loath to grant relief when defendants alleged technical errors rather than asserted their innocence.

Minton's deference to legislative judgment did not extend to race relations. He opposed all forms of government-sponsored discrimination, as evidenced by his vigorous support of the school desegregation cases. He considered *Brown v. Board of Education* (1954) to be the most significant case in which he participated. In his majority opinion in *Barrows v. Jackson* (1953), he extended the holding of *Shelley v. Kraemer* (1948), which forbade the judicial enforcement of restrictive covenants, by prohibiting courts from awarding damages to property owners who sued their neighbors for violating restrictive covenants.

Consistent with his judicial philosophy, however, Minton strictly interpreted the Constitution's state action doctrine, which limited the application of the Fourteenth and Fifteenth Amendments to discriminatory practices that were directly authorized by state legislatures or government officials. In *Brotherhood of Railroad Trainmen v. Howard* (1952), for example, Justice Hugo Black held that a white union, bargaining under the authority of the Railway Labor Act, could not infringe on the rights of other workers by persuading a railroad to replace black porters with the union's members. Minton's dissent, joined by Vinson and Reed, countered that the union, as a private association, could conduct negotiations in any manner it pleased. Similarly, in a lone dissent in *Terry v. Adams* (1953), he insisted that the preprimary elections conducted by the private Jaybird Democratic Association, which excluded black members, did not constitute state action, even though the Jaybird primary had governed the selection of local Texas leaders for half a century. Private discrimination, however objectionable, could only be forbidden by the courts if the government directly enforced it.

When his anemia forced Minton reluctantly to retire, he predicted that "there will be more interest in who will succeed me than in my passing." His remarks were prescient, as he left no judicial legacy. He had emerged as a leader of the Truman bloc, forging compromises that fostered the public's image of institutional stability, but his influence waned significantly after Earl Warren became chief justice. Minton's opinions lacked the elegant reasoning that characterizes great jurists, but, more important, as a proponent of judicial restraint, he lacked Frankfurter's ability to transcend the more doctrinaire aspects of the philosophy. Minton's jurisprudence sprang from his experience during the New Deal, when activist judges attempted to preserve a laissez-faire economy in the face of massive societal dislocation. By the time he reached the Court, however, his approach, particularly his reverence for precedent, deprived him of the opportunity to lead a Court that had begun to use activist principles to protect individual rights and liberties from government interference.

—*Eric W. Rise*

BIBLIOGRAPHY

Two book-length biographies of Minton have been published: Linda C. Gurgin and James E. St. Clair, *Sherman Minton: New Deal Senator, Cold War Justice* (1997); and William F. Radcliff, *Sherman Minton: Indiana's Supreme Court Justice* (1996). See also Elizabeth A. Hull's unpublished dissertation, "Sherman Minton and the Cold War Court" (New School for Social Research, 1977).

For an excellent discussion of Minton's career prior to joining the Court, which also examines the origins of his judicial philosophy, see David N. Atkinson, "From New Deal Liberal to Supreme Court Conservative," *Washington University Law Quarterly* (1975): 361. The most comprehensive account of Minton's tenure on the Court, written by one of his law clerks, is Harry L. Wallace, "Mr. Justice Minton—Hoosier Justice on the Supreme Court," *Indiana Law Journal* 34 (1959): 145, 377. While perhaps overly sympathetic to Minton, Wallace ably assesses his contribution to the jurisprudence of the Vinson Court. David Atkinson has published several law review articles examining Minton's views on specific constitutional issues, the most perceptive of which is "Justice Sherman Minton and the Protection of Minority Rights," *Washington and Lee Law Review* 34 (1977): 97.

Minton destroyed most of his papers, but a small collection of documents pertaining to his opinions is housed in the Harry S. Truman Library in Independence, Missouri.

NOTEWORTHY OPINIONS

United States ex rel. Knauff v. Shaughnessy, 338 U.S. 537 (1950)

United States v. Rabinowitz, 339 U.S. 56 (1950)

International Brotherhood of Teamsters v. Hanke, 339 U.S. 470 (1950) (Dissent)

Adler v. Board of Ed. of the City of New York, 342 U.S. 485 (1952)

Brotherhood of Railroad Trainmen v. Howard, 343 U.S. 768 (1952) (Dissent)

Terry v. Adams, 345 U.S. 461 (1953) (Dissent)

Barrows v. Jackson, 346 U.S. 249 (1953)

WILLIAM MOODY

Birth: December 23, 1853, Newbury, Massachusetts.

Education: Harvard College, A.B., cum laude, 1876; Harvard Law School, 1876–1877; read law with Richard Henry Dana.

Official Positions: City solicitor, Haverhill, 1888–1890; district attorney, Eastern District of Massachusetts, 1890–1895; U.S. representative, 1895–1902; secretary of the navy, 1902–1904; U.S. attorney general, 1904–1906.

Supreme Court Service: Nominated associate justice by President Theodore Roosevelt, December 3, 1906, to replace Henry B. Brown, who had retired; confirmed by the Senate, December 12, 1906, by a voice vote; took judicial oath December 17, 1906; retired November 20, 1910; replaced by Joseph R. Lamar, nominated by President William Howard Taft.

Death: July 2, 1917, Haverhill, Massachusetts.

Born and raised in Massachusetts's Merrimac valley, Moody excelled at physical, not mental, activity until his third year at Harvard. Although he never lost his love of sports—especially baseball—and the outdoor life, Moody became a man of some learning and an aggressive, able lawyer. In 1878 he began practicing corporate law in Haverhill. He soon entered local politics and became a typical Yankee Republican reformer. He was a protégé of Henry Cabot Lodge and, through Lodge, met Theodore Roosevelt. With their backing, he rose quickly, serving as a state district attorney (he was one of the prosecutors of Lizzie Borden), U.S. representative, secretary of the navy, and attorney general. In the latter office, Moody vigorously carried out Roosevelt's policies of punishing "bad" trusts under the Sherman Antitrust Act and rebating railroads under the Elkins Act of 1903. Roosevelt selected him for the Supreme Court in the hopes of making that body more receptive to the progressives' use of government power.

A key to Moody's jurisprudence is found in his dissent in the *First Employers' Liability Case* (1908). In a 5–4 decision, the Court struck down the 1906 Employers' Liability Act, which made all common carriers engaged in interstate commerce liable for injuries sustained at work by their employees. The majority—committed to the theory of dual sovereignty of state and nation—said the law was too broad and as such an interference with the states' right to control intrastate commerce through their police powers. Speaking of the Constitution's commerce clause, Moody wrote, "Its unchanging provisions are adaptable to the infinite variety of the changing conditions of our National life." Therefore, because "the forces of steam and electricity" had "so wonderfully aided" the development of interstate commerce, it was natural to Moody that the federal commerce power should also modernize to keep pace.

But, like many progressives, Moody did not intend to allow the central government to ride outside of all constitutional limits and obliterate the states. He supported the states' police power to regulate the economy and daily life. In *Tilt v. Kelsey* (1907), for example, Moody wrote the opinion that declared the states had the sovereign authority to determine rules for the succession of property upon death. Further, in *Twining v. New Jersey* (1908), Moody wrote the Court's opinion stating that the Fourteenth Amendment did not extend the Bill of Rights to the states. Moody assumed that state action would be enough to protect liberties; if people thought they did not, they should seek redress at the ballot box and not in the federal courts.

In his brief career on the bench, Moody showed himself a true Roosevelt Progressive. Illness, however,

William Moody

kept Moody from fulfilling the president's ambition for him. Almost as soon as he took his seat, Moody became seriously ill from infectious arthritis, and he participated in only two judicial terms. After 1909, his failing health kept him from attending the sessions. Following Congress's conferring upon him special retirement benefits, he resigned from the Court.

—*Richard F. Hamm*

BIBLIOGRAPHY

The Moody papers, dealing mostly with his pre-Court career, are housed at the Library of Congress. James F. Watts Jr., "William Moody," in Friedman and Israel, *Justices*, vol. 3, 1801, is a short but sensitive treatment of Moody's life and Court career.

NOTEWORTHY OPINIONS

Tilt v. Kelsey, 207 U.S. 43 (1907)

First Employers' Liability Case, 207 U.S. 463 (1908) (Dissent)

Twining v. New Jersey, 211 U.S. 78 (1908)

ALFRED MOORE

Birth: May 21, 1755, New Hanover County, North Carolina.

Education: Educated in Boston; studied law under his father; received law license, 1775.

Official Positions: Member, North Carolina legislature, 1782, 1792; attorney general, North Carolina, 1782–1791; trustee, University of North Carolina, 1789–1807; judge, North Carolina Superior Court, 1799.

Supreme Court Service: Nominated associate justice by President John Adams, December 4, 1799, to replace James Iredell, who had died, confirmed by the Senate, December 10, 1799, by a voice vote; took judicial oath April 21, 1800; resigned January 26, 1804; replaced by William Johnson, nominated by President Thomas Jefferson.

Death: October 15, 1810, Bladen County, North Carolina.

Alfred Moore is among the least-known justices ever to sit on the Supreme Court, and his lack of notoriety is well deserved. Although he played a small part in one of the most important decisions of the Court, *Marbury v. Madison* (1803), he himself wrote only one opinion during his four years as a justice.

Before his appointment to the Court, however, Moore had been a prominent North Carolina Federalist. After a notable career during the Revolutionary War, he served the state as a legislator and as attorney general. Most important, he successfully defended a state law that required the dismissal of all suits contesting the title of land confiscated from Tories. In doing so, he challenged the legitimacy of judicial review even though an initial verdict against him is often cited as a precedent for the *Marbury* decision. Moore's active support of the Federalists and his success as a treaty negotiator brought him to the atten-

tion of President John Adams, and when North Carolinian James Iredell died in 1799, Adams appointed Moore to succeed him.

The quasi-war with France provided Moore his only opportunity to draft an opinion. *Bas v. Tingy* (1800) arose out of the frequent seizure of American merchant ships by French privateers. A statute specified that the owner of an American ship captured by "the enemy" and recaptured after more than ninety-six hours had to pay one-half the value of the ship and its goods to the recapturer as salvage. But if the ship had not been taken by the "enemy," the owner only had to pay one-eighth the value as salvage.

The French had captured the American ship *Eliza*, and twenty days later an armed American vessel recaptured her. The Court had to decide whether to consider the French an enemy within the meaning of the act. Like his colleagues, who all issued their own opinions, Moore decided that a state of war did exist between the United States and France. "And how can the characters of the parties engaged in hostilities of war, be otherwise described than by the denomination of enemies," he asked rhetorically. The former owner of the *Eliza* had to pay half the value of the ship and its goods for salvage.

Moore's only other major judicial contribution came when tardiness forced him to miss the arguments in the *Marbury* case. As a result, he did not take part in the decision, and voiced no opinion on judicial review, even though he had resisted it as North Carolina attorney general. Chief Justice John Marshall, however, was criticized for going ahead with the case and not waiting for Moore and Justice William Cushing, who also missed the arguments.

Alfred Moore

Citing fears of ill health caused by the rigors of circuit riding, Moore resigned from the Court in 1804, creating the vacancy to which Thomas Jefferson appointed the first Republican justice, William Johnson of South Carolina. Moore spent the final years of his life helping to establish the University of North Carolina.

—*Michael Grossberg*

BIBLIOGRAPHY

There is practically nothing written on Moore other than the sketch by Leon Friedman in Friedman and Israel, *Justices*, vol. 1, 267.

NOTEWORTHY OPINION

Bas v. Tingy, 4 U.S. 37 (1800)

WILLIAM FRANCIS (FRANK) MURPHY

Birth: April 13, 1890, Sand Beach (now Harbor Beach), Michigan.

Education: University of Michigan, A.B., 1912, LL.B., 1914; graduate study, Lincoln's Inn, London, and Trinity College, Dublin.

Official Positions: Chief assistant U.S. attorney, Eastern District of Michigan, 1919–1920; judge, Recorder's Court, Detroit, 1923–1930; mayor of Detroit, 1930–1933; governor general of the Philippines, 1933–1935; U.S. high commissioner to the Philippines, 1935–1936; governor of Michigan, 1937–1939; U.S. attorney general, 1939–1940.

Supreme Court Service: Nominated associate justice by President Franklin D. Roosevelt, January 4, 1940, to replace Pierce Butler, who had died; confirmed by the Senate, January 16, 1940, by a voice vote; took judicial oath February 5, 1940; served until July 19, 1949; replaced by Tom C. Clark, nominated by President Harry S. Truman.

Death: July 19, 1949, Detroit, Michigan.

The appointment of Frank Murphy in 1940 gave President Franklin D. Roosevelt a crucial fifth vote on a Supreme Court that had been dominated for two decades by a reactionary "horse-and-buggy" approach to the Constitution. Roosevelt tried to reshape the Court as a New Deal agency, but several of his eight nominees, most notably Felix Frankfurter, shed their liberal politics and veered to the right once on the bench. Murphy, however, began and ended his entire public career as a consistent, committed liberal. He is arguably the most liberal—even radical—justice to serve on the Supreme Court. His judicial opinions, often written in dissent, swept aside technical "niceties" in a quest for justice and "human dignity." Often accused of voting with his heart, Murphy pleaded guilty to a visceral jurisprudence. "The law knows no finer hour," he wrote, "than when it cuts through formal concepts and transitory emotions to protect unpopular citizens against discrimination and persecution."

Unlike many of his colleagues, Murphy was no mystery man; one can find no disparity between his upbringing and his judicial philosophy. But differences existed within his family that help to explain the demons that afflicted Murphy during his entire life. Moreover, Murphy's Irish heritage affected him in two very different ways. His father was a small-town lawyer, a Democrat, and freethinker in the Republican bastion of northern Michigan. His great-grandfather was hanged by the British as an insurrectionist, and his father was jailed as a youth in Canada for Fenian sympathies. Murphy adopted his father's radical politics, but he also absorbed his mother's devout Catholicism. This was not just parish piety; she instilled in him an equally radical religious vision that would not allow Murphy, he later wrote, to "remain silent in the face of wrong."

The conflicts of Murphy's early years offer a clear guide to those of his judicial career. In high school and college, he loved debating and hated exams. He was popular, but had few close friends. He courted many women, but never married. Murphy was renowned for his generosity and equally noted for his egocentricity. He acted for the people and looked first at his press clippings. There was nothing about Murphy that was not calculated. He differed from judges who gave their votes to the government; his sympathies lay with those who "have been burned at the stake, imprisoned, and driven into exile in countless numbers for their political and religious beliefs."

Murphy viewed law and politics as inseparable, and he pursued an ambitious political career, with the White House as the ultimate goal. First elected as a Detroit criminal judge in 1923, he reformed an archaic system. Clarence Darrow, who tried a racially charged case before Mur-

William Francis (Frank) Murphy

phy, called him "the kindliest and most understanding man I ever happened to meet on the bench." Murphy courted labor and minority groups, and was elected Detroit's mayor in 1930. Faced with massive unemployment, he instituted a welfare program that strained city finances but alleviated poverty.

Murphy helped Franklin Roosevelt win the White House in 1932 and was rewarded with the post of governor general of the Philippines, where he became popular by supporting the independence movement and bringing money from Washington for jobs and welfare. The political bug lured him back to Michigan in 1936. His inauguration as governor was followed by immediate crisis, when militant autoworkers began sit-down strikes that company and local officials met with judicial injunctions. Murphy called out National Guard troops to maintain peace while he worked behind the scenes to head off industrial warfare. The irony of his success was that both sides accused him of favoring the other, and Murphy lost his reelection battle in 1938.

The next year Roosevelt appointed Murphy to head the Justice Department. His major achievement was to set up the civil liberties unit, whose lawyers dusted off unused federal laws to prosecute local officials who abused—and even murdered—blacks and labor organizers. Murphy's crusading zeal made enemies, many of them Democrats; moving him to the Supreme Court allowed Roosevelt to find a more pliable replacement as attorney general. Murphy did not want to join the Court. Feeling he lacked the legal skill for the job Roosevelt was forcing him to accept, he lobbied instead for appointment as secretary of war. "I am not too happy about going on the Court," he wrote a friend. "I fear that my work will be mediocre up there while on the firing line where I have been trained to action I could do much better." Although several senators agreed with Murphy's self-assessment, and others considered him too radical, Roosevelt's clout secured his confirmation without objection.

It is not surprising that Murphy arrived at the Court with an inferiority complex: he was joining legal luminaries such as Chief Justice Charles Evans Hughes, who presided with Jovian firmness; Harlan Fiske Stone, former Columbia law dean; Felix Frankfurter, who lectured his colleagues like the Harvard law students he had taught; and William O. Douglas and Hugo Black, dissimilar in temperament but liberal allies on the bench. Murphy, in fact, had more prior judicial experience—eight years as a criminal judge—than any sitting justice, but his knowledge of constitutional law was sketchy, and he had never written an appellate opinion, but neither had Stone, Frankfurter, Douglas, or Black before their appointments. Like most junior justices, Murphy learned by on-the-job training, assisted by colleagues and bright law clerks. More than most justices, he relied on his clerks to draft opinions, which caused some grumbling from those who considered him lazy.

Three years before Murphy joined the Court, the "constitutional revolution" of 1937 had ended the reign of the judicial reactionaries who struck down most of the New Deal recovery measures Roosevelt had pushed through Congress. In 1938 the Court began to shift its agenda from property rights to human rights. The famous "footnote four" of Justice Stone's opinion in *United States v. Carolene Products* (1938) proposed a "searching judicial inquiry" of laws that were challenged as violating any of "the first ten Amendments" or as discriminating against racial or religious minorities. Murphy embraced the so-called "strict scrutiny" doctrine and the related position that First Amendment rights occupied a "preferred place" in the Constitution.

New justices are allowed to pick their first opinion, and Murphy's choice reflected his concerns for labor and free speech. The case, *Thornhill v. Alabama* (1940), challenged a state law that banned virtually all picketing by union members. Judges had often agreed that even peaceful picketing was not speech, but a form of intimidation. Murphy broke new ground in extending the First Amendment to picketers. He made a point of citing the *Carolene Products* footnote, and he struck down the statute "on its face" as violat-

ing the First Amendment. He also took note of "the circumstances of our time" in holding that "the dissemination of information concerning the facts of a labor dispute must be regarded as within that area of free discussion that is guaranteed by the Constitution." Implicit in Murphy's opinion was his recognition that workers had fewer weapons in battles for public support than employers, who often controlled local newspapers. Picket signs helped to answer hostile news coverage and editorials.

Murphy's first opinion turned out to be one of his most influential and enduring. *Thornhill* has been cited in more than 300 opinions, and Justice Tom C. Clark wrote in 1969 that it was "the bedrock upon which many of the Court's civil rights pronouncements rest." Critics have complained that *Thornhill* was phrased too broadly and limited the power of officials to protect streets and sidewalks from disruption. But Murphy effectively buried the ancient doctrine that picketing was unlawful in any form.

Murphy's commitment to *Carolene Products* and its protection of minorities was shaken by a case decided six weeks after *Thornhill* in June 1940. With war clouds looming, the Court in *Minersville School District v. Gobitis* upheld the expulsion from public school of a Jehovah's Witness student who refused on religious grounds to salute the American flag. Only Stone dissented from Frankfurter's majority opinion, which said that "national unity is the basis of national security." Murphy had prepared a dissent but withdrew it to show his patriotic colors. Even more than Frankfurter, Murphy had a bad case of war fever. He shocked his colleagues by trading his judicial robe for a uniform in 1942, reporting for infantry training at Fort Knox.

This short army stint, however, did not keep Murphy from deserting Frankfurter's judicial platoon. Along with Douglas and Black, and a new recruit, Justice Wiley Rutledge, he joined Stone, now chief justice, in overruling *Gobitis* in 1943. Concurring in *West Virginia State Board of Education v. Barnette* (1943), Murphy answered Frankfurter in writing that "the real unity of America" rested not on coercion or conformity, but on religious freedom. "Reflection has convinced me," he added, "that as a judge I have no loftier duty or responsibility than to uphold that spiritual freedom to its farthest reaches." The *Barnette* case split the Court into hostile factions. Frankfurter felt betrayed and derided Murphy as a conspirator in a judicial "Axis" that undermined political and military authority. Changing his mind from *Gobitis* to *Barnette* did not mean that Murphy had no judicial compass; rather, it showed his growing ability to separate personal emotions from the Constitution's dictates. In this regard, he displayed greater maturity and discipline than Frankfurter, who stuck to his belief that even schoolchildren should support the war effort.

Murphy demonstrated his commitment to principle by consistently supporting the Jehovah's Witnesses, who bitterly attacked his beloved Catholic Church. He dissented when the Court upheld in 1944 a state law that barred minors from selling religious literature on public streets. Murphy cited the Witnesses in *Prince v. Massachusetts* as "living proof of the fact that even in this nation, conceived as it was in the ideals of freedom, the right to practice religion in unconventional ways is still far from secure." He noted that Witnesses "have suffered brutal beatings; their property has been destroyed: they have been harassed at every turn by the resurrection and enforcement of little used ordinances and statutes." Theological disputes aside, Murphy knew that Witnesses and Catholics had both suffered for their faith. "If Frank Murphy is ever sainted," one colleague said, "it will be by the Jehovah's Witnesses."

Even more than religious bigotry, Frank Murphy hated racism. As a criminal court judge, he knew that black defendants were treated more harshly than white defendants. And as mayor of Detroit, he saw the punishing impact of the Depression on minorities. During his army training in southern states, he saw the all-black chain gangs and the demeaning customs of segregation. Murphy wrote a friend that he was determined to redress the reality that "people of color" were denied "constitutional rights and any kind of social justice."

When Murphy was forced to choose, however, between his wartime fervor and revulsion at racism,

he succumbed to judicial paralysis. He faced this choice in *Hirabayashi v. United States* (1943), which produced a dramatic clash between the Constitution's "war powers" and its prohibition of racial discrimination. The case began with the Japanese attack on Pearl Harbor on December 7, 1941. More than 100,000 Americans of Japanese ancestry—two-thirds of them native-born citizens—became the victims of wartime hysteria and racism. Fueled by sensational (but false) reports of sabotage and espionage, military officials persuaded President Roosevelt to sign an executive order in February 1942 that authorized the removal of "any or all persons" from the West Coast. Congress backed the order with criminal penalties, and army troops herded the entire Japanese American population into "relocation centers" in isolated desert and swamp areas. Even liberals such as Earl Warren, then California's attorney general, supported this program of ethnic cleansing.

Only three young men, acting separately, had the courage to challenge the military curfew and exclusion orders that preceded the mass evacuation. They were arrested and convicted in brief trials, and then appealed their sentences to the Supreme Court. The justices first addressed the curfew orders in the cases of Gordon Hirabayashi, a University of Washington student, and Minoru Yasui, an Oregon lawyer and reserve army officer. Stone wrote for the Court in both cases, addressing the major issues in the *Hirabayashi* opinion in June 1943. "Distinctions between citizens solely because of their ancestry," he admitted, "are by their very nature odious to a free people whose institutions are founded upon the doctrine of equality." Wartime pressures, however, allowed officials to place "citizens of one ancestry in a different category from others." Stone blamed Japanese Americans for their plight: decades of discrimination resulted in "little social intercourse between them and the white population." The chief justice deferred to military authority and ignored his *Carolene Products* footnote on racial discrimination.

Murphy was appalled by an opinion he considered "utterly inconsistent" with American ideals, and he drafted a stinging dissent. He denied that the Constitution allowed "one law for the majority of our citizens and another for those of a particular racial heritage." And he said the internment of Japanese Americans "bears a melancholy resemblance to the treatment accorded to members of the Jewish race" by the Nazis. Frankfurter was offended by suggestions the Court was "behaving like the enemy" and pleaded with Murphy to withdraw his dissent. As he had in *Gobitis,* Murphy yielded. But his *Hirabayashi* concurrence retained the analogy to Nazi persecution and said the mass internment "goes to the very brink of constitutional power."

Again, Murphy repented his vote with a vengeance. But this time he remained in the minority. In December 1944 the Court upheld the military exclusion orders in *Korematsu v. United States.* Fred Korematsu was a shipyard welder in California who violated the exclusion order because he wanted to stay with his Caucasian fiancée, but someone recognized him and called the police. Black wrote for the Court in affirming his conviction. Like Stone, Black agreed that laws which "curtail the civil rights of a single racial group" were subject to "the most rigid scrutiny." And like Stone, he exempted from scrutiny military claims that Japanese Americans posed a security threat and that it was impossible to separate "the disloyal from the loyal" in this racial group.

Murphy was the only member of the liberal "Axis" to dissent in *Korematsu.* He charged the Court with plunging over the brink of constitutional power "into the ugly abyss of racism." His carefully documented opinion showed that belief in "racial guilt rather than bona fide military necessity" had motivated the officials who urged the internment program. Murphy quoted the West Coast army commander who said all Japanese Americans belonged to "an enemy race" and the farm leader who admitted "wanting to get rid of the Japs" so that "white farmers can take over and produce everything the Jap grows." And he accused the Court's majority of adopting "the cruelest of the rationales used by our enemies to destroy the dignity of the individual" and of opening the door "to discriminatory actions against other minority groups in the passions of

tomorrow." Murphy simply could not stomach what he called "this legalization of racism."

Murphy's dissent in *Korematsu* stands as his most powerful opinion. His marshalling of the facts—which Black ignored or distorted—belies charges that Murphy lacked the skills of legal craftsmanship. It should be noted that he won vindication four decades later when federal judges vacated the convictions in the wartime internment cases. The judge who cleared Gordon Hirabayashi added more documentation to Murphy's charges that racial bias had motivated government officials. He hoped these facts would "stay the hand of a government again tempted to imprison a defenseless minority without trial and for no offense." And the judge in Fred Korematsu's case echoed Murphy in writing, "The shield of military necessity and national security must not be used to protect governmental actions from close scrutiny and accountability." Murphy would have relished these posthumous tributes to his legal skills.

The bedrock principle of Murphy's view of the Constitution was that no person remained outside its protection, however unpopular or even hated. Communists, aliens, accused spies, even war criminals deserved all the rights of the most respected citizen. Murphy held government officials, from the police to the president, to the highest standards of behavior. For example, he dissented in 1945 from a decision overturning the federal conviction of a Georgia sheriff for beating a black prisoner to death. The Court held in *Screws v. United States* that a Reconstruction-era law making it criminal to act "under color of law" in depriving anyone of constitutional rights required strict proof of intent. Writing for the 5–4 majority, Douglas found insufficient evidence that Sheriff Claude Screws intended to deprive Robert Hall of a specific federal right when he killed the handcuffed prisoner with a tire iron.

Murphy was the only justice who voted to uphold both the law and the conviction. He faulted the majority for ignoring the clear language of the Fourteenth Amendment, "which firmly and unmistakably provides that no state shall deprive any person of life without due process of law." Robert Hall "has been deprived of the right to life itself," he wrote. "That right was his because he was an American citizen, because he was a human being." It required only "common sense" to understand that a police officer who has "beaten and crushed the body of a human being" has violated the clearest demand of the Constitution.

In two politically charged cases, Murphy protected an admitted Communist from denaturalization and an alleged party member from deportation. Federal officials tried in 1939 to strip William Schneiderman of American citizenship on grounds that his Communist activities showed he was not "attached to the principles of the Constitution" when he was naturalized in 1927. Opposed to loyalty tests in general, Murphy objected to this retroactive test in particular. Writing for the Court in *Schneiderman v. United States* (1943), he blasted the government for seeking "to turn the clock back twelve years" and to deprive Schneiderman of the "priceless benefits" of citizenship for acts that were perfectly lawful. Murphy would grant to every new citizen—even Communists—the right "to think and act and speak according to their convictions, without fear of punishment or further exile so long as they keep the peace and obey the law."

The government tried even harder to deport Harry Bridges, the controversial leader of West Coast maritime workers. Bridges came from Australia in 1920 and never applied for citizenship. He freely admitted his radical sympathies but denied Communist Party membership. Efforts to deport Bridges began in 1934 after a bloody waterfront strike in San Francisco, but several panels found no evidence he belonged to the party. In 1940 Congress passed a law allowing deportation of aliens who had at any time been "affiliated" with the Communist Party. Its sponsor proclaimed his "joy" that the government "should now have little trouble in deporting Harry Bridges and all others of similar ilk." Government witnesses at a new hearing testified that Bridges agreed with Communist policies, and he was again served with a deportation order. The Supreme Court reversed the order in *Bridges v. Wixon* (1945), ruling narrowly that pivotal witnesses had given "untrustworthy" testimony. But the Court declined to decide whether "affiliation" with the Communist Party could justify deportation.

Although he agreed with the outcome, Murphy was outraged at this evasion of the constitutional issue. He put his most passionate language into a concurring opinion. "The record in this case will stand forever as a monument to man's intolerance of man," he wrote. "Seldom if ever in the history of this nation has there been such a concentrated and ruthless crusade to deport an individual because he dared to exercise the freedom that belongs to him as a human being and that is guaranteed to him by the Constitution." The final sentence of his opinion set out Murphy's vision of the Constitution: "Only by zealously guarding the rights of the most humble, the most unorthodox and the most despised among us can freedom flourish and endure in our land."

Gen. Tomoyuki Yamashita was probably the "most despised" person who ever appealed to the Supreme Court. There was no doubt the Japanese troops he commanded in the Philippines had committed unspeakable atrocities, but there was considerable doubt that Yamashita ordered or even knew of these atrocities. An American military tribunal sentenced him to hang for violating the U.S. Articles of War. His appeal, prepared by U.S. Army defense lawyers, raised issues of due process, international law, and American treaty obligations. Stone urged the justices to take a "hands off" position on military authority. All but Rutledge and Murphy agreed, and Yamashita's execution quickly followed the Court's decision.

Even though his years in the Philippines had given Murphy a special sympathy for those who suffered "brutal atrocities" at the hands of Japanese troops, he still had a greater attachment to the Constitution. His dissenting opinion in *In re Yamashita* (1946) catalogued at length the procedural flaws in Yamashita's hasty trial. Due process guarantees applied to "any person" accused of crime. "No exception is made as to those who are accused of war crimes," Murphy wrote. Yamashita was "rushed to trial under an improper charge" and deprived of basic rights. Murphy put the Bill of Rights in universal terms:

The immutable rights of the individual ... belong not alone to the members of those nations that excel on the battlefield or that subscribe to the democratic ideology. They belong to every person in the world, victor or vanquished, whatever may be his race, color or beliefs. They rise above any status of belligerency or outlawry. They survive any popular passion or frenzy of the moment. No court or legislature or executive, not even the mightiest army in the world, can ever destroy them.

Not surprisingly, Murphy's last opinion was a dissent. And, not surprisingly, it dealt with another "despised" person, an accused Soviet spy named Gerhart Eisler, who had fled the country to avoid imprisonment. The Court voted to dismiss his pending appeal, but Murphy disagreed. The issues before the Court "did not leave when Eisler did" he said in *Eisler v. United States* (1949). Within weeks of this opinion, Murphy died of a heart attack. The inscription on his grave marker, in his Michigan birthplace, is simple: Frank Murphy/ Justice United States Supreme Court/ 19 July 1949.

But the final paragraph of Murphy's last opinion offered a fitting epitaph:

Law is at its loftiest when it examines claimed injustice even at the instance of one to whom the public is bitterly hostile. We should be loath to shirk our obligations, whatever the creed of the particular petitioner. Our country takes pride in requiring of its institutions the examination and correction of alleged injustice whenever it occurs. We should not permit an affront of this sort to distract us from the performance of our constitutional duties. I dissent.

—*Peter Irons*

BIBLIOGRAPHY

The Frank Murphy papers are in the Michigan historical collections, University of Michigan, Ann Arbor, and contain virtually all of Murphy's Court papers and correspondence. The Eugene Gressman papers, also in the Michigan historical collections, are a valuable supplement to Murphy's papers. Sidney Fine, *Frank Murphy: The Washington Years* (1984), is the definitive account of Murphy's Supreme Court career. Two prior volumes in this massive biography cover the earlier parts of his public life. See also J. Woodford Howard Jr., *Mr. Justice Murphy: A Political Biography* (1968), a biography that is less detailed but somewhat more critical than Fine's work. Harold Norris, *Mr. Justice Murphy and the Bill of Rights* (1965), includes many of Murphy's opinions.

Two worthwhile articles are Eugene Gressman, "The Controversial Image of Mr. Justice Murphy," *Georgetown Law Review* 47 (1959): 631, an admiring but insightful memoir by a former law clerk and longtime friend; and Archibald Cox, "The Influence of Mr. Justice Murphy on Labor Law," *Michigan Law Review* 48 (1950): 769, an excellent review of Murphy's labor opinions. More recent articles include T. J. St. Antoine, "Justice Frank Murphy and American Labor Law," *Michigan Law Review* 100 (2002): 1900; and M. J. J. Perry, "Justice Murphy and the Fifth Amendment Equal Protection Doctrine: A Contribution Unrecognized," *Hastings Constitutional Law Quarterly* 27 (2000): 245.

NOTEWORTHY OPINIONS

Thornhill v. Alabama, 310 U.S. 88 (1940)

West Virginia State Board of Education v. Barnette, 319 U.S. 624 (1943) (Concurrence)

Hirabayashi v. United States, 320 U.S. 81 (1943) (Concurrence)

Schneiderman v. United States, 320 U.S. 118 (1943)

Prince v. Massachusetts, 321 U.S. 158 (1944) (Dissent)

Korematsu v. United States, 323 U.S. 214 (1944) (Dissent)

Screws v. United States, 325 U.S. 91 (1945) (Dissent)

Bridges v. Wixon, 326 U.S. 135 (1945) (Concurrence)

In re Yamashita, 327 U.S. 1 (1946) (Dissent)

Eisler v. United States, 338 U.S. 189 (1949) (Dissent)

SAMUEL NELSON

Birth: November 11, 1792, Hebron, New York.

Education: Graduated, Middlebury College, 1813; studied law privately; admitted to the bar, 1817.

Official Positions: Postmaster, Cortland, New York, 1820–1823; presidential elector, 1820; judge, Sixth Circuit of New York, 1823–1831; associate justice, New York Supreme Court, 1831–1837; chief justice, New York Supreme Court, 1837–1845; member, Alabama Claims Commission, 1871.

Supreme Court Service: Nominated associate justice by President John Tyler, February 6, 1845, to replace Justice Smith Thompson, who had died; confirmed by the Senate, February 14, 1845, by a voice vote; took judicial oath February 27, 1845; retired November 28, 1872; replaced by Ward Hunt, nominated by President Ulysses S. Grant.

Death: December 13, 1873, Cooperstown, New York.

Samuel Nelson attended Middlebury College in Vermont, apprenticed in a law office in Salem, New York, and was admitted to the New York bar in 1817. He built a successful litigation and commercial law practice and served as postmaster in Cortland, New York, from 1820 to 1823. He then served for eight years on the state's sixth circuit, presiding over the suits in equity brought in the nine counties of the jurisdiction. From 1831 to 1837, he was an associate judge on the New York Supreme Court, becoming chief judge in 1836, a position he held until 1845 when he was sworn in as an associate justice of the U.S. Supreme Court.

Although he was President John Tyler's fourth nominee to fill the Court vacancy, Nelson proved a wise choice. In his twenty-seven years on the Court, Nelson was a prolific justice, producing 347 opinions (323 majority opinions, 19 dissents, and 5 concurrences). He wrote on a broad range of legal topics in these opinions, but his most noteworthy contribution

was the influence he brought to bear in resolving the difficult legal issues arising before and during the Civil War.

Originally, Nelson was to be the author of the majority opinion in *Dred Scott v. Sandford* (1857), but his proposed proslavery opinion held only that Missouri's slavery laws determined Scott's status after he returned from Illinois, a free jurisdiction in which he had resided with his master. Chief Justice Roger Brooke Taney believed that a stronger statement was needed to counter the antislavery dissents, and he took on the writing of the majority opinion. Taney went further than Nelson's more temperate views, holding the Missouri Compromise void and saying that neither people imported into the United States as slaves nor their descendants could ever be citizens of the United States. Nelson filed a separate concurrence.

Two years later Taney wrote for a unanimous Court in *Ableman v. Booth* (1859). Wisconsin's Supreme Court had released Sherman Booth, who had allegedly assisted a fugitive slave to escape from his pursuing master, after a hearing on a writ of *habeas corpus.* Taney's opinion characterized the state court's action as a great abuse of power. Yet Taney had joined a Nelson dissent in an earlier decision, *In re Thomas Kaine* (1852), in which Nelson had extolled the liberal use of the writ of *habeas corpus,* stating a preference "to follow the free and enlarged interpretation always given, when dealing with it by the courts of England." Indeed, "so liberally do the courts of England deal with this writ . . . that the decision of one court or magistrate upon the return to it, refusing to discharge the prisoner, is no bar to the issuing of a second, or third, or more, by any other court or magistrate having jurisdiction of the case."

Taking these opinions together, the views of Nelson and Taney seem to be far more lenient in the case of a fugitive from justice (Kaine had been arrested in the United States on a charge of murder committed in Ireland and examined before a U.S. commissioner) than in the case of an American citizen (Booth had been accused of assisting a fugitive slave to escape to freedom). Although numerous motives for the difference in perspective on the two kinds of fugitives might be defended, the cases' proximity to the Civil War undoubtedly bore some influence.

Nelson wrote a number of opinions regarding the capture of ships and their cargos as war prize. In the *Prize Cases* (1863), the majority held legitimate the July 1861 taking of four ships attempting to run a

Samuel Nelson

Union blockade that President Abraham Lincoln had declared the previous April. In a powerful dissent concurred in by Taney, John Catron, and Nathan Clifford, Nelson declared that only Congress, not the president, could declare war. Congress had not declared war in July 1861, and Nelson believed the seizures invalid.

In *The Circassian* (1864), a Union ship had captured a British merchant steamer close to Havana, Cuba, on May 4, 1862, on evidence that its ultimate destination was New Orleans, then under blockade. The majority opinion upheld the ship's capture as prize even though New Orleans had been taken by federal troops on May 2, 1862. Nelson dissented, claiming "the defect in the case, on the part of the captors is that no blockade existed at the port of New Orleans at the time the seizure was made."

The facts in *The Siren* (1868) were more complicated, involving a steamer captured by Union forces. While being taken to Boston, *The Siren* collided with a sloop, which sank with its cargo of iron. After *The Siren* was sold as lawful prize, the sloop's owners filed a claim against the proceeds for damages. The majority decided this claim should be honored, but Nelson dissented, stating that, under the principle of sovereign immunity, the sloop's owners could not sue the U.S. government. With its capture, *The Siren* had become government property, and the fact that it was later sold changed nothing.

Nelson joined with the majority in two other noteworthy Civil War cases, both concerning the jurisdiction and powers of military commissions during the war. In *Ex parte Vallandigham* (1863), a commission had imprisoned a civilian in Ohio for public speech disloyal to the Union. The Court held this decision was not reviewable and denied the writ of certiorari. But in *Ex parte Milligan* (1866), the Court reversed a military commission decision to hang an Indiana civilian convicted of various treasonous acts during "the late wicked Rebellion" and held that Lambdin Milligan deserved a jury trial in either state or federal court.

Samuel Nelson was a true craftsman in his work, with an "elevated conception of justice and of right" as stated in a letter from members of the Supreme Court bar after his retirement. In several respects he could be considered a precursor of his twentieth-century brethren on the Court: his opinions were lucid and logical; he frequently cited authority for specific points (Chancellor James Kent being one of his favorites); and his opinions were quite succinct by comparison with many other nineteenth-century judicial pronouncements. He was also a gentleman and would have been horrified by some of the personal attacks engaged in by late twentieth-century members of the Court toward each other.

Nelson's combined years of service on state and federal courts covered a half century of unprecedented change in America. Old age and failing health forced his retirement from the Court in November 1872, and he died a year later. Far less has been written about this quietly competent jurist than his more flamboyant and controversial judicial brethren. This omission probably says more about Supreme Court observers than it does about Justice Nelson.

—*Jenni Parrish*

BIBLIOGRAPHY

There is no full-length authoritative biography on Samuel Nelson and no single collection of his papers in existence. The following round out what little there is in print on the man. Edwin Countryman, "Samuel Nelson," *The Green Bag* 19 (1907): 329, which is probably the single best biographical source on Nelson to date; Richard Leach, "The Rediscovery of Samuel Nelson," *New York History* 34 (1953): 64, which includes excerpts from Justice Nelson's correspondence; Jenni Parrish, "Justice Samuel Nelson," *New York Notes* (1987), which is useful for discussion of cases during his tenure on the New York State Supreme Court. Numerous biographical directories include basic descriptions of Justice Samuel Nelson, including *Dictionary of American Biography,* vol. 13 (1928), 422.

NOTEWORTHY OPINIONS

In re Thomas Kaine, 55 U.S. 103 (1852) (Dissent)

Dred Scott v. Sandford, 60 U.S. 393 (1857) (Concurrence)

Prize Cases, 67 U.S. 635 (1863) (Dissent)

The Circassian, 69 U.S. 135 (1864) (Dissent)

The Siren, 74 U.S. 152 (1868) (Dissent)

SANDRA DAY O'CONNOR

Birth: March 26, 1930, El Paso, Texas.

Education: Stanford University, B.A., 1950, Stanford University Law School, LL.B., 1952.

Official Positions: Deputy county attorney, San Mateo, California, 1952–1953; assistant attorney general, Arizona, 1965–1969; Arizona state senator, 1969–1975; state senate majority leader, 1973–1974; judge, Maricopa County Superior Court, 1975–1979; judge, Arizona Court of Appeals, 1979–1981.

Supreme Court Service: Nominated associate justice by President Ronald Reagan, August 19, 1981, to replace Potter Stewart, who had retired; confirmed by the Senate, by a 99–0 vote, September 21, 1981; took judicial oath September 26, 1981; retired January 31, 2006; replaced by Samuel Anthony Alito Jr., nominated by President George W. Bush.

Justice Sandra Day O'Connor had an impressive career in public service long before becoming the first female member of the U.S. Supreme Court. She grew up on her family's Lazy B ranch, which sat on the Arizona-New Mexico border. She graduated magna cum laude from Stanford University and was third in her class at Stanford Law School—her long-time colleague, William H. Rehnquist, was first in the same class. After the large law firms offered her only legal secretary positions, she became a deputy county attorney in San Mateo, California, which was the beginning of her long career in public service. At the same time, she married fellow lawyer John Jay O'Connor III.

Between 1954 and 1957 the O'Connors were stationed in West Germany. John served in the U.S. Army Judge Advocate General Corps, and Sandra worked as a civilian lawyer specializing in contracts for the U.S. Army Quartermaster Corps. From 1957 to 1965 she focused on raising their three sons, Scott, Brian, and Jay, although she also maintained a private law practice in Maryvale, Arizona. John established a thriving law practice in Phoenix at the firm of Fennemore, Craig, von Ammon & Udall. Sandra became an Arizona assistant attorney general in 1965, and four years later she was appointed to the Arizona Senate after a sitting senator resigned to take an appointment in the Nixon administration. The citizens of Arizona subsequently elected her to two full terms, and in 1973 she became the Senate majority leader. She then sought and won her first judicial office as a Maricopa County trial judge on the Arizona Superior Court. O'Connor earned a wide respect as a very efficient trial judge, setting high standards for the lawyers who practiced before her. In 1979 she was appointed to the state's intermediate court of appeals, the Arizona Court of Appeals, and served in that capacity until President Ronald Reagan selected her as his first appointment to the U.S. Supreme Court. The president said:

> Judge O'Connor is, as I have come to know personally, a very warm and brilliant woman who

has had an outstanding career in Arizona. I know the Court and the nation will benefit both from her lifetime of work, service, and experience in the legal profession, and from her solid grasp of our Constitution, which she reveres. . . . Let me also say that Judge O'Connor's confirmation symbolizes the richness of opportunity that still abides in America—opportunity that permits persons of any sex, age, or race, from every section and every walk of life to aspire and achieve in a manner never before even dreamed about in human history.

Long before she began her service on the Supreme Court, O'Connor was passionately committed to the principle of federalism, or states' rights. For her, the constitutional system had established dual sovereignty, meaning that the state and federal governments were each sovereign and exercised distinctive powers. As an Arizona state judge, she dealt with the core areas of state regulation, including criminal, employment, contract, tort, and property law.

Sandra Day O'Connor

O'Connor's childhood taught her certain lessons about state and federal power that she brought with her to the Supreme Court, the most important of which was to distrust the federal government. From an early age, O'Connor was struck by the ineptitude of the federal government when it came to regulating the western ranch lands. She watched as an ever-larger federal bureaucracy made ranching more difficult.

She writes, "Problems that could have been resolved out in the field would be referred instead to the state office and then to Washington, D.C. Decisions would be made by people who had never been in the area where the problem arose and sometimes were lacking in common sense."

For O'Connor, there was a sharp contrast between the resourcefulness of the ranch owners and hands and the bumbling federal bureaucracy. Naturally, she came to believe in the inherent value of local and state control over public welfare, especially when the issue involved local resources—in other words, she saw, in action, the value of federalism. Her work as an Arizona state legislator and judge galvanized her respect for these principles, as she learned, in a very practical context, how federal and state governments relate. She would take away from those positions an innate respect for the states as sovereigns and lawmakers. Her firsthand experience dealing with state issues gave her a unique perspective among her peers on the Court as the first member of the Supreme Court with state legislative experience since Justice Stanley Reed was appointed in 1938. Reed had served as a member of the Kentucky House of Representatives from 1912–1916.

Although William Rehnquist did not have state legislative experience, he shared O'Connor's western preference for independent state power over an unaccountable and distant national government. Before O'Connor joined the Court, Rehnquist was usually relegated to dissents, one of which foreshadowed her stirring dissent in *Gonzales v. Raich* (2005), in which she emphasized the value of permitting the states to operate as fifty laboratories for experiment: "One of the great virtues of federalism is the opportunity it affords for experimentation and innovation, with freedom to discard or amend that which proves unsuccessful or detrimental to the public good." It should not be surprising that the two of them were instrumental in the Court's restoration of federalism as an important doctrine in constitutional law.

Ten years into her career at the Court, she memorably articulated the distinctive roles for the states and federal government in the constitutional scheme. In *New York v. United States* (1992), the Court was faced with a state challenge to the federal Low-Level Radioactive Waste Policy Amendments Act of 1985, which, among other provisions, mandated states to "take title," or assert ownership, to radioactive waste or to enact regulations dictated by Congress. Although the Court upheld most of the act in a 6–3 decision, it declared the "take title" provision unconstitutional, holding that Congress had overstepped its enumerated powers and violated the Tenth Amendment. From O'Connor's perspective, Congress's action was also fundamentally at odds with her view of the role of the states in the Constitution. For O'Connor, the states were not "mere political subdivisions" of the federal government; rather, they were independent sovereigns.

It had been suggested in a brief filed by several states that the states had acquiesced in the federal government's takeover of their power, and, therefore, there was no constitutional error, but O'Connor soundly rejected such a theory. In her experience, this would have wholly undermined the Constitution's division of governing power between state and federal governments. Her opinion elegantly illustrates her view of the state/federal relationship:

How can a federal statute be found an unconstitutional infringement of state sovereignty when state officials consented to the statute's enactment? The answer follows from an understanding of the fundamental purpose served by our Government's federal structure. The Constitution does not protect the sovereignty of States for the benefit of the States or state governments as abstract political entities, or even for the benefit of the public officials governing the States. To the contrary, the Constitution divides authority between federal and state governments for the protection of individuals.

By the time O'Connor joined the Supreme Court, the predominant federalism jurisprudence of the previous decades showed a Court unwilling to review federal statutes in terms of Congress's power to enact the law. The Court had abandoned one of the cardinal principles at the Constitutional Convention—Congress was to be an institution of enumerated, limited powers, and the states were intended to hold all other lawmaking capacity. The result of the Court's nonenforcement was that Congress came to view its power as plenary and legitimate within any arena of public policy. In fact, it ceased asking or wondering whether it had the power to enact any particular law and simply assumed that it did. When a majority of the Court held in the landmark case *United States v. Lopez* (1995) that Congress had overstepped its power under the commerce clause when it enacted the Gun-Free School Zones Act, it reintroduced the principle of enumerated powers, and O'Connor joined Chief Justice Rehnquist's majority opinion. O'Connor later explained that Congress went too far by enacting a strictly criminal statute aimed at noncommercial conduct. By overstepping its powers, Congress overtook the states' "role as laboratories for solutions to local problems."

When the Court was faced with another law that commanded the states do the federal government's bidding, O'Connor once again voted to hold the law unconstitutional on federalism grounds (*Printz v. United States*, 1997). The law in question was the provision of the Brady bill that required state and local law enforcement officers to perform background checks on prospective handgun purchasers, along with other designated tasks. O'Connor integrated her practical understanding of how the states operate with her belief in federalism in her concurrence. She asserted that the Brady act violated the Tenth Amendment by directly compelling state officials to administer a federal regulatory program, which made it a statute that "utterly fail[s] to adhere to the design and structure of our constitutional scheme."

Despite her devotion to a structural reading of the Constitution—which was evident by her repeated votes in favor of states' rights principles—she was not doctrinaire on the issue. When the Court faced the question whether Congress held the power under Section 5 of the Fourteenth Amendment to enforce the Americans with Disabilities Act against the states in contexts involving the deprivation of access to the courts, she voted to uphold Congress's power, despite impassioned dissents from Chief Justice Rehnquist and Justice Antonin Scalia (*Tennessee v. Lane,* 2004).

O'Connor believed in federalism as an essential and structural constitutional principle, but that did not mean she believed that state and local governments should be permitted to violate federal constitutional rules. For example, she voted with the majority in *Bush v. Gore* (2000), which held that Florida had violated the Fourteenth Amendment's equal protection clause through the state's unreliable voting system. And she railed in dissent against the widely unpopular decision in *Kelo v. City of New London* (2005), which gave state and local governments broad (one might even say unrestricted) authority to use the power of eminent domain in favor of developers and against private homeowners. She saw the potential for government abuse of power at every level, including the local. She observed that local governments, as a result of the *Kelo* decision, would have license to transfer property from those with fewer resources to those with more, and that this power was likely to benefit those who already wielded a disproportionate amount of political influence, such as large corporations and development firms. "The Founders," she noted, "cannot have intended this perverse result."

Her most memorable writing in the federalism arena came in her dissent in *Gonzales v. Raich.* The case addressed the question of whether the federal Controlled Substances Act trumped California's

Compassionate Use Act, which permitted in-state cultivation and administration of marijuana for medical purposes. This case was an opportunity for the conservatives on the Court to counteract the charge that they had championed states' rights just to suppress federal civil rights. California had chosen a liberal public policy, to be sure, so if the conservatives on the Court were willing to say federalism protected California in this case, they would go far to make the case that the reintroduction of federalism was a principled, not a political, move.

O'Connor's *Raich* dissent was joined only by Rehnquist and Justice Clarence Thomas. She castigated the majority, and, one imagines, Justices Scalia and Anthony Kennedy, in particular, for betraying the principled application of federalism principles:

> One of federalism's chief virtues, of course, is that it promotes innovation by allowing for the possibility that "a single courageous State may, if its citizens choose, serve as a laboratory; and try novel social and economic experiments without risk to the rest of the country." . . . Today the Court . . . extinguishes that experiment, without any proof . . . [of] a substantial effect on interstate commerce. . . . In so doing, the Court announces a rule that gives Congress a perverse incentive to legislate broadly pursuant to the Commerce Clause—nestling questionable assertions of its authority into comprehensive regulatory schemes—rather than with precision. That rule and the result it produces in this case are irreconcilable with our [prior] decisions.

Reinforcing the point that hers was a structural and a principled federalism jurisprudence, and not one based on policy preferences, she revealed that she probably would not have, if given the chance, voted for medical marijuana. But, she explained, that issue was left to the state legislature, and no federal power should have been permitted to interfere with this wholly intrastate regulation and activity.

It is remarkable that when O'Connor joined the Court, federalism was a doctrine in need of revival, but by the time she retired in 2006, it had become part of the fabric of the Court. The last two major federalism decisions during her tenure, *Tennessee v. Lane* and *Gonzales v. Raich,* were written by Justice John Paul Stevens, one of the liberal members of the Court, who applied the Court's federalism jurisprudence in a matter-of-fact fashion. Thus, by 2005 the doctrine was settled, and the Court would continue to inquire into whether Congress had exceeded its authority or improperly commandeered the states. It was an enormous achievement.

During O'Connor's tenure the Court was persistently split over the question of the separation of church and state. In 1962, nineteen years before she joined the Court, the establishment clause had been interpreted to prevent public school administrators and teachers from leading prayers in class. That case, *Engel v. Vitale,* triggered an animated debate over the parameters of government speech implicating religion, which continued to the very end of her service.

O'Connor will be remembered for introducing the principle that the government may not "endorse" religious viewpoints. Her first articulation of the principle appeared in *Lynch v. Donnelly* (1984), which held that the Pawtucket, Rhode Island, holiday display was not unconstitutional even though it included a crèche. O'Connor explained that the government should not be permitted to endorse, or stand behind, any particular religious content, because it sends a divisive message to those with different beliefs that they are disenfranchised. But when a city put together a holiday display including "a Santa Claus house, reindeer pulling Santa's sleigh, candy-striped poles, a Christmas tree, carolers, cutout figures representing such characters as a clown, an elephant, and a teddy bear, hundreds of colored lights, a large banner that read 'SEASONS GREETINGS,' " and the city's intent was to boost holiday shopping, the religious endorsement element was not present. When, however, a local government placed a crèche, by itself, within the county courthouse, the government's message of endorsement was unmistakable, divisive, and unconstitutional, as the Court held in *Allegheny County v. ACLU* (1989).

This view saw its full fruition in *Lee v. Weisman* (1992), which found that a nondenominational prayer at a public middle school graduation offended the establishment clause, because it violated "the Constitutional guarantees that government may not coerce anyone to support or participate in religion or its exercise." Moreover, "the degree of school involvement here made it clear that the graduation prayers bore the imprint of the State and thus put school-age children who objected in an untenable position." Kennedy's opinion for the Court did not literally adopt O'Connor's "endorsement" label in the case, but the test applied is indistinguishable. Kennedy wrote that "prayer exercises in public schools carry a particular risk of indirect coercion," because they take on a different meaning in a public school context, where it might appear that the state is endorsing a particular religious orthodoxy.

The endorsement test was a revolutionary approach that responded to the growth of pluralism in religious belief in the United States. Its solicitude for the sensibilities of those who do not share the government's religious message speaks to a world view that is embracing and inclusive. As with the federalism cases, O'Connor had a natural affinity for the "little guy" and little regard for those who abuse their political power to the detriment of outsiders.

But O'Connor's contribution to the establishment clause cannot be limited solely to her introduction of the endorsement test. As she demonstrated in her concurrence in *Board of Ed. of Kiryas Joel Village School Dist. v. Grumet* (1994), she was also unwilling to oversimplify the project of balancing the power between church and state. Rather, on her terms, the establishment clause decisions were not susceptible to a "grand unified theory" that would fit every case addressing the relationship between religion and the state. This is an accurate explanation of establishment clause jurisprudence, but it was a feature that infuriated Justice Scalia:

Unlike Justice O'Connor . . . I would not replace *Lemon* [*v. Kurtzman,* the governing establishment clause authority] with nothing, and let the case law "evolve" into a series of situation-specific rules ... unconstrained by any "rigid influence." ... The foremost principle I would apply is fidelity to the longstanding traditions of our people, which surely provide the diversity of treatment that Justice O'Connor seeks, but do not leave us to our own devices.

As in all of her jurisprudence—and despite Scalia's vitriol—O'Connor addressed each establishment clause case on its own facts and never sought to enunciate a rule that was broader than necessary. For her, the Constitution's "case and controversy" requirement, which forecloses advisory opinions, was part of the common law of constitutional law, which, at best, developed incrementally. For O'Connor, "The Court's role is uniquely reactive. It is the Constitution, after all, that limits our business to 'Cases or Controversies.' The business of the Court is to resolve controversies, not create them. That is how it should be. And, our docket reveals, that in fact is how it is."

A good example of her approach to cases in general was her concurrence in *Mitchell v. Helms* (2000). The case affirmatively answered the question whether parochial schools could receive computers from the federal government, and the various opinions nicely plot the map of establishment clause approaches on the Court during her service. The live question in the case was whether a religious organization might use such a computer for religious purposes, not just secular educational purposes, and whether this use would breach the line between church and state. A four-member plurality, Rehnquist, Scalia, Kennedy, and Thomas, saw no objection to such a scheme and only asked whether the government had a neutral principle at the time it provided the computers. If so, the transfer of ownership was permissible and the Court had no further role. For them, a later diversion of the computers from education to proselytization was irrelevant.

The dissenters, Justices David Souter, Ruth Bader Ginsburg, and Stevens, took an opposite approach, saying that the Court had "long held government aid invalid when circumstances would allow its diversion to religious education."

O'Connor, joined by Justice Stephen Breyer, staked out the middle. For them, the transfer of the computers to parochial schools occurred for the secular purpose of teaching children at a time when computers had become a crucial component to a good education. But if the computers were in fact diverted to religious purposes, they would revisit the constitutionality of the transfer. They were unwilling to find a violation in this case, because the years-long record in *Mitchell* had revealed little or no such diversion.

O'Connor's last words on the establishment clause as a justice appeared in the 2004 term's closing opinions in the Ten Commandments cases, *McCreary v. ACLU* (2005) and *Van Orden v. Perry* (2005). Both cases posed the question whether a government could display the Ten Commandments, but they were quite different on their facts. In this instance, the difference on the facts did not yield different outcomes—both of the displays, in her view, were unconstitutional.

McCreary, a case from Kentucky, presented a county intent on exhibiting the commandments in high-visibility areas inside the county courthouse. They were accompanied by public resolutions invoking Christ as "Prince of Ethics" and a declaration that they were the source of Kentucky law. *Van Orden*, which arose in Texas, concerned a large granite monument bearing the Ten Commandments standing on the Texas State Capitol grounds, along with many other monuments respecting the origins of law. The commandments monument had been donated in 1961 by the Fraternal Order of Eagles to help reduce juvenile delinquency. Therefore, the Kentucky case involved a clear government purpose to endorse religion, while the Texas case presented a more subtle endorsement. For O'Connor, however, both involved government adoption of a plain religious message.

Predictably, she voted to find the McCreary County courthouse display in violation of the establishment clause. But she also thought the Texas monument crossed the line, because of its "predominant purpose on the part of government either to adopt the religious message or to urge its acceptance by others." She was in the majority in the former, and the dissent in the latter. In the Texas case, Justice Breyer split ranks from those finding the *McCreary* display unconstitutional, because the Texas display was not so apparently intended to endorse religion.

Justice O'Connor was truly in the middle on the issue of abortion. Unlike her conservative colleagues, she believed in a woman's right to choose an abortion and that *Roe v. Wade* (1973) should not be overturned. Unlike her liberal colleagues, she believed the states should be given broad latitude to regulate abortion in many circumstances. In the end, her view evolved into the "undue burden" standard, which prevented the states from regulating abortion only in those circumstances when the law imposed a substantial burden on the right.

The Supreme Court decided *Roe v. Wade* just shy of a decade before O'Connor's appointment to the Court, and during her tenure she had a number of opportunities to address whether it should be upheld. The Court, and O'Connor in particular, was subjected to tremendous political pressure, and literally tons of mail aimed at persuading the justices to reaffirm or overturn *Roe*. Then in *Webster v. Reproductive Health Services* (1989), Chief Justice Rehnquist wrote a plurality opinion upholding Missouri's regulations on abortion and advocated reconsideration of *Roe*.

O'Connor supplied the fifth vote to uphold the Missouri regulations but wrote a separate concurrence, in which she expressed her opinion that the regulations did not conflict with the Court's precedents and therefore it was unnecessary to reexamine *Roe v. Wade*. Her decision to avoid answering the question of whether to overrule *Roe* triggered a condescending, angry, and frenzied attack from Scalia, who characterized O'Connor's approach as "irrational." As was typical of O'Connor—who raised the Court's level of professionalism to new levels—she did not respond in kind.

When the Court squarely faced the question whether it would overrule *Roe v. Wade* in *Planned Parenthood of Southeastern Pennsylvania v. Casey* (1992), O'Connor joined with Kennedy and Souter in a three-member plurality to find that the conditions precedent to overruling settled Supreme Court case law had not been satisfied. According to the plurality,

Roe remained workable; its factual underpinnings had not been sufficiently altered to justify overturning it; and, therefore, the "essential holding of *Roe*" should be upheld. But the plurality was not inclined to persist with the trimester framework initially introduced by *Roe* and, instead, adopted the "undue burden" standard O'Connor had adopted previously. Accordingly, the plurality joined the more liberal members of the Court (Stevens and Blackmun) to invalidate a provision of the law that required spousal notification before a woman could undergo an abortion.

Given her broad reading of the states' power to regulate abortion and her narrow reading of *Roe,* the liberal wing of the Court could not rely on O'Connor to vote to invalidate regulations that burdened (but in her view did not "substantially" burden) the right to choose. For example, in *City of Akron v. Akron Center for Reproductive Health* (1983), she wrote a dissent joined by Justices Rehnquist and Byron White, arguing that two regulations, one requiring a minor seeking an abortion to obtain the consent of one parent, and the other requiring hospitalization if an abortion occurred in the second trimester, did not impose undue constitutional burdens. In contrast, she concurred in *Hodgson v. Minnesota* (1990) to join the majority's holding that a two-parent notification provision, without judicial bypass, *was* an undue burden on the right to choose an abortion. In 2000 she voted to invalidate Nebraska's late-term (often called partial-birth) abortion statute because it lacked an exception for the life or health of the mother.

Less well-known than her judicial role is O'Connor's role as an unofficial U.S. ambassador advocating the rule of law all around the world. For her, the rule of law was the bedrock on which the success of the American constitutional experiment rested. She spoke passionately on the topic to the governments of Brazil, China, France, Germany, India, Kenya, Luxembourg, the Netherlands, Rwanda, and the countries in Eastern Europe. She was a founding chair of the American Bar Association's Central European and Eurasian Law Initiative.

O'Connor also viewed the 2001 terrorist attacks on the United States through the lens of the rule of law:

The events of September 11, 2001, and thereafter shattered our peace but not our faith in our institutions. We remain persuaded of the benefits of helping to shape a world in which democratic principles predominate in national governance, and in which the Rule of Law offers the best approach to secure freedom and equality for all people.

For her, racism and violence were constitutional dysfunctions that emphasized the indispensability of the rule of law for the constitutional order. "It is precisely because we believe deeply in the Rule of Law that we are repelled by its malfunction. Racism and violence are never excusable. Nor can democracy tolerate terrorism, abuse, and injustice."

Her work for the rule of law was hardly limited to the Western world. She met with twenty-eight Iraqi judges and Ministry of Justice officials in the Netherlands in May 2004, as part of a workshop on the rule of law. Her deep devotion to the principle was evident in her eloquent remarks delivered at the Southern Center for International Studies, where she marveled at "how deeply embedded rule of law principles" were in Arab countries. She said:

I left the conference with the conviction that the differences between nations with regard to their commitment to the rule of law are fewer and less important than the similarities. And it is in everyone's interest to foster the rule-of-law evolution. Again, the United States will be in the best position to assist in this development if, in its own treatment of foreign and international law, it has left a good impression on politicians and members of the legal profession in the countries in which the evolution is taking place.

In recognition of her devoted public service, the British Inns of Court established the Sandra Day O'Connor Award for Professional Service honoring an American Inn member. The award honors an "Inn member each year for exemplary service and to honor Justice O'Connor for being the paragon of professional service throughout her distinguished career while exemplifying legal excellence, civility, ethics and professionalism."

It is impossible to do full justice to all of Sandra Day O'Connor's achievements benefiting the United States and democracy worldwide in a short biography. Suffice it to say that the system of constitutional democracy here and elsewhere would be less healthy absent her energetic and passionate involvement.

—*Marci A. Hamilton*

BIBLIOGRAPHY

Justice O'Connor's early years are documented in *Lazy B* (2002), a memoir of ranch life, which she co-wrote with her brother, H. Alan Day. In *The Majesty of the Law* (2003), O'Connor provides an overview of life on the Court and devotes special attention to women and the law and the rule of law in developing countries.

Justice O'Connor has written on federalism in "Testing Government Action: The Promise of Federalism," in *Public Values in Constitutional Law,* ed. Stephen E. Gottlieb (1993); and in several law review articles: "Trends in the Relationship Between the Federal and State Courts from the Perspective of a State Court Judge," *William and Mary Law Review* 22 (1981): 801; "Our Federalism," *Case Western Reserve Law Review* 35 (1985): 1; and "On Federalism: Preserving Strong Federal and State Governments," *Court Review* 35 (1998). Good commentary on her perspective can be found in Erwin Chemerinsky, "Justice O'Connor and Federalism," *McGeorge Law Review* 32 (2001): 877.

Analysis focusing on Justice O'Connor's religion clause and reproductive freedom jurisprudence can be found, respectively, in Alan Brownstein, "A Decent Respect for Religious Liberty and Religious Equality: Justice O'Connor's Interpretation of the Religion Clauses of the First Amendment," *McGeorge Law Review* 32 (2001): 837; and Dorothy E. Roberts, "Sandra Day O'Connor, Conservative Discourse, and Reproductive Freedom," *Women's Rights Law Reporter* 13 (1991): 95, 100.

NOTEWORTHY OPINIONS

Lynch v. Donnelly, 465 U.S. 668 (1984) (Concurrence)

Webster v. Reproductive Health Services, 492 U.S. 490 (1989) (Concurrence)

Allegheny County v. ACLU, 492 U.S. 573 (1989) (Concurrence)

Hodgson v. Minnesota, 497 U.S. 417 (1990) (Concurrence)

Planned Parenthood of Southeastern Pennsylvania v. Casey, 505 U.S. 833 (1992)

United States v. Lopez, 514 U.S. 549 (1995) (Concurrence)

Printz v. United States, 521 U.S. 898 (1997) (Concurrence)

Tennessee v. Lane, 541 U.S. 509 (2004)

Gonzales v. Raich, 125 S. Ct. 2195 (2005)

Kelo v. City of New London, 545 U.S. __ (2005)

McCreary County v. ACLU, 545 U.S. __, 125 S. Ct. 2722 (2005) (Concurrence)

Van Orden v. Perry, 545 U.S. __ (2005)

WILLIAM PATERSON

<table>
<tr><td align="right">Birth:</td><td>December 24, 1745, County Antrim, Ireland.</td></tr>
<tr><td align="right">Education:</td><td>Graduated from College of New Jersey (Princeton), 1763; M.A., 1766; studied law under Richard Stockton; admitted to the bar, 1769.</td></tr>
<tr><td align="right">Official Positions:</td><td>Member, New Jersey Provincial Congress, 1775–1776; delegate, New Jersey State Constitutional Convention, 1776; New Jersey attorney general, 1776–1783; delegate, U.S. Constitutional Convention, 1787; U.S. senator, 1789–1790; governor, New Jersey, 1790–1793.</td></tr>
<tr><td align="right">Supreme Court Service:</td><td>Nominated associate justice by President George Washington, March 4, 1793, to replace Thomas Johnson, who had resigned; confirmed by the Senate, March 4, 1793, by a voice vote; took judicial oath March 11, 1793; served until September 9, 1806; replaced by Henry B. Livingston, nominated by President Thomas Jefferson.</td></tr>
<tr><td align="right">Death:</td><td>September 9, 1806, Albany, New York.</td></tr>
</table>

William Paterson left a major imprint on the United States judiciary, but it was based largely on his achievements before he was appointed to the Supreme Court. Paterson supported an independent judiciary at the Philadelphia Convention of 1787. His New Jersey Plan of Union proposed to amend the ineffective Articles of Confederation by adding "a federal Judiciary . . . to consist of a supreme Tribunal" and providing that acts and treaties established under the new Constitution "shall be the supreme law of the respective States . . . and that the Judiciary of the several States shall be bound thereby." Much of the rest of his life was devoted to implementing the "supreme law" clause he had introduced.

Two years later, as a member of the first U.S. Senate, Paterson was second only to Oliver Ellsworth as the principal author of the Judiciary Act of 1789, legislation that for a century provided the framework of the federal judiciary, and much of which is still determinative. The first nine sections of the manuscript, those that establish the structure of the federal courts, are in Paterson's hand. He argued strenuously in the Senate for lower federal courts, rather than leaving local jurisdiction entirely to state courts. Ironically, President George Washington attempted to withdraw Paterson's nomination the day after he had submitted it, because of the Judiciary Act. On February 28, the president wrote the to Senate: "It has since occurred that he was a member of the Senate when the Law creating that office was passed, and that the time for which he was elected is not yet expired. I think it my duty therefore, to declare that I deem the nomination to have been null by the Constitution." Paterson was, nevertheless, confirmed four days later.

Although Paterson had never previously been on the bench, he brought a wealth of courtroom experience to the Supreme Court. As attorney general for New Jersey from 1776 to 1783, he was accustomed to long horseback rides from court to court. This may have been the best possible preparation for the arduous circuit court duties that seemed to consume the lives of the justices; in 1800 Paterson complained of riding "over stones and rocks and mountains" to get to court in New Hampshire.

Paterson had compiled the *Laws of the State of New Jersey* and "Paterson's Practice Laws," a compendium of New Jersey procedures and practices in common law and chancery courts. Even though he did not take his seat until 1794, Paterson was the first holder of the second seat (intended to be that of the senior associate justice) to give substantive service. And he declined the opportunity for an early exit when Washington wished to appoint him as secretary of state in 1796.

Paterson's devotion to the integral part the judiciary would play in preserving the Constitution can be found in a lengthy charge to the federal grand jury in the Pennsylvania circuit court in 1795. There he

William Paterson

offered one of the finest and most extensive justifications for judicial review prior to *Marbury v. Madison* (1803). The superiority of the Pennsylvania Constitution to state legislation was at stake in *Van Horne's Lessee v. Dorrance* (1795), but Paterson's powerful argument would extend as well to federal legislation. "I take it to be a clear proposition," he declared, "that if a legislative act oppugns a constitutional principle the former must give way, and be rejected on the score of

repugnance. I hold it to be a position equally clear and sound that in such a case, it will be the duty of the court to adhere to the constitution and to declare the act null and void." He showed little concern for the tender feelings of legislatures. They are merely "creatures of the constitution; they owe their existence to the constitution, it is their commission and, therefore, all their acts must be conformable to it, or else they will be void." Lest the jury remain in doubt, he admonished that "there can be no doubt that every act of the legislature repugnant to the constitution is absolutely void." This powerful charge soon gained wide attention in pamphlet form. In *United States v. Lyon* (1799), Paterson informed the jury that the constitutionality of the Sedition Act was a matter for judges to determine, not juries.

Paterson had been a confirmed nationalist from the time during the Constitutional Convention that he had succeeded in establishing a secure place for New Jersey (and other small states) within the Union. His nationalism was shown in his first Supreme Court decision, *Talbot v. Janson* (1795), in which he ruled that state law could not affect U.S. citizenship: "Allegiance to a particular state is one thing; allegiance to the United States is another. . . . The sovereignties are different." A system of "sovereignties moving within a sovereignty" requires great care lest "a slight collision may disturb the harmony of the parts and endanger the machinery of the whole."

He went a huge step further in *Penhallow v. Doane's Administrators* (1795), declaring that the states had never been recognized as sovereign. He ridiculed the idea that the states could have any power of war and peace. He saw the United States as one great political body, with Congress "the directing principle and soul." Some in the gallery must have marveled at this imaginative paean to the repudiated Continental Congress: "Congress was the general, supreme, and controlling council of the nation, the centre of the nation, the centre of the union, the centre of force, and the sun of the political system."

As one of four Supreme Court justices who had participated in the writing of the Constitution, Paterson twice took advantage of his status as a Founding Father. He argued persuasively in *Hylton v. United States* (1796) that the direct tax clause of the Constitution was intended to apply only to a capitation tax and a land tax. He asserted that it was "obviously the intention of the framers of the Constitution, that Congress should possess full power over every species of taxable property, except exports," because they had been painfully aware of the failings of the requisition system under the Articles of Confederation. He took a further step in *Calder v. Bull* (1798). After remarking that the Constitutional Convention had intended that the *ex post facto* clause apply only to criminal cases, not to civil cases, he added that he, personally, felt differently, implying that this was an issue on which he had lost in the secrecy of the last few days of the 1787 convention. In the same session as *Hylton v. United States,* Paterson also participated in the vitally important *Ware v. Hylton,* but he added little to Justice Samuel Chase's masterful exposition.

As with most of the other Founding Fathers, Paterson strongly disapproved of political parties. Yet like so many of his peers, he too became extremely partisan. His intense respect for authority and stability, his aristocratic view of society, made him a natural ally of the Hamiltonian Federalists. He quickly displayed blatant federalism in circuit trials of several participants in the so-called Whiskey Rebellion. Trials under the Sedition Act of 1798 brought out the worst in him. Even his admiring biographer describes him as an unjust "hanging judge" who merited the abuse of his Republican critics in 1799 and 1800. Following

the prosecution of Rep. Matthew Lyon of Vermont for sedition in 1799, Paterson proceeded to rule before Lyon's counsel could present a defense. When the defendant's lawyer protested, he "politely sat down." But Paterson's instructions demolished Lyon's defense, and he was convicted within an hour, the first conviction under the Sedition Act. Paterson sentenced him to four months in jail and fined him $1,000. He likewise undermined the defense of Anthony Haswell, who had defended Lyon so strenuously that he, too, was convicted of sedition.

Paterson became a special hero to the high Federalists with a charge to the Portsmouth, New Hampshire, grand jury in May 1800. He branded the Jeffersonian Republicans as Jacobins who were "the disorganizers of our happy country, and the only instruments of introducing discontent and dissatisfaction among the well-meaning part of the Community." His admirers hoped to reward him by persuading or coercing President John Adams to appoint Paterson as Chief Justice Oliver Ellsworth's successor. The Federalist-dominated Senate briefly held up Marshall's confirmation in hopes that Adams would relent, but the president had no desire to reward someone who was so popular among those Federalists who had so persistently undermined his administration. Federalist friends sent Paterson spiteful remarks about Adams and his refusal to appoint him as chief justice. Such remarks would have merited prosecution for sedition if they had been supporters of Jefferson rather than of Hamilton.

"I will not nominate him," Adams declared. After offering the position again to John Jay and unsuccessfully sounding out other nominees, Adams finally turned to Secretary of State John Marshall, shortly before the position would have fallen to President Jefferson to fill. This decision was a dramatic turning point in American judicial history. If Paterson had been appointed, Thomas Jefferson would have been able to appoint a new chief justice in 1806, when Paterson died. Marshall, on the other hand, outlasted the Jefferson, Madison, Monroe, and John Quincy Adams administrations, and most of the Jackson administration as well. Paterson sent a warm letter of congratulations to Marshall and was a valued ally in the short time that they served together on the bench.

Ironically, nonpartisan statesmanship became the hallmark of Paterson's last few years on the Supreme Court. His last significant decision proved also to be his most important. In *Stuart v. Laird* (1803), he upheld the constitutionality of the Circuit Court Act of 1802. The seeming partisanship of the Judiciary Act of 1801, by which the lame-duck Congress attempted to create lifetime judicial sinecures for "deserving Federalists," while seeking the more worthy goal of relieving Supreme Court justices from their arduous circuit duties, caused President Jefferson to respond in kind. In addition to withholding some commissions from lesser lights such as William Marbury and others, the Republicans took the more important step of deleting the new circuit courts and, with them, the new circuit judges. The Supreme Court justices, all Federalists, received two concessions from the Republican Congress following the repeal of the Judiciary Act of 1801. Only one justice would be required in each circuit court, and the Supreme Court would meet for one four-week session each year, rather than for two sessions of two weeks each. These changes had the politically beneficial impact, from the Republican standpoint, of keeping the Court from convening until February 1803. Ironically, it was probably also fortunate timing for the justices. It gave them time to discuss the judicial reforms before ruling on whether Congress had acted constitutionally in removing judges who had theoretically been appointed for a lifetime tenure. Only Justice Chase insisted that the members should refuse to continue riding circuits.

Paterson ruled in *Stuart v. Laird* because Marshall had already ruled on the question on circuit. Paterson's four brief paragraphs agreed essentially with Marshall's findings. Paterson conceded that Congress could assign Supreme Court justices to circuit duty. They had performed such duties from the beginning, and this practice had "fixed the construction" so that it is "too strong and obstinate to be shaken or controlled." The question is at rest, he admonished, and it ought not now to be revived. Congress has the "constitutional authority to establish from time to time such inferior tribunals as they may think proper; and to transfer a cause from one tribunal to another." Paterson did not add, if he even knew it, that Chief Justice Jay had questioned the constitutionality of circuit riding in September 1790. The justices' wisdom in accepting a setback in their politics and in their personal comfort, rather than challenging the dominant Republicans, has been described as the ultimate "example of the nonpartisanship of the American judiciary." Just the week before, the Court had chosen a much less dangerous case, *Marbury v. Madison* (1803), through which to challenge Congress and the Jefferson administration.

Justice William Johnson, whose term overlapped with Paterson's for barely two years, unjustly described Paterson in 1822 as "a slow man" who "willingly declined the Trouble" of writing opinions—this despite the fact that Paterson, not Johnson, was the first to write a dissent from a Marshall opinion, in *Simms v. Slacum* (1805). Paterson was seriously injured in a carriage accident in 1804, was nearly immobile for weeks, and he missed both Court and circuit assignments. Severe illness forced him to leave the New York circuit in August 1806, where he was contending that the court should subpoena President Jefferson and Secretary of State James Madison, to answer allegations of defendants being prosecuted for participation in Francisco Miranda's attack on Venezuela. His departure left the field to district judge Matthias Tallmadge, who opposed this affront to the executive. Justice Paterson died shortly afterward at the home of his daughter in Albany, New York. Justice Johnson could scarcely have known the colleague whom he criticized for partisan reasons sixteen years later.

—*Donald O. Dewey*

BIBLIOGRAPHY

John E. O'Connor, *William Paterson, Lawyer and Statesman, 1745–1806* (1979), is admiring of Paterson's career, yet properly critical of his partisan decisions. His life is ably and briefly profiled in Michael Kraus's essay in Friedman and Israel, *Justices*, vol. 1, 163. Gertrude S. Wood's doctoral dissertation, "William Paterson of New Jersey, 1745–1806," (Columbia, 1933), was privately published in condensed form in 1940. Julian P. Boyd in Willard Thorpe, ed., *The Lives of Eighteen from Princeton* (1946), uses the Van Horne case to justify entitling his essay on Paterson, "Forerunner of John Marshall." Leonard B. Rosenberg's unpublished doctoral dissertation, "The Political Thought of William Paterson" (New School for Social Research, 1967) helps us understand his judicial career. For another look at the Sedition Act cases, see Williamjames Hull Hoffer, "William Paterson and the National Jurisprudence: Two Draft Opinions on the Sedition Law of 1798 and the Federal Common Law," *Journal of Supreme Court History* 36 (1997).

NOTEWORTHY OPINIONS

Penhallow v. Doane's Administrators, 3 U.S. 54 (1795)

Talbot v. Janson, 3 U.S. 133 (1795)

Hylton v. United States, 3 U.S 171 (1796)

Calder v. Bull, 3 U.S. 386 (1798)

Stuart v. Laird, 5 U.S. 299 (1803)

RUFUS WHEELER PECKHAM JR.

Birth: November 8, 1838, Albany, New York.

Education: Albany Boys' Academy; studied privately in Philadelphia; read law privately, admitted to the bar, 1859.

Official Positions: District attorney, Albany County, 1869–1872; corporation counsel, City of Albany, 1881–1883; judge, New York Supreme Court, 1883–1886; judge, New York Court of Appeals, 1886–1895.

Supreme Court Service: Nominated associate justice by President Grover Cleveland, December 3, 1895, to replace Howell E. Jackson, who had died; confirmed by the Senate, December 9, 1895, by a voice vote; took judicial oath January 6, 1896; served until October 24, 1909; replaced by Horace H. Lurton, nominated by President William Howard Taft.

Death: October 24, 1909, Altamont, New York.

Rufus Wheeler Peckham was born in 1838 into one of New York's oldest and most prominent upstate families. Although in his later years he relished the mantle of judicial impartiality, his life was filled with intense partisan furor, and there can be little doubt that this fact exercised a tremendous influence over Peckham's judicial philosophy. His father, also named Rufus Wheeler Peckham, was a Democratic Party stalwart who served in the House of Representatives and, like his son, on the New York Supreme Court and court of appeals. The younger Peckham was strongly influenced by his father's political and philosophical views and was so similar to his father in mannerisms and appearance that the two were occasionally confused by their contemporaries. Peckham's older brother, Wheeler H. Peckham, was a president of the state bar and himself a nearly successful candidate for a seat on the Supreme Court.

Peckham's judicial philosophy was strongly shaped by the two preoccupations of his pre-judicial career, namely, struggling with Tammany Hall for control of the state Democratic Party machinery and representing major corporate interests, particularly railroads. In the political arena, Peckham aligned himself closely with Grover Cleveland, who came to view Peckham as a principal ally. On the corporate stage, Peckham developed a reputation as a zealous, if not brilliant or inventive, advocate for the captains of industry. Although Peckham himself was never the target of charges of serious corruption, there can be little doubt that his excellent political connections were useful to his clients and contributed to his success in practice—judges in New York are elected, and in the second half of the nineteenth century these elections were fiercely partisan.

As the nineteenth century drew to a close, America's tycoons were under attack from an array of groups seeking to rein in the industrialists' unfettered control over the market and the workplace. Reformers sought to bust monopolies, develop more humane working conditions, end child labor, and protect consumers. To industry's defense rose Rufus Peckham, and great titans of industry such as George F. Baker, Jim Fisk, Jay Gould, James J. Hill, J. Pierpont Morgan, William Rockefeller, James Speyer, and Cornelius Vanderbilt became his clients, friends, and confidants.

Peckham's best known Supreme Court opinion is *Lochner v. New York* (1905), but the views in that case are stated much more vigorously in a dissent he wrote while on the New York Court of Appeals, to which he was elected in 1886 with Cleveland's solid support. In *People v. Budd* (1889), New York's efforts to fix rate levels for grain elevators were attacked as unconstitutional. The court upheld the statute. Peckham's impassioned dissent contains one of the clearest and earliest statements of substantive due process. Directing stinging criticism at his colleagues for their political partisanship, he observed that "all men, however great and however honest, are almost necessarily affected by the general belief of their times." Yet Peckham, even more than his colleagues, was driven by a political credo. He believed that allowing the government to intervene in the economy would "wholly ignore the latter and as I firmly believe the more firmly correct ideas which an increase of civilization and a fuller knowledge of the fundamental laws of political economy, and a truer conception of the proper functions of government have given us at the present day."

Curiously, Peckham saw the political controversy in terms of an almost Marxist class struggle. In his mind, the government could not be permitted to involve itself in a struggle between one "class" (impoverished farmers) against another (capitalist grain factors), because such involvement would lead to "a new competition for the possession of the government so that legislative aid may be given to the class in possession thereof in its contests with rival classes or interests in all sections or corners of the industrial world." For Peckham, the Constitution formed a bulwark against government interference in favor of the underprivileged: the statute was an abridgement of "the most sacred rights of property and the individual's liberty of contract" and was entitled to no presumption of validity. Freedom of contract and the takings clause invalidated such legislation, which, moreover, was "not only vicious in its nature, communistic in its tendency and in my belief wholly ineffective to permanently obtain the results aimed at, but illegal."

Rufus Wheeler Peckham Jr.

In 1895 the death of Justice Howell F. Jackson created a vacancy that President Cleveland was quick to fill with the nomination of his Albany protégé, Rufus Peckham. The confirmation process was uneventful. During his thirteen-year tenure on the Court, Peckham wrote 303 opinions, 9 dissents, and 2 concurring opinions, but only one opinion is generally still reckoned to be of importance, *Lochner v. New York* (1905).

From his arrival on the Court, Peckham belonged to its ultraconservative wing. He joined the majority in *Plessy v. Ferguson* (1896)—perhaps the Court's most pernicious case after *Dred Scott v. Sand-*

ford (1857)—endorsing the "separate but equal" doctrine, and he dissented in nearly all the cases, most notably *Holden v. Hardy* (1898) and *Jacobson v. Massachusetts* (1905), in which reform legislation was sustained. By 1905 Peckham was finally able to muster a 5–4 majority on the Court for his viewpoint.

In *Lochner*, the Court was presented with a challenge to New York's law limiting the number of hours that an employee could work in a bakery to sixty per week. Peckham declared that the right of employee and employer to contract freely for performance of labor is fundamental to the Fourteenth Amendment, and any state power of intervention narrowly circumscribed. If the state chooses to invoke its police power in a way that potentially infringes freedom of contract, the Court must inquire: "Is this a fair, reasonable, and appropriate exercise of the police power of the state, or is it an unreasonable, unnecessary, and arbitrary interference of the right of the individual to his personal liberty, or to enter into those contracts in relation to labor which may seem to him appropriate or necessary for the support of himself and his family?" So phrased, there could be little doubt as to the anticipated outcome. The effect of *Lochner* was to elevate the Supreme Court to the status of a super legislature authorized to reconsider the wisdom of legislation and to strike down offensive acts as an abridgement of the "sacred freedom of contract."

Peckham and his colleagues maintained that the Civil War amendments had one essential purpose: to further individual economic rights, particularly the freedom of contract. They simultaneously denied or undermined what clearly had been the major purpose of those amendments, to protect the fundamental civil and human rights of the recently emancipated slaves. In the hands of the Court's conservative majority, these constitutional provisions had the effect not only of frustrating the efforts of Progressive reformers to enact and enforce legislation protecting consumers, promoting health, and improving safety in the workplace, but also of offering no protection to black southerners feeling the oppressive hand of the Ku Klux Klan and its sympathizers in state government, or to individuals facing criminal procedures clearly at

odds with the Bill of Rights. Peckham was forthright in acknowledging that his purpose in introducing substantive due process was to protect America's industrial sector, the mainspring of America's economy, against the regulatory barrage of the Progressive movement. Peckham acknowledged a single exception—for women. In his paternalistic view, women were the "weaker sex" and required protection from the exploitation of men (*Muller v. Oregon*, 1908).

Peckham was also an active writer on cases challenging the Sherman Antitrust Act. His opinions in this area reveal strong sympathies for antitrust legislation for the protection of small business. In *United States v. Trans-Missouri Freight Association* (1897), he wrote:

It is not for the real prosperity of any country that such changes should occur which result in transferring an independent business man, the head of his establishment, small though it might be, into a mere servant or agent of a corporation selling the commodities which he once manufactured or dealt in, having no voice in shaping the business policy of the company and bound to obey orders issued by others.

In *Addyston Pipe & Steel Co. v. United States* (1899), he succeeded in breathing new life into the antitrust act by rejecting the argument advanced by manufacturers that proof of total monopoly was necessary to sustain an action. Higher prices alone constituted sufficient evidence, Peckham reasoned. Still, in the most important antitrust case of the period, *Northern Securities Co. v. United States* (1904), he sided with the conservative majority in urging a narrow reading of the act, so that it applied only against unreasonable restraints of trade.

A significant number of Peckham's other contributions on the Court were in the area of criminal procedure. With only a few exceptions, Peckham, the former Albany County prosecutor, revealed his disdain for the "mere technicalities" of criminal procedure that are the bedrock of the Bill of Rights (*White v. United States*, 1896). He was vehement in the conviction that the Bill of Rights protections of the criminal justice system, while grudgingly applicable in federal courts, should not apply to the states (*Maxwell v. Dow,* 1900).

Today, we know Peckham principally through the devastating critique of Oliver Wendell Holmes Jr., whose *Lochner* dissent is a dazzling example of judicial exposition. "The Fourteenth Amendment," he insisted, "does not enact Mr. Herbert Spencer's Social Statics"—a popular and widely read presentation of the doctrine of laissez-faire. Still, it took thirty years, the Great Depression, and the appointment of New Deal justices before the Court accepted this view and substantive due process fell into judicial opprobrium. By the 1950s it seemed that Peckham and his doctrine were useful to law professors only as an example of what the Supreme Court should not do.

In the 1960s and 1970s, however, scholars and activists looking for a creative way of addressing civil rights problems turned again to *Lochner*. Substantive due process, they reasoned, might be revived as a doctrinal basis for challenging state and federal laws that interfere with fundamental civil and human rights, such as the right to privacy, reproductive rights, and freedom from ethnic or religious discrimination. Reframed in this way, substantive due process continues to live as a credible constitutional doctrine, but the circumstances of the doctrine's birth under the parentage of Rufus Peckham do little to burnish it.

—*Scott Horton*

BIBLIOGRAPHY

There is no full-scale biography of Peckham, but shorter sketches include Richard Skolnik, "Rufus Peckham" in Friedman and Israel, *Justices,* vol. 3, 1685 (the most exhaustive treatment of Peckham's legal career); A. Oakey Hall, "The New Supreme Court Justice," *Green Bag* 8 (1896) (an interesting though somewhat fawning contemporary account of Peckham's career as a lawyer); and *Proceedings of the Thirty-Third Annual Meeting of the New York State Bar Association* (1910), 683–712 (professional reminiscences). A harshly critical dissection of judicial interventionism by the conservative Court of the Peckham era is Louis B. Boudin, *Government by Judiciary,* 2 vols. (1932), 2: 423–442. A more modern view is in Paul Kens, *Lochner v. New York: Economic Regulation on Trial* (1998).

NOTEWORTHY OPINIONS

White v. United States, 164 U.S. 100 (1896)

United States v. Trans-Missouri Freight Association, 166 U.S. 290 (1897)

Addyston Pipe & Steel Co. v. United States, 175 U.S. 211 (1899)

Maxwell v. Dow, 176 U.S. 581 (1900)

Lochner v. New York, 198 U.S. 45 (1905)

MAHLON PITNEY

Birth: February 5, 1858, Morristown, New Jersey.

Education: College of New Jersey (Princeton), A.B., 1879; A.M., 1882.

Official Positions: U.S. representative, 1895–1899; New Jersey state senator, 1899–1901; president, New Jersey Senate, 1901; associate justice, New Jersey Supreme Court, 1901–1908; chancellor of New Jersey, 1908–1912.

Supreme Court Service: Nominated associate justice by President William Howard Taft, February 19, 1912, to replace John Marshall Harlan, who had died; confirmed by the Senate, March 13, 1912, by a 50–26 vote; took judicial oath March 18, 1912; retired December 31, 1922; replaced by Edward T. Sanford, nominated by President Warren G. Harding.

Death: December 9, 1924, Washington, D.C.

Scion of a distinguished New Jersey legal family, Mahlon Pitney brought a wealth of political and judicial experience to the Court, having served in Congress, his state legislature, and the state supreme court. One of Pitney's principal specialties on the U.S. Supreme Court was tax law. His most famous tax opinion, still taught in law schools today, was *Eisner v. Macomber* (1920), in which the Court held that stock dividends were not taxable income within the meaning of the Sixteenth Amendment.

Yet it is for his decisions in labor cases that Pitney is best remembered. Pitney's opinions in a few high-profile cases earned him a reputation in some quarters as an antilabor reactionary. He wrote the majority opinion in *Coppage v. Kansas* (1915), declaring that a Kansas statute prohibiting an employer from requiring his employees to contract not to join a union impaired the employer's liberty of contract. His majority opinion in *Hitchman Coal & Coke Co. v. Mitchell* (1917) held that an employer was entitled to

an injunction prohibiting union organizers from recruiting employees working under such a contract. Pitney dissented in *Wilson v. New* (1917), which upheld a federal statute regulating the wages and hours of railroad workers, and he voted to strike down an Oregon law prescribing minimum wages for women in *Stettler v. O'Hara* (1917).

Yet for Pitney, the rights of property and contract frequently yielded to the police power of the state. For example, Pitney voted in *Bunting v. Oregon* (1917) and other cases to uphold maximum hour laws for both men and women; he voted to uphold statutes prohibiting payment of employees in company scrip and requiring at least semimonthly payment of employees in *Keokee Consolidated Coke Co. v. Taylor* (1914) and *Erie R. Co. v. Williams* (1914), respectively; and he dissented from the majority opinion in *Truax v. Corrigan* (1921), which struck down an Arizona statute prohibiting the issuance of injunctions against labor's peaceful picketing of an employer. Most notably, Pitney wrote a trilogy of opinions in 1917 upholding various state workmen's compensation statutes. In addition, he generally displayed a sympathetic attitude toward injured workers in cases arising under the Federal Employers Liability Act and the Safety Appliance Act.

Pitney's reputation as an antilabor judge was, however, enhanced by his opinions in *Paine Lumber Co. v. Neal* (1917) and *Duplex Printing Press Co. v. Deering* (1921). Dissenting in *Paine Lumber* and writing for the majority in *Duplex,* Pitney said that an employer whose product was being boycotted by a labor union was entitled to an injunction against the union under the antitrust laws. At the same time, however, he joined the Court's opinion in *Coronado Coal Co. v. United Mine Workers* (1922), refusing to invoke the Sherman Antitrust Act against the strike of a coal miners' local union. Moreover, throughout his tenure on the Court, Pitney applied the antitrust laws against business with equal zeal. Like many other justices of his period, Pitney brought to the Court the atomistic, competitive world view of nineteenth-century liberalism, which distrusted economic combinations of any kind.

Such liberalism did not yet fully embrace a solicitude for noneconomic civil liberties. Pitney consistently joined in the Court's opinions upholding convictions of wartime dissenters under the Espionage Act, and he wrote the majority opinion in *Pierce v.*

Mahlon Pitney

United States (1920), upholding the conviction of a clergyman for distributing an antiwar pamphlet. His opinion in *Frank v. Magnum* (1915) upheld against a due process challenge the conviction of a man whose trial had been dominated by a mob. Yet here again Pitney defies easy categorization. He joined the opinion creating the exclusionary rule for federal criminal cases in *Weeks v. United States* (1914); he voted to strike down a city ordinance mandating segregated housing in *Buchanan v. Warley* (1917); he joined the opinion in *Guinn v. United States* (1915), striking down Oklahoma's racially discriminatory scheme of eligibility; and his concurring opinion in *Newberry v. United States* (1921), contending for broad federal power to regulate primary elections for federal officials, anticipated the Court's invalidation of the racially discriminatory primary in the 1940s. Indeed, the complexity of Pitney's record exposes the folly of using vulgar political taxonomy as a means of explaining the judicial behavior of his era.

—*Barry Cushman*

BIBLIOGRAPHY

The standard biographical source on Pitney is Alan Ryder Breed, "Mahlon Pitney: His Life and Career—Political and Judicial" (unpublished senior thesis, Princeton University, 1932). David Levitan, "Mahlon Pitney—Labor Judge," *Virginia Law Review* 40 (1954): 733; and Michal R. Belknap, "Mr. Justice Pitney and Progressivism," *Seton Hall Law Review* 16 (1986): 381, offer valuable insights into Pitney's judicial career.

NOTEWORTHY OPINIONS

Coppage v. Kansas, 236 U.S. 1 (1915)

Frank v. Magnum, 237 U.S. 309 (1915)

Paine Lumber Co. v. Neal, 244 U.S. 459 (1917) (Dissent)

Hitchman Coal & Coke Co. v. Mitchell, 245 U.S. 229 (1917)

Eisner v. Macomber, 252 U.S. 189 (1920)

Pierce v. United States, 252 U.S. 239 (1920)

Duplex Printing Press Co. v. Deering, 254 U.S. 443 (1921)

Newberry v. United States, 256 U.S. 232 (1921) (Concurrence)

LEWIS FRANKLIN POWELL JR.

Birth: September 19, 1907, Suffolk, Virginia.

Education: Washington and Lee University, B.S., 1929; Washington and Lee University Law School, LL.B., 1931; Harvard Law School, LL.M., 1932.

Official Positions: Chairman, Richmond School Board, 1952–1961; member, 1961–1969, and president, 1968–1969, Virginia State Board of Education; president, American Bar Association, 1964–1965; president, American College of Trial Lawyers, 1968–1969.

Supreme Court Service: Nominated associate justice by President Richard Nixon, October 22, 1971, to replace Hugo L. Black, who had retired; confirmed by the Senate, December 6, 1971, by an 89–1 vote; took judicial oath January 7, 1972; retired June 26, 1987; replaced by Anthony Kennedy, nominated by President Ronald Reagan.

Death: August 25, 1998, Richmond, Virginia.

A reluctant nominee who had repeatedly removed himself from consideration, Lewis F. Powell Jr. ultimately yielded to the entreaties of Solicitor General Erwin Griswold, Attorney General John N. Mitchell, and Sen. Harry F. Byrd Jr., D-Va., in October 1971 to accept nomination by President Richard Nixon to succeed Justice Hugo L. Black. Given the ABA Committee on Federal Judiciary's highest rating as "the best qualified available," Powell was unanimously and enthusiastically approved by the Senate Judiciary Committee, and the full Senate followed suit briskly by confirming him 89–1 on December 6. The sole dissenter was a maverick one-term Democratic senator from Oklahoma, Fred R. Harris, who opposed the nominee as "an elitist who has never shown any deep feeling for little people."

Nothing could have been further from the truth. The sixty-four-year-old Powell, although to the manner born and destined to reap a very considerable fortune in his long and productive legal career, had dedicated significant aspects of his life to the socio-economic and political enhancement of the less fortunate; and his record on the bench amply and poignantly demonstrated his concerns for "little people." His jurisprudence was governed by his concern for fairness, compassion, equity, and a desire for genuine societal consensus. Powell quickly came to be regarded as the conscience of the Court on emotion-charged issues such as race and gender, as well as the omnipresent contentious questions of religion, suffrage, and criminal justice. He prevailed on the side of justice, as he interpreted it, by casting the decisive vote in 5–4 opinions in a host of closely contested cases. Law professor Herman Schwartz, writing in *The Nation,* called him "the most powerful judge of his time," and *U.S. News & World Report* noted that Powell's "courtly manner . . . failed to disguise the immense power he wielded."

Not all new members of the Court deliberately pattern themselves on predecessors, although often they evince jurisprudential commitments or practices that trigger comparisons. Powell, however, clearly and consciously endeavored to emulate the second John Marshall Harlan and, to a lesser degree, Felix Frankfurter. But Harlan was his judicial hero. Powell had known him personally, and he respected and admired him philosophically and jurisprudentially. In considerable measure, Powell's career on the Court reflected Harlan's approach to adjudication and intepretation—centrist, moderately to conservatively cautious, and historically aware. But given Powell's conscience-driven stances on pressing civil rights and liberties issues such as racial and gender discrimination and abortion, it is obvious that his jurisprudence was considerably less consistent than Harlan's. Powell more than occasionally violated Harlan's all but predictable embrace of Frankfurter's stance on judicial restraint, deference to the political branches of government, and all but commandment-like dedication to the principles of the separation of powers and of federalism. Powell's pragmatism, his "conscience" approach to adjudication, his bowing to a perceived need of "balancing of competing constitutional interests," were at least partly un-Harlanesque. His frequent ally, Justice Sandra Day O'Connor, captured that fact well when, in a *Harvard Law Review* tribute to Powell on his retirement, she contended that "at times he may have been willing to sacrifice a little consistency in legal theory in order to reach for justice in a particular case."

On the other hand, the Powell of the realm of economic proprietarian matters; of the suffrage, including reapportionment and redistricting; of criminal justice; of Tenth Amendment issues; of the reach of the federal interstate commerce power; and of access to the courts, especially the excessive utilization of the writ of *habeas corpus,* was vintage Harlan.

Arguably, the opinion for which Powell may well be most remembered is the "affirmative action" case of *Regents of the University of California v. Bakke* (1978), one that he himself viewed as seminal in the universe of racial discrimination. That he was given the assignment of writing the opinion would seem at first blush surprising, for although he had supported the central tenets of the public school desegregation case, *Brown v. Board of Education* (1954), he was no partisan of the all-out approach of activist jurists such as Earl Warren, William O. Douglas, or William J. Brennan Jr. As a gradualist and as a former state school board president, he consistently opposed mandated busing to achieve racial balance. And as a lifelong resident of Virginia, he was reluctant to have the judiciary become a (and certainly not *the*) leader in broad-scaled, imposed integration (as opposed to *Brown*-based desegregation). He expressed that view forcefully in pre-*Bakke* cases on race and the public schools such as *Keyes v. School District No. 1, Denver* (1973) and *Milliken v. Bradley* (1974), and in post-*Bakke* cases such as *Columbus Board of Education*

Lewis Franklin Powell Jr.

v. Penick (1979) and *Estes v. Metropolitan Branches of Dallas NAACP* (1980).

Yet Lewis Powell had had no truck with those in his state who had called for "massive resistance," a program designed to negate the holding in *Brown* and its implementation decision, *Brown II* (1955). Notwithstanding his place in Virginia's conservative establishment, he was opposed to continued segregation, and he publicly characterized the Byrd organization's anti–Supreme Court policy of "massive resistance" and "interposition" as "a lot of rot"—a strong statement for the normally kind and conciliatory Powell. It was he who mounted the opposition to those policies and ultimately succeeded in defeating them. As chairman of the Richmond Public School Board from 1952 to 1961, he provided the indispensable leadership for what proved to be the successful, disturbance-free desegregation of the city's public schools. It was not an easy task, but it earned him the support of the NAACP at the time of his appointment to the Court.

Bakke and its two components, known as *Bakke I* and *II*, reached the bench four years after the Court's failure to bite the proverbial bullet of "affirmative action/reverse discrimination" in *DeFunis v. Odegaard* (1974). In *DeFunis*, over Justice Douglas's eloquent dissent, the Court had mooted the issue because Marco DeFunis, already attending the University of Washington Law School under court order, would soon graduate. At the Court's conference following oral argument in *Bakke*, it became clear that neither Chief Justice Warren E. Burger nor Justice Brennan would be able to harness a majority, or even a plurality, for both aspects of the case. It fell to Powell to construct the two 5–4 opinions, and he accomplished it by creating an intriguing scenario. First, supported by the chief justice, John Paul Stevens, Potter Stewart, and William H. Rehnquist, he ruled that Alan Bakke—a rejected white applicant, who was more qualified to enter the University of California's Medical School at Davis than minority students who had been admitted on the basis of the 16 of 100 racial admissions quota established by the university— would have to be admitted because the racial quota

constituted a violation of the Fourteenth Amendment's equal protection clause. Powell's four supporters, however, wanted the issue to be settled on statutory grounds—namely, that Title VI of the 1964 Civil Rights Act specifically barred discrimination on the basis of race to any government-subsidized institution, such as the University of California. Powell, however, insisted on constitutional grounds, for he feared that accepting the statutory basis would too strictly harness affirmative action initiative and experimentation, which he favored and which he explained in the second prong of his opinion.

In that part (joined by Brennan, Byron White, Thurgood Marshall, and Harry Blackmun) Powell upheld on constitutional grounds—the same equal protection clause—the significant concept of using race as a plus. He admonished, however, that it could be used only when a university had a "substantial interest" in a diverse student body "that legitimately may be served by a properly devised admissions program involving the competitive consideration of race and ethnic origin." Therefore, over the angry objections of the Stevens group, the Powell-led majority in *Bakke II* in effect gave a green light to a host of innovative actions on the affirmative action/reverse discrimination front, and this despite his striking down of rigid racial or ethnic quotas.

The future proved the dissenters' dire prophecies to be generally correct. Indeed, Powell himself later proffered serious objections to the expansive interpretations given to what he had clearly intended to be a narrow holding. He was particularly disturbed by some of the Court's broad-gauged backing of the use of racial quotas in involuntary school busing—crying out in separate dissenting opinions in two leading cases, decided just one year after *Bakke*, that he was "profoundly disturbed" by this "creation of bad constitutional law." Yet although he had never intended his *Bakke* holdings to give warrant to what he now decried and although it is clearly possible to distinguish among and between sundry racial quota cases, there is no doubt that his Solomon-like resolution has resulted demonstrably in an embrace of *Bakke's* permissive, but very little of its restrictive, mandate.

Perhaps that is why, in an un-Harlanesque manifestation, Powell, in evident inconsistency with *Bakke*, supplied the decisive fifth vote in *United States v. Paradise* (1987), narrowly upholding an Alabama federal district judge's orders of 1983 and 1984 requiring Alabama to promote one black state trooper for each white state trooper until the state could develop an acceptable promotion procedure. Brennan's plurality opinion was joined in full by Marshall and Blackmun, with Stevens and Powell penning separate concurrences. Powell's vote in favor of promotion quotas represented a clear departure from his contrary stance in *Bakke*, a fact of which he seemed to take note by explaining that a rigid quota was proper in this instance because it was "short in duration" and the "effect of the order on innocent white workers is likely to be relatively diffuse." He also pointed to evidence that the state "had engaged in persistent violation of constitutional rights and repeatedly failed to carry out court orders." In effect, Powell's crucial vote meant that strict racial quotas in both promotion and hiring would likely henceforth be upheld by the U.S. Supreme Court—as indeed they have generally been to date, with some exceptions. Moreover, his careful balancing in *Bakke* was reaffirmed by the Court in *Grutter v. Bollinger* (2003), the University of Michigan Law School affirmative action case.

In no area of constitutional law and interpretation was Lewis Powell more influential than in that of First Amendment issues involving the religion clauses—"Congress shall make no law respecting an establishment of religion, or prohibiting the free exercise thereof." The first of these two phrases provided Powell with an unbroken string of triumphs. In the thirty leading cases that the Court decided during his tenure on the separation of church and state, he was on the winning side in every one of them. Nineteen of these found violations of the clause, and eleven sanctioned accommodation of sundry forms of government aid to religion. No other contemporary justice could boast of such a record. Fearful of the potentials of religio-political strife, he unfailingly sensed the appropriate stance for the good of society. Toward that end, and unlike several of his colleagues, he

firmly embraced Burger's triad requirement articulated in *Lemon v. Kurtzman* (1971) even more consistently and more closely than its own author. That triad, still in existence, albeit somewhat embattled, requires that aid to religion provided by the government: (1) must have a secular legislative purpose; (2) its principal or primary effect must be one that neither advances nor inhibits religion; and (3) it must not foster an excessive entanglement with religion.

Powell was therefore willing to join the 5–4 majority that sanctioned a Minnesota law providing for an across-the-board tax deduction of up to $500 for parents of all elementary and up to $700 of all secondary school children for bona fide educational expenses, identified as "tuition, secular textbooks and instructional materials, and transportation." Distinguishing *Committee for Public Education and Religious Liberty v. Nyquist* (1973), the majority opinion by Justice Rehnquist surprisingly gained Powell's vote, because Rehnquist claimed that the Minnesota law withstood separation of church and state challenges because it was "neutral" in design; it enabled parents of public school children as well as those in parochial and other private schools to avail themselves of the annual deduction (*Mueller v. Allen*, 1983).

On the other hand, Powell was in the 5–4 majority in *Grand Rapids School District v. Ball* (1985), which struck down a school board's authorization of public support for personnel, supplies, and materials furnished to private, mostly religious, schools. He joined another 5–4 majority in *Lynch v. Donnelly* (1984), which upheld the constitutionality of Pawtucket, Rhode Island's government-sponsored practice of displaying a crèche as part of a Christmas display in a park owned by a nonprofit corporation in the heart of the city's shopping district. But he was in full agreement with the 7–2 majority in *Edwards v. Aguillard* (1987), which declared unconstitutional Louisiana's "balanced treatment" statute that required the teaching of creationism to balance that of evolution in its public school curriculum. There, in a concurring opinion that was vintage Powell, he movingly elucidated Jefferson's and Madison's labors in quest of a full measure of religious freedom and an utter ban on religious establishment.

Justice Powell's prior experience as school board chairman provided him a well-informed and pragmatically enlightened viewpoint on the many delicate matters involving public education the Court faced during his tenure. His background and many written opinions on this issue established him as a kind of education authority on the nation's highest tribunal. This was true not only in the area of desegregation, where his careful balancing led to the flexible affirmative action compromise in *Bakke,* but in other areas of education law as well. His careful, case-by-case approach, and his distrust of broad, bright-line legal rules in complex subject areas, was as evident in Powell's education jurisprudence generally as it was in *Bakke.* But for all his balancing of competing constitutional interests in those cases, he never lost sight of the central purpose of the schools themselves, namely: education. He was particularly loath to let abstract principles interfere with the practical pursuit of this purpose.

Perhaps the most important of Powell's many written opinions in public school cases came in *San Antonio Independent School District v. Rodriguez* in 1973. The case was a class action challenging the manner in which the state of Texas supported its local public schools partly through local property taxes. The suit claimed that the state's method violated equal protection by discriminating against children in poorer districts. Powell's opinion for the 5–4 majority proceeded cautiously, demonstrating respect for established precedents, the traditional distribution of state and local authority, and the complexity of the subject. He refused to break new constitutional ground by declaring education a "fundamental right," and he declined the opportunity to launch a broad egalitarian legal revolution by declaring wealth a suspect classification. He was not persuaded that in an area as complex as education, levels of educational funding exactly paralleled levels of educational quality. Instead, Powell believed it was reasonable as well as constitutionally permissible for a state to establish a certain minimum funding level for local school districts, and to allow improvements beyond this level for those districts with the resources and the political will to fund them.

In reaching this conclusion, Powell sounded a common theme in his education jurisprudence. He emphasized that the kinds of complex decisions involved in state plans for funding education were precisely the kind that were most appropriate for resolution by those who have the local familiarity and the educational and administrative expertise to decide wisely. For this reason, these kinds of decisions were not appropriate for resolution by the courts, which, as he frequently pointed out, lack such familiarity and expertise.

Beyond obvious constitutional mandates and the manifest requirements of justice, Powell frequently showed a confirmed faith in the ways state or local authorities' political traditions had worked out their own modes of operation. He distrusted the ability of the federal courts to improve on these traditions by novel constitutional interpretations requiring broad federally mandated changes. His defense of local control over decisions affecting education was of a piece with his vigorous resistance to the court-ordered elimination of local political patronage and the old system of political parties.

Although Powell's jurisprudence in the education area emphasized local control, and although he did not agree that education was a fundamental right of constitutional proportions (and thus preserved his flexibility), he nevertheless adhered strongly to the position that an important function of the state is to make public education available to children. In his view, the balance of equal justice required that the state's responsibility for education weigh heavily against competing interests. He therefore concurred with Brennan's opinion for the Court in the remarkable case of *Plyler v. Doe* (1982), upholding the right of minor children of undocumented alien residents to receive a free public education, like all other children in Texas. Powell's concurrence, however, avoided the implication that education was a fundamental right, and instead emphasized the balancing of the practical concerns in the case, most especially the potential consequences of denying educational opportunity to thousands of children, many of whom were likely one day to become U.S. citizens. Powell also objected in principle to a state's penalizing resident children permanently because of their parents' immigration status, and he punctuated the point by indicating that he would take the same position if there were a similar complete denial of any other important state benefit, such as welfare assistance. He distinguished *Rodriguez* on this basis as well, pointing out that there was no question in that case of any child being denied an education, as there was in *Plyler*.

In yet another important equal protection case involving education, *Mississippi University for Women v. Hogan* (1982), Powell found himself in dissent when the Court ruled that a single-sex institution's admissions policy violated the Fourteenth Amendment's equal protection clause. Powell's opinion provides an important glimpse of his particular vision of the clause. For Powell, it was not a constitutional mandate for imposing an ideological uniformity of educational practice across the nation. Instead, it embodies a liberating spirit, which a wooden application would stultify. This view required a certain flexibility, careful attention to the facts of each case, and awareness of the potential consequences of a given decision. In *Rodriguez*, this had meant that beyond a basic minimum, the equal protection clause allows the state the freedom to experiment with educational funding formulas in accord with the will of the local electorate. Similarly, in his dissent in *Hogan*, Justice Powell stated that by

> applying heightened equal protection analysis to this case, the Court frustrates the liberating spirit of the Equal Protection Clause. It forbids the State from providing women with an opportunity to choose the type of university they prefer.

Instead of reading equal protection as both a protective and liberating aspiration, the Court had, in Powell's view, protected nothing of value by its decision, and had instead simply eliminated one desirable alternative for the women of Mississippi. In effect, the Court's decision violated Powell's jurisprudential principles by ignoring the facts in deference to an unenlightened and unfortunate application of theoretical legal principle.

Finally, as a former school administrator, Powell was always sensitive to intrusion into the affairs of school management by a judiciary ill-equipped to do so competently. He wrote the opinion of the Court in *Healy v. James* (1972) and agreed with his fellow justices in finding that a school administration had violated a student's First Amendment rights, but Powell trod very carefully. Instead of holding broadly that the school administrators had no authority to deny recognition to a controversial student organization, he proceeded "with special caution, recognizing the mutual interests of students, faculty members, and administrators in an environment free from disruptive interference with the educational process." He asserted that where the necessarily wide latitude for free expression threatens to collide with the equally necessary maintenance of order, the Constitution does not sweep one aside in deference to the other, but "strikes the required balance." Although it would not be unlawful for school administrators to deny recognition to the student group in order to maintain order and discipline, according to Powell, the school would have to make an adequate showing that the proposed organization would likely act beyond mere speech, by disrupting the school's ability to function in an orderly fashion. In the specific case at hand, no such showing had been made, and the case was remanded for further hearing.

In *Healy*, Powell struck a soon-to-be-classic balance, a balance that looked not only toward the Court's constitutional doctrine but also to the details of the case, the competing interests that would be affected by the decision, and the purpose of the institution under scrutiny. *Healy* was not an especially difficult case, but Powell showed in his opinion for the Court that he was no ideological warrior. His opinion foreshadowed his continued cautious and balanced jurisprudence, and his view that the most important elements in a given case lay not in any overarching theory, but in the facts and in the practical consequences involved.

Because the facts were paramount, Powell frequently expressed the view that those who were most intimately familiar with them should be allowed the latitude to make the relevant policies. For example, in his dissent in *Board of Education, Island Trees Free School District v. Pico* (1982), he found that the Court's interpretation of the First Amendment to prohibit a local school board from removing certain books from a school library was "a debilitating encroachment upon the institution of a free people." A school library, after all, was part of a school, and the people responsible for the education of the children should be allowed to decide what was appropriate for that education and what was not. Far from seeing it as government censorship, Powell viewed the book removal as an essential feature of educational policy. Therefore, like the selection of textbooks and the design of curriculums, these decisions should be for state and local school administrators to make, not for a federal court.

Similarly, Powell expressed the view that disciplinary regulations are best left to the states and local schools. He evidently did so not for ideological reasons, but because, on balance, he believed that such a disposition of responsibility would allow the schools to function best as educational institutions. He opposed requiring elaborate due process hearings prior to student suspensions, and he refused to extend the Eighth Amendment's cruel and unusual punishment prohibition to cover "paddling," or corporal punishment, in the public schools. Speaking for a 5–4 majority, as he did so often, Powell observed in *Ingraham v. Wright* (1977) that history, tradition, the common law, and the decisions of most of the states dealing with the question permitted corporal punishment and prohibited only the use of excessive or unreasonable force. Against this factual background, he was unwilling to find that the mere use of some corporal punishment in the schools was "cruel and unusual." Nor was he persuaded that the Constitution required additional procedural safeguards in administering nonexcessive punishment. It was certainly typical of his jurisprudence that in such cases Powell considered not only the rights of the persons who were complaining of harsh disciplinary measures, but also the important interests of other students and the local communities in an orderly school environment conducive to the school's purpose— providing students with an education.

Justice Powell's commitment to balancing societal and individual privileges and obligations under a written Constitution is appropriately illustrated by his approach to the universe of criminal justice. There, with an eye to the public's fear of burgeoning crime, he more often than not chose a "tough" stance on the side of what has often been characterized as the "peace forces" versus the "criminal forces." He frequently evinced sympathy with the difficult tasks confronting law enforcement authorities, perhaps recalling Justice Robert H. Jackson's admonition in a famed dissenting opinion that there is no obligation "to turn the constitutional Bill of Rights into a suicide pact" (*Terminiello v. Chicago*, 1949).

Profoundly committed to procedural due process and the basic prerogatives of a fair trial, he nevertheless would not embrace a jurisprudence that allowed defendants and their attorneys "to play a game with the courts." He was willing, for example, to provide his votes to trim excessive, multiple use of *habeas corpus* appeals arising from duly processed state cases such as *Stone v. Powell, Wolff v. Rice,* and *United States v. Janis,* all in 1976. Although not unsympathetic to claims of "unreasonable" searches and seizures (see his early contragovernment opinions for the unanimous Court in *United States v. United States District Court,* 1972, and similarly in *Almeida-Sanchez v. United States,* 1973), he had noteworthy limits. He was in the 1984 majorities that recognized a "good faith" limitation on the proscription of the introduction of illegally procured evidence in criminal proceedings, thereby narrowing the reach of the judicially created exclusionary rule in *United States v. Leon* and *Massachusetts v. Sheppard.* Similarly, he opted for the constitutionality of the composition of state juries that permitted convictions by 9–3, 10–2, and 11–1 verdicts in criminal cases (*Johnson v. Louisiana* and *Apodaca v. Oregon,* both 1972), while rejecting convictions by 5–0 and 5–1 juries in *Ballew v. Georgia* (1978) and *Burch v. Louisiana* (1979).

A personal opponent of capital punishment, he nevertheless remained true to his deferential approach to legislative power and consistently supported the option of capital punishment, provided due process of law had been followed. He was one of the four dissenters in *Furman v. Georgia* (1972), which seemed to outlaw capital punishment as then constituted, and he flayed the majority of five for what he viewed as a flagrant disregard of "the root principles" of precedent, judicial restraint, separation of powers, and federalism. His dissent proved to be prolegomenon to the Court's 7–2 reinstatement of the death penalty as a legitimate constitutional punishment, always provided the presence and application of due process of law. "We hold that the death penalty," Powell wrote in *Gregg v. Georgia* (1976) in the controlling opinion jointly written with Stewart and Stevens, "is not a form of punishment that may never be imposed, regardless of the circumstances of the offense, regardless of the character of the offenders, and regardless of the procedure followed in reaching the decision to impose it." To Powell, the death penalty was an appropriate "expression of society's moral outrage," if that was what the people's representatives determined to write into law. No matter what his personal feelings may have been on the subject, he recognized that retribution is not only permissible, but a fundamental resolve of an orderly societal rejection of "self-help to vindicate wrongs."

A close student of the purposes of the U.S. constitutional scheme, Powell remained acutely aware of its federal basis. He consistently and firmly rejected the notion that the Tenth Amendment ought to be regarded as a "mere truism," and that in the event of conflicts with the national government it should *a fortiori* be the loser. Indeed, time and again he admonished his colleagues and the polity that the Tenth Amendment was in effect not only part and parcel of the Bill of Rights, but an "essential" one. It was a view that, with but rare exceptions, he customarily shared during his time on the bench, especially with Rehnquist and O'Connor.

That view achieved a surprising victory in *National League of Cities v. Usery* (1976), in which a 5–4 majority led by Justice Rehnquist endeavored to establish a protective states' rights doctrine against federal intrusion. At best, the effort lasted a mere nine years, but it represented a view with which Powell was

wholly comfortable. In 1974 Congress had amended the Fair Labor Standards Act of 1938 to extend minimum wage and maximum hours provisions to cover all but a few employees of the fifty states and their sundry political substructures. A battery of cities and states joined the National League of Cities in a suit against the secretary of labor, alleging an unconstitutional application of Congress's power over interstate commerce to the detriment of the states' Tenth Amendment authority. The states had failed to prevail in the federal district court below, but they triumphed in the Supreme Court. Acknowledging the vast range of the congressional interstate commerce power, the majority nevertheless ruled that "there are limits upon the power of Congress to override state sovereignty even when exercising its otherwise plenary powers to tax or to regulate commerce which are conferred by Article I of the Constitution." And, the majority opinion concluded: "We hold that insofar as the challenged amendments operate to directly replace the States' freedom to structure integral operations in areas of traditional governmental functions, they are not within the authority granted Congress by Article I, § 8, cl. 3."

Justice Powell's satisfaction with the gravamen of the *Usery* decision would soon be vitiated, however, largely due to a rather rapid change of mind by Justice Blackmun, who had concurred separately in that case. Now, in two cases that dealt with the imposition of federal rules and procedures over state regulatory powers, one involving the monitoring of a state's gas and electric public utilities (*Federal Energy Regulatory Commission v. Mississippi*, 1982) and the other the question whether a state had a right to impose an age limit of sixty-five on its fish and game wardens (*EEOC v. Wyoming*, 1983), Powell found himself in dissent. He simply could see no constitutional justification for the expansive reading of the interstate commerce powers that drew majority approval in these two cases, without some clearly expressed congressional preemption.

Yet it would be the 5–4 vote in *Garcia v. San Antonio Metropolitan Transit Authority* (1985) that served as the vehicle for Powell's most passionate articulation of what he viewed as constitutionally applicable states' rights under the Tenth Amendment. Because of Blackmun's change of position, *Garcia* in effect overruled *Usery,* the slim majority holding that the federal government's minimum wage and overtime requirements for state and local employees was constitutionally justifiable under the commerce clause. Powell was neither amused nor persuaded by this dramatic, speedy overturning of the *Usery* precedent. Dissenting for himself, Chief Justice Burger, and Justices Rehnquist and O'Connor, Powell produced a major articulation for the federalist faith, commencing with the statement that he dissented because "I believe this decision substantially alters the federalist system embodied in the Constitution." He pointed out with passion that in the U.S. federal system "the States have a major role that cannot be pre-empted by the national government"; that the instant decision, like others of similar concerns, in effect reduced the Tenth Amendment to "meaningless rhetoric"; that it and its kindred rulings "eventually would eliminate the states as viable political entities." With uncharacteristic gloom he wrote a brief concluding separate paragraph that bears quoting:

> Although the Court's opinion purports to recognize that the States retain some sovereign power, it does not identify even a single aspect of state authority that would remain when the Commerce Clause is invoked to justify federal regulation. . . . As I view the Court's decision today as rejecting the basic precepts of our federal system and limiting the constitutional role of judicial review, I dissent.

Powell's defeat in *Garcia* was one of the few major losses he sustained during his distinguished career. His warm personality, wisdom, gentleness, and determination rendered him a highly successful consensus seeker and Court "marshaller," and he secured more victories in close cases than any of his contemporaries. To a considerable degree, that accomplishment materialized because, although instinctively deferential and a true devotee of the Frankfurter-Harlan jurisprudence of judicial self-restraint, he was willing to bend to attain what he viewed as necessities to achieve fairness and justice. He did not believe in "justice at any cost" or "justice *über alles,*" as did Douglas, Brennan, or Thurgood Marshall, but he felt that justice in certain realms was incumbent upon society, including such areas as affirmative action, abortion, aspects of privacy (within limits), and separation of church and state. Largely because of his willingness to bend principle in these and related "wrench" issues in order to do "the right thing," even if it had to be on an ad hoc basis, he carried the banner for progressive justice without in any sense pursuing a specific agenda, much less a radical one.

His instinct for what the people's conscience would both desire and need rendered him the pivotal justice during his years on the Court. The public, whether professional or lay, grew to understand the central role he played. He became without challenge the most popular and most revered member of the Burger Court. His decisive votes on the pressing issues of the day were the critical factor to the identity of his successor when age and ill health dictated his retirement in 1987. No wonder that the ensuing confirmation battle, initially involving U.S. Court of Appeals judge Robert H. Bork, would turn into one of the most protracted, and one of the ugliest, in two centuries of Supreme Court confirmation proceedings. The Powell "swing vote" devotees throughout the land feared that his successor would not be like the justice whom sundry retirement commentators labeled "the best justice." History may not accord him that accolade, but it assuredly will view him as a man of splendid acumen, towering influence, absolute integrity, a superb consensus builder, a consistent winner on fundamental issues, and a lovely, compassionate human being.

When all is said and done, Powell lived up to his views on "the role of the Court," which he had submitted as a prepared statement to the Senate Judiciary Committee's hearings on his confirmation in late 1971:

1. A belief in the separation of powers; that courts should not encroach on the prerogatives of the legislative and the executive branches.
2. A belief in the federal system of government.

3. An attitude of judicial restraint.

4. A respect for precedent, springing from a belief in the importance of continuity and predictability in the law.

5. The need to decide cases on the basis of law and fact before the court.

6. The responsibility of the Court to uphold the rule of law and to protect the liberties guaranteed by the Bill of Rights and of the Fourteenth Amendment.

Mr. Madison had expressed the fervent hope that the Supreme Court would be peopled by "giants." Lewis F. Powell Jr. proved to be one.

—Henry J. Abraham

BIBLIOGRAPHY

One of his former law clerks, John Calvin Jeffries Jr., wrote a superb biography of Powell: *Justice Lewis F. Powell, Jr.* (1994). For a fairly accurate prognosis of Powell's behavior on the Court at the time of his appointment, see A. E. Dick Howard, "Mr. Justice Powell and the Emerging Nixon Majority," *Michigan Law Review* 70 (1972): 445. Material on Powell can be found in Henry J. Abraham, *Justices, Presidents and Senators* (4th ed., 1999); Henry Abraham and Barbara A. Perry, *Freedom and the Court* (8th ed., 2003); Jacob W. Landynski, "Justice Lewis F. Powell, Jr., 'Balance Wheel of the Court,' " in Charles M. Lamb and Stephen C. Halpern, eds., *The Burger Court: Political and Judicial Profiles* (1987); and David M. O'Brien, *Storm Center: The Supreme Court in American Politics* (7th ed., 2005). The enduring importance of *Bakke* is explored in John Jeffries Jr., "Bakke Revisited," *Supreme Court Review* (2003): 1.

Among the many articles, see Gerald Gunther, "A Tribute to Lewis F. Powell, Jr.," *Harvard Law Review* 101 (1987): 409; Sandra Day O'Connor, "A Tribute to Lewis F. Powell, Jr.," *Harvard Law Review* 101 (1987): 409; Symposium: "Hon. Lewis F. Powell, Jr.," *University of Richmond Law Review* (1977); and Melvin I. Urofsky, "Mr. Justice Powell and Education: The Balancing of Competing Values," *Journal of Law and Education* 13 (1984): 581.

A special and affectionate portrait of Powell can be found in a book written by his first law clerk, J. Harvey Wilkinson III, *Serving Justice: A Clerk's View* (1974).

NOTEWORTHY OPINIONS

United States v. United States District Court, 407 U.S. 297 (1972)

Healy v. James, 408 U.S. 169 (1972)

Furman v. Georgia, 408 U.S. 238 (1972) (Dissent)

San Antonio Independent School District v. Rodriguez, 411 U.S. 1 (1973)

Keyes v. School District No. 1, Denver, 413 U.S. 189 (1973) (Concurrence and partial dissent)

National League of Cities v. Usery, 426 U.S. 833 (1976) (Concurrence)

Gregg v. Georgia, 428 U.S. 153 (1976)

Ingraham v. Wright, 430 U.S. 651 (1977)

Regents of the University of California v. Bakke, 438 U.S. 265 (1978)

Columbus Board of Education v. Penick, 443 U.S. 449 (1979) (Dissent)

Plyler v. Doe, 457 U.S. 202 (1982) (Concurrence)

Board of Education, Island Trees Free School District v. Pico, 457 U.S. 853 (1982) (Dissent)

Mississippi University for Women v. Hogan, 458 U.S. 718 (1982) (Dissent)

Garcia v. San Antonio Metropolitan Transit Authority, 469 U.S. 528 (1985) (Dissent)

United States v. Paradise, 480 U.S. 149 (1987) (Concurrence)

Edwards v. Aguillard, 482 U.S. 578 (1987) (Concurrence)

STANLEY FORMAN REED

Birth: December 31, 1884, Minerva, Kentucky.

Education: Kentucky Wesleyan University, A.B., 1902; Yale University, A.B., 1906; legal studies, University of Virginia and Columbia University (no degree); graduate studies, University of Paris, 1909–1910.

Official Positions: Representative, Kentucky General Assembly, 1912–1916; general counsel, Federal Farm Board, 1929–1932; general counsel, Reconstruction Finance Corporation, 1932–1935; special assistant to attorney general, 1935; solicitor general, 1935–1938.

Supreme Court Service: Nominated associate justice by President Franklin D. Roosevelt, January 15, 1938, to replace George Sutherland, who had retired; confirmed by the Senate, January 25, 1938, by a voice vote; took judicial oath January 31, 1938; retired February 25, 1957; replaced by Charles E. Whittaker, appointed by President Dwight D. Eisenhower.

Death: April 2, 1980, New York City.

Stanley Forman Reed entered this life at the end of December 1884, and did not depart it until after his ninety-fifth birthday, making him the longest-lived of all members of the Supreme Court. Described by those who knew him as a man of courtesy and geniality, he once told Justice Potter Stewart that he would not want to live his life over again, as "it could not possibly be as good the second time." But despite his good nature, Justice Reed was among the least likely of his brethren to favor rulings to broaden the rights of criminal defendants or protect citizens' constitutional rights against federal government encroachment.

Reed's judicial temperament was decisively shaped by his professional life prior to his elevation to the Court in 1938. After earning bachelor degrees at Kentucky Wesleyan University and Yale, Reed dabbled in state politics, serving a term in the Kentucky legislature as a Wilsonian progressive and helping to manage a congressional campaign for his friend Fred Vinson. He also built a thriving law practice in Maysville, Kentucky, based upon a select group of wealthy corporate clients. Yet it was only when he embarked on government service that Reed really made a name for himself. As counsel to the Federal Farm Board from 1929 to 1932, and as head of the Reconstruction Finance Corporation under Presidents Herbert Hoover and Franklin Roosevelt, Reed was part of a generation of federal administrators who believed passionately in the desire and the capacity of the government to improve American society and American life. He was serving as solicitor general when President Roosevelt appointed him to replace retiring justice George Sutherland. In marked contrast to Sutherland, Reed brought to the bench the characteristically buoyant faith of the New Dealer. It was a sensibility that would color Reed's opinions throughout his nineteen years on the Court.

In cases involving the scope of Congress's regulatory powers, therefore, Reed was usually prepared to defer to the government. The tone was set in one of his very first opinions, *United States v. Rock Royal Cooperative* (1939), in which Reed, writing for a sharply divided Court, found that the commerce clause permitted Congress to fix agricultural prices even where the transaction was complete before any interstate commerce took place. Another representative case was *Gray v. Powell* (1941), in which the petitioner questioned a finding by the Department of the Interior that it was subject to the price stabilization provisions of the Bituminous Coal Act. In rejecting this claim, Reed showed how reluctant he was to interfere with an administrative determination:

> Unless we can say that a set of circumstances deemed by the Commission ... [sufficient for its findings] is so unrelated to the tasks entrusted by Congress to the Commission as in effect to deny a sensible exercise of judgment, it is the Court's duty to leave the Commission's judgment undisturbed.

The important words here are "tasks entrusted by Congress." Where administrative agencies seemed to fail to live up to their congressional mandates, Reed was quick to uphold legislative intent. In *Power Commission v. Panhandle Eastern Pipeline Co.* (1949), the Court faced the issue of whether the Power Commis-

sion could, under the Natural Gas Act, void the lease of certain land containing natural gas deposits. In ruling against the commission, Reed found that nothing in the statute supported Justice Felix Frankfurter's view that this was a transaction that was subject to Congress's control. For Reed, a determination of what Congress meant to do was often dispositive of the issue involved, whether that issue was constitutional or one of identifying administrative prerogatives. Perhaps the best example of this aspect of Reed's jurisprudence is his majority opinion in *United States v. Kahringer* (1953), in which the Court permitted Congress to tax wagering activities that were traditionally the subject of state police powers. For Reed, it was "hard to understand why the power to tax should raise more doubts because of indirect effects than other federal powers." Few justices were as dependable a friend of government intervention in the economy as Reed.

Despite this record, Reed is usually considered a conservative. The reason for this view lies in that same progovernment temperament that influenced him in favor of progressive legislation. Reed joined the majority in *Korematsu v. United States* (1944), upholding the government's wartime mass internment of Japanese Americans. He wrote the Court's opinion in *United Public Workers v. Mitchell* (1947), upholding the Hatch Act, which barred federal employees from certain types of political activity. *United Public Workers* contains a revealing passage that neatly summarizes Reed's notion of the relationship

Stanley Forman Reed

between the Court and the other two branches of the federal government:

> Congress and the President are responsible for an efficient public service. If in their judgment, efficiency may best be obtained by prohibiting active participation by classified employees in politics as party officers or workers, we see no constitutional objection.

When President Harry S. Truman issued his order seizing the nation's steel mills, Reed joined Chief Justice Vinson in dissenting from the Court's opinion in *Youngstown Sheet & Tube Co. v. Sawyer* (1952), which declared that order unconstitutional. Reed recognized few limits to what Congress or the president might do, as long as they could articulate a justification based on national security. In writing for the majority in *Carlson v. Landon* (1952) that the Justice Department could detain Communist aliens without bail pending a determination of their deportability, Reed saw no need for the government to show any likelihood that the alien would skip bail or engage in espionage before the hearing. "The Attorney General's exercise of discretion [is] presumptively correct and unassailable except for abuse." He also joined Justice Tom C. Clark's dissent in *Cole v. Young* (1956) to the effect that federal employees ought to be subject to dismissal at any time "in the interests of national security," whether or not they were occupying sensitive positions at the time. And in *Joint Anti-Fascist Committee v. McGrath* (1951), Reed penned an unusually lengthy dissent asserting the power of the Justice Department to designate an organization as "Communist" for the purpose of determining the loyalty of federal employees, without any procedure for such an organization to contest that designation. In fact, throughout his tenure on the Court, Reed was a consistent supporter of the government and its antisubversion programs.

These habits of deference to federal authorities do not, however, support characterizing Reed as a believer in judicial restraint. Although he showed himself to be the archetypal New Dealer when a dispute involved the authority of the federal govern-

ment, he was somewhat less likely to uphold state or local regulations in the face of constitutional attack. When, for example, the issue involved prior restraints of free speech, Reed's was a dependable voice in favor of broadening First Amendment protections. In *Winters v. New York* (1948), the Court had to decide whether New York State could constitutionally bar the sale of sensationalistic "true crime" magazines. Reed found for the majority that such publications, though "of no possible value to society," were "as much entitled to the protections of Free Speech as the best of literature." The statute was struck down as unconstitutionally vague, provoking a dissent from Frankfurter, who called for much the same sort of deference to legislative judgment that Reed customarily displayed when construing federal law. Similarly, in *Joseph Burstyn, Inc. v. Wilson* (1952), Reed joined Clark's ruling bringing films under the protection of the First Amendment, and he wrote a brief concurrence stating that he saw no reason for banning from public view the movie in question.

Perhaps most compelling, Reed dissented from Frankfurter's majority opinion in *Beauharnais v. Illinois* (1952), in which the Court upheld an Illinois statute that prohibited the dissemination of material that portrayed certain classes of people as, among other things, "lacking in virtue." Reed, always a careful reader of statutes, had a field day with the imprecision of such phrasing, asking "are the tests of the Puritan or the Cavalier to be applied, those of the city or the farm, the Christian or the non-Christian, the old or the young?" In view of its rigorous insistence that states should not be in the business of banning the content of speech, however hateful it might be, the *Beauharnais* dissent may take on more significance as time goes on.

Moreover, as befitted a New Dealer, and in keeping with his roots in rural Kentucky, Reed was a dependable friend of the First Amendment rights of organized labor. In *Carpenters Union v. Ritter's Café* (1942), the Court upheld a Texas state court injunction against union members picketing in front of a restaurant that was refusing to hire union contractors. Reed could see no reason for such a restraint on picketing, writing that "so long as civil government is able to function normally for the protection of its citizens, such a limitation on Free Speech is unwarranted."

Here was the rub: where a litigant's free speech rights seemed to bear a distinct menace to the well-being of the public at large, Reed was often willing to uphold state and local enactments burdening that speech. He wrote the majority opinion in *Kovacs v. Cooper* (1949), upholding a local ordinance banning the broadcasts of "loud and raucous" messages via loudspeakers mounted on trucks on the grounds that people in their homes and businesses had a right to be protected from irritating noises. He also joined the majority in *Feiner v. New York* (1951), which held that police had acted constitutionally in arresting a rabble-rousing speaker for disorderly conduct, and in *Breard v. Alexandria* (1951), permitting traveling salesmen to be constitutionally banned from going door-to-door. As Francis William O'Brien has pointed out, such cases evince a concern on Reed's part for balancing the rights of the community against First Amendment guarantees to individuals.

O'Brien's view seems to find support in Reed's record on opinions addressing the First Amendment freedom of religion. In this area, Reed was a fairly consistent advocate of the right of communities to impose reasonable restrictions on religious activity for the good of the citizenry as a whole. In *Jones v. Opelika* (1942), Reed's majority opinion upheld a series of municipal regulations from around the country placing licensing fees on the sale or distribution of all printed matter, including religious tracts passed out door-to-door by Jehovah's Witnesses. For Reed, the sovereign power of state bodies "to ensure orderly living" justified such ordinances, as long as the transactions regulated were more in the nature of commercial activities than religious rites as such.

This commercial/religious ritual distinction may have seemed viable to Reed, but it suffered a major blow during the very next term, with Justice William O. Douglas's majority opinion in *Murdock v. Pennsylvania* (1943), in which a municipal ordinance obliging fund-raising Jehovah's Witnesses to pay the same licensing fee charged to all other solicitors was struck down as a denial of the plaintiffs' First Amendment freedoms. To Douglas, the licensing fee amounted to "a charge for the enjoyment of a right granted by the Federal Constitution." In his dissent, Reed fastened on what he felt to be the injustice of the majority's position removing from religious groups their obligation to help contribute to the maintenance of "the government which provides the opportunity for the exercise of their liberties." No "wall of separation" for Reed: religious bodies had their responsibilities to the general commonwealth, just like everyone else. It was no surprise when Reed was chosen to write the majority opinion in *In re Summers* (1945), which upheld the right of the Illinois bar to refuse membership to a conscientious objector whose scruples would not have permitted him to fulfill his statutory duty to serve in the state militia in time of emergency.

One of the most illuminating of Reed's pronouncements on the subject of religious liberty occurs in *Illinois ex rel. McCollum v. Board of Education* (1948), in which the Court struck down as a violation of the establishment clause a local public school program in which students could voluntarily receive religious instruction on school property and during school hours. Here the issue was no longer one of obliging religious bodies to bear their fair share of community burdens; rather, the controversy revolved around the extent to which these bodies could be prohibited from taking part in the life of the community's secular institutions. Reed, in the uncomfortable position of lone dissenter, argued eloquently that the long tradition of religious activity in America demanded that all faiths should have the opportunity to participate fully in the community: "Devotion to the great principle of religious liberty should not lead us into a rigid interpretation of the constitutional guarantee that conflicts with the accepted habits of our people." The important point for Reed remained the avoidance of any rigid wall of separation that would unnecessarily prohibit religious groups from either shouldering the burdens or enjoying the benefits of residence in an orderly, democratic society.

Was Reed, then, a communitarian? His First Amendment opinions can certainly be read to suggest as much, and to the extent that a tendency to subsume individual rights or needs to the greater good of the community was a part of the ethos of the New Deal, Reed probably merits the label. Yet his principles in this regard were not especially deep. We have already noted his reluctance to admit people to equal standing in the community whom the government for whatever reason had deemed "subversive," and he does not seem to have harbored a sense, so carefully developed by the Warren Court, that a healthy community demanded a zealous attention of law enforcement agencies to the constitutional rights of the accused.

In fact, Reed was less likely than other members of the Court to look favorably on claims that the confessions of criminal defendants had been coerced. His opinion in *Gallegos v. Nebraska* (1951), in which the defendant had been held in solitary conditions without bail for seven days before he finally confessed, is remarkable for the deference it shows to the deputy sheriff's testimony that no coercion was used. And in *McNabb v. United States* (1943), a case in which federal agents had clearly violated the law by not bringing the defendants into the presence of a magistrate prior to their confessions, Reed wrote a dissent that criticized Frankfurter's majority opinion for relying on this "technicality"; for Reed, the jury's determination that the confessions had been voluntary should have been dispositive. Although Reed often had in mind the need to protect the health of the community, his notion of what precisely that "health" consisted of did not always accord with more modern understandings.

Perhaps the best known of Reed's opinions in the area of constitutional rights was *Adamson v. California* (1947), in which the Court faced the issue of whether the Fourteenth Amendment incorporated the Fifth Amendment so as to bind it upon the states. The California statute under review permitted judges and attorneys to comment to the jury on the decisions of defendants not to testify in their own behalf. Reed, writing for the 5–4 majority, refused to apply the Fifth Amendment to invalidate this practice, relying on the sanctity of the federal system and on what

he believed to be the reasonableness of permitting the prosecution to bring defendants' failure to take the stand to the jury's attention. *Adamson* represented one of the last instances in which the Court interpreted the Fourteenth Amendment so narrowly, and it is a good example of Reed's characteristic lack of sensitivity to the rights of the accused. This stance might have arisen from his experiences as a practicing lawyer, which were largely limited to various sorts of corporate litigation and government service rather than the field of criminal law.

Given his professional background and his origins in the rural Kentucky of the late nineteenth century, it may be surprising that Reed had one of the best civil rights records on the Stone and Vinson Courts. He wrote the majority opinions in *Smith v. Allwright* (1944), invalidating the whites-only Texas Democratic primary, and in *Morgan v. Virginia* (1946), striking down a Virginia statute requiring segregated seating on buses passing through the state. Yet these opinions do not evince any deep-seated belief in integration on Reed's part. The result in *Smith* was mandated by the clear fact that the primary was conducted in large part by the state of Texas; it is doubtful that Reed would have voted as he did had the election been a purely private or informal affair. As for *Murphy,* Reed predicated his ruling squarely on the commerce clause and the inconvenience of rearranging bus seating every time the vehicle crossed the Virginia line, rather than on equal protection or due process grounds.

That Reed was no principled foe of segregation is demonstrated by his reaction to the momentous case of *Brown v. Board of Education of Topeka* (1954). After many months of studying the question of segregation's effects on the educational capabilities and job performances of African Americans, Reed still could not bring himself to believe that segregation was equivalent to discrimination and therefore a violation of the equal protection clause. Only after Vinson died and Reed realized that he would he the only dissenter in the ruling that Chief Justice Earl Warren was planning to hand down did Reed decide to join the majority. Warren had urged the justices to bring the important sanction of unanimity to a ruling that was bound to alter forever the fabric of American life. For Frankfurter, this act of selflessness on Reed's part was "the most lasting service" to the country that he performed during his tenure on the Court.

Reed retired from the bench in 1957, at the age of seventy-two. He went on to serve President Dwight D. Eisenhower for a brief term as chairman of the Civil Rights Commission, after which he spent the remainder of his days in his beloved Maysville, Kentucky. After Reed's death in 1980, Chief Justice Warren Burger wrote a memorial tribute in which he lauded Reed's judicial temperament and his personal generosity, noting that Reed had sent him a bottle of Kentucky bourbon every Christmas since his accession to the bench in 1969. In the end, Reed may be considered to have been the last of the New Dealers, embodying the goodness of heart and occasional intellectual inconsistency that this appellation implies.

—*Daniel L. Breen*

BIBLIOGRAPHY

John D. Fassett, a former Reed law clerk, has written a sympathetic biography, *New Deal Justice: The Life of Stanley Reed of Kentucky* (1994). An older but still useful treatment of his jurisprudence is F. William O'Brien, *Justice Reed and the First Amendment: The Religion Clauses* (1958), which views Reed as a pluralist. There is also an unpublished dissertation by Mark I. Fitzgerald, "Justice Reed: A Study of a Center Judge" (University of Chicago, 1950). Reed's relationship with Frankfurter is explored in two articles: John Fassett, "The Buddha and the Bumblebee," *Journal of Supreme Court History* 28 (2003): 165; and B. C. Canon, "Justice Frankfurter and Justice Reed: Friendship and Lobbying on the Court," *Judicature* 78 (1995): 224. Posthumous tributes to Reed can be found in volume 69 of the *Kentucky Law Journal*.

For general works on the Court in this era that examine Reed's role, see Jan Palmer, *The Vinson Court Era: The Supreme Court's Conference Votes* (1990); Michal Belknap, *The Supreme Court Under Earl Warren, 1953–1969* (2004); and Melvin I. Urofsky, *Division and Discord: The Supreme Court Under Stone and Vinson, 1941–1953* (1997). Some Reed papers reside in the Kentucky Historical Society in Lexington.

NOTEWORTHY OPINIONS

United States v. Rock Royal Cooperative, 307 U.S. 368 (1939)

Carpenters Union v. Ritter's Café, 315 U.S. 722 (1942) (Dissent)

Smith v. Allwright, 321 U.S. 649 (1944)

United Public Workers v. Mitchell, 330 U.S. 75 (1947)

Adamson v. California, 332 U.S. 46 (1947)

Illinois ex rel. McCollum v. Board of Education, 333 U.S. 203 (1948) (Dissent)

Winters v. New York, 333 U.S. 507 (1948)

Kovacs v. Cooper, 336 U.S. 77 (1949)

Beauharnais v. Illinois, 343 U.S. 250 (1952) (Dissent)

WILLIAM HUBBS REHNQUIST

Birth: October 1, 1924, Milwaukee, Wisconsin.

Education: Stanford University, B.A., 1948, M.A., 1948; Harvard University, M.A., 1950; Stanford University Law School, LL.B., 1952.

Official Positions: Law clerk to Supreme Court justice Robert H. Jackson, 1952–1953; assistant U.S. attorney general, Office of Legal Counsel, 1969–1971.

Supreme Court Service: Nominated associate justice by President Richard Nixon, October 22, 1971, to replace John M. Harlan, who had retired; confirmed by the Senate, December 10, 1971, by a 68–26 vote; took judicial oath January 7, 1972; nominated chief justice by President Ronald Reagan, June 20, 1986, to replace Warren E. Burger, who had retired; confirmed by the Senate, September 17, 1986, by a 65–33 vote; took judicial oath September 26, 1986; replaced as associate justice by Antonin Scalia; served until September 3, 2005; replaced by John G. Roberts Jr., nominated by President George W. Bush.

Death: September 3, 2005, Arlington, Virginia.

William Rehnquist grew up in Milwaukee and was educated at Stanford University, Harvard University, and Stanford Law School. After graduation, he served as a law clerk to Justice Robert H. Jackson and then entered into private practice in Phoenix, Arizona. In 1969, through his association with Deputy Attorney General Richard Kleindienst and his work as a Republican Party official in Phoenix, Rehnquist came to Washington as assistant attorney general for the Office of Legal Counsel. From this position, he was nominated to the Supreme Court where, in 1972, he was sworn in along with Lewis F. Powell. When he was sworn in as chief justice of the United States in 1986, he became only the third sitting justice to be so elevated.

Despite widespread disagreement with Rehnquist's views among many legal academics, few dis-pute that he was among the ablest and most learned justices ever to serve on the Court. With Powell's replacement of Hugo Black, the Republicans gained control of the Court for the first time since the New Deal, and they did not relinquish it during Rehnquist's tenure. Although Rehnquist was not able to achieve his most ambitious goals, such as overruling *Roe v. Wade* (1973) and *Miranda v. Arizona* (1966), he remained a highly influential member of the majority party throughout his tenure. He thus avoided the fate of Justices William Brennan and Thurgood Marshall, who, with their party in the minority, languished in dissent during their last years on the Court.

Justice Rehnquist's vision of the nation's constitutional structure was firmly rooted in the words and history of that document. He based it on three doctrines: strict construction of the Constitution and statutes, judicial restraint, and federalism or states' rights. He summarized this vision in a 1976 speech at the University of Texas:

> It is almost impossible . . . to conclude that the [Founding Fathers] intended the Constitution itself to suggest answers to the manifold problems that they knew would confront succeeding generations. The Constitution that they drafted was intended to endure indefinitely, but the reason for this well-founded hope was the general language by which national authority was granted to Congress and the Presidency. These two branches were to furnish the motive power within the federal system, which was in turn to coexist with the state governments; the elements of government having a popular constituency were looked to for the solution of the numerous and varied problems that the future would bring.

In other words, as he said in his dissent in *Trimble v. Gordon* (1977), neither the original Constitution nor the Civil War amendments made "this Court (or the federal courts generally) into a council of revision, and they did not confer on this Court any authority to nullify state laws which were merely felt to be inimical to the Court's notion of the public interest."

During his early years on the Court, despite the Republican majority, Rehnquist was often in lone dissent, espousing a view of states' rights and limited federal judicial power that many regarded as anachro-

nistic. For example, in *Weber v. Aetna Casualty and Surety Co.* (1972), *Sugarman v. Dougall* (1973), and *Frontiero v. Richardson* (1973), he resisted the view of the other eight members of the Court that the equal protection clause of the Fourteenth Amendment applied to, and required heightened scrutiny of, state-sponsored discrimination against illegitimate children, resident aliens, and women, respectively. Rather, he insisted that the Fourteenth Amendment was limited in its application solely to racial discrimination. In the criminal procedure area, he urged that *Mapp v. Ohio* (1961), which applied the exclusionary rule to the states, be overruled, but although he was clearly hostile to *Miranda*, he never directly argued that it should be overruled.

Still, even in his first years, Rehnquist was less likely to be in dissent than the liberal bloc of Brennan, Marshall, and William O. Douglas. Moreover, some of Rehnquist's early dissents, such as in *Memorial Hospital v. Maricopa Co.* (1974), *Cleveland Board of Education v. La Fleur* (1974), and *Fry v. United States* (1975), were to form the basis for majority opinions in the years to come. As Prof. Laurence Tribe of Harvard observed, "Even in lone dissent, he has helped define a new range of what is possible."

The 1975 term saw Rehnquist come into his own as the leader of the ever-shifting conservative wing of the Court. In that term he wrote the opinion in *Paul v. Davis* (1976), holding that reputation, standing alone, was not a constitutionally protected interest subject to vindication under Section 1983 of the Civil Rights Act

William Hubbs Rehnquist

of 1871, which allows an injured party to sue a government official. He also wrote for the 5–4 majority in *National League of Cities v. Usery* (1976), ruling that the Tenth Amendment limited Congress's power to regulate the states under the commerce clause; and for the 5–3 majority in *Rizzo v. Goode* (1976), holding that "principles of federalism" forbade federal courts from ordering a restructuring of state agencies in response to Section 1983 violations.

National League of Cities used an expansive reading of the Tenth Amendment to strike down a federal statute that regulated the wages and hours of state government employees, despite the fact that such regulation was concededly within Congress's commerce power. It showed that, when faced with a choice between judicial restraint/strict constructionism and states' rights, Rehnquist was prepared to aggressively defend the latter. The potential significance of this case was eroded by subsequent Court majorities, which first refused to follow and then overruled *National League of Cities* in *Garcia v. San Antonio Metropolitan Transit Authority* (1985).

Nevertheless, the Tenth Amendment continued to exert some limitation on Congress, as illustrated by *Gregory v. Ashcroft* (1991), holding that a federal statute will not be interpreted to restrict the autonomy of state and local governments unless Congress has plainly stated its intent to do so. Going further, in *New York v. United States* (1992), the majority held that the Tenth Amendment prohibited Congress from requiring a state to regulate private sector commercial activity in a case involving the disposal of radioactive waste. And, in *Printz v. United States* (1997), the Court invalidated that portion of the Brady Handgun Violence Prevention Act that required local police departments to do background checks on potential handgun buyers.

In 1995 and again in 2000, Rehnquist was able to strike further blows in favor of states' rights in *United States v. Lopez* (1995) and *United States v. Morrison* (2000), this time by limiting Congress's power under the commerce clause. In *Lopez,* the Court, for the first time since the 1930s, struck down an act of Congress for going beyond the commerce power. The Court,

per Rehnquist, held that the Gun-Free School Zones Act, which prohibited, among other things, the possession of a gun within a certain distance of a school, exceeded Congress's power because such possession did not "substantially affect" interstate commerce. In *Morrison,* the Court, again with Rehnquist writing, held the same for the Violence Against Women Act, despite congressional findings that such violence *did* have a substantial impact on commerce.

At the time, it was widely believed that these two cases were the first shots in a "federalism revolution," in which a major devolution of power from the federal government to the states was under way. This belief was tempered, however, by the Court's failure to strike down any additional acts of Congress on commerce clause grounds in the ensuing five years. Then, in *Gonzales v. Raich* (2005), a majority held that Congress had the power to prohibit possession of marijuana for medical purposes, despite a state statute allowing such possession. The majority did this despite the lack of any obvious connection with interstate commerce, much less a "substantial effect." Rehnquist joined Justice Sandra Day O'Connor in dissent, but it seemed that the federalism revolution had, at least for the time being, ground to a halt. Nevertheless, *Lopez* and *Morrison* stand as reminders to Congress that its commerce power is not unlimited, and it is likely that the doctrine established in those cases will be used again.

Rehnquist was more receptive to congressional assertions of power under the spending power. In *South Dakota v. Dole* (1987), Rehnquist, writing for the Court, upheld a condition on federal highway funds that required the states to prohibit the purchase of alcohol by anyone under the age of twenty-one. Similarly, in *New York v. United States,* Rehnquist joined the Court in upholding that portion of the radioactive waste statute that rewarded states for adhering to federal rules.

When dissenting, Rehnquist made his most telling points opposing the majority's efforts to enact "desirable" social policy with little support from the constitutional or statutory provisions they purport to be interpreting. An example is *United Steelworkers of*

America v. Weber (1979). In that case, Kaiser Aluminum Company and the United Steelworkers had devised a "voluntary" affirmative action plan under which half of available positions in an on-the-job training plan would be reserved for blacks. Excluded solely because he was white, Brian F. Weber filed suit based on Title VII of the Civil Rights Act of 1964. The statute provides that "it shall be unlawful for an employer . . . to fail or refuse to hire . . . any individual . . . because of such individual's race." The statute goes on to say that its provisions are not be interpreted "to require any employer . . . to grant preferential treatment to any individual or to any group because of the race . . . of such individual or group." Moreover, as a unanimous Court had recognized only three years before in *McDonald v. Santa Fe Trail Transportation Co.* (1976), the "uncontradicted legislative history" showed that Title VII "prohibited racial discrimination against the white petitioners . . . upon the same standards as would be applicable were they Negroes." Nevertheless, a 5–2 majority in *Weber* reversed the lower courts and found that discrimination against whites was not within the "spirit" of Title VII and consequently was not prohibited. In a bitter dissent, Rehnquist accused the majority of Orwellian "newspeak" and concluded that "close examination of what the Court proffers as the spirit of the Act reveals it as the spirit of the present majority, not the 88th Congress."

Similarly, in *Roe v. Wade,* in which the majority based a woman's right to an abortion on a constitutional "right to privacy" that arose not from the terms but from the "penumbras" of the Bill of Rights, Rehnquist wrote: "To reach its result, the Court necessarily has had to find within the scope of the Fourteenth Amendment a right that was apparently completely unknown to the drafters of the Amendment." Whatever the wisdom of the policies announced in these cases, it is difficult to disagree that Rehnquist's reading of the textual material in question was the more accurate one; that is, even if the drafters of the Bill of Rights or of the Fourteenth Amendment had agreed that there was a right to privacy that exceeded the precise terms of the Bill of Rights, they surely would not

have agreed that it included a constitutional right to an abortion.

It is ironic that Rehnquist, often condemned as a right-wing ideologue, was, in *Weber* and *Roe,* as in many other cases, advocating a view of the Court's role that had previously been vigorously advanced by the progressive members of the Court. In *Morehead v. New York ex rel. Tipaldo* (1936), for example, the dissenting opinion of Justice Harlan F. Stone, joined by Justices Louis Brandeis and Benjamin Cardozo, declared:

> It is not for the Court to resolve doubts whether the remedy by regulation is as efficacious as many believe, or better than some other, or is better even than blind operation of uncontrolled economic forces. The legislature must be free to choose unless government is rendered impotent. The Fourteenth Amendment has no more imbedded in the Constitution our preference for some particular set of economic beliefs, than it has adopted in the name of liberty the system of theology which we happen to approve.

If Rehnquist was not altogether successful in exempting states from *congressional* control, he often prevailed in his efforts to exempt state courts from *federal court* interference. To do this, he took the 1971 decision in *Younger v. Harris,* which counseled restraint by federal courts in enjoining ongoing state criminal proceedings, and extended it. In *Rizzo v. Goode* (1976) and *Fair Assessment in Real Estate Assn., Inc. v. McNary* (1981), he held that "principles of federalism" limited a federal court's ability to enjoin not just the judicial branch, but also the executive branch of state governments, and that this comity limitation was not confined to criminal proceedings. Nor, as he held in *Doran v. Salem Inn, Inc.* (1975), was it necessary that a state criminal proceeding predate a federal action for the federal action to be barred by principles of comity.

Another area in which Rehnquist enjoyed considerable success was in state action. The Constitution limits only action by government, not private individuals. Prior to 1972, however, the Court had taken a very broad view of who was a state actor and therefore subject to lawsuits alleging violations of the Constitution. In a series of cases beginning with *Moose Lodge No. 107 v. Irvin* (1972), Rehnquist wrote majority opinions finding that a variety of defendants, including private clubs with state liquor licenses, public utilities, and state-regulated nursing homes, generally were not state actors and could not be subject to lawsuits based on enforcement of constitutional rights. One common criticism of Rehnquist is that, in striking down acts of Congress under the commerce clause, for example, he stood for "judicial supremacy." His state action decisions, limiting the authority of the courts to interfere with the actions of private citizens and businesses, are inconsistent with this critique.

In criminal procedure, his views were driven by the same narrow view of the role of courts in a federal system, and he frankly admitted that his goal when he came on the Court was to "call a halt to a number of the sweeping rulings of the Warren Court in this area." In this he generally was joined by the other Nixon appointees and by Justice Byron White. Consequently, during the 1970s and 1980s the Court issued a series of opinions aimed at making it easier for the police to investigate crime and harder for defendants to upset their convictions because of police investigatory errors. For example, in *Rakas v. Illinois* (1978), the Court, speaking through Rehnquist, made it more difficult for a defendant to establish standing to litigate search and seizure violations, and in *United States v. Robinson* (1973), the scope of police searches incident to arrest was expanded. In *United States v. Leon* (1984), Rehnquist joined White's decision establishing a "reasonable good faith" exception to the exclusionary rule in search warrant cases. Rehnquist did not seek to overrule the fundamental rights to trial by jury, counsel, and appeal that had been applied to the states by the Warren Court, even though he consistently voted to limit them. Despite the feeling of most Court watchers that the Burger Court had *not* dismantled the major criminal procedure protections of the Warren Court, including the *Miranda* requirements and the application of the exclusionary rule to the states in

Mapp v. Ohio, in a 1985 interview, Rehnquist pronounced himself satisfied that the law was "more evenhanded now than when I came on the Court."

In 2000 Rehnquist surprised many by writing the opinion for the 7–2 majority in *Dickerson v. United States*, upholding *Miranda v. Arizona* against a 1968 congressional statute that purported to overrule it. This decision, however, said more about respect for precedent and resistance to congressional attempts to trench on the Court's constitutional turf than it did about Rehnquist's sudden agreement with *Miranda*. Indeed, Rehnquist showed his thinking four years later when he joined Justice Clarence Thomas in *United States v. Patane* (2004), holding that the physical "fruits" of a *Miranda* violation could be used against a defendant. But he dissented in *Missouri v. Seibert* (2004), in which the majority held that a second confession, obtained after the police deliberately violated *Miranda* in getting the first confession, must be excluded as a "fruit" of the original *Miranda* violation.

Dickerson also provides a good example of the power, albeit limited, of the chief justice over the rest of the Court. When the chief is in the majority after a case is discussed in conference, he assigns the majority opinion. If the chief is in dissent, the senior justice in the majority assigns the opinion. Had Rehnquist dissented in *Dickerson*, the result would have been 6–3, instead of 7–2, in favor of upholding *Miranda*. Justice John Paul Stevens, a long-time defender of *Miranda*, would have been the senior justice in the majority and likely would have assigned the opinion to himself. Stevens would have written a very broad opinion reaffirming the constitutional validity of *Miranda*, making it difficult to allow the fruits of *Miranda* violations to be admitted in future cases. By voting with the majority and assigning the opinion to himself, Rehnquist could write a narrow opinion that reaffirmed the bare *Miranda* holding while preserving the qualifications that the Court had established over the previous thirty-five years. In particular, *Dickerson* reaffirmed *Oregon v. Elstad* (1985), a decision from which Stevens had vociferously dissented. *Elstad* held that a nondeliberate violation of *Miranda* did not require suppression of a subsequent, warned, confession. *Elstad* provided the basis for *Patane*'s subsequent undercutting of *Miranda*.

In the area of federal *habeas corpus* for state prisoners, Rehnquist and his conservative colleagues advanced the dual goals of limiting federal court interference with state court adjudications and enhancing the finality of criminal convictions. The most significant holding in this line of cases is *Wainwright v. Sykes* (1977). Rehnquist, writing for a six-justice majority, held that failure to raise an issue at the appropriate stage of a state criminal proceeding barred the federal courts from considering that issue on *habeas corpus,* absent a showing of good cause for the failure and prejudice to his case by the defendant. *Sykes* overruled *Fay v. Noia* (1963), which had allowed new issues to be raised on federal *habeas* unless they had been deliberately bypassed by the defendant in state proceedings.

Sykes represents a significant diminution of the power of federal courts to interfere with state convictions. *Sykes* was reaffirmed in 1989 in *Teague v. Lane,* in which O'Connor, writing for the Court, held that "new" rules of criminal procedure generally should not apply retroactively on *habeas corpus* to defendants whose state convictions became final before the new law was established.

Then, in *Brecht v. Abrahamson* (1993), a 5–4 majority held, per Rehnquist, that for a prisoner to have his conviction reversed by a federal court on a writ of *habeas corpus,* as opposed to direct appeal, the burden is on the prisoner to show not only that there were constitutional errors at his trial, but also that those errors had a "substantial and injurious effect or influence in determining the jury's verdict." As White noted in dissent, the practical impact of this holding in most cases of "trial error" is that "a state court determination that a constitutional error . . . is harmless beyond a reasonable doubt has in effect become unreviewable by lower federal courts by way of habeas corpus."

Consistent with his federalism/judicial restraint stance, Rehnquist was the Court's leading advocate of a narrow interpretation of the restrictions imposed on states by the establishment clause of the First Amendment: "Congress shall make no law respecting an establishment of religion." He set forth his view in detail in a dissenting opinion in *Wallace v. Jaffree* (1985), in which the majority struck down Alabama's statutorily required "moment of silence" for "meditation or voluntary prayer" in public schools. Rehnquist rejected the "wall of separation between church and state" principle of *Everson v. Board of Education* (1947) that had been the Court's touchstone for forty years. Claiming that history did not support this rigid interpretation of the First Amendment, Rehnquist argued that the view of James Madison, the "architect of the Bill of Rights," as to the function of the establishment clause was simply "to prohibit the establishment of a national religion, and perhaps to prevent discrimination among sects." He did not see it as requiring neutrality on the part of the government "between religion and irreligion." Consequently, Rehnquist would have found no defect in a state statute that openly endorsed prayer, much less a "moment of silence."

Rehnquist's rejection of the "wall of separation" generally left him in dissent in the religion cases, with the exception of cases involving aid going directly to students. In *Zelman v. Simmons-Harris* (2002), a majority, per Rehnquist, agreed that vouchers to pay for private school tuition, granted directly to parents, and used for secular as well as religious schools, did not run afoul of the establishment clause, even though most of the vouchers went to religious schools. Similarly, in *Zobrest v. Catalina Foothills School District* (1993), Rehnquist spoke for a 5–4 majority in holding that the establishment clause did not prohibit a deaf student in a Catholic school from receiving the assistance of a state-funded sign language interpreter—just as a public school student would—even though that aide would be interpreting religious instruction and services for the student. As the dissent noted, this was the first time the Court had authorized "a public employee to participate directly in religious indoctrination."

In a similar vein, in *First National Bank v. Bellotti* (1978), Rehnquist, in sole dissent, refused to recognize a First Amendment free speech right for corporations, and in *Virginia State Board of Pharmacy v. Virginia*

Citizens Consumer Council (1976), he refused to recognize a First Amendment right for consumers to receive commercial information, even though he eventually gave up and agreed to First Amendment protection for commercial speech. Nevertheless, in the First Amendment area, as in all others, he generally gave the legislative branch, whether state or federal, greater freedom to plot its own course than his colleagues did.

Notre Dame law professor Richard Garnett has explained Rehnquist's narrow view of First Amendment protections in terms that apply to his attitude toward the scope of constitutional rights in general:

Rehnquist's work does not reflect skepticism or hostility toward the core values protected by the free speech clause, as some have charged, but instead reveals a careful appreciation of the fact that the translation and reduction of so many policy questions to free speech problems comes at a cost. After all, as the civic, social, and political territory covered by the free speech clause grows, the amount shrinks that is governed democratically and experimentally by the people and their representatives or that is left under the direction of private persons, groups, and institutions. One implication of the free speech takeover, Rehnquist seems to be warning us, is that difficult policy and other decisions depend increasingly on judges' evaluation of the abstract weight or worthiness of the government's interests, rather than on deliberation, compromise, and trial-and-error by and among citizens and politically accountable public officials.

When Chief Justice Warren Burger announced his retirement in June 1986, President Ronald Reagan nominated Rehnquist as his replacement and set off a firestorm of protest among liberals. Sen. Edward Kennedy, D-Mass., denounced Rehnquist as having an "appalling record on race," and liberal columnists branded him a right-wing extremist. A concerted effort was undertaken to find something in his past that might provide a basis for defeating the nomination. Assorted allegations were raised concerning contacts with black voters when he was a Republican Party official in Phoenix, the handling of a family trust, a memo he had written to Justice Jackson as a law clerk urging that the "separate but equal" doctrine not be overruled in *Brown v. Board of Education* (1954), and a racially restrictive covenant in the deed to his Phoenix house. The Senate correctly perceived that these allegations were either unproven or, if true, were "ancient history" and irrelevant to his fitness for the post of chief justice. Significantly, no serious charge of misconduct was raised as to Rehnquist's fourteen and a half years as an associate justice on the Supreme Court. In the end, after much sound and fury, he was confirmed, 65–33. If the 1975 term had seen Rehnquist "arrive" as a major force on the Court, it was the 1987 term, his second year in the center chair, that saw him mature as chief justice. In a speech given in 1976, he had discussed the role of chief justice, citing Charles Evans Hughes as his model:

Hughes believed that unanimity of decision contributed to public confidence in the Court. . . . Except in cases involving matters of high principle he willingly acquiesced in silence rather than expose his dissenting views. . . . Hughes was also willing to modify his own opinions to hold or increase his majority and if that meant he had to put in disconnected thoughts or sentences, in they went.

Following his own advice, in the 1987 term he achieved a high level of agreement with his fellow justices, ranging from 57.6 percent with Thurgood Marshall to 83.1 percent with Anthony Kennedy. His administrative abilities in the 1987 term won the praise of his colleague Harry Blackmun, who deemed him a "splendid administrator in conference." For the first time in years, the Court concluded its work prior to July 1. During that term, Rehnquist showed that he could be flexible, joining with the more liberal justices to subject the dismissal of a homosexual Central Intelligence Agency employee to judicial review and to support the First Amendment claims of *Hustler* magazine to direct off-color ridicule at a public figure.

Most significant, in *Morrison v. Olson* (1988) he wrote for a 7–1 majority upholding the special prosecutor legislation against a challenge by the Reagan administration. In a decision termed an "exercise in folly" by the lone dissenter, Antonin Scalia, Rehnquist held that the appointments clause was not violated by Congress's vesting the power to appoint a special prosecutor in a Special Division consisting of three U.S. court of appeals judges. Nor did the act violate separation of powers principles by impermissibly interfering with the functions of the executive branch. Although the act may have theoretical flaws, Rehnquist was correct in perceiving that a truly independent prosecutor was a necessary check on the many abuses of executive power, including criminal violations, that were occurring during the latter years of the Reagan administration. In upholding a check on those abuses, Rehnquist's opinion gained the concurrence of a substantial majority of his colleagues. His performance that term led the *New York Times*, which had opposed his elevation to chief justice, to praise him with faint damnation: "While he is certainly no liberal, or even a moderate, his positions are not always responsive to the tides of fashionable opinion among his fellow political conservatives."

Although the 1987 term showed that Rehnquist could be flexible as chief justice, that term and those that followed also showed him, in most instances, leading the Court (to the extent that any justice can be said to "lead" the Court) in a conservative direction. For example, in a series of close cases decided in the 1987 term ranging across the landscape of the Bill of Rights, the Court denied an equal protection challenge to user fees for school busing, denied a claim by Indians that a Forest Service logging road through a national forest would interfere with their free exercise of religion, denied food stamps to striking workers, allowed censorship of a school newspaper, upheld federal tort immunity for defense contractors, and allowed illegally discovered evidence to be used against a criminal defendant under the "independent source" exception to the exclusionary rule.

The following term showed that Rehnquist was still prepared to be flexible. For example, in *City of Canton v. Harris* (1989), he joined an opinion by White holding that a city could be liable for damages

under Section 1983 of the Civil Rights Act for poor training of police officers and that a new trial was not barred. Rehnquist chose not to join O'Connor, Kennedy, and Scalia, who, in a concurring and dissenting opinion, would have dismissed the plaintiff's case because she could not have met the "deliberate indifference" standard of proof. Such flexibility was rarely called for, however, as the conservatives prevailed most of the time.

In the leading case of the term, *Webster v. Reproductive Health Services* (1989), Rehnquist, consistent with his views of states' rights and strict construction of the federal Bill of Rights, joined by four others, upheld a Missouri statute that forbade public funding and the use of public hospitals for abortions. Rehnquist observed that "our cases have recognized that the due process clauses generally confer no affirmative right to government aid, even where such aid may be necessary to some life, liberty or property interests of which the government itself may not deprive the individual." Because a state is under no constitutional obligation to provide public hospitals at all, it is free to condition their use as it wishes. This notion, that beneficiaries of public largess must accept the "bitter [restrictions] with the sweet" was a hallmark of Rehnquist's jurisprudence since he first expressed it in *Arnett v. Kennedy* in 1974. He was, however, unable to convince O'Connor that it was time to abandon the "rigid" framework of *Roe v. Wade*, which gave a woman an absolute right to an abortion during the first trimester of pregnancy, despite his drafting of a compromise opinion that continued to recognize a limited constitutional right to abortion.

Subsequently, in *Planned Parenthood v. Casey* (1992), the Court did abandon the rigid trimester framework of *Roe* in favor of a test that considered whether or not a given regulation placed an "undue burden" on a woman's constitutional right to an abortion. This reaffirmation of the constitutional right to an abortion of a nonviable fetus left the chief justice largely in dissent, returning to the position that *Roe* should be overruled outright.

Rehnquist was not successful in getting a majority of the Court to overrule *Roe*, but substantial inroads have been made into that holding. *Casey,* in which the Court reaffirmed the state's power to prohibit abortions of viable fetuses, is a good example. In *Casey,* the Court upheld a twenty-four-hour waiting period and an "informed consent" restriction on abortions as well as a parental consent limitation on abortions for minors. The only provision struck down as unduly burdensome was a spousal notification requirement. This relatively tolerant attitude toward many state regulations, as well as the Court's position, stated by Rehnquist in *Rust v. Sullivan* (1991), which upheld the right of government to place restrictions on, or withhold, public funding for abortions, is a far cry from the broad right apparently conferred by *Roe,* as Blackmun's dissenting opinions consistently emphasized.

An interesting feature of Rehnquist's tenure as chief justice was the decline in overall activity of the Court. From the 1980 to the 1988 terms, the Court never decided fewer than 159 cases by written opinion, with the number ranging as high as 216 in the 1981 term. In the 1989 term, this number dropped to 151, and in the 1990 term to 129. By the 1999 term it had dropped to 81, and it was at 83 in the 2004 term. The downward movement took place even though the Court's docket steadily increased during this period, from 4,280 cases disposed of in the 1980 term, to 5,825 in the 1991 term, to more than 7,000 by 2004.

This trend cannot be attributed to any action or inclination by the chief justice alone; any time four justices vote to hear a case, certiorari will be granted, whatever the view of the chief. Nor can the trend be fully explained by the overwhelming Republican dominance of the Court (no more than two Democrats on the Court since 1990), because such a partisan Court might be eager to undo the work of prior Courts, and the Republicans have held this majority since 1972.

Because Republicans, at least in theory, generally take a dim view of government activism, it does seem likely that the predominantly moderate Republican appointees would be less likely to want to assert their will on the rest of the country, even if it took the form of reversing liberal trends. As the joint opinion of Justices O'Connor, Souter, and Kennedy in *Planned Par-*

enthood of Southeastern Pennsylvania v. Casey (1992) made clear, an allegiance to the principle of *stare decisis* is part of the conservative credo, even if a justice may disagree with an earlier case.

Another possible reason for a diminution of the Court's activity could be that Supreme Court action depends of the composition of the lower courts. This supposition is supported by the fact that only about 20 percent of all cases in which certiorari was granted from 1980 to 1992 were affirmed by the Court. Because the purpose of a certiorari grant is overwhelmingly to vacate or reverse a lower court decision, it follows that general agreement with the lower courts should lead the Supreme Court to grant fewer writs of certiorari. With Republicans dominating the lower federal benches for the last twenty or so years, it is perhaps not surprising that the Supreme Court has found less with which to disagree.

Rehnquist's level of activity declined even more than that of the Court itself. In the 1980 through 1982 terms Rehnquist averaged forty opinions (including dissents and concurrences) per term. By contrast, in the 1989 through 1992 terms he averaged twenty-one opinions annually and wrote only fourteen in the 2003 term. He continued to write his share of majority opinions, but the dissents and concurrences diminished; for example, in the 1979 term he wrote twenty-six dissenting opinions compared to four in the 1990 term and three in 2003. Thus he was much less likely to disagree with the majority than he was at the beginning of his tenure. He cast a dissenting vote in nineteen cases in the 1990 term compared to forty-nine in 1981, and compared to forty-two for Stevens in the 1990 term. Also, the marked diminution in his dissenting votes after he became chief justice may reflect his view, noted earlier, that the chief should attempt to exercise a moderating influence and dissent as infrequently as conscience will allow. Indeed, the number of Rehnquist's dissenting votes dropped off sharply after he became chief. Finally, it is likely that, after twenty years on the Court, he may have felt less need to express his individual views on particular cases, especially as he was also tasked with the additional duties the chief justice performs.

Although Rehnquist's judicial philosophy undoubtedly sprang from a staunch political conservatism, the principles of federalism and strict construction frequently prevailed, even when they led to a "liberal" result. For example, in *Pruneyard Shopping Center v. Robins* (1980), he wrote the opinion upholding state constitutional provisions that allowed political demonstrators to solicit signatures for a submission to the United Nations in a shopping center. He recognized "the authority of the state to exercise its police power or its sovereign right to adopt in its own Constitution individual liberties more expansive than those conferred by the Federal Constitution." Similarly, in *Hughes v. Oklahoma* (1979), he dissented when the Court invalidated a state's attempt to preserve its wildlife. And in *Pennell v. City of San Jose* (1988), he upheld the city's rent-control ordinance in the face of a due process challenge by landlords. In numerous criminal cases, such as *United States v. Muze* (1974) and *Ball v. United States* (1985), he voted to reverse criminal convictions on the ground that the government had failed to prove that the defendant's conduct had violated the terms of the (strictly construed) statute.

Despite an overall highly successful effort by Rehnquist to move the Court toward strict construction, judicial restraint, and states' rights, he did not prevail in a variety of important areas. As noted, his views as to the First Amendment's protection of commercial speech and the establishment clause did not generally win out. He could not overrule *Roe v. Wade*, although he succeeded in narrowing it considerably. Likewise, he was unsuccessful in overturning the two landmarks of the criminal procedure revolution, *Mapp v. Ohio* and *Miranda v. Arizona*. His strong states' rights views were rejected in *Gonzales v. Raich* (2005). He failed to strike down the use of affirmative action in a law school's admissions program in *Grutter v. Bollinger* (2004). And he could not resist the Court's invalidation of homosexual sodomy prohibitions in *Lawrence v. Texas* (2003). Still, you "can't win 'em all," and Rehnquist won more than he could have reasonably anticipated when he joined the Court in 1972.

Despite the national debate on abortion, it is unlikely that the country ever will be confronted with a constitutional problem of the magnitude of the legal discrimination against blacks, and the closely related problem of police abuse of the rights of criminal suspects, that faced the Warren Court. Consequently, it is also unlikely that the judicial activism displayed by the Warren Court to deal with these problems will be morally necessary or politically desirable in the future. Rehnquist's view of a more limited role for the federal Constitution—and therefore for the federal courts—in the politics of the nation may well be the wave of the future. Having reached its highest point in the 1960s, the rights revolution—already dying during the Burger Court years—terminated with the appointment of William Rehnquist as chief justice of the United States. It will not recur unless the Court swings further than it has in the opposite direction.

Rehnquist died on September 3, 2005, after suffering from thyroid cancer for an extended period. Despite his illness, his death was unexpected. The preceding July he had issued a press release indicating that he had no plans to retire and would resume his duties as chief justice in the fall. John G. Roberts, who had once clerked for Rehnquist, succeeded him as chief justice at the opening of the October 2005 term.

—*Craig M. Bradley*

BIBLIOGRAPHY

Rehnquist's views on the Court, the Constitution, and the role of the chief justice can be found in his book, *The Supreme Court* (2d ed., 2001); and in two articles, "Chief Justices I Never Knew," *Hastings Constitutional Law Quarterly* 3 (1976): 637; and "The Notion of a Living Constitution," *Texas Law Review* 54 (1976): 693.

Books that look at the broad spectrum of Rehnquist's career and jurisprudence are Craig M. Bradley, ed., *The Rehnquist Legacy* (2006); Peter Irons, *Brennan vs. Rehnquist: The Battle for the Constitution* (1994); and Sue Davis, *Justice Rehnquist and the Constitution* (1989).

Books analyzing the Rehnquist Court, rather than Rehnquist himself, include: Mark V. Tushnet, *A Court Divided: The Rehnquist Court and the Future of Constitutional Law* (2005); Earl Maltz, ed., *Rehnquist Justice: Understanding the Court's Dynamic;* Herman Schwartz, ed., *The Rehnquist Court: Judicial Activism on the Right* (2002); and

David G. Savage, *Turning Right: The Making of the Rehnquist Supreme Court* (1992). See also Symposium: "The Rehnquist Court," *Northwestern University Law Review* 99 (Fall 2004): 1–381.

NOTEWORTHY OPINIONS

Moose Lodge No. 107 v. Irvin, 407 U.S. 163 (1972)

Frontiero v. Richardson, 411 U.S. 677 (1973) (Dissent)

Cleveland Board of Education v. LaFleur, 414 U.S. 632 (1974) (Dissent)

Rizzo v. Goode, 423 U.S. 362 (1976)

Paul v. Davis, 424 U.S. 693 (1976)

National League of Cities v. Usery, 426 U.S. 833 (1976)

Trimble v. Gordon, 430 U.S. 762 (1977) (Dissent)

Wainwright v. Sykes, 433 U.S. 72 (1977)

First National Bank v. Bellotti, 435 U.S. 765 (1978)

United Steelworkers of America v. Weber, 443 U.S. 193 (1979) (Dissent)

Pruneyard Shopping Center v. Robins, 447 U.S. 74 (1980)

Wallace v. Jaffree, 472 U.S. 38 (1985) (Dissent)

South Dakota v. Dole, 483 U.S. 203 (1987)

Morrison v. Olson, 487 U.S. 654 (1988)

Rust v. Sullivan, 500 U.S. 173 (1991)

Brecht v. Abrahamson, 507 U.S. 619 (1993)

United States v. Lopez, 514 U.S. 549 (1995)

United States v. Morrison, 529 U.S. 598 (2000)

Dickerson v. United States, 530 U.S. 428 (2000)

Zelman v. Simmons-Harris, 536 U.S. 639 (2002)

JOHN GLOVER ROBERTS JR.

Birth: January 27, 1955, Buffalo, New York.

Education: Harvard University, B.A., summa cum laude, 1976; Harvard Law School, LL.B., magna cum laude 1979.

Official Positions: Law clerk to Justice William Rehnquist, 1980–1981; special assistant to attorney general, 1981–1982; associate White House counsel, 1982–1986; principal deputy U.S. solicitor general, 1989–1993; judge, U.S. Court of Appeals for the District of Columbia Circuit, 2003–2005.

Supreme Court Service: Nominated associate justice by President George W. Bush, July 28, 2005, to replace Sandra Day O'Connor, who announced her retirement on July 1, 2005; nomination withdrawn, September 6, 2005; nominated chief justice by President Bush, September 6, 2005, to replace Chief Justice William H. Rehnquist, who had died; confirmed by the Senate, September 29, 2005, by a 78–22 vote; took judicial oath September 29, 2005.

When John G. Roberts Jr. presided over his first session of the Supreme Court as chief justice on October 3, 2005, he looked as if he had been in the job for years. He was comfortable and confident and quickly joined in questioning the advocates before him in oral argument.

For Roberts, more than for almost every justice who served before him, the Supreme Court was familiar territory. Not only had he served as a law clerk to his predecessor, William Rehnquist, twenty-five years earlier, but also he had stood before the Supreme Court thirty-nine times as an oral advocate, answering instead of asking the questions. His entire life, some said, was preparation for becoming chief justice.

The seventeenth chief justice of the United States was born in New York State. His family moved to Long Beach, Indiana, when he was in fourth grade, and Roberts still considers himself a Hoosier. His father, an executive at Bethlehem Steel, sent young

John to private schools, including La Lumiere, a Catholic boarding school for boys. He was captain of the football team and quickly outpaced fellow students in academics. And as President George W. Bush pointed out when he nominated him, Roberts worked during the summers at his father's steel plant—not just in the white-collar offices.

Roberts entered Harvard College in 1973 with sophomore status and graduated summa cum laude in 1976. It was at Harvard, friends said, that he grew more conservative as he became disenchanted with protests against the Vietnam War. Roberts went on to Harvard Law School, where he became known as one of the school's hardest-working and most brilliant students. He served as managing editor of the *Harvard Law Review*. But fellow students also said Roberts was modest and soft-spoken, not overly impressed with himself. More conservative than most of his fellow Harvard law students, Roberts was not politically active. After graduating magna cum laude in 1979, Roberts eschewed private law practice, serving instead as a law clerk to Henry Friendly, a respected conservative judge on the U.S. Court of Appeals for the Second Circuit in New York City. Friendly was known for writing his own opinions and asking his clerks to test his positions in give-and-take discussions in his chambers.

From July 1980 to June 1981 Roberts clerked for Associate Justice William Rehnquist. Copies of memorandums Roberts wrote while a clerk, contained in Justice Harry Blackmun's papers, were unremarkable, betraying no political slant but solid legal analysis.

Few blockbuster cases were decided that term, except for *Dames & Moore v. Regan* (1981), when the Court was asked to ratify actions taken by former president Jimmy Carter as part of the agreement that ended the Iran hostage crisis. Carter had agreed to terminate suits against Iran and attachments of Iranian property, and several U.S. companies and banks challenged his power to do so. The case was handled on an expedited basis.

John Glover Roberts Jr.

Rehnquist wrote the unanimous decision, and some Court law clerks from that term say Roberts was instrumental in its drafting. The decision upheld the president's actions and gave broad deference to executive power based on several federal laws and on congressional acquiescence. "Where, as here, the settlement of claims has been determined to be a necessary incident to the resolution of a major foreign policy dispute between our country and another, and where, as here, we can conclude that Congress acquiesced in the President's action, we are not prepared to say that the President lacks the power to settle such claims," Rehnquist's opinion states. The ruling has been criticized as being far too deferential to presidential power in the absence of laws that authorize the president's actions.

Following his year with Rehnquist, Roberts worked from 1981 to 1986 for President Ronald Reagan's administration, first in the Justice Department and then in the White House, as the conservative legal revolution was getting under way. In the weeks before his September 2005 confirmation hearing, numerous writings by Roberts that were archived at the Reagan Presidential Library were made public. They showed him to be a confident young government attorney with conservative views. In one 1981 memo, for example, he referred to the "so-called" right to privacy.

While serving as a special assistant to Attorney General William French Smith, Roberts was part of the team advising then-Supreme Court nominee Sandra Day O'Connor as she prepared for her confirmation hearing. In a 1981 memorandum that was revealed during Roberts's confirmation hearing, he advised O'Connor not to respond to questions asking her views on hypothetical cases or real, nonpending cases. "The proposition that the only way senators can ascertain a nominee's views is through questions on specific cases should be rejected."

In 1986 Roberts left government service to become an associate, then a partner at Hogan and Hartson, a large and respected Washington, D.C., firm. Three years later he argued his first case before the Supreme Court, a double jeopardy case titled *United States v. Halper* (1989). He was appointed by the Court to argue in support of the lower court ruling. The Court ruled unanimously in his favor.

Roberts returned to government service in October 1989 as the principal deputy solicitor general under Solicitor General Kenneth Starr. That position is often described as the "political deputy," meaning that the person filling the position is a political appointee who comes and goes with administrations, unlike the other three or four deputies in the office who are career civil servants. It also means that the person is generally in tune with the views of the administration that hires him. Some former holders of the job say they had to fight the impression that they were White House moles who enforced political or ideological orthodoxy in an office that has a long-standing tradition of independence.

Those who worked with Roberts for the three years he had the position say that he was not a political enforcer. In fact, as others have argued, Roberts insisted that his presence as the political appointee served to insulate the civil servants in the office from political pressure. Roberts went on to explain that he, rather than the career deputies, would take the angry calls from others in the administration questioning the solicitor general's position in a given case. At a 2002 Brigham Young University conference on the role of the solicitor general, Roberts said, "It was my job, I thought, to explain to this person that although this particular position . . . may be causing you some political heartburn, here is why we have to do it: It is compelled by our obligation to represent long-standing institutional interests of the United States."

Roberts did affix his name to controversial positions during his tenure in the solicitor general's office. In the 1991 case *Rust v. Sullivan*, which involved the abortion-related advice that could be given at federally funded clinics, Roberts's brief in passing said, "We continue to believe that *Roe v. Wade* was wrongly decided and should be overruled. . . . The Court's conclusion in *Roe* that there is a fundamental right to an abortion . . . finds no support in the text, structure, or history of the Constitution."

It was in his position at the solicitor general's office that Roberts honed his advocacy skills, arguing fifteen cases before the Supreme Court. He became well-known for his straightforward manner and thorough knowledge of the cases he argued. He would prepare for argument by writing on index cards hundreds of questions he thought he might be asked, and then shuffling the cards so he could develop smooth transitions between subjects. Roberts has a calming tone of voice that seemed to reassure cautious justices that whatever position he was asking them to take was a small step, not a major departure from precedent.

That style suited Roberts's unassuming, soft-spoken nature, but he once confessed that he would change his style in an instant if it would win cases. "Impassioned rhetoric doesn't work with the Supreme Court," Roberts said in a 2000 interview. "If it did, I'd become impassioned."

As unassuming as Roberts was at that time, he also had a keen sense of humor, friends say. When Roberts was deputy solicitor general in 1990, he and a former Hogan and Hartson colleague, E. Barrett Prettyman Jr., were adversaries in *Lujan v. National Wildlife Federation,* a case that became a landmark decision narrowing the doctrine of standing. Prettyman's federation clients claimed they had standing to challenge Interior Department land management decisions because they used nearby land for recreational purposes. Roberts argued that was not an injury sufficient to achieve standing.

To research the case, Prettyman says, Roberts went out West to look over the public lands at issue. "He sent me a postcard from out there," Prettyman recalls. "He wrote that he had looked and looked for my client, but couldn't find her." Neither could the Supreme Court, it appears. The Court ruled, 5–4, that Prettyman's clients had no standing to sue.

Roberts returned to Hogan and Hartson in 1993, where he became one of the most sought-after advocates among the elite group of lawyers who specialize in arguing before the Supreme Court. He represented corporate clients and a wide range of others, including the states of Alaska and Hawaii and the Tahoe Regional Planning Agency. As highly regarded as he was, Roberts did not always win his cases. But he retained a sense of humor about his losses. Asked to explain why he lost *Digital Equipment Corp. v. Desktop Direct, Inc.* (1994) by a 9–0 vote, he replied, "Because there were only nine justices."

Solicitor General R. Ted Cruz of Texas, who clerked for Chief Justice Rehnquist in the mid-1990s, recalls that when he and his fellow clerks asked Rehnquist who he thought was the best lawyer currently practicing before the Court, John Roberts was Rehnquist's unhesitating reply. "For three young clerks that makes an impression," Cruz said. Later, during the 2000 presidential election dispute over voting in Florida, Cruz, who was working for the Bush campaign, recruited Roberts to work briefly on the legal issues involved.

In 1996 Roberts married Jane Sullivan, also a D.C. lawyer. They have two adopted children, Josephine and Jack.

Given Roberts's lucrative practice, he could have easily decided not to return to public service. But soon after George W. Bush became president in 2001, he included Roberts on his list of preferred appeals court nominees. Nomination politics were contentious early in Bush's first term, however, and it was not until January 2003 that Roberts was formally nominated to the U.S. Court of Appeals for the District of Columbia Circuit. During his Senate confirmation hearing, Roberts seemed to reject the notion that he would be a predictable judge, conservative or otherwise. He criticized the press for identifying judges according to whether they were appointed by Democratic or Republican presidents. "That gives so little credit to the work that they put into the case," he said. "They work very hard, and all of a sudden the report is, well, they just decided that way because of politics. That is a disservice to them."

Some Bush nominees were blocked or filibustered, but Roberts won broad support and was confirmed unanimously by voice vote in May 2003. He

settled into the D.C. Circuit and began producing well-written and largely noncontroversial opinions. His votes fell mainly on the conservative side, but that was not always the case. University of Chicago law professor Cass Sunstein called Roberts a judicial minimalist in his two years on the D.C. Circuit: "Judge Roberts's opinions thus far are careful, lawyerly and narrow. They avoid broad pronouncements. They do not try to reorient the law."

In a 2004 case, *Barbour v. Washington Metropolitan Area Transit Authority (WMATA)*, Roberts joined Merrick Garland—a Clinton appointee—in deciding that sovereign immunity did not bar a D.C. employee with bipolar disorder from suing the transit agency under federal laws barring discrimination against the disabled. But then came another WMATA case—which became known as the french fry case—that critics attacked as a sign of a certain hard-heartedness in Roberts's rulings. In *Hedgepeth v. WMATA* (2004), Roberts upheld the arrest, handcuffing, and detention of a twelve-year-old girl for eating a single french fry inside a D.C. Metro station. "No one is very happy about the events that led to this litigation," Roberts acknowledged in his written opinion, but he ruled that nothing the police did violated the girl's Fourth Amendment or Fifth Amendment rights.

Roberts also angered environmentalists in a 2003 case, *Rancho Viejo v. Norton*. Roberts wanted the full District of Columbia Circuit to reconsider a panel's decision that upheld a Fish and Wildlife Service regulation protecting arroyo toads under the Endangered Species Act. Roberts said there could be no interstate commerce rationale for protecting the hapless toad, which, he said, "for reasons of its own lives its entire life in California."

In another decision in June 2005, Roberts went even further than his colleagues in supporting the Bush administration in a case that pitted the government against veterans of the first Gulf War. In this case, *Acree v. Republic of Iraq*, American soldiers captured and tortured by the Iraqi government during the first Gulf War sued the Iraqi government in U.S. court and won nearly $1 billion in damages at the district court level. But once Saddam Hussein was toppled in 2003, the Bush administration wanted to protect the new Iraqi government from liability and intervened to block the award. Roberts, alone among the circuit judges who ruled with the government, said the federal courts did not even have jurisdiction to consider the victims' claim. He said Congress had plainly given the president authority to oust the courts' jurisdiction in these circumstances. "Give me English words over Latin maxims," Roberts wrote.

Justice Sandra Day O'Connor on July 1, 2005, announced plans to retire once her replacement was confirmed. Roberts soon found himself on the short list of potential replacements, although most pundits expected a woman to be appointed to replace the Court's first female justice. Bush did in fact nominate Roberts to replace O'Connor, and a summer of searching scrutiny of his record ensued. Thousands of documents from his years in government service were released, although the Bush administration, citing the need for confidentiality, resisted making public the memos Roberts wrote as deputy solicitor general. Liberal groups announced opposition to Roberts, but given his unimpeachable credentials, they faced an uphill battle.

Then, just a short time before Roberts's confirmation hearing was to begin, a startling development changed the dynamics overnight. Chief Justice William Rehnquist, who had been battling thyroid cancer, died on September 3. Suddenly, a Supreme Court that had been stable for eleven years would be dealing with one definite and one prospective vacancy. Within days, President Bush decided to withdraw Roberts's nomination as associate justice and resubmit it as a nomination for chief justice.

Even though the position of chief justice has more symbolic and historic importance, the switch may actually have eased Roberts's path toward confirmation. Now, instead of replacing O'Connor, who was considered the swing justice, Roberts would be replacing a like-minded conservative—his mentor, Rehnquist. As a result, it did not appear that he would change the balance on the Court appreciably. For her part, O'Connor agreed to stay on, as she had promised.

During four days of hearings, Roberts gave typically cautious answers. He declined to offer his views on specific issues or controversies that might come before him, at the same time insisting that his personal views on those issues would be irrelevant. In general terms, Roberts embraced the principle of *stare decisis*—respect for precedent—stating at one point that overturning a Court precedent is a "jolt to the system." But Roberts stopped short of saying whether that view would govern how he would vote on abortion rights or other issues. "I do not have an overarching judicial philosophy that I bring to each case," Roberts said. Roberts also seemed to express an expansive view of concepts such as "liberty," stating that they were meant to be given a broad meaning—a view at odds with at least one future colleague, Antonin Scalia.

With the Democrats divided on Roberts, on September 22, the Senate Judiciary Committee endorsed his nomination by a 13–5 vote. A week later, the full Senate confirmed his nomination, 78–22, a larger pro-Roberts margin than expected. "The Senate has confirmed a man with an astute mind and a kind heart," President Bush said later that day when Roberts was sworn in at a White House ceremony. John Paul Stevens, the senior associate justice, administered the judicial oath, symbolizing what appeared to be great enthusiasm among the sitting justices about their new chief.

As Roberts began his tenure as the youngest chief justice since John Marshall 200 years earlier, it appeared he might bring some changes to the Court, but not abruptly. He said during his confirmation hearings that he thought the Court could produce more decisions than it now does—around eighty—and that would be a popular move among lawyers who argue before the Court. Roberts was noncommittal about whether he favored allowing broadcast coverage of the Supreme Court, but it seemed possible that he might take that or other actions making the Court more accessible to the public. In his first months as chief justice, Roberts seemed to achieve a new level of harmony on the Court, as the justices issued opinions with fewer separate concurrences and dissents than in prior years. A relatively young and energetic man, with the prospect of serving for thirty years or more, had taken the helm of the Supreme Court.

In his first two opinions, Roberts spoke for unanimous Courts. In *Gonzales v. O Centro Espirita Beneficiente Uniao Do Vegetal* (2006), he ruled that the government had failed to show a compelling interest in preventing the Uniao Do Vegetal sect, a group with its origins in the Amazon rain forest, from importing hoasca, a hallucinogenic tea that it used in its rites. The case was fairly straightforward, involving a section of the 1993 Religious Freedom Restoration Act that had never been tested in the courts.

In the other case, *Rumsfeld v. Forum for Academic and Institutional Rights, Inc.,* the Court rejected a suit by a coalition of law schools protesting the Solomon Amendment, which required that any colleges or universities accepting federal monies had to allow recruiters from the armed services onto their campuses. The law schools claimed that the military's anti-gay policies violated their policies, which were in turn protected by the First Amendment. This argument convinced no judge, and Roberts, in the tone of a schoolmaster lecturing students on what the First Amendment covers and does not cover, dismissed the claim on the grounds that Congress has the power to require access to military recruiters on campuses that received federal funds under its power to raise and support armies as exercised through its spending powers.

—*Tony Mauro*

BIBLIOGRAPHY

There is no biography of Roberts, but he has written several articles that illuminate some of his views. Among them are: "In Memory of Rex E. Lee," *Brigham Young University Law Review* 1 (2003); "Forfeitures: Does Innocence Matter?" *Legal Times,* October 2, 1995; "The 1992–93 Supreme Court," *Public Interest Law Review* 107 (1994); "Riding the Coattails of the Solicitor General," *Legal Times,* March 29, 1993; "Oral Advocacy and the Re-emergence of a Supreme Court Bar," *Journal of Supreme Court History* 30 (2005): 68; "New Rules and Old Pose Stumbling Blocks in High Court Cases," *Legal Times,* February 26, 1990.

NOTEWORTHY OPINIONS

Gonzales v. O Centro Espírita Beneficiente União Do Vegetal, No. 04-1084 (2006)

Rumsfeld v. Forum for Academic and Institutional Rights, Inc., No. 04-1152 (2006)

OWEN JOSEPHUS ROBERTS

Birth: May 2, 1875, Germantown, Pennsylvania.

Education: University of Pennsylvania, A.B., 1895; LL.B., cum laude, 1898.

Official Positions: Assistant district attorney, 1903–1906; special deputy attorney general, Eastern District of Pennsylvania, 1918; special U.S. attorney, 1924–1930; umpire, Mixed Claims Commission, 1932; chairman, Pearl Harbor Inquiry Board, 1941–1942.

Supreme Court Service: Nominated associate justice by President Herbert Hoover, May 9, 1930, to replace Edward Terry Sanford, who had died; confirmed by the Senate, May 20, 1930, by a voice vote; took judicial oath June 2, 1930; resigned July 31, 1945; replaced by Harold H. Burton, nominated by President Harry S. Truman.

Death: May 17, 1955, West Vincent Township, Pennsylvania.

Owen Roberts grew up in Germantown, Pennsylvania, close to Philadelphia, where he passed a quiet, studious childhood. He graduated with honors from the University of Pennsylvania in 1895 following an undergraduate career that included membership in Phi Beta Kappa and an active part in the debate team. Three years later he earned a law degree from the same school, once again with honors.

Roberts achieved immediate success at the bar. He built one of the most successful private practices in Philadelphia by specializing in corporation law, especially railroads and banking, both of which figured prominently in the city's economy. Roberts was a member of the prestigious Philadelphia Law Academy, a leader of the Law Association of Philadelphia, and a part-time law teacher at his alma mater until 1919. As assistant district attorney during World War I, Roberts earned public attention for his successful prosecution of violators of the federal Espionage Act. His impeccable Republican credentials, strong ties to

business, and great courtroom success caught the attention of President Calvin Coolidge, who in 1924 appointed him as one of two special U.S. attorneys assigned to investigate the Teapot Dome scandals. Roberts became something of an overnight celebrity with the successful prosecution and then imprisonment of Warren C. Harding's interior secretary, Albert Fall. In 1930 Roberts briefly returned to his private practice.

Roberts's reputation as a federal prosecutor was critical to his appointment to the Supreme Court. President Herbert Hoover in 1930 had nominated Judge John J. Parker of North Carolina to the Court, but Parker's nomination stirred powerful resistance from labor and civil rights groups. When the Senate failed to confirm Parker, Hoover turned to Roberts, the heralded prosecutor of the Teapot Dome scandals, as a nominee above reproach. Although business and labor interests both raised questions about Roberts's candidacy, neither group was willing to wade into another bloody confrontation over a Supreme Court nominee. As a result, Roberts, who had no judicial experience and had not sought the appointment, won Senate confirmation without a dissenting vote.

Roberts probably did not belong on the Court. His personality matched his experience as a prosecutor and investigator. He was, as is true with any good prosecutor, analytical and inquisitive, and although studious and academically inclined, he was not a scholar and did not posses a philosophical or theoretical turn of mind, and by temperament was unsuited to the appellate bench. In addition, Roberts joined a Depression-era Court identified with entrepreneurial liberty and skepticism about the value of government regulation. Because the Court was deeply divided between warring liberal and conservative factions, Roberts became the swing vote, especially in the constitutional struggle over the legitimacy of the New Deal's economic reform measures. Roberts had never been enthusiastic about active government involvement in the economy; rather, he had frequently proclaimed, as did many Republicans of his era, the virtues of states' rights. He took

Owen Josephus Roberts

exception to many of the New Deal measures designed to regulate business and promote the rights of labor, believing that the Constitution lacked sufficient authority to sustain either action, but his positions were not anchored in any profound understanding of the issues. Roberts was in the unenviable position for an appellate judge of being neither doctrinaire nor theoretically well versed in the views he held.

Roberts's rulings in major New Deal cases left Court observers of his era puzzled, and scholars of today are still puzzled. He had no consistent jurisprudential principles, meaning that in conference and in speaking for the majority he was unpredictable and, some even charged (incorrectly), whimsical. Much of Roberts's judicial career turned on his reaction to Franklin D. Roosevelt's New Deal economic recovery program. Because Roberts was the swing vote, his views were especially important, yet he never developed arguments that clearly delineated them. For example, Roberts delivered the opinion of the Court in *Nebbia v. New York* (1934), in which the justices held that a state could regulate business activity in appropriate ways and at appropriate times, including, but not limited to, fixing prices. The issue in *Nebbia* was whether the New York State Milk Board had the authority to set the minimum and maximum prices at which milk could legally be sold. In a strong and detailed opinion, Roberts proclaimed that neither contract nor property rights were absolute; indeed, he held that such rights had to yield to the good of the public. Roberts insisted that if a state's laws had a rational relation to a legitimate state purpose, such as the public welfare, and were neither discriminatory nor arbitrary, those measures had satisfied the requirements of due process of law secured by the Fourteenth Amendment. Roberts ignored the larger economic issues raised by the desirability of preferring free, as opposed to regulated, markets. He seemed, therefore, to validate government intervention in the economy. Such was not the case, however.

As conservative opposition to the New Deal hardened, Roberts moved with it, at least initially. He joined with the conservative bloc to form a majority in *Panama Refining Co. v. Ryan* (1935), striking down Section 9c of the National Industrial Recovery Act. The act was the keystone of Roosevelt's economic recovery plan, but it was hastily drafted and of dubious constitutional authority. In *Schechter Poultry Corp. v. United States* (1935), Roberts enlisted with a unanimous Court to strike down the entire measure. He voted with the majority in *Louisville Bank v. Radford* (1935), which voided the Federal Farm Bankruptcy Act of 1934. He wrote the opinion for the Court in *Railroad Retirement Board v. Alton Railroad Co.* (1935). That case involved the Railway Pension Act, which made all persons who had worked for rail carriers within the preceding year eligible for pensions, including those discharged for cause. Roberts agreed with the carriers that no federally imposed pension plan could ever be considered within the powers conferred on Congress by the commerce clause. Finally, Roberts joined with the conservatives in *Carter v. Carter Coal Co.* (1935) to overturn the Bituminous Coal Act as an invasion by the federal government of powers of economic regulation reserved to the states.

Roberts delivered his most sensational (and controversial) opinion in *United States v. Butler* (1936). The case involved certain provisions of the Agricultural Adjustment Act of 1933 that authorized the federal government to raise farm prices by reducing production. The act was the New Deal's most important effort to ameliorate the depression in agriculture and raise farm prices by limiting production. Farmers who agreed to reduce crop acreage received benefit payments, the funds coming from a tax levied on the first processor of the commodities. William M. Butler, the bankruptcy receiver for a cotton processor, refused to pay the tax.

Roberts wrote for a 6–3 majority that overturned the act. He insisted that the only duty a judge had in such cases was "to lay the Article of the Constitution which is invoked beside the statute which is challenged and to decide whether the latter squares with the former." Roberts then proceeded to do just the opposite.

Roberts's decision did, however, settle a long-standing dispute concerning the taxing power of Congress. Article I, Section 8, authorizes Congress to levy taxes "to pay the debts and provide for the common defense and general welfare of the United States." The debate over the meaning of these words ran back to the beginning of the Republic, with James Madison and Alexander Hamilton taking different positions. Madison insisted that "general welfare" purposes were limited to those already authorized elsewhere in the Constitution; Hamilton claimed that the language amounted to an independent power to tax and spend, as long as it was done to promote the general welfare. Roberts accepted Hamilton's view and held the processing taxes justified.

He then proceeded, in a quite stunning turn of logic, to find the legislation unconstitutional. His majority opinion concluded that the question of whether Congress could raise and spend money was moot because efforts to regulate and control agricultural production clearly violated the Tenth Amendment's reservation of powers to the states. In essence, Roberts concluded that Congress could do what it wished with its taxing power, but that it could not apply that power in a way that interfered with local control of agriculture. The opinion came under harsh attack from the liberal wing of the Court. In a scathing rebuttal, Justice Harlan Fiske Stone called Roberts's ruling "a tortured construction of the Constitution" and condemned Roberts and the other conservatives for forgetting that "courts are not the only agency of government that must be assumed to have capacity to govern." "The only check," Stone continued, "upon our own exercise of power is our own sense of self-restraint."

Although Roberts was a moderate, centrist justice, his propensity to vote with the conservatives on many critical aspects of the New Deal fueled growing anger in Congress, the White House, and the public toward the Court. The criticism directed at Roberts was not altogether justified because he had, in fact, supported certain aspects of the New Deal. For example, in *Ashwander v. Tennessee Valley Authority* (1936), Roberts voted with the majority to uphold the power of Congress to establish the Tennessee Valley Authority to develop natural resources, control flooding, stabilize navigation on the Tennessee River, and generate electricity for a severely depressed regional economy.

As demands for reform of the Supreme Court grew, Roberts seemed to soften his attitude toward the New Deal. In 1937 he joined with the liberals to form a majority in *West Coast Hotel v. Parrish*, which upheld a Washington State minimum wage law for women. Although scholars have debated the extent to which Roosevelt's proposed "Court-packing" plan of the same year figured in Roberts's thinking, it is worth noting that he had reached his decision in *West Coast Hotel* before the president announced his plan. In this regard, Roberts's chief shortcoming was not that he succumbed to political pressure, but that he continued to follow an uncertain course in his general approach to the constitutional issues raised by the Depression and the New Deal response to it.

Even though the Court-packing scheme faltered in Congress, beginning in 1937 Roberts continued on a far steadier course on New Deal measures. He joined with the Court in sustaining the Farm Mortgage Act of 1935, the National Labor Relations Act of 1935, and the Social Security Act of 1935. Roberts explained his actions by insisting that these New Deal measures were better drafted and constitutionally sounder than earlier legislation. Roberts's critics, however, concluded that he simply found it easier to go along with the liberals than to endure the sharp criticism directed against him. In perhaps his most important reversal, he wrote the opinion for the Court in *Mulford v. Smith* (1939), which sustained the constitutionality of the second Agricultural Adjustment Act, finding this time that Congress did have the power, under the commerce clause, to regulate agriculture. So, in 1939 Roberts acknowledged what he had refused to recognize in 1936: the problems confronting agriculture were national in scope and required national legislative attention.

Roberts also influenced the Court's emerging civil liberties and civil rights agenda, but, once again, he trod an unpredictable path. For example, he wrote the opinion of the Court in *Grovey v. Townsend* (1935), which involved the constitutionality of the all-white Texas Democratic primary. R. R. Grovey, a black man, sued Albert Townsend, a state officer, for denying him the right to vote in the party's primary election. Roberts rejected Grovey's claim on the grounds that political parties were private organizations to which the equal protection clause of the Fourteenth Amendment did not apply. Roberts's opinion sustained the practice of excluding African Americans from voting in Democratic Party primaries. In *Smith v. Allwright* (1944), the Court overturned *Grovey*, and Roberts filed the only dissent. This dissent was unexpected, however, because six years earlier, in *Missouri ex rel. Gaines v. Canada* (1938), he had voted with the Court to invalidate the exclusion of African American students from the state's law school. In doing so, Roberts agreed with the majority that such legislation violated the equal protection clause of the Fourteenth Amendment. Finally, Roberts wrote the strongest dissent of his judicial career in *Korematsu v. United States* (1944). This case involved the constitutionality of the forced relocation of Japanese Americans during World War II. Roberts insisted that the orders issued to move Japanese Americans away from the West Coast were "a case of convicting a citizen as punishment for not submitting to imprisonment in a concentration camp . . . solely because of his ancestry."

In matters of civil liberties, Roberts followed an equally tortured course. In *Herndon v. Lowry* (1937), Roberts delivered the opinion of the Court that set aside the conviction of a black organizer of the Communist Party in Georgia for inciting insurrection. By making a distinction in this case between the "clear and present danger" and "bad tendency" tests for freedom of speech, Roberts advanced civil liberties. Three years later, Roberts also delivered the opinion of the Court in *Cantwell v. Connecticut* (1940). Newton Cantwell and his two sons were Jehovah's Witnesses convicted of violating a Connecticut law that pro-

scribed the act of soliciting money for religious, charitable, or philanthropic causes without the approval
of the secretary of public welfare. The Cantwells'
house-to-house solicitation included the loud playing
of records that described the books. Roberts took the
side of the Witnesses. He held that in balancing the
interests of an individual's freedom of religion and
the state's interest in preserving order, the Constitution meant to support the former over the latter.
Roberts argued that opinions expressed in such a way
as to provoke violence and disturb the public order
were subject to criminal liability, but that in this case
no such threat existed. In the same year, however,
Roberts also voted with the majority in *Minersville
School District v. Gobitis* to uphold a state-imposed
flag salute that the Witnesses refused to obey. Three
years later, in *West Virginia State Board of Education v.
Barnette* (1943), the Court reversed its direction and
declared flag salute statutes unacceptable, but Roberts
held in dissent to his position in *Gobitis*.

Roberts resigned from the Court in 1944. He left
angry at the direction taken by the liberal justices
President Roosevelt had installed. During his last
term on the bench, Roberts found himself almost
constantly at odds with the Court's Democratic
majority. He dissented fifty-three times, insisting that
he was the chief defender of precedent and legal stability. Roberts then returned to his alma mater to
become dean of the University of Pennsylvania Law
School from 1945 to 1951. He also chaired the security board of the Atomic Energy Commission.

Because Roberts had the temperament and experience of a prosecutor, his years on the Court left little
in the way of a substantive constitutional legacy. He
was philosophically opposed to the New Deal, but he
never developed a sustained jurisprudential position
within the Constitution to guide his opposition. The
very qualities of independence that made him a brilliant prosecutor weighed against his success as a
judge. He refused to allow himself to be classified as
either a conservative or a liberal. Such a position is
not unique in the history of the Court, but what
Roberts considered independence many of his critics
saw as unpredictable wavering that hindered rather

than helped the development of American constitutionalism. There is every reason to believe that
Roberts enjoyed the role of serving as the Court's
swing vote during the turbulent 1930s, but once President Roosevelt began to fill the bench with his
appointees, the Republican Roberts found himself
isolated, anachronistic in his views, and far less
important than he had been in the 1930s. As the new
justices moved on to fresh constitutional ground,
Roberts remained behind, and in so doing earned his
reputation as one of the Supreme Court's lesser lights.
—*Kermit L. Hall*

BIBLIOGRAPHY

Henry J. Abraham, *Justices and Presidents: A Political History
of Appointments to the Supreme Court,* (2d ed., 1985), provides a thoughtful analysis of Roberts's appointment to the
Court and his difficulties with the justices appointed by
Franklin D. Roosevelt. David Burner's sketch in Friedman
and Israel, *Justices,* vol. 3, 2253, is too generous in attempting to find a pattern to his jurisprudence. Augustus M.
Burns's portrait in Kermit L. Hall, ed., *The Oxford Companion to the Supreme Court of the United States* (2d ed., 2005),
is a careful overview of Roberts's career that highlights the
idiosyncratic nature of his jurisprudence. Paul E. Nelson's
unpublished dissertation, "The Constitutional Theory of
Mr. Justice Roberts" (University of Chicago, 1960), offers
the best argument available that Roberts had a strong theoretical understanding of both the judicial role and the Constitution. See also Louis Pollak, "Philadelphia Lawyer: A
Cautionary Tale," *University of Pennsylvania Law Review* 145
(1997): 495.

NOTEWORTHY OPINIONS

Nebbia v. New York, 291 U.S. 502 (1934)

Grovey v. Townsend, 295 U.S. 45 (1935)

Railroad Retirement Board v. Alton Railroad Co., 295 U.S.
330 (1935)

United States v. Butler, 297 U.S. 1 (1936)

Herndon v. Lowry, 301 U.S. 242 (1937)

Mulford v. Smith, 307 U.S. 38 (1939)

Cantwell v. Connecticut, 310 U.S. 296 (1940)

Korematsu v. United States, 323 U.S. 214 (1944) (Dissent)

JOHN RUTLEDGE

Birth: September 1739, Charleston, South Carolina.

Education: Privately tutored; studied law at the Middle Temple in England; called to the English bar February 9, 1760.

Official Positions: Member, South Carolina Commons House of Assembly, 1761–1776; South Carolina attorney general pro tem, 1764–1765; delegate, Stamp Act Congress, 1765; member, Continental Congress, 1774–1776, 1782–1783; president, South Carolina General Assembly, 1776–1778; governor, South Carolina, 1779–1782; judge of the Court of Chancery of South Carolina, 1784–1791; chief, South Carolina delegation to the Constitutional Convention, 1787; member, South Carolina convention to ratify U.S. Constitution, 1788; chief justice, South Carolina Court of Common Pleas, 1791–1795; member, South Carolina Assembly, 1798–1799.

Supreme Court Service: Nominated associate justice by President George Washington, September 24, 1789; confirmed by the Senate, September 26, 1789, by a voice vote; took judicial oath February 15, 1790; resigned March 5, 1791; replaced by Thomas Johnson, nominated by President Washington. Recess appointment as chief justice by President Washington, July 1, 1795; took judicial oath August 12, 1795; appointment rejected by the Senate, 14–10, December 15, 1795; service terminated December 15, 1795.

Death: July 18, 1800, Charleston, South Carolina.

John Rutledge dominated South Carolina politics in the 1770s and 1780s, serving as a delegate to the First and Second Continental Congresses and as the state's chief executive during the Revolutionary War. Rutledge was also elected to the Confederation Congress in 1782, was appointed a judge of the state court of chancery in 1784, and represented the state at the Constitutional Convention in 1787.

In 1789 President George Washington nominated Rutledge as one of the first six justices of the newly established U.S. Supreme Court. Rutledge accepted the commission and rode on circuit, but he did not attend any meetings of the Court before resigning in March 1791 to become chief justice of the South Carolina Court of Common Pleas. After four years of service as a state judge, Rutledge apparently had second thoughts about the desirability of a seat on the U.S. Supreme Court. Anticipating Chief Justice John Jay's resignation, Rutledge wrote to President Washington in June 1795, offering to replace him. Washington accepted with alacrity and issued a temporary commission, subject to the acceptance of the nomination by the Senate when it reconvened in December.

Chief Justice Rutledge participated in two cases during the August 1795 term of the Supreme Court, *United States v. Peters* and *Talbot v. Janson*. Both cases involved libels against ships accused of violating the Neutrality Act of 1794, which prohibited the arming of ships in American ports and barred American citizens from serving on foreign privateers. Rutledge announced the opinion in *Peters,* which involved the seizure on the high seas of an American schooner, the *William Lindsey,* by an armed corvette, the *Cassius,* commanded by a U.S. citizen acting under the authority of a French commission. The *Lindsey,* which had been carrying a cargo of British goods, had been taken before a French prize court in Port-de-Paix, Haiti. Because the *Cassius* was the property of the French government, the Court held, only a French tribunal had jurisdiction to decide the dispute.

Talbot v. Janson involved two ships, apparently acting in concert, that had taken as prize a Dutch brigantine. Although the captains of both ships were American by origin, both claimed to have adopted French citizenship. They also claimed that their ships were French, but the owner of the Dutch brigantine alleged that the true owners were Americans. The Court was unanimous in holding that the Dutch shipowner was entitled to restitution and damages, although each justice wrote a separate opinion. Rutledge, in a terse, three-paragraph opinion, eschewed any discussion of the vexing question of whether an American citizen could unilaterally expatriate himself. He based his decision on the grounds that one vessel had been illegally fitted out in the United States and that the other was actually American property. Rutledge did not mention the Neutrality Act but held that the capture violated the law of nations and the American treaty with Holland.

These two brief opinions are Rutledge's legacy as chief justice. Shortly after his nomination for the post (but probably before he had received word of it) he engaged in some intemperate criticism of the then-controversial Jay Treaty of 1794. Opposition to his appointment arose immediately, and when the Senate reconvened in December, it voted, 14–10, to reject his nomination.

—*Natalie Wexler*

John Rutledge

BIBLIOGRAPHY

No reliable full-length biography of John Rutledge exists. The best sources for treatment of his Supreme Court career are Leon Friedman, "John Rutledge," in *Justices,* vol. 1, 33; and the volumes of Maeva Marcus, ed., *The Documentary History of the Supreme Court of the United States, 1789–1800* (1985–).

NOTEWORTHY OPINIONS

United States v. Peters, 3 U.S. 121 (1795)

Talbot v. Janson, 3 U.S. 133 (1795)

WILEY BLOUNT RUTLEDGE JR.

Birth: July 20, 1894, Cloverport, Kentucky.

Education: University of Wisconsin, A.B., 1914; University of Colorado, LL.B., 1922.

Official Positions: Judge, U.S. Court of Appeals for the District of Columbia Circuit, 1939–1943.

Supreme Court Service: Nominated associate justice by President Franklin D. Roosevelt, January 11, 1943, to replace James F. Byrnes, who had resigned; confirmed by the Senate, February 8, 1943, by a voice vote; took judicial oath February 15, 1943; served until September 10, 1949; replaced by Sherman Minton, nominated by President Harry S. Truman.

Death: September 10, 1949, York, Maine.

Wiley Rutledge was the last of eight justices Franklin D. Roosevelt appointed to the Supreme Court and one of the most forward-thinking proponents of civil liberties and civil rights in the Court's history. With his colleague Frank Murphy, Rutledge was, on these issues, to the "left" of two other liberals on the Court at the time, Hugo Black and William O. Douglas. Rutledge served only six-and-a-half years; he died suddenly in 1949 at age fifty-five after a cerebral hemorrhage. But while he was there, he was the "conscience of the Court" among justices who, in addition to Black and Douglas, had become long-tenured giants: Harlan Fiske Stone, Felix Frankfurter, and Robert Jackson. Rutledge is best remembered as a dissenter who spoke to the future with a prophetic voice. So who was Wiley Rutledge, how did he get to the Court, and what did he accomplish there?

FDR once exclaimed to Rutledge, "Wiley, you have a lot of geography!" And indeed he did. He was born in small-town Kentucky, grew up in Tennessee, graduated from college at Wisconsin, began law school at Indiana, came down with tuberculosis and found treatment in North Carolina, got married and "chased the cure" while teaching high school in New Mexico, finished law school in Colorado, and briefly practiced and taught law in Boulder until he joined the law faculty, and eventually became dean, at Washington University in St. Louis. In 1935 he assumed the deanship of the University of Iowa College of Law.

The son of a Baptist preacher, Rutledge lost his mother to tuberculosis when he was nine and eventually learned that he might die of the disease himself. Rather than feeling sorry for himself, however, he developed a deep concern for others at the sanatorium worse off than he and, when he recovered, emerged as man of great empathy. As a young southerner, Rutledge had his share of racial prejudice. But he eventually outgrew it, influenced by his wife from Michigan, Annabel Person, who had been his Greek teacher at Maryville College in Tennessee, which he had attended before the University of Wisconsin. Religion was significant in Rutledge's life. From a Southern Baptist he became a Christian humanist, akin to a Unitarian, and focused on meeting human needs.

Politically, Rutledge was always a Democrat and, as early as his college years, stressed the rights of individuals over the demands of majorities. In St. Louis, Rutledge became a very public liberal, seeking reform of the criminal justice system and campaigning against the abuses of child labor and the power of public utility holding companies. In Iowa, he was particularly supportive of African American, Jewish, and female students. He urged support of legal aid to the poor and warned the legal profession against monopolizing services that laypersons could offer just as well at less cost. In 1937 Rutledge was one of the few law deans in the country to support FDR's "Court-packing" plan.

Largely because of efforts by Irving Brant, an editor of the *St. Louis Star-Times* and long-time friend of FDR, Rutledge—whom the president had never met—had been the runner-up each time in 1939 when Roosevelt named two of his friends, Frankfurter and Douglas, to the Supreme Court. Instead, Roosevelt appointed Rutledge to the U.S. Court of Appeals for the District of Columbia Circuit and, four years later, nominated him to the Supreme Court when Justice James F. Byrnes resigned.

Rutledge joined the Court, at age forty-eight, with an established jurisprudence and approach to decision making. He saw the Constitution, with its general terms such as "due process" and "commerce," as a flexible document adaptable to the needs of a

Wiley Blount Rutledge Jr.

changing society much like the evolution of the common law. As a legal realist, he freely acknowledged that in the difficult cases, where text, legislative history, and precedent supply no clear answer—and the opinion could be written coherently with different outcomes—every judge's values become part of the decision. The real dichotomy is not between activism and restraint, he believed, but between one judge's values and another's. As a man influenced by the sociological jurisprudence of Harvard Law School dean Roscoe Pound and the writings of Louis Brandeis, his values favored protection of the individual, the ordinary worker, and small business.

When Rutledge took his seat in February 1943, the Court still adhered to Justice Benjamin Cardozo's opinion in *Palko v. Connecticut* (1937), ruling that although the entire Bill of Rights applied in federal court, only a select few amendments were available in state courts, namely those "implicit in the 'concept of ordered liberty' "—more specifically, those " 'so rooted in the traditions and conscience of our people as to be ranked as fundamental.' " *Palko*'s formulation was reaffirmed, 5–4, in *Adamson v. California* (1947). Rutledge was among the four dissenters, who said that the entire Bill of Rights was incorporated in the Fourteenth Amendment and therefore applied in full in state courts. But Rutledge and Murphy went further than the other two dissenters, Black and Douglas, who had concluded that the Fourteenth Amendment incorporated the Bill of Rights and *no more*. Rutledge joined Murphy's dissent suggesting that the

Fourteenth Amendment might well guarantee additional rights—a telling observation as evidenced, for example, by the Court's eventual recognition of the right to privacy in *Griswold v. Connecticut* (1965).

Two years after *Adamson,* the Court held in *Wolf v. Colorado* (1949) that the Fourth Amendment protection against unreasonable searches and seizures was "implicit in the concept of ordered liberty" and therefore applicable to the states. But a majority, including Black, also agreed that the "exclusionary rule," barring admission of unlawfully seized evidence in federal court, was a mere evidentiary limitation that a legislature could negate, not a core protection of the Fourth Amendment. In dissent, Rutledge argued that the rule itself was inherent in the Fourth Amendment and so applicable in state courts through the Fourteenth. His view prevailed twelve years later in *Mapp v. Ohio* (1961) with the support of Black, who acknowledged that the "force" of Rutledge's dissent in *Wolf* had "become compelling."

A majority of the justices in the 1940s would not incorporate the Sixth Amendment right to counsel into the Fourteenth Amendment, but Rutledge pressed hard nevertheless in *Canizio v. New York* (1946) and in *Foster v. Illinois* (1947) and *Gayes v. New York* (1947), usually in dissent, to expand the right to counsel in state criminal proceedings as a matter of due process. Rutledge was particularly distressed in *Foster,* in which the Court held 5–4 that even though state law entitled the indigent defendant to a free lawyer, due process was not violated when the state failed to inform the defendant of that right and he entered a guilty plea without legal advice.

Rutledge also perceived other violations of due process in state courts. For example, Illinois appellate procedure for exhausting state remedies—as required before seeking federal court review of a state criminal conviction—was so byzantine, and tripped up so many petitioners, that Rutledge, in *Marino v. Ragen* (1947), called for accepting every criminal case presented to the Court from Illinois until the state changed its procedure. A year and a half later, the Court followed Rutledge's advice in *Young v. Ragen* (1949), and Illinois soon changed its ways.

Rutledge sided with criminal defendants 80 percent of the time compared to the Court's 52 percent during his tenure. Especially when the death penalty was involved, Rutledge would construe an ambiguous statute against the government or grant the defendant a generous interpretation of due process. Or he would even invoke the Court's inherent supervisory power over the administration of criminal justice as he did while dissenting, for example, in *Fisher v. United States* (1946), in which the Court rejected a diminished capacity defense in a District of Columbia murder case, and Rutledge himself could not find a violation of due process. He even relied, in dissent, on the Court's supervisory power in a noncapital conspiracy case, *Pinkerton v. United States* (1946), because he was not willing to affirm conviction of a coconspirator for particular criminal acts underlying the conspiracy that the coconspirator had not known about. To do so would "fracture the spirit" of due process, he said, by carrying vicarious responsibility too far.

These also were the days of the Jehovah's Witness cases, when Rutledge helped form a new majority that struck down, under the free exercise of religion clause of the First Amendment, the tax on religious literature in two companion cases, *Jones v. Opelika* (1943) and *Murdock v. Pennsylvania* (1943), and invalidated the compulsory flag salute in public schools in *West Virginia Board of Education v. Barnette* (1943) (overruling *Minersville School District v. Gobitis,* 1940). In only one instance did Rutledge reject a free exercise defense. In writing for the majority in *Prince v. Massachusetts* (1944), another Jehovah's Witness case, Rutledge upheld a Massachusetts statute imposing criminal fines on adults who allowed children to distribute religious literature on the street—a statute Rutledge perceived as a child labor, not a free exercise, regulation.

As to the First Amendment's establishment clause, the Court has never had a stronger statement supporting separation of church and state than Rutledge's dissent in *Everson v. Board of Education* (1947), in which the Court upheld state-subsidized bus fares to Catholic schools. In the next term, in *Illinois ex rel.*

McCollum v. Board of Education (1948), Black relied heavily on Rutledge's *Everson* dissent (as well as on his own majority opinion in *Everson*) to strike down a voluntary program of religious instruction during the school day on school premises. Years later, in his opinion invalidating a required school prayer, *Engel v. Vitale* (1962), Douglas, who had joined the majority in *Everson,* acknowledged that his task would have been easier if the majority had followed Rutledge in *Everson,* in which Rutledge had stated "durable First Amendment philosophy."

Aside from *Prince,* Rutledge supported a First Amendment defense in every case in which it was raised, whether for religion, press, assembly, petition, or speech. In doing so, he wrote in *Thomas v. Collins* (1945) as forceful an opinion supporting free speech as the Court has yet produced. There, the Court reversed, 5–4, the criminal contempt conviction of a union organizer who had ignored a court order not to address a mass meeting without obtaining a state-required "organizer's card." Frankfurter, in *Kovacs v. Cooper* (1949), criticized Rutledge's opinion as the most extreme statement yet written favoring a "preferred position" for First Amendment rights.

In dissent, Rutledge made the earliest pronouncements by a Supreme Court justice that discrimination based on gender and on poverty denied equal protection of the law. In *Goesaert v. Cleary* (1948), he found a denial of equal protection when the majority upheld a Michigan statute forbidding any female to tend bar unless she was the "wife or daughter of the male owner." And in *Foster v. Illinois,* in addition to finding a due process violation, Rutledge concluded that the state's failure to provide counsel for an indigent defendant violated the equal protection clause because wealth and poverty would "make all the difference in securing the substance or only the shadow of constitutional protection."

Rutledge also attacked discrimination based on blood line and race. In *Kotch v. Board of River Port Pilot Commissioners* (1947), he dissented from Black's opinion upholding a Louisiana system permitting a river pilots' association, required by law to guide Mississippi River boats near New Orleans, to choose all new pilots from among family and friends. And in *Fisher v. Hurst* (1948), he was the lone dissenter when the Court rejected Thurgood Marshall's petition for a writ of *mandamus* to compel Oklahoma's compliance with the Court's earlier mandate to provide the African American petitioner a legal education "as soon as it does for applicants of any other group." Rutledge interpreted the mandate to mean that the law school must be shut down entirely unless the petitioner was admitted, not left open to second- and third-year students (no longer "applicants") as the Oklahoma courts were allowing. Only in voting rights cases did Rutledge balk at an equal protection remedy. In *Colegrove v. Green* (1946) and *MacDougall v. Green* (1948), he joined colleagues who concluded that unequal voting districts and discriminatory signature requirements for getting a political party onto the ballot violated equal protection. But in each case, Rutledge withheld relief because he perceived that either proposed remedy—at large election or last minute access to the ballot—would create inequities of its own.

Rutledge was a major contributor to the Court's interpretation of the commerce clause. In a case of considerable notoriety, Michigan successfully prosecuted a charter boat company under the state's civil rights act for refusing to carry African American schoolchildren from Detroit to an amusement park on a Canadian island. In *Bob-Lo Excursion Co. v. Michigan* (1948), Rutledge wrote for a majority that upheld the conviction against a defense that the commerce clause, standing alone, forbade Michigan's interference with foreign commerce. In other, more common contexts, Rutledge's exhaustive concurring opinions on state taxation, *Freeman v. Hewitt* (1946) and *Memphis Natural Gas Co. v. Stone* (1948), and his majority opinion on coordinated regulation of commerce by Congress and the states, *Prudential Insurance Co. v. Benjamin* (1946), are the law today. When the Court considered a challenge to a statute expanding federal court "diversity" jurisdiction to include suits not only between citizens of different states, as specified in Article III of the Constitution, but also suits involving citizens of the District of Columbia and the territories, the Court upheld the statute, 5–4, in *National Mutual Insurance Co. v. Tidewater Transfer Co.* (1949). The majority cobbled together an opinion by Jackson, finding authority in the "District clause" (Article I, Section 8, clause 1), and an opinion by Rutledge, joined by Murphy, finding authority in Article III. Rutledge deemed the District of Columbia a state for this purpose, reflecting other instances, such as the Sixth Amendment right to a speedy criminal trial, where constitutional rights applicable to the states had been extended to the District of Columbia. Unlike the other justices, Rutledge and Murphy saw the availability of federal diversity jurisdiction as an access-to-justice (a civil rights) issue.

Rutledge was involved in most of the major decisions concerning World War II and its aftermath. In December 1944, when he had been on the Court less than two years, he joined the 6–3 majority in *Korematsu v. United States* (1944), which upheld the West Coast evacuation of 112,000 persons of Japanese ancestry, including 70,000 American citizens. He accepted "military necessity" based on threats of espionage and sabotage that were later proved untrue. He told his colleagues that he could perceive no principled distinction between that evacuation and the West Coast curfew, applied to the same population, which the Court had unanimously upheld a year earlier in *Hirabayashi v. United States* (1943). In short, he could find no basis for second-guessing the military—or his president—in wartime.

Rutledge is not known to have expressed regret about his vote in *Korematsu* during the short time he lived after he cast it, but he had anguished over what he felt he had to do, and all his votes after *Korematsu* on cases concerning the war went in the other direction, almost always in dissent. For example, Rutledge concluded that the naturalized citizenship of Nazi sympathizers and Communists could never be revoked (as permitted under the naturalization statute) for misrepresentation of loyalty to the United States *before* naturalization. It could be revoked, he said, only for actions "taking place afterward," as could also happen to native-born Americans. He therefore dissented in *Knauer v. United States* (1946). Joined only by Murphy, Rutledge rejected "two classes

of citizens, one superior, the other inferior" as if in "suspended animation" vulnerable to erasure. In another war-related dissent in *Yakus v. United States* (1944), Rutledge voted to declare unconstitutional a criminal price control statute that barred the accused from challenging the price ceilings while defending the accusation. Congress accepted Rutledge's analysis and amended the statute.

After the war, in *United States v. United Mine Workers* (1947), in which the prevailing justices relied on dubious precedent and questionable analysis, Rutledge voted to reverse the convictions of John L. Lewis and his union for criminal contempt of court in refusing to comply with a federal court order enjoining a national coal strike when President Harry S. Truman seized the mines. A year later, in *Ahrens v. Clark* (1948), Rutledge dissented from an opinion by Douglas, who rejected petitions for writs of *habeas corpus* by German nationals awaiting deportation from Ellis Island after hostilities had ceased. Douglas reasoned that the statute required the *habeas* petition to be filed in New York, where the prisoners were held, not in the District of Columbia, where the *Ahrens* petition had been filed. Rutledge stressed, to the contrary, that precedent called for filing the petition in a jurisdiction where the jailer could be found, which included the District of Columbia, home of the attorney general. Eventually, *Ahrens* was overruled: the Court's decision in *Rasul v. Bush* (2004)—holding that U.S. courts have jurisdiction over challenges to the legality of the detention of foreign nationals captured abroad while fighting for the Taliban and incarcerated at the U.S. Navy base at Guantánamo Bay, Cuba—is traceable to Rutledge's dissent in *Ahrens*.

In his most heralded opinion, *In re Yamashita* (1946), Rutledge dissented from the Court's deference to the military commission conviction of Lt. Gen. Tomoyuki Yamashita, the Japanese commander in the Philippines, who was sentenced to death for failure to prevent troops under his command from committing atrocities in Manila at the end of the war. Yamashita had been retreating with some of his forces more than 100 miles north of Manila, and, with communications in shambles, he claimed he did not know what his men were doing in Manila. No clear proof was found to contradict him. Rutledge concluded that in the absence of such knowledge, the general could not be held criminally responsible under the international law of war, a view adopted by military tribunals in Germany and elsewhere in the late 1940s, as well as in the U.S. Army Field Manual by 1956.

Rutledge also found violations of the Articles of War, the Geneva Convention, and Fifth Amendment due process. He rejected Chief Justice Stone's analysis for the majority, which held that the Geneva Convention applied only to prosecutions for offenses committed by prisoners of war *while prisoners*, not to alleged war crimes committed before capture. In 1949 the Geneva Convention was amended and eventually ratified by the U.S. Senate, adopting Rutledge's interpretation. As a result, the Geneva Convention now applies to prisoners of war charged with crimes committed before capture and grants them the same right to court-martial protection accorded members of the U.S. military. Significantly, if court-martial protection had been available to General Yamashita through the Articles of War or the Geneva Convention, as Rutledge had argued, that protection presumably would have satisfied due process. But Rutledge was dogged in his belief that the Fifth Amendment, as such, was also available to prisoners of war and that the Court should say so.

Rutledge's *Yamashita* dissent, along with Murphy's, had major impact. By preventing a unanimous Court in the first postwar trial by a military commission, Rutledge and Murphy offered lawyers and judges in upcoming war crimes trials credible and persuasive alternatives to the rules of law and procedure applied in *Yamashita*, alternatives that were eventually incorporated into U.S. military procedure and international treaty. The dissents also had a chastening impact on the press and the American public, as editorials reflected nationwide, and they energized the American liberal community to monitor the increasing number of war crimes trials around the world. And the dissents stood out as expressions of national conscience at a time when feelings of hate and revenge might otherwise have overwhelmed the nation.

Despite his vote in *Korematsu*, Rutledge was the "conscience of the Court" in the 1940s for three reasons. First, he characteristically insisted on due regard for the individual, pressing hard for expansive interpretation of the Bill of Rights. Second, he always gave principled, detailed reasons for his opinions based on meticulous examination of the facts; he would not twist the trial record for his own purposes. Third, because of the integrity of his elaborations, his colleagues took him very seriously, even in disagreement; he forced them to think more deeply than they otherwise might have. No other justice at the time exemplified all three of these attributes.

This period of great intellectual divide on the Court was also marked by an abundance of personal acrimony, perhaps the worst in the Court's history. Black and Jackson disliked and disrespected each other. The same was true of Frankfurter and Douglas. Justice Owen Roberts became upset with the Court's evolving jurisprudence and isolated himself, even refusing to shake hands before argument as was the custom. And several of Murphy's colleagues did not take him seriously. With the possible exception of Stone, only one justice—Wiley Rutledge—had both the intellectual and personal respect of all his colleagues. In a context of centrifugal forces, Rutledge was the Court's balance wheel. As the Court's most collegial member, he was a civilizing influence whose very presence called for integrity in the Court's work.

Because he served only six-and-a-half years, Rutledge's contribution necessarily was limited. He wrote only three significant majority opinions: *Prince*, *Thomas*, and *Prudential Insurance*. His impact as a justice—his opinions that helped reshape the law in the long run—came primarily in dissent or, occasionally, in a concurring opinion. For all the regard his colleagues accorded him, he was rarely asked to write a majority opinion in a close, highly contentious case. Writing was difficult for him; despite being an indefatigable worker, he took a long time to get his opinions done. And he often wrote opinions that were too long or too much like law review articles with material unnecessary to the decision to command a majority easily. He was assigned more than his share of the commercial and other less emotionally charged decisions where there was little disagreement.

In comparison with two highly regarded justices who had virtually the same length tenure as he did—Benjamin R. Curtis (1851–1857) and Benjamin Cardozo (1932–1938)—Rutledge never wrote a majority opinion with the precedential force of Curtis's in *Cooley v. Board of Wardens* (1851) or Cardozo's in *Palko v. Connecticut* (1937). On the other hand, numerous Rutledge dissents supplied significant momentum toward the Warren Court's virtually complete incorporation of the Bill of Rights, by way of *Palko,* in the Fourteenth Amendment. And although Curtis's contribution in *Cooley* facilitated regulation of interstate commerce by the states during a period of forty years when Congress declined to do so, Rutledge supplied the enduring rationale of *Prudential Insurance* for coordinating federal and state regulation of interstate commerce when both sovereigns had become active. Curtis's dissent in *Dred Scott v. Sandford* (1957) was one for the ages; but Rutledge's dissent in *Yamashita* was a courageous act as well, launching more enlightened standards of justice, international as well as national.

Ultimately, the story of Wiley Rutledge is the story of his genuine regard for all people, regardless of station. His friend Willard Wirtz, a law professor who later became secretary of labor, observed: "Wiley Rutledge, above almost all others, loved people and respected his fellow men. This was the quality of his great personal attraction and it was the core of his reputed liberalism." Referring to Rutledge, Hugo Black Jr. said: "I think he very well could have enlarged my father's heart." And a former law clerk of Justice Douglas from the 1940s, after a lifetime in the law, remarked: "If I were a defendant being tried by a single judge, I'd rather have Justice Rutledge than any judge I have known." Rutledge, in sum, was a hardworking, principled justice memorable for his rare combination of mind and heart.

—*John M. Ferren*

BIBLIOGRAPHY

The most comprehensive study of Justice Rutledge and his role on the Stone and Vinson Courts is John M. Ferren, *Salt of the Earth, Conscience of the Court: The Story of Justice Wiley Rutledge* (2004). An earlier biography, Fowler V. Harper, *Justice Rutledge and the Bright Constellation* (1965), focuses less on his life than on legal developments on the Court during his tenure. Important insights about Rutledge are found in essays by two of his law clerks: Louis H. Pollak, "Wiley Blount Rutledge: Profile of a Judge," in R. D. Rotunda, ed., *Six Justices on Civil Rights* (1983), 177; and John Paul Stevens, "Mr. Justice Rutledge," in A. Dunham and P. Kurland, eds., *Mr. Justice* (1958), 177.

A year after Rutledge died, two law reviews simultaneously published the same collection of articles, written in his honor by colleagues, law clerks, and other friends, covering his character as a person and a judge, as well as his contributions as a justice in specified areas, such as the commerce power and civil liberties: "A Symposium to the Memory of Wiley B. Rutledge (1894–1949)," *Indiana Law Journal* 25 (1950) and *Iowa Law Review* 35 (1950). A useful contemporary study is David M. Levitan, "Mr. Justice Rutledge," *Virginia Law Review* 34 (1948): (part 1), 393; (part 2), 526. Of the various publications by Rutledge himself, the most compelling may be a series of three lectures he gave at the University of Kansas in 1946 and published as Wiley Rutledge, *A Declaration of Legal Faith* (1947).

NOTEWORTHY OPINIONS

Prince v. Massachusetts, 321 U.S. 158 (1944)

Thomas v. Collins, 323 U.S. 516 (1945)

In re Yamashita, 327 U.S. 1 (1946) (Dissent)

Prudential Insurance Co. v. Benjamin, 328 U.S. 408 (1946)

Knauer v. United States, 328 U.S. 654 (1946)

Everson v. Board of Education, 330 U.S. 1 (1948) (Dissent)

Bob-Lo Excursion Co. v. Michigan, 333 U.S. 28 (1948)

Wolf v. Colorado, 338 U.S. 25 (1949)

EDWARD TERRY SANFORD

Birth: July 23, 1865, Knoxville, Tennessee.

Education: University of Tennessee, B.A. and Ph.B., 1883; Harvard, B.A., 1884, M.A., 1889; Harvard Law School, LL.B., 1889.

Official Positions: Special assistant to the U.S. attorney general, 1906–1907; assistant U.S. attorney general, 1907–1908; federal judge, U.S. District Court for the Middle and Eastern Districts of Tennessee, 1908–1923.

Supreme Court Service: Nominated associate justice by President Warren G. Harding, January 24, 1923, to replace Mahlon Pitney, who had retired; confirmed by the Senate, January 29, 1923, by a voice vote; took judicial oath February 19, 1923; served until March 8, 1930; replaced by Owen J. Roberts, nominated by President Herbert Hoover.

Death: March 8, 1930, Washington, D.C.

A member of the inaugural staff of the *Harvard Law Review*, Edward Terry Sanford practiced law in Knoxville, Tennessee, for sixteen years before being named special assistant to the attorney general for the fertilizer trust prosecution in 1905. In 1907 he was appointed assistant attorney general, and in 1908 he returned to Tennessee as a federal district court judge. Fifteen years later, President Warren G. Harding elevated Sanford to the U.S. Supreme Court.

Sanford brought to the Court a quiet moderation, a respect for precedent, and considerable erudition. Chief Justice William Howard Taft frequently turned to him to write important cases in technical areas such as bankruptcy and federal jurisdiction. Of all the justices of the Taft Court, Sanford was generally among the more hospitable to federal and state exercises of regulatory power. He voted to sustain federal regulation of grain exchanges and stockyards against substantive due process and Tenth Amendment challenges in *Chicago Board of Trade v. Olsen* (1923) and *Tagg Bros. & Moorhead v. United States* (1930). He voted with the majority in the landmark case of *Euclid v. Ambler* (1926), upholding a zoning ordinance against a substantive due process challenge. He dissented from the Court's holding in *Tyson v. Banton* (1927) that a New York statute regulating theater ticket brokers violated the due process clause; and he concurred in *Ribnik v. McBride* (1928), which struck down a statute regulating employment agency fees, only because *Tyson* was the controlling authority. Perhaps most notably, he joined Taft's dissent from the Court's opinion striking down the District of Columbia's minimum wage law for women in *Adkins v. Children's Hospital* (1923). Sanford was not a doctrinaire opponent of substantive due process, however. He joined the Court's opinions in *Meyer v. Nebraska* (1923) and *Pierce v. Society of Sisters* (1925), which recognized important noneconomic substantive liberties under the due process clause. Moreover, he joined Taft's opinion for a unanimous Court holding that a Kansas statute imposing a comprehensive system of labor regulation in certain industries violated the Fourteenth Amendment in *Chas. Wolff Packing Co. v. Court of Industrial Relations* (1923).

Sanford's days as an antitrust prosecutor showed in the trustbusting posture he struck in cases such as *Maple Flooring Manufacturers Assn. v. United States* (1925) and *Cement Manufacturers Protective Assn. v. United States* (1925). His record in antitrust cases brought against labor unions was mixed. He joined Taft's unanimous opinion in the second Coronado coal case (*Coronado Coal Co. v. Mine Workers,* 1925), upholding a verdict against the United Mine Workers union. On the other hand, he joined the majority opinion in *Leather Workers v. Herkert & Meisel Trunk Co.* (1924), holding that a local strike was beyond the reach of the Sherman Act. In *Bedford Cut Stone Co. v. Stone Cutters* (1927), his respect for precedent was again apparent: he concurred in the majority opinion upholding a verdict against the union for boycotting the company's store only because *Duplex Printing Press Co. v. Deering* (1921) was the controlling authority.

Sanford's positions in cases involving the constitutional rights of African Americans were typical of the legal thinkers of his day. He joined the majority opinion in *Moore v. Dempsey* (1923), holding that the conviction of black defendants in a trial dominated by a mob deprived them of due process. He also joined the Court's unanimous opinion in *Nixon v. Herndon* (1927), holding that a Texas statute prohibiting blacks from voting in the Democratic Party primary violated the equal protection clause. At the same time, he joined the Court's unanimous decision upholding segregated public education in *Gong Lum v. Rice* (1927) and wrote the Court's unanimous opinion in *Corrigan v. Buckley* (1926), holding that private, racially restrictive real estate covenants were constitutionally permissible.

Sanford is perhaps best known for his contributions to First Amendment jurisprudence. The presumption of constitutionality he indulged with respect to statutes regulating the economy he also extended to measures regulating antigovernment speech. Sanford's opinions in *Gitlow v. New York* (1925) and *Whitney v. California* (1927) upheld the prerogative of the states to criminalize advocacy of violent revolutionary action. Yet in both cases he advanced the novel and historically pivotal position that the due process clause of the Fourteenth Amendment applied the protections of the First Amendment against the state governments. In *Fiske v. Kansas* (1927), he overturned the criminal syndicalism conviction of a man whose only offense was membership in the Industrial Workers of the World, which had not been shown to advocate the violent overthrow of the government. And in *United States v. Schwimmer* (1929), Sanford dissented from an opinion upholding the denial of American citizenship to a pacifist who

Edward Terry Sanford

would not swear to bear arms in defense of the United States. Perhaps because of his persistently moderate position on the Court, Sanford occupies a sort of neutral zone in judicial history: neither sanctified nor vilified by historians of the Court.

—*Barry Cushman*

BIBLIOGRAPHY

There is no biography of Justice Sanford. Some useful material is contained in James A. Fowler, "Mr. Justice Edward Terry Sanford," *A.B.A. Journal* 17 (1931): 229; John W. Green, "Some Judges of the United States District Court of Tennessee (1878–1939)," *Tennessee Law Review* 18 (1944):

227; and "Proceedings in Memory of Mr. Justice Sanford," 285 U.S. xxxvii (1932). A small collection of Sanford's papers can be found at the University of Tennessee Library in Knoxville.

NOTEWORTHY OPINIONS

Gitlow v. New York, 268 U.S. 652 (1925)

Corrigan v. Buckley, 271 U.S. 323 (1926)

Whitney v. California, 274 U.S. 357(1927)

Fiske v. Kansas, 274 U.S. 380 (1927)

Ribnik v. McBride, 277 U.S. 350 (1928) (Concurrence)

United States v. Schwimmer, 279 U.S. 674 (1929)

ANTONIN SCALIA

Birth: March 11, 1936, Trenton, New Jersey.

Education: Georgetown University, A.B., summa cum laude, 1957; Harvard Law School, LL.B., magna cum laude, 1960.

Official Positions: General counsel, White House Office of Telecommunications Policy, 1971–1972; chairman, Administrative Conference of the United States, 1972–1974; assistant attorney general, Office of Legal Counsel, 1974–1977; judge, U.S. Court of Appeals for the District of Columbia Circuit, 1982–1986.

Supreme Court Service: Nominated associate justice by President Ronald Reagan, June 24, 1986, to replace William H. Rehnquist, who had been promoted to chief justice; confirmed by the Senate, 98–0, September 17, 1986; took judicial oath September 26, 1986.

Antonin Scalia was born March 11, 1936, in Trenton, New Jersey. He is the only child of an Italian immigrant father who became a professor of Romance languages at Brooklyn College and of an Italian American mother who taught public school. Scalia was educated at Georgetown University, where he graduated as valedictorian of his class in 1957, and Harvard Law School, where he served as Notes editor of the *Harvard Law Review* and from which he received his L.L.B. in 1960. He is married and the father of nine children.

Scalia practiced law in Cleveland, Ohio, until 1967, when he became professor of law at the University of Virginia. He joined the law faculty at the University of Chicago in 1977 and served there until his appointment to the D.C. Circuit by President Ronald Reagan in 1982. Often on leave from his academic posts, he served as general counsel for the Office of Telecommunications Policy, where he successfully negotiated a major agreement among industry groups that provided the framework for the growth of cable

television in the United States. He was chairman of the Administrative Conference of the United States, assistant attorney general for the Office of Legal Counsel, chairman of the ABA's Administrative Law Section, and chairman of the ABA Conference of Section Chairmen. With Murray Weidenbaum, he was founding coeditor of *Regulation*.

Since his elevation to the Supreme Court in 1986, Scalia has assiduously and consistently pursued a textualist jurisprudence. He argues that primacy must be accorded to the text, structure, and history of the document being interpreted and that the job of the judge is to apply the clear textual language of the Constitution or statute, or the critical structural principle necessarily implicit in the text. If the text is ambiguous, yielding several conflicting interpretations, Scalia turns to the specific legal tradition flowing from that text—to "what it meant to the society that adopted it." "Text and tradition" is a phrase that fills Scalia's opinions. Judges are to be governed only by the "text and tradition of the Constitution," not by their "intellectual, moral, and personal perceptions." As he remarked in his concurring opinion in *Schad v. Arizona* (1991): "When judges test their individual notions of 'fairness' against an American tradition that is deep and broad and continuing, it is not the tradition that is on trial, but the judges."

For Scalia, reliance on text and tradition is a means of constraining judicial discretion. He believes that "the main danger in judicial interpretation of the Constitution—or, for that matter, in judicial interpretation of any law—is that the judges will mistake their own predilections for the law." Faithful adherence to the text of a constitutional or statutory provision or, if that is ambiguous, to the traditional understanding of those who originally adopted it, reduces the danger that judges will substitute their beliefs for society's.

Scalia understands that the Constitution creates two conflicting systems of rights: one is democratic—the right of the majority to rule individuals; the other is antidemocratic—the right of individuals to have certain interests protected from majority rule. He relies on the Constitution's text to define the respective spheres of majority and minority freedom, and when that fails to provide definitive guidance, Scalia turns to tradition. He argues that tradition, not the personal values of the justices, is to tell the Court when the majoritarian process is to be overruled in favor of individual rights. He believes that by identifying those areas of life traditionally protected from majority rule, the Court can objectively determine

Antonin Scalia

which individual freedoms the Constitution protects. As he argued in his dissent in *Board of County Commissioners, Wabaunsee County v. Umbehr* (1996), "I would separate the permissible from the impermissible on the basis of our Nation's traditions, *which* is what I believe sound constitutional adjudication requires."

Scalia, therefore, would overrule the majority only when it has infringed upon an individual right explicitly protected by the text of the Constitution or by specific legal traditions flowing from that text. In his dissent in *United States v. Virginia* (1996), in which the Court proclaimed that the Virginia Military Institute's exclusively male admission policy violated the equal protection clause of the Fourteenth Amendment, he declared that the function of the Court is to "preserve our society's values, not to revise them; to prevent backsliding from the degree of restriction the Constitution imposed upon democratic government, not to prescribe, on our own authority, progressively higher degrees." The Court is not to "supersede" but rather to "reflect" those "constant and unbroken national traditions that embody the people's understanding of ambiguous constitutional texts."

In *Harmelin v. Michigan* (1991), Scalia's text-and-tradition approach was on full display. In it, he held that the cruel and unusual punishments clause of the Eighth Amendment does not prohibit the imposition of a mandatory term of life in prison without the possibility of parole for possessing more than 650 grams of cocaine. Announcing the judgment of the Court, he rejected the plaintiff's contention that his sentence was unconstitutional because it was "significantly disproportionate" to the crime he had committed. Scalia noted that "this claim has no support in the text and history of the Eighth Amendment." Concerning the text, he observed that "to use the phrase 'cruel and unusual punishment' to describe a requirement of proportionality would have been an exceedingly vague and oblique way of saying what Americans were well accustomed to saying more directly." Concerning history, he surveyed English constitutional history since the promulgation of the English Declaration of Rights, as well as eighteenth- and nineteenth-century American constitutional and legal history, to show that the cruel and unusual punishments clause was understood only "to outlaw particular modes of punishment," such as drawing and quartering, breaking on the wheel, flaying alive, not to require that "all punishments be proportioned to the offense." He was led, therefore, to argue that *Solem v. Helms* (1983), in which the Court had held that the Eighth Amendment does contain a proportionality guarantee, was "wrong" and should be overturned.

Although his textualist approach led Scalia in *Harmelin* to reject a criminal defendant's claim, it does not always. In *Coy v. Iowa* (1988), it led him to uphold the right of a defendant—a man convicted of two counts of engaging in lascivious acts with a child—literally to "be confronted with the witnesses against him" and to overturn his conviction because Iowa law allowed the two thirteen-year-old girls he was charged with sexually assaulting to testify behind a large screen that shielded them from the defendant. For Scalia, the text was unequivocal and governing:

"[s]imply as a matter of English" it confers at least "a right to meet face to face all those who appear and give evidence at trial." Simply as a matter of Latin as well, since the word "confront" ultimately derives from the prefix "con-" (from "contra" meaning "against" or "opposed") and the noun "frons" (forehead). Shakespeare was thus describing the root meaning of con-

frontation when he had Richard the Second say: "Then call them to our presence—face to face, and frowning brow to brow, ourselves will hear the accuser and the accused freely speak.

Scalia does not restrict his text-and-tradition approach to criminal procedural matters; rather, he applies it across the constitutional board. He applied it, for example, in *Pacific Mutual Life Insurance Co. v. Haslip* (1991) when he denied that the due process clause places limits on the size of punitive damage awards. He argued that due process is met if the trial is conducted according to the settled course of judicial proceedings. "If the government chooses to follow a historically approved procedure, it necessarily provides due process."

He has also applied his text-and-tradition approach to the religion clauses. It led him to conclude in his dissent in *Lee v. Weisman* (1992) that the establishment clause "was adopted to prohibit such an establishment of religion at the federal level (and to protect state establishments of religion from federal interference)" and that it did not bar nonsectarian prayers at public school graduation ceremonies. Likewise, in the Ten Commandments case of *McCreary County v. ACLU of Kentucky* (2005), it led him to respond to Justice David Souter's assertion that "the First Amendment mandates governmental neutrality between religion and nonreligion" and that it is therefore unconstitutional to "manifest a purpose to favor adherence to religion generally" by asking:

Who says so? Surely not the words of the Constitution. Surely not the history and traditions that reflect our society's constant understanding of those words. Surely not even the current sense of our society, recently reflected in an Act of Congress adopted *unanimously* by the Senate and with only five nays in the House of Representatives, criticizing a Court of Appeals opinion that had held "under God" in the Pledge of Allegiance unconstitutional.

And, concerning the free exercise clause, his text-and-tradition approach led him to conclude in his controversial majority opinion in *Employment Division, Department of Human Resources of Oregon v. Smith* (1990) that "as a textual matter," there is no need to provide a religious exemption to a generally applicable statute, and that

> to make an individual's obligation to obey such a law contingent upon the law's coincidence with his religious beliefs, except where the State's interest is "compelling"—permitting him, by virtue of his beliefs, "to become a law unto himself,"—contradicts both constitutional tradition and common sense.

Scalia believes deeply in the text-and-tradition approach. His duty, as he described it in his dissent in *Planned Parenthood of Southeastern Pennsylvania v. Casey* (1992), is to "read the text and discern our society's traditional understanding of that text." Discerning the original meaning is, he told the Senate Judiciary Committee during his confirmation hearings, "the starting point and the beginning of wisdom." Nevertheless, Scalia occasionally drifts from his text-and-tradition moorings. A glaring case in point is *Texas v. Johnson* (1989), the Texas flag-burning case, in which he joined in Justice William Brennan's majority opinion striking down Texas's ban on burning the American flag. It is true that during his Senate confirmation hearings Scalia defined speech as "any communicative activity," and by that definition flag burning was communicative activity protected by the First Amendment. What is problematic, however, is not that Scalia's conclusion does not follow logically from his premise, but the premise itself. No textual or historical evidence exists to support the contention that the society that adopted the First Amendment understood it to cover all communicative activity.

A second example of Scalia's straying from his text-and-tradition approach is his unquestioning acceptance of the incorporation doctrine, which is possibly explained by his reluctance to be perceived as a Don Quixote tilting at windmills. As he observed in *Albright v. Oliver* (1994): "Our decisions have included within the Fourteenth Amendment certain explicit substantive protections of the Bill of Rights—

an extension I accept because it is both long established and narrowly limited."

A third example, and perhaps the most difficult to explain, is Scalia's consistent embrace of the Court's "state sovereign immunity" jurisprudence. In his 1991 opinion for the Court in *Blatchford v. Native Village of Noatak,* he expressed the decidedly nontextualist view that the Eleventh Amendment bars all suits against a state in federal court, even though its text is much narrower and bars only suits "commenced or prosecuted against one of the United States by citizens of another State, or by the Citizens or Subjects of any Foreign State." By its terms, the Eleventh Amendment precludes individuals from bringing suit against states in the federal courts only when the basis of jurisdiction is state-citizen diversity; it says nothing about precluding suits against the states in federal court that are based on the existence of a federal question. Nevertheless, Scalia insisted that the amendment stood "not so much for what it says, but for the presupposition ... which it confirms"—that presupposition being the doctrine that a state cannot be sued in federal court without its consent. And, in seven cases since 1996, he has invariably joined majority opinions that openly dismiss textualism and repeat the words of Chief Justice William Rehnquist, first uttered in *Seminole Tribe of Florida v. Florida* (1996), that "a blind reliance upon the text of the Eleventh Amendment" would be "overly exacting."

Scalia believes that "the rule of law is the law of rules," which reflects the title of his Oliver Wendell Holmes Lecture delivered at Harvard Law School in 1989. He argues that where the text embodies a rule, judges are simply to apply that rule as the law. Where text and tradition fail to supply a rule, there is no rule. Therefore, there is no law for judges to apply to contradict the actions of the political branches and no warrant for judicial intervention.

In his book *A Matter of Interpretation,* Scalia succinctly spelled out both the origins of judicial policymaking and his reasons for rejecting it. Judicial policymaking arose, he noted, in the old common-law system in England, where judges, unconstrained by statutes or a written constitution, exercised the "exhilarating" function of making law. From there, it eventually spread to modern American law schools where impressionable "law students, having drunk at this intoxicating well," come away thinking that the highest function of the judge is "devising, out of the brilliance of one's own mind, those laws that ought to govern mankind. How exciting!" He noted a central problem with this approach: it is a "trend in government that has developed in recent centuries, called democracy." As Scalia insisted, "It is simply not compatible with democratic theory that laws mean whatever they ought to mean, and that unelected judges decide what that is."

As one committed to a text-and-tradition approach to constitutional interpretation, Scalia has vigorously resisted the tendency among a number of his colleagues on the Supreme Court to turn to foreign law and practices for guidance on the meaning of various provisions of the U.S. Constitution, especially the cruel and unusual punishments clause of the Eighth Amendment. In *Thompson v. Oklahoma* (1988), he paraphrased Chief Justice John Marshall's words and said, "We must never forget that it is a Constitution for the United States of America that we are expounding." And, in his dissent in the juvenile death penalty case of *Roper v. Simmons* (2005), he declared that "the basic premise of the Court's argument—that American law should conform to the laws of the rest of the world—ought to be rejected out of hand." He pointed out that "in many significant respects the laws of most other countries differ from our law." Not only do they lack "such explicit provisions of our Constitution as the right to jury trial and grand jury indictment," but they also reject "many interpretations of the Constitution prescribed by this Court itself." He reminded his colleagues that the Supreme Court's exclusionary rule, which excludes from introduction at trial illegally seized evidence, is "distinctively American" and "has been 'universally rejected' by other countries, including those with rules prohibiting illegal searches and police misconduct." England and Canada, he noted, rarely exclude evidence, and the Court majority's favorite international institution, the European Court of Human Rights, "has held that introduction of illegally seized evidence does not violate ... Article 6, § 1, of the European Convention on Human Rights."

Scalia was certain that the Court would be unwilling to conform to international opinion concerning the exclusionary rule; to read the First Amendment's establishment clause in the light of the practices of "the Netherlands, Germany, and Australia [all of which] allow direct government funding of religious schools"; to modify its abortion jurisprudence, "which makes us one of only six countries that allow abortion on demand until the point of viability"; or to "relax our double jeopardy prohibition" and "curtail our right to jury trial in criminal cases" because England now allows "the prosecution to appeal cases where an acquittal was the result of a judge's ruling that was legally incorrect" and "permits all but the most serious offenders to be tried by magistrates without a jury." He challenged the Court to "profess its willingness to reconsider all these matters in light of the views of foreigners" or to "cease putting forth foreigners' views as part of the *reasoned basis* of its decisions. To invoke alien law when it agrees with one's own thinking, and ignore it otherwise, is not reasoned decision making, but sophistry."

As a textualist, Scalia also totally rejects reliance on legislative history or legislative intent. He invariably criticizes his colleagues for turning to committee reports, floor speeches, and even colloquies between members of Congress to ascertain what a law means because, as he declared in *Thompson v. Thompson* (1988), they "are frail substitutes for a bicameral vote upon the text of the law and its presentment to the President." The Court's use of legislative history lends itself, he wryly observed in *Koons Buick Pontiac GMC v. Nigh* (2004), "to a kind of ventriloquism. The *Congressional Record* or committee reports are used to make words appear to come from Congress's mouth which were spoken or written by others (individual Members of Congress, congressional aides, or even enterprising lobbyists)."

Scalia argues that the Court is to interpret the text alone and nothing else. The law should be understood to mean what it says, and say what it means. Otherwise, as Scalia noted in his court of appeals dissent in *Illinois Commerce Commission v. Interstate Commerce Commission* (1984), compromise, so essential to the legislative process, "becomes impossible." "When there is no assurance that the statutory words in which [the compromise] is contained will be honored," both sides to a compromise "have every reason to fear that any ambiguity will be interpreted against their interests" in subsequent litigation. Likewise, if the law does not mean what it says and does not say what it means, citizens are left at a loss concerning how they should conduct themselves. As he said in *United States v. R. L. C.* (1992): "It may well be true that in most cases the proposition that the words of the United States Code or the Statutes at Large give adequate notice to the citizen is something of a fiction, albeit one required in any system of law, but necessary fiction descends to needless farce when the public is charged even with knowledge of Committee Reports."

When the Court departs from the text of the statute and considers the legislative history surrounding its passage, its exegesis, Scalia argues, undermines rather than fosters the "democratic process" and fails to cabin the discretion of judges. As he wrote in *A Matter of Interpretation,* citing legislative history is like "look[ing] over the heads of a crowd and pick[ing] out your friends." And such an exegesis removes any incentive for Congress to enact clearer statutes. Scalia believes that if Congress knows that the Court will focus only on the text of a statute and not its legislative history, it will be more diligent and precise in its drafting. He declared for the Court in *Finley v. United States* (1989):

> Whatever we say regarding ... a particular statute can of course be changed by Congress. What is of paramount importance is that Congress be able to legislate against a background of clear interpretive rules, so that it may know the effect of the language it adopts.

Scalia emphatically rejects legislative history and intent, yet he is described, and describes himself, as an originalist. On the surface, this contradiction suggests a tension: If it is a mistake to consult extrinsic evidence

of Congress's intentions as found in a law's legislative history, why is it appropriate for him to consult extrinsic evidence of the framers' intentions as found, for example, in *The Federalist*? The tension is heightened further as a result of Scalia's assertion in *Tome v. United States* (1995) that "the views of Alexander Hamilton (a draftsman) bear [no] more authority than the views of Thomas Jefferson (not a draftsman) with regard to the meaning of the Constitution."

The answer to that question is that Scalia is a particular kind of originalist. What he means by originalism is revealed by illustration in his Holmes Lecture: "If a barn was not considered the curtilage of a house in 1791, ... and the Fourth Amendment did not cover it then, unlawful entry into a barn today may be a trespass, but not an unconstitutional search and seizure." For Scalia, originalism is synonymous with the original meaning doctrine. He seeks the original meaning from the text of the document itself and from what it meant to the society that adopted it; at the same time, he ignores altogether the subjective preferences or intentions of those who wrote it. Moreover, for Scalia, originalism means applying that original meaning to the case at hand. His application of originalism in the context of the Fourth Amendment is clearly evident in his majority opinion for the Court in *Kyllo v. United States* (2001). *Kyllo* involved the warrantless use from a public street of a thermal-imaging device aimed at a private residence occupied by someone suspected of growing marijuana. The device detected relative amounts of heat within the residence and whether high-intensity lights were being used indoors. Scalia held its warrantless use was unreasonable and therefore constituted an unlawful search within the meaning of the Fourth Amendment. He declared:

> In the case of the search of the interior of homes—the prototypical and hence most commonly litigated area of protected privacy—there is a ready criterion, with roots deep in the common law, of the minimal expectation of privacy that *exists,* and that is acknowledged to be *reasonable.* To withdraw protection of this minimum

expectation would be to permit police technology to erode the privacy guaranteed by the Fourth Amendment. We think that obtaining by sense-enhancing technology any information regarding the interior of the home that could not otherwise have been obtained without physical "intrusion into a constitutionally protected area" constitutes a search—at least where (as here) the technology in question is not in general public use. This assures preservation of that degree of privacy against government that existed when the Fourth Amendment was adopted.

In his essay "Originalism: The Lesser Evil," published in 1989 in the *University of Cincinnati Law Review,* Scalia contrasted his originalism with nonoriginalism, which he defined as a method of interpreting the Constitution "not on the basis of what the Constitution originally meant, but on the basis of what judges currently [think] it desirable for it to mean." According to Scalia, the principal defect of nonoriginalism is "the impossibility of achieving any consensus on what, precisely, is to replace original meaning, once that is abandoned." He noted that nonoriginalists invoke "fundamental values as the touchstone of constitutionality" but observed that "it is very difficult for a person to discern a difference between those political values that he personally thinks important, and those political values that are 'fundamental to our society.' Thus, by the adoption of such a criterion judicial personalization of the law is enormously facilitated." He also observed that those values that are "fundamental to our society" can both expand and contract. Describing nonoriginalism as "a two-way street that handles traffic both to and from individual rights," he contrasted it with his originalism as displayed in *Coy v. Iowa,* in which he secured the confrontation rights of a criminal defendant against legislation passed by a state less concerned with the text and tradition of the Sixth Amendment than with the "emotional frailty of children and the sensitivity of young women regarding sexual abuse."

As an originalist, Scalia cites and quotes from *The Federalist* to reveal constitutional history—to show how those who drafted and ratified the Constitution saw its various structural provisions and principles as means for achieving the ends the Constitution was drafted to secure. He studies the framers, and especially *The Federalist,* not to find out what the framers, either individually or collectively, would have done if faced with a specific contemporary constitutional issue, but rather to understand (given the words they used) how the framers designed the Constitution to work and, on that basis, to ascertain how, institutionally, they intended for that issue to be addressed. What Scalia finds is that the framers generally and *The Federalist* in particular placed great emphasis on constitutional structure. During his confirmation hearings, he was asked by Sen. Strom Thurmond, R-S.C., why he thought the Constitution had endured for so long—why he thought it had come to be "the oldest existing Constitution in the world today." Scalia responded:

I think most of the questions today will probably be about that portion of the Constitution that is called the Bill of Rights, which is a very important part of it, of course. But if you had to put your finger on what has made our Constitution so enduring, I think it is the original document before the amendments were added. Because the amendments, by themselves, do not do anything. The Russian constitution probably has better, or at least as good guarantees of personal freedom as our document does. What makes it work, what assures that those words [in the Bill of Rights] are not just hollow promises, is the structure of government that the original Constitution established, the checks and balances among the three branches, in particular, so that no one of them is able to "run roughshod" over the liberties of the people as those liberties are described in the Bill of Rights.

The structure of the Constitution—especially separation of powers—and the need to preserve that structure was central to Scalia's dissent in *Morrison v. Olson* (1988) and his majority opinion in *Plaut v. Spendthrift Farm* (1995). Scalia's textualist jurisprudence generally demands deference to the popular branches, but not in separation of powers cases. As he pointed out in *Morrison,* the independent counsel case, in such cases, the "caution that we owe great deference to Congress's view that what it has done is constitutional . . . does not apply." He continued:

> Where a private citizen challenges action of the Government on grounds unrelated to separation of powers, harmonious functioning of the system demands that we ordinarily give some deference, or a presumption of validity, to the actions of the political branches in what is agreed, between themselves at least, to be within their respective spheres. But where the issue pertains to separation of powers, and the political branches are (as here) in disagreement, neither can be presumed correct. . . . The playing field for the present case . . . is a level one. As one of the interested and coordinate parties to the underlying constitutional dispute, Congress, no more than the President, is entitled to the benefit of the doubt.

Feeling no obligation to presume the constitutionality of the independent counsel statute, Scalia complained that Congress had "effectively compelled a criminal investigation of a high-level appointee of the President in connection with his actions arising out of a bitter power dispute between the President and the Legislative Branch." He further objected that Congress also removed "the decisions regarding the scope of [any] further investigation, its duration, and finally whether or not prosecution should ensue" from "the control of the President and his subordinates" and placed them instead in the hands of a "mini-Executive that is the independent counsel." Quoting the language of Article II, Section 1, clause 1, of the Constitution, providing that "the executive Power shall be vested in a President of the United States," Scalia declared, "This does not mean some of the executive power, but all of the executive power." He then proclaimed that "governmental investigation and prosecution of crimes is a quintessentially executive function" and that "the statute before us deprives the President of exclusive control over that quintessentially executive activity."

The Court majority's response conceded that the statute reduced the president's control but insisted that he preserved "sufficient control" to "perform his constitutionally assigned duties" and that it did not "interfere impermissibly with his constitutional obligation to ensure the faithful execution of the laws." Scalia's rejoinder was direct: "It is not for us to determine, and we have never presumed to determine, how much of the purely executive powers of government must be within the full control of the President. The Constitution prescribes that they all are." He accused the Court majority of replacing "the clear constitutional prescription that the executive power belongs to the President with a 'balancing test,' " and of abandoning the "text of the Constitution" as the "governing standard" in favor of "what might be called the unfettered wisdom of a majority of this Court, revealed to an obedient people on a case-by-case basis." For his part, Scalia preferred "to rely upon the judgment of the wise men who constructed our system, and of the people who approved it, and of the two centuries of history that have shown it to be sound."

Declaring that "if to describe this case is not to decide it, the concept of a government of separate and coordinate powers no longer has meaning," Scalia attacked his colleagues for their failure to abide by what "the text of the Constitution seems to require, . . . the Founders seemed to expect, and . . . our past cases have uniformly assumed." He sought to preserve separation of powers because, as he noted, "Without a secure structure of separated powers, our Bill of Rights would be worthless, as are the bills of rights of many nations of the world that have adopted, or even improved upon, the mere words of ours." Scalia's argument in *Morrison* is clear: by refusing in this case to defer to Congress and by steadfastly protecting constitutional structure, he can be restrained and deferential elsewhere—in other words, he is spared the need in other cases to protect constitutional rights that are better secured by structure than by judges.

In *Plaut,* Scalia declared for a seven-member majority that Congress violated separation of powers by "requiring the federal courts to exercise 'the Judicial Power of the United States' in a manner repugnant to the text, structure, and traditions of Article III." It did so when it passed a law requiring federal courts to reopen final judgments in private civil actions under the Securities Exchange Act for those plaintiffs whose suits for fraud and deceit in the sale of stock had been dismissed as time-barred because of an earlier Court decision that had the effect of reducing the length of time in which such suits could be filed. Scalia recognized that Congress was motivated by good intentions—the desire to assist defrauded shareholders hurt by the Court's earlier ruling. But he insisted: "Not favoritism, not even corruption, but power is the object of the separation-of-powers prohibition. The prohibition is violated when an individual final judgment is legislatively rescinded for even the very best of reasons, such as the legislature's genuine conviction (supported by all the law professors in the land) that the judgment was wrong." The doctrine of separation of powers, he contended, "is a structural safeguard rather than a remedy to be applied only when specific harm, or the risk of specific harm, can be identified. In its major features, it is a prophylactic device, establishing high walls and clear distinctions because low walls and vague distinctions will not be judicially defensible in the heat of interbranch conflict." In *Plaut*, Scalia likened what Congress had done to its widespread use of legislative vetoes declared unconstitutional in *Immigration and Naturalization Service v. Chadha* (1983) and asserted that "legislated invalidation of judicial judgments deserves the same categorical treatment accorded by *Chadha* to congressional invalidation of executive action." He concluded: "Separation of powers, a distinctively American political doctrine, profits from the advice authored by a distinctively American poet: Good fences make good neighbors."

Scalia's invocation of Robert Frost prompted Justice Stephen Breyer, who concurred only in the judgment and not in Scalia's opinion, to respond in kind: "As the majority invokes the advice of an American poet, one might consider as well that poet's caution, for he not only notes that 'Something there is that

doesn't love a wall,' but also writes, 'Before I built a wall I'd ask to know / What I was walling in or walling out.' " Breyer's selection of these particular lines from Frost highlights the chasm that exists between him and Scalia—and more generally between the Court and Scalia—concerning separation of powers. Unlike Breyer and most of Scalia's colleagues, Scalia loves the wall of separation of powers. He loves it because, as he said in his *Morrison* dissent, "without a secure structure of separated powers, our Bill of Rights would be worthless." He loves this wall and wants it kept high and strong because, as he noted in *Plaut*, "low walls . . . will not be judicially defensible in the heat of interbranch conflict." He also loves the wall of separation of powers, because, as he said in *Morrison*, it was built by and reflects the "judgment of the wise men who constructed our system, and of the people who approved it, and of the two centuries that have shown it to be sound." Additionally, unlike Breyer and those others, Scalia would never quote a passage that implies that it is his job to build the wall and, therefore, his task to decide what to wall in or wall out. True to his text-and-tradition jurisprudence, Scalia would argue that the justices are to secure the wall of separation of powers built by the framers, not wonder whether it is worthy of their love and certainly not replace it with one of their own design. The decisions of the framers concerning constitutional structure are for the justices to secure, not to alter or to second-guess.

Scalia's textualist approach is also apparent when he addresses questions pertaining to the other principal structural feature of the Constitution, federalism. He has opposed the Court's "negative" or "dormant" commerce clause jurisprudence, which serves as a major limitation on the power of the states, because, as he argued in *Tyler Pipe Industries v. Washington State Department of Revenue* (1987), it has "no foundation in the text of the Constitution." In his concurrence in that case, he observed that the commerce clause of Article I, Section 8, is an express grant of power to Congress, not to the Court, and that if the federal government is to eliminate state burdens on interstate commerce, it must be by an affirmative act of the Congress, exercising its enumerated power to do so, not by the Court, proceeding on the nontextualist premise that the commerce clause has also delegated to it the power to keep interstate trade free from restrictive state regulation. He relies on the text of the supremacy clause to justify Congress's power to preempt all state regulations that are incompatible with federal law, and he carefully studies the text of the federal law in question to determine, as he put it in *Puerto Rico Department of Consumer Affairs v. Isla Petroleum Corp.* (1988), whether the "statutory cat" has a "pre-emptive grin." If it does, he will give it full preemptive effect. But if it does not, or if it cannot be determined definitively from its text that it does, he will permit the states to regulate as they choose. And, as *Printz v. United States* (1997) and *Branch v. Smith* (2003) make clear, he relies on specific constitutional texts such as the take care clause of Article II, Section 3, or the times, places, and manner clause of Article I, Section 4, to determine whether federal commandeering statutes will be affirmed or struck, protecting federalism only when doing so is not incompatible with the words of these texts.

Scalia's textualist jurisprudence leads him to seek to understand the original meaning of the substantive rights found in the First Amendment and the equal protection clause and the procedural rights found in the due process clauses of the Fifth and Fourteenth Amendments and the criminal procedural provisions of the Fourth through Eighth Amendments. Accordingly, in his majority opinion in *Employment Division v. Smith* and his dissents in *Lee v. Weisman, McCreary County v. ACLU,* and *Locke v. Davey* (2004), Scalia has adopted what might be called a "no preferences, no privileges, no penalties" approach to the establishment and free exercise clauses; in his concurring opinion in *Barnes v. Glen Theatre, Inc.* (1991) and his dissent in *McConnell v. Federal Elections Commission* (2003), he has limited the free speech and press clauses to oral and written speech and not to expressive conduct unless the government has prohibited the conduct precisely because of its communicative attributes; and in his concurring opinions in *Adarand Constructors v. Pena* (1995) and *City of Richmond v. J. A. Croson* (1989) and in his dissenting opinion in

United States v. Virginia, he has interpreted the equal protection clause to ban only racial discrimination—but in all its forms, invidious or otherwise.

Scalia is often described as a judicial conservative who favors the government over the individual when the due process clauses and criminal procedural protections are involved. That description is, however, not true. By pursuing a text-and-tradition approach that seeks to understand the original meaning of these rights and then faithfully apply that meaning to the facts in the cases before him, he often comes down solidly on the side of the individual. His powerful dissent on behalf of the defendant in the due process case of *Rogers v. Tennessee* (2001); his strong Fourth Amendment opinions on behalf of criminal defendants in *County of Riverside v. McLaughlin* (1991) and *Kyllo v. United States* and customs employees in *National Employees Union v. Von Raab* (1989); his forceful confrontation clause opinions in *Crawford v. Washington* (2004) and *Coy v. Iowa;* and his passionate commitment to a defendant's Sixth Amendment right to have a jury determine every element of the crime charged in *Blakely v. Washington* (2004) are all examples.

With regard to other provisions, however, Scalia's textualist approach leads him to favor the government. He has held that the government can, consistent with the traditional understanding of due process, pass laws that allow for unlimited punitive damages in *BMW v. Gore* (1996); grant visitation rights to grandparents in *Troxel v. Granville* (2000); prevent suicide in *Cruzan v. Director, Missouri Department of Health* (1990); and criminalize homosexuality in *Lawrence v. Texas* (2003). And he has concluded that the government can have laws and procedures in place that impose successive punishments—so long as it do not engage in successive prosecutions—in *Department of Revenue of Montana v. Kurth Ranch* (1994); encourage confessions—so long as it does not compel them—in *McNeil v. Wisconsin* (1991); impose punishments that are disproportional to the offense—so long as it does not inflict certain cruel methods of punishment not regularly employed when the Eighth Amendment was ratified—in

Harmelin v. Michigan; and impose the death penalty on those convicted of murder regardless of age or mental retardation—so long as the defendant is subject to the jurisdiction of the adult courts and the punishment is either mandatory or the sentencing judge or jury has found at least one aggravating factor—in such cases as *Atkins v. Virginia* (2002), *Tennard v. Dretke* (2004), and *Roper v. Simmons* (2005).

And, if not most important, then certainly most controversial, his text-and-tradition approach allows the government to pass whatever laws it wishes concerning abortion. As he declared in his dissent in *Planned Parenthood of Southeastern Pennsylvania v. Casey:*

> The States may, if they wish, permit abortion on demand, but the Constitution does not *require* them to do so. The permissibility of abortion, and the limitations upon it, are to be resolved like most important questions in our democracy: by citizens trying to persuade one another and then voting. . . . The issue [is] whether [the power of a woman to abort her unborn child] is a liberty protected by the Constitution of the United States. I am sure it is not. I reach that conclusion . . . because of two simple facts: (1) the Constitution says absolutely nothing about it, and (2) the longstanding traditions of American society have permitted it to be legally proscribed.

In *A Matter of Interpretation,* Justice Scalia acknowledged that his textualist jurisprudence is regarded in "some sophisticated circles" of the legal profession as "simpleminded—'wooden,' 'unimaginative,' 'pedestrian.' " He rejected this characterization and denied that he was "too dull to perceive the broader social purposes that a statute is designed, or could be designed to serve, or too hidebound to realize that new times require new laws"; he merely insisted that judges "have no authority to pursue those broader purposes or to write those new laws." During his distinguished career on the Supreme Court, Scalia has remained faithful to the "text and tradition" of the written Constitution and has rejected the intellectual fads and novel theories of

interpretation that he sees as having the invariable effect of transferring power from the political branches to the judiciary. In so doing, he reminds his colleagues of the most important right of the people in a democracy—the right to govern themselves as they see fit and to be overruled in their governance only when the clear text or traditional understanding of the Constitution they have adopted demands it.

—*Ralph A. Rossum*

BIBLIOGRAPHY

Scalia spells out the principles and reasons for his textualist jurisprudence in Antonin Scalia, "The Rule of Law as a Law of Rules," *University of Chicago Law Review* 56 (1989): 1175; and Scalia, "Originalism: The Lesser Evil," *University of Cincinnati Law Review* 57 (1989): 849. In *A Matter of Interpretation: Federal Courts and the Law* (1997), Scalia further elaborates on his jurisprudential approach in his essay "Common-Law Courts in a Civil Law System: The Role of United States Federal Courts in Interpreting the Constitution and Laws," based on his 1995 Tanner Lectures on Human Values delivered at Princeton University; the book then provides commentaries on his essay by four prominent constitutional scholars (Gordon S. Wood, Laurence H. Tribe, Mary Ann Glendon, and Ronald Dworkin) and Scalia's replies to these commentators.

Michael H. Koby, "The Supreme Court's Declining Reliance on Legislative History: The Impact of Justice Scalia's Critique," *Harvard Journal on Legislation* 36 (1999): 369, is an excellent treatment of Scalia's objections to and successful critique of the use of legislative history in Supreme Court decisions. Hadley Arkes, "Scalia *Contra Mundum,*" *Harvard Journal of Law & Public Policy* 21 (1997): 231, provides an important analysis of the philosophical premises of Scalia's jurisprudence. Two recently published books offer brief but intelligent introductory essays on Scalia's textualist approach, followed by well-chosen samples of Scalia's opinions on a variety of topics—especially in the area of civil rights and liberties—that employ that approach: Kevin A. Ring, ed., *Scalia Dissents* (2004); and Paul I. Weizer, ed., *The Opinions of Justice Antonin Scalia* (2004). The only recent comprehensive treatment of Justice Scalia's understanding of constitutional and statutory interpretation and the role of the Court is Ralph A. Rossum, *Antonin Scalia's Jurisprudence: Text and Tradition* (2006).

NOTEWORTHY OPINIONS

Morrison v. Olson, 487 U.S. 654 (1988) (Dissent)

Coy v. Iowa, 487 U.S. 1012 (1988)

Employment Division, Department of Human Resources of Oregon v. Smith, 494 U.S. 872 (1990)

Harmelin v. Michigan, 501 U.S. 957 (1991)

Lee v. Weisman, 505 U.S. 577 (1992) (Dissent)

Planned Parenthood of Southeastern Pennsylvania v. Casey, 505 U.S. 833 (1992) (Dissent)

Plaut v. Spendthrift Farm, 514 U.S. 211 (1995)

Adarand Constructors v. Pena, 515 U.S. 200 (1995) (Concurrence)

United States v. Virginia, 518 U.S. 515 (1996) (Dissent)

Rogers v. Tennessee, 532 U.S. 451 (2001) (Dissent)

Kyllo v. United States, 533 U.S. 27 (2001)

McConnell v. Federal Elections Commission, 540 U.S. 93 (2003) (Dissent)

McCreary County v. ACLU of Kentucky, 545 U.S. __ (2005) (Dissent)

GEORGE SHIRAS JR.

Birth: January 26, 1832, Pittsburgh, Pennsylvania.

Education: Ohio University, 1849–1851; Yale University, B.A., 1853, honorary LL.D., 1883; studied law at Yale and privately; admitted to the bar in 1855.

Official Positions: None.

Supreme Court Service: Nominated associate justice by President Benjamin Harrison, July 19, 1892, to replace Joseph P. Bradley, who had died; confirmed by the Senate, July 26, 1892, by a voice vote; took judicial oath October 10, 1892; retired February 23, 1903; replaced by William R. Day, nominated by President Theodore Roosevelt.

Death: August 2, 1924, Pittsburgh, Pennsylvania.

His position on the U.S. Supreme Court was the only public office George Shiras Jr. ever held. Son of a prosperous Pennsylvania brewer, Shiras received his bachelor's degree from Yale University in 1853. After studying briefly at Yale Law School, he read law privately and won admittance to the bar in 1855. Quickly building up a lucrative practice, Shiras represented illustrious corporate clients such as Carnegie Steel and the Baltimore and Ohio Railroad. His aloofness from factional politics and his support by powerful men, including Andrew Carnegie, helped win his 1892 appointment and confirmation as associate justice.

Shiras joined the Court at a time of economic upheaval in the United States. Reform-minded Republicans and Democrats, as well as Populists, Socialists, and Progressives, all pushed for regulation of big business by both the state and national governments. Powerful corporate interests, supported by many lawyers and politicians, fought the new wave of business regulation. On the Court, Shiras tended to steer a middle course, often slow to approve of regulation, but not blindly supporting big business, either.

In the years just before Shiras joined the Court, justices had been using the due process clause of the Fourteenth Amendment to insist that states' regulation of business must be "reasonable" and that the courts could determine what was reasonable, striking down statutes that did not meet the test. Shiras, however, was slower than a number of his colleagues to strike down state statutes. One of his first important decisions was the majority opinion in *Brass v. North Dakota ex rel. Stoeser* (1894), dealing with state regulation of grain elevators. Previously, the Court had upheld such regulation if aimed at monopolistic situations. In *Brass*, however, North Dakota was regulating a system of elevators in which healthy competition was present. Shiras held that because the Court had earlier ruled that states had the right to regulate grain elevators, it was not for the judicial branch to examine myriad individual cases. The legislatures should weigh the different situations in each state, Shiras concluded. Four justices dissented angrily.

In other cases of state regulation of business, Shiras voted with the majority to uphold Utah's requirement of an eight-hour workday for miners in *Holden v. Hardy* (1898). He also wrote the majority opinion in *Knoxville Iron Co. v. Harbison* (1901), sustaining a Tennessee law that companies paying workers in scrip must be willing to redeem the scrip in cash.

Shiras was less friendly toward federal economic legislation, such as the Sherman Antitrust Act, the Interstate Commerce Act, and the federal income tax. The income tax case provided Shiras with his one moment of notoriety on the Court. In *Pollock v. Farmers' Loan & Trust* (1895), the Court divided 4–4 on some of the most important issues, and the justices decided to rehear the case when all nine members were present. Shiras was widely accused of changing his vote, from upholding the income tax at the first hearing to opposing it at the rehearing. Later evidence seemed to suggest that another justice, not Shiras, changed his vote. At any rate, Shiras did vote with the majority in the second *Pollock* case to strike down the tax. Recent historians regard that decision as contrary to well-established precedent, revealing a conservative Court fighting the new economic trends.

George Shiras Jr.

In the civil liberties arena, Shiras was one of the more liberal justices of his time. It is true that he voted to uphold state laws separating the races or denying rights to blacks in cases such as *Plessy v. Ferguson* (1896) and *Williams v. Mississippi* (1898). But in his majority opinion in *Swearingen v. United States* (1896), Shiras and four other justices refused to uphold the conviction of a populist editor accused of violating a federal obscenity law in one of his political editorials.

Arguably, Shiras's most important opinion was *Wong Wing v. United States* (1896). Congress had passed a series of laws limiting Chinese immigration and calling for the deportation of Chinese who were illegally in the country. Congress added a provision that U.S. commissioners (the federal equivalent of justices of the peace) could sentence Chinese aliens to hard labor prior to their deportation. Speaking for a unanimous court, Shiras held that the Fifth Amendment promise of trial by jury applied to aliens as well as to citizens. Wong Wing had not received a jury trial, and the Court overturned his sentence of a year at hard labor.

When Shiras retired in 1903, he was seventy-one years old and still in good health. In his eleven years on the Court, he had avoided extremism; he was a team player who generally sided with the majority, writing only fourteen dissenting opinions during his tenure. He died in 1924 at the age of ninety-two.

—*Stephen Cresswell*

BIBLIOGRAPHY

The fullest documentation of Shiras's life is contained in a book by his son and grandson: George Shiras III and Winfield Shiras, *Justice George Shiras, Jr., of Pittsburgh* (1953). An excellent treatment of the legal culture of Shiras's day is Arnold M. Paul, *Conservative Crisis and the Rule of Law: Attitudes of Bar and Bench, 1887–1895* (1960). See also Paul's solid treatment of Shiras in Friedman and Israel, *Justices*, vol. 2, 1577.

NOTEWORTHY OPINIONS

Brass v. North Dakota ex rel. Stoeser, 153 U.S. 391 (1894)

Swearingen v. United States, 161 U.S. 446 (1896)

Wong Wing v. United States, 163 U.S. 228 (1896)

Knoxville Iron Co. v. Harbison, 183 U.S. 13 (1901)

DAVID HACKETT SOUTER

Birth: September 17, 1939, Melrose, Massachusetts.

Education: Harvard College, B.A., 1961; Oxford University (Rhodes Scholar), 1961–1963; Harvard University Law School, LL.B., 1966.

Official Positions: Assistant attorney general, New Hampshire, 1968–1971; deputy attorney general, New Hampshire, 1971–1976; attorney general, New Hampshire, 1976–1978; associate justice, New Hampshire Superior Court, 1978–1983; associate justice, New Hampshire Supreme Court, 1983–1990; judge, U.S. Court of Appeals for the First Circuit, 1990.

Supreme Court Service: Nominated associate justice by President George H. W. Bush, July 25, 1990, to replace William J. Brennan Jr., who had retired; confirmed by the Senate, October 2, 1990, by a 90–9 vote; took judicial oath October 9, 1990.

David Souter was appointed in 1990 by President George H. W. Bush to be the 105th justice to serve on the U.S. Supreme Court. Born in Melrose, Massachusetts, a Boston suburb, Souter at age eleven moved with his parents to the small town of Weare, New Hampshire, to a home in which his grandparents had lived. The small town life helped shape Souter's vision of participatory democracy. As he recalled at his Senate confirmation hearing, "I would sit in the benches in the back of the town hall after school, and that is where I began my lessons in practical government." His father worked as a banker in nearby Concord, and Souter commuted to Concord High School. He met with considerable academic success, graduating from Harvard in 1961, earning a two-year Rhodes Scholarship, which he spent at Magdalen College at Oxford, and then receiving a law degree from Harvard Law School in 1966.

Souter returned to New Hampshire and worked in a private law firm for two years before joining the state attorney general's criminal prosecution staff. In 1971 Republican Warren Rudman, who had become the state's attorney general the year before, picked Souter to be his deputy and to run the day-to-day operations of the office. In 1976, when the moderate Rudman's term expired, Souter succeeded him as attorney general of New Hampshire, appointed at Rudman's urging by the very conservative Republican governor, Meldrim Thomson. These were the first occasions, but not the last, on which Rudman boosted the career of his protégé, Souter. Two years later, Souter was appointed to be a trial judge on the New Hampshire Superior Court. By 1983 the political landscape had changed; Rudman had been elected to the U.S. Senate in 1980, and another conservative Republican, John Sununu, had become governor in 1982, a combination of individuals that would play a major role in Souter's life. At Rudman's urging, Sununu elevated Souter to a seat on the New Hampshire Supreme Court, where he earned a reputation for possessing a powerful intellect, asking tough questions from the bench, and producing well-reasoned opinions. With Rudman on his side again, in 1990 Souter was nominated and confirmed to a vacancy on the U.S. Court of Appeals for the First Circuit.

Before he could finish setting up chambers in Concord, and after only one sitting on the circuit court, President Bush selected Souter to fill the vacancy created by the unexpected retirement of Justice William J. Brennan Jr. The Senate confirmed Souter, 90–9, and he took his seat on October 9, 1990.

An analysis of Justice Souter's record on the Supreme Court must proceed in two parallel universes. First is the real universe in which an examination of his years as a justice reveals an intellectual force whose voice of moderation, often expressed in dissent, is deeply rooted in his study of the Court and constitutional history, but whose passion for his own privacy makes him an enigma. In the second universe resides an individual who seems more like a caricature of Souter, described as the paradigm "stealth" nominee with no record or background; criticized as a witness who, at his confirmation hearings, told the Senate too little about himself or even misled senators; tarred and feathered by conservatives as one of their own who betrayed the cause and became a moderate to liberal member of the Court.

David Hackett Souter

In the real universe, however, David Souter represents a tradition of thoughtful, independent-minded New England Republican leaders whose brand of conservatism predated the influence of Sen. Barry Goldwater, R-Ariz., or President Ronald Reagan. This tradition may have been less apparent during Souter's tenure as state attorney general and state supreme court justice, but that is not surprising, as he was engaged in a far more modest task than that of a justice sitting on the U.S. Supreme Court. He was engaged in the job of enforcing the laws of his state, and that task lent itself naturally to a seemingly hard-nosed approach, one that appeared quite conservative.

Souter's tough-on-crime record did not give Republican conservatives enough to satisfy them that the appointment was a solid one. But when Souter appeared before the Senate Judiciary Committee, conservatives apparently heard the reassurances they were seeking and which, to this day, they use to accuse him of duplicity in his testimony. Fifteen years after Souter's appointment, the editorial page of the *Wall Street Journal*, for example, still says, "David Souter repudiated his confirmation testimony and joined the Court's liberal wing." But these subsequent critics may have simply heard what they wanted to hear, for they clearly missed the voice of moderation that Souter revealed during three days of testimony. He offered strong praise for Justice John M. Harlan, a member of the Warren Court, who, although often in dissent, became a model for a philosophy that embodied both judicial restraint and recognition of privacy and other due process notions. He paid poignant tribute to the very liberal Brennan's fight for individual rights. He said he recognized the existence of privacy and other unenumerated rights in the Constitution. And he described judging in most compassionate terms in his opening statement, when he said about judges generally, "Some human life is going to be changed in some way by what we do."

The David Souter who appeared before the Senate Judiciary Committee fell somewhere between a moderate Republican and an individual who, as a state court judge, had not confronted many of the major federal constitutional issues of the day. Senator Rudman understood clearly, when he urged President Bush to pick Souter, that this is what Souter was about; White House Chief of Staff John Sununu, when he assured the president and conservative allies that Souter was one of them, apparently did not fully comprehend the distinction between a conservative who bought into the Reagan-Bush political agenda and a judge who was conservative because of his respect for precedent, history, and tradition.

Was Souter the perfect "stealth" nominee, as he has been described? The term stems from comments by Republican senators after the 1987 defeat of Judge Robert Bork for a Supreme Court seat. They noted that Bork suffered from too long a record of writings and speeches that made him an easy target, and they said that future nominees would be chosen precisely because they had little or no paper trail. Souter had given few speeches and had done little or no writing outside of briefs and court opinions, but the idea that this record was an insufficient basis on which to judge him was a product of the times. In an earlier era, William Brennan had presented even less than Souter for the Senate to examine—a half dozen speeches, private law practice, and opinions written as a state supreme court justice—but no one described Brennan as a "stealth" candidate.

Did Souter carefully and deliberately reveal little of himself at his confirmation hearings? His praise for Harlan, Brennan, and unenumerated rights actually seems quite forthcoming. He expressed a belief that

the due process clauses of the Fifth and Fourteenth Amendments protect substantive rights and liberties, and he assured the Senate with apparent candor that he had no agenda for how to approach cases involving *Roe v. Wade* (1973) and the right to abortion.

As a justice, Souter has expressed his views most clearly and forcefully, and with some frequency, in cases involving federalism and religious freedom. He has often taken on the formidable task of countering the arguments of Antonin Scalia, perhaps the Court's most conservative justice, a role at which Souter has proved adept.

Ironically, however, his legacy may be defined by his part in a single abortion case, *Planned Parenthood of Southeastern Pennsylvania v. Casey* (1992). The case presented the first reconsideration of *Roe v. Wade* not only for Souter but also for Justice Clarence Thomas, who joined the Court in 1991. With these two new Republican appointees on the bench, abortion opponents hoped the moment had arrived when the Court would vote to overrule *Roe* and declare that abortion was not a constitutionally protected right. The case was watched closely and carried with it an air of drama and suspense that was unusual even for the Supreme Court.

According to several writers about the Court and confirmed by information found in Justice Harry Blackmun's papers, Souter played a leading role behind the scenes in saving the right to abortion in *Casey*. He brought together Justices Sandra Day O'Connor and Anthony Kennedy to prepare an opinion, signed by the three of them, that said the concept of abortion as a constitutional right should be reaffirmed. Although the three authors of the ruling did not identify who wrote which sections, Souter is generally credited with the third part of the opinion, which contains an extensive and sometimes eloquent defense of the right to abortion as a precedent that is entitled to the Court's and the nation's respect.

Among his arguments were two interesting and unusual points. He maintained that women had come to rely on the availability of abortion, not so much in the narrow, practical sense that it factored into specific decisions about intimate relations, but rather that it contributed to the sense of freedom and equality that women and society had developed in the decades since *Roe*. "The ability of women to participate equally in the economic and social life of the Nation has been facilitated by their ability to control their reproductive lives," Souter wrote.

His second argument was that the credibility of the Court would be permanently damaged if it appeared that the Court was overruling *Roe* because of public opposition or political pressure. He wrote:

> Where, in the performance of its judicial duties, the Court decides a case in such a way as to resolve the sort of intensely divisive controversy reflected in *Roe* and those rare, comparable cases, its decision has a dimension that the resolution of the normal case does not carry. It is the dimension present whenever the Court's interpretation of the Constitution calls the contending sides of a national controversy to end their national division by accepting a common mandate rooted in the Constitution.
>
> The Court is not asked to do this very often. . . . But when the Court does act in this way, its decision requires an equally rare precedential force to counter the inevitable efforts to overturn it and to thwart its implementation. . . . So to overrule under fire in the absence of the most compelling reason to reexamine a watershed decision would subvert the Court's legitimacy beyond any serious question. . . .
>
> A decision to overrule *Roe*'s essential holding under the existing circumstances would address error, if error there was, at the cost of both profound and unnecessary damage to the Court's legitimacy, and to the Nation's commitment to the rule of law.

This portion of the decision strongly reflects Souter's persona; it combines his fascination with the Court as an institution and his passion for constitutional history. The formation of the three-justice coalition was, itself, a bold move. In a separate opinion in *Casey*, Blackmun, *Roe*'s author, wrote, "Make no mistake, the joint opinion . . . is an act of personal courage and constitutional principle."

Yet the effort to save *and* settle *Roe* was not successful and to some extent alienated all sides. Abortion opponents were upset because the basic right to abortion was preserved, *Roe* was not overruled, and a provision in the Pennsylvania law requiring women to notify their spouses before obtaining an abortion was struck down. Abortion rights groups had mixed reactions: the trimester approach to abortion regulation was scrapped; O'Connor's test was implicitly adopted, asking whether an abortion regulation imposes an "undue burden" on a woman; and several provisions of the Pennsylvania law were upheld as posing no undue burden, even though earlier Supreme Court rulings had struck down virtually identical regulations.

This experience, so early in Souter's tenure, continues to shape the public's perception of him, despite his participation in nearly 1,000 cases since *Casey*. In fact, Souter's action in *Casey* may rank as the most visible, most public moment for an intensely private individual, who has created no other public image. The other justices travel around the country and the world, giving speeches at law schools and to bar groups, but Souter declines all such invitations except for meetings at the Court with visiting groups. It is not shyness that imposes this regime; in high school and college, he was described by friends and classmates as outgoing and fun-loving. Although a desire to be low-key and private undoubtedly plays a part, Souter also believes as a philosophical matter that justices should speak through their written Court opinions. So he does not give speeches, except on the most rare occasions, such as paying tribute to a colleague or addressing the judges of the First and Third Circuits, for which he is the circuit justice.

It is not just the absence of public speeches that makes Souter so enigmatic. He also eschews social Washington. Unless the justices are lunching together in their private dining room, he eats in his chambers—he is legendary for eating only a yogurt and an apple. He goes home at the end of the work day to jog and settle into a modest apartment, and he goes home to New Hampshire at the end of the Court term, not to be seen again in Washington until after Labor Day. He generally does not attend Washington parties or major, visible social functions. With his colleagues, he is gregarious and well-liked. Because he is a bachelor and has no family, other justices sometimes look out for his interests. For example, O'Connor included Souter in her family's Thanksgiving dinners.

But outside the Court family and close New Hampshire friends, Souter remains unknown, except for the occasional quirky episode. For example, when it was his turn to testify in Congress to explain the Court's budget in 1996, he declared his opposition to television cameras in the Supreme Court and told a House subcommittee, "The day you see a camera come into our courtroom, it's going to roll over my dead body." In an alarming incident, Souter was assaulted by a group of young men in May 2004 while jogging alone at night. The attack touched off a round of press stories about whether the justices had adequate protection. With Souter at the center of these reports, one can imagine that the publicity caused him as much anguish as the original assault.

Where does Souter fit in the Court on which he sits? Different measures can shed some light. Through his first fourteen years on the Court, according to annual charts prepared by the *Harvard Law Review,* Souter wrote a total of 275 opinions. Of these, 121, or 44 percent, were majority opinions for the Court. He wrote 154 dissenting and concurring opinions, or 56 percent of the total—32 percent in dissent and 24 percent concurring. These numbers suggest that Souter's influence may more often be in separate views than in speaking for the majority. The Harvard charts also show his voting patterns. For the ten-year period from 1994 through 2003, Souter voted most frequently with liberal justice Ruth Bader Ginsburg; over the ten years, they agreed on average 85.6 percent of the time. Justices Scalia and Thomas, who are often derided for their high degree of voting agreement, sided with one another 86.7 percent on average in the same period. This level of agreement with Ginsburg lends credence to the idea that Souter moved out of the middle of the Court, where he was in *Casey,* to the more liberal wing.

What has been Souter's impact substantively? If breathing new life into federalism was one of the hallmarks of the Rehnquist Court, Souter was one of the consistent doubters. He wrote frequent separate opinions in a series of federalism cases, accusing the majority of rewriting the Constitution's structural balance and sometimes of ignoring the lessons of history, as well.

For example, when the Court invalidated part of the Violence Against Women Act in *United States v. Morrison* (2000), Souter dissented and took Chief Justice William Rehnquist to task. The portion of the law struck down allowed individuals to sue their assailants for damages for gender-motivated violence. The majority faulted Congress for using its power over interstate commerce to regulate noneconomic activity with no showing that the activity involved commerce. But Souter argued that the majority was actually changing more than fifty years of precedent in two significant ways. First, the majority was not using the deferential "rational basis" test, because if they were, Congress had provided numerous studies and hearings that easily provided a rational basis, he said. Second, the Court appeared to be carving out a new category, noneconomic activity that was beyond the reach of Congress, even it affected interstate commerce. Resorting to his favorite tool, history, Souter said it was this kind of categorical carving out that led to a power struggle between President Franklin Roosevelt and the Court in 1937. "And yet today's decision can only be seen as a step toward recapturing the prior mistakes," Souter wrote.

Earlier, in *United States v. Lopez* (1995), Souter dissented when the majority struck down a federal law that made it a crime to have a gun within 1,000 feet of a school. Here, too, the Court relied on the view that possession of a gun near a school was not economic activity and did not have a substantial effect on interstate commerce. Souter wrote, "A look at history's sequence will serve to show how today's decision tugs the Court off course."

Souter's argument is not simply rooted in history for history's sake. Nor is it driven by any love for the power of Congress. It is based on his brand of conservatism—a somewhat restrained role for the judiciary, especially when the dangers of a more active role are well documented in ignominious episodes in the

Court's history. Souter's argument traces the first third of the twentieth century, when the Supreme Court second-guessed the economic judgments of state legislatures and found them faulty under the due process clause of the Fourteenth Amendment, and second-guessed the judgment of Congress and found it had exceeded its power to regulate interstate commerce. During this period, the Court abandoned restraint on its role and scrapped judicial deference to the elected representatives in the states and in Congress. In *Lopez*, Souter said, the Court was taking a "backward glance at both the old pitfalls." For Souter, both *Lopez* and *Morrison* came down to a simple question: Why would the Court abandon its judicial restraint when the danger to the Court and the country of doing so is well documented in history?

Souter objected to other facets of the Court's federalism movement. In *Printz v. United States* (1997), he and Scalia engaged in what might well have been an academic debate at a history conference, differing sharply over the meaning of *The Federalist* No. 27, written by Alexander Hamilton. In *Printz,* the Court struck down an interim requirement of the Brady Handgun Violence Prevention Act that required local law enforcement officers to conduct background checks on handgun buyers. Scalia said the law amounted to "federal commandeering" of state and local officials to turn them from independent officials into agents of the national government. Souter countered that No. 27 and other documentation persuaded him that the framers of the Constitution envisioned having the states occasionally help out with the implementation of federal law.

Not everyone on the Court can match wits with the strong intellect and often pointed rhetoric of Scalia, but, as was apparent in *Printz,* the less flashy, soft-spoken, and low-key Souter is more than able to hold his own, especially when analyzing the history of the Court and of the Constitution. Souter's canvass of history is often a powerful counterbalance to Scalia's invocation of the original meaning of the text or original intent of the framers; at the very least, this approach by Souter makes issues seem far more complex and multifaceted, rather than the straightforward

resort to original meaning Scalia and others use. Occasionally, Souter's wry sense of humor pokes through the otherwise serious rhetoric of Court decisions. In a majority opinion in *Sabri v. United States* (2004), Souter introduced a discussion of the congressional debate over a federal bribery law with the phrase, "For those of us who accept help from legislative history . . . ." He was poking fun at Scalia, who rejects the value of legislative history.

What may be Souter's most exhaustive historical work is a dissenting opinion in *Seminole Tribe of Florida v. Florida* (1996). Rehnquist ruled for a 5–4 majority that when Congress uses its commerce power to regulate, lawmakers do not have the authority to waive the sovereign immunity of states to make them liable for lawsuits for damages. Souter's review of the history of the Eleventh Amendment and of congressional efforts to waive state immunity occupies about eighty-five pages in the *U.S. Reports,* the official record of the Court's rulings. Souter declared with unusual dramatic flare that the Court "holds for the first time since the founding of the Republic that Congress has no authority to subject a state to the jurisdiction of a federal court."

Demonstrating an unmistakable passion for understanding the history of the power relationships defined by the Constitution, Souter decried the majority's preference for its own principle of sovereign immunity, which he said was not tied to any specific constitutional provision, over the actual language of the Constitution, which confers broad regulatory power on Congress with no specific exemption for the states. Souter said the majority was returning to the era of *Lochner v. New York* (1905), during which the Court elevated its own judgment of the wisdom of state legislative power over any role for the Court properly spelled out in the Constitution.

The issue in *Seminole Tribe,* Souter said, was the ability of "citizens to enforce federal rights in a way that Congress provides." He asked, "In the end, is it plausible to contend that the plan of the convention was meant to leave the National Government without any way to render individuals capable of enforcing their federal rights directly against an intransigent state?"

If judicial restraint and deference to Congress have been Souter's main motivations for his extensive participation in the federalism cases, his outspoken efforts in numerous cases to preserve the separation of church and state appear to be driven by a profound sense of the long history of the issue. Undoubtedly, his strongly held view also reflects his own religious upbringing in the Episcopal Church, although this is difficult to measure.

At times, his quarrel with the majority in religion cases sounds the same theme of ignoring the lessons of history that Souter has raised in the federalism cases. In *Agostini v. Felton* (1997), the Court overruled *Aguilar v. Felton* (1985), striking down a federal program under which New York City sent public school teachers into parochial school classrooms to provide remedial education. In 1997 the Court said the earlier ruling was inconsistent with the Court's subsequent easing of the separation required by the establishment clause of the First Amendment.

In dissent, Souter said the Court should adhere to a firm rule against government support of religion:

> The rule expresses the hard lesson learned over and over again in the American past and in the experiences of the countries from which we have come, that religions supported by governments are compromised just as surely as the religious freedom of dissenters is burdened when government supports religion. . . . The ban against state endorsement of religion addresses the same historical lessons. . . .
>
> The human tendency, of course, is to forget the hard lessons, and to overlook the history of governmental partnership with religion when a cause is worthy, and bureaucrats have programs. That tendency to forget is the reason for having the Establishment Clause (along with the Constitution's other structural and libertarian guarantees) in the hope of stopping the corrosion before it starts.

Souter has sounded this theme repeatedly in church-state cases, frequently writing separate concurring or dissenting opinions. As the Court has explored different, less-demanding standards for measuring how much church-state separation is required by the First Amendment, Souter has emerged as one of the principal defenders of the old order—keeping the wall of separation high, to use Thomas Jefferson's metaphor. In *Zelman v. Simmons-Harris* (2002), the Court upheld a Cleveland school voucher program that permitted students to use public funds to pay tuition at private, religious schools. In dissent, Souter acknowledged the sympathetic goal of boosting education for poorly taught Cleveland schoolchildren, and he said if there were ever an excuse for violating church-state separation, this might be it. "But there is no excuse," he declared. In *Mitchell v. Helms* (2000), the Court upheld a federal program that gave aid to states and localities to provide educational equipment to public and private schools; in Jefferson Parish, Louisiana, outside New Orleans, the funds for private schools went largely to religious schools and were used to buy computers and video equipment. In a lengthy dissent, Souter accused the Court of undermining the core principle that government should not provide aid to religion and especially not to support the religious mission of private schools.

The touchstone for Souter in these cases is a belief that government can and must be neutral toward religion, and he is frequently disturbed by the Court's apparent rejection of this principle. On occasion, however, he has been able to write for the majority and to make this point emphatically. In *Board of Education of Kiryas Joel Village School District v Grumet* (1994), Souter invalidated the New York legislature's creation of a separate school district for a strictly orthodox Jewish sect. He said the legislature could not create a governing district based entirely on the religious makeup of that district; this violated the principle of neutrality toward religion.

Justice Scalia wrote a strong dissent, suggesting that Souter had twisted the establishment clause so that an act of "religious toleration" by the New York legislature was transformed into the creation of an establishment. Scalia's dissent prompted an unusually feisty reply from Souter. Recalling a quote from Justice Benjamin Cardozo that the dissenter is like "the gladiator making a last stand against the lions," Souter wrote, "Justice Scalia's dissent is certainly the work of a gladiator, but he thrusts at lions of his own imagining."

Eleven years later, Souter wrote the majority opinion declaring unconstitutional the display of the Ten Commandments in two Kentucky courthouses. In *McCreary County v. American Civil Liberties Union* (2005), Souter got the chance to defend the Court's three-prong establishment clause test outlined in *Lemon v. Kurtzman* (1971): whether government action has a secular purpose, whether its effect advances religion, and whether there is excessive entanglement with religion. Throughout the Rehnquist Court, justices attacked the "purpose prong," suggesting that judges should not second-guess the motives of elected legislators. But Souter defended the purpose test as necessary to the paramount goal of maintaining government neutrality toward religion. In a companion case, *Van Orden v. Perry* (2005), the Court upheld the display of a Ten Commandments monument on the Texas state capitol grounds. Souter dissented, noting "the simple realities that the Ten Commandments constitute a religious statement, that their message is inherently religious, and that the purpose of singling them out in a display is clearly the same."

When a majority of the Court used free speech analysis to resolve two cases involving access by religious groups to student activity fees and access to public school facilities, Souter in dissent held fast to a clear vision of separation embodied in his establishment clause principles. In *Rosenberger v. Rector and Visitors of the University of Virginia* (1995), the Court upheld the use of student activity fees to pay printing costs for a religious student newspaper, finding that denial of funding by the University of Virginia would amount to viewpoint discrimination against freedom of speech about religious matters. Souter, however, saw it as a clear example of conduct forbidden at the very heart of the establishment clause: the use of public funds to support the dissemination of religious teachings. He relied heavily on the writings of James Madison to support his view. Souter pursued a similar dissent in *Good News Club v. Milford Central School* (2001). Where the majority saw free speech discrimi-

nation in the exclusion of a Christian club from after-school meetings, Souter saw a group that fully intended to engage in religious exercises on school property in direct violation of the establishment clause. Souter was not trying to shy away from confronting free speech issues; rather, he felt that the establishment clause was being violated.

When it comes to free speech, Souter has expressed himself forcefully on numerous occasions, showing particular concern with laws or regulations that reach too far, a problem referred to in free speech terms as "overbreadth." In an unusual solo dissenting opinion, he would have invalidated standards used by the National Endowment for the Arts (NEA) taking into account "decency and respect" for diverse views in awarding grants to artists. The Court upheld the standards in *National Endowment for the Arts v. Finley* (1998), but Souter declared in dissent that the provision was overbroad "and carries with it a significant power to chill artistic production and display." He also dissented when the Court upheld Congress's decision to require filtering devices on library computers to prevent children from exposure to sexually explicit material. In *United States v. American Library Association* (2003), Souter objected that the federal law reached so far that it would force libraries to engage in censorship by denying adults access to material to which they were entitled.

In another significant ruling, this one for a majority, Souter ruled that the organizers of Boston's annual St. Patrick's Day parade had a free speech right to decide to exclude a gay rights group from marching in the event. In *Hurley v. Irish-American Gay, Lesbian and Bisexual Group of Boston* (1995), Souter rejected the use of a Massachusetts public accommodations law to prohibit exclusion of the gay group from the parade. This "use of the state's power violates the fundamental rule of protection under the First Amendment, that a speaker has the autonomy to choose the content of his own message," Souter wrote in a simple but powerful statement. But Souter dissented when the Court ruled that the Boy Scouts could not be required under New Jersey's public accommodations law to keep working with a declared homosexual scoutmaster. In *Boy Scouts of America v. Dale* (2000), Souter said the problem with the majority's ruling was that the Boy Scouts had not demonstrated that they had an advocacy position on homosexuality with which the scoutmaster's presence would interfere.

Although Souter has often pushed the Court on specific issues in his dissenting opinions, another aspect of his dissents is driven by lawyerly analysis and the sense of procedural order that may derive from his experience as a trial judge and a state supreme court justice. From time to time, Souter chastises the Court for reaching and deciding issues that were not squarely presented by the briefs or that were not fully developed in the trial and appellate record in the lower courts. For example, in *City of Boerne v. Flores* (1997), the Court curtailed the power of Congress to pass laws using its power under Section 5 of the Fourteenth Amendment; the Court ruled that Congress could not rely on Section 5 to alter the Court's narrow interpretation of the free exercise clause of the First Amendment, as expressed in *Employment Division v. Smith* (1990). In a brief dissent, Souter said he doubted whether the *Employment Division* decision was valid, and he criticized the Court for ruling on Congress's actions without asking for full consideration of Scalia's opinion in that case.

Souter was even more adamant in *Missouri v. Jenkins* (1995), a school desegregation case from Kansas City, that the Court was deciding issues not raised or briefed in the case. The Court invalidated a district court order that the Kansas City schools should engage in extensive reforms to make them attractive not only to city residents but to students living in the suburbs as well. In dissent, Souter said the appeal to the Supreme Court only involved two specific portions of the desegregation order—teacher salaries and student testing—but the Court on its own decided to review the entire scope of the district court's desegregation remedy. "The Court's process of orderly adjudication has broken down in this case," Souter said.

Souter has had much to say, again in dissent, on the Court's consideration of race in voting district cases and in affirmative action. He weighed in on the

University of Michigan's undergraduate admissions affirmative action plan in *Gratz v. Bollinger* (2003). His dissent argued that the undergraduate plan was not an unconstitutional quota and that it was within the bounds of the Court's equal protection analysis; in particular, he faulted suggestions by the Justice Department that Michigan try the system that some other states were using to achieve diversity by guaranteeing space to students at the top of each high school class in the state. Those plans, Souter said, practice "deliberate obfuscation" because they avoid "saying directly what they are doing or why." Michigan's use of a point system, giving points for minority status among other factors, is more honest, he said. "I would be tempted to give Michigan an extra point of its own for its frankness. Equal protection cannot become an exercise in which the winners are the ones who hide the ball."

Souter was also a leading dissenter from the Rehnquist Court's tough treatment of racially drawn voting districts intended to benefit minorities by increasing their legislative representation. In cases spanning a decade, Souter criticized the Court for abandoning traditional equal protection clause analysis of race discrimination claims and creating a tough new standard that made it harder to justify districts drawn to enhance minority representation. He also faulted the Court for failing to articulate a clear standard. In dissent in *Bush v. Vera* (1996), he said:

> The result of this failure to provide a practical standard for distinguishing between the lawful and unlawful use of race has not only been inevitable confusion in statehouses and courthouses, but a consequent shift in responsibility for setting district boundaries from the state legislatures, which are invested with front-line authority by Article I of the Constitution, to the courts, and truly to this Court, which is left to superintend the drawing of every legislative district in the land.

Souter has been an active, mostly liberal participant in the Court's numerous criminal cases, in which his opinions—whether majority, concurring, or dissenting—rarely argue for major advances in the law; rather, they are typically very lawyerly, suggesting that the Court majority or the court below has misapplied existing rules to the circumstances of a particular case. Occasionally, he moves beyond this technical legal analysis to confront what he sees as an abusive practice. In a plurality opinion for the Court in *Missouri v. Seibert* (2004), Souter showed his frustration with police efforts to undermine the warnings of suspects in custody that were called for in *Miranda v. Arizona* (1966). The police practice he decried has an officer question a suspect in custody without warnings, obtain information that is inadmissible, then administer the warnings and use the earlier statements to get the suspect to repeat the earlier statements. Souter concluded, "The question-first tactic effectively threatens to thwart *Miranda*'s purpose of reducing the risk that a coerced confession would be admitted."

The abortion battle in *Casey*, early in Souter's tenure, was likely not the toughest case in which Souter participated. He was one of the dissenters in *Bush v. Gore* (2000), the 5–4 ruling in which the Supreme Court ended the Florida election recount and gave the presidency to George W. Bush. The case was divisive within the Court, and some observers argue that it tarnished the Court's stature in the country and the world. Souter's dissent made it clear that he thought the case should have been left in the Florida courts and Florida legislature to resolve. But, ever concerned about the Court as an institution, he was careful to avoid the inflammatory rhetoric that marked some exchanges among the justices, and he eschewed the gloomy prophecies of others about the Court's damaged standing.

—*Stephen J. Wermiel*

BIBLIOGRAPHY

Souter has not disclosed any provision for handling of his Supreme Court papers, and his penchant for privacy makes it possible that he may not make them public. The only full biography of Souter is Tinsley E. Yarbrough, *David Hackett Souter: Traditional Republican on the Rehnquist Court* (2005). It canvasses his pre-Court years and then runs through his Supreme Court tenure.

There are comparatively few scholarly articles on Souter, and most focus on specific issues. These include David L. Hudson Jr., "Justice Stevens, Justice Souter, and the Secondary Effects Doctrine," *University of West Los Angeles Law Review* 35 (2003): 48; Alan J. Meese, "Will, Judgment, and Economic Liberty: Mr. Justice Souter and the Mistranslation of the Due Process Clause," *William and Mary Law Review* 41 (1999): 3; Liang Kan, "Comment: A Theory of Justice Souter," *Emory Law Journal* 45 (1996): 1373; Liza Weiman Hanks, "Note: Justice Souter: Defining 'Substantive Neutrality' in an Age of Religious Politics," *Stanford Law Review* 48 (1996): 903; and David K. Koehler, "Comment: Justice Souter's Keep-What-You-Want-and-Throw-Away-the-Rest Interpretation of Stare Decisis," *Buffalo Law Review* 42 (1994): 859.

NOTEWORTHY OPINIONS

Planned Parenthood of Southeastern Pennsylvania v. Casey, 505 U.S. 833 (1992)

United States v. Lopez, 514 U.S. 549 (1995) (Dissent)

Hurley v. Irish-American Gay, Lesbian and Bisexual Group of Boston, 515 U.S. 557 (1995)

Rosenberger v. Rector and Visitors of the University of Virginia, 515 U.S. 819 (1995) (Dissent)

Seminole Tribe of Florida v. Florida, 517 U.S. 44 (1996) (Dissent)

Agostini v. Felton, 521 U.S. 203 (1997) (Dissent)

Printz v. United States, 521 U.S. 898 (1997) (Dissent)

United States v. Morrison, 529 U.S. 598 (2000)

Mitchell v. Helms, 530 U.S. 793 (2000) (Dissent)

Missouri v. Seibert, 542 U.S. 600 (2004)

JOHN PAUL STEVENS

Birth: April 20, 1920, Chicago, Illinois.

Education: University of Chicago, B.A., 1941; Northwestern University School of Law, J.D., magna cum laude, 1947.

Official Positions: Law clerk to Justice Wiley B. Rutledge, 1947–1948; associate counsel, Subcommittee on the Study of Monopoly Power, House Judiciary Committee, 1951; member, U.S. Attorney General's National Committee to Study the Antitrust Laws, 1953–1955; judge, U.S. Court of Appeals for the Seventh Circuit, 1970–1975.

Supreme Court Service: Nominated associate justice by President Gerald R. Ford, December 1, 1975, to replace William O. Douglas, who had retired; confirmed by the Senate, December 17, 1975, by a 98–0 vote; took judicial oath December 19, 1975.

John Paul Stevens served for five years as an appeals court judge, and before that he had spent two decades as a lawyer in Chicago with a specialty in antitrust matters. He was considered lawyerly, not ideological, and this reputation was one reason President Gerald Ford selected him for the Supreme Court in 1975. Ford had just assumed the presidency after the resignation of Richard Nixon, and he was not looking for a confirmation fight. The result was indeed painless: the Senate confirmed Stevens unanimously after two days of mild questioning. But Justice Stevens's career on the Court then followed a rather unusual path. He started out as a moderate conservative; he ended up the member of the Court considered most reliably liberal in many respects. Stevens was a centrist on the Burger Court, but a leader in dissent after William Rehnquist became chief justice. How are we to account for these changes?

Making sense of Stevens's trajectory requires us to draw some distinctions. First, we must distinguish between two sources of ideological movement: changes in the justice's views and changes in the views of those surrounding him. In Stevens's case both kinds of changes occurred to some extent. In certain areas—particularly those involving race and criminal procedure—the evidence suggests that his views did become less conservative as years went by. At the same time, when Stevens arrived at the Court, other justices—notably William Brennan and Thurgood Marshall—were obviously well to the left of him, as was reflected in their votes in capital cases and many matters under the equal protection clause. When those justices retired and were replaced by David Souter and Clarence Thomas, respectively, the entire Court moved to the right, and Stevens was moved to its leftmost edge.

Second, we need to distinguish between conservatism in substance and in method. During Stevens's tenure, "liberalism" generally was associated with certain types of substantive positions: broad views of federal congressional power, a willingness to recognize unenumerated constitutional rights through the doctrine of substantive due process, support for affirmative action but otherwise expansive readings of what the "equal protection of the laws" forbids, robust interpretations of the establishment clause, and solicitude for the rights of criminal defendants. Stevens was at odds with the conservative majorities of the Rehnquist years on many such issues. But conservatism also can refer to style or to judicial technique, and in this respect Stevens has been fairly conservative all along. His approach has been cautious, and he prefers small rather than large decisions. By examining Stevens's record in some areas of interest and controversy, we can ascertain the common threads in his style of decision making.

Stevens's handling of questions concerning race are a good place to start. During his early years on the Court, Stevens consistently voted to strike down affirmative action programs of various sorts. In one such case, *Fullilove v. Klutznick* (1980), he stated his position in remarkably strong language: "The very attempt to define with precision a beneficiary's qualifying racial characteristics is repugnant to our constitutional ideals." Moreover, he suggested in a footnote that the government ought to "study precedents such as the First Regulation to the Reichs Citizenship Law of November 14, 1935"—and then quoted from Nazi Germany's rules defining who was Jewish. If the case is taken in isolation, Stevens appears to be painting with a broad brush. But when we look at his decisions

as a group, a different style becomes visible: judgments based on details. In *Wygant v. Jackson Board of Education* (1986), for example, the Court forbade a school district to give preferential treatment to minorities in deciding which teachers to lay off. In dissent, Stevens argued that "a school board may reasonably conclude that an integrated faculty will be able to provide benefits to the student body that could not be provided by an all-white, or nearly all-white, faculty." But then in *City of Richmond v. J. A. Croson Co.* (1989), Stevens voted to strike down a program that required construction firms working for the city to give 30 percent of their subcontracts work to businesses owned by minorities. Stevens thought that in construction, unlike in education, there was no reason to think there were benefits to racial diversity.

This style of decision making, based on fine distinctions rather than broad principles, is characteristic of Stevens. But the cases also reflected an apparent movement to the left on substance. A few years after *Croson*, Stevens dissented from a decision striking down preferences that were similar in many ways to those at issue in *Fullilove* fifteen years earlier. He criticized the majority for delivering a "disconcerting lecture about the evils of government racial classifications" and said that its analysis "ignores a difference, fundamental to the idea of equal protection, between oppression and assistance." This made for a stark contrast with the lecture on the dangers of racial classifications Stevens had delivered in his *Fullilove* dissent. And then Stevens

John Paul Stevens

also may have become more liberal on racial issues in a merely relative sense. During the 1990s he dissented consistently from the Court's interpretations of the Voting Rights Act to limit the use of race in redistricting. His dissents contradicted nothing from his early career and may just have reflected the recent arrival of several members of the Court who were considerably to his right on matters of race and many other issues.

Another group of Stevens's decisions under the equal protection clause—those evaluating the lawfulness of discrimination between the sexes—shows a similar combination of fine-spun methods and results that are typically but not reliably liberal. In *Craig v. Boren* (1976), the Court held unconstitutional a law that prevented the sale of strong beer to males under twenty-one and to females under eighteen. Stevens dissented, suggesting that laws connected to physical differences between the sexes might be considered presumptively valid, and those not so connected might be presumptively invalid. The presumptions could then be rebutted with evidence bearing one way or the other on the link between the laws involved and the justifications for them, and this in turn would require detailed inquiries into the reasons the laws were passed. He voted to strike down laws distinguishing between the sexes in *Califano v. Goldfarb* (1977), where the Social Security act had distributed survivor benefits differently to widowers and widows; *Michael M v Superior Court* (1981), where the state's criminal penalties for statutory rape applied only to males; and *United States v. Virginia* (1996), where a state-supported military academy only admitted males. In *Miller v. Albright* (1998), however, he went the other way. The law in *Miller* gave citizenship to children born out of wedlock to American mothers and foreign fathers but imposed greater burdens on children born out of wedlock to American fathers and foreign mothers. Stevens held this reasonable because "the blood relationship to the birth mother is immediately obvious and is typically established by hospital records and birth certificates; the relationship to the unmarried father may often be undisclosed and unrecorded in any contemporary public record." The stylistic pattern is becoming apparent: Stevens makes no sweeping references to principle; instead the judge's role is to carry out detailed scrutiny of whether the application of the law to the facts of the case conforms to reason.

A similar "all things considered" approach is found in Stevens's decisions under the due process clause. In *BMW of North America v. Gore* (1996), the Court struck down a $2 million award of punitive damages against an auto company for retouching the paint on the plaintiff's car before he bought it. Stevens wrote the majority opinion and spoke of various "guideposts" suggesting that the award was excessive: the defendant's conduct had not been morally reprehensible; the ratio between the punitive damages and compensatory damages ($4,000) was lopsided, indeed "breathtaking"; and the criminal penalties applied to the same conduct were minor. The *BMW* analysis is classic Stevens: factors are considered that produce a judgment on the facts, the balancing will have to be repeated by other judges in other cases.

In a similar vein are Stevens's opinions in the Court's leading cases on whether the Constitution recognizes a "right to die." In *Cruzan v. Director, Missouri Department of Health* (1990), the Court held that the state could forbid the parents of a woman in a vegetative state to withdraw medical support from her. Stevens dissented, saying that "in answering the important question presented by this tragic case, it is wise not to attempt, by any general statement, to cover every possible phase of the subject," and that "Nancy Cruzan's liberty to be free from medical treatment must be understood in light of the facts and circumstances particular to her." He then argued that the state could not plausibly insist on prolonging Cruzan's life except on theological grounds, which it had no business doing. Seven years later the Court considered *Washington v. Glucksberg* (1997) and held that the Constitution does not protect a right to assisted suicide. Stevens wrote a concurring opinion, staking out his now-familiar preference for decision on the details:

Although, as the Court concludes today, [the] potential harms [cited by the state] are sufficient to support the State's general public policy against assisted suicide, they will not always outweigh the individual liberty interest of a particular patient. Unlike the Court of Appeals, I would not say as a categorical matter that these state interests are invalid as to the entire class of terminally ill, mentally competent patients. I do not, however, foreclose the possibility that an individual plaintiff seeking to hasten her death, or a doctor whose assistance was sought, could prevail in a more particularized challenge.

Stevens also has consistently supported abortion rights under the Constitution. Here his most characteristic work has come in assessing laws that require parental notification or consent when a minor seeks an abortion. At one point in his career, Stevens argued it was constitutional to require that a minor obtain consent from one of her parents before having an abortion, but only if a judicial bypass were an option. In another case, however, he took the position that the Constitution forbids a state to require notification of both parents before a minor has an abortion—and this regardless of whether there was a judicial bypass option. He found the distinction between these situations in considering "three separate but related interests—the interest in the welfare of the pregnant minor, the interest of the parents, and the interest of the family unit."

The same sort of particularism is found in Stevens's decisions concerning freedom of speech: his votes depended on an assessment of the value and context of the speech at stake. In *FCC v. Pacifica Corp.* (1978), the FCC had decided that a radio station violated federal law by broadcasting comedian George Carlin reciting his "seven dirty words" monologue. Stevens wrote:

The Commission's decision rested entirely on a nuisance rationale under which context is all-important. The concept requires consideration of a host of variables. The time of day was emphasized by the Commission. The content of the program in which the language is used will also affect the composition of the audience, and

differences between radio, television, and perhaps closed-circuit transmissions, may also be relevant. As Mr. Justice Sutherland wrote, a "nuisance may be merely a right thing in the wrong place—like a pig in the parlor instead of the barnyard." We simply hold that when the Commission finds that a pig has entered the parlor, the exercise of its regulatory power does not depend on proof that the pig is obscene.

The agency's style of decision—distinguishing between parlors and barnyards—was congenial to Stevens, and indeed it much resembled his own approach to these cases. This approach has sometimes made his decisions difficult to predict, but it has also produced noticeable trends, making him a less-reliable defender of free speech claims than some of his colleagues who adhere to broader principles. For example, Stevens voted against protecting those who burn American flags, and he has been a consistent vote to uphold restrictive campaign finance laws. He also argued against constitutional protection for "hate speech" in *R. A. V. v. City of St. Paul* (1992), arguing that "the concept of 'categories' fits poorly with the complex reality of expression," and that "the categorical approach does not take seriously the importance of context."

Three months after Stevens arrived at the Court, oral arguments were conducted in a series of cases testing the legality of death penalty statutes; the statutes had been passed in response to the Court's decision in *Furman v. Georgia* (1972). Stevens delivered joint opinions in the cases with Potter Stewart and Lewis Powell. The cases introduced a sort of regulatory regime for the death penalty and started the Court down a path of drawing fine distinctions between when executions were allowed and when they were not. The Court eventually would say, for example, that it is unconstitutional to instruct a jury that it can impose a death sentence if the defendant's crime was "outrageously or wantonly vile, horrible or inhuman" because the instruction is not sufficiently narrow. But it is permissible to give the death penalty to the perpetrator of a crime found "especially heinous, cruel, or depraved"—if those words are read to only cover crimes where the perpetrator "relishes the murder, evidencing debasement or perversion," or "shows an indifference to the suffering of the victim and evidences a sense of pleasure in the killing." Stevens did not always join these opinions, but they provide a sense of where his approach to capital punishment has led. He wanted detailed judicial supervision, not abolition or too much deference to the states; and details are what the Court has argued about ever since.

Stevens's tenure also has coincided with a line of decisions constricting the availability of writs of *habeas corpus,* and Stevens generally resisted the trend. In *Rose v. Lundy* (1982), the Court considered how federal judges should respond to "mixed" petitions from prisoners—petitions including some claims that had not been exhausted in state court. The majority held that such petitions must be dismissed, but Stevens dissented, saying that the district court

> had a duty to look at the context in which the error occurred to determine whether it was either aggravated or mitigated by other aspects of the proceeding. . . . The inflexible, mechanical rule the Court adopts today arbitrarily denies district judges the kind of authority they need to administer their calendars effectively.

This response was typical of Stevens's preference in interpreting *habeas corpus.* In *Murray v. Carrier* (1986), the question was whether a prisoner should be allowed to bring a claim in a *habeas corpus* proceeding when his lawyer inadvertently had failed to raise the issue on appeal in the state courts. The Court said that the prisoner must show he probably was innocent of the crime to overcome this default. Stevens, in a concurrence, said he would prefer "consideration, not only of the nature and strength of the constitutional claim, but also of the nature and strength of the state procedural rule that has not been observed." It is always a question of details.

The interesting thing about Stevens's detailed inquiries is that we might expect them to lead in unpredictable directions; after all, one never knows which way the details will point. But in practice they have led to some striking patterns. From fall 1994 through spring 1999, the Court decided 160 criminal matters of one sort or another. Fifty-one of them resulted in unanimous judgments; in the other 109 cases, Stevens voted for the defendant ninety-two times and for the government fifteen times. These votes were the opposite of those cast by Rehnquist, who voted for defendants sixteen times and for the government ninety-one times. They made Stevens considerably more friendly to defendants than, say, Stephen Breyer, who was one of the Court's only two "Democratic" appointees during this period; Breyer voted for defendants fifty-eight times and for the government forty-four times. In this area of the law Stevens seems to have made another ideological shift. From his arrival at the Court through the 1980–1981 term, he voted for the government in criminal cases 43 percent of the time; from the 1994 term through 1999, he voted for the government 26 percent of the time, while Rehnquist's votes for the government during the same period went from 80 percent to 75 percent.

By now a general picture of Stevens's style and substance should be clear enough for us to assess its implications and try to take his measure from the standpoint of jurisprudence. Distinctions of the sort Stevens tends to rely on can be hard to explain as interpretations of constitutional or statutory text; they become comprehensible only by reference to a different model—that of the common law judge. Most of the justices treat the Court's cases fairly openly as occasions for deciding large legal questions, but Stevens is likely to approach a case at the Supreme Court the same way he did as judge on the court of appeals, placing emphasis on the facts rather than relegating them to the background. This style has a distinguished jurisprudential pedigree; it puts one in mind of Oliver Wendell Holmes's description of the common law judge as one who "decides the case first and determines the principle afterwards." But it also can be a problematic strategy on the Supreme Court, because the Court generally only infrequently hears cases in any given area. So when Stevens makes narrow decisions, he is not necessarily postponing the remaining questions until another day; he more typically is delegating them to lower court judges.

Leaving so much for other judges to decide has costs and benefits. A cost of the approach is a lack of uniformity and predictability in the resulting decisions, especially when the Court hands down open-ended standards that leave trial and appellate judges a good deal of room for discretion. The lower court judges are less constrained as a result, and their rulings are less predictable than they otherwise might be. A benefit, however, is that delegation causes questions to be resolved in a dense factual context that may produce better decisions. As Stevens himself said it:

When we follow our traditional practice of adjudicating difficult and novel constitutional questions only in concrete factual situations, the adjudications tend to be crafted with greater wisdom. Hypothetical rulings are inherently treacherous and prone to lead us into unforeseen errors; they are qualitatively less reliable than the products of case-by-case adjudication.

Another consequence of Stevens's preference, which may be considered either a cost or a benefit, is that it makes trial judges very important and implies great trust in them. They are not merely given rules to apply; they are given legal principles or "factors" to bring to bear on their cases according to their own judgments. In this sense, Stevens shows humility, preferring to spread around the task of decision making among countless judges rather than assign himself the task of making big decisions once and for all. But this strategy also assigns a large role in lawmaking to judges generally. They are left with lots of supervising to do, and they end up giving detailed review to restrictions on abortion, to petitions for *habeas corpus,* to complaints about restrictions on speech, to punitive damage awards, and on and on.

Stevens's judicial style implies great respect—reverence, even—for the trial judges called upon later to make the sorts of judgments that his decisions require. Stevens once said that his former teacher, Leon Green, had a "special influence on my understanding of the law." He then described Green's view

that "any workable system of law depends as heavily on the quality of the persons who administer it as on the form that particular rules take." The same view was reflected much later in Stevens's dissent to *Bush v. Gore* (2000), in which he said he regarded the majority's lack of respect for the impartiality of judges as the most bothersome feature of its decision:

What must underlie petitioners' entire federal assault on the Florida election procedures is an unstated lack of confidence in the impartiality and capacity of the state judges who would make the critical decisions if the vote count were to proceed. . . . The endorsement of that position by the majority of this Court can only lend credence to the most cynical appraisal of the work of judges throughout the land. It is confidence in the men and women who administer the judicial system that is the true backbone of the rule of law.

This is not the sort of thing one likely would expect to hear from, say, Antonin Scalia, who regards the "backbone" of the rule of law as consisting of rules, not the people who apply them.

Stevens's judicial style reflects a preference for complexity, subtlety, and accuracy in individual cases over predictability, clarity, finality, and cheapness. Does this stance make him a "pragmatist," as some observers have claimed? It depends how the word is defined. Pragmatism in law can refer generally to a preference for facts and consequences rather than abstractions and theories, and so far this description seems to fit Stevens well enough. He has always cared about how a judicial decision would work in the real world. But pragmatism also can be defined as concern for what "works well" rather than with what comports with high principle, and saying whether this sense of the word describes Stevens is not so easy. The trouble is that, as federal judge Richard Posner has said, "The relevant consequences to the pragmatist are long run as well as short run, systemic as well as individual, the importance of stability and predictability as well as of justice to the individual parties." The first members of those couplets tended to get short shrift from Justice

Stevens. The problem is that notions of pragmatism founded on what "works" are not very informative by themselves. They have to be filled in with value judgments about what it looks like when law works well. So far as Stevens is concerned, a decision that sacrifices individualized accuracy for clarity and predictability does not work well; others might say that Stevens's own decisions are the ones that do not work precisely because they create too much unpredictability and high administrative costs. Assessing him as a pragmatist in this respect is a matter of deciding which sorts of consequences we value.

Stevens's version of pragmatism puts him at home in a significant school of thought in twentieth-century jurisprudence. It is the school that eschewed formalism and mechanical tests in favor of a style of analysis said to be "functional"—a position often identified with legal realism and, occasionally, pragmatism. Stevens's style has a family resemblance to other branches of those movements from the middle of the century—for example, with the interest-balancing approach to choice of law problems. Stevens's approach to judging did not really catch on for the same reason that the net benefits of the conflict of laws revolution were still controversial at the end of the century—not because either of the approaches reflected a want of pragmatism, but because in their pragmatism they struck a balance between priorities that was in questionable keeping with the mainstream values of the times, which weighted clarity, finality, predictability, and generality as more important virtues than those approaches did.

Meanwhile, Stevens also is an antipragmatist in a separate sense: from the time he arrived on the Court, he became a frequent issuer of separate opinions, and he never showed much interest in sacrificing a full airing of his views of a case to secure a majority. "His concern with procedural safeguards was frequently expressed in separate opinions. The number of such opinions in part reflects his deep interest in issues which were to him fundamental, but it also reflects a quality of integrity that is difficult to describe. . . . His conscience literally forced him to add the statement of the real basis for his vote." This might sound like a

description of Stevens in fact, it was an admiring description that Stevens wrote of Justice Wiley Rutledge, for whom he clerked after graduating from law school. Stevens evidently approved of Rutledge's ways, for he surpassed his former boss in the production of separate opinions. The large number of separate opinions seems to reflect a want of pragmatism more in the colloquial sense of "realpolitik" than in the jurisprudential sense; in the latter respect, it can be viewed as just another example of Stevens's insistence on getting every case decided precisely right on its facts, without overmuch concern for the side consequences.

A final matter to examine is the relationship between Stevens's methods and his politics. The natural question is whether his politics are a product of his method (or vice versa) or whether they are independent variables. I suggest that they are not independent, at least not all the time, and especially not in the criminal cases where Stevens most obviously staked out territory to the left of his colleagues during the 1990s. Granted, either preference—for abstract rules or for narrow standards—can be (and has been) made consistent with both conservatism and liberalism. But in Stevens's case, his preference for standards over rules seems to stem from a larger set of values: a heavy valuation of accuracy in individual cases; a sense that faith in the judgment of judges is justified, necessary, and to be counted upon, rather than the occasions for it minimized; and a comparatively low valuation of the clarity, finality, and low administrative costs that rules and generalizations provide. These values inevitably tend to produce decisions helpful to criminal defendants, because their cases so often amount to contests between the interests of accuracy and finality.

As noted, during the later years of the Rehnquist Court, Stevens rarely—but not never—voted for the government in criminal matters where the Court was divided. So when did he vote with the government? Most such cases involved the definition of some element of a crime—for example, whether a drug dealer "carries a firearm," and is therefore subject to extra criminal penalties, when he keeps it in the glove compartment of his car. When making decisions such as these, Stevens was not particularly likely to be helpful to defendants—yet Scalia was: he dissented in almost all of those cases where Stevens voted in a majority that favored the government's position. At first these outcomes might seem odd, for one does not usually think of Scalia as friendlier than Stevens to criminal defendants. But the pattern can be explained by reconsidering the values already noted. A decision about whether to define an element of a crime more or less favorably to a defendant does not play a part in the disagreement between Stevens and the conservatives; it is not obvious which decision about the gun in the glove compartment would be more likely to result in clarity, predictability, finality, low administrative burdens, fairness, or accuracy.

These considerations describe both the nature of Stevens's liberalism and the limitations of it. He is not the sort to make broad proclamations or offer surprising new innovations in favor of civil liberties. His style is fundamentally conservative, and his goal not so much to push back the power of the state as to produce the greatest possible accuracy and fairness in each individual case. That is why he prefers to regulate capital punishment—to micromanage it, we might say—rather than to abolish it as Brennan or Marshall preferred. He is a somewhat frustrating figure for both the right and the left because he does not entirely share the conventional values of either ideological wing.

Stevens took the seat previously occupied by William O. Douglas. The two men lend themselves to interesting and amusing comparisons. They ended up the ranking liberals on their respective Courts in both politics and seniority—rather more surprisingly in Stevens's case. Neither man was terribly interested in compromising his precise views to create a majority or otherwise build a coalition, and, as a result, both of them probably were less influential than they otherwise might have been. But nobody actually familiar with Stevens and Douglas is reminded of either by the other, and in fact they are very nearly opposites. Douglas showed little interest in the sorts of details that are a preoccupation for Stevens. Stevens is the judge's justice; Douglas was the "antijudge." Stevens is a lawyer; Douglas was a crusader. Taken together they

illustrate the great range of meanings "liberalism" can have when applied to a member of the Court and perhaps, finally, the uselessness of the term.

The two justices can, however, teach us something about legal realism. Douglas was a realist of the open variety. He once wrote of a formative moment soon after he joined the Court when the chief justice, Charles Evans Hughes,

> made a statement to me which at the time was shattering but which over the years turned out to be true: "Justice Douglas, you must remember one thing. At the constitutional level where we work, ninety percent of any decision is emotional. The rational part of us supplies the reasons for supporting our predilections."

Douglas went on to become famous for writing his preferences into the law without much fussing over details of doctrine or a close reading of the legal materials involved. Justice Stevens does not care for that approach, as is suggested by this language from one of his dissents:

> Some students of the Court take for granted that our decisions represent the will of the judges rather than the will of the law. This dogma may be the current fashion, but I remain convinced that such remarks reflect a profound misunderstanding of the nature of our work. Unfortunately, however, cynics—parading under the banner of legal realism—are given a measure of credibility whenever the Court bases a decision on its own notions of sound policy, rather than on what the law commands.

So Douglas seems an archrealist, and Stevens an antirealist. For all that, however, Stevens himself can be considered a nice study in the realist's claims. Here is the lawyerly judge, meticulously scrutinizing the facts and doctrine of each case, eschewing ideology, and frequently offering idiosyncratic reasoning and arguments—and yet arriving at results in most politically sensitive areas about as predictable as those reached by Rehnquist, who at times was accused of partisanship in rather blunt language. This pairing of meticulous method and consistent outcome shows how difficult it is for any justice to avoid seeing his decisions express his own values, and perhaps especially when he so persistently avoids the constraining force of rules. But if Stevens expresses his values through his decisions, he does so modestly. He plays the law game, and takes it very seriously; regardless of what he says, he generally says it in the language of picky, realist-hating analysis of doctrine and facts. This is admirable, for it means that on their way into his decisions, his values have to be transformed into a shape that constrains the scope of their consequences and leaves room for the values and choices of others. We learn from Stevens that what Hughes said to Douglas probably was true, but that judges do better by doubting and hedging against it than they do by trying to internalize it.

—*Ward Farnsworth*

BIBLIOGRAPHY

A good discussion of the intersection between Stevens's judicial style and his speech jurisprudence—and an excellent general discussion of Stevens—is Frederick Schauer, "Justice Stevens and the Size of Constitutional Decisions," *Rutgers Law Journal* 27 (1996): 543. A good book-length treatment of Stevens's constitutional work is Robert J. Sickels, *John Paul Stevens and the Constitution* (1988). For more on Stevens's role on the Court, see Stuart Taylor, "The Last Moderate," *American Lawyer* 48 (June 1990); and Norman Dorsen, "John Paul Stevens," *Annual Survey of American Law*, 1992/1993. And, for a fuller explication of the ideas discussed here, see Ward Farnsworth, "Realism, Pragmatism, and John Paul Stevens," in Earl Maltz, ed., *Rehnquist Justice: Understanding the Court Dynamic* (2003).

NOTEWORTHY OPINIONS

Craig v. Boren, 429 U.S. 190 (1976) (Dissent)

FCC v. Pacifica Corp., 438 U.S. 726 (1978)

Fullilove v. Klutznik, 448 U.S. 448 (1980) (Dissent)

Wygant v. Jackson Board of Education, 476 U.S. 276 (1986) (Dissent)

BMW of North America v. Gore, 517 U.S. 559 (1996)

Washington v. Glucksburg, 521 U.S. 702 (1997) (Concurrence)

Bush v. Gore, 531 U.S. 98 (2000) (Dissent)

POTTER STEWART

Birth: January 23, 1915, Jackson, Michigan.

Education: Yale College, B.A., cum laude, 1937; Yale Law School, LL.B., cum laude, 1941; fellow, Cambridge University, 1937–1938.

Official Positions: Member, Cincinnati City Council, 1950–1953; vice mayor of Cincinnati, 1952–1953; judge, U.S. Court of Appeals for the Sixth Circuit, 1954–1958.

Supreme Court Service: Recess appointment as associate justice by President Dwight D. Eisenhower, October 14, 1958, to replace Harold H. Burton, who had retired; nominated associate justice by President Eisenhower, January 17, 1959; confirmed by the Senate, May 5, 1959, by a 70–17 vote; took judicial oath October 14, 1958; retired July 3, 1981; replaced by Sandra Day O'Connor, nominated by President Ronald Reagan.

Death: December 7, 1985, Hanover, New Hampshire.

The life story of Justice Potter Stewart reads like that of many American upper-middle-class white, male, political success stories. Educated at the prestigious Hotchkiss preparatory school, Stewart earned undergraduate and law degrees from Yale University, graduating cum laude both times, studied in England at Cambridge University, served in the navy during World War II, and went on to work in a leading Midwestern law firm. The common adage "like father, like son" is perhaps more true of Stewart than any other contemporary political figure. Like his father before him, Stewart rose from Republican electoral city politics in Cincinnati to a position of prominence in the judiciary, but while his father's judicial service was limited to the Ohio Supreme Court (1947–1959), the younger Stewart went on to the U.S. Court of Appeals for the Sixth Circuit and the U.S. Supreme Court. Also like his father before him, Stewart was generally associated with the moderate forces

in the Republican Party. As a Supreme Court justice, he carved out a unique position as a centrist moderate, exhibiting the characteristics of both lawyer and politician and avoiding an ideological label.

Although he worked within an institution where an ideological "tag" is generally all that the public knows about a justice, Stewart was especially concerned that he not be labeled as either a liberal or a conservative. To him, those labels suggested a judge who acted upon his own economic, political, social, or religious values. In contrast, Stewart asked repeatedly that he be thought of as simply "a good lawyer who did his best." His justice-as-lawyer model suggested a jurist capable of applying objective legal reasoning to questions before the Court, uninfluenced by his own values. Even at the close of his career on the Court, Stewart succeeded in eluding the pigeonholers.

The most commonly used terms to describe Stewart—*moderate, neutral,* and *swing voter*—reflected his tendency to vote "liberal" in some cases and "conservative" in others and his propensity to defy prediction in specific cases. His decisions in cases on controversial subjects such as establishment of religion, pornography, equal protection of the law, and criminal defendants' rights show that he was an independent voice on the Court. While his colleagues over more than two decades tended to vote relatively predictably for or against expansive conceptions of individual rights, Stewart appeared to "swing" from the liberal to the conservative position from one case to another, and he often staked out a position substantively different from either.

Constitutional scholars, often frustrated in their attempt to pinpoint Stewart's ideology, and most content to discuss the justices as parts of coalitions or voting blocs within the Court, have either tended to ignore Stewart or have assumed that his positions were the result of inconsistent or random decision making. Careful analysis of Stewart's decisions, however, reveals that his unpredictable votes and uniquely fluid voting alignments with other justices were not the result of randomness or inconsistency. His patterns in fact reflected the importance of three principles in his "lawyerly" approach to constitutional interpretation. First, he placed great value on states' rights. Second, he demonstrated an equally strong commitment to narrow, nonanticipatory decision making. Third was his exceptionally strong concern about the preservation of judicial autonomy and authority. An appreciation of the significance of these

Potter Stewart

principles for Stewart explains many of his otherwise incomprehensible decisions.

The most significant substantive element in Stewart's jurisprudence was his commitment to states' rights. To most students of constitutional law, states' rights is a relic of America's darkest past, a constitutionalism that supported slavery, corporate oligopoly, and the inability of the federal government to deal with contemporary problems. The ideology of dual federalism, under which the Tenth Amendment stood as a positive restriction on national authority, was laid to rest in *United States v. Darby* (1941), when Justice Harlan Fiske Stone proclaimed, "The [Tenth] Amendment states but a truism that all is retained [by the states] which has not been surrendered." But Stewart, in contrast with the predominant legal thought of his time and with the Supreme Court on which he served, maintained a commitment to dual federalism, to the belief that states continued to retain substantial constitutional autonomy. Dissenting alone in *Perez v. United States* (1971), he concluded that loan-sharking was only a local business practice and therefore, despite its occurrence nationwide, not subject to congressional regulation. His Tenth Amendment reasoning was reminiscent of ideas largely abandoned by the Court during the presidency of Franklin D. Roosevelt.

Stewart also dissented against incorporating most of the Bill of Rights protections for defendants in state criminal proceedings. He viewed the imposition of these restrictions on the states as an interference with their conduct of their criminal justice systems. Because the operation of a criminal justice system was, for Stewart, an essential function of government, largely definitional of a sovereign state, he was extremely unlikely to favor abridging the autonomy of the states in this area. His votes in *Malloy v. Hogan* (1964), *Benton v. Maryland* (1969), and *Duncan v. Louisiana* (1968) against incorporation of, respectively, the privilege against self-incrimination, the ban on double jeopardy, and the right to a trial by jury, as well as his votes in *Escobedo v. Illinois* (1964), *Miranda v. Arizona* (1966), and *Gilbert v. California* (1967), against restrictions on police practices in the states, all spoke to his commitment to the autonomy of state government.

His reluctance to interfere with states' criminal justice systems extended to even those cases in which First Amendment rights were jeopardized. Despite his usual support for the free speech rights of demonstrators and alleged pornographers, in *Cameron v. Johnson* (1965) and *Gunn v. Committee to End the War in Vietnam* (1970), as well as in *Byrne v. Karalexis* (1969), *Perez v. Ledesma* (1971), and *Huffman v. Pursue, Ltd.* (1975), Stewart refused to enjoin states from enforcing their criminal laws against these defendants without definitive showings of bad faith by the state. He was not unsympathetic to their substantive claims to freedom of speech, but he did not believe that the federal courts ought to enjoin the states' routine law enforcement processes. In Stewart's view, the First Amendment issues raised in these cases were more appropriately resolved on appeal and not by preventing the constitutionally questionable prosecutions.

His commitment to states' rights also explains his limited support for voting rights claims that challenged poll taxes, literacy tests, malapportionment, and other state government practices that diluted the political strength of black voters. Although he upheld the jurisdiction of the federal courts over such cases and sustained the authority of the attorney general under the 1965 Voting Rights Act, he severely restricted the power of either to reject the state systems they scrutinized. A state's electoral system, like the enforcement of its criminal law, was to Stewart an

inherent feature of its sovereignty. He was, therefore, apt to sustain all but the most flagrant abuses and irrational policies.

In 1957 Stewart had given a speech recommending that most civil litigation be "returned" to the state courts. On the Supreme Court, however, he was largely alone in his views on federalism until President Richard Nixon selected four new justices, and federalism was once again in vogue. In 1976 Stewart and the four Nixon appointees formed a slim majority favoring the autonomy of state and local governments in *National League of Cities v. Usery*. That decision, which immunized state and local government from federal wage and hours legislation applicable to other employers, was the first of its type in nearly forty years. Similar coalitions then proceeded to "return" to the states a modicum of autonomy over their electoral and criminal justice processes. Therefore, while other justices were concerned with defining the privilege against self-incrimination or the constitutional principle of one person, one vote, Stewart was more concerned with deciding whether states should be required to respect either.

Perhaps most striking in Stewart's jurisprudence was his commitment to narrow, nonanticipatory opinions. His constitutional decision making was characterized by his narrowing of the issue, the decision, and the remedy. In contrast with contemporary exponents of judicial self-restraint, such as Felix Frankfurter and John Marshall Harlan, who believed in the Court limiting the kinds of cases it took, Stewart's restraint was in the manner of his resolution of the controversial cases of the day. It might be noted in this respect that Stewart, unlike Frankfurter, did not shy away from the Court resolving the legislative malapportionment dispute, and that it was only Stewart, joined in dissent by William O. Douglas, who believed that the Court should decide whether the war in Vietnam was constitutional. It was, rather, his very deliberate, step-by-step process of decision making that best defined his concept of "lawyering." "The law," he told me in a 1976 interview, "is a careful profession." During the same interview Stewart commented on the virtue of this approach. "No one," he said, "is wise enough to see around the next corner." By committing himself no further than was necessary to resolve the case before the Court, he retained considerable freedom in subsequent cases. His voting patterns may have been unique and unpredictable, but they were not inconsistent.

The hallmark of a Stewart opinion is that as much attention was paid to clarifying what was not being decided as what was. In *Furman v. Georgia* (1972), Stewart rejected the death penalty, as applied, because of its "freakish" imposition. Unlike William Brennan and Thurgood Marshall, however, he thought it "unnecessary to reach the ultimate question" of the unconstitutionality of capital punishment *per se*. Similarly, Stewart was seen as a supporter of the media when he voted against enjoining the publication of the Pentagon Papers. What received less attention was that unlike his more liberal brethren, he specifically left open the possibility of postpublication criminal charges against the *New York Times* and the *Washington Post*. He further allowed for legislation that would permit such injunctions in the future. And in *Virginia State Board of Pharmacists v. Virginia Citizens Consumer Council* (1976), Stewart concurred that commercial speech (advertising) was not "wholly outside" the protections of the First Amendment. He cautioned, nevertheless, that the Court must not be understood to be protecting fraudulent advertisement from state regulation. Because of his limited opinion in *Virginia State Board,* one year later in *Bates v. State Bar of Arizona* (1977), Stewart was free to dissent in support of the authority of the state to regulate the advertising of the legal profession.

Stewart's unique ability to narrow decisions and subsequently to see differences in seemingly similar cases made him a critical figure on the Court. His was often the tie-breaking fifth vote in controversial decisions. For example, distinguishing pretrial hearings from criminal trials with respect to the access of the press, in *Gannett Co. v. DePasquale* (1979), he wrote for a majority of five that judges may close hearings. In *Richmond Newspapers v. Virginia* (1980), however, he concurred with the Court's holding that trials must ordinarily be open. In *Cleveland Board of Education v.*

LaFleur (1974), he wrote the Court's opinion rejecting a mandatory five-month maternity leave policy for elementary school teachers, but shortly thereafter, in *Geduldig v. Aiello* (1974), he upheld discrimination against pregnancy in a state disability plan. Stewart wrote both the *Brewer v. Williams* (1977) and *Rhode Island v. Innis* (1980) decisions, distinguishing squad-car conversations by police designed to elicit information from the suspect-passenger from those that result in allegedly voluntary cooperation with the police. Finally, Stewart was the only justice to reject affirmative action programs sponsored by governments in *Regents of the University of California v. Bakke* (1978) and *Fullilove v. Klutznik* (1980), but to uphold a private plan fostered by Kaiser Aluminum Corporation in *United Steelworkers of America v. Weber* (1979).

Stewart also had an almost uncanny ability to seize the middle ground. He was uniquely prone to resolve constitutional battles with compromises. Such was his disposition of cases on interdistrict school desegregation, capital punishment, and gender discrimination. The conditions under which he would sustain such practices were more moderate than those of either the liberals or the conservatives. Oddly enough, his lone dissent against the proscription of school prayer in *Engel v. Vitale* (1962) reflected his moderate perspective. He viewed voluntary prayer in public schools as a compromise in which the free exercise of those who chose to participate did not burden those who declined to pray. Without evidence of coercion, he saw no need to interfere with this ubiquitous practice. In Stewart's jurisprudence, the skill of precision, characteristic of the lawyer, was, perhaps paradoxically, overlaid with the penchant for moderation and compromise, qualities one associates with the politician.

The third theme in Stewart's decisions that helps to explain many of his positions is his belief in the importance of America's judicial institutions for resolving conflict and his commitment to the integrity and autonomy of judges. These principles were not only demonstrated by his openness to the use of judicial institutions in areas that others would have preferred to avoid, but were also manifested in cases challenging the authority of the judiciary. In *Landmark Communications, Inc. v. Virginia* (1978), for example, Stewart concurred with the decision that the state could not punish the press for publishing information about a state judicial fitness proceeding. But in arguing in support of the power of the state to preserve the "quality of its judiciary," Stewart maintained that the state could punish anyone who leaked information about such proceedings.

As a justice, Stewart did not demonstrate any particular reluctance to reverse decisions of lower court judges when he disagreed with their conclusions, but he was especially prone to defend the judiciary from external challenges to their authority. His decision in *Walker v. Birmingham* (1967), upholding the contempt conviction of civil rights protesters who defied a judicial injunction against a march, is an excellent case in point. Despite Stewart's generally strong support for the First Amendment rights of protesters, and despite the clarity of the First Amendment abridgements that occurred in *Walker*, Stewart's concern about the autonomy of the judiciary eclipsed these constitutional considerations. In a clash between First Amendment rights and judicial power, the dictum that one does not disobey a judicial order prevailed.

Stewart's belief in the integrity and autonomy of the judiciary also influenced his positions in cases on criminal procedure. The manifestations of this persuasion were many. He stood foursquare behind the power of judges to hold in criminal contempt those who "misbehaved" in their courtrooms despite the due process questions raised by the summary quality of the procedures employed. He trusted their unilateral fairness. He also opposed expansion of the right to a trial by jury in state criminal cases. This position reflected not only his preference for states' rights, but also his trust of the judiciary and belief that a jury was not an essential element of due process of law. He dissented in *Duncan v. Louisiana* (1968) against the Court's requirement of trial by jury in serious state criminal cases, but he also dissented in *Apodaca v. Oregon* (1972), which allowed verdicts in state criminal cases to be reached by nonunanimous juries. A case tried by a judge alone satisfied Stewart's conception of due process, but a conviction by a divided jury did not. Similarly, in rejecting an expansion of due process guarantees to minors in cases such as *Kent v. United States* (1966), *In re Gault* (1967), *In re Winship* (1970), and *McKeiver v. Pennsylvania* (1971), Stewart maintained faith in the ability of juvenile court judges to protect the interests of their young charges and to render unnecessary the usual processes of the adversary system. It might also be noted that in the myriad cases brought by indigents who had been denied free transcripts of their trials, Stewart sided with only those convicts who had been refused the requested documents by someone other than a judge. Access to judicial determination of one's right to acquire such materials was all that Stewart was prepared to protect; judges alone remained free to decide whether or not to grant the convict's request.

Finally, with respect to his support for trial judges, he was deferential to their higher sentences after retrials, whereas more severe charges on a retrial by a prosecutor elicited no such presumption of legitimacy from Stewart. He trusted judges to set aside their irritation at having been reversed on appeal but assumed no similar magnanimity on the part of law enforcement. In sum, many areas of Stewart's jurisprudence are marked by his faith in the ethics and objectivity of the judiciary and his fervent belief in the importance of an autonomous judiciary to which deference and obedience are due.

No retrospective on a former justice would be complete without an assessment of the quality of his constitutional jurisprudence. Stewart rates high on intellect, lucidity, and judicial candor. His opinions are never difficult to decipher; they are short, crisp, and to the point. In this respect, he rivals the craftsmanship of John Harlan II and Robert H. Jackson.

Stewart's justice-as-lawyer role is, however, a problematic concept. It rests on the assumption that each clause of the Constitution has an unambiguous, objective meaning. If this were so, then one might apply the Constitution the way one would apply a commercial code: place the facts of the case alongside the applicable "rules" and automatically reach a "correct" legal conclusion. But this mechanical jurisprudence, so tenaciously embraced by, among others, Owen J. Roberts, is rarely possible. The Constitution's clauses on freedom of speech, due process of law, or equal protection do not admit of lexical definition. Few of its provisions do. The Constitution must be interpreted, and in order to do that a jurist must identify the values underlying the words. Stewart regularly shied away from constitutional theorizing, perhaps out of fear of its being misconstrued as the subversion of the true Constitution in favor of his image of it. But a justice must be at least a bit of a political theorist for his or her judgments to be persuasive.

Stewart's commitment to states' rights–oriented federalism significantly influenced his jurisprudence, but it was never clear that this commitment flowed from an appreciation of the values in the U.S. system of federalism. The federal division of power may be understood to (1) promote democracy by allowing decisions to be made by those who will be affected by them; (2) facilitate good governance by permitting problems to be resolved at the lowest level of government that is equal to the task; (3) encourage the solving of social problems by allowing states to be laboratories for experimentation; and (4) minimize the opportunity for oppressive government through the division of power. That being so, one would have great difficulty understanding why the restriction of individual rights under the Fourteenth Amendment was dictated by federalism. Except in rare instances, broadly defined individual rights are unlikely to interfere with the values that underlie federalism. Yet Stewart tended to begin every Fourteenth Amendment analysis with a presumption of state sovereignty.

The commitment to the narrow, nonanticipatory decision-making process, the element of the justice-as-lawyer model most characteristic of Stewart, is similarly problematic. A distinction must be drawn between the Court deciding no more than is before it in the case at bar, on the one hand, and choosing to resolve the case with the narrowest possible reasoning, on the other. The virtue of the former is clear. As Stewart said in an interview, issues not fully litigated in the adversary process should not be disposed of prematurely. When insufficient light is cast on an issue, the Court might well come to the wrong conclusion. But this kind of judicial restraint should not be confused with resolving a constitutional issue with the narrowest possible lawyerly reasoning. To resolve the case with the narrowest possible reasoning is to focus on the trees and perhaps miss the forest.

Excessively narrow reasoning breeds unpredictability in the law. One does not know how the Court will resolve the next case. It also provides little guidance for judges faced with similar or related cases in the lower courts; and that, in turn, promotes a lack of uniformity in the decisions made in different jurisdictions. Those are practical problems.

The philosophical problem is more serious. Resolving constitutional cases in the narrowest possible manner, like the concept of mechanical jurisprudence, suggests that the Constitution is simply a legal code requiring no theoretical exegesis and/or that the development of constitutional theory is to be avoided whenever possible. This philosophy deprives both the people and their political leaders of the opportunity to question and to debate the virtue of our constitutional system and legal values. Moreover, the failure to place constitutional questions in a broad context results in inequities in the disposition of cases.

The folly of excessive narrowness is particularly apparent in cases involving gender discrimination and discrimination against pregnant women. Because Stewart favored a nondoctrinal course, he would not define sex as a "suspect classification" when the four comparatively liberal justices voted to do so in 1973. As a result, the Court did not reach a uniform standard for reviewing such cases, and no reliable standard exists today; rather, the case law on the subject remains largely a patchwork. Similarly, the two constitutional cases on maternity leave, *LaFleur* and *Geduldig*, both written by Stewart, were resolved by entirely different reasoning and reached contrary conclusions. In the broad view, the issue in both was the constitutionality of the states' disfavor of pregnancy vis-à-vis other temporary "disabilities." In an even broader perspective, the issue was sex discrimination.

Given that it was Potter Stewart's reluctance to view sex discrimination, like race discrimination, as "suspect," that prevented the Court from doing so twenty years ago, it is perhaps a great irony of history that his retirement from the Court paved the way for the first appointment of a woman to the Supreme Court. On Stewart's announcement of his retirement in 1981, President Ronald Reagan announced the nomination of Justice Sandra Day O'Connor. After he retired, Stewart dedicated much of his time to family matters and to recording for the blind. He died in New Hampshire on December 7, 1985.

—*Gayle Binion*

BIBLIOGRAPHY

There is no biography, but a good brief sketch is by Jerold Israel in Friedman and Israel, *Justices*, vol. 4, 2921. One can examine Stewart's decisions in the context of the Court on which he sat in Leonard Levy, ed., *The Supreme Court Under Earl Warren* (1972); David Rohde and Harold Spaeth, *Supreme Court Decision Making* (1976); and Glendon Schubert, *The Judicial Mind Revisited: Psychometric Analysis of Supreme Court Ideology* (1974). Specific analyses of Stewart's jurisprudence include Gayle Binion, "Justice Potter Stewart on Racial Equality: What It Means to be a Moderate," *Hastings Constitutional Law Quarterly* 6 (1979): 853;

and "Justice Potter Stewart: The Unpredictable Vote," *Journal of Supreme Court History* (1992): 99. See also W. W. Greenhalgh, "In Defense of the "per se" Rule: Justice Stewart's Struggle to Preserve the Fourth Amendment's Warrant Clause," *American Criminal Law Review* 31 (1994): 1013. Two of the justice's articles worth looking at are: Potter Stewart, "The Role of the Federal Courts in the Administration of Justice," *Ohio Bar Journal* 30 (June 3, 1957): 480; and Stewart, "Robert H. Jackson's Influence on Federal State Relationships," *Record of the Association of the Bar of the City of New York* 23 (1968): 7.

NOTEWORTHY OPINIONS

Engel v. Vitale, 370 U.S. 421 (1962) (Dissent)

Walker v. Birmingham, 388 U.S. 307 (1967)

Duncan v. Louisiana, 391 U.S. 145 (1968) (Dissent)

Perez v. United States, 402 U.S. 146 (1971) (Dissent)

Geduldig v. Aiello, 417 U.S. 484 (1974)

Cleveland Board of Education v. LaFleur, 414 U.S. 632 (1974)

Virginia State Board of Pharmacists v. Virginia Citizens Consumer Council, 425 U.S. 748 (1976) (Concurrence)

Brewer v. Williams, 430 U.S. 387 (1977)

Bates v. State Bar of Arizona, 433 U.S. 350 (1977) (Dissent)

Gannett Co. v. DePasquale, 443 U.S. 368 (1979)

Rhode Island v. Innis, 446 U.S. 291 (1980)

HARLAN FISKE STONE

Birth: October 11, 1872, Chesterfield, New Hampshire.

Education: Amherst College, A.B., 1894, M.A., 1897; Columbia University, LL.B., 1898.

Official Positions: U.S. attorney general, 1924–1925.

Supreme Court Service: Nominated associate justice by President Calvin Coolidge, January 5, 1925, to replace Joseph McKenna, who had retired; confirmed by the Senate, February 5, 1925, by a 71–6 vote; took judicial oath March 2, 1925; nominated chief justice by President Franklin D. Roosevelt, June 12, 1941, to replace Charles Evans Hughes, who had retired; confirmed by the Senate, June 27, 1941, by a voice vote; took judicial oath July 3, 1941; served until April 22, 1946; replaced by Fred M. Vinson, nominated by President Harry S. Truman.

Death: April 22, 1946, Washington, D.C.

Harlan Fiske Stone, the son of New England farming parents, was born on the edge of the obscure village of Chesterfield, New Hampshire. During his eventful life he was a New York attorney, dean of Columbia Law School, and attorney general of the United States. He served twenty-one years on the Supreme Court. In fact, he was the only jurist in American history to occupy every seat on the Court—from the most junior associate justice's chair to the center seat of the chief justice. By the time of his death in 1946 he had become one of the best known and most beloved figures in American legal history.

As a boy, Stone was large for his age and excelled in sports, especially football. He had a sharp, methodical mind and developed into a first-rate student. Called "Doc" by his close friends, Stone was popular and a student leader at every level of his education. A rare flash of youthful temper, however, led to his expulsion from the Massachusetts Agricultural College in 1890. He then enrolled at nearby Amherst College. There Stone made the acquaintance of the young Calvin Coolidge, who would later nominate him to the nation's highest court. Prophetically, Stone's Amherst classmates predicted that "Doc Stone will take warning and proceed to be the most famous man in [the class of] '94."

After a brief stint as a high school teacher, Stone enrolled in Columbia Law School, where his diligence and acute intelligence led to more academic success and accolades from his professors. Graduating in 1898, Stone was admitted to the New York bar and went into practice with the New York City firm of Wilmer and Canfield. He also began teaching part-time at Columbia Law School. Stone relinquished his adjunct teaching appointment in 1905 to devote himself to his law practice, but in 1910 he accepted an appointment as professor and dean of the law school. As a teacher, Stone was enamored of the case method, which was then becoming the norm at the nation's most prestigious law schools. By all reports, he was a challenging, even inspiring, professor. As a dean he handled administrative work competently but without relish. One of the things that troubled him as a law school administrator was what he saw as "the influx to the bar of greater numbers of the unfit." This prejudice, fully consonant with upper-class thinking of the World War I period, would be abandoned during Stone's later years on the Supreme Court.

Dean Stone maintained the trust of the law faculty at Columbia, but he had great difficulty working with the autocratic university president, Nicholas Murray Butler. In 1923, smarting from a series of skirmishes with Butler and worn down by "administrivia," Stone resigned and accepted a remunerative position with the esteemed Wall Street firm of Sullivan and Cromwell.

Stone's reentry into private practice was short-lived. The very next year President Coolidge chose Stone to be attorney general. Stone came into the Justice Department with a mandate to eliminate the corruption permitted by his predecessor, Harry M. Daugh-

Harlan Fiske Stone

erty. Stone succeeded so well in cleaning up the "Daughteyism" in the department that some Democratic partisans believed his 1925 nomination to the Supreme Court was sparked by the Republican Party's desire to have him "kicked upstairs." Stone's most enduring legacy from his Justice Department tenure may have been his selection of the twenty-nine-year-old J. Edgar Hoover to head the recently established Federal Bureau of Investigation.

Stone was the first nominee to the Court to appear before a Senate confirmation hearing to answer questions. Despite charges that he was "J. P. Morgan's lawyer" (his firm had acted as counsel for the House of Morgan), Stone handled the senators' questions deftly and was confirmed by a vote of 71 to 6.

The Court that Stone joined in 1925 was headed by the affable William Howard Taft, who believed in "massing the Court." He attempted to present a unified judicial front by discouraging dissenting or concurring opinions. For his first term, Stone dutifully followed the lead of the chief justice and stifled any urges to dissent. To Court watchers of the mid-1920s, Stone looked to be another "safe Republican." His forte as a professor and attorney had been in financial matters, especially tax and patent law, and he could be counted on for solid opinions in complex but essentially uninteresting private law cases. In a Court that was coming to be dominated by constitutional issues, however, most legal experts predicted that Stone would act as a cipher for Taft.

During his second term on the Court, Stone began to slide away from Taft's shadow. He often refused to join the opinions of the chief justice and the Court's "Four Horsemen" (conservatives Pierce Butler, James McReynolds, George Sutherland, and Willis Van Devanter). In moving metaphorically to the left of the bench, Stone frequently found himself in league with two giants of Supreme Court history, Louis Brandeis and Oliver Wendell Holmes. The phrase "Holmes, Brandeis, and Stone dissenting" became a frequent litany at the end of opinions by Taft and the Four Horsemen. Some of these dissents, particularly in civil liberties cases, were among the most eloquently phrased statements in the Court's history. But most of the truly classic dissents of the period—in cases such as *Olmstead v. United States* (1928)—came from Brandeis or Holmes, not Stone.

As the silent partner in this triumvirate, Stone was generally overlooked or underestimated. It is true that he did not possess the epigraphical eloquence or the stark philosophical principles of Holmes, nor did he manifest the crusading zeal or prodigious commitment to factual documentation of Brandeis. Although Stone generally permitted his senior brethren to speak for him, he was a profound thinker with clear principles of his own. In his passion for judicial self-restraint in economic regulation cases, he was every bit the equal of Brandeis or Holmes. If Congress or the state legislatures devised a particular regulatory statute, Stone was loath to strike it down unless it was totally lacking in a reasonable legislative foundation. On the other hand, if the legislatures came up with a statute that impinged upon the civil liberties of selected Americans, Stone was as quick as his two esteemed colleagues to vote against its constitutionality.

Stone would not begin to speak regularly for the liberal dissenters on the Supreme Court until the 1930s. By then, Holmes had retired and was replaced by Benjamin Cardozo, and a new chief justice, Charles Evans Hughes, had taken Taft's place. Hughes had served on the Court from 1910 to 1916, but resigned to seek the presidency; in 1930 he became the first justice to return to the Court after a resignation. Like Taft, Hughes was interested in massing the Court around single majority opinions, but he was even less successful at it than Taft. In part, Hughes's failure to mold a unified Court was due to Stone's emergence as a consistent and strident opponent of judicial conservatism. In addition, unanimity on the Hughes Court was frustrated by the complexities of the Great Depression and the controversial New Deal legislation that demanded judicial review.

Although a lifelong Republican and private critic of the New Deal, Stone was seldom disposed to exalt his own policy preferences over those of the nation's elected representatives. One of Stone's greatest opinions, his dissent in *United States v. Butler* (1936), offers a good illustration of his judicial philosophy in full flower. The case involved the Agricultural Adjustment Act (AAA) of 1933, one of the most important pieces of legislation in the early New Deal. Speaking for the six-member Court majority in *Butler*, Justice Owen Roberts held that the AAA processing tax, which furnished revenue to underwrite crop subsidies and soil restrictions, was both an unconstitutional infringement on the states' rights to regulate agriculture as protected by the Tenth Amendment and an unreasonably broad reading of the clause in Article I that extends to Congress the right to "provide for the . . . general Welfare."

Stone believed that the majority in *Butler* read the Constitution much too narrowly. He maintained that courts should not question the means by which Congress elected to carry into operation its delegated powers. In a classic justification of judicial self-restraint every bit as eloquent as any ever uttered by Holmes or Brandeis, Stone submitted:

> The power of courts to declare a statute unconstitutional is subject to two guiding principles of decision which ought never to be absent from judicial consciousness. One is that courts are concerned only with the power to enact statutes, not with their wisdom. The other is that while unconstitutional exercise of power by the executive and legislative branches of the government is subject to judicial restraint, the only check upon our own exercise of power is our own sense of self-restraint. For the removal of unwise laws from the statute books appeal lies not to the courts but to the ballot and to the processes of democratic government.

Later in the opinion, he added: "It is a contradiction in terms to say that there is power to spend for the national welfare, while rejecting any power to impose conditions reasonably adapted to the attainment of the end which alone would justify the expenditure."

At the end of the 1935–1936 term, Stone wrote his sister to lament that during that year the Court's majority had been "narrow and obscurantic in its outlook." Referring to the term just completed as "one of the most disastrous in its history," Stone ventured the following: "I suppose no intelligent person likes very well the way the New Deal does things, but that ought not to make us forget that ours is a nation which should have the powers ordinarily possessed by governments, and that the framers of the Constitution intended that it should have."

Throughout the 1930s, Stone privately complained that Chief Justice Hughes kept him on what he termed "short rations," that is, assigning Stone the mundane financial cases while saving the juicy constitutional and public law cases for other justices. Perhaps Hughes was wary of Stone because he saw him as a rival for the Court's leadership. Stone, after all, had been widely touted as the perfect chief justice after Taft's departure, and many in the American legal community resented Hughes for resigning from the Court in 1916 to seek public office.

During the infamous "Court-packing" controversy of 1937, Stone was active behind the scenes. He told President Franklin Roosevelt privately that the bench needed more justices who shared the philosophy of Holmes, Brandeis, and Cardozo, but who could also express this philosophy cogently and bear their share of the Court's work. Yet he was definitely opposed to changing the size of the Court. Stone fumed when Hughes wrote a letter to Sen. Burton K. Wheeler, D-Mont., explaining that the Court was fully abreast of its business and did not need new blood. Stone objected to the propriety of a Court member, even the chief justice, rendering a public advisory opinion. He also was miffed that so few of the justices were consulted before the release of the letter. Partly as a result of the letter, the Court-packing bill failed. But, as is well known, the president ultimately had his way with the Court because of the defection of Roberts and, to a lesser extent, Hughes himself from the camp of those who feared the exercise of federal government power during the Depression.

One problem that Stone had with the "switch in time that saved nine" was that he was skeptical of the authenticity of Hughes's conversion. Stone believed that the chief justice had used the Court-packing issue to grandstand. He also saw that Hughes frequently assigned an opinion to himself when the Court overruled a pre-1937 decision, such as in *West Coast Hotel v. Parrish* (1937). This, Stone believed, made Hughes look good to the liberal law school elite. On the other hand, whenever the chief justice took the conservative position, which he did quite regularly, Stone saw that he silently hid behind the opinion of another justice.

For his part, Hughes learned of Stone's disapproval of the Wheeler letter, and he may have even detected Stone's skepticism regarding his change of position. Obviously, there was no love lost between Hughes and Stone. As a result, in the spate of opinions issued in the 1937 term that revivified the New Deal and the "little New Deals" of the states, Stone was assigned to write for the majority in only one case, *Carmichael v. Southern Coal & Coke Co.* (1937). In upholding the state of Alabama's unemployment compensation law, Stone wrote: "There is no warrant in the Constitution for setting the tax aside because a court thinks that it could have drawn a better statute or could have distributed the burden more wisely. Those are functions reserved for the legislature."

Between 1937 and 1943 retirements and deaths allowed President Roosevelt to remake the Court almost entirely, and he chose candidates whose New Deal credentials were unassailable. When Hughes retired in 1941, Roosevelt moved Stone to the center seat and selected Attorney General Robert Jackson to fill the vacancy created by Stone's elevation to chief justice. By the time of his death in April 1945, Roosevelt had filled every seat on the Court except the one occupied by Owen Roberts. The nation's highest court was now quite properly known as the "Roosevelt Court."

The ironies that would soon confront Stone and the Roosevelt Court were striking. The judicial self-restraint in the face of economic issues that Holmes, Brandeis, and Stone had argued for with varying degrees of passion and logic was now a reality. After 1937 the Court essentially accepted legislative economic regulation through state and federal statutes with only the most perfunctory degree of judicial review. But unanimity on economic regulation did not mean a successful "massing of the Court" on all issues. Civil liberties questions were arising as the Depression merged into another world war, and, if anything, they would prove to be even more divisive than economic questions. Issues such as freedom of expression, separation of church and state, and racial justice befuddled and divided the Roosevelt Court just as they continue to challenge the Supreme Court today.

Moreover, the staunch New Dealers appointed to the Court were bright, accomplished, opinionated, and far from timid. Stone referred to Hugo Black, William O. Douglas, and Felix Frankfurter as "wild horses." Stone's relations with the new justices, both before and after he became their chief, could only be described as strained. For example, he and Black got off on the wrong foot. In his first term, Black dissented far too much for Stone's taste. In addition, Black was openly political and confrontational in his opinions. Stone did not keep his feelings about Black's lack of proper judicial decorum to himself. Stone liked to talk to reporter friends, and he carried on a voluminous correspondence with members of the legal community. Apparently, Black learned of Stone's privately expressed dissatisfaction with his performance as a judicial rookie. Stone did not have the personal skills to smooth over the friction, and Black never forgot what he perceived to have been a personal slight. Sadly, the relationship of two great jurists, who shared so much in terms of philosophy, never recovered from a bad start.

One of Stone's greatest contributions to the Roosevelt Court and to American law generally came in what appeared, at first reading, to be an unimportant case, *United States v. Carolene Products Co.* (1938). The case involved a challenge to a federal law prohibiting the interstate transportation of "filled milk," which was skimmed milk mixed with animal fats. As might be expected, given that the case came to the Court after the judicial revolution of 1937 had severely undercut the economic judicial fiat, the Court found the statute constitutionally acceptable.

What made this decision memorable was its fourth footnote, perhaps the most famous footnote in all of Supreme Court history. In it Stone enunciated what many Court watchers believed had been true since 1937, that the Supreme Court would henceforth subject statutes dealing with civil liberties and racial issues to a much more searching examination than laws pertaining to economic matters. The footnote stated a clear double standard, but the Court in 1938 appeared to be able to live with it.

Because of its importance, the *Carolene Products* footnote deserves quoting at length:

> It is unnecessary to consider now whether legislation which restricts ... political processes which can ordinarily be expected to bring about repeal of undesirable legislation, is to be subjected to more exacting judicial scrutiny under the general prohibitions of the 14th Amendment than are most other types of legislation. ... Nor need we inquire whether similar considerations enter into the review of statutes directed at particular religious ... or national ... or racial minorities; ... whether prejudice against discrete and insular minorities may be a special condition, which tends seriously to curtail the operation of those political processes ordinarily to be relied upon to protect minorities, and which may call for a correspondingly more searching judicial inquiry.

In simple terms, this footnote ratified the economic self-restraint so identified with Holmes and Brandeis, while at the same time suggesting that statutes that on their face restricted civil liberties or the rights of racial minorities would be subjected to a standard of review more probing than that accorded to economic regulations. This footnote, while technically not part of the holding in *Carolene Products,* has been cited favorably by federal courts hundreds of times ever since, specifically in cases involving "suspect classifications" such as race, alienage, and gender.

Most legal historians have identified Hughes's opinion in *West Coast Hotel v. Parrish* as a watershed in American constitutional law. It was this opinion that announced the new orientation of Roberts and Hughes, which meant that the Court would no longer attempt to act as a superlegislature to review economic regulatory statutes. The *West Coast Hotel* decision, however, did not hint at the new judicial activism that would soon infuse the Court on civil rights and civil liberties questions. Stone's *Carolene Products* footnote, by contrast, looked both backward and forward. It also made clear that different standards of constitutional review would henceforth be exercised in economic regulation and personal rights cases. An argument can be made that Stone's *Carolene Products* footnote provides a better point of demarcation than *West Coast Hotel* for the shift to modern constitutional jurisprudence. Two Stone opinions, a dissent in 1940 and a majority opinion in 1941, while Hughes was still chief justice, offer apt illustrations of this new jurisprudence.

Stone's majority opinion in *United States v Darby Lumber Co.* (1941) warrants discussion first. Stone provided a brilliant and eagerly awaited legal construction of the 1938 Fair Labor Standards Act, arguably the last major piece of New Deal legislation. It is uncertain why Hughes, who generally preferred to keep for himself majority opinions reversing previous laissez-faire decisions, assigned the *Darby* opinion to Stone. In any case, Stone made the most of the opportunity.

Among other things, the Fair Labor Standards Act banned the interstate transportation of merchandise produced by companies that violated federal minimum wage, maximum hours, or child labor precepts. The statute was challenged in federal district court by a Georgia lumber manufacturer who maintained that the law impermissibly intruded into local (intrastate) manufacturing, something he felt was beyond the sweep of federal regulation. The lower court agreed with Darby Lumber, relying on the 1918 opinion in *Hammer v. Dagenhart,* in which the Court had been unwilling to construe the commerce clause of Article I to permit the regulation of manufacturing and held unconstitutional the Child Labor Act of 1916.

Reversing the lower court and overruling *Hammer v. Dagenhart,* Stone's majority opinion in *Darby*

continued to obliterate the specious distinction between manufacturing and commerce that the Court had set its guns against in *National Labor Relations Board v. Jones & Laughlin Steel Corporation* (1937). The goods produced and marketed by the lumber company, Stone concluded, were part of the stream of commerce and, therefore, could be banned under the commerce clause.

Stone's opinion also helped expunge from constitutional jurisprudence the doctrine of "dual federalism," a nineteenth-century conservative dogma that held that the Tenth Amendment sets an explicit limitation on the powers of Congress. In burying dual federalism, Stone insisted that the Tenth Amendment

> states but a truism that all is retained which has not been surrendered. There is nothing in the history of its adoption to suggest that it was more than declaratory of the relationship between the national and state governments as it had been established by the Constitution before the amendment or that its purpose was other than to allay fears that the new national government might seek to exercise powers not granted.

Stone's leading biographer, Alpheus T. Mason, declared that with the 1941 *Darby* opinion, Stone was "now recognized as the intellectual leader of the Court's center."

In the year before the *Darby* opinion, Stone had hardly seemed at the intellectual center of the Court. With his lone dissent in *Minersville School District v. Gobitis* (1940), he appeared to some Court watchers as if he had wandered off the left edge of the political spectrum. In retrospect, his dissent in *Gobitis* is now seen as one of his finest hours. The case arose when a group of Jehovah's Witnesses children balked at saluting the American flag in their Pennsylvania elementary school. The Witnesses were not anti-American, but their literal reading of the Old Testament compelled them to refuse to pay homage to a "graven image." They considered then and still do consider the flag to be such an image.

The Witnesses' principled stand in the late 1930s violated a compulsory Pennsylvania flag salute statute. Lillian and William Gobitas (the name was misspelled in Court records) were summarily expelled from school for refusing to salute the flag. The Witnesses' attorneys argued that the statute—a law passed in the midst of patriotic fervor as America prepared for war—was an unconstitutional infringement on the Witnesses' freedom of expression and, therefore, should be struck down as a violation of the First Amendment as held applicable to the states by the due process clause of the Fourteenth Amendment.

Frankfurter wrote the opinion for the 8–1 majority, which upheld the Pennsylvania law. As the Court's only Jewish member in 1940, Frankfurter was particularly sensitive to the rights of religious minorities. But he felt strongly that the country could legitimately ask it citizens for some minimal patriotic expression, such as the salute of the American flag. Frankfurter, a consistent judicial self-restrainer in civil liberties as well as economic regulation cases, provided a brilliant discourse on the power of a symbol such as the American flag. He argued, however, that while he might not favor flag salute legislation personally, he would not wish to inject his views between the people of a state and their elected representatives.

Frankfurter had tried mightily to secure Stone's vote for the majority in *Gobitis,* writing him a five-page letter that even used some of Stone's own language in the *Carolene Products* footnote against his position. Stone would not budge. Shortly before the opinion in *Gobitis* was to be announced in open court, Stone learned that Frankfurter planned to read from the bench his entire lengthy majority opinion. Stone debated whether he should simply announce that he dissented, as was the custom, or whether he should attempt to match Frankfurter's rhetoric by reading his opinion as well. Ironically, Frankfurter elected at the last minute not to read his opinion, merely announcing the result in the case. But Stone was so agitated that he decided to plunge ahead and read his dissent, doing so with a level of emotion rare for him.

In asserting that the Gobitas children were denied their freedom of speech and religion by the Pennsylvania law, Stone declared:

The guaranties of civil liberty are but guaranties of freedom of the human mind and spirit and of reasonable freedom and opportunity to express them. . . . If these guaranties are to have any meaning they must, I think, be deemed to withhold from the state any authority to compel belief or the expression of it where that expression violates religious convictions, whatever may be the legislative view of the desirability of such compulsion.

Stone later expressed chagrin that he was so carried away by emotion that he had read his entire dissent. But he was buoyed by praise from many quarters for expressing such a courageous opinion in the face of the uncritical patriotism of the country in 1940. The chairman of the American Civil Liberties Union, John Haynes Holmes, ventured that Stone's *Gobitis* opinion would "rank as one of the great dissenting opinions in American history." Editorials in 171 U.S. newspapers supported Stone's dissent; only a few joined company with Frankfurter.

Stone's apprehension about the lack of tolerance for religious differences was confirmed by the persecution of Jehovah's Witnesses in the immediate aftermath of the *Gobitis* decision. In the week of June 12–20, 1940, alone, the Justice Department received reports of "hundreds of attacks on the Witnesses." Among the many incident reports were the following: a Witnesses' Kingdom Hall in Maine was burned; a mob attacked a Witnesses' Bible meeting within a few miles of the nation's capital; and in Connersville, Indiana, a Witnesses' attorney was beaten and driven from town. The Justice Department attributed this wave of violence directly to the *Gobitis* decision.

The physical attacks eventually tapered off, but the Witnesses would continue to find their way to the Supreme Court to contest a variety of issues. In *Jones v. City of Opelika* (1942), the case involved the constitutionality of municipal ordinances levying a license tax on groups selling books and pamphlets door-to-door. The Witnesses took the position that such laws violated their First Amendment rights of freedom of expression and the free exercise of religion. The

Witnesses lost the case by a 5–4 vote. As expected, Stone dissented. But, in another dissent filed by Black, Douglas, and Murphy, something unheard of in Supreme Court history took place. These three justices, all of whom had voted with the majority in *Gobitis,* confessed that they had changed their minds about the constitutionality of flag salute statutes and now agreed with Stone on this issue.

The about-face of the three liberal justices in *Jones v. Opelika* persuaded the Witnesses to bring another case to federal court on the constitutionality of compulsory flag salute laws. This time the case came from West Virginia. In 1943, along with several other cases involving the Witnesses, the Court handed down the ruling in *West Virginia Board of Education v. Barnette,* which explicitly overruled *Gobitis.* The vote was 6–3, with Stone, the three recanting justices, and the recently appointed Wiley Rutledge and Robert Jackson in the majority. Stone graciously allowed Jackson to write the majority opinion. Frankfurter issued an impassioned dissent. The majority opinion, one of Jackson's best, echoed many of the arguments and even some of the phraseology in Stone's *Gobitis* dissent. In three short years, Stone as a lone dissenter had turned the Court around on a major civil liberties issue.

When Roosevelt named Stone chief justice, poet and essayist Archibald MacLeish wrote that the nomination was "so clearly and certainly and surely right it resounded in the world like the perfect word spoken at the perfect moment." And when the nomination came up for discussion in the Senate on June 27, 1941, Sen. George Norris, R-Neb., the last of the Progressives who had fought Stone's earlier appointment as an associate justice, delivered the only speech. He confessed his error in opposing Stone in 1925 and now strongly endorsed his elevation to the chief justiceship. A few moments later, Stone was confirmed unanimously by a voice vote of the Senate.

In the newly confirmed chief justice's obligatory letter thanking the president, Stone referred to himself as now having to shoulder "some burdens which John Marshall did not know." He could not have been more prophetic. Marshall, for example, did not even see a single dissent to any opinions of the Court (most of which he wrote himself) in his first three terms as chief justice. By contrast, the pace of dissent on the Stone Court was higher than at any previous time in American history.

The "wild horses"—Black, Douglas, and Frankfurter—now had a similarly rambunctious stablemate in Jackson. Stone basically tried to stay out of the way. Never one to hog the glory, he took pains to assign important majority opinions to each of his brethren. As a result, Stone did not issue any majority opinions during his tenure as chief justice to match the significance, for example, of his 1941 opinion in *Darby.*

In many ways, the chief justiceship was an unhappy denouement to an otherwise illustrious public life. Part of Stone's difficulty as chief justice was his tolerance for disagreement. In the minds of some Court colleagues, he let conferences over pending cases and petitions of certiorari continue far too long. The Stone Court did not generally observe the normal Court protocol of allowing the justices to speak in turn in ascending levels of seniority. As a result, the discussions went in many different directions. Frankfurter, the professor, may have enjoyed the lively exchanges, but more efficiency-minded justices chafed at the time seemingly wasted in conferences.

Another problem was that Stone did not have the ability or perhaps the inclination to massage the massive egos of some of his colleagues. As an associate justice, Stone kept to a strict schedule and dispatched routine work with amazing speed. He was troubled that others could not do the same, but he did not have the patience or tact to cajole them into more rapid activity. Jackson believed that Stone's problem was that he dreaded conflict. But because Stone was willing to permit dissension to continue and fester, he unintentionally abetted the already high degree of conflict that was inevitable given the positions and personalities of the "wild horses."

One example of the difficulty Stone had in uniting his Court can be seen in the deceptively simple matter of composing a farewell letter to Owen Roberts when he retired in 1945. Roberts was the only member of the Court in 1945 who had not been nominated by Roosevelt. At the end of the 1944–1945 term Roberts was not a happy justice. He had dissented fifty-three times that year, frequently with bitter and intemperate language. After he announced his plans to retire, Stone drafted a farewell letter couched in cautious, hardly generous language. Some justices signed it, some refused. Black drafted a second letter that was even less flattering to Roberts, and it too made the round of the justices. The negotiations over language continued for weeks. The Black draft eventually received six "votes." Although not satisfied with Black's draft, Stone used it substantially as the basis for his comments about Roberts at the Court's opening session in October 1945. This was a sorry episode that did no credit to the Stone Court.

Assessing the qualities and accomplishments of Harlan Fiske Stone is no easy matter. Published studies of judicial greatness have usually placed Stone in the "great" or "near great" category. Judged against the justices with whom he served, Stone should receive high but not top marks in most categories. For example, although he did not shine as brightly as his compatriots in judicial restraint, Holmes and Brandeis, his was a consistent and solid voice for respect of the legislative prerogative. He did not have the crusading zeal of Brandeis, Black, or Douglas, but he held strong principles and expressed them cogently at appropriate times: unlike the legal crusaders, he had an impeccable sense of judicial decorum. Judged against other academic lawyers who found their way to the Court, his scholarship was well above average but not of Frankfurter's caliber. As a legal writer he rose to brilliance on occasion, as in his *Darby* majority opinion or his *Gobitis* dissent, but his prose did not consistently sparkle as did that of Holmes and Cardozo. And as sensitive as Stone was to civil liberties, he failed to weigh in against the egregious treatment of Japanese Americans during World War II. Finally, as a chief justice, Stone was honest and solid but not as effective a consensus-builder as Taft or even Hughes.

The end of Stone's long public life came suddenly and with a measure of incongruity. On Easter Monday 1946 Stone was presiding over an opinion day session of the Court. He read a dissent in *Girouard v. United States*, a case addressing the question of whether a conscientious objector was entitled to citizenship. Ironically, Stone was dissenting to a majority view that wrote into law a position he had himself expressed in a previous dissent. Thus this eloquent practitioner of self-restraint and advocate of judicial consensus was in the anomalous position of dissenting from one of his own dissents. Stone's reasoning was complicated, but essentially he believed that Congress had acted to interpret the statute at issue, the Naturalization Act of 1940, in a way contrary to his earlier dissent. Ever sensitive to legislative prerogative, he felt bound to express his support for the wishes of elected representatives, even if that meant dissenting and going against a position he had advocated just a few years earlier.

At the end of his opinion in *Girouard,* as almost a fitting epitaph, he stated: "It is not the function of this Court to disregard the will of Congress in the exercise of its constitutional power." Following the disposition of this case, Black announced several opinions. Then Stone was scheduled to deliver three decisions. He paused for a long moment, then mumbled incoherently. Black, the senior associate justice, sensing that something was wrong, banged the gavel and ended the session. Stone was helped out of the chamber. He then collapsed in a Court washroom and was later taken home by ambulance.

Stone never regained consciousness. He died of a massive cerebral hemorrhage that evening, April 22, 1946. Three days later more than 2,500 people attended his funeral. Of the many stirring eulogies, perhaps that delivered by Sen. Alben Barkley, D-Ky., struck the most apt chord: "No Associate Justice or Chief Justice ... held a more abiding place in the affections of the American people and in the affections of all who knew him intimately and personally."
—*John W. Johnson*

BIBLIOGRAPHY

The Stone papers are in the Library of Congress. Stone's own writings include: *Law and Its Administration* (1915); "The Common Law in the United States," *Harvard Law Review* 50 (1936): 4; "Fifty Years Work of the Supreme

Court," *American Bar Association Journal* 14 (1928): 428; and "The Public Influence of the Bar," *Harvard Law Review* 48 (1934): 1. Stone's career has benefited from a masterful biography: Alpheus T. Mason, *Harlan Fiske Stone: Pillar of the Law* (1956), which makes extensive use of Stone's correspondence and other private papers. An affectionate portrait is Milton C. Handler, "Clerking for Justice Harlan Fiske Stone," *Journal of Supreme Court History* (1995): 113.

Useful on Stone's legal thought are Samuel J. Konefsky, *Chief Justice Stone and the Supreme Court* (1946); G. Edward White, *The American Judicial Tradition: Profiles of Leading American Judges* (1976), 215–229; Allison Dunham, "Mr. Chief Justice Stone," in Allison Dunham and Philip B. Kurland, eds., *Mr. Justice* (1964), 229–249; John P. Frank, "Harlan Fiske Stone: An Estimate," *Stanford Law Review* 9 (1957): 621; Noel T. Dowling, "Mr. Justice Stone and the Constitution," *Columbia Law Review* 36 (1936): 351; Learned Hand, "Chief Justice Stone's Conception of the Judicial Function," *Columbia Law Review* 46 (1946): 696; Herbert Wechsler, "Stone and the Constitution," *Columbia Law Review* 46 (1946): 793; Noel T. Dowling, "The Methods of Mr. Justice Stone in Constitutional Cases," *Columbia Law*

Review 41 (1941): 1160; and M. Galston, "Activism and Restraint: The Evolution of Harlan Fiske Stone's Judicial Philosophy," *Tulane Law Review* 70 (1995): 137.

Footnote Four has generated a literature of its own. See, for example, P. Linzer, "The Carolene Products Footnote and the Preferred Position of Individual Rights: Louis Lusky and John Hart Ely vs. Harlan Fiske Stone," *Constitutional Commentary* 12 (1995): 277; and M. Perry, "Justice Stone and Footnote Four," *George Mason University Civil Rights Law Journal* 6 (1996): 35.

NOTEWORTHY OPINIONS

United States v. Butler, 297 U.S. 1 (1936) (Dissent)

United States v. Carolene Products Co., 304 U.S. 144 (1938)

Minersville School District v. Gobitis, 310 U.S. 586 (1940) (Dissent)

United States v. Darby Lumber Co., 312 U.S. 100 (1941)

Jones v. Opelika, 316 U.S. 584 (1942) (Dissent)

Girouard v. United States, 328 U.S. 61 (1946) (Dissent)

JOSEPH STORY

Birth: September 18, 1779, Marblehead, Massachusetts.

Education: Attended Marblehead Academy; graduated from Harvard, 1798; LL.D., 1821; read law under Samuel Sewall and Samuel Putnam; admitted to bar, 1801.

Official Positions: Member, Massachusetts legislature, 1805–1808; speaker of the Massachusetts House, 1811; U.S. representative, 1808–1809; delegate, Massachusetts Constitutional Convention, 1820.

Supreme Court Service: Nominated associate justice by President James Madison, November 15, 1811, to replace William Cushing, who had died; confirmed by the Senate, November 18, 1811, by a voice vote; took judicial oath February 3, 1812; served until September 10, 1845; replaced by Levi Woodbury, nominated by President James K. Polk.

Death: September 10, 1845, Cambridge, Massachusetts.

Joseph Story was the youngest Supreme Court nominee in history, but he went on to become one of the commanding figures of American legal history. While writing a larger proportion of the Marshall Court's opinions than anyone other than John Marshall himself, Story created an extensive and crudite commercial, insurance, and admiralty jurisprudence in his capacity as circuit justice for the New England states. After 1829, as Dane Professor of Law, Story was the central figure of the antebellum Harvard Law School; the treatises he wrote in carrying out his professorial duties played a seminal role in the creation of a sophisticated, genuinely American jurisprudence. When one also notes Story's extensive occasional writings, his active (if usually unacknowledged) political activities, and his services as president of a bank and member of the Harvard Corporation, it becomes clear that Story was the busiest justice in the Court's history, as well as one of its best known.

Story's happy marriage, his love of learning and his gregariousness, his liberal attitudes about women, slavery, and the mistreatment of Native Americans, and his basic social conservatism all had their roots in his childhood and his parents. Story's parents came from privileged backgrounds, but his father's medical practice in the declining fishing village of Marblehead inculcated at an early date the lesson that public service is a duty. Dr. Elisha Story, one of the "Indians" at the Boston Tea Party, clearly was the major source of Joseph's youthful politics and a significant influence on his lasting ethical and theological beliefs. Joseph's mother, Mehitable Pedrick, was a strong-willed and voluble self-taught woman; she seems to have played a decisive role in shaping the future justice's personality.

Story attended Harvard College, graduating in 1798 with second honors in his class and a strong taste for belles lettres, an interest that reached its high point with his publication in 1802 of a volume of mediocre poetry entitled *The Power of Solitude.* After overcoming an initial dislike for the "dry and technical principles" of the law, Story became enamored of legal learning. Soon after his admission to the bar in July 1801, he wrote to a friend of his "love for my profession. The science claims me as a fixed devotee." Story was to remain a devotee of the law and of legal learning for the rest of his life.

During the first years of the nineteenth century, Story built what was by decade's end a prominent legal practice. At the same time, he was busily engaged in politics. Although in later life he often sought to downplay his early partisanship, the youthful lawyer was an enthusiastic Republican in a state and a profession then dominated by Federalists. His involvement in county Republican politics led to his rapid rise as his party gained political strength in Massachusetts. He was first elected to the Massachusetts legislature in 1805 and served an unexpired term as a Republican member of Congress from May 1808 to March 1809; he became speaker of the lower house of the state legislature in 1811.

Joseph Story

Politics and law converged in Story's work as a lobbyist and lawyer in the famous Yazoo affair, which stemmed from the wholesale corruption of the Georgia legislature and its sale of 35 million acres in the state's Yazoo area (now Alabama and Mississippi) at extremely favorable prices. The state's subsequent attempt to rescind the sales sparked a fifteen-year struggle in the courts and Congress over the validity of the rescission and the propriety of reimbursing third-party purchasers of the disputed real estate. Along with Robert Goodloe Harper, a well-known Maryland lawyer, Story successfully argued the purchasers' position in the great case of *Fletcher v. Peck* (1810), which held that the original land grants were irrevocable.

With the death of Justice William Cushing in September 1810, it was at last possible for the Republicans, in control of the presidency and Congress since 1801, to secure a majority on the Supreme Court. President James Madison's problem was to identify a suitable replacement for Cushing (a Massachusetts native) from among the small body of Massachusetts Republican lawyers. Madison's first selection declined; the Senate rejected the second; and the third, John Quincy Adams, preferred to remain a diplomat. Story's suitability for the appointment was suspect to some, particularly to ex-president Thomas Jefferson, who resented Story's role in Congress in terminating the embargo on international trade that Jefferson had used to retaliate against European attacks on American vessels. Over Jefferson's private objections—he wrote that Story was "unquestionably a tory . . . and too young"—Madison chose Story. Madison also nominated Gabriel Duvall to succeed Samuel Chase, who had died in mid-1811, and the nominees were confirmed on November 18, 1811.

With Madison's two appointments, the Court Story joined for the February 1812 term was made up of five Republicans and only two Federalists, but the Court already bore the impress of the views and personality of its Federalist chief justice. Story was in broad agreement with Marshall's nationalism and his preference for public consensus on the Court, and he quickly became Marshall's confidant and ally. Story's original Republicanism had always been more partisan than ideological, and in the 1810s he, like many younger Republicans, found less and less to dislike in Marshall's basic constitutional vision.

The War of 1812 began only a few months after Story took his seat, and much of his early judicial work both on the Court and as presiding judge of the federal circuit court for New England concerned matters arising from the war and related federal policies of trade restriction and embargo. The relevant bodies of law—admiralty and prize cases, the law of nations, the historical practice of belligerents—gave ample room for Story's love of recondite legal research, but his frequent disagreements with his colleagues did not arise solely on intellectual grounds. Circuit justice Story was, in a peculiarly personal sense, the representative of the nation and the federal government in a region torn by disagreement over the war and tempted to outright defiance of federal authority. Story's usual response was to assert an expansive view of the nation's rights as a belligerent.

The central doctrinal theme in Story's war-related jurisprudence was the existence and significance of implied federal power to carry out the war. On circuit, in *United States v. Bainbridge* (1816), Story held that Congress's power to create a navy implied the power to permit the enlistment of minors without their parents' permission: "Whenever a general power to do a thing is given, every particular power necessary for doing it is included." In *Brown v. United States* (1814), Story concluded that in the absence of express statutory authorization, the president had the implied power to prosecute the war by seizing enemy property found in the United States. Writing for the Supreme Court, Marshall reversed the decision. Indeed, on the question of confiscation, Story and Marshall frequently disagreed. Story maintained, and Marshall denied, the power to confiscate the property of American citizens resident in Britain despite their ignorance of the outbreak of war or their good-faith intent to return to the United States in the event of war (*The*

Venus, 1814), enemy goods consigned to American buyers prior to the war (*The Merrimack,* 1814), goods purportedly immune under a special license from the British vice-admiral (*The Julia,* 1814—compare Marshall's 1813 circuit decision in *United States v. The Matilda*—and neutral goods carried on a belligerent vessel [*The Nereide,* 1815]). In the latter case, Story delivered an elaborate 6,000-word dissent from Marshall's opinion in vindication of what he termed "the national rights, suspended upon" the power to confiscate the goods.

Story's solicitude for the "national rights" of the United States at war led him to defend implied judicial power as well. In *Houston v. Moore* (1820), Story dissented from a judgment upholding a state court-martial of a federalized militiaman on the ground that the federal courts implicitly had exclusive jurisdiction to try the case. He also repeatedly attempted to establish the existence of a broad, judicially developed federal common law of crimes. In *United States v. Hudson & Goodwin* (1812), decided a few weeks after Story took his seat, the Court endorsed the orthodox Republican view that federalism and separation of powers rendered illegitimate the exercise of criminal jurisdiction except in pursuance of a statute. No justice publicly dissented, but in an 1813 circuit opinion, Story stated that he "considered the point, as one open to discussion, notwithstanding . . . *Hudson.*" The opinion argued at length in support of a common law of offenses against the United States, at least within the scope of admiralty jurisdiction, but the government declined to support his views in the Supreme Court, and Story was unable to persuade his colleagues to reopen the issue (*United States v. Coolidge,* 1816). Story was more successful in sustaining judicial power to define criminal offenses under open-ended statutes. In *United States v. Smith* (1820), he carried all but one of his colleagues with him in concluding that a statute criminalizing piracy "as defined by the law of nations" was precise enough to meet what modern lawyers would call the requirements of due process.

Story, like other nationalists of the early Republic, saw deep connections between a strong federal government and the growth of commerce and industry. Even as he was defending the existence of broad, implied federal powers, Story spent his first years on the bench laying the groundwork for a law of business and commerce, expounded by the federal courts, that would favor growth and industry. In an early decision on circuit, *De Lovio v. Boit* (1815), Story wrote a seventy-page opinion holding that cases involving marine insurance contracts fell within the federal courts' exclusive admiralty jurisdiction. The subject matter of *De Lovio* was of great significance in the early nineteenth century, but Story's opinion went beyond insurance to sweep virtually everything afloat—"all maritime contracts, torts, and injuries"— within the federal sphere. Federal courts in admiralty cases sit without juries, and that aspect of *De Lovio* proved especially popular with New England business because, as Story noted in a letter, merchants "declare that in mercantile cases, they are not fond of juries." The publication of Story's circuit court decisions, which began in 1815, made his probusiness opinions available on a wider basis. On the Supreme Court as well, Story early on established an expertise in maritime, insurance, and commercial cases. In cases such as *Raborg v. Peyton* (1817), which extended the enforceability and therefore the utility of bills of exchange, Story consistently rejected older, anticommercial decisions, "made at a time when the principles respecting mercantile contracts were not generally understood," in favor of legal doctrines favoring the development and expansion of a market economy.

For Story, the nurturance of commerce and the protection of property were two sides of the same coin. In *Fairfax's Devisee v. Hunter's Lessee* (1813), Story for the Supreme Court reversed a Virginia court decision and held that British real property claims— and the interests of the American land speculators who purchased them—were protected from state expropriation laws under U.S. treaties with Britain. Story's first major constitutional opinion for the Court, *Terrett v. Taylor* (1815), displayed the centrality of property rights in his legal universe. *Terrett* held that land belonging to the colonial established church in Virginia was vested in the postwar Episcopal

Church, even though the Virginia legislature and courts had concluded that recognizing the church's claims violated the Virginia Constitution's guarantee of religious freedom. Story's opinion grandly, if rather vaguely, invoked "the principles of natural justice" and "the spirit and letter of the constitution" (without specifying which provision he had in mind). The actual basis of the decision was Congress's legislative jurisdiction over the land in question, which lay within Virginia's contribution to the District of Columbia.

The connection between the protection of vested rights and the encouragement of business became clear in Story's concurring opinion in *Trustees of Dartmouth College v. Woodward* (1819). Marshall's opinion for the Court held that the college's royal charter was protected against state interference by the Constitution's contracts clause. Story made explicit the applicability of the decision to business corporations and at the same time reassured state legislators concerned about creating inviolable corporate privileges by admitting the legitimacy of corporate charters reserving certain amending powers to the state.

Story's genuine distaste for the wheeling and dealing of partisan politics did not prevent him from becoming actively involved in the federal political arena almost from the beginning of his tenure on the Court, although his efforts were covert and generally directed toward the improvement and expansion of the federal judiciary. From 1813 on, Story was a confidant of Daniel Webster, then rising toward prominence as an orator in Congress and in oral argument before the Court. Story supplied Webster and other congenial members of Congress with legislative proposals dealing with the courts and later with constitutional arguments to rebut the states' rights views frequently voiced in Congress after 1820. After the conclusion of the War of 1812, Story prodded and cajoled his congressional allies to enact legislation extending the criminal powers of the federal courts, establishing a federal bankruptcy system, and vesting the judiciary with the full range of jurisdiction authorized under Article III. In private, Story commended his proposals to Republican legislators as a means of seizing the "glorious opportunity" the end of the war presented "for the Republican party to place themselves permanently in power."

Publicly, Story read Congress an elaborate lecture on the scope of federal court jurisdiction in his famous 1816 opinion in *Martin v. Hunter's Lessee. Martin* was the aftermath of Story's opinion in *Fairfax's Devisee.* Instead of obeying the Supreme Court's mandate, the Virginia court's judges unanimously declared unconstitutional the provision of the Judiciary Act giving the Supreme Court jurisdiction over state decisions. Story's rebuttal, that Supreme Court review of state decisions on federal law issues was consonant with text, history, and practice, was not surprising, but the way he announced it was dramatic. Story vindicated the Court's authority in terms that unequivocally repudiated traditional Republican rhetoric about states' rights. The Constitution, Story wrote, "was ordained and established, not by the states in their sovereign capacities, but emphatically . . . by 'the people of the United States.' . . . [The Constitution] is crowded with provisions which restrain or annul the sovereignty of the states in some of the highest branches of their prerogatives." He went on to instruct Congress on its obligation to extend federal jurisdiction to the limits of Article III in terms that amounted to a brief in support of the judiciary legislation he was then circulating among members of Congress.

The period from 1812, when Story joined the Court, to 1824 was the most productive in the Marshall Court's history. The Court's membership remained unchanged until Henry Brockholst Livingston's death in 1823, and the justices enjoyed, in the main, a remarkable degree of harmony in their private relations and in their public decisions. In all of this Story was an enthusiastic participant, but one with a distinctive voice. He endorsed the generous view of federal power announced by Marshall's great decisions in *McCulloch v. Maryland* (1819) and *Gibbons v. Ogden* (1824), but Story's own opinions in *Martin* and the war-related cases showed his nationalism to be less nuanced and more confrontational. Story's colleagues generally shared his probusiness orientation and admired his legal scholarship, but there too, Story sometimes took extreme positions or was too eager to advance his own views of the properly scientific understanding of the law. His most daring decision of the period, however, concerned the international slave trade, which Story on circuit declared an offense against the law of nations (*United States v. La Jeune Eugenie,* 1822). Story's opinion eloquently denounced the trade as "unnecessary, unjust, and inhuman" and "repugnant to the general principles of justice and humanity," but the decision went beyond existing international law and Marshall's notions of judicial prudence. Three years later, a Marshall opinion for the Court (*The Antelope,* 1825) gently but unequivocally repudiated Story's holding.

From his earliest days at the bar, Story was a scholarly lawyer, and as a judge he was able to indulge his interest in exploring what he described in an 1820 letter as an empire of reason. The first volume of Supreme Court reports covering cases decided after Story's appointment contained a separate page of "corrections and additions" to Story's opinions and a note by Story explaining a case that the Court decided by a *per curiam* order. After Henry Wheaton became the Court reporter in 1816, Story frequently wrote unsigned "themes" on legal questions that Wheaton obligingly included in the Court's reports. Story viewed his opinions, his extrajudicial writings, and even his political contacts with allies in Congress as part of an effort to make American law into a science in which an independent judiciary discovered and applied an orderly system of legal principles through the exercise of reason. Only if the law could be a science, Story believed, could it play the role he envisaged for it in the disorderly world of a democratic republic.

This vision of scientific law, and scientific lawyers, grew in salience as the Marshall Court's institutional and political environment began to deteriorate in the mid-1820s. Story's opinions for the Court in the period expanded on familiar themes. *Martin v. Mott* (1827), for example, broadly interpreted the president's exclusive authority to determine when state militia should be called into federal service, and *Wilkinson v. Leland* (1829) employed extravagant rhetoric about the "sacred" rights of private property on the way to reaching a narrow holding based on the construction of a state statute. *Van Ness v. Pacard* (1829) undermined the property law doctrine of "waste" by interpreting a traditional exception to favor social mobility and investment in the commercial and industrial use of real property. *The Thomas Jefferson* (1825) limited federal admiralty jurisdiction over torts to the ebb and flow of the tide, which denied it to the great body of river commerce, but the decision did not truly contradict Story's usual views. It left maritime contracts in federal court and was dictated, Story believed, by the very historical materials that he thought a scientific lawyer should consult to answer the question.

The continuity of the Court's decisions, however, was threatened by forces external to Story's legal science. The election of 1824, in which four Republicans vied for the presidency, shattered the postwar dominance of a nationalist Republican leadership that supported the Court. Andrew Jackson, the leader in the 1824 popular vote, and the victor in 1828, was in Story's eyes a military chieftain clearly unsuited for high office. The democratic and states' rights themes associated with Jackson were antithetical to Story's political beliefs, and Story was not referring only to the boisterous festivities that accompanied Jackson's inauguration when he described it as "the reign of King Mob triumphant." The posthumous publication of Jefferson's correspondence, with his caustic comments on the Court and on Story personally, lent prestige to ideological criticism of the Court. Moreover, changes in the Court's membership eroded the old practices of consensual decision making and, whenever possible, official unanimity. In *Ogden v. Saunders* (1827), for example, Marshall dissented publicly in a constitutional case for the first time in his tenure, and Story and Duvall joined the dissent.

In the stormy political waters of the Jackson years, Story strove to preserve the Court's institutional position while defending his political and constitutional values as best he could. He took an active role in pushing the Court toward its decision in *Worcester v. Georgia* (1832) that Georgia's attempt to assert jurisdiction over the Cherokee nation was a violation of the supremacy of federal constitutional and treaty

provisions, a decision that was at odds with Jackson's popular anti-Indian attitudes and that Georgia defied.

Story's behind-the-scenes political activity continued unabated. He was, for example, the principal draftsman of the federal crimes act Congress passed in 1825. When President Jackson vetoed a bill to renew the charter of the Bank of the United States in 1832 and, in the process, denied the finality of the Supreme Court's constitutional decisions, Story was the source of the legal reasoning Webster used to denounce the veto. Story probably played a similar role in the genesis of Webster's famous 1830 speech defending the unity and supremacy of the Union against South Carolina's claim that an individual state could "nullify" federal laws it deemed unconstitutional. The question of nullification put Story in the unaccustomed role of supporting Jackson. When South Carolina threatened to nullify an unpopular federal tariff act, Jackson responded with a proclamation as emphatically nationalist in tone and content as any state paper since Story's *Martin* opinion. Story publicly praised the president's proclamation as "among the ablest commentaries ever offered" on the Constitution's meaning; privately, Story noted that he was among Jackson's "warmest supporters . . . just as long as he maintains the principles contained" in the proclamation.

Story's most lasting defense of his vision of constitutional nationalism and legal science came about through the largess of the New England lawyer and senior statesman Nathan Dane. In 1829 Dane offered to endow a chair of law at the Harvard Law School with the express condition that Story be the first incumbent, if he were willing, and on August 25 Story was installed as the first Dane Professor of Law. Under the terms of the endowment, Story was to deliver and revise for publication lectures on a variety of subjects, and over the next sixteen years, Story wrote and published nine treatises. Several of them are classics of legal scholarship. The *Commentaries on the Constitution* (1833) restated the Marshall Court's constitutional legacy for a new generation, and Story ensured its wide influence by preparing an abridged edition for use as a college and law school text. The treatises on *Equity Jurisprudence* (1836) and *Equity Pleadings*

(1838) played a major role in Americanizing English equity, and the *Conflict of Laws* (1834) essentially created that area of law as a systematic area of study. All of the treatises reflected Story's energy, his love of abstruse historical and comparative learning, and his desire to bring order and system to American law. Through them, and through his lectures and personal contact with a law school student body that grew exponentially during his tenure, Story fruitfully pursued the same goal he sought in his opinions. Justice Story's prestige lent authority to Professor Story's legal science, and the professor's scholarship undergirded the justice's opinions and generalized their teaching.

John Marshall's death in July 1835 marked the end of an era for Story, personally and professionally. Story presided over the Court's next term because the Senate had not yet confirmed Marshall's successor, but Story suffered grief and loneliness from his chief's absence. Story wrote to a friend that he "missed the Chief Justice at every turn." But Marshall's passing was more than the death of a great and good friend, for Story feared that it marked the end of the Court as he and Marshall had known and revered it. The president chose Roger Brooke Taney to be the new chief justice, even though Taney's Democratic partisanship and Jacksonian ideology had prevented his confirmation when Jackson nominated him in early 1835 to be an associate justice.

When the Taney Court convened for the first time in January 1837, all but two of its members were Jackson appointees; when Congress increased the size of the Court to nine justices, Jackson and his handpicked successor, Martin Van Buren, filled those positions as well. Many Democrats hailed the changes in Court membership as an opportunity to reverse what they saw as the aristocratic and antidemocratic jurisprudence of the Marshall era. In an 1835 essay about the late chief justice, Jacksonian editor William Leggett praised Marshall's "spotless purity of life" but wrote pointedly that "we cannot but experience joy" that the Court would no longer be led by a judge who sought always "to strengthen government at the expense of the people." Story anxiously awaited a jurisprudential revolution.

Chief Justice Taney's first term appeared to confirm Story's worst fears, driving him almost to despair and to serious consideration of resignation from the Court, an idea he toyed with for the rest of his life. In a trilogy of constitutional decisions held over from Marshall's day, the Taney Court distanced itself dramatically from what Story and others believed was correct doctrine.

In *New York v. Miln* (1837), the Court upheld the constitutionality of a state law requiring the masters of ships arriving in the port of New York from outside the state to register all passengers and post bond that none would become wards of the city. The majority insisted that the Marshall Court's precedents on the scope of Congress's commerce power were distinguishable, but deliberately went on to make the provocative assertion that the states' police powers over "safety, happiness and prosperity" were "complete, unqualified, and exclusive." In lone dissent, Story argued that the law interfered with Congress's power to regulate commerce; he concluded with the remark that he had the consolation of knowing that it also had been Marshall's "deliberate opinion" that the law was unconstitutional for the same reason.

Briscoe v. Bank of the Commonwealth of Kentucky (1837) involved the validity of a state statute establishing a bank and authorizing it to issue notes that would be circulated as legal tender. The defendants maintained that the statute violated the Constitution's prohibition on state issuance of "bills of credit." When the Court first heard the case in 1834, Marshall and Story concluded that under the Court's 1830 decision in *Craig v. Missouri*, the notes were clearly unconstitutional, but in 1837 the Jacksonian justices brushed *Craig* aside and described the states' power to charter banks and define their powers as subject to "no limitation in the federal constitution." Story, once again the sole dissenter, insisted that *Craig* was controlling in an opinion the length of which he justified in part by his "profound reverence and affection for the dead" chief justice.

The third decision in "the revolution of 1837" pitted Story directly against Taney. *Charles River Bridge v. Warren Bridge* stemmed from a state grant to the Charles River Bridge Company to collect tolls for a substantial period as compensation for the expense of building and maintaining the bridge. In 1828, while the privilege was still in effect, the Massachusetts legislature authorized the Warren Bridge Company to build a toll-free bridge not far from the old bridge. With the value of its privilege nullified, the Charles River Bridge Company sued, claiming that the new charter violated the contracts clause. Taney's opinion for the Court refused to construe the original charter as affording the company a monopoly on the explicitly instrumental ground that recognizing such an implied monopoly would jeopardize the "millions of property, which have been invested in rail roads and canals. . . . We shall be thrown back to the improvements of the last century."

Story did not disagree with the desirability of encouraging economic development, but he thought Taney's reasoning bad law and bad economics. In a massive fifty-seven-page dissent joined by the other pre-Jackson holdover, Smith Thompson, and approved in substance by one Jackson appointee, John McLean, Story marshaled case law running back to the Middle Ages to show that the new charter was an unconscionable invasion of a recognized property right; it was Taney, he insisted, who was impeding investment by unsettling the reasonable expectations of the initial investors. Story's friend, the great New York jurist James Kent, wrote him that Taney's opinion "over-throws a great Principle of constitutional Morality" and proves that "we are to be under the reign of little Men." Story agreed; for him, *Charles River Bridge* showed the new Court to be the servant of politics rather than legal science. He was, he wrote a friend soon after the end of the 1837 term, "the last of the old race of Judges."

Story's despair was premature. After the drama of 1837, the Taney Court proved surprisingly moderate. The very next term, in *United States v. Coombs* (1838), Story for a unanimous Court gave an expansive interpretation to Congress's commerce power, and in general, the new justices proved uninterested in rolling back Marshall-era precedents on the scope of congressional or federal court authority. Indeed, the Taney Court was if anything more receptive than its predecessor to Story's interest in bringing the law into accord with the needs of business and commerce. In *Louisville Railroad Co. v. Letson* (1844), for example, the Court overruled an 1809 Marshall Court decision to hold that for the purposes of federal diversity of citizenship jurisdiction, a corporation was the citizen of the state that chartered it, not of all the states of which its shareholders were citizens. *Letson*, Story wrote, "gets rid of a great anomaly in our jurisprudence," and he could only be pleased that the decision significantly increased the number of cases involving commercial and industrial development that could be litigated in federal court. Story himself was, as always, busily involved in his discreet lobbying of Congress on behalf of his desired legal reforms. With Webster, Story drafted a bankruptcy bill that was enacted in 1841 during the brief dominance of nationalist Whigs in Congress. On the bench, Story gave the bankruptcy act a sweeping interpretation, holding in *Ex parte Foster* (1842) that the federal courts should enjoin state insolvency proceedings in order to protect the orderly administration of the federal statute. Story's aggressiveness had the unintended consequence of prompting Democratic and states' rights objections to the act, which was repealed in March 1843.

It was with the concurrence of all of his colleagues that Story wrote what was perhaps the most important opinion of his career. *Swift v. Tyson* (1842), which presented a question about the validity of a bill of exchange, was a diversity case, in federal court solely because the plaintiffs and defendants were residents of different states. The plaintiffs argued plausibly that the bill was valid under generally accepted commercial law principles, but the defendants cited New York state court decisions under which the bill was invalid. Section 34 of the Judiciary Act required federal courts to treat "the laws of the several states" as rules of decision in common law cases "where they apply" except in situations of conflict with federal law, but in *Swift* Story rejected its applicability. The statute's concern was with local laws and long-established local customs, not with "questions of a more general nature" such as the interpretation of contracts or the resolution of "questions of general commercial law." In cases presenting "general" questions, Story reasoned, "the state tribunals are called upon to perform the like functions as ourselves, that is, to ascertain upon general reasoning and legal analogies" the correct legal answers. *Swift*, in other words, posed a question of legal science, the answer to which was to be ascertained by the reasoned application of the whole body of the law. The federal courts would be acting contrary to legal principle if they blindly followed state decisions that they determined to be erroneous in the light of the law as a whole.

Swift v. Tyson was the mature expression of many long-standing themes in Story's jurisprudence: confidence in legal reasoning as an objective science, the desire to disseminate a progressive and systematic jurisprudence, and his belief in the centrality of the federal courts in the creation of a well-ordered market society. The decision was marvelously successful in the short run: federal and state court judges generally accepted with enthusiasm the concept of a general commercial law supervised by the Supreme Court, and so the doctrine of *Swift* was influential in the creation of a genuinely national law of business and commerce. In the twentieth century, the case came under mounting criticism: Justice Oliver Wendell Holmes argued, anachronistically and unfairly, that Story's opinion rested on a fallacious belief in "the common law" as a "brooding omnipresence in the sky" (*Southern Pacific Co. v. Jensen*, 1917), and in 1938 Justice Louis Brandeis for the Court overruled *Swift* as an "unconstitutional" decision in *Erie Railroad Co. v. Tompkins*. In fact, the disagreement between Story and his latter-day critics stemmed not from illogic on Story's part, but from the critics' acceptance of a thoroughgoing legal positivism alien to the mind-set of Story's era.

Story's last years were darkened by the lengthening shadow of slavery. In Marshall's day, the Court generally avoided that potentially explosive topic, but the Taney Court was unable or unwilling to stay out of the problems human slavery posed for American law and society. Story's personal abhorrence of the institution remained unchanged from his early slave trade opinion, but it was balanced by his concern for the preservation of the Union. In *United States v. The Amistad* (1841), all but one justice joined a Story opinion narrowly construing a treaty and thereby ensuring freedom for a group of Africans sold into slavery. In *Prigg v. Pennsylvania* (1842), the Court confronted the constitutionality of the federal Fugitive Slave Act and of a state personal liberty law under which Edward Prigg, a professional slave catcher, was indicted for kidnapping. Story's opinion for the Court upheld the federal statute and invalidated the state law and, by implication, all other state legislation interfering with the federal right to reclaim fugitive slaves. Four concurring opinions debated Story's ambiguous suggestions that Congress had exclusive power to enforce the federal right and that Congress could not require state officials to execute the federal legislation. (Story's opinion could be read, probably erroneously, to absolve the free states from anything beyond passive acquiescence.) For Story, *Prigg* was the unavoidable product of the original agreement to protect "the security of this species of property," which he termed "a fundamental article, without the adoption of which the Union could not have been formed." His opinion, therefore, was no more or less than his duty as a judge, but abolitionists saw the decision as proof of the moral bankruptcy of Story's legal science. When Story on circuit carried out *Prigg* by recognizing a slave owner's rights under the federal act, a critic labeled him "Slave-Catcher-in-Chief for the New England States."

By early 1845 Story's sense of isolation on the Court and his growing pessimism about the Court's work and the Republic's future finally persuaded him that the time had come to retire to full-time teaching at Harvard. He informed family, friends, and the university that he would resign from the bench in the winter, but after a strenuous summer tour on circuit, Story died on September 10, 1845.

—*H. Jefferson Powell*

BIBLIOGRAPHY

R. Kent Newmyer, *Supreme Court Justice Joseph Story: Statesman of the Old Republic* (1985), is the definitive biography and a magisterial achievement. There is, unfortunately, no edition of Story's extremely valuable personal papers, but Newmyer's biography lists their scattered locations. Gerald T. Dunne, *Justice Joseph Story and the Rise of the Supreme Court* (1970), an older, very readable narrative of Story's career on the Court, remains useful.

For a brilliant study of the later Marshall Court that is also an important contribution to Story scholarship, see G. Edward White, *The Marshall Court and Cultural Change, 1815–1835* (1988), a volume in the *Holmes Devise History*. Charles Warren, *The Supreme Court in United States History* (rev. ed., 1928), includes extensive discussions of Story's work and remains valuable despite its age.

Specialized studies relating to Story include: Tony A. Freyer, *Forums of Order: The Federal Courts and Business in American History* (1979), an important historical study of a central theme in Story's thought; H. Jefferson Powell, "Joseph Story's Commentaries on the Constitution: A Belated Review," *Yale Law Journal* 94 (1985): 1285, a thematic and rhetorical study of Story's great treatise on the Constitution; and Alan Watson, *Joseph Story and the Comity of Errors* (1992), which argues that a major element of Story's influential theory of the conflict of laws rested on a simple misunderstanding of his continental sources and that Story's error had dramatic consequences for American law. On this topic, see also G. B. Baker, "Interstate Choices of Law and Early American Constitutional Nationalism . . . ," *McGill Law Journal* 38 (1993): 454. A lesser-known Story opinion is examined in Jay Allan Sekulow et al., "The Story Behind *Vidal v. Girard's Executors:* Joseph Story, the Philadelphia Bible Riots, and Religious Liberty," *Pepperdine Law Review* 32 (2005): 605.

Story's slavery decisions have generated a number of comments. See Paul Finkelman, "Joseph Story and the Problem of Slavery: A New Englander's Nationalist Dilemma," *Massachusetts Legal History* 8 (2002): 65; and Finkelman, "Story Telling on the Supreme Court: *Prigg v.*

Pennsylvania and Justice Joseph Story's Judicial Nationalism," *Supreme Court Review* (1995): 247. See also B. Holden-Smith, "Lords of Lash, Loom, and Law: Justice Story, Slavery, and *Prigg v. Pennsylvania*," *Cornell Law Review* 78 (1993): 1086.

For Story's own writings, see especially his *Commentaries on the Constitution of the United States* (1987), a photographic reprint of Story's abridgement of his constitutional treatise, with a valuable introductory essay by Ronald D. Rotunda and John E. Nowak; and William W. Story, *Life and Letters of Joseph Story* (1851), written by Story's son. This two-volume work has all the predictable limitations of genre and bias but is an important source of the justice's letters and papers.

NOTEWORTHY OPINIONS

Fairfax's Devisee v. Hunter's Lessee, 11 U.S. 603 (1813)

Terrett v. Taylor, 13 U.S. 43 (1815)

Martin v. Hunter's Lessee, 14 U.S. 304 (1816)

Trustees of Dartmouth College v. Woodward, 17 U.S. 518 (1819) (Concurrence)

Houston v. Moore, 18 U.S. 1 (1820) (Dissent)

United States v. Smith, 18 U.S. 153 (1820)

Martin v. Mott, 25 U.S. 19 (1827)

Briscoe v. Bank of the Commonwealth of Kentucky, 33 U.S. 118 (1837) (Dissent)

New York v. Miln, 36 U.S. 102 (1837) (Dissent)

Charles River Bridge v. Warren Bridge, 36 U.S. 420 (1837) (Dissent)

United States v. Coombs, 37 U.S. 72 (1838)

United States v. The Amistad, 40 U.S. 518 (1841)

Swift v. Tyson, 41 U.S. 1 (1842)

Prigg v. Pennsylvania, 41 U.S. 539 (1842)

WILLIAM STRONG

Birth: May 6, 1808, Somers, Connecticut.

Education: Yale College, A.B., 1828, M.A. in law, 1832.

Official Positions: U.S. representative, 1847–1851; justice, Pennsylvania Supreme Court, 1857–1868.

Supreme Court Service: Nominated associate justice by President Ulysses S. Grant, February 8, 1870, to replace Robert C. Grier, who had retired; confirmed by the Senate, February, 18, 1870, by a voice vote; took judicial oath March 14, 1870; retired December 14, 1880; replaced by William B. Woods, nominated by President Rutherford B. Hayes.

Death: August 19, 1895, Lake Minnewaska, New York.

William Strong spent ten years on the Supreme Court bench in relative obscurity. As a skilled case writer and expert in patent and business law, he earned the respect of his judicial brethren, but Strong wrote few of the important cases that have shaped constitutional law, and his tenure has therefore stimulated little historical investigation. A product of his times, Strong was a conservative justice more concerned with private property rights than with civil rights.

The eldest of eleven children of a New England Congregational minister, Strong attended Yale, taught school while he read law, then returned to Yale to complete his legal training. He settled in Reading, Pennsylvania, mastered German, and quickly became a prominent railroad lawyer. He served two congressional terms as a "Locofoco" (Radical) Democrat (they were called Locofocos after a brand of matches). Strong then returned to private practice, and in 1857 he was elected to the Pennsylvania Supreme Court. A staunch unionist, Strong joined the Republican Party during his tenure on the state bench and earned a reputation for upholding Republican war measures.

Not content with serving the state, Strong also worked to advance the kingdom of God. He was a devout Presbyterian involved in numerous evangelical reform movements. Concerned that the Founding Fathers had omitted God from the Constitution, Strong headed the national reform movement to amend the preamble to acknowledge "Almighty God as the source of all authority and power in Civil government, the Lord Jesus Christ as the Ruler of all nations, and His revealed will as the supreme law of the land." Strong did not advocate a state church, but believed that law should adhere to Christian principles. His background provided the values he would bring to the Supreme Court: strong Christian principles, unionism, a probusiness outlook, and respect for private property.

Strong's appointment to the Supreme Court was surrounded with controversy. President Ulysses S. Grant appointed him and Joseph Bradley on the same day that the Court, in *Hepburn v. Griswold* (1870), declared the legal tender act unconstitutional as it applied to preexisting debts. Strong's support for legal tender on the Pennsylvania bench was well established, and consequently Grant was accused of "Court-packing." The timing was unfortunate, but it was to be expected that Grant would appoint justices who would uphold the Republican program. Within months, the Supreme Court dramatically reversed itself on the legal tender issue. Strong was chosen to write the opinion in *Knox v. Lee* (1871), the most important he would write during his tenure.

Because the authority to make Treasury notes legal tender was not an enumerated power, the right, if it existed, was an implied power. Chief Justice Salmon Chase and Strong both relied on John Marshall's classic explication of the elastic clause in *McCulloch v. Maryland* (1819) that any legitimate end "consistent with the letter and spirit of the constitution" was constitutional, but they reached different conclusions. Chase admitted that Congress possessed broad implied powers, but he ruled in *Hepburn* that the legal tender act violated the "spirit" of the Constitution by impairing the obligation of contracts (constitutionally forbidden to the states rather than the national government) and depriving creditors of their property without due process of law. Overturning *Hepburn,* Strong emphasized in *Knox v. Lee* the broad range of methods available to Congress for carrying out the enumerated powers. Because Congress had the power to coin money, it followed, for Strong, that it also had "the power to declare what is money."

William Strong

It was not the prerogative of the Court to judge the "degree of appropriateness" of the means Congress chose to achieve a legitimate end. Strong emphasized the wartime emergency as rationale for the currency law and made clear his understanding that Congress was not authorized to "make anything which has no value money." But Congress had power to enact laws that made "the government's promises to pay money . . . for the time being, equivalent in value" to that of hard money. As he generally voted to support vested property rights, Strong probably would not have sanctioned a legal tender act in ordinary times.

In Reconstruction matters, Strong was reluctant to follow through with Republican Party efforts to effect lasting change in the southern states. Speaking for a unanimous Court, Strong ruled in *Bigelow v. Forrest* (1870) that the Civil War confiscation acts conflicted with the Article III attainder of treason clause of the Constitution. Confiscated property could be held only for the life of the original owner; on his death it reverted back to his heirs. *Bigelow* effectively negated any long-term effects of the confiscation acts, although Strong upheld the validity of the laws in *Miller v. United States* (1871). In *Blyew v. United States* (1872), a test of the 1866 Civil Rights Act, Strong refused to allow removal of a murder trial to federal court even though the only witnesses, who were black, had not been allowed to testify in the Kentucky court. Because the victim was dead, Strong insisted, she had no rights at stake, and therefore the federal government lacked jurisdiction. Strong voted with the majority in the *Slaughterhouse Cases* (1873), which, although concerned with white butchers, defined national citizenship so narrowly that former slaves were left without the protection of the federal government for their basic rights. Overall, Strong appeared relatively unconcerned about federal protection of black citizens.

It was Strong, however, who spoke for the Court on two of the rare occasions when black Americans won legal victories. Three cases involving jury rights for black citizens were handed down on the same day in 1880. In *Ex parte Virginia*, Strong upheld the section of the Civil Rights Act of 1875 that pertained to jury selection—the only part of the statute left standing when the Court declared it unconstitutional in the *Civil Rights Cases* (1883) and he found a state judge who had routinely excluded blacks from jury duty guilty of violating the act.

In *Strauder v. West Virginia*, Strong declared a state statute that excluded blacks from jury duty invalid as a violation of the equal protection clause of the Fourteenth Amendment. He noted, however, that the issue was not whether some blacks sat on the jury, but whether "all persons of his race or color may be excluded by law, solely because of their race or color." It was the exclusionary statute that proved discrimination for Strong.

The third jury case, *Virginia v. Rives,* proved less benign and certainly more important over the years. Blacks were routinely barred from jury duty in Virginia, even in the absence of a discriminatory state law and therefore no official state action. Strong refused to acknowledge that the black citizens of Virginia were being denied a jury of their peers. Instead, he argued that juries composed entirely of whites did not indicate discrimination because of race or color. Even an all-white jury could be impartially selected. If there was no state law, there was no discrimination. This decision countenanced a practice that would have been unconstitutional if written into law, and it presented black citizens the difficult task of proving systematic exclusion from jury duty.

Strong's experience as a railroad lawyer was reflected in his actions on the Court. He voted with the minority against state regulation in *Munn v. Illi-*

nois (1877), for example, and, in the *State Freight Tax Case* (1873), he held a Pennsylvania state tax invalid as a breach of the commerce clause.

In 1877 Strong served on the electoral commission to settle the disputed presidential election of 1876. Like the other members, he voted his party preference, giving Rutherford B. Hayes a majority of one in the commission and securing the presidency for the Republican Party.

Strong retired from the Supreme Court in 1880, still in full possession of his physical and mental faculties. Apparently, he meant his resignation to serve as an example to the justices who were no longer up to the task. He spent his remaining years doing Christian benevolent work.

—*Lou Falkner Williams*

BIBLIOGRAPHY

There is, not surprisingly, no published biography of Strong. Stanley I. Kutler's sketch in Friedman and Israel, *Justices,* vol. 2, 1153, is the best single source of information on Strong's judicial career. Daniel G. Strong's unpublished dissertation, "Supreme Court Justice William Strong, 1808–1895: Jurisprudence, Christianity and Reform" (Kent State University, 1985), contains excellent information on Strong's early life and career that cannot be located elsewhere, but the chapter on the Supreme Court years is very weak on case analysis. Jon C. Teaford, "Toward a Christian Nation: Religion, Law and Justice Strong," *Journal of Presbyterian History* 54 (1976): 422, is concerned with Strong's religious ideas rather than his judicial career. Charles Fairman's two-volume work in the *Holmes Devise History, Reconstruction and Reunion* (1971, 1987), is the most exhaustive treatment of the Reconstruction Court and includes analyses of all of Strong's major opinions.

NOTEWORTHY OPINIONS

Bigelow v. Forrest, 76 U.S. 339 (1870)

Knox v. Lee, 79 U.S. 457 (1871)

Strauder v. West Virginia, 100 U.S. 303 (1880)

Virginia v. Rives, 100 U.S. 313 (1880)

Ex parte Virginia, 100 U.S. 339 (1880)

GEORGE SUTHERLAND

Birth: March 25, 1862, Buckinghamshire, England.

Education: Brigham Young Academy (University), 1879–1881; University of Michigan Law School, 1882.

Official Positions: Utah state senator, 1896–1900; U.S. representative, 1901–1903; U.S. senator, 1905–1917; chairman, advisory committee to the Washington Conference for the Limitation of Naval Armaments, 1921; U.S. counsel, Norway-United States arbitration, The Hague, 1921–1922.

Supreme Court Service: Nominated associate justice by President Warren G. Harding, September 5, 1922, to replace Justice John H. Clarke, who had resigned; confirmed by the Senate, September 5, 1922, by a voice vote; took judicial oath October 2, 1922; retired January 17, 1938; replaced by Stanley F. Reed, nominated by President Franklin D. Roosevelt.

Death: July 18, 1942, Stockbridge, Massachusetts.

George Sutherland may be best known as one of the conservative "Four Horsemen" (the others were Pierce Butler, Willis Van Devanter, and James McReynolds) who opposed Franklin Roosevelt's New Deal. In truth, he had a much more complex career on the bench than that nickname suggests. During his sixteen years as an associate justice, Sutherland wrote not only principled objections to progressive and liberal intrusions on cherished property and contract rights, but also impassioned defenses of the rights of the press and the accused. To his biographer, Joel Francis Paschal, Sutherland was consistently "a man against the state," a sobriquet Sutherland earned through a productive career on the Court. Although many of his opinions were overruled and disapproved as the Court drifted away from its laissez-faire moorings, the clarity and independence of his judicial contributions serve even today as examples of well-reasoned decision making.

In 1864 George Sutherland's Scottish father, newly converted to the Church of Jesus Christ of Latter-day Saints, moved the family from Buckinghamshire, England, to Utah Territory. His father soon left the new church, and Sutherland grew up a nonbeliever in Mormon-dominated Utah. He attended Brigham Young Academy (later University), leaving after three years to work as a railroad agent. He then took his legal education at the University of Michigan, where he studied with two jurists whose influence can be found in his Supreme Court writings: James Campbell, chief justice of the Michigan Supreme Court, and Judge Thomas Cooley, author of influential works such as the *Treatise on the Constitutional Limitations Which Rest upon the Legislative Power of the States of the American Union* (1868). In 1883 Sutherland married, moved back to Provo, and began law practice with his father (the partnership lasted but three years).

Ten years later Sutherland moved to Salt Lake City and was elected to the first state legislature in 1896. A Republican, he was elected to the U.S. House of Representatives in 1900 and to the Senate in 1904. He supported reform measures, including the Pure Food and Drug Act, held the protectionist line in tariff debates, and led the fight for federal workers compensation legislation for employees of interstate carriers. Sutherland refused to break with the Republican Party in 1912 and carried on the conservative struggle against Woodrow Wilson's progressive measures. In 1917 Sutherland, now in private practice in Washington, D.C., was elected president of the American Bar Association (ABA). In his presidential address, entitled "Private Rights and Government Control," Sutherland stated that when the choice was between individual freedom and the common good, "doubts should be resolved in favor of the liberty of the individual." In September 1922 Warren Harding tapped his friend and close adviser to fill the Supreme Court seat vacated when Justice John H. Clarke resigned.

It would not be long before Sutherland was called on to resolve the tension between public needs and private rights. The issue before the Court in *Adkins v. Children's Hospital* (1923) was the legitimacy of an act of Congress fixing minimum wages for working women and children in Washington, D.C. The legislation faced two challenges, one brought by the hospital that was paying wages below the statutory minimum and the other by a female elevator operator who, it was alleged, would lose her low-paying job if her employer had to comply with the act.

The statute was attacked as violative of "the freedom of contract included within the guaranties of the due process clause of the Fifth Amendment." Sutherland acknowledged that the freedom of contract protected by the Constitution was not absolute, but he could not fit this case into any of the exceptions recognized by the Court. Then, in a move that would set the tone for the next dozen years, Sutherland quoted generously and favorably from Justice Rufus Peckham's opinion in *Lochner v. New York* (1905), for nearly two decades the bête noire of progressives on and off the Court. Subsequent decisions of the Supreme Court, according to Sutherland, had distinguished but not overruled *Lochner*'s elevation of freedom of contract over the state's police power.

Viewed through the lens of substantive due process, Sutherland could not find the crucial link between ends and means: the statute "extracts from the employer an arbitrary payment for a purpose and upon a basis having no causal connection with his business, or the contract or the work the employee engages to do." In sum, the act was "so clearly the product of a naked, arbitrary exercise of power that it cannot be allowed to stand under the Constitution of the United States."

Reiterating the theme of his ABA address, Sutherland concluded by noting that far from being harmed, the public good was actually "exalted" by protecting individual liberties, "for surely the good of

George Sutherland

517

society as a whole cannot be better served than by the preservation against arbitrary restraint of the liberties of its constituent members." Sutherland's reinvigoration of *Lochner* and the due process clause provided the new conservative bloc on the Court—the Four Horsemen were complete when Sutherland arrived—with the intellectual leadership it needed to sustain its crusade against confiscatory, arbitrary, and unreasonable social and economic legislation.

Over the next few years, Sutherland expanded on the ideas introduced in *Adkins,* applying its principles in other regulatory contexts. In *Tyson & Brother v. Banton* (1927), a case concerning the validity of a New York statute forbidding the resale of theater tickets at a higher price, Sutherland refused to recognize that the economic activity at issue was "affected with a public interest" and thereby a legitimate area for state intrusion. In *Ribnik v. McBride* (1928), a New Jersey law regulating charges by employment agencies was the victim of Sutherland's analysis: "The interest of the public in the matter of employment is not different in quality and character from its interest in the other things enumerated [the procurement of food and housing and fuel]; but in none of them is the interest that 'public interest' which the law contemplates as the basis for legislative price control."

Sutherland was not an unswerving opponent of the state's police power, however, a point best demonstrated by reference to four cases involving state and local land-use regulation: *Village of Euclid v. Ambler Realty Co.* (1926), *Zahn v. Board of Public Works of City of Los Angeles* (1927), *Gorieb v. Fox* (1927), and *Nectow v. City of Cambridge* (1928). *Euclid* is a landmark decision in the long, intricate history of Anglo-American property law. In his opinion, Sutherland provides a conceptual link between the awkward, common-law, judicially controlled system of private and public nuisance in land management to the modern, comprehensive planning schemes found in a growing number of American central cities and suburbs. At issue was the height, area, and use-classification plan designed for a suburb of Cleveland. Ambler Realty asserted successfully in the federal trial court that the local ordinance violated the due process

clause and denied equal protection of the laws under the Fourteenth Amendment. Legend has it that after initially siding with the other three Horsemen, who dissented, Sutherland considered the positive effects such regulation would have on property rights and joined with the progressives on the Court to reverse the lower court holding. Other observers of the Court have suggested that the justices were more intrigued by the potential use of zoning to exclude outsiders from protected, single-family residential zones than anything else.

Whatever his motive, Sutherland set a standard of judicial deference accorded state and local officials that allowed for significant public regulation and control of land use for the next several decades. The law of nuisance provided "a fairly helpful clew" for the Court as it sought to determine where to draw "the line which . . . separates the legitimate from the illegitimate assumption of power." Also helpful to the Court were the findings of "commissions and experts" who had thoroughly studied zoning and concluded that there were clear health and safety benefits to the segregation of incompatible uses. The village of Euclid need not "demonstrate the wisdom or sound policy in all respects of those restrictions" on land use, however, for there was enough to prevent the Court from concluding "that such provisions are clearly arbitrary and unreasonable, having no substantial relation to the public health, safety, morals, or general welfare." This formula, unlike Sutherland's more demanding substantive due process analysis, remains relevant and controlling to this day for the great bulk of cases involving challenges to land use and environmental restrictions.

In *Zahn* and *Gorieb,* both times for a unanimous Court, Sutherland summarily dismissed objections to local zoning and setback schemes. In *Nectow,* however, Sutherland reversed the state court's dismissal of a challenge to a residential zoning classification that left the plaintiff with "no practical use" for his property. Sutherland concluded that there was a "serious and highly injurious . . . invasion of the property of the plaintiff." In other words, the line between the legitimate and illegitimate exercise of the police power, though hard to draw, had been crossed.

Sutherland could be equally protective of other civil liberties when the Court was faced with similar egregious invasions. *Powell v. Alabama* (1932) was the first of two cases to reach the Court involving the prosecution of the "Scottsboro Boys," nine African American teenagers accused of raping two young white women. Writing for the majority, Sutherland detailed the nightmarish nature of the case:

> The defendants, young, ignorant, illiterate, surrounded by hostile sentiment, haled back and forth under guard of soldiers, charged with an atrocious crime regarded with especial horror in the community where they were to be tried, were thus put in peril of their lives within a few moments after counsel for the first time charged with any degree of responsibility began to represent them.

A review of the shoddy performance of the attorneys for the defense convinced Sutherland that "defendants were not accorded the right of counsel in any substantial sense." Sutherland concluded that the defendants were denied their due process rights under the Fourteenth Amendment, as well as their Fifth Amendment–guaranteed right to counsel. Four years later, in *Grosjean v. American Press Co.* (1936), Sutherland cited *Powell* as he spread the protective cloak of the Fourteenth Amendment around the free speech and free press sanctions against federal intrusion found in the First Amendment, in the process invalidating a Louisiana tax on newspapers.

Sutherland's patience with performance of counsel was again tried in *Berger v. United States* (1935), a federal prosecution for uttering counterfeit notes. Here, it was the prosecutor who "overstepped the bounds of . . . propriety and fairness." Mixing the rhetoric of morality with the rules of sport, Sutherland advised the representative of the people that "he may prosecute with earnestness and vigor. . . . But, while he may strike hard blows, he is not at liberty to strike foul ones." In this case, prejudice to the defendant was undeniable, concluded the Court.

One of Sutherland's anti–New Deal cases can be seen as consistent with the sentiments expressed in *Powell* and *Berger*. In *Jones v. Securities and Exchange Commission* (1936), Sutherland compared the SEC's abuse of investigatory powers to the practices of the universally condemned Star Chamber.

In the area of social and economic regulation, as states explored ways to relieve the stresses caused by the severe economic crisis after the stock market disaster of 1929, Sutherland and his fellow conservatives held the line. In *New State Ice Co. v. Liebmann* (1932), the topic of the challenged state regulation was quite mundane, "an ordinary business," according to Sutherland. In 1925 the Oklahoma legislature had decided to require a license for the manufacture, sale, and distribution of ice, a license New State had not secured. Predictably, the majority found that such unreasonable regulation of a nonpublic business would not be tolerated under the Fourteenth Amendment. Sutherland offered skepticism about the ability of the state to innovate in crisis times. In a direct challenge to the dissenting Louis D. Brandeis's notion of a state laboratory to "try novel social and economic experiments," Sutherland baldly asserted, "It is plain that unreasonable or arbitrary interference or restrictions cannot be saved from the condemnation of that Amendment merely by calling them experimental." This exchange foreshadowed the jurisprudential conflict that would soon burden the Court and the nation.

Two years later, Sutherland found himself speaking for a minority of four, as the Court, led by Chief Justice Charles Evans Hughes, allowed Minnesota's mortgage moratorium legislation to survive its scrutiny in *Home Building & Loan Assn. v. Blaisdell* (1934). "While emergency does not create power," Hughes wrote, "emergency may furnish the occasion for the exercise of power." The majority found little guidance in the history of the framing of the contract clause, or in case law interpreting that constitutional stricture, turning instead to cases such as *Block v. Hirsh* (1921), in which the Court upheld temporary emergency rent control legislation. The Minnesota debtor relief legislation, according to the majority, did not violate the contract clause, the due process clause, or deny creditors equal protection.

Sutherland's response was a masterful blend of history, framers' intent, and judicial precedent. He furnished a riposte for each majority thrust, countering Hughes's assertion that the past furnished no answer with substantive historical footnotes and generous excerpts from relevant case law. This was just the first step down a dangerous hill, warned the four conservative justices: "He simply closes his eyes to the necessary implications of the decision who fails to see in it the potentiality of future gradual but ever-advancing encroachments upon the sanctity of private and public contracts."

Sutherland reached back to the darkest periods of Supreme Court history to amplify the point that the Constitution must "remain unaltered," lest it "become a mere collection of political maxims to be adhered to or disregarded according to the prevailing sentiment or the legislative and judicial opinion in respect of the supposed necessities of the hour." He quoted the words of Justice David Davis in *Ex parte Milligan* (1866) and Chief Justice Roger Taney in *Dred Scott v. Sandford* (1857)—two of the most widely assailed opinions in the chronicles of the Court—as if to strengthen the image of the conservative bloc as the last defenders of the Constitution in the face of a tyrannical majority.

"The present exigency," Sutherland told the suffering nation, "is nothing new." Then, condescendingly, in terms that suggested the victims were to blame, he instructed his readers that "the vital lesson that expenditure beyond income begets poverty, that public or private extravagance, financed by promises to pay, either must end in complete or partial repudiation or the promises be fulfilled by self-denial and painful effort, though constantly taught by bitter experience, seems never to be learned." The gap between Sutherland's personal and judicial philosophy and the activist agenda of the states and, soon, the federal government was striking. Shortly, matters would come to a head.

Two subsequent Sutherland opinions, issued ten months apart, best illustrate the shift by the "nine old men" that saved the New Deal and signaled the ascension of a new era of judicial deference to social and economic regulation. In *Carter v. Carter Coal Co.* (1936), Sutherland, for a majority of five, annulled the Bituminous Coal Conservation Act of 1935 (the Guffey Act), Congress's attempt to replace the regulatory controls that the National Recovery Administration had wielded prior to the Roosevelt administration's defeat in *Schechter v. United States* (1935). The new law created an administrative body, the Bituminous Coal Commission, to formulate regulations and set coal rates; the law also authorized coal taxes and mandated collective bargaining and other labor reform measures.

Sutherland conceded that the objects of the act were quite worthy, but cautioned that legislative means to accomplish these goals "must be appropriate, plainly adapted to the end, and not prohibited by, but consistent with, the letter and spirit of the Constitution." State sovereignty itself was endangered by the Guffey Act. If the federal government were given such extensive powers, in the future, states might be reduced "to little more than geographical subdivisions of the national domain." Not only was the tax an illegal penalty, but also Congress had no business intruding in the area of labor regulation for "the evils are all local evils over which the federal government has no legislative control. The relation of employer and employee is a local relation." There being no "interstate commercial intercourse" at issue, the labor provisions were invalid under the Constitution. Finally, notwithstanding statutory language to the contrary, Sutherland found that the violations noted in the opinion tainted the whole act, including the price controls.

Although wounded by decisions in cases such as *Schechter* and *Carter Coal*, the New Deal received a substantial boost six months later, in November 1936, when Roosevelt was reelected in a landslide. In March 1937, one month after the president introduced his ill-conceived "Court-packing" plan, the Court announced its opinion in *West Coast Hotel Co. v. Parrish* (1937), overruling Sutherland's holding in *Adkins*. Now that a majority of justices had abandoned substantive due process, the need to pack the Court vanished.

West Coast Hotel upheld a Washington State law that authorized the setting of minimum wages for women and children. Chief Justice Hughes deemed *Adkins* "a departure from the true application of the principles governing" state regulation of labor relations. Not surprisingly, Sutherland objected, strongly but respectfully. He invoked the words of Judge Campbell and Judge Cooley, his law school professors, for the notion of the immutability of the Constitution and the availability of the amendment process as a remedy when change was truly needed. "The judicial function," according to Sutherland, "did not include the power of amendment under the guise of interpretation." Sutherland referred his readers to the logic and rationale of his *Adkins* opinion, furnishing a long excerpt, as well.

Justice Van Devanter resigned from the Court two months later and was replaced by Hugo Black. Sutherland, expressing in his personal correspondence great satisfaction at the defeat of Roosevelt's Court packing plan, followed suit shortly thereafter.

If we focus only on substantive due process and the intransigence of the Four Horsemen, Sutherland's legacy seems thin indeed. If we direct our attention instead to the way he fashioned and presented his arguments, particularly in his opinions in *Euclid*, *Blaisdell*, *Powell*, and *United States v. Curtiss-Wright Export Corp.* (1936), which outlined the extraconstitutional nature of the conduct of the nation's foreign policy, we cannot help but be struck by Sutherland's mastery of the judicial craft.

—*Michael Allan Wolf*

BIBLIOGRAPHY

Joel Francis Paschal's biography, *Mr. Justice Sutherland: A Man Against the State* (1951), is a fine treatment of the justice's life, work, and philosophy before and during his term on the Court. It is far better than the more recent but highly ideological Hadley Arkes, *The Return of George Sutherland: Restoring a Jurisprudence of Natural Rights* (1994).

There are some interesting contributions in Sutherland's Supreme Court memorial, 323 U.S. v (1944), particularly Chief Justice Hughes's essay. Sutherland's papers are included in the manuscript division of the Library of Congress. A studious exploration of Sutherland, including insights from his defenders and critics, can be found in William M. Randle's "Professors, Reformers, Bureaucrats, and Cronies: The Players in *Euclid v. Ambler*," chapter 2 of Charles M. Haar and Jerold S. Kayden, eds., *Zoning and the American Dream* (1989). See also articles by S. R. Olken, "Justice George Sutherland and Economic Liberty: Constitutional Conservatism and the Problem of Factions," *William & Mary Bill of Rights Journal* 6 (1997): 1; and Olken, "The Business of Expression: Economic Liberty, Political Factions, and the Forgotten First Amendment Legacy of Justice George Sutherland," *William & Mary Bill of Rights Journal* 10 (2002): 249.

NOTEWORTHY OPINIONS

Adkins v. Children's Hospital, 261 U.S. 525 (1923)

Village of Euclid v. Ambler Realty Co., 272 U.S. 365 (1926)

Tyson & Brother v. Banton, 273 U.S. 418 (1927)

Zahn v. Board of Public Works of City of Los Angeles, 274 U.S. 325 (1927)

New State Ice Co. v. Liebmann, 285 U. S. 262 (1932)

Powell v. Alabama, 287 U.S. 45 (1932)

Home Building & Loan Assn. v. Blaisdell, 290 U.S. 398 (1934) (Dissent)

Berger v. United States, 295 U.S. 78 (1935)

Grosjean v. American Press Co., 297 U.S. 233 (1936)

Carter v. Carter Coal Co., 298 U.S. 238 (1936)

United States v. Curtiss-Wright Export Corp., 299 U.S. 304 (1936)

NOAH HAYNES SWAYNE

Birth: December 7, 1804, Frederick County, Virginia.

Education: Studied law privately; admitted to the bar in Warrenton, Virginia, in 1823.

Official Positions: Prosecuting attorney, Coshocton County, Ohio, 1826–1829; Ohio state representative, 1830, 1836; U.S. attorney for Ohio, 1830–1841; city councilman, Columbus, Ohio, 1834.

Supreme Court Service: Nominated associate justice by President Abraham Lincoln, January 22, 1862, to replace John McLean, who had died; confirmed by the Senate, January 24, 1862, by a 38–1 vote; took judicial oath January 27, 1862; retired January 24, 1881; replaced by Stanley Matthews, nominated by President Rutherford B. Hayes and renominated by President James A. Garfield.

Death: June 8, 1884, New York City.

Admitted to the Virginia bar in 1823, Noah Swayne soon after moved to Ohio because his Quaker-inspired opposition to slavery aroused resentment among his Virginia neighbors. In the 1850s his uncompromising antislavery position—he frequently defended fugitive slaves—made him switch from being a Jacksonian Democrat to the Republican Party. When Supreme Court justice John McLean died in Cincinnati on April 4, 1861, President Abraham Lincoln appointed Swayne as his successor, not only because of the entreaties of Ohio politicians but also because Swayne was a southerner by birth, a dedicated supporter of the Union, a proven opponent of slavery, and a successful corporation lawyer with close ties to the business community. He served as an associate justice for nineteen years.

Although Swayne wrote more than 350 majority opinions, only a few had any long-term constitutional importance. But Swayne did fulfill the expectations of the president and Republican Reconstruction members of Congress because he identified the national interest with the Republican Party and faithfully supported expansion of federal executive and legislative powers on a narrowly divided Court. Swayne voted with the majority in the *Prize Cases* (1863), which upheld the constitutionality of Lincoln's blockade of southern ports before Congress had officially declared war. In *Ex parte Vallandigham* (1864), he voted that the civilian courts could not review a trial by military court. In *Ex parte Milligan* (1866), he joined in a partial dissent that argued that Congress could determine that the Bill of Rights did not apply in crisis situations. In *Cummings v. Missouri* (1867) and *Ex parte Garland* (1867), he supported the constitutionality of post–Civil War loyalty oaths for teachers, lawyers, and ministers, and in *Texas v. White* (1869), he argued in dissent that the political reality of Texas having left the Union now made that state's future a question for

Congress to decide. He supported the constitutionality of the federal government's issuance of legal tender on the grounds that Congress's emergency powers were not restricted to wartime. In *The Cherokee Tobacco* (1871), Swayne along with the majority decided that Congress, not the courts, would have to protect Native Americans because Congress was not bound by treaties with the Indians. In all these cases, Swayne voted to broaden the powers of the national government.

As was expected from his background, Swayne was a consistent champion of the civil rights of freed slaves. Even while he served on the Court, Swayne lobbied for passage of the Fifteenth Amendment and campaigned for its ratification by Ohio. His broad interpretation of the Thirteenth Amendment was especially noteworthy. In *United States v. Rhodes* (1866), Swayne on circuit contended that the amendment not only abolished slavery but also abolished every manifestation of bondage. He maintained that the amendment was closely connected with the civil rights law, and the two

Noah Haynes Swayne

together transformed the federal system by establishing federal protection over everyone, at all times and in all places. He dissented against the Court's decision in *Blyew v. United States* (1872), which declared that because an old, blind, and murdered black woman could not profit from any verdict, there was no harm in Kentucky's exclusion of African American witnesses from the trial of her murderer. He voted with the majority in declaring unconstitutional West Vir-

ginia and Virginia statutes that excluded African Americans from jury service in *Strauder v. West Virginia* and *Ex parte Virginia*, both in 1880.

Civil rights were also utmost in Swayne's mind when he issued a sharp dissent in the historic *Slaughterhouse Cases* (1873). The majority, he contended, had distorted the Fourteenth Amendment by taking it out of its historical context and tortuously narrowing its scope. He maintained that as the first eleven amendments limited the federal government, so the three Civil War amendments directly restricted the power of the states. The federal government was now the protector of the "privileges and immunities" of each and every one of its citizens.

For all his interest in civil rights, Swayne's most important opinions were concerned with economic issues. In *Gelpcke v. Dubuque* (1863), he used the case of a municipal bond default to expand the Court's review power over state supreme court decisions, thereby increasing federal common law jurisdiction. Economics were also involved when Swayne delivered his most famous opinion on his last day on the Court. In *Springer v. United States* (1881), he upheld the Civil War income tax, arguing that it was not a direct tax because it fell not on persons, but on profits and income. His position died four years later when the Court overruled it in *Pollock v. Farmers' Loan & Trust Co.* (1895) but was resurrected during the Progressive Era.

Although chronically sick and mentally deteriorating during the 1870s, Swayne held on tenaciously until President Rutherford B. Hayes pressured him to retire. He left the Court on January 24, 1881, and died in New York City on June 8, 1884.

—*William Bosch*

BIBLIOGRAPHY

Swayne's life, character, and early Court activity are surveyed in David M. Silvers *Lincoln's Supreme Court* (1956).

His later career is related in Robert Fridlington's *The Reconstruction Court, 1864–1888* (1987).

NOTEWORTHY OPINIONS

Gelpcke v. Dubuque, 68 U.S. 175 (1863)

Slaughterhouse Cases, 83 U.S. 36 (1873) (Dissent)

Springer v. United States, 102 U.S. 586 (1881)

WILLIAM HOWARD TAFT

Birth: September 15, 1857, Cincinnati, Ohio.

Education: Yale University, A.B., 1878; Cincinnati Law School, LL.B., 1880.

Official Positions: Assistant prosecuting attorney, Hamilton County, Ohio, 1881–1883; assistant county solicitor, Hamilton County, 1885–1887; judge, Ohio Superior Court, 1887–1890, U.S. solicitor general, 1890–1891; judge, U.S. Court of Appeals for the Sixth Circuit, 1892–1900; chairman, Philippine Commission, 1900–1901; governor general of the Philippines, 1901–1904; secretary of war, 1904–1908; president of the United States, 1909–1913; joint chairman, National War Labor Board, 1918–1919.

Supreme Court Service: Nominated chief justice by President Warren G. Harding, June 30, 1921, to replace Chief Justice Edward D. White, who had died; confirmed by the Senate, June 30, 1921, by a voice vote; took judicial oath July 11, 1921; retired February 3, 1930; replaced by Chief Justice Charles Evans Hughes, nominated by President Herbert Hoover.

Death: March 8, 1930, in Washington, D.C.

Unique in the annals of American government, William Howard Taft was both president and chief justice of the United States. He brought to his role on the Supreme Court an unparalleled wealth of administrative experience, which deeply affected not only his personal jurisprudence but also the institutional development of the federal judiciary.

Taft was the son of a prominent Ohio lawyer, Alphonso Taft, who was attorney general and secretary of war during President Ulysses S. Grant's administration. Trading on family position and connections, after he graduated from law school in 1880, William Taft fashioned a meteoric career, rising from local prosecutor in 1881 to the presidency in 1909, with many prestigious positions in between. Taft's consummate ambition was, however, to be a Supreme Court justice. "I love judges and I love courts," he said

in 1911. "They are my ideals, that typify on earth what we shall meet hereafter in heaven under a just God." Ironically, Taft twice declined President Theodore Roosevelt's offers to appoint him to the Supreme Court, in 1902 and again in 1906, "giving up the hope and ambition of my life," he said, because he believed that the exigencies of duty—as governor of the Philippines and then secretary of war—required that he remain in his administrative posts. When as president he appointed Edward Douglass White as the successor to Chief Justice Melville Fuller, Taft ruefully mused, "It seems strange that the one place in the government which I would have liked to fill myself I am forced to give to another."

Taft's turn came a decade later, in 1921, when Chief Justice White died and Warren Harding nominated his fellow Ohioan to the center seat. The Senate confirmed him the same day. To the bafflement of the *New Republic*, Harding's choice was greeted with "almost universal acclaim." The *New Republic* wondered why "the very Progressivism which President Taft provoked," and which had sent him to a humiliating political defeat in 1912, did not "uncompromisingly" oppose his appointment to the Court. Its answer was "the present temporary triumph of reaction." And, no doubt, postwar disillusionment and Harding's sweeping return to "normalcy" marked Taft's natural conservatism as politically ascendant.

But Taft's national rehabilitation was also due to the notable grace and equanimity with which he had accepted the dismal results of the 1912 election, to his patriotic and nonpartisan support of President Woodrow Wilson during the world war and the campaign for the League of Nations, and to his joint chairmanship of a National War Labor Board (NWLB) that had supported union organizational rights to a degree unprecedented by any government agency. The latter was particularly important because, in his work as a state and federal judge, Taft had been known as the "father of the labor injunction," a device used by courts to crush union organizing efforts. Taft's stint at the NWLB did much to ameliorate that reputation and to ensure the remarkable national outpouring of goodwill that accompanied his confirmation to the Court.

Taft's predecessor as chief justice was known for his refusal to engage the political branches of government. But Taft, with his wealth of contacts and influence, with his years of executive and lobbying experience, immediately began to put his immense prestige to work to create support for a comprehensive and constructive program of judicial reform. He had long been concerned with the improvement of the judicial branch. In his first State of the Union address, for example, he had declared that "a change of judicial procedure, with a view to reducing its expense to private litigants in civil cases and facilitating the dispatch of business and final decision in both civil and criminal cases, constitutes the greatest need in our American institutions."

Accustomed to viewing the judiciary from a presidential perspective, Taft brought to his new position not only a new political energy and purpose but also the firm belief that courts were more than isolated decision makers; rather, they were fundamentally an administrative arm of the government whose particular task it was to dispense justice. He longed to instill "the common sense idea of applying to the disposition of business in the courts the same principle that is applied everywhere in the organization of men," which was "the application of . . . energies to a single purpose." For Taft it was evident that courts, like any bureaucratic organization, needed careful and constant supervision. He was the first to apply this insight to the federal judiciary, and for this he deserves to be honored as the father of modern judicial management.

The concept of judicial management underlay both of the major reforms that Taft achieved. The first was embodied in the Act of September 14, 1922, which

William Howard Taft

established a conference composed of the chief justice and the senior judges of the nine circuits, and which empowered Taft, with certain limitations, to reassign district court judges geographically to meet the needs of judicial business. Taft violated precedent by directly testifying for the bill before the Senate Judiciary Committee, but he viewed the reform as "one of the most important acts in the history of the judiciary."

The conference, the direct ancestor of the present Judicial Conference, was by law to implement the managerial task of compiling an annual "comprehensive survey of the condition of business in the courts of the United States" and recommending necessary or advisable changes. Taft's new statutory authority to transfer judges enabled him to oil "the judicial machinery" and "to mass the force of the judiciary where the arrears are greatest." In both respects, the 1922 act recognized federal courts as a single administrative unit and established rudimentary mechanisms through which the achievement of their institutional mission could be monitored and supervised. The result, wrote Felix Frankfurter and James M. Landis, was nothing less than "the beginning of a new chapter in the administration of the federal courts."

The second major reform legislation Taft achieved made a huge difference in the conduct of the Court. The Judges Bill of 1925 drastically reduced the mandatory appellate jurisdiction of the Supreme Court and instead allowed the justices to pick and choose the bulk of cases to review through the discretionary writ of certiorari. Underlying the act was a new vision of the function of the Supreme Court, which Taft had set forth in his second State of the Union message:

No man ought to have, as a matter of right, a review of his case by the Supreme Court. He should be satisfied by one hearing before a court of first instance and one review by a court of appeals. The proper and chief usefulness of . . . the Supreme Court of the United States is, in cases which come before it, so to expound the law, and especially the fundamental law—the Constitution—as to furnish precedents for the

inferior courts in future litigation and for the executive officers in the construction of statutes and the performance of their legal duties.

The technical jurisdictional provisions of the 1925 act were designed to implement Taft's view that the primary function of the Supreme Court was to supervise and administer the development of federal law, a function that required that the Court be ceded wide managerial discretion. The transformation, well recognized at the time, was "drastic."

Although Taft was unsuccessful in realizing his third major reform project—congressional authorization for the judicial promulgation of simple and uniform federal rules of civil procedure that merged law and equity—his executive ability and inclinations were everywhere evident in his actions as chief justice. He viewed himself as "the head of the judicial branch of Government," and he made every effort to "come into touch with the Federal Judges of the country, so that we may feel more allegiance to a team and do more teamwork." He actively sought to monitor and guide the selection and appointment of new federal judges, even of Supreme Court justices. He was determined to reduce delays and increase the efficiency of the Supreme Court, in fact achieving a significant reduction in the Court's backlog. Appalled at the inadequate space and resources available to the Court in its chambers within the Capitol building, Taft lobbied for and obtained congressional authorization and moneys for a new Supreme Court building, but he did not live to see it completed. Within the Court, Taft continually sought to promote "teamwork," to "mass" the Court so as give "weight and solidarity to its opinions." He was skillful at assigning opinions, reconciling differences, making conferences pleasant and efficient. During the eight full terms of Taft's tenure as chief justice, 84 percent of all written opinions were unanimous.

His success as an executive chief justice was manifest to all, and it is common to rank him with Oliver Ellsworth as one of the primary architects of the federal judicial system. But Taft's success as a writer of judicial opinions is something else again. Brandeis accurately but cruelly observed that Taft was "a first-rate second-rate mind." One might say that Taft had thoroughly mastered and been mastered by the clichés of his time and class. Few of his more than 250 opinions have survived as living presences in the law. One reason is that he was, as Taft himself was well aware, without auctorial "facility or the graceful literary style." But another reason is his tendency to accept the conventional as the given.

Taft's jurisprudence was dominated by a few major ideas: the importance of nationalism, the defense of property, the necessity for intelligent social management, and the enforcement of law and order. His idol was John Marshall, "the greatest Judge that America or the World has produced." And, in Taft's eyes, Marshall's great achievement was to set the Court toward a "liberal construction of the Constitution in conferring powers upon the National Government," against "the school of Jefferson" that would have "emphasized unduly the sovereignty of the States." Borrowing from Marshall's opinion in *Gibbons v. Ogden* (1824), Taft wrote to Harlan Fiske Stone in 1928 that the "power of Congress" over interstate commerce is "exactly what it would be in a government without states."

In the period before the New Deal, the extent of federal power over interstate commerce was a highly controversial subject, and among Taft's most successful and influential opinions were those that strongly supported the expansion of this federal power. His most important contribution concerned the question of when Congress could regulate intrastate commerce that threatened to obstruct or burden interstate commerce. In cases such as *Stafford v. Wallace* (1922) and *Board of Trade of Chicago v. Olsen* (1923), Taft made clear that "it is primarily for Congress to consider and decide the fact of the danger and meet it. This court will certainly not substitute its judgment for that of Congress in such a matter unless the relation of the subject to interstate commerce and its effect upon it are clearly non-existent." Taft was also highly nationalistic in his interpretation of the dormant commerce clause, which the Court used during the 1920s to strike down state legislation that "directly regulated"

or "unduly burdened" interstate commerce. In decisions such as *Hanover Fire Insurance Co. v. Carr* (1926) and *Compania General de Tabacos de Filipinas v. Collector of Internal Revenue* (1927), Taft made clear his determination to use the power of the Court to sustain and protect a national common market. Not surprisingly, he also supported a strong doctrine of federal preemption and a robust national federal common law.

Taft's concern to promote a national and uniform market was ultimately rooted in his conception of property rights. As a Yale undergraduate, Taft had been deeply influenced by the social Darwinism of William G. Sumner, and, for the remainder of his life, Taft accepted without question the principle that human conduct was naturally self-regarding. The challenge was to divert this selfishness into socially productive channels. The primary mechanism for this purpose was the institution of property, "the keystone of our society." To impair property rights was to threaten "our whole social fabric" by undercutting "the motive of enlightened selfishness that to-day is at the basis of all human labor and effort, enterprise and new activity." For Taft, therefore, property rights were to be regarded as uniform and universal, like human nature itself. Such rights were to receive national protection in the constitutional guarantees of the due process clause. Taft believed that "the corner stone of our civilization" lay "in the proper maintenance of the guaranties of the 14th Amendment and the 5th Amendment."

He therefore supported the Court's general program during the 1920s to limit the ability of governments to regulate property. Although he dissented in the infamous case of *Adkins v. Children's Hospital* (1923), in which the Court struck down a minimum wage law for women in the District of Columbia, he joined the many other similar cases in which the Court used the due process clause of the Fourteenth Amendment to invalidate social legislation. He generally stood against those, like Brandeis and Holmes, whom he believed were "in favor of breaking down the Constitution, or making it a mere scrap of paper."

In effect, the Court's aggressive reading of the due process clause during the 1920s created national criteria for the acceptability of progressive statutes. Taft was very concerned that access to federal courts be preserved so that these national criteria could be enforced through a centralized judicial system. So, for example, in *Terral v. Burke Construction* (1922), he wrote an opinion using the doctrine of unconstitutional conditions to prohibit states from imposing on foreign corporations the precondition that they waive the right to remove cases to federal courts. He also fought fiercely to preserve federal diversity jurisdiction when it was threatened by progressive senators such as George W. Norris, R-Neb., and David I. Walsh, D-Mass.

Although Taft was solicitous of property rights, he was also quite aware that the increased "mutual dependence" of modern industrial society required that property be regulated in a manner "appreciative of the change of conditions and the necessity for a liberal construction of the restrictions of the Constitution." He joined important and progressive opinions, such as *Village of Euclid v. Ambler Realty Co.* (1926), which upheld the constitutionality of city zoning, and *Miller v. Schoene* (1928), which upheld the constitutionality of confiscating infected trees. These opinions are facially inconsistent with Taft's commitment to preserve property rights, and they reflect a deep tension within his jurisprudence between that commitment and his evident appreciation of the necessary prerogatives of managerial expertise in contemporary society, an appreciation no doubt reinforced by his own executive experience.

The primary stratagem Taft employed to ease this tension was his effort in *Charles Wolff Packing Co. v. Court of Industrial Relations* (1923) to articulate a constitutional distinction between ordinary property, which was entitled to full constitutional protection, and property affected with a public interest, which could be subjected to extensive administrative control by the state. Using this distinction, Taft wrote several important opinions upholding the revolutionary efforts of the Transportation Act of 1920 to regulate the income and property of interstate railroads, as in *Dayton-Goose Creek Railroad Co. v. United States* (1924). Taft also used the distinction to uphold regulations of the insurance industry. Although the distinction was conceptually unstable—and therefore did not survive the constitutional revolution of the 1930s—it nevertheless illustrates Taft's sincere effort to reconcile his strong managerial bent with his equally sincere dedication to rather inflexible notions of property rights.

Taft's managerial propensity is evident in many aspects of his jurisprudence. It is most strikingly visible in opinions such as *United States v. Murray* (1928), *Federal Trade Commission v. Klesner* (1927), *Richmond Screw Anchor Co. v. United States* (1928), and *Girard Trust Co. v. United States* (1926), where he easily and masterfully assimilated the process of statutory interpretation into an intelligent and purposive social pragmatism. It is also apparent in Taft's grasp of the basic principles of administrative law and his clear understanding that executive agencies needed discretion and authority to function effectively. Representative opinions in this regard include *United States v. Stone & Downer Co.* (1927), *Federal Trade Commission v. Curtis Publishing Co.* (1923), *Federal Trade Commission v. Western Meat Co.* (1926), and *J. W. Hampton, Jr., & Co. v. United States* (1928). This same understanding underlay Taft's persistent commitment to an expansive interpretation of presidential power. Although some of Taft's opinions in this area—for example, the notorious *Myers v. United States* (1926)—are strident and overreaching, most, such as *McConaughey v. Morrow* (1923) and *Ex parte Grossman* (1925), are entirely convincing in their comprehensive insight into the pragmatic interrelationships among working government agencies.

Taft's view of the law as a purposive social instrument is also evident in his handling of the legal and constitutional dimensions of Prohibition. Taft had initially opposed Prohibition because he believed that it would be unenforceable and therefore create a cancerous disrespect for the law. With the enactment of the Eighteenth Amendment, however, Taft dedicated himself to establishing the legal mechanisms necessary for the social control of liquor. His most successful and long-lived opinion, *Carroll v. United States* (1925), completely reinterpreted received Fourth Amendment jurisprudence so as to enable effective supervision of the illegal transportation of liquor in cars and trucks. The same sustained determination and legal ingenuity is evident in other important Taft Prohibition opinions: *United States v. Lanza* (1922), *Samuels v. McCurdy* (1925), *Ford v. United States* (1927), and *Olmstead v. United States* (1928).

Throughout his tenure as chief justice, Taft advocated various reforms of the criminal law system to make it more efficient. He thought that the worst danger to the country was the "general spirit of lawlessness" loose in the land. Yet, for Taft, that spirit was not to be countered merely by more effective mechanisms of social control; equally important was the inculcation of fundamental norms of legality and fair procedure. Writing to the president of the Cincinnati Legal Aid Society, Taft said that he was strongly in favor of the movement to have public defenders appointed for indigent defendants. "The objection that it would delay matters is exactly the reason why I am in favor of it. Of course I think we ought to speed all prosecutions, but we ought not to speed them at the cost of saving from injustice many who are brought in charged with criminal offenses and not able really to defend themselves."

This commitment to fair procedures and respect for law is one of the foundational pillars of Taft's jurisprudence. In *Cooke v. United States* (1925), for example, Taft pioneered the effort to reconcile norms of due process with the administrative need of trial judges to use criminal contempt to retain control over their courtrooms. In *In re Gilbert* (1928), he delivered a stinging lecture to the bar about the need to scrupulously obey judicial regulation. And despite his evident commitment to the enforcement of Prohibition, he nevertheless struck down the widespread and effective technique of reimbursing the judges in mayoral "liquor courts" from fines they levied on Prohibition offenders. In *Tumey v. Ohio* (1927), Taft wrote:

> Every procedure which would offer a possible temptation to the average man as a judge to forget the burden of proof required to convict the defendant, or which might lead him not to hold the balance nice, clear and true between the

state and the accused denies the latter due process of law.

Taft's concern with societal lawlessness accounted for a good deal of his well-known hostility to prolabor legislation. For Taft, organized labor was as a class "distinctly arrayed against the Court":

> That faction we have to hit every little while, because they are continually violating the law and depending on threat and violence to accomplish their purpose. They are not content to depend only on organization, and the background of lawless trouble is always presented to give them an undue influence.

And to make matters worse, the "undue" influence of labor was for Taft often directed against the maintenance of necessary traditional property rights.

For these reasons, Taft had no doubt about the necessity of constitutionally striking down an Arizona law that prevented trial judges from issuing injunctions in labor disputes. As he noted in his notorious opinion in *Truax v. Corrigan* (1921), such injunctions were necessary both to protect property rights in an ongoing business and to prevent violence, because "peaceful picketing was a contradiction in terms." In his labor decisions, Taft tried to walk a narrow line between recognizing labor's right to organize (*American Steel Foundries v. Tri-City Central Trades Council*, 1921) and even encouraging employers to deal honorably with labor unions (*Pennsylvania Railroad Co. v. United States Railroad Labor Board*, 1923) and scrupulously striking down all organizing tactics that seemed to him lawless and coercive, such as picketing and the secondary boycott.

The intrinsic limitations of Taft's jurisprudence are perhaps most strikingly revealed in his labor decisions, for they are manifestly the product of a specific class ideology that identified traditional property rights and social arrangements with individualism and the centrality of personal responsibility and decision making. In his own managerial vision of the judiciary, Taft was able to transcend the notion that courts were merely individual decision makers and to glimpse the idea of judges as part of a larger and administered system of justice. But Taft never could come to see property and labor as similarly structured systems designed to achieve specific social goals. Property and labor were for him always anchored in the autonomous will of the particular person, from which vantage organized labor appeared as merely a local variant of "socialism," the systemic subordination of the individual. Taft was thus blinded to the directions the law would shortly take during the New Deal on many of the most significant constitutional issues of his day.

In this sense we can best appreciate Taft as a truly transitional figure. In his efforts at judicial reform, he was able to bring to bear a contemporary and pragmatic understanding of the mechanisms of social relations. He used this understanding to great effect in various aspects of his jurisprudence, most notably in opinions dealing with statutory interpretation, administrative law, and Prohibition. But in pervasive and important ways, he remained tied to a nineteenth-century naturalized and inflexible image of the person protected by universal and immutable property rights. For this reason, those who charged that the Supreme Court during the 1920s "had reached the zenith of reaction" made no exception for Chief Justice Taft.

—*Robert C. Post*

BIBLIOGRAPHY

The best primary source is the remarkable collection of William Howard Taft papers in the Library of Congress, which include about 750,000 items. The papers contain a rich trove of documents about Taft's personal philosophy and about the inner workings of the Court during his tenure as chief justice. Taft himself published numerous books and articles, the most important being *Popular Government: Its Essence, Its Permanence, and Its Perils* (1913); *Our Chief Magistrate and His Powers* (1916); *Liberty Under Law: An Interpretation of the Principles of Our Constitutional Government* (1922); "The Right of Private Property," *Michigan Law Journal* 3 (1894): 215; and "Three Needed Steps of Progress," *American Bar Association Journal* 8 (1922): 24.

The definitive biography of Taft remains Henry F. Pringle, *The Life and Times of William Howard Taft* (1939).

An interesting modern psychological biography, focusing on the presidential years, is Judith Icke Anderson, *William Howard Taft: An Intimate History* (1981). The best study of Taft's years on the Court is Alpheus Thomas Mason, *William Howard Taft: Chief Justice* (1964). For an excellent contemporary evaluation of Taft's judicial reforms, see Felix Frankfurter and James M. Landis, *The Business of the Supreme Court* (1927). See also D. F. Anderson, "Building National Consensus: The Career of William Howard Taft," *University of Cincinnati Law Review* 68 (2000): 323.

For good specific studies, see Peter G. Fish, "William Howard Taft and Charles Evans Hughes: Conservative Politicians as Chief Judicial Reformers," *Supreme Court Review* (1975): 123; Stanley I. Kutler, "Chief Justice Taft and the Delusion of Judicial Exactness—A Study in Jurisprudence," *Virginia Law Review* 48 (1962): 1407; and Kutler, "Chief Justice Taft, National Regulation, and the Commerce Power," *Journal of American History* 51 (1965): 651; Alpheus T. Mason, "The Labor Decisions of Chief Justice Taft," *University of Pennsylvania Law Review* 78 (1930): 585; Walter F. Murphy, "Chief Justice Taft and the Lower Court Bureaucracy: A Study in Judicial Administration," *The Journal of Politics* 24 (1962): 453; Robert C. Post, "Chief Justice Taft and the Concept of Federalism," *Constitutional Commentary* 9 (1992): 199; and Post, "Judicial Management and Judicial Disinterest: The Achievements and Perils of Chief Justice William Howard Taft," *Journal of Supreme Court History* (1998): 50.

NOTEWORTHY OPINIONS

Truax v. Corrigan, 257 U.S. 312 (1921)

Terral v. Burke Construction, 257 U.S. 529 (1922)

Stafford v. Wallace, 258 U.S. 495 (1922)

Federal Trade Commission v. Curtis Publishing Co., 260 U.S. 568 (1923)

Adkins v. Children's Hospital, 261 U.S. 525 (1923) (Dissent)

Charles Wolff Packing Co. v. Court of Industrial Relations, 262 U.S. 522 (1923)

Carroll v. United States, 267 U.S. 132 (1925)

Cooke v. United States, 267 U.S. 517 (1925)

Myers v. United States, 272 U.S. 52 (1926)

Tumey v. Ohio, 273 U.S. 510 (1927)

Olmstead v. United States, 277 U.S. 438 (1928)

ROGER BROOKE TANEY

Birth: March 17, 1777, Calvert County, Maryland.

Education: Graduated from Dickinson College, 1795, honorary LL.D.; read law privately.

Official Positions: Member, Maryland House of Delegates, 1799–1800; Maryland state senator, 1816–1821; Maryland attorney general, 1827–1831; U.S. attorney general, 1831–1833; acting secretary of war, 1831; U.S. secretary of the Treasury, 1833–1834 (appointment rejected by Senate).

Supreme Court Service: Nominated chief justice by President Andrew Jackson, December 28, 1835, to replace John Marshall, who had died; confirmed by the Senate, March 15, 1836, by a 29–15 vote; took judicial oath March 28, 1836; served until October 12, 1864; replaced by Salmon P. Chase, nominated by President Abraham Lincoln.

Death: October 12, 1864, Washington, D.C.

Roger Brooke Taney came from a wealthy and well-connected Maryland family that made its fortune in landholding, slaves, and tobacco. At age eighteen Taney graduated from Dickinson College in Pennsylvania, read law with Judge Jeremiah Chase in Annapolis, and began practicing in 1799. Initially a Federalist, Taney served in the state legislature for two years and broke with his party when it failed to support the War of 1812. In 1816 he won a five-year term in the Maryland Senate. At the expiration of his term, Taney moved to Baltimore where his law practice flourished. He also remained politically active and was elected Maryland's attorney general in 1827. Taney became a staunch supporter of Andrew Jackson and in 1828 chaired the Maryland central committee for Jackson's presidential campaign.

In 1831 Jackson appointed Taney U.S. attorney general, and Taney soon became one of Jackson's main advisers, helping shape administration policies on slavery and the rights of blacks, federal-state relations, and the Bank of the United States. Like Jackson, Taney had mixed and often seemingly inconsistent views on these issues.

During the nullification crisis Taney strongly supported Jackson's confrontation with South Carolina. On this issue Taney was a proponent of federal power in the tradition of Chief Justice John Marshall. When confronted with questions of slavery and the rights of free blacks, however, Taney deferred to state authorities and declined to assert any federal power. He argued that neither under the commerce clause nor the treaty power could the national government regulate slavery and race relations in the states.

Taney's deference to states' rights on issues of race and the rights of free blacks anticipated the views he later articulated in his famous—and infamous—opinion in *Dred Scott v. Sandford* (1857). As attorney general, Taney had to comment on the constitutional power of southern states to prohibit free blacks (from other states or the British Empire) from entering their jurisdiction. In his official "Opinion of the Attorney General," Taney asserted:

> The African race in the United States even when free, are everywhere a degraded class, and exercise no political influence. The privileges they are allowed to enjoy, are accorded to them as a matter of kindness and benevolence rather than right.... They are not looked upon as citizens by the contracting parties who formed the Constitution. They were evidently not supposed to be included by the term *citizens*.

Taney concluded that the Declaration of Independence was never meant to apply to blacks, who were, in the attorney general's mind, not entitled to the natural rights of "life, liberty, and pursuit of happiness."

This official opinion of Attorney General Taney demonstrates that the antiblack, proslavery views Chief Justice Taney expressed in *Dred Scott* were neither an aberration nor a function of the changing politics of the 1850s; rather, they were part of his lifelong ideology. This opinion was never published and therefore did not affect public debate, but it certainly bolstered Jackson's hands-off policy toward southern regulations of free blacks from the British Empire and the North.

When examined through the lens of *Dred Scott*, Taney's views on free blacks become extraordinarily significant. At the time he entered the cabinet, however, the most divisive political issue facing the nation was not the status of blacks, but the Bank of the United States. Taney wholeheartedly supported Jackson's war against the bank, and he helped the president draft the veto message that asserted its unconstitutionality. Jackson's veto was a direct rebuke to Marshall's opinion in *McCulloch v. Maryland* (1819) that the bank was constitutional. Taney's assistance to Jackson can be seen as the first step in his gradual dismantling of much of Marshall's jurisprudence.

After the bank veto, Jackson ordered two successive secretaries of the Treasury to begin withdrawing federal deposits from the Bank of the United States. When both refused to comply with his order, Jackson fired them and appointed Taney secretary of the Treasury. Taney immediately began removing deposits from the bank, and the following June the bank's supporters in the Senate retaliated by blocking his confirmation. Taney returned to his law practice in Maryland. On January 15, 1835, Jackson nominated Taney for the Supreme Court, to replace Justice Gabriel Duvall, who had retired. The Senate on March 3 once again refused to confirm Taney to office by postponing any action on it.

When Chief Justice Marshall died in July 1835, Jackson nominated Taney to succeed him. By the following spring, Jacksonians controlled the Senate, and on March 16, 1836, the Senate confirmed both Taney and Philip P. Barbour, who took Duvall's seat. Although appointed for his political loyalty, Taney also served another purpose. He was the Court's first

Roger Brooke Taney

Catholic, and his appointment helped solidify Catholic (especially Irish) support for the Democratic Party at a time when large numbers of Catholics were immigrating to the United States.

Taney's confirmation distressed the Whigs, who believed the new chief justice, along with Jackson's other appointments, would destroy the judicial and economic nationalism Marshall had created. By the time Taney became chief justice, Jackson had already placed John McLean, Henry Baldwin, and James Wayne on the Court. With the confirmation of Taney and Barbour, Jackson had a majority of justices. The additions of John Catron and John McKinley in 1837 created a Court with seven Jacksonian Democrats. If Taney wanted to, he apparently had the votes to dismantle Marshall's legacy.

Indeed, for all but the last two years of his tenure, Chief Justice Taney could count on a Democratic, states' rights, proslavery majority. From 1837 until 1862, only four Whigs served on the Court. Smith Thompson remained on the bench until 1843, and Joseph Story, Taney's only rival for intellectual leadership of the Court, until 1845. By the mid-1840s, McLean had abandoned Jacksonian principles and was on a political trajectory that took him to the Whig, Free Soil, and Republican parties. From 1851 to 1857 the Court included Benjamin Curtis, a conservative Whig from Massachusetts. President Abraham Lincoln nominated three Republicans to the bench in 1862, and a fourth in 1863, so that in his last two terms Taney no longer controlled the Court or its jurisprudence.

From 1837 to 1862 the Democratic-Jacksonian majority crafted opinions that were generally supportive of states' rights and slavery and skeptical of national power. In the areas of contract and commerce, Taney led a partial retreat from Marshall's nationalist jurisprudence, but in others, such as procedure, the Taney Court expanded on Marshall's foundation. On slavery, the Taney Court was never jurisprudentially consistent. Until 1861 Taney rejected states' rights when asserted by northerners opposed to slavery, while supporting southern assertions of power over slavery. Where federal power would protect slavery, Taney was a nationalist; but where the government

in Washington might threaten southern bondage, Taney supported a limitation of federal power. The unifying theme of Taney's jurisprudence on slavery, then, was protection of slavery. Indeed, he remained proslavery throughout his public career, despite having freed his own slaves in the 1810s and 1820s.

The Taney Court's slavery jurisprudence should not be surprising. In addition to the heavy presence of Democrats, until the Civil War the Taney Court always had a proslavery majority. From his appointment as chief justice to the outbreak of the war, the Court always had four northerners and four southerners plus Taney. The southern majority was enhanced by the fact that throughout this period at least two and sometimes three of the northerners were Democratic "doughfaces"—northerners with southern principles. Only McLean was openly antislavery, and his opposition to the "peculiar institution" was relatively mild. In Peter V. Daniel and John A. Campbell, the Court had two uncompromisingly proslavery justices, as well other slave-owning southerners whose jurisprudence reflected their sectional and economic interests. By the last antebellum decade, the Supreme Court had become, in the words of historian David Potter, "the very citadel of American slavery."

Initial Whig fears about Taney eventually proved to be overblown. He was not a radical, but his jurisprudence, especially on economic issues, was clearly different from Marshall's. Marshall generally favored sweeping federal powers over commerce and a strict interpretation of the limitations on the states in areas such as contract and currency. Taney's approach was far more flexible.

Charles River Bridge v. Warren Bridge (1837), decided during Taney's first term, set the tone for his economic jurisprudence. In 1785 the Charles River Bridge Company had obtained a state charter to operate a toll bridge between Boston and Cambridge. With no other bridge across the Charles River, the company had been enormously profitable, and by the 1830s the bridge was worth a half-million dollars. But the single bridge was also no longer adequate for the needs of Boston and its suburbs. In 1828 the Massachusetts legislature chartered the Warren Bridge

Company to build a second bridge across the river. Under its charter, the Warren Company could collect tolls to earn back the cost of building the bridge and a reasonable profit, but after that, the bridge would belong to the state. The Charles River Bridge Company argued that its charter implied it had a monopoly, and by granting a charter to the Warren Company, the state effectively violated the contract clause of the Constitution. Speaking for the Court, Taney concluded that "any ambiguity in the terms of the contract, must operate against the adventurers [stockholders] and in favor of the public."

Although Whigs disliked the result (Daniel Webster was the losing attorney, and Justice Story dissented), Taney's decision was not a radical departure from Marshall's economic jurisprudence. Taney simply recognized that the public good required a balance between private interests (the corporation) and the public need, as reflected by the legislature. The Taney Court followed the spirit of *Charles River Bridge* in subsequent cases—allowing states great flexibility in issuing corporate charters, but always reading those charters narrowly in order to protect the public good and the states. Thus the Taney Court had no difficulty in recognizing the right of the state to give companies tax breaks or the power of eminent domain, but in *West River Bridge v. Dix* (1848), the Court also upheld the right of the state to use eminent domain to take property from a corporation.

Taney's decision in *Charles River Bridge* and subsequent cases also reflected his states' rights proclivities. The *Charles River Bridge* opinion deferred to the needs of the states to promote economic development and to control local industries. In *New York v. Miln* (1837), the Court (in an opinion by Justice Barbour) upheld New York City's law requiring ships entering the port to provide detailed information about immigrant passengers. As with the contract clause, the Taney Court reshaped Marshall's nationalist commerce clause jurisprudence to give states more latitude in regulating their economies.

The Taney Court also expanded the power of states in *Briscoe v. Bank of the Commonwealth of Kentucky* (1837), which upheld the power of a state-chartered

bank to issue bank notes. This decision narrowed the implications of Marshall's opinion in *Craig v. Missouri* (1830), which had prohibited states from issuing paper money. Logically, if the Constitution prohibited a state from issuing currency, then surely a state could not charter a bank to do what the state itself could not do. McLean's opinion for the Court distinguished between a bank issuing notes and a state issuing currency. Carrying on Marshall's nationalist traditions, Story dissented.

The outcome of *Briscoe* dovetailed with Taney's role in dismantling the Bank of the United States three years earlier. In the 1830s the U.S. government did not print currency, but only minted a small amount of gold and silver coins, while the Bank of the United States issued bank notes that functioned as a national currency. But with the expiration of the bank's federal charter in 1836, the United States had no national currency. Had the Taney Court ruled differently in *Briscoe*, there would have been no currency in the United States, which might have forced the national government to once again charter a national bank.

Charles River Bridge, Miln, and *Briscoe* presaged other cases in which Taney and his colleagues supported state regulation and experimentation in commercial and economic areas. For example, in the *License Cases* (1847), the Taney Court upheld the right of Massachusetts, Rhode Island, and Connecticut to ban the importation of liquor. In the *Passenger Cases* (1849), the Court struck down, on commerce clause grounds, state laws taxing immigrants, but Taney, ready to defer to the states, dissented. In *Cooley v. Board of Wardens of Port of Philadelphia* (1852), the Court upheld a Pennsylvania law requiring that ships entering Philadelphia take on a local pilot. This decision also reflected Taney's general deference to the states, although Curtis wrote the opinion of the Court.

Despite his general sympathy for the states in economic regulation, Taney did not always limit federal power. Two cases dealing with corporations and interstate commerce suggest his flexibility on economic matters. On circuit, in *Warren Manufacturing Co. v. Aetna Insurance Co.* (1837), Taney upheld a Maryland law allowing a Connecticut company doing business in Maryland to be sued in Maryland. Furthermore, Taney held that a judgment against the company in the state court could then be enforced in a federal court. Although a victory for state power, this case also helped establish an atmosphere conducive to corporations doing business on a national scale. Under *Warren Manufacturing,* states would have some control over out-of-state companies and could count on the federal courts to help them enforce that control. This decision made it more likely that states would allow out-of-state companies to do business in their jurisdictions. Two years later, in *Bank of Augusta v. Earle* (1839), Taney further enhanced interstate business while at the same time recognizing the power of the states to regulate their economies. In this case, Taney held that a bank chartered in one state might do business in another unless specifically prohibited from doing so. This ruling did not destroy state power, but it left the states in the position of having to specifically ban out-of-state corporations from doing business in their jurisdictions.

In some commercial cases, Taney actually expanded on Marshall's judicial nationalism. In *Swift v. Tyson* (1842), Story, writing for a unanimous Court, held that the federal courts were free to develop their own common law for commercial litigation. This case allowed those engaged in interstate business to rely on general rules of commercial law and consequently limited the power of the states to create unique rules that might burden out-of-state litigants. And in *Propeller Genesee Chief v. Fitzhugh* (1852), Taney reversed the Marshall Court's earlier doctrine enunciated in *The Thomas Jefferson* (1825) to actually expand federal jurisdiction. In the 1825 case, Story, writing for the Court, had allowed the states to regulate traffic on inland waters. By 1852 this practice had developed into an impossible set of different and sometimes contradictory rules in the nation's water commerce. Taney concluded that federal admiralty jurisdiction extended to all navigable rivers and lakes, not just to those affected by "the ebb and flow of the tide." As law and history professor R. Kent Newmyer concluded: "In an explicitly pragmatic response to commercial necessity, Taney reversed Story's earlier ruling, declaring it mistaken law and bad policy, and extended the admiralty jurisdiction of federal courts over the whole system of

inland waterways. Marshall, who never liked the *Jefferson* decision, would surely have congratulated his successor." These decisions, which enhanced federal power, were imperative for the emerging national economy and did not significantly hamper the ability of the states to control their own economic affairs.

The antebellum Court rarely faced questions about politics and fundamental rights in the states. Three cases, *Permoli v. First Municipality of New Orleans* (1845), *Ex parte Dorr* (1845), and *Luther v. Borden* (1849), illustrate the way the Court under Taney's leadership avoided such questions. *Permoli* reaffirmed Marshall's holding in *Barron v. Baltimore* (1833) that the federal Bill of Rights did not apply to the states. *Permoli* questioned the right of the city of New Orleans to prohibit burial masses in certain Catholic churches in the city. Bernard Permoli was a Catholic priest who held a mass in his church in violation of a city ordinance. Catron, for a unanimous Court, dismissed the case for lack of a federal question on the ground that the Bill of Rights did not apply to the new states any more than it did to the old.

Ex parte Dorr and *Luther v. Borden* arose from the Dorr War, an extralegal attempt to bring about political reform in Rhode Island. In 1841 Rhode Island was still operating under its colonial charter, which prevented a substantial majority of the adult males from voting. In addition, malapportionment of the state legislature allowed a small minority of rural farmers to control the government and stifle all reform. Led by Thomas Dorr, reformers wrote a new constitution, elected a new government, and for a time Rhode Island had two competing governments. Dorr was forced to flee the state when the governor under the old charter called out the militia. Dorr was eventually arrested, convicted of insurrection, and sentenced to life in prison. In *Ex parte Dorr,* the Court overruled a petition for *habeas corpus* on the grounds that the federal government could not interfere in state criminal proceedings. A year later, the new governor of Rhode Island, who had gained office under a democratic constitution written by the Dorrites, pardoned Dorr.

In *Luther v. Borden,* Martin Luther, a Dorrite, sued Luther Borden, a state militiaman, for trespass for searching his home and arresting him during the uprising. Luther argued that Rhode Island had not had a republican form of government and that under Article IV, Section 4, of the Constitution, the Supreme Court had jurisdiction. Taney, writing for the Court, rejected Luther's arguments, concluding that the legitimacy of the old charter government was a "political question to be settled by the political power" of the people within the state.

In these cases, Taney declined to assert federal power over questions of politics and rights in the states. This stance was consistent with his beliefs about states' rights and limitations on the national government, but the subtext to these decisions, and to most of the Taney Court's decisions on interstate commerce, was slavery.

In their study of antebellum constitutionalism, *Equal Justice Under Law,* Harold M. Hyman and William M Wiecek refer to slavery as the "Nemesis of the Constitution." The characterization is apt, and, in terms of his historical reputation, no one suffered more from this nemesis than Taney. Had he died or left the bench in 1850, or even 1856, before his opinion in *Dred Scott,* he would be remembered as a great chief justice, well-liked by his colleagues and admired by the citizenry. But in his last fourteen years on the Court, Taney faced cases on slavery and the Civil War that left his reputation in tatters.

As an adult Taney personally divorced himself from slavery. That he did so is to his credit and distinguished him from southern presidents from George Washington to Andrew Johnson—none of whom freed their slaves in their lifetime. But Taney never divorced himself from his southern roots, his ideological support of slavery as an institution, or his beliefs in the racial inferiority of blacks. Throughout his career, Taney's jurisprudence was overwhelmingly proslavery and antiblack.

As chief justice, Taney's first major encounter with slavery came in 1841 in two cases, *United States v. The Amistad,* and *Groves v. Slaughter. Amistad* was the first great slavery-related cause célèbre to reach the Court. The *Amistad* was a Spanish schooner filled with African slaves, who had been illegally imported

to Cuba. While being transported from one part of Cuba to another, the slaves revolted, killing some of the crew and demanding that they be taken back to Africa. The remaining crew members sailed east during the day, but at night reversed course, heading north and west, in hopes of reaching a U.S. southern state. The craft was eventually boarded by the U.S. Coast Guard in Long Island Sound. Various suits arose over the status of the vessel and the slaves on it. Ultimately, the Supreme Court ruled that the blacks had been illegally taken from Africa, could not be held as slaves under Spanish or American law, and were to be returned to Africa. Story wrote for the Court, with Taney remaining silent. By 1841 even many proslavery advocates found the African trade to be immoral and a violation of natural law and most public law (but not international law). Taney's acquiescence in freeing the *Amistad's* slaves cannot be seen as antislavery.

On its face, *Groves v. Slaughter* (1841) also did not raise pro- or antislavery issues. Rather, it was essentially a commerce clause case—the only major slavery case to come before the Court that directly raised commerce clause issues. Mississippi's 1832 constitution prohibited the importation of slaves for sale. This was not an antislavery provision, but an attempt to reduce the flow of capital out of the state. Robert Slaughter, a professional slave dealer, had sold slaves in Mississippi and received notes signed by Moses Groves and others. Groves and his codefendants later defaulted on the notes, arguing that the sales of slaves in Mississippi were void. The suit was between slave sellers and slave buyers.

Speaking for the Court, Thompson held that the notes were not void because Mississippi's constitutional clause was not self-executing; absent legislation implementing the prohibition, the clause was inoperative. This result was reasonable based on commercial rules and consistent with the outcome in *Bank of Augusta v. Earle* (1839). In that case, Joseph B. Earle and other Alabamians had refused to honor bills of exchange they had issued on the grounds that they had been bought by an out-of-state bank, and out-of-state banks could not operate in Alabama. Taney had ruled that out-of-state banks could operate in any state in the absence of an explicit act of the legislature to the contrary. Similarly, in *Groves,* the Court held that the Mississippi purchasers could not hide behind a clause of the state constitution and refuse to pay the notes they had signed without an explicit statute in Mississippi banning slave sales. This result was "neutral" with regard to slavery.

Indicative of what would be his highly partisan approach to slavery throughout the rest of his career, Taney wrote a separate concurrence, insisting that the federal government had no power over slavery. This issue was not directly before the Court, but Taney did not want to leave any implication that Congress could regulate slavery under the commerce clause. He declared:

> The power of this subject [slavery] is exclusively with the several States, and each of them has a right to decide for itself whether it will or will not allow persons of this description to be brought within its limits from another State, either for sale or for any other purpose . . . and the action of the several States upon this subject cannot be controlled by Congress, either by virtue of its power to regulate commerce, or by virtue of any other power conferred by the Constitution of the United States.

On the other side of the question, McLean asserted in a concurrence that the free states could prevent the importation of slaves if they wished and that Congress could not interfere. Sounding much like Taney, McLean declared that "the power over slavery belongs to the States respectively. It is local in its character, and in its effects," and "each state has a right to protect itself against the avarice and intrusion of the slave dealer; to guard its citizens against the inconveniences and dangers of a slave population." He argued, "The right to exercise this power by a State is higher and deeper than the Constitution." In essence, both Taney and McLean agreed that a state might legally ban the importation of slaves. This principle supported northerners interested in keeping slaves out of their states and the southern desire to make

sure that the federal courts could not interfere with slavery on the local level.

In 1841, then, supporters and opponents of slavery on the Court were anxious to see the issue remain solely in the hands of the states. By 1842, however, Taney would no longer be content with that interpretation of slavery, unless it was a slave state making the determination.

In 1842 the Supreme Court heard *Prigg v. Pennsylvania,* its first case involving the fugitive slave clause of the Constitution. *Prigg* involved the constitutionality of a Pennsylvania personal liberty law requiring that slave catchers receive a proper writ from a state judge before removing any blacks from the state. Edward Prigg had seized a woman and her children without any state process and was subsequently convicted of kidnapping in Pennsylvania. In a sweeping victory for slavery, which shook to the core his antislavery reputation, Story struck down the Pennsylvania law, upheld the federal fugitive slave law of 1793, and further declared that slave owners had a constitutional right to seize their slaves anywhere they found them, without resort to any sort of legal process, as long as the seizure could be done without a breach of the peace. In reaching these conclusions, Story swept aside the facts of the case, which showed that at least one of the people Prigg seized had been born in Pennsylvania and was therefore free under that state's laws.

In his opinion, Story asserted that the federal government could not require state officials to enforce the federal fugitive slave law of 1793, although he urged them to do so as a matter of patriotism, moral obligation, and (unenforceable) constitutional duty. This holding was consistent with prevailing notions of federalism and states' rights, and Taney should have applauded it. Indeed, later in his career, in *Kentucky v. Dennison* (1861), Taney argued that the federal courts could not order state governors to enforce the criminal extradition clauses of the same 1793 law. But Taney did not endorse this view in *Prigg*. In a partial concurrence, Taney argued that state officials ought to be required to enforce the fugitive slave clause. This opinion was the beginning of

Taney's assertion of Marshall-like federalism to protect slavery.

In *Strader v. Graham* (1850), Taney once again spoke out on slavery. Jacob Strader was the owner of a steamboat that had transported Christopher Graham's three slaves to Ohio, where they disappeared. Under Kentucky law, a steamboat operator was liable for the value of any slaves who escaped by boarding the boat without written permission of the owner. Strader, however, argued that the blacks, who were musicians, were free because Graham had previously allowed them to go to Indiana and Ohio to perform. Speaking for a unanimous Court, Taney ruled against Strader, arguing that the status of the blacks could be decided only by Kentucky, which had ruled they were slaves. Kentucky was free to ignore the laws of Ohio and Indiana on this question. Taney declared that "every State has an undoubted right to determine the status or domestic condition of the persons domiciled within its territory" except as "restrained" by the Constitution. This wording certainly applied to fugitive slaves, whom the northern states could not declare free, but it also held open the possibility that slave owners had other federal rights to carry their slaves into the North or the federal territories. Part of this implication became explicit in *Dred Scott*.

Dred Scott was the slave of Dr. John Emerson, a military physician who had taken him to Fort Snelling, in present-day Minnesota. At the time, this part of the Louisiana Purchase was free territory under the Missouri Compromise. After Emerson's death, Scott sued for his freedom on the grounds that he had become free in Minnesota, and once free, always free. After nearly eleven years of litigation in state and federal courts, the Court decided the case in 1857. Although every one of the justices wrote an opinion, Taney's was the opinion of the Court. In his sweeping fifty-five-page opinion, Taney sought to settle the divisive political questions of slavery and race in favor of the South.

Three aspects of Taney's opinion made it infamous. First, in a tortured interpretation of the Constitution's clause on territorial jurisdiction in Article IV, Taney ruled the Missouri Compromise unconstitutional. On a totally unpersuasive textual analysis,

Taney struck down a major piece of congressional legislation that had been the keystone of sectional compromise for more than a generation.

Second, Taney ruled that under the Fifth Amendment's due process clause slaves could not be freed by federal law. In essence, Taney held that the slave was a protected species of property and that under the Constitution Congress could not deprive any citizen of this kind of property. This interpretation of the Constitution pleased the South and angered the North, but it also flew in the face of national law predating the Constitution, in which Congress had banned slavery from some federal territories. Moreover, the use of the Fifth Amendment seemed, to many northerners at least, cynical and ironic. It was that amendment, after all, that asserted that no person could be denied life, liberty, or property without due process of law. Taney stressed the "property" in slaves, and protected it, but ignored the obvious possibility that the amendment might ban slavery in all federal jurisdictions because slavery denied people liberty without due process.

Even more egregious than these two assertions was Taney's claim that blacks—even if free and allowed to vote in the states where they lived—could never be citizens of the United States and have standing to sue in federal courts. In a thoroughly inaccurate history of the founding period, Taney argued that at the adoption of the Constitution, blacks were not

included, and were not intended to be included, under the word "citizens" in the Constitution, and can therefore claim none of the rights and privileges which the instrument provides and secures to citizens of the United States. On the contrary, they were at that time considered as a subordinate and inferior class of beings who had been subjugated by the dominant race, and, whether emancipated or not, yet remained subject to their authority, and had no rights or privileges but such as those who held the power and Government might chose to grant them.

Taney concluded blacks were "so far inferior, that they had not rights which the white man was bound to respect."

If the chief justice hoped to end all controversy over slavery in the territories with this opinion, he seriously miscalculated. Northern anger over the opinion fueled the Republican Party and helped put Lincoln in the White House. Rather than acknowledge the complexity of slavery, Taney simply tried to sweep away the opposition to the institution, and he failed miserably.

Two decisions following *Dred Scott* showed the proslavery cynicism of Taney's jurisprudence. In *Ableman v. Booth* (1859), Taney rejected Wisconsin's attempts to remove from federal custody the abolitionist Sherman Booth, who had helped a fugitive slave escape. Taney refused to even consider the constitutionality of the new Fugitive Slave Law of 1850, even though it was substantially different from the law upheld in *Prigg* in 1842. Taney dismissed Wisconsin's states' rights arguments as though he had never heard of the idea and in his *Ableman* opinion endorsed a sweeping federal power to support slavery.

In *Kentucky v. Dennison* (1861), Taney changed his tune once again. The case was an attempt by the state of Kentucky to force Gov. William Dennison, R-Ohio, to extradite a free black named Willis Lago who had helped a slave woman escape from Kentucky. The obvious proslavery result would have been to side with Kentucky, which was consistent with Taney's opinions in *Prigg, Dred Scott,* and *Ableman,* all rejections of states' rights in favor of federal protections of slavery. But by March 1861, when the case was decided, seven slave states had already left the Union. Sympathetic to the southern cause, Taney avoided writing an opinion that would have given the federal government the power to force state governors to act. In an opinion reminiscent of Marshall's tactics in *Marbury v. Madison,* Taney castigated Dennison but refused to order him to act.

Taney remained on the Court until his death in 1864. During his last few years as chief justice he did everything in his power to thwart Lincoln's policies. In *Ex parte Merryman* (1861), Taney denounced the president for the military arrest of a Maryland man who was organizing Confederate troops, destroying bridges, and in other ways making war against the United States. Lincoln ignored Taney's fulminations and kept Merryman in Fort McHenry. Failing to recognize the nature of the Civil War, Taney dissented in the *Prize Cases* (1863) and opposed the taxation of judges' salaries to help pay for the war. He secretly drafted an opinion declaring conscription unconstitutional, but no case ever reached the Court in which he could use it.

At the time of his death, Taney was a minority justice, ignored by the president and Congress, held in contempt by the vast majority of his countrymen, and respected only in those places that proclaimed themselves no longer in the Union. Taney's obvious tilt toward the Confederacy showed that he had traveled far from the days when he had advised Andrew Jackson on how to suppress nullificationists. Indeed, he had become one himself in all but name.

Taney's reputation as a judge is mixed. When he died, few had anything good to say about him. Congress refused to appropriate money to put his bust in the Supreme Court chambers. Yet it is clear that his impact on the law was great. For the first twenty years of his tenure, he successfully guided the Court and helped develop important constitutional doctrines. Nevertheless, he is most remembered for *Dred Scott,* the most infamous decision in American constitutional history. *Dred Scott,* however, should be seen as only one in a series of decisions designed to strengthen slavery, protect the South, and, in the end, to undermine the cause of the Union after 1861. Taney was creative in finding legal solutions to questions about banking, commerce, and transportation, but he ultimately failed in creating a jurisprudence that could defend fundamental liberty and human rights. That failure will always overshadow his successes.

—*Paul Finkelman*

BIBLIOGRAPHY

The best biography of Taney remains Carl B. Swisher's classic *Roger B. Taney* (1935); but see also Frank Otto Gatell, "Roger B. Taney," in Friedman and Israel, *Justices,* vol. 2, 635, which provides a good short biographical sketch of Taney and discusses some of his opinions. For two opposing views of Taney, see James B. O'Hara, "Out of the Shadow: Roger Brooke Taney as Chief Justice," *Journal of Supreme Court History* (1998): 21; and Paul Finkelman, " 'Hooted Down the Page of History': Reconsidering the Greatness of Chief Justice Taney," *Journal of Supreme Court History* (1994): 83.

Harold M. Hyman and William M. Wiecek's *Equal Justice Under Law* (1982) is the best book available on the constitutional history of antebellum America. For the Court under Taney, see the comprehensive and classic, Carl B. Swisher, *The Taney Period* (1974), volume 5 of the *Holmes Devise History*. R. Kent Newmyer, *The Supreme Court Under Marshall and Taney* (1974), provides a good short history of the Court during Taney's service.

David Potter, *The Impending Crisis, 1848–1861* (1976) is a history of the years leading up to the Civil War, which puts many of Taney's opinions on slavery into historical context. On slavery and the legal system, see Paul Finkelman, *An Imperfect Union: Slavery, Comity, and Federalism* (1981), a study of the interstate movement of slaves, which includes detailed analyses of many Taney opinions, and Finkelman, *Slavery in the Courtroom* (1985). On the most infamous of Taney's opinions, see the prizewinning study by Don Fehrenbacher, *The Dred Scott Case: Its Significance in Law and Politics* (1978).

NOTEWORTHY OPINIONS

Briscoe v. Bank of the Commonwealth of Kentucky, 33 U.S. 118 (1837)

Charles River Bridge v. Warren Bridge, 36 U.S. 420 (1837)

Warren Manufacturing Co. v. Aetna Insurance Co., 29 Fed. Cases 294 (C.C.D. Conn. 1837)

Groves v. Slaughter, 40 U.S. 449 (1841) (Concurrence)

Prigg v. Pennsylvania, 41 U.S. 539 (1842) (Concurrence)

Luther v. Borden, 48 U.S. 1 (1846)

Strader v. Graham, 51 U.S. 82 (1850)

Propeller Genesee Chief v. Fitzhugh, 53 U.S. 443 (1852)

Dred Scott v. Sandford, 60 U.S. 393 (1857)

Ableman v. Booth, 62 U.S. 506 (1859)

Kentucky v. Dennison, 65 U.S. 66 (1861)

Prize Cases, 67 U.S. 635 (1863) (Dissent)

CLARENCE THOMAS

Birth: June 23, 1948, Pin Point, Georgia.

Education: Immaculate Conception Seminary, 1967–1968; Holy Cross College, B.A., 1971; Yale University Law School, J.D., 1974.

Official Positions: Assistant attorney general, Missouri, 1974–1977; assistant secretary of education for civil rights, 1981–1982; chairman, Equal Employment Opportunity Commission, 1982–1990; judge, U.S. Court of Appeals for the District of Columbia Circuit, 1990–1991.

Supreme Court Service: Nominated associate justice by President George H. W. Bush, July 8, 1991, to replace Thurgood Marshall, who had retired; confirmed by the Senate, October 15, 1991, by a 52–48 vote; took judicial oath October 23, 1991.

Justice Clarence Thomas was the great dissenter on the Rehnquist Court. While the mainstream conservatives on that tribunal largely tinkered with past Burger Court precedent, and Justice Antonin Scalia called for a wholesale rejection of liberal judicial decisions handed down during the 1970s, Thomas called for the overthrow of both Great Society and New Deal constitutional principles. His most noteworthy opinions consistently eschewed doctrinal arguments based on past precedents in favor of broad declarations about the original understanding of constitutional provisions and the core principles of the American constitutional regime. No other justice in American history has ever insisted on abandoning so many past judicial decisions in so many areas of the law.

Born in rural Georgia, Thomas was raised by his grandfather, whose penchant for hard work Thomas constantly celebrates. He attended private seminary schools, Holy Cross College, and Yale Law School. Feeling stigmatized and stereotyped because of his race in law school, Thomas began developing strong conservative commitments, a powerful anathema to

affirmative action in particular. After graduation, he served on the staff of John Danforth, the attorney general of Missouri, and did a brief stint in private practice. Thomas rejoined Danforth's staff when Danforth was elected to the Senate in 1980. Ronald Reagan appointed Thomas to the Department of Education and then as chair of the Equal Employment Opportunity Commission (EEOC), where he served for eight years. President George H. W. Bush nominated Thomas to the U.S. Court of Appeals for the District of Columbia Circuit in 1990 and to the Supreme Court in 1991.

The confirmation hearings provided little guidance as to how Thomas was likely to behave if confirmed. Prepared by Bush administration officials, Thomas combined vague bromides indicating sympathy toward the poor and a commitment to privacy in general, with a refusal to indicate his opinions on the constitutional issues of the day. Previous writings praising natural law, opposing abortion, and condemning affirmative action, he indicated, were mere speculations by a part-time philosopher. Responding to questions from Senate Democrats, Thomas declared he had never even thought about whether the Supreme Court in *Roe v. Wade* (1973) correctly ruled that the Constitution protected a right to an abortion. The hearings became sidetracked by claims that Thomas had sexually harassed a subordinate, Anita Hill, when at the EEOC. One consequence of Hill's allegations and the days of uncomfortable testimony was that when Thomas was confirmed by a 52–48 vote, the closest successful judicial confirmation vote in American history, he was already a polarizing figure. Liberals regarded Thomas as a perjurer, unfit for the Court. Conservatives saw him as a victim of left-wing racism. Thomas, a private person, limited his public appearances to friendly conservative audiences.

In his first years on the Court, Thomas typically voted with the conservatives, but in several cases he preferred the company of the moderate justices to Scalia's constitutional conservatism. His votes during his first year on the bench, in particular, gave hints that Thomas might be closer on many issues to Justices

Clarence Thomas

Anthony Kennedy and Sandra Day O'Connor than to Scalia. In *Richmond v. Lewis* (1992), a death penalty case, Thomas's concurring opinion asserted that precedent should govern, even though he thought the previous decisions were mistaken. Scalia's dissent would have overruled those precedents and denied relief. Thomas demonstrated a similar commitment to precedent in *Georgia v. McCollum* (1992). Chief Justice William Rehnquist and Justices Scalia, O'Con-

nor, and Thomas agreed that *Edmonson v. Leesville Concrete Co.* (1991) erroneously found state action whenever criminal defendants exercised peremptory challenges. Scalia and O'Connor called for the decision to be overruled. Thomas and Rehnquist insisted that the precedent be followed, particularly because Georgia did not ask for the case to be overruled. In *United States v. Fordice* (1992), Thomas endorsed the majority's conclusion that "a State does not satisfy its obligation to dismantle a dual system of higher education merely by adopting race-neutral policies for the future administration of that system." Scalia submitted the only dissent in that case.

Other opinions were less moderate. Thomas dissented in *Riggins v. Nevada* (1992), a case holding a criminal defendant's Sixth Amendment right to a fair trial was violated by the forced administration of antipsychotic drugs. While conceding that mandatory medication might have "deprived Riggins of a protected liberty interest in a manner actionable in a different legal proceeding," Thomas and Scalia concluded that "Riggins nonetheless had the fundamentally fair criminal trial required by the Constitution." In *Hudson v. McMillan* (1992), Scalia and Thomas were the only two justices who questioned previous judicial decisions holding that conditions of imprisonment might violate the Eighth Amendment. "For generations," Thomas's dissent declared, "judges and commentators regarded the Eighth Amendment as applying only to torturous punishments meted out by statutes or sentencing judges, and not generally to any hardship that might befall a prisoner during incarceration." This use of history to combat doctrine became a constant theme in Thomas's opinions.

Thomas seemingly began playing a leadership role in 1994 when he spoke for the Court in three cases of some constitutional significance. All three opinions gained strong support across the judicial spectrum. Two opinions discussed dormant commerce clause issues, matters concerning whether states may regulate interstate commerce in the absence of federal legislation. In *Associated Industries of Missouri v. Lohman* (1994), Thomas, speaking for an 8–1 majority, issued an opinion holding unconstitutional a Missouri use tax on goods purchased outside the state. That the tax discriminated against interstate commerce only in some state counties was constitutionally unimportant. Thomas's opinion, signed by every justice but Harry Blackmun, "rejected any theory that would require aggregating the burdens on commerce across an entire State to determine the constitutionality of a burden on interstate trade imposed by a particular political subdivision of the State." *Oregon Waste Systems v. Department of Environmental Quality* (1994) held that Oregon could not impose a surcharge on in-state disposal of waste imported from other states. Thomas gained the support of every justice but Rehnquist and Blackmun for his analysis in that case. In *FDIC v. Meyer* (1994), Thomas for a unanimous Court declared that the due process clause did not permit persons to sue federal agencies they believed violated their rights, only the federal official responsible for the alleged rights violation.

Thomas's concurring and dissenting opinions on racial matters before 1995 were often less moderate than his majority opinions. His concurring opinion in *Holder v. Hall* (1994), joined only by Scalia, asserted that the Voting Rights Act "reach[ed] only state enactments that limit citizens' access to the ballot." Insisting that justices should examine only the text of the Voting Rights Act and not the legislative debates responsible for that measure, Thomas declared that the federal government had left states free to structure government offices in ways that in practice prevented persons

of color from winning elections. That opinion was the first time that Thomas, as a justice, attacked the use of race as a criterion for making government decisions. The Court's voting dilution jurisprudence, he declared, relied on "questions of political philosophy, not questions of law" and had contributed to "the racial 'balkinization' of the Nation." "As a practical political matter," Thomas concluded, "our drive to segregate political districts by race can only serve to deepen racial divisions by destroying any need for voters or candidates to build bridges between racial groups or to form voting coalitions."

Although strongly worded, Thomas's concurrence in *Holder* did not go further than Scalia's frequent condemnations of race-based measures. Nor did Thomas appear to push the Court beyond Scalia in solo opinions issued in *Johnson v. Texas* (1993), *Graham v. Collins* (1993), and *Farmer v. Brennan* (1994). His concurring opinions in the first two cases called on the justices to reject past decisions protecting the procedural rights of persons sentenced to death. In *Farmer,* Thomas's concurrence rejected claims that "the Eighth Amendment regulates prison conditions not imposed as part of a sentence." Scalia did not join these opinions, but reasonable observers could conclude Thomas had Scalia's full support. Given that Scalia had dissented from the precedents Thomas would have overruled, Thomas's most important solo opinions written before 1995 could be interpreted as expressing agreement with Scalia rather than marking out new legal terrain.

The United States, the Supreme Court, and Thomas all lurched to the right after the 1994 midterm elections. The Republican Party landslide that year enabled the GOP to gain control of both the Senate and House of Representatives for the first time in more than forty years. The new Republican leadership in the House and Senate was far more sympathetic to Scalia's conservatism than to the moderate approach identified with O'Connor. The Court in 1995, perhaps emboldened by these political and electoral developments, began striking down an unprecedented number of federal laws passed by more liberal regimes and curtailing the powers of state governments to restrict campaign finance, regulate commercial speech, adopt affirmative action policies, and pass land-use regulations. Thomas endorsed this new activism, voting with the majority in all the major cases in which conservative justices declared state and federal laws unconstitutional. Still, the concurring opinions in these cases made clear that the conservative bloc was not internally united behind a common constitutional vision. Kennedy and O'Connor often indicated that they had no desire to significantly turn back the constitutional clock. Rehnquist and Scalia did not fully reveal their ambitions. Thomas alone insisted that the justices should make a full-scale assault on the New Deal constitutional order, that fundamental constitutional questions thought settled by the Hughes and Vinson Courts had to be reopened.

The new judicial revolution was heralded by *United States v. Lopez* (1995). That 5–4 decision, declaring the Gun-Free School Zones Act of 1990 unconstitutional, was the first time in more than fifty years that the Court rejected a claim of federal power under the interstate commerce clause. *Lopez* was followed by other decisions limiting federal power under the commerce clause: a series of cases beginning with *Printz v. United States* (1997) imposing federalism limits on all federal powers set out in Article I; a series of cases beginning with *Seminole Tribe of Florida v. Florida* (1996) prohibiting states from being sued in federal or state courts for violating otherwise valid exercises of Congress's Article I powers; and a series of cases beginning with *City of Boerne v. Flores* (1997) limiting congressional power under Section 5 of the Fourteenth Amendment to enforce the equal protection and due process clauses of Section 1. The conservative justices proved as willing to limit state and federal power in the service of individual rights. In 1993 *Shaw v. Reno* had suggested that race-based legislative districting might be suspect; in 1995 *Miller v. Johnson* declared unconstitutional any districting scheme where "race was the predominant factor." The Court in *Adarand Constructors, Inc. v. Pena* (1995) seemed to ring the judicial death knell for affirmative action.

Thomas agreed with the results in these cases but proclaimed their doctrinal foundations constitution-

ally inadequate. His concurring opinions exhorting greater judicial activism combined with his inability to gain votes for his constitutional views indicated that Thomas was jurisprudentially as far from the new conservative mainstream as were the liberal justices who repeatedly dissented from Rehnquist Court rulings. Thomas was the only member of the Rehnquist Five who did not announce the judgment of the Court in any major or landmark decision handed down from *Lopez* until *Bush v. Gore* (2000). He wrote the opinion for the Court only in cases of constitutional criminal procedure, where he usually rejected claims of individual right on doctrinal grounds, and on less politically charged constitutional matters such as the proper interpretation of the excessive fines clause of the Eighth Amendment (*United States v. Bajakajian*, 1998). For the most part, when Thomas wrote on constitutional matters, he wrote only for himself and his hopes for the future.

Lopez provided the first occasion for Thomas to distinguish himself from O'Connor, Kennedy, Scalia, and Rehnquist. Rehnquist's opinion for the Court repeatedly endorsed New Deal rulings such as *Wickard v. Filburn* (1942) that vested the national government with the power to regulate any "activity that substantially affects interstate commerce." The majority opinion merely insisted that the Gun-Free School Zones Act did not meet the constitutional standard established by past precedent. Congress, Rehnquist wrote, had not made the findings necessary to establish a substantial effect on interstate commerce. The three dissents in *Lopez* agreed with Rehnquist that Congress could constitutionally regulate any economic activity that had a substantial effect on interstate commerce, but they insisted that guns near schools have such an effect. Thomas challenged this consensus. His concurring opinion called on the justices to "reconsider our 'substantial effects' test with an eye toward constructing a standard that reflects the text and history of the Commerce Clause."

Thomas's concurrence in *Lopez* claimed that constitutional jurisprudence took a wrong turn during the New Deal when the Roosevelt Court interpreted the commerce clause as permitting any federal regulation that might have some impact on interstate commerce. Disdaining Rehnquist's effort to limit stricter commerce clause scrutiny to noneconomic activity, Thomas called for a return to pre–New Deal cases that distinguished commerce from production. "The term 'commerce,'" he insisted, was originally "used in contradistinction to productive activities such as manufacturing and agriculture." This constitutional language sharply restricted federal economic power. Although the framers were "well aware that agriculture, manufacturing, and other matters substantially affected commerce," Thomas continued, "the founding generation did not cede authority over all these activities to Congress." Whether these distinctions between different economic activities provided appropriate categories for describing contemporary economic practice was not constitutionally significant. "The boundary between commerce and other matters" that might "seem arbitrary or artificial to some," Thomas wrote, still constituted "a constitutional line that does not grant Congress power over all that substantially affects interstate commerce."

Other concurring opinions during the 1995 term provide more evidence that Thomas was less satisfied than Scalia with the speed at which the Rehnquist Court was moving to the right. In *Rosenberger v. Rector & Visitors of the University of Virginia* (1995), a 5–4 majority ruled that state universities had to fund student newspapers with religious perspectives when funding was available to all other student organizations. Kennedy's majority opinion said that state officials had engaged in unconstitutional viewpoint discrimination and that the establishment clause did not obligate state actors to discriminate against religious groups when distributing public benefits. Thomas would have the Court provide greater accommodation for religious groups. In his view, the Constitution both forbids government discrimination against religious groups when distributing public benefits and permits government to favor religion when making public policy as long as the policy is neutral between religious groups. His concurring opinion suggested that states could limit some benefits to religious groups as long as all religious groups were equally ben-

efited. Thomas found "much to commend" in the position that "the Framers saw the Establishment Clause simply as a prohibition on governmental preferences for some religious faiths over others."

Affirmative action was a second area in which Thomas expressed concern with possible limits on Rehnquist Court activism. He applauded the majority's holding in *Adarand* that "strict scrutiny applies to all government classifications based on race," but he wrote separately to reject suggestions in O'Connor's majority opinion that benign racial classifications might meet that standard. Largely supported by Scalia's concurrence, Thomas declared, "It is irrelevant whether a government's racial classifications are drawn by those who wish to oppress a race or by those who have a sincere desire to help those thought to be disadvantaged." In his view, "racial paternalism" was "as poisonous and pernicious as any other form of discrimination." The beneficiaries of such programs, he believed, would "develop dependencies or . . . adopt an attitude that they are 'entitled' to preferences." Thomas concluded that both hostile and benign discrimination violated fundamental regime principles. "The paternalism that appears to lie at the heart of [affirmative action]," he wrote, "is at war with the principle of inherent equality that underlies and infuses our Constitution."

Thomas more clearly separated himself from Scalia on racial issues in *Missouri v. Jenkins* (1995). The 5–4 conservative majority in that case ruled that federal courts could not order Missouri to fund magnet programs that might reduce segregation in public schools. Thomas's solo concurrence was the only opinion that questioned whether desegregation was a constitutional value. "It never ceases to amaze me," he declared, "that courts are so willing to assume that anything that is predominantly black must be inferior." Echoing views W. E. B. Du Bois had articulated during the 1930s, Thomas endorsed a restoration of black institutions, minus state-enforced segregation. He wrote: "Given that desegregation has not produced the predicted leaps forward in black educational achievement, there is no reason to think that black students cannot learn as well when surrounded by members of their own race as when they are in an integrated environment."

Printz v. United States (1997) provided Thomas with the opportunity to demonstrate his iconoclastic views on both federal power and individual rights. Scalia's majority opinion in that case ruled that the Tenth Amendment forbade federal legislation requiring state officers to implement federal gun laws. Thomas's concurrence maintained that the commerce clause was violated as well by the congressional effort to monitor local gun sales. Federal commerce power, he insisted, did not "extend to the regulation of wholly intrastate, point-of-sale transactions," even though the guns in question may have been shipped from state to state. Thomas further insisted that federal regulations concerning "purely intrastate sale or possession of firearms" might violate the Second Amendment. Alone, he hoped "this Court will have the opportunity to determine whether Justice Story was correct when he wrote that the right to bear arms 'has justly been considered as the palladium of the liberties of a republic.' "

The closest Thomas came to speaking for the conservative justices in a landmark case decided between 1995 and 2000 was his dissent in *U.S. Term Limits v. Thornton* (1995). Writing for the majority, Justice John Paul Stevens held that Arkansas could not constitutionally prevent the names of representatives seeking reelection who had served three terms and senators who had served two terms in Congress from appearing on the ballot. Stevens's opinion held that states could not prescribe additional qualifications for federal representatives beyond those laid out in Article I. Thomas, speaking for Rehnquist, Scalia, and O'Connor, disagreed with both the result and the theory of federalism underlying that ruling. Thomas's dissenting opinion was particularly notable for endorsing a theory of state sovereignty thought abandoned after the Civil War. Challenging doctrine dating from *McCulloch v. Maryland* (1819), he insisted that "the ultimate source of the Constitution's authority is the consent of the people of each individual State, not the consent of the undifferentiated people of the Nation as a whole." This compact theory of the

Constitution structured the appropriate interpretation of federal powers. Thomas maintained that because the states were the parties to the original Constitution, "the States can exercise all powers that the Constitution does not withhold from them." Given that Article 1 did not explicitly declare that the constitutional qualifications for representatives were exclusive, states were free to add whatever qualifications their citizens thought best.

That Thomas was estranged from the conservative bloc on many issues, and the liberal bloc on most, does not mean that he always stood alone during the Clinton presidency. He and Scalia typically took the same conservative positions on issues of constitutional criminal procedure, and they were often joined by the moderate conservatives and sometimes by the liberal justices. In *Mitchell v. Helms* (2000), for example, Thomas wrote for the judicial plurality, sustaining a Louisiana law permitting educational materials to be loaned to religious schools. "If a program offers permissible aid to the religious (including the pervasively sectarian), the areligious, and the irreligious," his opinion stated, "it is a mystery which view of religion the government has established." Thomas also took an active interest in free speech issues. He joined with Scalia and Rehnquist in efforts to strike down all regulations of campaign finance, but joined with the liberal justices in *McIntyre v. Ohio Elections Commission* (1995), a case finding a First Amendment right to anonymous speech. Thomas wrote for an 8–1 majority in *Rubin v. Coors Brewing Co* (1995), holding that the Constitution protected commercial speech and that a federal law prohibiting beer labels from indicating alcohol content did not satisfy the First Amendment standards laid out in *Central Hudson Gas v. Public Service Commission* (1980). That particular show of community spirit proved transient. The next year, in *44 Liquormart v. Rhode Island* (1996), Thomas urged the justices to abandon the *Central Hudson* test when determining whether governments could regulate truthful advertising. "I do not see a philosophical or historical basis," his solo opinion declared, "for asserting that commercial speech is of 'lower value' than 'noncommercial' speech."

Conservative expectations for the Supreme Court were not immediately realized after *Bush v. Gore* and the inauguration of a conservative chief executive. Although Scalia and Thomas enjoyed the strong support of a president whom they had helped put into office and, after 2002, solid majorities in both houses of Congress, conservative electoral victories in 2000, 2002, and 2004 were not matched by conservative judicial triumphs. The federalist revolution stalled; efforts to ban affirmative action failed; small judicial majorities began once again to chip away at the death penalty; and *Roe v. Wade* remained the law of the land. Worse, from a conservative perspective, O'Connor and Kennedy wrote majority and concurring opinions in *Lawrence v. Texas* (2003), the decision holding that states could not punish consensual homosexual sodomy. As the judicial revolution inaugurated in 1995 faded, Thomas found himself increasingly isolated, often even from Scalia and Rehnquist.

One measure of Thomas's isolation on the Court is the decline in the already low number of constitutional cases in which he announced the Court's opinion. Although Thomas has been on the Court since 1991, his majority assignments from 2001 to 2005 resembled those of a newly minted appointee learning the judicial ropes. He wrote the majority opinion in thirty-nine cases, but only nine involved constitutional issues. Nineteen of the twenty-three opinions for the Court Thomas wrote from 2003 to 2005 involved nonconstitutional matters. The only statutory case that captured national attention in which Thomas announced the judicial ruling was *United States v. Oakland Cannabis Buyers' Cooperative* (2001), a decision rejecting any medically necessary exception for marijuana in the Controlled Substances Act. Most of the constitutional issues on which Thomas wrote majority opinions were relatively minor, and concurrences by Kennedy or O'Connor sometimes further reduced the impact of his writing.

Thomas appeared to be in the judicial mainstream only during the 2001–2002 term. That spring he delivered the opinion for the Court in three fairly important constitutional cases. In *Board of Education v. Earls* (2002), Thomas compensated for O'Connor's

defection from the conservative bloc by picking up Justice Stephen Breyer's vote for his opinion sustaining the power of public schools to administer drug tests to all student participants in extracurricular activities. Breyer questioned whether the privacy interests were "negligible," but both he and Thomas agreed that the drug problem in schools was sufficiently troubling to make the mandatory and suspicionless drug testing reasonable. *Federal Maritime Commission v. South Carolina State Ports Authority* (2002) extended state sovereign immunity to administrative agency rulings. After declaring that "dual sovereignty is a defining feature of our Nation's constitutional blueprint," and that "an integral component of that 'residuary and inviolable sovereignty' . . . retained by the States is their immunity from private suits," Thomas concluded that administrative agency hearings were sufficiently judicial to warrant immunizing state agencies from federal administrative adjudications. Thomas also announced that the Court in *Ashcroft v. American Civil Liberties Union* (2002) had rejected a facial challenge to the Child Online Protection Act. The justices agreed that Congress could regulate pornography on the Internet but disputed whether regulatory standards could vary by community. Thomas, for a plurality, called for local standards. He insisted that "if a publisher chooses to send its material into a particular community, this Court's jurisprudence teaches that it is the publisher's responsibility to abide by that community's standard." Justice O'Connor's crucial concurring opinion disagreed. She suggested that a judicial majority would sustain a conviction only if the trial court adopted a national standard for determining what constituted proscribable pornography.

Thomas's continued penchant for solo opinions more clearly marked his isolation during the last years of the Rehnquist Court. No other justice signed fifty-three of the ninety-three concurring or dissenting opinions Thomas issued from 2001 to 2005. Two-thirds of his sixty concurrences and dissents in constitutional cases were solo. Again 2002 was the major exception, the only year in which a slight majority of Thomas's dissenting and concurring opinions in constitutional cases attracted at least one other justice. In some cases, Thomas did little more than endorse or provide an addendum to another opinion. For example, his dissenting opinion in *Lawrence v. Texas* described the Texas ban on homosexual sodomy as "silly," but not unconstitutional. Although Thomas's opinions in affirmative action cases reemphasized his belief that race-conscious measures designed to benefit persons of color were as pernicious as Jim Crow, the constitutional standards he applied in *Grutter v. Bollinger* (2003) and *Gratz v. Bollinger* (2003) were those that Scalia articulated in his separate opinions. At times, however, Thomas's solo opinions were not mere elaborations or endorsements of other opinions, but his laying out pieces of a constitutional vision alien to his colleagues.

Federal power was the area in which Thomas most often expressed frustration with the Rehnquist Court. His solo opinions from 2001 to 2005 continued to insist that the commerce clause did not permit the federal government to regulate agriculture, manufacturing, and production, while he offered three additional inroads into New Deal jurisprudence. Thomas's dissent in *Gonzales v. Raich* (2005), a California medical marijuana case, rejected reasonableness tests under the necessary and proper clause, suggesting instead the more demanding standard that "there must be an 'obvious, simple, and direct relation' between the intrastate ban and the regulation of interstate commerce." A federal ban on medical marijuana, he insisted, was constitutionally improper because that policy "encroached on States' traditional police powers to define the criminal law and to protect the health, safety, and welfare of their citizens." Thomas's solo concurrences in *Sabri v. United States* (2004) and *Cutter v. Wilkinson* (2005) rejected rationality tests under the spending clause in favor of requiring federal spending to have "an obvious, simple and direct relationship" with the end to be achieved. Thomas was the only member of the Rehnquist Court to question precedents on legislative delegation that date from before the New Deal. In *Whitman v. American Trucking Associations, Inc.* (2001), the other eight members of the Court debated

whether the delegation under review met the "intelligible principle" requirement set out in *J. W. Hampton, Jr., & Co. v. United States* (1928). Thomas announced he was "not convinced that the intelligible principle doctrine serves to prevent all cessions of legislative power." His opinion called for the justices to revisit questions of legislative delegation thought settled by the Hughes Court. No other Rehnquist Court justice accepted that invitation.

When constitutional issues raised by the war on terror came before him, Thomas remained isolated from his colleagues, but in these cases he endorsed fewer constitutional limitations on federal power than they did. *Hamdi v. Rumsfeld* (2004) raised questions about the extent to which federal statutes and the Constitution limited presidential power to declare an American citizen an "enemy combatant." Justices O'Connor, Scalia, and David Souter agreed that the Bush administration had unconstitutionally deprived Yaser Hamdi of his liberty by failing to give him any opportunity to rebut claims that he had affiliated with the Taliban. Thomas alone would have the executive completely unfettered. He insisted that the matter was "of a kind for which the Judiciary has neither aptitude, facilities nor responsibility and which has long been held to belong to the domain of political power not subject to judicial intrusion or inquiry." "Judicial interference in those domains," Thomas continued, "destroys the purpose of vesting primary responsibility in a unitary Executive." In his view, courts had no role to play when the nation was a war. "The Power to protect the Nation," he declared citing *The Federalist Papers*, " 'ought to exist without limitation.' "

Thomas also ventured further afield than any other Rehnquist Court justice on matters concerning the constitutional law of religion. Inspired by the work of Yale Law School professor Akhil Amar, Thomas began questioning "whether and how" the establishment clause "should constrain state action under the Fourteenth Amendment." His concurring opinion in *Zelman v. Simmons-Harris* (2003) suggested that "state action should be evaluated on different terms than similar action by the Federal Government." Thomas claimed that "while the

Federal Government may 'make no law respecting an establishment of religion,' the States may pass laws that include or touch on religious matters so long as these laws do not impede free exercise rights or any other individual religious liberty interest." The next year, Thomas bluntly declared that "the Establishment Clause is a federalism provision, which, for this reason, resists incorporation." State religious exercises were constitutional, his solo concurrence in *Elk Grove Unified School District v. Newdow* (2004) declared, as long as the state did not require participation by "tax or penalty."

This iconoclasm extended to the takings clause of the Fifth Amendment. In *Kelo v. City of New London* (2005), the other eight justices on the Rehnquist Court debated whether past precedents permitted localities to condemn property, with compensation, to facilitate economic development. Justices Ruth Bader Ginsburg, Kennedy, Stevens, Souter, and Breyer insisted that if, as previous decisions had held, land condemned for urban renewal satisfied the "public use" clause of the Fifth Amendment, then condemning land for economic development was constitutional. O'Connor's dissent, joined by Scalia and Rehnquist, distinguished *Kelo* from those precedents. Thomas's solo dissent proposed discarding one hundred years of precedent that he believed "replaced the Public Use Clause with a 'Public Purpose' Clause." Combining textual and historical arguments, he insisted that evidence that the taking produced public benefits was constitutionally not relevant. "The most natural reading of the Clause," he declared, "is that it allows the government to take property only if the government owns, or the public has a legal right to use, the property, as opposed to taking it for any public purpose or necessity whatsoever."

Any evaluation of a justice's jurisprudence reveals as much about the critic as the subject of criticism. That proponents of liberal judicial activism are more critical of Thomas than proponents of conservative judicial activism is hardly surprising. Whether Thomas engages in constitutional interpretation or legislates from the bench depends to a fair degree on whether one believes the Constitution properly inter-preted supports the New Deal/Great Society principles that he detests or imposes the sharp limits on federal power that he champions. How one evaluates Thomas's claim in *Stenberg v. Carhart* (2000) that judicial protection for abortion rights has "no historical or doctrinal pedigree" and is "illegitimate" depends on contestable assertions about the constitutional pedigree of reproductive choice.

Evaluating Thomas's jurisprudence is especially difficult because he practices originalism inconsistently and selectively. He is concerned with how constitutional language was understood at the time of framing only in some areas of constitutional law. He offers detailed investigations into the original meaning of constitutional provisions when writing on commerce and takings clause issues, but barely acknowledges history when voting to strike down bans on commerce speech or affirmative action policies. Law professor Scott Gerber provided a glimpse into this practice when he suggested that Thomas in race and speech cases is a liberal originalist committed to the original principles underlying the constitutional order, but a conservative originalist in criminal rights and federalism cases committed to the particular practices entrenched by the framers. What neither Thomas nor Gerber offers is any explanation as to why aspirational reasoning is appropriate in some cases, but not in others.

Thomas clearly is a judicial activist, if activism is defined by a willingness to strike down federal and state laws that a reasonable person might think constitutional. Professor Thomas Keck found that from 1994 until 2000 Thomas voted to strike down federal laws in twenty-five cases. This tied him with Scalia for the highest number of invalidations on the Rehnquist Court. This activism increased during the next half decade. Among the types of federal laws Thomas routinely votes to invalidate are restrictions on campaign finance, affirmative action policies, bans on commerce speech, efforts to limit state sovereign immunity, and federal efforts to expand individual rights, such as the Religious Freedom Restoration Act, which Thomas believes are beyond the power of Congress to enact. Although Thomas is no more activist than the other justices on the Rehnquist Court when judging the constitutionality of state laws, he still exercises judicial power aggressively. Affirmative action programs, land restrictions, state campaign finance restrictions, and local laws restricting commerce speech have been particular targets of his ire.

Thomas is also a judicial activist if activism is defined by a willingness to overrule past precedent. No Supreme Court justice in American history has been less constrained by previous judicial rulings. In three 1992 cases, he urged the Court to overrule or rethink basic confrontation clause doctrine (*White v. Illinois*), abandon heightened rationality in some areas of equal protection law (*Nordlinger v. Hahn*), and reverse past cases forbidding litigants to use race when exercising peremptory challenges (*Georgia v. McCollum*). He later urged justices to abandon the pervasive sectarian test and overrule past cases limiting state power to provide religious organizations with public benefits (*Mitchell v. Helms*, 2000); overrule those parts of *Buckley v. Valeo* (1976) that permit some regulation of campaign finance (*Nixon v. Shrink Missouri Government PAC*, 2000); overrule past decisions applying a balancing test to truthful commercial advertising (*Glickman v. Wileman Brothers & Elliott, Inc.* 1997); overrule decisions limiting punitive damages (*Cooper Industries v. Leatherman Tool Group, Inc.*, 2001); and rethink judicial decisions providing less protection to broadcast media (*Denver Area Educational Telecommunications Consortium v. FCC*, 1996).

He would overrule or rethink decisions holding that prison conditions may constitute cruel and unusual punishment (*Farmer v. Brennan*, 1994); decisions providing prisoners with some access to legal materials (*Lewis v. Casey*, 1996); the line of cases, beginning with *Griffin v. Illinois* (1956), providing some assistance to impoverished persons appealing criminal convictions (*M. L. B. v. S. L. J.*, 1996); virtually all limits the Supreme Court places on the capital sentencing process (*Graham v. Collins*, 1993); a decision, *Papachistou v. Jacksonville* (1972), declaring loitering statutes unconstitutionally vague (*City of Chicago v. Morales*, 1999); decisions providing notice of various remedies for persons whose property has

been seized during criminal investigations (*West Covina v. Perkins*, 1999); decisions forbidding adverse commentary on the exercise of Fifth Amendment rights (*Mitchell v. United States*, 1999); decisions claiming that the Fifth Amendment does not protect the production of incriminating evidence (*United States v. Hubbell*, 2000); and cases justifying some suspicionless roadblock searches (*Indianapolis v. Edmond*, 2000).

Thomas would overrule every judicial case providing constitutional protection for abortion rights (*Stenberg v. Carhart*, 2000) and reconsider every judicial decision using the due process clauses of the Fifth and Fourteenth Amendments to protect substantial freedoms (*Troxel v. Granville*, 2000). He insists that the entire commerce clause doctrine developed after the New Deal be reconsidered (*United States v. Lopez*, 1995), as well as modern decisions on legislative delegation (*Whitman v. American Trucking Associations*, 2001), the spending power (*Cutter v. Wilkinson*, 2005), and the necessary and proper clause (*Gonzales v. Raich*, 2005). Age provides little protection for past precedent. Thomas wants the justices to rethink past understandings of the privileges and immunities clause dating back to the *Slaughterhouse Cases* (1873) (*Saenz v. Roe*, 1999); not only overrule the Chase Court's decision in *Woodruff v. Parham* (1869), limiting to foreign trade the constitutional prohibition on state efforts to lay duties on imports or exports, but also abandon dormant commerce clause doctrine first developed by the Marshall and Taney Courts (*Camps Newfound/Owatonna v. Town of Harrison*, 1997); and rethink the Jay Court's decision in *Calder v. Bull* (1798), limiting the *ex post facto* clause to retroactive criminal legislation (*Eastern Enterprises v. Apfel*, 1998).

Thomas was the only justice on the Rehnquist Court interested in the constitutional scholarship of the 1990s. The other conservative justices largely limited their activism to the parameters marked out by the conservative academics opposed to the direction of the Burger Court. Thomas, by comparison, often relies on and cites more contemporary works, particularly those that support conservative judicial activism or justify greater state solicitude for religion. His solo concurrences in *Lopez* and *Raich* urged constitutionalists to incorporate the work of libertarians such as Randy Barnett and Richard Epstein into constitutional law. Thomas frequently advances new originalist positions only after those positions appear in scholarly works. Amar's *The Bill of Rights* (1998) seems to have inspired the justice's claim that the Fourteenth Amendment did not incorporate the establishment clause. Thomas first objected to the twentieth-century interpretation of "public use" after Eric Claeys published an essay in the *Northwestern Law Review* insisting that "public use" during the framing was limited to takings of property that would be used by the government or open to the entire public.

This effort to incorporate contemporary conservative scholarship into constitutional law is problematic. One difficulty is that Thomas often rejects a more general consensus among historians in favor of contrarian scholarship that favors preferred results. Although Thomas cites law professor (now federal judge) Michael McConnell's article in *Virginia Law Review* for the proposition that *Brown v. Board of Education* (1954) was consistent with the original understanding of the framers, he does not mention the far more voluminous legal and historical literature questioning this proposition. Prominent legal historians insist that the persons responsible for the Fourteenth Amendment supported race-conscious measures designed to benefit persons of color, and the dominant strain in contemporary Fifth Amendment scholarship suggests that in 1791 and 1868 "public use" was understood to refer to any taking that conferred a benefit on the public. Relying on the most conservative historical scholarship in different areas of constitutional law may result in a jurisprudence that does not add up to a coherent whole. Thomas appropriated Boston University law professor Randy Barnett's writings on the original understanding of federalism in *Gonzales v. Raich* when he insisted on a narrowly limited federal commerce power, but Barnett insists the same principles support the majority decision in *Lawrence v. Texas*. Amar's claim that the Fourteenth Amendment did not incorporate the establishment clause is embedded in a more general claim that the Fourteenth Amendment ought to be interpreted far more expansively than Thomas has been willing to do. Whether the conservative writings Thomas cites are part of a consistent jurisprudence or whether he merely cherry-picks whatever historical scholarship is available for supporting conservative results remains to be seen.

Great dissenters have had different fates on the Supreme Court. William Brennan and Thurgood Marshall during the 1980s became the fading voices of the *ancien régime*, defending Great Society constitutional visions that no longer had the power to command judicial or popular majorities. John Marshall Harlan and Oliver Wendell Holmes heralded the future. Their respective claims that "our Constitution is color blind" and that the government may regulate only speech that presents a "clear and present danger" became the unquestioned constitutional law of the land only after they left the bench. William Johnson and Peter Daniel represent paths not taken. Their views on natural law and judicial power were accepted by neither their judicial ancestors nor descendants. Thomas is not, as Justice Story described himself, "the last of the old race of judges." Whether he will be remembered as a prophet or a crank is for the future to determine.

—*Mark A. Graber*

BIBLIOGRAPHY

Scott Gerber, *First Principles: The Jurisprudence of Clarence Thomas* (1999), is the only scholarly analysis of the justice's opinions. The work is solid but focuses on Thomas's first year on the Court. Those interested in sympathetic popular biographies should read Ken Foskett, *Judging Thomas: The Life and Times of Clarence Thomas* (2004); or Andrew Peyton Thomas, *Clarence Thomas: A Biography* (2001). Those preferring criticism will enjoy Ronald Suresh Roberts, *Clarence Thomas and the Tough Luck Crowd: Counterfeit Heroes and Unhappy Truths* (1995); and John Greenya, *Silent Justice: The Clarence Thomas Story* (2001). The same partisan split characterizes accounts of the Thomas confirmation hearings. John Danforth, *Resurrection: The Confirmation of Clarence Thomas* (1994), is sympathetic; Jane

Mayer and Jill Abramson, *Strange Justice: The Selling of Clarence Thomas* (1994), is not.

Studies of the Rehnquist Court provide additional insight into the jurisprudence of Clarence Thomas and his status on the tribunal. The two best are Thomas M. Keck, *The Most Activist Supreme Court in History* (2004); and Mark Tushnet, *A Court Divided* (2005). Keck does an excellent job documenting Rehnquist Court activism. Tushnet highlights important differences between Thomas and Scalia. Mark A. Graber's essay on Justice Thomas in Earl Maltz, ed., *Rehnquist Justice: Understanding the Court Dynamic* (2003), focuses on Thomas's marginalization and his disdain for precedential reasoning.

NOTEWORTHY OPINIONS

United States v. Fordice, 505 U.S. 717 (1992) (Concurrence)

United States v. Lopez, 514 U.S. 549 (1995) (Concurrence)

U.S. Term Limits, Inc. v. Thornton, 514 U.S. 779 (1995) (Dissent)

Printz v. United States, 521 U.S. 898 (1997) (Concurrence)

Ashcroft v. American Civil Liberties Union, 542 U.S. 656 (2002)

Gonzales v. Raich, 545 U.S. ___ (2005) (Dissent)

Kelo v. City of New London, 545 U.S. ___ (2005) (Dissent)

SMITH THOMPSON

Birth: January 17, 1768, Dutchess County, New York.

Education: Graduated Princeton, 1788; read law under James Kent; admitted to the bar, 1792; honorary law doctorates from Yale, 1824; Princeton, 1824; and Harvard, 1835.

Official Positions: Member, New York state legislature, 1800; member, New York Constitutional Convention, 1801; associate justice, New York Supreme Court, 1802–1814; member, New York State Board of Regents, 1813; chief justice, New York Supreme Court, 1814–1818; secretary of the navy, 1819–1823.

Supreme Court Service: Recess appointment as associate justice by President James Monroe, September 1, 1823, to replace Henry Brockholst Livingston, who had died; nominated associate justice by Monroe, December 8, 1823; confirmed by the Senate, December 9, 1823, by a voice vote; took judicial oath February 10, 1823; served until December 18, 1843; replaced by Samuel Nelson, nominated by President John Tyler.

Death: December 18, 1843, Poughkeepsie, New York.

Smith Thompson served on the U.S. Supreme Court for twenty years. During that long tenure, he wrote more than eighty-five opinions, and states' rights served as the most significant theme of his judicial writing. Thompson consistently opposed the centralizing federalism of Chief Justice John Marshall.

Thompson came to the Court as a successful New York politician. After practicing law for several years, he became part of the Livingston faction. A string of political offices culminated in his appointment as state chief justice, replacing James Kent. His states' rights beliefs became clear in a decision upholding a state monopoly grant to steamboat promoter Robert Livingston that Marshall later overturned in *Gibbons v. Ogden* (1824), which held the monopoly violated federal commerce powers. Presi-

dent James Monroe appointed Thompson secretary of the navy in 1818, and while Thompson maneuvered for a possible presidential campaign, Monroe named him to the Supreme Court to fill the seat vacated by the death of his fellow New Yorker, Henry Brockholst Livingston. Thompson continued to be an active politician on the bench and even launched an unsuccessful campaign for governor of New York against Martin Van Buren in 1828.

Thompson's devotion to states' rights played a role in his appointment, and once on the bench, he opposed Marshall's centralizing tendencies. For example, Thompson joined the majority in *Ogden v. Saunders* (1827), in which the Court upheld the constitutionality of state insolvency statutes limiting debt liability contracted prior to the passage of the acts.

This decision overruled Marshall's holding in *Sturges v. Crowninshield* (1819). Thompson defended the acts as legitimate exercises of state bankruptcy authority held concurrently with federal bankruptcy power.

These commitments are also evident in his two most important decisions. In 1831 he dissented from Marshall's opinion in *Cherokee Nation v. Georgia*, which denied jurisdiction to hear the tribe's complaints against their forced removal. Along with Justice Joseph Story, Thompson disagreed with Marshall's assertion of federal control over the tribe and argued that the Cherokee should be considered a foreign nation with a right to be heard in the Supreme Court. Seven years later, in *Kendall v. United States* (1838), Thompson wrote the majority opinion upholding the power of the District of Columbia Circuit Court to order an officer of the executive branch to perform a ministerial duty. The case involved a suit for payment against the postmaster, and Thompson's opinion served to limit the autonomous authority of the president.

Thompson served on the Court and continued to dabble in politics until his death in 1843.

—*Michael Grossberg*

Smith Thompson

BIBLIOGRAPHY

Little has been written of Thompson, but see Gerald T. Dunne's sketch in Friedman and Israel, *Justices,* vol.1, 473.

NOTEWORTHY OPINIONS

Cherokee Nation v. Georgia, 30 U.S. 1 (1831) (Dissent)

Kendall v. United States ex. rel. Stokes, 37 U.S. 528 (1838)

THOMAS TODD

Birth: January 23, 1765, King and Queen County, Virginia.

Education: Graduated from Liberty Hall (Washington and Lee University), Lexington, Virginia, 1783; read law under Harry Innes; admitted to the bar in 1788.

Official Positions: Clerk, federal district for Kentucky, 1792–1801; clerk, Kentucky House of Representatives, 1792–1801; clerk, Kentucky Court of Appeals (Supreme Court), 1799–1801; judge, Kentucky Court of Appeals, 1801–1806; chief justice, 1806–1807.

Supreme Court Service: Nominated associate justice by President Thomas Jefferson, February 28, 1807, to fill a newly created seat; confirmed by the Senate, March 2, 1807, by a voice vote; took judicial oath May 4, 1807; served until February 7, 1826; replaced by Robert Trimble, nominated by President John Quincy Adams.

Death: February 7, 1826, Frankfort, Kentucky.

The youngest son of Richard and Elizabeth Richards Todd, Thomas Todd exemplified the American revolutionary ideals of civic virtue, independence of mind, and entrepreneurial zeal. As the author of a Supreme Court memorial explained in 1839, Todd's early experience with hardship—extreme poverty, the loss of both parents, a bankrupt guardian—fostered "that energy and enterprise which afterwards signalized his character."

These qualities emerged well before Todd's nomination to the Court. After a stint in the Virginia line late in the Revolution, he graduated from Liberty Hall and accepted a post as tutor in the household of his cousin, Harry Innes, an up-and-coming attorney. When Innes moved to Kentucky (then Virginia's westernmost county) in 1783 to become judge of the Supreme Court of Judicature for the Kentucky district, Todd accompanied the family as tutor and law clerk. No doubt in response to ripe opportunities pre-sented by chaotic land titling in "Kentucke," Todd mastered surveying, which was a lucrative sideline in emerging states, and land law—perhaps the most exacting (some would say arcane) legal specialization available to a nineteenth-century practitioner.

Within a few years, Todd had gained a reputation as a gifted businessman, lawyer, and penman; he also found Kentucky's Jeffersonian political culture entirely congenial. He served as clerk of the Kentucky House of Representatives from 1792 to 1801, as well as clerk of several conventions organized to negotiate the terms of the 1792 separation agreement between Kentucky and Virginia and draft a state constitution. Between 1801 and 1807 he served ably as associate justice and then chief justice of the Kentucky Court of Appeals. Todd had crossed the Appalachians with little more than ambition in his pocket; by 1807, when Jefferson tapped him for the federal bench—and, with it, the new Seventh Circuit—Todd had established a respected law practice, first in Danville as a circuit-riding frontier lawyer, then in the capital city of Frankfort, and a reputation for honesty and precision. He also had amassed a fortune, much of it through land agency and speculation.

Todd has yet to attract a biographer, partly because his written legacy seems thin. He produced only twelve opinions for the Court, mainly in land cases, including a *per curiam* opinion in *McKim v. Voorhies* (1812), which one authority wrongly terms a "statement" rather than an "opinion"; one narrowly procedural concurrence in an 1812 chancery case, *Wallen v. Williams*; and a little-known 1810 opinion, dissenting in part, in *Finley v. Lynn*. None of these rulings contributed directly to American constitutional law—the main avenue to judicial "greatness." In addition, because historians rarely consult the manuscript minute books of Todd's busy circuit court (shared with Judge Robert Trimble of Kentucky), where many learned opinions appear in politically explosive contract, taxation, and land cases, much of his legal writing escapes notice. To make matters worse, Todd missed five out of nineteen terms because of illness or misadventure, eschewed publicity, and left few private papers. Therefore, scholars wryly conclude, with G. Edward White, that Todd's "most conspicuous act" as a jurist was perhaps to "marry Dolley Madison's sister" in 1812.

These impressions are mistaken. First, as White also notes, Todd's colleagues viewed him as an invaluable "strategic member" of the bench and the quintes-

Thomas Todd

sential team player. Despite a Jeffersonian cast of mind, he staunchly supported Chief Justice John Marshall's judicial federalism when it mattered most—in rulings that devotees of states' rights objected to most strenuously; in the process, he antagonized friends and family in Kentucky. For example, he was absent from the Court in 1819, but nevertheless agreed with Marshall's opinion on the controversial question of state taxation of the Second Bank of the United States in *McCulloch v. Maryland,* as he did five years later in *Osborn v. Bank of the United States* (1824), an Ohio case appealed from Todd's own circuit, when Ohio refused to comply with *McCulloch*. Todd had been a charter bank stockholder; he apparently thought that the institution would benefit the capital-poor Republic, so long as stockholders elected Jeffersonian directors. Kentuckians disagreed. Between 1819 and 1825, Kentucky's new, aggressive Anti-Relief Party loudly denounced *McCulloch, Osborn,* and the "traitorous" Todd as sellouts to an aristocratic "Monied Hydra"; similar remarks filled newspaper columns in Tennessee, Ohio, and Missouri.

At the least, then, Todd was a disciplined, thick-skinned judge: although "bred in a different political school from that of the Chief justice," wrote Joseph Story, Todd "never failed to sustain those great principles of constitutional law on which the security of the Union depends. He never gave up to party, what he thought belonged to the country."

He also was a hardworking, substantial scholar and a savvy politician content to remain in the wings.

As Story and Marshall said repeatedly, Todd was a fount of specialized legal information and, as rebellion and antijudicial sentiment advanced in the West and South after 1819, a reliable source of political advice, notably about the objectives of seemingly lawless, contract-smashing state assemblies.

A few examples make the point: Todd quietly labored to shore up the Marshall Court's claim of jurisdiction under Section 24 of the Judiciary Act of 1789; to defend the sanctity of agreements—including treaties and interstate compacts, both of which mightily concerned Marshall—in several cases involving pacts between states or with Indian nations; and generally to advance Marshall's campaign for economic union and judicial control of economic development. In a little-read 1818 decision in *Robinson v. Campbell*, for example, Todd refused to allow Tennessee legislators to question, merely on the ground of shifting boundaries or inconvenience to settlers, the validity of titles originating in Virginia law and secured by an 1802 compact between Tennessee and Virginia.

To encourage stability in landholding and what he termed in *Robinson* "the purposes of justice," and perhaps to lend support (with Story) to the notion that virtuous republicans kept their promises, Todd leaned hard upon traditional English rules in land and contract cases and resisted legislative innovation whenever it seemed to limit the courts' ability to defend old, lawful claims of right against junior, merely equitable, or doubtful claims. In 1814 Todd insisted in *Vowles v. Craig*, a land case appealed from Kentucky, that a seller could not reclaim part of a tract once the land had been conveyed lawfully, even when the original survey was erroneous and the buyer received a windfall of 700 acres. Buyers should be able to rely on the terms of lawful agreements. In *Preston v. Browder* (1816), North Carolina land claimants pegged their hopes to a survey rendered illegal by a 1777 statute that expressly placed off limits Cherokee lands not yet ceded by treaty. Todd praised state legislators for insisting on cession in advance of surveys and refused to legitimize the specious claim. How, asked Todd in *Preston*, could Americans "parcel out vacant lands to industrious people" or provide an "easy subsistence for families" if they ignored sound laws, "provoking hostilities with . . . tribes" and "diminishing the strength of the country"? In an extensive republic, stability and prosperity depended on close attention to law and to collective as well as individual honor.

At the same time, Todd contributed heroically to the Story-Marshall campaign to stem corruptions of legal science in his native trans-Appalachian West, often by doing the spadework for subsequent constitutional interpretations. When the Panic of 1819 triggered a rash of emergency banking and contract measures, alongside Bank of the United States taxation bills, throughout the West and South, Todd and Trimble labored long and hard at circuit court sessions in Frankfort, Chillicothe, and Nashville to unhinge state debtor relief measures. Among these were "three-quarters" execution laws (postponing forced sales until buyers could offer at least three-fourths of the property's pre-panic value), replevy statutes (authorizing debtors, once creditors refused to accept emergency paper money in debt settlement, to offer a state-supported bond promising future settlement), and state-funded debtor banks in Tennessee, Missouri, and Kentucky.

Time and again, the two increasingly unpopular judges blasted relief laws as unconstitutional abrogations of the contracts clause and denounced currency issued by unstable debtor banks. Their incendiary 1819 and 1820 circuit court opinions in well-publicized actions of debt, such as *Bank of the United States v. Joshua Norvell* and *Bank of the United States v. James Morrison*, elicited extraordinary rage in the press as did pro-bank rulings in hundreds of additional debt cases docketed after 1819. Other decisions, such as *Wayman v. Southard* (1825) and *Briscoe v. Bank of the Commonwealth of Kentucky* (1834), eventually worked their way to the Supreme Court as tests of the constitutionality of emergency economic legislation and bills of credit issued by debtor banks; in the resulting "Kentucky Cases," Marshall reworked but did not fundamentally alter the research and arguments deposited in Seventh Circuit opinions.

Finally, Todd laid foundations for the Court's notorious opinions (Story's in 1821 and Story and

Bushrod Washington's in 1823, after the case was reconsidered) in another Kentucky land case, *Green v. Biddle,* which pronounced the state's compensatory occupant laws an abrogation of the 1792 separation agreement with Virginia and therefore a violation of the contract clause. In case after case on circuit, including dozens of suits brought by heirs of John Green, the plaintiff in *Green v. Biddle,* Todd beat back adverse, equitable claims of settlers and speculators in order to defend the legal right of out-of-state claimants. In an unpublished circuit court opinion in *John Green's Heirs v. Bernard Gittner* (1819), involving many of the parties named in Biddle's case, Todd took dead aim at allegedly unprincipled occupant laws and aggressive deployment of the rules of equity to defeat lawful claims, laying out many of the precedents to which both Story and Washington later referred. So reliant were they on Todd's work that Story, in a letter to Todd, referred to *Green v. Biddle* as "our opinion." Todd did not mindlessly oppose local control over land titling; rather, he abhorred what he took to be a rising tide of immoral disregard for the terms of promises, whether made by states or individuals.

Todd's contributions to American jurisprudence, in short, far exceed his reputation. Few judges were so fluent in the particulars of the common law, relevant treatises, and conflicts of law jurisprudence; Story said for good reason that Todd enjoyed "the legal confidence of all who knew him." Many of the memorable constitutional statements fielded by the Marshall Court before 1825–1826, when members began to soften legal purism and economic nationalism, commenced as land or contract disputes in Todd's Seventh Circuit. Todd stood at the ready with copious research and well-crafted opinions in hand. He entered public life as a foot soldier and perhaps died a foot soldier (albeit a wealthy one, with an estate exceeding $70,000). But this unassuming closet Jeffersonian was an indispensable member of Marshall's federalizing cavalry, devoted simultaneously to his chief justice and to the moral fabric of the Republic. Small wonder that his colleagues held him, to borrow the Supreme Court memorializer's elegant phrase, in "sacred regard."

—*Sandra F. VanBurkleo*

BIBLIOGRAPHY

There are no full biographies of Todd; for short sketches, see Fred Israel, "Thomas Todd," in Friedman and Israel, *Justices,* vol. 1, 407; Charles Lee Jr., "Thomas Todd," in John Kleber, ed., *The Kentucky Encyclopedia* (1992), 888; and "The Honorable Thomas Todd, Formerly Chief Justice of the State of Kentucky etc.," in 38 U.S. iii–viii, (1839), the best contemporary sketch and the official Court memorial.

On the Seventh Circuit, see Thomas Speed, *History of the United States Courts in Kentucky* (1896), a still solid descriptive account of an evolving federal judicial presence in nineteenth-century Kentucky; Mary K. Bonsteel Tachau, *Federal Courts in the Early Republic: Kentucky, 1789–1816* (1978), a pathbreaking study of personnel and practice of the earliest Kentucky bench; and Sandra F. VanBurkleo, " 'The Paws of Banks': The Origins and Significance of Kentucky's Decision to Tax Federal Bankers," *Journal of the Early Republic* 9 (1989): 457, a revisionist study of the milieu giving rise to relief parties, bank taxes, and controversial Seventh Circuit rulings.

For the Supreme Court during this period and Todd's contributions, see George Haskins and Herbert Johnson, *Foundations of Power: John Marshall, 1801–1815* (1981); and G. Edward White, *The Marshall Court and Cultural Change, 1815–1835* (1988), vols. 2 and 3 of the *Holmes Devise History.*

NOTEWORTHY OPINIONS

Vowles v. Craig, 12 U.S. 371 (1814)

Preston v. Browder, 14 U.S. 116 (1816)

ROBERT TRIMBLE

Birth: November 17, 1776, Berkeley County, Virginia.

Education: Bourbon Academy; Kentucky Academy; studied law under George Nicholas and James Brown; admitted to the bar in 1803.

Official Positions: Kentucky state representative, 1802; judge, Kentucky Court of Appeals, 1807–1809; U.S. district attorney for Kentucky, 1813–1817; U.S. district judge, 1817–1826.

Supreme Court Service: Nominated associate justice by President John Quincy Adams, April 12, 1826, to replace Thomas Todd, who had died; confirmed by the Senate, May 9, 1826, by a 27–5 vote; took judicial oath June 16, 1826; served until August 25, 1828; replaced by John McLean, nominated by President Andrew Jackson.

Death: August 25, 1828, Paris, Kentucky.

Robert Trimble had a tragically brief tenure on the U.S. Supreme Court. His sudden illness and death cut short what many of his contemporaries thought would be a very distinguished judicial career.

Trimble was born in Berkeley County, Virginia, in 1777. His father's Protestant ancestors had emigrated from Ireland to America for religious freedom. When Robert was two years old, the family moved to Kentucky, where they prospered at farming on Howard's Creek in Clark County. Robert was taught at home by his grandfather, but he also attended organized schools on the Kentucky frontier. He entered Bourbon Academy in 1795, but illness forced him to leave in less than a year. He then studied law in a class of nineteen students organized by Transylvania University. Kentucky's first attorney general, George Nicholas, taught the class and was succeeded after his death by James Brown. Trimble was admitted to the bar in 1803, the same year he married Nancy Timberlake.

Appointment to the U.S. Supreme Court capped Trimble's successful career as a Kentucky lawyer and jurist. Like many other judges, he repeatedly left the state bench to earn a higher income as a practicing attorney. Nevertheless, a flourishing and lucrative practice did not deter Trimble from accepting appointment by President James Madison as the federal district judge for Kentucky in 1817. Amid bitter battles over state-federal jurisdictional questions, Trimble supported the supremacy of the federal government, which led President John Quincy Adams to nominate Trimble to the Supreme Court on the death of Kentuckian Thomas Todd. Five senators voted against the nomination because of Trimble's belief in federal supremacy. On confirmation, he became Adams's first and only appointment to the Court.

During his brief two terms, Trimble agreed with Chief Justice John Marshall in the vast majority of cases. Of the 103 opinions delivered during those two sessions, he spoke for the Court sixteen times. Most of

Trimble's cases dealt with technical litigation and procedural matters. His most important opinion came in *Ogden v. Saunders* (1827), when he departed from his faith in federal supremacy. For the Marshall Court, this was an unusual case in that the four justices in the majority could not agree on a single rationale and instead issued *seriatim* opinions. Trimble's opinion upheld the constitutionality of a New York bankruptcy law against claims that by authorizing the discharge of the person of the debtor and the debtor's future property, the act violated the contract clause of the Constitution. Marshall, along with Joseph Story and Gabriel Duvall, dissented, claiming the act impaired the obligation of contract.

Trimble's other major decision came in connection with *The Antelope* (1827), in which the Court had also issued opinions in 1825 and 1826. In this case, the Court confronted the legality of the slave trade under international law. At stake was the fate of a cargo of slaves on a foreign ship seized by an American revenue cutter. Two years earlier the Court had ruled in the same case that no matter how reprehensible, the slave trade had not been outlawed and slave ships could not be seized. Trimble reinforced this decision by upholding the return of the slaves to their owners.

In his first opinion for the Court, *Montgomery v. Hernandez* (1827), Trimble spelled out a procedure that the modern Court still follows. He said that to obtain a hearing in the Supreme Court, for a violation of federal rights, one must first have raised that issue in the state court.

Trimble caught a "malignant bilious fever" and died shortly after his second term on the Court. Eulogies spoke of the great promise he had shown as a justice, and his colleagues mourned what had been the start of an illustrious career on the bench. Marshall wrote to Sen. Henry Clay of Kentucky, "I need not say how deeply I regret the loss of Judge Trimble. He was distinguished for sound sense, uprightness of intention, and legal knowledge. His superior cannot be found. I wish we may find his equal."

—*Michael Grossberg*

Robert Trimble

BIBLIOGRAPHY

The only biographical sketch of Trimble is by Fred L. Israel, in Friedman and Israel, *Justices,* vol. 1, 511.

NOTEWORTHY OPINIONS

The Antelope, 25 U.S. 546 (1827)

Montgomery v. Hernandez, 25 U.S. 129 (1827)

Ogden v. Saunders, 25 U.S. 213 (1827)

WILLIS VAN DEVANTER

Birth: April 17, 1859, Marion, Indiana.

Education: Indiana Asbury University (DePauw), A.B., 1878; University of Cincinnati Law School, LL.B., 1881.

Official Positions: City attorney, Cheyenne, 1887–1888; member, Wyoming territorial legislature, 1888; chief justice, Wyoming Territory, 1889–1890; assistant attorney general, Department of the Interior, 1897–1903; judge, U.S. Court of Appeals for the Eighth Circuit, 1903–1910.

Supreme Court Service: Nominated associate justice by President William Howard Taft, December 12, 1910, to replace Edward D. White, who became chief justice; confirmed by the Senate, December 15, 1910, by a voice vote; took judicial oath January 3, 1911; retired June 2, 1937; replaced by Hugo L. Black, nominated by President Franklin D. Roosevelt.

Death: February 8, 1941, in Washington, D.C.

Willis Van Devanter was born in Marion, Indiana, but migrated to the Wyoming Territory as a young man after completing his education at the University of Cincinnati Law School. He became involved in Wyoming politics as a member of a political machine run by Francis E. Warren, who was elected to the U.S. Senate shortly after Wyoming was admitted to the Union. Van Devanter's law practice represented a number of railroads, including the Burlington and the Union Pacific, experience that later contributed to his being labeled a tool of railroad interests. Through service as chief justice of the Wyoming Territory and as assistant attorney general in the Department of the Interior, Van Devanter became familiar with Indian rights and land claims that he also put to use during his tenure on the U.S. Supreme Court. He preceded his service on the Court with seven years on the U.S. Court of Appeals

for the Eighth Circuit, to which he was appointed in 1903 by President Theodore Roosevelt. Van Devanter was selected for the Supreme Court in 1910 as a result of heavy-handed lobbying by Senator Warren. Progressive politician William Jennings Bryan criticized Van Devanter's links with railroad interests and opposed the appointment.

As a member of the Court, Van Devanter lived a quiet existence, seldom making public appearances and writing few controversial opinions. His colleagues were glad to hand over to him cases in his areas of expertise, the unglamorous fields of public land law, admiralty, water rights, Indian claims, and corporation law. Van Devanter was regarded as skilled in handling procedural and jurisdictional disputes. Nevertheless, he was one of the least productive of the justices on the Court during his twenty-six years of service, writing only 346 opinions, 1 concurrence, and

4 dissents. His lack of output is generally attributed to a severe writer's block, but others point out that Van Devanter, while apparently skilled in discussing cases in conference, lacked any strong judicial philosophy that might have prompted him to take a leading role in writing opinions.

Van Devanter's knowledge of Indian life and customs was reflected in his opinion in *United States v. Sandoval* (1913), which some commentators have found suggestive of Justice Louis Brandeis, despite its patronizing tone. The case concerned the prohibition against bringing alcoholic beverages into an Indian community, in this case two pueblos held in fee simple. Van Devanter upheld the prohibition, citing studies of primitive Indian culture that ascribed to them an inferior intellect.

In his best-known opinion, *Second Employers' Liability Cases* (1912), Van Devanter reflected the progressive attitude that the exercise of broad government power was justified when the interests of the working public benefited. Congress had passed a law in 1906 making railroads liable for employees injured on the job. The Court overturned this law in 1908, and Congress responded with the Federal Employers' Liability Act, designed to correct the provisions of the first law that the Court found unconstitutional. Railroads responded to this second effort with more than 600 test cases, and Van Devanter's opinion was the result. He had first upheld the law in *Kieran v. Portland* (1912), which applied to injured railroad workers employed in interstate commerce.

The 1912 opinion concerned congressional power to make a railroad liable for an employee injured in interstate commerce through the actions of a fellow employee not working in interstate commerce. Van Devanter upheld the law, arguing that Congress could do whatever was necessary "to save the act of interstate commerce from prevention or intervention, or to make that act more secure, more reliable, or more efficient." He wrote that the purpose of the statute was to prevent negligence on the part of the railroad by imposing greater liability, and that was well within the powers of Congress in regulating interstate commerce. The result of the opinion was to assign greater responsibility to the railroads, do away with the "fellow servant" rule, and limit the use of the doctrines of contributory negligence, all goals of various groups within the Progressive movement.

Despite this opinion, Van Devanter remained loyal to the railroads, as was evidenced by numerous other rulings. For example, in *St. Louis, Iron Mountain and Southern Railway v. Wynne* (1912), he rejected an Arkansas law designed to impose heavy penalties on railroads when their trains killed wandering livestock. Van Devanter wrote that instead of providing an incentive for settling just claims, the statute antagonized the railroads by depriving them of recourse in cases of excessive fines. In *Burke v. Southern Pacific Railroad* (1914), Van Devanter's opinion strictly limited the power of the U.S. Land Office to divest railroads of land grants that had subsequently been found to have

Willis Van Devanter

valuable mineral deposits. And despite some assessments of his ruling in the *Second Employers' Liability Cases* as liberal, Van Devanter showed that his support for liability legislation was not unqualified. In *New York Central v. Winfield* (1917), he rejected the application of state liability statutes to railroads, arguing that the federal law was designed to be uniform, consistent, and to supersede state laws.

Under the leadership of William Howard Taft, who had appointed him and who joined the Court as chief justice in 1921, Van Devanter continued to be largely unproductive as a writer of opinions, but he served the Court in other ways. He became Taft's good friend and confidante, and one writer has suggested that perhaps the chief justice was content to have Van Devanter remain mute, so long as he voted with the conservative side and supported Justice George Sutherland's more scholarly opinions. Van Devanter is remembered during this period for his strong support of Taft's conservative leanings and for his contributions to Court reform in 1925.

One of Taft's goals for the Court was to streamline its operations and give it more control over its own jurisdiction. Several pieces of legislation to that end were introduced in Congress, culminating with the Jurisdictional Act of 1925. This law reduced the number of cases heard by the Court on appeal by broadening the justices' discretion in granting writs of certiorari. The statute also made judgments in the courts of claims and certain decisions in the courts of appeals final and allowed constitutional questions to continue to rise from state courts on writs of error. Van Devanter was the chief author of this portion of the reform legislation, and he put his reputed political expertise to use as the Court's representative before congressional committees holding hearings on the bill.

Van Devanter is also remembered for his authorship of one significant opinion, *McGrain v. Daugherty* (1927), which is considered the strongest among the small number of opinions he wrote in the 1920s. This ruling, reflecting Van Devanter's expertise in procedural matters, upheld the right of the Senate to arrest a person who had refused to honor a subpoena commanding his testimony in an investigation of the Jus-

tice Department. Van Devanter concluded that the Senate had acted properly because the investigation served a legitimate legislative purpose.

By the beginning of the 1930s, any judicial philosophy that Van Devanter had formulated could be described as strongly conservative, if not reactionary. His colleague Harlan Fiske Stone labeled him the "Commander in Chief of Judicial Reaction." He was not a supporter of civil liberties, and he opposed New Deal economic programs almost without exception. Although he wrote none of the important opinions, he could be counted among the majority in every ruling overturning President Franklin Roosevelt's recovery programs until his retirement in 1937. It has been suggested that Van Devanter delayed his retirement simply to remain on the Court as an opponent of Roosevelt.

Van Devanter's concern about infringements on economic liberties did not carry over to protection of individual rights. For example, in *Near v. Minnesota* (1931), a case testing the reach of freedom of the press, Van Devanter agreed with the minority's contention that a state "press gag" law should be upheld. A year later, he dissented from the Court's invalidation of the Texas white primary law in *Nixon v. Condon* (1932). He did, however, vote to extend the Sixth Amendment right to counsel in the infamous "Scottsboro Boys" case, *Powell v. Alabama* (1932).

Van Devanter achieved his greatest fame on the Court as one of the "Four Horsemen" who consistently opposed FDR's economic programs. He supported Sutherland's dissent in *Home Building & Loan Assn. v. Blaisdell* (1934), a mortgage moratorium case in which Chief Justice Charles Evans Hughes tentatively indicated that the Court might show some sympathy for emergency legislation designed to cope with the Depression. Van Devanter voted against the National Recovery Act, the Agricultural Adjustment Act, the Wagner Act, the first Frazier-Lemke Act, the Bituminous Coal Conservation Act (the Guffey law), and the gold clauses. In the spring of 1937 he worked with Hughes to thwart Roosevelt's proposed "Court-packing" plan, advising the chief justice to respond in writing, rather than send the justices to testify to, and to be questioned by, a congressional investigating committee.

Van Devanter retired in May 1937, soon after the Court issued its first opinions in support of the New Deal philosophy. He became the first justice to take advantage of a new law permitting members of the Court to retire at full pay. Some said he also timed his retirement to create the maximum embarrassment for the president, as it demonstrated that a little patience would have enabled Roosevelt to avoid the political fiasco engendered by his Court-packing proposal. After resigning from the Supreme Court, Van Devanter moved to New York where he presided in the U.S. district court until his death in 1941.

Historians have billed Van Devanter as an "unimaginative conservative" with strengths largely in negotiation and knowledge of judicial procedure. Brandeis, however, considered Van Devanter one of the most skillful members of the conference and compared him (favorably) to a Jesuit cardinal in his abilities. One study lists him as one of the eight "failures" in Court history because of the small number of opinions he produced and because he was not an identifiable leader among his colleagues. Others have suggested that Van Devanter has fared poorly with evaluators because he is best known as a reactionary conservative in a period dominated by liberal writers.

—*Rebecca Shepherd Shoemaker*

BIBLIOGRAPHY

There is no published biography of Willis Van Devanter. The best primary source for his judicial career are his professional papers, located in the Library of Congress. Most of the detailed studies of Van Devanter's career are unpublished dissertations. They include Lewis H. Gould, "Willis Van Devanter in Wyoming Politics, 1884–1897" (Yale, 1966); James O'Brien Howard, "Constitutional Doctrines of Mr. Justice Van Devanter" (University of Iowa, 1937); and Ronald F. Howell, "Conservative Influence on Constitutional Development, 1932–37: The Judicial Theory of Justices Van Devanter, McReynolds, Sutherland, and Butler" (Johns Hopkins, 1952).

Paul M. Hollinger has published two brief articles on aspects of Van Devanter's career: "The Appointment of Supreme Court Justice Van Devanter: A Study in Political Preferment," *American Journal of Legal History* 12 (1968): 324; and "Mr. Justice Van Devanter and the New Deal: A Note," *History* 31 (1968): 57. See also Barry Cushman, "The Secret Lives of the Four Horsemen," *Virginia Law Review* 83 (1997): 559; and W. H. Johnson, "Willis Van Devanter—A 'Re-examination,'" *Wyoming Law Review* 1 (2001): 403.

NOTEWORTHY OPINIONS

Second Employers' Liability Cases, 223 U.S. 1 (1912)

United States v. Sandoval, 231 U.S. 28 (1913)

New York Central Railroad v. Winfield, 244 U.S. 147 (1917)

McGrain v. Daugherty, 273 U.S. 135 (1927)

FREDERICK MOORE VINSON

Birth: January 22, 1890, Louisa, Kentucky.

Education: Kentucky Normal College, 1908; Centre College, A.B., 1909; LL.B., 1911.

Official Positions: Commonwealth attorney, Thirty-second Judicial District of Kentucky, 1921–1924; U.S. representative, 1924–1929, 1931–1938; judge, U.S. Court of Appeals for the District of Columbia Circuit, 1938–1943; director, Office of Economic Stabilization, 1943–1945; administrator, Federal Loan Agency, 1945; director, Office of War Mobilization and Reconversion, 1945; secretary of the Treasury, 1945–1946.

Supreme Court Service: Nominated chief justice by President Harry S. Truman, June 6, 1946, to replace Harlan F. Stone, who had died; confirmed by the Senate, June 20, 1946, by a voice vote; took judicial oath June 24, 1946; served until September 8, 1953; replaced by Earl Warren, nominated by President Dwight D. Eisenhower.

Death: September 8, 1953, Washington, D.C.

Fred Vinson was educated at Kentucky Normal School, obtained a law degree in 1911 from the law department of Centre College, and subsequently practiced law in Louisa and Ashland, Kentucky, including brief service as Ashland's city attorney and commonwealth attorney. In 1924 he was elected to the House of Representatives from Kentucky's Ninth District. He was defeated in 1928 but reelected to the House in 1930 and kept the seat in ensuing elections. Vinson was a powerful member of the House Ways and Means Committee and was chosen chairman of its tax subcommittee.

His judicial career began in May 1938, when President Franklin Roosevelt named him to the U.S. Court of Appeals for the District of Columbia Circuit. In 1942 Chief Justice Harlan Fiske Stone gave him the additional job of chief judge of the wartime U.S. Emergency Court of Appeals, a court especially cre-

ated to clear the backlog of war-related cases. Vinson resigned from the bench in May 1943 to become director of the Economic Stabilization Board. He then held a series of increasingly responsible executive positions. In March 1945 he was the federal loan administrator; from April to July, the director of the Office of War Mobilization and Reconversion; and then secretary of the Treasury. Before he became chief justice, the kind and affable Fred Vinson had exercised federal legislative, judicial, and executive powers.

Legal acumen and jurisprudential scholarship played no role in President Harry Truman's nomination of Vinson to be the nation's thirteenth chief justice; rather, the motivating factors were political philosophy and Vinson's personality—he was friendly, sociable, humorous, patient, relaxed, and respectful of others' views. Truman hoped that these attributes would unite the fractious Supreme Court.

Given the personalities and intellectual strengths of associate justices such as Felix Frankfurter, Hugo Black, William O. Douglas, and Robert Jackson, just reducing tension and dissension on the Court would have been a formidable task. Vinson, then fifty-six years old, did not succeed.

Any evaluation of Vinson's seven-year Supreme Court tenure must, therefore, rest on his judicial opinions, which were nourished by an intellect that eschewed theoretical grandeur. Instead, he thought in terms of specific problems and formulated responses designed to meet present contingencies, not unforeseen and unpredictable future events. His mind, ideas, and jurisprudence were, in this sense, pragmatic. Whether a longer tenure would have changed that judicial posture is doubtful. Vinson's opinions are devoid of any trace of John Marshall's statesmanship or Oliver Wendell Holmes's rhetoric. Moreover, their small number may render any such comparison grossly unfair. He was not the most insignificant chief justice—that title might be accorded to John Rutledge or Oliver Ellsworth—but Vinson's opinions have virtually disappeared.

In the realm of federal legislative powers, the lack of noteworthy opinions is not surprising, because Vinson was aligned with the victors. Following the 1937 "Court-packing" plan, the Court conceded virtually unlimited scope to the congressional commerce power. Sustaining the validity of economic legislation did not, therefore, require or permit memorable or original judicial opinions. It did, however, enable Vinson to endorse the concept, and promote the possibility, of national, rather than fragmented, power and policies. Expansion, not contraction, of the commerce clause was a constant refrain of Vinson's opinions. That concept is particularly evident even where Congress remained silent. On this aspect of the commerce clause's federalist dimensions, Vinson was hostile toward any state burdens on interstate or foreign commerce. Between 1937 and 1946 the Court had allowed some state regulation and taxation to operate on such commerce. Reflecting an antipathy to state encroachments on federal government domains, Vinson was unwilling to concede their constitutionality. Only after elaborate scrutiny of national needs and interests balanced against local benefits was there a possibility that state regulations and taxes might not be invalidated. Cases such as *Independent Warehouses v. Scheele* (1947), *Bob-Lo Excursion Co. v. Michigan* (1948), and *Breard v. Alexandria* (1951) exemplify this Vinson approach.

Presidential and federal executive power also received Vinson's constitutional imprimatur, as exemplified in his dissent in *Youngstown Sheet & Tube Co. v. Sawyer* (1952). By a 6–3 majority, the Court held that President Truman possessed no power derived from the Constitution, either as chief executive or as commander in chief, to seize and operate privately owned steel mills. Without congressional authorization, the president's actions were unconstitutional. Even before that seizure occurred, but as chief justice, Vinson had

Frederick Moore Vinson

privately advised Truman that in his opinion the Constitution permitted such a seizure, and Vinson restated that view in his dissent. The chief justice attributed to the framers an awareness "that there is real danger in Executive weakness." Crises and emergencies clearly exposed not only this peril but also the corresponding need for near omnipotence for the executive. On Vinson's assessment, these factors coalesced when Truman directed the secretary of commerce to take possession and operate the plants and facilities of specified steel companies.

Given American military commitments in Korea, this presidential action to avert a steelworkers' strike came at a time when "vigor and initiative," not "inertia," were necessary. To Vinson, the reasons were obvious: a serious emergency existed, and the nation's vital interests included the continuing production of steel. Vinson's response to critics, including those justices who perceived unbridled executive power resulting in executive tyranny and autocracy, was emphatic: "Those who suggest that this is a case involving extraordinary powers should be mindful that these are extraordinary times." For President Truman, Vinson's point "hit the nail right on the head." Others, however, saw Vinson's dissent as proof that he, despite being elevated to the pinnacle of the Supreme Court, remained in spirit and deed ensconced in the other branches of the federal government.

Vinson's Bill of Rights and Fourteenth Amendment opinions reinforced this perception. The evidence here is indisputable: individuals and their constitutional rights were, for the chief justice, subordinate to federal and state powers. Within the context of a larger perspective—the previous history of Supreme Court decisions on such rights—his views may conform with, rather than deviate from, the predominant trend of constitutional law. The small number of civil rights cases decided during the Vinson years—*Shelley v. Kraemer* (1948), *Hurd v. Hodge* (1948), *Sipuel v. Board of Regents of the University of Oklahoma* (1948), *McLaurin v. Oklahoma State Regents* (1950), and *Sweatt v. Painter* (1950)—may represent an aberration. But for those ensnared in the cold war and McCarthyism hysteria, Vinson's tenure

offered no protection against repressive congressional laws and committees, executive investigations, or criminal prosecutions.

The most notorious and, in terms of practical consequences, the most important Vinson opinion sustained, against First Amendment free speech challenges, the convictions of eleven U.S. Communist Party leaders, including Eugene Dennis. Their indictment under the 1940 Smith Act alleged a conspiracy to teach or advocate the forceful overthrow of the U.S. government and membership in an organization advocating such an overthrow. In his plurality opinion, Vinson transformed Oliver Wendell Holmes and Louis Brandeis's formulation and application of the clear and present danger test. The constitutionally protected realm of free speech could be legislatively invaded to the extent necessary to obviate dangers, provided its gravity and probability of occurring had been assessed.

Two immediate results ensued from *Dennis v. United States* (1951). First, the constitutionality of the Smith Act was upheld. Second, other federal prosecutions could and did successfully proceed against what government officials considered to be potentially subversive doctrines. Noncriminal sanctions and deprivations applied to Communists and others suspected of disloyalty were also constitutionally vindicated by Vinson's refutation of counterarguments premised on the Bill of Rights in cases such as *American Communications Association v. Douds* (1950), *Bailey v. Richardson* (1951), and *Joint Anti-Fascist Refugee Committee v. McGrath* (1951).

To what extent did these opinions rest on Vinson's view of the necessity to sustain and defer to exercises of national and federal authority? Some relative indication can be gleaned from his First Amendment free speech decisions involving, via the Fourteenth Amendment, state laws and regulations. At least on some occasions, he was prepared to invalidate local ordinances to vindicate assertions of individual rights. This civil libertarian posture is revealed in *Saia v. New York* (1948), *Niemotko v. Maryland* (1951), and *Kunz v. New York* (1951). However, other cases, such as *Kovacs v. Cooper* (1949) and *Feiner v. New York*

(1951), return Vinson's image to that of an authoritarian advocate.

In addition, within the criminal law context, despite some ambivalence, government interests in law enforcement, not individual rights and immunities, prevailed. This general stance is obvious in procedural and substantive criminal law issues in state and federal courts, where Vinson usually rejected Fourth Amendment claims, but the trend was not devoid of exceptions. Indeed, a 1940 Fourth Amendment Vinson opinion in the court of appeals (*Nueslein v. District of Columbia*) clearly indicated the possibility of such occurrences. Successful invocation of defendants' rights during the Vinson era are few, but do include *Niemotko, Jennings v Illinois* (1951), *Fowler v. Rhode Island* (1953), and *Brock v. North Carolina* (1953).

Even more tentative was Vinson's approach to cases under the First Amendment's establishment clause, which *Everson v. Board of Education* (1947) extended to the states. Two conclusions are obvious. First, Vinson was prepared to apply the Bill of Rights, at least to some extent, to the states with the consequential diminution of state authority and federalism implications. Second, *Everson* was only the beginning, not the end, of Supreme Court explorations among the religion clauses. Vinson's votes to allow school districts to reimburse parents for transporting their children to parochial schools in *Everson*, to invalidate a released time program in which the clergy taught religion in schools during school time in *Illinois ex rel. McCollum v. Board of Education* (1948), and to uphold a program that provided students with religious instruction outside school premises in *Zorach v. Clauson* (1952) are, therefore, not reliable guides as to how his views concerning federal and state authority, individual rights, and the judicial function might eventually have coalesced to reveal his posture in this aspect of First Amendment jurisprudence.

In stark contrast, it is usually suggested that no such equivocation surrounded Vinson's use of constitutional law to eliminate racial discrimination. Three categories of cases testing the equal protection clause are involved. The first is the invalidation of racial restrictions on Japanese pertaining to landholding and fishing rights in *Oyama v. California* (1948) and *Takahashi v. Fish and Game Commission* (1948). Second are the cases involving restrictive covenants that prevented African Americans from buying houses in white neighborhoods. In *Shelley v. Kraemer*, Vinson spoke for the Court to hold that state court enforcement of such private racial covenants constituted state action forbidden by the Fourteenth Amendment's equal protection clause. In *Hurd v. Hodge*, Vinson also applied that decision to the District of Columbia.

Doctrinally, these cases are among Vinson's most interesting, complex, and adventurous opinions. Even so, it is doubtful whether they reveal any significant new dimension to his decisions or decision-making process. Indeed, Vinson made a conspicuous effort to locate *Shelley* within the parameters of previous state action cases and to see the state action concept as a rigid limitation on, rather than a malleable entrance to, Fourteenth Amendment rights. Significantly, Vinson dissented in *Barrows v. Jackson* (1953) when all the other justices held that a state court's award of damages for breach of a racial covenant infringed the equal protection clause.

The third category of racial discrimination cases in which Vinson participated is state-segregated graduate education. State action in *Sipuel, McLaurin,* and *Sweatt* unconstitutionally denied African American university students equal protection of the laws. In one respect, these decisions simultaneously pointed in antithetical directions: the separate but equal doctrine was not rejected or abandoned, but, as a practical matter, the application of a rigorous equal facilities test eliminated the maintenance of racial segregation in state graduate and professional schools. Ultimately, that tension would be broken in *Brown v. Board of Education* (1954), but by then Vinson was no longer on the Court.

Compared to other justices, including chief justices, Vinson wrote few opinions. Moreover, it has been suggested "that Vinson did all his 'writing' with his hands in his pockets, outlining the general approach to his clerk[s] and then suggesting but few revisions in the draft." If that observation is correct, how and why he cast his vote in deciding cases may have been more influential and may be more reveal-ing than his written opinions. A further impediment to his reputation is the unevenness of quality, in prose and legal analysis, among his opinions. At best, they were succinct and precise; their clarity was bereft of irrelevant erudition and relentlessly drove toward a seemingly inevitable result. The worst were vacuous. Fine distinctions and silent avoidance of precedents are their dominant characteristics.

All of Vinson's perspectives, however, gained sus-tenance from a single premise: authority, not free-dom, ought to prevail when a choice had to be made. If, almost without exception, that choice dictated the constitutional validity of federal and state exercises of legislative, executive, and judicial powers, the result was to be celebrated as a victory for patriotism, not decried as a defeat of liberty. Whether or not Vinson's sentiments are endorsed, their promulgation has one virtue: the inevitable juxtaposition of the opposing view that mandates sacrificing the common good to individual rights and freedoms. That, especially for the Supreme Court, is the enduring American dilemma: when, where, and how majoritarianism or constitutionalism should be triumphant.

—*James A. Thomson*

BIBLIOGRAPHY

The Vinson papers are in the Margaret I. King Library at the University of Kentucky in Lexington. The only biography is James E. St. Clair and Linda C. Gugin, *Chief Justice Fred M. Vinson of Kentucky: A Political Biography* (2002). Other examinations of Vinson include Francis A. Allen, "Chief Justice Vinson and the Theory of Constitutional Govern-ment: A Tentative Appraisal," *Northwestern University Law Review* 49 (1954): 3; and John P. Frank, "Fred Vinson and the Chief Justiceship," *University of Chicago Law Review* 21 (1954): 212. The most critical view of Vinson is Fred Rodell, *Nine Men: A Political History of the Supreme Court from 1790 to 1955* (1955).

For analyses of the Vinson Court, see Melvin I. Urof-sky, *Division and Discord: The Supreme Court Under Stone and Vinson, 1941–1953* (1997); Jan Palmer, *The Vinson Court Era: The Supreme Court's Conference Votes: Data and Analysis* (1990); and Francis H. Rudko, *Truman's Court: A Study in Judicial Restraint* (1988).

For particular cases and issues, see Michal R. Belknap, *Cold War Political Justice: The Smith Act, the Communist Party, and American Civil Liberties* (1977); Maeva Marcus, *Truman and the Steel Seizure Case: The Limits of Presidential Power* (1977); and Clement E. Vose, *Caucasians Only: The Supreme Court, the NAACP, and the Restrictive Covenant Cases* (1967).

NOTEWORTHY OPINIONS

Shelley v. Kraemer, 334 U.S. 1 (1948)

Hurd v. Hodge, 334 U.S. 24 (1948)

Dennis v. United States, 341 U.S. 494 (1951)

Youngstown Sheet & Tube Co. v. Sawyer, 343 U.S. 579 (1952) (Dissent)

Barrows v. Jackson, 346 U.S. 249 (1953) (Dissent)

MORRISON REMICK WAITE

Birth: November 29, 1816, Lyme, Connecticut.

Education: Graduated from Yale College, 1837.

Official Positions: Ohio state representative, 1850–1852; representative to the Geneva Arbitration, 1871; president of the Ohio Constitutional Convention, 1873–1874.

Supreme Court Service: Nominated chief justice by President Ulysses S. Grant, January 19, 1874, to replace Chief Justice Salmon P. Chase, who had died; confirmed by the Senate, January 21, 1874, by a 63–0 vote; took judicial oath March 4, 1874; served until March 23, 1888; replaced by Melville W. Fuller, nominated by President Grover Cleveland.

Death: March 23, 1888, Washington, D.C.

Morrison Waite's appointment as chief justice of the United States was hardly auspicious. For one thing, Waite was nominated by President Ulysses S. Grant, renowned for heading one of the most corrupt administrations in American history. Moreover, Waite was not even Grant's first choice. Following unsuccessful attempts to place George H. Williams and Caleb Cushing on the Court, and after consideration of at least two others, Grant submitted Waite's name to replace Chief Justice Salmon P. Chase on January 19, 1874. Two days later an exhausted Congress confirmed the nomination. As Rep. Rockwood Hoar, R-Mass., observed, Waite had been "that luckiest of all individuals known to the law, an innocent third party without notice."

That Waite had been "without notice" prior to his appointment was fairly certain. He was born in Lyme, Connecticut, on November 29, 1816, to an established New England family that produced a number of lawyers, including his father, Henry, who served as chief justice on the state supreme court. Like his father and grandfather before him, Morrison attended Bacon Academy and Yale College. After graduation, he studied law in his father's office, but in 1838 moved to Maumee City, Ohio, where he continued his law studies with Samuel D. Young. He was admitted to the bar and began a law practice largely devoted to commercial and corporate transactions. In 1840 he returned briefly to Connecticut to marry Amelia C. Warner, a second cousin. Ten years later, Waite moved his family to Toledo and set up practice with his younger brother Richard.

Waite's political involvement during his years building a successful law practice was minimal. He served briefly on the Toledo City Council, sat for one term in the state legislature, and made an unsuccessful run for Congress in 1862. Thanks in large part to geographic circumstances, Waite was appointed by President Grant in 1871 to serve as counsel for the United States during the arbitration negotiations in Geneva over the Alabama claims from the Civil War. Following his return from Switzerland, he served as delegate and president of the Ohio Constitutional Convention, the position he held when nominated in January 1874 to the Supreme Court.

The membership of the Court that Waite was chosen to lead reflected a variety of abilities, personalities, and beliefs. Nathan Clifford was a Democratic holdover from the pre–Civil War period, and his age and increasing senility proved a constant challenge to Waite's patience and good nature. David Davis, President Abraham Lincoln's former political manager, harbored an ongoing desire for the presidency, as perhaps did Stephen J. Field of California. Intellectually, the two dominant forces on the Court were Samuel Miller and Joseph P. Bradley; the latter became Waite's most consistent ally, while the former would always resent the fact that Grant had not selected him to be chief justice. The rest of the Court consisted of Republican appointees of lesser talents: Noah H. Swayne, Ward Hunt, and William Strong. Although he was never a dominant intellectual force on the Court, Waite was an "adept" social and managerial leader, using his inherent graciousness and good cheer, along with his power as chief justice to assign opinions, to mold an unusually harmonious Court.

Morrison Remick Waite

Over the course of Waite's fourteen-year tenure as chief justice, the Supreme Court decided some 3,470 cases with opinions, of which Waite wrote 967. His tendency to go along with the Court's majority was evidenced by the fact that he dissented in only fifty-four cases or less than 2 percent. The large number of cases, as well as the variety of issues confronted, was due to the lack of discretion the Supreme Court could exercise over its docket during this period, rather than a testament to the Court's interests and work ethic.

Of all the public and private law issues that Waite and the Court encountered between 1874 and 1888, two were of paramount importance. One concerned the scope and meaning of the Reconstruction amendments, particularly as they affected the lives and future of the 3.5 million former slaves. The other, and to some extent related, issue was the role of government with regard to the growth of industrialism and the emergence of big business in late nineteenth-century America. Waite's contributions to the law in both of these areas are therefore the key to understanding his judicial philosophy and his role in American constitutional development.

Following the Civil War, Republicans in Congress passed measures intended to protect the economic, social, and political rights of blacks in the South who had recently been emancipated under the Thirteenth Amendment. As a further guarantee, Congress also enacted the Fourteenth Amendment, which forbade states to deprive any citizen of "life, liberty or property ... without due process of law," and which required states to grant to all citizens the "equal protection of the laws," as well as the "privileges and immunities" of all citizens. When this amendment proved insufficient to ensure the full participation of the freedmen in the political process of Reconstruction in the South, Congress passed the Fifteenth Amendment, which was ratified in 1870. Under this amendment, the right to vote could "not be denied or abridged by the United States or by any state on account of race, color, or previous condition of servitude." Sections in both the Fourteenth and Fifteenth Amendments gave Congress the authority to enforce the amendments' provisions "by appropriate legislation."

Following reports of ongoing terrorism directed against blacks attempting to vote or participate in political activities, in 1870 and 1871 Congress passed three measures known as the enforcement acts. These measures set out a wide variety of possible crimes directed against potential voters and provided the machinery for federal enforcement through the Department of Justice. On March 27, 1876, the Supreme Court announced two decisions dealing with convictions under these statutes, and Waite wrote the majority opinion in both. In *United States v. Cruikshank,* the Court reviewed the convictions of three men accused of massacring at least 105 blacks and three whites outside the Grant Parish courthouse in Colfax, Louisiana, on Easter Sunday, 1873. In overturning the convictions, Waite admitted that the right to assemble peacefully was constitutionally protected, and that under the Fifteenth Amendment Congress could protect this right from infringement on account of race. Indeed, Congress had done so in the enforcement acts. The problem was whether the indictments under which the defendants had been tried were sufficient in law, and Waite argued they were not, because they had failed to allege that the murders had been committed because of the victims' race. "We may suspect that race was the cause of the hostility," Waite concluded, "but it is not so averred."

In *United States v. Reese,* also announced that day, Waite went further and declared two sections of the May 1870 enforcement act unconstitutional. In overturning the convictions of two Kentucky election inspectors for refusing to allow William Garner, a citizen "of African descent," to vote, Waite held that the Fifteenth Amendment did not "confer the right of suffrage upon anyone." It prohibited states from discriminating or "giving preference" in exercising voting

rights on account of race, but the statutes under review did not specifically require this; hence they were invalid.

Waite's opinions in *Reese* and *Cruikshank* were just two of the Supreme Court rulings after 1873 that seemingly left the Reconstruction amendments and the various federal laws enforcing them "almost wholly ineffective" in protecting the rights of blacks in the South. In *Virginia v. Rives* (1880), the Court ruled that the absence of blacks on juries was not proof of racial discrimination. And most prominently, in the *Civil Rights Cases* (1883), the Court struck down the Civil Rights Act of 1875, which forbade racial discrimination in places of public accommodation. Yet a careful review of Waite's, and the Court's, opinions in other cases during these years suggests something other than outright hostility to the interests of African Americans. In *Strauder v. West Virginia* (1880), the Court struck down a state law requiring all-white juries as a violation of the equal protection clause of the Fourteenth Amendment. And that same year, in *Neal v. Delaware,* the Court held that state judges could not exclude blacks from jury duty.

Moreover, Waite supported strong congressional powers, particularly when it came to protecting voting rights. In three cases, *Ex parte Siebold* (1880), *Ex parte Clark* (1879), and, the most important, *Ex parte Yarbrough* (1884), the Court, with Waite's concurrence, upheld federal authority to protect voters from racially motivated infringement of their rights in state and local elections and under any circumstances in federal elections. This commitment to "preserving federalism," as one scholar has put it, entailed a willingness to accept broad national authority while recognizing the limits of that authority in light of state actions and prerogatives.

To that extent, Waite was neither ahead of nor behind the views of most moderate white northerners, or of southern leaders such as Sen. Wade Hampton, D-S.C., who accepted black social inferiority but retained a concern for the protection of the "free ballot and a fair count." Like many other white Americans of the time, Waite believed that the key to the future for African Americans in the South was education. He actively supported the Slater and Peabody Funds, two northern philanthropies set up to provide money for schools and colleges in the South for blacks, and he lobbied Congress (unsuccessfully) to provide federal funds for such efforts.

Waite's willingness to abandon blacks in the South to the mercy of their state governments, despite the due process and equal protection guarantees of the Fourteenth Amendment, reflected the increasing attention after 1874 to similar claims made by business owners in defense of their property interests. In the late nineteenth century industry and business in America experienced tremendous growth fueled by massive immigration, technological innovations, and government support on all levels. Changes resulting from this expansion were not entirely welcome, and various groups in American society, particularly farmers and labor, responded through organization and political action. At the same time, business and its attorneys discovered a federal judiciary that was willing to consider claims that economic regulation was unreasonable and, more important, unconstitutional.

Railroads were emblematic of late nineteenth-century industrialism and in the eyes of American farmers were the root cause of most of their troubles. During the late 1860s, farmer protest groups sprang up around the country, and in the Midwest they were particularly successful in capturing control of state legislatures. These states enacted a series of laws, known as the Granger laws, to regulate railroads and related businesses. In the landmark ruling *Munn v. Illinois* (1876), Waite, speaking for a 7–2 majority of the Court, upheld an 1871 Illinois statute regulating grain storage warehouses, known as grain elevators. Waite rejected the argument that the state regulations had deprived the elevator owners of their property without due process of law and sustained the laws as a valid use of state police power. Under this power, according to Waite, "The government regulates the conduct of citizens one towards another, and the manner in which each shall use his own property, when such regulation becomes necessary for the public good."

If government can regulate private property, under what circumstances could it do so? For Waite, those circumstances existed when "one devotes his property to a use in which the public has an interest." Ira Munn's grain storage elevators in Chicago were an important part of a vast national commercial network, and were therefore affected with a "public interest." Finally, Waite rejected the notion that the laws denied owners "reasonable compensation" and that in any case, what was or was not reasonable was a "judicial" matter to be decided in the courts. The power to fix maximum rates is implied in the power to regulate, he asserted. "We know that this is a power which may be abused; but that is no argument against its existence. For protection against abuses by legislatures the people must resort to the polls, not to the courts."

Scholars still debate the extent to which Waite's opinion in *Munn* was his own and not Justice Bradley's and the degree to which he misused the concept of public interest that English jurist Lord Hale had enunciated 200 years earlier. But Waite's decision in this case clearly reflects a number of themes that appeared throughout his career on the bench. Support for state regulation of business was certainly a principal theme. As a successful railroad and corporation attorney before he came to the Court, Waite was not unsympathetic to the interests and concerns of business. Moreover, as a Republican, Waite had little patience with the states' rights arguments of the pre–Civil War era. Yet he also recognized that changing times and economic circumstances required some limitations on corporate activity, and, along with a democratic faith in popular sovereignty, he believed that state legislatures should be the source of such limitations. In his view of state police powers, corporations, and the contract clause of the Constitution, Waite harkened back to Chief Justice Roger Taney's ruling in *Charles River Bridge v. Warren Bridge* (1836). For example, in *Wright v. Nagle* (1879), Waite allowed the state of Georgia authority to authorize new bridges for its rivers on the grounds that there was no "exclusive right to public franchises." And in *Stone v. Mississippi* (1880), Waite upheld a state ban on a previously granted lottery charter, arguing that "the legislature cannot bargain away the police power of the

State," a power that "extends to all matters affecting the public health or the public morals."

As he had in *Munn,* Waite found little merit in business owners' contention that economic regulation was a deprivation of their property rights under the due process clause of the Fourteenth Amendment or a violation of the contract clause of the Constitution. In *Railroad Company v. Richmond* (1878), he warned that "appropriate regulation of the use of property is not 'taking' property within the meaning of the constitutional prohibition." And in a number of decisions after 1878, the Waite Court upheld state regulation of railroad rates, culminating in 1886 with its ruling in *Stone v. Farmers' Loan & Trust Company.* In that case, the state of Mississippi had specifically granted the Mobile and Ohio Railroad Company the power to fix rates. Subsequently, the state had created a special commission with the power to determine reasonable rates and charges for railroads operating within the state. The railroad contended that this was a direct violation of its charter rights and a deprivation of its property without due process of law.

In rejecting the railroad's arguments, Waite noted that the "great purpose" of the statute was to "regulate in some matters of a police nature the use of railroads in the State." Citing *Munn* and the other railroad cases, he upheld both the states' power to regulate rates and their use of a commission in doing so. Even though the railroads were given authority to fix rates, such a grant was not a "renunciation of the right of legislative control so as to secure reasonable rates." Remarkably, Waite did make an important concession to the railroads in the case. The chief justice admitted that

> it is not to be inferred that this power of limitation or regulation is itself without limit. . . . Under pretense of regulating fares and freights, the State cannot require a railroad corporation to carry persons or property without reward; neither can it do that which in law amounts to a taking of private property for public use, without just compensation, or without due process of law.

Although not completely appreciated at the time, in the 1890s this statement provided the opening wedge for the Court to begin striking down the very kinds of economic regulation Waite was approving. With Waite gone, and the addition of the "new conservative" justices such as Horace Gray and David Brewer, the dissents of Justice Field in the Granger and railroad rate cases would become the basis of a new line of majority opinions striking down state economic and social regulations.

Waite's support for state regulatory authority also encompassed financial and debt obligations. To encourage and assist the construction of railroads, many states and localities had authorized large bond issues as a means of financing public improvements. When the economic benefits did not appear and those issuing the bonds were forced to assume an unwelcome debt, some states stepped in and attempted to repudiate or reduce the debt. Waite and the Court upheld these state actions. One example is *Louisiana v. Lumel* (1882), in which Waite cited the Eleventh Amendment's prohibition on suits by citizens of one state against another state in blocking a suit by an outside bondholder when Louisiana attempted such a repudiation in 1879. According to Waite, "The officers owe duty to the state, and have no contractual relations with the bond-holders. They can act only as the State directs them to act, and hold as the State allows them to hold."

As was true with respect to civil rights, Waite supported broad national regulatory authority over commercial matters, believing that the commerce power must "keep pace with the progress of the country." In 1866 Congress gave Western Union Telegraph Company the "right to construct, maintain, and operate lines of telegraph through and over any portion of the public domain of the United States." Shortly thereafter, the Florida legislature granted Pensacola Telegraph Company the right to construct and run telegraph lines in several northern counties that connected to other states. In *Pensacola Telegraph Company v. Western Union Company* (1878), Waite rejected an attempt by the Pensacola company to prevent Western Union's franchise from operating in those areas covered by its service. He declared that the authority of the government of the United States

> operates upon every foot of territory under its jurisdiction. It legislates for the whole nation, and is not embarrassed by State lines. Its peculiar duty is to protect one part of the country from encroachment by another upon the national rights which belong to all.

The state-chartered corporation, therefore, had to give way to a federally supported one.

Similarly, in the *Sinking Fund Cases* (1879), Waite supported significant national control over federally chartered corporations. He upheld congressional statutes requiring the Union Pacific and Central Pacific railroads to set up special funds explicitly reserved for the repayment of the debt on bonds issued by the federal government to enable the original construction of the railroads. In doing so, he cited the critical role railroads had come to play in national commerce, as well as the fact that as national corporations, they were subject to federal restrictions. Going back to *Munn*, Waite stated that both railroads were private corporations whose property is "to a large extent devoted to public uses." As such, these businesses were subject to regulation, including "regulations by which suitable provision will be secured in advance for the payment of existing debts when they fall due." Requiring the railroads to create these sinking funds was a kind of "deposit of security" intended to protect the public and ensure the "solvency" of the railroads themselves.

Waite's commitment to "preserving federalism" in the area of civil rights can therefore be seen as consistent with his economic views. In the 1890s and after, Justice Field's dissents became the basis for the Court's rejection of economic and social legislation, but Waite's view of state and national regulatory powers was never totally repudiated, even during the Progressive Era and the zenith of judicial activism in protecting corporate property rights from government interference in the 1920s. To that extent, his constitutional philosophy could be seen as part of the liberal tradition of American politics. At the same time, his faith in a legislative rather than judicial approach to solving the problems of an increasingly complex industrialized society would seem to place him in the "judicial restraint" tradition of modern-day conservatives.

According to Felix Frankfurter, Waite's opinions were generally "humdrum, matter of fact, dry lawyer's English." It was a characterization Waite himself would probably not have disputed. His strengths were his character and leadership and an ability to recognize his own limitations. The moderation that provoked disparaging evaluations of his abilities and beliefs during his tenure now seems more like the work of a judicial statesman in the tradition of other great chief justices such as John Marshall and Earl Warren. He most certainly helped restore the prestige of the Supreme Court to at least its stature before the "self-inflicted wound" of the *Dred Scott v. Sandford* decision in 1857. That he was devoted to his Court service is undeniable. In 1885 he suffered a breakdown, probably from overwork, but refused to retire. Three years later, he was still drafting opinions and leading the Court—almost literally up to the moment of his death from pneumonia on March 23, 1888.

—*Robert M. Goldman*

BIBLIOGRAPHY

The main body of primary source material is located in the Waite collection at the Library of Congress. Materials relating to the Supreme Court during Waite's chief justiceship are located in the Supreme Court records at the National Archives. Waite has not gone unnoticed by historians. C. Peter Magrath's *Morrison Waite: The Triumph of Character* (1963) is a well-balanced biography. The most comprehensive account of the Supreme Court during Waite's tenure can be found in Charles Fairman's contribution to the *Holmes Devise History, Reconstruction and Reunion, 1864–88*, part 2 (1987). For an appraisal of Waite as chief justice, see D. Grier Stephenson, "The Chief Justice as Leader: The Case of Morrison R. Waite," *William and Mary*

Law Review 14 (1973): 899; and a later revisiting of the issues, Stephenson, "The Waite Court at the Bar of History," *Denver University Law Review* 81 (2003): 449. A persuasive reevaluation of Waite's civil rights decisions is Michael Les Benedict, "Preserving Federalism: Reconstruction and the Waite Court," *Supreme Court Review* (1978): 39. Two older studies still worthwhile are Felix Frankfurter, *The Commerce Clause Under Marshall, Taney and Waite* (1937); and the chapter on Waite in Kenneth Umbreit, *Our Eleven Chief Justices* (1937).

NOTEWORTHY OPINIONS

United States v. Reese, 92 U.S. 214 (1876)

United States v. Cruikshank, 92 U.S. 542 (1876)

Munn v. Illinois, 94 U.S. 113 (1876)

Pensacola Telegraph Co. v. Western Union Co., 96 U.S. 24 (1878)

Wright v. Nagle, 101 U.S. 791 (1879)

Louisiana v. Lumel, 107 U.S. 711 (1882)

EARL WARREN

Birth: March 19, 1891, Los Angeles, California.

Education: University of California, B.L., 1912; J.D., 1914.

Official Positions: Deputy city attorney, Oakland, California, 1919–1920; deputy district attorney, Alameda County, 1920–1925; district attorney, Alameda County, 1925–1939; California attorney general, 1939–1943; governor, 1943–1953.

Supreme Court Service: Recess appointment as chief justice by President Dwight D. Eisenhower, October 2, 1953, to replace Chief Justice Fred M. Vinson, who had died; nominated by President Eisenhower, January 11, 1954; confirmed by the Senate, March 1, 1954, by a voice vote; took judicial oath October 5, 1953; retired June 23, 1969; replaced by Warren E. Burger, nominated by President Richard Nixon.

Death: July 9, 1974, Washington, D.C.

The constitutional mark left at the end of Earl Warren's nearly sixteen years as chief justice of the United States reflected the tremendous changes in American society during the 1950s and 1960s. These changes involved a significant expansion in the rights and liberties of individuals in the name of securing the goals of social and political equality. Warren's judicial legacy is striking in two important respects. First, the decisions of the Supreme Court under Warren contributed substantially to the expansion of the constitutional rights of Americans and to the expansion of the role of the federal government in enforcing and protecting those rights. Second, Warren's willingness to adapt and create legal doctrines to fit his ideological beliefs and commitments represented an enhanced role for the Court in superintending government decision making on an order of magnitude not seen since the New Deal. Especially significant during Warren's stewardship was the Court's role in eradicating vestiges of public and private discrimination, in expanding the scope of protections for individuals accused of committing crimes, in ensuring the rights of free expression and religious freedom, and in improving the processes of representation and democracy to ensure a more responsive and effective government. To his critics, Warren is responsible for a precipitous expansion of the powers of the judiciary. The Warren Court, they charge, replaced the will of the elective branches of government with the will of unelected judges and limited the discretion of local officials to establish procedures and policies free of second-guessing by the national judiciary.

Whether supportive or hostile to the outcomes and strategies of Earl Warren and the Court over which he presided, all agree that Warren played an enormously influential role as leader of a fractured institution during a critical period in American history. The revolution in American law wrought by the

Warren Court was, as journalist Anthony Lewis put it, a "revolution made by judges." And, like any revolution, this one had its leader—Earl Warren.

The bulk of Warren's pre-Court years were spent serving his home state of California. He grew up in the central California city of Bakersfield and received an undergraduate degree from the University of California, Berkeley, and a law degree from Berkeley's Boalt Hall School of Law. Warren enlisted in the army in 1917, but was not sent to fight overseas. He began his legal career as deputy city attorney with the city of Oakland and next was deputy district attorney for Alameda County. He served for fourteen years as the county's district attorney and in 1939 won election as California's attorney general. In 1942 he was elected governor of the state, a position he held until his appointment to the Court.

There is an incongruity between Chief Justice Warren's service in the cause of expanding the civil rights and liberties of American citizens and his participation in episodes in California history when rights and liberties were curtailed. As attorney general, Warren publicly, and rather hyperbolically, opposed the nomination of Berkeley law professor Max Radin to the California Supreme Court. In doing so, Warren engaged in the sort of Red-baiting that he would come to despise, asserting, without credible evidence, "that Radin constantly gives aid and comfort to Communists and other radicals."

In addition, Warren's service as attorney general and governor will forever be remembered for his deci-

Earl Warren

sion to order the evacuation of Japanese Americans from their homes and to intern them in various camps throughout the West. Decades later, Warren expressed regret for this decision, but at the time he vigorously defended the action. In a 1943 speech, Warren warned that "if the Japs are released, no one will be able to tell a saboteur from any other Jap." Accordingly, he said, "We don't propose to have the Japs back in California during this war if there is any lawful means of preventing it." By his actions, Warren "engineered one of the most conspicuously racist and repressive governmental acts in American history." And for this episode, his contributions over the course of his public life to the cause of social justice must always include a significant caveat.

As California's chief law enforcement officer, Warren was a vigorous crime fighter and effective administrator. He fought organized crime by prosecuting the fruits of its activities, including gambling, bootlegging, and graft. He ran for governor on a platform of good government and independence from special interests. He was a lifelong Republican, but received the Democratic nomination as well. Although it has become a commonplace to view Warren's pre-Court career as a Republican prosecutor as inconsistent with his commitment on the bench to the rights of accused, Warren was known to be fair in his law enforcement career to the rights of defendants as well as victims. He was, in the words of University of California professor Arthur Sherry, "keenly conscious of the risk of convicting an innocent person," and he scrupulously monitored his staff's law enforcement conduct. On balance, Warren's reputation after nearly two decades of service to California's citizens was as a solid, well-meaning, and rather nonpartisan public servant.

President Dwight Eisenhower also knew Warren as a prominent figure in national politics. Warren ran for vice president on the losing ticket in 1948 and was a candidate for the Republican Party's presidential nomination in 1952. Eisenhower had made a promise to appoint Warren to the Court, and he kept his promise when Chief Justice Fred Vinson died in September 1953.

Historians' judgment that Warren ranks behind only John Marshall as the greatest chief justice in the Court's history is based on Warren's performance as a leader of the Court during a time of tremendous social and political controversy. But scholars have struggled to carve out from Warren's decisions a discernible judicial philosophy and jurisprudential compass. In truth, Warren has never been regarded as a great jurist, as a judge who shaped the course of the law through his written opinions. One of Warren's biographers, G. Edward White, argues that Warren's judicial writings do indeed possess a coherent jurisprudential line. White claims that Warren "equated judicial lawmaking with neither the dictates of reason ... nor the demands imposed by an institutional theory of the judge's role, nor the alleged 'command' of the constitutional text, but rather with his own reconstruction of the ethical structure of the Constitution."

This "ethicist" approach to judging pointed to particular judicial results—quite liberal results—but it is less clear that such a description captures fully the structure of reasoning in Warren's decisions. Quite often, Warren's opinions are stolid and doctrinally underdeveloped. In other instances, notably *Brown v. Board of Education* (1954) and *Miranda v. Arizona* (1966), Warren relied on a body of empirical data and social science without adequately explaining the bases of this approach and the link between the empirical evidence and the stated doctrine. Nevertheless, Earl Warren does stand out as a great chief justice, one whom Justice William Brennan described as the

"Superchief," because of his performance as leader of the Court. Rather than exercising influence through an outpouring of carefully crafted judicial decisions, Warren was content to affect the course of the law chiefly through the powers of the office of chief justice and especially through his considerable interpersonal skills and political savvy. His most notable victories, namely *Brown, Miranda,* and *Baker v. Carr* (1962), reflect the work of a skillful judicial leader, one with a keen sense for politics as "the art of the possible."

The Supreme Court that Warren joined in 1954 was fractured by conflicts among strong judicial personalities. Warren's predecessor, Fred Vinson, had failed miserably at the task of contending with the fractious justices. Intimidated by the Court's most forceful members and intellectually underequipped, Vinson had died frustrated with his inability to shepherd his eight brothers through the minefield of cases of the postwar decade. By contrast, Warren proved remarkably able to deal with conflicts among his colleagues in his first years on the Court. His most challenging task was to bring together the alliances formed among the Court's intellectual leaders. This group included Felix Frankfurter, Robert Jackson, Hugo Black, William O. Douglas, and, later in Warren's tenure, Brennan and John Marshall Harlan. While Black, Douglas, and Brennan represented, across a range of cases, one faction, and Jackson, Frankfurter, and later Harlan represented another, each of these men was individualistic and even obstinate.

The mercurial Frankfurter, a former Harvard Law School professor and a judicial conservative, posed a special challenge to Warren, but, in his first few years on the Court, Warren successfully placated Frankfurter. "The Professor" at first admired Warren for his shrewd political instincts and his apparent willingness to learn the ropes from him, the more senior justice. By Frankfurter's final term on the Court in 1962, however, the relationship between the two men had soured, as Warren solidified his grip over the increasingly liberal Court majority.

Naturally, Warren's relationship with the justices who were more sympathetic to his ideological instincts posed less of a challenge. Black and Douglas were no less powerful personalities than Frankfurter and Jackson, but Warren could more easily turn their energies to furthering their jurisprudential agendas through written decisions. The two liberals remained rather cantankerous, however, even though they had a strong ideological ally in Warren. At times, Black's persistent squabbles with Jackson and Frankfurter were beyond Warren's ability to control. Douglas was frequently incorrigible as well. Ever the skilled politician, Warren remained wisely patient, waiting until Jackson and Frankfurter retired and taking advantage of both the considerable experience and intellect of Black and Douglas and of the qualities of the new justices to move the Court past internecine conflicts and in a more pronounced liberal direction.

By far the most important ally in this quest was Brennan, who served with Warren for thirteen years. Brennan is widely regarded as the intellectual catalyst of the Warren Court's doctrinal revolution. Warren soon found that he could count on Brennan to draft intellectually rigorous opinions defending results that jibed with Warren's preferences and philosophies. In cases such as *New York Times v. Sullivan* (1964), a landmark libel case, and *Baker v. Carr,* the reapportionment decision, Brennan fashioned creative rationales for expanding the scope of individual rights under the Constitution. The Warren-Brennan alliance was the key to the success of the Court's expansion of individual rights and of the role of the judiciary. Where Black and Douglas were idiosyncratic and often divisive in their temperament and in their jurisprudence, Warren and Brennan proved the perfect combination of political and intellectual skills mobilized in the pursuit of a doctrinal agenda.

Warren's ability as a leader was tested immediately upon his arrival at the Court. The justices had already heard arguments in a consolidated group of cases challenging the constitutionality of segregated public schools. The most ambitious of the claims raised by the appellants was the call for the Court to overrule *Plessy v. Ferguson* (1896), which had enunciated the "separate but equal" doctrine and had upheld the constitutionality of segregated public facilities. At conference following the oral argument in the first case to reach the Court in the spring of 1953, the justices were divided. On taking office, Warren presided over reargument in the case and then set out to manufacture a unanimous Court for the proposition that segregated public schools constituted an unconstitutional deprivation of the equal protection of the laws.

Scholars who have examined the decision-making process in the segregation cases agree that Warren's skills were crucial to securing assent by each justice to the ruling in *Brown*. He began by asserting in the conference that *Plessy* should be overruled. He worked on securing a unanimous result through conversations with the undecided justices and through circulation of the drafts of an opinion in the case. Warren's decision for the unanimous Court in *Brown* concentrated on taking the doctrinal legs out from under *Plessy*, relying on sociological data and on a forceful explication of the view, eloquently presented to the Court by NAACP lawyer Thurgood Marshall, that "separate is inherently unequal."

When the time came to fashion a decision in the remedial portion of the segregation disputes, Warren turned to Frankfurter and borrowed the famous phrase "all deliberate speed" to describe the time period in which local decision makers were obliged to desegregate the schools. Warren was also determined to secure a unanimous decision in *Brown v. Board of Education II* (1955). Ironically, although the cautious language of *Brown II* was intended to cabin the role of the federal judiciary in superintending local decisions, the result of the "all deliberate speed" standard was to thrust the federal courts continuously into disputes over the pace and scope of desegregation in various areas.

Warren's tone in *Brown II* was relatively mild, but he soon realized that he needed to lay down an unmistakably direct instruction to government officials to obey the Court's desegregation rulings. In *Cooper v. Aaron* (1958), the Court faced the defiance of a state official who believed the *Brown* decisions were not the law of the land. In response to the official's argument that the people of his state have a "right to have a doubt" concerning the legal effect of the Court's desegregation decisions, Warren declared that he had "never heard a lawyer say that the statement of a Governor as to what was legal or illegal should control the action of any court." Warren again secured unanimous agreement on the principle "that the federal judiciary is supreme in the exposition of the law of the Constitution." The Court's statement in *Cooper* proved a watershed in the effort of the federal government to confront local officials' unwillingness to carry out their desegregation responsibilities.

In his influential monograph on judicial review and constitutional theory, law professor John Hart Ely explains much of the Warren Court's constitutional jurisprudence as a coherent effort to respond through creative judicial intervention to failures in the political process, failures that had the effect of disenfranchising political minorities and impeding democratic processes. Ely's reconceptualization of the Warren Court's rights revolution moves attention away from what has often been seen as Warren's and his allies' tendencies to act on their own views of what the Constitution means; instead, Ely grounds the jurisprudence of the Warren Court majority in democracy and fair representation, regarding the Court in this era not as antidemocratic but, on the contrary, facilitative of democracy in its proper form. The strongest support for the thesis that the Supreme Court was, under Warren's strong leadership, democracy-enhancing and process-perfecting are the Court's opinions in the constitutional cases concerning representation and the political process.

Legislative apportionment in many ways represents the quintessential dispute over the proper role of the judiciary in ensuring fair representation. The Supreme Court revisited the constitutionality of various malapportioned legislative districts in the early 1960s against the backdrop of precedents holding apportionment to be a nonjusticiable political question. The lodestar decision was *Baker v. Carr,* a complaint from Tennessee that the vote of a rural voter was worth four times that of an urban voter. The Court declared that the apportionment issue was justiciable and therefore within the discretion of the federal courts to consider and resolve. Frankfurter had spelled out the contrary position in his opinion for

the Court in *Colegrove v. Green* (1946), and he reiterated it in his dissent in *Baker*. According to Frankfurter, reapportionment disputes were a political thicket that the Court should not enter. Such questions, he wrote, are properly political and therefore outside the appropriate range of judicial scrutiny. The decision in *Baker* was a decisive rejection of this "political question" theory. Although the Court majority declined to reach the merits of the constitutional argument in *Baker,* leaving that issue open for another two terms, what it did decide was that questions of fair representation raised by disputes concerning reapportionment and similar controversies were within the scope of the judicial function.

In *Reynolds v. Sims* (1964), the Court reached the merits of an apportionment scheme. *Reynolds* concerned Alabama's apportionment scheme, which had the same problem as Tennessee's plan. This predicament was common in the South, where black voters tended to be concentrated in cities and white citizens had a vested interest in ensuring that the current political structure continued. *Reynolds* and related cases that the Court had before it triggered Warren's instincts for political fairness and equality. "How long should we have to wait?" Warren asked Alabama's attorney, who attempted to reassure the justices that Alabama would correct its representational flaws in time. Warren wrote the opinion for the Court in *Reynolds,* declaring that "legislators represent people, not trees or acres" and announcing the "one man, one vote" rule mandating that state legislative districts represent an equal number of constituents.

The desideratum of the Court's apportionment decisions was to provide both a precedent for judicial intervention into the political arrangements of states and a bright-line rule for the construction of all legislative districts except the U.S. Senate. Friends and foes of the Warren Court's apportionment decisions shared the view that they were significant in their effects on the relationship between federal constitutional doctrine and local political decision making or, more simply, on the relationship between law and politics. What remains controversial to this day, however, is whether the enunciation of the one person, one vote rule as the strict criterion of fair apportionment represents the best way of correcting flaws in the political processes of states. The persistence of the *Reynolds* rule has restricted the states' abilities to experiment with alternative representational schemes that may improve the political process, while maintaining fair, if not numerically equal, representation. To Warren, however, the effects of the reapportionment decisions were transformative in just the right way. The decisions represented the critical point between the Court's efforts to limit the effects of race discrimination and the states' efforts to shut out minorities from effective participation in state political systems. Indeed, Warren suggested that had the Court decided *Baker v. Carr* early on, the desegregation decisions would have been unnecessary.

Judicial intervention in the name of securing fair representation was a major theme in Warren's jurisprudence throughout his tenure. Two important cases decided in his final term illustrate the scope of this philosophy. In *Powell v. McCormack* (1969), the Court considered whether the decision by the House of Representatives to unseat Rep. Adam Clayton Powell, D-N.Y., violated the Constitution. In his opinion for the Court, Warren explained the limited power of the House to discipline its members, stressing the right of the people to elect their representatives. *Powell* was a rare case in which the Court invalidated an internal decision of the legislature on what amounted to democratic "fairness" grounds.

In *Allen v. State Board of Elections* (1969), the Court considered what scope to accord to Section 5 of the Voting Rights Act of 1965. Section 5 provided that changes in state voting schemes be subjected to review by the Justice Department prior to taking effect. Warren's opinion for the Court rejected the view that the statute was limited to only those state enactments that prescribe who may register to vote. Warren wrote that the act "was aimed at the subtle, as well as the obvious, state regulations which have the effect of denying citizens their right to vote because of their race." Accordingly, he interpreted the act to subject to federal review any state voting enactment that "altered the election law of a covered State in even a minor way."

Powell and *Allen* demonstrate Warren's commitment to enforcing a vision of the Constitution in which fair representation is ensured through strict constitutional and statutory review. The basic underpinnings of these rulings, particularly *Baker* and *Reynolds,* have survived more or less intact, but the Burger and Rehnquist Courts proved far less willing than Warren and his allies to implement this vision of democratic fairness. Scholars writing at the time of the landmark Warren Court decisions of the 1960s confidently predicted that the Court would act to police the democratic process for unfairness and inequalities. The phrase "due process of lawmaking" was coined to capture the spirit of the Court's decisions to scrutinize closely the processes of government decision making and to strike down decisions that failed to measure up to a standard of fair representation. This spirit proved short-lived. Efforts to revive a sustained process-perfecting approach to judicial review are often grounded in a nostalgic appreciation of the Warren Court's commitments to procedural fairness in government. Contemporary constitutional jurisprudence, however, inspires little confidence that this commitment will be fulfilled.

Many believe that the Warren Court made its greatest mark in the area of individual rights and liberties. It is associated with a jurisprudence of robust personal freedom and searching scrutiny of government conduct that arguably infringes on this freedom. Criminal law, specifically the rights of the accused, is the most controversial area in which the Warren Court changed the distribution of authority and prerogative between the individual and the state. Reflecting his pre-Court commitment to fairness in law enforcement, Warren proved willing to look closely at police conduct and to consider whether the accused had been treated fairly. In such cases, observes G. Edward White, "Warren saw himself as vindicating an innate right of citizens to be presumptively free from the coercive mechanisms of government." In *Watkins v. United States* (1957), for example, Warren wrote an opinion for the Court in which he held that Congress, acting through the House Un-American Activities Committee, had improperly held

John Watkins in contempt of Congress for failing to disclose certain information. According to Warren, Congress had failed to provide the defendant with "a fair opportunity to determine whether he was within his rights in refusing to answer." Judicial redress for the failure of the government to provide a criminal defendant with due process was a common theme in Warren's constitutional jurisprudence.

The most famous of these criminal procedure decisions was *Miranda v. Arizona.* Ernesto Miranda had been arrested for kidnapping and rape and questioned without being advised as to his constitutional rights, including the right to have an attorney present during questioning. In an opinion another justice described as "entirely" Warren's, the chief justice relied on an elaborate description of historical and contemporary police practices, all with an eye toward persuading the reader that the requirements the Court imposed in this case, namely, the now well-known Miranda warnings, would not unjustifiably burden law enforcement officials. *Miranda* was the quintessential Warren opinion: it was far-flung, relying on a patched-together history and impassioned plea for fairness rather than a closely reasoned doctrinal story. And it unhesitatingly imposed substantial restrictions on government conduct. Although *Miranda* generated a storm of controversy at the time of the decision and for years after, Warren's approach to constructing a code of police conduct in the arrest and interrogation of suspects has largely been vindicated; most regard the criminal process as substantially fairer as a result of *Miranda.*

A far less generous reading is accorded Warren's work in the area of obscenity and the First Amendment, where his jurisprudence was of a piece with his thinking across the range of the Constitution's guarantees of individual rights. Often following Brennan's carefully constructed doctrinal rationales, Warren predictably voted to strike down various government restrictions on the First Amendment freedoms of expression and religion. When the issue was government restrictions on allegedly obscene speech, however, Warren fell out of step with the standard liberal tradition. He believed steadfastly in what he called "a

right of the government to maintain a decent society." Accordingly, he gave the government much latitude to prohibit the trafficking of allegedly pornographic materials. The concern in such cases, argued Warren, was with the conduct of the individual, not with the content of the material. In this way, Warren attempted to steer away from coaxing the Court into the position of ad hoc censor. He emphasized in his obscenity opinions that it was to local communities that the Court should delegate the principal role in combating obscenity and its effects. In the final analysis, Warren's struggle to carve out a special jurisprudence for obscenity was widely regarded as a failure. Simply, it became impossible to reconcile the Warren Court's commitment to freedom of expression and reluctance to play the role of censor through content-based restrictions on speech with the chief's unguarded hostility to pornography.

Warren also placed his stamp on the Court's expansive rights jurisprudence. In the constitutional rights area, perhaps more than any other, the Warren Court was committed to a capacious jurisprudence of rights and liberties under the Constitution. This approach reached its apotheosis in cases such as *Griswold v. Connecticut* (1965), in which the majority found a right to privacy in the penumbra of the Bill of Rights. The Court's expansive approach to construing the Constitution largely jibed with the public's view of the proper role of the Court and of the relationship between government conduct and individual rights, but many commentators felt uneasy with the Court's broad interpretations of the Bill of Rights. Indeed, the Court was continuously faced, in the later years of the Warren Court and beyond, with disputes that posed questions concerning how far these results and rationales could be pushed. Nevertheless, the Warren Court's constitutional jurisprudence proved resilient even after Warren left. Indeed, not one of the Warren Court's landmark civil liberties cases—not *Brown, Baker, Miranda,* or *Griswold*—has been overturned by judicial decision or constitutional amendment.

Where the Warren Court had perhaps its most lasting impact was with respect to the role of the judiciary in reviewing government decisions. Warren rarely explained in any detail his views concerning the appropriate role of the judiciary in the democratic system. His actions in creating an activist Supreme Court truly spoke louder than his words on the subject. His actions included a plethora of decisions in which the Court subjected decisions taken by institutions at all levels of government to searching scrutiny. Warren was untroubled with the expanding judicial role portended by the liberal direction of the Court's constitutional jurisprudence. He eschewed the cautious role commended by notable liberals such as Benjamin Cardozo and Oliver Wendell Holmes. Where there was a wrong to be corrected and a right to be vindicated, Warren was content to have the Court provide redress through the means available to it. His jurisprudence, as Prof. Martin Shapiro has labeled it, was decidedly a "jurisprudence of values," in which the right result took precedence over doctrinal clarity and consistency.

The Warren Court played a crucial, if overlooked, role in reshaping the distribution of powers among government decision makers at all levels of the federal system. Within the national government, this impact was felt through a changing scope of the Constitution's separation of powers. And with respect to the relationship between the national government and state and local governments, the impact of Warren Court decisions was felt in the area of federalism. Compared to other periods of American history, during the Warren years relatively few cases came before the Supreme Court that directly concerned an issue of separation of powers or of federalism. In the Warren years the disputes among institutions in the federal government, and among the federal, state, and local governments, ordinarily arose indirectly, that is, under the rubric of the Bill of Rights. Nevertheless, the effect of the Warren Court's jurisprudence in the constitutional area was to change dramatically the relationship among government institutions; in particular, it expanded the scope of the federal government's power to regulate under the Constitution's grants of authority.

The decisions in several civil rights cases decided in the 1960s contributed to this expanded federal role.

Following Congress's burst of civil rights legislation enacted in the mid- and late 1960s, the Court was faced with challenges to the legislature's constitutional power to pass laws directed at private and state government conduct. In every case, the Warren Court upheld Congress's constitutional powers. In the process, the Court created a jurisprudence in which legislative attempts to ameliorate the effects of segregation and discrimination were given the most capacious interpretations.

The difficulty with the Warren Court's approach was that in the rush to make emphatic the Court's commitment to furthering the cause of federal civil rights legislation and enforcement, it failed to establish doctrines of federalism that would clarify the limits of federal, state, and local power. In short, the Warren Court created a jurisprudence of civil rights without creating or maintaining a workable jurisprudence of federalism that would remain in place once state-federal disputes over civil rights were settled.

In a sense, this outcome was another consequence of the dilemma created by the Warren Court, in general, and Chief Justice Warren's approach to judging, in particular: the commitment to a set of particular results without the doctrinal underpinnings sufficient to resolve difficult problems that would arise later. In the area of individual rights and liberties, this dilemma was considerably less onerous; after all, the signal sent by the Warren Court was to stand committed to individual freedoms and to err on the side of protecting such freedoms even when the doctrinal pegs proved slippery. But with respect to disputes concerning the proper allocation of power among government institutions, the failure to establish coherent and persuasive doctrinal frameworks invited unique and difficult problems. Indeed, the controversies over separation of powers and federalism that loomed large in the Burger and Rehnquist Courts were partly a product of the questions left unanswered and the doctrinal anomalies left unresolved by the Warren Court.

The Court that Warren left in 1969 was dominated by a liberal, activist approach to judging in which a solid majority was committed to expanding the scope of individual freedoms even where the Constitution's text was less than clear and the Constitution's history indeterminate. Students of the Warren Court have provided analyses of the Court's decisions, as well as of Warren's individual decisions, suggesting that the Court's approaches were neither intellectually rudderless nor democratically illegitimate, but instead were grounded in creative, yet doctrinally respectable, interpretations of the Constitution's commands and the expressed views of Congress through its statutes. Critics have challenged the Warren Court's legacy both on the grounds that its jurisprudence, however ideologically appealing, is without adequate doctrinal anchors, and also because it represented a dramatic expansion in the powers of the unelected federal judiciary at the expense of the more democratic institutions: Congress, the president, and state and local governments.

In an essay written at the end of Earl Warren's tenure, Prof. Philip Kurland observed with respect to the Warren Court's legacy that "history has a nasty way of measuring greatness in terms of success rather than in terms of goodness." Kurland was suggesting that the future would regard the Warren Court's judicial revolution as a failure, however good its intentions, but history has been rather kind to the Warren Court. Public opinion was remarkably supportive of the Warren Court's decisions in the 1950s and 1960s, and historians continue to acknowledge their impact. Indeed, the triumph of the Warren Court was its success in leading the way toward a reconstructed constitutional system, a system in which the goals of equality and fair representation were expanded and protected against government encroachments. There had been other periods of judicial activism, and it is not at all clear that the Warren Court's activism was different in kind from the Marshall Court's of the early nineteenth century or the New Deal Court's of the 1930s. In fact, scholars have noted a different kind of activism—a conservative activism—in the decisions of the Court under William H. Rehnquist. The Warren Court stands out primarily for the goals it expounded and enshrined into constitutional law through its decisions and for its success in grounding

these efforts in the evolving public opinion of American society. As the public and legislative debate that led to the defeat of Judge Robert H. Bork's nomination to the Court in 1987 showed, the jurisprudence of the Warren Court had become part of the sensibilities of a substantial majority of Americans. If, as Kurland suggests, history measures greatness by success, then the legacy of the Warren Court was quite secure, at least at that point.

As for Earl Warren's particular role in constructing this legacy, it seems clear in retrospect that this judicial revolution required exactly the sort of chief justice he was. His ability to formulate judicial strategies, illustrated most famously in *Brown* and *Baker,* was impressive. It was largely due to his uncanny abilities to lead the Court in a liberal direction during a turbulent period that his reputation is as one of America's greatest chief justices.

—*Daniel B. Rodriguez*

BIBLIOGRAPHY

Earl Warren, *The Memoirs of Chief Justice Earl Warren* (1977), is rather disappointing in its treatment of his judicial career. His papers, in the Library of Congress, offer a somewhat more illuminating account of his tenure on the Court. The most important biography is G. Edward White's *Earl Warren: A Public Life* (1982). Its treatment of Warren's career is definitive, but White's thesis concerning the conceptual underpinnings of Warren's jurisprudence is somewhat idiosyncratic. The most recent full-scale biography is Edward Cray, *Chief Justice: A Biography of Earl Warren* (1997). Other biographies on Warren are rather unilluminating accounts of his political and/or judicial career. A useful collection of essays examining the decisions of the Warren Court is Leonard W. Levy, ed., *The Supreme Court Under Earl Warren* (1972), which includes an interview with Warren on the role of the Court and insightful essays by two of the Court's most prominent academic critics, Alexander M. Bickel and Philip B. Kurland. More sympathetic accounts of Warren's jurisprudence include Archibald Cox, *The Warren Court* (1968); and Anthony Lewis, "Earl Warren," in Friedman and Israel, *Justices,* vol. 4, 2721. John Hart Ely, *Democracy and Distrust* (1980), is the most important effort to construct a comprehensive theoretical defense of the Warren Court's constitutional jurisprudence against charges that the Court was merely political and theoretically ungrounded. For a competing view of the Warren Court's philosophy, see Martin Shapiro, *Law and Politics in the Supreme Court* (1964); and Shapiro, "Fathers and Sons: The Court, The Commentators, and the Search for Values," in Vincent Blasi, ed., *The Burger Court: The Counter-Revolution that Wasn't* (1983).

For books that incorporate more recent scholarly work, see Michal R. Belknap, *The Supreme Court Under Earl Warren, 1953–1969* (2004); Morton Horwitz, *The Warren Court and the Pursuit of Justice* (1998); Bernard Schwartz, ed., *The Warren Court: A Retrospective* (1996); Mark Tushnet, ed., *The Warren Court in Historical and Political Perspective* (1993); and especially Lucas A. Powe Jr., *The Warren Court and American Politics* (2000).

Many books and articles address specific Warren Court decisions. On the desegregation cases, the most notable treatment is Richard Kluger's *Simple Justice* (1975). An account that makes use of Earl Warren's papers is Mark Tushnet, "What Really Happened in Brown v. Board of Education," *Columbia Law Review* 91 (1991): 1867. Issues of the *Supreme Court Review* published during Warren's tenure contain many interesting discussion of the Warren Court's pivotal cases. See also the symposium, "The Jurisprudential Legacy of the Warren Court," *Washington & Lee Law Review* 59 (2002): 1055.

NOTEWORTHY OPINIONS

Brown v. Board of Education, 347 U.S. 483 (1954)

Brown v. Board of Education II, 349 U.S. 294 (1955)

Baker v. Carr, 369 U.S. 186 (1962)

Miranda v. Arizona, 384 U.S. 436 (1966)

Powell v. McCormack, 395 U.S. 486 (1969)

Allen v. State Board of Elections, 393 U.S. 544 (1969)

BUSHROD WASHINGTON

Birth: June 5, 1762, Westmoreland County, Virginia.

Education: Privately tutored; graduated College of William and Mary, 1778; honorary LL.D. degrees from Harvard, Princeton, and University of Pennsylvania.

Official Positions: Member, Virginia House of Delegates, 1787; member, Virginia convention to ratify U.S. Constitution, 1788.

Supreme Court Service: Recess appointment as associate justice by President John Adams, September 29, 1798, to replace James Wilson, who had died; nominated by Adams, December 19, 1798; confirmed by the Senate, December 20, 1798, by a voice vote; took judicial oath February 4, 1799; served until November 26, 1829; replaced by Henry Baldwin, nominated by President Andrew Jackson.

Death: November 26, 1829, Philadelphia, Pennsylvania.

A favorite nephew of George Washington and the heir to Mount Vernon at the death of Martha Washington, Bushrod Washington studied at the College of William and Mary, apparently from 1775 to 1778, and again in 1780, on the latter occasion as a law student of George Wythe. After military service in the Virginia campaign and the siege of Yorktown in 1781, he continued his legal education in Philadelphia from 1782 to 1784 under statesman and jurist James Wilson.

Admitted to the Virginia bar, Washington began the practice of law in his home county and also served in the state legislature and as a Federalist delegate to the Virginia convention for the ratification of the U.S. Constitution. After an unsatisfactory effort to relocate his practice in Alexandria, he moved to Richmond, where he had greater success. Washington and John Marshall frequently appeared as opposing counsel in cases before the Virginia Court of Appeals, and during

1797 Washington worked on an edition of his notes on cases heard by that court between 1790 and 1796.

By the time the two volumes of his notes were published in 1798 and 1799, President John Adams had offered him an appointment as associate justice of the Supreme Court to fill the vacancy created by the death of his law teacher, James Wilson. Washington withdrew his announced candidacy for a seat in Congress and accepted, becoming at age thirty-six the youngest appointee to serve on the Court to that point.

On receipt of his commission, Washington immediately departed for service on the circuit court that sat for the Carolinas and Georgia, and he took his seat on the Supreme Court for the first time in February 1799. He was virtually the only sitting justice of any intellectual vigor when Marshall accepted an appointment as chief justice in 1801 and began the transformation of the Court into the powerful body that it became. Washington served on the bench thirty-one years in all, twenty-eight of them in the heyday of the Marshall Court.

Given their existing friendship and agreement on many political and legal matters, the collaboration between the two Virginians was long and close. Indeed, Justice William Johnson, in an often quoted letter to Thomas Jefferson, who had appointed him, observed that Marshall and Washington "are commonly estimated as one judge." Johnson's implication, too readily accepted by many later historians, that Washington was a cipher without influence of his own on the Court, is assuredly an exaggeration. It is true that over his long tenure Washington disagreed with the chief justice only eight times. He wrote relatively few decisions, some eighty-one in all, of which only three were dissents. He also wrote two concurrences and seven *seriatim* opinions, most of the latter before Marshall joined the Court or when he was absent.

This record, however, has to be set in the context of the Marshall Court, for which the chief justice wrote many of the decisions and always sought as much unanimity as possible. Washington's activity was, even so, greater than that of most of the justices apart from Joseph Story and Johnson. Moreover, he generally agreed with Marshall and remained particularly committed to the principle that the justices should, whenever possible, resolve their disagreements before announcing a decision. Washington's fellow justices respected him for the learning and patience he brought to the discussions that preceded final decisions, as well as for his integrity and willingness to work hard on the Court's business.

Washington proved a particularly active judge on circuit, serving continuously after the Judiciary Act of 1802 on the Third Circuit, which included Pennsylvania and New Jersey. He was among the Federalist judges who vigorously enforced the Alien and Sedition Laws of 1798, although less vindictively than some of his colleagues. In the circuit court case of *United States v. Bright* (1809), he strongly upheld the right of federal courts to overrule the actions of a state by convicting a Pennsylvania militia general for obeying the governor's order to defy the Supreme Court decision in *United States v. Peters* (1809). In his last years, Washington published, with the assistance of Richard Peters Jr., the district judge who sat with him on the Third Circuit, four volumes of reports of cases decided in the court.

Of Washington's Supreme Court opinions, three—a concurrence, a majority opinion on a rehearing of a case, and a *seriatim* opinion—have particular significance for the history of the Marshall Court. They also effectively illustrate Washington's general agreement with the Court's efforts to strengthen the authority of the national government and its courts, guarantee the force of private contracts, and encourage the free flow of commerce. Yet they also show that Washington at times provided a moderating influence on those trends in an effort to accommodate political reality and permit a reasonable sphere of activity for the states.

Bushrod Washington

For example, in the well-known case *Trustees of Dartmouth College v. Woodward* (1819), Washington accepted the general conclusion of Marshall's majority opinion that New Hampshire violated the contract clause of the Constitution in its attempt to alter the colonial charter of the college by introducing public control through the governor's appointment of its trustees. Washington was, however, unhappy with the chief justice's opinion, which was written on broad principles and without any effort to find precedents for his decision. Washington wrote a concurring opinion, reaching the conclusion that the charter was indeed a valid contract, but by a more specific argument. Washington then went on to raise a second question: Does the contract clause protect the charter of a corporation? He concluded that the charter of a charitable institution, such as Dartmouth College, was so protected, but that noncharitable corporations were not. Washington was here contesting Story's concurring opinion, which explicitly included business corporations under the contract clause. Had Washington's view prevailed, the *Dartmouth College* decision might not have achieved its full significance as a guarantor of private incorporations.

In *Green v. Biddle* (1823), Washington managed, successfully this time, to moderate a decision of the Court without altering its substance. The case tested the force of the compact concluded between Virginia and Kentucky in 1792, by which Virginia consented to the formation of the new state from its territory, but required that all its previously issued private land titles remain valid. In 1797 Kentucky attempted to assert, by a so-called occupying claimant law, that if others had subsequently settled on lands without a legal title, but had improved them, the original owners would be required to forego rents and to pay reimbursement to such illegal occupants before they could recover possession.

In the original hearing in 1821, Story wrote a sweeping opinion, based on broad principles of natural law, that overturned the Kentucky legislation and aroused a storm of political protest. The Court agreed to a rehearing at the instigation of Henry Clay. On this occasion, Washington wrote an opinion that still upheld the validity of Virginia titles and the sanctity of private property, but on more legalistic grounds and by reference to the Court's authority under the contract clause. He also assured Kentuckians that they could still take lands for public use or resale, provided just compensation was paid the original owners. The opinion perhaps rested on somewhat shaky ground in trying to apply the contract clause to the interstate Kentucky-Virginia agreement, and it did not in the least assuage Kentucky interests. But it accorded with Washington's inclinations to provide maximum protection for property rights and limit state sovereignty.

Washington was, within limits, more sympathetic to state authority in his *seriatim* opinion in *Ogden v. Saunders* (1827), a decision involving the constitutionality of a state bankruptcy law. The Court had wrestled with this thorny question for some years, torn between a belief that under the Constitution, bankruptcy statutes were the sole preserve of Congress and a recognition that the Congress's persistent failure to pass such an act created an undesirable void. The justices were also divided as to whether bankruptcy laws were an impairment of the contract clause. In 1814 Washington had taken an extreme view in a circuit court decision in which he argued that the states lacked any constitutional power whatsoever to enact bankruptcy laws. Then, in 1819, a badly split Supreme Court achieved an outward show of unanimity by ruling in *Sturges v. Crowninshield* that state bankruptcy laws were permissible in the absence of action by Congress, but that the law under review was unconstitutional because it extended to debts contracted prior to the enactment of the legislation and thereby impaired the obligation of contract. Washington had accepted the decision, perhaps out of his desire for unanimity, but also because he may have changed his mind about state legislation in some circumstances.

Now, in *Ogden v. Saunders,* the Court, with a somewhat different membership, again disagreed on a state bankruptcy law that applied only to obligations incurred after its passage. Marshall, in the only minority constitutional opinion he ever wrote, insisted that the Constitution protected all contracts, past or future, and two justices voted with him in the minority. The four justices in the majority wrote separate and differing opinions, but upheld the validity of the law under review and, in one degree or another, the constitutionality of state bankruptcy laws generally. Washington's opinion was the most restrictive, essentially following the precedent of *Sturges*, that is, allowing such laws in the absence of an act of Congress and approving the present law because it applied only to future debts. As with many of his decisions, he had demonstrated his concern for attention to past precedent.

Through much of the 1820s, Washington suffered periods of illness that at times prevented his sitting either on circuit or in the Supreme Court. On other occasions, he rallied and was as active as ever. At his final session of the Court in early 1829, he wrote an unusually large number of opinions—six in all. He died in late November while in Philadelphia attempting, almost to the end, to carry out his circuit court duties. In his obituary in the *Reports* of the Supreme Court, John Marshall wrote, "No man knew his worth better or deplores his death more than myself."

—*Thad W. Tate*

BIBLIOGRAPHY

David Leslie Annis's dissertation, "Mr. Bushrod Washington, Supreme Court Justice on the Marshall Court" (Notre Dame, 1974), provides a full account of Washington's life and service on the Court; Albert Blaustein and Roy Mersky, "Bushrod Washington," in Friedman and Israel, *Justices*, vol.1, 243, is a good sketch; G. Edward White, *The Marshall Court and Cultural Change, 1815–35* (1988), volume 3 of the *Holmes Devise History*, 344–354, provides a perceptive account of Washington and deals fully with his post-1815 decisions; in the same series, George Lee Flaskins and Herbert A. Johnson's volume, *Foundations of Power, John Marshall, 1801–15* (1981), covers Washington's early years on the Court. For a more recent evaluation, see Daniel Faber, "Justice Bushrod Washington and the Age of Discovery in American Law," *West Virginia Law Review* 102 (2000): 735.

NOTEWORTHY OPINIONS

Trustees of Dartmouth College v. Woodward, 17 U.S. 518 (1819) (Concurrence)

Green v. Biddle, 21 U.S. 1 (1823)

Ogden v. Saunders, 25 U.S. 213 (1827)

JAMES MOORE WAYNE

Birth: 1790, Savannah, Georgia.

Education: College of New Jersey (Princeton University), 1808, honorary LL.B., 1849; read law privately; admitted to the bar January 1811.

Official Positions: Member, Georgia House of Representatives, 1815–1816; mayor, Savannah, 1817–1819; judge, Savannah Court of Common Pleas, 1820–1822; judge, Georgia Superior Court, 1822–1828; U.S. representative, 1829–1835; chairman, Committee on Foreign Relations.

Supreme Court Service: Nominated associate justice by President Andrew Jackson, January 7, 1835, to replace William Johnson, who had died; confirmed by the Senate, January 9, 1835 by a voice vote; took judicial oath January 14, 1835; served until July 5, 1867; replaced by Joseph Bradley, nominated by President Ulysses S. Grant.

Death: July 5, 1867, Washington, D.C.

James Moore Wayne was born about 1790 in Savannah, Georgia, the twelfth of thirteen children of Richard Wayne and Elizabeth Clifford. Raised on his family's rice plantation, Wayne enrolled at the College of New Jersey (now Princeton University) in 1804 at age fourteen and received his degree in 1808. He then studied law under the tutelage of several lawyers in Georgia and Connecticut, including Judge Charles Chauncey of New Haven. Admitted to the bar in 1811, Wayne entered law practice in Savannah.

During the next two decades, Wayne gradually gained national prominence through his work in Georgia state politics and in the judiciary. He served in the Georgia legislature and as a member of the Savannah Board of Aldermen. He was the mayor of Savannah for two years. Starting in 1819 he served first as judge on the Savannah Court of Common Pleas and then as judge on the local superior court. In

1828 Wayne was elected to the U.S. House of Representatives, where he served for three terms and garnered recognition as a leading Democrat and supporter of President Andrew Jackson, who nominated him to fill the U.S. Supreme Court seat vacated by the death of William Johnson.

As associate justice, Wayne developed a particular interest and expertise in admiralty cases, and many of his most distinctive opinions in his first two decades on the Court propounded his view of the expansive power enjoyed by Congress in its regulation of waterways. For example, in *Waring v. Clarke* (1847), Wayne wrote on behalf of the Court to accord broad federal admiralty jurisdiction in a case involving a ship collision nearly 100 miles up the Mississippi River, reasoning that such power should extend to sea waters flowing by tide or otherwise into rivers and ports. In the *Passenger Cases* (1849), the Court struck down two state laws levying taxes on ship captains for each immigrant carried. The Court said that the laws constituted improper incursions into congressional power over foreign commerce; and, in a separate concurring opinion, Wayne asserted that the laws were invalid because the commerce power was vested exclusively in Congress. He dissented in *Cooley v. Board of Wardens of the Port of Philadelphia* (1852), in which the Court announced the so-called "Cooley doctrine" of "selective exclusiveness" in balancing federal and state powers with regard to foreign and interstate commerce. Wayne said that the commerce clause demanded exclusive federal regulation of foreign and interstate commerce.

Wayne's tenure was also marked by personal conflict and ambivalence. He was a southerner and a slave owner, but he supported the Union cause during the Civil War. He regularly favored slave interests in his rulings on the Court, but voted with the majority in the momentous decision of *Dred Scott v. Sandford* (1857). Wayne agreed with Chief Justice Roger Taney's opinion, which held that Congress had the authority neither to prohibit the introduction of slavery into the territories nor to recognize as free a slave who had been brought into the territories. Nevertheless, Wayne refused to join the Confederacy or to leave the Court during the war. As a result, the Confederacy labeled him a traitor, charged him in a Confederate court with being an enemy alien, and confiscated his property in Georgia. In the *Prize Cases* (1863), Wayne joined the Court in upholding the constitutionality of President Abraham Lincoln's proclamation of a Union naval blockade of Confederate ports; yet, by the war's end, he voted to strike down Reconstruction measures such as the test oath laws in *Cummings v. Missouri* (1867) and *Ex parte Garland* (1867), and he refused to sit as circuit court judge in states under military Reconstruction rule.

Wayne died of typhoid on July 5, 1867, in Washington, D.C. Despite his repudiation of the Confederacy during the Civil War, he was buried in Savannah.

—*Margaret M. Russell*

James Moore Wayne

BIBLIOGRAPHY

The most comprehensive study to date of Wayne's life and work is Alexander A. Lawrence's *James Moore Wayne, Southern Unionist* (1943). Also of note are the following brief sketches: Alexander A. Lawrence, "Justice Wayne and the Dred Scott Case," *Proceedings of the Fifty-Seventh Annual Session of the Georgia Bar Association* (1940): 196; George G. Battle, "James Moore Wayne: Southern Unionist," *Fordham Urban Law Journal* 14 (1964): 42; and Warren Grice, "James M. Wayne," *Georgia Bar Association Proceedings* (1938): 179.

NOTEWORTHY OPINIONS

Waring v. Clarke, 46 U.S. 441 (1847)

Passenger Cases, 48 U.S. 283 (1849)

Cooley v. Board of Wardens of the Port of Philadelphia, 53 U.S. 299 (1851) (Dissent)

BYRON RAYMOND WHITE

Birth: June 8, 1917, Fort Collins, Colorado.

Education: University of Colorado, B.A., 1938; Rhodes Scholar, Oxford, 1939; Yale Law School, LL.B., magna cum laude, 1946.

Official Positions: Law clerk to Chief Justice Fred M. Vinson, 1946–1947; deputy U.S. attorney general, 1961–1962.

Supreme Court Service: Nominated associate justice by President John F. Kennedy, April 3, 1962, to replace Charles E. Whittaker, who had retired; confirmed by the Senate, April 11, 1962, by a voice vote; took judicial oath April 16, 1962; retired June 28, 1993; replaced by Ruth Bader Ginsburg, nominated by President Bill Clinton.

Death: April 15, 2002, Denver, Colorado.

Byron White holds the unique distinction of being the only former professional football player ever to sit on the U.S. Supreme Court. An athletic standout in several sports at the University of Colorado, White chose to play football for the Pittsburgh Steelers for one year after his 1938 graduation, before taking up a Rhodes scholarship to Oxford. The following year World War II broke out and White, along with many of the other American students in England, returned to the United States. He entered Yale Law School in 1939, and in his second year played pro football on weekends for the Detroit Lions. After service in the navy during the war, White completed his law degree at Yale in 1946, graduating magna cum laude, and then clerked for Chief Justice Fred Vinson. He entered private practice in Colorado, dabbling a bit in local politics, and probably would have stayed there for the rest of his life had not John F. Kennedy run for president in 1960.

White had met Kennedy years earlier, when the two were on the same ship to England. White was traveling to begin his studies at Oxford, and Kennedy to join his family (his father, Joseph Kennedy, was the U.S. ambassador to England). White agreed to chair the Colorado committee for Kennedy's presidential campaign, and after the election, White accepted an offer to become deputy attorney general in the Justice Department headed by the president's brother, Robert F. Kennedy. White apparently could have had other positions in the administration, but he wanted to be where the action was, and he expected that to be in Justice. He became Robert Kennedy's right-hand man, helped him put together the team that would run the department for the next three years, and was an indispensable adviser. There is no indication that White, who had been active in helping select lower court nominees, thought himself under consideration when Justice Charles Whittaker left the Court after a nervous breakdown. But John Kennedy had him in mind from the start and had no interest in considering other candidates. The president nominated White to the Court on April 3, 1962, and after pro forma hearings (the Judiciary Committee met for only ninety minutes) the Senate unanimously confirmed him on April 11 by a voice vote, dispensing with the usual rule of holding a nomination over for twenty-four hours after the committee vote. Five days later "Whizzer" White took the oath of office.

At the time of his appointment some conservatives grumbled that White, like most of the members of the Kennedy administration, was too liberal. When, later in his judicial career, White tended to vote with the more conservative bloc on the Court, commentators charged that he had betrayed the Kennedy legacy or that he had in fact been a conservative all the time. Yet White never saw himself as either a liberal or a conservative, but as a pragmatist, a man who assessed a problem and then tried to solve it. Law professor William Nelson, who clerked for White, argues that White always remained a Kennedy liberal, but that one had to understand what Kennedy liberalism meant—namely, pragmatism, egalitarianism, and individualism.

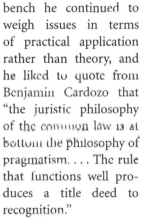

Byron Raymond White

According to Nelson, White never deviated from the Kennedy commitment to pragmatic social reform and an impassioned devotion to equality. White departed from more activist members of the Court, such as his close friend William Brennan, on individual rights, where he eschewed the idea of group rights in areas such as affirmative action. White's pragmatic side is apparent in criminal law cases, where he assessed how workable particular choices would be. In 1966 he dissented in *Miranda v.*

Arizona, which imposed the obligation upon police officers to inform detainees of their rights, arguing that constitutional decisions "cannot rest alone on syllogism, metaphysics or some ill-defined notions of natural justice." The Court had a duty to "inquire into the advisability of its end product in terms of the long-range interest of the country." White thought the Miranda warnings would not be effective and that the practice would hinder law enforcement; in this, he proved wrong. But throughout his tenure on the bench he continued to weigh issues in terms of practical application rather than theory, and he liked to quote from Benjamin Cardozo that "the juristic philosophy of the common law is at bottom the philosophy of pragmatism. . . . The rule that functions well produces a title deed to recognition."

This pragmatism made him, as much as any member of the Court, a fact-driven judge, for whom the specifics of a case, rather than a cast-iron doctrine, determine the outcome. As a result, commentators often criticized him as unpredictable or even arbitrary, when it would have been far more accurate to recognize that he was not doctrinaire. He paid close attention to the record, and if in one case he could uphold the Federal Communications Commission's authority against a First Amendment claim (*Red Lion Broadcasting v. FCC*, 1969), in another he could argue that the commission had exceeded its statutory powers (*FCC v. Midwest Video*, 1979). Law professor Monroe Price found that this antidoctrinaire trait did not make White a swing vote;

instead, he found that White's work reflected a determined effort to "maintain the sense that judges should not be pre-programmed and easily predictable, that their views and values evolve and that they must, therefore, maintain only a tentative and analytical approach to certain of the largest questions in the society." This approach reflected the legal realism in which White had been schooled at Yale, but it could, as some critics believed, also make him unpredictable.

Those who thought (or hoped) that White would join the four liberal activists on the Court—Earl Warren, Hugo Black, William O. Douglas, and Brennan—were quickly disappointed. Although White took his seat in mid-April 1962, the chief justice had held several cases over for reargument because of Whittaker's illness, and White not only heard these cases, but wrote three opinions before the Court adjourned. One of them, *Robinson v. California* (1962), involved a state statute criminalizing addiction to narcotics. A majority of the Court ruled the law unconstitutional because it punished a status rather than an act and therefore violated the Eighth Amendment ban against cruel and unusual punishment; Justice Douglas added a concurrence in which he argued that addiction was a disease, not a crime.

White's short dissent set a pattern for his later opinion writing. He accused the majority of misrepresenting the facts in the case and unnecessarily reaching a constitutional issue. The record indicated to him that Robinson had been tried for habitual use and by his own admission had shot up eight times the day before his arrest. No evidence had been presented that California would in fact prosecute a "helpless addict," and the majority, by invalidating the drug use that led to the addiction, cast doubts "upon the power of any State to forbid the use of narcotics under the threat of criminal punishment." In his concluding sentence he heartened those who believed the Court had become far too activist. "I fail to see why the Court deems it more appropriate to write into the Constitution its own abstract notions of how best to handle the narcotics problem, for it obviously cannot match either the States or Congress in expert understanding."

As his biographer, law professor Dennis Hutchinson, notes, White, the first law clerk to be appointed to the Court, had already dealt with the issue of federal court supervision of state criminal proceedings during his year clerking for Vinson. At that time he had subscribed to the belief that federal courts were poor instruments to oversee state criminal courts, and he continued to believe that during much of his career on the Court. But his voice on this matter was pretty much drowned out when later in 1962 Arthur Goldberg took Felix Frankfurter's seat and provided the liberal bloc with a solid five-man majority. During the October 1962 term, White dissented often, but in cases that had little lasting doctrinal significance. The following term, however, Warren assigned him the opinion in *Jackson v. Denno* (1964), and he staked out as his own the self-incrimination clause of the Fifth Amendment, which the Court just the week before had applied to the states in *Malloy v. Hogan* (1964). White dissented in *Malloy,* and in *Jackson* he set forth a fundamental principle in his criminal law jurisprudence, one that he would develop over the years—the content of a constitutionally protected right must be decided by an unbiased decision maker.

In *Jackson v. Denno,* the trial jury decided as a question of fact not only the guilt of the defendant, but also whether a confession had been given voluntarily. White concluded that this procedure did not provide a reliable measure of voluntariness, because the evidence of the crime and other evidence regarding the defendant's guilt would taint the jury's assessment of the confession. Here White ran up against his own reluctance to interfere with state procedures, but the risk of biased fact finders would have made decisions on voluntariness depend on the whims of juries and thus subvert a constitutional right. The decision voided practices in fifteen states and a number of federal circuits.

Although Warren joined White in *Jackson,* the two parted company in the most famous criminal law case of the Warren era, *Miranda v. Arizona.* The decision not only led White to issue a bristling dissent but also to publicly criticize the whole line of criminal justice decisions beginning with *Mapp v. Ohio* (1961).

He attacked specific provisions of the decisions in speeches to various bar associations, as well as the whole interpretation given by the Court in what has been called the "due process revolution." White did not believe that the meaning of the Bill of Rights had been set in stone by the founders, but that different meanings could be determined by future generations. Neither did he believe that judges were necessarily best suited to decide what he considered important public policy matters. As he told a friend, "The trouble with these liberals up here is that they think they have all the answers to social problems like crime and race, and what's worse, they're putting them into the Constitution."

White had been one of the leaders in the Kennedy administration's efforts to secure civil rights for blacks, and on the Court he proved a consistent vote in striking down overt discrimination against African Americans. He joined unanimous courts during the latter part of the Warren era and the first part of the Burger years to enforce the message that state-sponsored discrimination against blacks violated the Fourteenth Amendment's equal protection clause. Moreover, White was willing to go beyond school segregation; he wrote the majority opinions in *Reitman v. Mulkey* (1967) and *Hunter v. Erickson* (1969) striking down efforts by state and local governments to erect roadblocks to housing integration.

Initially, White favored some forms of affirmative action. In the landmark case *Regents of the University of California v. Bakke* (1978), he joined the plurality that upheld the race-quota program at the University of California at Davis Medical School, and he wrote separately to note his belief that "government may take race into account when it acts not to demean or insult any racial group, but to remedy disadvantage cast on minorities by past racial prejudice." In 1980 he again joined with a majority to uphold minority preference programs in federal purchasing in *Fullilove v. Klutznik*, and as late as 1990 he voted in *Metro Broadcasting, Inc. v. FCC* to endorse a federal program that sought to foster minority ownership of radio and television stations.

Despite these votes, White felt uncomfortable with affirmative action. Like many moderates, he questioned whether, absent evidence of prejudice against specific individuals, a generalized quota system would actually help minorities. At the time of the *Bakke* decision, he sent a memo to his colleagues expressing his anxieties that any race-sensitive program "in the end would often make race the determinative factor in administering a seemingly neutral set of qualifications." In *Bakke*, he had successfully urged a statutory rather than a constitutional basis for the decision to uphold the legitimacy of taking race into account, so that the decision of the Court would not be set in constitutional stone. Moreover, he believed that there were limits on which government agencies could in fact implement affirmative action programs. Although he was willing to allow the federal and state governments to do so, he drew a line when it came to municipal efforts. In *City of Richmond v. J. A. Croson Co.* (1989), he joined the majority in striking down a city program clearly based on the federal model in *Fullilove*.

Overall, there is no question that White continued the dedication that had marked his tenure in the Kennedy Justice Department to wiping out the badges of racial discrimination. As he did in school, housing, and affirmative action cases, he also voted consistently to protect minority voting rights. He voted with the majority in the cases leading up to and including *Reynolds v. Sims* (1964) that established the one person, one vote rule in legislative apportionment. Many commentators saw this case as pitting entrenched rural groups against the new urban majorities, but White and others recognized that in many states African Americans constituted a large part of those new urban majorities. The one person, one vote rule was an effective tool in increasing the voting power of blacks. In his opinion for a plurality in *United Jewish Organizations v. Carey* (1977) and his very last opinion, a dissent in *Shaw v. Reno* (1993), White supported the idea that efforts to draw legislative district boundaries "to provide minority voters with an effective voice in the political process" did not violate the Constitution.

White's reputation as a conservative stems primarily from his views on civil liberties. He never shared the Warren Court's liberal bloc's commitment to individual rights. Here again, those who claim that he changed his views after he went onto the Court misread White's original ideas, which included a strong belief in judicial restraint and deference to legislative policy decisions. The legal realists at Yale Law School had taught him that legal reasoning does little more than reflect the judge's preferences for one policy choice over another. If there were no principled constitutional reasons to strike down a statute, then judges should defer to the policy choices of the democratically elected branches.

Although he concurred in *Griswold v. Connecticut* (1965), the case that established the right to privacy, White opposed the whole notion of unenumerated rights or the use of the Fourteenth Amendment's due process clause to read new rights into the Constitution. He dissented in *Roe v. Wade* (1973), declaring that he could find nothing in the "language or history of the Constitution to support the Court's judgment" that the document supported a right to abortion. In White's view, the question of whether abortions are legal should be left to legislative judgment, and in all the abortion cases between *Roe* and his retirement from the bench in 1993, White consistently voted to give legislatures full scope to regulate or even forbid abortions. White also found nothing to support the right of homosexuals to engage in sodomy and said so in his majority opinion for the Court in *Bowers v. Hardwick* (1986). As to the claimed connection to earlier cases involving privacy, White noted that they were related to family rights, marriage, child rearing, and procreation, and none had "any resemblance to the claimed constitutional right of homosexuals to engage in acts of sodomy."

White's antipathy to claims of individual rights went far beyond his views on privacy but included some First Amendment issues and the rights of the accused. One reason the media labeled him a conservative was his refusal to read the First Amendment's freedom of the press clause expansively. In *Branzburg v. Hayes* (1972), White wrote for a 5–4 Court that refused to allow journalists to refuse to answer grand jury questions about confidential sources. Then in *Zurcher v. Stanford Daily* (1978), he spoke for a 5–3 Court in ruling that the press clause did not prohibit

reasonable searches of newsrooms when a proper warrant had been issued. In 1979 White again spoke for the Court in another opinion that the press saw as hostile to their rights. The First Amendment, White ruled in *Herbert v. Lando,* did not prevent a reasonable discovery request in a libel suit for outtakes and other unpublished editorial material. White also wrote the Court's unanimous opinion in *Red Lion Broadcasting Co. v. FCC* (1969), which affirmed the FCC's power over broadcast media in the face of a First Amendment challenge. Hutchinson writes that privately White "loathed" the press, a feeling that was clearly reciprocated. To give but one example, columnist Charles McCabe decried White as a "jock . . . named by a jock" to the Court, and he wrote that "17 years after his appointment, the former All-American is known chiefly as the Javert of the American press, [who] has pursued our editors and publishers with the cold fury of the pursuer of Jean Valjean."

In other matters relating to the Bill of Rights, White took a narrow view of the rights of protesters and of those accused of crimes. Given his time in the Justice Department, this stance should not be surprising. Like his boss, Robert Kennedy, White believed no quarter should be given to accused criminals, and, starting with his dissent in *Robinson v. California,* he for the most part disagreed with the Warren Court's expansive reading of the Fourth, Fifth, and Sixth Amendments. He dissented in *Escobedo v. Illinois* (1964), in which the majority invalidated a confession obtained at the police station from a suspect who had asked for his lawyer but was not allowed to see him. Two years later he voted against the majority position in *Miranda.* In *Berger v. New York* (1967), which placed limits on state wiretapping, White argued in dissent that wiretapping and other forms of eavesdropping constituted "irreplaceable investigative tools which are needed for the enforcement of criminal laws." Later on, in *Minnesota v. Dickerson* (1993), he supported the right of the police to seize contraband, without a warrant, when frisking a suspect.

As to the rights of the accused, here, too, White's votes could surprise. He voted with the majority in the landmark case *Gideon v. Wainwright* (1963), which imposed upon the states the requirement to provide counsel for indigents. He wrote the two leading opinions that applied the Fourth Amendment to legislative searches, *Camara v. Municipal Court* (1967) and *See v. Seattle* (1967). He joined with the majority in striking down the death penalty as then applied in *Furman v. Georgia* (1972), and he provided the fifth vote in *James v. Illinois* (1990) to stop the enlargement of exceptions to the exclusionary rule. At the end of his tenure, White wrote the majority opinion in *Helling v. McKinney* (1993), holding that the Eighth Amendment prevented prison officials from exposing prisoners to unreasonable health risks by placing them in cells with smokers. Where the record showed that a more expansive reading of a constitutional right could be warranted, White would vote to do so; other than that, he took a narrow view of how far the Bill of Rights protections extended.

A similar pattern is found in matters of free expression. In his early years on the bench, White often voted to protect the right of protesters. But cases such as *Edwards v. South Carolina* (1963) and *Brown v. Louisiana* (1966) involved young blacks protesting against segregation, and White—like the majority of the Court—could see the clear relation between the fight for civil rights and the need to protest discrimination. The furthest he seemed willing to go, however, was his vote in *Tinker v. Des Moines School District* (1969), permitting high school students protesting the Vietnam War to wear black armbands.

By the time of the *Tinker* decision, however, White had become less sympathetic to First Amendment claims of protesters. Although *Cox v. Louisiana* (1965) was a civil rights–related case, he voted to affirm the conviction of a minister who led a march to protest the arrest of students who had picketed segregated stores. The determining factor appears to have been that the site of the protest was the local courthouse, and White saw this as a breach of the peace. In later cases, whether in the majority or in dissent, White indicated that he had little tolerance for those who burned draft cards, wore clothing with objectionable language, or desecrated the flag. In taking this position, White resembled many liberals of his

age who valued civility and discourse as part of the rational processes of democratic government. He also shared the Kennedy faith in government as an effective tool for reform and, just as important, as a means of maintaining order.

As a result of his faith in government, he never shared the Warren Court's belief that government, even when it impinged upon individual rights, had to be restrained. From his Justice Department experience during years of civil strife (which then increased during the protests against the war in Vietnam), he believed that a strong and effective government provided the best means for social progress and the best protection against the forces of crime and disorder. As a result, he took a far more pragmatic approach to how government behaved than some of his brethren, who believed the Constitution set up immutable barriers to certain types of government action.

A good example of White's pragmatism is his dissent in *Immigration and Naturalization Service v. Chadha* (1983), decided about two-thirds of the way through his tenure. In this case seven members of the Court found that the so-called legislative veto, by which the vote of either the House of Representatives or the Senate could reverse an administrative decision, was a violation of separation of powers, in that a single house of Congress could undo an action taken by the executive in pursuance of a constitutionally enacted statute. Only White and William Rehnquist dissented, and White took the rare step of reading his dissent aloud. He told the audience gathered that day in the Court's chamber that it had been many years since he had done this, "but this is probably the most important case the Court had handed down in many years." The decision, he believed, was "destructive" and "clearly wrong and unnecessarily broad."

White advocated a flexible approach to the separation of powers. He believed the legislative veto had no more negative effect than if one house had rejected a private bill proposed by the executive (a bill dealing with a particular instance or individual rather than a broad policy), and that it was no worse for Congress to delegate authority to one of its houses than to delegate authority to an executive agency that it had created.

Because, in White's view, Congress had delegated so much authority to the executive, the legislative veto actually strengthened the balance of powers by imposing a counterweight to such excessive delegation.

Chief Justice Warren Burger's majority opinion in *Chadha* received harsh criticism in some academic circles, and privately even Burger conceded that "Byron has a forceful dissent in this case." White's dissent found a great deal of approval among those who admired his commonsensical approach to policy making and the realities of the give-and-take necessary between the different branches in the business of everyday governing. Judge Louis Oberdorfer, an old friend from law school and a colleague at Justice, believed that in no other decision could one find the essence of White's judicial philosophy. Others, however, found that the emphasis on what White saw as customary and usual reflected the general attitude of the Kennedy administration—that niceties, even constitutional niceties, ought not interfere with important policies.

On March 19, 1993, White informed President Bill Clinton that he would retire at the end of the current term. As White said to Harry Blackmun, "It's been a great ride." White, the last member of the Warren Court, died nine years after stepping down from the Court.

—*Melvin I. Urofsky*

BIBLIOGRAPHY

Dennis J. Hutchinson, himself a former clerk to White, has written the definitive biography, *The Man Who Once Was Whizzer White: A Portrait of Justice Byron R. White* (1998).

In 1987 the *University of Colorado Law Review* published a symposium to honor White on the twenty-fifth anniversary of his joining the Court. Among the articles that one should read are: William E. Nelson, "Deference and the Limits of Deference in the Constitutional Jurisprudence of Justice Byron R. White"; Pierce O'Donnell, "Common Sense and the Constitution: Justice White and the Egalitarian Ideal"; and Lance Liebman, "Justice White and Affirmative Action." In another issue devoted entirely to White, see especially Kate Stith-Cabranes, "Criminal Law and the Supreme Court: An Essay on the Jurisprudence of Byron White," *University of Colorado Law Review* 74 (2003): 1523. See also Victor S. Navasky, *Kennedy Justice* (1971); and Monroe Price, "A Justice of Studied Unpredictability," *National Law Journal,* February 18, 1980.

NOTEWORTHY OPINIONS

Robinson v. California, 370 U.S. 660 (1962) (Dissent)

Jackson v. Denno, 378 U.S. 368 (1964)

Miranda v. Arizona, 384 U.S. 436 (1966) (Dissent)

Reitman v. Mulkey, 387 U.S. 369 (1967)

Hunter v. Erickson, 393 U.S. 385 (1969)

Red Lion Broadcasting Co. v. FCC, 395 U.S. 367 (1969)

Branzburg v. Hayes, 408 U.S. 665 (1972)

Roe v. Wade, 410 U.S. 113 (1973) (Dissent)

Zurcher v. Stanford Daily, 436 U.S. 547 (1978)

Regents of the University of California v. Bakke, 438 U.S. 265 (1978)

Herbert v. Lando, 441 U.S. 153 (1979)

Immigration and Naturalization Service v. Chadha, 462 U.S. 919 (1983)

Bowers v. Hardwick, 478 U.S. 186 (1986)

Shaw v. Reno, 509 U.S. 630 (1993) (Dissent)

EDWARD DOUGLASS WHITE

Birth: November 3, 1845, Lafourche Parish, Louisiana.

Education: Mount St. Mary's College, 1856; Georgetown College (University), 1857–1861; studied law at University of Louisiana (Tulane) and privately; admitted to the bar in 1868.

Official Positions: Louisiana state senator, 1874; associate justice, Louisiana Supreme Court, 1878–1880; U.S. senator, 1891–1894.

Supreme Court Service: Nominated associate justice by President Grover Cleveland, February 19, 1894, to replace Samuel Blatchford, who had died; confirmed by the Senate, February 19, 1894, by a voice vote; took judicial oath March 12, 1894. Nominated chief justice by President William Howard Taft, December 12, 1910, to replace Melville Fuller, who had died; confirmed by the Senate, December 12, 1910, by a voice vote; took judicial oath December 19, 1910; served until May 19, 1921; replaced as chief justice by William Howard Taft, appointed by President Warren G. Harding.

Death: May 19, 1921, Washington, D.C.

Edward Douglass White, the ninth chief justice of the United States, was a southern gentleman, a Jesuit-trained Roman Catholic, and a man early acquainted with defeat. The son of a plantation owner, he attended Georgetown College (now University) until the Civil War ended his formal education. He joined the Confederate army, was promptly captured and imprisoned for several months. Far from becoming the stereotypical embittered southerner, with maturity White apparently gained some perspective on the defeat. "Young man," he once told a law clerk, "you'll be lucky when you're my age if you've only been a damned fool once."

After the war, White attended the University of Louisiana (Tulane) and read law in the New Orleans office of Edward Bermudez. White opened his own practice there and became active in Louisiana's Democratic Party. By 1874, when he was elected to the state senate, he had established one of the city's largest law practices. White's support of the successful candidate for governor two years later won him an appointment to the state supreme court, but he served for only a year because the Louisiana Constitution of 1879 established a minimum age of thirty-five for supreme court justices. White, then thirty-four, had to resign, start another law practice, and resume his political activity. He was elected to the U.S. Senate in 1888, but a partisan dispute over the state lottery kept him in Louisiana until 1891.

The tensions of White's early career may have contributed to the development of a nervous habit that made writing arduous in an era when nearly all professional work was done in longhand. For the rest of his life, White could not write unless he pressed the first finger of his right hand against his nose and held the pen between his thumb and second finger. There is no evidence, however, that this difficulty affected either the quantity or quality of his work.

When Justice Samuel Blatchford died in July 1893, President Grover Cleveland tried twice to name his replacement, but the Senate rejected both William Hornblower and Wheeler Peckham. Cleveland then tried the familiar ploy of nominating one of the Senate's own. In addition to being a senator, Edward White had other characteristics that made him eligible in Cleveland's eyes: he was a Democrat, and his opposition to a tariff bill gave Cleveland reason to want him out of the Senate. White took his seat in March 1894. A few months later, the forty-eight-year-old bachelor married Leita Montgomery Kent, the widow of a Washington lawyer. The marriage, like White's service on the Court, was by all accounts a happy association and lasted until his death.

White's appointment as chief justice in 1910 was a departure from custom in two ways. Except for John Rutledge, who served briefly as chief justice in 1795 until the Senate rejected him, White was the first associate justice to be promoted. White was also a Democrat appointed by a Republican president, William Howard Taft. But Chief Justice Melville Fuller's death coincided with so many Court vacancies that Taft may have felt it necessary to elevate a sitting justice to ensure continuity, and White's fellow justices thought highly enough of him to petition Taft to promote him. Moreover, the fact that three of Taft's six appointees to the Court were Democrats suggests that partisan loyalty mattered little to him. White's biographer, Robert Highsaw, suggests that the justice's high productivity may have impressed Taft, and that their views on most issues were compatible. A Taft biographer has suggested that White's age (sixty-five) also made him an attractive choice because Taft's greatest ambition was to be chief justice, not president. He was twelve years younger than White, and he may have acted in the hope that the position would be vacant after he left the White House and was still young enough to fill it. The fact that any such strategy on Taft's part was successful—President Warren Harding appointed him to succeed White—makes this conclusion tempting without much evidence to support it.

Two chief justices later, Robert H. Jackson wrote: "Never in its entire history can the Supreme Court be said to have for a single hour been representative of anything except the relatively conservative forces of the day." The Court on which Edward White served from 1894 to 1921 provides ample support for this generalization, whether we take "conservative" in its literal meaning or in its informal association with wealth, advantage, and privilege. White was at home in this intellectual environment, and attuned to the prevailing ideology of the day. Some cases from this period that strike us as infamous examples of this conservatism, like the endorsement of racial segregation in *Plessy v. Ferguson* (1896), may seem more important in retrospect than they did at the time. White concurred without opinion

Edward Douglass White

in *Plessy*. Although a single, unverifiable report states that he had been a member of the Ku Klux Klan, little information survives about his racial views.

The primary challenge that faced White and his colleagues was fashioning a judicial response to legislation aimed at controlling the effects of the concentration of wealth and the subsequent, if not consequent, abuse of power the industrial revolution had created. These laws fell into two general categories: efforts to retard the concentration of wealth and efforts to benefit workers facing employers far more powerful than they. Year after year, the Court confronted both kinds of laws.

The prevailing sentiment in the legal profession in the 1890s was adverse to this kind of legislation. At colleges and law schools, which were replacing the kind of apprenticeship White had served as the source of legal training, lawyers were exposed to the social Darwinism of professors such as Christopher Tiedemann, who urged generations of students to resist "the impulse of a generous nature . . . to call loudly for the intervention of the law to protect the poor wage-earner from the grasping cupidity of the employer [who] has acquired this superior position . . . through the exertion of his powers; he is above, and can to some extent dictate terms to, his employees, because his natural powers are greater." The justices were not immune from the socialization going on within their profession.

By the time White took his seat, the Court had developed an approach to these laws that was hostile without being suicidal. This hostility persisted, with some ups and downs, until 1937, when Franklin Roosevelt's threat to enlarge the Court brought about a judicial retreat from activism in economics that may or may not have been permanent.

However conservative White's general ideology was, it is not clear how fully he shared the social Darwinist ideology of his profession. His papers were destroyed after his death, and he was silent in many landmark cases. For example, he dissented without opinion in both *Lochner v. New York* (1905), which struck down a maximum working hours law, and *Bunting v. Oregon* (1917), which appeared to overrule

Lochner; he concurred without opinion in both *Muller v. Oregon* (1908), which upheld a maximum hours law for women, and in *Hammer v. Dagenhart* (1918), which invalidated Congress's attempt to discourage child labor. The opinions White did write—and his productivity was high—show that he took an active part in erecting and maintaining judicial barriers to progressive legislation. As chief justice, he took an equally active part in preventing judicial activism from becoming suicidal.

The "rule of reason," which severely limited the government's power to control monopolies, was White's primary contribution to constitutional law. The Sherman Antitrust Act of 1890 forbade all combinations "in restraint of trade or commerce among the several States, or with foreign nations." White concurred without opinion in *United States v. E. C. Knight Co.* (1895), which effectively derailed antitrust prosecutions for the rest of the nineteenth century by declaring that commerce did not include manufacture. Two years later, White was willing to go even further than the Court majority in weakening the Sherman Act. His dissent in *United States v. Trans-Missouri Freight Assn.* (1897) won three other votes, thus coming a single justice short of a majority.

White insisted that the Sherman Act could not be read literally because any contract restrained trade. "To define, then, the words 'in restraint of trade' as embracing every contract which to some degree produced that effect would be violative of reason, because it would include all those contracts which are of the very essence of trade." The common law, therefore, had evolved the "rule of reason," which ordained that "reasonable contracts cannot be embraced within the provisions of the statute." The Court's ruling, therefore, meant that "a law in favor of freedom of contract . . . is so interpreted as to gravely impair that freedom." White's doctrine still remained one vote short in 1904 in the famous *Northern Securities Co. v. United States*.

White's opportunity to write his doctrine into dogma—without precipitating a showdown with a trust-busting administration—came during his first term as chief justice. In *Standard Oil Co. v. United*

States (1911), the Court, by an 8–1 vote, ordered the dissolution of the Standard Oil trust. White again endorsed "the standard of reason which had been applied at the common law and in this country." He declared, "The criterion to be resorted to in any given case . . . is the rule of reason guided by the established law." Justice Oliver Wendell Holmes later remarked, "The moment I saw that in the circulated draft, I knew he had us. How could you be against that without being for a rule of unreason?"

As an exercise in judicial power, *Standard Oil* was an accomplishment worthy of John Marshall. By conceding a battle to the legislative and executive branches, White won both a campaign and a war. The impact of *E. C. Knight* and *Standard Oil* after 1911 defeated virtually all trust prosecutions. But "reasonableness" is in the eye of the adjudicator, and the rule of reason greatly expanded the Court's power, making it the arbiter of reasonableness.

As an exercise in constitutional interpretation, however, the rule of reason suffers from the defects of *Lochner* and its line of substantive due process cases. The *Standard Oil* doctrine edits both the statute and the Constitution by adding words not included in either, almost as blatantly as the opinion White joined in *Hammer v. Dagenhart,* which edited the Tenth Amendment by adding the word "expressly." Such free translation of text is neither unknown nor uniformly unwelcome today, but the typical defense of it, familiar after the famous footnote in *United States v. Carolene Products Co.* (1938), is not applicable in antitrust cases: the interest being protected is neither a specified constitutional right nor an excluded minority group. Instead, the White Court expanded judicial power to serve the interest of the privileged few, a group that, moreover, had lost a fair fight in the political arena.

Another judicial barrier to progressive legislation that White helped to fashion came from the Court's reading of the federal commerce power. In *Northern Securities,* Holmes's dissent promulgated the rule of reason, but White based his dissent on the doctrine of dual federalism: the proposition that national and state governments are each sovereign within their own spheres; the nonexercise by one government of its own power does not permit the other government to exercise the power, however innocuously; and the states retain all power not delegated to the national government. The power to regulate combinations such as the Northern Securities Company, White insisted, was "entirely distinct from the power to regulate the acquisition and control of such instrumentalities." Congress could do the latter, but the former power belonged to the states. Although White's dual federalism never commanded a Court majority, as his rule of reason did, he had some successes using it. He wrote for the Court in the 1908 *Employers' Liability Cases,* for example, holding that the commerce clause does not include the power to regulate employer-employee relations. *Hammer v. Dagenhart,* without an opinion from White, was perhaps the greatest victory for his dual federalism.

Constitutional scholar Edward S. Corwin credited White with resurrecting dual federalism, which had prevailed since the Taney Court but by 1904 seemed "about to pass into eclipse beneath the waxing orb of the commerce power." Perhaps, Corwin suggested, White's Jesuit education made him sympathetic to the doctrine by teaching him "its medieval counterpart, the dual jurisdiction over common territory of Church and State." It is also possible that the time and place of White's young manhood favorably disposed him toward state sovereignty. But the difficulty with these explanations is that White was not uniformly hostile to national usurpations of state power; he voted to limit national power when Congress attempted to bar articles from interstate commerce that were not inherently dangerous, but because they were associated with some practice Congress wanted to control.

If the possibility occurred to White that the corporations Congress tried to restrict might have been considerably more powerful than the states in which he situated the power to restrict them, he never indicated such awareness. At any rate, White was fighting a rearguard action. Dual federalism did not survive the New Deal; *United States v. Darby Lumber Co.* (1941) repudiated *Hammer v. Dagenhart.*

White's contributions to doctrine outside the area of economic regulation show that his jurisprudence was motivated no more by distrust of the national government than by deference to the states. The first, chronologically, of the two instances in which White succeeded in writing erstwhile minority opinions into law broadly interpreted Congress's power over acquired territories, and the resulting rule has proved more nearly permanent than either the rule of reason or dual federalism. The events of 1898, the year in which the Hawaiian Islands were annexed, the Spanish-American War ended, and the resulting Treaty of Paris ceded Puerto Rico, Guam, and the Philippine Islands to the United States, made future judicial involvement with questions concerning these territories a virtual certainty, and the Court's docket between 1901 and 1905 was thick with them.

Article IV of the Constitution left no doubt that Congress had the power to govern territories and to make states out of them, and the Louisiana Purchase of 1803 had effectively settled any doubts about Congress's power to acquire territory. The questions presented to the Fuller Court concerned an issue that had not yet been decided: the applicability of constitutional guarantees to territories. *Downes v. Bidwell* (1901) involved a statute that established a civil government for Puerto Rico and levied a tax on its exports to the United States. An importer insisted that the territory was a part of the United States and that the tax, therefore, violated the provision in Article I, Section 8, that all duties be uniform throughout the country. The Court upheld the law, but without a majority opinion. White was part of the 5–4 majority, but he refused to join Justice Henry Brown's opinion, which hinted that some constitutional guarantees might apply to territories without restriction. White's concurring opinion propounded the "Insular Doctrine," the theory that constitutional limitations on congressional powers applied to territories only after they were incorporated into and became an integral part of the United States. Four years later, White's doctrine claimed a majority in *Rasmussen v. United States* (1905), and in 1914 a unanimous Court accepted it in *Ocampo v. United States.*

White's Insular Doctrine has been called a new *jus gentium* (international law). It is similar to the Roman doctrine whereby usages common to different peoples were incorporated into the "law of nations" and applied to conquered territories, while the *jus civile* (civil law) applied only to Roman citizens. White invoked "the general rule of the law of nations" by which "the acquiring government fixes the status of the acquired territory." The majority decision in *Downes,* he wrote, therefore "rests on the erroneous assumption that the United States under the Constitution is stripped of those powers which are absolutely inherent and essential to the national existence." Puerto Rico "was not a foreign country since it was subject to the sovereignty of and was owned by the United States"; however, it "was foreign . . . in a domestic sense, because the island had not been incorporated into the United States, but was merely appurtenant thereto as a possession." Until Puerto Rico was incorporated—that is, when Congress said it had been—the uniform duty provision of Article I "was not applicable to Congress in legislating for Porto Rico."

Unincorporated territories were therefore in a kind of limbo: Congress's Article IV power to govern applied, but the limitations on Congress's power, including the Bill of Rights, did not. White's customary solicitude for business may have influenced his opinions in the Puerto Rico tax cases; he recognized that the imperialists wanted to retain their gains, and yet, at the same time, domestic interests wanted protection against an influx of duty-free sugar and tobacco from the islands. Here, as with the rule of reason, judgments of the quality of White's intellectual contribution to constitutional law and of the effectiveness of his leadership on the Court should be separated from any judgments about the wisdom or justice of his doctrines.

The protracted political controversy that culminated in *Virginia v. West Virginia* (1907) showed White as the arbiter of divisions of power among states and between the states and the national government. When Virginia seceded in 1861, the western part of the state refused to leave the Union. West

Virginia became a separate state two years later; it agreed to assume a fair share of Virginia's prewar debt, and Congress ratified the compact. West Virginia did not make good on its promise, however, and in 1907 Virginia brought suit. The Supreme Court ordered West Virginia to pay in 1915, but no money was forthcoming, and Virginia reinstated the suit. The Court faced the possibility that West Virginia might continue to defy direct orders. A state's obligation to obey the Court was already beyond dispute, but it was not clear how the Court could enforce its order. What was clear is that the state's defiance of an order would embarrass the Court.

White's opinion carefully avoided the dangers the case presented. He reaffirmed the principle "that judicial power essentially involves the right to enforce the results of its exertion" and went on to suggest that the remedies for defiance included not only judicial enforcement but congressional legislation. Neither Congress nor the Court had to act further: West Virginia paid its share of the debt.

A general evaluation of White's jurisprudence can easily describe what it is not. White was no Felix Frankfurter, with his concern for judicial self-restraint, nor a Hugo Black, with his literal reading of the constitutional text, nor an Antonin Scalia, with his jurisprudence of original intent. Although White may have practiced judicial restraint in the pragmatic sense of keeping the Court out of confrontations, he had no hesitation about holding the other branches of government to notions of fundamental principles of justice or "inherent" rights, concepts that come close to a "natural law" doctrine. This attitude was not unusual in the nineteenth century, when few were embarrassed to suggest that positive law incorporated higher law principles; the abolitionists, for example, had made similar arguments in opposing slavery. One difficulty with natural law arguments was that a consensus that fundamental principles existed was not accompanied by consensus on what constituted those principles, and these arguments, therefore, can be and have been advanced to defend contradictory positions.

As both justice and chief justice, White was an unambiguous success in his own time. His major opinions show impressive knowledge of law and a facility for creative reasoning, and the Court's votes show his skill at promoting consensus and keeping the Court out of trouble. But the fact that two of his doctrines, the rule of reason and dual federalism, did not survive his tenure even by a generation indicates that his ability to persuade his colleagues may have been greater than his ability to adapt doctrine to changing conditions. (The dual federalism concept did, however, reappear in the late twentieth century.) And assessment of the rightness or wrongness of his opinions, and of the directions in which he influenced the Court, will probably depend on the views of the observer.

Some commentators found evidence of White's Jesuit education in these decisions. The rule of reason and the Insular Doctrine reveal that far from limiting himself to any minimalist doctrine of constitutional interpretation, White freely drew on common law and Roman law to graft concepts onto the Constitution. White may well have been one of the last American judges to merit the description "natural law" jurist; he might even have welcomed the label and perhaps cheered Justice Clarence Thomas's advocacy of this doctrine.

Because White's success with the Insular Doctrine antedated his promotion, these cases show that his leadership on the Court did not depend solely on his position as chief justice, and neither did the intellectual manipulation in *Standard Oil* on which Holmes remarked. Any justice can do that sort of thing, and many have. But the chief justiceship enhanced White's opportunities to lead, as the formal powers of the position gave him ample occasion to exert informal influence. The presiding role allows the chief to set both agenda and tone; the chief's skill in performing these tasks influences the collegiality and productivity of the Court, for good or for ill. As Prof. David Danelski has written: "In terms of influence, then, the ideal chief justice is a persuasive, esteemed, able, and well-liked judge who perceives, fulfills, and even expands his role on the Court." Until White's last few years, when he stayed too long on the Court, his performance came close to this ideal.

Danelski borrows from small group studies to posit two types of leadership within the Court. The task leader "makes more suggestions, gives more opinions, and successfully defends his ideas more often than the others." The social leader "attends to the emotional needs of his associates" and typically "is the best-liked member of the conference." One individual can fulfill both these roles—Danelski argues that Charles Evans Hughes did—but the positions are to some extent contradictory; people who win arguments are not always liked.

There is no doubt that White acted as social leader. Even those who do not describe his abilities in superlatives attest to his personal charm. This consensus and the fact that the White Court included such luminaries as Holmes, Hughes, and Louis Brandeis might lead to the expectation that White would not have been task leader as well. But all the evidence suggests that he was. The high productivity, low dissension, and warm collegiality revealed in volumes of *United States Reports* and in individual memoirs attest to White's ability both to set tasks and stroke the egos of his colleagues.

Dissent was less common in the late nineteenth and early twentieth centuries than it is now, and unanimity remained the norm until Hughes's tenure as chief justice. Even the relatively contentious Fuller Court reached unanimous decisions in 70 percent to 75 percent of its cases in most terms. White had greater success than Fuller in achieving unanimity; his figures compare favorably with Taft's. In 1912, for instance, only 9 percent of the cases had dissents. Productivity also rose under White by roughly 40 percent. This pattern began to change in 1916; productivity decreased slightly from then on, and the dissent rate climbed as high as 25 percent. The presence on the Court of notorious combatants such as Brandeis, James McReynolds, and John Clarke probably combined with White's failing health to weaken his leadership. Soon after Taft took over, Brandeis remarked that "the judges go home [from conference] less tired emotionally and less weary physically than in White's day."

No one disputes that White was always well-liked, on and off the Court, but opinion about his performance is divided. Several years after his death, Justice

Holmes wrote, "If Hughes had been appointed then, . . . I think the history of the Court would have been better than it is." In 1970 a poll of legal scholars rated White among the "near great" Supreme Court justices but ranked Hughes among the "great" judges. Highsaw rates him lower than the panel did, attributing his subject's success to "the fact that, though he was far from a mediocrity, he was not such an outstanding man that he aroused any considerable opposition."

In one sense, White accomplished in *Standard Oil, Rasmussen,* and to a lesser degree in *Virginia v. West Virginia,* exactly what Hughes did in the "switch in time which saved nine" of 1937. Less dramatically—and perhaps, therefore, more successfully—than Hughes, White withdrew from disputes that the Court, lacking both the purse and the sword, was doomed to lose. Yet the observation White's biographer makes of his dual federalism, that it constituted a brilliant rearguard action, seems true in general of White's contribution to public law. The values he defended most, corporate power and imperialism, while far from obsolescent, seem not to have needed much judicial help. Brandeis—or even Holmes, who, we now know, had little more sympathy than White had for progressive legislation—might have acted on the need to interpret constitutional principles in the light of the immense socioeconomic changes occurring in his time and rendered obsolete verities such as the harmony of worker-employer relations assumed in Hamilton's *Federalist* 35 and uncritically endorsed in several White Court rulings. But White used his talents, jurisprudential and political, in the defense of values that seem less admirable now than they did in his time.

—*Judith A. Baer*

BIBLIOGRAPHY

The only biography of White is Robert B. Highsaw, *Edward Douglass White: Defender of the Conservative Faith* (1981), which, although biased toward its subject, is valuable for its clear presentation of constitutional doctrine. David J. Danelski, "The Influence of the Chief Justice in the Decisional Process," in Sheldon Goldman and Austin Sarat, eds., *American Court Systems: Readings in Judicial Process and Behavior*

(2d ed., 1989), 486–499, is the definitive study of the distinguishing features of White's position. Other works that are useful for understanding White and his Court include Dean Acheson, *Morning and Noon* (1965), Chapters 4 and 5, in which the former secretary of state, who clerked for Louis Brandeis from 1919 to 1921, presents a revealing picture of "our Court" under White; Edward S. Corwin, *The Twilight of the Supreme Court* (1934), a valuable analysis of the important constitutional issues of White's day; Mark DeWolfe Howe, ed., *The Holmes-Laski Letters* (2 vols., 1953), a valuable source of Holmes's trenchant opinions about his colleagues; and Stephen B. Wood, *Constitutional Politics in the Progressive Era* (1968), an explanation of the events, judicial and political, culminating in *Hammer v. Dagenhart.*

Two valuable studies of the White Court are William F. Pratt, *The Supreme Court Under Edward Douglass White,* *1910–1921* (1999); and Alexander M. Bickel and Benno C. Schmidt Jr., *The Judiciary and Responsible Government, 1910–1921* (1984), a volume in the *Holmes Devise History.*

NOTEWORTHY OPINIONS

United States v. Trans-Missouri Freight Assn., 166 U.S. 290 (1897) (Dissent)

Northern Securities Co. v. United States, 193 U.S.197 (1904) (Dissent)

Virginia v. West Virginia, 206 U.S. 290 (1907)

Employers' Liability Cases, 207 U.S. 463 (1908)

Standard Oil Co. v. United States, 221 U.S. 1 (1911)

Ocampo v. United States, 234 U.S. 91 (1914)

CHARLES EVANS WHITTAKER

Birth: February 22, 1901, Troy, Kansas.

Education: University of Kansas City Law School, LL.B., 1924.

Official Positions: Judge, U.S. District Court for the Western District of Missouri, 1954–1956; judge, U.S. Court of Appeals for the Eighth Circuit, 1956–1957.

Supreme Court Service: Nominated associate justice by President Dwight D. Eisenhower, March 2, 1957, to replace Stanley Reed, who had retired; confirmed by the Senate, March 19, 1957, by a voice vote; took judicial oath March 25, 1957; retired March 31, 1962; replaced by Byron R. White, nominated by President John F. Kennedy.

Death: November 26, 1973, Kansas City, Missouri.

Charles Evans Whittaker was no child of privilege, no great public servant, no brilliant legal scholar. His beginnings, his background, indeed his legal career all suggest a man of modest ambition, inauspicious achievement, and unremarkable intellect. Unfortunately, Whittaker's appointment to the Court did nothing to alter the character of his life; indeed, all the literature on this justice concludes that Whittaker was in every way unsuited for his exalted position. His indecision and intellectual torment drove him to retire after only five years on the bench.

Whittaker's early life retells the quintessential American rags-to-riches story. Born in rural Kansas, he dropped out of high school at sixteen and helped his father on the family farm. He went to work as an office boy for a Kansas City law firm and was admitted to a private night law school on the condition that he also finish high school. He practiced law for nearly thirty years, advising primarily Kansas City's major corporations. Whittaker's service as a federal trial and appellate judge positioned him well when President Dwight Eisenhower, looking for nominees with judicial experience, sought a replacement for Justice Stanley Reed.

Whittaker came to the Court too late to participate in the Warren Court's first activist phase, marked by its 1957 decisions providing constitutional protections to suspected Communist Party members, and he left before the liberal Warren Court came into its own in the mid-1960s. In a sense, Whittaker reflected the Court's uneasy transition from the conservatism that had long characterized the institution; his inconsistency and confusion mirrored the larger struggle taking place between proponents of judicial restraint such as Justices Felix Frankfurter and John Marshall Harlan and ardent civil libertarians such as Chief Justice Earl Warren and Justices Hugo Black, William O. Douglas, and William Brennan.

Except in cases dealing with outrageous police or prosecutorial conduct towards a particularly helpless defendant, Whittaker took a conservative position on most civil liberties issues. He was a legal technocrat rather than a judge; he narrowed the scope of constitutional questions to avoid framing great, enduring principles. His most impressive votes for broad constitutional rights came in two cases overturning provisions of the Naturalization Act, which stripped native-born Americans of their citizenship if they deserted the military during wartime (*Trop v. Dulles,* 1958) or if they voted in foreign elections (*Perez v. Brownell,* 1958). He was less certain of himself in cases dealing with the military's authority to court-martial civilians, taking a middle ground between the majority's decisions for the civilians and Frankfurter's arguments on behalf of the military. Whittaker said that the military ought to be able to prosecute employees but not dependents, a distinction he did not (or could not) justify in three 1960 cases, *Kinsella v. United States ex rel. Singleton, McElroy v. United States ex rel. Guagliardo,* and *Grisham v. Hagan.*

More typical of Whittaker's voting pattern were his plainly inconsistent votes in cases challenging the constitutionality of coerced confessions in murder cases. He sided with an uneducated black defendant in *Moore v. Michigan* (1957), but in *Thomas v. Arizona* (1958), he voted for the state even though the police had put a noose around the neck of a black man in the course of a twenty-hour interrogation. In cases involving civil liberties, Whittaker had the most conservative voting record of anyone on the Court during his tenure.

Charles Evans Whittaker

After three years on the Court, Whittaker was already paralyzed by the conflict between his conservative instincts, his occasional liberal leanings, and the pressure levied by the crush of Court work. His inability to produce an intellectually coherent rationale for his own decisions made him a "prize target" for Justice Frankfurter's relentless lobbying. His distress infiltrated even the most mundane cases. When Whittaker was unable to compose his majority opinion in a case involving the application of the Internal Revenue Code to the disbursement of a life insurance claim, Justice Douglas, who had already penned a dissent in the case, wrote it for him (*Meyer v. United States,* 1960).

After leaving the Court, Whittaker returned to his roots in corporate law by becoming counsel to General Motors. He also became an outspoken critic of the social protest movements waged by civil rights demonstrators and antiwar protesters during the late 1960s. His choice as a forum for his beliefs, the FBI Law Enforcement Bulletin, testifies as much as anything else to his law-and-order instincts.

—*Victoria Saker Woeste*

BIBLIOGRAPHY

A short biography is R. L. Miller, *Whittaker: Struggles of a Supreme Court Justice* (2002). Only a few law review articles specifically analyze his jurisprudence. For brief sketches, see Leon Friedman, "Charles Whittaker," in Friedman and Israel, *Justices,* vol. 4, 2893, which is probably the most complete existing account of Whittaker's record; and Michael Parrish's piece in Leonard W. Levy, Kenneth L. Karst, and Dennis J. Mahoney, *Encyclopedia of the American Constitution*, vol. 4, 2060 (1986). See also D. M. Berman, "Mr. Justice Whittaker: A Preliminary Appraisal," *Missouri Law Review* 24 (1959): 1. William O. Douglas, *The Court Years: 1939–1975* (1981), contains some useful information about Whittaker. Although Douglas objected to Whittaker's unreflected conservatism, he respected Whittaker personally, and the few Whittaker anecdotes here are told with warmth

and charity. Bernard Schwartz, on the other hand, in *Super Chief: Earl Warren and His Supreme Court—A Judicial Biography* (1983), provides an adoring portrait of Warren that describes Whittaker with contempt.

NOTEWORTHY OPINIONS

Perez v. Brownell, 356 U.S. 44 (1958)

Trop v. Dulles, 356 U.S. 86 (1958)

Meyer v. United States, 364 U.S. 410 (1960)

JAMES WILSON

Birth: September 14, 1742, Carskerdo, Scotland.

Education: Attended University of St. Andrews (Scotland); read law privately; admitted to the bar in 1767; honorary M.A., College of Philadelphia, 1776; honorary LL.D., 1790.

Official Positions: Delegate, first Provincial Convention at Philadelphia, 1774; member, Continental Congress, 1775–1777, 1783, 1785–1786; delegate, U.S. Constitutional Convention, 1787; Pennsylvania delegate to the Federal Convention, 1787; delegate, Pennsylvania convention to ratify U.S. Constitution, 1787.

Supreme Court Service: Nominated associate justice by President George Washington, September 24, 1789; confirmed by the Senate, September 26, 1789, by voice vote; took judicial oath October 5, 1789; served until August 21, 1798; replaced by Bushrod Washington, nominated by President John Adams.

Death: August 21, 1798, Edenton, North Carolina.

James Wilson was born on a farm in Scotland and educated at the University of St. Andrews, where he studied Latin, Greek, mathematics, logic, moral philosophy, ethics, and natural and political philosophy. As he was acquainted with the literature of the Scottish and English enlightenment, Wilson was well prepared to take an active part in revolutionary activities when he arrived in America in 1765. After a short time as a tutor at the College of Philadelphia, Wilson determined that studying law would more likely lead to his advancement, and he arranged to read law with John Dickinson, a prominent lawyer. Less than a year later, Wilson was ready to practice on his own, and he established himself in Reading. In 1770 he moved to Carlisle and in 1778, to Philadelphia, all the while expanding his clientele.

During these same years Wilson became involved in patriot politics. In 1774 he revised and published a pamphlet that he had written six years earlier, *Considerations on the Nature and Extent of the Legislative Authority of the British Parliament.* His radical view that Parliament had no legislative authority over the colonies contributed effectively to the patriot cause, and publication of it enlarged his reputation in America and England. In 1774 Wilson attended the Pennsylvania Provincial Convention as a delegate. He served several times as a member of the Continental Congress, where he was not an early supporter of independence. Yet Wilson was one of the three (out of seven) Pennsylvania delegates who signed the Declaration of Independence.

Wilson's private activities, in addition to his service in the Continental Congress, contributed to his belief that a more powerful central government was needed. As an attorney, he had an extensive admiralty practice and became convinced of the necessity to create a federal court supreme over state courts. His business dealings led him to take an active part in the establishment of the first national bank, the Bank of North America. When the bank was attacked in 1785, Wilson wrote a defense of it, *Considerations on the Power to Incorporate the Bank of North America,* in which he formulated arguments favoring the implied powers of Congress under the Articles of Confederation to charter a bank. Wilson also found time to pursue his own scholarly studies in political theory, history, and philosophy, and his preeminence in these fields was recognized by the American Philosophical Society, which elected him a member in 1786.

It was hardly surprising, therefore, that the Pennsylvania legislature appointed Wilson a delegate to the Federal Convention in 1787. By that time his views on government had become clear. In the convention he advocated popular election of both houses of Congress as well as of the executive, no property qualifications for voting, no restrictions on the admission of new states to the Union, the supremacy of the national government for the purposes of the new Union, the creation of a supreme court with judges appointed by the president and with the power of judicial review, and congressional authority to establish inferior federal courts. Wilson was a member of the Committee of Detail that prepared a draft of the Constitution. The convention did not adopt every measure that Wilson supported, but he did all in his power, as a member of the Pennsylvania Convention, to ensure the successful outcome of

James Wilson

the ratification contest. George Washington rewarded Wilson's efforts by nominating him to the Supreme Court.

Wilson's moment of glory as a Supreme Court justice came, oddly enough, while sitting as a circuit judge (a duty required by the Judiciary Act of 1789) in Pennsylvania in April 1792. There the court, by refusing to hear the petition of William Hayburn, a veteran of the Revolutionary War seeking a pension under the Invalid Pensions Act of 1792, exercised judicial review for the first time. The court wrote no opinion but instead sent a letter to President Washington explaining its actions. The court could not proceed, the judges declared, "because the business directed by this act is not of a judicial nature" and because, if, upon that business, the court had proceeded, its judgments ... might, under the same act, have been revised and controlled by the legislature, and by an officer in the executive department. Such revision and control we deemed radically inconsistent with the independence of that judicial power which is vested in the courts; and, consequently, with that important principle which is so strictly observed by the Constitution of the United States.

Known for giving long and learned grand jury charges while on circuit—Attorney General Edmund Randolph referred to him as "the professor"—

Wilson's few Supreme Court opinions, with the exception of *Chisholm v. Georgia* (1793), are short and unremarkable, except for their inherent interest as rulings of a justice who had helped to frame the Constitution. In each case he upheld the power of the national government: in *Hylton v. United States* (1796), Wilson, who had affirmed the constitutionality of the federal Carriage Tax Act while on circuit, merely reiterated his belief that the tax was valid. In *Ware v. Hylton* (1796), he enforced the supremacy clause of the Constitution by declaring that a federal treaty was superior to a state law.

Wilson wrote an extensive, learned dissertation in *Chisholm* that led him to the same conclusion as a majority of the Court, sustaining the right of a citizen of one state to sue a different state in the U.S. Supreme Court. After defining the concepts of sovereignty and statehood and describing the practice of other states and kingdoms, Wilson determined that nothing stood in the way of the Supreme Court's jurisdiction over the state of Georgia. The "general texture" of the Constitution also contributed to Wilson's view that the people of the United States formed a nation and instituted a national government with complete power to achieve the purposes of the Union, and that "with Regard to such Purposes," it would be incongruous for "any Man or Body of Men—any Person natural or artificial, . . . to claim successfully, an entire Exemption from the Jurisdiction of the national Government." But it was the language of the Constitution itself that in the last analysis convinced Wilson of the accuracy of his belief: "The judicial Power of the United States shall extend to Controversies between two States." Wilson asked, "Can the most consummate Degree of professional Ingenuity devise a Mode by which this 'Controversy between two States' can be brought before a Court of law; and yet neither of those States be a Defendant?"

James Wilson's exceptional intellectual promise, so evident throughout his career, should have made him a natural leader of the fledgling Supreme Court. But his preoccupation with financial affairs during the later years of his brief tenure on the bench—he even spent a short time in jail for debt in 1797—robbed him of the time and the stature to put his imprimatur on the Court's jurisprudence. Desirous of becoming the first chief justice in 1789—he actually wrote to President Washington on April 21, 1789, requesting the position—Wilson masked his disappointment at receiving a commission only as associate justice. When a vacancy occurred in the chief justiceship in 1795, and then again in 1796, Wilson hoped that he would be appointed. He was passed over both times, most probably because his speculation in western land had hurt his reputation. Wilson's frustration, coupled with constant worry about money, seriously affected his health, forced him to neglect his Supreme Court duties, and ultimately led to his death at age fifty-five.

—*Maeva Marcus*

BIBLIOGRAPHY

More has been written about James Wilson than any other of the first six justices, but little of it concerns his tenure on the Supreme Court. Grand jury charges given by Wilson while on circuit, as well as letters relevant to his Supreme Court service, can be found in the volumes of Maeva Marcus, ed., *The Documentary History of the Supreme Court of the United States, 1789–1800* (1985–). A useful, complete biography is Charles Page Smith, *James Wilson: Founding Father, 1742–1798* (1956). A concise, instructive, and authoritative essay about Wilson, written by Robert G. McCloskey, appears in Friedman and Israel, *Justices*, vol. 1, 79. See also D. W. Maxey, "The Translation of James Wilson," *Journal of Supreme Court History* (1990): 29.

NOTEWORTHY OPINIONS

Chisholm v. Georgia, 2 U.S. 419 (1793)

Hylton v. United States, 3 U.S. 171 (1796)

Ware v. Hylton, 3 U.S. 199 (1796)

LEVI WOODBURY

Birth: December 22, 1789, Francestown, New Hampshire.

Education: Dartmouth College, 1809; Tapping Reeve Law School, ca. 1810.

Official Positions: Clerk, New Hampshire Senate, 1816; associate justice, New Hampshire Superior Court, 1817–1823; governor, New Hampshire, 1823–1824; Speaker, New Hampshire House, 1825; U.S. senator, 1825–1831, 1841–1845; secretary of the navy, 1831–1834; secretary of the Treasury, 1834–1841.

Supreme Court Service: Recess appointment as associate justice by President James K. Polk, September 20, 1845, to replace Justice Joseph Story, who had died; nominated by Polk, December 23, 1845, confirmed by the Senate, January 3, 1846, by voice vote; took judicial oath September 23, 1845; served until September 4, 1851; replaced by Benjamin R. Curtis, nominated by President Millard Fillmore.

Death: September 4, 1851, Portsmouth, New Hampshire.

Levi Woodbury graduated from Dartmouth College in 1809, studied law under Judge Jeremiah Smith and at Tapping Reeve Law School in Litchfield, Connecticut, and began a law practice in 1812. During the War of 1812, Woodbury defended President James Madison's unpopular policies in his native New Hampshire. Before his appointment to the U.S. Supreme Court, Woodbury had an impressive public career, serving his state as a supreme court justice, governor, legislator, and U.S. senator. He was also secretary of the navy and secretary of the Treasury. In his political career, Woodbury was a loyal Democrat, a stalwart defender of Andrew Jackson's policies against the Bank of the United States, and a proponent of Manifest Destiny and Texas annexation. In September 1845 President James K. Polk appointed Woodbury to the Court, rewarding him for his service to the Democratic Party. Woodbury, however, was never terribly interested in the Court and, as a justice, remained an active presidential hopeful. He was seriously considered for the presidency in 1848, and, had he lived longer, it seems likely that Woodbury, not Franklin Pierce (New Hampshire's other great Jacksonian politician), would have been the Democratic nominee in 1852. His judicial opinions reflect his Jacksonian ideology and his presidential aspirations.

Polk appointed Woodbury to replace Joseph Story in the Court's traditional New England seat, but Woodbury was never a legal scholar and, therefore, not substantively a replacement for Story. Woodbury was pedantic, competent, and hardworking. In his six terms, he wrote more than 17 percent of all majority opinions (43 opinions in 244 cases) as well as 14 concurrences and dissents. But his hard work led to little of lasting value; his Court career was one of virtually unblemished mediocrity.

As a senator, Woodbury had criticized the Court for its "sleepless opposition . . . to the strict construction of the Constitution" and its support for "a diseased enlargement of the powers of the General Government and throwing chains over States-Rights." As a justice, Woodbury tried to reverse these trends. He wrote a separate opinion in the *License Cases* (1847), upholding state power to prohibit the sale of liquor that traveled in interstate commerce. Here Woodbury clearly articulated his overriding judicial philosophy: "I carry with me, as a controlling principle, the proposition, that State powers, State rights, and State decisions are to be upheld when the objection to them is not clear," and obviously not in conflict with the Constitution. Woodbury rejected the idea that state laws could be declared unconstitutional by "some remote or indirect repugnance to acts of Congress." A "potential inconvenience" was not enough "to annul the laws of sovereign States, and overturn the deliberate decisions of State tribunals." For Woodbury to overturn a state law, he had to see "an actual collision, a direct inconsistency" and a "clashing of sovereignties."

Levi Woodbury

Consistent with this ideology, he dissented in the *Passenger Cases* (1849), arguing that states could constitutionally regulate the entrance of immigrants into their jurisdictions. Woodbury wrote a fifty-five-page dissent (enormous at the time), arguing that since colonial times Massachusetts and other states had regulated immigration and that this regulation was fully constitutional. Similarly, in *Waring v. Clarke* (1847),

he argued in dissent that states had jurisdiction over navigable rivers within their boundaries.

A rare break from his states' rights views was Woodbury's majority opinion in *Planters' Bank v. Sharp* (1848). Here Woodbury wrote to strike down a Mississippi statute and state court decision under the contract clause. He noted that such a decision had to be reached with "no peculiar liberality of construction in favor of a corporation." He reiterated that a state "under its general legislative powers" could regulate or prohibit sales of certain kinds of property "or sales by certain classes of persons or corporations." In this case, however, Mississippi had chartered the bank, and therefore the state's subsequent statutory prohibition on the bank's normal business activities constituted an impairment of contract in violation of the Constitution.

Ironically, Woodbury's most famous and important opinion of the Court, *Jones v. Van Zandt* (1847), expanded federal power at the expense of the states. But this case involved slavery, and, like other Jacksonian Democrats, Woodbury supported southern interests on slavery, even when they clashed with other ideological interests. In 1843 Wharton Jones, a Kentucky slave owner acting under the Fugitive Slave Law of 1793, sued John Van Zandt, an Ohio farmer, for helping his slaves escape. Van Zandt argued that he had found the group of blacks walking on a road in Ohio, and he had presumed they were free because slavery was illegal in Ohio. Furthermore, when he gave them a ride in his wagon, he had not aided in their escape, and he argued that offering them a ride could not be considered concealment of a fugitive slave within the meaning of the federal law. Van Zandt claimed he had no "notice" that the blacks he offered a ride to were, in fact, slaves.

Woodbury rejected these defenses, asserting that "the Constitution itself" in the fugitive slave clause "flung its shield, for security" over slavery "and the right to pursue and reclaim" slaves and "within the limits of another State." This conclusion nationalized southern legal presumptions that all blacks were slaves and destroyed the free states' concept that all people were presumptively free. While enhancing the federal government's power to protect slavery, at the expense of northern states' rights, Woodbury reiterated the principles of Jacksonian–southern states' rights advocates that "the supposed inexpediency and invalidity of all laws recognizing slavery or any right of property in man" was "a political question, settled by each State for itself; and the federal power over it is limited and regulated by the people of the States in the Constitution itself, as one of its sacred compromises." This extraordinarily proslavery decision enhanced Woodbury's prospects as presidential candidate. It also accurately reflects his jurisprudence, which combined Jacksonian, proslavery, and states' rights principles with an overall goal of leaving the bench for the White House.

—*Paul Finkelman*

BIBLIOGRAPHY

There is no biography of Woodbury. Frank Otto Gatell, "Levi Woodbury," in Friedman and Israel, *Justices*, vol. 2, 843, provides a good short biographical sketch of Woodbury along with some of his opinions. Donald B. Cole, *Jacksonian Democracy in New Hampshire, 1800–1851* (1970), places Woodbury in the context of New Hampshire politics. W. D. Bader has written two articles attempting to rehabilitate Woodbury's reputation: "The Jurisprudence of Levi Woodbury," *Vermont Law Review* 18 (1994): 261; and "Justice Levi Woodbury: A Reputational Study," *Journal of Supreme Court History* (1998): 129.

Harold M. Hyman and William M. Wiecek, *Equal Justice Under Law* (1982), is the best book available on the constitutional history of antebellum America, while R. Kent Newmyer, *The Supreme Court Under Marshall and Taney* (1974), is the best short history of the Court during Woodbury's service. Carl B. Swisher, *The Oliver Wendell Holmes Devise History of the Supreme Court of the United States*, vol. 5 *The Taney Period* (1974), is a classic history of the Taney Court. Levi Woodbury, *The Writings of Levi Woodbury*, 3 vols. (1852), provides access to some of Woodbury's writings, most of which are political.

NOTEWORTHY OPINIONS

Jones v. Van Zandt, 46 U.S. 215 (1847)

Waring v. Clarke, 46 U.S. 441 (1847) (Dissent)

License Cases, 46 U.S. 504 (1847) (Concurrence)

Planters' Bank v. Sharp, 47 U.S. 301 (1848)

Passenger Cases, 48 U.S. 283 (1849) (Dissent)

WILLIAM BURNHAM WOODS

Birth: August 3, 1824, Newark, Ohio.

Education: Attended Western Reserve College for three years; graduated from Yale University, 1845.

Official Positions: Mayor of Newark, Ohio, 1856; Ohio state representative, 1858–1862; chancellor, middle chancery district of Alabama, 1868–1869; judge, U.S. Court of Appeals for the Fifth Circuit, 1869–1880.

Supreme Court Service: Nominated associate justice by President Rutherford B. Hayes, December 15, 1880, to replace William Strong, who had retired; confirmed by the Senate, December 21, 1880, by a 39–8 vote; took judicial oath January 5, 1881; served until May 14, 1887; replaced by Lucius Q. C. Lamar, nominated by President Grover Cleveland.

Death: May 14, 1887, Washington, D.C.

William B. Woods is remembered more for his role as a judge of the U.S. Court of Appeals for the Fifth Circuit than for his six years of active service on the U.S. Supreme Court. A native of Ohio and a Union veteran, Woods settled in Alabama after the Civil War and was active in Republican politics there. After his appointment to the Fifth Circuit Court, which encompassed states of the deep South, Woods was the first circuit judge to deal with acts of Congress designed to enforce blacks' political and civil rights. In conjunction with these laws, Woods was also called on to consider the meaning of the Fourteenth Amendment. Did the amendment's privileges and immunities clause protect citizens from the adverse actions of private citizens or only from harmful legislation? In collaboration with Supreme Court justice Joseph P. Bradley, who was assigned to the Fifth Circuit, Woods developed a sweeping view of the Fourteenth Amendment in several cases during Reconstruction.

In 1880 President Rutherford B. Hayes tapped Woods for the U.S. Supreme Court. The president was attracted by the idea of appointing a southerner, yet was reassured by Woods's status as a Union veteran. Ironically, while on the Court, Woods joined the majority in reversing his once broad interpretation of the Fourteenth Amendment. Undoubtedly, his most noted opinion is *United States v. Harris* (1883), which involved a prosecution under the Ku Klux Klan Act of 1871. The defendants allegedly had used violence to curtail blacks' civil rights by breaking into the jail where four black men were held, beating them, and causing the death of one. Woods held that Congress had overreached its powers in passing the law. Acts of Congress could not punish mob action in this kind of case; only state law could do that. The duty of the national government was simply to work against state laws that discriminated against certain classes of citizens. In the *Civil Rights Cases* (1883), Woods joined the majority in holding that the Fourteenth Amendment could not prevent private acts of discrimination, such as the refusal of a theater owner to sell first-class tickets to blacks.

In *Presser v. Illinois* (1886), Woods wrote for a unanimous Court an opinion that reinforced his new limited view of the Fourteenth Amendment. Herman Presser had been arrested for carrying arms in a private militia in violation of an Illinois law. He sought to have his conviction overturned on grounds that the Second Amendment granted the right to bear arms, and the Fourteenth promised to protect this right for all U.S. citizens. Woods's opinion, however, made it clear that the Second Amendment only prevented Congress from interfering with the right to bear arms; state governments traditionally controlled militias, and nothing in the Fourteenth Amendment warranted interference with state laws in this sort of case.

Woods was a workhorse while on the Court; he wrote some 160 majority opinions during his relatively short tenure, most of them dealing with real estate, mortgages, patents, and taxation. He dissented only

William Burnham Woods

eight times in six years. Illness struck suddenly in the spring of 1886, and one year later Woods died. His status as a forgotten justice is probably related to his short tenure and his tendency to side quietly with the majority. He may also have failed to win respect over the years because of his status as a "carpetbagger." In addition, his shifting interpretation of the Fourteenth Amendment gave him the appearance of having a muddled judicial philosophy.

—*Stephen Cresswell*

BIBLIOGRAPHY

On political matters and Woods's appointment, see Thomas E. Baynes Jr., "Yankee from Georgia: A Search for Justice Woods," *Supreme Court Historical Society Yearbook* (1978): 31, which also provides analysis of Woods's voting on the Court. A good overall treatment is Louis Filler, "William B. Woods," in Friedman and Israel, *Justices,* vol. 2, 1327.

NOTEWORTHY OPINIONS

United States v. Harris, 106 U.S. 629 (1883)

Presser v. Illinois, 116 U.S. 252 (1886)

SELECTED BIBLIOGRAPHY

Abraham, Henry J. *Justices, Presidents, and Senators: A History of the U.S. Supreme Court Appointments from Washington to Clinton.* New and revised ed. Lanham Md.: Rowman & Littlefield, 1999. This text explores the relationship of the justices to the presidents who appointed them and the political process of confirmation.

Cushman, Clare, ed. *The Supreme Court Justices: Illustrated Biographies, 1789–1995.* 2d ed. Washington, D.C.: Congressional Quarterly, 1995.

Friedman, Leon, and Fred L. Israel, eds. *The Justices of the United States Supreme Court: Their Lives and Major Opinions.* Revised ed. 5 vols. New York: Chelsea House, 1995 These volumes, in addition to short biographical entries, also have samplings from the justices' opinions.

Hall, Kermit L., ed. *The Oxford Companion to the Supreme Court of the United States.* 2d ed. New York: Oxford University Press, 2005. This book is one of the best one-volume reference works available on the Court and includes pieces on the justices.

Hall, Timothy L. *Supreme Court Justices: A Biographical Dictionary.* New York: Facts on File, 2001.

Johnson, Herbert A., ed. *The Chief Justiceships of the United States Supreme Court.* Columbia: University of South Carolina Press, 1997– . As of 2006, this series has six volumes in print, one out of print, and several others in development.

Katz, Stanley N., ed. *Oliver Wendell Holmes Devise History of the Supreme Court.* New York: Macmillan, 1971– . New York: Cambridge University Press, 2005– . The *History* is the larger and more comprehensive of two multi-volume histories of the Supreme Court (for the second, see Herbert A. Johnson, above). As of 2006, it is complete through Volume 9 (the White Court). Volume 12, covering the Stone and Vinson Courts, is also available, and volumes covering the Taft, Hughes, and Warren Courts are under preparation.

Savage, David. *Guide to the Supreme Court.* 4th ed. Washington, D.C.: CQ Press, 2004. The *Guide* is an excellent two-volume thematic reference on the Court.

Urofsky, Melvin I., and Paul Finkelman. *A March of Liberty: A Constitutional History of the United States.* 2 vols. New York: Oxford University Press, 2001. This text provides an overall view of the Supreme Court, its history, and the justices.

White, G. Edward. *The American Judicial Tradition: Profiles of Leading American Judges.* Expanded ed. New York: Oxford University Press, 1988. White provides thorough analysis as well as biographical information on some of most important members of the Court.

YEAR	CHIEF JUSTICE	SEAT 2	SEAT 3	SEAT 4
1789	Jay	Rutledge, J.	Cushing	Wilson
1790–1791				
1791–1793		Johnson, T.		
1793–1795		Paterson		
1795	Rutledge, J.			
1796–1798	Ellsworth			
1799				Washington
1800				
1801–1803	Marshall, J.			
1804–1806				
1807–1810		Livingston		
1811			(vacant)	
1811–1823			Story	
1824–1826		Thompson		
1826–1828				
1829				
1830–1834				Baldwin
1835				
1836	Taney			
1837–1841				
1841–1843				
1844		(vacant)		
1845		Nelson		(vacant)
1846–1851			Woodbury	Grier
1852			Curtis	
1853–1857				
1858–1860			Clifford	
1861				
1862				
1863–1864				
1865	Chase, S.P.			
1866–1867				
1868–1869				
1870–1872				Strong

. . . SUPREME COURT SEATS

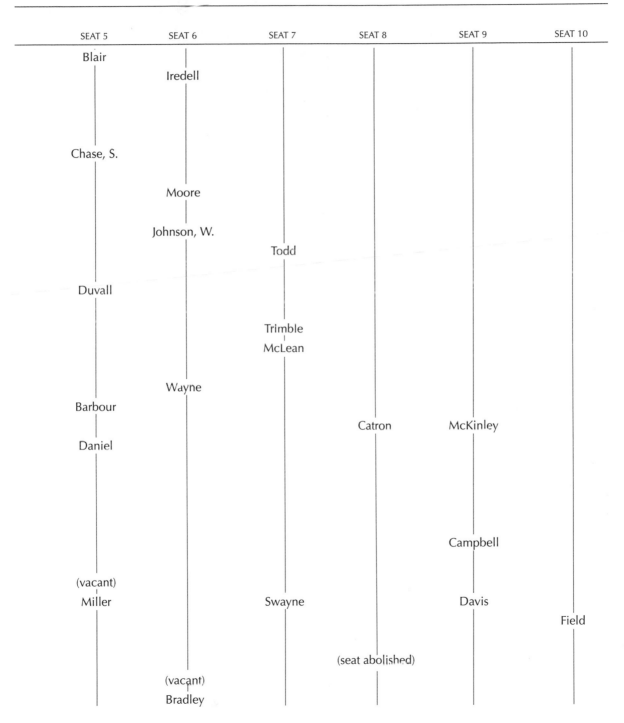

SEAT 5	SEAT 6	SEAT 7	SEAT 8	SEAT 9	SEAT 10
Blair					
	Iredell				
Chase, S.					
	Moore				
	Johnson, W.				
		Todd			
Duvall					
		Trimble			
		McLean			
	Wayne				
Barbour			Catron	McKinley	
Daniel					
				Campbell	
(vacant)					
Miller		Swayne		Davis	
					Field
			(seat abolished)		
	(vacant)				
	Bradley				

YEAR	CHIEF JUSTICE	SEAT 2	SEAT 3	SEAT 4
1873		Hunt		
1874–1877	Waite			
1877–1880				
1881				Woods
1882–1887		Blatchford	Gray	
1888				Lamar, L.
1888–1889	Fuller			
1889–1890				
1891				
1892				
1893				Jackson, H.
1894–1895		White, E.		
1896–1897				Peckham
1898–1902				
1903–1906			Holmes	
1907–1909				
1910				Lurton
1910–1911	White, E.	Van Devanter		
1912–1914				
1914–1916				McReynolds
1916–1921				
1921–1922	Taft			
1922				
1923–1924				
1925–1930				
1930–1931	Hughes			
1932–1937			Cardozo	
1937		Black		
1938				
1939			Frankfurter	
1940–1941				
1941–1942	Stone			Byrnes
1943–1945				Rutledge, W.
1945–1946				
1946–1949	Vinson			
1949–1953				Minton
1953–1954	Warren			
1955–1956				
1957–1958				Brennan
1959–1962				
1962–1965			Goldberg	
1965–1967			Fortas	
1967–1969				
1969	Burger		(vacant)	
1970–1971			Blackmun	

SEAT 5	SEAT 6	SEAT 7	SEAT 8	SEAT 9	SEAT 10
				Harlan I	
		Matthews			
		Brewer			
Brown					
	Shiras				
					McKenna
	Day				
Moody					
Lamar, J.		Hughes		Pitney	
Brandeis		Clarke			
	Butler	Sutherland			
				Sanford	Stone
				Roberts	
		Reed			
Douglas					
	Murphy				Jackson, R.
				Burton	
	Clark				
		Whittaker			Harlan II
		White, B.		Stewart	
	Marshall, T.				

YEAR	CHIEF JUSTICE	SEAT 2	SEAT 3	SEAT 4
1971–1975		Powell		
1975–1981				
1981–1986				
1986–1987	Rehnquist			
1988–1990		Kennedy		
1990–1991				Souter
1991–1993				
1993–1994				
1994–2005			Breyer	
2005–2006	Roberts			
2006–				

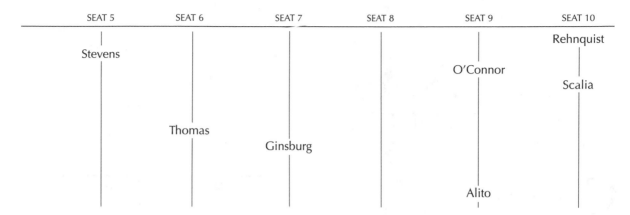

SUPPORTING PERSONNEL OF THE SUPREME COURT

Compared to the executive and legislative branches of the federal government, the Supreme Court employs few people and spends relatively little money. Although the number of Court offices and positions has grown, some are as old as the Court itself. About 470 people work for the Court, and its fiscal year 2006 budget for salaries and expenses was in the comparatively modest $60 million range.

The Court's statutory employees—clerk, marshal, reporter of decisions, and librarian—are appointed by the Court. The justices each select their clerks and other personal staff. The Court's administrative assistant is appointed by the chief justice, and all other court officers, such as the public information officer and the curator, are appointed by the chief justice in consultation with the Court.

CLERK OF THE COURT

The clerk of the Court is the Court's judicial business manager. The clerk ensures that the Court is able to carry out its constitutional duty, its judicial business, in orderly fashion. The office was established by the first formal rule of the Court, adopted in February 1790. Through the years, the clerk's duties have increased enormously. The clerk has a staff of about thirty people.

The responsibilities of the clerk of the Court include:

1. administering the Court's dockets and argument calendars;
2. receiving and recording all motions, petitions, jurisdictional statements, briefs, and other documents filed on the various dockets;
3. distributing those various papers to the justices;
4. collecting filing fees and assessing costs;
5. preparing and maintaining the Court's order list and journal, upon which are entered all the Court's formal judgments and mandates;

CLERKS OF THE COURT

Name	Term	State of Origin
John Tucker	1790–1791	Massachusetts
Samuel Bayard	1791–1800	Pennsylvania
Elias B. Caldwell	1800–1825	New Jersey
William Griffith	1826–1827	New Jersey
William T. Carroll	1827–1863	Maryland
D. W. Middleton	1863–1880	D.C.
J. H. McKenney	1880–1913	Maryland
James D. Maher	1913–1921	New York
William R. Stansbury	1921–1927	D.C.
C. Elmore Cropley	1927–1952	D.C.
Harold B. Willey	1952–1956	Oregon
John T. Fey	1956–1958	Virginia
James R. Browning	1958–1961	Montana
John F. Davis	1961–1970	Maine
E. Robert Seaver	1970–1972	Missouri
Michael Rodak Jr.	1972–1981	West Virginia
Alexander Stevas	1981–1985	Virginia
Joseph F. Spaniol Jr.	1985–1991	Ohio
William K. Suter	1991–	Virginia

6. preparing the Court's formal judgments and mandates;
7. notifying counsel and lower courts of all formal actions taken by the Court, including written opinions;
8. supervising the printing of briefs and appendices after review has been granted in *in forma pauperis* cases;
9. requesting and securing the certified record below upon the grant of review or other direction of the Court;
10. supervising the admissions of attorneys to the Supreme Court bar, as well as their occasional disbarments; and

11. giving procedural advice, by telephone, mail, and in person, to those counsel and litigants who need assistance or assurance as to the Court's rules and procedures.

To date, there have been only nineteen clerks of the Court. Four of them served for a quarter of a century or more: Elias B. Caldwell (1800–1825), William T. Carroll (1827–1863); J. H. McKenney (1880–1913), and C. Elmore Cropley (1927–1952). The first clerk, John Tucker, was selected on the third day of the Court's first session, February 3, 1790, to oversee the courtroom and library, manage subordinate employees, collect the salaries of the justices, and find them lodgings when necessary.

The 1790 rule that established the position of clerk prohibited him from practicing law before the Court while he was a clerk. In the early years the clerk performed many of the duties later taken over by the reporter and the marshal. So varied were the responsibilities of the early clerks that they were described as a combination business manager-errand boy for the justices and the lawyers who appeared before the Court.

MARSHAL OF THE COURT

The Judiciary Act of 1867 gave the Court authority to appoint a marshal, to remove a marshal, and to fix that official's compensation. Today the marshal oversees the operations of the Court building as its general manager, its paymaster, and its chief security officer. Before the office was created, these duties were performed either by the clerk or the marshal of the district in which the Court was located. Between 1801 and 1867, for example, the twelve men who served as marshal of the District of Columbia also served, informally, as marshal of the Court.

The present-day marshal attends all the Court's sessions, manages more than two hundred employees, supervises the federal property used by the Court, pays the justices and other employees, oversees telecommunications, orders supplies, and pays the Court's bills. The marshal, whose original duties were to keep order in the courtroom, also oversees the Supreme Court Police Force, which consists of a chief of police and about eighty officers. They police the building, grounds, and adjacent streets; they may make arrests and carry firearms. The marshal and the marshal's aides also receive visiting dignitaries and escort the justices to formal functions outside the Court.

During public sessions of the Court, the marshal (or a deputy) and the clerk–both dressed in morning coats or cut-aways—station themselves at opposite ends of the bench. At exactly 10 a.m., on a signal from the chief justice, the marshal pounds the gavel and announces: "The Honorable, the Chief Justice and the Associate Justices of the Supreme Court of the United States." As the justices take their seats, he calls for silence by crying "Oyez" ("Hear ye") three times and announces: "All persons having business before the Honorable, the Supreme Court of the United States, are admonished to draw near and give their attention, for the Court is now sitting. God save the United States and this honorable Court." During oral argument, the marshal or an assistant flashes the white and red lights to warn counsel that the time for presenting arguments is about to expire.

MARSHALS OF THE COURT	
Name	Term
Richard C. Parsons	1867–1872
John G. Nicolay	1872–1887
John Montgomery Wright	1888–1915
Frank Key Green	1915–1938
Thomas E. Waggaman	1938–1952
T. Perry Lippitt	1952–1972
Frank M. Hepler	1972–1976
Alfred Wong	1976–1994
Dale E. Bosley	1994–2001
Pamela Talkin	2001–

REPORTER OF DECISIONS

The reporter of decisions is responsible for editing the opinions of the Court and supervising their printing and publication in the official *United States Reports*. The reporter and the reporter's staff of nine check all citations after the opinions of the justices have been delivered, correct typographical and other errors in the opinions, and add the headnotes, the voting lineup of the justices, and the names of counsel that appear in the published version of the opinions.

The post of reporter of decisions had informal beginnings. The first reporter, Alexander J. Dallas (1790–1800), was self-appointed, and most accounts of the early Supreme Court indicate that as a lawyer he undertook the first reports as a labor of love and a public service. Dallas, who was also a journalist, editor, patron of the arts, and secretary of the Treasury (1814–1816), published four volumes of decisions covering the Supreme Court's first decade.

Dallas was succeeded unofficially by William Cranch in 1801. Like Dallas—who served as Treasury secretary while reporting on the Court's decisions—Cranch continued to sit as a judge and later chief justice of the circuit court in Washington, D.C.

Cranch's successor, Henry Wheaton, was the first reporter formally appointed by the Court, in 1816. John W. Wallace was the last reporter to have his name on the cover of the Court's published reports. The first ninety volumes of the reports were titled Dall. 1-4; Cranch 1-15; Wheat. 1-12; Pet. 1-16; How. 1-24; Black 1-2, and Wall. 1-23. After 1874 the name of the reporter of decisions appeared only on the title page of the reports.

As Augustus Garland noted, "The office of the Reporter is not a bed of roses. The work is constant, arduous and exacting. A failure to give full scope in the syllabus to the utterances of a judge brings wrath upon him." [1] Reporters Benjamin C. Howard (1843–1861) and John W. Wallace (1863–1875) felt the wrath of several justices.

REPORTERS OF DECISIONS

Name	Term
Alexander J. Dallas	1790–1800
William Cranch	1801–1815
Henry Wheaton	1816–1827
Richard Peters Jr.	1828–1843
Benjamin C. Howard	1843–1861
Jeremiah S. Black	1861–1862
John W. Wallace	1863–1875
William T. Otto	1875–1883
J. C. Bancroft Davis	1883–1902
Charles Henry Butler	1902–1916
Ernest Knaebel	1916–1946
Walter Wyatt	1946–1963
Henry Putzel Jr.	1964–1979
Henry C. Lind	1979–1987
Frank D. Wagner	1987–

LIBRARIAN

The Supreme Court library, which contains more than 450,000 volumes in print, microform, and electronic formats, is located on the third floor of the Court building. (A private library for the justices, with 65,000 volumes, is on the second floor. There are also small core libraries in each chamber plus an offsite annex library containing 50,000 books.) The main Supreme Court library's use is limited to Court personnel, members of the Court bar, members of Congress, their legal staffs, and government attorneys. Usually, however, the library will grant access to its books to members of the public or press who specify a particular research interest.

The library, which grew from a donation of 2,011 law books given to the Court by Congress in 1832, has the most complete available set of the printed briefs, records, and appendices of Court cases. It also contains all federal, state, and regional reports, federal and state statutory codes, legal periodicals, legal treatises, and digests and legislative and administrative source material. There are also special collections in international law, military law, British law, patent and trademark law, and Supreme Court history.

Since 1887, when the post of librarian was created, there have been eleven Court librarians. The library has a staff of about twenty-five professional librarians and lawyers.

LIBRARIANS OF THE COURT

Name	Term
Henry Deforest Clarke	1887–1900
Frank Key Green	1900–1915
Oscar Deforest Clarke	1915–1947
Helen C. Newman	1947–1965
Henry Charles Hallam Jr.	1965–1972
Edward G. Hudon	1972–1976
Betty H. Clowers (acting)	1976–1978
Roger F. Jacobs	1978–1985
Stephen G. Margeton	1985–1988
Shelley L. Dowling	1989–2003
Judith A. Gaskell	2003–

Source: David Savage, *Guide to the Supreme Court,* 4th ed. (Washington, D.C.: CQ Press, 2004), 880–884.

---

[1] Augustus H. Garland, *Experience in the Supreme Court,* quoted in Supreme Court Information Office, "The Docket Sheet" 13 (Summer 1976): 4.

CASE INDEX

SUBJECT INDEX

Main entries on Supreme Court justices are indicated by bold page numbers, and their pictures are indicated by italic page numbers.

PHOTO CREDITS

Names of photographers or painters appear in parentheses.

368 Library of Congress, Prints and Photographs Division
370 Collection of the Supreme Court of the United States
372 Collection of the Supreme Court of the United States
379 Collection of the Supreme Court of the United States
382 Collection of the Supreme Court of the United States
391 Collection of the Supreme Court of the United States
396 Collection of the Supreme Court of the United States
400 Collection of the Supreme Court of the United States
403 Collection of the Supreme Court of the United States
413 Library of Congress, Prints and Photographs Division
419 Supreme Court Historical Society (Dane Penland)
430 Supreme Court Historical Society (Steven Petteway)
436 Collection of the Supreme Court of the United States
441 Library of Congress, Prints and Photographs Division
443 Collection of the Supreme Court of the United States
450 Library of Congress, Prints and Photographs Division
453 Collection of the Supreme Court of the United States
465 Collection of the Supreme Court of the United States
468 Collection of the Supreme Court of the United States
478 Supreme Court Historical Society (Joseph H. Bailey, National Geographic Society)
487 Collection of the Supreme Court of the United States
494 Library of Congress, Prints and Photographs Division

504 Collection of the Supreme Court of the United States
514 Collection of the Supreme Court of the United States
517 Collection of the Supreme Court of the United States
523 Library of Congress, Prints and Photographs Division
526 Library of Congress, Prints and Photographs Division
533 Collection of the Supreme Court of the United States
543 Supreme Court Historical Society (Hugh Talman)
555 Collection of the Supreme Court of the United States
557 Collection of the Supreme Court of the United States
561 Library of Congress, Prints and Photographs Division
563 Library of Congress, Prints and Photographs Division
567 Collection of the Supreme Court of the United States
572 Collection of the Supreme Court of the United States
579 Collection of the Supreme Court of the United States
589 Library of Congress, Prints and Photographs Division
593 Collection of the Supreme Court of the United States
595 Collection of the Supreme Court of the United States
602 Collection of the Supreme Court of the United States
610 Collection of the Supreme Court of the United States
613 The Historical Society of Pennsylvania, Society Portrait Collection, C. B. Longacre
616 Library of Congress, Prints and Photographs Division
619 Collection of the Supreme Court of the United States